A New Reader's Guide to African Literature

Second, completely revised and expanded edition

Edited by
HANS M. ZELL, CAROL BUNDY
and VIRGINIA COULON

Associate editors
Donald Burness
Rita Giwa
Miranda North Lewis
Katrina Robinson

HEINEMANN
LONDON · IBADAN · NAIROBI

Heinemann Educational Books Ltd
22 Bedford Square, London WC1B 3HH
PMB 5205, Ibadan · PO Box 45314, Nairobi

EDINBURGH   MELBOURNE   AUCKLAND
HONG KONG   SINGAPORE   KUALA LUMPUR
NEW DELHI   KINGSTON   PORT OF SPAIN

ISBN 0 435 91997 0 (paper)
      0 435 91999 7 (cased)

© Hans M. Zell, Carol Bundy and Virginia Coulon 1983
First published 1971
Second, completely revised and
expanded edition first published 1983

c
l

Set in 9/10 Baskerville by
Microset (VAP) Ltd., Aylesbury, Bucks
Printed in Great Britain by
Biddles Ltd, Guildford, Surrey

CONTENTS

Biographies

Essential addresses

Index · 545

Acknowledgements

Many people have helped in shaping this new edition of the *Guide*. First and foremost I am greatly indebted to my two co-editors, Carol Bundy and Virginia Coulon, without whom a new edition would never have materialized. Other active contributors were Donald Burness, who covered lusophone African literature and prepared the biographies on these writers; Rita Giwa and Katrina Robinson who helped with the annotations and write-ups of many of the non-fiction items; and Miranda North Lewis, who compiled the directory of libraries with African literature collections. Acknowledgement must also be made of Helene Silver, who was the joint editor of the first edition, but who is now active in other areas.

Several people provided advice or help in various form: especially warm thanks go to Michael Chapman, Robert Cornevin, Bernth Lindfors, Paulette Lorderau, Alain Ricard, O-lan Style, Stephen Tooke, and Bob Townsend. Thanks are also due to the management and staff of Librairie Harmattan in Paris, the librarian at the Afrika Studiecentrum in Leiden; Françoise Meynard, Librarian at the Centre d'Etudes d'Afrique Noire; Cathérine Brisou, Librarian at the Centre d'Etudes Littéraires Maghrébine et Afro-Antillaise; and to Jacques Chevrier, Albert Gérard, Michel Hausser and Jan Kees van de Werk.

We are grateful to the many publishers who generously sent us examination copies of books, review extracts, or catalogue information. We cannot list them all, but particular thanks are due to: Allison & Busby, Rex Collings, East African Publishing House, Editions CLE, Editions Karthala, Evans Brothers, Faber & Faber, Fontana Books, French Literature Publications, Ghana Publishing Corporation, Guild of Tutors Press, Heinemann Educational Books, Heinemann Educational Books (East Africa), Hatier, Lawrence Hill, Kenya Literature Bureau, Librairie Populaire Bafoussam, Longman Group, Longman Kenya, Macmillan Education, Macmillan Press, Mambo Press, Nok Publishers International, Nouvelles Editions Africaines, Onibonoje Press & Book Industries, Oxford University Press, Oxford University Press Nairobi, David Philip, Popular Publications, Présence Africaine, Ravan Press, Routledge & Kegan Paul, Seven Seas Publishers, Schwiftinger Galerie Verlag, Three Continents Press, Twayne Publishers, Vantage Press, Waterville Publishing House, and Yale University Press.

Hans M. Zell
Oxford

Picture credits

The editors and publisher would like to acknowledge the following for photographs reproduced in this book:
William Collins & Sons for Camara Laye; Editions du Seuil for Sony Labou Tansi; Faber & Faber for Richard Rive and Amos Tutuola; Sandra Gatten for Kofi Awoonor; *The Guardian* for Dambudzo Marechera and Ngugi wa Thiong'o (photo: Frank Martin); George Hallett for Chinua Achebe, Mariama Bâ, Francis Bebey, Mongo Beti, Dennis Brutus, Cyprian Ekwensi, Buchi Emecheta, Nuruddin Farah, Bessie Head, Ahmadou Kourouma, Mazisi Kunene, Alex La Guma, Taban lo Liyong, Meja Mwangi, Sembène Ousmane, Lenrie Peters and Wole Soyinka; Jalabert for Tchicaya U Tam'si; Société Nouvelle Présence Africaine (Photo Sport) for Bernard Dadié; The Transcription Centre, London for Lewis Nkosi (photo: Bill Orchard).

Map of Africa

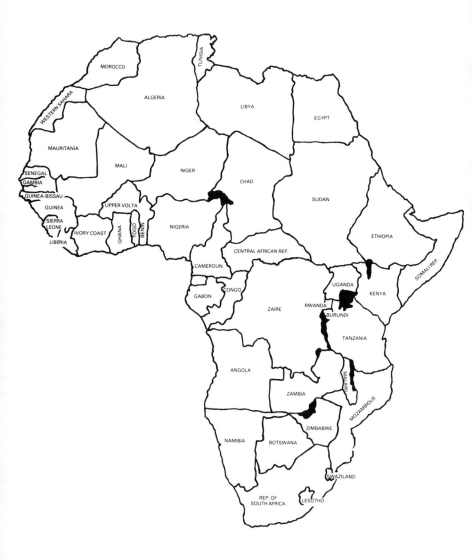

Preface to the second edition

More than ten years have elapsed since the first edition of this *Guide* was published. A great deal has happened to African literature during that decade. Gone are the days when the main themes of African writing were the experience of colonialism in Africa, or the issue of culture conflict. Writing today is very much centred on the contemporary scene; it has shifted from country to town, and the *urban* novel has emerged. More and more writing is concerned with social problems in Africa today, writers have become catalysts for social change, and there has been a great deal of radical, socially-committed writing. This is not to suggest that earlier writing was devoid of commitment, or lacked seriousness and political intent. Writing about the colonial experience was an historical necessity, it formed the roots for much of the African literature of the 1950s and 1960s, but today the *nature* of the commitment has taken on a different perspective.

The perception and role of literature has also changed quite dramatically. The issue of language, for one, has come even more into the forefront and has been much debated. A second generation of African writers has appeared, and a whole new crop of African critics have come forth. Names that did not appear in the first edition, exciting new dramatists in Nigeria like Femi Osofisan; outstanding new novelists such as Kole Omotoso, Nuruddin Farah, Sony Labou Tansi, Luandino Vieira, Dambudzo Marechera and Meja Mwangi; poets such as Mongane Wally Serote and Oswald Mtshali; all now appear prominently in this edition. The woman's voice in African literature has similarly blossomed: Buchi Emecheta has produced seven books since her first novel was published in 1972; Flora Nwapa has now written nine books and runs her own publishing company in Nigeria; in Bessie Head there is an eloquent voice of protest in Southern Africa; and Senegal's Mariama Bâ (who unfortunately died just as she was becoming known) was the first

winner of the Noma Award for Publishing in Africa, for her remarkable and compelling first novel *Une si longue lettre*, which has since been translated into no fewer than sixteen languages.

Many of the well-established writers of the 1960s, such as Wole Soyinka, Chinua Achebe and Ngugi wa Thiong'o, have greatly extended their output as well as their international reputations, and have confirmed their standing as major literary figures. Soyinka has produced a whole new range of plays, two new novels, as well as a delightful volume of autobiography. But today his main concern perhaps is that of the role of the writer and artist in society; he sees himself as a voice of reason and conscience, and he remains passionately outspoken against hypocrisy and corruption. Chinua Achebe has enjoyed wide international acclaim for his novels, and has since published a volume of poetry, one of essays and one of short stories, several children's books for a new Nigerian imprint, as well as writing prolifically on African writing, and editing a major new literary journal *Okike*. And Ngugi has followed up on his three earlier works with two further novels, as well as two volumes of essays which mark a new phase in his development as a writer. Ngugi has always had a long-standing commitment to the promotion of writing in the African languages, and he strongly believes that literature should be written in the language of the people, and that of the rural poor. His *Caitaani Mutharaba-Ini*, written in Gikuyu and published in 1981, is the first modern novel in that language. Ngugi has also been instrumental in raising political consciousness with his plays in Gikuyu. Like several other African writers he has found the theatre to be the genre which is most immediately accessible to the people. Ngugi's *Ngaahika Ndeenda* (I Will Marry When I Want) broke theatrical traditions by selecting actors among peasants and workers from a small village community, who were involved in all stages of the evolution of the script and in directing the play. It was performed to huge audiences and enjoyed enormous success but upset the authorities who were prompted to remove its performing licence. Ngugi himself was subsequently detained by the government for nearly a year.

The past decade has also seen some significant developments in the African book industries. The first edition of the *Guide* listed less than 50 books actually published in Africa. In the second edition the number amounts to several hundred. Output has increased dramatically, new companies are emerging all the time, and there is evidence of a great deal of imaginative entrepreneurial skill as well as rapid growth of some indigenous firms, particularly in Nigeria and in Kenya. In East Africa a recent phenomenon has been the proliferation of popular literature and mass paperbacks, many publishers having apparently suddenly awakened to the fact that money was to be made in such literature. Francophone Africa has witnessed the impressive start of Les Nouvelles Editions Africaines, a publishing undertaking set up with the enlightened support of two African governments and which, since its founding in 1972, has published over 300 titles, many in the literature area. Small presses whose publishing programmes include creative writing have also been established in Southern Africa. In Malawi, for example, Popular Publications in Limbe launched its 'Malawian Writers Series' in 1974. In South Africa, despite a repressive government and despite the restrictions imposed by the country's Publications Control Board, which is empowered to declare any book, film or object 'undesirable', there has been a marked increase in publishing activities during the past few years, accompanied by a sustained output by local writers, both black and white. Several small independent companies have sprung up, many of which are prepared to publish socially-committed literature and who actively encourage Black expression. The radical and anti-apartheid Ravan Press in Johannesburg is the most prominent among them, and they have somehow managed to survive despite various moves against them by the government. The Press has been prosecuted under the Suppression of Communism Act, their offices have been subjected to police searches, and among the many titles that have been banned are several issues of that unique literary and cultural magazine *Staffrider*.

Internationally, too, African literature has 'arrived'. In 1980 the Frankfurt Book Fair focussed on Africa, and this led directly to a great many more works of African creative writing being made available in translations in the major European languages. It also resulted in the establishment of a 'Society for the Promotion of African, Asian, and Latin American Literatures', providing a clearing house and a framework of promotion for Third World literature, and publicizing this literature in the Federal Republic of Germany and elsewhere in Europe. Many European publishers now have active lists of African writing in translation, among them Peter Hammer Verlag and Verlag Otto Lembeck in Germany, Edicões 70 in Portugal, Uitgeverij Corrie Zelen in Holland, Jaca Books in Italy, or Progress Publishers in the Soviet Union. If further evidence of the growing interst in African literature were neces-sary, one need only point to the *serialization*, in the Zürich *Tages-Anzeiger*, one of Switzerland's major dailies, of Hilary Ng'weno's *Der Mann aus Pretoria* (The Men from Pretoria), later published in book form by Unionsverlag in Zürich.

In Britain, Heinemann's pioneering 'African Writers Series' now faces stiffer competition in the form of several other series launched during the past few years – Longman's lively new 'Drumbeat' imprint, Nelson's 'Panafrica Library', and Macmillan's series of popular paperback fiction, 'Pacesetters', which was launched in 1977. In the meantime, Heinemann's 'African Writers Series' has grown to over 250 titles, with many new talented writers emerging all the time.

Inevitably, the volume of criticism and research tools on African literature has also grown enormously, as have collections of African writing, and studies on individual authors. For example, there are now eight individual studies on Chinua Achebe, five on Wole Soyinka, two on Peter Abrahams, and no less than eighteen on Leopold Senghor. Even more remarkable is the number of study and examination guides on African literature, and those providing 'Questions and Answers'. Study guides on Achebe's *Things Fall Apart* head the list, with twelve titles on this novel, followed by seven on Camara Laye's *L'Enfant Noir/The African Child*, and six on Wole Soyinka's play *The Lion and the Jewel*. There are even three study guides on John Ruganda's *The Burdens*, two of them published in Nairobi, and both in 1977! Bibliographic and reference tools have also proliferated, the most significant of which was perhaps Bernth Lindfors's *Black African Literature in English: a guide to information sources*, which provides a bibliography of more than 3,300 critical books and articles on over 400 African authors.

Finally, growing interest, both academic and public, in African writing is demonstrated in America by an active African Literature Association, which aims to promote the creative efforts of African writers and artists to a worldwide audience; and, in the United Kingdom, the Association for the Teaching of Caribbean and African Literature (ATCAL) recently held its fourth well-attended conference.

Confronted with these developments it soon became apparent that what was needed, a decade later, was something of a new book altogether, with different criteria for selection and a new approach to its overall organization. But despite being selective, the number of entries in the *Guide* has grown from the 820 in the first edition to over 3,000 in this new edition. The number of biographies now included has doubled and of course they are larger. Our plans were ambitious when we first commenced work on the second edition: not only did we want to provide full details of writing in English, French, and Portuguese, but we also

intended to list details of available *translations* of African literary works into the major European languages. Moreover, we wanted to feature at least a select listing of creative writing in the African languages. In the end, we had reluctantly to abandon these ideas, due to limitations of space, as well as time. In the new edition the objective, once again, has been to provide a practical, easy-to-handle, and typographically attractive handbook and reference tool – a *readable* bibliography – that does not pretend to be exhaustive, but aims to be as comprehensive as possible within its purpose and definitions of scope. There *are* some *lacunae*, however, even within this framework, particularly of some material published in Africa which we were unable to examine or which came to our attention too late for inclusion in the new edition.

The annotations, many of which have been completely rewritten, intend to guide the reader, not present critical evaluations, what an individual work is about, rather than its distinctive literary merits. The biographies aim to be both informative and lively, with insightful comments, assessment and quotes from critics and the writers themselves, culled from interviews and articles. About a hundred entries have been deleted from the first edition, as have a number of biographies. Two sections which appeared in the first edition have been dropped, 'A select list of periodical articles' and 'Politically committed writing'. However the section on children's books by African authors has been retained and considerably expanded. A new feature is a select listing of writing in Portuguese and the inclusion of some critical works on lusophone African literature, as is a similarly selective section of books on folklore and the oral tradition. The section on literary and cultural magazines has been much expanded. Another entirely new feature is an annotated directory of the major libraries in the USA, Canada, and in Europe that hold substantial African literature collections, giving details about access, loan and reference facilities, size of book and serials collections, and more.

Review extracts again supplement the synopses for many books, although we are only too well aware of the fact that inclusion of review extracts on certain books may well be rather arbitrary, particularly since we only quote reviews which are generally favourable. Users of the *Guide* should not interpret omission of review quotes on certain titles as being indicative that the book is insignificant, is not recommended for reading or for purchase, or has not been favourably reviewed. In many cases relevant reviews were simply not available, or we were unable to examine them. This applies particularly for African-published material. Reviews for these works, if they exist, are difficult to get hold of, and other than newspaper reviews and reviews in the *African Book Publishing Record*, African-published material still does not get sufficient review coverage.

Our overall policy has been to include review quotes provided we were in a position to examine at least two favourable reviews. One hastens to add of course that for many books we frequently found two, three or more reviews which were highly favourable, with the same number of reviews which were not favourable. For example, this is the case for the works of two much-maligned critics of African literature, the American

Charles Larson, and the Sierra Leonean Eustace Palmer. Their books have been warmly welcomed by some critics in the West, but, with few exceptions, have had generally scathing reviews from African critics. For example, Chris Wanjala, reviewing Palmer's *Introduction to the African Novel* in the journal *Dhana* says that it 'is yet another unfortunate addition to the twaddle on African literature by expatriates; it is a work most unwelcome for people who take our literature seriously' (making the somewhat embarrasing mistake of referring to Palmer as an 'expatriate'), whereas several Western critics reviewed the same book favourably elsewhere.

Considerable importance has again been put on the question of *availability*. Titles which we have ascertained to be out-of-print have been thus marked. Most UK and American entries have been checked against *British Books in Print* and its American and French equivalents, although it is of course entirely feasible that many titles for which we indicate prices may in fact be no longer available, or may be out-of-print by the time the new edition of the *Guide* appears. Keeping up-to-date with price changes proved to be a losing battle, however, and prices stated can only give an indication of the approximate price range.

Introduction

A New Reader's Guide to African Literature lists 3091 works by black African authors south of the Sahara writing in English, French and Portuguese. Reference material, critical works and anthologies (many by non-African authors) are also included, as is a section on children's books by African authors.

Arrangement

Books are listed in this order:
(i) Bibliographies and reference works (including bibliographies on individual authors)
(ii) Criticism and essays – General
(iii) Studies of individual authors (including study guides to individual books)
(iv) Folklore and oral tradition (a selective listing)
Thereafter titles are grouped under regional headings, covering fiction, drama and poetry from: English-speaking West Africa, Northeastern Africa, East Africa, Central and Southern Africa, Francophone Africa (again sub-divided by regions), and Lusophone Africa. Within divisions the arrangement is by country and alphabetically by author.

Multiple entries by the same author are listed in chronological sequence of publication date. However, English translations of, say, a francophone item or vice-versa, follow immediately after the listing of the work in its original edition, even though the publication date may be a later one than subsequent entries of works by the same author. Authors' names appear in bold face, but are not repeated for multi-entries by the same author. For titles lacking names of authors or editors, the first word of the title appears in bold, to avoid any possible confusion with the preceding entry. Many authors do, of course, appear under several different sections, and entries by the same author might well be found under creative writing, criticism, folklore, as well as children's literature. A complete author index is provided at the end of the volume.

Cut-off date

The cut-off date is *June 1981*, when the bibliography went to the typesetters. Nevertheless, we have included provisional details of books that were to appear during the second half of 1981. In those cases the entries consist merely of an author/title listing and lack an annotation. We have *not* included details of any titles that were scheduled for publication beyond 1981. [Publisher's note: the single exception to the above is the biography of Okot p'Bitek, which was updated following the death of this writer in July 1982]

Omissions and exceptions

It has not been easy to keep the *Guide* to manageable proportions. Regrettably, we have not been able to include the increasing volume of creative writing published in various African languages – this is an area which calls for an entirely separate bibliography. We have similarly not included the vast number of Onitsha market novels, popular pamphlet literature from Nigeria (and elsewhere in West Africa), which was largely published in the late 1950s and early 1960s. We have, however, included a sizeable number of works of popular fiction and mass-market paperbacks published more recently, both in West and in East Africa.

Our general policy has been to exclude a single, and only book by an author, say a volume of poetry privately printed and/or published, unless there have also been subsequent titles produced by commercial publishers.

The section on folklore and the oral tradition – i.e. collections of tales and fables, proverbs and sayings, traditional poetry, etc. – is strictly selective, and merely provides a sampling of the literature available. The section on lusophone African writing (and relevant critical studies) is similarly selective.

Finally, although this is a bibliography of *contemporary* African literature, some of the classic early works such as Olaudah Equiano's *Narrative*, or Thomas Mofolo's *Chaka* first published in translation in 1931, are included.

Bibliographic data and prices

We have aimed to provide as full bibliographic data as possible and, as for the first edition, we have felt that stress on availability to be desirable. In addition to bibliographic data, we give the names of publishers of both English and American editions (where two editions exist), together with their prices, name of series, editions, etc. Several books have gone through many editions; we list them all unless they are from the same publisher, in which case we list the most recent edition or reprint (reprints, as opposed to new editions, are not specifically indicated). Details of illustrative matter is not given, except in the section on children's books. A number of the most frequently cited publishers and series appear in the common abbreviated form as follows:

AWS   – African Writers Series
         (Heinemann)
CUP   – Cambridge University Press
EAPH – East African Publishing House
HEB   – Heinemann Educational Books
OUP   – Oxford University Press
SAL   – Studies in African Literature
         (Heinemann)

Unless otherwise stated, all books are published in paperback (soft cover/limp) format. Cloth or cased editions are indicated accordingly and, if two editions exist, the paper edition is given as 'p/b'.

We have provided details of prices whenever the information was available to us from publishers' catalogues, or bibliographic tools. As we have already pointed out in the preface, prices, in these inflationary times, do of course change all the time and, at best, prices give some indication of approximate price *range*.

Several publishers notified us of titles being out-of-print; others were checked against the various 'Books-in-Print' listings. If we were notified or otherwise ascertained that the books were no longer available, we have indicated this accordingly by the abbreviation 'o/p'. However, we have exercised considerable caution here. Several titles, appear without an indication of price: for them availability may be doubtful. On the other hand, it is of course always entirely feasible that certain out-of-print titles may well be reprinted or re-issued in the near future.

Prices are listed in the currency of the country of publication. Entries for African-published material frequently give both the local price as well as overseas Sterling and/or Dollar prices, where established. The list below provides approximate Sterling and Dollar equivalents for African currencies:

Country	Currency	Value of £ Sterling	Value of US $
Algeria	*A. Dinar*	7.4	4.2
Angola	*Kwanza*	62.9	30.2
Botswana	*Pula*	1.6	0.9
Burundi	*B. Franc*	164.3	90.0
Cape Verdi Is.	*C.V. Escudo*	64.7	36.5
Egypt	*E. Pound*	1.47	1.4
Eq. Guinea	*Ekuele*	377.7	213.5
Ethiopia	*E. Birr*	3.6	2.00
Franc Zone	*CFA Franc*	553.7	312.3
Gambia	*Dalasi*	4.0	2.2
Ghana	*Cedi*	4.9	2.7
Guinea	*Syli*	39.3	22.2
Guinea Bissau	*Peso*	70.0	39.5
Kenya	*K. Shilling*	19.0	10.7
Lesotho	*Loti*	1.9	1.0
Liberia	*L. Dollar*	1.7	1.0
Libya	*L. Dinar*	0.5	0.3
Madagascar	*M.G. Franc*	553.7	312.3
Malawi	*Kwacha*	1.7	0.9
Mali	*M. Franc*	1,107.5	624.6
Mauritania	*Ouguiya*	87.3	49.3
Mauritius	*Rupee*	19.1	11.2
Morocco	*Dirham*	10.4	5.8
Mozambique	*Metical*	53.2	30.0
Nigeria	*Naira*	1.2	0.7
Rwanda	*R. Franc*	168.0	92.8
Seychelles	*Rupee*	11.4	7.4
Sierra Leone	*Leone*	2.2	1.2
Somalia	*S. Shilling*	11.2	6.3
South Africa	*Rand*	1.8	1.00
Sudan	*S. Pound*	1.6	1.1
Swaziland	*Lilangeni*	1.8	1.0

Tanzania	T. Shilling	16.6	9.2
Tunisia	T. Dinar	0.9	0.5
Uganda	U. Shilling	150.0	78.0
Zaïre	Zaïre	10.1	5.7
Zambia	Z. Kwacha	1.6	0.9
Zimbabwe	Z. Dollar	1.3	0.7

(Source: *Financial Times*)

Reviews and annotations

A short synopsis or annotation is provided for most entries, accompanied by extracts from reviews on many titles. The annotations are descriptive, not critical; they are intended to place, not judge, the books. They have been prepared, as far as possible, from actual reading or examination of each book. In some cases we were unable to obtain or examine a copy of the book and have had to rely on publishers' blurbs alone. The annotations vary considerably in length – in some cases it may be no more than an indication whether the book is a work of fiction, a volume of verse, etc. A few entries have no annotation of any sort, but this does not necessarily reflect on the quality, or significance, of any one book. In many cases the disparity in length in annotations is due to the fact that we did not have a copy of the book available for examination.

The reviews originate largely from major literary magazines on African writing, from important scholarly journals, and from major newspapers. We have especially heavily relied on these periodicals and magazines:
The African Book Publishing Record (for African-published material)
Africana Journal (formerly *Africana Library Journal*)
African Literature Today
L'Afrique Littéraire et Artistique
Okike
Présence Africaine
Research in African Literatures (for critical works and folklore)
West Africa
World Literature Today (formerly *Books Abroad*)

World Literature Written in English

There are rather more review quotes on books in English, as there are more English-language journals reviewing African writing than there are in France or in francophone Africa. Our selection policy has been to include review extracts provided we were in a position to have read at least two favourable reviews. But in many cases no reviews at all were available, or we were unable to obtain them. Therefore, a considerable number of books which may well be important to many, or which may well have enjoyed favourable reviews, appear without any extracts, and it is stressed that omission of a review, *or* the inclusion of one or two extracts, does not necessarily reflect on the importance or literary quality of any title.

Children's literature

A selection of books for children and young adults, written by African authors, is included as a separate section. The annotations for children's books tend to be much briefer than for entries in the main bibliographic section.

Biographies

Supplementing the bibliographic sections, there are short biographical sketches on 95 of what arguably are the most prominent African authors of today. Fifty new biographies have been added for this new edition; existing ones have been extensively revised and updated, and a few have been dropped, where living authors have not published any further writing during the past decade.

We have again been led by the belief that the writers ought to *speak for themselves*: about their achievements, their ideologies, their commitment, the way they see their role as writers in society, and their views on African literature – its definition, its language, and its future directions. The biographies aim to be both informative as well as making for lively reading – they include many quotes, culled from articles and interviews, from critics and the writers themselves, speaking about their work and that of other African writers. We have taken great care to be as accurate as possible (considering the often contradictory sources) and present information that is reasonably up to date, but we should be grateful to hear of serious inaccuracies, so that these can be corrected in future editions of the *Guide*.

Magazines and periodicals

A great many new periodicals and magazines on African literature (some, alas, very short-lived) have commenced publication since the first edition of the *Guide* was published. This has necessitated a considerable expansion and revision of this section. Readers might well use the magazines section in conjunction with an entirely new feature in this second edition, the 'Directory of libraries with African literature collections' on page 525 – the latter will tell them which periodicals are available for examination in which libraries; it will also provide

them with information about how to gain access to these libraries and about their loan and reference facilities.

A listing of special issues on African literature by non-Africanist journals is also provided. However, if such special issues have been published in the form of a separate book or volume, and if they are available individually, then they have been included, as a monograph, in the main body of the bibliographic section.

Addresses

(i) The names and full addresses of all the publishers cited in the bibliographic sections are provided alphabetically by country on page 512. The exceptions are a small number of publishers whose addresses we were unable to trace and who presumably are no longer in existence.

(ii) Also included is a list of booksellers and dealers who carry sizeable stocks of African literature and/or who undertake mail orders. We suspect there are probably gaps in the USA section, and we would be pleased to hear from any dealer specializing in African literature or devoting considerable shelf space to the subject, in order that they may be included in subsequent editions.

BIBLIOGRAPHY

Bibliographies and reference works

Note: bibliographies and checklists of children's literature may be found in the children's section on p. 305

Abrash, Barbara comp. and ed.
Black African Literature in English, since 1952: works and criticism
New York: Johnson Reprint Corp., 1967. 92 pp.
A pioneering bibliography of creative works of literature by black African writers, along with selected relevant criticism. Amos Tutuola's *Palm-wine Drinkard* is taken as a starting point. Gives 463 entries, covering both books and periodical articles, together with a list of literary magazines. Includes listings of authors whose work has appeared in anthologies. There is an introductory essay by John Povey.
'. . . an invaluable list.'
Ezekiel Mphahlele – *Africa Today*

Aguolu, Christian C. comp.
Ghana in the Humanities and Social Sciences 1900–1971
Hamden, Ct.: Scarecrow Press, 1973. 212 pp. $12.50 cased
A bibliography of books and their reviews, articles and periodicals, theses/dissertations, conference papers and pamphlets, and official publications produced from 1900 to 1971, which also includes reprints of some classics published before 1900. The 'literature' section identifies works written by Ghanaians, and gives special attention to children's literature. There is a directory of publishers, printers, booksellers and book trade organisations in Ghana, plus a list (with annotations) of those newspapers and periodicals published elsewhere which carry substantial bibliographic material on the whole of Africa. Entries classified mainly by subject. Also contains a brief history of West African libraries.

Nigeria: a comprehensive bibliography in the humanities and social sciences, 1900–1971
Boston: G. K. Hall, 1973. 620 pp. $20.50 cased
Over 6,500 entries, 60% with annotations, arranged by subject in two main sections 'Africa' and 'Nigeria'. It is both selective and comprehensive in its coverage of items on all major humanities and social science topics. The literature sections include substantial entries on children's literature. Cites books, periodicals, newspaper articles, theses/dissertations, pamphlets, conference papers, official

publications, written by both Nigerians and non-Nigerians. There is a directory of major publishers, printers, booksellers, book trade organisations in Nigeria, plus selected periodicals published elsewhere which carry significant bibliographical material on Africa. Also a selected list of Nigerian newspapers and periodicals, and an introduction which outlines Nigeria's political history and her particular bibliographical problems.
'*Scholars and students engaged in Nigerian Studies will surely welcome Aguolu's bibliography as a significant contribution in the field of the humanities and social sciences. Athough other bibliographies on Nigeria are avaialable . . . Aguolu's book has a wider subject coverage.*'
R. A. Ukoh – *Research in African Literatures*

Amosu, Margaret comp. and ed.
Creative African Writing in the European Languages: a preliminary bibliography
Ibadan: Institute of African Studies, Univ. of Ibadan, 1964 (African Notes Bulletin Special Supplement). 35 pp. 50k
Lists works by 251 authors including South African writers 'irrespective of colour, whose work is clearly inspired (for better or for worse) by their relation to the African social and political situation of that country.' Now inevitably out-of-date, but as a preliminary bibliography still valuable. Notable for its inclusion of writings by North African authors.

Anafulu, Joseph C. comp.
Chinua Achebe: a preliminary checklist
Nsukka, Nigeria: Univ. of Nigeria Library, 1978 (Nsukka Library Notes, Special Issue, 3). 55 pp. ₦1.00 ($2.00)
Assembles all Achebe scholarship (books, periodical articles, theses, conference papers) known to the compiler at the time of publication. All editions of Achebe's novels, short stories, essays/palavers, interviews, poems, and children's literature are listed (some 155 items), followed by details of critical works, short notices, biographical material and bibliographies concerning the writer (amounting to a further 282 entries). Critical insights are arranged by heading, and there is an author index and list of sources too.
'. . . [a] commendable and urgent exercise in documentation by an African institution and compiler.'
Lemuel A. Johnson – *African Book Publishing Record*

Baldwin, Claudia

Nigerian Literature: a bibliography of criticism, 1952–1976
Boston: G. K. Hall, 1980. 147 pp. $19.50 cased
Contains criticism in English and French of 51 authors and 148 titles. One-sentence descriptive annotations are provided on some entries. The bibliography is limited to material 'available in United States libraries'.

Baratte-Eno Belinga, Thérèse

Ecrivains, cinéastes et artistes camerounais: biobibliographie
Yaoundé: Ministère de l'Information et de la Culture (distr. by Centre de Diffusion du Livre Camerounais), 1978. 217 pp.
A selective bio-bibliography of ninety-three important Cameroon francophone writers and artists. The entries, arranged alphabetically, give information on the lives and works of, and critical literature about, forty-six writers of prose, poetry and drama; sixteen journalists and critics; fifteen musicians; twelve painters and sculptors; seven actors; two film-makers. There is also a discography of works by the musicians/composers, and the critical literature on all the writers and artists listed includes interviews and reviews from Cameroon newspapers and periodicals.
'. . . extremely helpful to anyone interested in the modern arts in Cameroon . . . a fascinating cutural portrait of modern French-speaking Cameroon.'
Karen Keim – *Research in African Literatures*

Baratte-Eno Belinga, Thérèse; Chaveau-Rabut, Jacqueline; Kadima-Nzuji, Makala eds.

Bibliographie des auteurs africains de langue française
Paris: Nathan, 1979 (4th rev. ed.) (Classiques du Monde). 245 pp. FF69.00
Containing almost twice as many authors and entries as in the 3rd edition, this comprehensive bibliography covers not only creative writing but also literary history and criticism, bibliographies, collaborative works and anthologies (periodical literature is excluded). New categories include translations, and works in disc and cassette form. Gives prices. Arranged country-by-country, with indexes of authors, editors, discs and cassettes.

Beeton, D. R. comp. ed.

A Pilot Bibliography of South African English Literature (from the beginnings to 1971)
Pretoria: Univ. of South Africa, 1976 (Documenta, 14). 104 pp. R.4.75 (R5.75 overseas)
Provisional edition of a bibliography of South

African literature written in English, classified in three parts: Part 1 – bibliographies, criticism and collections; Part 2 – an A–Z listing of the writers, their works (first editions only) and major criticism; Part 3 – chronological and genre indexes, plus an appendix of names for further consultation. Covers creative writing by native-born citizens, visitors to, or foreign-born residents of South Africa, and brings together a selection of South African literature from a variety of bibliographical sources.
'The compilers have dealt fairly with the thorny problem of what constitutes South African English literature.'
G. E. Gorman – *African Book Publishing Record*

Blaise, Nicolas and Costisalla, Monique

Bibliographie des auteurs gabonais
Libreville: Institute Pédagogique National, Ministère de l'Education Nationale, 1975. 17 pp.
A short checklist of creative writing by authors from Gabon.

Bonneau, Richard

Ecrivains, cinéastes et artistes ivoiriens: aperçu bio-bibliographique
Dakar: Nouvelles Editions Africaines, 1973. 176 pp. CFA1,200
A reference book that represents the first attempt to provide complete bio-bibliographical information for writers, film-makers and artists from the Ivory Coast. More than eighty names figure here and most are writers. Each biography, compiled, except in a limited number of cases, through personal interview, includes a photograph and is followed by a bibliography of books and articles by and/or about the person concerned. Indexed.

Cohen, Karen comp.

South African English Poetry, 1937–1970, in the Johannesburg Public Library and the Gubbins Collection of Africana in the University of Witwatersrand Library, a bibliography 2 vols.
Johannesburg: Dept. of Bibliography, Librarianship and Typography, Univ. of the Witwatersrand, 1973. 467 and 384 pp. R50.00 set 2 vols.
Contains entries on works by white poets – *born* in South Africa or from (then) Rhodesia, plus listings of poems related to South Africa by other writers who visited the country or lived there. Volume 1 is the author index, while

volume 2 consists largely of a title and first-line index plus a short list of volumes of poetry, anthologies and other publications consulted. In mimeograph form.

Cordor, Henry S. ed.
Bibliography of Liberian Literature: a bibliographical review of literary works by Liberians
Monrovia: Liberian Literature Studies Programme, 1971.

Coughlan, Margaret
Folklore from Africa to the United States: an annotated bibliography
Washington D.C.: Library of Congress, 1976. 188 pp.
This selective listing of 190 books for adults and children aims to locate the origins of African tales and to show how they relate to tales in the United States and West Indies. Arranged under headings devoted to Sub-Saharan, West, Southern, Central and East Africa, the West Indies, and the United States, the items include references to well-known collections compiled in the late 19th and early 20th centuries by missionaries and government officials. The children's books are mostly European-American imprints.
'This bibliography will be most useful for those who are unfamiliar with Euro-American collections of African animal tales and are interested in learning about their Afro-American derivatives.'
Nancy J. Schmidt – *Research in African Literatures*

Davidson, Elizabeth comp.
Some English Writings by Non-European South Africans, 1928–1971: a bibliography
Johannesburg: Dept. of Bibliography, Librarianship and Typography, Univ. of the Witwatersrand, 1972. 54 pp. R1.50
Lists writings by non-whites in South Africa, covering novels, autobiographical novels, short stories, poetry, and some drama.

Duignan, Peter and Conover, Helen F. comp.
Guide to Research and Reference Works on Sub-Saharan Africa
Stanford, Ca.: Hoover Institution Press, 1972 (Hoover Institute Bibliographical Series, 46). 1,102 pp. $19.50 cased $8.95 p/b.
Gives details of 3,126 reference works on Sub-Saharan Africa, covering bibliographies, indexes, guides, dictionaries, abstracts, directories, encyclopaedias, histories, biographical works and specialized scholarly monographs. Also includes lists of periodicals and magazines, surveys of official publications,

a guide to publishers' and book dealers' catalogues, and a section on reprints. Annotations accompany practically all entries.
'. . . an essential purchase for all the larger university, college and public libraries, and it is also strongly recommended for the reference shelf of African studies scholars.'
Hans M. Zell – *Research in African Literatures*

East, N. B. comp. and ed.
African Theatre: a checklist of critical materials
New York: Africana Publ. Corp., 1970. 48 pp. $5.45
This bibliography draws together wide-ranging references to secondary materials related to African drama. It is divided into seven areas: Bibliographies; General; North; South; East; West; and films.

Ecole des Hautes Etudes en Sciences Sociales, Centre d'Etudes Africaines
Bibliographie des travaux en langue française au Sud du Sahara; Sciences sociales et humaines 1977–
Paris: CARDAN, C.N.R.S., 1979. 199 pp. (1977 vol.), 244 pp. (1978 vol.), 281 pp. (1979 vol.) FF80.00 ea.
An annual bibliography of writing in French in the field of the social sciences concerning Sub-Saharan Africa. Three volumes so far have appeared – for 1977, 1978, and 1979. Creative writing from Africa is not listed but critical writing is, as well as works on or about oral literature. There is a general category for literature and a country by country listing. The bibliography includes books that have appeared on the subject and articles compiled from more than three hundred publications.

Ferragne, Rev. M. comp.
A Catalogue of 1000 Sesotho Books
Roma, Lesotho: The Social Centre. 1974. 157 pp. R3.00 ($4.25)
The catalogue lists not only books, but many periodicals, newspapers, instructional and propagandist pamphlets, categorized according to type of publisher – church and missionary groups, religious and secular presses, government departments, bible societies. It is rich in Sesotho language publications, and whereas it contains a high proportion of religious material, there are also extensive listings of creative writing. Also included are reprints of two articles: 'Bibliographical Problems in Creative African Literature' (from *The Journal of General Education*, 19, No. 1, April

1967) and 'The Literature of Lesotho' (from
Africa Report 11, No. 7, 1966).
'. . . *very useful in alerting the reader to the existence
of the publications listed.*'
                    Daniel P. Kunene – *Research in
                                    African Literatures*

Ferreira, Manuel and Moser, Gerald
comps.
Bibliography of Portuguese-African Literature
Lisbon: Ediçōes 70 and Instituto de Alta
Cultura, forthcoming 1981.

Fontvieille, Jean R.
*Guide bibliographique du monde noir:
littéraire, ethnologie*, 2 vols.
Yaoundé: Univ. Féderale du Cameroun, 1971.
1,173 pp.
Volume 2 (entry numbers 4578 to 9279)
contains literature, ethnography bibliographies, and 200 pages of an index.

Ganz, David L. and Herdeck, Donald E.
comps.
*A Critical Guide to Anthologies of African
Literature*
Waltham, Mass.: Brandeis University; African
Studies Association, Literature Committee,
1973. 76 pp. $2.00
Fifty-nine anthologies of African literatures
are analysed. Also contains an introduction
explaining the guide's method, a 'worksheet'
for each anthology listed, a chart analysis and
'Masterlist of English Language Anthologies'.
'. . . *a valuable, time-saving reference tool which,
overlooking its sometimes questionable critical approach, will no doubt be of considerable use to those
following the phenomenal growth of publications in
the field of African literature.*'
          Rand Bishop – *Research in African Literatures*

Goldstein, Gillian
*Oswald Muyiseni Mtshali, South African Poet:
a bibliography*
Johannesburg: Department of Bibliography,
Librarianship and Typography, Univ. of the
Witwatersrand, 1974. 31 pp. R2.10
The author has assembled details of the
poetry, drama and polemical works of this
important young Black South African writer,
noted for his intensely political and confron-
tative tone. She shows us the extent of
Mtshali's reputation and commitment, gives
first-line references to his poems, full summaries of his writings in prose, and lists all
known critical works on his total output.
'*Goldstein has unearthed for us, the students and
scholars of African literature, an important corpus of
work, and from here we can proceed to the many
avenues and byways which she has so clearly indicated*

. . . *a valuable contribution to the ongoing work on
Mtshali's contribution to South African literature.*'
                    Cecil A. Abrahams – *Research in
                                    African Literatures*

Gorman, Gary E.
*The South African Novel in English since
1950: an information and resource guide*
Boston: G. K. Hall, 1978 (Bibliographies and
Guides in African Studies). 252 pp. $32.50
cased
A guide to bibliographical resources useful in
the study and acquisition of South African
fiction written by black and white authors since
1950. Aimed at librarians and students or
scholars, the book is in two parts. The first is a
survey of the development of the South African
novel, its form, style and content, with
approaches to its study and the bibliographical
problems likely to be encountered during such
an undertaking. The second contains the guide
proper: the bibliographical resources listed
are classified thus: 'Sources of biographical
data; General bibliographical guides; Selective
non-serial bibliographies; National bibliographies and selected serial bibliographies;
Periodical lists and periodical indices; Dissertations, theses and research in progress;
Bibliographies of African and South African
literature; Selected publishers and scholarly
societies.' The major sources in each category
are analysed and evaluated, with suggestions as
to how gaps might be filled. The volume is
completed by a bibliography of works cited
and consulted, and subject and author-title
indexes.
'. . . *Its consistent angle of approach – how this
resource will be useful to a worker in this field –
produces annotations that are always strictly relevant
. . . the guide is also invaluable to workers in related
fields that are not as yet blessed with such a
publication. His inclusion of sources from many
countries makes the book useful for researchers
everywhere.*'
                    Vivienne Dickson – *Research in
                                    African Literatures*
'. . . *a book of immense value to anyone interested in
the field.*'   G. D. Killam – *Africana Journal*

Görög, Veronika
*La littérature orale Africaine. Bibliographie
analytique*
Paris: Maisonneuve et Larousse, forthcoming
1981.

Harvard University Library
*African History and Literatures: classification
schedule, classified listing by call number,
chronological listing, author and title listing*
Cambridge, Mass.: Harvard Univ. Press, 1971

(Harvard Univ. Library: Widener Library Shelflist, 34). 600 pp. $35.00 cased

Herdeck, Donald E. ed.
African Authors: a companion to Black African writing vol. 1: 1300–1973.
Washington D.C.: Black Orpheus Press, 1973. 605 pp. $27.50 cased [company now defunct, and distribution of this title has been taken over by Gale Research Co.]
Contains almost 600 bio-bibliographies on black African writers and their works over nearly seven centuries. Includes 233 authors writing in 37 different indigenous African languages. This massive tome also contains maps, lists of publishers, journals, bookshops dealing with African works, and three critical statements by Gideon Magoaela, Lilyan Kesteloot and Abiola Irele. Also lists authors by genre, chronologically, by country of origin, and by language employed.
'... another treasury of factual data which no student of African literature can henceforth afford to ignore.'
     Albert Gérard – *Research in African Literatures*

Hobson, Mary Bonin
A Select Bibliography of South African Short Stories in English, 1870–1950
Cape Town: Univ. of Cape Town Library, 1972 (Bibliographical Series). 29 pp. 70c.
Covers short stories including folktales, adventure stories, animal stories, in an alphabetical sequence by authors.

Howard University Library
Dictionary Catalog of the Arthur B. Spingarn Collection of Negro Authors, 2 vols.
[Photographic reprint of catalogue card-index, 31,400 cards]
Boston: G. K. Hall, 1970. $150.00 cased
This collection of Negro authors is the result of fifty years of effort by Arthur B. Spingarn, a New York attorney and authority on Negro life and history, to assemble all significant writings by persons of African descent throughout the world. The bulk of the collection consists of more than 8,000 volumes. Among them there is a great deal of early Afro-American writing; slave narratives and biographies; works by Caribbean authors, Afro-Cuban and Afro-Brazilian poets, novelists and essayists, as well as African literature in the indigenous languages and in English and French.

Jahn, Janheinz comp. and ed.
A Bibliography of Neo-African Literature: from Africa, America and the Caribbean
London: Deutsch, 1965. 336 pp. o/p
New York: Praeger, 1965. 359 pp. o/p

Prior to the late Janheinz Jahn's *Bibliography of Creative African Writing* published in 1971, this was the most comprehensive and authoritative bibliographic source. Now out-of-print, it listed 1,184 works by African authors, noting both translations and country of origin for each writer.

Jahn, Janheinz and Dressler, C. P. comps.
Bibliography of Creative African Writing
Nendeln, Liechtenstein: Kraus-Thomson Organisation, 1971. 486 pp. $25.00 cased
Lists 2,868 entries of creative literature written in black Africa – all published books, performed plays and completed manuscripts from the 19th century to 1970. Bibliographies, secondary literature, anthologies, and creative works published in journals are included, as well as autobiographies, novels and narrative stories. Cites works of all authors who published before 1900; after that date only creative works are listed. Entries are arranged under five main headings: General, Western Africa, Central Africa, Eastern Africa, Austral (Southern) Africa. Includes works in indigenous languages, and lists and maps 49 of these languages. Also contains a section on 'forgeries' – works purporting to be by Africans but written by Europeans.
Jahn and Dressler's Bibliography of Creative African Writing *will automatically become a necessary reference tool for all scholars in the subject ... A noteworthy and welcome addition is the inclusion of references to review articles for authors and individual works.'*
     Edgar Wright – *Research in African Literatures*

Jahn, Jahnheinz; Schild, Ulla; Nordmann, Almut eds.
Who's Who in African Literature: biographies, works and commentaries
Tübingen, Germany: Horst Erdmann Verlag, 1972. 412 pp. £5.50 cased
A guide to African literature which brings together the biographies of over 400 sub-Saharan African writers. As well as giving comprehensive biographical data, the literary and other works of the writers are listed and reviews of their most important works are given by critics. The volume contains an index of countries and languages and is illustrated with photographs of the leading African authors.
'Jahn is usually ... precise and accurate ... discriminating in his choices ... another treasury of factual data which no student of African literature can henceforth afford to ignore.'
     Albert Gérard – *Research in African Literatures*

Kadima-Nzuji Mukala (Dieudonné)
Bibliographie littéraire de la République du Zaïre de 1931 à 1972
Lubumbashi: CELRIA (Centre d'Etudes des Littératures Romanes d'Inspiration Africaine), Université Nationale du Zaïre, 1973. 60 pp.
Z21.50
A short annotated bibliography of creative writing from the Zaïre Republic. Also includes criticism.

Lindfors, Bernth ed.
A Bibliography of Literary Contributions to Nigerian Periodicals 1946–1972
Ibadan: Ibadan Univ. Press, 1975. 231 pp.
₦6.00
Lists 4,137 literary contributions by over 1,200 authors to 177 Nigerian periodicals, covering scholarly and literary periodicals, religious, political, teachers', sports, radio, women's, youth, police and even military journals! Most of the authors are from Nigeria and other English-speaking West African countries, but writers from East and South Africa are also included, and there are works by African authors originally written in French and Portuguese, in English translation. Also includes a few Afro-American, West Indian, and European, authors.
'. . . a contribution of major importance to research tools for the study of African literature . . . the bibliography is clearly arranged, easy to use, and can serve as a model which should be copied for listing the literary contributions in periodicals in every African country.'
Nancy J. Schmidt – *World Literatures Written in English*

Black African Literature in English: a guide to information sources
Detroit: Gale Research Co., 1979 (Gale Information Guide Library; American Literature, English Literature, and World Literatures in English Information Guide Series, 23). 482 pp. $36.00 cased
A partially annotated bibliography of more than 3,300 critical books and essays on over 400 African authors, arranged in two parts. In the first, 2,221 numbered entries are arranged in 24 sections covering different types of genre and topical studies and reference sources – including bibliographies and interviews. Genre coverage ranges from fiction, drama, poetry and criticism, to autobiography, children's literature and popular literature, while topical studies include language and style, literature and commitment, folklore and literature, audience, craft of writing, per-

iodicals, publishing, censorship, research, teaching, organizations and associations, conferences, festivals. Part two treats critical studies of individual authors. Its 1,100 entries concern the works of over 400 African authors. The bibliography attempts to list all the important works produced on black African literature in English up to the end of 1976.
'. . . An outstanding piece of scholarship . . . an indispensable reference tool for anyone with a serious interest in African writing today.'
Hans M. Zell – *West Africa*
'. . . belongs in every university library and on the shelf of every serious scholar of African literature.'
Nancy J. Schmidt – *Africa Today*

McIlwaine, J. H. St. G. comp.
Theses on Africa, 1963–1975, accepted by Universities in the United Kingdom and Ireland
London: Mansell, 1978. 139 pp.
£13.50/$26.65 cased
Britain's Standing Conference on Library Materials on Africa (SCOLMA) initiated this reference work, which contains 2,231 entries – most of them referring to doctoral dissertations, accepted between 1963 and 1975. A separate index lists 124 earlier titles, and supplements the previous SCOLMA pre-1963 bibliography. Arranged by region and country, with subject subdivisions and an author index. Contains at least 55 titles of central interest to African literature researchers, with others on oral traditions, etc.
'This compilation, with its predecessor, is a "must" for all libraries with research interests in Africa; and all researchers in African literatures should know about it.'
Elizabeth A. Wiedenman – *Research in African Literatures*
'The easy accessibility to recent British theses by this book, hereto available only by rooting through several sources, will be a boon to Africanists.'
David Henige – *Africana Journal*

Mamonsono, Léopold P. and Bemba, Sylvain
Bio-Bibliographie des écrivains congolais: belles lettres, littérature
Brazzaville: Editions Littéraires Congolaises et Ministère de la Culture et des Arts de la République Populaire du Congo, 1979. 33 pp.
Resembles in format Baratte-Eno Belinga's Bio-Bibliography for Cameroon. Seventy-six authors (including 43 unpublished writers) are listed in alphabetical order with a short biography for each and a list of their (in most cases, published) works.

Mérand, Patrick and Dabla, Séwanou
Guide de littérature africaine: de langue française
Paris: L'Harmattan, 1979. 219 pp. FF40.00
An annotated bibliography of francophone African literature arranged alphabetically by author. A separate part contains a listing by country with a brief commentary on the state of creative writing in each. An introduction sums up the history of African writing in French in the twentieth century from Négritude and the movement of ideas leading up to it and on to post-independent writing. Also lists winners of the Grand Prix Littéraires de l'Afrique Noire from 1961 to 1978 and of the Grands Prix de Radio-France (for theatre) from 1967 to 1978. Includes a total of 1,000 entries, and is indexed by author and by title.
'En plus d'une recension bibliographique très étoffée, il signale les grands moments de la littérature noire . . . Un outil de travail indispensable pour tous ceux qui s'intéressent à la littérature africaine moderne. Un guide pour ceux qui, désireux de s'initier à cette littérature, ne savent pas toujours orienter leurs choix.' — *L'Afrique Asie*

Modern Language Association of America
MLA International Bibliography of Books and Articles on the Modern Languages and Literatures
New York: Modern Language Association of America, 1921– (three numbers annually, plus cumulative library edition in single cased volume)
Has included an annual bibliography of criticism on African literature since 1957. Over the years entries on African writing have grown very considerably and this is now probably the most comprehensive source on critical studies and folklore. The most recent annual volume (for 1979, published in 1980) lists a total of 1,200 literature references under the headings 'General and Miscellaneous', 'Bibliography', 'Folklore', and 'Literature', the last two sections with subheads by genre or topic and by countries.

Moser, Gerald comp.
A Tentative Portuguese-African Bibliography: Portuguese literature in Africa and African literature in the Portuguese language
University Park, Pa.: Pennsylvania State Univ. Libraries, 1970 (Bibliographical Series, 3). 151 pp. o/p
Divided into three sections – on Folk Literature; Art Literature (essays, novels, poems, stories, theatre); and History and Criticism of Literature. Each section is subdivided in turn

according to the five main geographical regions of Lusophone Africa. There is an author index with biographical notes, and photographs of such writers as Francisco José Tenreiro, Manuel Lopes, Costa Alegre and Tomás Vieira da Cruz.
'. . . his brief introduction is clear and contains a good deal of information . . . a good working list and an example of a bibliography that can claim to be reasonably complete as a first draft because restricted in geographical area and languages.'
Edgar Wright – *Research in African Literatures*

Mutiso, Gideon-Cyrus M. comp.
Messages: an annotated bibliography of African literature for schools
Upper Montclair, N.J.: Montclair State College Press, 1970. 97 pp.
A list of the holdings at Montclair State College, of all literary materials, written in English by Black writers, which are in print and available in the US. Oriented toward social science and Black Studies, the bibliography consists of three parts – Juvenilia, Literature, and a selective Africana list.

National Book League, London
Checklist: creative writing from Black Africa (sub-Saharan)
London: National Book League, 1971. 30 pp. 20p.
A short annotated listing in country order. Gives details of 126 titles currently in print.

Literature and the Arts of the Commonwealth
London: National Book League, 1972. 90 pp.
Prepared for the 1972 Commonwealth Book Fair, this annotated checklist gives details on 160 titles.

National Book League, London, and The Commonwealth Institute, London
The Development and Achievements of Commonwealth Literature
London: National Book League, 1978. 60 pp. 85p.
An annotated catalogue published to provide a permanent record of the 1978 Commonwealth Book Exhibition, covering fiction, drama, poetry, literary criticism and biography by Commonwealth authors, excluding British authors. Lists 560 items.

New, William H. comp.
Critical Writings on Commonwealth Literatures: a selective bibliography to 1970, with a list of theses and dissertations
University Park, Pa.: Pennsylvania State Univ. Press, 1975. 333 pp. $11.25

A selective bibliography, dealing primarily with literature written in English, which assembles 6,576 entries of critical writings on literatures from the British Commonwealth. There are sections on East and West Africa, South Africa and Zimbabwe (then Rhodesia), each divided into 'Research aids', 'General' and 'Individual authors'. Includes a list of theses and dissertations, plus an author index.
'. . . given the 1970 cutoff date, Professor New seems to have been thorough and consistent in his compilation . . . as a "guide and an aid to research, in a field of literary study that is only just recently attracting serious international critical attention" . . . this book will be of great value.'
    Alan J. Horne – *Research in African Literatures*

Obasi, John U. comp.
African Book List. The novel in Africa
London: Westminster City Libraries, n.d.
9 pp. free
A brief annotated listing of African fiction held at Westminster City Libraries.

Ojo-Ade, Femi
Analytic Index of Présence Africaine (1947–1972)
Washington D.C.: Three Continents Press, 1977. 194 pp. $22.00 cased
An index of the critical studies, essays, comments, conference papers, poems, short stories, messages, speeches, fragments of novels and even whole plays, which have appeared during the past 30 years in the important journal of black culture *Présence Africaine*. 4,705 entries are listed under author or subject. Subjects (43 of them) range from agriculture, anthropology, archaeology, to socialism, sociology, sport, theatre and urbanism. Texts by major writers, politicians and philosophers include those by Senghor, Césaire, Eric Williams, Sekou Touré, Nyerere, Sartre, Gide, Pierre Naville, Roger Bastide and Georges Balandier.

Páricsy, Pál comp.
A New Bibliography of African Literature
Budapest: Center for Afro-Asian Research of the Hungarian Academy of Sciences, 1969 (Studies on Developing Countries, 24). 108 pp. $1.80
Consists of two parts: Part I 'An additional bibliography to J. Jahn's *A Bibliography of Neo-African Literature from Africa, America and the Caribbean*; Part II 'A preliminary bibliography of African writing (from 1965 to the present)'. Part I lists 361 entries additional to the Jahn coverage of African writing. Part II lists 377 titles. Follows the Jahn style for bibliographic description.

Patten, Margaret D.
Ghanaian Imaginative Writing in English, 1950–1969: an annotated bibliography
Legon, Ghana: University of Ghana, Dept. of Library Studies, 1971 (Occasional Paper, 4). 60 pp. £1.00 ($3.25)
A classified listing of writings by 92 Ghanaian authors.

Philombé, René
Le livre camerounais et ses auteurs: une contribution à l'histoire littéraire du Cameroun avec notice bio-bibliographie
Yaoundé: Editions Sémences Africains, 1977. 304 pp.

Pichanick, J.; Chennells, A. J.; Rix, L. B. comps.
Rhodesian Literature in English: a bibliography (1890–1974/5)
Gwelo, Zimbabwe: Mambo Press, 1977 (Zambeziana, 2). 249 pp. Z$5.30
The first comprehensive attempt to list systematically the creative literature of Rhodesia-Zimbabwe written in English over a fifty-year period. Novels, short stories, verse, drama, by black and white writers are classified by genre, and listed alphabetically within those sections by author. Also covers all locally-published periodicals – about 120 titles.
'. . . thoroughly researched . . . faults notwithstanding . . . an essential addition to any academic or larger public library . . . contains a great deal of interest, such as early poems and short stories by Doris Lessing . . . in local periodicals during the 1940s.'
    O-lan Style – *Research in African Literatures*

Ramsaran, John
New Approaches to African Literature: a guide to Negro-African writing and related studies
Ibadan: Ibadan Univ. Press, 1970 (2nd ed.). 182 pp. ₦3.00
Introduces various aspects of African, Caribbean and Black American writing, followed by extensive book lists, details of critical articles, book reviews and a list of African language publications.

Rauter, Rosemarie and Mzee, Said comps.
Africana. An international exhibition of books at the 32nd Frankfurt Book Fair/Africana. Une exposition internationale de livres à l'occasion de la 32ème Foire du Livre de Francfort/Africana. Eine internationale

Buchausstellung anlässlich der 32. Frankfurter Buchmesse.
Frankfurt: Ausstellungs- und Messe-GmbH des Börsenvereins des Deutschen Buchhandels, 1980. 425 pp. DM12.00
The 1980 Frankfurt Book Fair focussed on publishing and book development in Africa. This catalogue provides a permanent record of an 'Africana' exhibition of books published on African topics by publishers in all parts of the world (outside Africa) in numerous languages. Pages 179–225 cover books on African literature, theatre, drama, dance, and music.

Rauter, Rosemarie and **Mzee, Said, comps.**
Printed and Published in Africa. An exhibition of books in print submitted by 200 African publishing houses at the 32nd Frankfurt Book Fair/Printed and Published in Africa. Une exposition de titres disponibles de 200 maisons d'édition africaines à l'occasion de la 32ème Foire du Livre de Francfort/Printed and Published in Africa. Eine Ausstellung lieferbarer Titel von 200 afrikanischen Verlagen anlässlich der 32. Frankfurter Buchmesse
Frankfurt: Ausstellungs- und Messe-GmbH des Börsenvereins des Deutschen Buchhandels, 1980. 233 pp. DM10.00
A catalogue of a further special exhibition held at the Frankfurt Book Fair in 1980 to coincide with Fair's accent on Africa in that year. The 'Printed and Published in Africa' display brought together almost 2,000 titles published by some 180 publishers in 29 African nations, and it included 350 items of African literature in English, French, Portuguese, and many in the African languages.

Roda, Jean-Claude
Bourbon littéraire: guide bibliographique des prosateurs créoles
Sainte-Denis: Bibliothèque universitaire de la Réunion, 1975 vol. 1: 74 pp. (poetry); vol. 2: pages 75 to 184 (prose writers)
Volume 1 is a chronological presentation of 27 poets from the Réunion with a bibliography and biography for each. It also contains details of critical books and articles about authors, and a bibliography of authors whose books are set in Réunion. Volume 2 covers 33 prose writers organized like the first volume.

Saint-André-Utudjian, Eliane comp.
A Bibliography of West African Life and Literature
Waltham, Mass.: Crossroads Press, 1977. 146 pp. $12.00

Catalogues the literary output of English-speaking West Africa, covering culture, literary criticism, poetry and a wide range of prose works – autobiographies, novels and stories, drama, chapbook literature. Includes an author index and additional sections for background studies and creative works. Contains some 4,000 entries.

Scheub, Harold comp.
African Oral Narratives, Proverbs, Riddles, Poetry and Song: an annotated bibliography
Madison, Wis.: University of Wisconsin; African Studies Program, [publ. as *Bibliography of African Oral Narratives*], 1971 (2nd rev. ed.). 160 pp.
Boston: G. K. Hall, 1977 (Bibliographies and Guides in African Studies). 393 pp. $42.00 cased
A revised and enlarged edition of the 1971 title *Bibliography of African Oral Narratives*, this new version contains around 2,800 entries on lore from the whole of Africa, culled from books, monographs, periodical articles, and accompanied in a good proportion of cases by annotations.
'... *deserves appreciation from those who need a scholarly bibliography hitherto lacking, of African oral literature and of the increasingly numerous studies in this field.*'
Véronika Görög – *Research in African Literatures*

Scheven, Yvette comp.
Bibliographies for African Studies, 1970–1975
Waltham, Mass.: Crossroads Press, 1977 (Archival and Bibliographic Series). 159 pp. $14.00
An annotated guide to 993 bibliographies in the social sciences and humanities, appearing as books, articles, or parts of edited volumes. The sections on literature and oral tradition list 84 items.

Bibliographies for African Studies, 1976–1979
Waltham, Mass.: Crossroads Press, 1980 (Archival and Bibliographic Series). 157 pp. $20.00
The continuation of the preceding item containing a further 809 entries, mostly with annotations, and arranged by topic and by country. Sections on literature and oral tradition list 48 bibliographies or bibliographical articles on African writers and writings.

Scott, Patricia E. comp.
James James Ranisi Jolobe: an annotated bibliography
Johannesburg: Dept. of African Languages, Rhodes Univ., 1973 (Communications Series, 1). 36 pp. 50c

An annotated bibliography that lists 60 titles, including critical material. English translations of the Xhosa titles are given. Also includes a 'Select bibliography of Xhosa novels, drama, and poetry, 1909–1959'.

Samuel Edward Krune Mqhayi, 1875–1945: a bibliographic survey
Grahamstown: Dept. of African Languages, Rhodes Univ., 1976 (Communications Series, 5). 49 pp. R1.00
A partially-annotated bibliography of works by and about Mqhayi: published and unpublished manuscripts, contributions to newspapers and anthologies, works in translation, arranged chronologically; critical and biographical works and field recordings relating to him. Includes general index and index to works.
'Scott succeeds in the formidable task of writing a readable bibliography. Because of the contextualizing details she supplies, it is not only richly rewarding to read her bibliography but, indeed, also quite fascinating.'
Daniel P. Kunene – *Research in African Literatures*

Southern Bantu Literature: a preliminary bibliography of secondary sources
Grahamstown: Dept. of African Languages, Rhodes Univ., 1977. 14 pp. 50c
Arranged in three sections – General survey, Southern Sotho, Xhosa – gives details about 90 items.

Style, O-lan comp.
Recent Zimbabwean Literature
London: The Africa Centre, 1981. 32 pp. £1.00
The Africa Centre in London and The National Arts Foundation of Zimbabwe presented a literature exhibition in April 1981, together with arts and artefacts. This catalogue – produced to provide a permanent record of the exhibition – indicates the range of the literature available, and the extent of Zimbabwean publishing. Shona, Ndebele and English language sections cover fiction, poetry, drama, children's literature and related studies. There are brief annotations to the entries, plus a supplement including entries on education, literary criticism, folklore, political and historical prose.

Syracuse University. Maxwell Graduate School of Citizenship and Public Affairs. Program of Eastern African Studies
Onitsha Publications
Syracuse, N.Y.: Maxwell Graduate School of Citizenship and Public Affairs, 1967 (Program

of Eastern African Studies, Occasional paper, 32) 24 pp. $2.50
A listing – though by no means exhaustive – of a unique type of African literature, Onitsha market publications. Compiled by Andre Niteki, it provides details of 77 titles and a list of publishers.

Travis, Carole and **Alman, Miriam** comps.
Periodicals from Africa: a bibliography and union list of periodicals published in Africa
Boston: G. K. Hall, 1977. 619 pp. $58.00 cased
Sponsored by the Standing Conference on Library Materials on Africa (SCOLMA), this bibliography lists more than 17,000 periodicals from all African countries except Egypt, and with selective inclusion of South African periodicals. Fourteen islands off the African coasts, and banned political movements publishing outside the continent also have their periodicals listed. The catchment date ranges from the late 19th century up to 1973. Most of the periodicals are written in English, but those written in Amharic, Arabic, Ewe, Hausa, Luganda, Malagasy, Somali and Swahili are also included. Classification is by country of publication, and there is a title index as well. The work includes journals, magazines, reviews, government periodicals, official bulletins, non-commercial newspapers, yearbooks, and transactions and proceedings of institutions.

University of Ife Bookshop Ltd.
Contemporary African Literature
Ile-Ife: Univ. of Ife Bookshop Ltd., 1971, 78 pp. 75k (40p/$1.00). (Supplement, 1972, 10 pp. free).
The catalogue of an exhibition of contemporary African literature organized by the University of Ife Bookshop Ltd., and held at Ibadan, Ile-Ife and Lagos from 25 November to 21 December 1971. Includes an introduction by Abiola Irele.

University of Malawi; Department of English
Theatre in Malawi 1970–1976
Zomba, Malawi: University of Malawi Library, 1977. 102 pp.

United States. Library of Congress, African Section
Africa South of the Sahara: index to periodical literature 1900–1970 4 vols.
Boston: G. K. Hall, 1971. 744 pp. $345.00 cased

This monumental index is based on citations assembled over several years of searching little-known or not-indexed domestic and foreign journals and bibliographic sources. Entries are arranged by geographical location (region or country), and then by author. Social-science biased, the index nevertheless contains in volume 1 generous listings of articles, critical studies, bibliographies on African creative literature – drama, folklore and oral literature, literature in general, the novel, and poetry. Volume 4 contains a 'Literary Index' listing some 3,000 citations of African literary works, many in small-circulation magazines published in African countries. These entries are presented in four sections: poetry, novels, plays and short stories.

'. . . *provides a fine complement to both the 1965 Jahn and the 1971 Jahn-Dressler bibliographies.'*

Eugene de Benko – *Research in African Literatures*

Warren, Dennis M.

The Akan Literature of Ghana: a bibliography
Waltham, Mass.: African Studies Association, 1972 (African Studies Association, Literature Committee, Occasional publication, 2). 46 pp.
A partially annotated bibliography of traditional and modern Akan literature, including folklore, plays, poetry, and songs. Lists 492 items.

Warwick, Ronald comp.

A Handbook of Library Holdings of Commonwealth Literature: United Kingdom and Europe
London: Standing Conference on Library Materials on Africa, 1977. (2nd rev. ed.) 123 pp. £2.25
A revised edition of the handbook compiled by Gail Wilson in 1971 for the Working Party on Library Holdings of Commonwealth Literature. Lists 'creative literature written in English by a national of any Commonwealth country other than the United Kingdom' and includes critical and reference works, biographies and collections of related interest – for example historical, sociological and political collections. Separate sections list library holdings in the UK and continental Europe alphabetically by place name.

'. . . *a welcome addition to the librarian's reference shelf, and it should be available in all institutions with an interest in Commonwealth literature.'*

Vibeke Stenderup – *Research in African Literatures*

Commonwealth Literature Periodicals: a bibliography, including periodicals of former Commonwealth countries, with locations in the United Kingdom
London: Mansell, 1979. 172 pp.
£22.00/$45.00 cased
A bibliography of British Commonwealth literature periodicals up to mid-1977, arranged geographically. The Africa section consists of a country-by-country list of titles, a general section, and three regional sections. Contains a title index, and there is an introduction by Arthur Ravenscroft (former editor of *The Journal of Commonwealth Literature*).

'. . . *a welcome addition to the basic research tools being made available of late to students and scholars of Commonwealth literature.'*

Robert E. McDowell – *Research in African Literatures*

Waters, Harold A. comp.

Black Theater in French: a guide
Sherbrooke, Canada: Editions Naaman, 1978 (Bibliographies, 2). 91 pp. Can$10.00
Waters provides an introduction to the theatre of francophone black writers from Africa and the Caribbean and includes the plot summaries of some 150 plays. In a separate part he lists plays under six main thematic headings: 'Revolt', 'Impartial', 'Conflict of the old and the new', 'No black orientation', and 'Moral'.

'. . . *a timely and nearly exhaustive tool for research that will no doubt prove invaluable to students and teachers of black theatre, in general, and of its francophone part, in particular . . . will fill a significant gap in every Africanist's library.'*

K. Muhindi – *Research in African Literatures*

'. . . *given the enormous gap which this modest guide fills, it is evident that the volume will become* the *basic bibliographic tool for scholars and teachers in the relatively small but growing area of francophone drama from the black world.'*

Thomas A. Hale – *Africana Journal*

Wilkov, A. comp.

Some English Writings by Non-Europeans in South Africa, 1944–1960
Johannesburg: Dept. of Librarianship, Univ. of the Witwatersrand, 1962. 36 pp. R1.10
Pages 13–20 cover literature, largely being contributions that appeared in *Zonk* and *Drum* magazine during the period covered.

Wolke, Irmtraud D. ed.

Fachkatalog Afrika/Subject Catalog Africa/Catalogue-matières Afrique: vol. 3: Literature
Munich: K. G. Saur, 1979. 358 pp.
£27.50/$50.00

The third in a series of twelve volumes listing the Frankfurt Municipal and University Library's collection on Africa, *Subject Catalog Africa* volume 3 lists its holdings of literature from the entire continent of Africa from the beginning of the 19th century. Entries are classified in three main sections – Traditional writings: stories, legends, folktales; Modern literature in African and European Languages; and Studies in literature of Africa.

Zell, Hans M. ed.
African Books in Print/Livres africains disponibles 2 vols.
London: Mansell, 1978 (2nd revised ed.).
1,036 pp. £52.50 set cased
Westview, Conn.: Meckler Books, 1978. $98.50 cased
Paris: France Expansion, 1978. FF00.00
Extensively revised and expanded, this second edition indexes over 12,000 items published in Africa, by author, subject and title. Covers material available at the end of 1977, from 37 African countries, written in English, French and 83 African languages. Includes an introductory essay on the publishing industry in Africa, with an A–Z directory of publishers and a list of government printers and publishing agencies.
'. . . *an impressive initiative into a long-neglected area.*'   – *Library Journal*
'. . . *a unique and versatile tool, equally valuable*

for acquisitions, reference, collection building, and research tasks in Africa area studies.'
Michael Keresztesi – *American Reference Books Annual*

The African Book World and Press: a directory/Rèpertoire du Livre et de la Presse en Afrique
Oxford: Hans Zell Publishers, 1980 (2nd rev. ed.). 285 pp. £35.00 cased
Munich: K. G. Saur Verlag, 1980. DM148.00 cased
Detroit: Gale Research Co., 1980. $75.00 cased
Paris: France Expansion, 1980. FF420.00
The second fully revised and substantially expanded edition of this directory provides comprehensive information (in English and French) on libraries, publishers and the retail book trade, research institutions with publishing programmes, magazines and periodicals, major newspapers, and printers throughout Africa. The new edition lists a total of 4,028 entries. Individual entries have also been expanded to include extra details on many organizations' scale of operations.
'*It is always a pleasure to pick up a new reference work one knows will prove dependable. Zell's publications give a good measure of that kind of satisfaction . . . essential for any library acquiring publications from Africa, and very useful for libraries with an interest in Africa.*'   – *Choice*
'. . . *an indispensable tool for anyone concerned with the African book trade.*'   – *Library Journal*

Criticism and essays: General

Abanda N'Dengue, Jean-Marie
De la négritude au négrisme: essai poly-phoniques
Yaoundé: C.L.E., 1970 (Point de vue, 1).
143 pp. CFA660
The author first presented the idea of 'Négrism', as a counter-point to that of Négritude, at the Festival of Negro Arts in Dakar in 1966. He defines it as being a 'fertile and balanced' synthesis of the cultural values of Black Africa and the Occident. The first part of the book is a revised version of his doctoral thesis on the image of Black Africa in French literature from 1920 to 1940.
'*Abanda Ndengue a exhumé un certain nombre d'auteurs français plus ou moins oubliés, mais fort interessants, depuis ceux qui versaient dans l'exoticisme facile ou qui faisaient l'apologie de la colonisation, jusqu'aux autres qui au contraire eurent le courage d'en condamner les aspects les moins reluisants.*'
Claude Wauthier – *Research in African Literatures*

Abdul-Hai, Muhammad
Conflict and Identity: the cultural poetics of contemporary Sudanese poetry
Khartoum: Khartoum Univ. Press, 1977 (Institute of African and Asian Studies Seminar Series, 26). 73 pp.
Describes and illustrates with examples the instrumental role of the Sudanese poet in forging a Sudanese national identity, especially since the late 1920s. Sections include 'The Fajr Group and After'; 'The Emigré Poets'; and 'The New Poetry' – the last synthesized from traditional roots and responses to the modern condition. An appendix gives the Arabic texts of verse cited in translation earlier in the book.

Achebe, Chinua
Morning Yet on Creation Day: essays
London: HEB, 1975 (SAL). 128 pp. £6.00 cased £2.50 p/b
New York: Anchor/Doubleday, 1975. 145 pp. $7.95 cased $2.50 p/b

These essays, articles, university lectures, conference addresses, letters to the editor, and travel notes are the only published collection of Achebe's non-fiction prose writing, and they represent nearly a decade and a half of his thinking on the subject of African writing and literature. Most of the pieces have been published elsewhere, including the much-quoted early articles (1965) 'The African Writer and the English Language' and 'The Novelist as Teacher'. These two essays belong to Part I which is devoted to Achebe's academic and theoretical writing. The opening essay on 'Colonialist Criticism' is also the most recent (1974). The writing in Part II is much more personal in tone, containing Achebe's statement on 'The African Writers and the Biafran Cause' (which he ardently defended) and his angry response to the attack made by fellow Nigerian, Tai Solarin, about his base commercial instincts in writing in a non-African tongue, and another response to Dame Margery Perham questioning her much-publicized refusal to support Biafra. Here, too, is a piece of Achebe's upbringing and early training ('Named for Victoria, Queen of England') as well as travel notes from his first visit to East Africa (1961).

'. . . To him the criss-cross of Africa and Euro-America is a place of "a certain dangerous potency; dangerous because a man might perish there wrestling with multi-headed spirits, but also he might be lucky and return to his people with the boon of prophetic vision".'

Nadine Gordimer – *The Times Literary Supplement*

'. . . Achebe's essays have significant implications for all contemporary writers and readers who seek a literature that is a vital part of their community. In addition, the student of African literature, and particularly of Achebe's fiction and poetry, will find invaluable, insights into the biographical detail and philosophical framework that have gone into their creation.'

C. L. Innes – *Research in African Literatures*

Literature and Society: an African view
Enugu, Nigeria: Fourth Dimension Publ. Co., 1980. 154 pp. ₦5.00.
Professor Achebe makes characteristically uncompromising statements about this important subject. The title essay is based on the text of a series of lectures which the Nigerian Broadcasting Corporation invited him to deliver in October 1975.

Achiriga, Jingiri J.
La révolte des romanciers noirs de langue française
Sherbrooke, Canada: Ed. Naaman, 1978 (2nd ed.) (Etudes, 2). 260 pp. Can$10.00

A three-part study, first published in 1973 and prefaced by Georges Ngal of the National University of Zaïre, on the theme of revolt in the novels of Francophone Africa. In part I he deals with the genesis of revolt in separate chapters devoted to Jean Malonga, Eza Boto, Abdoulaye Sadji, Camara Laye, Ferdinand Oyono and Mongo Béti. Part II covers novels in which revolt takes the form of *engagement* (Jacques Roumain, Sembène Ousmane, Bernard Dadié). Post-independent works in which the hero is characterized by internal conflict are discussed in Part III (Kane, Ousmane, Laye, Boni, Niane). There are also chapters on Daniel Ewandé and René Maran. He concludes with a review of the themes of revolt in the works he has discussed.

Actes du colloque 'Situation et perspective de la littérature négro-africain', Abidjan, 16–25 avril 1969
Abidjan: Université d'Abidjan, 1970 (Annales de l'Université d'Abidjan, Série D. Lettres, 1970, 3). 144 pp. CFA400
The proceedings of a colloquium held at the University of Abidjan from 16–25 April, 1969. Papers discuss the role and the condition of the writer in Africa and his means of expression as well as offering perspectives on black-African literature.

Actes du colloque sur la littérature africaine d'expression française, Dakar, 26–29 mars 1963
Dakar: Université de Dakar, Faculté des Lettres et Sciences Humaines, 1965 (Publ. de la Faculté des Lettres et Sciences Humaines, langues et littératures, 14). 276 pp.
Contains the proceedings of a conference on francophone African writing, held in Dakar, Senegal, in 1963. Includes papers on the novel, on poetry, and on Négritude. There are studies on three individual writers: Cheikh Hamidou Kane, Ferdinand Oyono, and Tchicaya U'Tam'si. Among the contributors are Camara Laye, Armand Guibert, Thomas Melone, Roger Mercier, Janheinz Jahn, Gerald Moore, Anthony Brench, and Dorothy Blair.

Adedeji, J. A.
The Theatre in an African University: Appearance and reality
Ibadan: Ibadan Univ. Press, 1980. 19 pp. ₦1.00
An inaugural lecture.

Adetuyi, V. T.
Notes on 'West African Verse' for School Certificate and G.C.E.
Ibadan: Onibonoje Press, 1972. 60 pp. 45k.

Adotevi, Stanislas

Négritude et négrologues
Paris: Union générals d'éditions, 1972 (10/18, 713). 306 pp.
A polemical book in which the author proposes to go behind the myths and the 'oratorical hallucinations' that the doctrine of Négritude has inspired. To be aware of African culture for Adotevi does not mean to stand in ecstasy before it but to 'radicalize' it, to give Africans the means to produce a new civilization.

African Literature Association

Artist and Audience: African literature as a shared experience (selected papers from the 1977 ALA meeting at the University of Wisconsin)
Washington D.C.: Three Continents Press, 1979. $22.00 cased $15.00 p/b
Reprints selected papers from this 1977 ALA meeting, which deal with a variety of African literatures in indigenous and European languages (Swahili, Arabic, French, English and Portuguese).

Agetua, John ed.

Interviews with Six Nigerian Writers
Benin City, Nigeria: Bendel Newspapers Corporation, 1976. 40 pp. ₦1.50
Transcripts of individual interviews (spiced with some biographical data), conducted by Agetua with six Nigerian writers in 1973. Serialized by the *Sunday Observer*, the interviews explore aspects of each writer's work – its aims, content and the variety of influences it synthesizes. Attitudes towards European literary forms are also discussed by the three poets (Tanure Ojaide, Okogbule Wonodi, Kalu Uka) two novelists (Flora Nwakuche, Chukwueneka Ike) and one dramatist (Ola Rotimi).
'Agetua's pamphlets about Nigerian writing are important. They reveal some truths about Nigerian writers that outsiders would not have access to, even if they were to interview these writers.'
Chris Wanjala – *Research in African Literatures*

Interviews with Six Nigerian Writers
Benin City, Nigeria: Bendel Newspapers Corporation, n.d. [1977]. 57 pp. ₦1.50
A further collection of transcripts of interviews between Agetua and six Nigerian writers and critics, conducted in 1973–4. (See also entry above). Like the first collection of interviews this volume contains biographical data and explores not only aspects of the intentions and style of each writer but also raises the question of the writer's role in building a strong African society. The writers are Soyinka, Tutuola, Kole

Omotoso, and 'Zulu Sofola, the critics Nwanyonye Obiechina, and Dan Izevbaye.
'. . . these interviews form a useful picture of a literature under pressure and in the process of change.'
Steven Jervis – *Research in African Literatures*

Alvarez-Péreyre, Jacques

Les Guetteurs de l'aube: poésie et apartheid
Grenoble, France: Presses Universitaires de Grenoble, 1979. 472 pp. FF69.00

Amoda, Moyiba ed.

FESTAC Colloquium, 1977: FESTAC colloquium and Black world development
New York: Third Press, 1979. 270 pp. $20.00 cased $8.95 p/b.
A general report and analysis of the Second World Festival of Black and African arts and culture. The Colloquium was attended by participants or representatives from over fifty countries. Its two-week duration saw reports and discussions on what had been accomplished since the first FESTAC in 1966, and outlines of an ambitious programme for the future.

António, Mário

Luanda, 'ilha' crioula
Lisbon: Agência-Geral do Ultramar, 1968. 163 pp. o/p
Six essays, in which Mário António studies precursors to modern Angolan writing. He devotes one chapter each to Cordeiro da Matta, the 19th century intellectual, António de Assis Junior, the novelist, Tomas Vieira da Cruz, the poet, and Oscar Ribas, the story teller and folklorist. The other two chapters explore lusotropicality, the cultural and linguistic integration that characterized Portuguese-Angolan relations in and around Luanda. A French translation *Luanda 'Ile' Creole* was published by Agência-Geral do Ultramar in Lisbon in 1970.

Anozie, Sunday O.

Sociologie du roman africain
Paris: Aubier, 1970. 268 pp. FF12.00
Anozie maintains that West African novels, in English and French, all belong to the same literary space, despite the extremely different geographic and historical background of each, and share a common literary characteristic – realism. The author's method consists in analysing thematic structure patterns of these novels by focusing on the central character which he sees as being defined or 'determined' by a particular social situation. Part I prepares the theoretical grounding for this analysis which is carried on in Part II. Part

III concludes with a discussion of the future of the West African novel, which for Anozie is developing 'messianic tendencies', meaning the hero is becoming more and more the model of a true social pioneer – a man with a practical vision and a clairvoyant mind.

'Il prend bien garde de ne pas séparer les romans écrit en anglais de ceux écrits en française montrant par là un souci réel de saisir le phénomène littéraire africain dans son ensemble et refusant un découpage linguistique arbitraire hérité de la colonisation.'

Alain Ricard – *Research in African Literatures*

Structural Models and African Poetics: Towards a pragmatic theory of literature
London: Routledge and Kegan Paul, 1981. 388 pp. £13.50 cased
Sets out to examine the relevance of structuralism and semiology to literary criticism in general, and to African poetics in particular. The author points out in his introduction that behind the rapidly growing body of African literature 'lies an immense and largely untapped reservoir of oral and vernacular tradition for which the proper tools of analysis and interpretation have yet to be found'. Professor Anozie argues that criticism of African literatures 'could use more method, and a more rigorous ordering of sense'. He aims to demonstrate that modern structuralism with its emphasis on linguistic models, and the possibility of harmonizing the methods and theories of structuralism with traditional African modes of thought and action, can provide a unique vantage point from which to approach this task.

Araujo, Norman
A Study of Cape Verdean Literature
Boston: Boston College, 1966. 225 pp. o/p
The most thorough study of Cape Verdean literature to date in English. Araujo, a descendent of Cape Verdeans, examines writers in Portuguese and Crioulo who express unique qualities of Cape Verdean life: repeated droughts, emigration, longing for home and a society in which the majority of the population is mulatto. Includes chapters devoted to three prose writers, Manuel Lopes, Baltasar Lopes and António Aurélio Gonçalves.

Awoonor, Kofi
The Breast of the Earth: a survey of the history, culture and literature of Africa south of the Sahara
New York: Anchor/Doubleday, 1975. 387 pp. $15.00 cased $3.95 p/b
A three-part study which sets African litera-ture, art, music and languages in the context of African history, culture, philosophy and religion. Part one deals with four different phases of African history, Part two examines traditional African literatures and other art forms, while Part three analyses contemporary African writing.

'. . . a book of experience: balanced, scholarly and instructional . . . The author indicates a profound perception of the nuances, subtleties and range of the elements of culture in art.'

Tayo Olafioye – *Africa Today*

'. . . an excellent introduction to the African continent. Kofi Awooner has brought to this work his skill as one of Africa's foremost writers, his knowledge as a scholar of comparative literature, and his experience as a teacher who has learned to speak to a very broad audience.'

Richard Priebe – *Books Abroad*

Ballard, W. L. ed.
Essays on African Literature
Atlanta, Ga.: Georgia State University, School of Arts and Sciences, 1973. (Spectrum: Monograph Series in the Arts and Sciences, 3). 195 pp.
Eight out of the nine essays in this monograph concentrate on types of Nigerian literary expressions, ranging from traditional oral literature to Soyinka's dramas. They cover Yoruba oral and written poetry, the Yoruba 'Opera', and Tutuola's use of English, African proverbs and Soyinka's rendering of them, and Cyprian Ekwensi and his relationship to his Onitsha market literature roots.

Balogun, S. I.
Notes and Exercises on 'Modern Poetry from Africa'
Ibadan: Onibonoje Press, 1967, 55 pp.
Background notes based on the West African Examinations Council's selections.

Banham, Martin and **Wake, Clive**
African Theatre Today
London: Pitman, 1976 (Theatre Today). 110 pp. £3.50 cased, $1.95 p/b
Presents a range of playwriting from East and West Africa in English, French, and Yoruba, together with critical commentary.

Barthold, B. J.
Black Time: Fiction of Africa, the Caribbean and the United States
New Haven, Conn. and London: Yale Univ. Press, 1980. 209 pp. £11.00 cased
Aims to provide a fresh view of the whole body of modern black fiction in the English-speaking world. Part I of the book provides a

necessary historical background; part II considers certain characteristic themes and forms in black fiction relating them to the writers' manipulation of time; and in part III, seven representative novels are discussed. The African novels analysed are Chinua Achebe's *Arrow of God*, Ayi Kwei Armah's *Why Are We So Blest?*, and Wole Soyinka's *Season of Anomy*.

Beier, Ulli ed.
An Introduction to African Literature: an anthology of critical writing
London and New York: Longman, 1979 (2nd rev. ed.). 304 pp. £3.50/$8.95
A new edition, revised and updated of Beier's acclaimed collection of critical writings on African, Afro-American and West Indian literature originally published in 1967. Its thirty articles include three new ones: Beier's 'Public Opinion on Lovers', Mphahlele's 'Writers and Commitment', and R. N. Egudu's 'Objebe Poetry'. The remaining twenty-seven present works by and about leading black writers, with the emphasis on Africa. They are organised into four sections: an account of six major oral traditions; Poetry; The Novel; and Drama. The bibliography has also been expanded and updated.
'. . . *the strength of the book is its original strength, that it is a collection of essays by individuals, sometimes radically in disagreement. There is fascination in this diversity.*'
Abena P. A. Busia – *West Africa*

Bengu, S. M. E.
Chasing Gods Not Our Own
Pietermaritzburg, South Africa: Shuter and Shooter, 1976. 170 pp. R5.25
An interpretation of the ways in which African cultural identity (as evidenced in literary works, some newspaper articles and editorials from Nigeria and Ghana from 1958 to 1974) influences African economic and political relations with the rest of the world.
'. . . *a strangely interesting performance. The brilliance of its statement of purpose stands opposed to its efforts at realization.*'
Lemuel A. Johnson – *Research in African Literatures*

Berrian, Brenda *et al*
Critical Perspectives on Women Writers from Africa
Washington D.C.: Three Continents Press, forthcoming 1981.
A collection of essays by well-known critics discussing major African women writers and their works.

Blair, D. S.
African Literature in French: a history of creative writing in French from West and Equatorial Africa
London and New York: CUP, 1976. 348 pp. £19.50/$42.00 cased £5.95 p/b (p/b publ. 1981)
A comprehensive analysis and historical survey of literature written in French from West and Equatorial Africa in all its manifestations. An introduction gives a background to the literature, with brief accounts of West African history, the colonial education system, and the rise of the Négritude movement. The book is then divided into four chapters on folk tales and historical legends in literature, drama, poetry, and the novel. Each chapter contains an introductory section and proceeds to discussions of individual authors and their works, giving summaries, critical analyses, and biographical details.
'*Students of African literature will find Dorothy Blair's comprehensive study a valuable resource. It is the most complete account yet written of the development of all genres of literature in French from West and Equatorial Africa, summarising and giving a critical analysis of the works of authors of note.*'
Janet MacGaffey – *ASA Review of Books*
'*This book is an excellent tool, solid and well documented, prepared by a literary historian who is able, if need be, to contest her sources. It is by far the most complete and up-to-date work in English or French dealing with the question.*'
Jacqueline Leiner – *Research in African Literatures*

Bol, V. P., and Allary, J.
Littérateurs et poètes noirs
Léopoldville: Bibliothèque de l'Etoile, 1964. 79 pp. o/p
This volume is divided into two sections: the first provides a basic introduction to French African writing; the second is a bibliographic essay which systematically lists creative writing by francophone African authors as well as that from English-speaking West and South Africa, the Caribbean and the Americas.

Booth, James
Writers and Politics in Nigeria
London: Hodder and Stoughton, 1981. 192 pp. £6.95 cased £3.95 p/b
Aims to provide a new perspective on Nigerian writing by examining the impact the various political upheavals in Nigeria during the last two decades have had on the content and style of some of the major Nigerian authors. An introductory chapter is followed by an exam-

ination of 'Literature and the politics of
language', and thereafter there are three
chapters on 'Democracy and the elite: T. M.
Aluko', 'Distress and difficulty: Chinua
Achebe', and 'The Artist and political commitment: Wole Soyinka'. A final chapter looks at
the likely future trends in Nigerian writing.

Brench, A. C.

*The Novelists' Inheritance in French Africa:
writers from Senegal to Cameroon*
London and New York: OUP, 1967 (Three
Crowns Book). 152 pp. o/p
The writings of Birago Diop, Camera Laye,
Ferdinand Oyono, Mongo Béti, Jean
Malongo, Bernard Dadié, Ake Loba, Cheikh
Hamidou Kane, and Sembène Ousmane are
examined both as works of literature and as
writing that came into being as a result of
historical events. Bibliographical and bio-
graphical notes accompany the text.

Writing in French from Senegal to Cameroon
London and New York: OUP, 1967 (Three
Crowns Book). 160 pp. o/p
Untranslated extracts from the work of the
novelists considered in the preceding entry,
intended to be representative of each writer's
work. The selection complements the essays in
The Novelists' Inheritance in French Africa, but it
may be used separately. Bibliographical, biographical, and introductory notes are provided
for each passage.

Brindeau, Serge *et al.*

*La poésie contemporaine de langues françaises
depuis 1945*
Paris: Ed. Saint-Germain-des-Prés, 1973.
927 pp. FF75.00
Pages 707 to 813 of this critical panorama of
poetry in French since 1945 are devoted to
black Africa. Edouard Maunick has written
this part, and poets are presented individually,
country by country. The same format is used
by Marc Rombaut for the section on poets
from the West Indies and the Indian Ocean
(pages 815 to 848). There is a bibliography for
these two sections pages 853 to 855 and a
general index of names included.
'... un bon instrument de travail. Il embrasse toutes
les communautes d'expression français ... il permet
... d'établir des points de recontre, de fixer des
dissemblances, de dégager les aspects originaux, et
d'entreprendre avec des horizons élargis des études
comparatives de littérature ou de poésie.'
Maurice A. Lubin – *Research in
African Literatures*

Brown, Lloyd W. ed.

The Black Writer in Africa and the Americas
Los Angeles: Hennessey and Ingalls, 1973
(Univ. of Southern California Studies in
Comparative Literature, 6). 229 pp. $9.50
cased $4.95 p/b
The papers in this volume were originally read
at the Fourth Annual Conference on Comparative Literature organized by the University
of Southern California in April 1970. They
examine many of the key issues raised in
considering black literature today – questions
of critical evaluation, aesthetics, educational
availability, cross-cultural influences within
the black world, etc.
'I must say ... how moving, and stimulating I find
all this – in a special way in which so much of the
polemics about the Black esthetic and so many
analyses of Caribbean literature have not done
before.'
Ezekiel Mphahlele – *Research in
African Literatures*

Bukenya, Austin L.

Notes on East African Poetry
Nairobi: HEB (East Africa), 1978 (Heinemann
Student's Guides, 18). 92 pp. K.shs.12.50/75p
A student's guide which gives details of
background and technique and has sections on
East African poetry and how to read and study
a poem. Detailed notes on *Poems from East
Africa* are included and an appendix is attached
giving questions and a suggested book list.

Burness, Donald

*Fire: Six Writers from Angola, Mozambique
and Cape Verde*
Washington D.C.: Three Continents Press,
1977. 143 pp. $15.00 cased ($6.95 p/b)
A critical study of the writings of Agostinho
Neto, Luandino Vieira, Geraldo Bessa Victor,
Mário António, Baltasar Lopes, and Luís
Bernardo Honwana. Frequent comparisons
are made between Lusophone African writing
and the literature of Francophone and
Anglophone Africa. An afterword by Manuel
Ferreira provides an overview of the literatures
of Portuguese-speaking Africa.
'Fire *should be warmly welcomed as a valuable
contribution to the study of Lusophone African writing
... All of them [the six writers] are, for different
reasons, important in their literary contexts and
worthy of the careful and enthusiastic attention
Donald Burness devotes to them.'*
Fernando Martinho – *World Literature Today*
'Donald Burness's privileged position as an Africanist

with a knowledge of Anglophone and Francophone as
well as Lusophone writing, affords him a comparative
perspective generally lacking in English-language
studies of Afro-Portuguese literature.'
                          Russell G. Hamilton – *Research in
                                        African Literatures*

Burness, Donald ed.
*Critical Perspectives on Lusophone Literature
from Africa*
Washington D.C.: Three Continents Press,
1981. 307 pp. $18.00 cased ($9.00 p/b)
A collection of twenty-two critical essays in
English and Portuguese on Lusophone African
Literature. Five of the essays by such critics as
Norman Araujo, Gerald Moser and José
Martins Garcia examine the works of individual writers, while eight others study specific
literary journals including *Claridade* and *Raízes*
from Cape Verde and *Mensagem* and *Cultura*
from Angola. Several of the essays, papers
presented at literary conferences, appear in
print for the first time. Bibliographical notes
accompany the text.

Burton, Samuel H. and
Chacksfield, C. J. H.
African Poetry in English
London: Macmillan, 1979 (Macmillan International College Editions). 154 pp. £5.95
cased £1.95 p/b
A step-by-step approach to the practical
criticism of African poetry from many different
parts of the continent. The methodical introduction to the poets' techniques and their
effects is aimed at upper secondary school
students in Europe as well as Africa.

Cartey, Wilfred
*Whispers from a Continent: the literature of
contemporary black Africa*
New York: Random House, 1969. 397 pp.
New York: Vintage Books, 1969. 397 pp.
London: HEB, 1971. 397 pp.
This is an in-depth survey of African writing in
the fifties and sixties.
'. . . his interpretation might be a very special one
since his vision as a West Indian combines a degree of
external detachment denied the African yet his sense
of identifying blackness grants him a more intimate
perception than the totally external European critic
. . . this book is the boldest attempt yet to survey the
field of African literature and it is an impressive and
able work that will become a significant reference.'
John Povey – *Africa Today*

'Cartey . . . responds to African literature with the
perception and intention of a poet.'
          Ezekiel Mphahlele – *Journal of Commonwealth
                                                Literature*

Chemain, Roger and Chemain-Degrange, Arlette
*Panorama critique de la littérature congolaise
contemporain*
Paris: Présence Africaine, 1979. 238 pp.
FF46.00
Through a panoramic critical view of contemporary novels, drama and poetry by 22 authors
of the People's Republic of the Congo, the
authors show that a national literature, whose
characteristics have been fashioned by the
history and social development of the country,
is very much alive and well. There is a
historical summary of the development of the
literature which pays due tribute to the
achievements of the pioneers, many of whom
published in the literary review *Liaison*, followed by critical assessments of the contributions made to Congolese literature by some of
its best novelists, militant dramatists and
poets.

Chemain-Degrange, Arlette
Emancipation féminine et roman africain
Dakar: Nouvelles Editions Africaines, 1980.
360 pp. CFA3,250
For Madame Chemain-Degrange black
women are never portrayed in the literature of
Francophone Africa for themselves but for
what they represent: a means of political
action by expressing a historical situation or a
projection of the personal or collective fantasies of the authors (who up to the date this
study ended, 1976, were male). By dividing her
book into two distinct parts, pre-independent
writing (including poetry, despite the word
'novel' in the title) she aims to determine if
independence has brought about any changes
in the literary image of women. In pre-
independent writing the images of women
serve (especially in poetry) to re-vitalize the
ancient black African cultures or to criticize
colonialism through the portraits of female
victims of colonialism. The portrait of peasant
women, however, show a beginning of awareness of women's condition. Although these
tendencies continue into post-independent
writing, a few authors (Kourouma, Ousmane,
Lopes) start to portray women as the incarnation, not of old values but new ones – as
positive forces out of which will come a new
Africa. Henri Lopes has written a long preface
which is a call to his fellow writers to divest

themselves of old male prejudices and 'conquer the new idea of the African woman'.

Chevrier, Jacques
Littérature nègre: Afrique, Antilles, Madagascar
Paris: A. Colin, 1979 (3rd rev. ed.) (U prisme, 36). 288 pp. FF41.00
The first part of Chevrier's introduction to the Francophone literature of black Africa, the Caribbean, and Madagascar covers the chronology of events from 1921 to the present and devotes separate chapters to developments in poetry, the novel, and theatre, each with lengthy-passages on a number of individual authors and their works. Part II, entitled 'Situation and Perspectives', evokes the social responsibilities of four men of letters (Senghor, Césaire, Rabemananjara, Fanon) and writes on the question of the passage from the oral to the written tradition and on the reader and the role of books in Africa.
'Redigé dans un style vigoureaux et limpide, cet ouvrage constitue un document précieux pour les étudiants, chercheurs et professeurs de littérature négro-africaine de langue française.'
Willy A. Umezinwa – *Research in African Literatures*

Chinweizu, and Jemie, Onwuchekwa
The West and the Rest of Us
New York: Random House, 1975. 520 pp. $15.00 cased $4.95 p/b
A massive, outspoken tract against the political, economic and cultural exploitation of the 'Third World' by the West, with the focus on Africa. Contemporary culture in Africa is seen to be hog-tied by the continent's political ties to the West, and Chinweizu regards many African politicians and intellectuals as conspirators, berating members of these elite groups for their brazen mimicry of European policies and art forms. Centuries of imperial domination, it is suggested, have totally severed African art from its roots and left their indelible stamp on criticism. Chinweizu calls for a new 'African Modernism' that may provide a model for a new indigenous African art and literature.
'African intellectuals are likely to respond with distinctly mixed feelings to The West and the Rest of Us. *Many ... will endorse its radical anti-imperialism while deploring its esthetics as bullying and reactionary, Chinweizu ... is at his best in exposing the political and economic dependency of contemporary Africa. His book is abrasive, insightful, dogmatic, exasperating, enlightening. Above all it is important and needs to be read.'*
Steven Jervis – *Research in African Literatures*

Chinweizu, and Jemie, Onwuchekwa; Madubuike, Ihechukwu
Toward the Decolonization of African Literature
Vol. I: African Fiction and Poetry and Their Critics
Enugu, Nigeria: Fourth Dimension Publ. Co., 1980. 320 pp. ₦6.50
Provides a sharp dissection of some of the dominant trends in contemporary African literature and literary criticism presenting European viewpoints, or, in the authors' terminology 'Eurocentric' views. They set themselves the task of 'probing the ways and means whereby Western imperialism has maintained its hegemony over African literature, and the effects of the hegemony upon the literary arts of contemporary Africa'. They set out, they state in their preface, to administer 'a timely and healthy dose of much needed public ridicule to the reams of pompous nonsense which has been floating out of the stale, sterile, stifling covens of academia and smothering the sprouting vitality of Africa's literary landscapes'.
'Chinweizu, Onwuchekwa Jemie, and Ihechukwu Madubuike, familiar with European viewpoints and methodologies have had the bold idea of exposing the inadequacy of the established approach ... To read Towards the Decolonization of African Literature *is to follow important arguments as they move towards significant conclusions.'*
Andrew Ekwuru – *South*
'To attack Toward the Decolonization of African Literature *will be considered imperialist; to admire it, paternalist. It conforms to what a large number of ordinary teachers of African literature, of both races, have been saying in their seminars for years, but it is good to see it written down in a manner that successfully combines academic evidence with a populist tone. This is the most vital work on African literature to appear in years.'*
Alastair Niven – *Times Literary Supplement*

Clark, John Pepper
The Example of Shakespeare
London: Longman. 1971. 113 pp. £1.15
Evanston: Northwestern University Press, 1970. 112 pp. o/p
A series of essays on African (largely Nigerian) poetry, which Clark had previously published in *Transition, Présence Africaine, Black Orpheus* and elsewhere. Most of the essays appear in their original form or with few changes, and under the following chapter headings: 'The legacy of Caliban: an introduction to the language spoken by Africans and other "natives" in English literature from Shakespeare to Achebe'. 'Themes of African

poetry of English expression'. 'The communication line between poet and public', 'Aspects of Nigerian drama', and 'Othello's useless scene'.

The Hero as a Villain
Lagos: Univ. of Lagos Press, 1978 (Inaugural Lecture Series). 20 pp. ₦1.00
An inaugural lecture delivered at the University of Lagos in January 1978, in which the Professor of English describes the Western literary concept of the 'hero' and sets it against traditional African concepts in order to show the most appropriate interpretation of the 'hero' for modern-day Africa.

Collins, Harold
The New English of the Onitsha Chapbooks
Athens, Ohio: Ohio University Center for International Studies, 1968 (Papers in International Studies, Africa series, 1). 17 pp. $1.00
This is a short survey of and bibliographic essay on the popular Onitsha market literature, which ranges from such colourful titles as *Why boys don't trust their girl friends; Money hard to get but easy to spend; Beware of harlots and many friends; Beautiful Maria in the act of true love; How to avoid enemies and bad company;* and *Trust nobody in time because Human being is trickish and difficult.*
'This mini-monograph does well to remind us that linguistic processes are still busily at work . . . that "colleges and books only copy the language which the field and the work-yard made".'
Joseph Jones – *Research in African Literatures*

Colloque *sur la Négritude*
Paris: Présence Africaine, 1972. 244 pp.
The papers of a colloquium sponsored by the Union Progressiste Sénégalaise in Dakar on April 12–18, 1971. Participants spoke on the relationship of Négritude to a great variety of cultural and non-cultural subjects: Greek and Roman civilization, humanism, literature, music, contemporary art, traditional African art, economic development, education, politics, the African personality, African law and modern law, science and mathematics, and black power. Léopold Sédar Senghor delivered the opening address and Léon Damas the closing address. The papers were also published in a special issue of Dakar's daily newspaper, *Le Soleil*, on May 8, 1971.

Colloque *sur littérature et esthétique négro-africaine Abidjan 1974*
Dakar: Nouvelles Editions Africaines, 1979. 358 pp. CFA6,300
The proceedings of a colloquium held at the Institut de Littérature et Esthétique Africaines of the University of Abidjan on December 10–15, 1974.

Cook, David
African Literature: a critical view
London: Longman, 1977. 254 pp. £6.50 cased £3.50 p/b. $15.50 cased $7.95 p/b
A collection of essays which present the author's personal views of African writing since the mid 17th-century. A broadly-based first section discusses the links and contrasts between African and European literature, and the feelings of African writers about social and critical ideals in their continent. Close-up studies of works by Achebe, Ngugi, Soyinka, Palangyo and Ekwensi are followed by investigations of different political and critical aspects of African literature as manifest in selected works by Oculi, Kenyatta, Fanon and Nkosi.
'. . . Professor Cook . . . faces each work or set quite squarely and with a depth of candor shot through with valuable perceptivity and insightfulness.'
Bu-Buakei Jabbi – *Research in African Literatures*
'Also stimulating is Cook's brief essay on African poetry, and the role that poetry plays as a popular medium on that continent . . . Cook's tour of African literature is bracing and stimulating . . . His book belongs in all libraries as an addition to more formal and less speculative histories.'   – *Choice*

Cook, Mercer G. ed.
Modern Black Novelists: a collection of critical essays
Englewood Cliffs, N.J.: Prentice-Hall, 1971 (Twentieth Century Views Series). 219 pp. $1.95
A selection of critical essays on contemporary Black novelists from Africa, America and the West Indies, with a selective bibliography of the writers and their works.

Cook, Mercer G. and Henderson, Stephen E.
The Militant Black Writer in Africa and the United States
Madison: Univ. of Wisconsin Press, 1969. 136 pp. $4.25
The two essays that make up this volume were originally delivered in shorter form as papers at the first meeting of a two-day symposium, 'Anger, and Beyond – The Black Writer and a World in Revolution', held in Madison, Wisconsin, in August 1968. In his paper 'African Voices of Protest', Professor Cook traces the development of black African literature through the works of representative African writers from the nineteenth century to

the present. He explores basic themes: independence, identity, African personality, and African socialism, and draws a parallel between the concepts of African 'Négritude' and the black American 'Soul'. The second essay, by Stephen Henderson, is entitled 'Survival Motion'; this is a study of the black writer and the black revolution in America.
'Mercer Cook's "African Voices of Protest" is certainly an excellent introduction for anyone wishing to read a basic introductory essay on the revolutionary aspects of contemporary black African writing.'
Charles Larson – *Research in African Literatures*

Cordor, S. M. H. ed.
Towards the Study of Liberian Literature: a critical anthology
Monrovia: Liberian Literature and Education Publ., 1973. 200 pp. $3.00 (mimeographed)

Cornevin, Robert
Le théâtre en Afrique noire et à Madagascar
Paris: Le Livre Africain, 1970. 335 pp. FF33.00
A history of theatre and theatrical forms in Africa from pre-colonial times to 1970. Chaper 1 talks about traditional drama in Africa (including puppetry). The book then takes up the study of school and mission-sponsored troops during colonial times and in particular Charles Béart's troop at the William Ponty Normal School. There are chapters on African theatre and black actors in Europe (1946–1960), on theatre in Africa in that same period, and on black theatre in French in Europe since independence. Concludes with a country by country survey (with a special chapter on Madagascar) and a discussion of current problems. Includes a lengthy bibliography and an index.

Littératures d'Afrique noire de langue française
Paris: Presses Universitaires de France, 1976 (SUP Littératures modernes, 10). 273 pp. FF49.00
The first hundred pages of Cornevin's history of the Francophone literature of black Africa deal with problems of definition, of quality, of publication, and evoke the place of Francophonie in the world. African oral literature is also considered here. The historical study proper follows a chronological order. 'The First Age' presents 19th-century precursors and the 20th century up to World War II, with specific chapters on the historical and political background to Négritude and on the concept and genesis of the Négritude movement. 'The Second Age' is devoted to the post-war flowering of African literature with chapters on Négritude and the nationalist period. There is a chapter on the winners of literary prizes

and a survey of the state of African literature country by country (including 2 Anglophone countries, Nigeria and Ghana). Concludes with a 15-page bibliographic guide which is a history of the criticism of African literature.
'... the strength of the book is ... in the broad framework within which African literature is discussed and in the thoroughness with which the discussion is documented.'
Nancy J. Schmidt – *Africa Today*

Costa Andrade, Fernando da
Literatura Angolana (Opiniões)
Lisbon; Edições 70, 1980 (Estudos Autores Angolanos, 5). 134 pp.
A collection of essays on Angolan literature and culture by one of Angola's important poets. The essays include six papers presented at international literary gatherings from 1963 to 1979 and three prefaces to works by other writers. Costa Andrade asserts that literature, struggle and revolution are tools of a nation seeking to create its own history. He argues that the generation of *Mensagem* differed from the Négritude school in that the former was rooted in Africa and that the Angolan writers did not constitute an intellectual elite isolated from the masses. Essays on Agostinho Neto and Pepetela and one on Angolan theatre are included.

Critique *et réception des littératures négro-africaines*
Paris: Afrique littéraire, 1978. 92 pp. FF20.00
A special issue of *Afrique Littéraire* (no. 50, 1978) containing the assembled papers of a colloquium hosted by the University of Paris III (Sorbonne Nouvelle) on March 10–11, 1978. Robert Cornevin outlined the history of literary criticism of writing in French from Africa, J. P. Makouta M'Boukou spoke about the amateurish methods of literary critics, and Y. E. Dogbé about the way criticism has influenced writers; M. Steins pleaded for a new approach to Négritude, M. Fabre presented René Maran as a critic of African literature, and R. Fayolle discussed the critical reception of Maran's *Batouala*. In other contributions Jacques Chevrier reviewed the attitudes of African writers towards the French language, finding changes in post-independent writing, and J. M. Grassin noted how omissions or inclusions in the major international encyclopaedias can influence literary reputations and set values. Finally, L. Mateso urged critics not to neglect the impact of the oral tradition on contemporary poetry and fiction, and A. Margarido reminded participants that critics should no longer ignore lusophone African literature.

Dathorne, Oskar R.
The Black Mind: a history of African literature
Minneapolis: Univ. of Minnesota Press, 1974.
538 pp. $25.00
An ambitious book, giving a broad survey of
all the major contemporary writers. Crucial
subjects that are often ignored in such works
are given extensive coverage. The volume
begins by studying the oral art of traditional
African literature, early written literature and
literature in vernacular languages and then
proceeds to trace the development of African
prose, poetry, drama, etc. (A shortened version
of *The Black Mind* is also available: next entry,
African Literature in the Twentieth Century.)
*'With swift broad strokes Dathorne sketches the scene
of oral poetry . . . skilfully and intuitively groups
francophone, anglophone, writers and those of
Portuguese expression separately. Briefly, he passes
judgements as he goes along, particularly when he is
dealing with writers who have produced substantial
work . . . It is so far the most invaluable single text as
a history of African Literature.'*
Ezekiel Mphahlele – *Journal of Commonwealth
Literature*
*'. . . an excellent overview of the scope of African
literature . . . A fine reference book for libraries.'*
Charles R. Larson – *Books Abroad*

African Literature in the Twentieth Century
Minneapolis: Univ. of Minnesota Press, 1975.
387 pp.
London: HEB, 1976 (SAL). 416 pp. £3.50
A condensed version of *The Black Mind: a history
of African literature* (see previous entry), this
book focuses on novels, plays and poetry
written this century in English, French and
Portuguese, throughout sub-Saharan Africa.
Also contains a review of indigenous writing
in nearly twenty African languages, and sets
the African literature written in European
languages in the context of the overall
development of African writing. Includes a
chapter on the Négritude writers.
*'Dathorne has produced a uniquely comprehensive
reference work of a type that no single author is likely
to attempt again, and he deserves our gratitude for
that'.*
G. A. Heron – *Research in African Literatures*

Depestre, René
Bonjour et adieu à la négritude
Paris: Robert Laffont, 1980. 260 pp.
A collection of articles published by Depestre
over the years grouped under two headings.
The first set of writings goes over the history of
Négritude as well as the criticism it has
engendered whereas the second set is devoted
to articles on black identity. This section
includes a discussion of the negrism movement

in Latin America, a critical evaluation of the
personality and the work of Jean Price-Mars, a
portrait of Césaire followed by an interview,
and several studies on Haïtian literature.

Désalmand, Paul
*Vingt-cinq romans clés de la littérature négro-
africain*
Paris: Hatier, 1981 (Profil formation, 361).
80 pp. FF12.00
A study guide to twenty-five key African novels
in French.

Dogbé, Yves-Emmanuel
Négritude, culture and civilisation: essai sur la
finalité des faits sociaux
Lomé: Ed. Akpagnon, 1980. 275 pp. FF64.00
This is the published form of the author's
doctoral dissertation which examines the
ideology of Négritude and its contributions to
philosophy, culture, and civilization.

Dudley, D. R., and **Lang, D. M.** eds.
The Penguin Companion to Literature vol. 4:
Classical and Byzantine, Oriental and African
Harmondsworth, England: Penguin Books,
1971 (Penguin Reference Books, R 37). 360 pp.
£3.75
Section four of this volume (pp. 333–360)
covers African literature, and consists of 114
short bio-bibliographies of the major African
writers, together with a list of recommended
reading.
*'. . . deserves high praise . . . enables the reader,
made weary and sceptical by too many subtle
arguments on négritude, to return to the poems and
novels of African writers and discover in them virtue
that transcends the historical moment.'*
Emile Snyder – *African Forum*

Duerden, Dennis
*African Art and Literature: the invisible
present*
New York: Harper and Rowe, 1975. 190 pp.
$10.00
London: HEB, 1977. 192 pp. £5.95 cased
Although contemporary African writers have a
history of Western-type education extending
back at least 150 years, many aspects of their
indigenous, pre-colonial cultures are still
powerfully if invisibly present today, and exert
irresistible influences on their work, linking
them firmly with their roots. This is Dennis
Duerden's argument in this scholarly book. He
shows how the sculpture, architecture,
furniture, craft and ritual objects, and the
stories and proverbs of oral tradition – which
all formed inseparable parts of the traditional
African way of life – help to shape what African

authors write today. He also shows how
modern African writing can be used as a means
of interpreting pre-industrial African art.
*'This is a most profound and original work ... a
complicated and persuasive study.'*
John Povey – *African Arts*

Echeruo, Michael J. C.
Poets, Prophets and Professors
Ibadan: Ibadan Univ. Press, 1977. 16 pp.
₦1.00
An inaugural lecture.

Egejuru, Phanuel A.
*Black Writers, White Audience: a critical
approach to African literature*
Hicksville, N.Y.: Exposition Press, 1978.
255 pp. $12.50
An analysis of the perennial problems that
beset the African writer working towards a
national literature: who is his audience, who is
his critic, how much do Western standards
influence subject matter consciously or unconsciously? Concentrates on novels by seven
writers from Anglophone black African countries, and ten from Francophone ones, and
includes interviews with Senghor, Ousmane,
Laye, Kane, Pathe Diagne, Achebe, Ngugi and
Mphahlele.

*Towards African Literary Independence: a
dialogue with contemporary African writers*
Westview, Conn.: Greenwood Press, 1980.
208 pp. $23.95
London: Greenwood Press, 1981
(Contributions in Afro-American and African
Studies). £14.95
Charts the developing trends in African
literature by a series of interviews with nine
African writers – Achebe, Senghor, Laye, Dib,
Diagne, Kane, Mphahlele, Ousmane, and
Ngugi. The interviews are topically arranged,
and the writers voice their feelings and
opinions on the socio-political issues that
influence contemporary African literature, and
discuss the philosophic and artistic intentions
of their own writing.

Egudu, Romanus N.
*Modern African Poetry and the African
Predicament*
London: Macmillan, 1978. 154 pp. £7.00
cased £3.00 p/b
New York: Barnes and Noble, 1978. 154 pp.
$8.50
Deals with the historical ideas which have
influenced modern African poetry (and
African literature in general) – colonialism,
Négritude, apartheid, and post-colonial

African politics. Covers poetry from West, East
and Southern Africa, stressing the thematic
and stylistic peculiarities of the poetry of each
of these regions.
*'[Egudu's] .. main concern is to show the "socio-
cultural and historical relevance of the various poems
discussed"... a useful book for African universities.'*
– *West Africa*

Four Modern West African Poets
New York: Nok, 1977. 152 pp. $10.00 cased
$3.95 p/b
A systematic analysis of the poetry of four
of West Africa's most important poets:
Christopher Okigbo and John Pepper Clark
from Nigeria, Kofi Awoonor from Ghana, and
Lenrie Peters from Gambia.
*'Egudu is particularly good in his graphic encapsula-
tion of John Pepper Clark's poetry ... penetrating on
Kofi Awoonor's human and poetic principles ...
rewarding in his summary of Lenrie Peter's best
poems.'* Andrew Salkey – *World Literature Today*

Eliet, Edouard
*Panorama de la littérature négro-africaine
(1921–1962)*
Paris: Présence Africaine, 1965. 268 pp. o/p
A critical anthology of French-African writing,
with extracts from the works of Rabéarivelo,
Senghor, Césaire, Fodeba, Rabemananjara,
Diop, Oyono, Dadié, Laye, Fanon, and others,
and an interpretation of the meaning of
Négritude.

Emenyonu, Ernest
The Rise of the Igbo Novel
Ibadan: OUP Nigeria, 1978. 212 pp. ₦8.00
A text based largely on the author's 1972 Ph.D
dissertation on 'The Development of Modern
Igbo Fiction: 1857–1966'. The first chapters
deal with Igbo literary origins and pioneer
writers, the missionary influence, and the
transition to writing in English, before concentrating on the two best-known Igbo writers in
English: Cyprian Ekwensi and Chinua Achebe.
Underlying the study is the question the
author asks in his introduction: 'Why are
most contemporary Nigerian novelists Igbo?'
Without attempting a direct answer, the author
acknowledges the contribution made by the
Igbo to Nigerian (and African) creative writing.

Eno Belinga, Samuel Martin
*Littérature et musique populaire en Afrique
noire*
Paris: Ed. Cujas, 1965. 259 pp.
Examines African music and literatures in the
context of their ancient traditions.

Enobo-Kosso, Martin
Zangali ou l'échec d'un amour
Yaoundé: Ed. Semences Africaines, n.d.
[1979?]. 60 pp. CFA600
Discusses the problem of the collision of
African and European cultures, in particular as
related to African literature.

Erickson, John D.
*Nommo: African fiction in French South of the
Sahara*
York, South Carolina: French Literature Publ.
Co., 1979. 285 pp. $17.00 cased
After an introduction and a preliminary
chapter on the history of Francophone African
literature and a discussion of the forces acting
on writers, Erickson devotes the rest of his
book to studies of individual works. There is a
section on short fiction and one on the novel.
Each chapter provides brief bio-bibliographical studies of the author of the work
analysed. There is also an extensive bibliography and an index.

Ezeokoli, V.
African Theater
New York: Nok, 1980. 190 pp. $18.50 cased
$5.95 p/b
Explores the aesthetic language and forms of
African drama in Nigeria and shows its
seminal influence on modern drama in the
West.

Ferreira, Manuel
A Aventura Crioula
Lisbon: Editora Ulisseia, 1967.
Lisbon: Plátano, 1973 (2nd rev. ed.) (Temas
Portugueses, 2), 442 pp.
A cultural study of Cape Verde with emphasis
on the following: the islands' bilingualism; the
morna as expression of the soul of Cape
Verde; and 'cabo-verdianidade', the assertion
of a Cape Verdean identity through literature.
Manuel Ferreira postulates that Cape Verde is
a melting pot of Afro-European values in
which a new type of mestiço or mulatto is
being formed. A preface by Baltasar Lopes and
a fifty-page bibliography of literary works add
to this study.

Literaturas africanas de expressão portuguesa
2 vols.
Lisbon: Instituto de Cultura Portuguesa, 1977
(Biblioteca Breve, 6–7). 142 pp. and 152 pp.
The initial volume contains a general introduction and sections devoted to the literary
accomplishments of Cape Verde, Guinea
Bissau, and São Tomé and Príncipe; the
second volume includes sections on Angola

and Mozambique as well as a 'final commentary'. In only 209 pages of actual text, Ferreira
sketches major and minor literary movements
and writers in Portuguese Africa. Both volumes contain extensive notations as well as
select bibliographies.
'*Com espírito e precisão Manuel Ferreira aborda
assuntos de suma importância na história das letras
lusófonas de Africa desde o século XIX até a
tumultuosa decada de 1960 . . . Mas o crítico não
para com a década de 1960, ele entra com
esclarecimentos no periódo da pós-indepedência
apontando tendências e correntes nas actuais literaturas africanas de expressão portuguesa.*'
Russell Hamilton – *África*

Ferres, John H. and **Martin Tucker** eds.
Modern Commonwealth Literature
New York: Ungar, 1977 (Library of Criticism
Series). 561 pp. $28.50
This work contains a set of critical excerpts
about the works of 139 writers, each excerpt
ranging in length from 200–400 words. The
excerpts provide a coverage of each author's
most important works and give a variety of
critical opinion. A bibliography is included
also.
'*As a class reference book and as a source of ideas for
students' papers, Ferres and Tucker will prove
admirable.*'
K. L. Goodwin – *Research in African Literatures*

Fonlon, Bernard
La poésie et le réveil de l'homme noir
Kinshasa: Presses Universitaires du Zaïre,
1978. 340 pp.
An analysis of poetry as a means of awakening
black consciousness. Lilyan Kesteloot adds a
preface.

Fouet, Francis and **Renaudeau, Régine**
Littérature africaine: l'engagement
Dakar: Nouvelles Editions Africaines, 1976.
406 pp. CFA2,540
A secondary-school textbook written to conform to the guidelines of the Senegalese
Ministry of Education, with chapters on the
birth and historical context of Négritude, on
the role of black writers in the affirmation of
cultural identity, on black African art, on
cultural and economic imperialism and the
intellectual combat of black peoples. Covers
thirty authors.

Gachukia, Eddah and **Akivaga, S.
Kichamu** eds
Teaching of African Literature in Schools vol. 1
Nairobi: Kenya Lit. Bureau, 1978. 250 pp.
K.shs.10.45 (£3.50/$8.10)
Nineteen papers presented at the African

Literature Conference held at Nairobi School in September 1974 are reprinted here. They include contributions by and about Ngugi wa Thiong'o and consider the nature and role of African literature in the Kenyan educational system. Among the issues examined are: the role played by literature in society, especially in colonial Africa; the role it should play in an independent country; and the type of literature best suited to fulfilling that obligation.

Geno, Thomas H. and Bostick, Herman F. eds.
The Working Papers of the 1972 Pre-Conference Workshop on Black Literature of French Expression, 20–22 November 1972, Atlanta, Georgia
New York: American Council on the Teaching of Foreign Languages, 1973. 29 pp.
Contains papers by 23 participants, and takes in the cultural background and highlights of African and Afro-Caribbean literature written in French. The presentations are arranged in eight categories: African religious orientation; Physical Africa; Art, music and dance; African history; Literature of West Africa; Literature of Central and Equatorial Africa; Caribbean Literature; and Pedagogy.
'The organizers are to be congratulated for taking on such an ambitious project.'
Thomas Cassirer – *Research in African Literatures*

Gakwandi, Shatto Arthur
The Novel and Contemporary Experience in Africa
London: HEB, 1977. 136 pp. £7.50 cased £2.50 p/b
New York: Africana Publ. Corp., 1980.
140 pp. £22.50 cased £12.50 p/b
An introduction to, and critical assessment of, twelve major novels from Africa in terms of the basic themes of colonialism, progress, nationalism, disillusionment, social commitment etc. All the novels were written during the last two decades: Oyono's *Houseboy*; La Guma's *Walk in the Night*; Achebe's *No Longer at Ease* and *A Man of the People*; Beti's *Mission to Kala*; Abrahams' *A Wreath for Udomo*; Aluko's *One Man One Matchet*; Soyinka's *The Interpreters*; Armah's *The Beautyful Ones Are Not Yet Born*; Duodo's *The Gab Boys*; Ngugi's *A Grain of Wheat*; and Ousmane's *God's Bits of Wood*. Through his critical assessment of the literary and social importance of these novels Gakwandi outlines the main concerns of African fiction, with particular emphasis on the parallel relationship between nationalism and modern African literature.
'. . . one of the best introductions to the African novel for the general reader. It contains a good bibliography

of other critical works on the African novel and is highly recommended for all libraries. – *Choice*
'. . . his treatment of individual works includes consideration of their formal strengths and weaknesses, and he displays an admirable determination to treat them as works of art rather than as mere social treatises.'
Robert L. Berner – *World Literature Today*

Gassama, Makhily
Kuma: intérrogation sur la littérature nègre de langue française
Dakar: Nouvelles Editions Africaines, 1978. 343 pp. CFA2,500
Kuma means 'word' in Bambara, and the author's task in this critical study-cum-anthology of poetry and the novel is to determine how successful African writers in French have been in moulding their ideas to their words. The Western writer, for Gassama, searches *what* to say, and the African writer *how* to say it. In Part I on poetry there are chapters on 'The Right Word' and on the way words are used in traditional poetry. Gassama then gives extracts from the verse of four Négritude poets (Damas, Césaire, Senghor, D. Diop) on the theme of 'Exil-Passion'. In the second part there is a discussion of how novelists use the different registers of expression, including *petit nègre* and pidgin (with extracts to illustrate each). The author then isolates the theme of the evocation of the world of the occult and superstitions in the novel (with extracts from C. A. Diop, Sadji, Pliya, Matiba, T. Niane, Kourouma and Ananou). A bibliography and an index of authors complete each section.

Geno, Thomas H. and Julow, Roy eds.
Littératures ultramarines de langue française: négro-africain, antillaise, québecoise, franco-américaine, comparée. Genèse et jeunesse
Sherbrooke, Canada: Ed. Naaman, 1974 (Collection Littératures, 3). 154 pp.
Can.$10.00
A collection of papers presented at the University of Vermont's 1971 conference at which it conferred an honorary doctorate upon poet-president Senghor. His address introduces a volume on different aspects of Black francophone literature from the West Indies, Canada, America and Africa too. There is also a section dealing with themes and issues common to literature from all these places.
'Some of the papers on Québécois literature . . . should also be of interest to readers primarily concerned with African literature, since they deal with themes and problems that are equally important in the African context.'
Thomas Cassirer – *Research in African Literatures*

Gérard, Albert S.

Four African Literatures: Xhosa, Sotho, Zulu, Amharic
Berkeley, Ca.: Univ. of California Press, 1971. 458 pp. $15.00/£5.20
A critical study and literary history of four indigenous literatures during the last 150 years since Africans were introduced to the techniques of writing. It shows the conflicts that arose between traditional African culture and Western technical advances.
'Most academic libraries will want this scholarly work, some for its particular African interest, but all for its glorious chronicle of the birth and growth of a new literature.' Robert Koester – *Library Journal*
'. . . an admirable effort . . . He has been able to focus sharply on these language areas.'
Ezekiel Mphahlele – *Journal of Commonwealth Literature*

Etudes de littérature africaine francophone
Dakar: Nouvelles Editions Africains, 1977. 174 pp. CFA1,500
A collection of articles published by Gérard between 1961 and 1974, mainly in Belgian academic journals. There are theoretical essays on the study of African literatures, on the origin and literary destiny of Négritude, and *Francophonie* in African letters, but also several individual studies of authors, including Rabéarivelo, Ousmane, C. H. Kane, Bolamba, and Béti.
'Albert Gérard has been and continues to be an outstanding literary critic. He has written cogently on the English romantics, on American literature and, for the past two decades on African literature . . . He writes with extraordinary breadth on the . . . francophone literatures of Africa . . . the student . . . can only be enriched by it.'
Rand Bishop – *Research in African Literatures*

African Language Literatures: an introduction to the literary history of sub-Saharan Africa
Washington D.C.: Three Continents Press, 1980. 370 pp. $22.00 cased $10.00 p/b
An attempt to deal with and discuss the *written* literatures of over sixty linguistic areas by this noted Belgian Africanist. The linguistic areas discussed include Akan, Twi, Rongo, Somali, Venda and Wolof. The volume includes language maps, bibliographies and detailed notes.

Githae-Mugo, Micere

Visions of Africa
Nairobi: Kenya Lit. Bureau, 1978. 198 pp.
A concise critical analysis of the works of four contrasting writers on Africa: Chinua Achebe, Ngugi wa Thiong'o, Elspeth Huxley and

Margaret Laurence. The author examines their fiction against the socio-political background of Africa and gives a brief biographical sketch of each novelist.
'. . . a somewhat unusual but good addition to the growing corpus of indigenous criticism of literature on Africa.'
Lemuel A. Johnson – *African Book Publishing Record*

African Language Literatures: an introduction to the literary history of Sub-Saharan Africa.
Harlow: Longman, 1981. 400 pp. £7.95
Washington D.C.: Three Continents Press, 1981. 400 pp. $35.00
A comprehensive, encyclopaedic survey of the development of African-language creative literatures. Gérard traces its growth from 14th century Ethiopian sacred writings through to the modern age and writing in the African languages today.

Gleason, Judith

This Africa: novels by West Africans in English and French
Evanston, Ill.: Northwestern Univ. Press, 1965. 186 pp. $8.25
A detailed analysis of twenty-five African novels, seventeen of them originally in French and eight in English. Styles and traditions are discussed in relation to their settings. Mrs Gleason groups her study under the following chapter headings: The styles of the conquerors; The heroic legacy in Africa; Village life; City life; and The inner life. A bibliography of books and articles is appended.
'This is a splendid book. Not only does it reveal the volume and vitality of West African fiction, but it is also a first-rate piece of literary criticism.'
Robert Cobb – *Africa Report*

Gordimer, Nadine

The Black Interpreters: notes on African writing
Johannesburg: Ravan Press, 1973. 76 pp. R2.00
This book consists of two sections. The first, 'Modern African fiction in English' defines African writing, traces its origins and directions; it identifies its five or so major themes, and comments on the central issue of politics as fate which runs through much of this literature. The second section is a selective paper on the work of new black poets writing in English in South Africa.

Goré, Jeanne-Lydie ed.
Négritude africaine, Négritude caraïbe
Paris: Université Paris-Nord, Centre d'Etudes Francophones, 1973. 160 pp.
A collection of the papers presented at the 1973 Colloqium on Négritude held at Centre d'Etudes Francophones, Paris. The theme of the colloquium attempted to show that there is not one version of Négritude but two, or even more, and in this case, African Négritude was contrasted with Caribbean Négritude – although still stressing the harmonious relationship between them. The papers deal with two main subjects: purely literary problems and the interplay of literature and ideology.
'All in all, this volume should leave some idea as to present thinking of the whole Négritude question.'
Keith Q. Warner – *Research in African Literatures*

Görög, Véronika
Noirs et blancs: leur image dans la littérature orale africaine: étude-anthologie
Paris: SELAF/CILF, 1976 (Langues et Civilizations à Tradition orale, 23) 477 pp. FF99.00
An extensive discussion and structural analysis of African narrative representations about the clash between the European colonialists and African peoples.
'. . . a very important book.'
Lee Haring – *Research in African Literatures*

Gouraige, Ghislain
Continuité noire
Dakar: Nouvelles Editions Africaines, 1977. 223 pp. CFA1,200
A critical study of the literature of the black diaspora based on the hypothesis that the destiny of black peoples on both sides of the Atlantic has been similar and has produced similar reactions.

Gowda, H. H. A. ed.
Essays in African Literature: Powre above powres
Mysore, India: Centre of Commonwealth Literature, Univ. of Mysore, 1978. 160 pp.
Brings together a wide ranging collection of essays on African writing. Contributors include Bruce King on 'Varieties of African literature', George Heron on Okot p'Bitek, Andrew Horn on drama in Uganda between 1962 to 1972, and Anniah Gowda on Soyinka.

Graham-White, Anthony
The Drama of Black Africa
New York: Samuel French, 1975. 220 pp.
A broad critical survey of African drama, with special attention given to Wole Soyinka and John Pepper Clark as examples of the 'literary' form and a chapter devoted to Herbert Ogunde as an exponent of the 'traditional' mode. The volume includes extensive footnotes, bibliography and a preface by Dapo Adelugba.
'. . . should serve as an excellent introduction to a field of investigation which is becoming more interesting not only to those concerned with African drama for its own sake, but also those who wish to deduce more general principles regarding the form and function of theatre in society.'
Donald Baker – *Research in African Literatures*

Grassin, Jean-Marie ed.
Mythe et littérature africaine: colloque afro-comparatiste de Limoges
Paris: l'Afrique Littéraire, 1979/1980. 119 pp. FF20.00
The assembled papers of the colloquium on myth and African literature that was held concurrently with the annual meeting of the French association of comparative literature in Limoges in 1977 have here been published in a double issue of *Afrique Littéraire* (nos. 54–55, 1979/1980). Robert Pageard spoke generally about myth in literature and eighteen other participants developed aspects of myth in tradition and contemporary African literature: the function and form of myth in African literature, the myth of tradition in Africanist literary criticism, traditional historical myths as they emerge in the media and in modern literature. There are four contributions on the use of myth in works by individual authors. Two other papers discuss myth in the literature of the French West Indies and the Cape Verde islands.

Gray, Stephen
Southern African Literature: an introduction
Cape Town: David Philip, 1979. 209 pp.
London: Rex Collings, 1979. 209 pp. £7.50
Gray identifies and assesses the different lines of development of literature written in English in the multilingual, multicultural subcontinent of Southern Africa. Includes a chapter 'The Emergence of Black English'. Among the generative themes traced are those of the Adamastor myth, the myth of the Hottentot Eve, the frontier, the hunter's paradise, the missionary-as-explorer, and landscape-as-presence.
'. . . He looks also at the emergence of black English, elucidates how social change and interchange effect

changes in language usage and literary forms, and reassesses established attitudes and practices, particularly that of editorially regularising manuscripts before publication . . . [an] . . attractively-presented volume illuminating and stimulating to read.'
                    Lionel Abrahams – *Rand Daily Mail*

Griffiths, Gareth
A Double Exile: African and West Indian writing between two cultures
London: Marion Boyars, 1978. 205 pp. £6.95 cased £3.95 p/b
New York: Humanities Press (distr.) $13.00
A comprehensive study of the major African and West Indian writers in the light of what Gareth Griffiths has chosen to call 'a double exile': 'Brought up in a culture radically different from that of England they have nevertheless chosen to write in English. They are therefore exiled culturally from the sources and traditions of that language and linguistically from the landscapes and peoples they write about'. Among the African novelists, the author discusses Achebe, Elechi Amadi, Ayi Kwei Armah, Ngugi, and Wole Soyinka, while from the West Indies, Michael Anthony, V. S. Reid, Andrew Salkey and V. S. Naipaul are treated among others.
'A Double Exile is thoughtful, well-written and poses to a certain extent the problems facing Africans and West Indians writing in English.'
                    – *West Africa*
'Distinguished for its analyses of novels and authors as well as for its interesting thesis. Recommended.'
                    – *Choice*

Gurr, Andrew and Calder, Angus eds.
Writers in East Africa: papers from a colloquium held at the University of Nairobi, June 1971
Nairobi: East African Lit. Bureau, 1974. 150 pp. K.shs.19.50 (£1.60/$4.00)
This is the second of two volumes which record some of the proceedings of the 1971 Festival of East African Writing. Based on the Writers' Workshop sessions which studied the problems of writers of different genres and works in progress, it includes contributions by Ali Mazrui, Jared Angira, Joe de Graft, Ole Kantai, Okello Oculi, and Okot p'Bitek. Central themes are the part played, and the contribution made, by literature to the quality of cultural life in East Africa, and there is a concerted search for local pointers to the ultimate standards and values guiding this life.
'. . . the most important question raised . . . is that it is necessary for African literary critics to come out with a criticism relevant to the African reality.'
                    Peter Nazareth – *Research in African Literatures*

Hale, T. A. a: d Priebe, R. O. eds.
The Teaching of African Literature: selected working papers from the African Literature Association
Austin, Texas: African Literature Association (distr. by Univ. of Texas Press). 1977. 331 pp. $20.00
A group of papers focusing on the teaching of African literature in the United States and around the world, selected from the inaugural and second meetings of the African Literature Association.

Hallett, George
African Writers Portfolio
London: HEB, 1981. Unpaged £3.95/$6.00
A portfolio of poster size (A3 format) portraits of sixteen of the best-known African authors by George Hallett, who has produced the cover photographs of many titles in Heinemann's 'African Writers Series'. The portraits included are those of Chinua Achebe, Mongo Béti, Dennis Brutus, Cyprian Ekwensi, Buchi Emecheta, Bessie Head, Mazisi Kunene, Alex la Guma, Meja Mwangi, Nuruddin Farah, Lenrie Peters, Tayeb Salih, Taban lo Liyong, Sembène Ousmane, Wole Soyinka, and the publishers have also added a photograph of Ngugi wa Thiong'o.

Hamilton, Russell G.
Voices from an Empire: a history of Afro-Portuguese literature
Minneapolis: Univ. of Minnesota Press, 1975. 450 pp. $17.95
The first extensive history of Lusophone African literature. Hamilton devotes five chapters each to the literatures of Angola, Mozambique and the Cape Verde Islands, and two chapters to writing from São Tomé and Príncipe. The works of individual writers are examined from political as well as aesthetic viewpoints. Numerous quotations, which are translated into English, and a select bibliography, citing hundreds of primary and secondary sources, are provided.
'Trata-se, com éfeito, da primeira tentativa de dar em livro, e de forma sistematizada, uma história global da literatura africana de expressão portuguesa. . . . São de destacar, pela sua penetração, as paginas dedicadas a Agostinho Neto, Craveirinha, Knopfli, J. F. Tenreiro, Jorge Barbosa.'
                    Fernando Martinho – *África*
'I would enthusiastically recommend Voices from an Empire *to all students of African literature, whatever the area of their own particular speciality. It is both pleasurable reading and an excellent reference book.'*
                    Janis L. Pallister – *Africa Today*

Heywood, Christopher ed.
Perspectives on African Literature: selections from the proceedings of the Conference on African Literatures at the University of Ife 1968
London: HEB (for Univ. of Ife Press), 1971 (SAL). 175 pp. £2.90
New York: Africana Publ. Corp., 1972.
192 pp. $17.50 cased $8.00 p/b
The thirteen essays reprinted from papers given at the Conference are presented here in four sections, each of which puts a different aspect of writing into critical perspective. The first 'Literature and criticism' includes contributions by Ngugi and Irele. The second concentrates on 'Language and style' when writing or translating into English. An examination of 'Particular forms' concentrates mainly on drama but also explores new popular fiction in Ghana, while 'Authors and their works' focuses on Soyinka, Laye, Peter Abrahams and David Rubadiri.
'. . . This collection is valuable for the variety of insights and opinions it presents, for the factual material offered and for the incidental references it makes to other literatures . . . the index is an important part of this book.'
G. D. Killam – *Research in African Literatures*

Papers on African Literature
Sheffield: Univ. of Sheffield; Dept. of English Literature, in assoc. with Africa Educational Trust, London, 1976.
Austin, Texas: Univ. of Texas Press, 1976.
127 pp. $20.00
A collection of eight papers presented at the Sheffield University 'Open Seminar Series' on African literature and art during 1975–76. The essays encompass various themes ranging from sex and politics in South Africa, folk tradition and a paper on Conrad's *Heart of Darkness*.
'On balance, Papers on African Literature *is a very worthwhile undertaking . . . The volume would be a useful supplement to one's personal collection of critical writing on African literature and should be placed near the top of any university's acquisition list.'*
Russell J. Linnemann – *Research in African Literatures*

Aspects of South African Literature
London: HEB, 1976 (SAL). 224 pp. £8.00 cased, £2.90 p/b
New York: Africana Publ. Corp., 1976.
207 pp. $15.50
A collection of papers from two conferences on South African writing held during 1975 in USA and UK, presented here in three sections: 'Yesterday', 'Transition' and 'Today'. Among these articles, critical assessments and historical surveys are essays by Alan Paton, Oswald Mtshali and Nadine Gordimer.
'A fine introduction by Christopher Heywood acknowledges that these papers sketch rather than study South African literature, but in lieu of more complete criticisms and scholarship in the field, this collection serves a necessary purpose – to begin.'
R. Moss – *World Literature Today*
'. . . a valuable study of the literature of this country, which has been curiously neglected by its own critics.'
John Povey – *ASA Review of Books*

Houannou, Adrien
Trois poètes béninois
Yaoundé: C.L.E. 1980. 119 pp. CFA1,200
An introduction to the works of three poets from Benin (formerly Dahomey) who have had an indelible influence on the literature of that country: Richard Dogbé, Eustache Prudencio and Agbossahessou. With an introductory essay, bio-bibliographies and studies of the principal themes of the poems included, this book is a literary study as well as an anthology.

Huntsberger, Paul E. comp.
Highland Mosaic: a critical anthology of Ethiopian literature in English
Athens, Ohio: Ohio Univ. Center for International Studies; Africa Program, 1973
(Papers in International Studies, Africa Series, 19). 133 pp. $4.00
Excerpts from Ethiopian literature, ancient and modern, are presented in English translation, and are accompanied by a critical overview of the literary tradition.

Irele, Abiola
The African Experience in Literature and Ideology
London: HEB, 1981 (SAL). 216 pp. $27.50 cased £5.95/$14.50 p/b
A collection of essays, spanning a period of some fifteen years and which were previously published in various journals, by a critic who has once been described as 'the commanding intelligence of modern African literary criticism'. Irele's approach to African literature has been commanded largely by the fact, 'that modern African literature offers a special challenge of *newness.*' A situation 'in which a new literature is being constituted as an exploration of a new area of experience and expression, [and] an important function of the critic becomes the determination of which works and which writers have value and meaning in relation to just such a situation'. The studies in the first part examine critical positions involved in the study and criticism of literature from Africa, and the question of

language. Part two considers Négritude and African nationalism, and the third section consists of individual literary studies, examining the works of Aimé Césaire, Réne Maran and Frantz Fanon in one essay; others discuss the development of the French African novel, as well as the works of three leading Yoruba writers, Fagunwa, Tutuola and Soyinka. The section concludes with an essay on Soyinka and the Nigerian crisis.

Ithier, Wasley
La littérature de langue française à l'île Maurice
Paris: Slatkine. 1981. 288 pp. FF130.00

Iyay, Kimoni
Destin de la littérature négro-africaine ou problematique d'une culture
Kinshasa: Presses Universitaires du Zaïre, 1975. 270 pp. FF12.70
Sherbrooke, Canada: Naaman, 1975. 270 pp.

Jabbi, B.-B.
West African Poems: fifteen analyses
Freetown: Fourah Bay College Bkshp. (distr.)
1974 (Outline Hints on African Literature, 2).
48 pp. 85c

Jadot, J. M.
Les écrivains africains du Congo belge et du Ruanda-Urundi: Une histoire, un bilan, des problèmes
Brussels: Académie Royale des Sciences Coloniales, Classe des Sciences Morales et Politiques, 1959 (Nouvelle série. Tome XVII, 2). 167 pp.
This study of the development of written literature in French in the former Belgian colonies of the Congo and Ruanda-Urundi starts by surveying the legal and institutional frameworks for the arts as conceived by the Belgians in their colonies, and then summarizes the role played by oral traditions before analysing developments in poetry, the novel, the short story, theatre, essay writing and journalism. Closes with a discussion of problems confronting would-be writers; economic and political problems (cultural domination) and problems relating to inspiration and language.

Jones, Edward A. comp.
Voices of Négritude: the expression of Black experience in the poetry of Senghor, Césaire and Damas
Valley Forge, Pa.: Judson Press, 1971. 125 pp. $4.95

Jones, Eldred D. ed.
African Literature Today
London: HEB, 1968–
New York: Africana Publ. Corp., 1968–
Nos. 1–4, 264 pp. £3.50/$14.95
The first four issues of this journal (later published as an annual survey) appeared between 1968 and 1970. They are combined in this omnibus edition with an index. Achebe, Armah, Beti, Brew, Clark, Ekwensi, Laye, Ngugi, Okigbo and Soyinka are some of the writers represented in articles and reviews.

No. 5 *The Novel in Africa*
1971. 156 pp. £1.95/$13.50
Emenyonu takes critics to task for inadequate research into the novelists' backgrounds, while Jack Moore questions the ideological bias in critics. *The River Between* (Ngugi), Soyinka's plays, Nzekwu's novels, the satire of Aluko and the language and action of Achebe's novels receive attention.
'What this number loses by concentrating on the novel is compensated for by the unity of focus and by the variety of critical approaches.'
    D. S. Izevbaye – *Research in African Literatures*

No. 6 *Poetry in Africa*
1973. 186 pp. £1.90 p/b/$17.50 cased
Okigbo, Brutus, Peters, Senghor and Soyinka are some of the poets included in this volume. Articles range from an examination of Algerian poetry to a consideration of obscurity and commitment in African poetry.

No. 7 *Focus on Criticism*
1974. 192 pp. £2.30 p/b/$17.50 cased
The critical debate on the search for an African aesthetic is taken up by Izevbaye, Iyasere, Emenyonu, Lindfors *et al*. In addition, Senghor, Ngugi, Oyono, Armah are the subject of articles.
'The views exposed are representative of the more important of the different approaches and schools of thought.'   – *British Book News*

No. 8 *Drama in Africa*
1976. 160 pp. £1.80 p/b/$16.50 cased
Nine essays by African and European critics as well as by African dramatists provide an overview of the present scope of drama in Africa, as well as giving an historical insight into its development.
'The awareness recorded in this impressive book adds self-analysis to critical analysis.'
                John Povey – *ASA Review of Books*

No. 9 *Africa, America and the Caribbean*
1977. 118 pp. £4.50/$18.00 cased £1.80 p/b
Cultural links between African and American

Blacks are identified in essays on the Haarlem Renaissance, on comparisons between Soyinka and LeRoi Jones and on Armah's response to America. Ideas of cultural universality are underpinned by comparisons with Irish nationalism, and Cuban and Haïtian literature.

'. . . *a collection of incisive and illuminating studies by well-known names.*'

Dubem Okafor – *Research in African Literatures*

No. 10 *Retrospect and Prospect*
1979. 266 pp. £7.50/$25.50 cased £3.50/$12.50 p/b
The seminal role of African writers in their societies is evident: this volume offers a reassessment of their writing. Ouologuem, Awoonor, Ngugi, Mphahlele, Rive, Ekwensi, Armah, and Nortje are examined in detail.

No. 11 *Myth, History and the Contemporary African Writer*
1980. 231 pp. £8.50/$00.00 cased £4.50/$0.00 p/b
Three essays by Okpewho, Iyasere and Kunene cover the theoretical area of myth, oral narrative and cosmology, in this volume which seeks to examine ways in which myth is germane to African writers and writing. The historical novel receives attention, as does Armah's vision of history. Relevant themes in the writings of Awoonor, Achebe, Amadi, and Soyinka are dealt with in the other essays.

'. . . *this volume is a useful source for further exploration into two vital themes – the agony and the ecstasy of being African in the 20th century.*'

C. C. Ihekaibeya – *South*

No. 12 *New Writing, New Approaches*
1981. 224 pp. £12.50 cased £5.50 p/b
New writers, or those who, for disparate reasons, have been somewhat neglected by the critics, receive attention: Okara, Serumaga, Kane, Ousmane, Rotimi, Munonye and Mariama Bâ are included.

Jordan, A. C.
Towards an African Literature: the emergence of literary form in Xhosa
Berkeley: Univ. of California Press, 1973 (Perspectives on Southern Africa, 6). 116 pp. $6.00
Twelve essays which originally appeared in successive issues of *Africa South* from 1958 to 1960, chart the development of Xhosa literature from preliterate times until the establishment of a written tradition from the point of view of an 'insider'. The first three chapters show the oral literature of the southern Bantu, including folktales, songs, poetry, riddles and proverbs. From chapter four the emphasis remains exclusively on the Xhosa tradition and the social forces that shaped its development.

'*In a field where there are few reliable publications, Jordan's account is unrivalled.*'

Jeff Opland – *Research in African Literatures*

'*An authoritative source for scholars, this book is also recommended for the lay reader interested in African literature.*' Claudia A. Baldwin – *Library Journal*

Kabongo, Bujitu
La littérature pour quoi faire?
Kinshasa: Ed. Critique Littéraire, 1975. 94 pp.
Questions the role of literary criticism and offers thoughts on the literature of Zaïre today. With a short bibliography.

Pour mieux comprendre la littérature au Zaïre
Kinshasa: Ed. de la Grue Couronnée, 1975. 156 pp.
Examines the different problems of the writer and the artist in Zaïre today.

Kahari, G. P.
The Search for Zimbabwean Identity: an introduction to the Black Zimbabwean novel
Gwelo, Zimbabwe: Mambo Press, 1980 (Mambo Writers Series). 160 pp.
The book presents an attempt to provide a systematic account of the development of the modern Zimbabwean novel in English. An introduction is followed by a detailed textual analysis of eight novels.

'*The book is recommended for anyone interested in the uses of Western literacy in contemporary African culture.*'

Gordon Douglas Killam – *The African Book Publishing Record*

Kayo, Patrice
Panorama de la littérature camerounaise
Baffousam, Cameroon: Librairie Panafricaine, 1978. 62 pp.
Kayo's survey aims to show the development and diversity of modern Cameroonian literature, taking into account the many languages in which it is written, by providing a bird's-eye view of the paths followed by its writers on the threshold of the country's third decade of independence.

Kennedy, J. Scott
In Search of African Theatre
New York: Charles Scribner's Sons, 1973. 186 pp. o/p
This book mainly concerns the theatre in Ghana and Nigeria and contains discussions and analyses of works by Clark, de Graft, Rotimi, Soyinka, Sutherland and others.

Kern, Anita
Women in West African Fiction
Washington D.C.: Three Continents Press,
1980. 300 pp. $17.00 cased $8.00 p/b
The author, long time resident in Nigeria, has
attempted to portray the image and treatment
of women in works by both male and female
African writers. Biographies of authors and a
bibliography are included.

Kesteloot, Lilyan
Négritude et situation coloniale
Yaoundé: C.L.E., 1970 (Point de vue, 6).
96 pp. CFA450
In English *translation*, see next entry.

Intellectual Origins of the African Revolution
(Trans. from the French by A. Mboukou)
Washington: Black Orpheus Press, 1972
(Dimensions of Black Intellectual Experience).
128 pp. $8.50 cased
A comprehensive survey and analysis of
African protest writing in French which
commences with the publication of *Batouala: a
True Black Novel* by René Maran from
Martinique in 1921. The book exposes the
brutalities and hypocrisies of colonialism and
makes ample use of quotations from African
writers, among whom are Alioune Diop,
Léopold Senghor and Aimé Césaire.
'. . . *a valuable book, one which offers insights into
the colonial situation, its mentality and its legacies.*'
Jean Kennedy – *Research in African Literatures*

*Les écrivains noirs de langue française:
naissance d'une littérature*
Brussels: Université Libre de Bruxelles,
Institut de Sociologie, 1965 (3rd rev. ed.).
340 pp. FB380.00
In English *translation*, see next entry.

*Black Writers in French: a literary history of
Négritude*
(Trans. from the French by E. C. Kennedy)
Philadelphia: Temple Univ. Press, 1974.
401 pp. $12.50
A history and analysis in great depth of black
African writing in French. The book grew out
of a doctoral thesis submitted to the University
of Brussels in 1961 and has been through seven
printings in the original French (the latest in
1977). The history of the Négritude movement is analysed in detail and there is
heavy emphasis on the writings of Aimé
Césaire (from Martinique), Léon Damas
(from Guyana), Frantz Fanon (also from
Martinique), Birago Diop, Léopold Senghor,
David Diop and Jacques Rabemamanjara. A
comprehensive bibliography is appended.
'. . . *very readable and a valuable sociological and*

literary document.' S. K. Dagbo – *African Affairs*
'*Chief of its virtues is the very full and careful
historical research into the genesis and intellectual
ambience of Négritude in the years 1928–48 . . . a
monument to critical understanding, scholarship and
imaginative sympathy.*'
Gerald Moore – *Research in African Literatures*

Killam, G. D. ed.
African Writers on African Writing
London: HEB, 1972 (SAL). 165 pp. £6.50
cased, £2.95 p/b.
A representative collection of essays, articles
and interviews by African writers concerning
their own and other people's writings. The
essays treat the political, social and cultural
problems of Africa and how they affect the
author's work. Among the range of subjects
discussed are the ideology of Négritude,
historical surveys of African literature and the
racial policies of South Africa. Contributors
include Chinua Achebe, Ama Ata Aidoo,
Nadine Gordimer, Camera Laye and Ali
Mazrui.
'*It is an admirable introduction to the study of
African literature, especially for those whose acquaintance with the subject is either recent or shallow.*'
Juliet I. Okonkwo – *Research in
African Literatures*

Kimoni, Iyay
*Destin de la littérature négro-africaine ou
problèmatique d'une culture*
Sherbrooke, Canada: Ed. Naaman, 1975
(Littératures, 4). 273 pp. Can $15.00
Kinshasa: Presses Universitaires du Zaïre, 1975
(Thèses en Sciences Humaines, 6). 273 pp.
Z6.20
A history of black writing from its Harlem
renaissance and Négritude origins – two
landmarks in the desire of black intellectuals to
have an autonomous culture. The historical
survey, itself, is written up in the first part, and
it is followed by a study of the factors
contributing to the achievement of autonomy
– the role of ethnographers and the surrealist
movement. Particular attention is given in Part
III to the way writers see their culture through
the novel form. The conclusion speaks about
the role of literature in the renaissance of
African culture. A lengthy bibliography and an
index are appended.

King, Bruce ed.
Introduction to Nigerian Literature
London: Evans in assoc. with the Univ. of
Lagos Press, 1971.
224 pp. o/p
New York: Africana Publ. Corp., 1972. $17.50
cased

The editor has brought together a collection of essays which attempt to identify the aspects of the writings of Nigerian authors – their failures as well as their triumphs. Particular reference is made to Edo, Yoruba and Hausa literature and there is also a study on Caribbean literature in relation to Nigeria and to Africa in general.

'This is an excellent book to recommend to students.'
– African Studies Review

Literatures of the World in English
London: Routledge and Kegan Paul, 1974.
225 pp. £6.00/$15.95
A collection of essays by ten critic-scholars each surveying one national literature in English: Australia, Brian Elliott; Canada, Peter Stevens; England, William Walsh; India, B. Rajan; Ireland, A. Norman Jeffares; Kenya, Douglas Killam; Nigeria, D. S. Izevbaye; South Africa, John Povey; United States, Bruce King; West Indies, Kenneth Ramchand. The book attempts to show that there is much to connect the thought, perception and expression of the many different peoples who read and write English.

'Having allowed his contributors freedom to explore each of their national literatures in a variety of approaches, he has put together a miscellany of often brilliant insights and comments . . . His book then is useful and valuable as an impressionistic outline and chart of the rich body of material selected for study.'
Martin Tucker *– Research in African Literatures*

King, Bruce and Ogungbesan, Kolawole eds.
A Celebration of Black and African Writing
Ibadan: OUP (in assoc. with Ahmadu Bello Univ. Press), 1975. 269 pp. ₦10.00 ($25.75)
A collection of nineteen essays which provide an introduction to the study of black literature in Africa, the Caribbean and the United States, showing how the shared political and economic experiences of black peoples led to the search for an authentic black and African culture. Essays devoted to Césaire, Wright, Ellison, Senghor, Laye, Ousmane, Achebe, Soyinka and Ngugi emphasize the rediscovery of traditional culture and the critique of Western cultural values as a constant theme in their work. There are also essays on U'Tamsi, Guillen, Damas and Wilson Harris, plus surveys of early black writing in South Africa, and recent writing in East Africa and Sierra Leone.

'The collection does offer practical examples of the kind of critical modes which are desirable and necessary in the study of black literature . . . the editor's stated goal is "to offer a panoramic view of the modern black and African cultural and intellec-tual heritage"; and this goal is comfortably achieved by the stronger studies.'
Lloyd W. Brown *– Research in African Literatures*

New English Literatures: cultural nationalism in a changing world
London: Macmillan, 1980 (Macmillan International College Editions; Macmillan New Literature Handbooks). 259 pp. £12.00 cased £4.50 p/b
A comparative study of literatures written in English in those nations which have emerged from the former British empire into new independence since the Second World War. A summary of literature in colonial society sets the scene for the investigation into why these new literatures developed when they did, how they related to local nationalism, to each other, and to world-wide English-speaking culture generally. Major authors – Achebe, Soyinka and the Ogun myth in the case of Nigeria, for example – are discussed, as the author explores the origins, themes and contexts of creative writing in each of the new nations covered. (A section on the West Indies discusses Naipaul, Harris, Walcott and Braithwaite).

Klíma, Vladimír
Modern Nigerian Novels
Prague: Oriental Institute, 1969. 204 pp.
London: C. Hurst distr. 1970 (Dissertationes Orientales, 18). 204 pp. £3.25
A survey of Nigerian fiction during the years 1954–66 and the context in which it developed. Topics discussed include art form and language, politics and literature; synopses of Nigerian novels and biographical notes on their authors are included.

'Modern Nigerian Novels will be of particular interest to the serious student of African literature, as well as to the comparatist for the light it sheds on the murky depths of cross-cultural criticism. On a different level, it can serve the more casual reader looking for insight into the backdrop of Nigerian novels.'
Rand Bishop *– Research in African Literatures*

South African Prose Writing in English
London: Hurst, 1971. 202 pp.

Klíma, Vladimír; Růžička, Frantisek; Zima, Petr
Black Africa. Literature and Language
Prague: Academia Publishing House, 1976. 310 pp. Kcs.115.00
Dordrecht, Netherlands: D. Reidel, 1976. 310 pp.
A comprehensive survey of the literature of

black Africa from its beginnings to the present day. Combining linguistic methods with literary analysis, it focuses attention on oral tradition and folklore and deals with writing in the European (French, English, Portuguese) as well as African languages from all parts of the continent. There is information about cultural life in Africa and the influence of African elements on European languages is analysed. Includes a chapter on literary criticism.

'This book deserves close consideration for its objectives and its methods, for their advantages and shortcomings . . . The diversity of interests among the members of the team accounts for the wide-embracing quality of the book.'
Albert S. Gérard – *Research in African Literatures*

Krog, E. W. ed.
African Literature in Rhodesia
Gwelo, Zimbabwe: Mambo Press, 1966.
236 pp. 50c
The papers from the National Creative Writers Conference, held at Ranche House College, Salisbury, in 1964, on the topic of the vernacular literature of Rhodesia. In addition to a series of critical essays on a variety of subjects, there are detailed analyses of major Shona novels and poems and novels in Ndebele.

Larson, Charles R.
The Novel in the Third World
Washington D.C.: Inscape, 1976. 201 pp.
$16.00
A discussion of ten novels by writers from African countries, India, and other Third World nations. They include Ouologuem's *Bound to Violence* and Bessie Head's *A Question of Power,* and are discussed in an order that 'reflects the development of the Third World novel'.

The Emergence of African Fiction
Bloomington, Ind.: Indiana Univ. Press, 1972 (distr. by Three Continents Press, Washington D.C.). 305 pp. $15.00 cased $5.00 p/b
London: Macmillan, 1978 (2nd rev. ed.), (Macmillan International College Editions).
312 pp. £2.95
An individual approach to the development of African fiction since Amos Tutuola's *Palm-Wine Drinkard* of 1952, with substantial sections on Laye, Achebe, Soyinka, Ngugi wa Thiong'o, Peter Abrahams, Lenrie Peters, Armah, and Ekwensi. The origins and development of Onitsha Market literature are also examined, and the author shows how all the writers with whom he deals have forged a new, African mode of writing, suggesting the

inadequacy of Western literary criticism to an appreciation of the new fiction.

'Occasionally, if inconsistently, Larson offers some insightful and illuminating observations on African literature in general . . . but most importantly, he treats the literature as art, a consideration African fiction has long deserved.'
Solomon Ogbede Iyasere – *African Literature Today*

Panorama du roman africain
(Trans. from the English by Alain Ricard)
Paris: Ed. Inter-Nationales, 1974 (distr. by Hachette, Paris). (Nouveaux horizons, L97).
350 pp.
A French translation of the preceding entry (available in Africa *only*.)

Laurence, Margaret
Long Drums and Cannons: Nigerian dramatists and novelists
London: Macmillan, 1968. 208 pp.
New York: Praeger, 1969. 208 pp.
Long Drums and Cannons – a title adapted from Christopher Okigbo's poem 'Heavensgate' – is a critical interpretation of the works of modern Nigerian dramatists and novelists; it is 'an attempt to show that Nigerian prose writing in English has now reached a point where it must be recognized as a significant part of the world literature'. The first five chapters are devoted to an analysis and appreciation of works by Soyinka, Clark, Achebe, Tutuola, and Ekwensi. Chapter six, 'Other Voices', deals with Aluko, Amadi, Nwankwo, Nwapa, Nzekwu and Okara. An epilogue and bibliography by the author completes the volume.

'. . . the value of the volume lies in its commendable unity and the assistance it might give to the student who wishes to arrive at the center of Nigerian works without too much pain. The plots are there, fully described for him, and the judgments are never too risky or adventurous to be off center.'
Lewis Nkosi – *Africa Report*

Lebel, Roland
Etudes de littérature coloniale
Paris: Peyronnet et Cie., 1928. 216 pp. o/p
One of the earliest volumes in which mention is made of black African writing in French (pages 157–168), although the greater part of the work is devoted to the writing of French people living in France's colonies, or to works which simply evoke the exotic colonial setting.

Le livre du pays noir
Paris: Ed. du Monde Moderne, 1928. 251 pp.
o/p

Leiner, Jacqueline
Imaginaire – langage – identité culturelle – négritude: Afrique, France, Guyane, Haïti, Maghreb, Martinique
Tübingen, West Germany: Gunter Narr Verlag, 1980 (Études littéraires françaises, 10).
167 pp. DM44.80
Paris: Jean Michel Place, 1980.
A critical study of literature written in French by writers concerned with the legacy of French colonialism: Fanon, Malek Haddad, Albert Memmi, Léon-Gontran Damas, René Depestre, Césaire, Camara Laye, Senghor and Malraux. There are three main themes: Language and identity; Language – the imaginary world and Négritude; Literature – language and cultural identity. This last section contains transcripts of interviews with Memmi, Laye, Césaire and Senghor, in which each writer discusses the problems of expressing a cultural identity in a colonial language.

Leusse, Hubert de
Afrique occidentale: heurts et malheurs d'une rencontre. Les romanciers du pays noirs
Paris: Ed. de l'Orante, 1971. 296 pp.
Focuses on the theme of acculturation in the African novel as seen through the study of the student-heros of Camara Laye (Fatoman, the happy child of *L'enfant noir* and the 'good student' of *Dramouss*), of Ouologuem (Kassoumi, the 'mad student' of *Le devoir de violence*), of Dadié (Climbié, the 'disappointed student'), of Kane (Samba Diallo, the 'desperate student' of *L'aventure ambiguë*), and of a number of other authors and their works. Evokes in his conclusion the problems of education and the need to search for a new social equilibrium which he feels can be supplied by an ideology like Négritude.

Lézou, Gérard Dago
La création romanesque devant les transformations actuelles en Côte-d'Ivoire
Dakar: Nouvelles Editions Africaines, 1977. 259 pp. CFA1,900
Begins with a discussion of how the Eburnean novelist conceives of the notion of time and milieu and then devotes a section to how the different Africans are portrayed in the novel – colonial Africa, traditional Africa, Africa of myths, developing Africa. A third part evokes the land of the white man in the novel and speaks about the relationship between the writer and his reader and the writer and his people. Outlines the prospects of the novel form in the Ivory Coast in conclusion.

Lillis, K. M.
African Literary Appreciation
London: Hodder and Stoughton, 1975.
144 pp. £1.50
Presents a series of passages of African prose and poetry, together with a range of questions on each extract. The aim of the book, which is intended for students taking GCE Advanced level courses or English courses in their first year at university, is to provide stimuli which will encourage students to think precisely about what they read and write, and to be accurate and sensitive in their use of language.

Lindfors, Bernth; Munro, Ian; Priebe, Richard; Sander, Reinhard eds.
Palaver: interviews with five African writers in Texas
Austin, Texas: Univ. of Texas Press, distr., 1972 (Occasional Publications, African Literature, 3). 63 pp. $2.50
Transcripts of interviews with Chinua Achebe, John Pepper Clark, Dennis Brutus, Ezekiel Mphahlele, and Kofi Awoonor, assembled from 1969 to 1971. Each writer had been invited to the university campus at Austin to deliver a public lecture and meet with African literature classes. The lively question forums and private interviews which followed these lectures are recorded here. Issues discussed include not only the views of each author on his own writing and current African problems, but also the role and influence of the writer in African society and the concept of Négritude.

Lindfors, Bernth ed.
Dem-say: interviews with eight Nigerian writers
Austin, Texas: Univ. of Texas Press, distr., 1974 (Occasional Publications in African Literature, 9). 79 pp. $2.50
The ninth occasional publication by the African and Afro-American Studies and Research Center contains transcripts of interviews with Michael J. C. Echeruo, Obi Egbuna, Cyprian Ekwensi, John Munonye, Gabriel Okara, Kole Omotoso, Ola Rotimi, and Kalu Uka, recorded in Nigeria in 1972–3.
'... offers some poignant revelations about each writer's background and psyche, his definition of literature, the relationship between literature and life, thought on the Nigerian situation, and the much publicized civil war ... The interviews are a meticulously wrought whole; they are interrelated components which owe their oneness to the sincerity and genuine commitment of the eight writers concerned'.

Femi Ojo-Ade – *World Literature Written in English*

Lindfors, Bernth and Schild, Ulla eds.

Neo-African Literature and Culture: essays in memory of Jahnheinz Jahn
Wiesbaden, West Germany: B. Heymann, 1976 (Mainzer Afrika Studien, 1). 352 pp. DM68.00
A collection of 28 essays in honour of the late Jahnheinz Jahn presented at the Symposium held at the Mainz Institut für Ethnologie und Afrika-Studien. Written in English and French the essays include not only personal tributes like Ulla Schild's 'Bibliography of the works of Jahnheinz Jahn' but also critical and historical examinations of aspects of the development of literature forms in East, West and South Africa and the West Indies this century.

Lindfors, Bernth ed.

Critical Perspectives on Nigerian Literatures
Washington D.C.: Three Continents Press, 1976. 300 pp. $15.00
London: HEB, 1979 (Critical Perspectives Series). 304 pp. £4.95
A sampling of critical essays, with emphasis on the oral tradition, devoted to Nigerian literatures that originally appeared (with one exception) in *Research in African Literatures*. The three major literatures – Yoruba, Hausa and Igbo – and the most important authors writing in English – are covered in some detail. Includes a select bibliography of critical writing on Nigerian literatures.
'. . . illustrates the coming of age of the body of criticism represented and especially the healthy development of this discipline among Africans themselves . . . Lindfors' extensive bibliography . . . is particularly complete regarding African periodicals and African theatre.'
            Harold Collins – *ASA Review of Books*
'The book is encouraging. It is exemplary of a move from overly generalized studies on African literature to more specialized commentaries. For both teacher and student this volume can serve as a useful tool.'
            Janis A. Mayes – *World Literatures Written in English*

Mazungumzo: interviews with East African writers, publishers, editors and scholars
Athens, Ohio and London: Ohio Univ. Center for International Studies, 1980 (Papers in International Studies, Africa series, 41). 179 pp. $16.00/£7.80
These interviews with thirteen East African writers, editors, and publishers were recorded in 1976, and they offer 'a sample of the collective energy that has produced a distinctive regional African literature in less than two decades.' Among the writers interviewed are Taban lo Liyong, David Maillu, Meja Mwangi, Peter Nazareth, Grace Ogot, Okot

p'Bitek, and Chris Wanjala. Lindfors also provides biographical notes and a bibliography.

Lintsen, E.

Study Guide: African novels
Tabora, Tanzania: Tanzania Mission Press, 1975 (Study Guide Series). 16 pp. T.shs.1.00.

Littératures *de langue française hors de France: anthologie didactique*
Sèvres, France: Féderation Internationale des Professeurs de Français, 1976 (distr. by Ed. Duculot, Gembloux, Belgium). 704 pp.
Includes extracts of the works of thirty-three authors from black Africa, Madagascar, and Mauritius with a brief bio-bibliography for each author. A chronological table at the end of the volume relates literary and cultural landmarks to the principal political and economic events in Africa and the Indian Ocean, beginning in the mid-nineteenth century. There is a general index of authors anthologized. Alain Ricard has written the historical introduction to the section on Africa.

Littératures *d'expression française: négritude africaine, négritude caraïbe*
Paris: Ed. de la Francité, 1973. 159 pp.
The assembled papers of a colloquium held at the Centre d'Etudes francophones (Université Paris-Nord) on January 26–27, 1973. Part I presents papers of a more historical or descriptive nature with discussions of the ecological sources of black African literature; on the passage from the oral to the written tradition, of race and literary history, of the factors influencing the novel genre in francophone Africa, of the teaching of African literature in Africa, of nineteenth-century precursors, of surrealism and black poetry, as well as individual contributions on René Maran, Eugène Derain, and of Málagasy, Togolese and Gabonese writing. The presentations in Part II are more polemical in nature, questioning the myths of Négritude, wondering if there is only one Négritude, affirming the dangers of Négritude or criticizing Négritude as a revolutionary concept.

Littératures *ultramarines de langue française: genèse et jeunesse. Littératures négro-africaine, antillaise, québecoise, franco-américaine et comparee*
Sherbrooke, Canada: Ed. Naaman, 1974. 160 pp. Can$10.00
Papers from a colloquium held at the University of Vermont at Burlington on June 14 and 15, 1971, including the opening address by

Léopold Sédar Senghor (who also prefaced the bound volume). Among contributions are papers by Irene Jackson on Négritude ('Morale d'un phénomène'), by Eric Sellin on Ouologuem and Kourouma ('Le nouveau roman africain') and by Gilbert Sherman on Kane's *L'aventure ambiguë* and its impact on black Americans.

Little, Kenneth
The Sociology of Urban Women's Image in African Literature
London: Macmillan, 1980. 174 pp. £12.00
Totowa, N.J.: Rowman and Littlefield, 1980.
174 pp. $27.50
Summarizes and analyses the plots of some forty novels and short stories involving women, covering largely West African fiction. Certain characterizations (and stereotypes) of women emerge, which are brought together into these chapter headings: 'Girl friends and good-time girls', 'Wives', ' "Free" women', 'Mothers', 'Courtesans and prostitutes', and ' "Political" women and workers'.

Liyong, Taban lo
Thirteen Offensives against Our Enemies
Nairobi: East African Literature Bureau, 1973.
124 pp. K.shs.9.50 (£1.00/$2.50)
In his unique style, Taban lo Liyong presents his interpretations of modern African issues arising from the colonial and neo-colonial presence. These interpretations take the form of essays, poems, responses to criticism and other tracts, and include discussions of the intellectual and the role of the creative artist in contemporary Africa. They are presented in the form of the 'Thirteen battles' which Africa must undertake against her enemies within and without, and are spiced with humour, irony and anger.

The Last Word, Cultural Synthesism
Nairobi: EAPH, 1969. 210 pp. K.shs.30.00
cased K.shs.8.00 p/b. ($5.80 cased $2.60 p/b)
The first critical commentary on African literature to be published in East Africa, this is a collection of essays some of which have previously appeared in *Transition, Busara, Africa Report* and elsewhere. Contents include Taban lo Liyong's thoughts on Tutuola and the subject of Négritude. There is a commentary on Okot p'Bitek's *Song of Lawino*; reviews of Ngugi's *Weep not Child* and David Cook's anthology *Origin East Africa*. Among other chapter titles are 'Tibble, Tutuola, Taban and Thugs', 'Negroes are not Africans', and 'African Students in Washington D.C.'.
Taban's books, especially The Last Word *rank among the most seriously discussed East African*

books, only months after their appearance . . . one of the most outspoken commentaries on black people published in Africa up to the present.'
A. S. Bukenya – *Mawazo*
'With this slim book of essays he introduces himself as a powerful voice, a spectacular and audacious intelligence . . . His work is contentious, irreverent, and exciting . . . He writes on what interests him – and that, often, is what angers him: American arrogance, African self-indulgence, intellectual slackness, pettiness . . . His book is a Magna Carta for African greatness.'* Basil Busacca – *Africa Report*

Lubin, Maurice A.
Afrique et politique
Paris: La Pensée Universelle, 1973. 156 pp.
Washington D.C.: Three Continents Press, distr. $5.00
A study of twelve African politicians and their writings. Chapter one affirms that political writing in Africa today is a literary genre like any other and must not be neglected by students. This volume was the result of a class that the author taught at Howard University.

Madjri, Dovi J.
Sociologie de la littérature togolaise
Lomé: Ministère de la Culture, 1975. 175 pp.
The five chapters in this work devoted essentially to contemporary Togolese literature treat oral literature, the changes brought about by the urban culture, religious and social influences, literary characters and social change, and the relationship of literary creation to literary genres. Includes a dictionary of Togolese authors and a bibliography. Robert Cornevin has written a postface.

Madubuike, Ihechukwu
The Senegalese Novel: a sociological study of the impact of the politics of assimilation
Washington D.C.: Three Continents Press, 1980. 270 pp. $18.00 cased $7.00 p/b
Most Senegalese novels (with the exception of Bakary Diallo's *Force Bonté*, Paris, 1926), have been called passive or non-militant as far as their attitudes to colonialism are concerned. However, Madubuike argues that most Senegalese writers did indeed challenge the tenets of the politics of assimilation and were critical of the colonial administration.

Maes-Jelinek, Hena ed.
Commonwealth Literature and the Modern World
Brussels: Didier, 1975. 182 pp.
Contains 17 papers delivered at a conference on Commonwealth literature held at the University of Liège in April 1974. Contributions on African writing include 'Towards a

history of South African literature' by Albert Gérard; 'The Nigerian Civil War in Nigerian literature' by Arthur Ravenscroft; and 'Wole Soyinka talking through his hat' by Bernth Lindfors. The latter is an article on Soyinka's public entertainment programmes on Nigerian radio some twenty years ago, which demonstrates that radio stations in Africa frequently hold remarkable collections of important materials.

'*As a compendium of ideas on [the] peculiar position of Commonwealth literature in the modern world, and as an anthology of reflections on individual writers, this volume should serve well in university courses which are bringing readers and Commonwealth writers together.*'
　　　　　Robert E. McDowell – *Research in African Literatures*

Mahood, M. M.
Colonial Encounter
London: Rex Collings, 1977. 228 pp. £4.75
Presents critical studies of six books by writers from the British Commonwealth, including Achebe's *Arrow of God*.

Makouta-Mboukou, Jean-Pierre
Introduction à la littérature noire
Yaoundé: C.L.E., 1970 (Point de vue, 2).
164 pp. o/p
In English translation, see next entry.

Black African Literature: an introduction
(Trans. from the French by A. Mboukou).
Washington D.C.: Black Orpheus Press, 1973
(Dimensions of Black Intellectual Experience).
161 pp. $9.50 cased $2.95 p/b
Guides the reader through the heritage of oral literature, the concept of Négritude, and the topics which inspired the emerging Black African literature. Focuses on Oyono's *Houseboy*, Laye's *The Dark Child* (*The African Child*), Kane's *Ambiguous Adventure* and Roumain's *Masters of the Dew*, and calls for more 'complimentarity' between writing from Africa and the West.

Introduction à l'étude du roman africain de langue française
Dakar: Nouvelles Editions Africaines, 1980.
350 pp. CFA3,250
Yaoundé: C.L.E., 1980. 350 pp. CFA3,250
In this study the author endeavours to relate the francophone African novel to its political and philosophical intentions as well as to traditional African literary genres. He reviews what has been said on the subject of the blending of cultures (*métissage culturel*) and on

the problem of authenticity and looks at the hero in the novel. In a second part he discusses the origins of the novel genre in African writing, the linguistic problem it raises and its political role. A survey of other writing enables him to speak generally about the problems confronting authors and to note that certain genres, like autobiography and the diary, have been neglected by writers. In his preface he takes African writers to task for having written very little on the theory of their art, thus being consumers rather than producers of literary theory.

Makward, Edris, and Lacy, Leslie eds.
Contemporary African Literature
New York: Random House, 1972. 469 pp.

Manganyi, Noel Chabani
Mashangu's Reverie and other essays
Johannesburg: Ravan Press, 1977. 106 pp.
R5.90 cased R4.50 p/b
The essays in this book are concerned with violence. The title essay was written while Manganyi was at Yale and 'there is a sense in which the fragments which formed themselves into the story . . . are autobiographical'. Mashangu was a visiting fellow at an east coast Ivy-League university; the essay is a loosely knit account of his introspection and the surfacing of pent-up rage at racial indignities previously suffered. This essay is followed by a clinical appraisal of the feelings of love and hate that were its basis; while other essays explore the attitudes of black South Africans to the victory in Mozambique of Frelimo, and there is a philosophical appraisal of university education in South Africa.

'*While this collection of autobiographical essays does not rank with such South African classics as* Road to Ghana *and* Home and Exile *in style or content, it does gives the reader an insight into the complexity of an individual South African intellectual, and perhaps more important, it gives a sense of the "eclipse of reason" which permeates much of South African life.*'
　　　　　Randall L. Davenport – *World Literature Today*

Massa, Daniel ed.
Individual and Community in Commonwealth Literature
Valetta, Malta: Malta Univ. Press, 1979.
241 pp. M£3.00
Contains the papers presented at the A.C.L.S. Spring 1978 conference. Concerning African writing, there are essays on Ngugi, Bessie Head, Jared Angira, Soyinka, and Alex La Guma. Other contributions are Bernth Lindfors's 'Indigenous performance in alien

communities', and Cecil Abrahams's 'Literature and commitment'.

Mbele, Majola ed.
Viewpoints. Essays on literature and drama
Nairobi: Kenya Lit. Bureau, 1980. 102 pp.
K.shs. 22.50 (£2.90/$7.35)
A collection of six essays which previously appeared in *Umma*, the literary magazine from the Department of Literature at the University of Dar es Salaam. It includes two contributions on African theatre: 'African theatre a call for change' by James Birihanze, and 'On the social function of modern African theatre and Brecht'.

Mbwil a Mpaang, Ngal
Tendences actuels de la littérature africaine d'expression française
Kinshasa: Ed. Mont Noir, 1973 (Objectif, 80). 62 pp.

Melone, Thomas
De la négritude dans la littérature négro-africaine
Paris: Présence Africaine, 1962. 141 pp. o/p
Examines the philosophy of Négritude through an analysis of the major writings by French-African novelists and poets.

Melone, Thomas ed.
La littérature africaine à l'âge de la critique
Paris: Gallimard, 1972. 198 pp.
A special issue of *Diogène* (no. 80, October–December 1972) prepared by Thomas Melone and his research team at the Federal University of Cameroun in Yaoundé. Articles by Thomas Melone ('Cheikh Hamidou Kane et la folie'), by Louis-Marie Ongoum ('Mythe et littérature en Afrique'), by Joseph-Marie Awouma ('Le mythe de l'âge, symbole de la sagesse dans la société et la littérature africaines'), by Jourdain-Innocent Noah ('Les contes béti du Sud-Cameroun: le cycle de Kaiser'), and by Pierre Tchoungui ('Imagologie et ethno-psychologie littéraires: le Cameroun dans le miroir de ses écrivains'). Introduction by Roger Caillois.

Melone, Thomas *et al.*
Mélanges africains
Yaoundé: Faculté des Lettres, Equipe de Recherches en Littérature Africaine Comparée, 1973. 376 pp. CFA3,000
Fifteen articles (thirteen in French, two in English) by professors and researchers of African literature present critical viewpoints of the great stages and writers of Africa and the West Indies: Négritude; Senghor, Césaire, Maran, Mongo Béti, C. H. Kane; the recurrent

myths of oral literature; the anglophone diaspora in Kenya, Nigeria, the U.S. Looks at both general issues and specific works.

Mérand, Patrick
La vie quotidienne en Afrique noire à travers la littérature africaine d'expression française
Paris: L'Harmattan, 1977. 240 pp. FF49.00
Illustrates the daily life of Africans by quoting from works of Francophone African literature. Arranged thematically with chapters on nature and environment; birth and early childhood; school; marriage; married life and women's condition; daily life; professional life; leisure; communication and the media; family, community, country; illness; death; the idea of God. With a bibliography of literary works.

Michaud, Guy ed.
Négritude: traditions et développement
Brussels: Ed. Complexe, 1978. 184 pp.
The proceedings of two colloquiums organized by the Centre d'Etude des Civilisations of the University of Paris-X in 1976 and 1977. An article of Mongo Béti criticizes ethnocentrism and the notion of tradition and another by L. V. Thomas speaks about the relationship of oral and written elements in African literature. Guy Michaud concludes the volume.

Milbury-Steen, Sarah L.
European and African Stereotypes in Twentieth-Century Fiction
London: Macmillan, 1980. 200 pp. £15.00
An examination of images of Europeans and Africans depicted in novels published between 1921 and 1976. All are set in West Africa with the exception of one which is set in Central Africa, and include not only French and English colonial works but also anglophone and francophone West African ones. The book is in two parts – devoted to how Europeans look at Africans, and vice versa. Each part traces the origins of the stereotypes – in the writings of 'racial theorists', colonial adventures and administrators on the one hand, and in oral traditions on the other – and discusses works which preserve, contradict or transcend them.

Mmadu, C.
Guide to African Poetry
Onitsha, Nigeria: University Publishers, 1977. 95 pp. ₦1.50

Moore, Gerald ed.
African Literature and the Universities
Ibadan: Ibadan University Press (for Congress for Cultural Freedom), 1965. 152 pp. ₦3.50

The record of two seminars held at the University of Dakar and at Fourah Bay College, the University of Sierra Leone, in March and April 1963. The conferences grew out of a conviction that university initiative throughout Africa was needed to ensure the introduction of African literature to first-degree arts courses. There are papers on the African novel, poetry and Négritude, with a record of lively and at times heated discussions among the participants. These included Ezekiel Mphahlele, Janheinz Jahn, Camara Laye, Sembène Ousmane, Eldred Jones, Davidson Nicol, and many others.
'. . . one of Gerald Moore's best contributions to African literary studies . . . the meetings, and the resulting book shed new light on the communications gap and the differences in approach between the two leading intellectual and literary traditions in contemporary Africa.'
Ellen Conroy Kennedy – *Africa Report*

The Chosen Tongue: English writing in the tropical world
London: Longman, 1969. 222 pp. illus.
New York: Harper and Row, 1970. 222 pp.
A critical examination of English writing of tropical Africa and the Caribbean. In Moore's words, 'quite apart from their common use of English, these areas have direct historical, cultural and ethnic links with one another.' The study is grouped around four central themes: 'The Islands', 'The Continent', 'The City', and 'Guinea'. Its literary achievements are evaluated in the light of the historical, geographical, social and cultural backgrounds that have helped to shape its development.
'. . . a work which from start to finish impresses with its structural and thematic unity . . . should be read, I warmly recommend, for its scholarly excellence and perceptive critical insights into the literature it surveys, however disturbing its undercurrent of linguistic nationalism.'
Sunday O. Anozie – *The Conch*
'. . . Taking Moore's new book together with Seven African Writers, his work is the most rigorous and sensitive criticism yet written on African and Caribbean authors. Moore's commentary is informative and sensible in content, and eminently readable in expression.'
R. W. Noble – *West Africa*

Twelve African Writers
London: Hutchinson, 1980 (University Library for Africa). 327 pp. £12.60 cased £4.95 p/b
Bloomington: Indiana Univ. Press, 1980.
327 pp. $22.50 cased
A critical introduction to twelve of Africa's most significant and well established contemporary authors, whose work represents Anglophone and Francophone writing and drawn from West, East and Southern Africa. The richness and range of the continent's writing is demonstrated in studies of Senghor, Ezekiel Mphahlele, Ousmane, Laye, La Guma, Achebe, Tchicaya U'Tamsi, Okot p'Bitek, Mongo Béti, Soyinka, Awoonor, and Ngugi. The book is a revised, updated and expanded edition of *Seven African Writers*, originally published in 1962 by Oxford University Press. But it is, as Professor Moore states, 'largely a new book, with different standards of selection, presentation and approach; not a work which could usefully be conceived of as a revision of one which had served its purpose in a different way.' A bibliography and recommendations for further reading are included.
'. . . a major contribution not only to the evaluation of the work of the individual writers but also towards the assessment of African literature generally.'
Kole Omotoso – *Africa*

Morell, Karen L. ed.
In Person: Achebe, Awoonor, and Soyinka at the University of Washington
Seattle: Univ. of Washington; Institute for Comparative and Area Studies, African Studies Program, 1975. 163 pp.
Edited transcripts of three lectures by these eminent writers, presented at the University of Washington's African Studies Program annual seminar in Spring, 1973. Achebe's 'Africa and her Writers', Soyinka's 'Drama and the Revolutionary Ideal' and Awoonor's 'Tradition and Continuity in African Literature' are accompanied by selected segments of the lively audience responses and class discussion that followed the lectures.
'The idea of including discussions in the text is a rather innovative one . . . gives us a glimpse of the human side of three major African writers . . . We are offered new insights into each writer's works and are also able to feel the pulse of a certain sector of the American literary public.'
Femi Ojo-Ade – *Research in African Literatures*

Moser, Gerald M.
Essays in Portuguese-African Literature
University Park, Pa.: Pennsylvania State Univ., 1969 (Pennsylvania State Univ. Studies, 26).
88 pp. o/p
One of the first critical works in English devoted to Lusophone African writing. Moser presents three general essays, 'The Origins of an African Literature in the Portuguese Language', 'The Social and Regional Diversity of African Literature in the Portuguese Language' and 'Africa as a Theme in Portu-

guese Literature'. In his fourth essay, 'Castro Soromenho, an Angolan Realist', Gerald Moser studies 'the first Portuguese writer to do justice to the African'. In so doing he shows that Soromenho's life as well as his writing opposes a brutal colonialist dictatorship.

Mouralis, Bernard
Individu et collectivité dans le roman négro-africain d'expression française
Abidjan: Université d'Abidjan, 1962 (Annales de l'Universite d'Abidjan, Série D.-Letttres, 2). 168 pp.
A thematic study of the individual and the group in more than sixty Francophone African novels, with an extensive bibliography for the period up to 1967. The author devotes a section to a survey of the different forms of the group in the novel (traditional and modern) and pays particular attention to the style and structure of the works. He points out that because of the great social changes that have taken place in Africa since the forties a study of this theme could be useful in trying to define the specific characteristics of the African novel.

Mourão, Fernando
A Sociedade Angolana através da Literatura
São Paulo: Editora Atica, 1978 (Ensaios, 381) 157 pp.
This study of Angolan society and literature focuses on two subjects: the literary world in Luanda over a period of more than a century and the career and work of the novelist Castro Soromenho.
'Etnicidade e diversidade cultural são alguns dos conceitos implícitos na obra de Soromenho e evidenciados na sua leitura por Fernando Mourão.'
Carlos Serrano – *África*

Mphahlele, Ezekiel
Voices in the Whirlwind, and other essays
New York: Hill and Wang, 1972. 192 pp. $5.95 cased $2.45 p/b
London: Macmillan, 1972. 192 pp. £2.95
Dar es Salaam: Tanzania Publ. House, 1973. 224 pp. T.shs.20.00

Mutiso, Gideon-Cyrus M.
Socio-political Thought in African Literature
London: Macmillan, 1974. 182 pp.
New York: Barnes and Noble, 1974. 182 pp.
Gideon Mutiso aims to 'examine the social and political perceptions of African creative writers concerning the past, the transitional present and the future of African society'. This he does through a three-part analysis of African literature written in English from 1945 to 1967: Part One concerns 'Non-literary content in literature'; Part Two 'Group and

individual identity in the African context'; and Part Three 'African identity in the world context'.

Naaman, Antoine and Painchaud, Louis eds.
Le roman contemporain d'expression française
Sherbrooke, Canada: Université de Sherbrooke, Faculté des Arts, 1971. 350 pp. FF43.60
The collected papers of a colloquium held at Sherbrooke on October 8–10, 1970. Includes two papers, one by Georges Ngal and another by Hassan el Nouty, which survey the state of literature in Francophone Africa and Madagascar.

Nantet, Jacques
Panorama de la littérature noire d'expression française
Paris: Fayard, 1972 (Les grandes études littéraires). 285 pp. FF41.50
A systematic examination, state by state, of the literature of black Africa, Madagascar, and the Caribbean. For Africa, the entries are re-grouped along ancient historical and cultural lines: the ancient empire of Mali and its extensions, (the Mossi kingdom, the Fon empire and its extensions, the Fangs, etc.). Nantet summarizes briefly the history of each country by presenting the historical works of African authors and then looks at contemporary creative writing for each.
'... the best and most thorough literary history of black French literature to date ... it probably will be a long time before a more authoritative work will replace it.'
Harold A. Waters – *Research in African Literatures*

Nazareth, Peter
Literature and Society in Modern Africa: essays on literature
Nairobi: East African Literature Bureau, 1972. 223 pp. K.shs.45.00 cased, K.shs.19.50 p/b (£3.60/$9.00 cased £1.80/$4.50 p/b)
Evanston, Ill.: Northwestern Univ. Press [publ. as *An African View of Literature*], 1974. 223 pp.
A collection of essays, dissertations, reviews and letters, written by Nazareth between 1962 and 1968, and revised for inclusion in this volume. Its greater part consists of critical writings on works by East and West African authors – Ngugi wa Thiong'o, Barbara Kimenye, Murray Carlin, David Rubadiri, Wole Soyinka and Charles Mangua – but Conrad, V. S. Naipaul and R. K. Narayan are also included.
'... sometimes some of the essays ... are superficial.

At other times the essays have the freshness of outlook which makes reading rewarding, as in the essay on the politics of Wole Soyinka'.

Kole Omotoso – *Afriscope*

The Third World Writer: his social responsibility
Nairobi: Kenya Lit. Bureau, 1978. 202 pp. K.shs.27.00 (£2.50/$5.20)

The critical and exploratory essays and speeches in this book lay bare the issues facing Third World writers today, and show how some of them have succeeded or failed in dealing with them positively. The social responsibility of writers like Ngugi, Okot p'Bitek, or Ebrahim Hussein, is shown to be an enormous task in the face of cultural and economic colonialism, but it is possible to fight these evils with words, as a detailed analysis of Lambert Mascarenhas' novel *Sorrowing Lies my Land* reveals. Includes a section 'The Third World radicalisation of Graham Greene'.

'Nazareth has added a mark on his crown which he earned when he wrote his first critical essays in Literature and Society in Africa. *His insight, field of reference and ideological biases are more pronounced in* The Third World Writer.'

Senda Wa Kwayera – *Africa*

'This collection will draw a variety of responses, and because of the force with which Nazareth makes his argument, none is apt to be tepid.'

John Cooke – *World Literature Today*

N'Diaye, Papa Guèye
Manuel de littérature africaine: classe de première
Paris: Présence Africaine, 1978. 224 pp. FF29.00

The extracts in this classroom text for the older secondary school student are classed into two themes: *déracinement* ('uprooting') and *engagement* ('commitment'). Within these major headings there are subdivisions on the temptations of urban life, the way to Europe, culture conflict, the metamorphosis of the individual, the affirmation of cultural identity, the trial of colonialism, revolt and liberty, political, social and religious changes. Passages come from the works of the familiar names in Francophone African literature.

Neto, Agostinho
On Literature and National Culture
Luanda: Angolan Writers Union, 1979 (Cadernos lavra e oficina, 20), 30 pp. 20 Kwanzas (70c)

The English translations of three speeches of Angola's poet-president given from 1975–1979 were published in this small volume in conjunction with the Sixth Conference of Afro-Asian Writers held in Luanda from 26 June to 3 July, 1979. Neto sees the writer as a cultural agent working for the improvement of humanity. Moreover, Angolan writers, in particular, must bring together diverse elements in order to define and articulate a dynamic culture devoid of stereotypes. By tracing the history of the people's struggle for political and psychological freedom from colonialist domination, President Neto reflects a commonly held Angolan belief – that society is not static and therefore the literature of the society will reflect changing conditions.

New, William H.
Among Worlds: an introduction to modern Commonwealth and South African fiction
Erin, Canada: Press Procépic, 1975. 287 pp. $13.95 cased $6.95 p/b

An assessment of the literary traditions of the British Commonwealth outside Britain, which shows how a comparison of cross-colonial influences on the novel can yield rich results. It includes chapters which present an overview, as well as more detailed analyses of selected works, of fiction from East, West and South Africa.

'. . . (New's) interest is as much in the comparative framework as in scholarly analyses of particular national traditions or in in-depth assessments of specific works . . . his brief critical comments are often extremely concentrated and suggestive.'

Helen Tiffin – *Research in African Literatures*

Ngal Mbwil a Mpaang
Tendances actuelles de la littérature africaine d'expression française
Kinshasa: Ed. du Mont Noir, 1972 (Essais, 2). 64 pp.

Surveys contemporary African literature and then concentrates on the theme of revolt. There are also essays on René Maran, Aimé Césaire, and on Shakespeare and African theatre.

Ngandu Nkashama, P.
Comprendre la littérature africaine écrite
Issy-les-Moulineaux: Ed. Saint-Paul, 1979 (Les classiques africaines, 881). 128 pp. FF24.00

A critical outline of the novel, poetry and theatre in Africa today.

Ngugi wa Thiong'o
Homecoming: essays on African and Caribbean literature, culture and politics
London: HEB, 1972 (SAL). 176 pp. £2.50 Westport, Conn.: Laurence Hill, 1973. $6.50 cased $3.95 p/b

Thirteen essays and talks, given between 1962 and 1970, examine key issues: the nature of African culture (focusing on Kenya); the African writer's duty to attest to their cultural integrity; and the role of racial consciousness in the creativity of the Caribbean writer. Ngugi looks in detail at the works of Achebe, Soyinka, Aluko, and p'Bitek, and suggests ways for the heritage of Africa to be maintained in a modern culture which is true to its roots.

'... its tone, and the ideas which it sketches, are splendidly refreshing ... The clarity with which he writes stems from complete conviction and from two prime sources of authority ... he offers not dogma, but his own experience ... He is, secondly, a subtle and resolute Marxist humanist.'

Angus Calder – *New Statesman*

'... it is indeed most refreshing to hear from an African writer who is not only aware of the continental implications of African literature, but does in fact also demonstrate a formidable knowledge both of Caribbean and Black American literature ... must clearly be considered an achievement of the first magnitude.'

Stanley Macebuh – *Okike*

Writers in Politics. Essays
London: HEB, 1981 (SAL). 142 pp. £7.50 cased £2.95 p/b
Ngugi's second collection of essays, written between 1970 and 1980, reflect some of the issues that dominated his mind in the seventies, and which he sums up in the question: 'what's the relevance of literature to life?'. This period also saw Ngugi, in his own words, 'being hauled from the professorial heights at the University of Nairobi to a dungeon in Kamiti maximum security prison.' This collection gives notice of Ngugi's declared political commitment, as reflected in the title. It is called *Writers in politics* because, as Ngugi wa Thiong'o says in his preface, 'literature cannot escape from the class power structures that shape our everyday life.' The essays are grouped under three headings: 'Literature, Education: The struggle for a patriotic national culture', 'Writers in politics', and 'Against political repression'.

'... having them [the essays] together in one volume makes the collection an invaluable guide to the thought of one of Africa's most uncompromising exponents of cultural independence.'

John Chileshe – *The African Book Publishing Record*

Detained: a writer's prison diary
London: HEB, 1981 (AWS, 240). 256 pp. £7.50 cased £2.25/$6.00 p/b
In December 1978 Ngugi was imprisoned without trial by the Kenya Government, and

detained for a year. His prison diary was written whilst he was serving sentence, and here he describes the degradation and humiliation of life behind bars. Ngugi also reflects on life and politics in contemporary Kenya, and gives his views on the way forward for the people of Kenya.

'This is the Ngugi wa Thiong'o of Petals of Blood, the advocate of the exploited peasants. His vehement resentment of colonialism and its hangover comes out repeatedly in this book.'

Kikaya Chadaka – *Africa*

Nichols, Lee
Conversations with African Writers
Washington D.C.: United States International Communication Agency, Voice of America, 1981. 302 pp. free
Contains the transcripts of 'Voice of America' interviews with 26 African authors from English-speaking Africa. Many of the well-established writers are represented, but there are also interviews with lesser-known authors. The interviews cover aspects of the authors' life, how and why they started writing, their hopes and aspirations, together with their views on the role of the writer in Africa today and the problems and prospects for the future of African literature. Excerpts from each author's work are included also, and photographs and biographies accompany the published interviews.

African Writers at the Microphone: Lee Nichols (VOA) interviews 80 African authors
Washington D.C.: Three Continents Press, forthcoming 1981.

Niven, Alastair ed.
The Commonwealth Writer Overseas: themes of exile and expatriation
Brussels: Didier, 1976. 324 pp.
A collection of 23 papers and some original poems, given at the conference of the European branch of the Association for Commonwealth Literature and Language Studies (ACLALS) held in Stirling, Scotland, in April 1975. The essays treat a vast array of subjects relating to the conference's theme of 'exile and expatriation' in the works of writers from all parts of the British Commonwealth. Papers on African writers deal with Dennis Brutus, Achebe, Conton, Armah, Soyinka, Kahiga, and Mofolo.

'A few of the contributors attempt to pin down ... "the essence of Commonwealth literature". But ... perhaps the most valuable papers ... are those which address themselves to specific writers or works.'

Ian Munro – *Research in African Literatures*

Nkosi, Lewis
Home and Exile
London: Longman, 1965. 136 pp.
A collection of essays on three major themes: 'Home', meaning South Africa; 'Exile' and Nkosi's encounter with New York; and 'Literary'. The latter covers essays on Africa in Negro-American poetry; 'Black power or souls of black writers'; a survey of modern African drama; an account of the African writers' conference in Kampala in 1962; a review of Mphahele's *The African Image*; and an article on fiction by black South Africans.
'. . . *Lewis Nkosi has produced a slim but superb book.*'   William A. Payne – *Africa Report*

The Transplanted Heart
Benin City, Nigeria: Ethiope Publ. Corp., 1975. 161 pp. ₦3.00
The twenty essays in this volume treat three themes: politics in South Africa; travel – in Paris and America – and music, writers and books, analysing recent developments in these three forms of communication in South Africa.
'*The third section of the book I find most informative because one hears so little about other South African writers such as Bosman.*'
Kole Omotoso – *African Book Publishing Record*

Tasks and Masks: themes and styles of African literature
London: Longman, 1981. 256 pp. £12.00 cased £4.95 p/b
Lewis Nkosi sees the two major preoccupations of modern African literature as the social and political 'tasks' it must have as the mouthpiece of the people, and the detailed examination of the 'masks' of African culture. Commenting on the perennial problems of using a colonial language, he compares new and old views of Négritude, discusses the role of history in the African novel, and traces the search for modernism in the new African novel. Protest and commitment are seen as the most powerful themes of South African literature, and a panoramic look at modern African poetry reveals the changing themes and styles of its pioneers and its modern exponents.

Nordmann-Seiler, Almut
Le littérature néo-africaine
Paris: Presses Universitaires de France, 1976 (Que sais-je, 1851). 124 pp. FF16.80
A basic introduction to African writing in French.

Nwoga, Donatus I. ed.
Literature and Modern West African Culture
Benin City, Nigeria: Ethiope Publ. Corp., 1978. 148 pp. ₦3.00 (£2.00)

A collection of papers read at the 1972 conference 'Literature and Modern West African Culture' at the University of Nigeria, Nsukka. Presented in four sections, dealing with major issues facing African literature today, individual themes and authors: 'The writer and commitment'; 'The traditional literary artist and his society'; 'The writer and the West African past'; and 'The writer and the West African present'.
'. . . *a most welcome publication . . . represents an important contribution to the growing body of critical writing on African literature.*'
Abiola Irele – *The African Book Publishing Record*

Obiechina, Emmanuel
Literature for the Masses: an analytical study of popular pamphleteering in Nigeria
Enuga: Nwamife, 1971. 84 pp. 80k.
A book about Onitsha Market Literature which contrasts the ideas and attitudes of the pamphlet writers with those of 'intellectual writers' of Nigeria. The subject matter of the pamphlets is divided into categories (like 'love and marriage', 'adventure', 'political dramas') and there is a chapter on the influence of the study of English literature on pamphlet authors. Newspaper and cinema influence is also discussed.
'*It is encouraging to find a serious study of Onitsha literature by a Nigerian academic, which analyses its content, and puts it in a social context.*'
West Africa

Onitsha Market Literature
London: HEB, 1972 (AWS, 109). 182 pp. £1.95
New York: Africana Publ. Corp., 1972. 182 pp. $14.95 cased $5.95 p/b
The cheaply printed pamphlets and novelettes for which Onitsha is famous cover a wide variety of topics and are an important and dynamic genre of West African popular literature. Obiechina presents selections from twenty-three of these pamphlets which represent favourite themes ranging from political dramas, stories of love and adventure (with strongly moral overtones), to compilations of advice and illustrations of local custom. An introduction sets pamphleteering in its general context, outlines readership and content, and summarizes the many influences – which come from sources as diverse as oral tradition and the cinema – which have influenced its form and content. Includes a bibliography of Onitsha market literature.
'. . . *the best introduction to the pamphlets . . . a useful source for students of African literature and an affectionate tribute to the pamphleteers.*'
Don Dodson – *Research in African Literatures*

An African Popular Literature: a study of Onitsha pamphlets
Cambridge: CUP, 1973. 283 pp. £12.00 cased
£4.95 p/b
An exploration of the main themes and major conditioning influences on Onitsha market literature. Relates its emergence to the rise of newspaper publishing, writing by American-trained journalists, the influx of Indian and Victorian drug-store pulp magazine fiction, cinema and television. Favourite themes are romantic love and advice to the lovelorn. Includes a bibliography and three complete works in facsimile.
'. . . *the most detailed and comprehensive analysis of this large and growing literature . . . Dr. Obiechina's work is notable for its subtle and detailed analysis of specific texts, its attention to linguistic style and to socio-economic attitudes.*'   — *Africana Journal*

Culture, Tradition and Society in the West African Novel
Cambridge: CUP, 1975 (African Studies Series, 14). 304 pp. £16.50 cased £5.95 p/b
Obiechina relates the West African novel to its cultural and social environment in order to determine those factors which produced it. A brief survey of the literatures present in pre-colonial and colonial West Africa notes the works of expatriate writers like Waugh, Haggard, Conrad and Greene, and the status and importance of the oral traditions of West African society. Seventeen West African novels – mainly by Nigerian authors – are critically examined under the topic 'Domestication of the novel in West Africa', which comments on the ways in which each author's work has been influenced by the West African environment, and the unique literary traditions of the region.
'. . . *Whether he is writing on attitudes to nature or the uses of language, the meaning of magic or the development of character, Obiechina's insights are as far-reaching as they are profound.*'
Peter Thomas – *Books Abroad*
'*Minor defects notwithstanding, Professor Obiechina's study is an excellent* vade mecum *for a reading of the West African novels.*'
Harold Collins – *World Literatures Written in English*

Ogunba, Oyin and **Irele, Abiola** eds.
Theatre in Africa
Ibadan: Ibadan Univ. Press, 1978. 244 pp.
₦7.00
A collection of ten essays on traditional and modern drama in Africa, mostly by African critics who aim 'to create an African aesthetic consciousness . . . which could serve as a counterpoint to a Western-oriented thought

system which is notorious for masquerading as "universal".' Part 1 focuses on tradition, in African festival drama and Yoruba travelling theatre – 'Alaringo'. Part 2 surveys modern drama in West, East, Southern and Fran-cophone Africa, as well as in the Arabic north. Part 3 concentrates on Nigerian drama and the works of Soyinka, J. P. Clark, Wale Ogunyemi, Zulu Sofola, and Ola Rotimi.
'. . . *the book gives a solid overview and provides some interesting new material for the specialist . . . Well written and clearly documented by extensive fieldwork, the essays explore in detail both the form and the social context of traditional theatre.*'
Richard Priebe – *African Book Publishing Record*

Ogungbesan, Kolawole ed.
New West African Literature
London: HEB, 1979 (SAL). 128 pp.
£4.95/$15.95 cased £1.95/$5.95 p/b
Ten studies on anglophone and francophone writing, most of them on individual authors (Soyinka, Rotimi, Okai, Peters, Ouologuem, Kourouma, Ousmane and Bebey) by critics who, with two exceptions, are themselves West Africans. The volume aims to show that the African writer is a committed artist, that his art is the result of his search 'for an appropriate response to the political moment of his society.'
'*This book is [Ogungbesan's] memorial . . . a tribute to a devoted scholar [and] a landmark on the road to African literary studies . . . All of the contributions . . . have . . . a marked tendency to side with the arresting and experimental and against the sloppily conventional . . . there is a ruthless clarity, a biting turn of phrase, and breadth and depth of allusion which doubtless reflects the editor's own.*'
Robert Fraser – *West Africa*

Ogunbiyi, Yemi ed.
Drama and Theatre in Nigeria. A critical source book
Lagos: Nigerian Magazine Special Publ., Federal Ministry of Social Development, Youth, Sport and Culture, 1981, 521 pp.
₦12.00 (£9.50/$19.00) cased ₦9.00
(£7.00/$14.00) p/b
Presents an overview and critical look at Nigerian theatre from its earliest day – 'a look at the theatre as a movement and the nature and growth of such a movement', as the editor says in his introduction. It includes thirty-one articles, of which about two-thirds have earlier appeared in other journals (fifteen from *Nigeria Magazine*) the rest were specially com-missioned for this book.
'*The book provides a splendid survey and overview of*

Nigerian theatre . . . draws a fine balance between materials from traditional theatre and literary theatre . . . highly recommended.'

G. D. Killam – *The African Book Publishing Record*

Olney, James

Tell Me Africa: an approach to African literature
Princeton, N.J.: Princeton Univ. Press, 1973. 334 pp. $17.50 cased $4.45 p/b
Mr Olney approaches African fiction through the insights afforded by a study of African autobiographies. Treated in chapters which include 'The children of Gikuyu and Mumbi'; 'Ces pays lointains'; 'Love, sex, procreation'; 'Pornography, philosophy, history'; 'Politics, creativity, exile'; the autobiographies lead into interpretations of novels by Ngugi, Laye, Achebe, Ouologuem, Mphahlele, Abrahams, Mokgatle, Hutchinson, Matshikiza, Modisane, Awoonor, Soyinka, Armah and others.
'. . . a fine book, full of sensitive and illuminating commentaries on African autobiographies and novels'
Charles R. Larson – *Research in African Literatures*

Omotoso, Kole

West African Narrative: notes
Ibadan: Onibonoje Press, 1968. 52 pp. 70k.
Notes and questions on Paul Edwards's anthology.

The Form of the African Novel: a critical essay
Akure, Nigeria: Fagbamigbe Publishers, 1979. 80 pp. ₦1.50
A systematic attempt to define exactly what constitutes the form and 'Africanness' of the African novel through an analysis of the relationship between the novel and the social situation from which it takes its factual inspiration. Developing countries constitute a particular environment, and the author's role as social activist necessarily affects his relationship to the form he chooses. Kole Omotoso discusses the ways in which the novelist can manipulate his medium to take part in revolutionary change, perhaps relinquishing it for another, more populist medium. He concludes that three main units make up the form of the African novel: the form of oral narratives; the conventional form of the European novel; and the language and literary tradition of the non-African language used by the writer. A large number of printer's errors unfortunately mar the book.

Ortová, Jarmila

Etude sur le roman au Cameroun
Prague: Oriental Institut in the Publishing House of the Czechoslovak Academy of Sciences, 1971 (Dissertationes Orientales, 30). 221 pp.
An introductory chapter presents the Francophone African novel but the focus of this study is on the Cameroonian novel. There is a chapter on the historical, political and religious background to Cameroonian literature and individual studies of Béti, Oyono, and the post-independent novel.

Owomoyela, Oyekan

African Literatures: an introduction
Waltham, Mass.: Crossroads Press, 1979. 148 pp. $10.00
A basic introduction to African creative writing for newcomers to the field, which aims 'to provide the general reader with the essential facts about the development and features of African literature.'

Pagéard, Robert

Littérature négro-africaine d'expression française
Paris: Le Livre Africain, 1966. 140 pp. o/p
Paris: L'Ecole, 1979 (4th rev. ed.). 192 pp. FF58.00
An expanded and revised edition of the original 1966 volume that gives the history and analysis of contemporary African writing in French. The author considers creative writing as well as political and historical literature from the early colonial days to the present time. Bio-bibliographical notes are included in an appendix.

Palmer, Eustace

An Introduction to the African Novel
London: HEB, 1972 (SAL). 224 pp. £2.50
New York: Africana Publ. Co., 1972. 224 pp. $8.00
A critical evaluation by an African critic of the African novel. Dr Palmer examines twelve novels by Ngugi, Achebe, Laye, Amadi, Armah, Béti and Okara, singling out Chinua Achebe and Ngugi for particular attention.
'. . . the first closely argued critique of the African novel. The author demonstrates the relative importance of each of the novels analysed essentially from the artistic point of view.'
Adeola James – *African Literature Today*

The Growth of the African Novel
London: HEB, 1979 (SAL). 352 pp.
£9.50/$26.95 cased £4.95/$13.95 p/b
Palmer defines the standards best suited to evaluating the African novel – standards which

take into account both artistry and social relevance, and which reject a purely sociological approach. He then presents individual studies of twelve masters of African fiction, writing in English and French: Tutuola, Ekwensi, Achebe, Aluko, Soyinka, Armah, wa Thiong'o, Mwangi, Béti, Oyono, Ousmane, Ouologuem. An extensive bibliography is included.
'. . . *a good study of the works of the well-established masters, and a fine introduction to writers whose works have appeared more recently.*'
Abena P. A. Busia – *West Africa*

Páricsy, Pál ed.
Etude sur la littérature africaine contemporaine
Budapest: Afro-Asian Research Centre, Academy of Sciences, 1971. 98 pp.
Contains contributions by Dennis Brutus on the character of the tortoise in oral literature, by Tibor Keszthelyi on Négritude and African literatures in Hungary, by Bernth Lindfors on Achebe and the Nigerian novel, and by Páricsy on the history of drama in West Africa.

Studies on Modern Black African Literature
Budapest: Center for Developing Studies (distr. by Kultura), 1971. (Studies on Developing Countries, 43). 156 pp. £1.50

Parker, Carolyn A. ed. *et al.*
When the Drumbeat Changes: Selected papers from the 1978 meeting of the African Literature Association
Washington D.C.: Three Continents Press, 1981. $22.00 cased $14.00 p/b
Brings together papers from sixteen African literature scholars, writing on T. M. Aluko, Kofi Awoonor, Camara Laye, Bessie Head, Chinua Achebe, Arlindo Barbeitos, Luandino Vieira, Christopher Okigbo, Dennis Brutus, and others. There is also a critical introduction and a bibliography of sources.

Parker, Kenneth ed.
The South African Novel in English: essays in criticism and society
London: Macmillan, 1978. 202 pp. £12.00
New York: Africana Publishing Co., 1978. 202 pp. $23.95
Nine critical essays by six authors (all South Africans, some in exile) discuss authors or novels representative of South African literature written in English.

Peters, Jonathan
A Dance of Masks: Senghor, Achebe, Soyinka
Washington D.C.: Three Continents Press, 1978. 310 pp. $18.00 cased $7.00 p/b

A comprehensive approach to the works of three of Africa's greatest authors, who between them have produced a rich corpus of poetry, prose and drama.

Pieterse, Cosmo and **Munro, Donald** eds.
Protest and Conflict in African Literature
London: HEB, 1969. 192 pp. £2.50
New York: Africana Publishing Corp. 192 pp. $10.50 cased $7.50 p/b
An attempt to define and analyse some of the impulses and features that characterize African literature as a *genre* inspired the series of talks and discussions which were held in 1968 at the Africa Centre in London, the main substance of which form the contents of this volume. The series 'sought to popularize the growing body of what is generally called African literature while at the same time trying to avoid discussions consisting mainly of meaningless generalities.' The essays range widely from the politics of Négritude to protest against apartheid, and from cultural conflict to satire of the elite. Contributors include: Gerald Moore, Clive Wake, James Ngugi, Dennis Brutus, Jeannette Macaulay, and many others.
'. . . *a welcome addition to the accumulating criticism of African literature . . . these studies indicate new directions in the study of the theme of African literature.*'
Pio Zirimu – *Mawazo*

p'Bitek, Okot
Africa's Cultural Revolution
Nairobi: Macmillan Books for Africa, 1975. 108 pp. K.shs.15.00
A collection of essays (some previously published in periodicals and newspapers) written between the period 1964 to 1971, which plead for the regeneration of African culture, and for Africa to re-examine herself critically – 'she must discover her true self, and rid herself of "apemanship". For only then can she begin to develop a culture of her own.' Ngugi wa Thiong'o contributes an introduction.
'*An ephemeral but enthusiastic book of criticism . . . He is often mistaken about the facts of English social and literary history, but his zest to encourage a living literary culture in Africa is contagiously expressed.*'
Bill Noble – *The Times Educational Supplement*

Popkin, Michael ed.
Modern Black Writers
New York: Ungar, 1978 (Library of Literary Criticism). 561 pp. $25.00
An introduction to 81 modern black writers from Africa, the United States and the Caribbean, through selected excerpts from

significant critical writing by and about them. *'. . . his selections . . . are resourcefully and imaginatively culled and make entertaining and informative reading for someone setting out to acquire a knowledge of the criticism of each author . . . a valuable and readable contribution to the study of its subjects.'*

Arnold Rampersad – *Research in African Literatures*

Press, John ed.
Commonwealth Literature; unity and diversity in a common culture
London: HEB, 1965. 223 pp. o/p
Extracts from the proceedings of a conference held in Leeds, September 1964. Papers include: 'The Use of English in Nigeria', by J. O. Ekponyong, 'Nationalism and the Writer', by Eldred Jones, and, 'The Novelist as Teacher', by Chinua Achebe.

Preto-Rhodas, Richard A.
Négritude as a Theme in the Poetry of the Portuguese-Speaking World
Florida: Univ. of Florida Press, 1970 (Univ. of Florida Humanities Monograph, 31). 85 pp. $2.00
Preto-Rodas' study is somewhat dated because in the decade following its publication, new directions in the poetry of Portuguese speaking Africa have been explored. In his preface the author points out his survey attempts to situate the works of black Lusophone writers within the larger context of modern Négritude. The chapter, 'Négritude in Brazilian poetry: from "Whitening" to affirmation', illustrates that black poets from Brazil share with their Lusophone African counterparts a need to assert their Négritude.

Priebe, Richard O. and Hale, Thomas A. eds.
Artist and Audience: African literature as a shared experience
Washington D.C.: Three Continents Press and African Literature Association, 1979. 203 pp. $22.00 cased $14.00 p/b
A selection of thirteen papers presented at the Third Meeting of the African Literature Association, held at the University of Wisconsin, Madison, from 23–26 March 1977. Each paper examines a different aspect of communication in African literature – traditional or modern. The literature is discussed as a mouthpiece of the social and political ideologies of Africa, and the critical problems

raised by writing in non-indigenous languages are examined.

Prosper, Jean-Georges
Histoire de la littérature mauricienne de langue française
Port-Louis, Mauritius: Ed. de l'Océan Indien, 1978. 346 pp.
A pioneering history of writing in French from Mauritius from the eighteenth-century to the present. Prosper's panorama has an exhaustive survey of authors (including mention in the appendix of authors writing in Hindi and English, and French authors who have found inspiration in the island), plus chapters on printing and publishing in Mauritius (printers are listed in the appendix) and on literary circles in the island. Literary journals and magazines, published from as early as 1773, are also listed in the appendix. There is a complete bibliography of Mauritius authors writing in French and their works (published and unpublished) and a supplementary bibliography of anthologies and bibliographies devoted to literature from Mauritius (only twelve items, an indication of the vacuum this reference work has filled).

Reboullet, André and Tétu, Michel eds.
Guide culturel: civilisations et littératures d'expression française
Paris: Hachette et Les Presses de L'Université Laval, 1977. 380 pp.
Pages 258 to 310, prepared by Jacques Chevrier, survey writing in French in black Africa followed by an extensive bibliography compiled by Hélène Bruley. In a subsequent section (pages 310–339) Jean-Louis Joubert writes on the role of French in the Indian Ocean.

Réception *critique de la littérature africaine et antillaise d'expression française*
Paris: Ed. Jean-Michel Place, 1979. 274 pp. FF90.00
A double issue of *Oeuvres et critiques* (Vol. III, no. 2 and Vol. IV, no. 1, 1979) containing the papers of a colloquium on the role of the critic in African literature held at the Sorbonne on March 10–11, 1978. Apart from a theoretical article by Michel Hausser warning of ideological readings of African literature, most of the contributions survey the state of critical writings with reference to specific authors or literatures: Haïtian literature, Mongo Béti, Césaire, René Depestre, René Maran. There are also papers reviewing the way certain

national schools of criticism have seen particular authors or literatures.

Rial, Jacques

Littérature camerounaise de langue française
Laussane: Payot et la Commission Nationale
Suisse pour l'UNESCO, 1972. 95 pp. SF15.00
A presentation of Cameroonian literature in French with an introductory chapter surveying the role played by Cameroonian authors in the Négritude movement. Subsequent chapters cover the first generation of authors (1952–60) with the works of Béti and Oyono and post-independent writing and later authors like Bebey. Rial points out the role played by local book publishers (like C.L.E.) and notes the intense intellectual and literary activity and the presence of literary magazines (*Abbia, Ozila, Le Cameroun littéraire*) which has stimulated writers. A chapter is also devoted to the Cameroonian school of literary criticism with scholars like Melone, Ngendue, and Fouda. Contains numerous photos of authors.

Ricard, Alain

Livre et communication au Nigéria
Paris: Présence Africaine, 1975. 136 pp.
FF31.00
A sociological study of books and book publishing in Nigeria. The author first defines the reading public, gives a linguistic profile of Nigerians and relates economic development to literacy, then goes back in history to retrace the role played by missionaries in codifying local languages, particularly Yoruba (which produced the best-seller, *Igbo Olodumare* by D. O. Fagunwa). He outlines writing in English, the Onitsha authors and Tutuola on the one hand, the intellectuals or 'interpreters' on the other. The concluding chapter deals with the role of the media in Nigeria in developing a national culture.

Rive, Richard

Writing Black: an author's notebook
Cape Town: David Philip, 1981. 192 pp.
R13.50 cased
Richard Rive traces his development as a black South African writer from his childhood days in the slums of Cape Town's District Six, to his studies at Magdalen College, Oxford and Columbia University in New York. He discusses his position as a black writer in South Africa and describes his travels in various parts of the world. There are also accounts of his meetings with other African writers, including Chinua Achebe, Wole Soyinka, Lewis Nkosi and Ezekiel Mphahlele.

Roscoe, Adrian

Mother is Gold: a study in West African literature
London and New York: CUP, 1971. 274 pp.
£3.40/$21.50 cased £4.95/$10.50 p/b
A critical survey of West African literature (written in English or in translation), with special emphasis on the development of Nigerian literature since the early 1950s. The 'cultural collision' and the resultant fusion of traditional forms of modern modes has produced in that country a body of original, dynamic and 'African' writing, as the selections of Nigerian poetry, drama, novels, prose, children's and popular writing, and the writings of politicians and journalists demonstrate.
'. . . an exciting general work which is capable of stimulating deeper, more concentrated studies. The great merit of Professor Roscoe's work is its success in indicating the immense potentialities of African literary studies, the numerous facets and openings waiting anxiously to be explored.'
E. N. Obiechina – *Research in African Literatures*

Uhuru's Fire: African literature east to south
London and New York: CUP, 1977. 292 pp.
£17.50/$36.00 cased £5.95/$12.50 p/b
A synoptic view of verse, prose and drama from East to South Africa illustrated by in-depth examination of key figures in their development; Ngugi, Kibera, Palangyo, Alex La Guma, Nazareth, p'Bitek, Oculi, Buruga, lo Liyong, Brutus, Rubadiri and others. Chapters cover 'Language problems: English and the vernaculars'; 'Developments in verse' (on East and Central Africa); 'Aspects of South African verse'; 'Prose' (East Africa); 'Central and South African prose'; and 'A footnote on drama'.
'. . . deserves to be widely read for durable insights into some of the writers Roscoe chooses to examine . . . Moreover . . . any serious study of works from East, Central and South Africa is doubly welcome.'
Edwin Thumboo – *ASA Review of Books*
'Roscoe is at his best when examining individual writers . . . His skill in picking out the essential qualities of these writers is often brilliant.'
Ursula A. Barnett – *World Literature Today*

Rutherford, Anna ed.

Common Wealth
Aarhus, Denmark: Akademisk Boghandel, 1972. 207 pp. D.kr.23.50 (£2.20)
A collection of papers presented by academics and creative writers at the Conference on Commonwealth Literature held at Aarhus University, Denmark, from 26 to 30 April 1971. Includes papers on literary aspects of the African novel: Peter Young's 'Mechanism to

medium: the language of West African literature in English'; Bernth Lindfors's 'Characteristics of Yoruba and Igbo prose styles in English'; and Gerald Moore's 'The writer and the cargo cult'.

Sartre, Jean-Paul
Black Orpheus
(Trans. from the French by S. W. Allen)
Paris: Présence Africaine, 1963. 65 pp.
FF20.00
An English translation – here published separately – of Sartre's introductory essay to the Senghor anthology published in 1948. This is a manifesto of Négritude and the black soul.

Schild, Ulla ed.
Modern East-African Literature and its Audience
Wiesbaden, Germany: B. Heymann, 1978
(Mainzer Afrika Studien, 4) 155 pp. DM36.00
A collection of seven critical essays (presented at a symposium in memory of Jahnheinz Jahn) on East African prose, poetry and drama. The emphasis is on the connections that these modern literatures have with the past, showing how the contemporary forms have developed characteristics unique to the East-African environment. The essays are by Chris Wanjala, G. Kamenju, Ulla Schild, M. Schipper-de Leeuw, E. Kezilahabi, A. Abdalla, and E. Dammann.

Afrikanische Literatur: Perspektiven und Probleme
Stuttgart: Institut für Auslandsbeziehungen, 1979 (Materalien zum Internationalen Kulturaustausch, 8). 207 pp.
A special double issue (and here published separately) of the journal *Zeitschrift für Kulturaustausch*, which presents a wide-ranging collection of essays on African literatures in English, French, and German. The essays are original statements of opinion – about Jahn's Muntu-concept; problems of readership or the place of African literature in German universities, for example, or summaries of particular fields – francophone literature; anglophone literature of the seventies; the literatures of Cape Verde, São Tome and Principe; children's book publishing; and a contribution on 'African writers and their publishers'.
'... *these two volumes reflect in their range the energy and enthusiasm of their editor. The inclusion of essays on literatures in the main African languages as well as on those in all the relevant European ones distinguishes this work from comparable productions.*'
                    Nelson Wattie – *Kunapipi*

Schipper-de Leeuw, Mineke
Le blanc et l'occident au miroir du roman négro-africain de langue française (des origines au Festival de Dakar, 1920–1966)
Yaoundé: C.L.E. 1973 (Etudes et documents africains). 261 pp. CFA1,500
Assen: Netherlands: Van Gorkum for Vrije Universiteit, Amsterdam, 1973. 261 pp. D.Fl36.00
A study of the white man as he appears in works of African literature between 1920 and 1966. Contains profiles of civil servants and colonial officials, white settlers, school teachers, missionaries, women. A chapter is devoted to the Occident and the Westernized African. There is a bibliography, an index, and a chronological table of authors, works and themes.

Text and Context: methodological explorations in the field of African literature
Leiden, Netherlands: Afrika-Studiecentrum, 1976 (African Perspectives, 1). 160 pp.
An issue (available separately) of the semi-annual journal *African Perspectives* presenting a collection of twelve essays on the theory and criticism of African literature, which reflect a growing interest in the sociology of literature and with structuralism.
'... *most of the essays are important contributions to the theory and criticism of African literature.*'
            Rand Bishop – *Research in African Literatures*

Les mots sont comme des oeufs
Yaoundé: C.L.E., 1980. 180 pp.
An analysis of African literature through a study of a selected number of major works.

Senghor, Léopold Sédar
Liberté I: Négritude et humanisme
Paris: Seuil, 1964. 446 pp.
The first volume of what will be Senghor's collected writings. *Liberté I* and *Liberté III* are on cultural subjects, and *Liberté II* (*Nation et voie africaine du socialism*, Paris: Seuil, 1971) and *Liberté IV* (*Socialisme africain et démocratis*, not yet published) on political and economic matters. This first volume contains speeches and articles published by Senghor between 1937 and 1963 on a number of subjects relating to culture and literature. There are articles on the aesthetics of African literature, on the contribution it has made to world culture, on black-American literature, and on individual authors, both African and non-African (Camara Laye, Lamine Diakhaté, Lamine Niang, Birago Diop, Peter Abrahams, U'Tamsi, Victor Hugo, Camus, Saint-John Perse, René Maran). Senghor also writes here on questions of

métissage and assimilation, and there are articles on Guinea's national ballet troup, on UNESCO, on the Sorbonne and Négritude, and on *malégassitude*.

Les fondements de l'africanité ou négritude et arabité
Paris: Présence Africaine, 1967. 107 pp. o/p
In English *translation* see next entry.

The Foundations of 'Africanité': or Négritude and Arabité
(Trans. from the French)
Paris: Présence Africaine, 1967. FF34.00
The text of a speech given at the University of Cairo on February 16, 1967 when Senghor was awarded an honorary doctorate. He speaks about ethnic and cultural factors (including reference to physical anthropology) which link African, Arabic and Berber peoples.

La parole chez Paul Claudel et chez les négro-africains
Dakar: Nouvelles Editions Africaines, 1973. 55 pp. CFA550
The text of a talk given by Senghor at the International Conference of the Friends of Paul Claudel held in Brangues, France on July 27, 1972. Senghor writes that Claudel is the French poet who influenced him the most. He is struck by the singular world vision which inspired both Claudel and African poets – catholicism for Claudel and African cosmology for Africans.

Liberté III: Négritude et civilisation de l'universel
Paris: Seuil, 1977. 576 pp.
The articles in this volume were published in different magazines and periodicals between 1961 and 1974 and contain contributions to what Senghor calls the '*civilisation de métissage culturel*' or '*Civilisation Universel*', a term borrowed from Teilhard de Chardin. There are writings on aspects of Négritude, on return to origins, on the teaching of French and African history, on 'Africanism', on African pre-history, on *francophonie* and *anglophonie*, on black literary criticism, on individual writers and artists (Picasso, Claudel, Chagall, Günter Grass, Malik Fall, Appolinaire), on cultural institutions in Africa (the Musée dynamique in Senegal, art at the University of Ife), and on different civilizations (German, Mediterranean, Latin American).

La poésie de l'action
Paris: Stock, 1980. 360 pp. FF61.00
Senghor the man of letters and Senghor the head of state: images of each are revealed in this volume which is the result of Senghor's conversations with the Tunisian writer, Mohammed Aziza.

'*C'est donc entre deux Africains qui se cherchent et se trouvent, malgré l'écart des générations, entre deux écrivains francophones, que le dialogue s'engage en souplesse, voire à bâtons rompus, mêlant à la courbe d'une carrière politique l'aventure d'une pensée.*'
Jacqueline Piatier – *Le Monde*

Silveira, Onésimo
Consciencialização na Literatura Caboverdiana
Lisbon: Casa dos Estudantes do Império, 1963. 32 pp. o/p
[Available in Burness, *Critical Perspectives on Lusophone Literature from Africa*, see page 18]
In this essay Silveira argues that the Claridade Movement and the writers of its generation were inadequate and insufficient, for instead of being rooted in Cape Verdean culture as they were claiming, they were elitists, inspired by European rather than African traditions.

Smith, Rowland ed.
Exile and Tradition: studies in African and Caribbean literature
London: Longman, and Dalhousie Univ. Press, 1976. (Dalhousie African Studies). 190 pp. £6.00 cased £2.50 p/b
New York: Africana Publ. Co., 1976. 190 pp. $18.00 cased $7.00 p/b
A collection of thirteen essays, originally read at two conferences held at Dalhousie University, Nova Scotia, in 1973 and 1974. They cover a wide range of topics, but share two main unifying themes: the traditions unique to African cultures and the sense of alienation that arises from the imposition of Western codes and values thereon. Essays include works by established authors and critics like Soyinka, Achebe, Nadine Gordimer, G. D. Killam, Kofi Awoonor, D. I. Nwoga and Daniel Kunene.

'. . . contains valuable and insightful essays on the various aspects of African literature. Clearly . . . a welcome addition to the study and appreciation of African literary culture and tradition.'
Solomon O. Iyasere – *ASA Review of Books*

Société Africaine de Culture
Premier congrès international des écrivains et artistes noirs. Compte rendu complet 2 vols.
Paris: Présence Africaine, 1956/57. 408 pp. 363 pp.
The complete proceedings and individual papers submitted to the first international conference of Negro writers, held in Paris, September 19–22, 1966, issued here as two special numbers of the journal *Présence Africaine*, nos. 8/9/10 and 14/15.

Deuxième congrès des écrivains et artistes noirs, Rome, 26 mars–1 avril, 1959 [Proceedings] 2 vols.
Vol. 1: L'Unité des cultures négro-africaines, 435 pp. FF13.00
Vol. 2: Responsabilité des hommes de culture, 368 pp. FF12.00
Paris: Présence Africaine, 1959.
Two special issues of Présence Africaine, nos. 24/25, and nos. 27/28, covering the proceedings of the second congress of Negro writers held in Rome, April 1959.

Colloque sur l'art nègre 1ᵉʳ Festival mondial des arts nègres, Dakar, 1–24 Avril, 1966.
Colloque 'Function et signification de l'art nègre dans la vie du peuple et pour le peuple' (30 Mars–9 Avril) 2 vols.
Paris: Présence Africaine, 1967 (vol. 1). 645 pp. o/p
Paris: Présence Africaine, 1971 (vol. 2). 285 pp. FF59.00
The complete proceedings of the First Festival of Negro Arts held in Dakar, Senegal, April 1966.

Colloquium on Negro Art
1st World Festival of Negro Arts.
Function and significance of the African Negro art in the life of the people and for the people.
Paris: Présence Africaine, 1968. 599 pp., 272 pp. FF80.00, FF59.00
The English translation of the Colloquium. Articles on literature include: 'Oral literature' by G. Calame-Griaule: 'African oral literature' by John Mbiti; 'Negro-African oral literature' by Basile-Juléat Fouda; 'Meaning and function of the traditional Negro-African theatre' by Bakary Traoré; 'Modern Negro-African theatre' by Wole Soyinka; 'Black writers in a troubled world' by Langston Hughes; and 'Modern African poetry' by Lamine Diakhaté.

Le Théâtre négro-africaine: actes du colloque d'Abidjan 1970
Paris: Présence Africaine, 1971. 249 pp. FF47.00
The collected papers of a colloquium on African theatre held at the University of Abidjan from April 15–29, 1970. Thirty-one papers discussed the genesis of African theatre, sources of inspiration, dramatic techniques, the impact on the public, and universality. Participants included Barthélémy Kotchy, Lilyan Kesteloot, Harris Memel-Fote, Bakary Traoré, Alphamoye Sonfo, Christophe Dailly,

Bernard Mouralis, Mario de Andrade, Thomas Melone, Janheinz Jahn and Issa Sido.

The African Critic and his People as Producers of Civilization
Paris: Présence Africaine, 1977. 550 pp. FF88.00
A collection of papers in English and French given at a colloquium of the same name organized by the Society of African Culture and the Federal University of Cameroon, and held at the University of Yaoundé from 16 to 21 April 1973. The papers represent a wide variety of approaches to all aspects of the colloquium's title, and each is accompanied by a summary in English or French.
'. . . there is first-rate material to be found here . . . Also of real benefit, especially to the unilingual reader, will be the synopses in English or French accompanying each article.'
Rand Bishop – Research in African Literatures

Soyinka, Wole
Myth, Literature and the African World
London and New York: CUP, 1976. 168 pp.
£12.00/$25.00 cased £4.95/$11.95 p/b
A book of essays that comprise the lectures Soyinka gave when he held a year's appointment as Fellow of Churchill College, Cambridge, in 1973 and was simultaneously Visiting Professor at Sheffield University. Soyinka's aim in these four lectures, to which a fifth, much earlier essay is appended, is to contribute to what he calls 'African self-apprehension' both for foreigners or 'aliens' (whose theorizing on Africa derives from their own, not an African world view) and for 'the alienated African'. A first essay on ritual archetypes explores the contribution made to contemporary Nigerian theatre by Yoruba cosmology and in particular the deities, Sango, Obatala and Sango. In his second piece, 'Drama and the African world-view' he affirms that the differences of European and African drama result from two different world visions. Westerners have a compartmentalizing habit of thought which selects aspects of human emotion and even scientific observations and 'turns them into separatist myths'. African creativity, on the other hand, results from 'a cohesive understanding of irreducible truths'. He cautions at the same time against the 'red herrings' of criticism. Differences between Western and African theatre are not questions of style, form or audience participation (or even noise level, he adds jokingly). In the two following essays Soyinka examines African literature, through reference to selected works, as manifestations of 'social vision', with its religious and secular counterparts. He prefers

this term to that of 'literary ideology', which apart from the Négritude movement, he feels is not a characteristic of African writing. The volume closes with a revised version of 'The fourth stage', an article which originally appeared in 1969 in *The Morality of Art* edited by D. W. Jefferson.

'By the breadth of his scholarship, his profound and intimate knowledge of African culture, his familiarity with African and European literature and the quality of intellect which he brings to bear on all this matter, Soyinka forces one to grapple with unfamiliar ideas and ways of thinking – and to look afresh at previously unconsidered accepted commonplaces.'
— *Race and Class*

Taiwo, Oladele

An Introduction to West African Literature
London: Nelson, 1967. 192 pp. o/p
The first part of this book describes aspects of African life and culture that feature prominently in West African writing; oral traditions are then discussed and an attempt is made to relate them to the way of life of West African people. The author tries to determine to what extent they influenced contemporary literature in West Africa. In the second part characteristics of the major literary forms – the novel, poetry and drama – are discussed, and Négritude is considered in some detail. Part three, lastly, consists of a detailed analysis of four well-known works by West African authors: Camara Laye's *The African Child*, Cyprian Ekwensi's *People of the City*, Chinua Achebe's *No Longer at Ease*, and Wole Soyinka's *The Lion and the Jewel*.

'. . . the author has succeeded admirably in producing what he intended: a simple book of critical exposition for a first course in African literature.'
John Povey – *Africa Report*

Culture and the Nigerian Novel
London: Macmillan, 1976. 235 pp. £4.95 cased £2.45 p/b
New York: St. Martin's Press, 1976. 235 pp. $16.95 cased
A critical analysis of the Nigerian novel and of the impact of historical and cultural influences on the Nigerian novelist. The works of Tutuola, Achebe, Okara and Nwankwo, among others, are discussed and a short critique of each novelist is given.

'Taiwo's work is a significant contribution to the study of literature arising in the various regions of Africa.'
Ernest F. Dunn – *ASA Review of Books*
'Oladele Taiwo's book is certainly worth reading, as it is very rich in ideas and highly stimulating for further research.'
Vládimir Klimá – *Research in African Literatures*

Tollerson, Marie S.

Mythology and Cosmology in the Narratives of Bernard Dadié and Birago Diop
Washington D.C.: Three Continents Press, forthcoming 1981.

Traoré, Bakary

Le théâtre négro-africain et ses fonctions sociales
Paris: Présence Africaine, 1958. 160 pp. o/p
In English *translation*, see next entry.

The Black African Theatre and its Social Functions
(Trans. from the French and with an introduction by Dapo Adelugba)
Ibadan: Ibadan Univ. Press, 1972. 125 pp. ₦2.10
An introduction to the variety of theatre to be found in the parts of West Africa formerly governed by France, with particular reference to the theatricality of ceremonies and rituals such as the age-group ceremony, circumcision rites, hunting rites, etc. The work of Keita Fodeba, poet, playwright, dancer, choreographer and theatre director is extensively discussed. To the English translation, Dapo Adelugba has added an article 'Current trends in the African theatre' written by Traoré for *Présence Africaine* and also a brief preface and some short commentary on the text.

'Dapo Adelugba has done an excellent job of careful and accurate translation, capturing both the letter and the spirit of the original . . . he has earned our gratitude for his very sound translation and for the careful scholarship and integrity of his introduction and commentary.'
Herb Shore – *Research in African Literatures*

Tucker, Martin

Africa in Modern Literature: a survey of contemporary writing in English
New York: Ungar, 1967. 316 pp. $10.50
A study that 'differs in scope from other works of literary criticism on African writing in that it is an attempt to survey literature about Africa written in English in the twentieth century, and thus treats American and English writers, as well as Africans, as an integral part of "African literature" as a whole.' In effect, the book – arranged in terms of regional settings: West, East, Central and South Africa respectively – includes detailed analyses of the works of Joyce Cary, Joseph Conrad, Graham Greene, Elspeth Huxley, and several other European and American writers. African literature by West Africans is comprehensively surveyed in a separate chapter. There is a detailed reading list.

'. . . this is a book on which literary historians and literary critics alike will come to depend . . . will

become a standard for those who wish to know where African literature has been and where it may well be going.'   Robert Cobb – *Africa Report*

Udoeyop, N. J.
Three Nigerian Poets. A critical study of the poetry of Soyinka, Clark and Okigbo
Ibadan: Ibadan Univ. Press, 1973. 166 pp.
₦2.00
A critical appraisal of the works of three of Nigeria's most well-known poets. The volume is divided into sections, consisting of a general introduction on the traditions that influenced the poets, an essay on each poet's work, and a concluding examination of each poet's literary theories.
'. . . a welcome addition to the growing body of criticism on African literature . . . Udoeyop is good at tracing themes, analyzing imagery and determining points of view.'   – *Books Abroad*

Ugboma, Paul
Critical Notes on Some West African Poems
Calabar, Nigeria: Scholars Press, 1980.
111 pp.   ₦3.00.
Examines a selection of poems by a number of leading West African writers and presents a model of critical analysis required of candidates at the WASC, GCE and Grade II Teachers Certificate examinations.

Umezinwa, A. Wilberforce
La religion dans la littérature africaine
Kinshasa: Presses de l'Université du Zaïre, 1975. 185 pp. Z4.86
The author examines the impact of religious forces – traditional, Christian, Muslim – on the literatures of Africa.

Université Paris Nord, Centre d'Etudes Francophones
Les littératures d'expression française: négritude africaine, négritude caraïbe
Paris: Ed. de la Francité, 1973. 159 pp.
A collection of papers presented at the two-day event organized by the university and held on 26 and 27 January 1973.

Viatte, Auguste
Histoire comparée des littératures francophones
Paris: Nathan, 1980. 215 pp.
Contains chapters on African literature in French (the anti-colonialist struggle of Dadié, Béti, and Oyono), on Négritude, and on the literature of the Indian Ocean.

Vincent, Theo ed.
The Novel and Reality in Africa and America
Lagos: United States Information Service, 1974. 39 pp.
This is the complete, edited transcript of a symposium held at the University of Lagos on 26 January 1973. The subject was 'Appropriateness or the Suitability of the Novel Form for Expressing American and African Reality'. The speakers were ten distinguished writers and critics (J. P. Clark, John Updike, Cyprian Ekwensi, Elechi Amadi, Kole Omotoso, Dan Izevbaye, Abiola Irele, Michael Echeruo, Ime Ikiddeh, and Theo Vincent) who presented their interpretations and thoughts on the main topic, and responded to questions put to them afterwards.

von Grunebaum, G. E.
French African Literature: some cultural implications
The Hague: Mouton, 1964 (Publ. of the Institute of Social Studies, Series Minor, vol. 5). 41 pp. Dfl.5.00
An appreciation of the African writer 'd'expression française', with an emphasis on the works of Aimé Césaire and Léopold Senghor as well as some Maghrebi authors.

Walsh, William
Commonwealth Literature
London: OUP, 1973. 150 pp. o/p
The Africa section in this selective survey of English literatures from the British Commonwealth looks at the work of Olive Schreiner, Achebe, Soyinka, Tutuola, John Pepper Clark, Ngugi, T. M. Aluko, Ekwensi and Okigbo with briefer glances at Ama Ata Aidoo and Armah.
'For Africanists who stray outside his African chapter there are discoveries to be made. For non-Africanists who stray into his African chapter there is a sane and delightful introduction to the central writers.'
Jack Healy – *Research in African Literatures*

Walsh, William ed.
Readings in Commonwealth Literature
London: OUP, 1973. 448 pp. £2.95
A collection of essays on British Commonwealth literature with a section on Africa containing surveys, studies of individual authors, and statements from practising writers. Its topics include 'Novels of disillusion', 'Nigerian drama in English' and 'Problems of criticism', with closer studies of Tutuola and Soyinka, and an essay by Achebe.
'. . . this will remain a good book to browse in for a long time to come.'
Joseph Jones – *Research in African Literatures*

Wanjala, Chris L. ed.
Standpoints on African Literature: a critical anthology
Nairobi: East African Lit. Bureau, 1973.
389 pp. K.shs.80.00 cased K.shs.33.50 p/b
(£4.60/$11.60 cased, £2.80/$6.90 p/b)
A collection of critical essays from East Africa which stress the necessity for political and sociological involvement of the literary critic and which attempt to demonstrate the difficulty of using critical methods imported from a foreign culture. The book has an introduction by Angus Calder in which he says that it is the job of the African critic to 'strive actively to reform popular taste . . . we need critics to purge our minds and to prescribe the means to cultural health.'
'. . . Standpoints *suggests that East African criticism is well aware of the several locations of "language" and "life", but that it is at present finding the journey between these two points less than smooth.'*
Robert J. Green – *Research in African Literatures*

The Season of Harvest: a literary discussion
Nairobi: Kenya Lit. Bureau, 1978. 234 pp.
K.shs.50.00 (£3.65/$9.15)
Wanjala shows us the vitality and variety of East African literature during the 1970s in discussions of major issues and writers. Among the issues are the questions of the writer's approach as a direct result of his intentions – is there a commitment to East Africa or to materialism – what is the role of the writer in that society? Among the writers discussed are Ngugi wa Thiong'o, Okot p'Bitek and Taban lo Liyong, and two new writers of popular literature David G. Maillu and Charles Mangua.

For Home and Freedom
Nairobi: Kenya Lit. Bureau, 1980. 267 pp.
K.shs.50.00 (£3.65/$9.15)
This book was originally produced as the author's doctoral thesis for the University of Nairobi, and should be regarded as the more detailed sequel to *Season of Harvest* (see above). Its subject is alienation – as East African writers have analysed and depicted it. Wanjala attempts to distinguish the real causes of alienation from those suggested by these writers, and shows how their solutions to the problem of achieving cultural synthesis are accordingly off-centre. In the present neo-colonial environment, which features strongly in East Africa he thinks, a harmonious solution will be difficult to achieve.

Warren, Lee
The Theater of Africa: an introduction
Englewood Cliffs, N.J.: Prentice-Hall, 1975.
112 pp. $6.95
A volume aimed at the newcomer to the world of African theatre and African culture which contains chapters on storytelling, ritual drama, puppetry, folk opera and the concert party as well as illustrations of productions.

Waslay-Ithier, J. J.
La littérature de langue française à l'île Maurice
Paris: Librairie M. Lac, 1930. 288 pp. o/p
Paris: Slatkine, 1981. 288 pp.
A re-issue of the 1930 history of writing in French from Mauritius covering the period 1507 to 1929.

Wästberg, Per ed.
The Writer in Modern Africa
Stockholm: Almqvist and Wiksell (for Scandinavian Inst. of African Studies), 1968.
123 pp. Sw. Kr.25
New York: Africana Publ. Corp., 1969.
123 pp.
The proceedings of the African Scandinavian Writers' Conference sponsored by the Scandinavian Institute of African Studies, held at Häselby Castle near Stockholm, February 6–9, 1967. In his foreword, Per Wästberg describes this volume as 'a collage of voices from Africa . . . a confrontation of temperaments, the outcome of which is not measured in tangible results. Views, not facts.' Among the contributions in this collection are Wole Soyinka's paper 'The writer in a modern Africa state', and there are childhood memories by Dan Jacobson, Dennis Brutus, James Ngugi, and George Awoonor-Williams. Other contributors include Lewis Nkosi, Mbella Sonne Dipoko, Eldred Jones and Kateb Yacine, the Algerian poet and novelist. Each paper is followed by a general discussion.
'. . . is one of the most valuable documents available for those of us who are concerned with African literature.' John Povey – *African Studies Review*
'. . . remarkable for two or three contributions of exceptional sanity and directness.'
Gerald Moore – *Research in African Literature*

Wauthier, Claude
L'Afrique des africains: inventoire de la négritude
Paris: Seuil, 1977 (3rd and enlarged ed.)
(Collection l'Histoire immédiate). 370 pp.
FF65.00
The third edition of a title first published: 1964. For an English *translation*, see next entry.

The Literature and Thought of Modern Africa
London: HEB, 1978 (2nd revised and enlarged
ed.). 416 pp. £8.50 cased £3.20 p/b
Washington D.C.: Three Continents Press,
1978. $18.00 cased $8.00 p/b
A revised and enlarged second English-
language edition of the original work first
published in French in 1964 (see above). A
wide-ranging survey of the literary history of
African writing south of the Sahara, before
and after independence, it embraces creative
writing and politically committed literature in
English, French and Portuguese. The emphasis
is still on the modern trend of African
nationalist thought but the presses and
journals and other matters seminal to the
growing stream of African literature are also
covered. The writers are discussed under topics
which range from customs and traditions to
racial prejudice in sexual relations. Over 150
of them are cited, many of them are quoted,
and there is in addition a 700-item bibliography.
'... [Wauthier] examines almost every aspect of
black African culture and thought: the staggering
multiplicity of dialects and the use of European
languages ... the cultural and political significance
of both African religions and Islam and Christianity;
the relation of folklore to African belles lettres;
questions of African identity, including ... Négritude; the relation of African politics to literature,
and so on. The postface deals particularly with the
effect of national independence upon African writers
and with the fact that their work frequently reflects
deep disillusionment with the regimes that have
displaced colonial rule.'
         Robert L. Berner – *World Literature Today*

Wilhelm, Peter and **Polley, James A.** eds.
Poetry South Africa
Johannesburg: Ad. Douker, 1976. 150 pp.
R8.95
A volume containing ten essays selected from
the 'Poetry '74' conference proceedings which
formed part of the University of Capetown's
1974 Summer School programme, outlining
the present situation and providing background material to the new poetry now being
published. Also contains an extensive poetry
bibliography compiled by Cherry Wilhelm.

Wright, Edgar ed.
The Critical Evaluation of African Literature
London: HEB, 1973 (SAL). 179 pp. £2.90
A collection of seven essays which discuss some
of the more important elements of the
dialogue between literature and criticism,
showing how contemporary critical approaches can be employed and modified in the

study of African literature. African writing is
still deeply affected by two main elements: the
special complexity of African cultural and
linguistic backgrounds, and the importance of
the oral literary tradition. Essays by Wright
himself, Peter Young, Eldred Jones, John
Povey, W. J. Howard, Dan S. Izevbaye and
Clive Wake examine aspects of the work of
Soyinka, Ekwensi, Ngugi wa Thiong'o,
Christopher Okigbo, and J.-J. Rabéarivelo, as
well as the problem of the critical approach to
this literature.
'... any scholar or critic of African literature must
reckon with the assertions of this collection of essays
when analysing African literature, which ... poses a
special set of extremely complex cultural and
linguistic problems that absolutely cannot be dis-
regarded.'   – Janis L. Pallister – *Africa Today*
'... boldly attempts to assail the basic issue of
methodology ... provides the explication and
illumination of the work of several major African
writers by some well-read and perceptive critics.'
         John Povey – *ASA Review of Books*

Yoder, Carroll
*White Shadows: a dialectical view of the
French African novel*
Washington D.C.: Three Continents Press,
1980. 260 pp. $16.00 cased $7.00 p/b
A volume documenting the assumptions and
attitudes of the French in two centuries of
contact with West Africa. Attention is given to
the work and throught of early French writing
set in Africa, the rise of racism, the evolution
of Négritude, and, finally, new directions since
independence.

Zirimu, Pio and **Gurr, Andrew** eds.
*Black Aesthetics: papers from a colloquium held
at the University of Nairobi, June 1971*
Nairobi: East Africa Lit. Bureau. 1973.
216 pp. K.shs.42.00 cased K.shs.17.00 p/b
(£3.40/$4.90 cased £1.60/$4.00 p/b)
The colloquium formed part of the Festival of
East African Writing held at Nairobi University
in 1971. The eleven papers presented in this
book include contributions by Alan Ogot, Ali
Mazrui, Cyrus Mutiso and Angus Calder, and
concern the part played by literature in society
and its contribution to the quality of East
African life. Topics include aesthetic dualism,
Négritude, beauty, black identity, historicity
and the political role of the artist.
'... should be read ... by those who are bothered or
affected by the low place that has been given to the
black man's values and culture; and ... by those who
are concerned to know what role literature and art
play in society.'   H. Odera Oruka – *Joliso*

Criticism: Studies of individual authors and individual works

Adelusi, O.
Things Fall Apart: notes
Ibadan: Onibonoje Press, 1966. 96 pp. 85k
A short examination guide providing notes and questions on Achebe's novel.

Agetua, John ed.
When the Man Died: reviews and interviews on Wole Soyinka's controversial book
Benin City, Nigeria: Bendel Newspaper Corp., 1975. 47 pp. ₦1.00
A short volume containing a number of reviews of *The Man Died*. All are by Nigerians except for one by Conor Cruse O'Brien. The reviews are followed by a reprint of 'The writer in a modern African state' and the text of an interview given by Soyinka to the editor in Accra in 1974.
'Taken together, the reviews and the paper put Agetua in a position to produce a curious but effective book.'
James Gibbs – *Research in African Literatures*

Critics on Chinua Achebe, 1970–76.
Benin City, Nigeria: Bendel Newspaper Corp., 1977. 46 pp. ₦1.00
The book contains four short chapters of already published criticism on *Arrow of God*, *Morning Yet on Creation Day*, *Girls at War* and *Beware Soul Brother*. Part two contains an interview with Chinua Achebe. In his preface, the author states that the book 'brings together some of the best critical essays on Achebe's recent work'.
'The interview [with Achebe] makes this small book a must for specialists in African literature and for Achebe "fans".'
John J. Figueroa – *African Book Publishing Record*

Anozie, Sunday O.
Christopher Okigbo: creative rhetoric
London: Evans, 1972 (African Writers and Their Work). 160 pp. £2.60 cased £1.45 p/b
New York: Africana Publ. Co.,1972. $16.50 cased $7.95 p/b.
The life of the Ibo poet who was killed in action at the age of thirty-five during the Nigerian civil war, including analyses of his poetry and the new direction it was taking in both theme and structure, at the time of his death.
'... a warmly readable and understanding account of Okigbo the man ... and an exposition of his work that is both exhaustive and enlightening.'
Peter Thomas – *Research in African Literatures*

Bâ, Sylvia W.
The Concept of Négritude in the Poetry of Léopold Sédar Senghor
Princeton, N.J.: Princeton Univ. Press, 1973. 316 pp. $13.50
A study of the reciprocity of Senghor's poetry and his concept of Négritude. Includes the key chapters 'The basis of Négritude: black African ontology' and 'The expression of Négritude: black African psychophysiology' in which African world views are used as the bases for analysing Senghor's poetic sensibility and his recurrent themes and images.
'... a comprehensive investigation of the various facets of Négritude both as formulated by Senghor and as the objective manifestation of an essential African spirit in the lived complex of sociological realities, and explicit attitudes of African man ... These facets are examined and discussed in direct relation to the poetic expression of Senghor himself.'
Abiola Irele – *Research in African Literatures*

Bailey, Diana
Ngugi wa Thiong'o The River Between
London: Rex Collings in association with the British Council, forthcoming 1981.

Bamgbose, A.
The Novels of D. O. Fagunwa
Benin City, Nigeria: Ethiope Publishing Corp., 1974. 132 pp. ₦2.00
A critical study of Fagunwa's five novels which presents as essential background the features of Yoruba rural life and the wide variety of literary sources that they draw upon. Includes plot summaries, analyses of major themes, characterization, Fagunwa's famed didacticism, and his use of language and allegory.
'... a distinguished Yoruba linguist's informative critical study of the novels (more accurately romances) of Chief Fagunwa.'
Harold Collins – *Research in African Literatures*

Banham, Martin
Wole Soyinka's The Lion and the Jewel: a critical view
London: Rex Collings in association with the British Council, 1981 (Nexus Books, 2). 36 pp. £1.00
Offers an introduction to this Soyinka play, evaluating the work and explaining its context and background. There are also extracts from criticism, and giving Soyinka's own views on his work and on drama in Africa. Points for

discussion, hints on teaching, and a select reading list are included as well.

Barnett, Ursula A.
Ezekiel Mphahlele
New York: Twayne, 1976 (Twayne's World Author Series, 417). 195 pp. $9.95
A comprehensive study of the noted South African writer tracing his career as teacher, critic, novelist, poet and essayist and his life in exile in Nigeria, France, Kenya, Zambia and, ultimately, U.S.A. Themes of poverty, isolation, estrangement and the evils of apartheid are explored and Mphahlele's writings are chronologically discussed.
'Barnett is at her best when she is transcribing biological material . . . In these sections she presents us neatly organized and fully comprehensible material.'
Cecil A. Abrahams – *Research in African Literatures*
'In sum, the work is thorough, serious and careful, though its conclusions are debatable and reflect a pervading bias that might be characterized as the South African white liberal stance.' – *Choice*

Benoît, Norbert
Loÿs Masson
Paris: Nathan et Ed. de l'Océan Indian, 1981. 96 pp. FF15.00
A critical survey of the writing of the Mauritius author with extracts from his works, biographical details and a bibliography.

Bestman, Martin T.
Sembène Ousmane et l'esthétique du roman négro-africaine
Sherbrooke, Canada: Ed. Naaman, 1981 (Coll. Etudes, 27). 352 pp. Can. $20.00

Bibliothèque Nationale, Paris
Léopold Sédar Senghor
Paris: Bibliothèque Nationale, 1978. 143 pp.
The catalogue of an exhibition on Senghor held at the Bibliothèque Nationale in Paris in 1978.

Boucquey de Schutter, Eliane
Jacques Rabemananjara
Paris: Seghers, 1964 (Poètes d'aujourd'hui, 112). 192 pp.
A critical presentation of the verse of the Malagasy poet with extracts from his writings.

Boudry, Robert
Jean-Joseph Rabéarivelo et la mort
Paris: Présence Africaine, 1971 (2nd ed.). 84 pp. FF18.00
Unravels the threads of Rabéarivelo's life and times which led this Malagasy poet to commit suicide at the age of 35 on 22 June 1937. The author, a personal friend of Rabéarivelo's, brings his own insights to bear on this analysis of the man, his talent, and his times, showing how total alienation placed him in a 'no-man's-land' between the culture of his own country and that of the colonial power, whose language he used so powerfully and whose yoke he unceasingly fought to throw off. Includes extracts from Rabéarivelo's *Journal* in which he recorded his day-to-day life, and an anthology of his poems.

Britwum, Kwabena
Oyono's Une vie de boy
Benin City, Nigeria: Ethiope Publ. Corp., 1974. 133 pp. ₦2.50
A study guide aimed at French literature students at college or university in English-speaking countries. It contains the 1956 Editions René Julliard text, with an introduction and notes by Kwabena Britwum.
'Britwum . . . relates Oyono to other writers of literary history and the present and judges Une vie de boy along with Oyono's other prose fiction.'
David K. Bruner – *Research in African Literatures*

Brown, N.
Notes on Wole Soyinka's Kongi's Harvest
Nairobi: HEB (East Africa), 1973 (Heinemann Students' Guide). 48 pp. K.shs.6.00/75p
A guide for secondary school students which includes sections on Soyinka's life, a summary of the play, characterization, style, theme, study questions and a list of related books.

Carroll, David
Chinua Achebe
London: Macmillan, 1980 (2nd revised ed.) (Macmillan Commonwealth Writers Series). 192 pp. £8.95 cased £3.50 p/b
New York: St. Martin's Press, 1980. 192 pp. $16.95 cased
In this revised and extended version of the first edition, originally published in 1970, David Carroll updates his appreciative survey of Achebe's work to take into account the material published by him since then. The short stories (*Girls at War and Other Stories*) and poems (*Beware, Soul Brother*) are discussed in an additional chapter, while the essays (*Morning Yet on Creation Day*), plus Achebe's continued examination of the role of writer and critic in Africa in both essay and interview format, are explored in a revised introduction and conclusion. Among the issues Carroll explores are how Achebe uses these qualities manifest in the works written around the time of the Biafran War, to best effect in today's political realities.

He reveals and illustrates some of the innovations of Achebe's fictional writings and shows how his fusion of language and fictional technique becomes his greatest strength. The bibliography – listing all his main works and a selection of the major criticism – has also been updated.

'Mr. Carroll writes most interestingly and understandingly of Achebe's work.'

Edward Blishen – *The Times Educational Supplement*

'[the new edition] . . . shows, as before, a fine critical intelligence applied to the works of black Africa's finest novelist.'

Robert M. Wren – *Africana Journal*

Notes on Chinua Achebe's Arrow of God
Beirut and London: Longman York Press, 1980 (York Notes, 92). 78 pp. 90p
A study guide to Achebe's novel, providing an introduction to the text, a summary of the plot, together with critical commentary and hints for study, including specimen questions and answers.

Chakava, Henry
Notes on Meja Mwangi's Kill Me Quick
Nairobi: HEB (East Africa), 1976 (Heinemann Students' Guides, 11). 50 pp. K.shs.6.00/75p
This students' guide summarizes the novel and gives comments and characterization, themes, style and weaknesses in the novel. There is a section giving projects to be undertaken by the student which may give a deeper understanding of the novel, and context questions, essays and a book list are also included.

Charrier, Monique
L'Enfant noir de Camara Laye
Paris: Hachette, 1980 (Lectures pour les collèges, niveau 2, 20), 62 pp.
Extracts of Camara Laye's *L'Enfant noir* adapted for use by francophone secondary school children.

Chevrier, Jacques
Une vie de boy – Oyono: analyse critique
Paris: Hatier, 1977 (Profil d'une oeuvre, 54). 79 pp.
Chevrier's guide to Ferdinand Oyono's *Une vie de boy* is aimed at the university level student. The first chapter contains a brief biography of Oyono and notes on the historical and literary context of his works as well as a detailed plot summary of *Une vie de boy*. The other chapters present a study of chapters in the novel (the hero, minor characters, whites), of themes (racism and segregation, the breakdown of human relationships in colonial society, the loss of illusions concerning the past and the present), and of Oyono's literary technique – the autobiographical novel. The guide closes with a chapter on the meaning of Oyono's novel. There is a bibliography and a list of themes for further study.

'Chevrier does well . . . his judgments are provocative and significant.'

David K. Bruner – *Research in African Literatures*

Chinua Achebe: Arrow of God et ses critiques
Paris and Montpellier: Société d'Etudes des Pays du Commonwealth, Centre d'Etudes Afro-américaines et du Tiers Monde anglophone (Université de Paris III), Centre d'Etudes et de Recherche sur les Pays d'Afrique Noire Anglophone (Université Paul-Valéry, Montpellier), 1979. 196 pp. FF30.00
A combined issue of *Echoes du Commonwealth*, no. 5, 1979–80, and *AFRAM Newsletter*, no. 9. This volume of critical writings on Achebe's *Arrow of God* was brought out to help prepare French university students for the *agrégation* in English which, in 1980, included Achebe's novel as a set book. Three of the nine articles are in English (Douglas Killam writing on Achebe's aims in *Arrow of God*, Denise Bonneau on Achebe's language, and Bruce King on the revised edition of *Arrow of God*). There is also the transcription of a round table on Achebe held at the CERPANA in Montpellier in October 1979. Other contributors are Robert Mane, Michel Fabre, Jacques Leclaire, Elaine Amaizo, Denise Coussy, and Thomas Melone.

Clark, Ebun
Hubert Ogunde: the making of Nigerian theatre
Ibadan: University Press Ltd., 1979. 190 pp.
₦15.00 cased ₦5.00 p/b
A study of the formation (in 1944) and development of one of the most important influences on Nigerian theatre today – the Hubert Ogunde professional theatre company, using Nigerian newspapers, Ogunde's personal papers, and interviews as primary sources. The development of this very popular and innovative group is described from historical and theatrical points of view. Ogunde's political activism is emphasized through a discussion of his relationship to the 1940s nationalist movement and his encounters with censorial colonial authorities.

Collins, Harold T.
Amos Tutuola
New York: Twayne Publishers, 1969 (Twayne's World Authors Series, 42). 146 pp. o/p
A critical study and analysis of Tutuola's work. Harold Collins traces his early life, the beginnings of his writing career, the reception

of his work in Nigeria, and concludes with an appreciation of Tutuola's literary powers. Notes, references and a select bibliography are included.

'Professor Collins has collected and put forward the most comprehensive details on Tutuola and his novels that I have come across.'
Donatus I. Nwoga – *Research in African Literatures*

Dada, S.
Notes, Questions/Answers on Weep not, Child
Ibadan: Aromolaran, 1957. 60 pp. ₦1.20
An examination guide to Ngugi's novel.

Daniels, Russell
Peter Abrahams – Tell Freedom
London: Longman, 1981 (Longman Guides to Literature). 86 pp. 90p
This study guide ia aimed at 'O' level English literature candidates, and it takes the student through Abrahams's novel (the Allen and Unwin abridged school edition, edited by W. G. Bebbington), providing background to the text and biographical details about Peter Abrahams. Key themes and episodes are pinpointed, and a final section provides suggestions on how to interpret and tackle the different sorts of essay questions set by examiners.

Diakhaté, Lamine
Lecture libre de Lettres d'hivernage et d'Hosties noires de L. S. Senghor
Dakar: Nouvelles Éditions Africaines, 1976. 72 pp. CFA750
A presentation of two of Senghor's volumes of verse written by a man who is a friend and a disciple.

Dibba, Ebou
Camara Laye – The African Child
London: Longman, 1980 (Longman Guides to Literature). 49 pp. 90p
A study aid prepared for use by 'O' level English literature candidates, which provides a background to Laye's novel, with summaries of individual chapters. Key themes and episodes are highlighted, and a final section gives some guidance on the sort of essay questions students will be expected to answer in the examination.

Dunn, T. A.
Notes on Chinua Achebe's Things Fall Apart
Beirut and London: Longman York Press, 1981 (York Notes, 96). 62 pp. 90p
This study guide provides an introduction to the background of Achebe's novel, a summary

of the plot, commentary on the text, together with hints for study, including specimen questions and answers.

Dussutour-Hammer, Michèle
Amos Tutuola: tradition orale et ériture du conte
Paris: Présence Africaine, 1978. 158 pp. FF31.00
For Michèle Dussutour-Hammer, Tutuola is the craftsman-artist who paradoxically 'writes bad English but who uses it well'. Her study is based on the observation that Tutuola and his works belong at some half-way point between written and oral forms of language, that although Tutuola adheres loosely to traditional Yoruba story-telling conventions that he does more than simply transcribe his tales. He invents his identity as a writer and makes the tales his own by creatively rewriting them. This is the conclusion of the first five chapters of this book. The other chapters analyse closely how Tutuola has dealt with a certain number of story-telling conventions like gods and monsters, the travelling hero, the theme of punishment. Plot summaries of all of Tutuola's works are found in the appendix and there is an 18-page thematically arranged bibliography.
'Dussutour-Hammer is at her wittiest and most amusing in her discussion of Tutuola's monsters, those "trump cards in these tales of horror".'
Harold Collins – *Research in African Literatures*

Edições 70
Luandino: José Luandino Vieira e a Sua Obra
Lisbon: Edições 70, 1980 (Signos no. 32). 323 pp.
A collection of critical essays on the work of Luandino Vieira by sixteen scholars from Europe, Africa and the United States. This volume also includes interviews with Luandino and a bibliography.

Edorhe, P.F.
Weep Not, Child: notes
Ibadan: Onibonoje Press, 1970. 48 pp. 70k
Notes, questions and answers on Ngugi's novel. An examination guide.

Emenyonu, Ernest
Cyprian Ekwensi
London: Evans, 1974 (Modern African Writers Series). 151 pp. £2.60 cased £1.40 p/b
A chronological study of this versatile and prolific Nigerian author whose works include plays for radio and television, short stories and novels. The volume begins with a general account of Ekwensi's background leading to a consideration of his early writings and includes

chapters on 'Children's literature', 'Collections', *Jagua Nana* and *Burning Grass, Beautiful Feathers,* and *Iska.*
'*As the first book-length study of Ekwensi, Emenyonu's . . . is a bold first: it is complete, thoroughly researched, and will likely remain for a long time the most carefully documented biographical and critical source-book on Ekwensi . . . It is a not-to-be-missed scholarly work for critics, students, and teachers of African literature.*'
Charles E. Nnolim – *African Literature Today*
'*. . . the general reader will certainly appreciate the biographical data and descriptive passages offered . . . Emenyonu has introduced Cyprian Ekwensi as one of the pioneers of West African fiction.*'
Vladimir Klima – *Research in African Literatures*

Erapu, Laban
Notes on Francis Imbuga's Betrayal in the City
Nairobi: HEB (East Africa), 1979 (Heinemann Students' Guides, 15). 44 pp. K.shs.7.50/75p
A study guide which begins with a profile of Imbuga and his writing and contains sections on plot summary, characterization, theme, language and questions on the play.

Notes on Wole Soyinka's The Lion and the Jewel
Nairobi: HEB (East Africa), 1975 (Heinemann Students' Guides, 6). 44 pp. K.shs.6.00/75p
A student's guide which, in addition to sections on Soyinka's life and work, plot summary, characterization, symbolism and imagery, etc., gives suggestions for work, questions and a book list.

Notes on John Ruganda's 'The Burdens'
Nairobi: HEB (East Africa), 1977 (Heinemann Students' Guides, 12). 36 pp. K.shs.6.00/75p
This study guide gives a biographical outline of Ruganda, a plot summary of the play with commentary on themes, characterization, and language and style. Suggestions for work, questions, and a reading list are included also.

Folorunso, C. O.
Notes on The African Child
Ibadan: Aromolaran, 1970. 100 pp. ₦1.00
An examination guide, with questions and answers, on Camara Laye's novel.

Fraser, Robert
The Novels of Ayi Kwei Armah
London: HEB, 1980 (SAL). 128 pp.
£4.95/$15.95 cased £1.95/$5.95 p/b
The five novels of Ayi Kwei Armah, *The Beautyful Ones Are Not Yet Born, Fragments, Why Are We So Blest?, Two Thousand Seasons* and *The Healers,* which were published during the

period 1968–1978 are discussed in separate chapters in a book which is 'both an estimate of a writer and an essay in the evolution of a literary form'. The first chaper is devoted to a biography of Armah – placing his life and work in the political and social context of his time. The works are interpreted in logical sequence, the earlier novels being analysed in the light of the later ones, leading to the emergence of Armah as a novelist committed to the cause of cultural reconstruction in Africa.
'*. . . Fraser's interest in tracing Armah's emergence as "the craftsman of the plural voice" gives his book a refreshing wholeness.*' Abena Busia – *West Africa*

Gachukia, Eddah
Notes on Ngugi wa Thiong'o's The River Between
Nairobi: HEB (East Africa), 1976. (Heinemann Students' Guides, 8). 32 pp. K.shs.6.00/75p
A guide for the secondary school student which comprises a biography of Ngugi wa Thiong'o, chapter summaries, dominant themes, characterization and style of the novel, and also includes questions and a book list.

Gale, Steven H.
Chinua Achebe's No Longer at Ease: a critical commentary
New York: Monarch Press, 1975. 94 pp. $1.25
A critical study guide to this popular Nigerian novel which contains a biography, an extensive bibliography and cites many of Achebe's own pronouncements in interviews and publications.
'*[Steven Gale] . . covers a lot of ground and his research is as complete as anyone would wish.*'
Charles E. Nnolim – *Research in African Literatures*

Garrot, Daniel
Léopold Sédar Senghor: critique littéraire
Dakar: Nouvelles Éditions Africaines, 1978. 154 pp. CFA1,250
An analysis of a lesser known facet of Senghor – Senghor the literary critic – based mainly on an exegesis of the first volume of Senghor's collected writings on the subject of culture and literature, *Liberté I: Négritude et Humanism.* Garrot first examines how Senghor relates literature to ethnic and sociological considerations. The author then takes up the study of the principal themes of Senghor's critical apparatus – love, exile and the kingdom of childhood – followed by a discussion of what for Senghor constitute the fundamental elements of a genuine negro-African style – image and rhythm. The annexe contains Senghor's

answers to the author's questionnaire. There is also a bibliography of works by and on Senghor and on works of literary criticism.

Gibbs, James
Study Aid to Kongi's Harvest
London: Rex Collings, 1973. 56 pp. 35p
A guide for the student and teacher which examines the structure and meaning of Soyinka's play. Included in the text is an explanatory letter from the playwright.
'*Perhaps the most thorough and penetrating of any essay to date on* Kongi's Harvest.'
    Richard Priebe – *Research in African Literatures*

Critical Perspectives on Wole Soyinka
Washington D.C.: Three Continents Press, 1980. 350 pp. $18.00 cased $9.00 p/b
London: HEB, 1981 (Critical Perspectives Series). 274 pp. £3.95 p/b
Presents a selection of essays and reviews on the work of Wole Soyinka over the last twenty years. It includes critical assessments of the plays, and a substantial section of the book is devoted to Soyinka's collections of poetry. There are also articles on *The Interpreters* and *The Man Died*. James Gibbs provides an introduction to the volume, as well as an extensive, 20-page bibliography on Soyinka.

Gikandi, Simon
Notes on Camara Laye's The African Child
Nairobi: HEB (East Africa), 1980 (Heinemann Students' Guides, 18). 46 pp. K.shs.7.50/75p
A secondary school guide which outlines the novel and includes chapter summaries, themes, characterization, language etc. There is a section on 'Major flaws' in *The African Child* and questions and a book list are appended. Notes on the use of the guide and a summary of Laye's life, including his political beliefs, are also included.

Githaiga, Anna
Notes on Flora Nwapa's Efuru
Nairobi: HEB (East Africa), 1979 (Heinemann Students' Guides, 16). 48 pp. K.shs. 7.50/75p
In addition to sections on plot, characterization and themes, this students' guide also includes a section on 'Flaws in the novel', a comprehensive list of questions, and hints on answering examination questions.

Grant, Jane W.
Ama Ata Aidoo – The Dilemma of a Ghost
London: Longman, 1980 (Longman Guides to Literature). 49 pp. 90p
Intended for 'O' level English literature candidates, this study guide provides a back-

ground to Aidoo's play, discussing its structure, language and characterization. Key themes and episodes are examined, and in the final section the different aspects of the play are brought together in examination-type questions.

Gray, Stephen
Sources of the First Black South African Novel in English
Pasadena: California Institute of Technology; Munger Africana Library, 1976 (Munger Africana Library Notes, 37). 28 pp. $2.00
An interpretation of Plaatje's use of phrases and concepts from Shakespeare and Bunyan to *Mhudi*, which shows how he sought, through this method, to confront and deflate the bubble of 'colonial cultural arrogance'.

Guibert, Armand
Léopold Sédar Senghor: l'homme et l'oeuvre
Paris: Présence Africaine, 1968. 180 pp. illus. o/p
A critical study of Senghor's work, in which, after a detailed introduction, there are extracts from his poetry, prose and political writings, an interview with Senghor, quotations from book reviews, and a bibliography.

Léopold Sédar Senghor
Paris: Seghers, 1969 (Poètes d'aujourd'hui, 82). 189 pp. FF6.00
Presents a biography of Senghor, a study of his poetry, and a selected number of his poems, together with a glossary and a chronological table relating the events of Senghor's life to recent African and colonial history.

Heron, G. A.
Notes on Okot p'Bitek's Song of Lawino and Song of Ocol
Nairobi: HEB (East Africa), 1975 (African Students' Guides, 5). 42 pp. K.shs.6.00 (75p)
A student's guide dealing with the first two songs of Okot p'Bitek which contains sections on the argument of the poems, characterization, imagery and symbolism. Some suggestions for work and a list of questions are included.

The Poetry of Okot p'Bitek
London: HEB, 1976 (SAL). 163 pp. £5.00 cased £2.50 p/b
New York: Africana Publishing Co., 1976. 163 pp. $17.50
A critical assessment of the works of one of the leading contributors to African literature. The author's knowledge of the Acoli language and his understanding of the importance of Acoli oral traditions enable him to evaluate p'Bitek's

poetry against the backdrop of social change. The development of the poet's best known work, *Song of Lawino*, is described and the published poem is compared with the English version.

'It is a pioneering work in which the author draws on a large store of details of p'Bitek's life as an individual and as a cultural evangelist on the East African scene to illuminate certain aspects of his poetry.'
Samuel O. Asein – *Research in African Literatures*
'Heron's understanding of the importance of Acoli oral traditions to Okot's work and his excellent analysis of literary technique in Song of Lawino *and* Song of Ocol *make the book a success.'*
Laura Tanna – *ASA Review of Books*

Heywood, Christopher
Chinua Achebe's Things Fall Apart
London: Rex Collings in association with the British Council, forthcoming 1981.

Hoyet, D.
Francis Bebey
Paris: F. Nathan, 1979. 79 pp. FF12.40
A critical appreciation of Bebey's writings accompanied by extracts from his works. Includes biographical details and a bibliography.

Hymans, Jacques Louis
Léopold Sédar Senghor: an intellectual biography
Edinburgh: Edinburgh University Press, 1971. 312 pp. £4.00 cased
A book that attempts to retrace Senghor's intellectual wanderings between two civilizations and three historical eras. Part I entitled 'The Early Years' covers the period 1906–29, Part II ('The Discovery of Négritude') 1929 to 1948, and Part III ('From Poetry to Politics') from 1937 to 1970. The appendix includes a short chronology of Senghor's life and an exchange of letters between Senghor and the author. Senghor had read the original manuscript in 1964, in French, which was the author's doctoral dissertation for the *Doctorat en Etudes Politiques* from the Sorbonne.

Innes, C. L. and Bernth Lindfors eds.
Critical Perspectives on Chinua Achebe
London: HEB, 1979 (Critical Perspectives Series). 315 pp. £2.90
Washington D.C.: Three Continents Press, 1978. 320 pp. $18.00 cased $9.00 p/b
A collection of essays reprinted from various sources on the works and career of one of Africa's leading novelists in English. The

volume contains five general studies followed by more detailed analyses of Achebe's four novels and his poetry. Introductory notes on the life of Achebe and an extensive bibliography of works on and about him are included.
'The volume at present is a frontrunner in Achebe studies. The essays perceptively interpret Achebe's writing and reveal a variety of critical sensibilities.'
G. D. Killam – *Africana Journal*

Jabbi, B. B.
Achebe: Things Fall Apart (notes)
Freetown: Fourah Bay College Bookshop, distr., 1974 (Hints on African Literature, 1). 59 pp. Le1.10
Yet a further study and examination guide to Achebe's novel.

Jones, Eldred D.
The Writings of Wole Soyinka
London: HEB, 1973 (SAL). 190 pp. £2.25
Boston: Twayne Publishers [publ. as *Wole Soyinka*], 1974 (Twayne's World Author Series). $7.95
A detailed critical analysis of Soyinka's plays, poetry and fiction by this renowned West African critic. In discussing the plays (from *The Swamp-Dwellers* to *Madmen and Specialists*) the poetry (in *Idanre and Other Poems*; *Poems from Prison* and *Requiem*) and the novel *The Interpreters*, Jones shows how Soyinka's powerful imagery is a complex fusion of elements from his Yoruba and Christian background and his experience of European literature. Close analysis of the individual works illustrates Soyinka's sensibility, commitment and acute social awareness.
'. . . an admirable and illuminating guide . . . a measured and perceptive comment on almost a decade-and-a-half of Soyinka's work.'
Martin Banham – *African Literature Today*
'. . . bound to appeal to a wide cross-section of readers – from academic scholars to students in schools and colleges, from literary aestheticians to the general reader – for it is lucid, well-written and, at the same time, simple.'
Dapo Adelugba – *Research in African Literatures*

Kadima-Nzuji, Mukala
Jacques Rabemananjara: l'homme at l'oeuvre
Paris: Présence Africaine, 1981. 186 pp.
The format in this volume is similar to all those in 'L'homme et l'oeuvre' series. There is a biography of Rabemananjara, extracts from his poetry, his theatre, and his political and cultural writings (including two theoretical essays on poetry), and two interviews with the writer (both dating from early 1976). The book ends with extracts of critical reviews, a glossary

of Malagasy works, and a bibliography. Includes eight pages of photographs.

Kane, Mohamadou
Birago Diop: l'homme et l'oeuvre
Paris: Présence Africaine, 1971 (Collection Approches). 231 pp. FF36.00
Details of the life and work of this Senegalese writer, who was equally at home with poetry, short stories or drama, introduce the reader to subsequent sections which concentrate on critical commentaries of selected poems and short stories. Diop is placed in the context of contemporary West African creative writing, and the book closes with a transcript of an interview with him and excerpts from critical writings on his work.

Kahari, G.
The Imaginative Writings of Paul Chidyausiku
Gwelo, Zimbabwe: Mambo Press, 1975. 175 pp. Z$2.25

The Novels of Patrick Chakaipa: a critique in English and Shona
Salisbury: Longman, 1972. 110 pp. Z$1.75

Kemoli, Arthur
Notes on Achebe's Things Fall Apart
Nairobi: HEB (East Africa), 1975 (Heinemann Students' Guides, 9). 44 pp. K.shs.6.00/75p
A secondary school guide containing background material to Chinua Achebe and his work, chapter summaries, characterization, themes, and style. Working exercises and a book list are also included.

Killam, G. D.
An Introduction to the Writings of Ngugi
London: HEB, 1980 (SAL). 128 pp. £2.95/$8.50
A critical analysis of Ngũgĩ's novels, short stories and plays and the background and influences, both literary and other, which have shaped his writing. An attempt is made, through reference to the novels, to show how Ngugi transforms his experience and views on the function of art into literature. Particular attention is paid to Ngugi's involvement with the Kenyan independence movement and the problems to be faced in the post-independent state.
'. . . a useful survey of the development of a novelist who has written one of the best of all studies of the impossibility of human heroism ("A Grain of Wheat").'
Edward Blishen – *The Times Educational Supplement*

The Writings of Chinua Achebe: a commentary
London: HEB, 1977 (2nd revised ed.) (SAL). 132 pp. £2.25
Originally published as *The Novels of Chinua Achebe* in 1969, this revised edition retains practically all of the critical commentary devoted to Achebe's four novels and the copious extracts from his writings which characterized the first edition. Additions discuss revisions to *Arrow of God* and there is an updated conclusion to Killam's thoughts on *A Man of the People*, as well as an expanded commentary on the short stories and comments on Achebe's recent publications.
'. . . It is little wonder that the book has been the most useful single critical work on Achebe's novels for all classes of readers on both sides of the Atlantic.'
Robert M. Wren – *Research in African Literatures*

King, Adele
The Writings of Camara Laye
London: HEB, 1980 (SAL). 141 pp. £7.50/$21.00 cased £3.90/$10.50 p/b
A detailed study of the late Camara Laye's four novels, short stories and essays. In addition to a detailed analysis of themes, autobiographical elements and techniques, attention is paid to the influence of European literature and African arts on Laye's prose style and his aims as a writer. Interpretations of his work by previous critics are discussed and a full picture of Laye's life, including the reasons for his exile from Guinea, are given.
'. . . particularly interesting because based to some extent on interviews with the exiled author.'
Edward Blishen – *The Times Educational Supplement*

Kitonga, E.
A Study Guide to John Ruganda's Play The Burdens
Nairobi: OUP, 1977. 48 pp. K.shs.6.50
This study aid presents introductory background to Ruganda's play, a summary of the plot, notes and commentary, together with comprehension and essay questions.

Lebaud, Geneviève
Léopold Sédar Senghor ou la poésie du royaume d'enfance
Dakar: Nouvelles Editions Africaines, 1976. 104 pp. CFA600
Traces the psychological journey, with its components of exile and solitude, that led Senghor the poet into the search for his African heritage, a search that led ultimately to the publication of a major work, *Chants d'ombre*, and later, *Ethiopiques*.

Leusse, Hubert de
Léopold Sédar Senghor l'Africain
Paris: Hatier, 1969. 254 pp.
Part I of this text designed for use in the classroom analyses Senghor's poetry through a certain number of themes (the poet of the family and of the land of the blacks, the poet of love and friendship, the poet of the invisible). Part II is a study of Senghor's poetic style from the point of view especially of its rhythm and music. Concludes with two chapters on the poet's aims ('Le surréel', 'La Négritude'). The postface is devoted to *Elégie des alizés*.

Des 'Poèmes' editions aux 'Lettres d'hivernage'
Dakar: Nouvelles Editions Africaines, 1976.
96 pp. CFA450
Paris: Hatier, 1976. 96 pp.
A biography of Léopold Senghor – as a child, an adolescent, the statesman, the man of letters, and the poet – followed by an analysis of *Poèmes* and *Lettres d'hivernage* and a discussion of Senghor's sources of inspiration.

Lindfors, Bernth ed.
Critical Perspectives on Amos Tutuola
London: HEB, 1980 (Critical Perspectives Series). 284 pp. £4.95
Washington D.C.: Three Continents Press, 1975. 332 pp. $18.00 cased $9.00 p/b
An appraisal of the literary reputation of Amos Tutuola seen through the eyes of international critics. As Bernth Lindfors states in his introduction: 'Tutuola is one of the most controversial of African authors and his six books have drawn reactions ranging from delirious enthusiasm to amused indifference to undisguised contempt. He is the kind of writer who attracts ardent fans and equally ardent foes, but his writing does not seem to be much affected by what critics say about him.' The criticisms and reviews are grouped chronologically for ease of reference.
'Overall, I would reckon Critical Perspectives on Amos Tutuola *an indispensable tool for the study of this strangely fascinating author.'*
Robert M. Wren – *Africana Journal*

Mahlasela, B. E. N.
Jolobe: Xhosa poet and writer
Grahamstown, South Africa; Rhodes Univ., Dept. of African Languages, 1973 (Working Paper 3). 36 pp. 50c

Mbock, Charly Gabriel
Le monde s'effondre de Chinua Achebe
Yaoundé: Buma Kor, 1978. 109 pp. CFA450
A study guide to Achebe's *Things Fall Apart* for the Francophone reader in Africa. Contains Achebe's biography and a chapter by chapter

summary of his first novel, followed by a critical analysis of the novel from the points of view – as an ethnographic document (including the religious problem in a separate chapter), as a study in characterization (the struggle between modernists and traditionalists), and as a document of oral literature. There are also review quotes on *Things Fall Apart*, suggested questions for discussion, and a selective bibliography.
'. . . a work of general introduction and intelligent synthesis . . . extremely helpful both to teachers and students of African literature in French medium universities and secondary schools.'
Patrick Scott – *African Book Publishing Record*

Comprendre Ville cruelle d'Eza Boto
Issy-lesMoulineaux, France: Ed. Saint-Paul, 1981 (Les classiques africains, 853). 96 pp. FF19.00
A study guide to Eza Boto's *Ville cruelle*.

Melady, Margaret Badum
Léopold Sédar Senghor: rythme et reconciliation
South Orange, N.J.: Seton Hall University Press, 1971. 68 pp.
Begins with a biographic sketch of Senghor and then discusses the moulding of Senghor's ideas, touching on the influences of Césaire, the journal *Légitime Défense*, Teihard de Chardin, black American literature, and surrealism. The theory of rhythmic images and techniques in Senghor's poetry is developed in a separate chapter. Melady calls Senghor the 'poet of reconciliation' because he is concerned with bridging cultures and pursuing the Universal Civilization. Contains an extensive bibliography.

Melone, Thomas
Mongo Béti: l'homme et le destin
Paris: Présence Africaine, 1971. 285 pp. o/p
Béti's first four novels (*Ville cruelle, Le pauvre christ de Bomba, Mission terminée, Le roi miraculé*) provide the matter for this volume of criticism. Melone calls these works 'pagan', meaning they are profoundly rooted in the Cameroonian soil and traditions. They analyse the different phases of 'a situation that Béti has never lived, through the fault of the colonial order'. For this reason Melone considers Béti's novels as being the expression of an 'incomplete initiation rite'.

Chinua Achebe et la tragedié de l'histoire
Paris: Présence Africaine, 1973. 310 pp. FF62.00
A two-part study of Achebe and his fiction. A general introduction evokes Achebe's place in

Nigerian letters and comments on Achebe as critic, with special attention being given to Achebe and black South African writers as proponents of the African Personality in opposition to the doctrine of Négritude. A first part views Achebe's four novels historically, as a study of the ancient order and 'the death of Africa' (*Things Fall Apart* and *Arrow of God*) and the new order, or 'the failure of a civilization' (*No Longer at Ease* and *A Man of the People*). This part also includes a chapter on Achebe's days at the University of Ibadan and his student writings and another on Achebe's short stories. Part II analyses the structure, setting, and style of Achebe's works. In a chapter on Achebe's language Melone calls his fiction a 'pedagogical poem' and he points out not only Achebe's use of proverbs and allegorical writing (when speaking about the past), but also his use of ugly or grotesque images (when writing about the present).

Mercier, Roger and Battestini, M. and S. eds.

Mongo Béti: écrivain camerounais
Paris: Nathan, 1964 (Littérature africaine, 5). 64 pp. FF12.00
A critical appreciation and analysis of Béti's work. Includes a bibliography and extracts from reviews

Ferdinand Oyono: écrivain camerounais
Paris: Nathan, 1964 (Littérature africaine, 8). 62 pp. FF12.00
A critical appreciation and presentation of Oyono's works, with extracts from his novels and from book reviews. Includes biographical details and a bibliography.

Seydou Badian: écrivain malien
Paris: Nathan, 1968 (Littérature africaine, 10). 64 pp. FF5.60
A critical study and appreciation of Badian's writings, with extracts from his works and from book reviews. Includes biographical details and a bibliography.

Olympe Bhély-Quénum: écrivain dahoméen
Paris: Nathan, 1974 (Littérature africaine, 4). 64 pp. FF7.70
A critical presentation and appreciation of Bhély-Quénum's fiction, with extracts from his writings and from book reviews. Includes biographical details and a bibliography.

Bernard Dadié: écrivain ivoirien
Paris: Nathan, 1964 (reprinted 1978) (Littérature africaine, 7) 63 pp. FF7.70
A critical presentation and appreciation of Dadié's work, with extracts from his writings

and from book reviews. Includes biographical details and a bibliography.

Birago Diop: écrivain sénégalais
Paris: Nathan, 1964 (Littérature africaine, 6). 64 pp. FF12.00
A critical presentation and appreciation of Diop's writing, together with a biography, a bibliography, and extracts from book reviews.

Cheikh Hamidou Kane: écrivain sénégalais
Paris: Nathan, 1964 (Littérature africaine, 1). 64 pp. FF12.00
A critical commentary on Kane's writing including biographical details, a bibliography and glossary, and extracts from book reviews.

Camara Laye: écrivain guinéen
Paris: Nathan, 1964 (Littérature africaine, 2). 64 pp. FF12.00
A critical appreciation and presentation of Camara Laye's writings, with extracts from his works, a bibliography, extracts from reviews, and a biographical feature.

L. S. Senghor: poète sénégalais
Paris: Nathan, 1965 (reprinted 1978) (Littérature africaine, 3). 63 pp. F7.70
A critical appreciation and presentation of Senghor's verse, with extracts from his works, a bibliography, extracts from reviews and a biographical sketch.

Mezu, S. Okechukwu

Léopold Sédar Senghor et la défense et illustration de la civilisation noire
Paris: Didier, 1968. 232 pp. FF30.00
In his introduction Mezu criticizes studies of Senghor that have been too sociological and have seen Senghor only as the mouth-piece for Négritude and black civilization. In this study he attempts to bring Senghor, as an individual, back into the picture. He examines, therefore, the different sources of influence on Senghor and his works, including the traditional milieu and his family background, his French education (both religious and classical), and his life as a politician. The author underlines the way these elements have been integrated into a whole. Contains twenty-two pages of bibliography.

The Poetry of L. S. Senghor
London: HEB, 1973 (SAL). 160 pp. £6.50 cased £2.25 p/b
A 'companion' to the existing collections of Senghor's poems, which discusses them largely in chronological order so that the reader can trace the developments in the poet's imagination and style. With this aim in mind we are

presented with detailed commentaries of the more important poems in each collection. Senghor's aesthetics are discussed and his achievement is related to the literary and intellectual milieu throughout Africa.

'. . . *a sensitive response to the complexities of expression . . . through which Senghor carries the themes of his poetry and enlarges for use their human scope.'*
   Abiola Irele – *Research in African Literatures*

Milcent, Ernest and Sordet, Monique
Léopold Sédar Senghor et la naissance de l'Afrique moderne
Paris: Seghers, 1969. 273 pp.
Provides a biographical study of Senghor, then discusses his political philosophy and the contributions he has made in shaping modern Africa.

Mills, Peter
Notes on Chinua Achebe's No Longer at Ease
Nairobi: HEB (East Africa), 1974 (Heinemann Students' Guides, 2). 31 pp. K.shs.6.00/75p
Aims to increase the student's knowledge, understanding and enjoyment of *No Longer at Ease* by presenting information, comment and questions in eight sections. Gives information about the author's life and work, and presents a synopsis of the novel; thereafter examines its style and structure, and outlines the characters and their relationships with one another. Also includes context and essay questions and a further reading list.

'. . . *covers a lot of ground in a short compass and provides a sort of critical balance by pointing out weaknesses in the construction of* No Longer at Ease.'
   Charles E. Nnolim – *Research in African Literatures*

Minyona-Nkodo, Mathieu-François
Comprendre Le vieux nègre et la médaille de Ferdinand Oyono
Issy-les-Moulineaux, France: Ed. Saint-Paul, 1978 (Les classiques africaines, 850). 72 pp.
FF14.00
Provides the student with a key to the world of Oyono's *The Old Man and the Medal*, with a plot summary and a critique of its characters, language, style and significance. Includes subjects for study and a bibliography.

Comprendre Les bouts de bois de dieu de Sembène Ousmane
Issy-les-Moulineaux, France: Ed. Saint-Paul, 1979 (Les classiques africaines, 851). 95 pp.
FF18.00
A presentation of Ousmane as a writer and a film-maker. Discusses the historical context of

his novels as well as his characters and their roles. Contains extracts from key passages in his works.

Moody, H. L. B.
Kofi Awoonor's This Earth my Brother
London: Rex Collings in association with the British Council, forthcoming 1981.

Moore, Gerald
Wole Soyinka
London: Evans, 1978 (2nd ed.) (Modern African Writers Series). 187 pp. £4.50
New York: Africana Publ. Co., 1972 (1st ed.). $14.50 cased $6.75 p/b
This new edition has been updated to include works written by Soyinka since his release from prison in the early 1970s. Through a critical analysis of his varied output, Moore relates Soyinka's ten plays, three political reviews, two novels, several volumes of poetry and major critical essays to the writer's life, illustrating the extent of his political commitment. He also shows how powerfully Soyinka expresses issues central to the Yoruba world-view in a sophisticated use of the English language, and the major role he has played in the development of modern Nigerian drama.

'. . . *shows that Soyinka evaluates his own role as an artist in society through the leading characters of his major plays . . . an excellent and useful introduction to this flamboyant writer and his complex work.'*
   Ulli Beier – *Sydney Morning Herald*
'. . . *an intelligent and thoughtful analysis, commenting on virtually everything Soyinka has written since the first London production of the* Swamp Dwellers.'
   James Lampley – *Africa*

Moulin, Charles
Loÿs Masson
Paris: Seghers, 1962 (Poètes d'aujourd'hui, 88). 212 pp.
An introduction to the verse of the Mauritius poet who died in Paris in 1969. Includes extracts from some of his works.

Mouralis, Bernard
Comprendre Mongo Béti écrivain
Issy-les-Moilineaux, France: Ed. Saint-Paul. 1981 (Les Classiques Africains, 854). 136 pp.
FF19.00
A guide to the writing of Mongo Béti.

Nesbitt, Rodney
Notes on Elechi Amadi's The Concubine
Nairobi: HEB (East Africa), 1974 (Heinemann Students' Guides, 4). 44 pp. K.shs.6.00/75p
Aims to increase the student's knowledge, understanding and enjoyment of *The Concubine* by presenting information, comment and

questions in fifteen sections. These provide details of the author's life, a general summary of the novel and its purpose, an appreciation of some of the characters and of style and language. Includes a critical appreciation of the novel, projects context questions and essays, and a short list of further reading. Aimed at the senior school – or junior undergraduate – student.

Notes on Peter Abrahams's Mine Boy
Nairobi: HEB (East Africa), 1975 (Heinemann Students' Guides, 7). 52 pp. K.shs.6.00/75p
Aims to increase the student's knowledge, understanding and enjoyment of *Mine Boy* by presenting information, comment and question in eleven sections. These provide details of the author's life, the background to the novel, a summary of its development, purpose, style structure, language, and appreciation of its characters and themes. Also included are context questions and essays, and a bibliography to direct the student's further reading.

Niven, Alastair
Elechi Amadi's The Concubine: a critical view
London: Rex Collings in association with the British Council, 1981 (Nexus Books, 1). 32 pp. £1.00
Offers an introduction to Amadi's narrative method, and the language, theme, and characterization of *The Concubine*, together with extracts of some criticism on the work. Also included are points for discussion and questions for classroom debate, and a select reading list.

Nnamonu, Silas
Ferdinand Oyono – The Old Man and the Medal
London: Longman, 1981 (Longman Guides to Literature). 40 pp. 90p
A study aid for 'O' level English literature candidates, which takes the student through Oyono's novel, providing historical and literary background, pinpointing key episodes and central themes. A final section gives some advice on the sort of essay questions students should be prepared to answer in the examination.

Ogunba, Oyin
The Movement of Transition: a study of the plays of Wole Soyinka
Ibadan: Ibadan Univ. Press, 1975. 235 pp. ₦5.90 cased ₦3.50 p/b
This systematic study of eight Soyinka plays analyses their themes, and the ways in which Soyinka presents them dramatically.
'. . . *a good example of the application of*

sociocultural and aesthetic approaches to modern African literature, and it is a handbook for the teacher of dramatic literature and a guidebook for the director.'   Romanus Egudu – *Books Abroad*
'. . . *undoubtedly fills a need in present Soyinka criticism and will be a valuable companion to all students of the plays. Its meticulous attention to details of synopsis, characterization, and action will also be of great assistance to producers, in Africa and elsewhere.*'
          Gerald Moore – *Research in African Literatures*

Ogungbesan, Kolawole
The Writing of Peter Abrahams
London: Hodder and Stoughton, 1979. 156 pp. £6.50 cased £3.25 p/b
New York: Africana Publ. Co.: 1979. $24.50 cased $12.50 p/b
In his analysis of Abrahams's writings over a period of forty years, Ogungbesan shows how the author deals with the universal themes of relationships between black and white, political independence and spiritual freedom – issues which are ever-present in his birthplace, South Africa. An introduction describes Abrahams's literary development, his perfection of the 'dialectical political fable' and his influence on succeeding novelists.
'. . . *Refreshingly objective and unpretentious, the book presents an Abrahams whose career is impressive for its lifelong adherence to destroying racism.*'
          – *Choice*
'*We have needed a more comprehensive appraisal of his [Abrahams's] work than that available in isolated journal articles, and this is achieved in this excellent and balanced book . . . this is fundamentally a work of rigorous literary criticism, avoiding the shallow sociology by which much African writing has been judged.*'   John Povey – *Africana Journal*

Ogunmola, M. O.
Study Notes on Chinua Achebe's Things Fall Apart
Ibadan: Alliance, 1970. 41 pp. 40k
Notes, question and answers on Achebe's novel.

Okafor, Dubem
Nationalism in Okigbo's Poetry
Enugu, Nigeria: Fourth Dimension Publ. Co., 1980. 96 pp. ₦3.50
A study of Christopher Okigbo's poetry which examines its social significance and its political undertones.

Onibonoje, Biodun
The African Child: notes, Q/A
Ibadan: Onobonjoe Press, 1973 (Examination Aid Series). 52 pp. ₦1.00
Intended to help pupils working for the West

African School Certificate GCE ('O' level) examinations, this booklet outlines the Négritude movement, Camara Laye's position within it, a short biography of him. It also has chapters dealing with traditional belief, characterization and narrative technique, as well as a summary of the plot, followed by questions and answers on the novel.
'... *this little booklet, if properly used as a companion to the careful reading of* The African Child, *can enhance the high school reader's understanding of the novel.*'
Frederic Michelman – *Research in African Literatures*

The Lion and the Jewel: notes, Q/A
Ibadan: Onibonoje Press, 1974 (Examination Aid Series). 141 pp. ₦1.10
Provides help for pupils working for the West African School Certificate GCE ('O' level) examination, giving background information about the themes and settings of this Yoruba play, with summaries of the plot, characterization, plus a brief biography of its author, Wole Soyinka.

Houseboy: notes, Q/A
Ibadan: Onibonje Press, 1976 (Examination Aid Series). 68 pp. ₦1.00
Aims to assist pupils working for the West African School Certificate GCE ('O' level) examinations, by presenting a summary of the plot, characterization, and historical circumstance of Ferdinand Oyono's novel. Onibonoje concentrates on social protest, moral lessons and a political exposé of Oyono's major themes.

The Rhythm of Violence: notes, Q/A
Ibadan: Onibonoje Press, 1976 (Examination Aid Series). 79 pp. ₦1.10
Intended for pupils working for the West African School Certificate GCE ('O' level) examination, this booklet gives an interpretation of Lewis Nkosi's play, together with comprehension exercises, questions and answers.

Osiboye, S.
Notes, Questions/Answers on The Lion and the Jewel
Ibadan: Aromolaran, 1975. 64 pp. ₦1.20
An examination guide to Soyinka's play.

Osinowo, O.
Notes, Questions/Answers on Things Fall Apart
Ibadan: Aromolaran, 1970. 80 pp. ₦1.30
A study and examination guide to Achebe's novel.

Osman, Gusine Gawdat
L'Afrique dans l'univers poétique de L. Sédar Senghor
Dakar: Nouvelles Editions Africaines, 1979. 277 pp. CFA2,500

Parasuram, A. N.
Minerva Guide to Things Fall Apart
Madras: Minerva Publishing House, 1967. 96 pp.
The above item, and the following ones, all provide short critical commentary on various African novels, together with sample questions likely to be set in examinations.

Minerva Guide to The River Between
Madras: Minerva Publishing House, 1970. 106 pp.

Minerva Guide to The African Child
Madras: Minerva Publishing House, 1970. 88 pp.

Minerva Guide to Mission to Kala
Madras: Minerva Publishing House, 1970. 99 pp.

Minerva Guide to No Longer at Ease
Madras: Minerva Publishing House, 1971. 118 pp.

Minerva Guide to Mine Boy
Madras: Minerva Publishing House, 1971. 111 pp.

Minerva Guide to Down Second Avenue
Madras: Minerva Publishing House, 1972. 116 pp.

Minerva Guide to Danda
Madras: Minerva Publishing House, 1973. 110 pp.

Minerva Guide to The Old Man and the Medal
Madras: Minerva Publishing House, 1973. 91 pp.

Minerva Guide to Meja Mwangi, Kill Me Quick
Madras: Minerva Publishing House, 1977. 147 pp.

Minerva Guide to John Ruganda, The Burdens
Madras: Minerva Publishing House, 1977. 112 pp.

Parsons, E. M.

Notes on Wole Soyinka's The Jero Plays
London: Methuen, 1979 (Methuen Study-aid
Series). 41 pp. 75p
An introduction, with textual notes, to
Soyinka's *The Trials of Brother Jero* and *Jero's
Metamorphosis*, together with a critical appraisal
of the plays, suggested questions, and a
suggested reading list.

Petersen, Kirsten Holst

*John Pepper Clark's Selected Poems: a critical
view*
London: Rex Collings in association with the
British Council, 1981 (Nexus Books, 3). 32 pp.
£1.00
Provides an introduction to Clarke's verse
collection *A Reed in the Tide*, with an appreciation and analysis of the individual poems.
There are also extracts from interviews in
which Clark comments on his own work, as
well as extracts of some critical comment on
his poetry. Points for discussion and questions
for classroom debate are included too,
together with a reading list.

Quillateau, C.

Bernard Binlin Dadié: l'homme et l'oeuvre
Paris: Présence Africaine, 1967 (Collection
Approches). 176 pp. o/p
In this critical study of Dadié's work, there is a
detailed introduction, excerpts from his poetry
and prose, an interview, quotations from book
reviews, and a bibliography.

Rauville, Camille de

Chazel des antipodes: approche et anthologie
Dakar: Nouvelles Editions Africaines, 1974.
118 pp. CFA550
Introduces the work of the Mauritius writer
and painter who was born in 1902 and
includes many of his writings that have been
long out of print.

Ravelonanosy, G.

Jacques Rabemananjara: écrivain malgache
Paris: Nathan, 1970 (Littérature malgache, 3).
63 pp. FF7.70
A critical presentation and appreciation of
Rabemananjara's works, with extracts from his
writings and book reviews devoted to him.
Also includes biographical details and a
bibliography.

Ravenscroft, Arthur

Chinua Achebe
London: Longman (for British Council), 1969
(Writers and their Work Series, 209). 40 pp.
30p
A brief appreciation and critical commentary
of Achebe's four novels, with introductory

biographical notes and a select bibliography.
'. . . a fine, balanced study, pervaded with insight
and common sense. It treats Achebe and his novels
with the respect and solid critical standards of
judgment that such an important artist and his works
deserve . . . what impresses above all is Ravenscroft's
perceptive and repeated insistence that Achebe refuses
in any of his novels to simplify what are in reality
complex questions of history, politics, religion and
morality.'
                        Donald J. Weinstock – *Research in
                                           African Literatures*

Ricard, Alain

*Théâtre et nationalisme: Wole Soyinka et LeRoi
Jones*
Paris: Présence Africaine, 1972. 235 pp.
FF47.00
For the author, the comparison of the theatre
of the Nigerian Wole Soyinka, and the black
American, LeRoi Jones, is that of two theatrical worlds which are both marked by racial
conflicts, claims of cultural identity, and
political myths. Theirs is a theatre of cultural
nationalism. The four middle chapters show
how cultural nationalism permeates the very
theatrical tools, themselves: language, use of
space, genre (reinterpretations of history
through epic and satirical elements), theme
(use of religious elements). Before that Ricard
devotes a chapter to studying the critical
myths which are of no help in understanding
Soyinka and Jones (Négritude, neo-African-
ness according to Jahn, Black Consciousness),
and two chapters of general remarks on black
American theatre and Yoruba theatre. The
book closes with two separate chapters defining the nationalism of Soyinka and Jones.
There are chronological tables, plot summaries and a bibliography in the appendices.

Robson, Clifford B.

Ngugi wa Thiong'o
London: Macmillan, 1979 (Macmillan
Commonwealth Writers Series). 164 pp. £8.50
cased £2.50 p/b
A comprehensive study of Ngugi's writings,
including *Petals of Blood* and the little-studied
plays and short stories in *This Time Tomorrow*,
The Black Hermit and *Secret Lives*. Offers insights
into his literary, philosophical and stylistic
contributions to contemporary African writing.

Schaettel, M.

Léopold Sédar Senghor: poétique et poésie
Lyon: Eds. l'Hermès et Centre d'Etudes sur
l'Humanisme et la Communication, 1977.
41 pp.

Scott, Patricia E.

Mqhayi in Translation

Grahamstown: Rhodes University, Dept. of African Languages, 1976 (Communications, 6). 47 pp. R1.00

An introduction to this important Xhosa literary figure, including 'A Short Autobiography of Samuel Krune Mqhayi', 'The Death of Hintsa and the Dismissal of Sir Benjamin D'Urban'.

Tillot, Rennée

Le rythme dans la poésie de Léopold Sédar Senghor

Dakar: Nouvelles Editions Africaines, 1979. 168 pp. CFA1,250

Towa, Marcien

Léopold Sédar Senghor: négritude ou servitude?

Yaoundé: C.L.E., 1971 (Point de vue, 7). 120 pp.

In English *translation*, see next entry.

The Myth of Négritude

(Trans. from the French by Barbara Beck) Washington D.C.: Black Orpheus Press, 1973. 115 pp. $8.50

A critical reading of Senghor which attempts to trace his ideas and put them into their historical and sociological context.

Turkington, Kate

Chinua Achebe: Things Fall Apart

London: Edward Arnold, 1977 (Studies in English Literature, 66). 64 pp. £1.95

A critical analysis of Achebe's novel, presented in four sections: 'Okonkwo's Society'; 'Structure and Theme'; 'Characterization' and 'Language and Style'.

'. . . *Turkington is particularly good at drawing attention to ironies in tone, structure, and style within the novel.*'

C. L. Innes – *Research in African Literatures*

Valette, Pierre

Jacques Rabéarivelo: écrivain malgache

Paris: Nathan, 1967 (Littérature malgache, 1). 63 pp. FF7.70

A critical presentation of Rabéarivelo's writing with extracts from his works and from book reviews, and including biographical details and a bibliography.

Flavien Ranaivo: écrivain malgache

Paris: Nathan, 1968 (Littérature malgache, 2). 63 pp. FF7.70

A critical appreciation of the writing of Ranaivo with extracts from his works and book reviews, a biographical sketch and a bibliography.

Van Niekerk, Barend

The African Image in the Work of Senghor

London; C. Hurst (distr.). 1970. 140 pp. £3.90

Vieyra, Paulin Soumanou

Sembène Ousmane: cinéaste, lère période 1962–1971

Paris: Présence Africaine, 1972. 245 pp. FF41.00

Ousmane, the film-maker, with a biography, a technical summary of his films (*Borom Sarret, Niaye, La Noire de, Le Mandat, Tan, Emitai*), and a chapter on Ousmane as director. There is also an interview with Ousmane and the reproduction of an article he wrote on filmmaking and literature in Africa plus extracts of critical reviews of his films.

Wade, Michael

Peter Abrahams

London: Evans, 1972 (Modern African Writers Series). 220 pp. £2.95

New York: Africana Publ. Corp., 1972. $8.00

A critical analysis of the novels of Peter Abrahams – tracing the development of his ideology and the nature of his commitment to individual and political freedom – a commitment consolidated in *A Night of their Own* and *This Island Now*, Abrahams last two novels.

Wren, Robert M.

Achebe's World: the historical and cultural context of the novels of Chinua Achebe

Washington D.C.: Three Continents Press, 1980. 221 pp. $18.00 cased $7.00 p/b

London: Longman, 1981. 208 pp. £9.00 cased £4.95 p/b

A detailed study, through both oral and written roots, of the historical and cultural settings of Achebe's major fiction. Also included are a glossary of Igbo terms and proverbs found in his novels, some photographs, and maps.

Chinua Achebe – Things Fall Apart

London: Longman, 1980 (Longman Guides to Literature). 56 pp. 90p

A study aid for 'O' level English literature candidates, which takes the student through Achebe's novel, pinpointing key episodes and characters and central themes. A final section gives some advice on the sort of essay questions which students are likely to be expected to answer in the examination.

Collections

Abrahams, Lionel and **Saunders, Walter** eds.
Quarry '76: new South African writing
Johannesburg: Ad. Donker, 1976. 196 pp.
R4.50
The '76 edition of this annual paperback anthology of South African writing includes contributions from Jillian Becker, Ahmed Essop, Nadine Gordimer, Geoffrey Haresnape, Bessie Head, Essop Patel, Peter Rodda and Peter Wilhelm.

Quarry '77: new South African writing
Johannesburg: Ad. Donker, 1977. 172 pp.
R4.50
The second annually published volume of this paperback anthology of South African writing contains work by literally dozens of writers. Among the contributions is prose by Giles Hugo, Don Mclennan and Peter Wilhelm; poetry by Patrick Cullinan, Stephen Gray, Wopko Jensma, Chris Mann, Mike Nicol, Motshile Nthodi and David Wright. Joan Hoffman contributes a 'forceful chronicle on Soweto' and Peter Horn an essay on the poetry of Wopko Jensma.

Quarry '78: new South African writing
Johannesburg: Ad. Donker, 1978. 160 pp.
R4.50
The third in the series of annually published paperback anthologies of South African creative writing contains poetry, prose, essays and literary discussions by well-known as well as up-and-coming writers. With its preceding volumes (*Quarry '76* and *'77*) it focuses on new trends in South African writing today.

Achebe, Chinua *et al.*
The Insider: stories of war and peace from Nigeria
Enugu, Nigeria: Nwamife Publishers, 1971.
124 pp. 75k
Madness, politics and war are the themes of this collection of nine stories which features tales by Achebe, Flora Nwapa, Samuel Ifejika, Arthur Nwankwo and five younger writers. It is the sort of madness that sends an unemployed school drop-out on a murderous rampage, the madness that contaminates an innocent bystander. It is the sort of politics that favours political imperatives over competence, that goes to any length to make sure a favoured candidate wins. As for the war, it is that lived by civilians and soldiers alike: the war that puts a village in agony; that prevents a 14-year-old soldier from finding his way home; that forces a company of men to keep on fighting unaware hostilities had ended; that breeds a particular kind of opportunist, like the crafty young man who thought he could avoid recruitment with forged papers proclaiming him a supplies trader.

Achebe, Chinua and **Okafor, Dubem** eds.
Don't Let Him Die: an anthology of memorial poems for Christopher Okigbo 1932–67
Enugu, Nigeria: Fourth Dimension Pub. Co., 1978. 54 pp. ₦1.80
This slim volume of verse has a preface by Chinua Achebe in which he says: 'He [Okigbo] was not only the finest Nigerian poet of his generation but I believe . . . he will also be recognized as one of the most remarkable anywhere in our time.' It contributes, in verse form, to Okigbo's personality, poetry, life and death, by authors who include Achebe, Kofi Awoonor, J. P. Clark, and Wole Soyinka. There are also two poems in Igbo.
'. . . *this commemorative anthology testifies to the high regard in which he [Okigbo] and his work are held by his fellow writers . . . should be in every serious collection of modern African literature.*'
Patrick Scott – *The African Book Publishing Record*

Ademola, Frances ed.
Reflections
Lagos: African Universities Press, 1965.
123 pp. 75k
This anthology of prose, drama, poetry and essays from Nigeria features all of the major contemporary Nigerian writers. In addition there are also contributions by some less prominent and less well established authors such as John Ekwere, David Owoyele, Ralph Opara and Mabel Segun. The foreword is by Dr Nnamdi Azikiwe.

Allen, Samuel ed.
Poems from Africa
New York: Crowell, 1973. 205 pp. $4.50

Alvarez-Péreyre, J.
Poètes engagés sud-africains
Grenoble: Maison de la Culture de Grenoble, 1979. 54 pp.
An anthology of poetry by six South African writers; four black – James Matthews, Oswald Mtshali, Wally Serote, Sydney Sepamla, and two white – Wopko Jensma and Peter Horn. The tone is one of a continued exposé of the depravity of apartheid.
'*En meme temps qu'il découvre cette poésie engagée, le lecteur apprend ainsi l'essentiel de ce qu'il faut*

savoir sur le système de discrimination raciale sud-africain.'
Claude Wauthier – *Research in African Literatures*

Andrade, Mário de ed.
Antologia da Poesia Negra de Expressão Portuguesa
Paris: P. J. Oswald, 1958. 107 pp. o/p
(reprinted by Kraus Reprint, Nendeln, Liechtenstein, 1970. SF21.00)
This comprehensive anthology covers a period from the late nineteenth century to the mid-1960s and includes poems by African writers without overt political commitment such as Mário António and Bessa Victor, although most of the selections are by militant poets including the white Angolan António Jacinto. Andrade's various anthologies of Lusophone African poetry reflect an inconsistent sense of the value of particular writers. In his *Caderno de Poesia Negra de Expressão Portuguesa* published in Lisbon in 1953 in collaboration with Francisco José Tenreiro, he excludes Cape Verdean poets, for he doesn't feel they express an African identity. In the 1958 collection six Cape Verdean poets are included. There are several revised or altered anthologies edited by Andrade: *Letteratura Negra*, published in Rome by Editori Riuniti in 1961; *La Poésie Africaine d'Espression Portugaise* published by P. J. Oswald in Paris in 1969; *Antologia Temática de Poesia Africana – I – Na Noite Grávida de Punhais* published by Sá da Costa in Lisbon in 1976 with a second edition in 1977.

Angoff, Charles and Povey, John eds.
African Writing Today
New York: Manyland Books, 1969. 304 pp. $6.95
The major portion of this volume comprises the special African number of *The Literary Review*. It introduces a largely new generation of African writers, though Sarif Easmon, Eldred Jones, Ama Ata Aidoo, Taban lo Liyong, Kofi Awooner and Joe de Graft are among more familiar names included. John Povey provides an introductory essay, 'The quality of African writing today', which is followed by short stories, verse and a novella 'Under the Iroko Tree' by Joseph Okpaku. Biographical notes supplement the text.

Anthologie *de la littérature Gabonaise*
Québec: Beauchemin, 1978. 357 pp.
Initiated by the Institut Pédagogique National in Libreville (and first published by them in four 'provisional' editions between 1975–1976), this anthology contains poetry, short stories, oral literature, legends and epic poems by Gabonese writers.

Anthologie *de la poésie Nigérienne: Préface de Boubou Hama*
Arquian, France: Cercle International de la Pensée et des Arts Français, 1971. 132 pp.
Contains verse by poets from the Niger Republic, including Johnson Willian Yacoley, Omar Cissé, Souley Douramane, Boubou Idrissa Maiga, Thomas Koumako, Djerma Abdou, Mahamadou Halilou Sabbo, Aliou Saidou and others.

Awoonor, Kofi and Adali-Mortty, G.
Messages: poems from Ghana
London: HEB, 1970 (AWS, 42). 190 pp. £1.95/$5.00
A selection from the work of Major Ghanaian poets, including Joe de Graft, A. Kayper Mensah, Ayi-Kwei Armah, Amu Djoleto, Ellis Ayiteh Komey, Cameron Duodo, Kojo Gyinaye Kyei, Kofi Sey, Frank Kobina Parkes, Efua Sutherland, E. A. Winful, and verse by Kofi Awoonor himself. There are biographical notes on the authors.
'Many of the poems in this volume are variations on familiar themes – childhood, nationalism, racial injustice, and the devaluation of Europe . . . Pathos, humour, satire, rage, and even protest, are all present . . . a balanced picture of what has been done and what is being done, with glimpsed promises of what is to come.'
D. S. Izevbaye – *African Literature Today*

Azuonye, Chukwuma ed.
Nsukka Harvest: poetry from Nsukka, 1966-72
Nsukka: Odunke Publications, 1972 (Odunke Publications, 1). 40 pp. 50k
A slim collection of verse by writers at the University of Nigeria campus at Nsukka.

Baker, Houston A. ed.
Reading Black: essays in the criticism of African, Caribbean and Black American literature
Philadelphia, Pa. and Ithaca, New York: Philadelphia Univ. Press and Cornell Univ; African Studies and Research Center, 1976. (Monograph Series, 4). 58 pp. $4.00
A collection of essays – by Soyinka, Saunders Reading, Addison Gayle, Jr., Houston A. Baker, Ezekiel Mphahlele and Edward Brathwaite – which continues the debate on the issue of the Black Aesthetic and the fundamental question of alternative approaches to the criticism of Black literature.
'. . . at its best Reading Black achieves occasional insights which manage to rise above the limitations of

both sides of the issue . . . The two papers by Ezekiel Mphahlele and Edward Brathwaite are the most solid contributions . . . because they recognize the essential complexities of the Black writer's ambience and materials, without sacrificing their sense of the critic's ethnic and cultural motives.'
Lloyd W. Brown – *Research in African Literatures*

Banham, Martin ed.
Nigerian Student Verse, 1959
Ibadan: Ibadan Univ. Press, 1960. 36 pp. o/p
This small early anthology represents the best verse written by undergraduates of the University College of Ibadan, originally published in the student magazine *The Horn*.

Banks-Henries, A. D. comp.
Poems of Liberia (1836–1961)
London: Macmillan, 1966. 133 pp. o/p
A cross-section of the works of Liberian poets writing during the nineteenth and twentieth centuries.

Bassir, Olumbe ed.
An Anthology of West African Verse
Ibadan: Ibadan Univ. Press, 1957. 80 pp. o/p.

Beeton, D. R. and Saunders, Walter eds.
Twenty-three South African Poems
Johannesburg: Ravan Press, 1979. 24 pp. 89c/75p
An anthology of poems by some of South Africa's finest poets, from Roy Campbell to Mongane Wally Serote. It is intended for use by first-year undergraduates.

Beier, Ulli ed.
African Poetry: an anthology of traditional African poems
London and New York: CUP, 1966. 80 pp. £2.20/$10.95 cased $4.95 p/b
The poems in this book (which is intended as a school reader), are from widely different ethnic groups and cultures, including those of the Yoruba and Ewe of West Africa, the Zulu and 'Bushmen' of South Africa, the Galla and Swahili of East Africa, and the ancient Egyptians, and are arranged by themes such as Death, Sorrow, War, Love, People and Animals. There are notes on the poems and sources are cited, and line drawings by Susanne Wenger.

Black Orpheus; an anthology of new African and Afro-American stories
London: Longman, 1964. 160 pp. o/p
New York: McGraw-Hill, 1965. 156 pp. o/p
Sixteen stories representing the three main streams of African and Afro-American fiction,

grouped under three main sections entitled 'New Realities', 'Tradition', and 'Experiments'.
'. . . interesting, illuminating, and at times touching and troubling.'
Thomas Parkinson – *Journal of the New African Literature and the Arts*

Political Spider: an anthology of stories from 'Black Orpheus'
London: HEB, 1969. (AWS, 58). 118 pp. £1.75p
New York: Africana Publishing Corp., 1969. 118 pp. $5.45
Many of the best-known names in African writing made an early appearance in the pioneering magazine *Black Orpheus*. This selection gathers together some of their stories and extracts from novels. Most were written in English but there are also translations from the Yoruba, French and Portuguese.

Three Nigerian Plays
London: Longman, 1967. 89 pp. o/p
Three plays from Nigeria in which each author interprets an aspect of his traditional background. Two of the plays – *Moremi* by Duro Ladipo and *Born with the Fire on his Head* by Obotunde Ijimere – are based on Johnson's *History of the Yorubas*, whilst *The Scheme* by Wale Ogunyemi is based upon an incident that happened during the author's childhood. All three authors endeavour to express themselves in a language that owes much to classical Yoruba poetry. Ulli Beier provides an introduction and notes.
'. . . all three plays have a strong structure that lends inevitability to the events they record. One is surprised to learn that only Ladipo's Moremi has been performed, for the others appear to have a strong poetic and dramatic authority that acting would ignite into bold theatre.'
John Povey – *Africa Report*

Belvaude, Catherine and Dakeyo, Paul eds.
Aube d'un jour nouveau: 21 poètes sud-africains
Paris: Eds. Silex, 1981. 134 pp. FF40.00
An anthology of twenty-one South African poets.

Berry, John P.
Africa Speaks: a prose anthology with comprehension and summary questions
London: Evans, 1970. 128 pp. £1.95
An introduction to modern African literature with prose selections chosen for their subject interest, literary merit and suitability for language study. Selections represent the work

of thirty authors from all over black Africa, and are followed by questions and exercises with emphasis on comprehension and summary work. Gives practical hints in answering the new method English Language questions at 'O' and School Certificate Level now set by examination boards in East and West Africa.

Blackburn, Douglas; Horsfall, Alfred; Wanjala Chris L. eds.
Attachments to the Sun
London: Edward Arnold, 1976. 108 pp. £1.20
A collection of verse for secondary school students, by both famous and lesser-known African poets, as well as by West Indian and Latin American ones.

Bown, Lalage ed.
Two Centuries of African English: a survey and anthology of non-fictional English prose by African writers since 1769
London: HEB, 1973. (AWS, 132). 224 pp. £1.95/$4.00
This anthology contains extracts from a wide variety of writings from twelve countries, and demonstrates some of the ways in which Africans have used English since the language was first imported to that continent. Special sections assemble extracts illustrating the use of English as spoken word, in political tracts and didactic writings, biography, autobiography and travel texts.

Brooks, Charlotte K. ed.
African Rhythms: selected stories and poems
New York: Washington Square Press, 1974. 238 pp.

Butake, Bole
Thunder on the Mountain
Yaoundé: Buma Kor, 1981 [?] 145 pp.
An anthology of poetry by Cameroonian authors for use in secondary schools. Includes notes on the poets at the end of the volume.

Butler, F. G. and Mann, C. eds.
A New Book of South African Verse in English
Cape Town: OUP, 1979. 256 pp. R9.30

Carlos, Papiniano, ed.
As Armas Estão Acesas nas Nossas Mãos – Antologia Breve da Poesia Revolucionária de Moçambique
Porto, Portugal: Edicões A Pesar de Tudo, 1976. 102 pp. 55 escudos
This collection of Mozambican revolutionary poetry contains thirty-seven poems and a preface. Many of the poems celebrate the lives and deeds of heroes killed during the liberation struggle.

Cartey, Wilfred ed.
Palaver: modern African Writings
Camden, N.J.: Nelson, 1970. 224 pp. $6.95
This anthology for young readers is an invitation to *palaver*, a getting together to chat, to discuss things, to confer, or to argue. Twenty-six African authors are represented with selections from poetry, drama, folk myths, and the novel. Each of the six parts is introduced by the editor with background information on the authors and the selections.

Caverhill, Nicholas ed.
Recueil des textes Africains: an anthology of modern African writing in French
London: Hutchinson, 1967. 178 pp.
A collection of self-contained extracts from modern African authors writing in French. The first half of the anthology is made up primarily of traditional African folk-tales and some character sketches, while the second half contains passages describing African childhood and education. There are biographical details on the authors, and a vocabulary.

Cazziol, Roger J.
Douze auteurs Africains: a direct method reader with oral practice
London: Nelson, 1971. 88 pp. 40p

Cendrars, Blaise
Anthologie nègre: folklore des peuplades africaines
Paris: Au Sans Pareil, 1927. 400 pp. o/p
Paris: Ed. La Sirène, 1931. 327 pp. o/p
Paris: Corréa, 1947. 364 pp. (revised and corrected)
Paris: Buchet-Chastel, 1972 (Le livre de poche, 3370). 416 pp. FF4.30
Paris: Buchet-Chastel, 1979. 350 pp. FF60.00
The definitive edition of the first anthology of black-African writers that was originally published in 1920.

Centre Africain de Littérature
Quatre poètes du Kivu
Kinshasa: Centre Africain de Littérature, 1974. 32 pp.
An anthology of the verse of Cikuru-Ngashala Batumike, Nate-Ngu Mongala Vuru-Torote-Nzapa, Ntambuka Mwene-C'Shunjwa and Nyantabana-Ro-Ki-Simba-Nzarih.

Promesses: anthologie provisoire d'une jeune littérature zaïroise
Kinshasa: Centre Africain de Littérature/Presses Africaines, 1975. 144 pp.
Contains extracts of the works of eighteen young Zaïrois authors.

Chevrier, Jacques ed.
Anthologie africaine
Paris: Hatier, 1981 (Monde noir poche, 9).
159 pp. FF24.00
The extracts in this anthology of the prose
writing from Francophone Africa are presented by theme: the ambiguities and hardships of the colonial society, the period of
uneasiness, between tradition and revolt, and
disillusionment. The volume includes works
written as recently as 1979. The major names
of the first generation of writers are here but
also those of people who began publishing in
the seventies: M. M. Diabaté, Fantouré,
Monénembo, Sassine, Lab'Ou Tansi and
Mariama Bâ. Indexed by theme.

Clark, E. and Manley, D. comps.
Poetry
Lagos: Pilgrim Books, 1973 (African Reader's
Library, 20). 113 pp. 60k
An anthology for middle-school children, of
poems new and old from Africa and the rest of
the world on themes such as village life,
travels, moods, ideas, nature and man's
inventions.

Clark, Leon E. ed.
Coming of Age in Africa: continuity and change
New York: Praeger, 1969 ('Through African
Eyes' unit 1). 106 pp.
One in a series of books established to develop
curriculum materials for the study of other
cultures. Its aim is to let Africans speak for
themselves and to let students think for
themselves. This first volume contains contributions by Luis Bernado Honwana and
Anna Apoko, extracts from Okot p'Bitek's
Song of Lawino, Laye's *African Child*, and poetry
by Kwesi Brew, Ismael Hurreh (from Somalia)
and Léopold Senghor.

Collins, Marie
Black Poets in French
New York: Charles Scribner's Sons, 1972.
165 pp. $3.95

Cook, David ed.
*In Black and White: writings from East Africa
with broadcast discussions and commentary*
Nairobi: East African Literature Bureau, 1976.
169 pp. K.shs. 25.90 (£2.20/$5.50)
A collection of nineteen edited transcripts
from a series of broadcasts made on Radio
Uganda between December 1964 and July
1969. It includes prose, poetry and drama,
selected with the help of Ngugi wa Thiong'o,
with an appreciation and analysis by David
Cook, and the discussions with the young

writers which formed an integral part of each
broadcast. Extracts from works by Grace
Ogot, Okello Oculi and Ngugi himself are
included.
'. . . several of the broadcasts centre on authors who
have not become well-known, even in East Africa, but
this therefore makes the collection even more useful,
since in some cases these may be the only serious
critical reactions to minor writers.'
Alastair Niven – *The African
Book Publishing Record*

Origin East Africa – a Makerere anthology
London: HEB, 1965 (AWS, 15). 200 pp. o/p
Short stories, one-act plays, poetry and articles
by a group of young East Africans who were
all, at one time or another, students at
Makerere University College. Most of the
contributions come fron Kenya, Tanzania,
Uganda and Malawi, but there are also
writings by a Nigerian, an Englishman and two
Americans.
'. . . what appeals most in all these works is a
"naturalness" which is not a free gift but the result of
awareness . . . this is an excellent selection.'
Michel Ligny – *Présence Africaine*

Cook, David, and Lee, Miles eds.
Short East African Plays in English
London: HEB, 1968 (AWS, 28). 148 pp.
£1.75/$4.00
In this collection of ten plays by a number of
lesser-known dramatists from East Africa,
there are five short plays, one adaptation, and
four sketches – three of them translations from
East African vernacular languages. Several
have been successfully performed by the
Makerere Travelling Theatre and have been
broadcast by a number of radio stations in
East Africa.

Cook, David and Rubadiri, David eds.
Poems from East Africa
London: HEB, 1971 (AWS, 96). 218 pp.
£1.75/$3.00
A sampling of the work of fifty poets writing in
English in East Africa, which illustrates their
diversity of styles and interests. Moods range
from lyricism to strident calls for economic
and political justice; Cook and Rubadiri have
selected examples from the most renowned of
East African poets as well as from some
relatively unknown ones.
'. . . a blend of that gentle, modest lyricism that is a
feature of East African writing and an agressive,
abrasive voice that calls attention to economic and
political injustices both inside and outside Africa.'
Robert J. Green – *Books Africa*

Cordor, S. M. H. ed.
An Anthology of Short Stories by Writers from the West African Republic of Liberia
Monrovia: Liberian Literature and Education Publications, 1974. 341 pp. $5.95 cased $3.95 p/b

The Writings of Roland T. Dempster and Edwin J. Barclay: a prose and poetry collection of two leading Liberian poets
Monrovia: Liberian Literature and Education Publications, 1975. 288 pp. $5.00

Croft, J. ed.
Aureol Poems
Freetown, Sierra Leone: Fourah Bay College Bookshop, 1970. 24 pp. 24c

Cuingnet, Maguy
Poésie du monde noir: renaissance négro-américaine, Haïti, Antilles, Afrique, Madagascar
Paris: Hatier, 1973. 160 pp.
An anthology of poetry from the Black Diaspora for secondary schools with a short biography of authors listed. Each poem is briefly annotated and followed by study questions.

Damas, Léon-Gontran
Latitudes françaises: poètes d'expression française
Paris: Seuil, 1947. 328 pp. o/p
One of the earliest anthologies (in addition to Blaise Cendrars' *Anthologie nègre* dating from 1920) in which can be found the works of Francophone poets from black Africa, the Indian Ocean, and the West Indies.

Dathorne, Oscar Ronald ed.
African Poetry for Schools and Colleges
London: Macmillan, 1969. 166 pp. 80p
The poetry selections contained herein were 'chosen to show their varied approaches to writing verse'. They cover oral poetry, 'made up of all that is sung, chanted, or declaimed', poetry in the vernacular languages (in translation), early poetry in English and French, and contemporary verse. The second portion of the book is reserved for extensive notes on the poems themselves, accompanied by biographical details on the authors, and indexes of first lines, translators and authors.

Dathorne, Oscar Ronald, and **Feuser, Willfried** eds.
Africa in Prose
Harmondsworth, England: Penguin Books, 1969 (Penguin African Library, AP 24). 384 pp. 80p

A collection of forty-four extracts of writing from the entire African continent, providing a view of African prose from the early twentieth century to the present day. The editors' aim is 'to show that there is a recognizable prose tradition that goes back to the beginning of this century', and therefore they include several pieces not available elsewhere. There is an introduction by the editors, who also give biographical notes, and a brief commentary accompanying each extract.

Denny, Neville comp.
Pan African Short Stories
Walton-on-Thames: Nelson, 1966. 240 pp. £1.45
A broad and varied sampling of modern African writing south of the Sahara by authors 'pre-occupied with the experience of individual Africans adjusting themselves to life in a continent where the pace of change is faster than that which any other people have ever known.' There are stories by Efua Sutherland, Grace Ogot, Cyprian Ekwensi, Chinua Achebe, Gabriel Okara, James Ngugi, Alex la Guma, William Conton, and several others, with exercises and notes on each story.
'. . . the exercises form by far the most important part of the book. The intelligently framed questions and suggestions, even if some are twice removed from the immediate contexts of the stories, will stimulate critical reading and appreciation, and encourage practice.'　　　Theo Vincent – *Black Orpheus*

Diboti, Ekoa M., and **Dogbeh, Richard** eds.
Voix d'Afrique: echos du monde – livre de lecture
(Cours moyen et 1er cycle du second degré)
Paris: Inst. Pédagogique Africain et Malgache, 1965. 256 pp. FF9.00
A reader for primary schools in Africa. Extracts from African (and some French) novels and poetry are used to illustrate scenes from everyday life in Africa – school, family, playtime, sports, hunting etc. – and also provide descriptions of the country, its traditions, its legends and its heritage.

Dick, John B. ed.
The Cambridge Book of Verse for African schools
London and New York: CUP, 1966. 120 pp. £2.25
An anthology of English poetry that includes a section of poems by modern African poets.

Dick, John B.
African Forum
London and New York: CUP, 1968. 101 pp.

Comprehension and composition exercises aimed primarily at senior classes in African secondary schools 'to help each pupil to think and talk and write more fluently about his own experience, his own society, his own ideas and the ideas of others.' Extracts from the writings of a variety of African writers from Thomas Mofolo and Samuel Johnson to Camara Laye and Wole Soyinka are included.

Dickinson, Margaret ed.
When Bullets Begin to Flower
Nairobi: EAPH, 1972. 131 pp. K.shs 12.00 ($3.60)
One of the first collections of political poetry from Lusophone Africa to appear in English. There is a particularly rich sampling of Mozambican verse including selections from Marcelino dos Santos, Jorge Rebelo and José Craveirinha.

Dix *nouvelles de . . . Trimite Bassori, Patrice Ndedi Penda, Alain le Breton, Guy Menga, Bilal Fall, Donatien Ganvo, Anana Devi Nirsimloo, Flavien Bihina Bandolo, Dovoedo Amen Tayo, Daniel Valadon*
Paris: Agence de Coopération Culturelle et Technique/O.R.F.T., 1973. 223 pp.
Ten short stories by these authors from the Ivory Coast, Cameroons, Mauritius and Benin, printed under the auspices of the 1972 French Radio Competition for the best short story written in French.

Dix *nouvelles de . . . Flavien Bihina Bandolo, Patrice Ndedi Penda, Maliza Mwina Kintende, Jean Gérard Théodore, André Nyamba, Maoundoé Naindouba, Papa Samba Kebe, Martial Malinda, Abdourahmane Soli, Dramane Gnanou*
Paris: Agence de Coopération Culturelle et Technique/Radio-France, 1975. 223 pp.
Ten short stories by these writers from the Cameroons, Zaïre, Mauritius, Upper Volta, Senegal, Niger and Congo, printed under the auspices of the 1973 Radio Competition for the best short story written in French.

Dix *nouvelles de . . . M'Baye Gana Kebe, Sada Weinde N'Diaye, Abdoua Kanta, Chantal Wiene, Netonon Djekery, Liliane Berthelot, Cheikh C. Sow, Georges Révigne-Ngote*
Paris: Agence de Coopération Culturelle et Technique/Radio-France Internationale, 1977. 223 pp. FF12.00
Ten short stories by these authors from Senegal, Niger, Mauritius, Chad, and Gabon, printed under the auspices of the third Radio

Competition for the best short story written in French.

Djoleto, Amu and **Kwami, Thomas** comps.
West African Prose
London: HEB, 1972. 192 pp. 95p/$3.00
Brings together selections from the work of fourteen West African authors. Each passage is briefly set in the context of the whole novel. Intended for classroom use, especially in teacher training colleges, adult classes and secondary schools, it also includes topics for discussion that are aimed to help sutdents think and talk about the main points made by the authors.

Dogbé, Yves-Emmanuel ed.
Anthologie de la poésie togolaise
Le Mée-sur-Seine, France: Ed. Akpagnon, 1980. 223 pp. FF8.00/CFA2,500
An anthology of thirteen contemporary Togolese poets writing in French. In his preface, Dogbé underlines the linguistic problems of Togo (having been colonized by three European powers – the Germans, the British, and the French) which may explain why Togolese authors have come comparatively late to the contemporary literary scene. But he also recalls the writing in Ewé that exists and notes how many unpublished manuscripts in French he has come across, which may suggest that there is not a lack of authors, but of publishers.

Drachler, Jacob ed.
African Heritage: an anthology of black African personality and culture
New York: Crowell, 1962. 256 pp. o/p
New York: Macmillan, 1964. 286 pp. $3.95
London: Collier-Macmillan, 1969 (New ed.). £1.45
Divided into three main themes, 'African Voices', 'Afro-American responses', and 'Through the Eyes of Others', this volume presents a great deal of material, ranging from four tales from Togoland and songs from Dahomey, to articles by Melville and Frances Herskovits' 'Creative Impulses in Dahomean Poetry' and Thomas L. Hodgkin's 'The African Renaissance'.
'. . . one of the most significant anthologies.'
                    Dorothy Porter – *African Forum*

Duerden, Dennis and **Pieterse, Cosmo** eds.
African Writers Talking:
London: HEB, 1972 (SAL). 205 pp. £2.95
New York: Africana Publishing Corp., 1972. $19.50 cased $10.50 p/b

A selection of interviews from the historic collection of recordings made by the Transcription Centre, London between 1962 and 1969, and which provide insights into this important decade in the development of African literature written in English. Discussions with Achebe, Ama Ata Aidoo, Awoonor, Dennis Brutus, J. P. Clark, Ekwensi, Mazisi Kunene, La Guma, Ezekiel Mphahlele, John Nagenda, Ngugi, Christopher Okigbo, Okot p'Bitek, Richard Rive, Soyinka, and Efua Sutherland show the shifts in emphasis from definition to commitment to increased critical awareness which marked that decade. Aminu Abdullahi, Mphahlele, Lewis Nkosi and Robert Serumaga are among the interviewers. Topics covered by the two last-mentioned make sure that the reader not only has a grasp of the literary background to the work of each writer, but also an insight into his/her philosphy and working methods.

'... considerable illumination of the developing consciousness in men like Achebe, Okigbo, Awoonor, Ngugi and Soyinka; consciousness about their own work, the nature of the art in which they work, and ... their obligation to be ... teachers, stimulators and even admonishers of their societies.'
Times Literary Supplement
'African Writers Talking is really worth reading.'
Thomas Decker – West Africa

Editions du Mont-Noir
Poésie vivante I
Kinshasa: Ed. du Mont-Noir, 1971 ('Objectif 80', série jeune littérature, 7). 37 pp.
Contains the poems of Kabatantshi, Kabongo, Lomain-Tshibamba and Mweya.

Poésie vivante II
Kinshasa: Ed. du Mont-Noir, 1972 ('Objectif 80', série jeune littérature, 13). 49 pp.
The verse of eight poets: Gatambira, Kakesa, Latere, Maloba, Masa-ma-Mateka, Melady-Badum, Ndelo Nzungu, Ruduri Kwezi.

Edwards, Paul comp.
Through African Eyes 2 vols.
London: CUP, 1966. 122 pp. 126 pp. £1.95 each
A sampling of African writing in the form of prose extracts. This collection includes less familiar early authors of the eighteenth and nineteenth centuries, in addition to well-known contemporary writers, such as Peter Abrahams, Chinua Achebe, Amos Tutuola, Camara Laye, Abioseh Nicol, Cyprian Ekwensi, Mongo Béti, Ezekiel Mphahlele, and a great many more.

Modern African Narrative:
London: Nelson, 1966. 204 pp.
An anthology 'with a difference' in that it includes works by white South Africans such as Nadine Gordimer and Dan Jacobson, Doris Lessing from Zimbabwe, and a contribution by the Egyptian novelist Waguin Ghali. There is an extract from Kariuki's *Mau Mau Detainee*. Other authors represented in this collection are Peter Abrahams, Chinua Achebe, Cyprian Ekwensi, Ezekiel Mphahlele, James Ngugi, and Abioseh Nicol, among others. Each passage is preceded by an introduction.
'This collection is to be recommended for whetting the appetite for modern African literature.'
J. D. – West Africa

West African Narrative:
London: Nelson, 1966. 256 pp. o/p
This selection of prose writings by West Africans is designed especially for school use. The earliest piece of writing comes from Equiano's autobiography, published in 1789, and the most recent from the pen of Frances Selormey, a short story entitled 'The witch'. All the writing is narrative, ranging through fiction, history and biography. Although most of the passages were originally written in English, translations from Hausa, Tiv and French literature also appear. There is a general account of writing in West Africa, and each writer's work is introduced by critical and explanatory notes.

Ekwensi, Cyprian ed.
Festac Anthology of Nigerian New Writing
Lagos: Cultural Division, Federal Ministry of Information, 1977 (Nigeria Magazine special publ.). 246 pp. ₦2.50 ($8.00)
The emphasis of this anthology, which is an outgrowth of the Second World Black and African Festival of Arts and Culture held in Lagos in 1976, is on previously unpublished writing – short stories, poetry and criticism – of young Nigerian writers although there are a few new pieces by established writers like Achebe, Munonye, Tutuola, Nwekwu, Rotimi and Gbadamosi. The bulk of the contributions were furnished by the English departments and literary journals of Nigerian universities. In his preface Ekwensi expressed the hope that the anthology would become an annual affair but to this date no new volume has been published.
'The anthology contains a literary feast in eight courses.'
Oyekan Owomoyela – Research in African Literatures
'The book is a useful addition to any library with an interest in developing its holdings in Third World literatures.'
Choice

El Kholti, Mohamed and **Senghor,
Léopold Sédar** *et al.*
*Les plus beaux récits de l'Union française et du
Maghreb*
Paris: La Colombe, 1947. 456 pp. o/p
An anthology of writing by the inhabitants of
French holdings throughout the world. Pages
165–264 on black Africa are written by
Senghor. He presents extracts from African
oral literature and ancient texts in Arabic as
well as the modern writings of Maximilien
Quenum, Paul Hazoumé, Birago Diop, René
Maran, Césaire, Damas, and the students at the
William Ponty School. Writings from
Madagascar, mainly ancient genres, can be
found on pages 373–451.

Etherton, Michael ed.
African Plays for Playing 1
London: HEB, 1975 (AWS, 165). 144 pp.
£1.75/$14.00
This is the first of a two-volume anthology of
African plays in which the emphasis is on
production. It contains three plays: 'The
Invisible Bond' by Nuwa Sentongo, 'Amavi' by
Jacob Hevi, and 'Rakinyo' by 'Segun Ajibade,
the first two being accompanied by brief
production comments.

African Plays for Playing 2
London: HEB, 1976 (AWS, 179). 122 pp.
£1.75/$4.00
This is the second of a two-volume anthology
of African plays in which the emphasis is on
production. It contains three plays: 'Monkey
on the Tree' by Uwa Udensi, 'Black Mamba
Two' by Godfrey Kabwe Kasoma, and 'The
Tragedy of Mr No-Balance' by Victor Eleame
Musinga, with brief production notes.

Falq, J. and **Kane, M.**
Littérature africaine: textes et travaux
Paris: F. Nathan, 1974. 352 pp. FF81.00
A school text for the secondary level that
conforms to the syllabus adopted by the
Conference of Ministers of Education of
Francophone African countries in Madagascar
in 1972. The extracts of the works of the major
names in African writing in French are
presented thematically: daily life, structures of
society, family, human condition and African
wisdom, historical and legendary people, the
supernatural and the sacred, the metamor-
phoses of traditional society, colonial society
as seen by Africans.

Feinberg, Barry ed.
Poets to the People
London: George Allen and Unwin, 1974.
83 pp.

London: HEB, 1980 (2nd enlarged ed.) (AWS,
230). £1.95
A much enlarged edition of an anthology of
South African protest poems originally published in 1974 by George Allen and Unwin.
The volume contains contributions from
twenty-one South African poets, including
Dennis Brutus, Mazisi Kunene, Arthur Nortje
and Keorapetse Kgositsile.
'. . . eloquently echoes the torment and hope of
those struggling against South Africa's citadel of
inhumanity.'   Nene Mburu – *Africa*

Ferreira, Serafim ed.
Resistência Africana
Lisbon: Dabril Editora, S.A.R.L., 1975
(Universidade de Povo, 2). 132 pp.
This volume of Lusophone African poetry is
preceded by a ten-page essay, 'A Poesia Como
Arma Politica', Ferreira has selected over
seventy poems from thirty poets.

Ferreira, Manuel
*No Reino de Caliban – Antologia Panorâmica
da Poesia Africana de Expressão Portuguesa*
2 vols.
Lisbon: Seara Nova, 1975 (Vol. 1), 1976
(Vol. 2). 328 pp. and 488 pp.
Volume I is devoted to Cape Verde and
Guinea-Bissau; volume II is devoted to
Angola, São Tomé and Príncipe. An introductory essay of forty-seven pages, 'Uma Aventura
Desconhecida', provides essential historical
information of Lusophone African poetry.
Manuel Ferreira, a noted novelist, critic and
professor of African Literature at the University of Lisbon, asserts in his introduction the
existence of 348 specific works of poetry in
Portuguese-speaking Africa and includes 138
poets in his three-volume anthology. The
proposed third volume, dedicated to Mozambique, has not yet been published. Ferreira
offers an introduction to the poetry of each
country and includes a brief biography, a
photo and list of publications for each poet.
After each poem, Ferreira cites the journal or
book in which the poem first appeared as well
as the date of publication. There are also essays
on important literary journals, newspapers
publishing African poetry, and poetry in Cape
Verdean 'crioulo' language. Manuel Ferreira
usually provides an ample selection from each
poet, anywhere from five to fifteen poems.
'*Ferreira does provide new and important information: for instance, he points out that Marcelo Veiga
of São Tomé and Príncipe is not a minor poet as was
previously thought. In fact . . . he is the pioneer of an
authentic Négritude poetry in Lusophone Africa.*'
Donald Burness – *Research in African Literatures*

Feuser, Willfried F. ed.

Jazz and Palm Wine and Other Stories
London: Longman, 1981. 256 pp. £1.60
A collection containing works by Tchicaya U
Tam'si, Sembène Ousmane, Birago Diop,
Camara Laye and Emmanuel Dongala. The
stories range from the retelling of oral
tradition, African mystery, social satire and
fables. The volume also includes samples of
the modern short story told in traditional vein.

Finn, D. E. ed.

Poetry in Rhodesia
Salisbury: College Press, 1968. 80 pp. Z$1.00

Five *Plays from Zambia*

Lusaka: Zambia Cultural Services, 1975.
106 pp. K2.30
A collection of five short plays on varying
themes. The titles are: 'Hunter of God'; 'A
Clod for a Relative'; 'The Misfits'; 'The
Bridge' and 'That Which you Have'.

Fouet, Francis and Renaudeau, Régine

*Classe de première: littérature africaine (choix
de poèmes)*
Dakar: Nouvelles Editions Africaines, 1976.
408 pp. CFA2,350 (F47.00)

Fraser, Robert ed.

*Reading African Poetry: an introduction for
schools*
London: Collins Educational, 1975. 96 pp.
£1.50
A selection from the best of African poetry
designed for use in African secondary schools.
The poems, accompanied by some photographs, are arranged under topics such as 'The
Old Ways', 'The Ancient Gods', 'Rain', 'The
Coming of the White Man', etc., and an
introduction to each topic explains and guides
the reading of the poems.

Freeman, Richard A.

*Okoyai Aumgbomo. Seeds of Poetry: poems in
Ijo and English*
Ibadan: University of Ibadan; Institute of
African Studies, 1972 (Bi-lingual Literary
Works, 5). 62 pp. ₦1.85

Fremont. I. V.

Stories and Plays from Africa
Nairobi: OUP, 1968. 48 pp. K.shs. 3.00

Gibbs, James ed.

Nine Malaŵian Plays
Limbe: Popular Publ., 1977 (Malaŵian
Writers Series, 3). 171 pp. K2.60
The plays are by Innocent Banda, Chunga,
Kalikwembe, Kamlongera, Mosiwa, Mvula,
and Ngo'mbe. They are intended for
performance in schools and colleges, so the
casts and themes are modest. Three deal with
modern topics, and six have more traditional
themes.
'. . . an interesting introduction to drama in Malawi,
and all the plays would work well as theatre . . .
Banda is the most talented dramatist in the book, with
a sharp eye for social problems and skilful use of
language.'
Peter Nazareth – *World Literature Today*
'It will take some time before these young playwrights
make the international African drama scene, but one
must be immensely grateful to James Gibbs for
bringing out this volume.'
Sola Oyadiran – *African Book Publishing Record*

Gordimer, Nadine, and Abrahams, Lionel eds.

South African Writing Today
Harmondsworth, England: Penguin Books,
1967. 264 pp.
A collection of South African poetry, prose
and drama, by both white and black South
African writers. Among the latter are Dennis
Brutus, Alex La Guma, Todd Matshikiza,
Ezekiel Mphahlele, Nathaniel Nakasa, Lewis
Nkosi, and Can Themba. There is an introduc-
tion by Anthony Sampson.

Gourdeau, Jean-Pierre

*La littérature négro-africaine d'expression
française*
Paris: Hatier, 1973. 159 pp. FF11.55
The texts in this anthology of the writing of the
major names in francophone literature of
Africa and the Caribbean have been chosen to
bring light on the individual way each author
deals with a theme which concerns them all –
the return to origins. Authors included are:
Césaire, Senghor, Hampaté Bâ, Dadié,
Ousmane, Lopes, Oyono, Ouologuem,
Fanon, and Birago Diop.

Gray, Stephen ed.

*A World of their Own: Southern African poets
of the seventies*
Johannesburg: Ad. Donker, 1976. 176 pp.
R3.95
An anthology of poetry containing the works
of sixteen well-known South African poets
with contributions from Guy Butler, David
Farrell, Wopko Jensma, Douglas Livingstone,
Sipho Sepamla, Mongane Wally Serote and
Mark Swift among others. There is an
introduction by A. P. Brink.
'. . . all the poets represented here are very much
worth reading, and make up what is the best –

although not the most representative – collection of English South African poetry available.'
    Barend J. Toerien – *World Literature Today*

On the Edge of the World: Southern African stories of the seventies
Johannesburg: Ad. Donker, 1974. 196 pp.
R3.95
A collection of twenty stories by both famous and lesser-known writers from all racial groups in South Africa. The stories seek to portray something of the life in South Africa today and contributors include Yvonne Burgess, Ahmed Essop, Sheila Fugard, Nadine Gordimer, Bessie Head, Alan Paton, Sheila Roberts and Adam Small.
'This is an ideal collection of material for readers looking for an introduction to South African short fiction of the 70s.'
    Charles Larson – *Books Abroad*

Green, Robert ed.
Just a Moment, God! An anthology of prose and verse from East Africa
Nairobi: East African Literature Bureau, 1970. 206 pp. K.shs. 11.00 (£1.20/$3.20)
The first efforts of a group of young and as yet inexperienced writers from Eastern Africa, most of them students from the University College in Nairobi are brought together in this collection. The book takes its title from the opening poem, which explores the theme of God's inhumanity.

Greenville-Grey, Wilfred
All in an African Lifetime
New York: Friendship Press, 1971. 48 pp.
$1.50

Harris, Rodney H.; Shapiro, Norman R.; Harris, Micheline, F. eds.
Palabres: contes et poèmes de l'Afrique noire et des Antilles
Glenview: Scott, Foresman, 1973. 287 pp.
$5.50
Aimed at the secondary-school student, this collection of tales and poems provides a representative sampling of new African literature in French and its older Caribbean counterpart. Grammatical explanations and facing-page definitions are supplied for easy reference.

Hazareesingh, Kissoonsingh ed.
Anthologie des lettres mauriciennes
Port Louis, Mauritius: Eds. de l'Océan Indien, 1978. 192 pp. RS60.00
An anthology of creative writing from Mauritius.

Henderson, Gwyneth ed.
African Theatre: eight prize-winning plays for radio
London: HEB, 1973 (AWS, 134). 192 pp.
£1.95/$4.00
Wole Soyinka, Martin Esslin and Lewis Nkosi chose the prize-winning plays in the 'African Theatre' competition launched by the BBC's African Service in 1972. 'Make like Slaves' by Richard Rive took first prize, while second and third prizes went to plays by Khalid Almubarak Mustafa and Jagjit Singh. They are reprinted here with the remaining prize-winning plays by Charles C. Umeh, Derlene Clems, and Ken Tsaro-Wiwa.
'. . . a panorama of contemporary Africa in all its human vitality and resilient humour . . . its plays easily adaptable for the stage, African Theatre is.a lasting contribution to African literature.'
    A. D. Amateshe – *Dhana*

Henderson, Gwyneth and Pieterse, Cosmo eds.
Nine African Plays for Radio
London: HEB, 1973 (AWS, 127). 192 pp.
£1.95/$5.00
Nine plays selected from those broadcast over a period of ten years by the BBC 'African Theatre' programme (part of the BBC African Service) form this collection. Written by Yemi Ajibade, Gabriel Roberts, Derlene Clems, Jeanne Ngo Libondo, Fela Davies, Laban Erapu, Kuldip Dondhi, Gordon Tialobi and Robin White, these plays are a direct and vivid extension of the great African oral tradition. Producer's notes and recommendations show how they can easily be transferred to stage production or more intimate methods of presentation.

Hillion, Joel; Niang, Sada; Tamburini, Jean eds.
Elsewhere in Africa: pages d'auteurs africains anglophones 3 vols.
Paris: Hatier, 1978 95 pp., 93 pp. and 95 pp.
FF13.20 each
An anthology of anglophone African authors.

Horsfall, Alfred
Africa I: comprehension and composition
London: Edward Arnold, 1972. 96 pp. 42p
Extracts for comprehension taken from the works of African writers which can be linked to the experience of school-children. Aimed at the secondary-school pupil.

Howlett, Simone
Lectures africaines pour l'étude du français
Paris: Présence Africaine, 1975. FF17.00

Huet, Michel ed.
Afrique africaine
Lausanne: Clairefontaine, 1963. 145 pp.
SFr40.20
Includes texts by Senghor, Amadou M'Bow, F. N'Sougan Agblemagnon, Max Falade, J.-B. Obama, and H. M. A. Ontiri.

Hughes, Langston ed.
An African Treasury: articles, essays, stories, poems by black Africans
New York: Crown, 1960. 207 pp. o/p
London: Gollancz, 1961. 207 pp. o/p
New York: Pyramid Books, 1961. 192 pp.
$1.50
An extensive selection of African writing – from articles by Tom Mboya, Ezekiel Mphahlele and Peter Abrahams to stories and poetry by Efua Sutherland, Richard Rive, Abioseh Nicol, Wole Soyinka and many others; also included are speeches of Kwame Nkrumah,, Efik folk tales, and letters in the Lonely Hearts column of Johannesburg's *Drum* magazine, all reflecting the voice of the new Africa.

Hughes, Langston, and Reygnault, Christiane eds.
Anthologie africaine et malgache
Paris: Seghers, 1962. 307 pp. FF18.50
Short stories, essays and poetry. The majority of contributions by English-speaking authors (in French translation) are drawn from Langston Hughes's *An African Treasury*. These are supplemented by original French writings by Camara Laye, Ferdinand Oyono, Ousmane Socé, Bernard Dadié, Birago Diop, David Diop, Sekou Touré, and several others.

Hughes, Langston ed.
Poems from Black Africa
Bloomington, Ind: Indiana University Press, 1966. 158 pp. $6.50 cased $1.75 p/b/£1.05 p/b
Poetry from all parts of Africa. Its emphasis lies on English-speaking poets, but it also includes contributions from the Congo, Madagascar and Senegal (in translation) and three poems by Valente Malangatana from Mozambique. A section on oral tradition appears too. Langston Hughes contributes a foreword and biographical notes on the authors.

Ikiddeh, Ime comp.
Drum Beats: an anthology of African writing
Leeds: E. J. Arnold, 1968. 155 pp.
A collection of African narrative prose, intended for school level and aimed primarily at young people outside the African continent.

All extracts – many of which relate to childhood experiences – are from the major works of the most popular African authors, but the compiler has also included some writings by lesser-known writers. In making his selection Ime Ikiddeh places high value on variety – of setting, theme and style. Introductory and biographical notes accompany each contribution.

Institut Pédagogique Africain et Malgache
Ce que dit le vent: recueil de poésie pour l'enseignement africain et malgache
Paris: Istra, 1964. 127 pp. FF4.50

Institut Pédagogique National
Ecrivains, artistes et artisans gabonais
Monaco: Ed. Paul Bory, 1966. 95 pp.
Published for the 1966 World Festival of Black Arts in Dakar, Senegal.

Irele, Abiola ed.
Lectures Africaines: a prose anthology of African writing in French
London: HEB 1969. 118 pp. o/p
Introduces francophone African writing through a selection of extracts from novels and stories by Birago Diop, Bernard Dadié, Camara Laye, Sembène Ousmane, Ferdinand Oyono, Mongo Béti and Cheikh Hamidou Kane. Each extract is preceded by a critical commentary and a brief biography of the author.

Justin, Andreé
Anthologie africaine des écrivains d'expression française
Paris: Institut Pédagogique Africain, 1962. 190 pp. o/p

Kariara, J. and Kitonga, E. eds.
An Introduction to East African Poetry
Nairobi: OUP, 1977. 144 pp. K.shs.25.00
A collection of poems written in and about East Africa and aimed at secondary school students. The anthology contains comprehensive commentaries and introductory notes intended to aid understanding and enjoyment and is organized around the themes of 'Love and marriage', 'Yesterday, today and tomorrow', 'Politics, polemics and poetry' and 'Loss'. A series of photographs enhance the volume.
'. . . *a unique first, a textbook of solid scholarly merit and a joy for the general reader.*'
Andrew Salkey – *World Literature Today*

Kayo, Patrice
Anthologie de la poésie camerounaise du langue française
Yaoundé: Ed. Le Flambeau (Distributed by Centre Diffusion du Livre Camerounais), 1977. 89 pp. CFA1,500 ($7.50)
Presents thirty-two poets, including many new names in Cameroon letters.

Kayper-Mensah, A.W. and **Wolff, H.** eds.
Ghanaian Writing
Tübingen, Germany: Horst Erdman Verlag, 1972. 288 pp. DM18.00 (£2.75/$6.50/FF29.00)
This volume portrays Ghana as seen through the eyes of her own writers as well as through the eyes of German authors. It contains a selection of essays, poems, short stories, and folklore, and also includes works by up-and-coming writers.

Kemoli, Arthur ed. *Pulsations: an East African anthology of poetry*
Nairobi: East African Literature Bureau, 1971. 182 pp. K.shs.16.00 (£1.50/3.75)
This anthology of poetry has been assembled under the auspices of the publisher's 'Students' Book Writing Scheme' which encourages talented young East African writers to develop their skills by publishing collections of the most outstanding work. Eight poems by students from the Kyambogo National Teacher's College keep company with selected poems by Mauri Yambo, Sam Mbure, Roderic R. Roberts, Tom Simpson, Bahadur Tejani, Jared Angira and Amin Kassam.

Kennedy, Ellen C. ed.
The Négritude Poets: an anthology of translations from the French
New York: Viking Press, 1975. 284 pp. $15.00
This volume contains the works of twenty-seven poets covering a geographical area extending across Africa, to the Caribbean and the Indian Ocean. The countries represented are Haiti, French Guiana, Martinique, Guadeloupe, Senegal, Mali, Zaïre, Ivory Coast, Cameroon, Congo-Brazzaville, the Malagasy Republic and Mauritius. The central theme of most of the poems is some aspect of the 'Black experience' and they represent every shade of political opinion from religious conservatism to revolutionary communism. Preceding the selections from each poet's work is a biography and literary commentary by the editor.
'. . . Ellen Conroy Kennedy's Négritude Poets *is a truly outstanding work – a valuable contribution to black literary studies. It is attractive in format and highly readable, and it is especially recommended for students of black literature who do not read French.'*
Edward A. Jones – *Research in African Literatures*

Kente, Gibson *et al.*
South African People's Plays
Edited by Robert Kavanagh
London: HEB 1981 (AWS, 224). 192 pp. £2.95
A selection of experimental and workshop plays which portray the political situation in South Africa which led to the Soweto uprisings in 1976. The four plays – two of which were banned in South Africa – are by Gibson Kente, Credo V. Mutwa, Mthuli Shezi, and by the Workshop '71 Theatre Company. The collection attempts to give the reader some understanding of what these performances meant in South Africa herself, and Robert Kavanagh provides introductory notes which describe the context, meaning and stage history of each play, together with production information.

Kesteloot, Lilyan
Neuf poètes camerounais
Yaoundé: C.L.E., 1972. 111 pp. CFA350
The nine poets in this anthology of Cameroonian verse are Elolongué Epanya (a cousin of David Diop), Yondo, Nyunai, Charles Ngandé (a catholic priest), Jean-Louis Dongmo, Okala Alene, Ernest Alima, René Philombé, and Leon-Marie Ayissi. The oldest of these writers was born in 1930. Madame Kesteloot has supplied a general introduction and a brief presentation for each poet.

Anthologie négro-africaine
Verviers: Geráud et Cie, 1967.
Verviers: Marabout, 1976 (2nd ed.) (Collection Marabout Université, 129). 432 pp.
A critical panorama of black prose writers, poets and dramatists of the 20th century.

Kgositsile, Keorapetse ed.
The Word is Here: poetry from modern Africa
New York: Doubleday, 1973 (Anchor Books, 51). 173 pp. $7.50 cased, $2.95 p/b
A selection of contemporary African poetry containing works by p'Bitek, Rubadiri and David Diop, and others,

Klein, Pierre comp.
Anthologie de la nouvelle sénégalaise (1970–1977)
Dakar: Nouvelles Editions Africaines, 1978. 188 pp. CFA1,200
Twenty-three short stories by mostly unknown young writers from Senegal that record the problems of contemporary Africa – misery, unemployment, social inequality (modern elites and the traditional caste system), polygamy gone out of control.

Komey, Ellis Ayitey and Mphahlele, Ezekiel eds.

Modern African Stories
London: Faber, 1964. 227 pp.
London: Faber, 1966. 227 pp. £1.25
An anthology of twenty-five stories, contributed by such authors as Ghana's Christina Aidoo and South Africa's Can Themba. Other contributions come from Nigeria, Sierra Leone and Kenya.

'. . . *in imaginative literature in English, West Africa has produced a cultural protest, East Africa a political protest and South Africa a racial protest. Any collection should, in some measure, reflect these genres. This the present one does, more successfully than any of its predecessors.*'
O. R. Dathorne – *Black Orpheus*

Krige, Uys and Cope, Jack eds.

The Penguin Book of South African Verse
Harmondsworth, England: Penguin Books, 1968. 331 pp. o/p
The first section of this anthology covers original writing in English by white South Africans; the second, translations from the Afrikaans; and the third section presents translations from African languages – Bushman, Hottentot, Sotho, Xhosa and Zulu – both traditional and contemporary verse. S. D. R. Sutu, S. E. K. Mqhayi and B. W. Vilakazi are some of the contributors. The editors provide an introduction and biographical notes on the authors.

Kwakwa, B. S. ed.

Ghanaian Writing Today
Accra: Ghana Publishing Corp., 1974. 184 pp.
₵4.50 ($4.50)
Presents a selection of the most important writings by contemporary Ghanaian authors.

Anthology of Poetry
Accra: Ghana Publishing Corp., 1974. 160 pp.
₵1.25 ($1.50)

Laranjeira, Pires

Antologia da Poesia Pré-Angolana (1948–1974)
Porto, Portugal: Afrontamento, 1976. 106 pp.
Selections from fifteen Angolan poets with special emphasis on João-Maria Vilanova and David Mestre, two modern writers. Agostinho Neto and António Jacinto are also well represented. In his substantial preface Laranjeiro proposes 1948 as the birth date of what he calls pre-Angolan poetry, poetry committed to an African Angola, since it was in that year the militant cry 'Vamos descobir Angola' was first heard. A glossary of Kimbundu words, a

bibliographic and chronological table, and short biographical sketches of the poets appear at the end.

Larson, Charles R. ed.

African Short Stories: a collection of contemporary African writing
New York: Macmillan, 1970. 210 pp.
A selection of twelve short stories from seven African countries including contributions from Sembène Ousmane, Abioseh Nicol, Amos Tutuola, Birago Diop, Barbara Kimenye, Alex La Guma, James Ngugi, Cameron Duodo, and Ezekiel Mphahlele.

Modern African Short Stories
Glasgow: Fontana/Collins, 1971. 192 pp. 70p
The twelve stories in Larson's collection have been culled from periodicals and existing books of short stories. Three are from South Africa, where, Larson maintains, there are more skilled short story writers than on the rest of the continent: Mphahlele, La Guma and Matthews. Their stories are a vehicle for protest. Ousmane's 'Black Girl' and B. Diop's 'Sarzan' were translated specifically for this book. A couple of the tales are traditional – Tutuola's 'The Complete Gentleman' and Sentongo's 'Mulyankota'. The rest are deliberately modern and the writers are from West and East Africa – Nicol, Kimenye, Bemba, Aidoo and Ngugi.

Opaque Shadows and Other Stories from Contemporary Africa
Washington D.C.: Inscape, 1975. 158 pp.
$12.50 cased
More short stories from Africa.
'*With this second collection of short stories, Charles Larson continues to play a pioneering role in making African literature accessible to a widening audience.*'
Thomas A. Hale – *World Literature Today*

Lecherbonnier, Bernard

Initiation à la littérature négro-africaine
Paris: Nathan, 1977. 108 pp. FF12.40

Le Sénégal *écrit: anthologie de la littérature sénégalaise contemporaine*

Tübingen, West Germany: Horst Erdmann Verlag, n.d. [1975]. 508 pp.
Dakar: Nouvelles Editions Africaines, n.d. [1975]. 508 pp.
An anthology of contemporary literature from Senegal with an introduction by Gisela Bonn and a foreword by Léopold Sédar Senghor.

Lennox-Short, Alan ed.
English and South Africa
Johannesburg: Nasou, 1973. 180 pp. R3.95
A collection of short stories from South
Africa, including works by Abrahams, Rive,
Mphahlele, and others.

Lillis, K. M. ed.
Four African Plays
Nairobi: Longman Kenya, 1974. 80 pp.
K.shs.7.00

Lindfors, Bernth ed.
South African Voices
Austin, Texas: University of Texas Press, distr.,
1975 (Occasional Publications in African
Literature, 11). 64 pp. $2.50
Poems by Mphahlele, Brutus, Pieterse,
Mtshali, Serote, Kgositsile, and Kunene, read
by the poets in 1975 to mark the fifteenth
anniversary of the Sharpeville massacre.
*'Much as this poetry speaks to the plight of those back
home and of the poet who stands outside the
barricaded door because he is banned from his native
audience. . . . There is a strange kind of decorum,
subdued philosophical though apocalyptic tone running through the verse.'*
Ezekiel Mphahlele – *Okike*
*'This is a distinguished, energetic collection dedicated
to the strength of South African voices, some new,
some, as in Mphahlele, familiar to us in prose.'*
William D. Elliot – *World Literature
Written in English*

Liswaniso, Mufalo ed.
Voices of Zambia
Lusaka: National Educ. Co. of Zambia, 1971.
151 pp. K1.20
The short stories in this volume have largely
been culled from the publications of literary
groups that sprang up in Zambia after
independence. The themes covered are disparate, many dealing with the cross-currents of
lives split between villages and city.

Littératures *de langue française hors de
France: anthologie didactique*
Sèvres, France: Fédération Internationale des
Professeur de Français, 1976. 704 pp. FF62.00
Pages 15 to 156 are devoted to Francophone
authors from black Africa, Madagascar and
Mauritius. The thirty-three writers presented
are all major names in African literature.
There is a short biography and bibliography
for each followed by an extract from one of
their works. Alain Ricard has provided a
historical introduction to this section of the
anthology.

Litto, Frederic M. ed.
Plays from Black Africa
New York: Hill and Wang, 1968. 316 pp.
A collection of six plays, each preceded by an
introduction and notes on the authors, 'formed with the double intention of introducing
the playreading public to the best (by Western
standards) dramatic writing in Africa today
and providing theatre companies with a
selection of highly stageable plays from
Africa.' The plays are Lewis Nkosi's *Rhythm of
Violence,* John Pepper Clark's *Song of a Goat,*
Alfred Hutchinson's *The Rain-killers,* Efua
Sutherland's *Edufa* – all these also published
separately elsewhere – together with *The Jewels
of the Shrine* by James Ene Henshaw, and
Ghanaian Henri Ofori's *The Literary Society.*

Lonoh Malangi Bokelenge ed.
La marche du soleil: poésie militante zaïroise
Kinshasa: Centre Africain de Littérature, 1974.
40 pp.
This volume of militant verse contains poetry
by Bokeme Sha Ne Molobay, Elebe Lisembe,
Ipoto Embele-Wanya, Kanika Mwana Ngom-
bo, Lonoh Malangi Bokelenge, Musangi
Ntemo, and Mwamb'a Musas Mangol.

Lomax, Alan and Abdul, Raoul eds.
3000 Years of Black Poetry
New York: Dodd, Mead, 1970. 261 pp.
A wide-ranging anthology of Black voices,
from Akhenaton in the Egypt of the fourteenth
century B.C. to Langston Hughes, Gwendolyn
Brooks and Leroi Jones. African poetry is
represented by the early traditional songs and
verse of the Hottentots, Susus, Ewés, Yorubas
and Zulus, to contemporary poetry from the
pens of Senghor, David Diop, Bernard Dadié,
Paulin Joachim, Gabriel Okara, Christopher
Okigbo, Wole Soyinka, Lenrie Peters, and a
host of other writers.

Mabala, Richard S.
Summons: poems from Tanzania
Dar es Salaam: Tanzania Publ. House, 1980.
150 pp. T.shs.25.00
This is the first collection of verse written in
English by Tanzanian poets. It brings together
the work of a new generation of thirteen
Tanzanian writers, whose poetry reflects their
country's policy of socialism and self-reliance.
But there are also poems about ordinary
human situations and about the search of the
poets for personal happiness and meaning in
their lives.

Machin, Noel ed.
Winds of Change: modern short stories from black Africa
London: Longman, 1977 (Structural Readers Series, Stage 5). 90 pp. 43p
Simplified stories by Chinua Achebe, Camara Laye, Jomo Kenyatta, Amos Tutuola, Alex La Guma, James Ngugi and others, with exercises in comprehension and structure, intended for the adolescent reader.

African Poetry for Schools 2 vols.
London: Longman, 1979. 120 pp., 140 pp. 95p (vol. 1) £1.05 (vol. 2)
Intended for school children at junior secondary level, this collection brings together a representative sampling of African traditional and modern verse. The book is illustrated with many photographs and line drawings to capture the mood of the poems, and there are also teacher's and pupil's notes.

McLoughlin, T. O. comp.
New Writing in Rhodesia
Gwelo, Zimbabwe: Mambo Press, 1976 (Mambo Writers, Series 2). 146 pp. Z$1.15
This collection provides an outlet for new literary talent and comprises twenty-nine poems, ten short stories, and a three-act play, by young writers, Black and White.

Mamonsono, Léopold P. ed.
Aubes nouvelles
Brazzaville: Ed. Héros dans l'Ombre, 1976 139 pp.
An anthology of young Congolese poets.

Mamonsono, Léopold P.
La nouvelle génération de poètes congolaise: anthologie de la jeune poésie congolaise
Brazzaville: Ed. Héros dans l'Ombre, 1978. 196 pp. CFA3,500

Marquard, Jean ed.
A Century of South African Short Stories
Johannesburg: Ad. Donker, 1978. 368 pp. R14.50 cased R7.95 p/b
A collection of short stories with a comprehensive introduction and short biographies of the writers. Included in the volume are contributions from Bessie Head, James Matthews, Richard Rive and Can Themba, among others. Due to 'banning orders' the works of Ezekiel Mphahlele, Alex La Guma and Lewis Nkosi are excluded.

Masegabio, Nzanzu Mabele ma Diko
Le Zaïre écrit: anthologie de la poésie zaïroise en langue française
Kinshasa: Ed. Dombi Diffusion, 1977. 96 pp. Contains the verse of thirty-one poets from Zaïre.

Le Zaïre écrit: anthologie de la poésie zaïroise de langue française
Tübingen, West Germany: Horst Erdmann Verlag, 1976. 255 pp. cased
A German published re-issue of the preceding entry, in expanded form.

Matthews, James ed.
Black Voices Shout!: an anthology of poetry
Athlone, South Africa: BLAC Publishing House, 1974. 69 pp. R1.75
Austin, Texas: Troubadour Press, 1976. 76 pp. Poems by Serote, Matthews and others are included in this anthology, as well as a tribute to Timol (pushed to his death during interrogation).
'. . . a volume wherein the true inner feeling of the Blacks is painted in words.'
Leonard Koza – *African Arts*
'. . . the poetry is graceful and fine, a tribute to human endurance and grandeur.'
David Dorsey – *World Literature Today*

Mirrer, Martin comp.
Modern Black Stories, with Study Aids
Woodbury, N.Y.: Barron's, 1971 (Barron's Educational Series) 196 pp. $1.75

Momodu, A. G. S. and Schild, Ulla eds.
Nigerian Writing
Tübingen, West Germany: Horst Erdmann Verlag, 1976. 324 pp.
A sampling of contemporary Nigerian writing by both established and lesser-known authors.

Moore, Gerald and Beier, Ulli eds.
Modern Poetry from Africa
Harmondsworth, England and Baltimore: Penguin Books, 1963 (Penguin African Library, AP 7). (rev. ed.) 1968 192 pp. 95p/$2.95
A revised and considerably expanded version of a popular anthology that draws on sixteen countries to present the work of African poets writing in English, French and Portuguese (the latter two in translation). Substantial coverage is given to the poetry of John Pepper Clark, Kofi Awoonor, Christopher Okigbo and Wole

Soyinka. The poetry of Négritude too, gets a fair share, notably the works of Léopold Senghor, David Diop, Birago Diop, and the Congolese poets Tchicaya U Tam'si and Antoine-Roger Bolamba. There is an introduction, notes on the authors, and an index of first lines.
'The editors' introduction ... is among the most informative pieces written on the modern literature of Africa south of the Sahara.'
                          R. W. Noble – *West Africa*

Moore, Jane A. eds.
Cry Sorrow! Cry Joy!: selections from contemporary African writers
New York: Friendship Press, 1971. 224 pp.
$2.75

Mphahlele, Ezekiel ed.
African Writing Today
Harmondsworth, England: Penguin Books, 1967. 347 pp. o/p
An anthology 'intended to give the intelligent reader a map of themes and styles of African writing in the metropolitan languages – English, French and Portuguese'. It provides a wide cross-section by authors from fifteen different countries, and is especially strong on writings from Nigeria, Senegal, South Africa and Mozambique. There is a brief introduction and biographical notes on each author.
'European and African readers alike should delight in Ezekiel Mphahlele's anthology of African prose and poetry, releasing us as it does from the agonized neuroticism of much European writing to which we have become addicted ... should be read by all who are in danger of despairing over the future of African literature.'   Lenrie Peters – *African Affairs*

Muchemwa, K. Z.
Zimbabwean Poetry in English: an anthology
Gwelo, Zimbabwe: Mambo Press, 1978
(Mambo Writers Series, 4). 175 pp. Z$2.40
A selection of poetry by Black Zimbabweans from their first creative contact with the English language up to the present day. Among others, some themes of the poems are tradition, rural life, the changing word, and love and death. In his introduction, the editor says that 'This volume attempts to introduce readers to a culture, the sensitivity of which, as it finds expression in poetry, has not until now been available in any coherent way.'

Mudimbe, V. Y.
Poésie vivante 2 vols.
Lumumbashi, Ed. du Mont Noir, 1972 (Coll. 'Objectif 80' sér. Jeune Littérature, 7 and 13). 36 pp./48 pp. 30k each
Two slim volumes of verse by young writers

from Zaïre, including P. Kabatantshi, P. O. Musangi, I. H. Kabongo, E. F. Mweya, and V. Y. Mudimbe

Mushiete, Paul
La littérature française africaine: petite anthologie des écrivains noirs d'expression française
Leverville, Zaïre: Bibliothèque de l'Etoile, 1957. 40 pp. o/p

Mutloatse, Mothobi ed.
Forced Landing
Johannesburg: Ravan Press, 1980, 216 pp.
R2.85
London: HEB, [publ. as *Africa South: Contemporary Writings*] 1981 (AWS, 243). 224 pp. £1.95
A collection of stories, articles, pleas and polemic, once banned in South Africa – and some culled from magazines such as *The Classic* and *Staffrider* – make up a representative review of what black South African writers have to say about their people and their country. Much of the writing is of a politically committed nature, and contributors include James Matthews, Bessie Head, Ahmed Essop, Bob Leshoai, Miriam Tlali, Sipho Sepamla, Mongane Wally Serote, Desmond Tutu, and Mothobi Mutloatse himself.

Mutswairo, Solomon M.
Zimbabwe: prose and poetry
Washington D.C.: Three Continents Press, 1974. 276 pp. $16.00 cased $9.00 p/b
An English translation of the first Zimbabwean-language novel *Feso* together with an anthology of twenty-five poems by four poets in dual Zezuru-English text. The translation of both the novel and the poetry have been undertaken by Mutswairo. *Feso* portrays African life and customs and political institutions prior to colonial rule in Zimbabwe. The poetry covers themes ranging from love to nursery poems.
'In spite of the difficulties encountered in translating the book ... [it] is still a literary masterpiece which must engage not only scholars in African literature but all those who seek a better understanding of traditional African customs and politics.'
                          Henry V. Moyana – *Africa Today*

Ndiaye, Papa G.
Manuel de littérature africaine
Paris: Présence Africaine, 1978. 224 pp.
FF29.00
A selection of poetry, prose, drama, assembled from the works of African, Caribbean and Malagasy writers, organized under three main themes: The uprooting of traditional African

life; The battle for cultural identity; The political, social and religious varieties of Independent Africa. Intended for upper secondary-school children, the manual contains notes, questions on content and expression, themes for group work and research, which follow each excerpt.

'... conforme au programme ... adopté par la conférence des ministres de l'education nationale des états africains francophone réunis à Madagascar au mois de février 1972 ... l'auteur concu l'appareil pédagogique avec une supplesse qui sauve-garde la liberté de réflexion et une variété qui permet aux élèves de s'initier à un certain nombre d'exercices destinés à parfaire leur connaissance de la langue et à affirmer leurs qualités d'analyse et de synthèse.'

Bingo

Nkamgnia, Samuel
Confidences par les ondesi
Yaoundé: Ed. Sémences Africaines, 1979. 80 pp. CFA750
A collection of poems by Francophone African authors originally broadcast on radio.

Nolen, Barbara ed.
Africa is People: first-hand accounts from contemporary Africa
New York: Dutton, 1967. 270 pp. o/p
Thirty-four selections culled from books, journals, interviews, and eyewitness accounts. The editor places emphasis on autobiographical narratives by African writers, and she includes extracts from R. W. Cole's *Kossoh Town Boy,* Mbonu Ojike's *My Africa,* Camara Laye's *The Dark Child,* Noni Jabavu's *Drawn in Colour,* and Legson Kayira's *I Will Try.* Additional contributions are by Chinua Achebe, Peter Abrahams, Ulli Beier, Léopold Senghor, as well as other African, American and European scholars and journalists. Each selection is prefaced by a brief lead-in, which introduces the author and places the excerpt within its context.

Africa is Thunder and Wonder: contemporary voices from African literature
New York: Charles Scribner's Sons, 1972. 270 pp. $7.95
A collection of poetry and prose from all parts of the African continent, covering such themes as human problems, epic tales of heroes and the conflict between black and white. An introduction to the author and his background precedes each selection.
'... skilfully handled and edited ... provides an excellent introduction to the complete works ... striking illustrations by talented African-born artists are in perfect harmony with the text.'
Janet Polacheck – *Library Journal*

Nwoga, Donatus, I. ed.
West African Verse: an annotated anthology
London: Longman, 1965. 239 pp. £1.65
A comprehensive selection of West African verse primarily designed for candidates for WAEC School Certificate examinations in English Literature. Early poets include Gladys May Casely-Hayford, Raphael Armattoe, Dennis Osadebay, and Michael Dei-Anang, and contemporary authors are represented by Gabriel Okara, John Pepper Clark, Wole Soyinka, Léopold Senghor, and Bernard Dadié among others. Following each poem are notes designed to help in analysis and appreciation. Difficult words and words used in a special sense are defined and interpretations of meaning and comments on poetic technique are discussed. Finally, questions are asked with the purpose of aiding individual study. Biographical notes on each author are provided.

Okola, Lennard ed.
Drum Beat: East African poems
Nairobi: EAPH, 1967. 160 pp. K.shs.7.50 ($2.60)
'A modest attempt to bring out in its full freshness and flavour a representative collection of contemporary East African poetry.' The anthology includes verse not only by East African indigenous writers but also poetry by non-African authors who were either born in East Africa or have lived there at one time or another. Mr Okola provides brief biographical notes and an introduction, and there is an index of titles and first lines.

Okpaku, Joseph ed.
New African Literature and the Arts 3 Vols.
New York: Third Press, 1973. 224 pp. $10.00 cased $5.95 p/b each.
Three anthologies which bring together poetry, fiction, essays, criticisms and reviews as well as art reproductions, by leading black writers and artists. The series attempts to provide an ongoing acquaintance with current African literary trends and development.
'[The volumes] boast an array of new talent, and the confidence with which Mr. Okpaku goes on record is delicious.'
New York Times

Osahon, Naiwu; Williams, Lari; Bamijoko, Abu
The Music of the Message
Lagos: Third World First Publ., 1980. 65 pp. 75k
This is the text of the poetic performance of the three authors who are members of a group called 'Original Poets' whose aim is to read, dramatise and sing their works. First heard at the University of Lagos in June 1977.

**Oti, Sonny; Wartemberg, Nanabenyin
Kweku; Sofola, Zulu**
Three West African Plays
Ibadan: OUP Nigeria, 1977. 95 pp., 75 pp.
and 82 pp. ₦6.50
A combined volume containing three plays
which have also been published separately –
Oti's *The Old Masters*, Sofola's *The Sweet Trap*
and Wartemberg's *The Corpse's Comedy*.

**Ouologuem, Y.; Pageard, R.;
Demidoff, M. T.**
Introduction aux lettres africaines
Paris: Ed. de l'Ecole, 1973. 268 pp. FF45.00
A school text for the study of French literature
in Africa. Despite the title, extracts are not only
from the works of African authors, but also
include French writers like Gide, Loti, Verne,
Hugo, Voltaire, La Fontaine and Molière, and
French translations of Tolstoï, Richard Wright,
Kipling and the Bible. In an introduction
Ouologuem justifies this approach by saying,
'nous avons pensé qu'il n'était de famille
qu'humaine, c'est-à-dire, sans frontières'. The
passages are arranged thematically: the family,
the world of childhood, images of the country,
the sea, great people, technical progress,
humour and wit. The extracts from La
Fontaine and Molière are not found under any
heading but constitute sections in themselves.

Packman, Brenda ed.
*Etoiles africaines: morceaux choisis de la
littérature de l'Afrique noire*
London: Evans, 1968. 72 pp. 30p o/p
Introducing some of the major works of
African writing in French, using extracts from
several novels, this collection is aimed at
students who have outgrown juvenile readers
but who are not yet ready to embark upon full-
length novels.

Paoli, Pia ed.
L'Afrique des grands lacs: l'amour et la guerre
Paris: Seghers, 1978. 359 pp. FF50.00
An anthology of writing from anglophone East
Africa in French translation.

Pereira, Ernest ed.
Contemporary South African Plays
Johannesburg: Ravan Press, 1977. 293 pp.
R7.50
A selection of plays (all by South Africans
writing in English) which won prizes in the
1975 Olive Schreiner Award. Four complete
plays are reprinted here: *A Rhino for the
Boardroom* by Douglas Livingstone; *Ritual 2387*
by Ian Ferguson; *An Enquiry into the Voyage of the
Santiago* by Don Maclennan; and *An Evening at

the Vernes by Stephen Gray. Excerpts from
three other plays are also included: *Weekend* by
Sheila Roberts; *Lines Draw Monsters* by Benjamin Leshoai; and *Framework* by Peter
Wilhelm. (Other prize-winning plays were
ommitted because of South African censorship
laws. They are *Confused Mhlaba* by Khayalethu
and *God's Forgotten* by Pieter-Dirk Uys.) Includes a select bibliography of recent plays,
their history and criticism.
'. . . four plays and more or less self-contained
fragments of three others . . . reveal both the vitality
and the wide range of drama being produced in South
Africa.'
                Robert L. Berner – *World Literature Today*

Pieterse, Cosmo ed.
Ten One-Act plays
London: HEB, 1968 (AWS, 34). 304 pp.
£2.25/$6.50
Ten plays – four from West Africa, by Pat
Maddy, Femi Euba, Ime Ikiddeh and Kwesi
Kay; three from East Africa, by Ganesh Bagchi
(born in India) and Kuldip Sondhi (contributing two plays), and another three from South
Africa, by Athol Fugard, Alfred Hutchinson
and Arthur Maimane. There is an introduction
by the editor, notes on the plays, and
directions for producing them.
'The editor has projected himself into the interesting
notes he has made on each play, but these tend to be
an aid to literary analysis rather than production
points.'   Michael Etherton – *Books Abroad*

Eleven Short African Plays
London: HEB, 1971 (AWS, 78). 256 pp.
£1.95/$5.00
This collection includes 'Ancestral Power' and
'Lament', by Kofi Awoonor, 'God's Deputy',
by Sanya Dosunmu, 'The Scar', by Rebecca
Njau, 'Resurrection', by Richard Rive. 'Overseas', by Mbella Sonne Dipoko, 'The Magic
Pool', by Kuldip Sondhi, 'This Time Tomorrow', by James Ngugi, and David Lytton's,
'Episodes of an Easter Rising', Cosmo Pieterse
contributes his own play, 'Ballad of the Cells',
and provides an introduction and biographical
notes on the authors.

Seven South African Poets
London: HEB, 1971 (AWS, 64). 144 pp.
£1.75/$5.00
A collection of poetry by exiled South African
writers, delineating the inhumanity of
apartheid. The volume includes verse by
Dennis Brutus, C. J. Driver, Keorapetse
Kgositsile, Timothy Holmes and Ismail
Choonara.
'The one thing that strikes one very forcibly about
these poets is the complete absence of hysteria, the

great reserve and the withholding of passionate outburst, which give the poems their power and convince the reader, very deeply of the reality of the suffering they tell of – the suffering of imprisonment in South Africa, and all the other forms of deprivation apartheid brings with it.'

Clive Wake – *African Literature Today*

Five African Plays
London: HEB, 1972 (AWS, 114). 217 pp.
£1.95/$5.00
The five full-length plays collected in this volume display a wide variety of subject matter and treatment. 'Abiku' by Nigerian Femi Euba is a two-part play for television; 'The Drug' by Sierra Leonean Gaston Bart-Williams makes use of experimental techniques and was originally produced for radio, 'The Cell' by Harold Kimmel conveys the oppression of South Africa; 'Laughter and Hubbub in the House' by Ghanaian Kwesi Kay examines cultural conflicts symbolised by a murder; and *Houseboy*, Michael Etherton's dramatization (in English) of Ferdinand Oyono's powerful novel *Une Vie de Boy*, describes the brutal treatment meted out by a corrupt colonial administration in French Cameroun.

Short African Plays
London: HEB, 1972 (AWS, 78). 112 pp.
£1.95/$5.00
An anthology containing works by Ngugi, Kofi Awoonor, David Lytton, Mbella Sonne Dipoko and others.
'*Represented in this . . . collection are writers from Ghana, Nigeria, Sierra Leone, Kenya, Cameroon and South Africa, and it offers a fair example of the great creative energy active in African theatre today*'.
André P. Bruik – *Books Abroad*

Pieterse, Cosmo *et al.*
Present Lives, Future Becoming
London: Hickey Press, 1974. 96 pp. o/p
A South African landscape in words and pictures. Cosmo Pieterse in prose and poetry, and George Hallett, Wilfred Paulse, Clarence Coulson and Gavin Jantjes in their photographs capture in this book the texture and realities of everyday life for the coloured community in South Africa.

Radford, W. L.
African Poetry for Schools
Nairobi: EAPH, 1970. 68 pp. K.shs.6.00 ($2.00)
An anthology aimed primarily at pupils in the upper classes of primary school and in the first and second years of secondary school in Africa. The author provides an introduction, along with detailed notes and teaching suggestions.

Rancourt, Jacques
Poètes et poèmes contemporains: Afrique, Antilles
Paris: Agence de Coopération Culturelle et Technique and Ed. Saint-Germain-des-Prés, 1981. 200 pp. FF60.00
A critical anthology of poetry in French from Africa, Mauritius, and the Caribbean that has been written since 1950.

Reed, John, and **Wake, Clive** eds.
A Book of African Verse
London: HEB, 1964 (AWS, 8). 119 pp.
£1.50/$2.50
A wide-ranging selection of verse by thirty African poets from eleven countries. It includes some translations by the editors of poems originally written in French. The book features a critical introduction, biographical notes on each poet, twenty pages of notes on the poems, and an index of first lines.
'*. . . this verse anthology appeared soon after the Beier/Moore one and is a useful companion as only six poems are duplicated. Reed and Wake are not so much concerned with modern verse. There is some poetry in the traditional manner.*'
O. R. Dathorne – *Bull. of the Assoc. for African Literature in English*

French African Verse
London: HEB, 1972 (AWS, 106). 240 pp.
£2.50/$6.50
This collection of verse covers the period from the late 1930s to 1970 in chronological order of publication. It contains representative selections from the works of twenty-three authors, including both prominent writers such as Léopold Senghor and David Diop, as well as younger poets of the post-independence period. The editors have translated the poems into English verse and also provide an introduction and a bibliography. Each French original has a parallel English translation.

Reygnault, Christiane
Trésor africain et malgache: anthologie
Paris: Seghers, 1971 (2nd ed.) (Nouveaux Horizons). 249 pp.
A new edition of an anthology originally published in 1962, which was a translation of the Langston Hughes collection (see p. 83).

Ridout, Ronald and **Jones, Eldred** eds.
Adjustments: an anthology of African and Western writing
London: Edward Arnold, 1966. 164 pp. o/p
An attempt to put the work of African writers side by side with works from other traditions,

such as those of Jack London and Richard Parker. Contains extracts from works by two Sierra Leonean writers, Sarif Easmon and William Conton; and from Achebe's *No Longer at Ease;* and Ngugi's *Weep not, Child.*

Rive, Richard ed.
Modern African Prose
London: HEB, 1964 (AWS, 9). 230 pp.
£1.60/$4.00
An anthology of contemporary writing by Africans in English – covering both established as well as lesser-known authors – and intended primarily for use in schools and by students. One of the early endeavours of its kind, it includes extracts from novels and complete short stories by nineteen writers; eight from South Africa, eight from West Africa and three from East Africa. There are notes and an introduction by the editor.

Quartet: new voices from South Africa
New York: Crown, 1963. o/p
London: HEB, 1964 (AWS, 14). 150 pp.
£1.80/$4.00
A collection of sixteen stories by Alex La Guma, James Matthews, Richard Rive and a white South African writer, Alf Wannenburgh. The stories are arranged around four central themes, on which each author contributes a story: 'Without Justice', 'The Dispossessed', 'The Possessed', and 'The Outsider'. There is an introduction by Alan Paton, who considers this anthology 'a milestone in the history of South African literature'.

Robinson, William R. ed.
Nommo: an anthology of modern black African and black American literature
New York: Collier-Macmillan, 1972. 501 pp.
$7.50

Rombaut, Marc
La nouvelle poésie négro-africaine d'expression française
Brussels: Centre d'Etude et Documentation Africaine, 1972 (Cahiers du CEDAF, 5). 80 pp.

La poésie négro-africain d'expression française: anthologie
Paris: Seghers, 1976. 333 pp. FF36.00
Selected poems of sixty-six francophone poets from Africa, the Indian Ocean, and the West Indies. In a 50-page introduction Rombaut traces the history of the Négritude movement in the form of a screen-play 'starring' Senghor, Césaire, and Damas, and then goes on to discuss the early opponents of Négritude as

well as the latter-day generation of francophone African poets who are seeking to liberate themselves, in Rombaut's words, from the 'worn-out themes' of both the colonial and independence eras. Includes an extensive bibliography of general works and works by the poets anthologized.

Roth, Willard E.
No More the Round Mud Hut: voices of young Africa
New York: Friendship Press, 1971, 48 pp.
$1.50

Rothenberg, Jerome ed.
Technicians of the Sacred: a range of poetries from Africa, America, Asia, and Oceania
New York: Doubleday (Anchor Books), 1969.
520 pp $4.95

Royston, Robert ed.
To Whom it May Concern: an anthology of black South African poetry
Johannesburg: Ad. Donker, 1975. 96 pp.
R2.95
London: HEB [publ. as *Black Poets in South Africa*], 1974 (AWS, 164). 96 pp. £1.95
A collection of the works of some of the most well-known black poets in South Africa, presenting an insight into the poets' attitudes and outlooks and their anti-apartheid political commitments. Contributors include Mongane Wally Serote, Mandlenkosi Langa, Njabulo S. Ndebele, Mafika Pascal Gwala, Oswald Mtshali and Sipho Sepamla.
'There is a brute reality about the language which erodes niceties and projects the black psyche with hard hitting force. The correctness of the images makes the poems what they are: unmistakably local.'
Vrinda Nabar – *The Times of India*

Rutherford, Anna and **Hannah, Donald** eds.
Commonwealth Short Stories
London: Edward Arnold, 1971. 256 pp.
New York: Africana Publ. Corp., 1971 (distr.)
$19.50 cased $9.50 p/b
London: Macmillan, 1979 (2nd ed.) (Macmillan International College Editions). 255 pp.
£5.95 cased £3.80 p/b
Intended for students and readers new to the field, this selection of short stories from the Commonwealth contains contributions by Tutuola, Achebe, Ngugi and Mphahlele. Each story is preceded by a short critical introduction to its writer's main themes. Contains brief bio-bibliographical data.

Rutherford, Peggy, ed.
Darkness and Light: an anthology of African writing
Johannesburg: Drum Publications, 1958.
208 pp.
New York: Grosset [publ. as *African Voices*], 1959 (Universal Library, 105). 208 pp. $8.95
This is one of the very first anthologies of African writing published. It features folk tales, short stories, extracts from novels, and poetry, including a variety of contributions by lesser-known authors. The editor provides an introduction and biographical notes on each writer.

Sainville, Léonard ed.
Anthologie de la littérature négro-africaine: romanciers et conteurs négro-africains 2 vols.
Paris: Présence Africaine, 1963 and 1968.
456 pp. 644 pp. o/p
A comprehensive early anthology of new-African writing, with extracts from works by African, Caribbean and North American authors. Although there are brief extracts from writings by Nigerian and other English-speaking writers, this anthology puts heavy emphasis on francophone African literature.

Sangster, E. G. ed.
To Know My Own
Tema, Accra: Ghana Publishing Corp., 1971.
101 pp. ₵1.50.
A collection of poetry by young Ghanaian writers.

Sangster, E. G. and Quashie, C. K. A. eds.
Talent for Tomorrow. 5th anthology: creative writing from the training colleges and secondary schools of Ghana
Tema, Ghana: Ghana Publishing Corp., 1972.
234 pp. ₵1.20
An anthology of the best entries in a series of annual creative writing competitions among secondary schools in Ghana.

Schrey, Kurt ed.
African Authors of English Expression
Frankfurt: Diesterweg, 1966 (Diesterwegs neusprachliche Bibliothek). 60 pp. DM2.60

Senanu, K. E. and Vincent, T. eds.
A Selection of African Poetry
London: Longman, 1976. 224 pp. £2.70
An anthology aimed primarily at candidates for the West African School Certificate, which, on a more general level, attempts to emphasize the importance of poetry in the cultural heritage of Africa. The volume includes traditional poetry, works by 'established' poets, and contains poems by six authors whose work has not yet been widely anthologized. A section on 'How to Use the Anthology' provides a general commentary on each poem, explains difficult words, lines and devices and provides practical work based on key questions.

'Very few anthologies of African poetry in the past have taken the pain to include traditional poetry in their texts and to emphasize the emotional as well as aesthetic break such a cultural gap could lead to in the appreciation of poetry by the students. It is here that lies the first and perhaps the most important merit of the book of Senanu and Vincent . . . a good work which sets out to accomplish its stated goal within the scope of its narrow ambitions.'
Ihechukwu Madubuike – *Research in African Literatures*

Senghor, Léopold Sédar ed.
Anthologie de la nouvelle poésie nègre et malgache de langue française, précédée de Orphée noir par Jean-Paul Sartre
Paris: Presses Universitaires de France, 1977 (4th ed.) (Collection Pays d'Outre Mer). 228 pp. FF100.00
The fourth edition of Senghor's pioneering anthology of Black poetry from Africa, Haïti, Guadeloupe, Martinique, Guyana, and the Malagasy Republic, includes Sartre's famous introductory essay 'Orphée noir' in which he defines the concept of Négritude.

Sergeant, Howard ed.
Commonwealth Poems of Today
London: John Murray, 1967. 288 pp. £1.95 cased £1.50 p/b
An anthology of some 250 poems from Commonwealth countries, including verse from the Gambia, Ghana, Kenya, Malawi, Nigeria, Rhodesia, Sierra Leone, South Africa, Tanzania, Uganda and Zambia.

Poetry from Africa
Oxford and New York: Pergamon Press, 1968 (Commonwealth and Int. Library: Pergamon poets, 2). 108 pp. o/p
A selection from the work of Gabriel Okara, Gaston Bart-Williams, Kwesi Brew and David Rubadiri, accompanied by biographical notes.

New Voices from the Commonwealth
London: Evans, 1968. 208 pp. o/p
Reflecting the cultural diversity of the Commonwealth, this volume includes a substantial portion of poetry from African countries, by established as well as little-known African poets.

African Voices
London: Evans, 1976 (2nd ed.). 160 pp. £1.95
The work of forty-five contemporary African
poets is represented in this collection. Works
from the major African writers such as Wole
Soyinka, John Pepper Clark, Christopher
Okigbo and Gabriel Okara are included. The
anthology also includes writings by poets who
are less well-known outside their own countries.

How Strong the Roots: poems of exile
London: Evans, 1981. 96 pp. £3.95
A collection of verse which explores the theme
of origin and exile and the continuing search
for identity. The poems, many published for
the first time, come from poets who have
experienced exile in its various forms at first
hand, and include writers from Nigeria, South
Africa, and the Caribbean in addition to other
countries.

Shapiro, Norman R. ed. and trans.
*Négritude: Black poetry from Africa and the
Caribbean*
New York: October House, 1970. 247 pp.
$7.50 cased $4.95 p/b
Presents all the major exponents of Négritude
in the original French, with parallel English
translations. Includes verse by Aimé Césaire,
Léon Damas, Léopold Senghor, Tchicaya U
Tam'si, Bernard Dadié, Joseph Bognini, and
many others.
'. . . there is enough outstanding poetry for everybody,
some of it superb.'   *Africa Report*

Shelton, Austin J., jr. ed.
*The African Assertion: a critical anthology of
African literature*
New York: Odyssey Press, 1968. 273 pp. $5.00
p/b
This critical anthology of sub-Saharan African
writing contains extracts from both poetry and
prose drawn from a wide variety of African
literature. There is an introduction by the
editor and the book concludes with a section
'Readings, topics and questions for further
study', followed by a suggested reading list.
'. . . an excellent anthology . . . will serve well at the
core of survey courses in African literature.'
          Robert McDowell – *Africa Today*

Shore, Herbert I. and
Shore-Bos, Megchelina eds.
*Come Back, Africa: fourteen stories from South
Africa*
Berlin: Seven Seas Books, 1968. 202 pp.
A panorama of the South African way of life
seen through the stories of fourteen South

African writers. Among the contributors are:
Alex La Guma, William Modisane, Ezekiel
Mphahlele, Lewis Nkosi, Alan Paton and
Richard Rive. Herbert Shore provides an
introduction; 'A note on South African life
and letters'.

Sørensen, Lennart
*African Literature: an anthology of African
texts*
Kristianstad, Sweden: Hermods, 1971. 168 pp.

Sørensen, P. Husum ed.
Seven African Stories
Copenhagen: Gyldendal, 1974. 112 pp.

Soyinka, Wole ed.
Poems of Black Africa
London: Secker and Warburg, 1975. 378 pp.
£4.75 cased
London: HEB, 1975 (AWS, 171). 384 pp.
£2.25
New York: Hill and Wang, 1975. 378 pp. $4.95
An extensive anthology of verse edited by one
of Africa's major poets and containing works
by both established and new poets. Traditional
as well as modern poetry is included and there
are biographical notes on the authors. There is
an introduction by Wole Soyinka.
'The faultless choice of poems produces an anthology
of lasting virtue as a voice of Africa.'
          Ursula A. Barnett – *World Literature Today*

**Soyinka, Wole; Maine, Abbey;
Kabtihimar, Tesfaye**
Palaver: three dramatic discussion starters
New York: Friendship Press, 1971. 39 pp.

St. John-Parsons, Donald ed.
*Our Poets Speak: an anthology of West African
verse*
London: University of London Press, 1966.
64 pp. 60p
New York: Africana Publ. Corp., 1971. 64 pp.
$4.50
An anthology primarily aimed at young
readers in secondary schools in Africa. The
poems were deliberately selected to vary widely
in theme and style, and in the measure of their
success. Among the poets represented are well-
known names such as Abioseh Nicol, and
Frank Parkes, in addition to those whose
works appear for the first time: Jacob Standley
Davies and Simon Pederek, from Sierra Leone
and Ghana respectively, are among the latter.
The editor's approach is 'let the poets speak
for themselves', and the text aims to promote
enjoyment, appreciation and constructive
criticism. There are notes on the poems, brief

biographies of the authors, an index of first lines, and the selection is preceded by an introduction by O. R. Dathorne and a foreword by Eldred Jones.

Stokes, Olivia Pearl
The Beauty of Being Black: folktales, poems and art from Africa
New York: Friendship Press, 1971. 64 pp.
$2.50 p/b

Tati-Loutard, Jean-Baptiste
Anthologie de la littérature congolaise d'expression français
Yaoundé: C.L.E., 1977 (2nd ed.). 253 pp.
CFA 1,500
A selection of pioneering prose, poetry and drama designed to demonstrate Congolese cultural awareness during the past twenty years. Among the writers included in this collection are Tchicaya U Tamsi, Guy Menga, Makouta-Mboukou, Tati-Loutard himself and many others. A brief biography accompanies the work of each writer.
'. . . this anthology with its well done introductions to each author . . . answers a real need for collected Congolese literature and is highly recommended for all libraries where francophone literature is taught.'
Janis L. Pallister – *African Book Publishing Record*

Tibble, Anne ed.
African-English Literature: a survey and anthology
London: Peter Owen, 1965. 304 pp. £5.00
New York: October House, 1965 (1969 p/b ed.) 304 pp. $2.95
Preceded by a brief historical outline, the first part of this anthology offers a short survey of the most important written prose and poetry of Africa south of the Sahara. The second part of the book provides a selection of African-English prose and poetry, accompanied by a bibliography. It covers the output of thirty-seven African writers, from both English- and French-speaking African nations.

Tong, R.
African Helicon
London: Evans, 1981 (2nd ed.). 128 pp. £1.30
An anthology of poetry for schools with sections on animals, people and places, mystery and drama. The second edition contains a selection of verse by African poets.

Trask, W. R. comp. and ed.
Classic Black African Poems
New York: Eakings, 1971. 61 pp. $3.95

Troupe, Quincy and **Schulte, Rainer** eds.
Giant Talk: an anthology of Third World Writing
New York: Random House, 1975. 546 pp.
$20.00 cased $6.95 p/b
A collection of texts from authors of diverse backgrounds: African, Asian, American-Indian, Afro-American, and Euro-American. Among African writers represented are Achebe, Diop, Okigbo, p'Bitek, and Senghor.
'*This massive anthology is most timely. It should especially serve to let some fresh, non-imperialist air into the lungs of African literature in English . . . an important work superbly done.*' Chinweizu – *Okike*

Tubman, William V. S.
Liberian Writing: Liberia as seen by her own writers as well as by German authors
Tübingen, West Germany: Horst Erdmann Verlag, 1970. 238 pp. DM 18.00
The first comprehensive anthology to present an almost-complete survey of Liberian literature, past and present.

Turner, Darwin, T. comp.
Voices from the Black Experience: African and Afro-American literature
Lexington, Mass.: Ginn, 1972. 280 pp.

Urruty, Jean
Poètes mauriciens 3 vols.
Port Louis, Mauritius: Royal Printing, 1972, 1973. 122 pp., 135 pp., 145 pp.

Vaillant, Florence ed. and trans.
Poètes noirs d'Afrique du Sud: voix noires de l'Afrique blanche
Paris: Présence Africaine, 1975. 190 pp.
FF33.00
Except for the verse of Adam Small most of the poetry in this volume of black South African writers in French translation comes from previously published works like *To Whom It May Concern*, *Cry Rage*, Mtshali's *Sounds of a Cowhide Drum* or Seroto's *Yakhal'Inkomo*. The thirteen poets represented here belong to the young generation that has come to the scene since 1965.
'. . . there is good work here by the best poets . . . The French translations are good but sometimes arbitrarily amplify, explain and even add to the original.'
Barend J. Toerien – *Books Abroad*

Vatsa, Mamman J.
Voices from the Trench
Enugu, Nigeria: Fourth Dimension Publ. Co., 1978. 154 pp. ₦2.00
An anthology of the verse of Nigerian soldier-poets.

Vézinet, P. and **Désamais, R.** eds.
Pages africaines 5 vols.
Paris: Hatier, 1963–66: 79 pp., 79 pp., 72 pp.,
87 pp. and 95 pp. FF12.00 ea.
An anthology of traditional and contemporary
African writing in five volumes.

Vézinet, P. ed.
Poésie africaine
Paris: Hatier, 1969. 96 pp. FF12.00
An anthology of African poetry (from traditional and contempory sources) to illustrate
the themes of Négritude that are outlined in
the preface – return to origins, joy, love,
suffering and death, liberation of man are
some of the themes. The volume was prepared
with the help of a group of African teachers.

Vyas, Chiman L.
A Collection of Zambian Verse 2 vols.
Lusaka: Zambia Cultural Services, 1971/72.
32 pp., 34 pp. 25n ea.

Wake, Clive ed.
*An Anthology of African and Malagasy Poetry
in French*
London and New York: OUP, 1965. 181 pp.
o/p
Following a detailed introduction, this an-
thology presents, among others, the works of
Rabéarivelo, Senghor, Rabemananjara, Diop,
Dadié, U Tam'si, Bognini, Bebey and Ranaivo.
Notes on each poet and an index of first lines
supplement the text.

Wanjala, Chris L. ed.
Faces at Crossroads: a 'Currents' anthology
Nairobi: East African Literature Bureau, 1971.
216 pp. K.shs.14.25 (£1.40/$3.50)
A collection of stories and poems gathered
from the publications of the Writers' Workshop started at the University of Nairobi in
1968. It has an introduction by Angus Calder
in which he says: 'Here are faces at crossroads,
new faces for the most part, but distinct and
recognisable; and the roads lead in many
directions.'

Singing with the Night
Nairobi: East African Literature Bureau, 1974.
86 pp. K.shs.13.00 (£1.30/$3.20)
An anthology of East African verse.

*The Debtors: a collection of plays from East
Africa*
Nairobi: East African Literature Bureau, 1977.
155 pp. K.shs.20.55 (£1.80/$4.55)
Five plays by young and promising East
African playwrights are assembled in this

anthology. They are *The Debtors* by Kopa
Tarimu; *There were Strings on Magere's Shield* by
Ochieng-Konyango; *The Question of Bride Price*
by Wilfred Rimba; *In Search of a Wife* by
General T. K. Ulimwengu; and *The Positive
Volunteers* by Francis M. Kamau. The collection
is aimed at schools as well as the general public
and contains plays of widely-different lengths
and complexity, in a variety of different modes
of presentation.

Washington, Mary Helen
*Any Woman's Blues: stories of contemporary
black women writers*
London: Virago Press, forthcoming 1981.

Watts, Margaret E. ed.
*The New Generation: prose and verse from the
secondary schools and training colleges of
Ghana*
Accra: State Publishing Corp., 1967. 58 pp.
₵1.00
A collection of prize-winning entries from the
second creative writing competition organized
by the Ghana Association of Teachers of
English. Kofi Awoonor, who contributes a
small preface, says of them: 'Some of the
stories in this book bear a certain mark of
genius, some may be derivative; but they all
have the simple stamp of innocence'.

Weaver, Roger and **Bruchac, Joseph** eds.
*Aftermath: an anthology of poems in English
from Africa, Asia, and the Caribbean*
Greenfield Center, New York: Greenfield
Review Press, 1977. 257 pp. $4.00
Primarily aimed at an American audience, this
anthology includes poetry by well-known
writers such as Edward Braithwaite, Andrew
Salkey, Kofi Awoonor, Dennis Brutus, and
Wole Soyinka, as well as lesser-known names.

White, Margaret B. and **Quigley, Robert
N.** comps.
*How the Other World Lives: Third World
stories, poems, songs, prayers and essays from
Asia, Africa, and Latin America*
Maryknoll: Orbis Books, 1977. 425 pp. $4.95
An anthology which aims to provide insights
into the cultural backgrounds of Third World
peoples. The volume includes many contributions from Africa and contains sections on
poetry, stories, essays, journals and novellas.

White, Jo Ann ed.
African Views of the West
New York: Messner, 1972. 207 pp. $5.95
A collection of excerpts from some of the

major works of African writers and statesmen reflecting the broad spectrum of African reactions to the impact of Westerners and Western civilization upon Africa.

Wolfers, Michael, ed. and trans.
Poems from Angola
London, HEB, 1979 (AWS, 215). 128 pp.
£2.25/$5.50
This volume, the first in the 'African Writers Series' devoted to poetry from a Lusophone African country, contains selected works from twenty-two Angolan poets.

Zabala, Pam and **Rossell, Chris** eds.
African Writing: a thematic anthology
London: Collins Educational, 1974. 127 pp.
£1.20
An anthology of African texts and photographs built round five universal themes 'Conflict', 'Schooldays', 'Women', 'The Seven Ages of Man', and 'Folklore and Customs'. Intended to 'whet the appetite of secondary school students for the vast range of good African literature now available to them', the selections are made up of both prose and poetry. Each text is preceded by a short explanatory introduction and followed by a number of questions.

Folklore & Oral tradition – a selection

This section provides a *selection* of books on African folklore. It includes collections of folk-tales and fables, proverbs and sayings, folk drama, rhymes and verse and traditional poetry, as well as critical monographs on folklore, the oral tradition and African oral epics. Bibliographies on African folklore may be found in the main 'Bibliographies and Reference works' section on p. 1–12.

Space restrictions have prevented us from providing more that a sampling of the available literature. We have not included, for example, the many special-

ist volumes on African folklore and mythology published by the Centre d'Etudes Ethnologiques-Branche Anthropos (CEEBA), further details about which can, however, be obtained from B.P. 19, Bandundu, Zaïre Republic.

Also not included are titles that appear in the collection 'Grandes Figures Africaines', co-published by Editions ABC in Paris, Nouvelles Editions Africaines in Dakar, and Editions C.L.E. in Yaoundé, which present fictionalised accounts of the major names of African history.

Abdulaziz, Mohamed H.
Muyaka: 19th century Swahili popular poetry
Nairobi: Kenya Literature Bureau, 1979.
340 pp. K.shs.54.00 (£5.00/$9.00)
A collection of Swahili poems from the nineteenth century, presented in roman script versions of Swahili accompanied by English translations. There is also an extensive introductory historical profile of political, social and economic life in Mombasa at the time, which is essential for an understanding of the poems.
'. . . the book has immense value for linguists, historians, and sociologists. It is highly recommended for academic libraries.'
Greta D. Little – *African Book Publishing Record*

Abehikin, Laurent Mama
Akoun
Paris: Présence Africaine, 1980. 174 pp.
FF24.00
An Akan epic tale told by a grandfather around the fire.

Abimbola, Wande ed. and trans.
Ifa: an exposition of Ifa literary corpus
Ibadan: OUP, Nigeria, 1976. 256 pp. ₦7.50
cased ₦4.00 p/b
A scholarly discussion of the Ifa system of divination based on the author's Ph.D. thesis. The book draws on the personal knowledge of Wande Abimbola, who is an apprentice diviner.
'*Although book-length studies of the latter topic [Ifa divination] have been written, Abimbola provides a succinct description which is essential for understanding Ifa poetry in its cultural context.*'
Nancy J. Schmidt – *World Literature Today*

Ifa Divination Poetry
New York: Nok Publishers, 1977. 177 pp.
$12.50 cased $4.95 p/b
Ifa divination is most important among the Yoruba of South-Western Nigeria and the eastern Benin Republic. This volume contains myths, legends and folk-tales which the diviner recites to his clients in verse form and which

shed light on the Yoruba world view. The verses describe the conflicts between gods, witches and other powers such as Death, Loss, Curse, Disease, Imprisonment and Affliction.

Sixteen Great Poems of Ifa
Niamey: Centre d'Etudes Linguistique et Historique par Tradition Orale, 1975. 470 pp. CFA1,140

African Way of Life Club, Kachebere
Bantu Wisdom
Lusaka: Neczam, 1972. 128 pp. K1.40
Five-hundred traditional proverbs of Central Africa are gathered in this volume with English translations and explanations of their meaning.

Aghali-Zakara, Mohamed and Drouin, Jeannine
Traditions touarègues nigériennes: Amerolqis, héros civilisateur pré-islamique, et Aligurran, archétype social
Paris: L'Harmattan, 1980. 120 pp. F45.00
Two tales of the Kel Tamajag Tuareg people of Niger, published both in the original and in French; they are stories of a pre-Islamic folk hero and a social archetype.

Ahmed, Said Bakari bin Sultani
The Swahili Chronicle of Ngazija
(Ed. and trans. by Lyndon Harries)
Bloomington, Ind.: African Studies Program, Indiana University, 1977. 134 pp. $5.50
A volume which utilizes oral tradition and myths to create a work of historical scholarship which links older, traditional chronicles to modern historiography.

Ajuwon, Bade
Funeral Dirges of Yoruba Hunters
New York: Nok Publishers, 1978. 200 pp. $16.50 cased $5.95 p/b
A bilingual edition, Yoruba/English, of the funeral dirges of Yoruba hunters of Nigeria. The volume is presented with an introduction and notes.

Allen, J. W. T.
Tendi
London: HEB, 1971 504 pp. £8.50 p/b
New York: Africana Publ. Corp., 1971. 502 pp. $54.50 cased
A collection of six classical narrative Swahili poems. English translations and a detailed critical apparatus are provided.

Amadu, Malum
Amadu's Bundle
(Collected by Gulla Kell, trans. by Ronald Moody)
London: HEB, 1972 (AWS, 118). 96 pp. £1.60/$3.00
A collection of Fulani stories of love and djinns which come from northern Cameroun and Nigeria. The anthology also includes riddles and songs which exist only in the verbal tradition and some essays written by Malum Amadu at the request of Gulla Kell.

Amon d'Aby, François-Joseph
La mare aux crocodiles: contes et légendes populaires de Côte-d'Ivoire
Dakar: Nouvelles Editions Africaines, 1973. 123 pp. CFA600
Forty traditional tales from all parts of the Ivory Coast which the author recorded on his official trips (he is a civil servant) around the country. With illustrations by J. C. Bedia.

Andreski, Iris comp.
Old Wives' Tales: life stories of African women
New York: Schocken Books, 1971. 190 pp. $2.45
A collection of twenty-six autobiographies by Ibibio women of ages ranging from 50–100 years, who have led a mainly rural life in and around the Uyo area. Some accounts are accompanied by a short commentary by the editor.
'. . . the life-stories are interesting to read and valuable to have.'
Simon Ottenberg — *Research in African Literatures*

Andrzejewski, B. W. and Lewis, I. M. comps.
Somali Poetry
London and New York: OUP, 1964 (Oxford Library of African Literature). 178 pp. o/p
Texts and translations illustrating different styles of verse, song and the works of the greatest Somali poets. The editors, a linguist and an anthropologist, aim to provide a true image of Somali pastoral life and oral tradition.
'. . . their task has not been to recreate an oral tradition dependent on sounds extremely stylized and alien to unacquainted ears, but to introduce and describe the poetry in its cultural setting. The great value of this book is the success with which it accomplishes just that.'
Ellen Conroy Kennedy — *Africa Report*

Arewa, O. and Shreve, G. M.
The Genesis of Structures in African Narrative.
Vol. 1: *Zande trickster tales*
New York: Conch Magazine, 1975. 300 pp.
$20.00
A collection which attempts to demonstrate the existence of an orderly narrative structure in Zande trickster tales.

Armstrong, Robert *et al*. trans.
Iyèrè Ifá
Ibadan: Institute of African Studies, 1978.
141 pp. ₦2.50
The transcription of a performance of Ifá chanting which took place in 1965 at Oshogbo.

Awoonor, Kofi
Fire in the Valley: Ewe folktales
New York: Nok Publishers, 1973. 150 pp.
$10.00 cased $3.95 p/b
A collection of tales of a mythical and legendary world, many of which star the trickster 'Spider'.

Guardians of the Sacred Word: Ewe poetry
New York: Nok Publishers, 1974. 110 pp.
$10.00 cased $3.95 p/b.
An introduction to Ewe culture and traditional forms of Ewe poetry exemplified by the works of three living poets.
'It is likely that Awoonor, a fine poet in his own right, has obtained insights into his own feelings of loneliness and ennui through his experiences with these venerable traditional poets.'
Charles Dameron – *Books Abroad*

Awua-Asamoah, A. K.
Some Akan Fables
Accra: Waterville Publ. House, 1976. 68 pp.
60pes.
A collection of seven fables from the Akan of Ghana.

Awouma, Joseph-Marie
Contes et fables du Cameroun
Yaoundé: C.L.E., 1976 (Culture et tradition-initiation à la littérature oral, 1). 72 pp.
CFA600
This book aims to initiate the reader to the characteristics and the aims of the different genres of oral literatures.

Contes et fables: étude et compréhension
Yaoundé: C.L.E., 1979. 155 pp. CFA1,200
A study of African tales and fables. In the first part the author speaks about the origin and morphology of tales and fables, characters, and the art of story telling. The second part

presents the texts themselves, classed thematically and structurally.

Ayissi, Leon-Marie
Contes et berceuses Beti
Yaoundé: C.L.E., 1966. 94 pp. CFA420
The author's childhood memories are reflected in this small collection of traditional tales and lullabies.

Bâ, Amadou Hampaté and Dieterlen, Germaine
Koumen: texte initiatique des pasteurs peuls
Paris and The Hague: Mouton and Ecole Pratique des Hautes Etudes, 1961 (Cahiers de l'homme: Ethnologie, Géographie, Linguistique, nouvelle série, 1). 196 pp.
Amadou Hampaté Bâ collected this Fulani initiation tale from Ardo Dembo, a master storyteller from the district of Linguère in Senegal. In Fulani cosmology Koumen is the mythical shepherd of the principal deity, Tyanaba, the rightful owner of all cattle, and as such is the depository of all initiation secrets. This text relates how Silé Sadio became the first man to reach the highest initiation level and become a *silatigi*, or chief priest. A thirty-page introduction outlines the organization of Fulani society and the role of initiation in their pastoral economy.

Bâ, Amadou Hampaté and Kesteloot, Lilyan
Kaïdara: récit initiatique peul
Paris: A. Colin, 1968 (Classiques africains, 7).
184 pp. FF45.60
This second Fulani initiation tale comes from the people of the Ferlo and Mâcina in eastern Senegal and has recently been made into a film in France. It belongs to a literary genre called *janti*, which are long tales centred around human or divine personages, and tells the story of the man, Hammadi's, quest for Kaïdara, the god of wealth (gold) and knowledge. Bâ collected the tale and produced a prose version first which he rewrote in verse for publication. Bilingual text (Fulani-French) on facing pages with an introduction and notes.

Bâ, Amadou Hampaté; Kesteloot, Lilyan and Seydou, Christiane
L'éclat de la grande étoile suivi de *Bain rituel: récits initiatiques peuls*
Paris: A. Colin, 1974 (Classiques africains, 15).
152 pp. FF82.40
The theme here is the initiation into the secrets of power. Hammadi of the preceding text has long been dead but will resuscitate when

Kaïdara returns – announced by a great star – to give him the ultimate revelation. Meanwhile, secular power is in the hands of the young king, Diôm Dièri, Hammadi's grandson, who can only learn to govern by submitting to the teachings of his *silatigi*. This text is a sequel to *Kaïdara*, belonging to the transition period in Fulani history when the people become sedentarized and power gradually shifts from the *silatigi*, or religious chief, to the *laamiido*, or secular chief or king. Bilingual text on facing pages with an introduction and notes.

Bâ, Amadou Hampaté
Kaydara
Dakar: Nouvelles Editions Africaines, 1978. 112 pp. CFA1,500
This is a prose version of Bâ's famous Fulani initiation text previously published in verse. An English translation is shortly to be published by Three Continents Press, Washington D.C.

Babalola, S. A.
The Content and Form of Yoruba Ijala
London and New York: OUP, 1966 (Oxford Library of African Literature). 410 pp. o/p
Examines a type of oral poetry in the culture of the Yoruba-speaking people of Western Nigeria. The first part of this study is a critical introduction to Ijala, while the main body of the book is an annotated, classified anthology of Ijala poems, with the complete original texts facing the translations.

Baissac, Charles
Le folklore de l'île Maurice
Paris: Maisonneuve Larose, 1968 (2nd ed.). 494 pp. FF73.00
Legends, tales, songs, riddles and proverbs collected among the black creole peoples of Mauritius in the middle of the nineteenth century. This is a re-issue of the original volume, published in 1888.

Bamanan Nsiiriw
Contes bambara du Mali vol. 2
Paris: Publications Orientalistes de France, 1979. 111 pp. FF13.50
Bambara tales in the original Manding version. Veronika Görög has translated them into French (see *Contes Bambara du Mali I*, page 110).

Barat, Christian; Carayol, Michel; Vogel, Claude eds.
Krike Krake: recueil de contes créoles réunionnais
Saint-Denis, Réunion: Centre Universitaire de

la Réunion, 1977 (Travaux de l'Institute d'anthropologie sociale et culturelle de l'Océan Indian, 1). 109 pp.
Creole tales from Réunion.

Bascom, William
Ifa Divination: communication between gods and men in West Africa
Bloomington, Ind.: Indiana University Press, 1969. 575 pp. $20.00 cased
This volume is the result of more than thirty year's study. In the first section the author describes the apparatus, techniques and belief systems of Ifa and gives an analysis of the role of the diviner although the main portion of the book consists of texts of the diviner's verses which represent Ifa's message to the client. The verses are presented in Yoruba and are accompanied by a translation on the facing page.
'*Ifa Divination will stand as one of the most complete studies of divination in the literature; for students of oral literature it will be known as an exemplary study of the institutional context of verbal art. In either guise, it will have few equals as a work of scholarship.*'
Richard Bauman – *Research in African Literatures*

African Dilemma Tales
The Hague: Mouton, 1975. 175 pp.
A paper presented at the IXth International Congress of Anthropological and Ethnological Sciences held in Chicago in September 1973, with a preface by the series general editor Sol Tax. The author examines the social context of dilemma tales which, in this study, come from more than one-hundred African languages. A list of references and a two-page index of ethnic names is given.
'*. . . this book is a very interesting and useful document for students of African literature, folklore, and anthropology as well as for teachers and educators.*'
Sayyid Hurreiz – *Research in African Literatures*

Baumbach, E. J. M. and Marivate, C. T. D. eds.
Xironga Folk-Tales
Pretoria: Univ. of South Africa Press, 1973. 199 pp. R7.90
This volume is published in a limited edition of 1000 copies and the editors state that: 'This anthology presents a number of Xironga folk stories which the authors have recorded, exactly as they were told by different narrators, during a visit to the Lourenco Marques area'. The book also contains a series of wood-cut illustrations by Raymond Andrews.

Beard, Peter ed.
Longing for Darkness: Kamante's tales from "Out of Africa"
New York: Harcourt Brace Jovanovich, 1975. 302 pp. $19.95
Recollections of days on a Kenya coffee farm which give a Kikuyu view of people and events during the years 1914 to 1931. Kamante worked as a cook for Karen Blixen (Isaak Dinesen) and the volume gathers together his memories and observations during these years. The book also contains a collection of animal fables which are illustrated by Kamante. The manuscript is reproduced on lined paper instead of being set in type and contains many photographs.
'This is a beautiful book, a magnificent book, a valuable book, and possibly a unique book.'
Blair Rouse — *Research in African Literatures*
'The book ... is a production that re-creates an Africa that may never have existed but which has nevertheless sustained African and non-African dreamers and visionaries alike. The book is of another age, or really of no age at all, an ageless time.'
Martin Tucker — *Okike*

Beier, Ulli ed.
The Origin of Life and Death: a collection of creation myths from Africa
London: HEB, 1966 (AWS, 23). 96 pp. £1.10/$2.50
The creation myths in this collection originate from all over Africa and from many different languages. They provide a cross-section of the amount, variety and vitality of the form of the traditional story.
'... a perfect little gem ... will serve as an invaluable reference book for the student of African culture.' Charles Larson — *Africa Report*

Yoruba Poetry: an anthology of traditional poems
London and New York: CUP, 1970. 126 pp. £5.95
A collection of traditional African verse brought together by Ulli Beier. There are notes on the poems and an introductory essay entitled 'On translating Yoruba poetry'. Illustrated with line drawings.

Yoruba Myths
Cambridge: CUP, 1980. 88 pp. £5.95 cased £1.95 p/b
A collection of myths compiled and introduced by Ulli Beier which illustrate the religion and thought of the West African Yoruba people. The myths are interspersed with line drawings by Georgina Beier of Yoruba motifs, taken from shrines, beadwork and ceremonial objects.

Beling-Nkouba
Contes du Cameroun
Yaoundé: C.L.E., 1978. 156 pp. CFA900
Among the 'heroes' of these traditional Beti and Bulu tales from southern Cameroun we find Kulu the Tortoise, Bémé the Boar, Zé the Panther and Mian the Antelope.

Ben-Amos, Dan
Sweet Words: story-telling events in Benin
Philadelphia: Institute for the Study of Human Issues, 1975. 93 pp. $6.95
Attempts to portray story-telling as an organic part of the history, geography and daily life of the peoples of the Benin area. An English translation is placed side by side with the original Bini text.

Bhalo, Ahmad Nassir bin juma
Poems from Kenya
(Trans. and ed. by Lyndon Harries)
Madison: Univ. of Wisconsin Press, 1966. 244 pp.
The poems of a young Swahili poet in the original Swahili, with English translations. In his introduction, the translator outlines the complex traditions which form a framework for the poetry.

Biebuyck, Daniel P. and Mateene, Kahombo
Anthologie de la littérature orale nyanga
Brussels: A.R.S.O.M., 1970. 363 pp.
A collection of pieces from Nyanga oral tradition including the epic of the Maiden, tales, true stories, extraordinary facts and events, praise poems, riddles, proverbs, sayings, and songs.

Biebuyck, Daniel P. and Mateene, Kahombo C. eds. and trans.
The Mwindo Epic from the Banyanga (Congo republic)
Berkeley, Cal.: Univ. of California Press, 1972. (P/b. reissue of ed. orig. publ. 1969). 213 pp. $2.45
An African epic from the eastern part of the Congo Republic outlining the culture of the Nyanga people. In the past the Nyanga were strongly influenced by Pygmy culture and they themselves attribute the origins of their epic texts to this earlier association. The epic traces customs, institutions, activities, behaviour patterns, value and material objects which are of significance to the Nyanga and includes every literary form in both prose and poetry.
'The editors have themselves accomplished a linguistic tour de force in providing the original Nyanga text with tonal markings and regular distinction of the

seven-vowel system . . . African oral literature is enriched immeasurably by this edition of a masterly work.'
Lyndon Harries – *Research in African Literatures*

Binam Bikot, Charles
Contes du pays des rivières: contes du Sud-Cameroun
Paris: Conseil International de la Langue Française, 1977. 149 pp.
Tales from southern Cameroon, in bilingual text, which the author collected and translated in collaboration with Bot Ba Njok under the direction of Emmanuel Soundjock.
'. . . *a welcome contribution to published folklore. It is an attractive book with clear print and appealing illustrations.'*
Philip A. Noss – *Research in African Literatures*

Binam Bikot, C. and Soundjock, E.
Les Contes du Cameroun
Yaoundé: C.E.P.E.R., 1977. 264 pp. CFA400
A volume designed for use in secondary schools in Africa with the purposes of assisting in the instruction of the French language and providing students with literature which is relevant to their cultural experiences and background. Twenty-four tales are presented with vocabulary aids, exercises and footnotes with background information.
'From the point of view of a textbook, this is a useful and well-conceived volume.'
Mark DeLancey – *African Book Publishing Record*

Bird, Charles S. ed.
The Songs of Seydou Camara Vol. 1: *Kambili*
Bloomington, Ind.: African Studies Center, 1974. 120 pp. $4.50
Kambili is a hunter's epic tale from the Manding-speaking peoples of West Africa. The volume gives a general description of the life of Seydou Camara and of his development as a bard and continues with an outline of a bard's relationship with a hunter's society and of the societies themselves. Some aspects of cosmology are defined.
'The good introduction and extensive notes, as well as the colorful and lively translation make this volume a must for any student of Manding folklore and anthropology.'
John William Johnson – *Research in African Literatures*

Bosek'llolo-Baleka Lima
Les marais brulés: contes
Kinshasa: Centre Africain de Littérature, 1973. 40 pp. 50k
Four tales in a traditional vein with a preface by Elebe Lisembe. Contains 'The rat with 4

tails', 'The squirrel and the nut', 'Nk'Ekolo, the armless, legless child' and an African 'seven-in-one-blow' tale.

Bouc, Hadji ed.
Demb ak Tey (Cahiers du mythe)
Dakar: Centre d'Etudes des Civilisations, 1975. 59 pp.
A multi-faceted look at a multi-ethnic tale presented in Wolof, Peule and French versions. Symbols of the tale in the five cultures in which it is found are discussed, with a list of proverbs applicable to the plot and interviews and essays with scholars and laymen.
'The interviews and essays are invaluable for any scholar and all foreigners . . . An exemplar for the proper study of a folk-tale.'
David Dorsey – *Books Abroad*

Boucharlat, Alain
Le commencement de la sagesse. Devinettes rwanda
Paris: SELAF, 1975 (Tradition orale, 14). 175 pp. FF60.00
Rwanda riddles.

Burness, Donald
Shaka, King of the Zulus, in African Literature
Washington D.C.: Three Continents Press, 1976. 192 pp. $15.00 cased $9.00 p/b
A presentation of the Shaka legend in verse, fiction, and drama, with special essays by Jordan K. Ngubane on Shaka's political/social ideas and by Daniel P. Kunene on Shaka in South African vernacular literature.
'Burness has done a major service in bringing together for the first time diverse material on Shaka . . . His is not a mean achievement.'
Kolawole Ogungbesan – *Research in African Literatures*

Calame-Griaule, Geneviève ed.
Le thème de l'arbre dans les contes africains
vol. 1
Paris: SELAF, 1969 (2nd ed.) (Bibliothèque de la SELAF, 16). 92 pp.
A three-part study on the theme of trees in African and Haïtian folk-tales. Mrs Calame-Griaule writes on 'L'arbre au trésor' ('The Treasure Tree'), a West-African tale in which a hero successfully passes a test and finds a treasure, whereas another only finds fakes; Louis Mallart-Guimera supplies a series of ethnographic data concerning the Oven tree among the Evuzok in southern Cameroon; and Laënnec Hurbon analyses the role played by different trees in Haïti as the locus of tests which ultimately decide on matters of innocence (and, therefore, life) or guilt (and death).

There is a general introduction by Geneviève Calame-Griaule.

Le thème de l'arbre dans les contes africains vol. 2
Paris: SELAF, 1970 (Bibliothèque de la SELAF, 20). 137 pp.
The second volume contains 'L'arbre justicier' by Veronika Görög-Karady (tales in which a tree has a part in the atonement for an evil deed), 'L'arbre et le mariage' by Asia Popova (tales in which a tree attempts marriage to a human being or in which the tree is the intermediary in a courtship), and 'L'arbre ancestral' by John D. Studstill (analysis of tales in which trees symbolize traditional wisdom and play the role of arbiters). Madame Calame-Griaule has again written a general introduction.

Le thème de l'arbre dans les contes africains vol. 3
Paris: SELAF, 1974 (Bibliothèque de la SELAF, 42-43).212 pp. FF100.00

Cantell, J. V.
Folk-Tales from Mpondoland
Pretoria: Univ. of South Africa Press, 1978. 155 pp. R11.50
A collection of folk-tales with text in English and Mpondo, supplemented by a glossary of critical Mpondo words and interjections and exclamations.
'This book is an attractively packaged volume of twenty Mpondo folk-tales. Striking illustrations by Gert le Grance add considerably to the author's efforts to preserve the atmosphere of the original tales ... a valuable book for linguists, folklorists and anthropologists.
Greta D. Little – *African Book Publishing Record*

Caroyol, M. and Chaudenson, Robert
Les aventures de Petit Jean
Paris: EDICEF, 1978 (Coll. fleuves et flamme). 112 pp.
Tales in Creole from the Indian Ocean, with French translations.

Cauvin, Jean
La parole traditionnelle
Issy-les-Moulineaux, France: Ed. Saint-Paul, 1980 (Les classiques africains, 882). 87 pp. FF20.00
A complementary volume to the following entry. Here the author discusses how to read oral texts as well as evoking problems of comparison. A bibliography is appended.

Comprendre les contes
Issy-les-Moulineaux: Ed. Saint-Paul, 1980 (Les classiques africains, 883). 101 pp. FF22.00
Studies problems of methods of collection, transcription and interpretation of oral literature.

Centre Culturel du Collège Libermann
Herméneutique de la littérature orale
Douala, Cameroun: Collège Libermann, 1976. 150 pp. CFA1,250
The papers of a colloquium on oral literature organized at Yaoundé in September, 1975 by professors at the University of Yaoundé members of the Society of Jesus. Among the themes discussed: oral literature as a system with its own norms; the role of myths in the Negro-African consciousness; initiation names of the Sarh in Chad; the future of oral literature; oral literature: doomed to die.

Cissoko, S.M. and Sambou, K.
Recueil des traditions orales des Mandingues de Gambie et de Casamance
Yaoundé: C.E.L.T.H.O., 1974. 270 pp. CFA350
An anthology of folk-tales from the Mandingos of Gambia and Senegal.

Colin, Roland
Les contes noirs de l'Ouest Africain, témoins majeurs d'un humanisme
Paris: Présence Africaine, 1957. 206 pp. o/p
Study of traditional African literature, with a preface by Léopold Senghor.

Cope, Trevor ed.
Izibongo: Zulu praise poems
Collected by James Stuart and transl. by Daniel Malcolm
London and New York: OUP, 1968 (Oxford Library of African Literature). 240 pp. o/p
These Zulu eulogies or praise poems resemble odes in that they praise important persons, and epics recording great events. The poems in this selection cover the period from 1750 to 1900, and record the growth of the Zulu state from numerous independent tribes, and its subsequent disintegration. An introduction and annotations are provided for each poem, as well as a short account of Zulu history, social and cultural life, traditional literature, and the function, nature and content of praise poems. The Zulu originals are faced by English translations.
'... Dr Cope's literary analyses are detailed and informative ... printed as parallel Zulu and English texts, the poems themselves are most impressive; the startling imagery, imaginative wordplay and de-

liberate alliteration, together with such devices as understatement and the "contrary twist" at the end of stanzas, all effectively heighten the emotional content.'
J. M. Guy – *African Affairs*

Coupez, A. and Kamanzi, Thomas eds.
Littérature courtoise du Rwanda
London and New York: OUP, 1969 (Oxford Library of African Literature). 238 pp. o/p
The complex and refined poetry of Rwanda has been transmitted orally since the seventeenth century. The editors of this volume have recorded much of this heritage, and it is presented here in the original Rwanda and in French translation. The introduction and notes are also in French.
'. . . makes an excellent introduction not only to the literature of Rwanda but also to its civilisation.'
West Africa

Courlander, Harold
Tales of Yoruba Gods and Heroes
New York: Crown Publishers, 1973. 243 pp.

A Treasury of African Folklore
New York: Crown, 1975. 617 pp. $15.95
A study of various myths and their histories, which gives an introduction to each of the several traditions and cultures which are surveyed. The volume includes myths and oral traditional tales told in the languages of the Hausa, Kanuri, Yoruba, Zulu, Amharic, Mbundu, 'Hottentot' and Shangan peoples.
'. . . even with its flaws, the volume is one of the few comprehensive and reliable studies in the field.'
Martin Tucker – *Okike*

Crowley, Daniel J. ed.
African Folklore in the New World
Austin: Univ. of Texas Press, 1977. 98 pp.
$8.95 cased $3.95 p/b
A collection of essays in which contributors attempt to show that the narratives and song styles of Africa persist with little change in the New World; and how basic stories from West Africa were passed on through oral tradition and, although changed in some details, can still be traced back to the originals.

Curtis, Susheela ed.
Mainane-Tswana Tales
Gaborone, Botswana: United Congregational Church of Southern Africa, 1975 (distr. by the Botswana Book Centre, PO Box 91, Gaborone). 70 pp. £1.80
A collection of twenty-eight stories telling of the time when animals were still able to speak, about the spirits which plagued them and of happenings long ago.

Dadié, Bernard B.
Le pagne noir: contes africains
Paris: Présence Africaine, 1955 (repr. 1970).
160 pp. FF14.00
A collection of sixteen traditional tales featuring animals (spider, tortoise, iguana, bat) but also people: 'The Black Cloth', a sort of African Cinderella story, and 'The Man Who Wanted to be King'.

Damane, M. and Saunders, P. B. eds. and trans.
Lithoko: Sotho praise poems
Oxford: OUP (Oxford Library of African Literature), 1974. 306 pp. £9.00 cased
Two hundred years of Sotho history are covered in this anthology of traditional poems.

David, Raul
Contos Tradicionais da Nossa Terra
Luanda: União dos Escritores Angolanos, 1979 (Cadernos lavra e oficina, 22). 21 pp. 20 Kwanzas (70c)
Four traditional Umbundu fables narrated in a lively tone by the author, who has lived in the interior of his country and devoted much time to studying oral literatures. The tale of the tortoise and the antelope offers a fresh version of the well-known tortoise-hare confrontation.

de Dampierre, Eric ed. and trans.
Poètes Nzakara, vol. 1
Paris: A. Colin, 1963 (Classiques africains, 1).
224 pp. FF55.10
Traditional poetry of the Nzakara people of the Upper Ubangui, in bilingual text (Nzakara-French) with a long presentation by de Dampierre.

Dantioko, Makan
Contes et légendes soninké
Paris: Edicef, 1978 (Fleuve et flamme, 8).
150 pp.
A French translation of twenty Soninké tales and legends from the border region shared by Senegal, Mauritania and Mali and published in a series sponsored by the Conseil International de la Langue Française.

Deng, Francis Mading
The Dinka and their Songs
London: OUP, 1972 (Oxford Library of African Literature). 310 pp. £6.50

Dinka Folktales: African stories from the Sudan
New York: Africana Publ. Corp., 1974.
204 pp. $24.50 cased
A collection of twenty-one tales in English translation with commentaries, which are

concerned with traditional values and the social order.
'. . . *most of the tales unfold in a subtle and intricate fashion and therefore bear rereading.*'
                    C. Dameron – *Books Abroad*

Derive, Jean
Collecte et traduction des littératures orales. Un exemple négro-africain: les contes ngbaka-ma'bo (R.C.A.)
Paris: SELAF, 1975 (Traditions orale, 18).
256 pp. FF83.00
A volume on the methodology of collecting and translating oral literatures using the example of Ngbaka-ma'bo tales from the Central African Republic.
'*Derive's painstaking fieldwork and sophisticated reasoning are of the highest order, especially as all the philosophy is directed to the solving of practical problems; his argument is cogent and convincing.*'
        Lee Haring – *Research in African Literatures*

Derive, Marie-Jose and Jean, Thomas, Jacqueline M. C. with collaboration by Mavode, Marcel
La crotte tenace et autres contes ngbaka-ma'bo de Republique Centrafricaine
Paris: S.E.L.A.F., 1975 (Tradition orale, 13).
228 pp. FF90.00
A collection of nine tales from the Central African Republic which were translated and transcribed using the methods outlined in the author's previous work. Two 33rpm records are included.
'*Whether considered linguistically, ethnographically or literarily,* La Crotte tenace *is the most scrupulous and successful work I have seen.*'
        Lee Haring – *Research in African Literatures*

Diabaté, Massa Makan
Si le feu s'éteignait
Bamako: Ed. Populaires du Mali, 1967.
145 pp.
Traditional tales.

Janjon et autres chants populaires du Mali
Paris: Présence Africaine, 1970. 112 pp.
FF20.00
Traditional poetry told to the author by his uncle, the griot Kélé Monson Diabaté, including the *Janjon,* or praise-poem, in honour of the emperor Sunjata. Winner of the 1971 'Grand Prix Littéraire de l'Afrique'.

Diagne, Léon Sobel
Contes sérères du Sine
Dakar: Nouvelles Editions Africaines, 1978.
231 pp. o/p

Tales of the Serer people in Senegal (region of the Sine) in bilingual text (French-Serer). Lilyan Kesteloot has written the preface.

Dieterlen, Germaine ed.
Textes sacrés d'Afrique noir
Paris: Gallimard. 1965 (Collection UNESCO d'Oeuvres Representative, Serie africaine).
288 pp. FF17.50
Traditional texts, with a preface by Hampaté Bâ.

Diop, Birago
Contes et lavanes
Paris: Présence Africaine, 1963. 257 pp.
FF15.00
Dakar: Nouvelles Editions Africaines, 1980.
CFA1,900 cased
Diop's first rendering of folk-tales, collected from the rich oral tradition and literary heritage of his ancestors. The Dakar edition is an offering of NEA's new book club, 'Club Afrique Loisirs'.

Les contes d'Amadou Koumba
Paris: Fasquelle, 1947. o/p
Paris: Présence Africaine, 1961. 191 pp.
FF15.00
This collection of traditional folk tales from Senegal was awarded the Grand Prix Littéraire d'Afrique Noire in 1964. The stories were told to Diop by Amadou, this family's griot, the traditional story-teller and keeper of oral tradition. Amadou had first heard them at his grandmother's hut.
'. . . *B. Diop joue ses personnages avec une grande sûreté des gestes et d'intonation. Il s'agit de véritables spectacles aux dialogues animés.*'
        Léopold Sédar Senghor – *L'Afrique et L'Asie*

Les nouveaux contes d'Amadou Koumba
Paris: Présence Africaine, 1967 (3rd ed.).
176 pp. FF15.00
Diop's second collection of traditional folk stories, handed down by word of mouth and inspired by his household 'griot'. This edition has a forward by Léopold Senghor. First published in 1958.
'. . . *everything in this very delicate work is marvellous . . . must it be repeated for the benefit of those who have not yet understood, that the significance of Negro-African literature lies in the disinterment of abolished Negro cultural values.*'
        Olympe Bhêly-Quenum – *Présence Africaine*

Tales of Amadou Koumba
London and New York: OUP, 1966 (Trans. from the French by Dorothy S. Blair). 134 pp.
o/p
Amadou's tales presented in English, fourteen

of them from the original collection, and five translated from *Les nouveaux contes d'Amadou Koumba*. Dorothy Blair has provided a foreword and a glossary of local terms.

Contes choisis
(Ed. by Joyce A. Hutchinson)
London and New York: CUP, 1967. 176 pp.
A school edition, including stories from both collections of the Amadou Koumba tales, in the original French, with extensive footnotes in English. In the introduction there is an analysis of the 'conte' in African literature, and Diop's treatment of it, together with an appreciation of his work. The introduction stresses that the 'conte' or folk-tale is a vital part of the oral tradition of African peoples, and fundamental to an understanding of African literature.
'. . . *a useful introduction to Birago Diop's short stories which are part of the drive to help restore the African's self-confidence by bringing to light a glorious past which had either been denigrated or overlooked. Diop achieves these objectives by his qualities as a story teller.*'
S. K. Dabo – *African Affairs*

Contes d'Awa
Dakar: Nouvelles Editions Africaines, 1977. 40 pp. CFA550
A further collection of five illustrated folk-tales which includes stories of Leuck the Hare, Bouki the Hyena and Sarvet the Egret.
'*The colour illustrations contribute to the attractiveness of the volume . . . This good collection by one of Africa's outstanding short story writers is recommended for public libraries.*'
Gloria Reinbergs – *African Book Publishing Record*

Dogbé, Yves-Emmanuel
Fables africaines précédé de La puissance des mots
Le Mée-sur-Seine, France: Ed. Akpagnon, 1980. 108 pp. FF26.00/CFA2,400
Originally published by L'Harmattan, Paris, in 1978, this collection of fables is dedicated to 'La Fontaine, Florian, Anouilh and the father of us all – Aesope'. Begins with an essay on the power of words – and in particular, those of the poet – to accomplish miracles.

Doob, Leonard ed.
Ants Will not Eat your Fingers: a selection of traditional African poems
New York: Walker, 1966, 127 pp.
This collection of traditional African poems in translation utilizes a wide variety of sources. They are presented in alphabetical arrangement by ethnic group. The book, the editor

says, 'makes no trivial claim that the verses are typical of the society from which, out of context, they have been ripped; that the societies are representative of sub-Saharan Africa; or that the translations are faithful or scholarly.' A complete list of sources is appended.

Dorson, Richard M. ed.
African Folklore
Bloomington, Ind.: Indiana Univ. Press, 1972. 587 pp. $12.50 cased
New York: Doubleday/Anchor, 1972. 587 pp. $3.50 p/b
A general essay by the editor introduces a collection of sixteen papers presented at the Conference on African Folklore held at Indiana University's Folklore Institute in 1970. The papers are grouped into sections of 'Traditional Narratives'. 'Traditional Verbal Genres', 'Folklore and Literature', 'Tradition and History', 'Traditional Poetry' and 'Traditional Ritual'. Part three of the volume comprises verbal art texts from the Sudan, Ghana, Liberia, Mali, Cameroun, Gabon and South Africa.
'. . . *with the scope and general format of Dorson's survey article, the excellent papers, and the translated texts, we have a very worthwile introductory text to the study of African verbal art.*'
Philip M. Peek – *Research in African Literatures*

Dugast, Idelette
Contes, proverbes et devinettes des Banen du Cameroun
Paris: SELAF, 1975 (Tradition orale, 12). 575 pp. FF187.00

du Toit, Brian M.
Content and Context of Zulu Folk Narratives
Gainesville: Univ. Press of Florida, 1977. 86 pp. $3.00
An attempt to define African thought systems through the medium of Zulu folklore.

Dzokanga, A.
Chansons et proverbes lingala
Paris: EDICEF, 1978. 162 pp.
The author collected and transcribed these Lingala songs and proverbs from Zaïre with the help of Anne Behaghel.

Echeruo, Michael and **Obiechina, Emmanuel E.** eds.
Igbo Traditional Life, Culture and Literature
Buffalo, N.Y.: Conch Magazine, 1971. 218 pp. $10.00 cased $4.00 p/b
The purpose of this special edition of *The Conch* (111/2, 1971) is stated by the editors to be 'a

comprehensive and authoritative review of Igbo traditional life and culture.' It contains several essays, two critical reviews, an annotated bibliography, and an introduction to and commentary on the status of Igbo studies.

Editions C.L.E.

Contes du Nord-Cameroun: recueillis par les élèves du Lycée de Garoua et illustrés par le Club de Dessin Unesco du Lycée
Yaoundé: C.L.E., 1970. 155 pp.
A collection of thirty-one folk-tales representing seven little-known African cultures of North Cameroun. The coloured illustrations are a combination of African art styles and Western media.
'*Unesco is to be congratulated for encouraging students to express themselves both in print and in picture.*'
George R. Horner – *Research in African Literatures*

Effimbra, Georges

N'Goi: contes de mon village
Paris: L'Ecole, 1975 (Contes de la gazelle, 7). 63 pp.
A collection of Baoulé tales.

Egudu, Romanus N. and Nwoga, Donatus I.

Poetic Heritage: Igbo traditional verse
Enugu, Nigeria: Nwamife Publishers, 1972. 137 pp. ₦2.50
London: HEB, 1972 [publ. as *Igbo Traditional Verse*] (AWS, 129). 74 pp. £1.95/$5.00
A collection of Igbo poetry, in both traditional and current forms, translated into English. Presented in seven sections according to whether they are praise, invocation, incantation, dance, relaxation, satirical or lamentation poems, the verses range from serious to light-hearted in mood, and provide an introduction to the folklore of this part of Nigeria. The poems are preceded by a summary of their cultural background – which covers religion, magic and magicians, festivals, moonlight plays, and Igbo rites of passage.
'. . . *indispensible reading for anyone interested in either Igbo poetry – written or oral – or the numerous dialects of Igbo.*'
Rems. N. Umeasiegbu – *Research in African Literatures* '

Egudu, Romanus N.

The Calabash of Wisdom and Other Igbo Stories
New York: Nok Publishers, 1974. 141 pp. $10.00 cased $3.95 p/b
An illustrated volume of thirty folk-tales which range from origin stories, trick stories, contest and didactic stories.

Ekwulo, S. A.

Elulu Ikwere: Ikwere proverbs
Port Harcourt, Nigeria: Rivers State Council for Arts and Culture, 1975 (Rivers Bilingual Series, 1). 39 pp. ₦1.00
A collection of 200 proverbs which are divided into four categories: about human beings; the poor; animals; and plants in the forest.
'*The present publication is a modest but valuable start to a series of bilingual pamphlets and books that will record and make available oral literature from the Niger delta.*'
Robert M. Wren – *Research in African Literatures*

Eligwe, Obioma I.

Beside the Fire: two modern Igbo tales
Washington D.C.: Three Continents Press, 1974. 83 pp. $3.00
Modern renderings of two African folk-tales on the nature of good and evil. In his introduction the author states that the stories are 'told in the old days, but the ideas are contemporary and the situations or events are happening today.'
'*The main assets of the book are its presentation and its attempt to embody the live storytelling situation, maintaining the continuity of performance in the smooth transition from one tale to another. African literature study will certainly benefit from such works.*'
Helen Chukwuma – *Research in African Literatures*

Eno-Belinga, Samuel Martin

Introduction générale à la littérature orale africaine
Yaoundé: Université de Yaoundé, 1977. 113 pp.
The first is a three-part series of texts on African oral traditions and literatures.

L'explication de texte dans la littérature orale africaines
Yaoundé: Université de Yaoundé, 1977. 57 pp.

L'esthétique littéraire dans la littérature orale africaine
Yaoundé: Université de Yaoundé, 1977. 45 pp.

Comprendre la littérature orale africaine
Issy-les-Moulineaux, France: Ed. Saint Paul, 1978 (Les classiques africains, 80). 144 pp. FF19.00
A study of oral literature as a living tradition with its specific problems – problems of language, of translation, but also of style and

aesthetic inspiration. Also raises the issue of classification.

L'Epopée camerounaise – mvet: Moneblum ou l'homme bleu
Yaoundé: C.E.P.E.R., 1978. 287 pp. CFA1,500
Eno Belinga has recorded and translated an epic narrative in the *mvet* tradition from Bulu-Ngôé in southern Cameroon as received by the famous hard, Danial Osomo. The central character is not the 'blue man' of the title but Mekui-Mengömö-Ondo, part-man, part-spirit, who is banished from his homeland for violating custom but who returns successfully after defeating Efen-Ndön, a powerful supernatural being. In bilingual text (Bulu-French) with photographs of the performances.
'The book is important for the quality of the Bulu text and the French translation. It is a welcome addition to the primary documentation that is gradually becoming available on the extensive epic tradition . . . of a group of people living in Cameroun, Gabon, and Guinea.'
                    Daniel P. Biebuyck – *Research in African Literatures*

Eno-Belinga, Samuel Martin and **Minyono Nkodo, Mathieu-François**
Poésies orales
Issy-les-Moulineaux, France: Ed. Saint-Paul, 1978 (Les classiques africains, 451). 79 pp. FF9.00
An anthologie of oral poetry in French translation with questions and exercises for classroom work.

Equilbecq, F. V.
Contes populaires d'Afrique Occidentale.
Précedes d'un essai la littérature merveilleuse des noirs
Paris: Maisonneuve et Larose, 1972 (Les littératures populaires de toutes les nations, nouvelle série, 17). 520 pp. FF65.00

Evans-Pritchard, E. E. ed.
The Zande Trickster
London and New York; OUP, 1967 (Oxford Library of African Literature) 240 pp.
£5.00/12.50 cased
These tales from the Azande people of the Central African Republic all concern a character called Ture. Ture is a trickster and tries to fool everybody, but often only succeeds in fooling himself. Chapter I gives a brief account of the Azande. Chapter II outlines when, how, and where the tales were collected, and finally, Chapter III contains the stories themselves.

Faik-Nzuji, Madiya Clémentine
Enigmes Luba-Nshinga: étude structurale
Kinshasa: Ed. de l'Université de Lovanium, 1970. 168 pp.
A collection of two hundred riddles from villages between the Lulua and Lubilash rivers. The text is given in Luba and in a French translation and the socio-cultural aspects of the Luba riddle are examined.
'Miss Faik-Nzuji's handling of her texts is excellent. As a means of classification and as a study of the interrelations of the parts of riddles, her structural analysis succeeds well.'
                    Lee Haring – *Research in African Literatures*

Lenga et autres contes d'inspiration traditionelle
Lubumbashi: Ed. Saint-Paul, 1977. 78 pp.
Seven tales in a traditional vein.

Kasal, chant héroïque luba: étude
Lubumbashi: Presses Universitaires du Zaïre, 1974. 252 pp.
Eleven heroic poems, in bilingual text, of the Bakwa-Dushni, Luba peoples of Kassai.
'Une telle étude, non seulement sauve une partie d'un patrimone culturel qui rèsquait de pènir, mais apporte sa contribution à une véritable renaissance africaine.'   – *Présence Africaine*

Devinettes tonales tusumwinu
Paris: SELAF, 1976 (Bibliothèque de la SELAF, 56). 92 pp.
Tone riddles are one of the most popular genres of oral literature among the Luba and the Luluwa of central Zaïre. Part I of this volume presents a study of the genre from a corpus of 200 tone riddles which appear in the original and in French in Part II.

Finnegan, Ruth ed. and trans.
Limba Stories and Storytelling
London and New York: OUP, 1967 (Oxford Library of African Literature). 364 pp. o/p
The Limbas are rice farmers living in the hills of northern Sierra Leone. This volume is devoted to certain aspects and examples of Limba oral literature. The stories are treated as a form of literature in their own right, worthy of study in literary terms. In her introduction to this collection, Dr Finnegan comments:
'. . . they have no one simple message – there is after all, no reason to assume that the Limba, any more than we ourselves, see life as a simple matter. The stories are a complex medium through which comments can be variously expressed or implied.'
'. . . outstanding quality . . . Dr Finnegan lived and worked among the Limba and collected her im-

pressions in situ. Her comments reflect her understanding of the total situation.'
Eldred Jones – *Sierra Leone Studies*

Oral Literature in Africa
London and New York: OUP, 1970 (Oxford Library of African Literature). 58 pp. £13.50 $27.00 cased
A volume in which the author traces the various approaches of mid-nineteenth century collectors of oral traditions and gives an account of nineteenth century attitudes to those traditions. The difficulties of translation and interpretation are demonstrated.
'Dr. Finnegan's book will serve as more than a mere introduction in many quarters. The author deserves credit for compiling such an informed vade-mecum covering such a wide range and geographic area.'
Vernon A. February – *Journal of Commonwealth Literature*

Oral Poetry: its nature, significance and social context
Cambridge: CUP, 1977. 312 pp. £7.50 cased
The author, in the introduction to the book indicates the scope: 'This book is about oral poetry – its nature and its social context and significance – treated comparatively. It considers, therefore, examples such as unwritten Tatar epics, Eskimo lyrics, Malay love songs, South African praise poems to traditional chiefs or modern personalities, Nigerian election songs, or Anglo-American ballads, old and new. It is intended not as a comprehensive survey of oral poetry throughout the world but as a general introduction to oral poetry and to the range of controversies and problems in its study.' Finnegan extends her study to treating the approaches to oral poetry, its composition, style and performance, its transmission and publication, the position of the poets, the audience and the relationship of the poetry to society.

Fortier, Joseph ed.
Dragon et sorcières: contes et moralites du pays Mbai
Paris: A. Colin, 1974 (Classiques africains, 14). 365 pp. FF146.00
A collection of tales about parents and children and husbands and wives in which witches play the role of a catalyst. The stories are arranged thematically with linguistic and cultural annotations.

Fuja, Abayomi ed.
Fourteen Hundred Cowries
London and New York: OUP, 1962. 172 pp.
Thirty-one traditional stories from Yoruba-

land, mostly concerned with ancient beliefs. Originally written in verse-form and recited by Yoruba story-tellers, they are here retold by the editor.

Gbadamosi, Bakare, and Beier, Ulli eds.
Not Even God is Ripe Enough
London: HEB, 1968 (AWS, 48). 64 pp. £1.00/$3.00
'Not even God is ripe enough to catch a woman in love' is the theme of one of twenty Yoruba stories translated into English in this volume. Among others are: 'Every trickster will be fooled once'; 'A young man can have fine cloth like an elder but he can never have rags like an elder'; 'When life is good for us, we become bad'; and 'He who shits on the road will meet flies on his return'.
' . . . the stories are built around old Nigerian proverbs but the language and vigorous style of the narrator of these tales, Bakare Gbadamosi, is very present, immediate, modern.'
Bessie Head – *The New African*

Gbagbo, Laurent Koudou
Soundjata: Lion du Manding
Abidjan: C.E.D.A., 1978. 95 pp. CFA645
A popular version of the legend of the thirteenth century ruler of the Manding.

Gecau, R. N.
Kikuyu Folk-tales
Nairobi: Kenya Literature Bureau, 1970 (2nd ed.). 152 pp. K.shs.12.75, (£1.30/$3.30)
A collection of folk-tales chosen to give some insight into aspects of Kikuyu life and to expose the meanings that lie behind the apparent simplicity of the stories.

Gleason, Judith
Orisha: the gods of Yorubaland
New York: Atheneum, 1971. 121 pp.
A study of Yoruba religion and mythology, illustrated by Aduni Olorisa.

A Recitation of Ifa, Oracle of the Yoruba
New York: Grossman Publishers, 1973. 338 pp. $15.00
This work deals with one series of particular recitations – a requested performance series by an Ifa priest.

Goody, Jack
The Myth of the Bagre
London and New York: OUP, 1972 (Oxford Library of African Literature). 410 pp. o/p
The Bagre myth originated among the LoDagea peoples of Northern Ghana. The Bagre Society controls the telling of the myth

which is divided into two cycles: the White
Bagre tells of the discovery of staple crops and
harvesting and the Black Bagre is concerned
with the origin of man, technological discoveries and offers explanations of man's
relationship to the divine.
'. . . this major contribution to African literature. The
Bagre myth is the most extensive ever to have been
recorded in tropical Africa, and in this book Prof.
Goody gives us both the original and an English
translation, together with extensive explanatory
notes.'   West Africa

Une récitation du Bagré
Paris: A. Colin, 1981 (Classiques africains, 20).
FF125.00
Oral literature of the Dagara of Ghana in
trilingual text (Dagara, English, French).

Görög, Veronika
Contes bambara du Mali vol. 1
Paris: Publications Orientalistes de France,
1979. 119 pp. FF13.50
Volume I of this work contains the French
translation of these Bambara tales. Volume II,
authored by Bamanan Nsiiriw (see page 100),
contains the tales in the original Bambara
version.
'. . . twenty-four tales presented in Bambara and in
a highly readable French translation . . . can easily be
read without continued need for ethnographical
commentary.'
                    Daniel P. Biebuyck – *Research in
                              African Literatures*

Görög, Veronika *et al.*
Histoires d'enfants terribles
Paris: Maisonneuve et Larose, 1980 (Les
littératures populaires de toutes les nations,
nouvelle série, 27). 301 pp. FF130.00
An analysis of the theme of the terrible child
in four African cultures (Bambara-Malinké,
Dogon, Samo, Tyokosi) with an anthology of
twenty-nine tales. In most of these tales the
child hero has been set apart at birth by a
distinguishing characteristic.

Guerra, Henrique
Três Histórias Populares
Lisbon: Ediçoes 70, 1980 (Autores Angolanos,
29) 73 pp. 140 escudos
Three popular tales in which objective reality
and fantasy are combined to capture the spirit
of oral story telling. These are moral as well as
political fables, punctuated with etymological
and ethnological insights. The author introduces the volume with a nine-page preface
in which he explores the development of

modern Angolan writing in light of traditional
oral literatures.

Guma, S. M.
*The Form, Content and Technique of
Traditional Literature in Southern Sotho*
Cape Town: Balkema, 1967 (Hiddingh-Currie
Publ., 8). 215 pp. R3.50
A systematic review of traditional literature in
Southern Sotho. It provides a detailed analysis
of the various *genres*, with a view to establishing
their form and technique.

Hama, Boubou
Merveilleuse Afrique
Paris: Présence Africaine, 1971. 277 pp.
An essay on the Djerma-Songhai world
concept followed by a collection of stories and
legends and an imaginary dialogue between an
African and a Frenchman.

Contes et légendes du Niger
Paris: Présence Africaine, 1972-76.
Vol 1: 214 pp. FF31.00; Vol 2: 152 pp. o/p;
Vol 3: 153 pp. o/p; Vol 4: 140 pp. o/p; Vol 5:
135 pp. FF31.00; Vol 6: 108 pp. FF31.00

Harries, Lyndon
Swahili Poetry
London and New York: OUP, 1962. 326 pp.
o/p
A descriptive survey illustrating the themes and
prosodic forms of early Swahili poetry, with
texts transliterated from the adapted form of
the Arabic script. The content is grouped
around 'The technique of composition', 'The
linguistic medium', 'The Utenzi verses', 'Long-
measure verse', 'The quartain', 'Miscellaneous
verse', and 'Hotuba juu ya Ushairi', and
concludes with textual notes.

Hiskett, Mervyn
A History of Hausa Islamic Verse
London: School of Oriental and African
Studies, Univ. of London, 1975. 274 pp. £7.00
The author shows the relationship of Hausa
Islamic written verse to oral indigenous forms,
and explains the many functions – religious,
political, historical, astrological – it had in
society.
'. . . represents more than a decade of work by
Mervyn Hiskett to bring to light the extensive
manuscripts deposited in Northern Nigeria, and to
study the main historical periods and themes of this
unknown, if not hidden, literature.'
    Alain Ricard – *Journal of Modern African Studies*

Holas, Bernard

Contes Kono: traditions populaires de la forêt guinéenne
Paris: Maisonneuve et Larose, 1975. 342 pp.
The folklore of the Kono people from the region of Nzérékore in Guinea that was collected between 1948 and 1960. Contains fables and riddles as well as tales relating to the creation of man and the origin of Kono customs.

Huntingford, G. W. B. ed. and trans.

The Glorious Victories of 'Amda Seyon, King of Ethiopa', together with the history of the Emperor and Ceôn, otherwise called Gâbra Mazcâl
London and New York: OUP, 1965 (Oxford Library of African Literature). 186 pp. o/p
Specimens of early Ethiopian literature. The text translated here is part of a royal chronicle writen in the ancient Ge'ez language in the fourteenth century A.D. The editor supplements the text by explanatory notes and commentaries.

Illunga Bamuyeja, and Musasa B. Dibwe

Deux Griots de Kamina: Chants et poèmes
Kinshasa: Centre Africain de Littérature, 1974. 32 pp. 50k CFA250 (mimeographed)
The poetry of two writers from Zaïre.

Innes, Gordon ed. and trans.

Kelefa Saane: his career recounted by two Mandinka bards
London: School of Oriental and African Studies, Univ of London, 1978. 118 pp.
A study of an heroic epic originating in the Gambia. Following the introduction, which contains an essay by Lucy Doran on the musical aspects of the epic, there is an entire text composed by Bamba Suso and a fragment composed by Shirif Jebate. A synopsis of the plot is given in the original Mandinka, with English translation and comprehensive notes.
'. . . a welcome addition to the growing body of reliable texts becoming available to serious students of African oral folklore . . . Innes's book is acceptable to even the most sceptical critic with holistic interests in folklore, specifically heroic epic.'
John William Johnson – *Research in African Literatures*

Innes, Gordon

Sunjata: three Mandika versions
London: School of Oriental and African Studies, Univ. of London, 1974. 326 pp. £7.00
Each version of the Sunjata epic is preceded by a short biography of the bard and is followed by comprehensive notes. The introduction is in

eleven parts which includes sections on Sunjata, the griots, the audience and the modes.

Kaabu and Fuladu: historical narratives of the Gambian Mandinka
London: School of Oriental and African Studies, Univ. of London, 1976. 320 pp. £7.50

Issa, Adamou and Labatut, Roger

Sagesse de Peuls Nomades
Yaoundé: C.L.E., 1974. 68 pp. CFA480
Traditional texts of the Fulbe (Peuls), a nomadic people, which give them a common identity, despite their distribution over a wide geographical area. Part I includes proverbs from Dageeja Bibbe, Fulbe peoples of Northern Nigeria and Cameroun. Part II is a study of the oral texts which are principle factors in uniting the group.

Isaak, Tchoumba Ngouankeu

Autour du lac Tchad (contes)
Yaoundé: C.L.E., 1969. 181 pp. CFA450
Folk-tales from the diverse ethnic groups of Cameroon and Tchad, which the author wrote during his time in jail as a political prisoner.

Jablow, Alta

Gassire's Lute: a West African epic
New York: Dutton, 1971. 48 pp. $4.50
An introduction to the concept of poetic oral history aimed at young people with three-tone drawings by Leo and Diane Dillon.
'. . . this poetic rendering of African history is a welcome addition to books of African folklore for young people, which are often so simplified and universalized that there is no indication of their African origin or oral narratives being a living art.'
Nancy J. Schmidt – *Research in African Literatures*

Jahadhmy, Ali ed.

Plays in Swahili.
(Trans. by Suzanna Bushnell)
Madison, Wisc.: College of Printing and Typing Co., 1969. 141 pp.
A bi-lingual (English/Swahili) collection of plays.

Anthology of Swahili Poetry
London: HEB, 1977 (AWS, 192). 101 pp. £1.95/$4.00
This verse collection is divided into three sections comprising selections from the work of Shaaban Robert, classical poetry and miscellaneous poems. The subject matter of the poetry ranges from romance and tragedy to valour and comedy. Parallel English translations are given throughout.

Johnson, John W.

Heellooy Heelleellooy: the development of the genre heello in modern Somali poetry
Bloomington, Ind.: Indiana University Press, 1974 (Indiana Univ. Publications, Africa Series, 5). 209 pp.
Unlike traditional poetry, in Somalia and elsewhere, the *heello* only originated in the mid-1950s. The author presents certain aspects of the social and political history of Somalia from 1941–2 until 1969.

Johnson, John W. ed and trans.

The Epic of Sun-Jata according to Magan Sisoko
Bloomington, Ind.: Folklore Publications Group, Indiana Univ., 1979 (Monograph Series, 5). 280 pp. in two parts. $5.00
A translation of the recording of the Sunjata epic made by the bard from Mali, Magan Sisoko, with annotations and an introduction. The Maninka transcription of the recording is not included, but a copy can be obtained by arrangement with the editor.
'... the work of a highly competent bard and I warmly welcome this addition to the number of authentic texts based on oral performance that have become available in recent years ... Johnson has I know, a large collection of Sunjata texts and I hope that this is merely the first of a series of similar authentic, readable, well annotated – and affordable – texts.'
      Gordon Innes – *Research in African Literatures*

Johnston, H. A. S. ed. and trans.

A Selection of Hausa Stories
London and New York: OUP, 1966 (Oxford Library of African Literature). 292 pp. o/p
A collection of fairy tales, proverbs, animal stories, supplemented by historical legends and a number of 'true' stories collected from the rich oral tradition of the Hausa's. The editor provides a lengthy introduction and an appendix of the original Hausa versions of the stories.

Jordan, A. C. ed. and trans.

Tales from Southern Africa
Berkeley: Univ. of California Press, 1973. 320 pp. $12.95 cased $3.95 p/b
A collection of thirteen Xhosa stories retold by a Xhosa novelist and linguist, with an introduction and notes by Harold Scheub.
'This work provides a much needed and rich resource in the field of traditional oral art. It is a volume which will both instruct and delight.'
      Carrol Lasker – *Africana Journal*

Towards an African Literature: the emergence of literary form in Xhosa.
Berkeley: Univ. of California Press, 1973. 116 pp. $6.00

The Wrath of the Ancestors
(Trans. from the Xhosa by Phyllis Ntantlala Jordan)
Lovedale, South Africa: Lovedale Press, 1940 (reissued 1965). 250 pp.
Washington D.C.: Three Continents Press (distr.) $9.00
A translation (by Jordan's wife) of *Ingqumbo yeminyanya*, considered a classic of modern Xhosa writing, and which depicts the life of an oppressed people.

Kaba, Alkaly

Contes de l'Afrique noire: deux récits d'adventures ensorcelantes
Sherbrooke, Canada: Ed. Naaman, 1973 (Création, 3). 80 pp. Can$4.00
Entitled 'Tales from Black Africa: Two Bewitching Adventures', with illustrations in colour.

Kagame, Alexis

Introduction aux grands genres lyriques de l'ancien Rwanda
Butare, Rwanda: Ed. Universitaires du Rwanda, 1969 (Muntu, 1). 324 pp. FR600
A collection of traditional verse from Rwanda, in Kinyarwanda and parallel French translation, with commentary and explanatory notes.

Kamara, B.

Two Hunting Tales
Banjul, The Gambia: Oral History and Antiquities Division, 1980. 57 pp. D4.50 ($4.50)
Two folk-tales from the Gambia translated by D. S. Goering.

Kamera, W. D.

Tales of Wairaqw of Tanzania
Nairobi: Kenya Literature Bureau, 1976. 104 pp. K.shs.14.75 (£1.70/$3.50)
An anthology of folk-tales from the Iraqw people of Tanzania.

Kane, Mohamadou

Essai sur les contes d'Amadou Coumba
Paris: A. G. Nizet [published as *Les contes d'Amadou Coumba: du conte traditionnal au conte moderne d'expression française*], 1969 (Université de Dakar, Faculté des Lettres et Sciences Humaines, Langues et littératures, 16). 244 pp. o/p

Dakar: Nouvelles Editions Africaines, 1981
(2nd ed.) 249 pp.
A re-issue of the 1969 study of Birago Diop's
Tales of Amadou Koumba.

Kanié, Léon Maurice Anoma
Quand les bêtes parlaient aux hommes
Dakar: Nouvelles Editions Africaines, 1979.
64 pp. CFA550
The heros of these tales are the familiar
animals of African folklore — the fish, the
serpent, the spider, the tortoise, the panther —
but there are also men in them. The volume
closes with a number of fables of La Fontaine
which have been translated into the creole of
the Ivory Coast.

Kambale Kavutirwaki`
Contes fokloriques Nandé
Tervuren, Belgium: Musée Royal de l'Afrique
Centrale, 1975. 563 pp.

Kane, Thomas L.
Ethiopian Literature in Amharic
Wiesbaden, West Germany: Otto
Harrassowitz, 1975. 304 pp.
A study of Ethiopian literature in Amharic
which only began to be used in written form at
the turn of the century. In chapter one the
author presents a history of Amharic literature
and in chapter two, catalogues the main types
of Amharic writing. A further chapter discusses
the reflections of traditional Ethiopian culture
in modern writing and a final chapter deals
with the language question.
*'For those wishing to become acquainted with, or to
know more about one of Africa's most extensive native
literatures, this book is de rigeur.'*
    Jack Fellman — *Research in African Literatures*

Kavanagh, Robert and Quangule, Z. S.
The Making of a Servant and Other Poems
(Trans. from Xhosa by Kavanagh and
Quangle)
Johannesburg: Ophir/Ravan Press, 1974.
19 pp. RO.75/$1.50
Ophir Publications, Pretoria, initially pro-
duced this slim volume of eight traditional
Xhosa poems, dealing mainly with the land.

Kayo, Patrice
Fables et devinettes de mon enfance
Yaoundé: C.L.E., 1978. 60 pp. CFA300
A collection of fables and riddles which invites
child and adult alike into a journey to the
sources of traditional Cameroonian wisdom.

Kesteloot, Lilyan ed.
L'épopée traditionnelle
Paris: Nathan, 1971 (Littérature africaine, 11).
64 pp. FF11.00
Contains extracts from a selected number of
epic tales, each preceded by a short commentary. There are passages from the Fulbe epics
of *Sundiata* and *Silamaka* (versions published by
Niane and Hampaté Bâ and Madame
Kesteloot), from the Fang Mvet, the Douala
legend of Djeky la Njambé, from the French
version of Mofolo's *Chaka,* from the Royal
Chronicle of the Bushong of the Kuba. Except
for the Douala epic all have been previously
published in the full version. The introduction
underlines the characteristics of the epic tale —
history, imagination, and art — and recalls the
fundamental difference between the epic genre
(history which is imaginatively and creatively
presented by the teller) and the chronicle (a
straightforward recital of historical facts).
Concludes with essay questions for use in the
classroom.

La poésie traditionelle
Paris: Nathan, 1971 (Littérature africaine, 12).
64 pp. FF12.00
A complementary volume to the preceding
entry, on other traditional African verse forms.
A general introduction points out the stylistic
features of oral poetry (use of images, symbols,
metaphors, rhythm, repetition, alliteration
and stress). The extracts concern more than ten
countries and twenty ethnic groups from West
to Central Africa, and they are presented by
theme rather than by genre: childhood,
initiation, love and marriage, treason, society,
work, religion, blessings, mourning, and
wisdom. Some are followed by suggested
questions for classroom discussion.

Da Monzon de Ségou: épopée bambara 2 vols.
Paris: Nathan, 1978. 126 pp., 144 pp.
The epic tale of the Bambara empire that ruled
over Ségou in what is now known as Mali for
two centuries, beginning in the mid-seven-
teenth century. The two volumes contain the
French version of twelve episodes of the epic
recorded by Madame Kesteloot and her
collaborators and as recited by four different
griots on a number of different occasions.
Volume one includes a 30-page introduction
and geneological tables of the dynasty of the
kings of Ségou.

Kibulya, H. M.
Folk-Tales of Bwamba
Nairobi: Kenya Literature Bureau, 1976.
86 pp. K.shs.13.50 (£1.60/$3.30)

A collection of traditional stories from the Bwamba people of Uganda.

Kientz, Albert
Dieu et les génies: récits étiologiques sénoufo
Paris: SELAF, 1979 (Traditions orales, 30).
274 pp. FF89.00

Kilson, Marion
Rôyal Antelope and Spider: West African Mende tales
Cambridge, Mass.: The Press of the Landgon Associates, 1976. 374 pp. $10.00
A collection of one hundred Mende tales and an analysis of the Mende storytelling tradition based on a survey of Mende literary and cosmological ideas. The author states that the work is 'intended as a contribution to the continuing tradition of sociological concern with African oral literature.'

Knappert, Jan
Traditional Swahili Poetry: an investigation into the concepts of East African Islam as reflected in the Utenzi literature
Leiden: Brill, 1967. 264 pp. Dfl.45
The author aims to reconstruct Swahili concepts of life and death, their outlook on the world and other aspects of their ideology, as seen in their literature.

Myths and Legends of the Swahili
London: HEB, 1970 (AWS, 75). 212 pp.
£1.50/$4.00
A sampling from the great wealth of Swahili writing, both secular and religious. In this collection 'an attempt has been made in each case to tell the story in such a manner that is meaningful to an English-reading public, without losing in any way the typical Swahili flavour of the narrative.'

Swahili Islamic Poetry 3 vols
Leiden: E. J. Brill, 1971. Dfl.55.00 (v.1)
Dfl.30.00 (v.2) Dfl.55.00 (v.3)
A collection of Swahili Arabic liturgical texts in translation. Volume 1 'Introduction; the Celebration of Mohammed's Birthday; Swahili Islamic Cosmology'; volume 2 'The Two Burdas'; volume 3 'Mi'rai and Maulid'.

An Anthology of Swahili Love Poetry
Berkeley, Calif.: Univ. of California Press, 1972. 200 pp. $3.50 p/b
A collection of 'classical' Swahili lyrical verse. The original Swahili texts are given with English translations and each poem is given a full commentary which clarifies points of language and supplies information on the cultural background.

Myths and Legends of the Congo
London: HEB, 1971 (AWS, 83). 218 pp.
£1.75/$4.50
Tales from ten districts in the Congo have been collected, either by Flemish missionaries or in the course of the author's own research. Explanatory notes accompany the text.
'. . . the comparative folklorist should be pleased to add this collection to his material, and those who are fascinated by absorbing stories should be delighted by this book.'
                              Winifred Lambrecht – *Research in African Literatures*

A Choice of Flowers
London: HEB, 1972 (AWS, 93). 202 pp.
£1.95/$5.50
Knappert fills a gap in published Swahili poetry by providing a collection of 'modern lyrical verse in the "classical" tradition.' There are English translations and ethnographic notes on custom.

Four Centuries of Swahili Verse: a literary history and anthology
London: HEB, 1980. 352 pp. £10.50 cased
£4.95 p/b
A scholarly history and anthology of four centuries of Swahili poetry, which presents a collection of verse discovered by the author during twelve years of researching into the manuscripts and oral traditions of the East Coast of Africa. The book is illustrated with a selection of the original texts written in Arabic script, with parallel English translations.

Koelle, Sigismund Wilhelm
African Native Literature: or, Proverbs, Tales, Fables and Historical Fragments in the Kanuri or Bornu language
Graz, Austria: Akademische Druck- und Verlagsanstalt, 1968 (Reprint of ed. London, 1854). 434 pp. $10.50 cased
A reprint – with a new introduction by David Dalby – of a study aimed to present the reader with both unaltered specimens of oral Kanuri literature and the structure of one of West Africa's most important languages. Sigismund Koelle, who was at Fourah Bay College in Freetown for five years, is also the author of the monumental *Polyglotta Africana,* a collection of some two hundred African vocabularies.

Kouadio Tiacoh, Gabriel
La légende de N'Zi le grand guerrier d'Afrique
Abidjan: C.E.D.A., 1976 (2nd ed). 101 pp.
CFA500
An Akan legend about the extraordinary destiny of a slave.

Kraft, Charles H.
A Hausa Reader: cultural materials with helps for use in teaching intermediate and advanced Hausa
Berkeley: Univ. of California Press, 1974.
525 pp. $15.00
Consists of excerpts from thirteen published Hausa works, of which five or six are still unobtainable. The editor has added tone and vowel length which are essential for the foreign student.
'. . . it was clearly Dr. Kraft's main purpose to teach language, and his secondary one to say something about the culture of the Hausas, not to produce a literary anthology, and in achieving these purposes he has given us a useful textbook, for which teachers of Hausa may be grateful.'
Neil Skinner – *Research in African Literatures*

Kunene, Daniel P.
The Works of Thomas Mofolo: summaries and critiques
Los Angeles: African Studies Center, Univ. of California, 1967 (Occas. Papers, 2). 28 pp. 50c
A critical appreciation of Mofolo's writings. *Moeti oa Bochabela* (East-Bound Traveller), *Pitseng,* and his most significant piece, *Chaka,* are reviewed in some detail.

The Heroic Poetry of the Basotho
London and New York: OUP, 1972 (Oxford Library of African Literature). 203 pp.
£5.00/$12.00 cased
A study of poetic rhetoric among the Basotho of South Africa.
'. . . an impressive application of grammarians' analytical procedures to the description of Sotho oral traditional praise-poetry.'
David E. Bynum – *Research in African Literatures*

Kunene, Mazisi
Zulu Poems
London: André Deutsch, 1970. 96 pp. £1.50
New York: Africana Publishing Corp., 1970.
96 pp. $9.75 cased $5.50 p/b
A collection of poems – with accompanying notes – several of which the author originally wrote in Zulu. In his introduction Kunene stresses that 'these are not English poems, but poems directly evolved from a Zulu literary tradition'.

Emperor Shaka the Great: a Zulu epic
London: HEB, 1979 (AWS, 211). 438 pp.
£7.50/$25.00 cased £2.95/$6.50 p/b
Kunene has translated his own epic praise-song based on oral sources from Zulu into English. It comprises seventeen sections, spanning Shaka's life, his military organization, and his conquests.

Anthem of the Decades
London: HEB, 1981 (AWS, 234). 312 pp.
£3.50/$11.50
An oral epic poem on Zulu cosmology is translated by Kunene; a publisher's reader acclaims its originality: 'While its wellspring of inspiration derives from the traditional boasts and Zulu cosmology it is not a pastiche, an imitation or a compilation. It is an original creation, carried by a majestic and some ways unfettered imagination, yet an imagination harnessed to reason and structure. The structure gives it coherence and power.' The three sections, The Age of the Gods, The Age of Fantasy and The Age of the Ancestors indicate the scope of the epic. There are extensive introductory notes on symbols, religious beliefs, Zulu concepts and the performance of oral poetry.

Kuyate, M.
Alhaji Mohammed Farang Njie
(Ed. by B. K. Sidibe and J. Kenrick)
Banjul, The Gambia: Oral History and Antiquities Division, 1980. 72 pp. D5.00 ($5.00)
A hero tale.

Kuyate, S.
Kelefa Saane
(Ed. by A. Trilling)
Banjul, The Gambia: Oral History and Antiquities Division, 1980. 80 pp. D5.00 ($5.00)
A popular hero tale from the Gambia.

Laurence, Margaret ed.
A Tree for Poverty: Somali poetry and prose
Kampala: Eagle Press for the Somaliland Protectorate, 1954. 146 pp.

Lebeuf, Jean Pierre and Lacroix, P. F.
Devinettes peules: suives de quelques proverbes et exemples d'argots (Nord-Cameroun)
Paris: Mouton, 1971 (Cahiers de l'Homme, nouv. sér., 12). 71 pp.
The riddles, proverbs and slang words in this volume were collected among young boys, aged nine to thirteen, in Garoua and Maroua in northern Cameroon. They are catalogued by subject and include such headings as 'The Animal Kingdom', 'The Body', 'Tools and Weapons', 'Utensils', 'Home and Village', 'Plants'.

Lienhardt, P. A. ed. and trans.
The Medicine Man
London and New York: OUP, 1968 (Oxford Library of African Literature). 216 pp. o/p

A translation of Hasani Bin Ismail's 'Swifa Ya Nguvumali', a modern Swahili ballad, which gives an account of a murder investigation in Tanzania, in the poet's own neighbourhood. The villagers summoned not only the police but also the 'medicine man' Nguvumali, whom some regarded as a fraud and others as possessed of magical powers. The editor provides an introduction and discusses the social and cultural background of the poem.

Lindfors, Bernth
Folklore in Nigerian Literature
New York: Africana Publishing Corp., 1974. 192 pp. $19.95
Lindfors, in this collection of essays, looks at the function of folklore in Nigerian literature. An examination of the three main approaches to oral art covers the impressionistic, the anthropological and the interpretive methods. Further essays range from a discussion of the oral traditions of Tutuola, to Achebe's use of proverbs. Soyinka's skills at extracting 'literary mileage out of African oral art', Ekwensi's use of oral techniques, and the Onitsha chapbooks receive attention. Finally, Lindfors examines Yoruba and Igbo prose styles in English.
'*[Lindfors] stylistic gems . . . convey among other things, an intellectual joie de vivre, a spirit of intellectual adventure which is an integral part of the critical mode of this highly intelligent young pioneer in Africanist literary criticism.*'
    Harold R. Collins – *World Literature Written in English*

Lindfors, Bernth ed.
Forms of Folklore in Africa: narrative, poetic, gnomic, dramatic
Austin, Texas: Univ. of Texas Press, 1977. 281 pp. $13.95 cased $5.25 p/b
Brings together new work by folklorists in Africa, Europe and America. The articles, from past issues of the journal *Research in African Literatures*, cover the major genres of this rich and diverse field.

Liyong, Taban lo
Eating Chiefs: Lwo culture from Lolwe to Malkal
London: HEB, 1960 (AWS, 74). 128 pp. £1.25p/$3.00
'Forty-five bits and pieces' – a representative collection of Lwo verse and folk literature, with an introduction and a series of explanatory notes. The author says of it 'I have been not so much interested in collecting traditions, mythologies or folk-tales. Anthropologists have done that. My idea has been to create literary works from what anthropologists

collected and recorded. It is my aim to induce creative writers to take off from where the anthropologists have stopped.'

Liyong, Taban lo ed.
Popular Culture of East Africa: oral literature
Nairobi: Longman Kenya, 1972. 158 pp.
The results of an assignment given to students in Liyong's Nairobi University literature class, to record a wide variety of traditional lore from their own memories, form the core of this book. It is presented in two parts. The first outlines the oral traditions of the Luhya, Kalenjin, Maasai and Bakiga, while the second records myths, legends, customs, folk-tales, songs, poems, hymns, names and nicknames, proverbs, riddles, puns and tongue-twisters.
'. . . *the fresh publication of a number of new folklore texts . . . is an important event, and the book will be welcomed by all persons interested in African folklore and literature. Its emphasis on East African culture unity is timely and much needed.*'
    Lee Haring – *Research in African Literatures*

Longchamps, Jeanne de
Contes malgaches
Paris: Ed. Erasme, 1955. 229 pp.
Seventeen tales from all parts of Madagascar with a brief note for each describing the region in which it was collected and the story-teller. Followed by a bibliographic study on Malagasy folklore and ethnographic notes on the tales in this volume by Paul Delarue.

Luneau, René
Chants de femmes au Mali
Paris: Luneau Ascot, 1981. 192 pp.
Women's songs from Mali: songs about excision, about pride in overcoming the ordeal, about approaching marriage.

Maalu-Bungi, Crispin
Contes populaires du Kasaï
Kinshasa: Ed. du Mont-Noir, 1974. 107 pp. 70k
Folk-tales from Zaïre in bi-lingual Lingala and French text.

Mahlasela, B. E. N.
A General Survey of Xhosa Literature from its Early Beginnings in the 1800s to the Present
Grahamstown: Dept. of African Languages, Rhodes Univ., 1973 (Working Paper, 2). 12 pp.
A study of oral and written Xhosa literature. (See also this author's study of the Xhosa poet and writer James Ranisi Jolobe on p. 65.)

translator, and teacher – Reverend J. J. R. Jolobe.

Mama Abéhikin, Laurent
Akoun: récit du Fokwé
Paris: Présence Africaine, 1980. 174 pp.
A novel based on one of the epic traditions of the Akan.

Mbiti, John ed.
Akamba Stories
London and New York: OUP, 1966 (Oxford Library of African Literature). 250 pp. o/p
A selection of fables and tales representing the rich oral tradition of the Akamba people that make up one-ninth of Kenya's total population. The editor has selected 78 from his collection of some 1,500 stories. It is socially compulsory among the Akamba to learn the art of story-telling; anyone who cannot narrate stories is ridiculed and considered a 'good-for-nothing', since he is unable to do what is considered the most elementary thing on earth. The editor describes this sociological background in an extensive introduction.
'. . . *very good bed-time reading. But of course they are much more than that. Ethnologists, and those who study the structure of myth, will find plenty to engage their interest.*' F. B. Welbourn – *African Affairs*

Meye, François
Le récit de la forêt
Monte-Carlo: Ed. Paul Bory, n.d. [1970]. 94 pp.
Many of these short stories have the colonial setting of Gabon in the 1930s. Others are in a more traditional vein and, according to the author, aim to 'contribute to a better knowledge of moral and philosophic traditions of the Fang people'. There are two essays in the appendix, one on Emane Töle, the last Fang warrior, and the other on Fang family structure.

Meva'a M'Eboutou, Michel
Les aventures de Koulou-la-tortue
Yaoundé: C.L.E., 1972. 61 pp. CFA230
Thirteen tales taken from the oral literature of the Bulu of Cameroon.

Mefana, Nkulngui
Le secret de la source
Yaoundé: C.L.E., 1972. 64 pp. CFA350
Tales and fables to be told around the fireside.

Mfomo, Gabriel E.
Soirées au village: contes du Cameroun
Paris: Karthala, 1981. 136 pp. FF36.00
Folk-tales from Cameroon.

Mfouo-Tsially, Gilbert
Casse-tête congolais pour Berto: Enigmes avec solutions présentées sous formes d'histoires
Paris: P. J. Oswald, 1970 (distr. by L'Harmattan, Paris). 91 pp. FF18.00
The subtitle calls this collection 'riddles and their solutions, presented in the form of stories'.

Mimpiya Akan Onun
Les belles aventures d'Angile la Tortue
Issy-les-Moulineaux, France: Ed. Saint-Paul, 1977 (Classiques africains, 711). 96 pp. FF13.00
Traditional fables from Zaïre. The central figure of the title tale is Tortoise, a familiar animal hero of African folklore.

Mohamadou, Eldridge and Mayssal, Henriette
Contes et poèmes Foulbés de la Bénoué
Yaoundé: C.L.E., 1965. 84 pp. o/p
Folk stories and traditional poems – in the original Foulbe text with parallel French translation – collected by students in the northern areas of Cameroon, and here translated by a Cameroon linguist.

Mombeya, Tierno Mouhammadou Samba
Le filon du bonheur éternel
Paris: A. Colin, 1971 (Classiques africains, 10). 202 pp. FF69.40
The Fulani version of sacred Islamic poetry used by Islamic scholars in the Fouta-Djalon in the nineteenth century, collected and translated by Alfa Ibrahim Sow and appearing in trilingual text (Fulani/French/Arabic). Includes a short Fulani-French vocabulary.

Morris, Henry ed.
The Heroic Recitations of the Bahima of Ankole
London and New York: OUP, 1964 (Oxford Library of African Literature). 160 pp.
£3.75/$8.95 cased
A study of the heroic poetry of a pastoral people of Uganda. The recitations are praise poems describing – in highly exaggerated terms – the composer's heroism in battle and the beauty of his cattle. An introductory essay on the Bahima and their poetry precedes the recitations.

Mortimer, Mildred P. comp.
Contes Africains
(Ed. by Michel Benamou)
Boston: Houghton-Mifflin, 1972. 224 pp. $2.80
A collection of stories and legends by Bernard

Dadié, Birago Diop, Joseph Brahim Seid and Camara Laye aimed for classroom use.

'Calvin Burnett's illustrations, based on authentic works of African tribal art, add a touch of local color to the texts and help create an attractive book which second and third year teachers of French would do well to consider as a means of diversifying their classes.'

Keith Q. Warner – *Research in African Literatures*

Mufuta Kabemba, Patrice ed.
Les chants Kasala des Luba
Paris: A. Colin, 1969 (Classiques africains, 8). 293 pp. FF55.10
A study of the funeral songs of the Luba of the Eastern Kasaï region in Zaïre which are not properly speaking 'songs' at all, as generically defined by the Luba, Part I presents Luba society and analyses the functions of the Kasala within the society and its relationship to other literary genres whereas Part II presents the texts themselves, in the original, with French translation on facing pages. Includes a selective bibliography.

Musala, Claude
Contes des savanes et des forets
Paris: La Pensee Universelle, 1972. 154 pp. Folktales from Zaïre.

Mushang, M. T.
Folk tales from Ankole
Kampala: Adult Education Centre, 1970. 143 pp. U.shs.10.00

Mushieté, Mahamwe
Quand les nuages avaient soif: contes, chantes et proverbes de la savane
Kinshasa: Ed. du Leopard, 1968. 140 pp.

Mvungi, Martha
Three Solid Stones
London: HEB, 1975 (AWS, 159). 112 pp. o/p
The author heard these stories, or variations thereof, when she lived among the Hehe and Bena people of southern Tanzania. The twelve tales, in addition to providing entertainment, also fulfil a social function: ascriptive norms are conveyed through their moral treatment of subjects such as love, obedience, jealousy and the like.
'The author has retold them in a clear and engaging

manner that both children and adults will enjoy. For the student, they provide a valuable insight into East African culture.'

R. E. Mosberger – *Books Abroad*

Mwakasaka, C. S.
The Oral Literature of the Banyakyusa
Nairobi: Kenya Literature Bureau, 1979. 169 pp. K.shs.32.50 (£6.25/$2.50)
A volume containing mostly traditional stories but with some that deal with migrant labour, recent political events and some problems of modernization.

National Press of Guiné-Bissau
'N Sta Li, 'N Sta Lá
Bolama, Guinea-Bissau: Imprensa Nacional, 1979. 79 pp.
This book of riddles, a collection of popular oral culture, is bilingual. The riddles and their answers are in Crioulo; the introduction and a conclusion with an explanation of the riddles are in Portuguese. This book is the first in a series in commemoration of the centenary of National Press. It is also the first book published in Crioulo by that press.

Ndebe, Barnabus S.
Tales from Bandiland
Newark: Department of Anthropology, Univ. of Delaware, 1974. 192 pp.
A collection of mythical stories, didactic tales and tales that offer no answers collected from among the Bandi people of northwestern Liberia.
'Although this first publication of Bandi literature offers only a glimpse into the values and experiences of this Liberian group, it is a commendable start.'
Amelia Fitzjohn – *Research in African Literatures*

N'Diaye, Bokar
Veillées au Mali
Bamako: Ed. Populaires, 1970. 223 pp. MF700
A book of traditional tales in which we find the familiar animals associated with many African tales – the hyena, the hare, the ostrich, and the tortoise.

Ndong Ndoutoume, Tsira
Le mvett
Paris: Présence Africaine, Vol. 1, 1970. 159 pp. o/p
Paris: Présence Africaine, Vol. 2, 1975. 320 pp. FF66.00
In Fang culture *Mvett* refers both to an oral epic tradition and to the small string instru-

ment which is played during the tale and the word serves here as a generic title to a particular legend: that of the Chief of Flames who goes on crusade to destroy all metal as a source of suffering and who is opposed in this by the Chief of Storms whose daughter later falls in love with the Chief of Flames. Volume I contains a long introduction by the author who explains how he 'returned to sources' to write the book and to learn to play the mvett.

Nguema, Zwé
Un mvet: chant épique fang
Paris: A. Colin, 1972 (Classiques africains, 9). 494 pp. – 3. 45-rpms FF118.90
Herbert Pepper recorded this Fang epic song in 1960 in Anguia in Gabon. It was sung by the bard Zwè Nguèma non-stop from 8 p.m. to 6 the following morning. A first transcription was made and published in mimeographed form by ORSTOM. It was later re-transcribed by Paul and Paule DeWolf for the Classiques Africaines series. Includes three 45-rpm records.

Niane, Djibril Tamsir
Soundjata ou l'épopée mandique
Paris: Présence Africaine, 1960. 156 pp. FF14.00
In English *translation,* see next entry.

Sundiata: an epic of old Mali
(Trans. from the French by G. D. Pickett)
London: Longman, 1965. 96 pp. o/p
London: Longman, 1979 (2nd ed.). 112 pp. 95p
Niane's story of Sundiata, founder and hero of the mediæval Mandingo empire, one of the great African kingdoms of the late middle ages, was first published in English by Longman in 1965 and has been reissued in the Drumbeat series. The author collected the tale from a griot, a traditional story-teller called 'Belen-Tigui', who, Niane explains in his preface, is a very respected gentleman. Griots learn the art of historical oratory through long years of touring from village to village in Mali to hear the teaching of great masters.

Njururi, Njumbu
Agikuyu Folk Tales
London and New York: OUP, 1966. 120 pp. o/p
Twenty-five stories and legends from the Agikuyu people of Kenya, now more commonly known as Kikuyu.

Tales from Mount Kenya
Nairobi: Transafrica Publ. 1975. 128 pp. K.shs.12.50

Nkamgang, Sop Martin and Kayo, Patrice
Les proverbes Bamiléké
Yaoundé: Ed. Le Flambeau, 1976 (2nd ed.) 42 pp.

Nkamgang, Sop Martin
Contes et légendes du Bamiléké 2 vols.
Yaoundé: Impr. Saint-Paul, 1968/69. 110 pp.

Norris, H. T.
Saharan Myth and Saga
London and New York: OUP, 1972. 240 pp. £8.00/$20.50 cased
A collection of the sagas of the Sanhaja Berber peoples who lived in Mauritania and southern Morocco in early mediaeval times which combine tribal chronicle, history, genealogy and myth.
'For readers who . . . are not specialists in Western Saharan history or literature but who have interests in that or contiguous areas, Saharan Myth and Saga *presents a challenging opportunity to plunge in deeper than the popular accounts of Saharan "discovery" and travel by Westerners of the past two centuries.'*
Jeanette Harries and Dustin Cowell – *Research in African Literatures*

Noye, Dominique
Blasons peuls: éloges et satires du Nord-Cameroun
Paris: Geuthner, 1976. 192 pp. FF65.00

Le menuisier et le cobra
Paris: Luneau Ascot, 1980. 190 pp. FF48.10
Fifteen Fulbe tales from northern Cameroon with a preface by Christiane Seydou.

N'Sanda Wamenka and Tashdjian, Alain
Contes du Zaïre
Paris: Conseil International de la Langue Française/EDICEF, 1975. 119 pp.
A collection of tales from Zaïre.

Nyacka, D. and Mben Mben, J.
Basógól bá zkal lé . . . (As the elders Say)
Douala: Collège Libermann, 1977 (2nd ed.) (Langues nationales, 5). 288 pp. CFA900 (mimeographed)
An anthology of Basaa literature for use in secondary schools. Contains tales, extracts from epic poems, proverbs and games. The texts have been translated into French and are published with vocabulary notes and study questions. A cassette recording is available.

Nyembezi, C. L. S.
A Review of Zulu Literature
Pietermaritzburg: Univ. of Natal Press, 1961. 10 pp. o/p

Ogbalu, F. C.
Fireside Igbo Folklore
Onitsha, Nigeria: Univ. Publ., 1979. 60 pp.
₦1.50
A volume of Igbo folk-tales and lore.

Ogieriaikhi, E.
Edo Literature
Lagos: Univ. of Lagos Bookshop (distr.), 1973
(Edo Literature Series, monographs, 2). 33 pp.
60k

Ogunmola, K.
The Palmwine Drinkard. A Yoruba opera
(Trans. from the Yoruba by Robert Armstrong
et al.)
Ibadan: Inst. of African Studies, Univ. of
Ibadan, 1972 (Occasional publ., 12). 118 pp.
₦2.10   cased   ₦1.25   p/b
This Yoruba opera is based on the novel by
Amos Tutuola. It is also available as a two-disc
recording, as *Nigerian Cultural Records* (nos. 3
and 4).

Okeke, Uche
Tales of Land and Death: Igbo folk tales
New York: Doubleday, 1971. 114 pp. $8.50
cased $3.95 p/b

Okiri, K.
So They Say
Nairobi: East African Lit. Bureau, 1970.
164 pp. (£1.00/$2.50)
Luo folk-tales.

Okpewho, Isidore
The Epic in Africa
New York: Columbia Univ. Press, 1979.
288 pp. $19.50 cased
A comparative study of the oral epic form in
Africa, discussed and analysed within the
framework of the poetics of oral performance.

Omoleye, Mike
Great Tales of the Yorubas
Ibadan: Omoleye Publ. Co., 1977. 59 pp.
₦2.00
A collection of twelve short stories from
Yorubaland. In his preface the author gives a
brief account of the Yoruba people and of the
role of folk-tales among them.

Mystery World Under the Sea
Ibadan: Omoleye Publ. Co., 1979. 51 pp.
₦2.00
Three 'strange-but-true' stories of people who
claim to have had contact with the spirit world
or with aliens from outer space.

Onyango-Ogutu, Benedict and **Roscoe,
Adrian E.** eds.
Keep My Words: Luo oral literature
Nairobi: EAPH, 1974. 159 pp. K.shs.15.00
($5.00)
A collection of the oral literature of the Luo
people, pastoralists, who have now settled on
the shores of Lake Victoria.
'. . . a valuable contribution to the study of Luo oral
literature. It is a fascinating anthology in its own right
and deserves to be studied by anyone who is interested
in comparative traditions of oral literature.'
                      Clement A. Okafor – *Research in
                                       African Literatures*

Opland, Jeff
*Anglo-Saxon Oral Poetry: a study of the
traditions*
New Haven and London: Yale University
Press, 1980. 289 pp. $20.00
'. . . a persuasive refutation of several central
assumptions of much oral-formulaic scholarship on
medieval poetry during the past three decades. It is
also a major study of Xhosa and Zulu oral traditions
. . . Anglo-Saxon Oral Poetry is not about the
poems that have survived from Anglo-Saxon times
but about those that have not. It is about the poetry
that was never written down, the unrecorded oral
poetry.'
                      Thomas Cable – *Research in
                                       African Literatures*

Ortova, Jarmila *et al.*
*L'art de la parole dans la culture de l'Afrique
au sud du Sahara*
Prague: Oriental Institute, Univ. of Prague,
1971. 80 pp.
A first article by Madame Ortova speaks about
the art of oral literature in black Africa. It is
followed by a chapter on the influence of oral
literature on written literature in Ghana by
Francis Boakye Duah and one on the educational role of oral literature among the Besi
Kongo by M. P. Gonçalves.

Paulme, Denise
*La mère dévorante: essai sur la morphologie des
contes africains*
Paris: Gallimard, 1976. 321 pp.
A collection of ten essays, seven of which have

been published elsewhere. The first two, on the morphology of the African folk-tale and on oral tradition and social behaviour, serve as an introduction to the following studies which analyse, from a structural point of view, eight archetypal African tales. Includes an extensive bibliography.

'Written in an admirably straightforward and fluid French . . . an ideal introduction to the great corpus of French works on this subject.' West Africa

p'Bitek, Okot
Horn of My Love
London: HEB, 1974 (AWS, 147). 182 pp.
£1.95/$5.00

A wide range of the poetry of the Acoli (a people living on the Ugandan-Sudanese border) has been assembled by p'Bitek in this anthology, dealing with love, war, death, and satire. In Part I we are given descriptions of the occasions for the songs. Parallel texts in English and Acoli follow, while the third part encompasses a miscellany of topics. It considers poets as historians; descriptions of the praise names; and an analysis of the themes of the poems.

'. . . it is a book of poetry to be handled and enjoyed rather than a ponderous headstone placed on the living body of a popular art. It can be read with equal enjoyment . . . by Acolis relishing the felicities of the original languages and by English readers relishing the muscularity of Okot p'Bitek's translations.'
Gerald Moore – *Times Literary Supplement*

Hare and Hornbill
London: HEB, 1978 (AWS, 193). 80 pp.
£1.25p/$3.00

Thirty-two African folk-tales told by p'Bitek in an effort to rectify the inevitable mistakes that non-Africans have made in the past when transcribing the tales.

'The field of African folklore is vast, and extensive reading is necessary before the task of comparative study can begin. p'Bitek's collection, though he has made no attempt to exhaust his subject and though this edition lacks scholarly apparatus, is a model for this enormous task.'
Robert L. Berner – *World Literature Today*

Postma, Minnie
Tales from the Basotho
Austin: Univ. of Texas Press, 1974 (American Folklore Society Memoir Series, 59). 177 pp.
$8.50

A collection of twenty-three stories which have been translated by Susie McDermid.

Robinson, C. H.
Specimens of Hausa Literature
Farnborough, England: Gregg International Publ., 1969 (Reprint of ed., Cambridge, 1896). 134 pp. £10.00/$24.00

Rodegem, F. M. ed. and trans.
Anthologie rundi
Paris: A. Colin, 1973 (Classiques africains, 12). 417 pp. FF156.60

This volume offers a panorama of Rundi oral literature in bilingual text (Rundi-French) selected for the most part from the ten mimeographed volumes which the author has published in Rwandi under the title *Patrimoine culturel rundi*. The two parts – Poetry and Prose – are further subdivided by genre. Poetic genres, for example, are classified as 'noble' and 'popular' and in the first we find pastoral praise poems, incantations, and odes. The three chapters on prose include tales, fables, legends, riddles, and sections on humour and rhyming sequences. Indexed by genre with two maps and a bibliography.

Ribas, Oscar
See Section Lusophone Africa, p. 298

Rivièrre, Jean-Claude
Littérature orale cemuhi 2 vols
Paris: SELAF, 1977. 1,300 pp.
Vol. I: *Mythes, contes et poèmes*
Vol. II: *Textes historiques et cérémoniels.*

Ross, Mabel H. and Walker, Barbara K.
'On Another Day': tales told among the Nkundo of Zaïre
Hamden, Conn.: Archon Books, 1979. 596 pp.
$35.00

Ninety-five tales from the Nkundo (or Mongo) peoples of Zaïre, together with an extensive introduction discussing the themes and motifs of Mongo story telling.

Ruelland, Suzanne
La fille sans mains
Paris: SELAF, 1973 (Bibliothèque de la SELAF, 39-40). 209 pp.

An analysis of nineteen different versions of the tale of the 'Girl Who Had No Hands'.

Ruelland, Suzanne and Caprille, Jean-Pierre
Contes et récits du Tchad: la femme dans la littérature orale tchadienne
Paris: EDICEF, 1978. 121 pp.

A collection of tales about women gathered among different ethnic groups in Chad. There are stories about maidens, about wives and mothers, about wives with unfaithful husbands, about strong women, and about 'animal wives'.

Rugamba, Cyprian
Chansons rwandaises: mélodie et textes comprises
Butare: Institut National de Recherche Scientifique, 1979. 298 pp.
The text and music for twenty-five songs inspired by traditional rhythms that have been aired over Radio-Rwanda with the French translation.

Schapera, I. ed. and trans.
Praise Poems of Tswana Chiefs
London and New York: OUP, 1965 (Oxford Library of African Literature). 256 pp. o/p
This collection of poems in Tswana (using Sotho orthography with parallel English translations), are traditional eulogies of the rulers of four Tswana chiefdoms in the former Bechuanaland protectorate, now Botswana.
'... this book is more than a sampling of archaic tradition interesting only to the anthropologist; it is a living record of the Tswana people.'
John Povey – *Africa Report*

Scheub, Harold
The Xhosa 'Ntsomi'
London and New York: OUP, 1975 (Oxford Library of African Literature). 312 pp.
£15.00/$33.00 cased
Scheub attended several thousand *Ntsomi* performances in the Xhosa-speaking parts of South Africa in the course of his research. The *Ntsomi* is a performing art form in which the narrator expands upon a traditional tale, song, chant, or saying. The book falls into two parts. First, the author analyses the transmission, composition, themes and techniques involved in *Ntsomi* recitals. A second section consists of the text and translations of forty taped performances, collected in 1967 and 1968.

Seid, Joseph Brahim
Au Tchad sous les étoiles
Paris: Présence Africaine, 1962. 103 pp. o/p
A collection of folk stories, fables and legends based on local oral traditions and set in the Kotoko-Kanem area to the west and south of Lake Chad.

Seydou, Christiane ed. and trans.
La geste de Ham-Bodêdio ou Hama le Rouge
Paris: A. Colin, 1976 (Classiques africains, 18). 420 pp. – 2 45rpm records. FF143.30
The legend of the king of the Peul empire in pre-Islamic Mali. Bilingual text (Peul-French) on facing pages with two records.

Contes et fables des veillées
Paris: Nubia, 1976. 300 pp. FF60.00
A French translation of Peul tales and fables from Mali and Niger.

Sidibe, B. K.
Sunjata
Banjul, The Gambia: Oral History and Antiquities Division 1980. 80 pp. D5.00 ($5.00)
An epic tale from the Gambia.

Simagha, Diaowe; Doucoure, Lassana; Meillassoux, Claude
Légende de la dispersion des Kusa
Dakar: I.F.A.N., 1967 (Initiations et Etudes Africaines, 22). 137 pp.
A Soninke epic.

Simon, Pierre [pseud. for Dabire, Pierre]
Les aventures de Dari l'araignée: contes Dagaras
Bobo-Dioulasso, Upper Volta: Impr. La Savane, 1972. 62 pp.
Dagaras tales from Upper Volta: the aventures of Dari, the Spider.

Singano, Ellis and Roscoe, Adrian A. eds.
Tales of Old Malawi
Limbe, Malawi: Popular Publ. and Likuni Press, 1980 (2nd rev. and enlarged ed.) (Malawian Writers, 1). 106 pp. K1.90
A collection of thirty Malawian folk-tales translated into English, with an additional section of 140 riddles and their answers, complete with their Chichewa translations.

Sissoko, Fily-Dabo
Sagesse noire, sentences et proverbes malinkes
Paris: Ed. de la Tour du Guet, 1955. 63 pp. o/p
A collection of Malinke proverbs, sayings and stories.

Sissoko, Kabine
La prise de Dionkoloni: un épisode de l'épopée bambara
Paris: A. Colin, 1975 (Classiques africains, 16). 184 pp. FF58.50
An epic tale of the Bambara collected and presented by Gérard Dumestre and Lilyan Kesteloot.

Skinner, Neil ed. and trans.
Hausa Readings: selections from Edgar's 'Tatsuniyoyi'
Madison: Univ. of Wisconsin Press, 1968. 279 pp.
A selection of thirty-two pieces taken from Major Edgar's *Lifafi na Tatsuniyoyi na Hausa*,

with English annotations provided by the editor and translator. They are etiological tales, tall tales and proverbs, riddles and folk history. For Frank Edgar's complete collection see following entries.

Hausa Tales and Traditions vol. I
London: Cass, 1969. 440 pp. £16.00 cased
New York: Africana Publishing Corp., 1969. 440 pp. cased
A *magnum opus* of Hausa folk literature, *Lifafi na Tatsuniyoyi na Hausa* was originally collected, compiled and translated in three volumes by Major Frank Edgar, a British Administrative Officer in Northern Nigeria from 1905 until 1927. The collection embraces fables, history, riddles, songs, poems, proverbs, letters and religious and legal items.
'*As one of the few extensive collections of African tradition that have been made to date, the contribution of Edgar and Skinner cannot be overestimated. It offers a diverse sample of Hausa tradition with broad possibilities for comparative purposes, a fact which is particularly important in view of the wide range of Hausa influence among neighbouring peoples.*'
Philip A. Noss – *Africa Report*

Hausa Tales and Traditions, vols. II and III
Ann Arbor: Univ. Microfilms International for the Univ. of Wisconsin Press, 1977. [Produced and distributed on demand only.] approx. $850
Volume II of this massive work consists of fables and Volume III is made up of historical fragments and traditions. Each volume is itself divided into distinct subject groups.
'*What Skinner has so impressively done is, as one has come to expect from his previous work, far more than a translation of Edgar's original thousand and more pages of printed text.*'	*West Africa*

An Anthology of Hausa Literature in Translation
Madison: Univ. of Wisconsin, African Studies Program, 1977 (Occasional Paper, 7). 189 pp. $4.00
After categorizing about twelve different genres of Hausa literature, Prof. Skinner presents examples of each in translation, spanning almost a thousand years of Hausa literature and ranging from preliterate folk-tales and precolonial poetry up to the plays, prose and poetry of our modern era (1920-1960). An introductory analysis and further reading list is included in each section, and there is also a composite bibliography.
'*. . . here is a text that is at once a boon for the teacher and a joy for the taught.*'
A. H. M. Kirk-Greene – *Research in African Literatures*

Smith, P. ed.
Le récit populaire au Rwanda
Paris: A. Colin, 1976 (Classiques africains, 17). 432 pp. FF87.00
An anthology of thirty popular tales from Rwanda presented in the original and in French on facing pages. The selection was made from the more than 600 texts that were recorded by two Rwanda students, S. Bizimana and S. Rwerinyange. They are divided into three parts called 'fables', 'legends' and 'tales' and are preceded by a 106-page introduction which deals with the place of popular story-telling in the context of oral literature in Rwanda.

Socé, Ousmane
Contes et légéndes d'Afrique noire
Paris: Nouvelles Editions Latines, 1962, 157 pp FF15.00
A volume of folk-tales and legends.

Sow, Alfâ Ibrahim
La femme, la vache, la foi: écrivains et poètes du Fouta-Djalon
Paris: A. Colin, 1966 (Classiques africains, 5). 376 pp FF55.10
Folk-tales from Guinea.

Chroniques et récits du Fouta-Djalon
Paris: C. Kincksieck (in cooperation with the Centre National de la Recherche Scientifique), 1968 (Langues et littératures de l'Afrique noire. 3). 262 pp.

Stefaniszyn, Bronislaw
African Lyric Poetry in Reference to the Ambo Traditional Poem-Songs
Portland, Ore.: The HaPi Press, 1974. 208 pp. The volume is divided into three parts. In Parts I and II the author attempts to set the research within a theoretical framework. Part III consists of a cultural and social analysis of Ambo song texts.

Sy, Amadou Abel ed.
Seul contre tous 2 vols.
Dakar: Nouvelles Editions Africaines, 1978. 167 pp. and 61 pp. o/p
Two epic tales of the fishermen of the Fouta Toro as sung by Guélaye Fall. A bilingual edition (French-Fulbe) with an introduction to the culture of the Toucouleur people of northern Senegal.

Tchicaya U Tam'si, Gérald Felix
Légendes africaines
Paris: Senghers, 1980 (2nd ed.). 240 pp. FF43.00

A new edition of the volume that was first published in 1969 containing extracts from fourteen African legends and folk-tales with an introduction and explanatory notes on each passage. U Tam'si provides the first story, and this is followed by extracts from the works of Thomas Mofolo (*Chaka*), Djibril Niane (*Soundjata*), Ousmane Socé (*Karim*), Blaise Cendrar from France, and five passages form the writings of the ethnologist Leo Frobenius, all origin-ally published in German. Mercer Cook provides a preface.

'. . . *Empreintes tantôt de poésie, tantôt de violence, tantôt de fantasie, tantôt de mystère, ces légendes sont vivantes et variées. Leur principal mérite est surtout leur caractère original.*'

C. J. – *L'Afrique Littéraire et Artistique*

Tersis, Nicole
La mare de la vérité: contes et musique zarma
Paris: SELAF-ORSTOM, 1976 (Traditions orales, 19). 130 pp.
Music and folk-tales of the Zarma of Niger. Available with two recordings (33 rpm).

Thomas, Jacqueline M. C.
Contes, proverbes, devinettes ou énigmes, chants et prières Ngbaka-Ma'Bo
Paris: Klincksieck/SELAF, 1970 (Langues et littératures de l'Afrique Noire, 9). 908 pp.
An anthology of oral literature from the Central African republic including tales, proverbs, riddles and songs along with a linguistic study and an analytical index of characters, places, and things. Contains a bibliography.

Tiendrébéogo, Yamba
O Mogho! Terre d'Afrique!
Ouagadougou: Larhallé Naba, 1964. 206 pp.
Mossi tales and fables from Upper Volta, edited and presented by P. Arozena.

Contes et dictons du pays Mossi
Paris: L'Arbre du voyageur, 1980 (Contes de la gazelle, 13) (distr. by L'Ecole, Paris). 62 pp.
More Mossi tales and sayings.

Tinguidji, Boûbacar
Silâmakla et Poullôri: récit épique Peul
Paris: A. Colin, 1972 (Classiques africains, 13). 280 pp + 3 45 rpm records. FF98.80
The text plus recording of a Peul epic poem from Mali and Upper Volta as sung by Boubacar Tinguidji, a *mâbo*, or court singer to the sound of his *hoddu* or lute. It is the legend of the extraordinary destiny of two half-brothers, one a nobleman and the other a slave, who were born the same day in the same compound, and their struggle against Bambara domination in the late eighteenth century. Silâmaka dies but his brother and slave, Poullôri, lives on to inherit his master's power and become the sky hero whose thundering army brings rain. The text, which Christiane Seydou has edited, appears in the original and in French on facing pages and is accompanied by three records.

Todd, Loreto
Some Day Been Dey: West African Pidgin folktales
London and New York: Routledge and Kegan Paul, 1979. 186 pp. £5.95/$14.25
A collection of Pidgin narratives from Cameroon, together with descriptions on the use of Pidgin in social situations. The title, *Some Day Been Dey* is a popular opening formula in Pidgin folk-tales, meaning 'There was a day', a near-equivalent to 'Once upon a time'.

'. . . *an excellent and representative collection . . . I was delighted to find a scholar who appreciated the social and linguistic significance of Pidgin and clearly has learned to love it the way many Cameroonians do.*'

Bernard Fonlon – *Research in African Literatures*

Touré, Sada Moussa
Les premières guinéades: contes et légendes de chez nous
Conakry: Sily-Editions, 1961. 80 pp.
Tales and legends from Guinea.

Towo-Atangana, Gaspard, and Towo-Atangana, Françoise
Nden-bobo, l'araignée toilière (conte Béti)
Yaoundé: C.L.E., 1966. 36 pp.
Nden-Bobo, the name given to a spider's web, plays an important role in the daily life of a people living in the Béti region of Cameroon. This volume presents a transcription and translation from an original chant in the Eton language. The authors also provide an introduction and explanatory notes.

Traoré, Issa Baba
Contes et récits du terroir
Bamako: Editions Populaires, 1970. 224 pp.
MF1035
Twenty-seven traditional tales from Mali.

Traoré, Sadia
A l'écoute des anciens du village
Bamako: Editions Populaires, 1972. 104 pp.
MF685
Tales from Mali. The title reads, 'Listening to village elders'.

Travelle, Moussa
Proverbes et contes bambara
Paris: Geuthner, 1923 (2nd ed. 1977). 240 pp.
A volume of Bambara tales and proverbs, with French translation, which also contains a brief outline of Bambara and Malinké customary law. Maurice Delafosse has furnished a preface.

Trilling, Alex ed.
Ngansu Masing
Banjul, Gambia: Oral History and Antiquities Division, 1980. 63 pp. D5.00 ($5.00)
A popular hero tale from the Gambia.

Tsala, T.
Minkana Beti (Beti proverbs)
Douala: Collège Libermann, 1975 (Collection langues nationales, 3). 315 pp. CFA900 (mimeographed)
A collection of 300 Beti proverbs in bilingual text (Ewondo-French), extracts from Father Tsala's *Mille et un proverbes beti* and destined for secondary school usage. Also available in cassette recording.

Ugochuckwu, C. N.; Meniru, T.; Oguine, P. eds.
Omalinze: a book of Igbo folk tales
Ibadan: OUP Nigeria, 1979. 200 pp. ₦4.00
Sixty-three folk-tales, together with an introductory essay on the folk-tale as a genre of traditional literature.

Umeasiegbu, Rems Nna
The Way We Lived
London: HEB, 1969 (AWS, 61). 139 pp. £1.25/$3.50
An anthology of Ibo customs and stories, grouped under two major themes, 'Customs' and 'Folklore'.

Ask the Storyteller: an introduction to Igbo folklore
Buffalo, N.Y.: Black Academy Press, 1972. 160 pp. $7.95

Vatsa, Mamman J.
Nupe Dance Poems
Enugu, Nigeria: Fourth Dimension Publ. Co., 1980. 24 pp. ₦1.50
Traditional dance poems, in both Nupe and English, recited at births, weddings and other celebrations.

Vilikazi, Benedict W.
Zulu Horizons
(Trans. by F. Friedman)
Johannesburg: Witwatersrand Univ. Press, 1973 (new ed.). 144 pp. R10.00 cased
English version of Zulu poems, lyrics and praise songs derived from historical events.
'. . . a representative poet who is able to carry traditional material into the future, as well as write from immediacy with individual flair and freshness.'
Sam Bradley – *Africana Journal*

Vyas, C. L.
Two Tales of Zambia
Lusaka: NECZAM, 1973. 56 pp. 70n
Two stories about Sulwe, the most cunning animal of all and the romantic legend of Kapepe.

Folktales of Zambia
Lusaka: NECZAM, 1974. 96 pp. K1.20
More Zambian folk-tales and legends, heard and recorded in villages.

Whiteley, W. H. comp.
A Selection of African Prose, 2 vols.
Vol. 1: *Traditional oral texts*
Vol. 2: *Written prose*
London and New York: OUP, 1964 (Oxford Library of African Literature). 216 pp., 194 pp. £5.00 cased (vol. 2) (vol. 1 o/p)
An anthology of African prose initiated by UNESCO as the first in a series of anthologies. The first volume, *Traditional Oral Texts,* presents a selection from the oral tradition, representative both from a geographical point of view and from that of genre. Volume two provides a sampling of material written up to 1963 by African authors from different parts of the continent.
'Nowadays new anthologies are always coming out of Africa, but this present work is remarkable both for the great variety of material it has assembled together and for the manner in which Dr Whiteley has approached his task. It is only too easy to compile an anthology which may do credit to the editor's scholarship, or his industry, or his sense of mission but which remains lifeless and unreadable, Dr Whiteley has produced a lively and very readable book.'
Chinua Achebe – from the *Foreword*

Yede N'Guessan Gossey *et al.*
La légende de Momondieri
Abidjan: C.E.D.A., 1980. 78 pp.
A traditional tale as told by the story teller Yede N'Guessan Gossey from a village near Dabou in Ivory Coast and translated by E. Armand and R. Lanes.

ENGLISH-SPEAKING AFRICA
WEST AFRICA

Cameroon
(see also Francophone Africa)

Asong, L.T.
The Last Man to Die
Yaoundé: Buma Kor, 1980. 126 pp. CFA850
The hero of this first novel by a young
Cameroonian author is a talented artist who,
in his search for success, loses all sense of
being. A sort of Dr Faust–Mephistopheles plot
in an African setting.

Ba'Bila Mutai
A Second Chance
Calabar, Nigeria: Scholars Press, 1981.
130 pp. ₦2.50
A first novel by a young Cameroonian who
won a BBC short-story award in 1979.

Dipoko, Mbella Sonne
A Few Nights and Days
London: Longman, 1966. 184 pp.
HEB, 1970 (AWS, 82), 184 pp. £1.50/$4.00
The few nights and days in this novel cover the
life of an African student living and working in
Paris. He seduces a French girl, later on falls in
love with her, and they decide to get married.
The girl's parents reluctantly give their consent, provided that they stay in France, while
the boy's parents, on the contrary, insist that
he should return home. In collusion with his
prospective father-in-law, the boy secretly
leaves France without telling the girl and
thereby unwittingly occasions the ultimate
tragedy. The girl commits suicide when she
discovers the plot.
'. . . Dipoko is equally at home in English and French
. . . He is one of the few African writers who has
comfortably bridged the gap between two very
different cultural milieus . . . a fine piece of writing.'
Lewis Nkosi – *Africa Report*
'. . . a different type of African novel, smaller in
scope, egocentric, non-tribal, and almost (dare we say
it?) non-African. Mr Dipoko appears to be moving
away from the type of novel that critics have come to
expect of African writers . . . the characters in the
book are not grown up and they are cruel and spiteful.
But, what the hell, it's a novel not a religious parable
and it really doesn't matter if he is showing us more
than he thinks he is. That is one virtue, one bonus, of
the well-made novel and probably a reason for the
success of most novels.'
Paul Theroux – *Transition*

Because of Women
London: HEB, 1969 (AWS, 57). 178 pp.
£1.50/$3.00
The author describes this novel as 'a study in
pleasure and change. The story of a woman
who dreams of founding a large family. The
novel tries to show the deep joy there is in
women.'
'. . . an effective study of sex and society in the
Cameroons . . . Dipoko does not indulge in the
excessive anthropology that burdens many African
novels, but he enriches his narrative with evocative
images of the vital and vigorous life of the
Cameroons.'
Robert E. Morsberger – *Books Abroad*

Black and White in Love
London: HEB, 1972 (AWS, 107). 72 pp.
£1.95/5.00
These poems of love, doubt, hope and anger
are Dipoko's first published collection
although some have been published previously
in the pages of *Transition* and *Présence Africaine*
and in anthologies like *West African Verse*,
Modern African Poetry and *African Writing Today*.
Most of these poems have been extensively rewritten and the author considers this to be the
definitive version.

Jumbam, Kenjo
The White Man of God
London: HEB, 1980 (AWS, 231). 151 pp.
£1.40/$4.50
A tale of childhood in a Christian family in
Cameroon in the early days of colonialism. For
the boy, Tansa, there are good times, but also
bad ones – like being punished for participating in 'pagan' rituals. His parents are
loving but unbending on matters of Christian
principle, despite the occasional outburst from
Grandma Yaya who is still unconverted but
who accepts baptism on her deathbed, a
triumphant victory for the family. For
Christians life evolves around the church and
Big Father, the white missionary and his strict
teachings, but there is also Father Cosmas, a
younger, more tolerant priest with winning
ways.

Kewai Nyamgha
Spectres on Scale
Calabar, Nigeria: Scholars Press, 1980. 43 pp.
₦1.50

The poetry of a Cameroonian who is a student in the Department of Theatre Arts at the University of Calabar.

Rattles on Their Pinna
Calabar, Nigeria: Scholars Press, 1980. 56 pp.
₦1.50
Another volume of verse.

Maimo, Sankie
Sov-Mbang the Soothsayer
Yaoundé: C.L.E., 1969. 58 pp. CFA200
Elements of satire, folk-tale and biblical legend are interwoven in this play, which presents the clash of the traditional with the modern in Cameroon society.

The Gambia

Kinteh, Ramatoulie
Rebellion
New York: Philosophical Library, 1968. 79 pp.
A three-act play by a Gambian woman writer. The plot is centred around Nysata, a girl from a typical African home in a patriarchical society, and her father, chief Lamin Kuyateh, who is converted from his conservative views to a more progressive way of thinking.

Peters, Lenrie
Poems
Ibadan: Mbari, 1964. 44 pp. o/p
Lenrie Peters's first volume of verse.

The Second Round
London: HEB, 1965 (AWS, 22). 192 pp.
£1.50/$4.50
In his first novel, Lenrie Peters relates the story – through the person of Dr Kawa, a young doctor returning home after several years at medical school in England – of emotional and mental disintegration, and of family hate and disloyalty in Freetown society.
'. . . *a distinguished and memorable work of imagination.*'
Gerald Moore – *East Africa Journal*
'. . . *the most impressive title Heinemann has added to its African writers series in a long time . . . has outreached a whole generation of young African novelists.*' Charles Larson – *Africa Report*

Satellites
London: HEB, 1967 (AWS, 37). 112 pp.
£1.95/$4.00
Contains twenty-one poems from the Mbari

collection and an additional thirty-four previously unpublished poems.
'*Lenrie Peters has an uncommonly sophisticated talent . . . his imagination roams over a limitless area of the earth.*' *West Africa*

Katchikali
London: HEB, 1971 (AWS, 103). 70 pp. o/p
Peters wanders from the dream world of a child in the title poem, to poetry on medicine, sport, war, politics, love, anger.

Selected Poetry
London: HEB, 1981 (AWS, 238). 160 pp.
£2.75/$9.00
Selections from *Satellites* and *Katchikali* represent about half the contents of this anthology, the rest is new poetry.

Ghana

Abruquah, Joseph W.
The Catechist
London: Allen and Unwin, 1965. 202 pp. o/p
Tema, Ghana: Ghana Publ. Corp., 1971.
202 pp. ₵1.00 ($1.00)
A biographical novel describing the life of the writer's father, a dedicated and loving man desirous to see his daughters well married and determined that his sons enjoy a better education than he had.

The Torrent
London: Longman, 1968. 280 pp.
Portrays a boy, Josiah Afful, growing up in Ghana, from his life in Nzima village to secondary school at Cape Coast: from the shelter of a family background to the problems common to adolescence, in school, sex and personal relationships.
'*Mr Abruquah's critical insights into educational policies and practices transferred to the first African secondary schools from English public schools are lively and entertaining.*' R.W.N. – *West Africa*

Agyemang, Fred
Accused in the Gold Coast
Tema, Ghana: Ghana Publ. Corp., 1972.
98 pp. ₵1.50 ($1.00)
The lives of four Europeans who lived on the Gold Coast are depicted in this book.

Aidoo, Ama Ata
The Dilemma of a Ghost
London: Longman, 1980 (New ed.). 50 pp.
95p
New York: Collier-Macmillan, 1971. 93 pp.
$1.25

The plot of this play centres on the difficulties encountered by a black American girl who marries into a Ghanaian family, and the tensions and conflicts that ensue between the girl and her husband's family.

'... *the directness and poetic qualities of Miss Aidoo's art make the play a very interesting, and, quite often, moving experiment indeed.*'

Mbella Sonne Dipoko – *Présence Africaine*

Anowa
London: Longman, 1980 (New ed.). 72 pp. 85p
Washington D.C.: Three Continents, $9.00 cased $4.00 p/b
A symbolic play based on an old Ghanaian legend: The beautiful Anowa refuses the suitors chosen by her parents and decides to marry the man of her own choice. The action is set in Ghana towards the end of the nineteenth century.

'*In societies and times where questions like the position of women, childbearing, child adoption, divorce – indeed the whole business of man/woman relationships – need examination (and where not?) this play can find a place.*'

Eldred D. Jones – *African Literature Today*

No Sweetness Here: a collection of short stories
London: Longman, 1979 (New ed.). 134 pp. 95p
New York: Doubleday, 1971 (with an introduction by Ezekiel Mphahlele). 240 pp.
Contemporary Ghana sets the background for this collection of eleven short stories. They explore the tensions and conflicts between the rural and urban societies in modern Ghana.

'*Ama Ata writes with transparent honesty: behind it there is the feeling, the same as in the novels of Ayi Kwei Armah, of being near to tears. She and Armah are in the front rank of the literary talents that have come to the fore in recent years in Ghana.*'

K.W. – *West Africa*

Our Sister Killjoy: or reflections from a black-eyed squint
London: Longman, 1981 (New ed.). 134 pp. £1.25
New York: Nok Publishers, 1977. 137 pp. $7.95 cased $3.95 p/b
Our sister, or Sissie as she is known, on a scholarship trip to Europe, discovers herself and examines her attitudes to the West. This is Aidoo's first novel and bears a 1966 copyright. Divided into three sections, the novel deals firstly with Sissie's stay in a German youth hostel and her friendship with a lonely young housewife who is intrigued with her foreignness. In London next, Sissie antagonizes many

people with her bluntness and nagging, earning herself the soubriquet which is the title of the book. The third part is in the form of a long explanatory letter written on the flight home; considering and analysing some of the faults of independent Africa.

'*It is a witty, experimental work whose main point is a stylish dismissal of characteristic attitudes of both the white world and the black middle class.*'

Faith Pullin – *British Book News*
'... *she is a sensitive and committed writer with a recognizable personal style and a clearly-defined niche as a social critic; but* Our Sister Killjoy *is not the really major work she must be capable of creating.*'

Anita Kern – *World Literature Written in English*

Aidoo, Kofi
Saworbeng: a collection of short stories
Tema, Ghana: Ghana Publ. Corp., 1977. 114 pp. ₵4.00
Eleven short stories, some of which have been read on the BBC Africa Service. The tales are basically grounded in village life, showing the tensions caused by forced marriages, witch doctors, and the introduction of Christianity.

Ampofo-Opoku, K.
Abidjan Girl and Other Stories
Accra: Waterville Publ. House, 1978 (3rd ed.) 92 pp. ₵5.00
Popular short stories.

Ansah, W. K.
The Denizens of the Street
Tema, Ghana: Ghana Publ. Corp., 1971. 103 pp. ₵5.50 cased ₵1.25 p/b/$1.25
A novel.

Anyidoho, Kofi
Elegy for the Revolution
New York: Greenfield Review Press, 1978. 48 pp. $3.00
Over two dozen of Anyidoho's poems, some already published in journals, are gathered here. In them he explores some of the failures of the revolution ushered in by military coups.

'*The collection of poems is an interesting one. If the subject is somewhat limited and the topic one often rehearsed, Kofi Anyidoho's poetic statements are at least germane and often expressed in freshly designed metaphors.*'

David K. Bruner – *World Literature Today*
'*There are dramatic colours in his lines, actions and feelings, joining and jostling down a page of what amounts to part of Ghana's recent social history.*'

O.C-F. – *West Africa*

Armah, Ayi Kwei

The Beautyful Ones Are Not Yet Born
Boston: Houghton Mifflin, 1968. 215 pp.
London: HEB, 1969 (AWS, 43). 200 pp.
£1.25/$3.50
New York: Macmillan, 1969. 180 pp. $1.95
The misspelled title of this novel derives from
an inscription on an Accra bus. It tells the
story of a railway freight clerk – a story of
greed and corruption, of squalor and decay –
and, foremost, it is a study of politics and
politicians in a newly independent African
nation. The Macmillan paper edition has an
introduction by Ama Ata Aidoo
'. . . Armah has taken the predicament of Africa in
general, Ghana in particular, and distilled its despair
and hopelessness in a very powerful, harsh,
deliberately unbeautiful novel.'
Eldred D. Jones – *African Literature Today*
'. . . what is impressive about The Beautyful Ones
is the way in which it expresses the disillusion and
cynicism engendered in Ghana in the last years of
Nkrumah, which his fall only seemed to compound.'
West Africa

Fragments
Boston: Houghton Mifflin, 1970. 287 pp.
London: HEB, 1974 (AWS, 154). 287 pp. o/p
cased £1.95 p/b
New York: Collier-Macmillan, 1974. 296 pp.
$1.95
The main theme of Armah's second novel is
the shattered spiritual vision of a young
African returning home after five years in
America. He finds his homeland's society
materialistic and eager to adopt Western ways
and values, and soon sees himself surrounded
by career-minded and corrupt people.
'The novel, while a powerful moral indictment of the
present state of his country makes its force felt through
symbolism, not direct propagandistic means.'
Martin Tucker – *The New Republic*
'. . . Ghana has the most sophisticated reading public
in black Africa. Now in Ayi Kwei Armah, it has a
novelist of matching sophistication and skill.'
M. M. Mahood – *Saturday Review*

Why Are We So Blest?
New York: Doubleday, 1972. 288 pp. $6.95
London: HEB, 1974 (AWS, 155). 288 pp. o/p
cased £2.25 p/b
Nairobi: EAPH, 1974. 234 pp. K.shs.14.00
A revolutionary cause brings three people
together. The story is related by Solo, with
extracts from notes by the other two protagonists. Solo is an African intellectual
crippled by sensitivity to surroundings; Modin
a West African who has abandoned his studies
at Harvard to join in revolution; and Aimée,
an American who has demonstrated her
shallow revolutionary dedication while bed-

ding her way through East Africa. The novel
explores the sensibilities of the two men, and
looks at their predicament – rejecting both
white society and traditionalism, yet unable to
gain entrance to the revolution.
'Armah goes beyond an indictment of his own country
to a radical critique of the cant of commitment and
black power . . . Armah's own vision is darker than
Achebe's, but in truth-telling surely no 'betrayal' of
Africa: his derisively caricatured American academics
and philanthropists and the pitying portrait of
Modin's American mistress hungry for a vicarious
mission complete a double indictment.'
M. Thorpe – *English Studies*
'On an ethical level we can in fact see it as a carefully
planned attack on all racism, but aesthetically we can
also apprehend it as a sensitive exploration into the
minds of three alienated individuals and the web of
relationships which created their respective sensibilities.'
Richard Priebe – *Books Abroad*

Two Thousand Seasons
Nairobi: EAPH. 1973. 312 pp. K.shs.15.00
($6.00)
London: HEB, 1979 (AWS, 218). 206 pp.
£2.25
Chicago: Third World Press, 1979. $6.95
An epic – political, historical, and fantastical –
of the Ghanaian people. The 'two thousand
seasons' is the length of time prophesied for
the rape of Africa by colonialism and neo-
colonialism. Asserting the nullity and evil of
whiteness, Armah proposes that creative
energy permitted the survival of Africans. The
whiteness covers the first wave of invaders
(decadent Arabs, 'predators from the desert')
as well as the Europeans ('destroyers from the
sea').
'. . . and I would make bold to say that this novel
marks a definite stage in the development of the novel
in Africa and hints at the possible contributions the
African novelist can make to the traditional form.
Unlike Soyinka, Kwei Armah is unlimited to time and
space. The whole sweep of black history and myth is
his canvas.'
Kole Omotoso – *Afriscope*
'. . . the work remains a passionate often beautiful
testament of socio-racial faith. Kwei Armah's
spokesmen are persuasive visionaries of the future of
the continent.'
Bai Kisogie – *Transition*

The Healers
Nairobi: EAPH, 1978. 377 pp.
K.shs.25.00/$6.00
London: HEB, 1979 (AWS, 194). 309 pp.
£5.50 cased £1.95 p/b
The Healers are groups of people living in
close communication with nature who are
adept at healing in the customary sense, but
who also possess a symbolic insight into the
most distinctive ill of the African people – the

fragmentation of society. Set in the last century, the novel traces incidents in the fall of the great Ashanti kingdom to the imperialist forces. The young man Densu, refusing a kingship, wanting to join the Healers, and helping in the army, links the areas of activity. The disarray caused by the rivalry between people, greed of the kings, and disunity between peoples prevents any determined defence against the white army.

'*A historical novel that Walter Scott, and Lukács, would warm to. The focus – in the fall of Ashanti to its rulers' hubris, and to the technology and economic spell of Victorian imperialism – allows for the self-contradiction and sweaty feel of people in a fragmenting time.*'   N.H. – *Tribune*

'*It seemed hardly possible that Armah's commitment could be pushed further, but so it has, towards a more general and specifically African reading public.*'

S. Nyamfukudza – *New Statesman*

Armah, E. O.

A Custom Broken
Tema, Ghana: Ghana Publ. Corp., 1978.
87 pp. ₵3.50

A winner of the Ghana Library Board Award, this book is concerned with the effects of a change in tradition. Ayi allows his son to enter the laundry trade, rather than insist on his following him into the palm-wine trade.

Asalache, Khadambi

A Calabash of Life
London: Longman, 1967. 166 pp.

A story of love, intrigue and war, set in a royal village in the land of the Vatirichi in western Kenya in pre-colonial days. Its hero Shiyuka, whose family has lost the chieftainship, narrates the novel.

Asare, Bediako

Rebel
London: HEB, 1969 (AWS, 59). 160 pp.
£1.25/$3.00

The story of a man and his wife reacting against their tribe and a conservative fetish priest, over leaving the traditional tribal village of Pachanga.

'*. . . tells the story of a sad and dying village and its survivors. It relates the movements of Ngurumo, a young man with a vision, who leads his people through a maze of local fetish priests, rites and terrors across a dangerous forest and into a land that is green, bright and open . . . The struggle of young Ngurumo against deeply maintained tribal customs is sincere, if at times it seems contrived . . . The story is simple and the language unpretentious, and the impact of change and hope gives strength and quality to the novel.*'   Sheila Wilson – *Africa Report*

The Stubborn

Nairobi: East African Lit. Bureau, 1976.
162 pp. K.shs.20.90 (£2.20/$4.70)

Okello lands in trouble twice because he stubbornly resists his parents' advice. On the first occasion, he is led astray by a deviant young orphan: they run away to Nairobi and end up in prison. Okello's mortification leads him to study so hard that he emerges from medical school in glory – only to wed unwisely. Even then, he is saved by divorce.

'*The main themes are science versus superstition and the value of counsel from elders. Asare's main intended audience in this pulpit fiction is 15–18 year olds of East African ruling classes, though some graphic scenes . . . might extend the appeal to a broader readership.*'

Stephen H. Arnold – *African Book Publishing Record*

Ashong-Katai, Selby

Confessions of a Bastard
Tema, Ghana: Ghana Publ. Corp., 1976.
122 pp. ₵4.00 ($3.00)

Tales by a young writer commenting on society.

A Sonata of Broken Bones
Tema, Ghana: Ghana Publ. Corp., 1978.
67 pp. ₵4.00

Poems on a wide range of themes written while Ashong-Katai was an undergraduate at the University of Ghana.

Assan, Afari

Christmas in the City
London: Macmillan Educ., 1978. 112 pp. 80p

A morality tale about city boys introducing Ben Boham to Accra. His fantasies are shattered when they steal his money and become involved in deception and crime.

Awoonor-Williams, George
[Awoonor, Kofi]

Rediscovery and other poems
Ibadan: Mbari, 1964. 36 pp. o/p

Kofi Awoonor's first volume of verse.

'*. . . the work of this young Ghanaian poet is coolly rational.*'   O. A. – *Black Orpheus*

Awoonor, Kofi

Night of my Blood
New York: Doubleday, 1971. 95 pp.

The poems in this anthology, although ranging in subject matter, are thematically a lament for the neglect of his ancestors, his gods, and traditional culture, when Western creeds were

accommodated. The poet seeks a rediscovery
of a true African identity.
*'In his elegy for Okigbo, as well as in many of the
other poems . . . Kofi Awoonor has truly earned the
right to that vacated position.'*
Richard Priebe – *African Studies Review*
*'. . . felt observations flow out naturally in the forms
he has chosen, in stately rhythms. The lyricism is
enchanting; there are no gimmicks of punctuation, no
obscure allusions, no freak-outs. His themes are soul-
deep in African identity; his voice is gentle and
painfully honest.'*
Jon M. Warner – *Library Journal*

This Earth, My Brother . . .
New York: Doubleday, 1971.
London: HEB, 1972 (AWS, 108). 183 pp.
£1.75/$4.00
Using a combination of narration and sub-
chapters of poetic prose, Awoonor paints 'an
allegorical tale of Africa', set in post-Independence Ghana. The action covers key points in
the life of the lawyer, Amamu, psychologically
and professionally cut off from Africa; it
chronicles influences and events that are
germane to his life pilgrimage – a search for a
meaningful identity for himself and his people,
combining past and present.
*'. . . an expressionistic work taking us swiftly from
continent to continent, from country to country. But
one never loses track of the author. He is a persuasive
and ubiquitous narrator who shares and illuminates
even the most trivial experience through his own eyes.'*
Jan Carew – *New York Times Book Review*
*'. . . a writer who is textually exciting. Kofi Awoonor
can do what we journeymen of letters hate ourselves
for being unable to do: he can be his own man
stylistically, yet summon at need nearly any rhythm or
resource of the language.'*
Basil Busacaa – *Africa Report*

Ride Me, Memory
Greenfield Center, N.Y.: Greenfield Review
Press, 1973. 48 pp $1.25
Awoonor records here his experience of
America in poetry.
'. . . a major new volume by a celebrated writer.'
Robert Fraser – *West Africa*

The House By The Sea
Greenfield Center, N.Y.: Greenfield Review
Press, 1978. 78 pp. $3.00
The poems in this collection are grouped in
two sections: 'Before the Journey' and 'Homecoming'. They are the bitter fruits of the
author's year in a Ghanaian prison.

Azasu, Kwakuvi
Streams of Thought
Accra: Mpaba Educ. Publ., 1974 (distr. by
Univ. Ghana Bkshop.). 105 pp. ₵2.50
Poems.

Bediako, K. A.
Don't Leave Me Mercy
Accra: Anowuo Educational Publ., 1966.
119 pp.
'Echoes from Owusu's marriage life. Richly
entertaining and educative,' reads the sub-title
of this novel.

A Husband for Esi Ellua
Accra: Anowuo Educational Publ., 1968.
179 pp.
A popular novel.

Blay, J. Benibengor
Emilia's Promise and Fulfilment
Accra: Waterville Publ. House, 1967 (New
ed.). 134 pp. ₵3.90
One of several items of popular literature.

Earlier Poems
Aboso, Ghana: Benibengor Book Agency,
1971. 68 pp. 50pes

African Drums
Aboso, Ghana: Benibengor Book Agency,
1972. 51 pp. 50pes

Dr. Bengia Wants a Wife
Aboso, Ghana: Benibengor Book Agency,
1972 (3rd ed.). 18 pp. 20pes

Love in a Clinic
Aboso, Ghana: Benibengor Book Agency,
1972 (4th ed.). 20 pp. 20pes

Parted Lovers
Aboso, Ghana: Benibengor Book Agency,
1972 (3rd ed.). 23 pp. 20pes

Be Content with your Lot
Aboso, Ghana: Benibengor Book Agency,
1973 (5th ed.). 28 pp. 20pes

Stubborn Girl
Aboso, Ghana: Benibengor Book Agency,
1973 (3rd ed.). 20 pp. 20pes

Boateng, Yaw
The Return
London: HEB, 1977 (AWS, 186). 120 pp.
£1.50
New York: Pantheon Books, 1977. 118 pp.
$6.95
Melding fiction and history, Boateng's first

novel is set in Ghana of the early 1800s. The Muslim Jakpa seeks to kill Seku Wattera, the brave and popular warrior. As his personal motives are unfolded, we are presented with an historical perspective of his and Wattera's past: the gruesome realities of the slave trade. Personal vendettas and regional wars are the divisive elements sustaining the European stranglehold on the slave trade.
'An interesting first novel.'   A.M. – *West Africa*
'Even without the valuable historical background, this would be an interesting novel . . . Boateng is indeed a promising new writer.'
Richard Cima – *Library Journal*

Brew, Kwesi
The Shadows of Laughter
London: Longman, 1969. 76 pp.
A verse collection of forty-six poems, many of them hitherto unpublished. This is Kwesi Brew's only published volume, although his verse has been very widely anthologised.

Broni, Kofi
Beads from the Drumskin of my Forehead
London: Afro-Presse, 1972. 32 pp. 75p
Poems from Ghana, 1964–1972.

Cab-Addae, K.
A Lover's Dilemma
Legon: Adwinsa Public., 1978. 84 pp. ₵5.00
Popular fiction.

Cantey, R. A.
The Mystery of a Cockcrow
Tema, Ghana: Ghanaian Publ. Corp., 1971. 48 pp. 40pes
A play in three acts, set in a small village in Ghana, illustrating the unhappy implications of maternal inheritance.

Casely-Hayford, Joseph E.
Ethiopia Unbound: studies in race emancipation
London: C. M. Philipps, 1911. 211 pp. o/p
London: Frank Cass, 1969 (Reprint: Africana Modern Library) 215 pp. £11.00 cased
This is one of the earliest literary works from Africa and the first West African 'novel'. Its hero and protagonist is a man from the Gold Coast who goes to London to prepare himself for a legal career and who finally returns to his native country, but now finds himself a stranger there. He is saddened and angered by what he discovers in his homeland. The result is this book which, containing a great deal of historical, literary and philosophical references, is principally an early declaration of Négritude and an attempt to rally all black people to the defence of their culture, their achievements and racial pride. It is also an appeal for unity and national regeneration to the people of West Africa, based on the concept of *Ethiopianism*, i.e. the crystallization of religious and political notions with Ethiopia, which at that time was (with Liberia) the only independent nation in colonial Africa.

De Graft, J. C.
Sons and Daughters
London and New York: OUP, 1964 (Three Crowns Books). 53 pp. £1.50
The major characters of the play, the children of Aaron Ofosu, try to fulfil their ambitions against their father's wish; it is a drama of the tensions that result from the clash of two generations.

Through a Film Darkly
London: OUP, 1970 (Three Crowns Books). 70 pp.
First performed at the Ghana Drama Studio, Accra, this new play explores the racial tension underlying the lives of two married couples, and the cause of the hero's hatred of Europeans.
'Aside from the rather melodramatic ending, de Graft gets at a very important aspect of racial tensions. He points out how hard it is to remain "tough" and preserve one's humanity in a world dominated by white values.'   Reinhard Sander – *Books-Abroad*

Beneath the Jazz and Brass
London: HEB, 1975 (AWS, 166). 134 pp. £1.80/$5.00
These poems fall into three sections: love poetry constitutes most of the first section; in the second, de Graft moves to political themes; while in the third these two modes are combined.
'. . . a perceptive and worthwhile contribution to the corpus of West African poetry for the period out of which it grew.'
Clive Wake – *African Literature Today*

Muntu
Nairobi: HEB, 1977. 90 pp. K.shs.12.50
Muntu, an epic play, was commissioned for the All Africa Conference of Churches in 1975. Using symbolic characters, de Graft has incorporated the history of Africa into a thematic whole. He starts with the creation and the natural harmony of the people. The exploitation of the slave trade and the Scramble for Africa bring division in the land, the perpetuation of which he traces through the struggle for independence and its aftermath.
'Joe de Graft must be given credit for evoking a new symbolism about the existence of the African man. He

must be hailed for going back to his roots and incorporating oral traditional forms in his drama to give his vast subject unity.'
Simon Gikandi – *Africa*

Dei-Anang, Michael Francis
Okomfo's Anokyo's golden stool: a play in three acts
Ilfracombe, Devon: Stockwell, 1960. 54 pp.
o/p
This play is based on the traditional story of the Ashanti golden stool.

Wayward Lines from Africa
London: United Society for Christian Literature, 1964. 47 pp. o/p
(Reprinted in *Early West African poetry and drama*. Nendeln: Liechtenstein, Kraus reprint, 1970. $15.00)
A volume of verse.

Ghana Semi-tones
Accra: Presbyterian Book Depot, 1962. 28 pp.
o/p
Accra: Waterville Publ. Co., 1964. 28 pp.
20pes
A collection of eighteen new poems.

Dei-Anang, Michael Francis and **Warren, Jaw**
Ghana Glory: poems on Ghana and Ghanaian life
London: Nelson, 1965. 69 pp. o/p
In this joint collection two poets, a Ghanaian and an Englishman, combine their talents to present great moments of Ghana's history in narrative verse. Kwame Nkrumah has provided a foreword.

Dei-Anang, Michael Francis and **Dei-Anang, Kofi**
Two Faces of Africa
Accra: Waterville Publ. House, 1965. 124 pp.
o/p
Buffalo, N.Y.: Black Academy Press, 1972.
250 pp. $8.25 cased $4.25 p/b
Poems by father and son.

Djoleto, Amu
The Strange Man
London: HEB, 1967 (AWS, 41). 279 pp.
£1.50/$4.00
The funeral of his brother is the point of departure for the story of old Mensah, a respected member of his village community. In this account of his life, his boyhood in the village is retraced through school under a tyrannical headmaster to a minor position in the civil service, his problems with his own

family and his success as a businessman in the last days of the Gold Coast and the early days of Ghana.

Money Galore
London: HEB, 1975 (AWS, 161). 182 pp.
£1.95/$4.00
Teaching falls some way short of providing Kafu with the rewards he expects from life, and so he decides to enter politics. This ambition is realised through the support of corrupt people – and once in power Kafu becomes involved in unscrupulous financial transactions, neglects his wife, and relies increasingly on alcohol. His descent to the bottom is inevitable.
'Packed with telling portraits of manipulating civil servants, skimping building contractors, bent businessmen, coercive women and bewildered victims, this inventive, irreverent book is as sharp as a quince, and richly satisfying.' Jeremy Brooks – *Sunday Times*
'. . . he treats his satiric objects in a good-humoured, but not a light-hearted, manner.' British Book News

Duodo, Cameron
The Gab Boys
London: Deutsch, 1967. 208 pp. o/p
Glasgow: Fontana/Collins, 1969. 201 pp.
85p/$1.25
The gab boys – so called because of their gaberdine trousers – are the sharply dressed youngsters that idle and lurk about a Ghanaian village, mistrusted and considered delinquent by their elders. This is the story of one of them, a boy who runs away from village life, and after a series of adventures and setbacks finds a new life in Accra.

Egblewogbe, E. Y.
Victims of Greed
Tema, Ghana: Ghana Publ. Corp., 1975.
120 pp. ₡3.00 ($3.00)
A tragic tale of the obstacles to the love of young Gina and Foli, born to different clans. The traditional rituals and ceremonies provide the background to the main action.

The Wizard's Pride and Other Poems
Tema, Ghana: Ghana Publ. Corp., 1975.
40 pp. 95pes
Poems ranging from light-hearted to serious, with subject matter including thoughts on the beauty of nature as well as on love and death.

Ephson, I. S.
Tragedy of False Friends
Legon: Univ. of Ghana Bkshop, 1979. 191 pp.
₡8.00
A moral tale.

Equiano, Olaudah

*Equiano's travels: his autobiography. The
interesting narrative of the life of Olaudah
Equiano or Gustavus Vassa the African*
Abridged and edited by Paul Edwards
London: HEB, 1966 (AWS, 10). 192 pp. £2.25
New York: Praeger, 1967. 196 pp. $6.95
First published in 1789, this autobiography by
an African slave is a pioneering work. It is a
tale of high adventure and exploration:
describing Equiano's first encounter with the
white man, the terrors of the slave ships,
cruelty and injustice, and the constant dangers
and humiliations that made up the life of a
slave. But he also writes of his friendships with
English ladies, who taught him, of shipmates
who cared for him, and of a master who valued
his intelligence and integrity. Paul Edwards
has provided an introduction on Equiano as a
writer and personality, and adds comprehensive explanatory notes to the text.
*'. . . important as an attempt to foster an informed
pride in the origins of an increasingly productive
literature in English . . . a sensitive abridged edition
of an historically interesting, often compelling
narrative . . .'*
                    Peter Young – *African Literature Today*

Eshun, J. O.

Adventures of the Kapapa
Tema, Ghana: Ghana Publ. Corp., 1976.
115 pp. ₡3.00/$3.00
A book of science-fiction involving the scientist, Afful, and the Kapapa Craft which
operates on anti-gravitational principles.

Hihetah, Robert Kofi

Painful Road to Kadjebi
Accra: Anowuo Educational Publ., 1966.
194 pp.
Presenting a picture of Ghanaian rural society,
this novel recounts the story of Ewe, a man
imprisoned in a manner everyone believes to
be a miscarriage of justice.

Johnevi, Eta

Roses for Sondia
Accra: Johnevi Publ., 1973. 208 pp.
A coup in a fictitious African country, with the
conspirators eluding justice.

Kayper-Mensah, Albert W.

The Dark Wanderer
Tübingen, Germany: Horst Erdmann Verlag,
1970. 136 pp. DM13.80 (£2.00/$5.00)
Poems which have their inspiration not only in
the poet's native Ghana, but also in Germany
where he was a diplomat.
'The verse has the competence and easy flow to be

*expected of a practised writer, but its main strength is
its concreteness.'*
                    D. S. Izevbaye – *African Literature Today*

The Drummer in Our Time
London: HEB, 1975 (AWS, 157). 103 pp. o/p
A substantial volume of poems from a
Ghanaian poet sensitive to people both
personally and historically.
*'The work of a mature poet of cosmopolitan
background,* The Drummer in Our Time *is a
significant contribution to the literature of Ghana and
of Africa.'*   Richard F. Bauerle – *Books Abroad*

Sankofa: Adinkra poems
Tema, Ghana: Ghana Publ. Corp., 1976.
36 pp. ₡1.20/$1.20
Indigenous Ghanaian symbols are depicted,
with a short poetic explanation to accompany
each symbol.

Proverb Poems
Tema, Ghana: Ghana Publ. Corp., 1978.
69 pp. ₡3.50

Konadu, Asare

Wizard of Asamang
Accra: Waterville Publ. House, 1964. 129 pp.
Popular fiction.

The Player who Bungled his Life
Accra: Waterville Publ. House, 1965. 81 pp.
o/p

Come Back Dora
Accra: Anowuo Educational Publ., 1966.
218 pp.
'A husband's confession and ritual,' reads the
subtitle of this fictitious account of funeral
practices among the Akan society in central
Ghana.

Shadow of Wealth
Accra: Anowuo Educational Publ., 1966.
160 pp.
A business executive's search for a mistress,
ultimately upsetting the entire administration
of his company.

Night Watchers of Korlebu
Accra: Anowuo Educational Publ., 1967.
99 pp.
A popular novel of the African world of spirits,
of the juju man, his powers, and his hold on
the village community.

A Woman in her Prime
London: HEB, 1967 (AWS, 40). 116 pp.
£1.25/$4.00
Set in a Ghanaian society that considers it a

grave misfortune for a woman to have reached middle age without having borne children, this novel describes the plight of such a woman, who remains childless despite three marriages.

Ordained by the Oracle
London: HEB, 1969 (AWS, 55). 160 pp. £1.65/$3.00
A reissue, under a new title, of *Come Back Dora,* a novel that portrays a man's agony at the sudden death of his wife, and the long days and nights of ritual that follow.
'Even with the inadequacies of characterization and dialogue, the novel is an informative account of tribal death rites.' Patricia Saxon – *Books Abroad*

Kwarteng, J.S.
My Sword is my Life
Tema, Ghana: Ghana Publ. Corp., 1973. 96 pp. ₵1.50/$1.50
The historical struggles between the Ashanti and the Fanti provide the background to this novel, which illustrates the sufferings of the victims of war. The intrepid Kwasi Bota and his fellow men are captured by the Fantis. Their escape provides the climax of the story.

Kyei, Kojo
The Lone Voice
Accra: Ghana Univ. Press, 1969. 190 pp. ₵1.50 (75p/$1.50)
Poems borne of the poet's wish to portray the Ghana he knows, and a record of responses to a stay in the States.

Ghana: the road tomorrow
Tema, Ghana: Ghana Publ. Corp., 1978. 89 pp. ₵4.00
Poems.

Kyei, Kojo and Schreckenbach, Hannah
No Time to Die
Accra: Catholic Press, 1976 (distr. by Univ. Ghana Bkshop.). 80 pp. ₵7.00
Poems based on slogans on the mammy lorries of Ghana.
'... more than a mere collection of poems that drowns our sorrows in bemused laughter. It is also an interesting collection of the down-to-earth philosophy of the average Ghanaian.'
S. O. Duodu – *Afriscope*

Marshall, Bill
Stranger to Innocence and Shadow of an Eagle
Tema, Ghana: Ghana Publ. Corp., 1969. 46 pp. 35pes
The first play involves a clash between the townsfolk and a priest who, with his family, tries to understand an enigma in the guise of a

stranger. The enigma is explained shortly before the stranger's death. The second play hinges on a drunken father who is mismanaging the family farm. When Bimpo, the runaway son, returns he finds his mother still nagging, his sister with an illegitimate child, and his father unable to stop drinking.

Son of Umbele
Tema, Ghana: Ghana Publ. Corp., 1973. 80 pp. ₵1.00
This play, first staged in America, takes place in a village where the fisherman's daughter is the victim of local belief in traditional myths. Joshua, arriving from town, breaks the power of the myth.

Bukom
London: Longman, 1979. 118 pp. 80p Washington D.C.: Three Continents Press, distr. $4.00
A glimpse into the lives of Ataa Kojo and his family in seedy Bukom. Kojo would dearly love to have a flush toilet, and pursues this objective without regard to the consequences for his family.
'. . . a lovely, funny novel set in Accra.' – *Tribune*

Permit for Survival
Accra: Educational Press, 1981. 120 pp.
Marshall's latest novel is set in contemporary Ghana, and centres on the case of Joseph Jonathan Kofi Kuma who, at the prime of his life, finds himself in the bizarre situation of being confronted by the publication of his own obituary in the national press! His subsequent efforts to secure official certification of his existence, and to extricate himself from the bureaucratic maze, turns into something of an ordeal.

Obeng, R. E.
Eighteenpence
Ilfracombe, Devon: Stockwell, 1943. 180 pp. o/p
Birkenhead: Willmer Bros., 1950. 167 pp. o/p
Tema, Ghana: Ghana Publ. Corp., 1972. 146 pp. ₵2.50
Among the very first West African novels to appear in English, *Eighteenpence* chronicles the life of Obeng-Akrofi; it also documents the judiciary and legal systems of the Gold Coast (now Ghana) during the colonial days.

Ofoli, Nii Yemoh
The Messenger of Death
Tema, Ghana: Ghana Publ. Corp., 1979. 168 pp.
Why do all Niiboi's and Aayoo's children die?

Is it anything to do with the grandfather's warning that Aayoo's family has contained witches? We follow Niiboi's efforts to establish the identity of the witch.

Okai, John
Flowerfall
London: Writers Forum, 1969 (Writers Forum Poets, 25). 25 pp.
A sampling of five poems by a young Ghanaian writer.
'... *a group of poems neither esoteric nor non-African. In spite of sometimes clumsy craftsmanship, the book is promising for its wide frame of reference and lively music.*' June Hankins – *Books Abroad*

Oath of the Fontomfrom and Other Poems
New York: Simon and Schuster, 1971.
1958 pp. $6.95
Of these poems, K. Orraca-Tetteh has written 'there is more to Okai's verse than its music. Besides the music there is the arresting, startling imagery ... to which earlier critics have paid very scant attention.'

Okai, Atukwei (John)
Lorgorligi Logarithms
Tema, Ghana: Ghana Publ. Corp., 1974, 146 pp. ₵8.00/$5.00 cased
The first collection of Okai's poetry to appear in Ghana. Lyrical love poems, poems on Soweto and Nkrumah and other political themes, accompany the title poem. This (from the Ga word Lorgorligi) tackles the problem of the reality of life and is revolutionary verse, in theme and form.
'*The best poems in the later sections of the volume are as fine as anything which has come from Ghana to date. Okai is rapidly emerging as one of Africa's most talented young poets.*'
        Charles R. Larson – *Books Abroad*
'*I believe that Atukwei Okai is a poet of great sensibility with a capacity to produce verse which will endure.*'   P.W. – *West Africa*

Oppong-Affi, A. M.
The Prophet of Doom
Tema, Ghana: Ghana Publ. Corp., 1980.
123 pp.
The village of Amanfoso is divided by the teaching of the new preacher, Prophet Kofi and his Church of the New Covenant. He leads his followers to a remote spot, where they lead a life of denial, only to discover at the end of the year that the prophet has himself been amassing their wealth.

Owusu, Martin
The Sudden Return and other plays
London: HEB, 1973 (AWS, 138), 144 pp.
£1.75/$4.00
Owusu has drawn on existing African dramatic traditions in these five plays. 'The Sudden Return' is based on the belief that the sacrifice of life can bring wealth. The Ashanti-Dekyira war provides material for the second play. 'The Mightier Sword'. Two further plays are based on the Ananse tradition, and 'Anane' derives similarly from the story-telling tradition.
'*Here is a gorgeous texture: song, proverb, and myth blended together as in a rich kente. Here too is a remarkable awareness of the presence and needs of an audience ...*'
        Robert H. Fraser – *African Literature Today*

Parkes, Frank Kobina
Songs from the Wilderness
London: Univ. of London Press, 1965. 64 pp.
A selection of poems by Frank Parkes, the former President of the Ghana Society of Writers. In this volume he writes primarily of the destiny of the new Africa.
'... *Mr Parkes is one of the fine poets writing today about Africa and the world.*'
        Mbella Sonne Dipoko – *Présence Africaine*
'... *a landmark not only in Ghanaian poetry but in African poetry as a whole.*'
        M. Bulane – *The New African*

Sebuava, Joseph
The Inevitable Hour
New York: Vantage Press, 1980. 188 pp. $6.50
Set in the coastal region of south-east Ghana, this novel traces the career of Sedofia, who is a successful shallot farmer, but whose domestic life is a shambles.

Sekyi, Kobina
The Blinkards
London: Rex Collings, 1974. 160 pp. £3.00 cased
London: HEB, 1974 (AWS, 136). 148 pp.
£1.25/$4.00
Washington D.C.: Three Continents Press, 1974. $8.00
A comedy of manners originally written and staged in 1915. By lampooning the *nouveaux riches* of the day – who seek to copy uncritically anything English – Sekyi asserts his loyalty to traditional customs and speech, and provides a devastating attack on the cultural consequences of colonialism. The play uses a mixture of English and Fanti (for which a translation is provided).

Selormey, Francis

The Narrow Path

London: HEB, 1967 (AWS, 27). 184 pp.
£1.25/$1.25 (also available in Heinemann's
Windmill Series, 193)
New York: Praeger, 1968. 190 pp.
In this semi-autobiographical novel of
Selormey's childhood he recounts Kofi's upbringing in a village on the coast of Ghana
during the nineteen-twenties. Kofi's father,
headmaster of a Catholic mission school, is a
strict disciplinarian who brutally punishes the
boy to keep him on 'the narrow path' of right
behaviour.
*'... Selormey writes with great freshness and
simplicity; his tale moves swiftly and involves the
reader completely in the hero's painful pilgrimage.
His honesty is also frequently disarming ...
altogether this is a distinguished addition to African
autobiography.'*

Gerald Moore – *The Journal of
Commonwealth Literature*

Sutherland, Efua Theodora

Edufa

London: Longman, 1969. 72 pp. 80p
Washington D.C.: Three Continents Press,
$9.00 cased $4.00 p/b
A play based upon the conflict between
traditional belief and modern circumstances.
The hero faces a personal crisis caused by the
conflict between an education into an alien
culture on the one hand, and his African
cultural instincts on the other.

Foriwa

Tema, Ghana: Ghana Publ. Corp., 1967.
67 pp. ₡1.00
The action of this three-act play, first
performed in Akan at the Ghana Drama
Studio in 1962, takes place in a dilapidated
street in Kyerefaso; a small Ghanaian town.

The Marriage of Anansewa

London: Longman, 1980 (New ed.). 96 pp.
95p
Washington D.C.: Three Continents Press,
1980. $9.00 cased $4.00 p/b
The traditional cunning of Ananse is the basis
of this comic drama in which Ananse plans to
win rapid wealth by falsely betrothing his
daughter to four chiefs simultaneously.
Sutherland believes that the development of
theatre should be rooted in the artistic
sensibilities of the people.
*'There are a great many humorous stage shenanigans,
and Sutherland has made exceptional use of folk
materials. With its colorful use of dance and mime,
one can assume that* The Marriage of Anansewa
would be a pleasure to see staged.'

Charles R. Larson – *Books Abroad*

Wartemberg, Nanabenyin Kweku

The Corpse's Comedy

Ibadan: University Press Ltd., 1977. 86 pp
London: OUP, £2.25
Mr Hagan, a wealthy man refuses to allow his
daughter to marry Stanley because *he* wants
Stanley's mother, a widow, as a second wife,
his Christian beliefs notwithstanding. The only
way the two young lovers can marry is to
convince everyone that Mr Hagan has died.
The result is comic confusion. Has also been
published in the anthology *Three West African
Plays*.

Yirenkyi, Asiedu

Kivuli and other plays

London: HEB, 1980 (AWS, 216). 154 pp.
£2.10/$7.00
Yirenkyi, who teaches drama in Ghana and has
won the John Golden award for play-writing
at Yale, has a selection of five plays in this
compilation. The three-act 'Kivuli' is a
domestic tragedy: Kumi Mensah is driven to
antagonize the children of his first marriage
and to embark on a ruinous land case by his
demanding young wife. 'Blood and Tears' and
'Lovenet' are farces involving marital deception. 'Amaa Pranaa', a 'folk-story', dramatises
a situation where a girl is wooed by a lion in
the guise of a man. 'Firefly' is a short
rendering about a supposed witch.
*'Though Yirenki's characters are easily recognized,
they are entertaining. They reveal the playwright's
overriding passion, his "function": to criticize
contemporary African society for its great loss – an
increasing violation of traditional ways.'*

Randall Davenport – *World Literature Today*

Guinea
(see also Francophone Africa)

Modupe, Prince

I was a Savage

London: Museum Press, 1958. 168 pp. o/p
New York: Praeger [reissued as *A Royal
African*], 1969. 188 pp.
Living in the U.S. for the greater part of his
life, married to an American girl, Modupe,
who was born in French-speaking Guinea,
wrote this autobiographical novel in English.
He narrates his childhood life as a Sousou boy
on the slopes of the Fouta Djalon mountains;
his many adventures from the birth ceremonies and the initiation rites to his eventual
escape from bush life for good. Elspeth
Huxley has contributed a foreword.

Liberia

Corder, S. M. H.
The African Life. A collection of short stories.
Monrovia: Liberian Literary Publ., 1975.
230 pp. $3.50

Dempster, Ronald Tombekai
The Mystic Reformation of Gondolia
London: Dragon Press, 1953. 71 pp. o/p
Subtitled as 'being a satirical treatise on moral
philosophy'.

To Monrovia Old and New
London: Dragon Press, 1958. 13 pp. o/p
A booklet of patriotic verse in praise of
Monrovia, the capital of Liberia.

A Song out of Midnight
London: Dragon Press, 1959. 42 pp. o/p
A volume of verse produced as a souvenir for
the Tubman-Tolbert inauguration on 4 January 1960.

Moore, Bai T.
Ebony Dust
Monrovia: Author, n.d. [1965?] 111 pp.
A verse collection. Its main theme is Africa,
but the author's impressions of America –
where he was educated – Europe, and Asia are
reflected in several other poems.

Murder in the Cassava Patch
Monrovia: Author, 1968 [privately printed;
N. V. Drukkerij Bosch, Holland] 64 pp.
The mutilated body of Tene, the daughter of a
well-known Liberian family from Bendabli, is
discovered in a cassava patch, to the horror of
the entire community. A kind of 'detective'
story from Liberia.

Nigeria

Abdulkadir, 'Dandatti
*The Poetry, Life and Opinions of Sa'adu
Zungur*
Zaria: Northern Nigerian Publishing Co.,
1974. 109 pp. ₦1.55 p/b
A bilingual volume (Hausa-English) of the
verse of the most prominent Hausa poet in the
mid-twentieth century in Northern Nigeria.
The son of an Arabic scholar, Sa'adu was,
himself, educated in the colonial system and
played an important role in post-war nationalist movements in Nigeria. His poetry,
although containing references to Islam, deals
essentially with the political and social themes

of his day. Contains a chapter on Sa'adu
Zungur's life history and a brief bibliography
as well as a critical analysis of individual
poems.

Achebe, Chinua
The Sacrificial Egg, and other stories
Onitsha: Etudo Ltd, 1962, 32 pp. o/p
The five short stories collected in this volume
were written between 1952 and 1960. They are
introduced by Michael Echeruo.

Things Fall Apart
London: Heinemann, 1958. 185 pp. £1.75
cased
London: HEB, 1962 (AWS, 1). 187 pp. £1.25
p/b (also available in Heinemann's New
Windmill Series, 162)
New York: Astor Honor, 1959. 215 pp.
Greenwich, Conn.: Fawcett, 1969 (Premier
Book, T 450). 192 pp. $1.95
The first of Achebe's four novels derives its
title from W. B. Yeats' 'The Second Coming'.
It is set in the eastern part of Nigeria and
revolves around a double tragedy: that of its
hero Okonkwo and that of his village,
Umuofia. Though his entire life was dominated by fear, the fear of failure and weakness,
Okonkwo was 'one of the greatest men of his
time'. Through hard work and determination,
Okonkwo becomes a prosperous and respected member of the Umuofia community, as well
as being considered a great warrior. Though
deep down Okonkwo is not a cruel man, he
nevertheless acts thus with his son and wives.
Afraid of being thought weak, it is his own
machete that delivers the final blow to
Ikemefuna, a child hostage he had reared for
many years until the Oracle had decided he
must die as tradition demanded. This is
followed by his accidentally killing a clansman
of Umuofia. As a result Okonkwo and his
family are banished for seven years, and he
finds refuge in the village of his wife's mother,
Mbanta. During his exile, awaiting the return
to his clan, Okonkwo sees the arrival of the
first Christian missionaries. When he finally
returns to Umuofia, Okonkwo finds that, here
too, the Christians have built churches and
entrenched themselves in his society.
Okonkwo's opposition to them and the
colonial administrators brings him to murder
the white man's court messenger who tries to
stop a meeting of the clan. But he finds himself
alone in this warlike action; the villagers are
too divided to follow his example, and,
completely alienated from his people, he
decides to take his own life.
'Not since Mister Johnson *has a novel about West
Africa written in English shown such love and*

warmth for its subject as this first novel by a young Nigerian author.'   Diana Speed – *Black Orpheus*

'. . . *breaks new ground in Nigerian fiction . . . many books and anthropological treatises have told about the power of religious superstition, but here is one which forcefully but impartially gives us the reasons.'*   Mercedes Mackay – *African Affairs*

No Longer at Ease

London: Heinemann, 1960. 170 pp. £2.10 cased
London: HEB, 1963 (AWS, 3). 176 pp. £1.25 p/b
New York: Astor Honor, 1960. 170 pp.
Greenwich, Conn.: Fawcett, 1969 (Premier Book, T 449). 159 pp. $1.95

Generally regarded as a sequel to Achebe's first novel, *Things Fall Apart*, the central character of *No Longer at Ease* is the grandson of Okonkwo. Obi, having been granted an education in England by the Umuofia Progressive Union, returns to Lagos, where he obtains the prestigious position of Secretary to the government's Scholarship Board. In this new position he sets out with high principles and idealism, but shortly accumulates a series of debts: his loan from the Umuofia Union must be repaid, money is required at home to pay taxes and bills, and he is altogether living too extravagantly to manage prompt payments. Further complicating his life is Obi's love for Clara, a nurse whom he met on his homeward journey to Nigeria. However, Clara is an *osu*, considered an outcast because of her descent from slaves within the Ibo community. The Union and his father alike disapprove of his relationship and his mother threatens to kill herself should her son go ahead and marry this *osu*. As pressures mount, Obi's moral and intellectual opposition to bribery gives way and he succumbs to corruption. The results, ultimately, bring a sad and humilating end to a promising career.

'. . . *the writer has a fine gift for narrative and he never forces an issue or evades a conclusion. He has a flat unemotional style which brings its own reality. His characters are alive, but secondary to the settings which produce them, and these settings explain their actions. I have not yet read a book which brings the Lagos scene so vividly to life, revealing the circumstances which almost automatically lead to corruption.'*   Mercedes Mackay – *African Affairs*

'*Obi Okonkwo, the hero of this novel, is not an unusual type. We all know dozens like him. He is not as unforgettable a character as his grandfather the warrior Okonkwo, the hero of* Things Fall Apart. *But then this new novel is about the new Nigerian middle class, and like most bourgeoisies in the world*

the Nigerian one does not produce particularly colourful and memorable characters. The strength of the novel does not lie in its characterization but in its brilliant description and analysis of situations and conflicts . . . Mr. Achebe has gained a new confidence. He presents Nigerian life as it is – no need to justify or explain it.'
      Omidiji Aragbabalu [pseud. for Ulli Beier] –
                                    Black Orpheus

Arrow of God

London: Heinemann, 1964. 304 pp. £2.90 cased
London: HEB, 1965 (AWS, 16). 296 pp. £1.40
New York: John Day, 1967. 287 pp.
New York: Doubleday, 1969 (Anchor Book, A 698: with an introduction by Kenneth Post) 266 pp. $3.50

Achebe's third novel is set in the Ibo villages of Umuaro in Eastern Nigeria in the nineteen-twenties, a time when colonialism was firmly entrenched. At the centre of the novel is Ezeulu, old and dignified chief priest of Ulu, the traditional God of his Umuaro people. Ezeulu, struggling for power, finds that his authority as spiritual leader is considerably strengthened when a war he has been trying to prevent between his people and a neighbouring community is brought to a halt by a British District Officer, Captain Winterbottom. Though the latter is totally ignorant of tribal customs and beliefs, Ezeulu is greatly impressed by the knowledge and power of the white man. As a result he decides to send his son Oduche to the white man's mission school, to learn the secrets of such strength and 'to be my eyes and ears among the whites'. Ultimately, however, this gives cause for conflict, as the son, now converted to Christianity and over zealous in his freshly acquired new religion, attempts to kill the python of Idemili, the secret animal of traditional religion. After this, Ezeulu turns to oppose the colonial administration of the white man, but his obstinacy and pride bring tragedy in the end.

'. . . *more substantial than either of Achebe's two earlier works – more complex than* Things Fall Apart *and hence lacking the endearing simplicity of that novel. Its great contribution is its shift of emphasis from the clash of Africa with the outside world to the internal tensions of Africa itself, a clash which seems to be absent in much African writing . . . his novel is a human novel. His success in bringing out the general humanity above the Africanness of his themes is what gives him a high place among African writers.'*
      Eldred Jones – *The Journal of Commonwealth Literature*

'. . . *Achebe has done more than depict an African*

society, to determinate a moment of its history . . . this novel is very important. Not only is it the most serious African novel in English up to now; it can also be added to the author's two preceding masterpieces in order to reveal, in striking unity, the personal vision of a lucid artist.' Abiola Irele – *Présence Africaine*

A Man of the People
London: Heinemann, 1966. 166 pp. £3.90 cased
London: HEB, 1966 (AWS, 31). 176 pp. £1.35
New York: John Day, 1966. 167 pp.
New York: Doubleday, 1967 (Anchor Book, A 594: with an introduction by Kenneth Post). 141 pp. $1.95
A satirical farce and *exposé* of a corrupt government and the cult of personality in an African state after four years of independence, once described by Achebe himself as 'a rather serious indictment – if you like – on post-independence Africa'. The novel revolves around the affable Chief, the Honourable M. A. Nanga, and Odili, a former pupil of Nanga's. A 'bush' politician, semi-literate and half-witted, Nanga suddenly finds himself elevated to the new post of Minister of Culture while Odili, a young intellectual, is a member of the country's new elite. Odili, who serves as the narrator of the story, possesses a strong sense of idealism and hopes to create a better way of life for his country's people. However, he is soon introduced to the manipulations of power and fraudulent government; after accepting an invitation to be Nanga's guest in the capital city he himself enjoys the luxurious life lived by senior members of government. In the denouement of the novel, Odili becomes Nanga's political and social rival and his opponent for election as a member of parliament. The story climaxes in a military coup, now reminiscent of the army take-over in Nigeria in January 1966.
'. . . a vivid, free-moving, aggressive, partly impressionistic satirical comedy on contemporary Nigeria . . . the novel beautifully dramatises the multiple conflict |of | the intemperate intellectual idealism of a young college graduate . . . a most enjoyable novel.'
Joseph Okpaku – *Journal of the New African Literature and the Arts*
'. . . does not have the poise of Achebe's earlier novels. It has the necessary stridency of a tract. The fact is that Africa needs this kind of novel at this time as much as Victorian England needed Hard Times. Yet take it out of its immediate environment, retaining the essential message, and its general applicability is frightening.'
Eldred Jones – *The Journal of Commonwealth Literature*

Beware, Soul Brother and Other Poems
London: HEB, 1972. (AWS, 120). 72 pp. £1.95
Enugu, Nigeria: Nwamife, 1973. 68 pp. ₦1.20
New York: Anchor/Doubleday [published as *Christmas in Biafra and Other Poems*], 1973. 92 pp. $5.95 cased $2.50 p/b
Unable to write fiction during the Nigerian Civil War, Achebe turned to poetry as a means of expressing his distress and published a shorter form of this first collection of verse in Nigeria in 1971 with Nwankwo-Ifejika, later re-writing and re-arranging extensively for the second edition. Winner of the 1972 Commonwealth Poetry Prize.
'It is when Achebe writes about the unrecorded, unmourned, private tragedies of ordinary people that he engages our feelings in the fullest measure.'
Ime Ikiddeh – *Présence Africaine*
'Unlike many Nigerian poets who have written on the civil war, Achebe is actively involved in the traumatic events he describes and the strength of his talent lies in his ability to make vivid what he has experienced.'
John Agetua – *New Nigerian*

Girls at War and Other Stories
London: HEB, 1972. (AWS, 100). 128 pp. £1.25
New York: Doubleday 1973. 129 pp. $5.95
Several of the thirteen stories in this collection were written and published as early as twenty years before but others appear here for the first time, including three stories about the Biafran conflict. One of these, the title story, is about a young woman involved in the Biafran war effort whose ideals, and morals, vanish as the war drags on.
'. . . yields valuable insight into the development of the author's narrative stye as well as into the thematic concerns which were later to shape his major works. But this apart, the stories are a delight in their own right.' Ifeanyi A. Menkiti – *Library Journal*

Things Fall Apart
London: Pitman, 1978. 148 pp. £1.75
A Pitman New Era Shorthand Edition of Achebe's classic novel, edited by G. U. F. Ejiogu. Read Achebe and learn shorthand at the same time!

Adebiyi, T. A.
Two Kinds of Love
Lagos: Daystar, 1967. 31 pp. 10k

The Brothers
Ibadan: Fagbamigbe, 1980. 180 pp. ₦2.00
A novel.

Adeniyi, Tola
Soul Fire and Other Poems
Ibadan: Progresso Publishers, 1973. 50 pp.
50k
Twenty-nine poems written between 1967 and
1972. The themes range from politics (China's
admission to the U.N. and the police shooting
of an Ibadan student) to more personal
subjects.

*The Lunatic and Other Features: an epitome of
our golden age*
Lagos: Deto Deni Educational Productions,
1976. 77 pp. ₦1.00
These tongue-in-cheek essays thinly disguised
as pieces of fiction were first published as the
'Aba Saheed Series' in the *Daily Times* (Lagos)
in 1975, and comment on the political events
of the day that led to the downfall of General
Gowon.

Adenle, Tola
Love on the Rebounce
Ibadan: Onibonoje Press, 1979 (ALS, 21).
84 pp. ₦1.80
Spurned by Ife, Debola goes to London to try
and finish her education and gets involved
with Tony, a Nigerian medical student, a
relationship which also ends unhappily. Returning to Nigeria, she and Ife re-discover one
another.

Adetuyi, V.
All is Not Lost
Imo-Ilesha: Ilesanmi Press, 1972. 80k

Adewoye, Sam A.
The Betrayer
London: Macmillan Educ., 1979. 108 pp. 80p
Dishonest lovers always get their just deserts.
Olayemi, the only son of doting parents, is as
vain and unscrupulous as he is handsome.
Girls flock around him but he chooses Bimpe
for a fiancée, only to abandon her when he
goes abroad to study – thanks to her parents'
generous financial aid. His fortunes can only
fall and his maligned sweetheart's rise.

Adedoyin, Kunle
The Rape of Manhood
Hicksville, New York: Exposition Press, 1977.
78 pp. $5.50
A play.

Agbada, J. Obi
No Need to Cry
Ibadan: Fagbamigbe, 1980. 190 pp. ₦1.80
(£1.10)
A novel.

Agunwa, Clement
More than Once
London: Longman, 1967. 220 pp.
New York: Humanities Press, distr. $1.50 p/b
The tragi-comic story of Nweke Nwakor, a
struggling, illiterate businessman in Onitsha –
the book itself is perhaps reminiscent of
Onitsha market literature – who almost
achieves the opulence of his dreams and
ambitions.

Ajuba, Emeka
Mish–Mash and Other Stories
Ibadan: Onibonoje Press, 1978 (ALS, 20).
60 pp. ₦1.00
The title tale in this collection of seven short
stories sets the tone for the others. It is about
a young man desperate for employment who
finally gets a well-paying job as 'farm manager' in what turns out to be a rich man's
private zoo. He almost loses all when the
animals stage a hunger strike!

Aka, S. M. O.
Mid-day Darkness
Ibadan: Onibonoje Press, 1973 (ALS, 4).
136 pp. ₦1.50
Twin brothers choose two different ways of
life. Paul, the scholarly one, goes away to
university to study agriculture, and Peter, the
happy-go-lucky one, into the army, where he
manages to turn the civil war period to his own
personal profit, 'buying back' from his family
the consideration that had always been Paul's
– until the day he is found out.

My Father's Car
Benin City: S. M. O. Aka and Bros. Press,
1976. 68 pp. ₦1.00

College Days of John Ojo
Ibadan: Onibonoje Press, 1978. 116 pp.
₦1.25
Young John leaves for Provincial College of
Teachers amidst a hearty village send-off but
his arrival is more numbing than the cold
water 'baptism' older students reserve for
newcomers. Getting an education is not so
pleasant but the results may be worth it. A
school reader with notes and questions.

Cheer Up, Brother
Benin City, Nigeria: S. M. O. Aka and Bros.
Press, 1979. ₦2.00

Akinyele. J. I.
The Spoilt Child
Imo-Ilesha: Ilesanmi Press, 1972. 76 pp. 80k

Akpan, Ntieyong Udo
The Wooden Gong
London: Longman, 1965. 118 pp. o/p
A novel of changing times set in an Eastern Nigerian village in the middle colonial period. Wise Chief Inam's leadership is beginning to be questioned, not only by the Christian Spiritualists that are gaining ground in the village, but also by the members of the secret Mfina society that traditionally had been the cohesive force in the village. Inam is arrested by the colonizer and accused of condoning the reprehensible activities of the overzealous Spiritualists. He is soon released, but the village goes into decline and the Chief dies mysteriously some time later. It is the end of an era.
'. . . Akpan's story brings in social change, the mushroom of growth of new churches, local custom, the clash with the colonial administration and, guiding everything, the tradition and power of the tribal secret society. At times the story reads rather like a simpler version of Achebe's *Arrow of God but it has its own interest.'*   Edgar Wright – *Transition*

Alily, Valentine
The Mark of the Cobra
London: Macmillan Educ., 1980. 92 pp. 80p
Nigeria's only remaining Special Service Agent, SSA2 Jack Ebony, is pitted against Ca'fra Osiri Ba'ra, alias the Cobra, a multi-millionaire with a sinister plan for controlling the world, thanks to his monopoly of solar weaponry.

Aluko, Timothy Mofolorunso
One Man, One Matchet
London: HEB, 1965 (AWS, 11). 208 pp.
£1.25/$2.50
A story taking place in a cocoa community in Western Nigeria's Yorubaland. It tells of the conflict between a zestful, greenhorn district officer and a 'black whiteman', the un-scrupulous and conceited politician, journalist and agitator Benjamin Benjamin, who stirs up a land dispute between two Yoruba com-munities.
'For another conflict story, full of a clear and objective understanding of the problems of the period, written with marvellous lucidity, and full of humour without irritating belaboured flowery language, I recommend One Man, One Matchet.'
Nunasu Amosu – *Black Orpheus*

Kinsman and Foreman
London: HEB, 1966 (AWS, 32). 208 pp.
£1.25/$3.00
In this novel Titus Oti, a recent engineering graduate from the University of London, returns home to his family in a small town in Western Nigeria to take up a post in the public works department. Here he clashes with his shrewd and corrupt kinsman, the P.W.D. foreman Simeon, who has been with the department for many years, a pillar of society and now head of the family.
'. . . an amusing but penetrating vignette of modern life in a Yoruba village written lightly, in a simple polished style, by one who understands his people well.'   M. N. – *West Africa*
'. . . I strongly recommend this book: it is very eventful and well written with economy of style and a great sense of the ridiculous.'
Anne-Louise Edwards – *The New African*

One Man, One Wife
London: HEB, 1967 (AWS, 30). 208 pp.
£1.25/$3.00
The title is only one of the themes alluded to in Aluko's first novel which was first published in Lagos in 1959 by Nigerian Printing and Publishing Co. The book offers a satirical study of, among other things, Christian practices in a Yoruba village in late colonial times. The characters include Teacher Royasin, the catechist who is disgraced for sexual dallying and who goes on to set up a thriving business as a public letter writer, and old Joshua, one of the pillars of the church until he announces his intention to take on a second wife, young Toro. Joshua dies, struck by thunder, the night he renounces Christianity before the elders – the revenge of Shango, it is said, for his having led the life of a thief, unknown to the others. Toro refuses being 'inherited' by Joshua's son Jacob and Jacob sues her poor mother to recover the bride price. In the end, however, he receives a divine revelation and becomes a prophet, declaring young ladies shall henceforth choose their own husbands.

Chief the Honourable Minister
London: HEB, 1970 (AWS, 70). 160 pp.
£1.75/$4.50
A satirical study of a schoolmaster turned politician. Alade Moses, a brilliant educator, is elected to parliament and appointed Minister of Works without being consulted. He has serious misgivings but attacks the job with high hopes. Forced to toe the party line he is gradually worn down by political expediency and two bitter court cases, which he loses, initiated by the opposition. The novel ends with a military take over and Moses is killed in flight.
'. . . Aluko presents a foreboding view of the future of democratic nationalism in the Third World.'
Molly McIntosh – *Books Abroad*

His Worshipful Majesty

London: HEB, 1973. (AWS, 130). 192 pp.
£1.75/$4.00

With the introduction of local government reforms, the Oba of Aiye, is henceforth to have an advisory council, chaired by Barrister Morrison. The old monarch, however, continues to behave in the autocratic ways of his predecessors and clashes with Morrison are inevitable – until Morrison dies under mysterious circumstances and the Oba sends off a letter to the King of England asking for the Governor and the Resident to be recalled. In doing so the aged monarch signs his own warrant of destruction.

'Though the work as a whole may not be a finely wrought novel, Aluko has again shown himself to be a master of hyperbole and an important chronicler of the cultural changes in West Africa that were brought about by European colonialism.'

Richard Priebe – *Books Abroad*

Amali, Samson O. O.

Selected Poems

Ibadan: Univ. Bookshop Nigeria Ltd. distr., 1968. 129 pp.

Worlds Within Worlds and Other Poems

Ibadan: Univ. Bookshop Nigeria Ltd. distr., 1970. 49 pp.

God Poems

Ibadan: Univ. Bookshop Nigeria Ltd. distr., 1970. 25 pp.

Poems. A Conversation

Ibadan: Univ. Bookshop Nigeria Ltd. distr., 1971. 11 pp. 50k p/b

The Leaders

Ibadan: Institute of African Studies, Univ. of Ibadan, 1972 (Occasional publication, 30). 123 pp. ₦1.00 p/b

A bi-lingual play in Idoma and English.

Onugbo Mloko: a play

(Trans. by R.G. Armstrong and Samson O.O. Amali)

Ibadan: Institute of African Studies, Univ. of Ibadan, 1972 (Bi-lingual literary works, 3). 64 pp. ₦1.15 cased 55k p/b

A play based on a traditional Idoma ancestral story which Amali recorded at Otukpo and later creatively rewrote in Idoma. It tells of the tragic rivalry of two brothers, Onugbo and Oko. Onugbo had promised his dying father to look after his younger brother, but one day in a fit of jealous anger he takes Oko's life because he had become the greater hunter of the two.

Amadi, Elechi

The Concubine

London: HEB, 1966 (AWS, 25). 288 pp.
£1.25/$3.00

The fatal loves of a woman in an Eastern Nigerian village. Its heroine, the remarkable widow Ihuoma, is a virtuous, beautiful, gentle, near-perfect woman, respected by the entire village community, but one who brings suffering and death to men who court her.

' . . . by any account it is a most accomplished first performance . . . Amadi's style is lucid, unpretentious and direct. He writes with the ease and assurance of a man who enjoys writing. It is difficult to find flaws in this small masterpiece.'

Eustace Palmer – *African Literature Today*

The Great Ponds

London: HEB, 1969 (AWS, 44). 224 pp. £1.25
New York: John Day Co., 1969. 217 pp. $6.95

A battle between two village groups in Eastern Nigeria waged over the ownership and fishing rights of the pond of Wagaba, provides the focus of this novel.

'Elechi Amadi's achievement [is] . . . that he depicts the naïvety and superstition of a simple community without making the community in any way look . ridiculous.' Davis Sebukima – *Mawazo*

Sunset in Biafra

London: HEB, 1973 (AWS, 140). 192 pp.
£1.50/$4.00

The civil war diary of a man who was caught in the cross-fire of Biafran and Federal troops. A career officer in the Nigerian army, Amadi had resigned his commission just before the outbreak of the war and returned home to the Rivers area of the Niger Delta, an Ikwere enclave in Iboland. He was imprisoned for a time by Biafran forces but managed to pass through the Federal lines.

'To read Amadi's Sunset in Biafra *is to be in Biafra: witnessing the wanton rape of women detainees; rank corruption in all its sordid nakedness; surviving on two fistfuls of gari a day; stalked by death from all directions. . . . Above all, it is to read a master of prose at his magnificent best.'*

Dan Agbese – *Sunday Times* (Lagos)

' . . . a fascinating personal account of Amadi's life during the Biafran War.'

Charles Larson – *Books Abroad*

Peppersoup and The Road to Ibadan

Ibadan: Onibonoje Press, 1977. 76 pp.
₦1.50

Amadi's first two published plays. *Peppersoup*, which was first staged in 1974, is a light comedy about a jobless musician's dilemma in choosing between his Nigerian and his English girlfriend. *The Road to Ibadan* has a much graver tone. It tells of the growing love between a Federal army captain and a refugee, a student nurse, in a battle-front setting during the civil war.

The Slave
London: HEB, 1978 (AWS, 210). 160 pp.
£1.25/$3.00
Is Olumati, like his father, an *osu* (a slave of the god Amadioha), and hence a social outcast? In allowing the young man to return to his ancestral village to rebuild his father's compound, the elders of Eliji appear to have no doubts about his real status. But Olumati will have to contend with a more subtle and much greater force: the hostility of a local family who reactivate an old land dispute and the refusal of a beautiful young girl to marry him. In the end he admits defeat and returns to the shrine where he had spent his earlier years.

Dancer of Johannesburg
Ibadan: Onibonoje Press, 1978 (ALS, 19).
46 pp.   ₦1.00
The central characters of Amadi's most recent play are Bello, a Nigerian diplomat on the eve of posting, and Matiya, a black South African dancer working in a night club in Port Harcourt with whom Bello has fallen in love – until he learns that she is a spy for the racist regime. And what is the real identity of the undercover agent for the African High Command Intelligence Service whose daring plan brings about the fall of Johannesburg?

Anametemfiok, Emman T.

Sunset Smiles
Calabar, Nigeria: Scholars Press, 1980.
102 pp.   ₦1.50 p/b
Poetry in five parts: 'Listening to Incense', 'Desires', 'Oak Rains', 'Sunlight Shards', and 'Dusk Harvestide'. This volume was written while the author was in his final year in the English and Literary Studies Department at the University of Calabar. He is the founding editor of *Drumbeats* magazine and also co-edits the *Obodom Review*.

Aniebo, I. N. C.

The Anonymity of Sacrifice
London: HEB, 1974 (AWS, 148), 144 pp.
£1.60/$2.50
Two Biafran soldiers, British-trained Captain Onwura and his subordinate, Sergeant Agumo, are in theory fighting the same battle – the strategic defence of Awka between Enugu and Onitsha. The real combat, however, is in the intense rivalry that separates Onwura, the careful analyst, from Agumo, a man of action.

The ironies of war turn Agumo into a hero overnight and his ambition and desire for greatness take over and lead him to commit a fateful deed.
' . . . *a tight, dramatic story, tautly told . . . the moral earnestness of the author is as admirable as it is clear'.*
                         Peter Thomas – *Books Abroad*
'*The novel can be classified as an anti-war novel but it is more about human nature than about war. The war only provides the setting for the dramatic enactment of passions that be deep in man.'*
                         Kirpal Singh – *Dhana*

The Journey Within
London: HEB, 1978 (AWS, 206) 256 pp.
£1.95/$5.00
The marital 'ordeals' of two couples in pre-World War 'II Port Harcourt: Nelson and Ejiaka, the more traditional couple whose marriage endures despite Nelson's affair with a local barkeeper; and Christian and Janet, the urbanized, educated couple whose marriage fails. 'Marriage', says Janet, 'is a battle of the sexes'.

Anyasodo, Umunnakwe P.

Ebolachi: Have You Survived the Night?
Detroit: Harlo Press, 1975. 168 pp. o/p

Archibong, Francis M.

Pain of Exile
Calabar, Nigeria: Scholars Press, 1980. 51 pp.
₦1.75
A volume of verse.

Areo, Agbo

The Director
London: Macmillan Educ., 1977. 128 pp. 80p
How can a driver's apprentice who was expelled from high school turn into the managing director of a vast Ibadan business concern? It takes no small share of ambition and unscrupulousness, neither of which young Akinduro lacks. The law, however, eventually catches up with him.

The Hopeful Lovers
London: Macmillan Educ., 1979. 132 pp. 80p
Beautiful, serious-minded Roseline Momoh knows her university studies will go smoother if the task of husband-hunting could be completed rapidly. By luck she attracts the attention of Tade Eji, a young medical student, and the couple become engaged. Tade sees no reason, however, to dismiss his other girl-friends. His weakness for women leads him astray when he completes his medical degree

and is sent to a hospital in the north – and Roseline's fond hopes are dashed to the ground.

Are, Lekan
Always a Loser
New York: Vantage Press, 1976. 132 pp. $6.95

Balewa, Alhaji Sir Abubakar Tafawa
Shaihu Umar
(Trans. from the Hausa by Mervin Hiskett)
London: Longman, 1968. 80 pp.
A novel by the first Federal Prime Minister of Nigeria, who was killed during the military coup of January, 1966. The book tells the story of a distinguished teacher, Shaihu Umar, and is a portrayal of a Hausa family in an Islamic society. It is set at the end of the last century, at a time when civil war and slave-trading plagued the country. A short introduction to the novel is provided by the translator.

Begho, Mason Amatotsero
The Trio: Peter, Edema and Oni
Lagos: Daily Times Publ., n.d. [1973] 82 pp.
Three boys born a day apart in the early twenties to families of different faiths (Christian, Animist, Muslim) in Mid-Western Nigeria grow up and are educated together.

Bennett, Bob
The Deep End of the Night
Lagos: Third World First Publ., 1978. ₦1.00
Poetry on the theme of black self-denigration.

Besong, Bate
Polyphemus Detainee and Other Skulls
Calabar, Nigeria: Scholars Press, 1980. 44 pp.
₦1.20
A collection of verse that draws inspiration from a number of sources ranging from the topical to the mythical. Besong, who recently graduated with honours in English from the University of Calabar, counts T. S. Eliot, Christopher Okigbo, and Wole Soyinka as his poetic mentors. Ime Ikiddeh has written an introduction for this volume.

Boyo, T. O.
Somolu Blues
Ibadan: Fagbamigbe, 1981. 190 pp. ₦1.80
A novel.

Chinweizu
Energy Crisis and Other Poems
New York: Nok Publ., 1978. 68 pp. $6.95
cased $2.95 p/b

A collection of satirical verse. In his preface the author offers 'apologies . . . for contaminating [his] poems with allusions to such coarse and disreputable affairs as peace, reason, love, fidelity, democracy, statesmanship.'

Clark, John Pepper
Poems
Ibadan: Mbari, 1962. 51 pp. o/p
' . . . *poetry that makes heavy reading, but which is moving because it is always nourished by immediate experience and because the author's harassed, tormented and irrepressible personality is present in every line.'* Ulli Beier – *Black Orpheus*

Song of a Goat
Ibadan: Mbari, 1962. 43 pp. o/p
A play.

America, their America
London: Deutsch, 1964. 221 pp. o/p
London: HEB 1969 (AWS, 50). 224 pp. £1.95
New York: Africana Publ. Corp. 1969. 224 pp.
A sharp indictment of the sins of American society against John Pepper Clark, who spent the academic year 1962-3 as a Parvin Fellow at Princeton University.
' . . . *the strength lies in the message. Clark disagrees with the values of American society – the brazen capitalism, the exploitation of the Negroes, the power of the all-conquering dollar that forces a playwright to mutilate his plays to get financial backing . . . the Negro is not spared either. The Afro-American who has suddenly discovered his Africanness and goes for the ostentatious displays of African masks, imitations or originals, is called to order.'*
A. Bolaji Akinyemi – *West Africa*

Three Plays
London and New York: OUP, 1964 (Three Crowns Books). 134 pp. 95p/$1.35
Three verse plays: *Song of a Goat* (previously published separately by Mbari; *The Masquerade*: and *The Raft* – its characters, four lumbermen adrift on the river Niger.

A Reed in the Tide
London: Longman, 1965. 64 pp. 70p
A collection of thirty-three poems. Clark says in a personal note 'on the poet presenting himself': 'For me, the feeling is not unlike that of undergoing surgery – and surgery at my own hands too! What to cut, and what to save out of a body of poems that has come to represent more or less part of my own self, will always remain with me an unsettled issue.'

Ozidi
London and New York: OUP, 1966. 128 pp.
£1.25/$1.15
Taking place in the Ijo region of Nigeria, this
play is based on the Ijo saga of Ozidi, which
used to be told in seven days to dance, music
and mime. The myth – here recreated by Clark
– tells the tale of a posthumous son, Ozidi,
born and raised to avenge his father's murder,
and killed in a war by his own comrades.
*'Clark has remained true to his source and set down
for a much wider audience a most remarkable
dramatic experience . . . has offered to the theatre one
of the most fascinating works to have been created in
Nigeria in recent years.'*
Martin Banham – *Journal of Commonwealth
Literature*

Casualties: poems 1966/68
London, Longman, 1970. 62 pp.
New York, Africana Publ. Corp., 1970.
62 pp.$6.50 cased $4.95 p/b
London: Longman (2nd ed.), 1979. 72 pp. 80p
p/b
A collection of verse from the 1966–68 period,
largely concerned with the Nigerian Civil War.
It is a lament for the casualties, living and
dead, of a war that bewildered the world.
'Of the poetry written during the war, J. P. Clark's
Casualties *is among the most substantial volumes.
Clark was safely outside the war area, but his poetry
shows he was not emotionally out of it'.*
Ime Ikkiddeh – *Présence Africaine*
*'The poetry of John Pepper Clark . . . has greatly
matured; his style and use of language have grown
simpler and more effective. The casualties . . . are not
only the killers and the men they killed . . . we are all
casualties.'*   Louis Barron – *Library Journal*

Clark, John Pepper ed. and trans.
The Ozidi Saga
Ibadan: Ibadan Univ. Press in association with
OUP, 1977. 408 pp. ₦16.00 cased ₦14.00
p/b
This is the result of a fifteen-year undertaking
to record the epic tale of the Ijo people of the
Niger River delta. The original version which
has been edited down into book length,
normally takes seven full days to perform.
Clark provides an 'Introductory essay' which
explains how he chose this version over the
different ones available and tells the story of
his and his collaborators' long years of
collecting, filming and recording in addition
to providing complete background material
on the epic itself. In bi-lingual text (Ijo-
English).
'The value and interest of this book reside in the first

*place in the importance of the text now made
available . . . But the significance of Clark's presentation . . . derives essentially from his translation . . . This is certainly a poet's translation.'*
Abiola Irele – *The African Book Publishing Record*
*' . . . I am little interested in . . . "tribal" scholar-
ship. These strident efforts to establish appropriate
African equivalents to European cultural forms seem
to me to spring from an unconscious racial inferiority
in many of our compatriots. In place of that tedious
thesis, Clark here provides empirical proof and his is
a labour of love. Thus, the thing to emphasize here is
not its "ethnic imperative" but its accomplishment as
art.'*   Femi Osofisan – *Positive Review*

A Decade of Tongues
London: Longman, 1981. 104 pp. £1.75
The poet, himself, made the selection of the
verse in this anthology, most of which was
written in the period 1958–1968 and previously published in the Mbari edition of *Poems*,
long out-of-print, and in *A Reed in the Tide* and
Casualties. Some earlier and later work are also
included, however.

Dada, Olubandele
Poems of Penetration
New York: Vantage Press, 1971. 93 pp. o/p

Dina, Ishola O.
Sango Would Thunder Them
Calabar, Nigeria: Scholars Press, 1980. 56 pp.
₦1.50   p/b
The first book of verse of a recent graduate in
English of the University of Calabar. His
poems have appeared in several publications
in Nigeria and he co-edits *Drumbeats*, a literary
journal, and *Obodom Review*.

Echoes of Blood Tears
Calabar, Nigeria: Scholars Press, 1980. 72 pp.
₦1.50
A second volume of poetry.

Echebima, Godson N.
Two African Plays: No Time for Love and *A
Piece of Kolanut*
Ijesu-Ode, Nigeria: Kola-Sanya, 1977. 57 pp.
₦1.00   (£1.50)

Echeruo, Michael J. C.
Mortality
London: Longman, 1968. 66 pp.
A volume of poetry.
'It is refreshing to encounter a new poet with as firm

a sense of his own possibilities as Michael Echeruo. His gifts are for relaxed irony and the more concentrated expression of his own identity in opposition to a sordid generation . . . he displays most clearly the influence of the late Christopher Okigbo.'

Gerald Moore – The Conch

Echewa, T. Obinkaram

The Land's Lord
London: HEB, 1976 (AWS, 168). 160 pp.
£1.95
New York: Hill and Co., 1976. 145 pp. $6.50 cased

A philosophical novel set in colonial Nigeria and centred around three characters: Father Higler, a Catholic priest full of self doubt, Philip, his cook-steward, and Ahamba, a fetish priest. Winner of the 1976 English-Speaking Union Prize.

'Echewa's use of language is always fresh and often nothing short of spectacular . . . an outstanding first novel . . . a profound philosophical dialogue between paganism and Christianity and, by extension, between Africa and the West.'

Charles Larson – *World Literature Today*

Egbe, R. N.

The Orphan Child and Other Stories
Ibadan: Onibonoje Press, 1978. 49 pp.
₦1.50

Six stories for the classroom with suggested questions and activities and a glossary of difficult English words.

Egbuna, Obi B.

The Anthill
London and New York: OUP, 1965 (Three Crowns Books). 60 pp. 75p

Only the apex of an anthill can be seen above the ground: its foundations lie several layers deeper. The plot of this play is built to the same plan. It centres on an African art student with an obsession for painting anthills, his English friend and their Cockney landlady.

Elina
London: Faber, 1964 [publ. as *Wind Versus Polygamy*] 128 pp. o/p
Glasgow: Fontana/Collins, 1980 (2nd ed.). 126 pp. 95p

This is Egbuna's first novel which was originally published by Faber in 1964 under the title *Wind Versus Polygamy*. In a 'little village in the heart of New Africa' beautiful young Elina is being pressured to choose between two equally unacceptable suitors – a villainous old hunter and a rich Councillor. The Paramount Chief, a traditional ruler but a modern thinker, intervenes and wisely settles the matter in a surprise ending which finds the Chief in a courtroom being tried, retroactively, for violating the new law against polygamy. The author has also written a version for the stage and for radio.

' . . . entertains immensely . . . Mr Egbuna has written a remarkable novel.'

Mbella Sonne Dipoko – *Présence Africaine*

Daughters of the Sun and Other Stories
London: OUP, 1970. 106 pp. 60p

Four short stories set in contemporary Africa: an elderly catechist challenges the power of the village 'Divinity' with terrible results; a right-wing white settler clashes with a Black Power leader; an American medical student discovers that a 'witch doctor' has powers greater than his own; the title story, however, evokes the Africa of legend.

' . . . engrossing, compulsive reading . . . expertly told and the narrator takes an obvious relish in capturing that strangely elusive but persuasive power which Africa possesses.' N. R. – *West Africa*

Emperor of the Sea and Other Stories
Glasgow: Fontana/Collins, 1974. 127 pp. 95p

Contains three stories – the title story which has a traditional cast; 'Rivers Can't Speak' about a young man who is tricked by an old man with nine wives, and 'Some Come Home' about an Afro-American who pricks the political conscience of some African oil workers.

'This is one of the best collections of short stories by an individual African writer to come along in some time.'

Charles Larson – *Books Abroad*

'Egbuna's prose and narrative style is gripping and refreshing, enhanced by the sureness with which he uses the English language.' – *Afriscope*

The Minister's Daughter
Glasgow: Fontana/Collins, 1975. 96 pp. 95p

As the minister relaxes in his luxurious heavily-guarded residence in the company of his white mistress a poor, young student dares to disturb his peace to request the scholarship he needs to continue his education. Treated violently by the minister the young man is befriended by his daughter, the lovely intelligent Nneka. Meanwhile, a plot is being hatched to overthrow the corrupt, self-interested regime which the minister represents. All the events take place in the course of one sultry tropical afternoon.

Diary of a Homeless Prodigal
Enugu, Nigeria: Fourth Dimension Publ. Co.,
1978. 128 pp. ₦2.50
Egbuna's *Diary* is the record of a man who
returns home to Nigeria only to find himself
an exile in his own country. The first half of
the book deals with his own sensations on
homecoming; the second treats his recollections of the past and his attempt to define
himself. The *Diary* forms an extended analysis
of Black and White relationships, taking up
where a previous non-fiction work, *Destroy This
Temple*, ends. It includes a biographical sketch
and an introduction by R.W. Sander.

*The Rape of Lysistrata and Black Candle for
Christmas*
Enugu, Nigeria: Fourth Dimension Publ. Co.,
1980. 180 pp. ₦2.50
Short stories that touch on the human
condition of love, hate, passion, and prejudice.

The Madness of Didi
Glasgow: Fontana/Collins, 1980. 224 pp.
£1.35
When Dr Francis Didi, a former priest and
college professor, walks into his village in
Eastern Nigeria, inhabitants think they are
seeing a ghost. Had he not died in Britain
thirty years previously? He is an enigmatic
man with a mysterious past who stirs everyone's passions. Men like Chief Ndumezay and
the members of the Board of the college where
he teaches consider him a dangerous subversive but to his students he is a hero. No one
will ever be the same after his short, tragic stay,
and least of all young Obi, for whom he has
become 'Uncle Didi' and the girl, Nkechi, who
harbours a secret, herself.

Egudu, Romanus
Spine of Darkness
New York: Nok Publ. 1980. 62 pp. $6.95 cased
$3.95 p/b

Ekwensi, Cyprian
When Love Whispers
Yaba, Nigeria: Chuks, 1947. 44 pp. o/p
This short novel recounts various mishaps to
Ashoka, a young lady in distress.

People of the City
London: Dakers, 1954. 237 pp. o/p
London: HEB 1963 (AWS, 5). 156 pp. £1.35
Evanston: Northwestern Univ. Press, 1967.
156 pp. o/p
Greenwich: Conn., Fawcett, 1969 (Premier
Book, T 454). 207 pp. 75c
City life in Lagos today as viewed through the
eyes of a young crime reporter and dance-

band leader, with the action of the book
centring round the three women in his life. It
is a social commentary, in which Ekwensi
portrays the many problems – corruption,
bribery and depotism – that face a large and
overcrowded West African city. Simultaneously, the novel also represents an attack
on the government, the politicians and the
landlords.
'. . . *Posterity will thank Tutuola for recording a
phase of West African life before it disappears for
ever. Judgement may be harsher on Mr Ekwensi in
the final analysis, but now, in this day and age, he
has something important to contribute . . . This is the
first time that we have seen life in the Big City from
the West African point of view . . . no European
could have quite the same spontaneous affection for
the warm teeming mass of humanity spilling out into
the city streets.'* Elizabeth Bevan – *Black Orpheus*

Jagua Nana
London: Hutchinson, 1961. 192 pp. o/p
London: Panther Books, 1963. 144 pp.
Greenwich: Conn., Fawcett, 1969 (Premier
Book, T 455). 159 pp.
London: HEB, 1975 (AWS, 146). 192 pp.
£1.25/$4.00
Chronicles life in the city of Lagos – its night-
clubs with their high-life music, its bars, its
political intrigue. The heroine is Jagua Nana,
described as 'an ageing African beauty'. Jagua
is a former market woman from Onitsha, but
now of independent means. She is a shrewd
and colourful prostitute who, despite her
advancing age, manages to hold her own
against her younger rivals.
'. . . *conveys an excellent picture of Lagos . . . Jagua
is a magnificent woman. She may be a harlot, but she
is also an impressive woman full of warmth and
charm . . . The ending rings false, but it should not
blind us to the considerable talent of the author. This
book is infinitely more successful than* People of the
City.'   Ulli Beier – *Black Orpheus*

Burning Grass
London: HEB, 1962 (AWS, 2). 160 pp.
95p/$2.50
A story of the Fulani, a nomadic tribe in
Northern Nigeria. When the grass is burnt on
the plains, the cattlemen move south towards
the banks of the Niger. An old man, Mai
Sunsaye is afflicted with 'sokugo', the wandering sickness, and his experiences involve him
with those of the herdsmen.

Yaba Roundabout Murder
Lagos: Tortoise Series book [?], 1962. 55 pp.
o/p
A detective story that tells how a smart
inspector of police catches ,a murderer by

pretending to make advances to the murderer's wife.

Beautiful Feathers

London: Hutchinson, 1963. 159 pp. o/p.
London: HEB, 1970 (AWS, 84). 159 pp.
£1.50/$3.00

Ekwensi's fourth major novel, again set in Lagos, concerns Wilson Iyari, a young druggist, married and the father of three children. He attempts to found a political party – the Nigerian Movement for African and Malagasy Solidarity – to assert a desire for Pan-Africanism. Iyari is a successful man in politics, renowned throughout the city and popular with the girls, but his marriage is a failure.

'. . . *an excellent document on the Nigeria of today; one can compare it with the famous* Mister Johnson *by Joyce Cary.*' Michel Ligny – *Présence Africaine*

Iska

London: Hutchinson, 1966. 222 pp. o/p
London: Panther Books, 1968. 208 pp.

The heroine of this novel is Filia Enu, a beautiful Ibo girl brought up in Northern Nigeria whose short marriage to a Hausa civil servant (which she rushed into over the objections of both families) comes to an end when he is killed in a Hausa-Ibo brawl. Filia goes to Lagos and becomes a successful model and through her acquaintance with politicians and journalists begins learning the sad reality of politics in Nigeria of the mid-sixties. She dies mysteriously after a three-day disappearance, seemingly the victim of political thugs. The end is tragic, but her life and her example inspire her fiancé, a journalist, to abandon his cynical attitude towards public affairs.

Lokotown and other stories

London: HEB, 1966 (AWS, 19). 160 pp.
£1.50/$4.00

These nine short stories reflect the glitter, bustle, gaiety and seediness of Nigerian city life.

Restless City and Christmas Gold: with other stories

London: HEB, 1975 (AWS, 172). 112 pp.
£1.50/$4.00

The fifteen stories in this collection cover the time span from pre-independent Africa of the fifties through the era of independence (see 'Height of Freedom') and on to the present day in which human resources of the highest level are practically indispensible to development (see 'The Indispensible'). Several of these stories deal with the tragic, commercial and spiritual aspects of Christmas in West African cities and others contain the genesis of later novels and novellas. The lead story 'Restless City' comes from the manuscript of an unpublished novel.

'*Lagos oppresses the reader with its greed and violence . . . but this picture of the Devil's taking the hindmost is somehow excused by the Xmas tales, whose touch is as light and gentle as the Lagos days are harsh and brutal.*' H. P-J. – *West Africa*

Survive the Peace

London: HEB, 1976 (AWS, 185). 192 pp.
£1.60/$4.00

James Odugo, radio-journalist for Biafra, , survives the war, including several harrowing evacuations, only to be killed in the aftermath by armed robbers masquerading as soldiers and just as his fiancée is about to give birth to their child. Much of the novel is devoted to vignettes of the many forms of 'survival' Biafrans resorted to: the 'attack traders' and profiteers of all sorts, the flight of refugees, the resourcefulness of young wives who do not hesitate to take up with Federal soldiers in exchange for food and money.

'. . . *the odyssey of James Odugo's struggle to stay alive and to do his duty to family and friend., through the lawless chaos that inevitably follows a fratricidal war, is far more than a carefully paced and emotionally involving adventure story.*'
Jeremy Brooks – *The Sunday Times*
'*Within a simple and spare framework, Ekwensi has crammed a tremendous amount of information concerning the situation in the immediate period following the Biafran collapse.*'
Juliette I. Okonkwo – *Okike*

Divided We Stand

Enugu, Nigeria: Fourth Dimension Publ. Co., 1980. 234 pp ₦2.75

Set during the Nigerian Civil War years, Ekwensi's latest novel was written during the heat of the battle and kept for eleven years before being published. It traces the sufferings of the Chika family who return to Iboland from Northern Nigeria, comprising Pa Chika who would not be torn away from his roots, Ma Chika who single-handedly captures an armed Nigerian soldier, Issac Chika, correspondent of the Consolidated Press Agency, and his sister Selina of the Red Cross, who had once been in love with the formidable Nigerian soldier, Garuba Zaria, whose Operation Vietnam is launched to capture 'the Igbo heartland'.

Ekwuru, Andrew

Songs of Steel
London: Rex Collings, 1979. 160 pp. £4.95
cased
Walton-on-Thames: Nelson 1980. 160 pp.
£1.25 p/b
Ekwuru's novel of Abigail, a young mother of
three, widowed early in the Biafran war, is a
tale of the day-to-day lives of people caught up
in a devasating war that levels homes, shatters
families and sends survivors fleeing. But the
war has its paradoxes, too, straining certain
human relationships and reinforcing others.
Even the concept of 'enemy' is not a simplistic
one – as shown by scenes of enemy troops
fraternizing on the front lines. Abigail returns
home at the end of the war, having lost her
mother and her children, one by one, and
feeling certain that 'although the fighting was
over, the conflict still remains.'
'In this powerful novel, Andrew Ekwuru manages to
move us, both intellectually and emotionally, and does
it with simplicity.'   Edgar White – *Africa*

Going to Storm
Walton-on-Thames: Nelson, 1980. 148 pp.
£1.25
Ekwuru has completely changed his style and
theme in this second novel. It is written in
pidgin and paints a picture of low life in an
Eastern Nigerian town. The hero is Samson
Dike, a former policeman, who has become a
cloth merchant. In a world of deceit and
bribery, this handsome man stands out above
the others for his good sense and strong moral
fibre – which, however, does not always
include faithfulness to his good wife, Matilda!

Emecheta, Buchi

In the Ditch
London: Barrie and Jenkins, 1972. o/p
London: Allison and Busby, 1979 (2nd rev.
ed.). 128 pp. £4.95 cased, £1.95 p/b
Buchi Emecheta's first novel, autobiographical
in nature, recounts the struggles of Adah, a
Nigerian mother of five who is separated from
her husband, to raise her children in the slums
of North London while continuing work on a
degree in sociology. The 'Ditch' is the name
she and her neighbours give to the smelly run-
down council-house estate where the welfare
services have, at last, consented to re-locate her
and her children.
'. . . Miss Emecheta makes her characters live; but
her talent lies in her descriptions of hopelessness and
in her ability to convey the similarities and differences
between the culture and outlook of her white
neighbours and herself.'   D. W. – *West Africa*

Second-Class Citizen
London. Allison and Busby, 1974. 174 pp.
£5.95 cased
New York: George Braziller, 1975. 175 pp.
$6.95
Glasgow: Fontana/Collins, 1977. 192 pp. 75p
p/b
Emecheta continues Adah's story, here going
back in time to tell of her upbringing and early
education in Lagos as the daughter of poor
parents, her marriage to Francis and the birth
of her first two children, the family's move to
England where Francis becomes a student and
begins to show his true nature – that of a
brutish, lazy man who puts his wife to work,
enjoys humiliating her – and keeps her
pregnant. Slowly, painfully Adah discovers her
condition as second-class citizen, that of a
woman *and* a Black, and makes the courageous
decision to leave her husband and raise her
children alone.
' . . . harrowing in its piercing observations of Ibo
male attitudes and of English treatment of black
immigrants.'   D. Nelson – *West Africa*
' . . . this unpretentious, shocking, but splendidly
undepressing story.'
     Marigold Johnson – *Times Literary Supplement*

The Bride Price
London: Allison and Busby, 1976. 168 pp.
£5.95 cased
New York: George Braziller, 1976. 168 pp
$6.95
Glasgow: Fontana/Collins, 1978. 168 pp. 75p
p/b
Emecheta's third novel is her first one to have
a Nigerian setting – the Ibo town of Ibuza in
the early fifties. Aku-nna, its young heroine,
elopes with the schoolteacher (a member of a
slave caste) her uncle had refused to let her
marry and dies in childbirth. The tragic ending
is seen as the unavoidable consequence of her
bride price not having been paid. Winner of
the 1978 *New Statesman* Jock Campbell Award
for this and the previous novel.
'Throughout the novel, the author exhibits a great
sense of control over the story and its elements, giving
the reader a sharp picture of the place of the woman
in Ibo society of the time.'
     Kenneth Cripwell – *The Times Educational*
                              Supplement
' . . . a compelling and most moving novel.'
     Peter Tinniswood – *The Times*

The Slave Girl
London: Allison and Busby, 1977. 179 pp.
£5.95 cased
New York: George Braziller, 1977. 179 pp.
$7.95
Glasgow: Fontana/Collins, 1979. 190 pp. 75p
p/b

Beloved and pampered Ojebeta, her parents' only surviving daughter, is suddenly orphaned at the age of seven and sold to distant relatives, the Palagadas, by her older brother. She spends the next nine years as a virtual slave, knowing few joys and little affection, only returning home to Ibuza when 'Ma' Palagada dies. Marriage and a new 'master' – a husband – await her, but she will have the pleasure at age 35 of watching her husband return the price originally paid for her and of becoming a 'free' woman.
'Buchi Emecheta tells the distressing story with lucidity and restraint, and gets wonderfully well into the young mind of Ojebeta . . . a touchingly simple book, unsentimental and yet not afraid to record feeling.' M. Seymour-Smith – *Financial Times*
' . . . coherent, compact and convincing.'
Anita Kern – *World Literature Today*

The Joys of Motherhood
London: Allison and Busby, 1979. 224 pp.
£5.95 cased
London: HEB, 1980 (AWS, 227) 224 pp. £1.75
Nnu Ego, a chief's daughter from Ibuzu, finds herself in Lagos one day married to a most unlikely husband, an ugly, white-man's domestic servant, after a first childless village marriage. She will finally know the 'joys' of motherhood, giving birth over the years to nine children (seven survive), but it is a tale of hardship in a hostile urban environment and the title is, in fact, ironic. Nnu Ego spends long years raising the children alone when her husband is drafted during World War II and she must endure the presence of a second wife, a 'bad' woman, when he returns. She dies a lonely death, unattended by her children, two of whom she had struggled to send abroad to study. But what a magnificent funeral she will have!
'Buchi Emecheta has a way of making readable and interesting ordinary events. She looks at things without flinching and without feeling the need to distort or exaggerate. It is a remarkable talent . . . This is, in my opinion, the best novel Buchi Emecheta has yet written.' K.M. – *West Africa*
'Buchi Emecheta has a growing reputation for her treatment of African women and their problems. This reputation will surely be enhanced by The Joys of Motherhood.' A. N. Wilson – *The Observer*

Destination Biafra
London: Allison and Busby, forthcoming 1981.
A fictionalized story based on the Nigerian Civil War.

Naira Power
London: Macmillan, forthcoming 1981.
A fast-moving novel about contemporary Nigeria.

Double Yoke
London: Ogwugwu Afor (7 Briston Grove, London N8 9DX), forthcoming 1981.
Buchi Emecheta's latest novel to be published under her own imprint. It recounts the story of Nko, a Nigerian-born undergraduate and her boyfriend Ete Kamba, who are faced with the double yoke of tradition, and that of modernity.

Enahoro, Peter
You Gotta Cry to Laugh!
Cologne: Aquarius Books, 1972. 159 pp. £1.25
A series of tongue-in-cheek essays in which the author explores such subjects as 'Discovering Your Race' ('If you hear a voice whispering to you, "We Shall Overcome" . . . you know you belong to the black race'), 'Black God-White God' ('the Black God lacks credibility, he should have commissioned a ghostwriter like the White God'), and the GIR (Great Itinerant Revolutionary). He also gives advice to out-of-work black writers ('just mention drums . . . and legends') and talks about 'The Superior Race', 'The White Liberal', 'Your True Friend'.

Enekwe, Ossie Onuora
Broken Pots
Greenfield Center, New York: Greenfield Review Press, 1977. 39 pp. $3.00
Poetry.

Come Thunder
Enugu, Nigeria: Fourth Dimension Publ. Co., 1981. 144 pp. ₦2.25
A novel which recounts the opening stages of the Nigerian Civil War.

Esapebong, William
Mysterious Afrika
Yaoundé: Buma Kor, 1978. 80 pp.
Mysticism, superstition and belief that 'Africa is the beginning and the end, the fall and the rise of men' run through Esapebong's poems.

Eze, Esenta E.
The Cassava Ghost
Benin City, Nigeria: Ethiope Publ. Co., 1974. 147 pp. ₦1.35
A play in three acts about the historical revolt of market women in Aba in 1929.

Fagunwa, D. O.
The Forest of a Thousand Daemons: a hunter's saga
(Trans. from the Yoruba by Wole Soyinka)
London: Nelson, 1968. 160 pp. 30p illus.
A free translation of the late Chief D. O.
Fagunwa's novel *Ogboju Ode Ninu Igbo
Irunmale*, which has gone into many editions in
its original Yoruba. It is an adventurous tale
with a strong element of 'quest', and sheds
light on the myths of the Yoruba people of
Western Nigeria, whose culture has a very long
history. Wole Soyinka, who is responsible for
this translation, supplies some introductory
notes and a glossary of Yoruba and unfamiliar
words.
*'Fagunwa's tale is allegorical and as in all allegory
the intention is both to teach and to entertain . . . each
daemon represents a combination of three levels of
comprehension: a realistic figure, a supernatural
entity and an allegorical emblem . . . Fagunwa's
action is rendered by Soyinka with such effectiveness
that the novel often comes alive to sweep us into its
dance.'*   R. W. Noble – *West Africa*

Fatilewa, Tunji
Torrents of Soweto
Ibadan: Pat-Del Publ., n.d. [1978] 22 pp.
₦1.60   p/b
An anti-apartheid play inspired on the 1976
Soweto riots and centred around a group of
students led by Ndaba Diko who are involved
in guerilla activities against the South African
regime.

Fowowe, Oyeleke
Who Has Blood?
Ile-Ife, Nigeria: Pan-African, 1972 (Pocket
Poets, 5.) (distr. by Univ. of Ife Bookshop
Ltd.). 39 pp. 60k p/b
Many of the poems in this collection grew out
of the Nigerian Civil War experience.

Garba, Mohamed Tukur
The Black Temple
London: Macmillan Educ., 1981. 112 pp. 80p
An ambitious young man from the country
becomes involved in the Black Temple, a secret
society operating in Lagos involved in murder
and blackmail. A popular thriller.

Gbadamosi, Rasheed
Echoes from the Lagoon
Ibadan: Onibonoje Press, 1973 (ALS, 5).
95 pp.   ₦1.20
Tanko Arowolo, the poor young man, and
Comfort Erinla, the rich girl, live along a
Lagos lagoon, in close proximity to one
another, but in completely different worlds.

Then a chance encounter brings them
together. But Tanko enlists in the army and
goes off to fight in the civil war only to return
and find that his world has disappeared and
that the basis of his relationship with Comfort
needs to be redefined.

Behold My Redeemer
Ibadan: OUP Nigeria, 1978. 43 pp. ₦1.00
This two-act play opens first in a sinister
mental institution which combines Western
and African psychiatric practices. An African
psychiatrist with a penchant for playing God
attempts a new 'cure' for two of his patients –
a former professor of anthropology and an ex-
student nurse. He matchmakes them and sends
them off to rediscover their African origins in
a model village. The experiment ends in-
conclusively as the young woman is led back to
the institution.

Gbulie, Ben
Figments and Nothing
Enugu, Nigeria: Fourth Dimension Publ. Co.,
1978. 224 pp. ₦2.25
Gbulie's novel is woven around beliefs and
practices in Igboland. The strange death of an
Ogbanje (a twin) leads to unforseen results
when he mysteriously reappears to his cousin.

Henshaw, James Ene
Children of the Goddess, and other plays
London: Univ. of London Press, 1964. 128 pp.
66p
Three plays for reading and production by
schools, amateur and professional groups.
Children of the Goddess, a three-act play in a
nineteenth-century setting, tells the story of the
establishment of Christianity in a Nigerian
village, and the struggles between the local juju priest and the Reverend Donald McPhail
and his wife. The other two are one-act plays:
Companion for a Chief, a melodrama, and *Magic
in the Blood*, a comedy, centring round the
drunken, inefficient members of a local village
court at Udura. Details on stage direction are
included.

Medicine for Love: a comedy in three acts
London: Univ. of London Press, 1964. 108 pp.
75p
Monogamy, polygamy, medicine-men, tradition and the African are the subjects of this
play. Ewia, the central character, is a local
election candidate whose committee is attempting to secure his unopposed return by
bribing rival candidates into withdrawing their
nominations. The second motif concerns

Ewia's troubles with three prospective wives sent to him by relatives.
'. . . *a spirited and highly amusing satire which touches on more serious matters . . . an excellently constructed play.'*
Peter Kennard – *Bull. of the Assoc. for African Literature in English*

This is Our Chance: plays from West Africa
London: Univ. of London Press, 1964. 95pp. 50p
This is Our Chance, The Jewels of the Shrine (awarded the Henry Carr Memorial Cup in the All Nigeria Festival of the Arts in Lagos, 1952), and *A Man of Character*, the three plays appearing in this volume, are based on different aspects of African culture and tradition. Written in simple style and with equally simple plots, in one or two acts, these plays are primarily intended for secondary schools and training colleges in West Africa. There is a preface by the author, and notes on production are given.

Dinner for Promotion
London: Univ. of London Press, 1967. 103 pp. 80p
A three-act comedy about an ambitious young man-about-town, a newly rich and touchy businessman, and a quarrelsome sister-in-law. James Henshaw includes notes on production and an introductory article entitled 'The African writer, the audience and the English language'.

Enough is Enough
Benin City, Nigeria: Ethiope Publ. Corp., 1976. 103 pp ₦1.50
A play about six detainees and their guards in the last days of the Nigerian Civil War.

Ibizugbe, S. O.
The Mysterious Ebony Carver
Benin City, Nigeria: Ethiope Publ. Corp., 1979. ₦2.50
A popular suspense novel about a gang of criminals who produce large quantities of fake works of art and flood the market with them.

Ibukun, Olu
The Return
Nairobi: EAPH, 1970. 272 pp. k.shs.9.50 ($3.20)
Ebun Odanogun, the hero of the novel, is a favoured descendant of a Yoruba chief and therefore destined for a position of leadership in his village. But as the son of one of the first Christian converts he attends the missionary school, winning a scholarship to study abroad. Upon return five years later he discovers that it

is possible to assimilate Western education and his African culture.

Ifejika, Samuel U.
The New Religion
Enugu: Nwamife Publ., 1973. 192 pp. ₦1.80
London: Rex Collings, 1973. 192 pp. o/p
In Ifejika's first novel two educated men get caught up in 'the new religion of quick money'. One is a veterinary doctor who succumbs to the temptation of posing as a medical doctor when an epidemic of cholera breaks out shortly after the civil war. His arrest and suicide follow, serving as a lesson for his friend Professor Ikemba, a man of similar aquisitive instincts.
'. . . *a scathing commentary on life in postwar Nigeria . . . a highly rewarding novel.'*
Charles Larson – *Books Abroad*
' . . . *holds promise of greater things to come.'*
Dubem Okafor – *Afriscope*

Igbozurike, M. Uzo
Across the Gap
Ibadan: Onibonoje Press, 1977 (ALS, 13). 76 pp. ₦1.20
The light-hearted tale of a son who has always been the bane of his father's existence – until he manages to graduate from college, get a well-paying job and marry his childhood sweetheart without paying the bride price.

Ighavini, Dickson
Death is a Woman
London: Macmillan Educ., 1981. 160 pp. 80p
Is there any relationship between the three men that have been found dead in the street in Port Kano? When Police Chief Mack sets out to investigate the latest wave of murders it seems that each question he asks raises another.

Bloodbath at Lobster Close
London: Macmillan Educ., 1980. 160 pp. 80p
Outwardly prosperous and successful, Frank Jirinde is the export manager of a large Nigerian oil company. But shady episodes in his past life make him vulnerable to blackmail by an underworld syndicate.

Ijimere, Obotunde [pseud.]
The Imprisonment of Obatala, and other plays
(Trans. from the Yoruba by Ulli Beier)
London: HEB, 1966 (AWS, 18). 124 pp. £1.25/$3.00
Three verse plays from Western Nigeria originally written and performed in Yoruba and translated into English blank verse by Ulli Beier. Contains *The Imprisonment of Obatala,*

based on a Yoruba myth; *Everyman*, an adaption of Hugo von Hoffmannsthal's version; and *Woyengi*, founded on an Ijaw tale.

Ike, Vincent Chukwuemeka
Toads for Supper
London: Harvill Press, 1965. 192 pp. o/p
Glasgow: Fontana/Collins, 1966. 192 pp.
£1.25
The severe setbacks and complications in the life of an undergraduate, engaged to three girls simultaneously. He is accused by one of being the father of her child, and is expelled by the university authorities. How Amadi, the hero of this story, got himself into this situation, and his efforts to extricate himself from it, provide the subject of this novel.
'Mr Ike not only has a fine comic touch, but a talent for invoking interesting details and the right metaphor. Authentic African imagery and sayings add to the richness of his prose.'
Lewis Nkosi – *Africa Report*
'Perhaps the most redeeming thing about this novel is that it has no axe to grind. It is just a book – a look at life. No message . . . At once sad and frequently more than a little humorous. Toads for Supper *is excellent fare.'*   O. R. Dathorne – *Black Orpheus*

The Naked Gods
London: Harvill Press, 1970. 280 pp. o/p
Glasgow: Fontana/Collins, 1971. 254 pp.
£1.25
Ike's second novel satirically views the attempts made by British and American expatriates to gain control of an African university. At the centre of this campus comedy are Toogood, the honest and diligent British registrar of Songhai University; Professor Brown, his friend; and Julie Toogood, the registrar's frustrated wife, who falls into the clutches of an ambitious West African, Dr Okoro. The latter, sporting a worthless Ph.D. from an American university, aims at becoming vice-chancellor of Songhai upon retirement of the reigning vice-chancellor, an American, bewildered by Africa. He is challenged for the post by another African professor, a hen-pecked man with an ambitious wife, who is the favourite candidate of the Britains.
'Mr Ike presides with glee over a fast-moving plot . . . He has a nice eye for the complementary forms of condescension practised by his expatriates . . . all the intrigues have a familiar ring'
Gerald Moore – *Okike*
'[Ike] has an impressive personal knowledge of university life which he has turned, in part, to satirical end in his writing.'
Oyin Ogunba – *West African Journal of Modern Languages*

The Potter's Wheel
Glasgow: Fontana/Collins, 1974. 222 pp.
£1.25
Obu is spoiled and petted by a mother who despaired of ever having a male child. When he reaches nine his father decides it is time to make a man out of him. He is sent off to school in a distant town where he must earn his keep as houseboy to Teacher Zaccheus Kanu and his wife. Their spartan routine and strict discipline cannot fail to strengthen Obu's character. A satire of Nigerian educational practices.

Sunset at Dawn
Glasgow: Fontana/Collins, 1976. 255 pp.
£1.25
Ike's novel of the Nigerian Civil War is told from the Biafran point of view. Its main character is Dr Kanu, a high-level Biafran official, and his wife, Fatima, a Northerner, who is evacuated to her husband's village soon after their son is killed in a bombing attack. Her contact with the villagers and her work with refugees make a fervent Biafran of her, giving her courage to withstand yet another tragedy – the loss of her husband. Many other characters are present too, however, and the novel has a documentary quality to it.
'. . . not only a novel but a history of a war . . . Mr Ike gives the impression he is scrupulously fair, though passionately committed.'
D. A. N. Jones – *Times Literary Supplement*
'. . . a kind of kaleidoscopic narrative of the struggle.'
Charles Larson – *World Literature Today*

The Chicken Chasers
Glasgow: Fontana/Collins, 1980. 185 pp.
£1.25
The definition of 'chicken chasers': the elite of African universities who chase after power and privilege, who are not so interested in things academic as they are in 'cute little things', the young girls they have no trouble collecting despite balding hair and thickening waistlines. The locus of this novel is a world the author knows well: African cultural institutions. Ike writes here of the intrigues and base motives (including sexual ones) that are behind the move to unseat a brilliant, capable man from his position as secretary-general of the imaginary 'African Cultural Organization' during the annual meeting of the organization at a plush coastal resort in the state of Plassas.

Expo 77
Glasgow: Fontana/Collins, 1980. 192 pp.
£1.25
A detective story on an out-of-the-ordinary theme. 'Expo 77' is the code name of a vast

network of leaked examination papers that has the National Examinations Board and its upright director, Dr Buka, very worried.

Ikejiani, Okechukwu
Nkemdilim
New York: Vantage Press, 1975. 322 pp. o/p

Iroh, Eddie
Forty-Eight Guns for the General
London: HEB, 1976 (AWS, 189). 218 pp.
£1.75/$5.00
Like Aniebo's *Anonymity of Sacrifice* Eddie Iroh's novel focuses on the main actors in the Nigerian Civil War – the soldiers themselves. Forty-eight mercenaries, led by Colonel Rudolf, a Frenchman, are flown in to help the Biafrans but become a law unto themselves, threatening mutiny and plotting to hold the Biafran General for ransom. They ultimately fail, thanks to Sandhurst-trained Colonel Charles Chumah.

Toads of War
London: HEB, 1979 (AWS, 213). 144 pp.
£1.75/$4.00
Iroh's second war novel, of a proposed trilogy, leaves the battlefront for the civilian sector – Owerri town where a select group, ranging from bureaucrats to clergymen, are getting rich on blood money and the black market in the final days of Biafra. A former soldier, Kalu Udim, who has lost a hand at the front, falls in love with the mistress of his boss, a relief official who makes sure that incoming parcels contain dresses and perfume for the young woman as well as food for refugees. Matters come to a dramatic climax when Kalu tries to resolve affairs with an automatic pistol.
'Iroh takes a rather bitter look at the suffering and degradation of the vast majority during the 1960s, and contrasts it with the affluence and high living of the black market profiteers, indulging in night-long orgies against the background of ceaseless cannon-fire.
– *New African*
'. . . by dual narration and by projecting Kalu's own bitterness into the presentation of events, Iroh has made Toads of War *more compelling, as well as sharpening our anticipation of the novel promised to complete his trilogy on the war.'*
Geoffrey Parker – *British Book News*

Iyayi, Festus
Violence
London: Longman, 1979. 316 pp. £1.50 p/b
Washington D.C.: Three Continents Press,
$9.00 cased $4.00 p/b
A story of the stark contrasts between the rich and corrupt and the poor and the wretched in a modern African state, as portrayed by two couples – Ofufun and Queen, prosperous hotel proprietors, and Idemudia, the day-labourer they employ for a time, and his wife, Adisa. When Idemudia falls ill and is hospitalized Adisa has no recourse but to let Ofufun seduce her in order to get money for the medical expenses. According to the novel violence occurs 'when a man is denied the opportunity of being educated, of getting a job, of feeding himself and his family properly, of getting medical attention quickly and promptly . . .'
'. . . an embittered indictment against the corruption and misery of life in oil-rich Nigeria . . . must win full marks for its accuracy and truth.'
Dillibe Onyeama – *Books and Bookmen*
'. . . [a work] of originality and talent.'
K. M. – *West Africa*

The Contract
London: Longman, forthcoming 1981.

Johnson, L.
No Man's Land
Ibadan: Fagbamigbe, 1980. 198 pp. ₦1.80
A novel

Jemie, Onwuchekwa
Voyage and Other Poems
Ile-Ife, Nigeria: Pan African, 1971 (Pocket Poets, 2). (distr. by Univ. of Ife Bookshop Ltd.). 28 pp. 60k

Kalejaiye, Oladipo
The Father of Secrets
Palo Alto, Calif.: Zikawuna Books, 1978.
31 pp. $2.50
A play set in Yorubaland sometime during the Nigerian Civil War: a herbalist robs Salawu of a month's wages in pretending to cure his sick daughter. Followed by a two-page essay on African drama.

Kasaipwalova, John
Reluctant Flame
Ile-Ife, Nigeria: Pan African, 1971 (Pocket Poets, 1). (distr. by Univ. of Ife Bookshop Ltd.). 10 pp. 30k

Kor, Buma
Searchlight
Yaoundé: Buma Kor, 1975. 40 pp. CFA300
($1.50)
Contains the author's early poems.

Ladipo, Duro
Three Yoruba Plays: Ọba koso, Ọba mọrọ, Ọba waja
(English adaptation by Ulli Beier)
Ibadan: Mbari, 1964. 75 pp. o/p
The texts of three popular Yoruba folk operas, here translated by Ulli Beier.

Selections from Ọba koso
(Trans. by Robert Armstrong)
Ibadan: Univ. of Ibadan, Inst. of African Studies, 1966, 39 pp.
Selected passages from Ladipo's play in English translation.

Ọba Ko So: The King Did not Hang
(Transcribed and translated by R. G. Armstrong, Robert L. Awujoola, and Val Olayemi).
Ibadan: Inst. of African Studies, Univ. of Ibadan, 1972. 149 pp. ₦1.10
Duro Ladipo's popular opera here with texts in English and Yoruba.

Maimo, Sankie
Sov-Mbang the soothsayer
Yaoundé: Centre de Diffusion du Livre Camerounais, 1978 (2nd ed.). 70 pp. CFA480
A play.

Menkiti, Ifeanyi
Affirmations
Chicago: Third World Press, 1971. 24 pp. $1.00
Twenty-one poems on the black experience.
'. . . a tone of debunking laughter . . . a steady march of indictments . . . aimed at punching holes in the oppressor's mystique.'   Chinweizu – Okike

Mezu, S. Okechukwu
Behind the Rising Sun
London: William Heinemann, 1970. o/p
London: HEB, 1972 (AWS, 113). 241 pp.
£1.95/$5.00
Originally published in a hardcover edition in 1970 by William Heinemann Ltd. this is the earliest novel to have appeared about the Nigerian Civil War. Written from a Biafran point of view (the title refers to the Biafran battle emblem), it opens in Europe where Biafran representatives, from the safe luxury of hotel rooms, negotiate for arms and supplies with unscrupulous European businessmen. Part two, however, brings to the forefront Freddy Onuoha and his companion, Titi, who risk their lives to fly home and participate more meaningfully in the struggle, and their story is set against the sobering realities of war-

time – bombings, evacuations, fleeing refugees.
'. . . dispels the idealistic illusions and emphasizes the patina of cynicism that surrounded the best intentions of the "patriots".'
Keith Carter – Times Literary Supplement

Momodu, A. G. S.
The Course of Justice, and Other Stories
Ibadan: Onibonoje Press, 1973 (ALS, 1). 98 pp. ₦1.20

The Daughter-in-law and Other Stories
Benin City, Nigeria: Ethiope Publ. Corp., 1979. 109 pp. ₦2.00

Munonye, John
The Only Son
London: HEB, 1966 (AWS, 21). 202 pp.
£1.25/$2.50
Set in Eastern Nigeria in the twenties when the first Christian converts were being made. A young widow nearly loses her mind when she learns her young son, Nnanna, has been attending the mission school in secret and plans to convert. One of her main reasons for refusing to remarry was to raise the boy in the best village traditions and have him initiated so he could return triumphantly to his father's village and show his people how wrong they were to have neglected her and her son when her husband died. She recovers her senses in the end when she decides to remarry. Nnanna, however, refuses to follow his mother to her new husband, preferring instead to become the houseboy of a white priest in a far-off town.
'. . . Munonye has, to begin with, offered the reader an immediately compelling relationship, that of a mother – a widowed mother – with her only son . . . an altogether successful first novel.'
Don Carter – African Literature Today

Obi
London: HEB, 1969 (AWS, 45). 224 pp.
£1.20/$3.00
A sequel to The Only Son. Nnanna does return to his father's village many years later, but as Joe, the ex-mission boy, married to Anna, a convent-educated orphan. Joe and Anna earn the respect and admiration of all, including Joe's mother, not only for their wealth (the savings from Joe's former job as a Forest Officer) but for their 'modern ideas', and they settle down to what they expect to be a peaceful existence. Fate, however, decides otherwise. Just as Anna learns she is pregnant after years of barrenness, Joe is exiled from the village for being indirectly responsible for the death of a kinswoman. The title comes from

the Ibo word for a man's homestead. It is the homestead Joe comes home to rebuild and then loses.

The Oil Man of Obange
London: HEB, 1971 (AWS, 94). 224 pp.
£1.75/$4.50
Bad luck plagues Jeri. First, he loses his land and then his wife dies, leaving him with five young children to raise. Determined to keep his children in school, he struggles desperately to earn their fees by trading palm-oil, pedalling a long and difficult road each day with cans of palm-oil balanced precariously on his bicycle. He has an accident and cannot work for a time, and then his bicycle is stolen. At last the struggle becomes too great for him.

A Wreath for the Maidens
London: HEB, 1973 (AWS, 121). 288 pp.
£1.95/$2.50
Unlike other civil war novels, Munonye's book does not aim to be documentary. The setting is a fictional African country and the author tells the story of the breaking up of a nation. Two intellectuals, Roland and Biere, observe and comment on the ills that beset their country soon after independence. Roland blames what he calls the 'Imperator' and Biere the local politicians. They feel compelled to participate in the birth of the new secessionist state but soon learn that the evils they denounced are growing up in their midst.

A Dancer of Fortune
London: William Heinemann, 1974. o/p
London: HEB, 1975 (AWS, 153). 265 pp.
£1.75/$4.00
Munonye takes a comic look at business practices in an African town and at the economic resourcefulness that poverty and unemployment engender. It is the portrait of Ayasko, a picaresque hero, who makes his living dancing for sellers of patent medicine in the market place as a means of attracting customers. While masquerading as a simpleton he cunningly plays off competitors by selling his services to the highest bidder. In this way he gradually builds up his own 'practice'. His ways are as devious as those of the others, but he remains to the end a much more likeable character, in part because he is a good husband and father.
'. . . a happy work, its hero a fascinating scamp.'
    Robert L. Berner – *Books Abroad*
'. . . shrewd observation of character . . . Whether one reads this book for a taste of Nigeria, for a smirk at the antics of his characters or for something meatier, John Munonye will not let one down.'
    D. S. – *West Africa*

Bridge to a Wedding
London: HEB, 1978 (AWS, 195). 228 pp.
£1.95/$5.00
In this novel Munonye completes the trilogy he had begun with *The Only Son* and *Obi*. Joe Kafo, now a prosperous lumber trader, lives in the town of Sankia with Anna, his wife, and their six children. They are a happy family, but all ties have been cut with Joe's village (here called Mudi) and the children carefully shielded from their father's tragic secret. The novel ends with reconciliation, however, as Rose, Joe's eldest daughter, marries the son of another Mudi man.

Ndu, Pol
Golgotha
Ile-Ife, Nigeria: Pan African, 1971 (Pocket Poets, 4).
(distr. by Univ. of Ife Bookshop Ltd.). 34 pp.
60k

Songs For Seers
New York: Nok Publishers, 1974. 35 pp. $5.95 cased $2.95 p/b
The poetry in Ndu's second collection invites comparison to that of his fellow Ibo, the late Christopher Okigbo, to whom the title poem is dedicated. It is ironic, too, that Ndu, like Okigbo, died while still young, killed in an accident in 1976. Many of the poems in this volume carry the scars of the Nigerian Civil War.
'. . . a poet with a substantial endowment. Like Okigbo he is impressive in the quality of his vision and in his command of the resources of the culture in which he writes.'   Samuel Allen – *Okike*
'. . . an important young poet.'
    Harold Collins – *Books Abroad*

Njoku, Charles
The New Breed
London: Longman, 1974. 166 pp. £1.15
Told in autobiographical form, Njoku's novel relates the coming-of-age of Patrick Uzoma, a young man who reaches manhood in post-independent Nigeria. The fifties were for him a period of childish *insouciance* and schoolboy pranks, and his memory of the struggle for nationhood is that of the clinking of glasses in the family home as his lawyer father entertains his political friends. But the independence coincides with Pat's increasing self-awareness. It is the realization that he belongs to a 'new breed' of African, one whose education has included Achebe and Soyinka and not just Dickens, who has dared question his strict Catholic upbringing and who no longer feels the compulsiveness of his father's generation to master the English culture.

Njoku, John E. Eberegbulam
Refund My Bride Price
New York: Vantage Press, 1976. 101 pp. o/p
A dispute arises between two families over a
broken engagement that has to be settled in
court. The young man and woman who fall
'out' of love are Nwala Ojo, the educated son
of a poor peasant, and Jerry, the daughter of a
more well-to-do family who goes off to
England to study nursing and marries a doctor
there.

The Dawn of African Women
Hicksville, N.Y.: Exposition Press, 1977.
96 pp. $5.00

Nwakoby, Martina Awele
A Lucky Chance
Ibadan: Macmillan Nigeria, 1980. 96 pp.
₦2.00

A House Divided
Enugu, Nigeria: Fourth Dimension Publ. Co.,
1981. 184 pp. ₦2.25
A tragic story of ethnic intolerance and
parental bigotry.

Nwala, T. Uzodima
Justice on Trial
Ibadan: Onibonoje Press, 1973 (ALS, 3).
163 pp. ₦1.50
A tale of the infamous career of a Biafran war
hero turned armed robber who gets his just
deserts. As the grandson of a fearless Ibo
warrior who was defeated by the British at the
turn of the century and the son of a ruthless
smuggler, 'Major' Ituk is a violent man by
inheritance and by upbringing. And for a time
he unites Nigeria – in crime.

Nwankwo, Nkem
Danda
London: Deutsch, 1964. 208 pp. o/p
London: Panther Books, 1967. 154 pp. o/p
London: HEB, 1969 (AWS, 67). 208 pp.
£1.60/$5.50
Described as an 'alakalogholi', a good-for-
nothing, Danda lives in the Ibo village of
Aniocha, in Eastern Nigeria. He travels about
the villages, playing his flute, shocking the
'establishment', charming the women and
outraging his patriarchal father.
'. . . Nwankwo's gift for dramatic dialog, his ability
to capture atmosphere and idiom, as well as his
warmth and talent for sketching humorous scenes,
leads one to look for the second novel in preparation.'
Thomas Cassirer – *African Forum*

My Mercedes is Bigger than Yours
London: André Deutsch, 1975. 177 pp. £3.25
cased
London: HEB, 1975 (AWS, 173). 176 pp.
£1.95/$3.00
Glasgow: Fontana/Collins, 1976. 160 pp.
£1.00
A novel which takes a satirical look at a certain
social type in present-day Nigeria in whom an
elitist education has bred weak morals and a
passion for luxury. Onuma buys a golden
Jaguar on credit, takes a leave of absence from
his rather dubious 'public relations' job in
Lagos and makes a big entry into his village
after a 15-year absence. Then he has an
accident and his money supply dries up. The
women begin to shun him and his parents
ignore him. His fortunes soar when he goes
into politics and gets to drive a little Volkswagen but he ends up backing both sides in the
election campaign when he is unable to choose
between the two candidates – the man who had
employed him and his mother's relative. He is
beaten up but escapes by driving away in the
Mercedes belonging to the cousin he has just
shot.
'. . . gentle, finely judged satire . . . [Nwankwo] is
passionately concerned about the values that are
warring with each other in his country, but he does not
allow his own feelings to distort the faultless
cautionary tale he has constructed.'
Jeremy Brooks – *The Sunday Times*
'. . . this enormously intelligent and sophisticated
novel.'
John Fletcher – *The International Fiction Review*

Nwanodi, Okogbule Glory
Icheke and Other Poems
Ibadan: Mbari, 1965. 31 pp. o/p
A poetry collection in which the major poem,
'Icheke', derives its name from a local bird,
symbolically interpreted as seer or prophet.

Nwapa, Flora
Efuru
London: HEB, 1966 (AWS, 26). 288 pp.
£1.25p/$3.00
Efuru is a beautiful and respected woman.
However, she has been chosen by the goddess
of the lake, Uhamiri, to be one of her
worshippers. In effect, this means that
although she will be rich, she will never be able
to marry or have children successfully. This
novel was the first to be published by a woman
writer in Nigeria.

Idu
London: HEB, 1969 (AWS, 56). 218 pp.
£1.50/$3.00
A woman's desire for having children is the

basic theme of this novel, set in a small Nigerian town, where the life of an individual is intricately involved with that of the entire community. After she finally succeeds in giving birth to a boy, she becomes much closer to her husband, Adiewere. When the latter dies mysteriously she follows his death with her own suicide.

This is Lagos and Other Stories
Enugu, Nigeria: Nwamife Publ., 1971. 117 pp. ₦2.00

Six of the nine tales in Flora Nwapa's first collection focus on young women in urban Africa. There are characters like Bishi who refuses to be an easy conquest for men; like Soha, who comes to Lagos to study and secretly marries the Yoruba boyfriend who gets her pregnant much to the objection of her family; like Agnes who steals a newborn to try to save her childless marriage; and like Ozoemena, the young widow who refuses to be pressured by her mother into letting an older man finance her return to school. Two of these stories, however, touch on the Biafran crisis through the account of a soldier's return home to the East when life in the North becomes impossible for Ibos, and the death of a young student-soldier early in the war.

'[Nwapa] *looks at the problem of her sex from a passionate and yet realistic and intimate angle.*'
Tony Nnaemeka – *Daily Times* (Lagos)

Never Again
Enugu, Nigeria: Nwamife Publ., 1976. 80 pp. ₦2.00

This short novel – Flora Nwapa's third – evokes the evacuation of the town of Ugwuta in Eastern Nigeria after its fall to Federal troops during the Nigerian Civil War and its subsequent recapture by Biafran troops. The narrator is Kate, an educated woman who had taken refuge with her family in her home town after fleeing Enugu. She describes how fear of the enemy is compounded by fear of one's fellow Biafran – the fear of being arrested as a saboteur if one made preparations to flee as the enemy approached or if one dared to hint that the war was a folly because of Biafra's unpreparedness.

'. . . *gives the reader a realistic glimpse into the tensions of the war on a basic level.*'
Anita Kern – *World Literature Written in English*

Wives at War and Other Stories
Enugu, Nigeria: Nwamife Publ., 1980. 96 pp. ₦2.00

Flora Nwapa's most recent collection of stories.

One is Enough
Enugu, Nigeria: Flora Nwapa Co., forthcoming 1981

Nwoko, Demas
Children of Paradise. A dance play
Ibadan: New Culture Studios, 1981 (Theatre Production Series), 47 pp. ₦5.00

This is the first title in a series of published plays in a practical format, to enable the reader to envisage them staged, rather than as bland or academic texts. Nwoko's 'dance play' presents an allegory of the rape of Africa by white imperialists. The text is interspersed with ink sketches, and photographs taken during the three months of rehearsals before the first performance of the play during FESTAC 1977. There are also cut-out/pull-out patterns for making the costumes of the different characters, together with music for the songs in the play, all aimed to provide as much guidance as possible as to the practicalities of production.

Nwosu, T. C.
The Blind Spots of God
Lagos: Cross Continent Press, 1976. 37 pp. ₦1.25

The personal tragedies of the Nigerian Civil War provide the themes for these six stories which are written in a philosophical cast.

Poems about Love and Women
Lagos: Cross Continent Press, 1976. 120 pp. ₦3.00 p/b

Sirens of the Spirit
Lagos: Cross Continent Press, 1976. 136 pp. ₦2.50

A Game Of Blood and Other Plays
Lagos: Cross Continent Press, 1976. 145 pp. ₦2.50

Nzekwu, Onuora
Wand of Noble Wood
London: Hutchinson, 1961. 208 pp. o/p
New York: New American Library 1966 (Signet books D 2788). 142 pp.
London: HEB, 1970 (AWS, 85). 268 pp. £1.75/$5.00

Peter Obiesie, a Lagos magazine-editor, aims to strike a balance between his traditional society and the Western civilization in which he was brought up and educated. Searching for a wife, he decides to marry a schoolteacher from his own tribe. However, Nneka, his bride-to-be, is under the curse of *iyi ocha*, said to bring doom to anyone under its spell. Although the two of them perform lengthy and costly rites to absolve the girl from the curse, Nneka discovers that a vital white stone was missing in the ceremony. This causes her to commit suicide before the wedding.

Highlife for Lizards
London: Hutchinson, 1965. 192 pp. o/p
A domestic comedy about the trials and tribulations of Agom, the wife of Udezue. Her happy marriage turns sour after a few years when her barrenness forces her husband to take a second wife, thus disrupting the household and bringing in the proverbial lizards of the title. But Agom ends blessed with children and wealth – from her prosperous oil-trading business – and she and Udezue grow old peacefully together.

Blade Among the Boys
London: Hutchinson, 1962. 191 pp. o/p
London: HEB, 1972 (AWS, 91). 160 pp.
£1.75/$5.00
A novel about the dilemma of a young man caught between church and family. Patrick's mother is a fervent Catholic but she refuses to sanction her son's desire to be a priest, evoking an Ibo man's responsibility to marry and have children. He persists in his plans, breaking first his engagement and eventually all family ties, but will be unable to carry them out when his ex-fiancée manages to seduce him out of spite. One of the *leitmotifs* of the novel is the intolerance and racism of Catholic missionaries.

Odu, M. A. C.
Tears of the Fathers
Lagos: Cross Continent Press, 1977. 160 pp.
₦3.00   p/b

Oduyoye, Modupe
Statements
Ibadan: Daystar Press, 1980. 30 pp.
Twelve poems first made available for the Frankfurt Book Fair in October 1980.

Ofeimun, Odia
The Poet Lied
London: Longman, 1981. 96 pp. 95p
These poems, Odia Ofeimun's first published collection, present 'a common front born out of a refusal to accept the social reality of the moment'. They were written, he says, 'to strengthen my resolve and to activate in others this refusal to accept what deserves to be changed'.

Ogali, Agu Ogali
Coal City
Enugu, Nigeria: Fourth Dimension Publ. Co., 1978. 128 pp. ₦2.25
Ogali's first full-length novel is based on two of his Onitsha pamphlets, *Eddy the Coal-City Boy* and *Caroline the One-Guinea Girl*. It is the story of the lives and loves of the rising elite of Enugu, set against the background of politics, wealth and corruption. There is an introduction and biographical sketch by Richard Sander and Peter Ayers.

Tales For a Native Son
Enugu, Nigeria: Fourth Dimension Publ. Co., 1978. 110 pp. ₦1.30
In this collection of Igbo folk tales and lore Ogali tries to help young Uka make sense out of the conflicting versions of life given by his wise old father, on the one hand, and Western education, on the other. Gradually he comes to discover the significance of his own culture. Includes a biographical sketch and an introduction by R. W. Sander, P. K. Ayers and H. O. Chukwuma.

Fireside Folk-tales
Onitsha, Nigeria: Univ. Publ. Co., 1978.
83 pp.   ₦2.00

Talisman for Love
Onitsha, Nigeria: Univ. Publ. Co., 1978.
85 pp.   ₦2.00

The Juju Priest
Enugu, Nigeria: Fourth Dimension Publ. Co., 1978. 142 pp. ₦2.25
The stormy history of a representative Igbo community, closely patterned after the author's own home town, from the arrival of the first Christian missionaries to the nationalist period and the founding of a syncretic religion, the National Church of Africa combining Christianity and the spirit of the Juju Priests. The protagonists are Dimgba and Nweresi who had been doomed to be sacrificed to the Goddess of Iyinta but are saved and raised by the missionaries, later marrying and returning home to their village as missionaries, themselves. As they declare war on traditional religion and everything African the author's point of view begins to change. Ogali documents the collapse of morals and the weakening of family bonds that follow in the struggle of the two religious forces, the local one and the imported one. With a foreword by Reinhard Sander and Peter Ayers.

Veronica My Daughter and Other Onitsha Plays and Stories
Washington, D.C.: Three Continents Press, 1980. 376 pp. $15.00 cased $7.00 p/b
The first complete collection of the stories, plays and non-fiction of one of the most prolific and successful of the Onitsha chapbook writers. Two of Ogali's best-selling plays are included here: 'Veronica My Daughter' (250,000 copies sold in Nigeria since 1956) and 'Patrice Lumumba' (80,000 copies sold). In the former play an educated young woman refuses to marry the wealthy older man her illiterate father has chosen for her. Edited and presented by Reinhard Sander and Peter Ayers.

Ogieriakhi, Emwinma

Oba Ovonramwen, and Oba Ewuakpe
London: Univ. of London Press, 1969. 92 pp.
Two short historical plays based on the history of the Benin Empire, which fell in 1897. The first play is set in Benin City, when it was invaded by the British in the late nineteenth century. The second play, *Oba Ewuakpe*, characterizes the famous Oba, who reigned from A.D. 1700 to 1711 in a time of social unrest when the people revolted at the sacrifice of human beings for the purpose of giving fitting burial for Ewuakpe's dead mother.

Ogundimu, 'Dele

Fragments
Ibadan: Onibonoje Press, 1976. 52 pp. 65k
A collection of verse and aphorisms.

Ogunniyi, 'Laolu

Candle in the Wind
Ibadan: Onibonoje Press, 1977 (ALS, 14). 75 pp. ₦1.50
Dotun and Moji, two Nigerian students in England, plan to marry. Then tragedy occurs: Dotun dies after an operation for a brain tumor. But he leaves behind a meaningful legacy – a manuscript disproving the racist arguments of an American scientist, and the baby Moji is expecting. A play that was first performed in 1976.

Fateful Eclipse
Ibadan: Onibonoje Press, 1975 (ALS, 8). 87 pp. ₦1.50
The inability of an Englishwoman to adapt to life in Lagos where her Nigerian husband has brought her. A play that was first screened over Western Nigerian Television in 1975.

Riders on the Storm
Ibadan: Onibonoje Press, 1975 (ALS, 10). 71 pp. ₦1.50

In contrast to the previous play, the author's black-white couple here ride through their marital storm – the revelation that Dolu, the Nigerian husband, has another woman – and renew their love for one another. Previewed on Western Nigerian Television in 1974.

Oguntoye, Jide

Too Cold for Comfort
London: Macmillan Educ., 1980. 158 pp. 80p (₦1.30)
Kolade's marriage to the beautiful Hannah is not the bliss one might expect. Hannah is obsessed by Christian ideals of morality and purity and refuses to give in to the temptations of the flesh. The marriage sours as Kolade begins to look elsewhere and events take a tragic turn before Hannah is brought to her senses.

Ogunyemi, Wale

Ijayo War in the Nineteenth Century: a historic drama
Ibadan: Orisun Acting Editions, 1970. 66 pp.
A play about the war of rivalry in Yorubaland between Ijaye – led by the its Lord, the warrior-chief Kurunmi – and Ibadan in the mid-nineteenth century.

Eshu Elegbara
Ibadan: Orisun Acting Editions, 1970. 55 pp.
A play based on the Yoruba creation myth. The principal characters are Obatala, the creator god, Orunmila, the god of divination, Ogun, the god of iron and war, Shango, the god of thunder, and Eshu, the god of mischief.

Obaluaye: a music-drama
Ibadan: Univ. of Ibadan, IAS, 1972 (Bi-lingual literary works, 4). 83 pp. ₦1.95 cased ₦1.05 p/b
Ogunyemi's only play in Yoruba is intended as a multi-media production. Obaluaye, the God of smallpox takes revenge over a Yoruba chief who has converted to Christianity by unleashing an epidemic on his village. The play was produced at the Fifth Ife Festival of the Arts. In bilingual text (Yoruba-English).

Kiriji
Lagos: Pilgrim Books, 1976 (Drama from Africa series, 1). 76 pp. ₦1.50
Ogunyemi continues here to exploit the dramatic possibilities of African history. *Kiriji* is a play of epic proportions that is based on another of the Yoruba wars of the nineteenth century, that of Ibadan-Ekitiparapo from 1878 to 1886. It was first performed at the IAS in

Ibadan in 1971 and was taken on tour by the
Department of Theatre Arts of the University
of Ibadan in January, February and March
1972.
'. . . a welcome contribution to the drama of
Nigeria.'
                          Kole Omotoso – *The African Book*
                                          Publishing Record

The Divorce
Ibadan: Onibonoje Press, 1977 (ALS, 16).
118 pp.   ₦1.50
For this play Ogunyemi has switched from
historical drama to domestic comedy. Sanmi,
an agricultural officer, and his wife, Tayo, used
to be a happy couple until Michael comes into
Tayo's life. Who Michael really is and what his
exact relationship to Tayo is provide the comic
matter of this play which manages to save a
husband and a wife from the threat of divorce
just in time. The play was written in 1974 while
the author was at the Theatre Workshop of the
University of Leeds and was first performed in
Ibadan in 1975 by the troupe of the Department of Theatre Arts of the University, the
Unibadan Masques.

Ogwu, Sulu
The Gods are Silent
Ibadan: Onibonoje Press, 1975. (ALS, 7).
228 pp.   ₦2.50
A novel set in contemporary Lagos which
shows how the remnants of the superstitions of
the past can ruin a marriage which should have
been a happy one. Musa, the electronics
technician, recovers from the shock of finding
his fiancée in the arms of his best friend thanks
to the beautiful, and pure, Sheri. They marry
but their union soon heads for trouble as
Sheri, a fervant Catholic, becomes convinced,
with the help of her aunt and a juju man, that
a spirit husband is responsible for her
infertility. Then Sheri disappears mysteriously,
reappearing two years later with Musa's young
son. Their reunion, unfortunately, is short-
lived as tragedy awaits Sheri and the child.

Ojaide, Tanure
Children of Iroko and Other Poems
Greenfield Center, N.Y.: Greenfield Review
Press, 1973. $1.50

Okafor, Dubem
My Testaments
Onitsha, Nigeria: Univ. Publ. Co., 1981.
58 pp.   ₦2.00
A volume of verse grouped thematically under

headings such as 'Love', or 'Exile', that aim to
record the poet's 'moments of intense significance in [his] life'.

Okara, Gabriel
The Voice
London: Deutsch, 1964. 157 pp. o/p
London: Panther Books, 1969. 107 pp. o/p
London: HEB, 1970 (AWS, 68: with an
introduction by Arthur Ravenscroft).
127 pp. £1.35
New York: Africana Publ. Corp., 1970.
127 pp.
The first novel from the pen of Gabriel Okara,
The Voice is an experiment in translating
Okara's Ijaw dialect, its idioms and forms, into
English. Poetic in structure, it is the story of
Okolo's search for 'it'. Okolo's quest brings
him into contact with hostile antagonists as
well as empathetic allies; he is pitted against
the apathy of the ordinary people as he tries to
jolt them with the question 'have you got
"it"?' Essentially a political parable, the
complex meaning of 'it' is arrived at through a
cumulative process as each individual encountered by Okolo adds a new dimension of
meaning to the cryptic question. Arthur
Ravenscroft, in his introduction to this new
edition, provides the reader with a cogent
analysis.
'. . . ranks among the best of new African novels.'
                          Wilfred Cartey – *African Forum*
'. . . an interesting and imaginative piece of writing . . . Mr Okara has considerable narrative skill:
his story has the simplicity of a parable and the
poignancy of an epitaph. Much of the effect of the
language derives from his use of vernacular English
and from the interplay of vernacular English and
standard English.'
           M. Macmillan – *The Journal of Commonwealth*
                                                        Literature

The Fisherman's Invocation
London: HEB, 1978 (AWS, 183). 64 pp.
£1.95/$5.00
This is Okara's first published collection of
verse although many of the poems have been
published individually and cover twenty years
of production. The ten new poems in the
volume reflect the poet's experiences during
the Nigerian Civil War and the ghastly
tragedies he observed. Winner of the 1979
Commonwealth Poetry Prize.
'His poetry is visionary, delicately balanced opposed
impulses, is lyrical even to the point of dance and
incantation . . . The publication of this volume is a
long overdue occasion to be celebrated by lovers of
poetry the world over.'
                          Geoffrey Parker – *British Book News*

Okigbo, Christopher

Heavensgate
Ibadan: Mbari, 1962. 39 pp. o/p
Poetry.
'*Okigbo is chiefly a poet for the ear and not for the eye. We cannot see much of his poetry . . . But we can hear his verse, it fills our mind like a half forgotten tune returning to memory. Everything he touches vibrates and swings and we are compelled to read on and to follow the tune of his chant, hardly worried about the fact that we understand little of what he has to say.*'
Ulli Beier – *Black Orpheus*

Limits
Ibadan: Mbari, 1964. unpaged. o/p
Contains two long poems, 'Siren limits', and 'Fragments out of the deluge', both of which originally appeared in *Transition* magazine.
'*Christopher Okigbo's poetry is all one poem; it is the evolution of a personal religion.*'
O. R. Dathorne – *Black Orpheus*

Labyrinths with Path of Thunder
London: HEB, 1971 (AWS, 62). 88 pp. £1.95
New York: Africana Publ., 1971. 88 pp. $1.75
This posthumous collection brings together Okigbo's verse collections *Heavensgate* (1962), *Limits* (1964), and *Silences* (1965) – originally published separately by Mbari – together with *Distances* (1964), and a postscript, *Path of Thunder*. In his introduction the poet states that 'Although these poems were written and published separately, they are, in fact, organically related.'

Okolo, Emma

The Blood of Zimbabwe
Enugu, Nigeria: Fourth Dimension Publ. Co., 1979. 160 pp. ₦2.25
A novel of political intrigue and espionage set in Nigeria, Zambia, and Zimbabwe.

No Easier Road
Enugu, Nigeria: Fourth Dimension Publ. Co., 1981. 176 pp. ₦2.25
A fast-paced novel which portrays the get-rich-quick syndrome, leading to violence and crime.

Okoro, Anezi

Dr Amadi's Postings
Benin City, Nigeria: Ethiope Publ. Corp., 1975. 171 pp. ₦1.00
For young Dr Amadi, a British-trained physician, practising medicine in Lagos is a far-cry from his student days in London. First, there are the patients themselves, the sheer numbers of them who must be treated in record time, and then there are the occupational hazards: the ministers whose every whim must be obeyed and who have a strong dislike for young doctors with minds of their own; the Lagos girls who prey on handsome bachelors; and a prospective father-in-law, a powerful man, who does not like the idea of his daughter, a Yoruba girl, marrying an Ibo. But it all ends well.

Okoro, Nathaniel

The Warriors
Enugu, Nigeria: Fourth Dimension Publ. Co., 1981. 180 pp. ₦1.50
An entire Nigerian village is taken over by a band of disgruntled youths. A popular novel.

Okoye, Ifeoma

Behind the Clouds
London: Longman, forthcoming 1981.

Okoye, Mokwugo

Sketches in the Sun
Enugu, Nigeria: Nwamife Publ., 1975. 140 pp. ₦1.60
A collection of short stories that raises questions of human nature within the context of modern society.

Glimpses of Wisdom
Enugu, Nigeria: Fourth Dimension Publ. Co., 1979. 290 pp. ₦13.00 cased
A book of philosophical writings that attempts to integrate the strands of African thought with the world philosophical tradition going back to Confucius and Plato. By invoking the teachings of myth and folklore, biology, dreams, depth psychology, art, morality, politics and cosmology, he gives the reader 'glimpses of wisdom' on the nature of Man and the Universe.

Okpewho, Isidore

The Victims
London: Longman, 1979 (2nd ed.). 208 pp. 95p
New York: Doubleday-Anchor, 1971.
The victims of this novel of unrelieved tragedy are the Obanna family, a polygamous household, torn apart by hatred and envy brought on by Obanna, himself, a drunken good-for-nothing. But victimizing also occurs at every level of this man-eat-man society and the author hints at the main culprit – poverty. First published by Longman in 1970.
'*. . . probes remorselessly into the realities of polygamy and in doing so illuminates aspects of the human condition that few writers in any age or culture are able to deal with so well . . . a superior work of fiction that places Okpewho in the standard of contemporary African writing.*'
Jan Carew – *New York Times Book Review*

The Last Duty
London: Longman, 1981 (2nd ed.). 243 pp.
£1.50

Okpewho's story of Aku, a young woman who commits adultery while her husband is in prison for collaboration during a civil war (place names are imaginary but it is obviously Nigeria) is no ordinary tale of unfaithfulness. It is the tale of a loving wife and mother left with no means of support who is pushed beyond endurance by circumstances she cannot control. The novel is narrated in turn by six major characters.

' . . . a novel which will repay several readings.
                          Anita Kern – *World Literature Today*
' . . . the author explores with dramatic and compelling earnestness the reactions of the characters to their different interpretations to the varying themes of honour, integrity, conscience, personal good, self-respect and truth.'   Bozimo – *Afriscope*

Okpi, Kalu
The Smugglers
London: Macmillan Educ., 1977. 141 pp. 80p
Kaska, a ruthless criminal, has just been released from prison and is planning a vast smuggling operation. The only man who can outwit him is Jonnie Malu, who agrees to return to his former job in the Special Services, after three years in journalism. Malu has the full resources of the 'S' Squad at his disposal, including lovely inspector Ada Molo, but Kaska has Nigeria's entire crime syndicate behind him, as well as international contacts.

On the Road
London: Macmillan Educ., 1980. 150 pp. 80p
Jonnie Malu once again answers the 'S' Squad's call for help. This time it is to find out who is behind the rash of daring armed robberies perpetrated against Nigeria's most prestigious financial institutions.

Okri, Benjamin
Flowers and Shadows
London: Longman, 1980. 261 pp. £1.25
Must the sins of the father be visited on the son? On the verge of manhood, Jeffia Okwe, an intelligent and sensitive boy, wakes up from his pampered existence in the wealthy Lagos suburb of Ikoyi to discover the extent of his father's ruthless business dealings. As the errors of Jonan Okwe's past resurface – in the shape of a hated brother – his whole family is sucked into a maëlstrom out of which mother and son will be the only survivors. This is the first novel of a young Nigerian who was not yet twenty when he wrote this work.

' . . . the strengths of the book – its moral conviction,

and the carefully observed descriptions of the business world of Nigeria, are evidence of a genuine talent.'
                                                   New Statesman

The Landscapes Within
London: Longman, 1981. 180 pp. £1.50
The hero of Okri's second novel is a lonely artist whose paintings express his protest against the squalor and humanity that surround him. His home and family, his youthful ambitions, his tender love for his neighbour's wife, all are trampled and torn by the harsh intrusion of reality.

Olusola, Segun
The Village Headmaster
Yaba, Nigeria: Ariya Productions, 1977.
96 pp. ₦2.00
This is the transcript of a popular Nigerian television series. Includes biographical sketches of the leading actors and of Olusola, the serial creator.

Omotoso, Kole
The Edifice
London: HEB, 1971 (AWS, 102). 128 pp.
£1.95/$4.00
Dele, a Nigerian student in the United Kingdom, marries Daisy, an English girl, and takes her home to Africa where the marriage slowly disintegrates as Dele becomes interested in politics – and in another white girl. Told in two parts, from the point of view of both Dele and Daisy.

' . . . creative and honest writing.'
                          D. W. – *West Africa*
'What Kole Omotoso has done remarkably well is that he has experimented with unconventional, slightly anti-novel style.'   *Daily Times* (Nigeria)

The Combat
London: HEB, 1972 (AWS, 122). 96 pp.
£1.75/$4.00
Omotoso's second novel is meant as a parable of the Nigerian Civil War. Two 'brothers' challenge one another to a duel over the paternity rights to a child each one claims to have sired ten years previously with a young market girl, since turned prostitute. Their private quarrel turns into an international affair as the major powers take sides. Meanwhile, the object of the conflict, the child, lies dying, neglected by all.

'Kole Omotoso's writing is elegant, serious, ironic.'
                          Paddy Kitchen – *The Scotsman*
' . . . it gradually changes from comedy through satire to a doom-laden atmosphere of inescapable tragedy . . . brilliantly written'
                          Maurice Wiggin – *The Sunday Times*

Miracles and Other Stories
Ibadan: Onibonoje Press, 1973 (ALS, 2).
95 pp. ₦1.20
Children are the main protagonists in these six stories but they are not stories for children. 'Isaac', the third tale, seems to be an earlier version of one episode of *The Combat*.
'Omotoso's world in these stories is one without hope, one where each person seems a victim, one from which there is no redemption'
Cheryl Dash – *World Literature Written in English*

Fella's Choice
Benin City, Nigeria: Ethiope Publ. Corp., 1974. 111 pp. 80k
Called 'the first Nigerian detective novel', Omotoso's fourth book has Inspector Fella Dandogo pitted against the South African Secret Service who have a plan for weakening Nigeria (and thus, all of black Africa) by flooding the country with counterfeit currency.

Sacrifice
Ibadan: Onibonoje Press, 1974 (ALS, 6).
103 pp.   ₦1.80
When Mary is seduced by a photographer who had promised marriage, she turns to the only profession that will allow her to raise her son decently – prostitution. Years later the son, now a medical doctor, finds himself unable to come to terms with his mother's socially unacceptable means of existence and gradually pushes her to the brink of disaster.

The Curse: a play
Ibadan: New Horn Press, 1976. 32 pp. 75k
In this short satirical play wealth is a curse which blinds people to such feelings as loyalty, devotion and brotherhood. Man's only desire is to acquire riches and power at the expense of his fellow. Servants only too willingly take the master's place – and eliminate each other for top position. The master here is Chief Alagba and the servants are Gbolaro and Moyegun.

The Scales
Ibadan: Onibonoje Press, 1976 (ALS, 11).
104 pp. ₦1.80
Chief Daniran, a wealthy businessman with powerful connections, has a diabolic plan to increase his earnings which involves recruiting beggars and maiming them further. Unable to get official action against him, Barri Jogunde, of Nigeria's Third Division, sets up a private militia, 'The Gentlemen of Courage and Conviction', the GCC, and proceeds to restore the meaning of justice.

Shadows in the Horizons: a play about the combustibility of private property
Ibadan: Sketch Publ. Co., 1977. 44 pp. 75k
The title of this 4-act play is taken from Okigbo's *Elegy for Alto* and it was first staged at the University of Ife in May, 1977. The scene is a public layby on a motorway in present-day Nigeria. Amidst a servants' revolt property owners flee to protect their lives and their possessions. Alliances form, break-up and reform as the rich plot against one another and are themselves subjected to an inquest by the 'Citizen Judges'. Atewolara, a rich security man, outwits them all and takes over as dictator-king. It is but a short-lived triumph. The people (the servants) have the last word.
'As in his novels . . . Omotoso's satirical writing is characterized by wit and understanding . . . an important and powerful play.'
Donald Burness – *African Book Publishing Record*

Oni, D.
Gods are Parasites: a play
Ilesha, Nigeria: Fatiregun Press, 1979. 111 pp.
₦2.00

Onyeama, Dillibe
Nigger at Eton
London: Leslie Frewin, 1972. o/p
London: Satellite Books, 1976. 239 pp. 90p p/b
The author spent four years, from 1965 to 1969, at England's most famous school. In this story of his life there, he tells of bigotry, colour prejudice, homosexuality, violence, snobbery and alleged voodoo practices.

Sex is a Nigger's Game
London: Satellite Books, 1976. 151 pp. £3.75 cased
The erotic account of an Eton-trained Ibo, Child Uka, who is cut off from his wealthy parents by the Biafran war and forced to fend for himself in England, ending up with a menial job in a hotel with lodgings in the basement, a descent from 'heaven to hell', as he puts it.

Juju
London: Satellite Books, 1976. 143 pp. £4.00 cased
New York: Archer Editions, 1980. 143 pp. $10.00 cased
The chronicle of supernatural events covering seventy years in the life of an Ibo community. The diabolic nature of Beatrice Nwokedi survives through her son, Romanus, who relentlessly torments Comfort, the wife of his childhood friend. Thanks to the old man, Chuka, his evil aims are ultimately foiled.

The Return: homecoming of a negro from Eton
London: Satellite Books, 1978. 112 pp. £3.50 cased
This is a sequel to Onyeama's first book. He describes what it is like going home to Nigeria after eighteen years of 'Anglicisation' starting in 1959 at the age of eight. The Nigeria he discovers is one of poverty, deprivation, corruption and chaos, very unlike the exotic images the Western media deliberately propagate.

Secret Society
London: Satellite Books, 1978. 128 pp. £4.50 cased
London: Sphere Books, 1979. 127 pp. 75p. p/b
The Leopard Men, a secret Ibo society from out of the past that specialized in brutal attacks on the colonizer as a means to defend their traditional way of life, suddenly emerge in London years later for one specific last mission – avenging the death of a young Ibo woman at the hands of a white hunter. Veronica Jenkins, a beautiful Englishwoman, is the unwitting lure that leads the Leopard Men to their prey.

Onyeberechi, Sydney
Africa: melodies and thoughts
New York: Vantage Press, 1979. 86 pp. $4.95 cased
This collection of verse grouped into six parts – 'Personal', 'Struggle,' 'Philosophical', 'Excitement,' 'Satire,' 'On Africa' – reveals the author's concern with Africa as a unity as well as his deep feelings about his own Ibo culture and his recognition of the shortcomings of the Western world. There are also poems on a more personal level.

Onyekwelu, Fidel Chidi
The Sawabas: black Africa's mafia
New York: Vantage Press, 1979. 125 pp. $6.95 cased
A ruthless gang of criminals led by Mighty Joe, Thinker, Big Boy and the bloodthirsty Governor Hey have practically taken over Nigeria and the police are unable to stop them. One daring exploit follows another and the newspapers demand action. A police thriller set in the mid-sixties.

Oparandu, Ibe
The Wages of Sin
London: Macmillan Educ., 1980. 100 pp. 80p
Obi Chike, a twenty-one year old Political Science student falls hopelessly in love with a beautiful but notoriously promiscuous fellow student called Ojiji. Ignoring the advice of his friends and relatives, Obi strives to reform her,

but for all his efforts their relationship is doomed to end in tragedy.

Osahon, Naiwu
The Climate of Darkness
Lagos: Di Nigro Press, 1971. 115 pp. 50k
An angry account of an educated black man's encounter with racial discrimination in Great Britain, written as a novel.

Sex is a Nigger
Lagos: Di Nigro Press, 1972. 188 pp. 65k p/b
London: John Calder, 1980. 192 pp. £5.95 cased
The erotic memoirs of an African student in Scandinavia.

Fires of Africa: poems and articles
Lagos: Di Nigro Press, 1973. 84 pp. ₦1.25
Poems and essays about the black experience.

No Answer from the Oracle
Lagos: Third World First Publ. 1978 (2nd ed.). 75 pp. ₦1.00
Two plays that were originally published in 1976 by Di Nigro Press, Lagos. The title play is concerned with the falsification of values resulting from the Westernization of African communities.

Shadows
Lagos: Third World First Publ., 1980. 98 pp. ₦1.25
Short stories about the intrigues, pressures and headiness of life in rapidly developing urban Nigeria.

Poems for Young Lovers
Lagos: Third World First Publ., 1980 (2nd ed.). 90 pp. 75k
A collection of poetry for younger readers that was first published in 1974 by Di Nigro Press.

From the Fringe
Lagos: Third World First Publ., 1980. 100 pp. ₦1.00
A play about a man and a woman that takes on eerie dimensions.

A Life for Others
Lagos: Third World First Publ., 1980. 150 pp. ₦4.95

A Nation in Custody
Lagos: Third World First Publ., 1980. 115 pp. ₦5.00
Osahon's story of the son of a poor peasant who grows up to be the owner of a beer parlour is also an essay on Nigeria's current political predicament.

Nigeria

Osofisan, Femi
Kolera Kolej
Ibadan: New Horn Press, 1975. 113 pp. 80k
Osofisan's first novel is a satire of post-independent politics in Africa. An African university becomes a sovereign state when an epidemic of cholera breaks out in its midst: granting independence is an easy way for the mother country to rid itself of a problem. Chaos sets in as the young nation embarks on a path of repression, and to mask the real problems authorities launch an authenticity campaign. Opponents continue to be brutally dealt with and among them are the Poet who up to then had been a cynical observer. A *coup d'état* throws the campus into the hands of a self-declared monarch but in the prisons voices can be heard singing the Poet's songs. The novel has been adapted for the stage by the University of Ibadan Theatre Arts Department.
'. . . *a departure from the usual format of novel writing associated with African writers.*'
Kole Omotoso – *Afriscope*

A Restless Run of Locusts
Ibadan: Onibonoje Press, 1975 (ALS, 9). 51 pp. ₦1.20
This play dates back to the author's undergraduate days at the University of Ibadan and shows his concern about political violence. Sanda Adeniyi goes into politics to avenge his brother, a candidate for elections who was cruelly attacked by thugs of the opposing party, but ends up using the same methods he had condemned.

The Chattering and the Song
Ibadan: Ibadan Univ. Press, 1977. 57 pp. ₦1.50
Taking the form of a play within a play, *The Chattering and the Song* brings together a group of intellectuals and artists who aspire to remake the world. Among them are Sontri, an official of the revolutionary Farmers' Movement, and his bride-to-be, Yajin. On the eve of their wedding they and their friends act out a playlet, set in the past, in which a young man revolts against the oppression of a traditional monarch. As the playlet reaches its climax Sontri and Yajin are arrested by Mokan, an undercover agent and Yajin's spurned suitor. This is but a temporary set-back to the Movement. There is hope for their release and, meanwhile, others emerge to carry on the Movement's work. The play is dedicated to both Wole Soyinka and Christopher Okigbo and was first published in a provisional edition by New Horn Press in 1976.
'*There is innovation in* The Chattering and the Song, *as well as acknowledged borrowing from Africa's leading playwright.*'
Gerald Moore – *Afriscope*

Who's Afraid of Solarin?
Calabar, Nigeria: Scholars Press, 1978. 83 pp. ₦1.50 p/b
Osofisan's newest play, subtitled 'A Dramatic Creation after Gogol's *The Inspector General* in honour of Dr Tai Solarin, Former Public Complaints Commissioner for Ogun, Oyo, and Ondo States', is a comedy of errors based on a case of mistaken identity. In a town somewhere in Nigeria local officials shudder with fear. Solarin, the dreaded Public Complaints Commissioner has arrived and will inevitably discover how each has misused public funds. The man they prostrate themselves before, however, is Isola Oriebora, a petty thief on the run from Lagos, and his real identity is only revealed at the end when he has absconded with a pocket-full of bribe money – leaving behind the diary in which he has recorded everything, and a broken heart, that of Celia, the Pastor's daughter.

Oti, Sonny
The Old Masters
Ibadan: OUP, Nigeria, 1977. 95 pp. £1.95
When Mazi Oni-Okoro dies his nephew vows to entomb him with all the honours a man of his rank deserves in the Ibo community, meaning that seven fattened slaves are to be buried alive with him. Old Daniel, a member of the slave caste and a converted Christian, revolts not only against this custom but also against all the forms of discrimination that ritual slaves must accept in the Ibo society, like rules against marrying outside the caste (and Chidi, a young slave, and Oni-Okoro's niece are in love and wish to marry). Daniel appeals to the only possible source of help, the colonial authorities and the missionaries, but traditions hold firm and tragedy cannot be averted. A play set in eastern Nigeria in the early days of colonialism. See also *Three West African Plays* (p. 90).

Ovbiagele, Helen
Evbu, My Love
London: Macmillan Educ., 1980. 150 pp. 80p
Evbu leaves her village on the eve of her wedding and goes to Lagos in hopes of pursuing her education – and of meeting up with Jide Jones, the student doctor who had lured her to the city. She falls low for a while when she is constrained to earn her living as a good-time girl but in time she triumphs over misfortune – and the loss of Jide who turns out to be shallow and dishonest.

Oyewole, D.
Seven Short Stories
Zaria, Nigeria: Northern Nigerian Publ.
House, 1969. 54 pp. 50k
Seven stories that portray life in modern
Nigeria, occasionally in satirical form.

Rotimi, Ola
The Gods are Not to Blame
London: OUP, 1971. 80 pp. 85p
Rotimi's version of the myth of Oedipus has
Yoruba King Odewale as the central figure.
The play premiered at the first Ife Festival of
the Arts in 1968 and was awarded the first prize
in the *African Arts* competition in 1969.

Kurunmi: an historical tragedy
London: OUP Nigeria, 1971. 94 pp. 80k
London: OUP, distr. £1.50
The mid-nineteenth century witnessed a con-
flict of succession in the Yoruba empire of
Oyo. The dying monarch, the Alafin, wished
to reverse tradition and give his throne to the
Crown Prince who, in theory, had to commit
suicide when the Alafin died. The Lord of
Ibadan, who was also the Alafin's Prime
Minister, supported this move, but Kurunmi,
the Lord of Ijaiye and the Alafin's General-
issimo, fought to uphold tradition – and lost.
First performed at the second Ife Festival of the
Arts in 1969.

Ovonramwen Nogbaisi
Ibadan: OUP Nigeria, 1974. 96 pp. ₦2.00
London: OUP, distr. £4.95
A historical tragedy about the ruler of the
Benin empire who was crushed by the British
in 1895. Not always treated kindly by colonial
historians, Oba Ovonramwen comes across in
Rotimi's play as a man threatened externally
and internally – by the commercial ventures of
the white man and by political unrest in his
own empire. Published jointly with Ethiope
Publishing Corporation of Benin City.

Our Husband Has Gone Mad Again
Ibadan: Univ. Press Ltd., 1974. 86 pp. ₦1.40
London: OUP, distr. £1.95
Rotimi's best known play is a comedy that was
produced for the first time at the Yale School
of Drama under Director Jack Landau. A
former military Major and a member of an old
Lagos family, Rahman Taslim Lejoka-Brown,
takes to politics – and runs into problems,
among which are his two wives, plus a third
one arriving from America who knows nothing
about the other two. Many pidgin expressions
are used and a glossary is provided at the end,

as well as the score for five songs used in the
production.
' . . . a wildly hilarious comedy.'
                    Robert M. Wren – *Africa Report*
'Though Rotimi's greatest appeal is in his mastery of
physical theatrical craftmanship, his play reads
marvellously well.'
          Stephen H. Arnold – *African Book Publishing
                                                      Record*

Holding Talks
Ibadan: Univ. Press Ltd., 1979. 42 pp. ₦1.25
London: OUP, distr. £1.95
Rotimi's most recently published play, written
several years previously, is a theatrical experiment, very different in style from his other
plays. Characters and setting are only vaguely
identified. The author says, 'I meant it to be a
play of universal applicability.'

Safo, D. B.
The Search
Ibadan: Onibonoje Press, 1977 (ALS, 12).
76 pp. ₦1.50
An old man dares to take back his sick
daughter from the shrine where she has been
sent when he hears she is to be sacrificed. He
then attempts to have her cured by missionaries of a Christian sect but that, too, fails. In
the end his search takes him to a city hospital.

Segun, Mabel
Friends, Nigerians, Countrymen
Ibadan: OUP, Nigeria, 1977. 74 pp. ₦1.20
Contains the text of a number of broadcasts
satirizing Nigerian mores which were aired
over the Nigerian radio system between 1961
and 1974. Segun treats such subjects as the use
of dash, polygamy, Nigerian traffic conditions,
the legal system, and how to get a job.
' . . . she chaffs with a light touch . . . It is the kind of
book that gets passed around and that one likes to go
back to eventually re-enjoy.'
    Anita Kern – *World Literature Written in English*

Sikuade, Yemi
Sisi
London: Macmillan Educ., 1981. 112 pp. 80p
A romantic love story, in which a shy young
couple who have difficulty in coming to terms
with the world find happiness together and
eventually marry.

Sofola, 'Zulu
The Disturbed Peace of Christmas
Ibadan: Daystar Press, 1971 56 pp. ₦1.00
($1.80)
Titi and Ayo, in the roles of Mary and Joseph,

are the stars of the Youth Club's yearly Christmas pageant. The play is nearly ruined, however, when it is discovered that Titi is carrying Ayo's child and her father will not hear of her marrying the young man. Sofola's first play.

Wedlock of the Gods
London: Evans, 1972. 56 pp. 90p
Sofola's second play is a tragedy in a traditional setting. Ogwoma is widowed young and refuses to marry her dead husband's brother as custom would have it. She breaks a taboo by violating the period of mourning and becomes pregnant by her lover, a man she had wanted to marry in the first place but who could not afford the bride price. Ogwoma's mother-in-law will obtain revenge for what she views not only as sacrilege but as murder. The play was first performed at the University of Missouri in 1971.

The Wizard of Law
London: Evans, 1975. 44pp. 80p
This farce deals with the mounting troubles which beset a penniless old lawyer when he practises trickery to obtain nine metres of lace material for his frustrated wife.

The Sweet Trap
Ibadan: OUP Nigeria, 1977. 76 pp. ₦1.30
Set on the campus of a Nigerian university, this is a domestic comedy about Mrs Clara Sotubo's revolt against her husband over the matter of her annual birthday party which he has decreed may not be organized that year.

Old Wines are Tasty: a play
Ibadan: Univ. Press Ltd., 1981. 64 pp. ₦1.95

Sowande, Bode
Farewell to Babylon and Other Plays
London: Longman, 1979. 128 pp. £1.25 p/b
Washington D.C.: Three Continents Press, 1979. 128 pp. $9.00 cased $4.00 p/b
The first two plays in this collection of three have political themes. *The Night Before* has a group of young men at a drinking party on the eve of their university graduation reminiscing about their student days and wondering if their political ideals, which had cost the lives of some of their classmates, will withstand the inroads of time. In the title play, set twelve years later, two former student friends, now dedicated to opposing allegiences, clash in a fateful encounter which leads to a *coup d'état*. *A Sanctus for Women*, the third play, is based on a traditional myth.

Soyinka, Wole
Three Plays
Ibadan: Mbari, 1963. 118 pp. o/p
Contains *The Swamp-Dwellers*, *The Trials of Brother Jero* and *The Strong Breed*. See *Five Plays*.

A Dance of the Forests
London and New York: OUP, 1963 (Three Crowns Books). 89 pp. 95p/$3.95
First performed as part of the Nigerian Independence Celebrations, October 1960, this play is generally considered to be Soyinka's most complex and difficult to understand. The play takes place on the eve of a great festivity as the mortals of a tribe gather and call up ancestral spirits, who prove entirely unworthy of the great occasion.

The Lion and the Jewel
London and New York: OUP, 1963 (Three Crowns Books). 70 pp. 95p/$3.95
Rivalry in a polygamous marriage is the theme behind this comedy set in the Yoruba village of Ilunjinle. The main characters are Sidi (the jewel), the village belle; Baroka (the lion), the crafty and powerful 'Bale' or chief of the village; Lakunle, a Western-influenced modern young teacher; and Sadiku, the eldest of Baroka's wives.
'The play is Soyinka's most fully realized as far as dramatic effectiveness and poetic evocativeness are concerned and his most delightful in characterization.'
Susan Yankowitz – *African Forum*
' . . . might almost be outrageous if it were not so healthily sensual and amoral! The play is full of fresh and vivid imagery . . . this is a thoroughly enjoyable play.'
Peter Nazareth – *Transition*

Five Plays
London and New York: OUP, 1964 248 pp. o/p
Contains *A Dance of the Forests*, *The Lion and the Jewel* and the three plays earlier published in the Mbari collection. Of the latter three, *The Swamp-Dwellers* contrasts the superstitions and archaic traditions in the backward swamplands with the evils, corruption and exploitation of life in the big city of Lagos. *The Trials of Brother Jero*, a short, light-hearted comedy, satirizes the way of life of certain sectarian cultists in Nigeria. Lastly, *The Strong Breed* centres upon a New Year's celebration in a small village; a time at which traditional custom dictated the villagers' selection of an outsider as carrier of their sins – to carry away last year's sins in order to pave the way for a new year of purity and peace.
'Wole Soyinka is a highly accomplished playwright . . . My only criticism of his dramatic technique concerns his somewhat overfree, and somewhat

confusing, use of flashback scenes . . . But this is a minor technical criticism of Soyinka's work. I have no doubt whatever that he is a master-craftsman of the theatre and a major dramatic poet.'

Martin Esslin – *Black Orpheus*

The Interpreters
London: Deutsch, 1965 (2nd ed. 1972).
251 pp. £3.25 cased
London: Panther Books, 1967. 254 pp. o/p
London: HEB, 1970 (AWS, 76, with an introduction and notes by Eldred Jones). £1.50
New York: Macmillan, 1970. (With an introduction by Leslie Alexander Lacy).
276 pp. $1.50
New York: African Publ. Co., 1972. 251 pp. $17.50 cased

Soyinka's first novel (which has gone into many editions) spotlights a small circle of young Nigerian intellectuals – a journalist, a lecturer, an engineer, a civil servant and an artist – living in present-day Lagos, trying to come to terms with themselves. They have grown up together as close friends, and after leaving the university, they still meet from time to time in university common-rooms, at parties, and above all, in night-clubs and bars, in an effort to 'interpret' themselves and the society of traditional and modern Nigeria.
'*The quality of writing is very high. Soyinka has an extraordinarily strong visual imagination. He has the ability to see things superimposed on one another . . . a really brilliant novel in which Soyinka's talents as a poet, playwright and an extraordinarily sensitive writer of prose, are all fused.*'

Eldred Jones – *Bull. of the Assoc. for African Literature in English*

The Road
London and New York: OUP, 1965 (Three Crowns Books). 101 pp. 95p/$3.95
The 'road' is a highway in Nigeria near its capital city, Lagos. The chief characters in this play are the people who live and work on the road – truck drivers, mammy-wagon drivers, their passengers, touts and corrupt policemen.

Idanre, and other poems
London: Methuen, 1967. 88 pp. £1.75
New York: Hill and Wang, 1968. 88 pp. $3.95
This poetry collection features the long poem 'Idanre', written especially for the Commonwealth Arts Festival of 1965; it is a creation myth of Ogun, the Yoruba god of iron. The other poems range from a meditation on the news of the October massacres in Northern Nigeria in 1966, to love poems and a self-mocking lament 'To my first white hairs'.
'. . . *he displays here a prodigal command of language which one sees seldom; successions of*

brilliant images disciplined with the lyric form . . . the whole is strikingly relevant to the present fortunes of the society in which he lives.'

Elizabeth Isichei – *African Affairs*

Kongi's Harvest
London and New York: OUP, 1967 (Three Crowns Books). 96 pp. £1.25/$3.95
Soyinka's most recent play deals with conflict between the cunning President Kongi of Isma, a fictitious West African nation, and its spiritual leader King Danlola. It is set during a harvest festival arranged as the official start of a five-year plan.
'. . . *a hugely entertaining piece . . . Soyinka writes with ease and wit . . . the play consolidates Soyinka's position as one of the most promising talents of the contemporary theatre.*'

Martin Banham – *Journal of Commonwealth Literature*

Poems from Prison
London: Rex Collings, 1969. 4 pp. 50p
Soyinka managed to smuggle two poems out of prison in Nigeria: 'Live Burial' and 'Flowers for my Land'. The poems arrived in London with a letter to his publisher-friend, Rex Collings, in which Soyinka wrote: 'I've written a few of these, about the only creative writing that successfully defies philistinic strictures. And nihilistic moods.'

The Trials of Brother Jero, and The Strong Breed: two plays
New York: Dramatists' Play, 1967. 67 pp.
A special acting edition with notes on production.

Three Short Plays
London and New York: OUP, 1969 (Three Crowns Books). 128 pp. o/p
The Swamp-Dwellers, *The Trials of Brother Jero* and *The Strong Breed*, previously included in *Five Plays*. Both editions now out of print, and superseded by the two-volume *Collected Plays*.

A Shuttle in the Crypt
London: Rex Collings, 1971. 144 pp. £3.50 cased £1.50 p/b
New York: Hill and Wang, 1972. 89 pp. $6.95 cased $2.65 p/b
Whereas Soyinka offers in *The Man Died* the factual record of his imprisonment during the Nigerian Civil War, this volume constitutes his poetic record of those long months behind bars.
'*The poems are an expression of deep sympathy and an identification with the weaknesses and suffering of humanity as the poet mourns over the "little victories*

and the great loss" involved in the sad drama of
human history.'

Arthur Gakwandi – *Dhana*

Before the Blackout
London: Rex Collings, 1971. 68 pp. £1.50
This volume contains many of the sketches that
were first performed in Soyinka's satirical
revue of the same name at Ibadan University in
1965 and that deal with political events of the
day. First published in Ibadan in an Orisun-
Acting Edition.
' . . . an injection of Soyinka wit and style and Royal
Court professionalism into the sort of Yoruba political
plays made popular by such companies as Hubert
Ogunde.'

K. W. – *West Africa*

Madmen and Specialists
London: Methuen, 1971. 77 pp. £1.75 p/b
New York: Hill and Wang, 1972. 118 pp. $2.45
p/b
Soyinka's eighth play and first published work
after the Nigerian Civil War has close links to
the Theatre of the Absurd. It centres on three
members of one family: the once good Dr
Bero, who has taken on evil proportions in his
work for the regime's Medical Corp; the Old
Man (Bero's father), the philosopher-cum-
madman of the play who has tricked
authorities into adopting his macabre cult of
'As' without knowing what it means; Si Bero,
the doctor's sister, who has allied herself to the
healing forces of nature through two old
herbalists. The setting is glossed over, referred
to as 'out there,' where deeds of horror are
taking place, and 'down here,' meaning the
doctor's research lab. Crowds of maimed
beggars intervene throughout. Also available
in *Collected Plays*, volume 2.
' . . . a nightmarish image of our collective life as it
appears to a detached and reflective consciousness.'

Abiola Irele – *Sunday Times* (Lagos)
' . . . a masterpiece which may prove to be his finest
play . . . bound together by the satiric wit we saw in
Soyinka's earlier work, though here that wit has
matured and developed a far more refined edge.'

Richard Priebe – *Books Abroad*

The Strong Breed
London: OUP, 1964. o/p
London: Rex Collings, 1971. 40 pp. £1.50p/b
The Strong Breed centres upon a New Year's
celebration in a small village. According to
custom the villagers must select an outsider to
carry away last year's sins in order to pave the
way for a new year of purity and peace. Also in
Collected Plays, volume 1.

The Man Died
London: Rex Collings, 1972. 318 pp. £5.00
cased
Harmondsworth, England: Penguin Books,
1975. 320 pp. 85p. p/b
This is Soyinka's story of his arrest and
imprisonment by the Federal Authorities at the
beginning of the Nigerian Civil War. Accused
of supporting the Biafrans (Soyinka admits to
having gone to see Ojukwu to persuade him
not to take up arms), although never formally
charged or tried, he spent almost two years in
detention, largely in solitary confinement,
from August 1967 to 1969.
*The man we discover behind bars is not whimpering
in self-pity; he is loftily outraged.'*

Peter Enahoro – *Africa*
'Whatever one's political stand concerning the
contents . . . one cannot but be taken by the writing.
Soyinka is still Africa's greatest weaver of words.'

Kole Omotoso – *Afriscope*

Camwood on the Leaves
London: Methuen, 1973. 44 pp. £1.25
New York: Third Press, 1974.
Subtitled 'a rite of childhood passage, for
radio' this play explores the tensions of
adolescent awakening set against the internal
conflict of generations in a modern Yoruba
family and against pressures of European
Christianity on the traditional cultural patterns
of West African life. These tensions are
expressed here in terms of a conflict between
the Reverend Erinjobi, a severe minister, and
his son, Isola, who revolts against his father's
religion as well as his authority and who asserts
his own independence and that of the girl
whose lover he has become. First broadcast by
the Nigerian Broadcasting Corporation in
November 1960.

Three Plays
London: Rex Collings, 1973. 120 pp. £3.00
Includes *The Swamp-Dwellers*, *The Trials of
Brother Jero* and *The Strong Breed* which were
part of the original 1964 edition published by
OUP and entitled *Five Plays*. The *Swamp-
Dwellers* contrasts the superstitions and archaic
traditions in the swamplands of the Niger delta
with the evils, corruption and exploitation of
life in the big city of Lagos. *The Trials of Brother
Jero*, a short, light-hearted comedy, satirizes
the prophet figures of Christian syncretic sects
in Nigeria. Also printed in *Collected Plays*,
volume 1.

The Jero Plays
London: Methuen, 1973. 95 pp. £1.50
Contains *The Trials of Brother Jero* and its sequel,
Jero's Metamorphosis, which is here published for

the first time. In it the 'prophet' Jeroboam
emerges as a gifted union organizer when he
manages to unite his competitors and thwart a
government attempt to cleanse the beach of all
the dubious brethren, who ply their trade
there, in order to construct in its place a public
execution area. Also available in *Collected Plays*,
volume 2.
'*The* Trials *reveals the guillibility of men and the
qualities necessary for survival in Jero's spiritual
jungle . . . or anywhere else . . . The* Metamorphosis *shows a mature, deft and subtle playwright,
an imagination fertilized by harrowing experiences
and a humanity of vision which triumphs over
cynicism and despair.'*
James Gibbs – *Books Abroad*

The Bacchae of Euripides
London: Methuen, 1973. 108 pp. £1.75
New York: W. W. Norton, 1974. 112 pp. $6.95
cased $1.95 p/b
Soyinka has used existing translations to
rewrite the Greek tragedy but has formed the
original chorus into a slave chorus who praise
Dionysus. Rather than a merrymaker, the
Greek god, himself, has been transformed into
a deity who can alleviate the people's suffering
and there are parallels with the Yoruba deity,
Ogun.

Season of Anomy
London: Rex Collings, 1973. 320 pp. £4.00
cased
New York: Third Press, 1974. 320 pp. $10.00
Walton-on-Thames: Nelson, 1980. 320 pp.
£2.75 p/b
Soyinka's second novel takes its hero, Ofeyi,
on a quest for his abducted mistress, leading
him through a land wrecked by a repressive
regime and a cynical, acquisitive elite. Place
names are imaginary but the novel is clearly an
allegory for the upheavals that Nigeria has
known since independence.
'*The rewards of* Season of Anomy *are of a kind we
have come recently to expect from Mr Soyinka – an
unrelenting determination to count the cost of
Nigeria's tragic years.'* Times Literary Supplement
'*Soyinka skilfully interweaves a number of elements –
reality and fantasy, the literal and the allegorical, the
modern and the classical, African nature myths and
rituals and European archetypal allusions – into a
compact whole.'*
Eustace Palmer – *World Literature Written
in English*

Collected Plays vol. 1.
London and New York: OUP, 1973. 314 pp.
£1.95/$3.95
Contains *A Dance of the Forests, The Swamp-
Dwellers*, and *The Strong Breed* from *Five Plays*,

the original 1964 edition, now out-of-print,
plus *The Road* and Soyinka's adaption of *The
Bacchae of Euripides* which was staged by the
National Theatre in London in 1973. (For
more details see earlier entries of individual
plays.)

Collected Plays vol. 2.
London and New York: OUP, 1974. 282 pp.
£1.95/$4.50
Included here are *The Lion and the Jewel, Kongi's
Harvest*, the two Jero plays and *Madmen and
Specialists*.

Death and the King's Horseman
London: Methuen, 1975. 77 pp. cased £2.25
New York: W. W. Norton, 1975. 77 pp. $6.95
When a Yoruba king dies he must be
accompanied to his eternal abode by his
horseman, the Elesin Oba. In Soyinka's play,
based on events that took place in Oyo,
ancient Yoruba city in Nigeria in 1946, the
District Officer prevents the Elesin from
committing ritual suicide and Olunde, Elesin's
Western educated son, takes his own life in his
stead. In the production notes Soyinka underlines that the confrontation in the play is
metaphysical. The colonial factor is merely a
catalytic incident, and there is a hint in the play
that the Elesin's hesitation before death
facilitated his arrest.
'. . . *a text of great subtlety in which Soyinka both
consolidates and innovates . . . Elesin is in the
tradition of Soyinka's richest characters.'*
James Gibbs – *Books Abroad*

Ogun Abibiman
London: Rex Collings, 1976. 24 pp. £1.95
Washington, D.C.: Three Continents Press,
1976. $4.00
A three-part poem, inspired by President
Samora Machel of Mozambique's declaration
of intent to war against the Smith regime of
Rhodesia. In it the Yoruba deity Ogun is
viewed as a revolutionary archetype for all of
Africa and the Zulu king, Shaka, is a central
figure. The word 'Abibiman' comes from the
Akan and means 'the Black Peoples or
Nation'.

Opera Wonyosi
London: Rex Collings, 1980. 125 pp. £2.25
p/b
Boomington: Indiana Univ. Press, 1981.
125 pp. $12.95 cased $4.95 p/b
Soyinka has here transformed Brecht's *Threepenny Opera* into a cynical satire on contemporary Nigerian life, portraying greed, corruption, and social injustice.
'*When Soyinka uses satire it is creatively engaging.*

Sharp wit serves as a very effective weapon to confront the conscience of his audience.'
Kwesi Owusu – *Africa*

Aké: the Years of Childhood
London: Rex Collings, 1981. 230 pp. £7.50 cased
The story of the first twelve years of Soyinka's life – the only volume of autobiography he will ever publish, he claims. Soyinka had a secure and happy childhood and the pages of his book are peopled with characters such as Wild Christian (his mother), Essay (his father), and the bookseller whose wife was one of the little boy's early allies.
'Soyinka's autobiography celebrates and transcends its immediate landscape and represents a shared communal life which ultimately belongs to humanity. And because it succeeds – and succeeds well – Aké: the Years of Childhood *is a gift.*
Ben Okri – *West Africa*
'. . . without doubt one of the best books on African childhood . . . one marvels at the sharpness of the author's memory which goes as far back as three years old . . . This is a book that should replace some of the school text books that are irrelevant to African students.' Lionel Ngakane – *Africa*

Sule, Mohammed
The Undesirable Element
London: Macmillan Educ., 1977. 121 pp. 80p
Despite the death of her father, 16-year old Bintu is a star student with a bright future. Her plans include university studies and marriage to the son of her father's closest friend, a young lawyer. On the eve of her fiancé's return from England she gets into trouble.

The Delinquent
London: Macmillan Educ., 1979. 130 pp. 80p
Sale is the only son of Alhaji Abubakar, a wealthy businessman in Kano who, unlike his neighbours, has remained monogamous. Pampered by his mother he grows into rebellious manhood.

Thorpe, Victor
The Worshippers
London: Macmillan Educ., 1979. 156 pp. 80p
Who belongs to the mysterious Crocodile Society and what are their ultimate aims? Paul Okoro, journalist for the Ibadan *Western Echo,* and his lovely fiancée, Aimie, risk their lives to discover the truth – and to rescue Aimie's brother, John, from their fiendish jaws.

The Instrument
London: Macmillan Educ., 1980. 154 pp. 80p
A terrible crime wave has hit Nigeria. People are terrorized, the government is puzzled by a sudden increase in the number of brutal murders, and there has been a mysterious spate of gold thefts. Once again Paul and Aimie Okoro battle against the sinister forces of darkness.

Stone of Vengeance
London: Macmillan Educ., 1981. 120 pp. 80p
Chief Akintade is rich, respected, powerful – and frightened by a chain of events which seem to point to his death. Can Paul Okoro get to the bottom of his secret fears before it is too late?

Tutuola, Amos
The Palm-wine Drinkard, and his dead palm-wine tapster in the Deads' Town
London: Faber, 1952. 125 pp. o/p
New York Grove Press, 1953. 130 pp. o/p
London: Faber, 1962. 125 pp. £1.75
Westport: Conn., Greenwood Press, 1970 (Reprint of ed. New York, 1953). 130 pp.
'I was a palm-wine drinkard since I was a boy of ten years of age. I had no other work more than to drink palm-wine in my life. In those days we did not know other money, except cowries, so that everything was very cheap, and my father was the richest man in our town. My father got eight children and I was the eldest among them, all the rest were hard workers, but I myself was an expert palm-wine drinkard. I was drinking palm-wine from morning till night and from night till morning. By that time I could not drink ordinary water at all except palm-wine. But when my father noticed that I could not do any more work than to drink, he engaged an expert palm-wine tapster for me; he had no other work more than to tap palm-wine every day.' Thus begins this adventurous and folkloristic tale by Amos Tutuola, the first West African writer whose work was published in London by a major British publisher. Heavily influenced by Yoruba oral tradition, *The Palm-wine Drinkard* is a journey of the imagination into 'Deads' Town' – a never-never land of magic, ghosts and demons, unknown creatures and supernatural beings. The book might well have gone by unnoticed but for a rave review entitled 'Blithe Spirits' by Dylan Thomas, who had this to say:
' . . . a brief, thronged, grisly and bewitching story . . . written in English by a West African . . . nothing is too prodigious or too trivial to put down in this tall, devillish story.'
Dylan Thomas – *The Observer* (London)

My Life in the Bush of Ghosts
London: Faber, 1954. 174 pp. o/p
London: Faber, 1964. 174 pp. £1.65
New York: Grove Press, 1970 (Evergreen
Book, E-559). 174 pp. $2.95
An African fantasy – the people's beliefs about
the spiritual world and what happens to a
mortal who wanders into the 'bad bush' and
the world of ghosts. The American paperback
re-issue has an introduction by Geoffrey
Parrinder.
'. . . is the expression of ghosts and of African terror,
alive with humanity and humility, an extraordinary
world where a mixture of Western influences are
united, but one always without the least trace of
incoherence.'
                    Oumar Doduo Thiam – *Présence Africaine*

Simbi and the Satyr of the Dark Jungle
London: Faber, 1955. 136 pp. o/p
This is the fairy tale of Simbi, a rich girl and
only child, and the most beautiful girl in the
village. Despite the warnings of her over-
possessive mother, Simbi escapes from her
home only to experience poverty, punishment,
and starvation. After a great many misfortunes
she finally manages to return to her mother
and finds that life at home is better after all.

The Brave African Huntress
London: Faber, 1958. 150 pp. o/p
New York: Grove Press, 1970 (Evergreen
Book, E-560). 150 pp. $2.95
Narrates a brave huntress's search for her four
brothers, kept imprisoned by the hostile
pigmies.

Feather Woman of the Jungle
London: Faber, 1962. 132 pp. o/p
London: Faber, 1968. 132 pp. o/p
An old chief reminisces and entertains the
people of a Yoruba village with tales of his
adventures for ten memorable nights; notable
characters in these stories include the Feather
Woman, the Queen of the River, the Goddess
of the Diamonds, and the Hairy Giant and
Giantess.

Ajaiyi and his Inherited Poverty
London: Faber, 1967. 235 pp.
Again strongly influenced by Nigerian folklore, this story recounts the tale of Ajaiyi and
his loyal sister Aina, who set out after the death
of their parents to make a living on their own.
In his effort to get out of debt, Ajaiyi seeks the
help and counsel of an assortment of witches,
witch-doctors and wizards.

The Palm-wine Drinkard: opera by Kola
Ogunmola, after the novel by Amos
Tutuola
(Transcribed and translated by R. G.
Armstrong, Robert L. Awuloola, and Val
Olayemi)
Ibadan: Inst. of African Studies, Univ. of
Ibadan, 1972 (Bi-lingual literary works, 2).
153 pp. ₦1.25
The stage version of *The Palm-wine Drinkard* in
the original Yoruba, with parallel English
translation, as first performed in the Arts
Theatre of the University of Ibadan, in April
1963, with Kola Ogunmola taking the leading
role as the Drinkard. The Yoruba text here is
keyed to R. C. Abraham's *Dictionary of Modern
Yoruba,* and words and usages that do not
appear in it are explained in notes, unless the
English translation makes their meaning sufficiently clear.

The Witch Herbalist of the Remote Town
London: Faber, 1981. 205 pp. £6.95 cased
£2.95 p/b
The brave hunter of the Rocky Town sets off
on a six years' quest to find the witch herbalist
in the Remote Town who will give him the
medicine to make his barren wife pregnant. It
is a hazardous journey, and on his way he
meets such characters as the Abnormal Squat-
ting Man of the Jungle – who has a belly which
farts out air so cold that it paralyses all life for
miles around – and he overcomes such
problems as the Crazy Removable-Headed
Wild Man. He finally gets his medicine, but on
the way home is overcome by thirst, and he
sips a drop of the impregnating soup. His wife
drinks the rest and duly becomes pregnant –
but so does he! This is Tutuola's latest work
after an interruption of fourteen years.
'Mr Amos Tutuola is back, after depriving us of the
lovely poison for 14 years . . . he is as intoxicated and
intoxicating as ever. Tutuola is the real thing: not just
a teller of tales, but a maker of myths.'
                              Robert Nye – *The Guardian*

Uka, Kalu
Earth to Earth
Greenfield Center, N.Y.: Greenfield Review
Press, 1972. 26 pp. $1.00
A volume of verse.

Colonel Ben Brim
Enugu, Nigeria: Fourth Dimension Publ. Co.,
1978. 200 pp. ₦2.50
A novel that analyses the post-war fate of a
man who had fought in the Nigerian Civil
War. It is narrated by three of his former
colleagues: Major Koko, commanding in the
Bori region; Major Eugene Birigbo, comman-

ding in the Alaocha region; and Major Mike Chece, commanding in the Ibgwa area. The Colonel had earned the sobriquet of 'Brim' among fellow officers and men because of his prowess, insight and bubbling personality. By the disastrous end of the war this effervescent temperament had been dulled into what seemed like stark madness and the three friends try to discover why this had happened.

A Consummation of Fire
Enugu, Nigeria: Nwamife Publ., 1981. 208 pp. ₦2.80
An experimental novel that explores the political dilemma of a young African republic as violence and dissension tear it apart. Party leaders wrangle while the former colonial power intervenes to set up a pattern of government which, in reality, works against the interest of the emerging republic.

Ukoli, Neville M.
Home to the River: a play in two acts
Benin City, Nigeria: Ethiope Publ. Corp., 1975. 58 pp. ₦1.20
A tragedy of love in a traditional setting in the early days of colonialism. Odiete, a young man of strong character, is blindly in love with Isio, a maiden from a feuding clan believed to be possessed by the water god. While Odiete is away learning the ways of the white man Isio is sent to be his father's wife as a peace offering.

Ulasi, Adaora Lily
Many Thing You No Understand
London: Michael Joseph, 1970. 189 pp.
Glasgow: Fontana/Collins, 1973. 160 pp. 75p
A paramount chief dies and is buried with the heads of twenty men as custom dictates. But the brother of one of the victims complains. Thus begins a game of cat and mouse between colonial authorities (the novel is set in 1935) and Obieze III, the new chief, ending unfortunately in an ambush for Mason, a District Officer on the eve of retirement with eighteen years of service behind him. Mason had advised his young, naïve assistant not to pursue the investigation but is drawn into it in spite of himself.

Many Thing Begin for Change
London: Michael Joseph, 1971. 192 pp.
Glasgow: Fontana/Collins, 1975. 156 pp. 75p
Affairs take a different turn in this novel, a sequel to the previous one. As Mason's disappearance is being investigated by the District Commissioner, an African reporter carries on his own investigation about murder and secret society doings in the mining town of Amaku and Obieze II is revealed to be the culprit behind both.
'She writes skilfully, conveying the atmosphere of slight misunderstanding often present in a colonial situation.' M. N. – *West Africa*

Who is Jonah?
Ibadan: Onibonoje Press, 1978 (ALS, 17). 126 pp. ₦2.50
An expatriate with a dubious occupation is brought to the Mission Hospital with fatal head wounds. As he dies he pronounces the names of Jonah Isu and his son. When the police are brought in the body has disappeared from the morgue. What are the motives for his death?

The Man From Sagamu
Glasgow: Fontana/Collins, 1978. 124 pp. 75p
On the eve of the annual Oshun Festival, Olu Agege disappears. He is Sagamu's strangest citizen whose birth, forty years previously, was attended by a bizarre omen. Some suspect foul play, others breathe a sigh of relief, but everyone is vaguely worried. This includes Mr Whitticar, the Resident Officer, and the *Oba* who both agree that something must be done.

Umelo, Rosina
The Man Who Ate the Money
Ibadan: Univ. Press Ltd., 1978. 100 pp. ₦1.20
A collection of twelve short stories, five of which have won prizes in literary competitions in Nigeria and in the United Kingdom. Among the character portrayals there are Uche, whose wife has six daughters; Ihunanya, who lost her son during the Nigerian Civil War; Ekwueme, the man who knew too much; and Stephen, who went to England to get the Golden Fleece.

Felicia
London: Macmillan Educ., 1978. 128 pp. 80p
Felicia returns to her village from Red Cross Service in the Nigerian Civil War with a tragic secret and a private joy.

Umobuarie, David O.
Black Justice
Ibadan: Univ. Press Ltd., 1976. 195 pp. ₦2.50
London: OUP, distr. £4.00
Three stories illustrating the justice of traditional African society based on tales which the author heard his father tell. *Ughulu* is the story of a monarch who sought too much power; *Oisoikolo* relates the story of an ill-fated pair of lovers; *Isilua* is the tragedy of a queen.

Uzodinma, Edmund Chukuemeka Chieke
Brink of Dawn: stories of Nigeria
Ikeja, Nigeria: Longman Nigeria, 1966.
120 pp.
Short stories.

Our Dead Speak
London: Longman, 1967. 135 pp.
New York: Humanities Press, distr. $1.25
A series of mysterious events threatens a village
in Eastern Nigeria in this tale of murder and
revenge.

Vasta, Mamman J.
Will Live Forever
Enugu, Nigeria: Nwamife Publ., 1977. 35 pp.
₦1.00
A book of poetry dedicated to Africa's
freedom fighters.

A Bird That Sings for Rain
Enugu, Nigeria: Fourth Dimension Publ. Co.,
1978. 75 pp. ₦1.00
A volume of verse that shows the poet's
concern for his country, the contrasts it offers
and its varied traditions.

Ufuoma
Enugu, Nigeria: Fourth Dimension Publ. Co.,
1980. 32 pp. ₦1.50
The title poem concludes this collection. The
concern it shows with the revitalization of
Nigerian spiritual life is typical of the volume
as a whole.

Williams, Lari
Drumcall
Enugu, Nigeria: Fourth Dimension Publ. Co.,
1978. 80 pp. ₦1.50
The texts of the poetic dramatizations which
the author, who is a poet, playwright and
actor, has performed throughout the United
Kingdom.

They Stole the Night
Lagos: Third World First Publ., 1978. 95k
Poetry.

Wonodi, Okogbule
Dusts of Exile
Ile-Ife, Nigeria: Pan African, 1971 (Pocket
Poets, 3). (distr. by Univ. of Ife Bookshop
Ltd.). unpaged 60k
Poetry.

Yari, Labo
The Climate of Corruption
Enugu, Nigeria: Fourth Dimension Publ. Co.,
1978. 176 pp. ₦2.25
Naïve and vulnerable, Sule was brought up in
Kaduna as a strict Muslim. When his parents

move to Lagos he prefers to stay back but soon
falls into bad ways. Then with a new-found
resolution he decides to join his parents in
Lagos. The shock of what he finds there drives
him to drink.

Moonstruck and Other Stories
Enugu, Nigeria: Fourth Dimension Publ. Co.,
1981. 120 pp. ₦2.25
Rural Nigeria provides the setting for this
collection of short stories.

Yusuf, Ahmed Beita
The Reckless Climber
Ibadan: Onibonoje Press, 1978 (ALS, 18).
206 pp. ₦3.00
A poor young Pullo man, an anti-hero, climbs
to dizzying heights of wealth and power,
thanks to cunning – and luck. He inherits his
patron's fortune and marries his daughter with
his consent, but her heart is made of stone. In
consolation he turns to Islam and vows to
reform his life. Set against a background of
Muslim culture in contemporary Northern
Nigeria.

Zewi, Meki
Two Fists in One Mouth
Enugu, Nigeria: Fourth Dimension Publ. Co.,
1978. 80 pp. ₦1.50
A short play about the pranks and intrigues of
the younger generation. The introduction and
staging notes show the author had school
productions in mind.

The Lost Finger
Enugu, Nigeria: Nwamife Publ., 1979. 104 pp.
₦2.40
A folk opera centred around the myth of
Wentu, a female seer, who sells her finger to
the gods for the power to see visions. Wentu's
daughter falls in love with Obaladike, an
itinerant warrior, but he prefers the chief's
daughter. In trying to force Obaladike to love
her daughter, Wentu resorts to misusing her
powers.

Sierra Leone

Cheney-Coker, Syl
Concerto for an Exile
London: HEB, 1973 (AWS, 126). 40 pp.
45p/$2.50
Poems of agony and anger – encompassing the
church, race, love, his exile.
*'It would seem to me that this poetry is both
distinctive and individual.'*
          M. J. Salt – *African Literature Today*
'Out of our quarrel with others, said Yeats, we make

rhetoric, out of our quarrel with ourselves we make poetry. Cheney-Coker is a superb example of this truth: he courts the risks of rhetoric, but in his best poems he avoids it by containing his quarrel with the world within the greater quarrel with himself.'

Robert L. Berner – *Books Abroad*

The Graveyard Also Has Teeth
London: HEB, 1980 (AWS, 221). 128 pp.
£1.95/$6.50
The poet's first volume, *Concerto for an Exile*, is printed here, in addition to new poetry revolving around themes of grief and knowledge.
'The poetry . . . is all gold, and its authenticity arises partly from a necessary maturing of style and partly, and relatedly, from an access of self-knowledge.'

Robert Fraser – *West Africa*

Conton, William
The African
London: Heinemann, 1960. 224 pp. o/p
Boston: Little Brown, 1960. 224 pp. o/p
New York: New American Library (Signet Books D 1906), o/p
London: HEB, 1964 (AWS, 12). 224 pp.
£1.35/$3.00
One of the earlier West African novels. Writing in the first person, Conton tells the story of Kisimi Kamara, who is awarded a scholarship by his government to study in England. While exploring the Lake District, he meets a white South African girl whom he falls in love with. However, colour prejudice puts an end to their affair. Shocked and embittered, Kisimi returns home to dedicate his energies to the struggles for independence of his country, and eventually rises to power as a nationalist leader.
' . . . a very promising first novel . . . perhaps the best thing about the book is that the author has a rich sense of humour, and is also a fine philosopher.'

Mercedes Mackay – *African Affairs*
' . . . Mr Conton is such an excellent writer . . . that overall faults must be forgiven. This is a delightful book to read and Conton's feel for language is charming.'   Erisa Kironde – *Black Orpheus*

Easmon, R. Sarif
Dear Parent and Ogre
London: OUP, 1964. 108 pp. 75p
A 'drawing-room' three-act play about the conflicts between the old generation and the young, between traditional class distinction and modern classlessness.
' . . . peaches from Lake Como, moonlight on the Riviera, raffish Frenchmen and confetti, champagne and joloff rice on a moonlit beach – these are the stock-in-trade of this rather slick, West Endish play, yet there is no denying that the characters not only fit

into it, but they would be inconceivable in any other setting.'   Elow Gabonal – *Black Orpheus*

The Burnt-out Marriage
London: Nelson, 1967. 240 pp.
Against a background of village life a progressive chief and his even more progressive wife struggle to assert themselves. However, they conflict with one another and with the traditional framework of tribal society.

The New Patriots
London: Longman, 1965. 90 pp.
A modern comedy and morality play in three acts concerning the relationship between two political leaders and a powerful, well-bred widow with a heart of gold, whom they both wish to marry.

The Feud
London: Longman, 1981. 304 pp. £1.75
Short stories involving love, murder, the supernatural, and set in Africa and Europe.

John, Harry B. A.
Collected Poems
New York: Vantage Press, 1976. 41 pp.

Johnson, Lemuel
Highlife for Caliban
Ann Arbor, Michigan: Ardis Publ., 1973.
156 pp. $1.95.

Hand on the Navel
Ann Arbor, Michigan: Ardis Publ., 1978.
75 pp. $8.95 cased $2.95 p/b
These poems, Johnson purports, are from the pen of Corporal Bundu, who returned, crazed, to Freetown after the World War. Written in free verse, they present images of death and the trappings of war.

Maddy, Yulisa Amadu
Obasai and other plays
London: HEB, 1971 (AWS, 89). 184 pp.
£1.95/$6.50
Firmly rooted in tradition, these four plays employ ritual, chants and songs. 'Gbana-Bendu' and 'Obasai' are satirical, while 'Allah Gbah' is a melodrama and 'Yon Kon' explores the relationships of inmates in a gaol. They have been performed in various parts of Africa.
' . . . an exciting experience for the reader, and for the theatre-goer.'   F. A. – *West Africa*

No Past, No Present, No Future
London: HEB, 1973 (AWS, 137). 181 pp.
£1.95/$4.50
Rigid constraints in Sierra Leone (depicted as

Bauya in the book) cause three young friends
to throw away academic opportunity and to
become involved in corruption. When they
finally realize their ambition of getting to
London, their friendship is destroyed as each
flounders in his own neurosis. The future is as
bleak for them as is their present, and as was
the past.

*'Maddy . . . could teach his elders a thing or two
about writing with pace and vivid imagery, in this
tale of the growth and disintegration of a relationship
among three West African boys.'*
                     Clancy Sigal – *Sunday Times*
*'Maddy's previous work has been with drama – he
teaches acting in London – but this novel is more
successful than his published plays.'*
                     Charles Larson – *Books Abroad*

Mustapha, Muktarr
Thorns and Thistles
London: Paul Bremen, 1971. 24 pp.
Poems on African philosophy, dealing with
traditional Gods and ancestors.
*'This compulsive, powerful, and so far the best
collection of published poems by a Sierra Leonean.'*
                     Lans Joe Sasay – *West Africa*

Nicol, Abioseh [pseud. for Nicol, Davidson]
The Truly Married Woman, and other stories
London and New York: OUP, 1965 (Three
Crowns Books). 128 pp.
'Most of these stories are placed in colonial
pre-independence Africa with its emphasis on
pensionable jobs in government service, official decoration, and black and white keeping
their distance,' writes the author. The two tales
in the preceding entry are included, together
with the title story, 'The Judge's son', 'Love's
own tears', and 'Life is sweet at Kusmansenu'.

Two African Tales
London and New York: CUP, 1965. 75 pp.
£1.30/$3.50
In the 'The Leopard Hunt' a white European
officer puts pressure on a local subordinate to
take part in a hunt. The African gets killed and
local agitation results. The second story, 'The
Devil at Yolahun Bridge', concerns Sanderson,
a district officer posted near the Kissy hills in
Sierra Leone, and his encounter with the
visiting engineer from headquarters, who
turns out to be an African, Olayemi Egbert
Jones, the builder of a Yolahun Bridge.
*'[the tales] . . . reveal an abundance of what
William Dean Howells called the "cheerful realism of
the commonplace". In doing so, they provide insights
which are rare and which are to be cherished.'*
                     Robert F. Cobb – *African Forum*

Rowe, Ekundayo
No Seed for the Soil and other stories
New York: Vantage Press, 1968, 67 pp.
A collection of five short stories, all set in
Freetown.

Taylor, Wilfred H.
Black Melody
Walton-on-Thames: Outposts Publ., 1971.
16 pp.
Poems.

Till We See Again
Walton-on-Thames: Outposts Publ., 1971.
16 pp.
A further slim volume of verse.

A Poet's Palette
London: Regency Press, 1971. 58 pp.
A privately published edition of poetry.

Black Discord
Walton-on-Thames: Outposts Publ. 1973.
28 pp.
Twenty-eight short poems reflecting on events
in Africa.

NORTHEASTERN AFRICA

Ethiopia

Boruett, William Kibiegon
Give the Devil his Due
Nairobi: EAPH, 1969. 92 pp. K.shs.6.00/$2.00
Short stories and tales narrated to the author
by his Kalenjin elders in Kenya.

Gabre-Medhin, Tsegaye
*Oda-Oak Oracle: a legend of black peoples,
told of gods and God, of hope and love, and of
fear and sacrifices*
London and New York: OUP, 1965 (Three
Crowns Books). 54 pp.
Based partially on traditional Ethiopian
sources, this play develops the theme of fear in
the conflict between superstition and reason.
Ukutee, betrothed to Shanka, is under a curse,
interpreted by the oracle of the sacred Oda-
Oak to mean that her first-born son should be
sacrificed to the ancestral spirits.

Collision of Altars
London: Rex Collings, 1977. 80 pp. £1.95
Washington, D.C.: (distr.) Three Continents
Press, $5.00
The sixth century Auxumite Empire is the
setting for this historical drama. The pro-
tagonists of the four faiths of Christianity,
Judaism, Islam, and the ancient Ethiopian
religion are at the centre of the scene in their
struggle for influence when King Kaleb falls.

Lemma, Menghista
The Marriage of Unequals: a comedy
London: Macmillan, 1970. 96 pp.

Sellassie, Sahle
Shinega's Village: scenes of Ethiopian life
(Trans. from the Chaha by Wolf Leslau)
Berkeley: Univ. of California Press, 1964.
112 pp. $5.95
The first work written in Chaha, a heretofore
unwritten Ethiopian dialect, and translated
into English. It is in the form of autobiographical sketches – a fictionalized memoir
of village life in Ethiopia during the past two
decades.

The Afersata
London: HEB, 1969 (AWS, 52). 96 pp. o/p
The inhabitants of the thirty villages of
Wudma had no police force to investigate the
burning down of Namaga huts. But the
villagers had their own way of finding out –
through their ancient institution of the
'Afersata', the traditional Ethiopian way of
investigating crimes.

Warrior King
London: HEB, 1974 (AWS, 163). 150 pp.
£1.50/$4.00
Delving into nineteenth century Ethiopia,
Sellassie traces the fortunes of of Kassu Hailu,
a young man born into poverty and obscurity
who rises to become Emperor Teowodros II.

Firebrands
London: Longman, 1979. 174 pp. 95p
Washington, D.C.: Three Continents Press,
1979. 174 pp. $9.00 cased $4.00 p/b
The dramatic events of 1974 in Ethiopia
provide the climax to Sellassie's third novel in
English. Focusing on one particular case, that
of Bezunah and his family, he portrays the
widespread corruption existing in imperial
Ethiopia, and the division between the city and
the drought-stricken countryside. When the
Revolution of 1974 gains momentum Sellassie
notes with cynicism the dynamics of revolution, with people blatantly changing al-
legiances as demanded by expediency.
'. . . an engagingly naïve, political novel describing
the corruption in high places in Haile Selassie's
Ethiopia just before the revolution.'   Tribune

Worku, Daniachew
The Thirteenth Sun
London: HEB, 1973 (AWS, 125). 173 pp.
£1.95/$2.50
The contradictions between ancient Christianity and the prevalent superstitions in pre-
revolutionary Ethiopia are the background for
Worku's novel. A young educated Ethiopian
and his sister accompany their father, a dying
nobleman, on his last pilgrimage to a mountain shrine.
'With the publication of this novel, Daniachew
Worku emerges as a commanding presence on the
anglophone literary scene.'
Charles Larson – *Books Abroad*

Somalia
(See also Francophone Africa)

Farah, Nuruddin
From a Crooked Rib
London: HEB, 1970 (AWS, 80). 182 pp.
£1.50/$3.00
Farah's first novel – and the first Somali novel
to be written in English – is situated in Italian
Somaliland before independence. An arranged
marriage to an older man appals the young
nomadic girl, Ebla, who flees with a passing
camel train to Belete Wene, the first town she
has seen. She seeks refuge with a cousin and his
wife, who is heavily pregnant, effectively
becoming their servant. When the cousin
needs money he sells Ebla to a cattle broker.
She determines to flee again, and elopes with a
government official from Mogadiscio. He
leaves for a three-month study tour of Italy
shortly after their marriage; in his absence
Ebla enters a so-called marriage with a wealthy
man whom she discards when her husband
returns.
'Despite occasional stylistic awkwardness, From a
Crooked Rib *creates a valid and lively picture of a
Somali woman's world when she is caught up in a
conflict between her own goals and those her culture
dictates for her.'*   David F. Beer – *Horn of Africa*
'. . . fast-paced and always absorbing.'
Charles Larson – *Books Abroad*

A Naked Needle
London: HEB, 1976 (AWS, 184). 181 pp.
£1.95/$6.00
Koschin, a 'proud, fanatical, and poor'

Somalian teacher, is shaken when Nancy telegrams that she is coming to Mogadiscio from England. Two years have elapsed since they parted, and he is deeply uncertain about their relationship. The problems of cross-acculturation are illustrated for him by two friends, one successfully married to a foreigner, the other not. The backdrop to the personal involvement is post-revolutionary Somalia.

'The intelligence, sensitivity, and linguistic adventure of this novel make it a considerable achievement in any terms.'   C. J. Driver – *The Guardian*
'For the outside observer of political development in the Horn of Africa, Farah's novel offers a personal dimension to the ongoing Somali revolution.'
          Richard W. Sander – *World Literature Today*

Sweet and Sour Milk
London: Allison and Busby, 1979. 237 pp. £5.95 cased
London: HEB, 1980 (AWS, 226). 240 pp. £1.95/$5.00
Loyaan is drawn into the mysterious circumstances surrounding his brother's death when the state accords him a hero's tribute. As his brother's actual opposition to the one-party Soviet-backed Somalia emerges, Loyaan uncovers mounting state brutality. The action is enmeshed with the tensions created by the dichotomy between traditional forms of power and that vested in the modern state.

'Inside the framework of a plain, gripping (and it must be said, occasionally less than plausible) thriller, Nuruddin Farah achieves intensity by seemingly seeing, sensing, assessing and explaining everything at the same time.'   Hilary Bailey – *The Guardian*
' . . . not only is it beautifuly written and constructed, it also informs one, in the most vital sense of the word, of what it is like to live under the intolerable pressures of a tyrannous regime, whatever its political persuasion.'   Leonie Rushforth – *Bananas*

Sardines
London: Allison and Busby, 1981. 237 pp. £7.95 cased
London: HEB, 1982 (AWS, 252). 256 pp. £2.50
The central character of this novel, Medina, has been lifted out of the pages of *Sweet and Sour Milk*. She is a professional, strong-minded journalist whose writing has been banned in Somalia. She has left her rather weak husband, Sameter, who has compromised himself by accepting the post of Minister of Construction in the government. By leaving the household, Medina also escapes her fiercely traditional mother-in-law who threatens to circumcise Medina's young daughter, Ubax. A wide mesh of dilemmas and conflicts, her own as well as

those of her family and friends, is woven into the story, which ends on an unexpectedly quiet domestic note.
'So articulate a Third World voice deserves to be listened to, particularly as he writes like a novelist rather than a preacher.'
          Norman Shrapnel – *The Guardian*

Mumin, Hassan Sheikh
Leopard Among the Women
(Trans. by B. W. Andrzejewski)
London: OUP, 1974. 230 pp. £5.50
The main characters in this play – a merchant, his domineering wife, his daughter, and the eponymous hero – are vehicles for the playwright's concern about the new urban values which are eroding traditional ones. Specifically, he examines the ease with which marriages are broken in towns 'where the traditional safeguards for women and children are disappearing.'
' . . . the play unlocks the richness of Somali drama to a wider audience.'   F. A. – *West Africa*
'On one level the play relates to the African situation in particular in that it illustrates the fragility of modern marriages when traditional safeguards are no longer operating; but the essential question is whether marriage is possible at all.'   *British Book News*

Sudan

Fadl, El Sir Hassan
Their Finest Days
London: Rex Collings, 1969. 122 pp.
Washington, D.C.: Three Continents Press, 1969. $8.00
This book consists of two long short stories. The first, 'Their Finest Days,' is based on the Sudanese revolution of 1964, when the military regime in Khartoum was overthrown and the country returned to civilian rule. The second story, 'Barabbas down the Cross,' portrays the revolutionary period through the eyes and personal experiences of a young partisan.

Salih, Tayeb
Wedding of Zein, and other stories
(Trans. from the Arabic by Denys Johnson-Davies)
London: HEB, 1968 (AWS, 47: p/b edn 1969). 120 pp. £1.35/$4.00
A translation of 'Urs az-Zain wa sab'qisas', three traditional stories about the people in the remote Sudanese villages along the banks

of the Niger. Zein is a modern-age, monstrous-ly ugly buffoon, an object of both ridicule and affection. The story opens with the astounding news of his forthcoming marriage to the most sought-after girl of the village. The two other stories are 'The doum tree of Wad Hamid' and 'A handful of dates'.

Season of Migration to the North
London: HEB, 1969 (AWS, 66). 169 pp.
£1.95/$4.00
Narrates the life of Mustafia Sa'eed, who returns from a sordid environment in London to a village near the river Nile.
'*Salih is a masterly Sudanese writer with an oceanic, almost Jungian vision, profound and yet entirely matter of fact, without a false note or wrong emphasis.*' Jill Neville – *Sunday Times*

EAST AFRICA

Kenya

Akare, Thomas
The Slums
London: HEB, 1981 (AWS, 241). 182 pp.
£1.95/$6.50
The slums of Nairobi provide the home and hunting grounds of Eddy and the characters who populate the novel. An internally derived view of life in the slums is presented in an unsentimental manner. Life is cheap – drug-taking, drinking and prostitution are the norm, relationships are accordingly re-evalu-ated. The causes of poverty – corruption of the ruling elite, the workings of international politics – are perceived quite clearly by the slum dwellers.

Alot, Magaga
Heat of the Moment
Nairobi: Kenya Lit. Bureau, 1978. 60 pp.
K.shs.11.30 (£1.15/$2.90)
Dan, a Kenyan recently returned from study-ing in the United States, is the focal character of this play. His relationships with people variously representing traditional and chang-ing 'modern' culture highlight the struggle for identity in societies which are in a state of transition.
'*What Alot shows best is the contrast, amusing or painful, between the American style of Dan's Nairobi life and the traditional Africa of his upbringing.*'
M. G. Bloom – *African Book Publishing Record*

Angira, Jared
Juices
Nairobi: EAPH, 1970. 59 pp. K.shs.6.00
($2.40)
Poems encompassing not only traditional themes, but also abstract concepts, are infused with a moral awareness, with a concern for an imperfect environment.
'*Angira's sounds and people, simultaneously familiar and yet unique, meet in verse that is deceptively casual.*' John Povey – *African Arts*
'*. . . for a poet so young he speaks with a strikingly old voice.*'
Bahadur Tejani – *African Literature Today*

Silent Voices
London: HEB, 1972 (AWS, 111). 88 pp.
£1.95/$5.00
Angira writes of his anthology of poetry: '*Silent Voices consists of crude voices gasping in the dark, of voices trapped in between despair and existence, of voices caught up in a maze but always seeking to get through. They are voices from rusty tincans of the slums, seeking an outlet into the gay city, they are voices corked up in empty gourds. They are the searching voices that must achieve their goals in a strange silent quietness, quietness that defeats the drums. . . . Here is a conglomeration of voices.*'

Soft Corals
Nairobi: EAPH, 1973. 156 pp. K.shs.10.00
($3.20)
Angira's second collection of poetry, involving themes of self-interest and preservation, and the nature of life.

Cascades
London: Longman, 1979. 143 pp. £1.25
Washington, D.C.: Three Continents Press,
$4.00
The poet sums up his intentions thus: '*Cascades are poems about man as an individual first, who yearns to be understood before he is lumped on to the conveyor belt, the group on whose behalf philosophies are propounded, the guinea pig in the laboratory who seeks to be heard, at least before the experiments start.*'
'*The poems are a commentary – witty, sad, often cynical – on his own personal experiences and on modern society.*' Elizabeth Thomas – *Tribune*
'*Angira's poetry constitutes tremendous energy and movement and violent action – symbolising the violence of life and the passions of Man, as inspired by oppression, achievement and greed.*'
Dillibe Onyeama – *Paperbacks*

The Years Go By
Nairobi: Bookwise Ltd., 1980. 105 pp.
K.shs.20.00
Angira moves away from introspection to a more critical view of society in this volume of poetry.

Asalache, Khadambi
Sunset in Naivasha
London: Eothen Books, 1973. 59 pp. £1.25
A collection of meditative poetry on exile, including two long poems: 'Sunset in Naivasho' and 'Homecoming'.

Buruga, Joseph
The Abandoned Hut
Nairobi: EAPH, 1969. 112 pp.K.shs.24.00 cased K.shs.6.00 p/b ($5.80 cased $2.40 p/b)
A long poem in the p'Bitek style written by the author as 'a reaction to a common belief among some of the educated men and women that all that is tradition is bad'.

Buyu, Mathew
A Thousand Fireflies
Nairobi: Longman Kenya, 1974. 66 pp.
K.shs.7.25
A sad love story.

Chiume, W. K.
The African Deluge
Nairobi: Kenya Lit. Bureau, 1978. 136 pp.
K.shs.21.95 (£1.90/$4.80)
A gory account of the ancient and learned kingdom of Bayettia being tricked into supplying slaves to traders.

Gatanyu, James
The Battlefield
Nairobi: EAPH, 1967. 52 pp. K.shs.6.00 ($1.50)
A play that deals with the political situation just before Kenya's independence, and portrays the hopes and the intrigues of rival politicians.

Gatheru, Reuel John Mugo
Child of Two Worlds
London: Routledge and Kegan Paul, 1964. 215 pp.
New York: Praeger, 1964. 216 pp. o/p
New York: New American Library, 1972. 222 pp. $6.90
London: HEB, 1965 (AWS, 20). 230 pp. 95p.
'This is the story' writes Professor St Clair Drake in his introduction (to the American edition) 'of a young African for whom the dream of an education in America became a

compelling desire.' Mugo Gatheru's autobiography describes his tribal upbringing in Kikuyu country, his encounter with the West, and then his experience in schools in India, Lincoln University in Pennsylvania, and New York University, where he obtained a degree of Master of Arts, and finally in London, where he went to study law.
'... this extraordinary sensitive book could well become required reading in introductory courses in African culture.' Mary H. Lystad – *Africa Report*

Gicheru, Mwangi
Across the Bridge
Nairobi: Longman Kenya, 1979. 176 pp.
K.shs.16.50
Trouble lies in store for Chuma when he falls in love with the daughter of his wealthy master. His desperate desire for instant wealth, to be able to marry her and keep her in fitting style, leads him to the world of crime.
'... an excellent contribution to the genre of the picaresque novel.'
Emmanuel V. Seko – *African Book Publishing Record*

See also section 'Popular Fiction in East Africa', p. 194

Higiro, Joy
Voice of Silence
Nairobi: East African Lit. Bureau, 1975.
62 pp. K.shs.6.75 (£1.25/$2.70)
Joy Higiro's anthology includes poems on nature, as well as on themes of sentiment and black consciousness. The First Makerere Arts Festival Song of 1968 is included.

Hinga, Edward
Sincerity Divorced
Nairobi: East African Lit. Bureau, 1970.
112 pp. K.shs.5.50 (£1.10/$3.00)
Njamiki, to clear her conscience, dictates her life story to her husband, Hinga. Her revelations shock him: her inordinate snobbishness, her many affairs and her drunkenness, her complicity with her villainous lover in a plot to murder Hinga. Njamiki's sincerity destroys Hinga's love, and he drives her and their baby daughter out of his house.

Out of the Jungle
Nairobi: East African Lit. Bureau, 1973.
78 pp. K.shs.19.50 cased K.shs.7.50 p/b
(£1.75/$4.40 cased 90p/$2.25 p/b)
Kiamba, born to the Kikuyu, grows up in a traditional way, and the novel shows his passage towards becoming a freedom fighter.

Ibingira, Grace
Bitter Harvest
Nairobi: EAPH, 1980 (Modern African Library, 36). 157 pp. K.shs.15.00

Imbuga, Francis
The Married Bachelor
Nairobi: EAPH, 1973.(African Theatre 3) 60 pp. K.shs.8.50 ($2.00)
A dramatic rendering of two conflicts: one between a young man and a woman, each with an illegitimate child; the second involves the disagreement between the young man and his father over circumcision.
' . . . a good portion of the play is light humour. The result is more than satisfactory – a fine addition to the EAPH African Theatre series.'
Charles R. Larson – *Books Abroad*

Betrayal in the City
Nairobi: EAPH, 1976. 77 pp. K.shs.15.00 ($3.20)
Kenya's entry for the Second World Black and African Festival of Arts and Culture, held in Lagos in 1977.

Game of Silence
Nairobi: HEB, East Africa, 1977. 54 pp. K.shs.12.50
Raja is the chief protagonist in this play about the problems of a society which has the political elite alienated from the masses. Because he questions the role of education and the constituents of elitism, because he does not play the 'game of silence', he is a danger to the state and must be detained. The action is a mixture of reality, fantasy, and dream.

The Fourth Trial
Nairobi: East African Lit. Bureau, 1979 (2nd ed.). 76 pp. K.shs.10.10 (£1.05/$2.70)
A dramatic rendering of the conflict between a husband and his wife whose babies die. Is it her fault, as he thinks? Or is it the gonorrhoea he picks up from prostitutes? The second play, 'Kisses of fate', shows the meeting of youths overseas and what happens when they delve into their histories.
' . . . Francis Imbuga attempts in this volume of two plays to portray conflicts in cultural, social, and marital relations in this changing and complex world.'
William Ochieng – *Afriscope*

The Successor
Nairobi: HEB East Africa, 1979. 66 pp. K.shs.13.50
A play set in fictitious Masero in 'semi-modern' times seeks to examine ambition and what it does to people. The Emperor Chonda must choose a successor; Chief Oriomura must eliminate the emperor's favourite, Jandi. Using people as pawns, he embarks on a ruthless plot, but is himself checked.

Juma, Para
Portrait of Apartheid
Nairobi: EAPH, 1979. 286 pp. K.shs.20.00 ($4.50)
Onalo Magyo leaves Mombasa in search of further education. He arrives in South Africa, and becomes a victim of apartheid with all its ramifications of horror and violence. Hope for humanity materializes in the form of a young white woman, Betty Borner. Their love and marriage is the symbolic force for hope against tyranny and repression.

Kahiga, Samuel
The Girl From Abroad
London: HEB, 1974 (AWS, 158). 90 pp. £1.50/$2.50
June Mwihaki had been a scraggy school girl when Matthew Mbathia had last seen her. Her poise, beauty and intelligence now bowl him over when he meets her upon return from study in the United States. He is determined to marry her – but has not reckoned on the cultural changes she has undergone.
'Mr Kahiga has a sharp eye for significant detail and contrasts vividly the respective attractions of city and country life. His control of mood is sure, ranging from scenes of social comedy to the painful and moving encounters of the lovers endeavouring to build a relationship in which their needs and expectations are radically different.'
British Book News

Flight to Juba
Nairobi: Longman Kenya, 1979. 201 pp. K.shs.20.00
To be young in Africa today – Kahiga explores themes of youth in this collection of short stories. A detective, sailor, pilot, caddy, and an insurance agent are some of the characters who provide adventure and glamour.
' . . . it is certainly not difficult to see why his work should appeal to a large audience, particularly to readers who like their fiction seasoned with a dash of suspense and who do not insist too strongly that literature should examine or even reflect life as most people know it. Kahiga's characters are young, beautiful and usually rich: marvellous lovers, great drinkers, world travellers, businessmen on the make, detectives, television producers and actors.'
Ursula Edmands – *African Book Publishing Record*

When the Stars are Scattered
Nairobi: Longman Kenya, 1979. 140 pp.
K.shs.19.50
A love story involving Ricky, a young chemical
engineer, and two Muslim sisters. It is set in
Mombasa. His love for them is thwarted by
their different religion, their strict and unques-
tioning morality, which he respects but cannot
empathise with.
*'Sam Kahiga's short novel is not a major work of art,
but it might give some insight into the empty and
alienated life of urban, middle class East Africa.'*
                        Thomas O'Toole – *African
                        Book Publishing Record*

See also section 'Popular Fiction in East Africa',
p. 194

Katigula, Barnabas
Groping in the Dark
Nairobi: East African Lit. Bureau, 1974.
89 pp. K.shs.12.50 (£1.50/$3.10)
Katigula, one time editor of *Darlite*, is
concerned with the moral dilemmas of people
caught between traditionalism and modernity.
In close-up, Toma's wish to take a second wife
clashes with Christianity, and his son's desire
to be a writer and to map his own life provokes
familial anguish.

Kibera, Leonard and Kahiga, Samuel
Potent Ash
Nairobi: EAPH, 1968. 160 pp. K.shs.8.50
($2.60)
A collection of eighteen short stories.
'The stories in Potent Ash *which I have most
admired are those in which the inherent conflicts are
least clouded by an over-sophisticated sensibility.
These reveal two talented young writers who one
hopes will now experiment in longer forms of fiction,
especially perhaps in a couple of fully contemporary
novels.'*   Arnold Kettle – *East Africa Journal*

Kibera, Leonard
Voices in the Dark
Nairobi: EAPH, 1970. 180 pp. K.shs.12.50
($2.60)
In this, his first novel, Kibera probes in
fragmented fashion a Kenyan city after Independence. The central character, a playwright,
is a yardstick of the problems of the new
inequality which has arisen after – and despite
– the struggle for Independence.
'So far, Kibera's Voices in the Dark *is the leading
work in East Africa to come out strongly on the
alienation of the common man and the drunken riches
of the political élite. It is a masterpiece in style, and
a really difficult book for the lazy reader.'*
                        Chris L. Wanjala – *Joliso*
'Kibera is a tough, lyrical writer, but that is by no

*means all. He also writes superb dialogue and is a
deft satirist.'*
        Paddy Kitchen – *Times Educational Supplement*

Kibwana, John
Grand Race
Nairobi: Kenya Lit. Bureau, 1979. 74 pp.
K.shs.19.00 (£1.60/$4.00)
The Grand Race – a motor rally race – about
which Sasa has become obsessed, echoes the
race for wealth and possessions to which he is
also committed, becoming tyrannical in the
process. Conflict develops in this three-act play
between Sasa and his crew men, one of whom
turns out to be a police spy, the other a cripple
who is morbidly preoccupied with the spread
of leprosy, symbolic of greed and inhumanity.

See also section 'Popular Fiction in East Africa',
p. 194

Kithiniji, Gerald
Whispers at Dawn
Nairobi: East African Lit. Bureau, 1976.
143 pp. K.shs.23.70 (£2.05/$5.15)
Poems, sensory and intellectual, in categories
encompassing social, political, and academic
themes as well as love poetry.

Kittobe, Jem
Black Jesus and other poems
Nairobi: East African Lit. Bureau, 1978.
58 pp. K.shs.13.10 (£1.30/$3.25)
A short collection of poems on observations of
life and people.

Kulet, Ole
Is It Possible?
Nairobi: Longman Kenya, 1971. 156 pp.
K.shs.14.40
Lerionka is a young Maasai boy who is sent to
school by the colonial government, despite his
father's opposition.

To Become a Man
Nairobi: Longman Kenya, 1972. 141 pp.
K.shs.13.00
Leshao has to resolve the dichotomy of living
in a traditional society and having a Western-
style education. To prove the worth of his
education to his father, he aims to replace the
cattle his father had to sacrifice. Conflict
threatens when his father insists that he should
not buy them, but instead undergo the rites by
which to become a man.
*'Ole Kulet's stories could be called anthropological
studies of the Maasai. Drawing on a rich cultural
background, he dishes to us stories well prepared and
spiced with sweet tasting Maasai proverbs.'*
                        Muli Wa Kyendo – *Busara*

Likimani, Muthoni
What Does A Man Want?
Nairobi: East African Lit. Bureau, 1974 (2nd
ed.). 209 pp. K.shs.18.25 (£2.20/$4.15)
In verse form Likimani reflects on the
difficulties various women have in understanding their men and in ensuring that they
remain faithful.

They Shall be Chastised
Nairobi: East African Lit. Bureau, 1974.
233 pp. K.shs.12.50 (£1.50/$3.10)
The author, herself daughter of one of the first
Anglican ministers in Kenya, has tried to assess
the impact of missionaries on the life of a
village in Kenya. Beginning with some of the
first recruits to the mission, she points out the
advantages accruing to them, while also
demonstrating the psychological and moral
confusion to which they were subject. Circumcision, polygamy, and tribal rites were
anathema to the missionaries, who were
oblivious to the disruption of village and
family life that their stern attitudes caused.

Maillu, David G.
Kadosa
Machakos, Kenya: David Maillu Publ., 1979.
190 pp. K.shs.25.00
A fast moving tale involving the occult.
*'This is very far from being a lurid piece of Onitsha
style writing. Maillu is a highly competent storyteller
with a broad but vigorous ability in characterization.'*
Alastair Niven – *African
Book Publishing Record*

For Mbatha and Rabeka
London: Macmillan Educ., 1980. 149 pp. 80p
Love between Mbatha and Rabeka starts in
childhood and grows despite opposition and
difficulties. When illness takes Rabeka from
the countryside to Nairobi different perspectives of life open up to her. She becomes
dissatisfied with the limitations in Mbatha and
plans to marry the wealthier Mawa. Mbatha's
reactions, Mawa's financial downfall, and
Rabeka's true realization of the situation
complete the tale.

The Equatorial Assignment
London: Macmillan Educ., 1980. 156 pp. 80p
Secret agent Benni Kamba is involved in
penetrating the organization which is trying to
assume control of the African continent by
placing puppet presidents in all the states.

See also section 'Popular Fiction in East Africa',
p. 194

Mangua, Charles
Son of Woman
Nairobi: EAPH, 1971. 180 pp. K.shs.35.00
cased K.shs.12.50 p/b ($8.00 cased $3.20 p/b)
Dodge Kiunyu, son of a prostitute, reared in
the slums of Nairobi, is delivered by chance
into mission hands, education, and finally
Makerere University. He marries his foster
sister, an ex-prostitute, and meets his father
dying in a prison hospital. Drinking, womanizing, violence, corruption, and frequent
changes of employment are the basic ingredients of this picaresque novel: it depicts
human weaknesses as well as strengths. The
first printing, of 10,000, sold out in six
months.
'Because of the irreverent character of Dodge Kiunyu,
Son of Woman is more than just a work of erotic
fiction.' Peter Nazareth – *Busara*
'. . . Charles Mangua is well on his way to becoming
an important African novelist.'
Charles R. Larson – *Books Abroad*

A Tail in the Mouth
Nairobi: EAPH, 1972. 287 pp. K.shs.12.00
($3.20)
Samson Moira begins his life on the land and
will end it there. The intervening years
encompass varied activities: would-be priest,
home-guard turned forest-fighter, taxi-driver.
He is imprisoned for a murder he did not
commit, drinks heavily, causes his wife's death,
and is on the brink of becoming a thief when
he is saved. Man as tool of circumstances –
whether it be the Mau Mau Rebellion or
modern urban life – is what Samson's life
demonstrates. The novel was awarded the 1973
Kenyatta Prize for Literature.
'The novel is exciting because of the language.'
Peter Nazareth – *Busara*

Mbiti, John S.
Poems of Nature and Faith
Nairobi: EAPH, 1969. (Poets of Africa series).
92 pp. K.shs.24.00 cased K.shs.4.00 p/b ($4.00
cased $2.00 p/b)
John Mbiti is the author of several books and
articles on African religion. This is his first
poetry collection.

M'Imanyara, Alfred M.
Agony on a Hide
Nairobi: EAPH, 1973. 116 pp. K.shs.9.50
($3.00)
The fates of two families who intermarry are
traced over three generations in this novel.
Mutema, a village leader, starts the narrative
which ends with Mparu's adaptation to life in
Nairobi.

Mude, Dae Mude
The Hills are Falling
Nairobi: Transafrica, 1979 (New Writing Africa, 2). 296 pp. K.shs.30.00

Galge is a young man from Marsabit District who is successful in modern terms. He benefited from the sacrifices his family endured to educate him, finally receiving training in the United States and returning to a remunerative job. Mude is concerned with the moral, emotional, and financial problems now confronting Galge. Demands are not only constantly presented by his direct family, but also by unknown relatives and a greedy father-in-law, all in the name of African socialism. The tribal elders feel entitled to pontificate too. The hero is forced to consider whether he should personally provide support for people who are the victims of poverty and the social system.

Mudida, Francis
The Bottle Friends
Nairobi: Kenya Lit. Bureau, 1980. 111 pp. K.shs.10.50 (£1.80/$3.85)

When imprisoned for drunken driving, Aniluga analyses his downfall: his excessive drinking, his parasitical friends and the lure of prostitutes being the major factors.

Mugambi, J. N. Kanyua
Carry it Home
Nairobi: East African Lit. Bureau, 1974. 89 pp. K.shs.10.50 (£1.80/$3.85)

Mugambi adds this collection of poetry to publications on religion and philosophy. His poems constitute various responses to religious and cultural imperialism.

Mugo, Micere Githae
Daughter of my People, Sing!
Nairobi: East African Lit. Bureau, 1976. 60 pp. K.shs.8.40 (£1.20/$2.40)

Some of the poetry in this anthology has been published in *Fiddlehead*, the Canadian literary journal.

The Long Illness of Ex-Chief Kiti
Nairobi: East African Lit. Bureau, 1976. 82 pp. K.shs.13.30 (£1.60/$3.30)

The first play in this book, set during the Emergency in Kenya, shows ex-Chief Kiti suffering psychologically from the position he occupies – that of a collaborator rejected by his children. The second play, 'Disillusioned', shows that colour prejudice was practised by the nuns in an East African mission.

'The two plays are an addition to what has been

written on culture conflict and the destructive presence of the white man in East Africa.'
Chris Wanjala – *Afriscope*
(See also p. 190)

Mugot, Hazel
Black Night of Quiloa
Nairobi: EAPH, 1971. 91 pp. K.shs.7.50 ($2.60)

A story of love and betrayal between Hima and a white stranger who takes her to England.

Muli wa Kyendo
Surface Beneath
Nairobi: Longman Kenya, 1981. 125 pp. K.shs.20.00

A campus novel, set partly at the University of Nairobi and partly in Berlin. It is a novel about disillusion and alienation, and traces the plight of a Kenyan student who has left Kenya to study African literature at the Freie Universität in West Berlin.

Mulwa, David
Master and Servant
Nairobi: Longman Kenya, 1979. 206 pp. K.shs.16.50

The strange relationship between Hamad, the servant with a mysterious past, his joyless master, Kyanzo, and Kyanzo's sad wife Eileen, is observed through the disingenuous eyes of the young boy protagonist. The child learns of Hamad's past tragedy, the hopeless love he bears for Eileen, and unwittingly hastens the dénouement.

'This work shows promise for the continuing evolution of the novel in Kenya, as well as for the future development of Mulwa as a writer of sensitivity and depth.'
Thomas O'Toole – *African Book Publishing Record*

Muruah, G. K.
Never Forgive Father
Nairobi: East African Lit. Bureau, 1972. 319 pp. K.shs.30.00 cased K.shs.15.00 p/b (£3.00/$6.50 cased £1.50/3.50 p/b)

A long novel which examines modern urban morality. In particular, we follow the fall of Karinki, who re-encounters a girl for whose prostitution he may initially have been responsible. In trying to make amends, he wrecks his marriage and his life.

Mutiso, G. C. M.
Akina?
Nairobi: Kenya Lit. Bureau, 1978. 107 pp. K.shs.20.50 (£1.70/$4.25)

Free verse and prose are combined in three main sections: Identity, Re-collections and

Journeys in Diaspora. Mutiso is a political scientist, and perhaps it is not surprising that (as he says) 'politics seems to have taken the conceptual centre stage'. The style is eclectic, influenced by haiku, African oral traditions, the modern Russian poets, and some Latin American writers.

Mutiso, M.
Sugar Babies
Nairobi: Transafrica, 1975. 144 pp.
K.shs.12.50
A novel in blank verse.

Mwagiru, C.
The Day the Music Died and Other Stories
Nairobi: Transafrica, 1978 (New Writing, Africa 1). 129 pp. K.shs.20.00
An urban sensibility pervades this collection of short stories. Social hypocrisy, the vagaries of success, the new role of women, and recidivism are some of the themes.

Mwangi, Meja
Kill Me Quick
London: HEB, 1973 (AWS, 143). 151 pp.
£1.25/$3.00
Living in dustbins and scavenging for food, Maina and Meja soon learn that their ambition and idealism, fostered at school, are useless. When all attempts at finding employment are exhausted, and shame prevents their returning home, they drift deeper and deeper into crime.
'*Meja Mwangi's writings can help effect social change by changing the consciousness of the people.*'
Peter Nazareth – *Afriscope*

Carcase for Hounds
London: HEB, 1974 (AWS, 145). 134 pp.
£1.50/$3.00
Personal antagonism lends a particular savagery to the efforts by Captain Kingsley, former District Commissioner, to rout General Haraka who is leader of a Mau Mau company in the Laikipia district. The difficulties faced by the unwieldy colonial army are highlighted by the Mau Mau's swift mobility over forbidding terrain, and the fierce loyalty Haraka commands. Winner of the 1974 Kenyatta Prize for Literature.
'*The story never flags; Mwangi's ability to develop a fast-paced narrative is his major accomplishment. . . . A prolific young writer of considerable talent.*'   Charles R. Larson – *Books Abroad*

Taste of Death
Nairobi: EAPH, 1975. 258 pp. K.shs.12.00
($3.20)
Mwangi's concerns are centred on the Mau Mau struggle in this novel.

Going Down River Road
London: HEB, 1976 (AWS, 176). 215 pp.
£1.75/$4.00
Ben's life in Nairobi is hard – on temporary employment, drinking in sleazy bars, living in squalor. Hope visits him briefly when he moves in with the glamorous Wini, but is rudely dispelled when she departs, leaving with him the otherwise nameless Baby, her child.
'*Mwangi's exploration of urban problems is if anything, more detailed, more sensitive, and ultimately more convincing than anything that Ekwensi has ever written.*'
Eustace Palmer – *African Literature Today*
'*Mwangi's sense of the comic aspects of situations that are inherently painful indicates a detached and sophisticated approach to the problems of a developing economy and a developing country.*'
Faith Pullin – *British Book News*

The Bushtrackers
Nairobi: Longman Kenya, 1979. 208 pp.
K.shs.20.00/£1.25
The ugly world of poaching, mixed with gun-running, the gang protection racket, and the Mafia – such is the setting, based upon a film, with screenplay by Gary Strieker of Mwangi's novel. John Kimathi and Frank Burkell are the game-rangers who become embroiled with Al Haji's ruthless gang.

The Cockroach Dance
Nairobi: Longman Kenya, 1979. 383 pp.
K.shs.30.00
Dusman Gonzaga lives in Dacca House – a once opulent residence converted to mean lodgings for many who share one cold shower and a blocked toilet. Dusman is considered lucky to have a job; he is a meter reader. When he reacts against the degradation of Dacca House and the monotony of his job he is considered insane.
'*This novel is a valuable contribution to African literature, because it exhibits the Dickensian condemnation of human degradation, lest the society be anaesthetized against human exploitation.*'
Emmanuel V. Seko – *African Book Publishing Record*

Mwaniki, Ngure
The Staircase
Nairobi: Longman Kenya, 1979. 117 pp.
K.shs.12.50
A profile of life in urban Kenya emerges from the twelve short stories of this collection: the frustrations, corruption, inhumanity that are the result of the division between rich and poor, urban and rural.
'*Mwaniki's attitude towards his country and towards his writing suggests a degree of commitment to both*

which should make his further development interesting to watch.'

Ursula Edmands – *African Book Publishing Record*

Mwaura, Joshua N.

Sky is the Limit
Nairobi: East African Lit. Bureau, 1974.
254 pp.`K.shs.16.50 (£2.40/$5.00)
Looking simultaneously at father and son, Mwaura portrays the difficulties each encounters. The father, Ngarachu, is shaken by the changing traditions in his village; his lordly domestic rule is being whittled away. His son Mwangi is plagued with self doubts until he realizes the strength of mind over matter and rises to become a cabinet minister.

He Man
Nairobi: East African Lit. Bureau, 1977.
180 pp. K.shs.23.15 (£2.00/$5.05)
Kuria - sugar-daddy, tycoon, smuggler – rises rapidly and becomes ruthless, immoral, and extremely wealthy. We follow his unsalubrious adventures to acquire money and women.

Mwaura, M.

The Renegade
Nairobi: East African Lit. Bureau, 1972.
K.shs.10.00 (£1.70/$4.20)
The problems and conflicts involved in rearing children are examined.

The Flame Tree
Nairobi: Transafrica, 1977. 34 pp. K.shs.10.00
A novel.

Ng'Ombo, C.

Road to Murugwanza
Nairobi: EAPH, 1967. 150 pp.

Ngubiah, Stephen

A Curse from God
Nairobi: East African Lit. Bureau, 1970 (2nd ed.). K.shs.20.00 (£1.65/$4.15)
Karagu, with two wives, fourteen children, and no land, is troubled. His problems are exacerbated by famine and the repression of the Kikuyu, and he becomes a violent drinker heading for destruction.
'For the writer it is the choice between polygamy and monogamy, the traditional Gikuyu and the neo-Christian values, that tears apart the life of Karagu, the central character. The writer is decisively pro-Christian, for monogamy and against tradition.'
Bahadur Tejani – *African Literature Today*

Ngugi wa Thiong'o

Weep not, Child
London: HEB, 1964 (AWS, 7). 160 pp.
£1.25/$3.00
New York: Macmillan, 1969 (with an introduction by Martin Tucker), 184 pp.
The first novel in English to be published by an East African writer. *Weep not, Child* won a special award at the Festival of Negro Arts in Dakar in 1965, and is now one of the most popular of African novels. Divided into two parts, the first is set in the period just before the Emergency in Kenya and the rise of Mau Mau; the second deals with the Emergency itself in the life of a Kenyan family. Its central figure is Njoroge, whose dream of an education is destroyed when his father, Ngotho, a traditional Kikuyu, is arrested as a Mau Mau suspect and tortured by his former employer. Young Njoroge finds himself drawn into the struggle for Kenyan independence and the tragedies that are involved. The title of the novel is from Walt Whitman's poem 'On the beach at night'.
'. . . worth reading for its picture of African family life in Kenya, for its insight into, for instance, the ordinary African's bewilderment and indifference to the great European wars.'
D. E. S. Maxwell – *Black Orpheus*
'. . . important for three reasons: its historical place – the first novel in English by an East African; its setting or subject – Kenya during the Emergency; and its treatment of that subject or setting.'
M. M. Carlin – *Transition*

The River Between
London: HEB, 1965 (AWS, 17). 174 pp.
£1.25/$2.50
A novel of conflict between old and new, between Christianity and African traditional religion. Set in pre-independence Kenya, it tells the story of Waiyake and his love Nyambura, separated by the different beliefs and backgrounds of their families, living in two villages separated by 'the river between' – the river Honia.
'. . . seems to suggest that the solution to the problem of African versus European culture might not at all be synthesis, but rather a return to older values. The author seems to be arguing that evolution of the culture, rather than revolution, is the preferred method of change. This novel can be read as an interesting source-book on this one aspect of culture change, as well as a literary work more notable for its structuring images than for its story.'
Austin Jesse Shelton, Jr. – *Africa Report*
'. . . the conclusion is vague, giving the impression that the author is not certain how to gather together neatly the threads of plot in relation to his theme. But one can point out these limitations because the novel

will stand criticism; it is a successful one that makes a striking impression by its sincerity and ability.'
Edgar Wright – *Transition*

A Grain of Wheat
London: HEB, 1967 (AWS, 36). 280 pp.
£1.35/$3.00
Ngugi takes us back to the days immediately preceding Kenya's independence in 1963. The action centres around five main characters: Mugo, a local farmer and a hero in the eyes of the villagers, Mumbi and her carpenter husband Gikonyo, John Thompson, a British district officer, and the local petty clerk Karanja. Mugo is asked to deliver the main speech during the local Uhuru celebrations to be held in honour and memory of his friend Kihika, who was hanged by the colonial administrators. He refuses to make the speech, and though this is interpreted as an act of modesty, he turns out to be a traitor – the man who betrayed Kihika to his death. It is an attempt to identify, in terms of its characters, the racial, moral and social issues that made up pre-independence Kenya.

The Black Hermit
London: HEB, 1968 (AWS, 51). 96 pp.
£1.35/$3.00
The published version of a play first produced by the Makerere College Students Dramatic Society at the Uganda National Theatre in November 1962. Its central character is Remi, termed a 'black hermit' because he leaves his village tribe for the university.
'. . . probably the best of James Ngugi's published writings; and this is saying a great deal. The contrast between Country and City is effectively symbolized by the free verse spoken in the former and the prose of the latter.'   F. B. Welbourn – *African Affairs*

This Time Tomorrow
Nairobi: East African Lit. Bureau, n.d. [1970].
50 pp. K.shs.10.00 cased K.shs.5.50 p/b
(£1.50/$3.00 cased 80p/$2.00 p/b)
Three short plays by Ngugi: 'The Rebels', 'The Wound in the Heart' and the title play which was first broadcast by the BBC African Service in 1967. The basic concern of all three plays is the disruption caused to lives by colonialism, and the tragic problems created by the resultant conflicting sets of ethics.

Secret Lives: and other stories
London: HEB, 1975 (AWS, 150). 144 pp.
£1.50
Westport, Conn.: Lawrence Hill, 1975.
144 pp. $6.95
Of this collection of short stories, Ngugi says:
'. . . the stories in this collection form my creative autobiography over the last twelve years and touch on ideas and moods affecting me over the same period. My writing is really an attempt to understand myself and my situation in society and in history.' They fall into three categories: the first, 'Of Mothers and Children', deals with the kind of tragedies affecting women in pre-colonial Kenya. 'Fighters and Martyrs' examines problems created by the arrival of Europeans – facets of the Mau Mau struggle in particular. The glamour, shoddiness, loneliness of city life in post-independence Kenya provide the themes for 'Secret Lives', the third part.
'An accomplished book, remarkably free from rancour.'   Leonard Barras – *Sunday Times*
'Both for the serious student of African literature and the keen lover of African interpretation of his own existence, the book is a companion he should not miss.'
Jeff Mbure – *African Arts*

Petals of Blood
London: HEB, 1977 (AWS, 188). 352 pp.
£3.95 cased £1.95 p/b
New York: Dutton, 1978. 345 pp. $9.95 cased $4.95 p/b
As this long, complex and highly praised novel opens, a trio of prominent and corrupt Kenyans have been burnt to death in a brothel. Inspector Godfrey arrests three men – Munira, Karega, and Abdulla – and the prostitute-turned-madam, Wanja. In a series of flashbacks, the history of the previous years is gradually revealed. Munira had arrived in the village of Ilmorog twelve years before, as headmaster of the tiny school. Abdulla, once a Mau Mau fighter, now embittered and lame, was storekeeper and barman in the village; he employed Wanja as barmaid when she arrived, having inexplicably left the city life. Karega, a younger man, taught for Munira until the latter – jealous of his subordinate's relationship with the vibrant Wanja – dismissed him. When Karega returns to Ilmorog, he does so as a committed trade unionist. The lives of these four are interlocked with one another – and also with the community of Ilmorog. It is they who lead the abortive deputation to the MP in the city; it is they who revive the brewing of potent Theng'eta. Ironically, this traditional and local drink becomes the very symbol of the transformation of Ilmorog.
    When the Trans-Africa Highway arrives, a new Ilmorog ('a sprawling town of stone, iron, concrete and glass') is flung up; and none of its new enterprises is more profitable than the Theng'eta Brewery. Its chief beneficiaries (Mzigo, Chui, and Kimeria) are men of the new elite of businessmen and politicians; by the end of the novel it is clear that each of the four

suspects had abundant reason to have sought revenge on the three dead men. In fact, it is Munira who eventually confesses to the act of arson. The concluding passage carries a message of political redemption and hope. Karega, detained in prison as a communist, learns of the militancy being shown by the workers of Ilmorog: 'and he knew he was no longer alone.'

'. . . a book supremely well worth reading, and one which will repay rereading. Ngugi . . . is already acknowledged as one of the giants of African literature and his new novel underlines his stature.'
P. B. – *Africa*

'It's a wilfully diagrammatic and didactic novel which also succeeds artistically because of its resonant characterisation and deadly irony.'

Andrew Salkey – *World Literature Today*

'. . . Ngugi writes with passion about every form, shape and colour which power can take. A political novel, yes, but you have to add at once "among other things", since what is so compelling about its political fervour is exactly that it does always set politics among other things.'

Christopher Ricks – *Sunday Times*

Devil on the Cross
London: HEB, 1982 (AWS, 200). 256 pp.
£7.50/$21.00 cased £2.25/$6.00 p/b
Wariinga is sacked for refusing to sleep with her boss, and evicted from her shanty for refusing to pay exorbitant rent. She is also saved from throwing herself under a bus on the way back to Ilmorog, the scene of his previous novel *Petals of Blood*. This remarkable and symbolic novel centres around her tragedy and uses it to tell a story of contemporary Kenya faced with the 'satan of capitalism'.

The novel was written secretly in prison on the only available material – lavatory paper. It was discovered when almost complete but unexpectedly returned to Ngugi on his release. Such was the demand for the original Gikuyu edition that it reprinted on publication.

Ngugi wa Thiong'o and Mugo, Micere Githae
The Trial of Dedan Kimathi
Nairobi: HEB, 1976. 85 pp. K.shs.12.50
London: HEB, 1977 (AWS, 191). 86 pp.
£1.50/$4.00
Dedan Kimathi was a Field-Marshal in the War of Liberation in Kenya. He was caught, taken to trial and hanged. Mugo and Ngugi, having researched their material thoroughly first, have produced an imaginative interpretation of the trial in dramatic form. Using fluid movements, they seek to place the main action in the context of the long resistance of the

Kenyan people to oppression (beginning in the 15th and 16th centuries when they attempted to resist the Portuguese). The play, with the use of symbolic figures, shows how Dedan Kimathi and his followers were fighting not only imperialism, but also the concomitant powers behind it: banking, industrialism, religion, the black political collaborators. The ending, though it means the death of Kimathi, is a celebration of the victory of his beliefs.

'To be sure drama is not history and cannot seek to replace history. But to the extent that this all-engrossing play is grounded on concrete historical reality, to the extent that it begins, even within the limitations of its own framework, to help fill some of the gaps in the history of African revolutionary struggles, it is most welcome.'

Yemi Ogunbiyi – *Positive Review*

'The character of Kimathi has too long been wrapped up in awe, mystique and charisma without our people fully comprehending why. The Ngugi/Micere play puts the facts bare and affords us even greater understanding of why so many shed blood that we night be free.'   Seth Adagala – *Sunday Nation*

Ngugi wa Thiong'o and Ngugi wa Mirii
I Will Marry When I Want
London: HEB, 1982 (AWS, 246). 128 pp.
£1.95/$5.50
This is the renowned play which was developed with Kikuyu actors at the Kamiriithu Cultural Centre at Limuru. It proved so powerful, especially in its use of song, that it was banned and was probably one of the factors leading to Ngugi's detention without trial. The original Kikuyu edition went to three printings in the first three months of publication.

Nguya, Lydiah Mumbi
The First Seed
Nairobi: East African Lit. Bureau, 1975.
242 pp. K.shs.25.00 (£2.00/$5.00)
Kigaruri begins to question the efficacy of traditional sacrifices to ensure the safety of cattle on the day that his father is killed trying to prevent Mathai raiders from taking all his cattle. The fortunes and life of Kigaruri, living in pre-colonial Kikuyuland, are traced by Nguya in her first novel. The dominant theme is the necessity for Kigaruri to continue the male lineage. When neither his first wife, stolen from the Mathais, nor his second wife, married to him against her will, produce a son, he again flouts tradition by arranging for a son-in-law to live with him and become his heir. A new seed is planted – a new morality suggested.

Ngwabe, Victor
An Echo from the Past
Nairobi: Kenya Lit. Bureau, 1978. 154 pp.
K.shs.21.50 ($4.70)
Under the pretext of being asked to find an eloped couple, Vincent – a young man from a mission school – and Bill, an English linguist, set off to remote Basa. They are both subjected to a totally different cultural environment: Vincent appreciates the vitality of a non-Christian culture; Bill is forced to abandon his preconceived prejudices on closer understanding of a different set of ethics.
'If the first three chapters of the book are somewhat disjointed, stereotyped in their character portrayals and lacking in sustained interest, the next five chapters are an insightful, albeit eclectic, exploration of African culture in the uncorrupted villages of Kenya before Uhuru.'
Cecil Abrahams – *African Book Publishing Record*

Ng'weno, Hilary
The Men from Pretoria
Nairobi: Longman Kenya, 1975 (Crime series). 172 pp. K.shs.12.50/95p
A hunt to reach a political defector from South Africa involves South African agents, Kenyan security services, and the famous journalist 'Scoop' Nelson.
'If Hilary Ng'weno is willing to take the writing of fiction seriously . . . he may emerge as one of the important East African novelists.'
Peter Nazareth – *World Literature Written in English*

Njau, Rebeka
Ripples in the Pool
Nairobi: Transafrica, 1975. 168 pp.
K.shs.20.00
London: HEB, 1978 (AWS, 203). 152 pp.
£1.75/$4.00
Trouble is anticipated when idealistic Gikere takes Selina, the prostitute he has married, to live in his village. As the three main characters – Gikere, Selina, and the corrupt politican Munene – strive to fulfil their personal ambitions they ignore the symbolic life-giving power of the pool, quiet but menacing.
' . . . the work of an exceptionally gifted and articulate writer. . . . The characters, who span the whole tapestry of rural life in Africa, are portrayed with a depth and spicy richness that illuminates with shocking clarity aspects of rural society heretofore largely unexplored by African writers.'
Pius Omole – *Afriscope*

The Hypocrite
Nairobi: Uzima, 1980. 64 pp. K.shs.7.00/$1.00
Short stories which embody themes of hypocrisy, jealousy, ingratitude, and injustice.

Odaga, Asenath
Thu Tinda!
Nairobi: Uzima, 1980. 137 pp.
K.shs.18.00/$2.15
African tales incorporating traditional narrative style with the author's own originality.

Ogana, Billy Wandera
Hand of Chance
Nairobi: East African Lit. Bureau, 1970. 144 pp. K.shs.12.00 (£1.30/$3.25)
A young man and woman are confronted by the problems called into being by the changes in their traditional way of life.

Days of Glamour
Nairobi: East African Lit. Bureau, 1975. 109 pp. K.shs.15.80 (£1.80/$3.70)
Ogana gives us four vignettes of life in East Africa. In the title story, Grace is beautiful and capitalizes on her liberation until she finds that it is too late – there is no one left to marry her. In 'Grief, Rumour and Violence' crowd reactions to the murder of a prominent politician are portrayed. The final two stories show how a young English schoolmaster cannot adapt to Africa; and the problems besetting a young lad who sets out to visit his sister.

Ogot, Grace
The Promised Land
Nairobi: EAPH, 1966. 194 pp. illus.
K.shs.11.00 ($2.60) Cleveland: World Publ. Co., (Meridian Books), 1970 192 pp.
Subtitled 'a true fantasy', this novel is the story of Luo pioneers in Tanzania, and portrays the atmosphere and social tensions of rural life in Western Kenya.

Land without Thunder
Nairobi: EAPH, 1968. 204 pp. K.shs.30.00 cased K.shs.9.50 p/b ($5.80 cased $2.60 p/b)
Short stories of traditional life in the rural areas of East Africa – the villagers' life, fears, superstitions, and customs.
' . . . undoubtedly, a remarkable contribution to East African literature.' Neera Kent – *Busara*
' . . . by any standards, Grace Ogot is a very good writer of short stories; and her themes range from traditional occasions, through mission hospitals in colonial days, to the problems of sophisticated Africans at an Egyptian airport and the tragedy of young girls in contemporary Nairobi . . . she manages to write

from the inside of traditional Luo society, so that it comes to life in a wholly new way.'

F. B. Welbourn – *African Affairs*

The Other Woman and other stories
Nairobi: Transafrica, 1976. 150 pp.
K.shs.15.00
Nine short stories which concentrate on the problems of life: infidelity, illness, maliciousness, and how people cope with them.
'The stories themselves are such terrific inventions with several layers of suggestiveness as can be the result only of a rare imaginative activity, and the language is lucid and fresh.'

Romanus Egudu – *World Literature Today*

The Graduate
Nairobi: Uzima, 1980. 72 pp.
K.shs.14.00/$1.80
Questions of a woman's role, people's links with their mother country, are some of the themes in the story of the graduate who goes to America and returns home to find things have changed.

The Island of Tears
Nairobi: Uzima, 1980. 84 pp.
K.shs.15.00/$2.00
Short stories which range from the effects of a father's affairs on his family to incidents in New York. The title story commemorates the death of Tom Mboya.

Okello, C.
The Prophet
Nairobi: Uzima, 1980. 150 pp.
The situation in Etiak town after a coup, when the guerrillas and then the pastor are to be shot, concerns all Christians, in the opinion of Okello.

Okoboi, F.
The Final Blasphemy
Nairobi: Kenya Lit. Bureau, 1978. 181 pp.
K.shs.26.10 (£2.20/$5.55)
Ten years in the Civil Service find Joe Fakin still struggling to come out on his salary, while corrupt colleagues lead opulent lives. Temptation beckons, Joe gets involved in smuggling drugs and ivory, and becomes part of a vast network of corrupt government officials.

Oludhe-Macgoye, Marjorie
Murder in Majengo
Nairobi: OUP, 1972. 140 pp. K.shs.13.00

Song of Nyarloka and other poems
Nairobi: OUP, 1977. 64 pp. K.shs.12.00
(£1.95)
A woman who has journeyed to her new home earns the Luo form of address, 'Nyarloka'.

While observing the process of her transformation and adaptation, Oludhe-Macgoye points to aspects of Kenyan society.

Owino, H.
A Man of Two Faces
Nairobi: Kenya Lit. Bureau, 1979. K.shs.13.50
(£1.25/$3.10)
The protagonist, Okure, returns to East Africa after six years of study abroad. He rejects his family and faithful girl friend to wed unwisely; is imprisoned for procuring abortions; and even in jail cannot resolve the cultural conflict of which he is victim.

Ruheni, Mwangi
What a Life!
Nairobi: Longman Kenya, 1972. 161 pp.
K.shs.13.75/95p
Ruheni examines life for a young man in an East African city. He is fortunate enough to get a scholarship to study in England, enabling him to get a good job on his return, but temptations keep getting in his way.

The Future Leaders
London: HEB, 1973 (AWS, 139). 215 pp.
£1.95/$4.00
When Reuben Ruoro leaves Makerere University, he expects instantaneous success. A combination of colonial prejudice and lack of maturity on his part earns him a rapid dismissal. A teaching post which drops into his lap and stolen money which drops into his hands add further to his experience, so that when he is finally interviewed for a government job, he makes the grade.
' . . . this novel will certainly give another boost to African literature as a whole.'

C. I. Datondji – *Présence Africaine*

What a Husband!
Nairobi: Longman Kenya, 1974. 208 pp.
K.shs.13.75/95p
Things seem to happen to Dennis Kinyua – marriage, wife trouble, mistresses, unwitting involvement in gem-smuggling, counter-involvement with the police. These urban adventures are interspersed with accounts of an idealized village set up by the freedom-fighters to which Dennis is taken.

The Minister's Daughter
London: HEB, 1975 (AWS, 156). 186 pp.
£1.50/$4.00
Jane Njeri hasn't the resources to cope with life in Nairobi, having had a rigidly religious and repressive childhood upcountry. She becomes a tool in the hands of schemers out for sex and money. Her moral re-education is slow, but

she ends up wiser and better able to rectify her mistakes.

'Characterized by a deliberate sinister interplay between the forces of chance on the one hand and sheer human contrivance on the other, The Minister's Daughter *is an absorbing story told in the true spirit of a thriller without the cheapness of one.'*

Ejiet Komolo – *Dhana*

'Mwangi Ruheni is a gentle humorist who extends the rare warmth of his understanding even to his wickedest characters. It's very difficult to pin down in a few words the exact nature of his originality. He has an odd knack of being able to imply the nature of a milieu through the cadences of his prose.'

Jeremy Brooks – *Sunday Times*

See also section 'Popular Fiction in East Africa,' p. 194

Wachira, Godwin
Ordeal in the Forest
Nairobi: EAPH, 1967. 200 pp. K.shs.9.00 ($3.20)
Describes the effects of the Mau Mau Emergency in Kenya on the social structure of the Kikuyu people. The story deals with four young Kenyans whose education abruptly ends with the outbreak of the emergency. Nundu, its principal character, is transformed from a mischievous schoolboy to a courageous and dedicated forest fighter.

Waciuma, Charity
Daughter of Mumbi
Nairobi: EAPH, 1969. 96 pp. K.shs.8.00 ($2.60)
Describes the seven years Emergency period in Kenya through the eyes of an adolescent Kikuyu girl, and her reactions to the chaos that surrounds her.

Waithaka, Peter and Mbure, Sam
Flash Points
Nairobi: East African Lit. Bureau, 1976. 71 pp. K.shs.10.00 (£1.10/$2.70)
Two poets share this anthology of verse. Many of Peter Waithaka's poems urge moral commitment; there are also a number of nature poems. Sam Mbure explores contemporary issues with some irony.

Waititu, S. N. and Obasa, Y. G.
Sleepless Nights
Nairobi: East African Lit. Bureau, 1975. 64 pp. K.shs.5.75 (£1.30/$2.75)
Fourteen poems by Obasa, essentially Romantic, including love poems, descriptions, and serenades. Waititu's poetry – twenty-nine poems are included here – explore and reflect upon his emotions.

Wambakha, O.
The Way to Power
Nairobi: East African Lit. Bureau, 1975. 206 pp. K.shs.16.80 (£2.30/$4.70)
Mwele and Chido reap the benefits of independence by being offered jobs in the government. Mwele, a poor student, is lazy and incompetent yet receives promotion from friends. Chido stagnates, his brilliance ignored. Having reached the top, Mwele ruthlessly ejects so-called squatters from his farm, echoing colonial behaviour to his grandfather.

The Closed Road to Wapi
Nairobi: Kenyan Lit. Bureau, 1978. 275 pp. K.shs.36.85 (£3.00/$7.35)
Sanyo, a young man, fervently believing that socialism will bring post-independence equality to the common man, is foil to a tale of corruption. While punctiliously observing the forms of democracy, the government and the opposition use every means at their disposal for their own personal gain. Elections are rigged; officers of law are tools for dishonesty; even expulsions from the country are manipulated and court cases withdrawn. When Sanyo discovers that his uncle – a senator, an ardent advocate of socialism – is party to these malpractices, he finds life unbearable.

Wangusa, J.
Salutation: Poems 1965-75
Nairobi: Kenya Lit. Bureau, 1977. K.shs.9.00 (£1.20/$3.05)
Poems.

Watene, Kenneth
My Son for My Freedom
Nairobi: EAPH, 1973 (African Theatre, 4). 105 pp. K.shs.8.50/$2.60
The title play is set during the Mau Mau Emergency; it shows the position Kikuyu people were forced into, declaring their allegiance to either Christianity or nationalism, neutrality being unacceptable. When this involves the death of a son, as it does for Gaceru, the decision is traumatic. Two short plays complete the volume: 'The Haunting Past' deals with the generation gap; and 'The Pot' centres on drunkenness and its consequences.
'Draft rather than finished works, youthful exercises rather than mature accomplishments, they display a promising boldness of approach and some indications of subtlety.' James Gibbs – *Books Abroad*

Dedan Kimathi
Nairobi: Transafrica, 1974. 97 pp. K.shs.8.50
A dramatic rendering of events in the forest hideout prior to the arrest of the famous Field-

Marshal, Dedan Kimathi, during the Mau Mau rebellion.

Sunset on the Manyatta
Nairobi: EAPH, 1974. 263 pp. K.shs.15.00 ($5.00)
Watene presents a study of the alienation of a young Maasai boy from his culture and home through the process of education. A lengthy apprenticeship in Germany engenders a sense of solitude, exacerbated by instances of prejudice. His return to Africa leads him to a realization that the past must be integrated with the present and future.

Wegesa, Benjamin S.
Captured by Raiders
Nairobi: EAPH, 1969. 89 pp. K.shs.7.50 ($2.50)
The plight of a young Bukusu girl is the subject of this short novel. Nanjala is captured by a group of Tondo warriors in a raid upon her village and taken with them to their mountain home.

Yambo, Mauri
Flame Hands
Nairobi: EAPH, 1975. 79 pp. K.shs.9.00/$3.00
Yambo's first collection of poetry contains a revolutionary fervour in his dealing with the topics of colonialism and the future of Africa.
'At his best Yambo creates sharp concrete images and informs his poetry with hope for the future.'
Richard Priebe – *World Literature Today*

Man Without Blood
Nairobi: East African Lit. Bureau, 1975.
76 pp. K.shs.10.65 £1.30/$2.80
A volume of verse.

Popular Fiction in East Africa

The following entries list a number of works of popular, widely-selling light fiction. They are published in series form: as Afromance, Comb, Heartbeat, and Spear books. Heinemann's description of the Spear series is generally applicable to the works below: they 'have been selected for their punch, romantic flavour, earthy style, racy content and quick-fire interest.'

Afromance Series
Nairobi: Transafrica Books

Bobito, J.
Prescription: love
1975. 32 pp. K.shs.2.50
Kise, M.
Love and Learn
1975. 32 pp. K.shs.2.50

Sousi, D.
Hesitant Love
1974. 32 pp. K.shs.2.50
Love Music
1974 32 pp. K.shs.2.50

Comb Books
Nairobi: Comb Books
Kibwana, J.
Utisi
1974. 128 pp. K.shs.12.50($2.50)
Maillu, D. G.
Unfit for Human Consumption
1973. 93 pp. K.shs.6.00($1.20)
After 4.30
1974. 220 pp. K.shs.13.00($3.00)
My Dear Bottle
1974. 167 pp. K.shs.12.00($2.40)
Troubles
1974. 187 pp. K.shs.10.00($2.00)
The Kommon Man pt. 1
1975. 290 pp. K.shs.15.00($3.00)
The Kommon Man pt. 2
1975. 300 pp. K.shs.15.00($3.00)
The Kommon Man pt. 3
1976. 259 pp. K.shs.15.00($3.00)
Dear Daughter
1976. 59 pp. K.shs.6.00($1.20)
Dear Monika
1976. 64 pp. K.shs.6.00($1.20)
No
1976. 148 pp. K.shs.10.00($2.00)
Kadosa
1977. 190 pp. K.shs.15.00($3.00)
Maina, A. and Maillu, D. G.
One by One
1975. 125 pp. K.shs.12.00($2.40)
Mote, J.
The Flesh pt. 1
1975. 361 pp. K.shs.25.00($5.00)
Mwiwawi, A. M.
The Act
1976. 76 pp. K.shs.6.00($1.20)
Nanjala, E.
The Boyfriend
1976. 140 pp. K.shs.12.00($2.40)
Njue, P. N.
My Lovely Mother
1976. 97 pp. K.shs.10.00($2.00)
Ojienda, F.
The Native
1975. 176 pp. K.shs.15.00($3.00)

Heartbeat Books:
Nairobi: EAPH

Obondo-Okoyo, T.
A Thorn in the Flesh
1976. 159 pp. K.shs.12.50($3.60)

Onyango-Abuje, J. C.
Fire and Vengeance
1975. 132 pp. K.shs.10.00($3.20)

Spear Books
Nairobi: HEB East Africa (distr. in the U.K. by Tinga Tinga)

Alot, Magaga
A Girl Cannot go on Laughing all the Time
1975. 64 pp. K.shs.10.00 (90p)
Dawood, Yusuf
No Strings Attached
1978. 132 pp. K.shs.17.50(90p)
Erapu, Laban
Queen of Gems
1978. 144 pp. K.shs.15.00(90p)
Gicheru, Mwangi
The Ivory Merchant
1976. 88 pp. K.shs.10.00(90p)
Kahiga, Samuel
Lover in the Sky
1975. 88 pp. K.shs.10.00(90p)
Kalitera, Aubrey
A Taste of Business
1976. 106 pp. K.shs.10.00(90p)
A Prisoner's Letter
1978. 144 pp. K.shs.15.00(90p)
Ndii, Ayub
A Brief Assignment
1976. 90 pp. K.shs.10.00(90p)
Owino, Rosemarie
Sugar Daddy's Lover
1975. 80 pp. K.shs.8.00(90p)
Ruheni, Mwangi
The Mystery Smugglers
1975. 120 pp. K.shs.8.00(90p)
The Love Root
1976. 104 pp. K.shs.9.50(90p)

Tanzania

Hussein, Ebrahim N.
Kinjeketile
Nairobi: OUP, 1970 (New Drama from Africa, 5). 64 pp. K.shs.5.25 ($1.10)
This play is based on the 1904 *maji-maji* Rebellion, when Tanzanians sought to expel German colonists. The playwright seeks to make the play relevant to contemporary audiences by extrapolating meaningful parallels between the war and the problems of modern Tanzania.
'*Writing for a non-conventional theater, Hussein has*

employed techniques which challenge the actor, the producer, and also the audience.'
Ntangilege Green – *Books Abroad*

Mbise, Ismael R.
Blood on our Land
Dar es Salaam: Tanzania Publ. House, 1974. 127 pp. T.shs.16.00 (£1.50/$3.00)
Based upon a land case taken before the United Nations in 1951, this novel is partly autobiographical, partly fictionalized history. Mbise presents 'two ages' in Meru (in northern Tanzania): firstly, the 'age of clubs and spears that liberated the Meru land in 1896', and secondly the forced eviction of the village at the hands of the colonial government and the United Nations.
'*Written by a Meru . . . tells the story from the people's point of view. Thus there is neither condescension nor sentimentality in his fictional re-creation of great events.*'
Stephen H. Arnold – *Books Abroad*

Mkufya, W. E.
The Wicked Walk
Dar es Salaam: Tanzania Publ. House, 1977. 132 pp. T.shs.16.00 (£1.50/$3.00)
Some of the social problems of the neo-colonial period – prostitution, corrupt management – and the attempts of young people to deal with these problems, form the themes of this novel set in contemporary Dar es Salaam. Nancy cannot resist the temptation of money, and succumbs to the advances of a wealthy and immoral old man. Her mother, forced through necessity to become a prostitute, and the worthy young man who loves her, are both left desolate.
'*Politically bold and artistically solid . . . introduces a new talent and a turning point in English language literature from Tanzania.*'
Stephen Arnold – *World Literature Today*
'*Humility, respect for workers, democratic norms of behaviour – these are the qualities which official documents seek to encourage among Tanzania's leaders, yet the reality is different. Mkufya portrays this reality with brutal frankness.*'
Shabanji Opukah – *New African*

Mwambungu, Osija
Veneer of Love
Nairobi: East African Lit. Bureau, 1975. 152 pp. K.shs.16.50 (£1.80/$3.80)
Using the literary device of recounting his life story to a young woman, the author embarks on a long account of his schooling (begun in Tanzania in 1941). Interspersed in the history are reflections on friendship, sex, marriage, and colonialism.

Mwanga, Abel K.
Nyangeta: the name from the calabash
Nairobi: East African Lit. Bureau, 1976.
98 pp. K.shs.15.75 (£1.80/$3.75)
We follow the lives of the members of
Nyangeta's family, who lived on the shores of
Lake Victoria. Their chronicle is embellished
with descriptions of traditional ceremonies
attending birth, circumcision, marriage and
death.
*'The novel presents a portrait of traditional life which
is neither sentimentalized nor glorified, and this was
plainly the author's major purpose.'*
James C. Armstrong – *African Book
Publishing Record*

Nchimbi, B. R.
The Black-Eaters
Dar es Salaam: Tanzania Lit. Bureau, 1977.
Poetry.

Palangyo, Peter
Dying in the Sun
London: HEB, 1969 (AWS, 53). 136 pp.
£1.50/$4.00
The story of a man's love-hate relationship
with his dying and unloved father, of a family
struck by death in a village in the arid interior.
The son, Ntanya, goes through a difficult
personal time trying to resolve the hatred for
his father, the man who killed his mother.
*'Peter Palangyo has written the most profound
description I have yet read of an African man's
journey into the world of hallucinations and mental
torture . . . moreover there is an awareness of place,
of the valley and the fields and the colours of things;
and the story is set in a family and a village where
daily affections and tensions realistically surround
Ntanya's crisis.'*   Patricia Howard – *Mawazo*

Ruhumbika, Gabriel
Village in Uhuru
London: Longman, 1969. 202 pp.
Dar es Salaam: Longman Tanzania, 1973.
T.shs.9.50
Tells what 'Uhuru' – freedom and independence – meant to the people in a remote village
in Tanzania accustomed to the immediate
authority of their tribal chief and village
headman. A glossary of East African words
used in the story is included in an appendix.

Sokko, Hamza
The Gathering Storm
Dar es Salaam: Tanzania Publ. House, 1977.
176 pp. T.shs.20.00 (£2.75/$4.00)
The parallel stories of two families in the small
village of Bulembe, in post-independence
Tanzania, shows that Uhuru has not brought

the anticipated changes, and that exploitation
continues under different guises.

Uganda

Akello, Grace
My Barren Song
Arusha/Tanzania: EAPH, 1980. 140 pp.
The title poem and 'The Barred Entry' are two
long dramatic poems using narrators and
participants. There are 56 other poems, which
stress the reversal of the normal and through
which Idi Amin stalks.
*'Her vision is bleak and sustained; it is not only social
and political but also metaphysical . . . Grace Akello
is one of the most important women poets to have
emerged from Africa.'*
Peter Nazareth – *World Literature Today*

Bakaluba, Jane J.
Honeymoon for Three
Nairobi: EAPH, 1979. 192 pp. K.shs.12.00
($3.20)
A popular novel which dramatizes the conflicts
in modern African marriages.

Bukenya, Austin
The People's Bachelor
Nairobi: EAPH, 1972. 176 pp. K.shs.11.00
($2.60)
The author scrutinizes education, politics and
sex on an East African university campus,
viewing the problems as symptomatic of those
confronting the new African elite.
*' . . . a satirical novel that puts Africa's new
universities squarely in the dock. The author,
brilliantly humorous, bitingly frank, attacks the
artificial pretentiousness of African campus life and at
the same time grimly forces the reader to compare this
with the harsh realities just beyond the cloisters.'*
– *Afriscope*

The Bride
Nairobi: EAPH, n.d. 88 pp. K.shs.15.00
($3.50)
A play.

Byomuhangi, Fabian
The Whirlwind
Nairobi: Longman Kenya, 1981. 136 pp.
K.shs.23.00
A moral tale of a bright village school boy who
goes wrong. He does well at school and is a
natural leader, but is expelled for leading a
demand for reform. He drifts into the big city
to seek a living, and is driven by desperation
into a life of decadence.

Carlin, Murray
The Thousand
Nairobi: OUP, 1970 (New Drama from Africa, 3). 86 pp.

Not so Sweet Desdemona
Nairobi: OUP, 1970. (New Drama from Africa, 2). 68 pp.

Ibingira, Grace
Bitter Harvest
Nairobi: EAPH, 1980. (Modern African Library, 36). 157 pp. K.shs.15.00
Eight years after independence, in an African country, for which one reads Uganda, the opposition is vocal, the people disillusioned, the regime corrupt. This novel traces the obliteration of the opposition, mock trials, the degradation and ill-treatment meted out by the brutalized secret police of the regime. When the young army officers eventually overthrow the tyranny, one is left wondering what hopes there are for peace.

Kalimugogo, Godfrey
Dare to Die
Nairobi: East African Lit. Bureau, 1972. 178 pp. K.shs.42.00 cased K.shs.15.00 p/b (£3.50/$5.00 cased)
Four short stories are collected in this anthology, thematically linked by the different aspects of injustice.

The Pulse of the Woods
Nairobi: East African Lit. Bureau, 1974. 160 pp. K.shs.15.70 (£1.80/$3.70)
Tura leads his villagers from their drought-stricken land to the fertile Cocezo, where they tame the forest and raise crops successfully. The greed for more land on the part of a white farmer who has established himself some miles away threatens their security, but they have learned to fight, and his takeover bid is pre-empted.

Pilgrimage to Nowhere
Nairobi: East African Lit. Bureau, 1974. 154 pp. K.shs.14.00 (£1.60/$3.40)
Kalimugogo has captured the intrinsic sadness of the generation gap. Old widowed Bwengye cannot accept the fact that Kwita, his only son, has broken irrevocably from the life of the village with its taboos and traditions. He sets out to find his son, unaware that Kwita is a notorious drunkard, pimp, and murderer. When they eventually meet, Bwengye is stricken: he realises that his son cannot be contained in the village.

Trials and Tribulations in Sandu's Home
Nairobi: East African Lit. Bureau, 1976. 164 pp. K.shs.21.50 (£2.30/$4.75)
Sandu is obsessed with the worry that his wife Sara and son Daudi are pilfering items from his shop. Elaborate means are devised to exclude them, but to satisfy his own greed. Wife and son, meanwhile, do all they can to over-indulge themselves. In this, his fourth novel, Kalimugogo's main concerns are for characterization and an understanding of human foibles.
'Very different from his previous books, this novel reveals the versatile Ugandan writer as a master of comic situation, dialogue, and characterization.'
Stephen Arnold – *African Book Publishing Record*

The Department
Nairobi: East African Lit. Bureau, 1976. 157 pp. K.shs.18.00 (£2.00/$4.10)
A lampoon of the absurdities of bureaucracy and big business, with an underlying serious appraisal of the dehumanizing effects of the system.

The Prodigal Chairman
Nairobi: Uzima, 1979. 195 pp. K.shs.18.00
Crime and suicide are the results of evil and corruption in high places, when a top executive gets caught in the power politics race.

Kimenye, Barbara
Kalasanda
London and New York: OUP, 1965 (Three Crowns Books). 110 pp. illus.
A collection of short stories telling of incidents in the life of a typical Buganda village.
'. . . as a documentary account of village life it contains much that is vividly true . . . provides an entertaining diversion for anyone who enjoys village gossip.' Hebe Welbourn – *Transition*

Kalasanda Revisited
London and New York: OUP, 1966 (Three Crowns Books). 110 pp.
A further collection including tales of characters familiar from *Kalasanda*, and introducing some new arrivals.

Liyong, Taban lo
Fixions and other stories
London: HEB, 1969 (AWS, 69). 76 pp. £1.75/$4.00
'Fixions', the short story that supplies the title to this collection, is a satirical tale on the subject of foreign aid. The additional eight stories provide a combination of parables,

moral tales, folklore, satire, and literary innovations.

Meditations in Limbo
Nairobi: African Book Services (distr.), 1970. 72 pp. K.shs.6.50

Frantz Fanon's Uneven Ribs: poems more and more
London: HEB, 1971 (AWS, 90). 148 pp. £1.95/$5.00
lo Liyong ranges through time as well as space in these poems: subject matter, allusions, references arise from Africa, Europe, and America.
'In form and expression he is among the very "freest" verse writers, defying all rules and guides.'
    Timothy Wangusa – *African Literature Today*
'Whether the East African future belongs to those who appear to relish and capitalize on social inequities or to revolutionary zeal cannot yet be determined, but there can be no doubt that the latter has found in Liyong its authentic voice.'
    Robert J. Green – *Books Abroad*

The Uniformed Man
Nairobi: East African Lit. Bureau, 1971. 69 pp. K.shs.8.70 (£1.00/$2.40 p/b)
In the preface, Taban lo Liyong gives a philosophical and discursive framework to his book. 'We do not live in a time that has an intrinsic unity to it such as the Renaissance or classical Greece had. Hence, in a fragmented world, we should be dealing with fragmented images.' He proceeds to present six episodes or short stories in this manner; building up an understanding by showing different facets of the whole.

Another Nigger Dead
London: HEB, 1972 (AWS, 116). 72 pp. £1.95/$5.00
Poetry of diverse themes and moods; an account of his marital breakdown in poetic prose, and an abstruse fantasy in prose constitute this anthology.
'Sometimes, publication notwithstanding, Mr Taban lo Liyong's thoughts remain his private property . . . in other places, the sacred river bursts the measureless caverns of his mind, and it all comes pouring out.'
    Eldred Durosimi Jones – *African Literature Today*
'We know what to expect: provocative role player – clown in that profound Shakespearean sense of the fool who speaks the truth, lightning conductor flashing sudden dangerous revelation, ironic cynic-philosopher-teacher – and all these characters exposed in a scarifying mad cataract of words that tumble out . . . the latest work of this quite extraordinary writer.'   John Povey – *African Art*

Ballads of Underdevelopment
Nairobi: East African Lit. Bureau, 1976. 172 pp. K.shs.15.95 (£1.80/$3.70)
The cover proclaims: 'For Taban lo Liyong, the best thing for a man of thought is simply to laugh in order not to cry. With the idealism in him gone underground, he had no choice, but to wear a mask of cynicism in order to tolerate a dozen great years of folly, incompetence, loss of idealism, Africa's return to the dark continent.' He does this with a combination of stories, poetry and aphorisms. Book one consists of the Ballads of Underdevelopment; Book two, Thoughts Divine, presents 'a new mythology'; and Book three contains nearly 500 aphorisms.
'Many of the poems in this collection are unprintable; others kept me howling as I read through the volume . . . lo Liyong – the Tom Stoppard of Africa – is a master of the fractured proverb, the verbal surprise.'
    Charles R. Larson – *World Literature Today*
'The cutting edge of concern is always present. lo Liyong is a social critic who puts his art at the service of his fellows.'
    G. D. Killam – *African Book Publishing Record*

Meditations of Taban lo Liyong
London: Rex Collings, 1978. 160 pp. £6.50 cased
After a period of study at Howard University, where he was a contemporary of Stokely Carmichael, Taban went to the writers' workshop at Iowa University to 'learn to express his own thoughts in his own way'. *Meditations* is the result of that period. He claims it is a funeral dirge, too, occasioned by the death of his father. The subject matter ranges from sex to religion, from politics to the family, in short prose sections, comprising one man's attempt to find an essential wholeness.

Lubega, Bonnie
The Outcasts
London: HEB, 1971 (AWS, 105). 88 pp. £1.50/$3.00
Karekyesi and his family live as outcasts from the village. They tend the cattle lovingly and stink of the dung and urine they drink and wash in. Unsupervised, they cull the best calves and steal milk and butter. When the super-cilious and arrogant villagers dismiss Karekyesi, he leaves victorious, a wealthy man.
'Bonnie Lubega, a Ugandan journalist, tells this mildly comic story with simplicity and economy.'
    Bernth Lindfors – *Books Abroad*
' . . . dedicated to the "fertilizers" of East Africa's so-called literary desert, is a purely African novel which plunges the reader into the miserable and pathetic

world of Baganda village herdsmen and leaves him
there to draw his own conclusions on mankind.'
Aloys U. Ohaegbu – *Présence Africaine*

Mazrui, Ali
The Trial of Christopher Okigbo
London: HEB, 1971 (AWS, 97). 160 pp.
£1.95/$4.00
New York: Third Press, 1972. 145 pp. $5.95
Mazrui, an East-African political scientist, has
imagined a novel in which Christopher
Okigbo, the poet who was killed in action
during the Nigerian Civil War while fighting
for the Biafrans, is tried posthumously for
putting his interests as an Iboman above those
of his poetry and the pan-African ideal. The
trial is conducted in 'After-Africa' and set in a
soccer stadium attended by thousands of
spectators. Okigbo's 'Counsel for Salvation' is
Hamisi, a Kenyan Muslim killed in an
automobile accident who is, himself, on trial
for the sin of miscalculation in the 'Herebefore'. The 'Counsel for Damnation' is a
Ghanaian whose sin in the 'Herebefore' was
impatience. Among the witnesses called forth
to speak about the proper relationship
between politics and art are African political
figures and famous English authors.
'[*The novel*] *becomes its own best proof that important
political questioning and art are not mutually
exclusive . . . a fine and unusual piece of fiction.*'
The New York Times Book Review
'*Mazrui's angle of vision in the conflict is so special
and so challenging to partisan views that it is not
likely to get lost in the crowd.*'
R. F. Bauerle – *Books Abroad*

Mukasa, Ham
Sir Apolo Kagwa Discovers Britain
London: HEB, 1975 (AWS, 133). 160 pp.
£2.50/$5.00
In the year 1902 the Ugandan Prime Minister,
Sir Apolo Kagwa, and his secretary Ham
Mukasa were invited to the coronation of King
Edward VII in London. Their reactions to the
boat trip, what they saw in England, and
whom they met are carefully chronicled by
Mukasa. Taban lo Liyong provides editorial
comment. It was published originally in 1904
by Hutchinsons as *Uganda's Katikiro in England*.
'*Altogether a refreshing, and sobering, read for ex-
imperialists.*' David Williams – *Sunday Times*

Nakibimbiri, O.
The Sobbing Sounds
London: Longman, 1975. 118 pp. 95p
A comic account of the anti-hero's sexual
adventures from youth to maturity.
'*In a superficially unserious and apparently simple
novel, Nakibimbiri has succeeded in highlighting,*

very frankly, some of the serious social problems of his
society in a narrative style well suited to this theme.'
Kadiatu Sesay – *African Literature Today*

Nazareth, Peter
In a Brown Mantle
Nairobi: East African Lit. Bureau, 1972.
157 pp. K.shs.19.60 (£2.20/$4.70)
A novel dealing with post-independent Africa,
and analysing the political systems.
'*Nazareth's cool, analytical presentation is not vivid
enough for a fully successful novel, but his balance,
and his insight, are impressive.*'
Angus Calder – *The Scotsman*

Two Radio Plays
Nairobi: East African Lit. Bureau, 1976.
36 pp. K.shs.7.40 (95p/$2.20)
Two plays, 'The Hospital' and 'X', originally
produced for the British Broadcasting Corporation African Service.

Ntiru, Richard
Tensions
Nairobi: EAPH, 1971. 111 pp. K.shs.7.50
($2.60)
The tensions and paradoxes of life are
reflected in this collection of poems. It was
highly recommended for the Commonwealth
Poetry Prize for 1972.
'*. . . is still a young poet with, one hopes, his best
verse ahead of him.*'
James Burns – *Books Abroad*
'*This fine work will not only create tensions in the
hearts of the readers, but it will be a handbook for
those who want to know the East African society
through and through, today.*'
Chris Wanjala – *Dhana*

Oculi, Okello
Prostitute
Nairobi: EAPH, 1968. 132 pp. K.shs.10.00 p/b
($5.80 cased $2.60 p/b)
A poetic novel, part literary, part social
commentary. It portrays the life of a prostitute
in a squalid environment.

Orphan
Nairobi: EAPH, 1968. 104 pp. K.shs.7.00
($2.40)
'You are going to watch a village opera
performed. You will see each character walking along a path. All paths crisscross at a
junction. An orphan boy is seated crosslegged
at the junction, writing pictures of animals in
the sand. Today the people who talk in these
pages all pass through this junction. Each of
them notices the orphan boy,' writes the
author in his prologue.

Kanta Riti
Kampala: Uganda Publ. House, 1974. 45 pp.
U.shs.3.00

Malak
Nairobi: EAPH, 1977. 68 pp. K.shs.8.00/$2.00
A long political poem which examines the African experience (the 'screams of millions of the historically skinned . . . '), and which presents the case of the Third World against its oppressors.
'*This is not an easy poem by any count, but as an impression of the contradictions that constitute the history and reality of the African continent, it is worth the time and effort.*'   Simon Gikandi – *Africa*

Kookolem
Nairobi: Kenya Lit. Bureau, 1978. 73 pp.
K.shs.11.35 (£1.15/$2.10)
The unapproachable Kooklem – meaning 'crying is blunt' – and her husband, the crippled Nyenyi are the subjects of this tale. There is no plot as such: events, such as the intervention by Kookolem's father in the tobacco planting, the death of Kookolem's nine children, are woven into a whole.

Osinya, Alumidi [pseud.]
The Amazing Saga of Field Marshal Abdulla Salim Fisi (or How the Hyena Got His!)
Nairobi: Joe Magazine/Transafrica Publ., 1976. 131 pp. K.shs.16.00
London: Rex Collings, 1977. 132 pp. £1.25
The format of animal 'How' and 'Why' stories is borrowed for Osinya's satirical appraisal of what one assumes is Uganda under Idi Amin. Amin, the hyena, overthrows the leopard Obote, and the moral and physical rape of 'Animal Falls Park' continues in this fabulous vein.
'*The simple plotting never strays far from international press allegations . . . Recommended for all university and major public libraries.*'
Douglas Oliver – *The African Book Publishing Record*

p'Bitek, Okot
Song of Lawino
Nairobi: EAPH, 1966. 216 pp. illus.
K.shs.30.00 cased K.shs8.50 p/b ($5.80 cased $3.00 p/b)
Cleveland: World (Meridian Books M. 285), 1969. 216 pp. $3.25
This was one of the first major poetry collections to come from East Africa. 'Translated from the Acoli by the author who has thus clipped a bit of the eagle's wings and rendered the sharp edges of the warrior's

sword rusty and blunt, and also murdered rhythm and rhyme,' writes p'Bitek.
'*. . . a powerful impression of richness and plenty, after the thin lyrics and slender short stories which East African English so often produces. Mr Okot has so much more to say and the reason, surely, is that he said it first in the language which most perfectly expresses it . . . the publishers have produced an attractive volume, sure to be dog-eared or purloined before long.*'   Gerald Moore – *Transition*

Song of Ocol
Nairobi: EAPH, 1970. 86 pp. K.shs.10.00 ($3.00)
The husband's reply to Lawino's claims in *Song of Lawino* receives voice.

Two Songs
Nairobi: EAPH, 1971. 184 pp.
K.shs.9.50/$3.00
Two long poems, 'Song of Prisoner' and 'Song of Malaya' are combined in this volume which won the inaugural Kenyatta Prize for Literature in 1972. The prison is a symbol for Africa, and assuming various guises, the prisoner laments the betrayal perpetrated by some of his fellow countrymen.The Swahili word for prostitute provides the title for the next poem, wherein the hypocritical standards applied to prostitutes receive the attention of the poet.
'*This* [Song of Prisoner] *is a savagely urgent and fierce poem dredged out of desperation and disappointment. It is not a happy poem. It is a brilliant one.*'   John Povey – *African Arts*
'*. . . Okot's latest compositions are a demonstration of the amount of matter a truly creative hand can pack into a very brief space.*'
Bahadur Tejani – *African Literature Today*

Song of a Prisoner
New York: Third Press, 1971. 124 pp. $4.95 cased $1.95 p/b
One of the 'Two Songs' in the preceding entry.

Song of Lawino and Song of Ocol
Nairobi: EAPH, 1972. 225pp. K.shs.10.00 ($3.00)
A combined edition of the two poems.
'*Together,* Song of Lawino *and* Song of Ocol *constitute a heated debate over the future of Africa. In graphic metaphor and with dramatic intensity, p'Bitek presents the conflict between the new and the old, and in the process reveals a remarkable sensitivity to the values of both.*'
Richard F. Bauerle – *Books Abroad*

p'Chong, Cliff Lubwa
Generosity Kills and The Last Sacrifice
Nairobi: Longman Kenya, 1975. 63 pp.
K.shs.6.75

Both these plays have their roots in the Acoli culture. The first illustrates an Acoli proverb; in it a village woman is literally killed through her generosity in giving the chief a new drink she has invented. The omens of death before a hunt are indeed significant, as the second play shows.

Words of My Groaning
Nairobi: East African Lit. Bureau, 1976.
59 pp. K.shs.10.60 (£1.15/$3.00)
Verses rooted in an African poetic tradition. Some deal directly with man's relationship to nature, while others are urban in theme.

Ruganda, John
The Burdens
Nairobi: OUP, 1972 (New Drama from Africa, 8) 81 pp. K.shs.8.25
The second place in the 1972 Kenyatta Prize for Literature (Language section) was awarded to this play. Wamala, once Minister, was fortunate to be imprisoned and not executed for plotting against the government. The play starts after his downfall, when poverty and humiliation dictate the lives of Wamala and his family.
'He . . . developed a very taut language to reveal the betrayal of Africa by the new bourgeoisie.'
                         Peter Nazareth – *Busrara*

Black Mamba
Nairobi: EAPH, 1973. (African Theatre, 2). 120 pp. K.shs.9.00 ($3.00)
Two plays, 'Black Mamba' and 'Covenant with Death', are housed in this volume. 'Black Mamba' is a satirical exposé of the private life of a professor who gets involved with prostitutes. The second play covers the barrenness and subsequent alienation of childlessness.

The Floods
Nairobi: EAPH, 1980. (African Theatre, 7). 110 pp. K.shs.15.00/$3.50
Ruganda's play is experimental in form, and the content is both literal and symbolic. The flood warning on a small island on Lake Victoria is a hoax, perpetrated by Bwogo, the head of the secret police, in an effort to have his inconveniently pregnant mistress drowned with all the other islanders in the rescue boat. When Bwogo discovers that Nankya has not gone, he is disquieted, and the ensuing dialogue involves a recapitulation of their past and the economic and political determinants to relationships. A fisherman, Kyeyune, who also refused to leave, is an embodiment of the victimization that ordinary people suffer under military and oligarchic rule.

Rugyendo, Mukotani
The Barbed Wire and other plays
London: HEB, 1977 (AWS, 187). 112 pp.
£1.95/$5.00
Three socially committed plays are grouped in this book. Poor peasants defy a rich landowner who usurps their land in 'The Barbed Wire'. Rugyendo has sought to revivify drama in 'The Contest' by using a form of traditional heroic recitation. The third play, 'And the Storm Gathers', reveals the effect a military coup has upon a small village.
'People who are uncomfortable with didacticism in art will find more than a whiff of it in these plays. But a point central to them is the awareness of the strict imperatives we must follow if we are to break out of "the circle of our own damnation". These rich and well-written plays show the way on the artistic side of the struggle.'
                         N. B-E. – *West Africa*

Sebukima, Davis
Son of Kabira
Nairobi: OUP, 1972. 124 pp. o/p.
A novel.

The Half-Brothers
Nairobi: EAPH, 1974. 280 pp. K.shs.12.50 ($3.50)
The story of the escalation of sibling rivalry into murder, set in a police state where political malpractices abound.
'The pace of the narrative is intense, yet what begins as an extremely promising political satire ends as a rather sentimental account of life in a police-run state.'   Charles R. Larson – *Books Abroad*

Growing Up
Nairobi: East African Lit. Bureau, 1976.
132 pp. K.shs.13.50 (£1.60/$3.30)
These short stories are divided thematically into three parts. 'The Innocent Years' covers the world of the child – governed by fears, superstitions, and vulnerable to adult authority. 'The Love Years' and 'The Serious Years' deal with adolescence and some problems of marriage.

Seruma, Eneriko [pseud. for **Kimbugwe, Henry S.**]
The Experience
Nairobi: EAPH, 1970. 96 pp. K.shs.8.50 ($2.60)
This first novel has certain sociological undertones, and the author describes it as 'an expressionistic painting of contemporary Africa'.

The Heart Seller
Nairobi: EAPH, 1971. 125 pp. K.shs.8.50
($2.60)
A collection of short stories set in both Africa
and America. The author views people – their
emotions, weaknesses, strengths, and foibles –
with detachment. Two of the tales – 'The
Calabash' and 'Love Bewitched' – have won
the East African Literature Bureau and
Deutsche Welle's creative writing competitions
respectively.
'. . . impressive collection by a well known Ugandan
writer.'   E. A. Green – *Books Abroad*

Girl of God
Nairobi: Transafrica, 1975. 120 pp.
K.shs.10.00

Serumaga, Robert
Return to the Shadows
London: HEB, 1969 (AWS, 54). 176 pp.
£1.75/$5.00
New York: Atheneum, 1970. 176 pp. $4.95
A novel that deals with political realities in an
independent African nation. Joe Musizi, lawyer and businessman, a member of the upper
class, and his servant Simon, are forced to flee
their home after a military take-over.
'*Return to the Shadows is not an exceptionally
brilliant novel; nor is the writer wholly unique. But
there are traits which reveal that soon the author will
come out with a fine masterpiece.*'
                    Pat Amadu Maddy – *West Africa*

The Elephants
Nairobi: OUP, 1971 (New Drama from Africa,
6). 58 pp. K.shs.7.00
A two-act play which revolves around David, a
young research fellow whose childhood was
shattered by the death of his parents; Maurice,
a refugee whom David nurtures and shelters;
and Jenny, an American who threatens to
disrupt their relationship.

Majangwa and *A Play*
Nairobi: EAPH, 1974. 100 pp.
K.shs.9.50/$4.00 [Originally publ. as *A Play* by
Uganda Publ. House, 1967. 56 pp.]
Majangwa and his wife, Nakirijja, consider
their life as street entertainers. Poverty dictates
their debased act, but there is a wider
condemnation of the urban audiences who pay
to watch. *A Play* deals with the misery of a
haunted middle-aged man on the verge of
insanity.
'*They are derivative and uncertain but contain hints
of a pungent theatrical imagination and an acute
feeling for the theatre.*'
                    James Gibbs – *Books Abroad*

Tejani, Bahadur
Day After Tomorrow
Nairobi: East African Lit. Bureau, 1971 (2nd
ed.). 145 pp. K.shs.14.70 cased K.shs.6.00 p/b
(£1.40/$3.50 cased 85p/Z$2.00 p/b)
Samsher disappoints his parents when he
rejects the role of trader, traditional in his
family. He is frustrated by the alienated and
isolated lives led by the Indians in Kampala,
and seeks to transcend the prevailing racial
hostility between blacks and Indians, to find a
sense of identity in Africa. By becoming a
teacher and by falling in love with a Ugandan
woman he comes nearer his goal.

Zirimu, Elvania Namukwaya
When the Hunchback Made Rain
Nairobi: EAPH, 1975. 88 pp. K.shs.10.00
($3.00)
A two-act play, first produced in Kampala in
1970, which involves God, his emissary the
Hunchback, and man. Also included is a
briefer work, 'Snoring Strangers'.
'*In her collection she presents bleak images of the
human situation and employs a wide range of
dramatic resources.*'
                    James Gibbs – *World Literature Today*
'*The playwright does bring into focus the very real
controversial moral and legal issues of today.*'
                    D. K. Mayanja – *Dhana*

CENTRAL & SOUTHERN AFRICA

(and Mauritius)

Botswana

Sesinyi, Andrew
Love on the Rocks
London: Macmillan Educ., 1981 160 pp. 80p
In this popular novel, Pule Nkgogan, driven
out of his village by family conflicts, tries to
start a new life in the city. After many set-backs
he at last finds happiness with a young girl
called Moradi, only to discover that breaking
with the past is harder than he imagined.

Lesotho

Leshoai, Bob
Wrath of the Ancestors and other plays
Nairobi: EAPH, 1972. 72 pp. K.shs.6.00
($2.00)
The Rendezvous, the first of three plays, inverts
the solemnity of a funeral by having the coffin
contain smuggled liquor. The church is the
setting for *Revolution*, where a black cleaner
confronts successfully a white policeman and a
black collaborating priest, whom he kills.
Wrath of the Ancestors involves conflict between
the rightful chiefs in Africa and those usurpers
backed by the colonial power.
'... Wrath of the Ancestors *stands alone as an
essential entertainment better still than most other
African plays.'* George Menoe – *Busara*
*'Their true energy can only be released in production
– and it is quite obvious that they can be explosive in
their exuberance.'* André

Brink – *Books Abroad*

Malawi

Banda, Tito
Sekani's Solution
Limbe: Popular Publ. 1979 (Malaŵian Writers
Series, 5). 112 pp. K.1.30 ($1.55)
The problems of having to provide a bride
price are increased for Andreya when his
parents are killed and he has to finance the
education of his brothers. Sekani herself ends
the deadlock when she wins a beauty competition and, flaunting tradition, pays her own
bride price.
*'Tito Banda has a strong power of observation. The
manner in which he recreates the differing attitudes of
characters in different social classes, describes and
builds the life style of people in divergent rural and
urban atmospheres with their own language – jargon
or otherwise – and how he paints the general scenery,
demonstrate this ability.*
Zulani Lance Ngulube – *Malawi News*

Chimombo, Steve
The Rainmaker
Limbe: Popular Publ. 1978 (Malaŵian Writers
Series, 4). 51 pp. 80t (95c)
Chimombo has dramatized a myth, central to
Malaŵian oral history, about the origins of a
religious cult centred around M'bona. The
rainmaker, Kamundi, fails to bring rain; a
youth, M'bona, succeeds – but he effects his
own death by so doing as he is accused of
having invoked an evil magic. His death brings

him martyr status. In the Introduction, Dr
Schoffeleers dates the rise of this separatist cult
to the beginning of the seventeenth century.
The play contains a mixture of dialogue and
chants by masked dancers.
*'The play itself, like so many African art works,
refuses to fit comfortably into the definitions of
Western categories. There are songs and dances,
dramatic scenes and mimes, realistic scenes, declama-
tory segments and a bewildering, but somehow
acceptable, interweaving of English and African
language usage.'* John Povey – *African Arts*

Kachingwe, Aubrey
No Easy Task
London: HEB, 1966 (AWS, 24). 240 pp.
£1.45/$4.00
A story that tells of the political struggles of a
British colony with a while minority, moving
towards independence. It focuses around the
emotional and political awakening of a young
journalist, the son of a village pastor, who is
offered a job on a newspaper in Kawacha, the
capital of the colony.
*'Mr Kachingwe writes in an easy style with a
remarkable power to create lively and dramatic
scenes ... I enjoyed very much reading this first
novel from a Malawi writer.'*
Sunday O. Anozie – *Présence Africaine*

Kayira, Legson
I Will Try
London: Longman, 1965. 251 pp. £1.05
New York: Doubleday, 1965. 251 pp.
New York: Bantam Books (Bantam SP 188),
1967. 216 pp.
London: Longman. 1969 (abridged ed.).
192 pp. 65p
The autobiography of a determined young
man who walked 2500 miles across Africa in
pursuit of an American education. The major
part of the book recounts his experiences
during the first two years it took him to travel
from Nyasaland (now Malawi) to Khartoum in
the Sudan. When he finally reached the U.S. he
attended Skagit Valley Junior College in
Washington, and later the University of
Washington.

The Looming Shadow
London: Longman, 1968. 143 pp. 95p.
New York: Doubleday, 1969. 143 pp.
New York: Macmillan, 1970. 143 pp.
A novel of village life in Central Africa some
thirty years ago. A feud between Musyani and
Matenda, two villagers, erupts into accusations
of witchcraft and attempted murder.
*'... Mr Kayira adopts no particular attitude
towards his story of village intrigue, but handles*

everyone with detached amusement and considerable felicity of style.'

Gerald Moore – *African Literature Today*

Jingala

London: Longman, 1969. 160 pp. 95p
Washington, D.C.: Three Continents Press, $4.00
New York: Doubleday, 1969. 160 pp.
The name given this novel is that of its principal character, an elderly widower and retired tax-collector whose son wishes to become a priest. In the ensuing conflict, Jingala totally opposes this plan as he wants his son to continue to belong to himself and to the remote village in which they live. The story revolves around this conflict.

The Civil Servant

London: Longman, 1971. 216 pp. £1.75
Chipewa – the civil servant of the title – is tempted, for the basest of reasons, into having an affair with Isabella. When Isabella's miner husband is killed, her infidelity is proclaimed to be the cause of his death. She too dies while searching for Chipewa; he then suggests that he and his wife adopt Isabella's son.

The Detainee

London: HEB, 1974 (AWS, 162). 172 pp.
£1.75/$4.00
In this the fifth novel by Kayira, Napolo, a simple, honest old villager, seeks medical aid in a distant town. He is befriended by a young teacher whose tales of people disappearing at night and being murdered by the Young Brigands, under the dictatorship of Sir Zaddock, he finds hard to credit. When he is duped into going to a rest camp, and discovers that it is the notorious Snake camp, and that he is not free to leave, he is bewildered and angry. His eventual escape, after apparent drowning, leaves him poor, hungry, and in a foreign country.
'Kayira tells this disturbing story with precision and care. The movement and characters seem Kafkaesque.'

Charles F. Dameron – *Books Abroad*
'Kayira's well-written novel is a compelling indictment of dictatorship wherever it occurs and provides a warning that is as timely as it is universal.'

Choice

Lipenga, Ken

Waiting for a Turn
Limbe: Popular Publ. 1981 (Malaŵian Writers Series, 6). 122 pp. K.2.00
Of the thirteen short stories in this collection,

some have already won the author prizes in writing competitions.

Mapanje, Jack

Of Chameleons and Gods
London: HEB, 1981 (AWS, 236). 80 pp.
£1.95/$6.50
A compilation of ten years of poetry writing is represented in this collection – ' . . . turbulent years in which I have been attempting to find a voice (or voices) as a way of hanging on to some sanity. Obviously where voices are too easily muffled, this is a difficult task to set oneself.'

Phiri, Desmond Dudwa

The Chief's Bride
London: Evans, 1968. 62 pp. 90p
In a remote African village in the land of Abanturika young Tamara does an unheard of thing in refusing to marry the chief. By the end of act two of this play, however, when she finally accepts his hand, she has taught him a lesson about 'democratic marriage'. First performed in Dar es Salaam in 1964.

Rubadiri, David

No Bride Price
Nairobi: EAPH, 1967. 180 pp. K.shs.10.00
($3.00)
The story of Lombe, a young, ambitious and promising civil sevant, just promoted to the rank of Principal Secretary in a government department. He moves about in his new world with uncertainty, and falls foul of his Minister, who has him framed on a false charge. The novel also attempts to present some of the conflicts arising between the East African Indian and the indigenous population.

Zeleza, Paul

Night of Darkness: and other stories
Limbe: Popular Publ. 1976 (Malaŵian Writers Series, 2). 217 pp. K.3.00/$3.57
Zeleza has ranged far in the topics for this collection of twenty-two short stories. He covers scenes of town life, people's idiosyncrasies, vignettes of village life, some humorous, others tragic. The content is essentially human and non-political.
'The age of the author, seen against the background of the variety of narrative techniques employed in this collection, makes for a pleasant surprise. At twenty-two this is an impressive achievement whatever the faults of sentimentality or shallowness. These will have time to correct themselves in the years ahead.'

Kole Omotoso – *African Book Publishing Record*

Mauritius
(see also Francophone Africa)

Asgarally, Azize
The Hell-Hot Bungalow
Port-Louis: Dawn Printing Co., 1967. 83 pp.
A play about a family quarrel which takes on dramatic proportions and incites the members to fundamental change. The play was not allowed to be staged when first published and when authorized later became an immense success.

Blood and Honey
Port-Louis: Ioyster Publ., 1973.
A U.N.E.S.C. experiment whereby all news broadcasting stops for a day is halted when a race riot breaks out in New York. A play.

The Chosen Ones
Port-Louis: Ioyster Publ., 1969. 85 pp.
The time span of the author's third play ranges from the first days of man on the earth to the twentieth and thirtieth centuries.

South Africa

Abrahams, Peter
Dark Testament
London: Allen and Unwin, 1942. 160 pp. o/p
Nendeln, Liechtenstein: Kraus Reprint, 1970. 160 pp. SFr.24.00
A volume of short stories that were the first published works of Peter Abrahams.

Song of the City
London: Crisp, 1945. 180 pp. o/p
A novel.

Mine Boy
London: Crisp, 1946. 183 pp. o/p
London: Faber, 1954. 252 pp. o/p
New York: Knopf, 1955. 252 pp. o/p
London: HEB, 1963 (AWS, 6). 252 pp.
New York: Macmillan, 1970. 250 pp. £1.25 $3.00
This early novel of Peter Abrahams relates the story of Xuma, the boy from the country thrown into a large South African industrial city, and the impact on him of the new ways and values of the radically different world he encounters there. It was one of the first books that drew attention to the condition of black South Africans under a white régime, and the dehumanizing machinery of apartheid.

Wild Conquest
New York: Harper, 1950. 309 pp. o/p
London: Faber, 1951. 382 pp. o/p
Harmondsworth, England: Penguin Books, 1966. 252 pp. o/p
New York: Doubleday, 1971. 357 pp.
A novel about the Great Trek of the Boers to the land of the Matabele – their struggles, their motives, and their hopes and fears.

Return to Goli
London: Faber, 1954. 224 pp. o/p
Essays.

Tell Freedom
London: Faber, 1954. 311 pp. £1.30
New York: Knopf, 1954. 370 pp.
New York: Macmillan, 1970. 304 pp. $1.95
London: Allen and Unwin, 1978. (abridged school ed.) 224 pp. £2.25
Subtitled 'Memories of Africa', this autobiographical novel narrates the first twenty-two years of a talented boy who grows up in the slums of Johannesburg. It tells of his childhood, of his striving for an education, and his desperate attempts to escape from South Africa to the United Kingdom. The American paperback edition has an introduction by Wilfred Cartey, and the Allen and Unwin abridged school edition is edited by W. G. Bebbington.

A Wreath for Udomo
London: Faber, 1956. 309 pp. o/p
New York: Knopf, 1956. 356 pp. o/p
London: Faber, 1965. 309 pp.£1.60
A novel that deals with nationalism and politics in West Africa; a novel about African leaders – revolutionaries one moment and government ministers the next. Udomo, the hero of the novel, newspaper man and nationalist leader of his people of 'Panafrica', is imprisoned for sedition, yet elected whilst in prison, and then leads his people into independence. However, his position as a nationalist leader is not an entirely easy one: he is betrayed and accused of trying to do away with traditional ways of life, and to bringing more expatriates into the country than there had been during his country's days under colonial rule.

A Night of their Own
London: Faber, 1965. 269 pp. o/p
New York: Knopf, 1965. 236 pp. o/p
A story about the motives and tensions within the racial struggle in South Africa; about the role played by Indians in the underground

resistance movement, and their fight against apartheid.

'. . . *although unnecessarily long discussions about South African problems sometimes slow down the pace of the narrative* A Night of their Own *comes off as an exciting, suspenseful story which gathers momentum as it proceeds. A large measure of the success of the novel is due to Abrahams' clear understanding and sympathetic depiction of the plight of the Indian community in South Africa.'*
                 Bernth Lindfors – *Africa Report*
'*Peter Abrahams' narrative power and superb sensitivity bring out so vividly the characters, individually and collectively.'*
                 Nunasu Amosu – *Black Orpheus*

This Island Now
London: Faber, 1966. 255 pp. o/p
New York: Knopf, 1967. 305 pp.
New York: Macmillan, 1971. $1.95
During his term of office, President Moses Joshue so altered the political structure of the Caribbean island he led to independence that his death produced a crisis. This novel reveals the various elements – money, colour, family and custom – underlying the political conflicts and power struggles that follow.

The Path of Thunder
New York: Harper, 1948. 278 pp. o/p
London: Faber, 1952. 262 pp. o/p
Set in lovely and tranquil Quiet Valley, this is the story of a romance between Lanny, a 'coloured' South African, and Sarie, a white South African girl, a couple who dared to love each other despite the menacing shadow of the South African government's racial policy of segregation.

Banoobhai, Shabbir
Echoes of My Other Self
Johannesburg: Ravan, 1980. 52 pp. R3.60
Some of the poems in this volume have already appeared in *Bolt, Staffrider, New Classic, Contrast, Ophir* and *Unisa English Studies.*

Biko, Steve
I Write What I Like
Ed. by Aelred Stubbs
London: HEB, 1979 (AWS, 217). 160 pp.
£1.75
New York: Harper and Row, 1979. 160 pp.
$8.95
A selection of Biko's writings has been compiled by Aelred Stubbs, an Anglican priest who knew the author from the mid 1960s until his death in police detention in 1977. It includes a letter he wrote when president of SASO, a union of black students, and the monthly 'I write what I like' newsletters by

'Frank Talk' written by Biko for SASO Publications. In these, he examines various issues: the stance and role of liberals, African culture, the negative self-image of black children, the position of politicians like Buthelezi and Matanzima – and asserts the need for a positive approach of 'Black Consciousness'. This concept is further developed in conference papers and in submissions made during the SASO/BPC trial. Other documents include a memo from Biko to American senator Dick Clark, and a striking interview entitled 'So I said to them "Listen" . . . '

Boetie, Dugmore with **Simon, Barney**
Familiarity is the Kingdom of the Lost
London: Cresset Press, 1970. 189 pp.
New York: Dutton, 1970. 189 pp.
This novel, autobiographical in nature, recounts the story of a one-legged, black South African ex-convict in a small African town near Johannesburg. The author, Dugmore Boetie, who died of lung cancer in 1966, was persuaded to produce this book by Barney Simon, Editor of the South African magazine *The Classic.* Nadine Gordimer provides a preface to the book.
'. . . *a lively book, funny enough to make one laugh aloud.'*   Susan Anderson – *Books Abroad*

Bruin, John [pseud. for **Brutus, Dennis**]
Thoughts Abroad
Austin, Texas: Troubadour Press, 1970. 28 pp.
$1.50
Poems on the themes of exile, alienation, and identity.
'. . . *the importance of the poems lies in the lucid, passionate reflections of a political exile in ironically greater comfort and distress, greater success in vain, greater alienation in communing and commuting world-wide as he fights mankind's most vicious tyranny today.'*   D. Dorsey – *Books Abroad*
'. . . *impressive, vigorously impassioned, so suggestively brimming with the woes of an orphan, tragically mature, showing tears turned to blood.'*
                 Kalu Uka – *Okike*

Brutus, Dennis
Sirens, Knuckles and Boots
Ed. by Dennis Williams
Ibadan: Mbari, 1963. unpaged [43 pp.]o/p
Dennis Brutus was awarded a Mbari prize for poetry in 1962. This is his first collection, published while he was imprisoned in South Africa. Inevitably, many of the poems are protest literature, but there are also love poems, erotic poetry, and poems on other subjects.
'*Dennis Brutus' language and themes are almost*

prosy. But there is a maturity of feeling and above all a precision of phrase, that lifts this verse far above the common protest cry coming from South Africa.'
                    Ulli Beier – *Black Orpheus*

Letters to Martha, and other poems from a South African prison
London: HEB, 1969 (AWS, 46). 57 pp.
£1.50/$3.00
Poems chiefly of Brutus's experiences as a political prisoner on Robben Island off Cape Town. On release from prison Dennis Brutus was served with banning orders which made it criminal to write anything, including poetry, which might be published. To avoid the banning orders these poems were written as 'letters' to his sister-in-law Martha, after his brother had been sent to Robben Island prison.
'Letters to Martha is a handful of poems which are artistically competent and intellectually meaningful . . . sharply descriptive, these short poems bring out the horror, the misery, the loneliness, the humiliation – but above all, the horror of the South African prison cell . . . Brutus is dignified, self-controlled, almost urbane even when the pain is at its worst . . . many poems and political statements have been written in our time and before: Brutus' poems are among the best, the most important.'
        Sam C. Nolutshungu – *The New African*

Poems from Algiers
Austin, Texas: African and Afro-American Research Institute, 1970 (Occasional Publ., 2). 27 pp.
These poems arose from Brutus's visit to Algeria in 1969 to the First Pan-African Cultural Festival. He examines his right to be called an 'African voice', looking at the 'variousness' of Africa and his position within that framework.

China Poems
Austin, Texas: African and Afro-American Research Institute, 1970 (Occasional Publ., 10). 27 pp.
Twenty-eight poems, the fruits of the poet's visit to the Republic of China in 1973 – a celebration of the people and values he encountered there. He employs the Haiku form as a model. Ko Ching Po's translations accompany the verse.
'Brutus's earlier verse explored the finest nuances of grammar, image, and association; these poems achieve daring leaps of logic. They are exquisite and brief.' David Dorsey – *Books Abroad*
'It is the ability of these poems to astonish and betray us that makes them successful.'
                    Bernth Lindfors – *World Literature Written in English*

A Simple Lust
London: HEB, 1973 (AWS, 115). 176 pp.
£1.95/$5.00
New York: Hill and Wang, 1973. 176 pp. $7.95
An anthology comprising not only new unpublished poetry but also four previously published books: *Sirens Knuckles Boots, Letters to Martha, Poems from Algiers*, and *Thoughts Abroad*. His poems from *Seven South African Poets* and others that appeared in numerous journals are also included. The poems, of varying moods, cover the themes of oppression, apartheid, inhumanity, and the problems of exile.
'For those of us who want to understand the situation in South Africa, A Simple Lust *is indispensable.'*
            Cecil A. Abrahams – *Canadian Journal of African Studies*
'His mind is subtle and the poems do not yield up their secrets at once.'
                    M. M. Feeney – *Africa Digest*

Strains
Austin, Texas: Troubadour Press, 1975. 44 pp.
$1.95
Thirteen years of growth have resulted in these poems of revolution and liberation.
'Brutus the champion of justice and beauty is still here with us.' Ezekiel Mphahlele – *Okike*
'Strains is a consummate poet's exercise book.'
                    David Dorsey – *Books Abroad*

Stubborn Hope
London: HEB, 1978 (AWS, 208). 97 pp. £1.95
Washington, D.C.: Three Continents Press, 1978. 98 pp. $6.00
A substantial number of the poems in this volume were written in South Africa, or in the period immediately after the poet's exile from South Africa in 1966. The themes are a continuation of previous concerns, with a more meditative tone. Selections from *China Poems, Strains,* and *South African Voices* are represented.
'Brutus's new poems bear witness to a decade of struggle and show a new sense of history. The poet now allows himself the luxury of new themes and styles.' Hal Wylie – *Africa Today*
'. . . a collection of poems which are at once delicately sensitive and intellectually precise.'
            David K. Berner – *World Literature Today*

Carim, Enver
Golden City
Berlin: Seven Seas Publ., 1968. 166 pp.
New York: Grove Press, Inc., 1969. 141 pp.
Images of life as an Indian in South Africa swirl through the mind of Houran, in prison after celebrating his farewell from the country. Violence, parties, drugs, too much drink, and girls are the ingredients of a life where one's

future is determined by skin colour; where 'the future joys of becoming a man . . . flicker and cool, and a vast waste drags everywhere'; where racial stratification serves to fragment politically, and to leave only 'the blisters in the soul'.

A Dream Deferred
London: Allen Lane, 1973. 206 pp. £2.75 cased

Planned simultaneous attacks on key cities are the prelude to a hoped-for revolution in South Africa. Carim provides a close-up study of one small group of revolutionaries, exploring their motives and the implicit guilt of the white hostages they hold.

'Mr Carim's first success . . . lies in objectifying his own feelings and refusing to play to the prima facie sympathy his subject arouses. His second lies in eschewing the format and easy effects of the political thriller.'   Times Literary Supplement
'A horrible, frightening book, A Dream Deferred *marks the début of a gifted writer who has the compassion of the truly imaginative.'*
                                                  British Book News

Dangor, Achmat
Waiting for Leila
Johannesburg: Ravan, 1981. 140 pp. R4.50

For these six short stories Dangor was awarded the 1980 Mofolo-Plomer Prize. The author writes harshly about people being brutalised and about the people who are hurt by the poverty, inhumanity and landlessness that is the lot of the blacks in South Africa. In the title story he describes the destruction that was wrought not only on property in the notorious clearance of District Six (where the 'Cape Coloureds' were evicted to make way for white settlement), but also on the psyche and souls of the residents. A poignant tale of a relationship between a priest and a prostitute both destroyed by the system, a man being hunted by the police, the response of a 'coloured' man returning from abroad – tales showing how violence is an intrinsic and inevitable feature of life for the dispossessed.

Dhlomo, Herbert
The Girl who Killed to Save
Lovedale, South Africa, Lovedale Press, 1935. 46 pp. o/p
A play.

Valley of a Thousand Hills
Durban: Knox, 1941. 42 pp. o/p
A long poem, in praise of the magnificent scenery in the Natal Province of South Africa.

Dhlomo, Rolfes Reginald
An African Tragedy
Lovedale: South Africa, Lovedale Press, 1928. 40 pp. o/p

Dike, Fatima
The First South African
Johannesburg: Ravan, 1979 (Ravan Playscripts, 4). 48 pp. R2.75

In this second play Fatima Dike chronicles the fortunes of Zwelinzima, 'a man who looked like a white man, who had the heart of a black man, and was a "Coloured"'. 'What' (asks Dike) 'is that man?' The play depicts the insanity inherent in such a situation, the practical difficulties of finding work in a segregated society, and culminates in tragedy.

Dikobe, Modikwe
The Marabi Dance
London: HEB, 1973 (AWS, 124). 118 pp. £1.50/$4.50

The Mabongo family and many others share Molefe yard, a slum in Johannesburg in the 1930s. The frustrations and conflicts of people with their roots in tribal villages, but who have been forced to work in cities, is epitomized by Martha and her family. She has the choice of marriage to a country cousin, with all the hardships village life entails for a woman, or a more precarious relationship with George, the glamorous pianist at the notorious *marabi* parties. This is the only work by Dikobe, who himself grew up in the kind of area he describes.

'Dikobe's novel is an impressive piece of writing, rich in its creation of character types – a jarring slice of ghetto life, whose existence is always locked between pathos and destruction.'
                              Charles Larson – Books Abroad
'Dikobe stands out on a literary scene strewn with morbid white psyches: with no stylistic flourish beyond comparisons culled from the plants and animals of the South African land, he brings out the vitality of characters very ordinarily involved in the hard struggle of living, surviving, dying, giving birth and hoping against all odds.'
                          Catherine Glenu – Staffrider

Essop, Ahmed
The Hajji and Other Stories
Johannesburg: Ravan 1978. 120 pp. R5.85 (£2.50)

This collection of 22 short stories – some published previously in literary journals – was the winner of the 1979 Olive Schreiner Award. In the Foreword, Lionel Abrahams suggests its gist and range: 'The stories centre on the vivid aromatic world of Johannesburg's Indian community in Fordsburg, with its unique blend of religious, political, cultural and economic preoccupations. This is not to suggest that the interest is defined by a racial line. Characters of every South African extraction occur in Ahmed Essop's pages, and this is merely an element in a pattern of contrasts based on age, temperament, income, education, and above all occupation – among others, waiters, philosophers and shopkeepers, housewives, journalists, gangsters and soldiers, tarts, servants and mystics, a government inspector and a Molvi find roles in these stories.'

'*Part of Ahmed Essop's art is to reach out and highlight individuals and individuality in the community : . . the writer's individual note is struck in every one of these compelling stories. He is able to speak for Fordsburg and is yet somehow independent of it and thus able to speak to all of us.'*

Tony Voss – *Reality*

'*Essop has an observant eye and a gift of description. There is a healthy balance between involvement and detachment and the sense of an enquiring imagination constantly recharging itself.'*

Jean Marquard – *Staffrider*

The Visitation

Johannesburg: Ravan, 1980. 98 pp. R5.60 cased R3.60 p/b

Essop, in his first novel, provides glimpses of the characters from his short stories, centred on Mr Sufi, a merchant in trouble.

Fugard, Athol; Kani, John; Ntshona, Winston

Sizwe Bansi is Dead

London: OUP, 1974. 128 pp. £1.25

A play devised by the trio, revealing the fabric of life in South Africa.

Govender, Ronnie

The Lahnee's Pleasure

Johannesburg: Ravan, (1980. Playscripts, 5). 42 pp. R2.75

A comedy – with a satirical depth – illuminating some of the attitudes of the Indians in Natal.

Gwala, Mafika Pascal

Jol'iinkomo

Johannesburg: Ad Donker, 1976. 72 pp. R3.75 (£2.50/$5.95)

Jol'iinkomo is the first book of poetry by Gwala, whose work had previously appeared in *To Whom it May Concern* and many literary journals. He explores and illustrates the life of blacks in South Africa through a wide range of themes. Gwala sums up his intentions as follows: 'Jol'iinkomo means bringing the cattle home to the safety of the kraal and the

village elders. Jol'iinkomo is also to say I should bring some lines home to the kraal of my Black experience.'

Head, Bessie

When Rain Clouds Gather

London: Gollancz, 1969. 188 pp.
Harmondsworth: Penguin Books, 1971 o/p
New York: Simon and Schuster, 1968. 188 pp. $5.95
London: HEB, 1972. 192 pp. £1.15 (New Windmill Series, 168)

This novel follows the life of a black South African nationalist and idealist who – after serving two years in a South African prison for alleged subversive activities – flees his native country and escapes across the border into Botswana. Here, in the company of an English agricultural expert, he seeks to revive the poverty-stricken village of Golema Mmidi, by introducing modern methods of farming techniques, despite heavy opposition from a local chief who wants to preserve the old system.

'*With love and a searching perceptiveness which sometimes unearths hidden beauties, Bessie Head offers her insights into a characteristically African dilemma.'*

T. R. Wright – *Books Abroad*

Maru

London: Gollancz, 1971. 127 pp. £1.20
New York: McCall, 1971. 127 pp. $4.50
London: HEB, 1972 (AWS, 101). 127 pp. £1.80/$4.00

At the centre of this novel is the tension and conflict caused in a Botswana village by the arrival of a new teacher, Margaret Cadmore. Well educated, she is the protégeé of an eccentric English missionary, and she is taken for a 'Coloured'. When she corrects the mistake and claims to be a member of the Masarwa – a despised tribe of Bushmen used as slaves by the local inhabitants – she creates havoc in the village, either by drawing supporters to herself or creating enemies. Maru, the young chief, and his close friend Moleka both fall in love with Margaret: the plot involves plotting, betrayal, breakdown and marriage.

'*What comes through is Bessie Head's own passionate loathing of intra-racial prejudice, specifically that of Bantu against Bushman, which is not rendered any prettier by the white man against all non-white humanity in South Africa.'* – *British Book News*

A Question of Power

London: Davis Poynter, 1974. 206 pp. £3.00 cased
London: HEB, 1974 (AWS, 149). 206 pp. £1.95/$4.00

New York: Pantheon Books, 1973. 206 pp.
$6.95
Elizabeth, a 'Coloured' South African, living in
exile in Botswana, is the protagonist of this
novel. She and her young son live in a co-
operative community where she works on an
experimental garden. Her interaction with the
other members of the co-operative, and her
sense of fulfilment and pride in her garden, are
threatened by a nervous breakdown. Her
nights are filled with the horrific embodiment
of two men, figments of a mind trying to cope
with the immorality and degradation of past
life in South Africa. Her sanity and strength
are put to the severest tests, her behaviour is
unpredictable; she must cope with racial
prejudice rising in herself. Exorcised, she
survives the ordeal, and returns to the
sanctuary of her garden.
*'This novel is a small mine of insight into religion,
sex, sociology, psychology and morality from which
patient and receptive readers will be retrieving
treasures of new understanding for decades to come.'*
                    Lionel Abrahams – *Rand Daily Mail*
*'In her concern with women and madness, Bessie
Head has almost single-handedly brought about the
inward turning of the African novel.'*
                    Charles Larson – *Books Abroad*

The Collector of Treasures
London: HEB, 1977 (AWS, 182). 128 pp.
£1.75/$3.00
Cape Town: David Philip, 1978. 129 pp. R7.50
This is a carefully sequenced collection of short
stories that delve into many aspects of life in
Africa. Ms Head has refashioned myths, and
examined the problems of Christianity and
traditional religions, customs, and witchcraft.
The last four stories deal with the breakdown
of family life in Botswana, and the chaos left by
colonialism on older patterns of life. Her
linking theme is the status and position of
women in Africa, the hardship of being 'an
inferior form of life', of being used as sexual
objects, and the difficulty of bringing up
children in extreme poverty.
*'The strength of Ms Head's writing is that she refuses
to take up a sentimental or nostalgic attitude to the
changes and upheavals in the recent history of
Botswana.'* Faith Pullin – *British Book News*
*'Bessie Head's short stories have an extraordinary
simplicity and breadth of vision, a tolerant acceptance
of things as they are, which, if applied by a European
writer inside the structure of a European novel,
would cause her to be hailed as a new humanist saint,
a Tolstoy, a Gorki.'* Hilary Bailey – *The Tribune*

Hutchinson, Alfred
Road to Ghana
London: Gollancz, 1960. 190 pp. o/p

New York: John Day, 1960. 190 pp. o/p
An autobiographical account that tells of the
treason trials, Alfred Hutchinson's attempts to
escape from South Africa, and the travelogue
of his flight by train and by plane that
eventually brought him to Ghana, by way of
Zambia, Malawi, and Tanzania. Doris Lessing
has described the book as 'a record of brutality
and stupidity' and 'also one of the most
exciting and moving adventure stories'.

The Rain-Killers
London: Univ. of London Press, 1964. 80 pp.
35p
The tensions between the traditional and new
ways of thought in a small village community
form the core of this four-act play set in
Swaziland.

Jabavu, Noni
Drawn in Colour: African contrasts
London: John Murray, 1963. 261 pp.
New York: St Martin's Press, 1962. 208 pp. o/p
This is a picture of the life the author lived
among her Xhosa people in South Africa, and
her visit to a sister in Uganda. She says, 'It is a
personal account of an individual African's
experiences and impressions of the differences
between East and South Africans in their
contact with Westernization.'

*The Ochre People: scenes from South African
life*
London: John Murray, 1963. 261 pp. £2.50
New York: St Martin's Press, 1963. 261 pp. o/p
The author returns home to her Xhosa people
in this autobiographical account of her visits to
her family at Middledrift, to an uncle at
Confluence farm in Pondoland, and to 'Big
mother' in Johannesburg.

Kgositsile, Keorapetse
Spirits Unchained
Detroit: Broadside Press, 1969. 23 pp. $2.00
Poems from an exiled South African who fuses
the experiences of blacks in Africa and
America.

For Melba
Chicago: Third World Press, 1970. 24 pp.
$1.00
Keorapetse Kgositsile has been exiled from
South Africa since 1961, and there is a political
basis to these love poems to his wife, Melba.
*'Most of the poems are . . . sound, as is the overall
structure which sets the poet's love for Melba into an
analogical configuration with the needs of all black
peoples, the black nation.'*
                    Christopher Scott – *Books Abroad*

My Name is Afrika
New York: Doubleday, 1971. 96 pp.
A third volume of poetry with over fifty poems, in which he attacks institutionalized hypocrisy.

The Present is a Dangerous Place to Live
Chicago: Third World Press, 1974. 34 pp. $1.95
Poems about himself and fellow blacks, directed mainly at Afro-Americans.
'... *a work of profound human value, a work totally bereft of jive and sham, a work, finally, which lives precisely because it is engaged in the quest for human emancipation and dignity.*'
　　　　　Kiarri T-H. Cheatwood – *Ch'Indaba*
'*Kgositsile's volume is largely a brooding pessimistic book.*'　　　　　Ezekiel Mphahlele – *Okike*

Herzspuren
Kirchberg, West Germany: Schwiftinger Galerie-Verlag, 1981. 80 pp. DM14.00
Poems in German and English, dedicated to the women involved in the struggle for the liberation of South Africa. With illustrations by Dumeli Feni.

Kunene, Daniel P.
Pirates Have Become our Kings
Nairobi: EAPH, 1978. 91 pp. K.shs.15.00 ($3.50)
An exile from South Africa, Kunene writes poetry with a wide range of themes, but with a predominantly political basis.

A Seed Must Seem to Die
Johannesburg: Ravan, 1981. 88 pp. R3.95
Although still resident in the States, Kunene has had this second anthology of poetry published in South Africa. He has dedicated it to the children throughout the world who have been robbed of their childhood by tyranny.

La Guma, Alex
A Walk in the Night
Ibadan: Mbari, 1962. 90 pp. o/p
A short story.

And a Threefold Cord
Berlin: Seven Seas Books, 1964. 173 pp.
A grim presentation of the degradation of human life under apartheid in the slums of a South African city, a ghetto perched on the edge of Cape Town. The community is depicted through the story of one family, the Pauls, and we follow them in their struggle to keep alive. The book was written during the author's house arrest in 1963.
'... *La Guma's work is a considerable achievement.*'
　　　　　Robert McDowell – *Africa Today*

A Walk in the Night
London: HEB, 1967 (AWS, 35). 144 pp. £1.25
A new version of the original Mbari edition, now expanded to include six additional short stories. The feature story, 'A walk in the night', follows Michael Adonis, a coloured boy fired from his job for talking back to his white foreman. The story is set in Cape Town's toughest quarter, District Six, with its spivs, thugs, whores and derelicts 'doomed for a certain term to walk in the night'.
'... *although the story is both sordid and tragic, it makes refreshing reading after the revolving-door discussions of "what is African literature" that are unavoidable among those who care about literature in Africa ... A Walk in the Night is truly a slice of life.*'　　　Anthony M. Astrachan – *Black Orpheus*
'... *the book is short, the story is moving and readable, Alex La Guma's effort is well worth a large circulation. It should take its place on the shelves along with Alan Paton's* Cry the Beloved Country *and Doris Lessing's* Five.'
　　　　　Joseph Muwanga – *Transition*

The Stone Country
Berlin: Seven Seas Books, 1967. 169 pp. DM3.00
London: HEB, 1974 (AWS, 152). 172 pp. £1.50/$4.00
Dedicated 'to the daily average of 70,351 prisoners in South African gaols in 1964', La Guma's third novel presents another phase of life in South Africa, based on his experiences in prison, when he was jailed for illegal activities against the state.

In the Fog of the Seasons' End
London: HEB, 1972 (AWS, 110). 181 pp. o/p cased £1.95/$5.00 p/b
New York: Third Press, 1973. 181 pp. $6.95
The novel traces the paths of two political activists in South Africa. La Guma uses narrative 'flash-back' technique, picking up incidents and people in the past that formed or influenced his main characters, until their political commitment is no longer a matter of choice, but the only way forward in life. A strike is the focus of the book, and as action radiates from this, some of those involved are fearful and drop out; others become more committed. Elias Tekwane, one of the main protagonists, is tortured to death in a prison cell. Beukes, the other, leads a frightened, lonely life working for an undergound organization.
'*Anyone who has lived and worked in South Africa, on reading this novel, will feel a cold trickle of sweat down his back.*'
　　　　　Bob Leshoai - *East Africa Journal*

'This book unequivocally sides with hurt people against the race-based class which hurts them. It is propaganda, and so it should be. But it is humane, careful, and very moving; it is propaganda for the truth, and a work of art.'

Angus Calder – *New Statesman*

Time of the Butcherbird
London: HEB, 1979 (AWS, 212). 128 pp.
£1.95/$4.00

A small Karroo town is the setting of the narrative, woven from three strands of conflicting moralities and communities. The first is the black community on the outskirts of the town. Mineral deposits have been discovered on their ancestral lands, and it merely takes an official document to order the community's removal. Resistance is led by the chief's sister (' . . . it is better to retain dignity in hell than to be humiliated in their heaven'). Secondly, the town's respectable Afrikaners – typified by Hannes Meulen, the prospective parliamentary candidate – are strict in their own morality, and oblivious to the cruelty they inflict on the blacks: 'I would rather be accused a thousand times of being a racist than of being a traitor to the cause of the white man.' Thirdly, the English travelling salesman, Stopes, and his wife, are seen as morally bankrupt, and insensitive to the tragedy and conflict surrounding them. An agent of this tragedy is Murile, bent on private vengeance, but increasingly involved in opposition to the enforced removal of his people.

'He is a taut and disciplined writer – there are echoes of Hemingway . . . The complexity of life in South Africa comes clearly across.' K. M. – *West Africa*

Madingoane, Ingoapele
Africa My Beginning
Johannesburg: Ravan, 1979. 29 pp. R1.50
London: Rex Collings, 1980. 29 pp. £1.75

Madingoane is primarily an oral poet, writing and reciting his work for the group *Mihloti*. The first edition of these poems – now banned in South Africa – sold out immediately in Soweto.

Maimane, Arthur
Victims
London: Allison and Busby, 1976. 231 pp.
£3.95 cased

Philip Mokono's feelings of rage at being constantly humiliated by white people in South Africa finally vent themselves in the rape of a white woman. Both Philip and Jean, the woman he rapes, are profoundly affected. She will not accept an abortion, even though this decision loses her her husband, family and friends, for she has longed to be pregnant and

her husband is sterile. She bears a baby girl and goes to live in Doornfontein, the twilight area where whites and blacks exist in uneasy proximity. Her life is now a prison: rejected by the whites, she is regarded by blacks as an easy target for their advances. Philip does not find the rape the cathartic experience he had expected it to be; he is deeply disturbed, and eventually filled with remorse. The author portrays both Philip and Jean as the victims of their country's colour bar.

'As a work of social realism, a documentary on a hidden society, it is an effective book. But it deserves to be raised above such criteria of "authenticity" and be accepted as an impressive work of fiction.'

James Davie – *Glasgow Herald*

'An accomplished novel . . . Part of the novel's success comes from Arthur Maimane's sure handling of many different facets of his society. He is equally at ease in describing shebeen life and interracial cocktail parties.' Faith Pullin – *British Book News*

Manaka, Matsemela
Egoli: city of gold
Johannesburg: Ravan, 1980. 28 pp.

Two migrant mine workers who come to Egoli – Johannesburg – reveal, through this play for two actors, the horror of the migrant labour system.

Mandela, Zindzi
Black as I Am
Los Angeles: Guild of Tutors Press, 1978.
120 pp. $6.75

Zindzi, daughter of the imprisoned African National Congress leader Nelson Mandela, composed these poems at the age of sixteen. Written in free verse form, they mirror her experiences in South Africa – the deprivation and iniquities that a black child suffers. The poetry is accompanied by photographs on parallel themes, by Peter Magubane, a South African photographer of international reputation.

'In many of the poems of this young writer there is a special kind of truth. It derives from the deep experience that comes from being born in South Africa. Understandably there is little enough laughter in these poems, but that the human spirit can retain such a possibility is the justification and strength of Zindzi Mandela's writing.'

John Povey – *African Arts*

Matshikiza, Todd
Chocolates for my Wife: slices of my life
London: Hodder and Stoughton, 1961.
128 pp.

An autobiographical account by Matshikiza – who won fame through his successful musical *King Kong* – of his life in London.

'. . . *a marvellous book; its spontaneous inspiration
and deep originality have immediately placed it well
above those written by story-tellers or professional
novelists.*'   Salem Okonga – *Présence Africaine*

Matshoba, Mtutuzeli
Call Me Not a Man
Johannesburg: Ravan, 1979. 198 pp. R2.50
London: Rex Collings, 1980. 208 pp. £4.95
cased
London: Longman, 1981. £1.50 p/b
Matshoba started writing in 1976, compelled
by the horrific events in Soweto in that year.
These short stories have as their subject matter
black housing problems, the appalling conditions of convict labour, the Immorality Act,
a visit to Robben Island. He justifies his
writing thus: 'I want to reflect through my
works life on my side of the fence, the black
side: so that whatever happens in the future, I
may not be set down as "a bloodthirsty
terrorist". So that I may say: "These were the
events which shaped the Steve Bikos and the
Solomon Mhlangus, and the many others
who came before them and after them."'
(*Introduction*, p. x)
'*These are among the best South African short stories
that I have read for a long time . . . I wish that his
narrative gift should never lose its supremacy over the
didactic and the polemical.*'
                    Alan Paton – *Cape Times*
'*Matshoba's style is perhaps less refined than that of
Ezekiel Mphahlele or Alex La Guma, but his
sharpness and humour make him a pleasure to read.*'
        Katharine Robertson – *New Statesman*

Seeds of War
Johannesburg: Ravan, 1981. 96 pp. R3.50
The story of Mhlaba, a migrant worker,
involves the trauma of resettlement policies
destroying homes and families, and the
emotional crises they cause.

Matthews, James (also Thomas, Gladys)
Cry Rage!
Johannesburg: Spro-cas Publ./Ravan, 1972.
80 pp. o/p
Poems.

The Park and other stories
Athlone, South Africa: BLAC Publ. House,
1974. 102 pp. R1.75
Short stories.

Pass Me a Meatball, Jones
New York: Simon and Schuster, 1977. 44 pp.
Poems written while under detention in 1976.

Images
Athlone, South Africa: BLAC Publ. House,
1980.

Johannesburg: Ravan, 1980. R.6.00
Matthews's verses are accompanied by George
Hallett's photographs, presenting the tragedy
of life in South Arica as well as the dignity and
beauty.

Mda, Zakes
We Shall Sing for the Fatherland
Johannesburg: Ravan, 1980 (Ravan
Playscripts, 6). 64 pp. R2.75
This collection comprises three plays which
incorporate both the past and the future,
indicating some of the problems blacks face
now and will face in the future. Besides the title
play, *Dark Voices Ring* and *Dead End* are the
plays which have already received an award.

Mekgoe, Shimane Solly
Lindiwe
Johannesburg: Ravan, 1978 (Ravan
Playscripts, 3). 38 pp. R2.75
This is a musical play in two acts, inspired by
'*Lindiwe* – the conflict at the meeting point of
tribal tradition and custom and the cruelty of
the demands of commercial and industrial
western-style society.' It shows a family combining traditional and Western ways to overcome their problems.
'*Here, then, is popular art, art of the people, in a rich
and lively vein. Those of us who do not live in Soweto
can learn a lot from it.*'   Colin Gardner – *Reality*

Mofolo, Thomas
Chaka: an historical romance
(Trans. from the Sesuto by F. H. Dutton)
(Reprint of edn London, 1931)
London and New York: OUP, 1967. 214 pp.
£5.95/$15.50 cased 65p/$1.50 p/b
New translation by Daniel P. Kunene
London: HEB, 1981 (AWS, 229). 160 pp.
£1.95/$6.50
Recreates the career of Chaka, chief and
founder of the Zulu nation. The author,
Thomas Mofolo, born about 1875, was a
Musuto, a native of Basutoland, and wrote in
Sesuto, the language of his people.
'*. . . an insightful description of Zulu culture and
values.*'
            Sylvia Moeno – *African Studies*
'*The style, even in translation, bears the mark of
genius. And that is merely the outer form. The inner
content is of compelling interest.*'
        Ayi Kwei Armah – *Transition/Ch'Indaba*

Mopeli-Paulus, Atwell Sidwell, and Lanham, Peter
*Blanket Boy's Moon: based on an original story
by A. S. Mopeli-Paulus, chieftain of
Basutoland*

London: Collins, 1953. 320 pp. o/p
New York: Crowell [publ. as *Blanket Boy*] 1953.
309 pp. o/p
The story of Monare, who leaves his native
Basutoland to work in the mines of Johannesburg. After his return home he becomes a
fugitive from justice after having been involved
in a ritual murder.

Mopeli-Paulus, Atwell Sidwell, and Basner, Miriam
Turn to the Dark
London: Cape, 1956. 287 pp. o/p

Motsisi, Casey
Casey and Co: selected writings of Casey 'Kid' Motsisi
Ed. by Mothobi Mutloatse
Johannesburg: Ravan, 1978. 133 pp. R3.85
Motsisi was a reporter on *Drum* with Nat
Nakasa and Can Themba. He wrote also for
the *Classic* and *The World:* this latter newspaper
is now banned, and hence Motsisi's pieces for
it were not considered for inclusion in this
book. The articles, short stories and sketches
selected by Mutloatse include some of the
famous 'bugs' columns from *Drum,* in which
the journalist deployed an insect's eye-view to
pointed effect. The tough, lively and unsentimental vision of life on the Witwatersrand
that comes through the writing is neatly
characterized when Mutloatse dubs Motsisi
'Africa's Damon Runyon'.

Mphahlele, Ezekiel
Man Must Live, and other stories
Cape Town: African Bookman, 1947. 60 pp.
o/p
Ibadan: Ministry of Educ., 1958. 60 pp. o/p
Ezekiel Mphahlele's first published collection
of short stories.

Down Second Avenue
London: Faber, 1959. 222 pp. o/p
Berlin: Seven Seas Books, 1962. 222 pp. o/p
London: Faber, 1965. 183 pp. £2.25
New York: Doubleday, 1971.
Both an autobiographical novel and a social
commentary on a childhood in the crowded
back streets of a ghetto area in Pretoria, South
Africa.
'. . . is at once a personal anecdote and a social
comment, a factual statement, and a cry from the
heart . . . as a tale of childhood and of unique society
in Africa* Down Second Avenue *makes fascinating
reading; as a measure of human being outraged it
cannot fail to move the least committed reader to
compassion and a deep and lasting anger and a
thankfulness that he was not born into that part of
Africa where, by the chance of birth, he is either*

oppressed or oppressor.'
Diana Speed – *Black Orpheus*
'. . . a brilliant contribution to what is a new genre of
our intensely race-conscious century – the autobiography as a vehicle of protest . . . Mr Mphahlele
shows himself in this work to be master of literary
montage.'* Robert McDowell – *Africa Today*

The Living and the Dead, and other stories
Ibadan: Ministry of Education, 1961. 66 pp.
o/p

In Corner B
Nairobi: EAPH, 1967. 208 pp. K.shs.9.50
($3.50)
A collection of twelve short stories capturing
the atmosphere and tensions that make up life
in present-day South Africa. The lead story,
'Mrs Plum in Corner B', portrays a 'liberal'
white woman and her obscure physical attachment to her dogs, amidst a world of iniquities.

The Wanderers
New York: Macmillan, 1971. 320 pp. $6.95
London: Macmillan, 1972. 315 pp.
This four-part novel revolves around Timi, a
black South African journalist who seeks to
expose South African injustice; around the
narrative of a liberal white South African
journalist, his friend; around the political
situation in Africa observed by Timi in exile in
Nigeria; and around Timi's frustration, as an
exile teaching in Kenya, with his life, with
Africa, and with his son.
'Mphahlele, a humane, dedicated and compassionate
man, has used his novel, for all its structural
limitations, as a vehicle through which he can present
the issues with which his own life has confronted him.'
John Povey – *African Studies Review*
'The book is certainly worth reading for the reportorial
view it gives of life as an exile.'
Barney McCartney – *East Africa Journal*

Mphahlele, Es'kia (Ezekiel)
Chirundu
Johannesburg: Ravan, 1979. 158 pp. R5.85
Walton-on-Thames: Nelson, 1980 (Panafrica
Library). 220 pp. £1.50
Westport, Conn: Lawrence Hill, 1981. $12.00
cased $5.95 p/b
Chirundu is Minister of Transport in an
independent African country. He simultaneously faces charges of bigamy (brought by
Tirenje, his first wife) and a transport strike led
by his nephew Moyo. Chirundu is finally
destroyed by the evidence of one and the strike
organized by the other: he is imprisoned and
his house burns down. The novelist further
examines Chirundu's political career and
morality through the cases of Chieza and Pitso,

two refugees from southern Africa detained without trial on Chirundu's orders. The startling decision by one of these men to return to police custody and certain torture in South Africa serves as a particularly severe indictment of Chirundu and the form of rule he represents.

'Chirundu *may be fragmented in structure, but few recent African novels have examined a more crucial central issue. Although set in fictional Africa, the questioning of South African judicial principles is implicit throughout.*'

Alastair Niven – *African Book Publishing Record*

'*It is a very stimulating novel, on the surface not very eventful, but gathering a certain momentum that lasts after the final page has been turned.*'

H. B. – *West Africa*

The Unbroken Song

Johannesburg: Ravan, 1981. 328 pp. R6.95

Mphahlele's selected writings are gathered in this book, of which the writer says: 'This, my people, is my unbroken music. In years to come, when this will be an undivided house and we'll be done spilling blood and guts, and justice and peace and plenty will be what a decent house should contain, we shall most of us remember the history of these times ... the unbroken music of our communal experience.'

Mqayisa, Khayalethu
Confused Mhlaba

Johannesburg: Ravan, 1974. 42 pp. 50c

A play in nine scenes dealing with Hlubi's return from 15 years' imprisonment on Robben Island. He is greeted with a mixture of responses; these range from his son's confusion, his wife's bitterness, and the fear and rejection by some friends to the brave acceptance by others.

Mtsaka, Makwedini Julius
Not His Pride

Johannesburg: Ravan, 1979 (Ravan Playscripts, 1). 52 pp. R2.15

This play combines the present discord among three people determining the inheritance of a dead man (father, husband, and brother to them) with digressions ('in the midst of our troubles we can still afford to indulge our story telling habits') on the historical betrayal of black South Africans by white settlers.

'*With its cast of three, its simple setting and its spirited combination of humour and protest it will have an enduring appeal on the stage, although I doubt whether it will survive as a work of much literary value.*' Alastair Niven – *African Book Publishing Record*

Mtshali, Oswald Mbuyiseni
Sounds of a Cowhide Drum

Johannesburg: Renoster Books, 1971. 69 pp. R1.50

London and New York: OUP, 1972. 71 pp. 90p

New York: Third Press, 1972. $2.45

In her introduction to this anthology of poems, Nadime Gordimer sums up: 'he has forgotten nothing of the black man's rural past, nor does he turn historical tragedy into costume drama ... But he is also – preeminently – the poet of the black Johannesburger, a Villon of Soweto ... ' The success of Mtshali's poetry – which sardonically revisits many aspects of the black experience in South Africa – may be gauged by first edition sales of 16,000 copies and two subsequent editions in the following year.

'*His short poems – vivid, colloquial, evocative, ironic, yet compassionate – depict the sorrows and desperation of the shattered, detribalized victims of apartheid. They tell more about a black man's attempts to survive in a world made by white men than many a long treatise.*'

Louis Barron – *Library Journal*

'*... there is no ranting, only the acid calm of the more coldly accurate perception. ... He is a poet of irony and a poet of the image brilliantly executed.*'

John Povey – *African Arts*

Fireflames

Pietermaritzburg: Shuter and Shooter, 1980. 63 pp. R7.50

Mtshali's second anthology is dedicated to the schoolchildren of Soweto; it contains tributes to the heroes of South Africa, poems of anger for the people of South Africa, and poems written while he was in America. The book is banned in South Africa.

'*... his sustained performance in the new book is an important landmark of African literary history.*'

Es'kia Mphahlele – *Rand Daily Mail*

Mzamane, Mbulelo
Mzala

Johannesburg: Ravan, 1980. 185 pp. R3.50

London: Longman, 1981. £1.50 [publ. as *My Cousin Comes to Jo'burg*]

Short stories, showing the resilience of people in adapting to township life.

The Children of Soweto

London: Longman, forthcoming 1981.

Soweto, 1976, is the setting for Mzamane's novel.

Nakasa, Nathaniel N.
The World of Nat Nakasa

Ed. by Essop Patel

Johannesburg: Ravan/Bataleur, 1975. 125 pp.
R3.85 cased

'This collection was prompted by a brief
meeting with the late Nat Nakasa in London.
On a crisp morning over cups of coffee, he
asked "What happens to the writings of a man
when he is dead and gone?" In response to
that question, I have compiled this book . . . '
(from the *Introduction* by Patel). Some of the
writings of Nat Nakasa, who worked as a
journalist for *Drum, Golden City Post,* and the
Rand Daily Mail, and who founded and edited
Classic have been collected here. The pieces
range from accounts of life in Johannesburg
and the Rand, to sharply observed vignettes of
the daily life of blacks, commentaries on the
rural Transkei and Zululand, and pen-
portraits of prominent individuals. Together,
they ask (and try to answer) Nakasa's own
questions: 'Who am I? Where do I belong in
the South African scheme of things? Who are
my people?' (p. 77).
'His journalism retains vitality because it expresses a
personal struggle, heroic without heroics, to retain
dignity and humanity and to tell the truth in spite of
the good reasons for fear that might be able to silence
him, but not change his understanding.'
                                    Rose Moss – *Books Abroad*

Ngcobo, Lauretta G.
Cross of Gold
London: Longman, 1981. 289 pp. £1.75
With their father imprisoned on Robben
Island, and their mother having fled to
Botswana following the Sharpeville massacre,
the two young boys Mandla and Temba, are to
join their mother illegally. When she is shot
crossing the border to meet them, they set off
for Sharpeville to collect their belongings
before returning to their grandparents' reserve. Mandla is arrested for not having a
permit, and begins to get the sense, which
increases daily, of being a non-citizen in the
country in which he was born. Imprisoned,
and then sent off to a convict farm, the lad is
subjected to depravity and inhumanity.
Ngcobo traces his life, his realization of what it
means to be black in South Africa: the hunger,
the powerlessness, and the brutalization that
people suffer. Once politicized, Mandla cannot
but be commited to the struggle and to seeking
out the collaborator who shot his mother.
Ngcobo has also projected the action into the
future.

Ngubane, Jordan
Ushaba The Hurtle to Blood River
Washington D.C.: Three Continents Press,
1979. 323 pp. $15.00 cased $7.00 p/b
An epic account of the beginning of the race

war in South Africa, and Afrikaner colonialism. The narrative also includes reflections on religion, philosophy and economics.

Nkosi, Lewis
The Rhythm of Violence
London and New York: OUP, 1964 (Three
Crowns Book). 76 pp.
A three-act play set in Johannesburg in the
early 1960s dealing with the personal and
ideological struggles between black and white
South Africans, the brutality of the police and
the problems arising from attempts at racial
co-operation.

Nortje, Arthur
Dead Roots
London: HEB, 1973 (AWS, 141). 160 pp.
£1.95/$5.00
Nortje is another of the South African exiles
who have committed suicide. He did so while
working for a degree in Oxford, where many
of these poems were written. This substantial
volume of poetry includes poems he submitted
to Heinemann as well as a number collected
from friends after his death.

Nthodi, Mothshile wa
From the Calabash
Johannesburg: Ravan, 1978. 67 pp. R4.75
Nthodi has woven a long, narrative poem in
free verse around twenty of his own woodcuts.
Together they celebrate the life cycle in a
Ndebele village as uKambiri and uNomaseko
undergo their initiation rites, marriage, and
parenthood.

Peteni, R. L.
Hill of Fools
London: HEB, 1976 (AWS, 178). 160 pp.
£1.35/$3.00
Cape Town: David Philip, 1976. 160 pp. R3.60
Traditional animosity between two villages in
the Ciskei often results in formal faction
fighting. Zuziwe, a Hlubi girl, falls in love with
Bhuqa, a hot-headed young Thembu. Their
love ends tragically, blighted not only by the
traditional hostility between their clans but
also by the South African pass laws.
'Stark, in language none too supple, this story sounds
faithful to custom. With one part of his mind, Mr.
Peteni would prefer that this were not so, but he also
has the public story-teller's delight in village strengths
and joys . . . '
              David Pryce-Jones – *Sunday Times*
' . . . achieves a certain charm, a definite sense of
beauty, linking it to other pastorals. Peteni – who at
age sixty has just published his first novel – ought to
serve as inspiration for late bloomers across the
continent.'   Charles R. Larson – *Books Abroad*

Pieterse, Cosmo

Echo and Choruses: 'Ballad of the Cells' and selected shorter poems
Athens, Ohio: Ohio Univ. Centre for International Studies, 1974 (Papers in Internat. Studs., Africa Series, 22). 66 pp.
A long poem set in a cell in a Pretoria gaol, where Looksmart Ngudle is being interrogated, and a collection of short poems.

Plaatje, Solomon Thekiso

Mhudi: an epic of South African native life a hundred years ago
New York: Negro Univ. Press, 1970. 225 pp. $9.50
Johannesburg: Quagga Press, 1975. 165 pp.
Johannesburg: Ad. Donker, 1975. 168 pp. R9.00 cased
London: Rex Collings, 1976. 165 pp. £6.00
London: HEB, 1978 (AWS, 201). 188 pp. £1.50
Washington D.C.: Three Continents Press, 1978. 188 pp. $4.00
Probably the first novel in English by a black African, Mhudi was written in 1917 and published in 1930 in South Africa (Lovedale Press). The Barolongs – a Tswana people – were reduced to vassal status by Mzilikazi and the Matabele (Ndebele); in 1830 they killed one of Mzilikazi's tax collectors and invoked his vengeance. Their flight, to present day Lesotho, provides the circumstances for the hero, Ra-Thaga, to meet Mhudi by saving her from a lion. The Barolong combine with the Voortrekkers to drive the Matabele out of the area, but are then betrayed by the Voortrekkers.
'. . . grips the reader and remains in the mind. The strength of Sol Plaatje's personality and his political intelligence shine through.' K. M. – *West Africa*
'The harshest of realities take on a grandeur and beauty that are wonderfully old-fashioned.'
Paula Holmes – *Africa Report*

Rive, Richard

African Songs
Berlin: Seven Seas Books, 1963. 149 pp. o/p
A collection of short stories.

Emergency
London: Faber 1964. 251 pp.
New York: Macmillan, 1970. 250 pp. $2.75
The main action of this novel takes place in and around Cape Town between the 28th and the 30th of March, 1960. Through a series of flashbacks it traces the events that led to the shootings in Sharpeville and Lange, the growing conflict that culminated in the day a state of emergency was declared, and how the situation affects the life of Andrew Dreyer, a young coloured school teacher, who is having an illegal affair with a white girl in violation of the immorality act. Ezekiel Mphahlele adds an introduction to the American paperback reissue.

Selected Writings
Johannesburg: Ad. Donker, 1976. 184 pp. R7.95 (£5.25/$12.50)
Stories, plays, essays, some of which have already appeared in journals, are here collected together.
'Though the stories and plays in this selection are probably of minor importance, the essays make the book a valuable South African document.'
Robert L. Berner – *World Literature Today*

Sepamla, Sipho

Hurry up to it!
Johannesburg: Ad. Donker, 1975. 72 pp. R3.75 (£2.50/$5.95)
Sepamla's first published collection of poetry, in which he explores the condition of being black in South Africa.
'A new and already mature poetic voice, that of Sepamla, now rings out with an enviable sureness of diction. Publication within South Africa probably obviates the shrillness that sometimes mars the poems of political exiles . . . but has not prevented Sepamla from mercilessly exposing the injustices of the white regime.' Barend J. Toerien – *Books Abroad*

The Blues Is You In Me
Johannesburg: Ad. Donker, 1976. 72 pp. R3.75 (£2.50/$5.95)
Poems by the joint winner of the 1977 Pringle Award.

The Soweto I Love
Cape Town: David Philip, 1977. 53 pp. £1.50
London: Rex Collings, 1978. 53 pp. £1.50
Washington D.C.: Three Continents Press, 1978, $4.00
Sepamla's anger, frustration, and compassion for his fellow blacks following the riots in Soweto in 1976 gain voice in these poems.
'The simplicity of these poems should encourage people to understand violence not only in the reactions of oppressed peoples, but more importantly the violence that pervades the system of social organization, of which apartheid is merely an extreme expression.' N. B-E. – *West Africa*
'These poems are extremely dignified, never resorting to abuse and seldom to polemic, with an eye for landscape and toil. They are well crafted and written in the manner of plain speech, but almost every poem has intensity and feeling.'
Alastair Niven – *African Book Publishing Record*

The Root is One
Cape Town: David Philip, 1979. 142 pp.
R12.60
London: Rex Collings, 1979. 131 pp. £4.95
cased
Sepamla is already known as a poet, but this is
his first novel. It traces events through six days
in a township typical of those near Johannesburg; they are catastrophic days as the
inhabitants are to be forcibly removed to
another township. Juda Baloyi is manipulated
by white agitators to help organize a protest, at
which he is told not to appear. His feelings
that he is betraying his people are exacerbated
by his father's support of the administrators,
and the subsequent lynching of the old man.
As pressure mounts, Juda betrays his close
friend Spiwo to save himself; as his guilt
becomes unbearable, he takes his own life.
'*Sepamla achieved this without use of covert
sociology . . . the reader does not need this knowledge
to appreciate the intense humanity – or inhumanity –
which Sepamla delivers through a full-bodied prose
written in a poetic continuum.*'
Ad'Obe Obe – *West Africa*

Serote, Mongane Wally
Yakhal'Inkomo: Poems
Johannesburg: Renoster Books, 1972. 52 pp.
R1.75
Washington D.C.: Three Continents Press,
1974. $5.00
Serote is one of the group of young black poets
who have flourished in South Africa in recent
years, against heavy odds. His poems deal with
his personal experience, his emotional
responses forming the basis of them. The title
means 'cry of cattle at the slaughter house'.

Tsetlo
Johannesburg: Ad. Donker, 1974. 64 pp. o/p
A second volume of verse.

No Baby Must Weep
Johannesburg: Ad. Donker, 1975. 64 pp.
R3.75 (£2.50/$5.95)
The wide-ranging implications of being young
and black in a South African township are
captured in this long poem. It is in the form of
a monologue to a silent mother.
'. . . he becomes one of the few contemporary African
writers to raise the kind of sustained poetic voice
which one finds, for example, in Césaire's Return to
My Native Land.'
Thomas A. Hale – *World Literature Today*

Behold Mama, Flowers
Johannesburg: Ad. Donker, 1978. 88 pp.
R3.95 (£2.75/$6.25)
While Serote was in the United States he wrote

the long poem that comprises most of this
book. A series of shorter poems, also of
frustration and anguish, completes the work.

To Every Birth Its Blood
Johannesburg: Ravan, 1981. 368 pp. R7.95
London: HEB, 1983 (AWS, 263) forthcoming
Serote's first novel is of epic proportions, in
which we meet people from Alexandra Township at different periods in their lives. The links
that bind people are gradually uncovered, in
friendships, gangs and in political groups.

Small, Adam
Black Bronze Beautiful
Johannesburg: Ad. Donker, 1975. 64 pp.
R3.75 (£2.50/$5.95)
Hitherto, Adam Small has written in
Afrikaans. For this work, a celebration of
blackness in an address to a black woman who
merges with the image of the African conti-
nent, Small has chosen English.
'*On the whole the sequence must be regarded as a
remarkable contribution to imaginative self-awareness
in the Southern Africa of the late seventies.*'
Colin Gardner – *Reality*

Themba, Can
The Will to Die
London: HEB, 1972 (AWS, 104). 128 pp.
£1.50/$3.00
Can Themba was one of the group of brilliant
young journalists on *Drum* in the 1950s and
1960s. He subsequently became associate
editor of *Drum* and *Golden City Post,* and was a
founder of the journal *Classic.* This collection
of short stories is culled from his journalism,
and reflects the violent yet rich life in the
Johannesburg township of Sophiatown. His
work is banned in South Africa.
'. . . he echoed Ernest Hemingway's romanticism of
violence . . . He lent to his thoughts the same vivd
imagery, sharp staccato rhythm of the township
language of the urban tsotsi, because he himself was
the supreme intellectual tsotsi of them all, always, in
the words of the blues singer, "raising hell in the
neighbourhood".'
Lewis Nkosi – (from the Introduction)
'. . . subtle protest literature . . . in the sense that it
is a social documentary of the predicament of the black
man.'   Ricky Masagbor – *Nigerian Observer*

Tlali, Miriam
Muriel at Metropolitan
Johannesburg: Ravan, 1979. 95 pp. R2.95
London: Longman, 1979. 190 pp. 95p
Washington D.C.:Three Continents Press,
1979. $9.00 cased $4.00 p/b
Muriel is an efficient and intelligent black
woman working in a white-owned hire-

purchase store. Although she suffers no major calamity, she recounts the constant slights and insults suffered by black staff and customers; while her abilities are made use of, she gains none of the privileges accorded to her less able white colleagues. The moral dilemma of seeing customers manipulated out of money they cannot afford finally makes her reject the job, despite the consequences her family must endure.

'It is a slight book, and there are moments when it lapses into elementary journalism. But it is transparently honest; what must have been a strong temptation to sensationalize events is firmly resisted. And in the end it leaves the reader with a lasting and clear impression of the small Johannesburg shop and the people within it.' K. M. – *West Africa*

'Tlali's novel, based on her own experiences, describes simply and without sensationalism the plight of the South African Black struggling to find and keep a place in a society where white is always right.'
M. S. Wallace – *Time Out*

Amandla
Johannesburg: Ravan, 1980. 294 pp. R3.95
A story of a family set in 1976 – during the eruption of Soweto. *Amandla* – power – is the cry of the people. Banned in South Africa.

Williams, Neil Alwin and **Johennesse, Fhazel**
Just a Little Stretch of Road and *The Rainmaker*
Johannesburg: Ravan, 1979. 133 pp. R5.10
Published as one volume, works by two young writers examine the quality of their lives in South Africa. Williams has written a novella about childhood in Johannesburg, where children grow up quickly: they confront death, rape, and drunkenness, and have to live with the scars. The writing captures Williams' conviction that 'time has been running out – that we are well past the midnight hour' and the urgency of his continuing to 'write in the hope that there is still time.' Johennesse is a poet, whose work has been published in *Staffrider* and *New Classic*.

'Neil has not only mastered the language he uses. He expresses virtuosity itself . . . The hard-hitting lines of Fhazel – lines that don't easily lyricize – prove that one cannot deny the fact that blacks are doing much to save the English language in Southern Africa.'
Mafika Gwala – *Staffrider*

Zwelonke, D. M.
Robben Island
London: HEB, 1973 (AWS, 128). 160 pp. £1.95/$4.00
The author of this novel was himself imprisoned on Robben sland, the grim penal centre near Cape Town. Running through descriptions of life there – the hard labour, meagre diet, arbitrary punishments, the entertainments devised by the prisoners – is an account of Bekimpi, an imprisoned Poqo leader. His refusal to talk to his interrogators leads to severe punishment and ultimately to his death. His determination not to be a sellout is extremely important to the other Poqo prisoners on the Island.

Swaziland

Lukhele, Senzenjani
Tell Me No More
Mbabane, Swaziland: Macmillan Boleswa, 1980. 101 pp. 80p
London: Macmillan Educ., 1980.
Gugu's interference in a village affair is magnified and misinterpreted. She is banished by her adoptive father, flees to Manzini to shelter with relatives. Her father, Cele, has committed a grave error of custom in not fulfilling his role of adoptive father satisfactorily, and a fracas and court case ensue.

Zambia

Banjayamoyo, Storm
Sofiya
Lusaka: National Educ. Co. of Zambia, 1979 (Library Series, E4). 213 pp. K4.00
The expensive tastes of the beautiful Sofiya ruin the young salesman in love with her. If he cannot satisfy her demands there are plenty of men who can!

Chima, Richard
The Loneliness of a Drunkard
Lusaka: National Educ. Co. of Zambia, 1973. 36 pp. 60n
Twenty poems on a variety of topics.

Chipasula, F.
Visions and Reflections
Lusaka: National Educ. Co. of Zambia, 1972. 52 pp. 25n
Poems.

Kasoma, K.
Fools Marry
Lusaka: National Educ. Co. of Zambia, 1976. 48 pp. K.1.20

Marital unfaithfulness, drunkenness, and deceit are the ingredients of this play.

Masiye, Andreya S.

Before Dawn
Lusaka: National Educ. Co. of Zambia, 1971.
144 pp. K2.50
Karumba is born in a thunderstorm. His name – which means 'whirlwind' – presages future turmoil. His hardships when his mother dies, his unhappy attempts at working for the white man, and finally his conscription for war service are set in the context of a village disrupted by changing *mores*.

The Lands of Kazembe
Lusaka: National Educ. Co. of Zambia, 1973.
53 pp. 75n
Masiye has adapted an 1873 publication of the Royal Geographical Society to write this historical play. It dramatizes the journey of the Portuguese under Lacerda in 1798, from Beira to Angola, through the kingdom of Mwaata Kazembe.

Mulaisho, Dominic

The Tongue of the Dumb
London: HEB, 1971 (AWS, 98). 264 pp.
£1.95/$4.00
This, Mulaisho's first novel, is set in 1949. The dissatisfaction felt by the Kaunga peple at the white man's insistence on schooling, banishment of lepers, the demand for hut tax and an insensitive insistence on Western modes, is heightened by natural disasters. The chief succumbs to the DC's demands, knowing that imprisonment is the consequence of refusal. The scheming, ambitious councillor Lubinda manipulates the discontent, and by insidious means has the chief, Mpona, declared a witch. Mpona is saved from the death due to witches by the timely return of a young mute, who has been cured by a simple operation agreed to by the chief.

The Smoke That Thunders
London: HEB, 1979 (AWS, 204). 288 pp.
£1.95 ($5.00)
This is the second novel by Mulaisho, Economic Advisor to President Kaunda. He has located it in a fictitious British colony, between the former Rhodesia and Zambia. The Governor, Sir Elwyn Baker, is being pressed by various groups who wish to assume power. Most powerful at the outset are the white settlers – fervently anti-black, led by Sir Ray Norris – whose interests intermesh with those of the mining company. The company's directors seek stability at any cost, financial or

moral. The A.rican nationalist party, the PALP, is under considerable pressure as its members disagree on policy, its leader is imprisoned and tortured, and the party is banned. The nationalist leaders are frustrated in attempts to negotiate peacefully, and their victory is eventually achieved through mounting violence when they take control of the now independent state.
'*Mr Mulaisho's strength is that he succeeds in giving an in-depth portrait of a society in crisis and enables the reader to gain a necessary understanding of its complexities.*'   Faith Pullin – *British Book News*
'*Here we are in the hands of a narrator whose skill has matured and sympathies extended. . . . Not once does the prose crack or dialogue ring false.*'
K. Natwar-Singh – *Financial Times*

Mulikita, Fwanyanga M.

Shaka Zulu
London: Longman, 1967. 74 pp. 65p
A play about the great Zulu leader, Shaka (or Chaka), who, with his predecessor Dingiswayo, was the founder of the Zulu nation. The events of the play cover many years and are linked by chroniclers, who also serve to give accounts of battles and events that cannot be shown on stage.

A Point of No Return
London: Macmillan, 1968. 112 pp.
Lusaka: National Educ. Co. of Zambia, 1968.
112 pp. 60n
'Human caterpillars were eating away the leaves of his family', 'A Doctor of Philosophy changes his mind', 'A baby reforms a notorious thief' are some of the eleven short stories in this collection. The author was Zambia's first Ambassador to the United Nations.

Musonda, Kapelwa

The Kapelwa Musonda File
Lusaka: National Educ. Co. of Zambia, 1973.
140 pp. K1.00
A collection of newspaper articles by a well-known Zambian satirist falls into five main categories: culture, business, politics, family life, and urban life.
'*Although readers with first-hand experience of independent modern Africa will have greater delight in these amusing tales, such experience is not necessary for the enjoyment of a lively depiction of the day-by-day Zambian scene.*'
J. Burns – *Books Abroad*

Muyuni, Joseph

A Question of Motive
Lusaka: National Educ. Co. of Zambia, 1978.
89 pp. K1.50

A popular novel involving a famous doctor, pregnancy, and revenge murders.

'It has all the sensational ingredients of the thriller but also contains incidental comments that are of interest on the nature of contemporary society in Zambia.'

Faith Pullen – *African Book Publishing Record*

Phiri, G.
Ticklish Sensation
Lusaka: National Educ. Co. of Zambia, 1978 (rev. ed.). 140 pp. K2.50
Originally published in 1973, this is an account of an adolescent's search for the 'ticklish sensation' in love and life.

Victims of Fate
Lusaka: National Educ. Co. of Zambia, 1974. 156 pp. K2.20
A novel involving an unmarried mother, fatherless child, and a 'married bachelor'.

Phiri, Matsautso
Soweto: flowers will grow
Lusaka: National Educ. Co. of Zambia, 1979. 97 pp. K2.00
Phiri has delved into past oppression in South Africa in the writing of this play. Luthuli, Mandela, Sisulu, and Biko are the heroes of black resistance to apartheid; the villains are Western capitalism, Calvinism, Afrikanerdom. The play has a dirge-like effect; the characters are largely symbolic; the whole is a tribute to the culmination of resistance so far in South Africa – the Soweto uprising of 1976.
'It was a moving, sensitive and delicate depiction and portrayal of "black struggle" especially in Soweto.'
J. S. Mojapela – *Rand Daily Mail*

Saidi, William
The Hanging
Lusaka: National Educ. Co. of Zambia, 1979 (Library Series, E1). 176 pp. K4.00
Saidi, a journalist, has chosen a violent and fast-moving milieu for a thriller af political intrigue. Meke, the young reporter assigned to cover a murder trial, is caught between two political factions battling for power. His having an Afrikaner girl friend complicates the issues still further.
' . . . multi-influenced but inspired popular fiction narrative.'
Lemuel A. Johnson – *The African Book Publishing Record*

Samuel, J. M.
I Remember!
Lusaka: National Educ. Co. of Zambia, 1973, 34 pp. 25n

A collection of short poems, based on personal observations.
' . . . a minor but worthwhile contribution to the small but growing literature of Zambia.'
James Burns – *Books Abroad*

Sibale, G.
Between Two Worlds
Lusaka: National Educ. Co. of Zambia, 1979 (Library Series, E2). 160 pp. K4.00
Accusations of impotence, coupled with his poverty, drives Chifutu from his village to the city. Far from his fortunes improving, however, Chifutu sinks even lower in the world.

Simoko, Patu
Africa is made of Clay
Lusaka: National Educ. Co. of Zambia, 1975. 77 pp. 50n
An anthology of poems.

Simukwasa, W.
The Coup
Lusaka: National Educ. Co. of Zambia, 1978 (Library Series, E3). 96 pp. K3.00
A thriller involving Pungwa, the Zambian secret agent working for the Organization for African Unity.

Tembo, L.
Poems
Lusaka: National Educ. Co. of Zambia, 1972. 28 pp. 20n

Vyas, C. L.
The Falls and Other Poems
Lusaka: Zambia Cult. Serv., 1968. K1.00

Wind is the Messenger: a collection of poems.
Lusaka: Zambia Cult. Serv., 1973. K1.00

Zulu, Patrick C.
A Sheaf of Gold
Lusaka: Unity Press Ltd., 1971 37 pp.
A collection of poems.

Zimbabwe

Banana, Canaan S.
The Gospel According to the Ghetto
Geneva: World Council of Churches, 1974 (distr. in the U.K. by Third World Publ., Birmingham) 18 pp. £1.10 Gwelo, Zimbabwe: Mambo Press, 1980.
The President of Zimbabwe's poetry seeks to integrate the Christian philosophy with the experiences of those who have been oppressed.

The Woman of my Imagination
Gwelo, Zimbabwe: Mambo Press, 1980.
Fiction, drama and didacticism combined.

Chimsoro, S.
Smoke and Flames
Gwelo, Zimbabwe: Mambo Press, 1978
(Mambo Writers Series, 3). 53 pp. 85c
Poems.

Chingono, Julius
Flags of Love
Harare: Gazebo, 1981. 21 pp.
Poetry in English and Shona.

Chipunza, A.
Svikiro
Harare: Longman, 1981. (Zimbabwe Writers
Series). 68 pp. Z$1.20
A play.

Dube, H.
State Secret
London: Macmillan Educ., 1981. 80p
A fast moving popular novel.

Kadhani, Mudereri
Quarantine Rhythms
Aberdeen: Palladio Press, 1976. 53 pp. £1.45
Poems by a 24-year old Zimbabwean who was
imprisoned under the Smith regime.

Katiyo, Wilson
A Son of the Soil
London: Rex Collings, 1976, 147 pp. £3.50
cased
Washington D.C.: Three Continents Press,
1976. $7.00
The background to the story of Alexio is
sketched by Katiyo at the outset: ruthless
settler exploitation is followed by white
domination in what was Rhodesia. When
Alexio's father dies, his quiet village life ends;
he is eventually sent to school with a cousin in
Salisbury, a rude awakening to a white world.
His bitter childhood ends when a friend is
murdered by police, and he is detained. To be
reissued shortly in the Longman 'Drumbeat'
series.
'. . . the plain and moving story of a black child
growing up in Zimbabwe.'
M. Sullivan – *Sunday Telegraph*
'Told with a total lack of bitterness, it is often a
painful and harrowing story.
Rhodri Jones – *Times Educational Supplement*

Going to Heaven
London: Rex Collings, 1979. 139 pp. £4.95
cased
London: Longman, 1982. £1.50

Set in pre-independence Rhodesia, this sequel
to *A Son of the Soil* follows Alexio Shonga's fate
after he leaves school. The razing of his village,
the death of his wife and child, and the
political persecution he suffers, cause him to
flee Rhodesia. His eventual arrival in London
presents him with different problems of
identity and alienation. To be reissued shortly
in the Longman 'Drumbeat' series.
'Beautifully written, the traumatic experiences in the
flawed heaven of England are conveyed in simple if
racy style which compels the reader's attention.'
Ad'Obe Obe – *Africa*

Marechera, Dambudzo
The House of Hunger
London: HEB, 1978 (AWS, 207). 160 pp.
£1.75
New York: Pantheon Books, 1978. 167 pp.
$7.95 cased $3.95 p/b
Marechera, for this title, was joint winner of
the 1979 Guardian Fiction Prize. It is a
collection of short stories; the title story covers
half the length, being a montage of memories,
impressions and ideas about life and people in
a township in what was then Rhodesia.
Violence is a way of life, permeating relationships between friends and family. Smith's
UDI, the guerilla war, the effects of discrimination and apartheid are the backdrop to the
picture created. Using different perspectives in
the rest of the stories – variously that of poet,
journalist, exiled academic – he builds up
images of the problems of identity and
alienation for a people who are tyrannized and
deprived of their true identity.
'The stories in The House of Hunger are rather
uneven in quality. But it is rare to find a writer for
whom imaginative fiction is such a passionate and
intimate process of engagement with the world. A
terrible beauty is born out of the urgency of his vision.'
Angela Carter – *The Guardian*
'Marechera has in him the stuff and substance that go
to make a great writer.'
Doris Lessing – *Books and Bookmen*

Black Sunlight
London: HEB, 1980 (AWS, 237). 128 pp.
£2.60/$8.50
Using a mixture of fantasy and fiction, the
author has created a nebulous sequence of
events and states of mind. The protagonist, a
photographer, is caught between photo-
graphing the violence in his country, and
being involved in it. He is accepted by a
political organization, the Black Sunlight
Group, after rescuing one of their members. A
visit to their headquarters in the Devil's End
Caves and his personal and political trauma
are presented in fragmented and macabre

fashion.

'Marechera's talents are not modest.'
James Lasdun – *New Statesman*

Mungoshi, Charles L.

Coming of the Dry Season
Nairobi: OUP, 1972. 68 pp. o/p
Harare: Zimbabwe Publishing House, 1982,
Z$2.50
Ten short stories.

Waiting for the Rain
London: HEB, 1975 (AWS, 170). 192 pp.
£1.95/$3.00
Harare: Zimbabwe Publishing House, 1981,
Z$3.45
Lucifer, a talented artist, takes leave of his family before setting off for England. The action, concentrated into one week-end, covers the tensions between varying members of his family. We are also made aware of the gap for him between his educated rationality and the deep-seated superstitions and traditions of his family. Mungoshi was awarded the Rhodesian P.E.N. prize of 1976 for this novel, his first in English.
'That impartial eye, balanced against the passionate involvement in their land and culture of the characters it observes, is what gives this remarkable book its almost visionary double dimension.'
Jeremy Brooks – *Sunday Times*
'Rarely has an African writer composed such a powerful story about family turmoil and the generation gap . . . Mungoshi explores the multiple relationships among his main characters with the maturity of an accomplished writer.'
Charles R. Larson – *Books Abroad*

The Milkman Doesn't Only Deliver Milk:
selected poems
Harare: Poetry Society of Zimbabwe, 1981
(Mopani Poets, 5). 32 pp. Z$2.60
Mungoshi's poetry is bound with Colin Style's *Musical Saw* (Mopani Poets, 6).

Mutswairo, Solomon

Chaminuka: Prophet of Zimbabwe
Washington D.C.: Three Continents Press, 1978. 150 pp. $14.00 cased $5.00 p/b
Set in the mid-nineteenth century, this historical novel involves Chaminuka's efforts to preach friendship to the invading forces of the Ndebele.

Mapondera: Soldier of Zimbabwe
Washington D.C.: Three Continents Press, 1978. 150 pp. $14.00 cased $5.00 p/b
An historical novel about the Shona warrior turned freedom fighter in the late nineteenth-century struggle against colonialism.

Ndhlala, Geoffrey C. T.

Jikinya
Harare: Macmillan Zimbabwe, 1979. 118 pp.
Z$2.40
When Chedu ventures across the mountains he comes across a smouldering settler homestead, burnt in the Shona uprising of the last century, and a white baby – the sole survivor. She is named Jikinya, adopted by his family, and grows up in peace and happiness until the arrival of a young explorer, John Brown, who unwittingly brings destruction and tragedy to the village. The background to the action is a description of a people in harmony with nature. John Brown is faced with an African philosophy of life as complex and sincere as any he has found in the Western world.

Nyamfukudza, S.

The Non-Believer's Journey
London: HEB, 1980 (AWS, 233). 128 pp.
£1.95/$6.50
Amidst the complex moral decisions that war-torn Zimbabwe demands, Sam 'the teacher' is lethargic. He perceives the hollowness of the political meetings in the towns, the bitter sacrifices the peasants make for the war, the astuteness of the politicians, he sympathizes with 'the boys' – as the freedom fighters are called – but he will not actively help them. The action is encompassed within a weekend when Sam returns to his village, for the funeral of an uncle, killed by the guerillas for supposedly being a collaborator. The denouement involves Sam in a guerillas' meeting when he is asked to smuggle medical supplies to them.
'Nyamfukudza has talent to such an exent that, even in this his first novel, he has been able to dispense with a hero, and produce, in Sam, a plausible anti-hero.'
Michael Simmons – *South*
'. . . this is a novel that reaches through the story of a privileged educated son to the fundamental conflicts inherent in the loyalties that men owe because of upbringing or education in the modern world.'
G. Parker – *British Book News*

Samkange, Stanlake

The Mourned One
London: HEB, 1975 (AWS, 169). 160 pp.
£1.95/$3.00
The title derives from the name of Muchemwa the mourned one – the central figure in the book. Samkange purports that the narrative was written by 'Ocky' (Muchemwa) while awaiting execution in Salisbury jail in the 1930s. Muchemwa looks back over his life: rescued from a river death by a missionary, reared in European ways, and only finding out about his own background with difficulty. He visits his home village, meets his family, and

reflects on the feelings and experiences involved in this visit. As his life becomes less sheltered, he encounters more and more racial animosity and absurdity. His education fits him to become a teacher; while at the mission school it is claimed by a white colleague and friend that he has raped her. The evidence is inconclusive, but Muchemwa is sentenced to hang.

'Mr Samkange writes with the wit and authority that comes from a loving understanding of his subject; and, because he knows European culture so intimately too; he has that sharp double vision which gives an almost stereoscopic effect to so much African writing.'
Jeremy Brooks – *Sunday Times*
'There is some delicate fun and the Missions are regarded in an ambivalent way which tells the reader much more than would come out of any factual report.'   Naomi Mitchison – *Times Higher Educational Supplement*

Year of the Uprising
London: HEB, 1978 (AWS, 190). 160 pp. £1.50/$3.00
It is 1896 in Zimbabwe. Samkange has again melded history and fiction to set the scene for the great uprising ov the Matabele and Mashona. The distress felt by the people at the treatment meted out by white settlers and Zulu police under Rhodes's company is exacerbated by cattle disease, drought, and locusts. Word is spread that the settlers must be resisted by force of arms, and the uprising spreads quickly, and Rhodes finds it hard to quell. The African fighters are hard to pin down, and the Company faces ruin if the rebellion continues. Rhodes manages to sue for peace in time, but basically the settlers have learned nothing from the uprising.
'. . . it makes a fascinating book, like all of Samkange's writing, but (again like other books by this author) it has its difficulties and discouraging moments for some readers.'   K. M. – *West Africa*

Sithole, Ndabaningi
The Polygamist
New York: The Third Press, 1972. $6.95 cased $4.95 p/b
London: Hodder and Stoughton, 1972. $1.90
London: Sphere Books, 1978. 192 pp. 85p
A lengthy debate on polygamy is sustained in this novel, written while the author was imprisoned during Ian Smith's regime. The wealthy headman. Dube, is a traditionalist who supports his seven wives adequately, although not entirely to their satisfaction. Change, in the guise of his son who returns from studying and who wants a monogamous marriage, is initially threatening.
'Sithole offers a colourful evocation of life in a Rhodesian tribal village, which at the same time suggests some of the political parallels confronting the emerging nations as they seek to retain their traditions in the face of "progress".'   Publishers Weekly

Roots of a Revolution
Oxford: OUP. 1977. 142 pp. £3.50 cased
One of the books written by Sithole while in prison during the Smith regime. It consists of eleven short stories or 'scenes', set in the Rhodesia of the late 1950s and early 1960s. The articulate and forceful John Mayo – a highly educated nationalist leader – appears in several of the pieces, and his attitudes and urgings are clearly shared by the author.

Zimunya, Musa B.
Zimbabwe Ruins
Harare; Poetry Society of Zimbabwe, 1979, (Mopani Poets, 4). 32 pp. Z$2.60
This volume is bound with D. E. Borrell's *A Patch of Sky* (Mopani Poets, 3).

Thought Tracks
London: Longman, forthcoming 1981
A collection of poetry.

FRANCOPHONE AFRICA

WEST AFRICA

Benin

Agbogba, Paul Adanhoumey
Tam-Tams et flambeaux: poèmes
Cotonou: Ed. du Bénin, 1970 (Balafon, 3).
96 pp.
Poetry, with a preface by Eustache Prudencio.

Agbossahessou [pseud. for Martins Gutenberg]
Aï di a: j'ai vu
Yaoundé: C.L.E., 1969. 106 pp. o/p
Prose poems, in four parts, praising the African landscape and the people and the animals living in it. Contains a lexicon of terms used.

Les haleines sauvages
Yaoundé: C.L.E., 1972. 94 pp. CFA450
A collection of poems, some in prose, evoking a great diversity of themes such as Aziza, the muse of Africa, the yam harvest, an African child's Christmas, the death of a friend's wife, and procreation.

Alapini, Julian
Le petit Dahoméen
Avignon: Presses Universelles, 1950. 285 pp.
The story of a little boy from Dahomey.

Acteurs noirs
Avignon: Presses Universelles, 1965. 189 pp.
A collection of short plays.

Almeida, Fernando d'
Au seuil de l'exil
Paris: P. J. Oswald, 1976 (Poésie/prose africaine, 16) (distr. by L'Harmattan, Paris).
55 pp. FF15.00
A collection of the verse of a committed poet. His themes are protest, nostalgia for the homeland, pity and contempt for Africa's tyrants and her servile population.
'. . . his language is restrained, dignified . . . Though pleasing, this poetry never displays the personal anguish, the feeling of loss and bitterness of other poets who live in exile.'
C. H. Bruner – *World Literature Today*

Bhêly-Quénum, Olympe
Le chant du lac
Paris: Présence Africaine, 1965. 153 pp.
FF24.00

A dying man, a veteran of World War II and Dien-Bien-Phu on a boat returning to Africa swears that the gods of the lake who keep his people in fear and bondage will be vanquished. For the home-coming students listening to him he is a hero, but for the people of his lake-side village in Dahomey he is a murderer who had to be exiled years before, and his words are sacrilegious. It is the pre-independence era, nationalism is in the air and the village is torn by conflicting political parties. Are not the gods of the lake who harass them symbols of a past that must be renewed and of their own lack of unity? This novel won the Grand Prix Littéraire d'Afrique Noire in 1966.
'. . . portrays an African community held in the grip of animism . . . Bhêly-Quénum combines humour and psychological penetration with a talent for evocative description; and the extraordinary richness of levels in this novel – its blending of folk legend, social criticism, symbolism, and allegory – makes it stand out among modern African fiction.'
Thomas Cassirer – *African Forum*

Liaison d'un été et autres récits
Paris: Ed. SAGEREP, L'Afrique Actuelle, 1968 (Dossier littéraire, 2). 241 pp.
A collection of short stories.

Un piège sans fin
Paris: Présence Africaine, 1978. 253 pp.
FF47.00
This is a reissue of the original edition published by Stock in 1960, now out of print. In English *translation*, see *Snares Without End*.

L'initié
Paris: Présence Africaine, 1979. 251 pp.
FF47.00
Bhêly-Quénum's third published novel was originally written in 1964 but held back by the author for fifteen years because of its 'sensitive' subject matter. It is about Kofi-Marc Tingo who is both a French-trained medical doctor and a traditional healer as an initiate to the Ogboni cult. He is as concerned to preserve what is valid in the past as he is to rid his country of harmful superstitions, such as the black magic of old Djessou, whose 'clients' include the country's leading politicians.
'. . . interesting, lyrical in places, and highly dramatic towards the end when Djessou gets paid back in his own thunderous coin.' N. B.-E. – *West Africa*
'C'est un beau livre, un livre témoignage sur une époque charnière de l'évolution du continent noir.'
Afrique Contemporaine

Snares Without End
London: Longman, 1981 (Drumbeat, 23).
204 pp. £1.50
Washington D.C.: Three Continents Press.
$6.00
Set among the planters and herders in the
north of Dahomey under colonial rule, this
novel is the tragic tale of a man who is
implacably pursued by bad luck. Suspected of
unfaithfulness by his wife he is unable to prove
his innocence. Nor can he explain a fortuitous
encounter that would seem to confirm his
guilt. The English edition contains a short
glossary of terms used.
'... a fresco from Dahomey, full of reality and
lyricism.'   Andrée Clair – *Présence Africaine*

Les mille hâches
Paris: Hatier, (Monde noir poche). 160 pp.
forthcoming 1981.
Short stories.

Dogbeh, Richard

Les eaux du Mono
Vire, France: Lec-Vire, 1963. 59 pp. o/p
(Reprinted in *African Poems in French*. Nendeln,
Liechtenstein: Kraus Reprint, 1970. $27.00)
Poems.

Rives mortelles
Porto-Novo, Benin: Silva, 1964. 36 pp. o/p
(Reprinted in *African Poems in French*. Nendeln,
Liechtenstein: Kraus Reprint, 1970. $27.00)
Poems.

Voyage au pays de Lénine
Yaoundé: C.L.E., 1967. 96 pp. o/p
Richard Dogbeh visited Russia in 1966 at the
invitation of the Union of Soviet Writers. This
is his account of his impressions of that visit.

Cap liberté
Yaoundé: C.L.E., 1969. 76 pp. o/p
A verse collection, including a long dramatic
poem.
'*Depuis le poème d'ouverture "Salut Lagos"
jusqu'au poème final "Ballade Macabre" écrit en
souvenir de Daniel, l'Etranger sacrifié à la liberté du
Dahomey, Richard Dogbeh évoque la grandeur et la
misère du monde noir, sans jamais perdre l'espoir de
jours meilleurs pour l'homme enfin libre.*'
                         Afrique Littéraire et Artistique

Hazoumé, Paul

Doguicimi
Paris: G. P. Maisonneuve et Larose, 1978.
510 pp. FF40.00
First published in 1935 this work has again
become available after having been long out of
print. Drawing heavily upon traditional and
oral literature, this historical novel – set in pre-
colonial Dahomey – narrates the events of an
expedition of the kings of Abomey against the

Mahi tribe, through the adventures of a
Dahoman princess.

Hountondji, Victor M.

Deux filles . . . Un rêve fugitif: nouvelle, suivi
de *Les vertiges de Persu Grand-Vet: Poèmes en
prose*
Cotonou: Ed. A.B.M., 1973. 69 pp.
A short story followed by prose poems.

Couleur de rêve
Paris: La Pensée Universelle, 1977. 159 pp.
A short story and poems.

Joachim, Paulin

Un nègre raconte
Paris: Ed. Bruno Durochor, 1955. 16 pp. o/p
Poetry.

Editorial africain
Strasbourg: Imp. des Dernières Nouvelles,
1967. 180 pp. o/p
A collection of poetry with a preface by Joseph
Ki-Zerbo.

Anti-grâce
Paris: Présence Africaine, 1967. 64 pp.
FF20.00
A poetry volume.

Mêlé, Maurice

Harmonies dahoméennes
Porto Novo: Ed. Danito, 1965. 16 pp.
Poetry.

Danhômey: drame
Porto Novo: Imp. Rapidex, 1965. 16 pp.
A play, set in the 17th century, that tells how a
foreign prince became the monarch of
Danhômey by slaying Dan, the dragon, the
god of the land, and thus winning the hand of
the princess of Abomey.

Pliya, Jean

*Kondo, le requin: drame historique en trois
actes*
Cotonou: Ed. du Bénin, 1966. 112 pp. CFA125
Paris: O.R.T.F./D.A.E.C., 1969 (Répertoire
théâtral africain, 4). 112 pp. o/p
The central figure in this historical play, which
was first published in Bénin in 1966, is
Béhanzin, the last king of Abomey, whose
defeat by the French in the early twentieth
century opened the coast of Dahomey to
colonization. Béhanzin's royal symbol was
Kondo, the shark. Winner of the 1967 Grand
Prix littéraire de l'Afrique Noire.
'*Ici l'oeuvre théâtral, qui se veut d'abord document,
atteint à une intensité "subversive". Loin d'être une
exaltation de la grandeur de l'Afrique passée, elle
devient une critique du pouvoir, quel qu'il soit, dans
l'Afrique aujourd'hui.*'
         Alain Ricard – *Afrique Littéraire et Artistique*

La secrétaire particulière
Cotonou: Librarie Notre Dame, 1970. 102 pp.
Yaoundé: C.L.E., 1973. 96 pp. CFA520
A satirical play about the corruption and
inefficiency of African civil-servants. Mr.
Chadas has no use but for the most 'private' of
secretaries, such as the beautiful, incompetent
Nathalie. A new girl, Virginie, refuses to play
this game. Then Nathalie gets pregnant and
discovers her services are no longer needed.
Chadas, the villain, eventually gets his just
deserts – a prison sentence.

L'arbre fétiche: nouvelles
Yaoundé: C.L.E., 1971. 92 pp. CFA600
Four short stories. In the title story, which was
awarded a prize by the journal, *Preuves*, a man
dies for daring to cut down a sacred Iroko tree
to make way for a new road, and the theme of
'Le guardian de nuit' is the tragic consequence
of black magic. In contrast, the other two
stories are tales of hope: a poor peasant gets
an unexpected benefactor and a hungry boy an
unexpected present.

*Le chimpanzé amoureux, Le rendez-vous, La
palabre de la dernière chance*
Issy-les-Moulineaux, France: Ed. Saint-Paul,
1977 (Classiques Africains, 713). 95 pp. FF16.00
Three short stories.

Prudencio, Eustache
Vents du lac: poèmes I
Cotonou: Ed. du Bénin, 1967. 104 pp.
Poetry.

Ombres et soleils: poèmes II
Cotonou: Ed. du Bénin. 1968. 84 pp.
The author's second collection of verse.

Violence de la race: poèmes III
Cotonou: Ed. A.B.M., 1971 (2nd ed.). 135 pp.
The word 'violence' in the title of this
collection of thirty poems refers, says the
author, to 'intensity with which the poet sings
of his country and its realities'. Contains a
letter to the author by Léopold Sédar Senghor.

Tidjani-Serpos, Nouréini
Agba'Nla: poèmes
Paris: P. J. Oswald, 1973 (distr. by
L'Harmattan, Paris). 80 pp. FF16.00

Cameroon
(see also English-speaking Africa)

Abelar, Georges
Fils de paysan
Yaoundé: Ed. Semences Africaines, 1979.
70 pp. CFA600

A play which focuses on the problems of poor
peasants in trying to educate their children.

Abessolo, Théophile Bikoula
L'épopée d'Abogo, la femme-homme
Yaoundé: Ed. Semences Africaines, 1977.
21 pp. CFA250
An epic poem, written for the International
Women's Year, telling how Abogo came to the
rescue of her people.

Ahanda, Assiga
*Société Africaine et High Société: petite
ethnologie de l'arrivisme*
Libreville: Ed. Lion, 1978. 91 pp.
Vincent and Mathilde return home from
abroad and find their country changed. How
materialistic everyone has become! Success is
measured strictly in monetary terms. One is
expected to build an expensive home in the
village to honour the clan. But the two are
honest and hard-working and resist pressures
to do like everyone else.

Ahanda Essomba, Honoré-Godefroy
Le fruit défendu
Yaoundé: C.L.E., 1975. 145 pp. CFA630
A long-awaited son is finally born. Unfortunately, he is as stubborn as he is
intelligent, persisting in his desire to marry his
cousin (six times removed), which is nothing
less than incest. The entire extended family will
be called upon to settle the matter.
*'Well written and easy to read . . . The characters are
carefully developed.'*
           Philip A. Noss – *Books Abroad*
*'. . . donne à débattre deux thèmes: celui du conflit
entre la tradition et la modernité, et celui de
l'education des enfants. Si le premier thème manque
d'originalité, il rajeunit par la façon dont il est
traité.'*
           Charly-Gabriel Mbock – *Cameroon Tribune*

Akoa, Dominique
Survivances du clocher
Paris: P. J. Oswald, 1977 (Poésie/prose
africaine, 24) (distr. by L'Harmattan, Paris).
100 pp. FF20.00
A young Cameroonian relives his childhood in
the country.

Alima, Ernest
Si tu veux vivre longtemps
Issy-les-Moulineaux, France: Ed. Saint-Paul,
1977 (Classiques africaines, 715). 44 pp.
FF13.00
Twenty-one poems divided into four chapters:
'Toi,' 'L'autre', 'Femmes,' 'La vie.'

Aliou, Mohammadou Modibo
Sur les chemins de la Sa'IIRA
Paris: Ed. Saint Germain-des-Prés, 1979.
42 pp. FF25.00
A collection of poetry in five parts, or 'songs'.

Awona, Stanislas
Le chômeur: une tragi-comédie en cinq actes
Yaoundé: Centre d'édition et de production
des manuels, 1968. 64 pp. CFA200
A play about an educated young man who
finds himself unemployed because he refuses
to accept positions 'below' him. His friends of
less education, on the other hand, have
become successful civil servants, after climbing
to the top from humble beginnings. All ends
well, however.

Ayissi, Léon-Marie
Les innocents
Yaoundé: C.L.E., 1969 (C.L.E. Théâtre, 2).
48 pp. o/p
A tragedy in five acts centring around a
conflict between the clan and the idea of
romantic love.

Bebey, Francis
Le fils d'Agatha Moudio
Yaoundé: C.L.E., 1967. 208 pp. CFA800
In English translation see next entry.

Embarras et Cie: nouvelles et poèmes
Yaoundé: C.L.E., 1968. 117 pp. o/p
A collection of eight short stories, each of
which is supplemented by a poem.
'. . . Francis Bebey a donné a ce nouvel ouvrage un
rythme a la fois concerté et naturel . . . chacun des
poèmes est une respiration, une variation lyrique sur
un thème plus ou moins clairement évoqué par
l'anecdote précédente.'
Revue française d'études politiques africaines

Agatha Moudio's Son
(Trans. from the French by Joyce Hutchinson)
London: HEB, 1971 (AWS, 86). 160 pp. o/p
Westport, Conn.: Laurence Hill, 1973. 160 pp.
$5.95 cased $2.95 p/b
The hero of this novel (or fable) is Mbenda, a
young man from a fishing village at the mouth
of the Wouri river. In obedience to local
tradition, he marries the girl his father chose
for him on his deathbed, though his heart
longs for another, Agatha Moudio. The novel
won the Grand Prix Littéraire de l'Afrique
Noire 1968. Has also appeared in German,
Italian and Dutch translations.
'. . . un authentique roman, avec des personnages
bien vivants pris dans le mouvement alerte d'une
action méticuleusement construite: et surtout le
sourire qui plane sur les lèvres de Bebey, la malice qui

*brille dans ses yeux, sa plume, très efficace, les
restitue fidèlement.'* – Abbia
'. . . du début au coup de théâtre de la fin, se fablieu
camerounais est un petit chef-d'oeuvre de burlesque
tendre.'
Revue française d'études politiques africaines

Trois petits cireurs
Yaoundé: C.L.E., 1972. 62 pp. CFA210
Mamou, Abdel, and Nyassa, three little
shoeshine boys wait for customers in front of a
hotel in a big African city. They scuffle and
fight all day long – but pool their resources
every night according to a strict moral code.
One day, however, they are caught stealing a
wallet from a parked car by an important
looking African customer. It all ends well
when the identity of the man is revealed. A tale
for young and old alike.

La poupée ashanti
Yaoundé: C.L.E., 1973. 220 pp. CFA630
In English *translation*, see next entry.

The Ashanti Doll
(Trans. from the French by Joyce Hutchinson)
London: Rex Collings, 1977. 192 pp. £3.95
London: HEB, 1978 (AWS, 205). 192 pp.
£1.75
Spio, a young government worker, falls in love
with Edna, the illiterate but beautiful granddaughter of Mom, a leader of the market-
women of Accra. While developing this
romance, the novel explores the role of the
Accra market-women in the country's economy and their influence on its government.
'. . . a series of amiable but shrewd social observations.' John Povey – *African Arts*
'. . . a happy, if lightweight African tale.'
Kenneth Harrow – *World Literature Today*

Le Roi Albert d'Effidi
Yaoundé: C.L.E., 1976. 196 pp. CFA1,200
Three villages in present-day Cameroon vie for
political representation through their 'sons':
Albert, the 'King' of businessmen; Bikounou,
a government worker; Toutouma a railway
worker and trade-unionist. Added to that is
the romantic rivalry of Toutouma and
Bikounou who are also vying for the hand of
Albert's daughter.
'Francis Bebey has several unique talents evident in
Le Roi Albert d'Effidi. He handles deftly the
cultural transition in Cameroon from colonized status
to emerging independence. His satire is genial, his
characters fallible and lovable.'
Charlotte Bruner – *World Literature Today*
'Ce troisième roman de Francis Bebey . . . est
pourtant, à l'instar des deux autres, une perle
littéraire. Langue à la fois élégante, sobre et précise,

architecture textuelle rigoureuse, . . . phrases rythmées et nimbées d'un halo de poèsie.'
Fame Ndongo – *Cameroon Tribune*

Nouvelle saison des fruits
Dakar: Nouvelles Editions Africaines, 1980. 49 pp. CFA600
A collection of verse that shows Bebey's concern about the difficult choices confronting Africans today – choices of culture, of society.

Concert pour un vieux masque
Paris: L'Harmattan, 1980 (Encres noites, 6). 80 pp. FF28.00
A long poetic text relating the journey of an old mask from Africa to Brazil and to ultimate death in a museum showcase.
'Dans son récit, tout se mêle, la vie quotidienne et le surnaturel, Duke Ellington et le général Leclerc, un marabout tueur et le gouverneur général Félix Eboué . . . On lit le texte avec passion.'
Lucien Roux – *Le Nouvel Observateur*

Bengono, Jacques
La perdrix blanche: trois contes moraux
Yaoundé: C.L.E., 1966. 92 pp. o/p
Subtitled 'Three Moral Tales'.

Beti, Mongo [pseud. for Biyidi, Alexandre]
Le pauvre Christ de Bomba
Paris: Laffont, 1956. 371 pp. o/p
Paris: Présence Africaine, 1976. 285 pp. FF41.00
Beti's first novel, published by Laffont in 1956 and reprinted by Krauz in 1970, has again become available in a Présence Africaine edition. In English *translation*, see next entry.

The Poor Christ of Bomba
(Trans. from the French by Gerald Moore)
London: HEB, 1971 (AWS, 88). 224 pp. £1.75
In Bomba the girls who are being prepared for Christian marriage live together in the women's camp. Gradually it becomes apparent that the local churchmen have been using the girls for their own purposes. Set in a remote district of Cameroon in 1938 and written in the form of a diary by the 'boy' of Reverend Father Superior Drumont, this novel, despite comic overtones, is a sharp indictment of white missionary activities in Africa.
'In spite of the serious depth of the novel – its exploration of themes of racial and ethical incompatibility – comedy is always present in even the most dramatic scenes.' *Times Literary Supplement*
'. . . seen through the loving and wondering eyes of a priest's acolyte, Denis, whose comments unconsciously reveal a number of sad truths. . . . The book is extremely funny, with several scenes of ludicrous slapstick.'* Kenneth Williams – *West Africa*

Mission terminée
Paris: Corrêa, 1957. 257 pp. o/p
Paris: Buchet-Chastel, 1972 (2nd ed.) 256 pp.
A re-issue of the 1957 novel published by Corrêa. In English *translation* see next entry.

Mission to Kala
(Trans. from the French by Peter Green)
London: HEB, 1964 (AWS, 13). 192 pp. £1.25
Originally published in English as *Mission Accomplished* by Macmillan of New York and Muller of London in 1958, Mongo Beti's second novel was awarded the Prix Sainte-Beuve. Jean-Marie Medza, a young student who has failed his exams returns to his village in southern Cameroon to find his prestige and standing among the inhabitants intact. He becomes involved in a delicate task – to bring back a villager's wife who has run off with a man from another tribe and fled to relatives at Kala. When Jean-Marie reaches Kala he is well received, but the woman he seeks is away. Whilst patiently waiting for the woman's return he is generously entertained. His mission is eventually successful and he returns home. But he finds himself unable to come to terms with his family, particularly because of his father whom he abhors, and he leaves home for good.

Le roi miraculé: chronique des Essazam
Paris: Corrêa, 1958. 255 pp. o/p
Paris: Buchet-Chastel, 1972 (2nd ed.). 255 pp.
In English *translation* see next entry.

King Lazarus
(Trans. from the French by Peter Green)
London: Muller, 1960. 191 pp. o/p
London: HEB, 1970 (AWS, 77). 192 pp. £1.75
New York: Macmillan, 1977. 256 pp. $1.50
The Chief of Essazam, a powerful pagan king and spiritual leader of his people, is miraculously saved from a severe sickness, ostensibly by being 'baptized' by his old aunt with the aid of several jugs of water. The local missionary Le Guen is quick to put the King's recovery to use for his own purposes, and persuades the Chief to let it be believed that he has returned from the dead, to renounce his tribal ways and adopt Christianity. The repercussions that ensue are highly complicated.
Mongo Beti is one of the most entertaining and accurate of African satirists, and King Lazarus (Le roi miraculé) *is that rarity, a genuinely humorous novel . . . Both the author and his African characters are good at making fun of themselves, deflating pomposity, loquacious oratory, and concern for prestige.'* Robert E. Morsberger – *Books Abroad*

Perpétue ou l'habitude du malheur: roman
Paris: Buchet-Chastel, 1974. 304 pp.
In English *translation*, see next entry.

Perpetua and the Habit of Unhappiness
(Trans. from the French by John Reed and
Clive Wake)
London: HEB, 1978 (AWS, 181). 224 pp. £1.95
A young man's investigation of his sister's
death takes him throughout an imaginary
African country where the misery of the
inhabitants contrasts sharply with the life of
luxury of the head of state, Baba Toura, and
his ministers. Essola has spent six years in a
concentration camp for dissident activities and
on his release discovers that his sister,
Perpetua, has died mysteriously. She had, in
fact, died in childbirth, after having been 'sold'
for the bride price she would fetch to a man
whose pettiness, mediocrity and lack of
scruples are the very symbols of the regime.
*'While the novel suffers in sound characterization, the
poetic quality of the language cannot be denied . . . reaffirms the author's literary stature.'*
                               Victor Carrabino – *Books Abroad*

Remember Ruben
Paris: Union Générale d'Editions, 1974 (Coll.
10/18, 853). 320 pp.
In English *translation*, see next entry.

Remember Ruben
(Trans. from the French by Gerald Moore)
London: HEB, 1980 (AWS, 214). 272 pp. £3.40
Ibadan: New Horn Press. 1980
Washington D.C.: Three Continents Press,
1980
Ruben is the leader of the opposition to the
party chosen to be the successors of the
colonial government. He dies, killed by the
forces of order just before independence. This
novel is the precursor to *Perpetua and the Habit
of Unhappiness* and deals with a historical figure,
Ruben Um Nyobé, founder of the Union of
the Cameroonian People.

La ruine presque cocasse d'un polichinelle
Paris: Eds. des Peuples Noirs, 1979. 320 pp.
FF54.00
Taking up where *Remember Ruben* leaves off,
Beti's latest work, part fable, part allegory,
follows a pair of unlikely revolutionaries who
are soon joined by a young student, more
knowledgeable in books than in guerilla
practice, on a sort of 'long march' with the
ultimate aim of liberating a far-off province of
the young republic. On the way they are able
to assess, one after the other, the symbols of
oppression of all black peoples. The novel was
first serialized in the journal that Beti edits in
Paris, *Peuples Noirs, Peuples Africains*.

Boto, Eza [pseud. for Biyidi, Alexandre
also known as Beti, Mongo]
Ville cruelle
Paris: Les Editions Africaines, 1964. 221 pp.
o/p
Paris: Présence Africaine, 1972. 220 pp.
FF15.00
Set in Southern Cameroon in the 1930s this
novel relates the adventures of Banda, a young
peasant, who learns the sobering realities of
urban life in colonial Africa – which includes
dishonest African traders and white exploiters.
Then he meets Koumé who is being hunted for
beating a white man to death and offers him
and his sister, Odile, asylum in his village. But
Koumé dies accidentally en route and Banda
discovers the money he had stolen from the
white man which he gives to Odile after
resisting the temptation to keep it. Later Banda
receives a reward for having found the suitcase
lost by a Greek trader. Eventually Banda and
Odile will marry and go off to settle in the
town of Fort Nègre.

Dakeyo, Paul
Barbelés du matin
Paris: Eds. Saint Germain-des-Prés, 1973,
76 pp.
A collection of poems denouncing the exploitation and suffering of black peoples. Written
in honour of his people and 'to the memories
of its martyrs while awaiting liberty.'

Chant d'accusation, suivi de: Espace carceral
Paris: Eds. Saint Germain-des-Prés, 1978.
83 pp.
Another book of verse exploring the same
themes as the previous volume with a preface
by the West Indian poet, Alfred Melon-Dégras.

Le cri pluriel
Paris: Eds. Saint Germain-des-Prés, 1976.
84 pp.
Poems evoking the misery and servitude of
African peoples all over the continent made
particularly acute by the drought, with a
preface by Tidjani-Serpos Noureini and followed by the text of a lecture by Pierre
Fougeyrollas on 'The challenge of the drought
and the class struggle in Sahelian Africa'.

Soleils fusillés
Paris: Droit et Liberté, 1977. 159 pp.
Poetry

J'appartiens au grand jour
Paris: Ed. Saint Germain-des-Prés, 1979.
120 pp. FF50.00
Poetry.
'. . . composé de paysages à l'eau forte. L'acide

traverse le papier. La pluie le déchire. La voix est traversée d'inflexions métalliques. Rien n'y est sublimé, ni ne tend au sublime.'

Jean F. Brierre – *Afrique Nouvelle*

Deeh Segallo, Gabriel
Temps mort en Arcifa
Bafoussam, Cameroon: Libraire Populaire, 1979. 42 pp. CFA250
A play.

Désiré, Naha
Sur le chemin de suicide
Yaoundé: Ed. du Demi-Lettre, n.d. [1979]
100 pp. CFA450
An autobiographical novelette, which recounts the author's involvement with Jehovah's Witnesses in Benin, the resulting prosecution leading to his exile in Cameroun and his decision to commit suicide.

Le destin a frappé trop fort
Yaoundé: Ed. Populaires, 1980. 126 pp.
CFA650
An idealistic, imaginary account of a school dropout who, through the device of elaborate dreams and fantasies conveys to his readers melodramatic scenes from the South African liberation struggle as well as his daily experiences.

Dikolo, Jean-Pierre
Athlètes à abattre: une aventure de Scorpion l'Africain
Paris: A.B.C., 1976. (Archives secrètes du B.S.I., 3). 119 pp. FF6.00
One in a series of popular detective novels.

Main blanche sur la ville: une aventure de Scorpion l'Africain
Paris: A.B.C., 1976 (Archives secrètes du B.S.I., 5). 93 pp. FF6.00

Machines à découdre: une aventure de Scorpion l'Africain
Paris: A.B.C., 1976 (Archives secrètes du B.S.I., 6). 95 pp. FF6.00

Le Scorpion noir contre les tortionnaires rhodésiens
Paris: A.B.C., 1976 (Archives secrètes du B.S.I., 10). 111 pp. o/p

Djoupe, Martine
Terre desséchée
Bafoussam, Cameroon: La Librairie Populaire, 1979. 28 pp. CFA475
Poetry.

Djoussi, Mathieu
Les enfants du pauvre: mélodrame en 3 actes
Bafoussam, Cameroon: La Librairie Populaire, 1979. 26 pp. CFA300
A melodrama: 'The Poor Man's Children.'

Dooh-Bunya, Lydie
La brise du jour
Yaoundé: C.L.E., 1977. 350 pp. CFA2,000
An unhappy love story between Zinnie and her cousin, Patrick, who know that relationships between cousins are taboo. The two were raised in the same household and their love grew over the years but they were finally separated when they went to different secondary schools.

Douala, René
Le seigneur de la terre
Yaoundé: C.L.E., 1980. 63 pp.
A play set during colonial times evoking questions of tradition and modernity and of the roles of the old and the young.

Doukouré, Abdoul
Le déboussolé
Sherbrooke, Canada: Ed. Naaman, 1978.
96 pp.
Can$5.00 FF30.00
An African student, accused of fomenting strikes at the university in his country, flees to Paris where he is befriended by a young Frenchman and involved in the life of the counter culture (sex, alcohol, drugs) for which he is hardly prepared.

Doumba, Joseph-Charles
Guide pratique pour la réflexion
Yaoundé: C.L.E., 1980.
A collection of poetry and political writings.

Monsieur le Maire
Issy-les-Moulineaux, France: Ed. Saint Paul, 1978 (Les Classiques Africains, 717). 103 pp.
FF16.00
Contains fictitious letters addressed to the mayors of nine big African cities in which the correspondent evokes the problems of urban Africa.

Eno Belinga, Samuel-Martin
Masques nègres
Yaoundé: C.L.E., 1972. 64 pp. CFA400
Poetry.
'La poésie d'Eno Belinga n'est pas cérébrale. Elle tolère à peine qu'on l'étudie. Elle se vit.'
Charly Gabriel Mbock – *Cameroon Tribune*
'. . . semble trouver sa place de choix dans cette catégorie d'oeuvres rigouresement édifiées qui défient

l'éphémère pour s'établir non dans la promesse mais dans l'accomplissement, dans la permanence.'
Fernando d'Almeida – *L'Afrique Littéraire et Artistique*

La prophétie de joal suivi de *Equinoxes*
Yaoundé: C.L.E., 1976. 64 pp. CFA530
A collection of verse.
'This entire work vibrates with the hopes and fears of a young poet troubled by the tumultous nature of African politics . . . brings the African predicament into sharp focus, its hopes and fears, its contradictions and its frustrations . . . through a language that is at once incisive as well as biblical. Eno Belinga believes that the true poet must make use of his talent and that if he didn't he would suffer the same fate as the unproductive servant in the parable of the talents.'
Kole Omotoso – *African Book Publishing Record*

Ballades et chansons camerounaises
Yaoundé: C.L.E., 1974. 56 pp. CFA400
The poet's love for his country, Cameroon, and its people is the theme of this second collection by a man who is a geologist and a high-level civil servant and who is also well-known for his works on musicology.

Epanya Yondo, Elelongue
Kamerun! Kamerun!
Paris: Présence Africaine, 1960. 96 pp. o/p
Poems, appearing in indigenous Cameroon languages, each with a French translation.

Epassy, Antoin
Les asticots
Paris: O.R.T.F.-D.A.E.C., 1972 (Répertoire théâtral africain, 13) (distr. by Nouvelles Editions Africaines, Dakar). 121 pp. CFA300
A play that was a runner-up in the 1970 Interafrican Theatre competition sponsored by the French broadcasting corporation. In an African village where evil forces and treachery seem to have increased since the coming of the white man a mother struggles to save her two children. One has a wound that refuses to heal and the other has been bitten by a serpent. Bad luck pursues the poor woman to the very end.

Epée, Valère
Transatlantic Blues
(Trans. from the French by Samir M. Zoghby)
Yaoundé: C.L.E., 1972. 64 pp. CFA360
A dramatic poem in bilingual text (English-French) about slavery in the Americas.

Etoundi-M'Balla, Patrice
Lettre ouverte à Soeur Marie-Pierre
Yaoundé: C.L.E., 1978. 169 pp. CFA1,650
A journalist and former seminarian writes a

letter to Reverand Sister Marie-Pierre, who is none other than Pauline Akogo, a young woman he has loved since adolescence and to whom he was once engaged. A tale of disappointed love with a bitter-sweet ending.

Evembe, François Borgia
Sur la terre en passant
Paris: Présence Africaine, 1966. 111 pp. o/p
Evembe's novel, the journal of a dying man, won the 1967 Grand Prix Littéraire d'Afrique Noire along with Jean Pliya (for *Kondo le requin*). The central figure is an educated young man who is poor because jobless, but also too sick to work, and who dies amidst general indifference.

Evemba Njoku'A'Vemba (Evembe, François Borgia)
Tempête: recueil de poèmes
Victoria, Cameroon: Pressbook, 1976 (distr. by Centre de Diffusion du Livre Camerounais). 56 pp.

Ewandé, Daniel
Vive le Président: la fête africaine
Paris: Albin Michel, 1968. 224 pp. o/p
A novel of independence politics with a portrait of a 'good' president.

Ikelle-Matiba, Jean
Cette Afrique-là
Paris: Présence Africaine, 1963. 241 pp.
Recounts the life of Franz Momha during the German colonial days in the Cameroons in the late nineteenth century. The book was awarded the Grand Prix Littéraire de l'Afrique Noire in 1963.
'. . . un document de premier ordre qui fera date.'
– *Afrique Contemporaine*

Karone, Yodi [pseud.]
Le bal des caïmans
Paris: Karthala, 1980. 230 pp. FF45.00
A prison, somewhere in an independent African country, complete with torture chambers and dank detention cells, a trial which is a parody of justice, and a stadium readied for a public execution – these are the focal points of this novel by an African author writing under a pseudonym. The detainees: a motley group of men who have been arrested on false charges and made to confess, including Father Jean, a simple-minded priest relieved of his pastorship and who has been leading a hermit's existence in the forest. And then there is Adrien, the only 'guilty' one of the lot. A graduate in philosophy from a French university and the author of 'revolutionary' tracts, he has dedicated his life to an ideal and accepts his execution as inevitable. This is the first

novel published by Karthala, a new Paris-based publishing house specializing in books on the West Indies and Africa.

Kayo, Patrice

Hymnes et sagesse: poèmes
Paris: P. J. Oswald, 1970. 27 pp. o/p
Poetry.

Paroles intimes: poèmes
Paris: P. J. Oswald, 1972 (distr. by
L'Harmattan, Paris). 37 pp. FF12.00
Another collection of verse.
'Poésie ouverte sur l'univers solennelle, adulée par une cavalerie d'heureuses images-clés, traversée d'un dynamisme de l'espoir, telle est . . . la noble et envoûtante poésie de ce chantre.'
Fernando d'Almeida – *La Presse du Cameroon*

Une gerbe: à la mémoire de R. Um Nyobe
Yaoundé: Association des Poètes et Ecrivains
Camerounais, n.d. (Semences, 1). 4 pp.
A poem in memory of the leader of the Cameroonian Revolutionary Party who was killed just before independence and who also inspired Mongo Beti's *Remember Ruben*, see p. 230.

Kayor, Franz

Les dieux trancheront ou la farce inhumaine
Paris: P. J. Oswald, 1971 (Théatre africain, 16)
(distr. by L'Harmattan, Paris). 90 pp. FF16.00
In this historical tragedy, the Sultan of Bamoun who is fighting off German penetration is betrayed by one of his sons (who is killed in battle). The Germans are defeated and the King and his court 'rearrange' events so they will have a loftier ring to them in his subjects' memory.

Koungne, Tueno

Dzeudié se mariera-t-il?
Yaoundé: Ed. Semences Africaines, 1979.
70 pp. CFA600
A play centred around the difficulties a young man has in present-day Africa to find a wife who suits him – and his family.

Kud-Az-Eh

Perles de rosée
Yaoundé: Ed. Semences Africaines, 1979.
70 pp. CFA600
Poetry.

Kum'a N'Dumbe III, Alexandre

Cannibalisme
Paris: P. J. Oswald, 1973 (Théatre africain, 21)
(distr. by L'Harmattan, Paris). 85 pp. FF17.00
A play around the themes of colonialism and racism.

Kafra-Bitanga: tragédie de l'Afrique
(Trans. from German by Yvette Revellin)
Paris: P. J. Oswald, 1973 (Théâtre africain, 22)
(distr. by L'Harmattan, Paris). 82 pp. FF16.00
A denunciation of neo-colonialism showing how a people's revolution can be made to serve foreign interests. The characters have roles rather than names: the President, the Ambassador, the Oil Man, etc. The play was first written in German.
'The play reads well and seems ideally suited to radio or television performance.'
Peter Thomas – *Books Abroad*

Lisa la putain de . . .
Paris: P.J. Oswald, 1976 (Théâtre africain, 29)
(distr. by L'Harmattan, Paris). 96 pp. FF17.00
In a bar in the district of Mozart in Douala, Lisa, the beautiful prostitute, meets Dragon Sauvage. He is the leader of a band of thieves but also a man of principle who is revolted against the corruption and excesses of the police. Moreover, he never steals from the people. When he and his men get in trouble Lisa comes to their rescue by pressuring one of her powerful 'clients.'
'The action in this play moves quickly. The fusion of dance, music, poetry and prose is successful . . . the presentation is novel and entertaining.'
Mildred P. Mortimer – *World Literature Today*

Le soleil de l'aurore
Paris: P. J. Oswald, 1976 (Théâtre africain, 30)
(distr. by L'Harmattan, Paris). 96 pp. FF17.00
Independence comes to an unnamed African country. But it is a puppet regime, devoted to the former colonial power, and the authentic nationalists are brutally wiped out. The people will revolt, however, and a truly independent regime will be set up. Another play, in militant overtones, on the theme of neo-colonialism.

Amilcar Cabral ou la tempête en Guinée-Bissau: pièce document
Paris: P. J. Oswald, 1976 (Théâtre africain, 31)
(distr. by L'Harmattan, Paris). 106 pp. FF20.00
A play that traces Cabral's role in the struggle for independence of Guinea-Bissau.

Nouvelles interdites
Lyon, France: Federop, 1978. 150 pp. FF32.00
Short stories.

Kuoh-Moukouri, Thérèse

Rencontres essentielles: roman
Adamawa, Cameroon: Imp. Edgar, 1969.
127 pp.
A young Cameroonian couple (he is a doctor) meet and marry in Paris. Then come their first quarrels. Despite her 'modern' life-style, the wife's solution is a traditional one: her

husband needs a mistress (in other words a second wife). But she will not be able to prevent her own jealousy. The author is the founder of the Union of African and Malagasy women.

Manga-Mado, Henri-Richard
Complaintes d'un forçat
Yaoundé: C.L.E., 1971. 120 pp. o/p
Three tales about the harsh reality of forced labour during colonial days in the Cameroon: the construction of the railroad at Njock; a rubber plantation at Dizangué; and a gold mine at Bétaré-Oya.

Manguélé, Daniel Etounga
La colline du fromager
Yaoundé: C.L.E., 1979. 96 pp. CFA900
Having spent more than ten years in Europe in the period in which his country gained independence, Frederic Ntam, an engineer, returns to Africa accompanied by his French wife and child. Despite his qualifications he cannot find work for he lacks the necessary political contacts. Discouraged, he resolves to return to France, but makes a last-minute decision to settle in his village and cultivate the land.

Matip, Benjamin
A la belle étoile. Contes et nouvelles d'Afrique
Paris: Présence Africaine, 1962. 93 pp.
Short stories and tales from Africa.
'... elle fait appel à des resources verbales et poétiques d'une très rare qualité. Le style est sobre, l'écriture rapide, émaillée de notations d'une précision foudroyante. N'oublions pas, enfin, l'humour de Matip, un humour acide qui atteint parfois les sommets de l'ironie.'   Jeune Afrique

Laisse-nous bâtir une Afrique
Paris: Ed. Afriscope, 1979. 205 pp.
A three-act play about ancient Africa confronted with the cruel realities of the post-independence era. The play was first performed in 1961 under the title, *Le jugement suprême*, and again in 1970 at the University of Yaoundé.

Mba Evina, Jean
Politicos: comédie en cinq actes
Yaoundé: C.L.E., 1974. 64 pp.
Politicos, an illiterate peasant, thinks he can have an easier life by entering politics. But he enters prison, instead. A comedy in five acts.

M'Bafou Zetebeg, Claude Joseph
La couronne d'épines
Paris P. J. Oswald, 1973 (distr. by L'Harmattan, Paris). 79 pp. FF17.00
Poetry.

Mbock, Charly-Gabriel
Quand saigne le palmier
Yaoundé: C.L.E., 1978. 140 pp. CFA1,430
A psychological novel in a traditional setting. The village chief, Bitchoka Nyemb, is impotent and accepts the supreme humiliation to have an heir. His brother, Lién, fathers a son for him with his first wife, Sondi. Their secret is sealed in a blood pact under the palm tree. The son grows and looks more and more like his real father. The village guesses the truth and begins mocking the chief. Half-crazed by the turn of events, the chief tells all to his 'son' and sets about to punish his wife and his brother for adultery. It will end in tragedy for all.
'Mbock narre des faits cruels que se déroulent dans un univers typiquement traditionnel sans embellissement, sans falsification, mais avec réalisme ... et absence totale de complaisance.'
                    Fame Ndongo – Cameroon Tribune

La croix de coeur
Yaoundé: C.L.E., 1980. 300 pp.
A novel that raises the questions confronting an African Christian.

L'exile de Song Mboua
Yaoundé: Buma Kor, forthcoming 1981.
A novel.

Médou Mvomo, Rémy
Africa ba'a
Yaoundé: C.L.E., 1969. 181 pp. CFA900
Kambara leaves his dying village, Africa ba'a, for the city, symbolically named Necroville, only to discover that it is not a Promised Land. Jobs are hard to find and he supports himself as a 'boy' while preparing a civil service examination. Just as he learns he has passed, he realizes his place is in the village. The ideas and new methods he brings home with him give his people new life and hope.
'... a trait au thème de la désillusion qui a suivi l'indépendence, mais alors que d'autres auteurs se sont le plus souvent contentés de démolir en flétrissant ou en ridiculisant leurs méchants ou ineptes concitoyens, Mvomo a voulu construire en prêchant un ruralisme à même de faire fi de la mauvaise gestion des affaires à l'échelle nationale.'
                    Emeka P. Abanime – Afrique
                              Littéraire et Artistique

Mon amour en noir et blanc
Yaoundé: C.L.E., 1971. 109 pp. o/p
Amboise, a young Cameroonian student and Genviève, a French girl, are in love but must contend with the hostility and prejudice of both of their parents.

Le journal de Faliou
Yaoundé: C.L.E., 1972. 180 pp. CFA700
Sixteen months in the life of Faliou, a young
Cameroonian, father of three children, as he
comes to Douala to try to earn enough money
as a dance band musician to continue his
studies. Sixteen months of failure. He gets
work but loses it just as fast and he loses his
wife, his mistress, and his friends as well.
'Rémy Médou-Mvomo . . . s'affirme à 35 ans avec ce
troisiéme roman-récit comme peut-être le plus
intéressant auteur africain francophone de la nouvelle
génération.' Guy Kouassi – *Fraternité Matin*
4 Sept. 1973

Les enchaînés
Dakar: Nouvelles Editions Africaines, 1979
(Répertoire théâtral africain, 27). 142 pp.
CFA500
Yaoundé: C.L.E., 1979. 142 pp. CFA600
A play that was a runner-up in the 1973
African Theatre Competition in France. Zibi,
the village teacher, is appointed First Secretary
of the 'Ministry of Planning and Various
Affairs' and sets out living in a grand manner.
But when Betamoto, the rich merchant who
had loaned him money, begins pressuring him
for repayment Zibi suddenly realizes he is
chained up for life. A comic climax involving
his daughter, Juliette, and Betamoto's son,
Diamara, luckily turns his chains to gold.

Méyong, Békaté

Manes Sauvages
Paris: P. J. Oswald, 1975 (distr. by
L'Harmattan, Paris). 39 pp. FF13.00
Poetry.

Mokto, Joseph-Jules

Ramitou mon étrangère
Yaoundé: C.L.E., 1971. 139 pp. o/p
This novel centres on the theme of inter-ethnic
marriage. A young Bamiléké man and a young
Bamoun woman marry over their parents'
objections.

Mongo, Pabé [pseud. of Bekolo Bekolo, Pascal]

Innocente Assimba: comédie en quatre actes
Yaoundé: C.L.E., n.d. [1970] (CLE théâtre, 8).
48 pp. o/p
A play.

Un enfant comme les autres
Yaoundé: C.L.E., 1972. 58 pp. CFA230
Fifteen tales about growing up in a traditional
milieu.

Bogam Woup
Yaoundé: C.L.E., 1980. 120 pp.
Bogam Woup, a former soldier, thinks he has

a 'divine mission' to save his people from
misery and primitivism. He manages to be
appointed to a village chieftainship and bases
his political career on the fine art of bluffing.

Monondjana, Hubert

Vice versa: comédie en deux actes
Bafoussam, Cameroon: La Librairie Popu-
laire, 1975. 37 pp. CFA300
A play.

Mveng, Engelbert

Mon amour pour toi est éternel
Paris: Mame, 1963. 27 pp.
The first book of verse of Father Mveng, a
Jesuit priest, who is best known for his works
on African art and his history of Cameroon.
Illustrated by the author.

Lève-toi amie, viens
Dakar: Librairie Clairafrique, 1966. unpaged
Another book of verse illustrated by the
author.

Balafon
Yaoundé: C.L.E., 1972. 100 pp. CFA450
The poems in this collection show a great
thematic diversity. Some are of Christian
inspiration and others refer to the author's
travels, both in Africa and around the world –
China, New York, Moscow, Ostende.

Mvolo, Samuel

Les fiancés du grand fleuve
Yaoundé: C.L.E., 1973. 200 pp. CFA690
A love story, the fictionalized account of the
author's encounter with his wife, a traditional
princess, and at the same time an evocation of
Cameroon of the forties when the ways of the
past were still very much alive.

Na Bato, Nigoué

*Métamorphose suivi de Renégat: poésie
primaire, poèmes, chants, lettres et nouvelles*
Paris: P. J. Oswald, 1972 (distr. by
L'Harmattan, Paris). 109 pp. FF19.00
A collection of poetry and short stories.

Nanga, Bernard

Les chauves souris
Paris: Présence Africaine, 1980. 203 pp.
FF42.00
The author's first novel is set in a Cameroo-
nian village in the post-independent era.
Among the themes evoked are the self-centred
African elites, the problem of women and the
younger generation as well as the issue of local
chieftainships.

Ndam Njoya, Adamou
Daïrou IV
Yaoundé: C.L.E., 1973. 52 pp. CFA270
In this historical tragedy, a monarch dies for attempting to disregard the role played by ancestral spirits in designating rulers.

Ndedi-Penda, Patrice
Le fusil
Paris: O.R.T.F.-D.A.E.C., 1970 (Répertoire théâtral africain, 8) (distr. by Nouvelles Editions Africaines, Dakar). 119 pp. CFA300
Old Ndo has just received a much-envied medal as the best cocoa-planter in the region and sets off to Douala to sell his crop and buy a rifle. But he has neither an identity card nor an arms permit, and Douala, as everyone knows, is full of thieves. Ndedi-Penda's comedy won the listeners' prize in the 1969 Interafrican Theatre Competition organized by Radio France.

La nasse
Yaoundé: C.L.E., 1971. 156 pp. o/p
This novel is a criticism of marriage customs which leave no place for individual choice. Colette wants to marry Charles but must accept her family's choice, a civil servant and much older man, who has won them over with costly presents. The title – the fishing basket – symbolizes the trap the young people are caught in.

Ndeng Monewosso, James
Pris entre deux forces
Paris: La Pensée Universelle, 1975. 253 pp. FF27.90
A novel about the downfall of an educated young man who had been his village's brightest hope. He disappoints home people first when he goes off to France – to study agronomy. Then he marries a Frenchwoman, even though he has a local wife. Upon his return he settles in the capital and cuts all contact with his village, until he is forced to take his first wife in as a servant, unknown to his French wife. Things will go from bad to worse.

Fanatisme criminel
Paris: La Pensée Universelle, 1978. 128 pp. o/p
A novel about a religious zealot who staunchly refuses to help those who do not share his beliefs – with tragic consequences for himself and for the members of his family.

Ndie, Jacob
La place de la femme
Bafoussam, Cameroon: La Librairie Populaire, n.d. [1978?]. 50 pp. o/p
A comedy on the theme of the traditional role of women.

Ndika, Epala
La mort en silence
Yaoundé: C.L.E., 1980. 72 pp.
A collection of verse that attempts to show that man is capable of the deepest love, even when surrounded by hunger and misery.

Ndzaagap, Timothée
La fiancée du prêtre
Yaoundé: Semences africaines, 1974. 28 pp.
A play.

La fille du roi à menti: comédie en 3 actes
Bafoussam, Cameroon: La Librairie Populaire, 1976. (2nd rev. ed.) 42 pp. CFA300
A three-act play: *The King's Daughter Has Lied.*

Amoureuses flammes
Bafoussam: La Librairie Populaire, 1977. 24 pp. CFA350
In his preface to this volume of verse the author writes, 'All these thoughts evoke the same theme: love. But in this word has more than one meaning. But in this collection I mean love of mankind and love of the opposite sex. I have lived some of these experiences and I have chosen to express them through poetry.' '*Habitués à une poèsie engagée où l'appel à la violence est la note dominante, nous avons été réconfortés de recontrer une poèsie suave, doucereuse.*'
> Maurice A. Lubin – *African Book Publishing Record*

Ngo Mai, Jeanne
Poèmes sauvages et lamentations
Monte Carlo: Palais Miami, 1967 (Les cahier des poètes de notre temps, 362). 111 pp. o/p

Poèmes sauvages et lamentations
Paris: Poètes de Notre Temps, 1967. 110 pp.
This collection of poems and thirteen lamentations on the subject of Isaiah was the first book to be published by a Cameroonian woman.

Nguedam, Christophe
Murmure et soupir
Paris: P. J. Oswald, 1972 (distr. by L'Harmattan, Paris). 37 pp. FF14.00
Poetry.

Chemins du monde: poèmes
Paris: P. J. Oswald, 1973 (distr. by L'Harmattan, Paris). 51 pp. FF14.00
Poetry.

Paroles de semence – Grains de philosophie: poèmes
Paris: P. J. Oswald, 1975 (distr. by L'Harmattan, Paris). 55 pp. FF14.00
Poetry.

Njoya, Rabiatou
Toute la rente y passe. Ange noir, ange blanc
Yaoundé C.L.E., n.d. (CLE Théâtre, 13).
11 pp. and 24 pp. o/p
Two comedies: *The Money Is All Eaten Up* and
Black Angel, White Angel.

La dernière aimée
Yaoundé: C.L.E., 1980.
A tragi-comedy about a man who falls in love
with his daughter-in-law.

Nkamgnia, Samuel
La femme prodigue: comédie en deux actes
Yaoundé Éd. A.P.E.C., 1971 (A.P.E.C.-
Théâtre, 1). 34 pp.
A play about marriage that was first published
by C.L.E. in 1968 and that has been reissued
by the Cameroonian Writers Association.

Jeunesse et patrie: Poémes
Yaoundé: Ed. Saint-Paul, n.d. [1969]. 41 pp.
Patriotic poems for use in secondary schools.

Chemin de tous les coeurs: poèmes
Yaoundé: Imp. Saint-Paul, 1973. 116 pp.
A collection of verse that won the 1973 prize
for francophone African poetry.

Nkeunbang, Etienne-Magellan
Boumba: poèmes
Yaoundé: Ed. Semences Africaines, 1979.
38 pp. CFA500
Poems on the theme of apartheid.

Noume, Etienne B.
Angoisse quotidienne
Yaoundé: Ed. Le Flambeau, 1979. 31 pp.
CFA400
A posthumous volume of poetry. The author
died in 1970 at the age of twenty-six.

Nyunai, Jean-Paul
La nuit de ma vie
Paris: Debresse, 1961. 48 pp.
(Reprinted in *African poems in French*. Nendeln,
Liechtenstein, Kraus Reprint, 1970. $27.00)
Poems.

Pigments sang
Paris: Debresse, 1963. 31 pp.
(Reprinted in *African poems in French*. Nendeln,
Liechtenstein, Kraus Reprint, 1970. $27.00)
Poems.

Chansons pour Ngo Lima
Monte Carlo: Palais Miami, 1964 (Les cahiers
de poètes de notre temps, 251). 29 pp. o/p

Le mot et la chose
Nkongsamba, Cameroon: Imp. Protestante,
1980. 39 pp. CFA500
Poetry.

10 poèmes traduits du me an
Nkongsamba, Cameroon: Imp. Protestante,
1980. 24 pp. CFA300
A further volume of verse.

Nzouankeu, Jacques Mariel
Immortalité
Paris: Ed. de la Nef, 1957. o/p
A collection of sonnets.

Le souffle des ancêtres: nouvelles
Yaoundé: C.L.E., 1965. 107 pp. o/p
Four traditional stories around the theme of
human clashes with mystic forces.

Obama, Jean-Baptiste
Assimilados
Paris: O.R.T.F.-D.A.E.C., 1972 (Répertoire
théâtral africain, 11) (distr. by Nouvelles
Editions Africaines, Dakar). 80 pp. CFA300
A play set in Angola which won the 1970
Interafrican Theatre Competition organized
by Radio France. Mukoko, the official praise-
singer in a Portugese work camp far up the
Congo, stays away for months at a time. In
order to feed her children Ngola, his beautiful
wife, becomes the mistress of a Portuguese
colonial administrator. He fathers her son who
will become a Portuguese citizen, the *assimilado*
of the title.

Omog, Paul
Où est le vrai amour?
Yaoundé: Ed. Semences Africaines, 1979.
60 pp. CFA550
A play about the problems of young people.

Omo Ya Eku
La prison sous le slip d'Ebela: roman
Paris: La Pensée Universelle, 1976. 217 pp.
FF30.00
A novel: *Imprisoned in Ebela's Underpants*.

Oto, James D.
Ngonrogo-le-fou: pièce en 11 tableaux
Yaoundé: C.L.E., [n.d.] (CLE Théâtre, 12).
31 pp. o/p
A play: 'Ngonrogo, the Madman'

Owono, Joseph
Tante Bella
Yaoundé: Au Messager, 1959. 295 pp. o/p
The conditions of women in Africa are evoked
in this novel set in pre-colonial days. Bella is
taken away from her mother at the age of six to
pay for the debt her father contracted when he

married her mother. As a grown woman she is handed over from husband to husband by her family as she is successively widowed.

Oyono, Ferdinand

Une vie de boy
Paris: Juillard, 1956. 183 pp. o/p
Paris: Presses Pocket, 1970 (Presses pocket, 791). 187 pp. FF8.50
A paperback re-issue of the original 1956 edition. In English *translation*, see next entry.

Houseboy
(Trans. from the French by John Reed)
London: HEB, 1966 (AWS, 29). 144 pp. £1.25
New York: Macmillan [published as *Boy*], 1970. 150 pp. $1.75
Written in the form of a diary, this novel describes Toundi Joseph's experiences as a steward in the household of a French District Commissioner in Cameroon, the 'Commandant du Cercle' Robert Decazy, and his wife Madame Decazy. It presents a critical and satirical view of colonial administrators and Christian missionaries. Edris Makward contributes an introduction to the American edition.
'. . . humour and brutality are depicted with the same simplicity and unpretentiousness which give the reader of this novel a feeling that the author's description has been faithful to his observation.'
Eldred Jones – *Bull. of the Assoc. for African Literature in English*
'. . . John Reed's English translation – with which I have nothing at all to quarrel – will surely enable non-French speaking readers to come to terms good humouredly with this masterpiece of anti-colonialist satire.' Sunday O. Anozie – *Présence Africaine*

Le vieux nègre et la médaille
Paris: Juillard, 1956. 211 pp. o/p
Paris: Union Générale d'Editions, 1974 (10/18, 695). 192 pp. FF13.00
Dakar: Nouvelles Editions Africaines, 1980 (Club Afrique loisirs, 3). CFA1,900 cased
First issued by Juillard in 1956, Oyono's novel is currently available in the paperback edition published in Paris and in a hard-cover book club edition on the African continent published by Nouvelles Editions Africaines. In English *translation* see next entry.

The Old Man and the Medal
(Trans. from the French by John Reed)
London: HEB, 1969 (AWS, 39). 167 pp. £1.25
New York: Collier Books, 1971. 191 pp. $1.50
The English edition of Oyono's satire on colonialism was first published by Heinemann in 1967 in a hard-cover volume. The central figure is Meka, an old cocoa farmer, a devoted Christian and God-fearing man. His two sons

have died fighting for the white man, and the Catholic mission has taken his land. He has always been loyal to the white man and is, in their eyes, a 'good native'. As compensation for his services to France he is to receive a medal. When the great day of his decoration, 14th July, arrives, Meka is early but the Governor General is late. Waiting in the hot sun for the ceremony to commence, Meka's attitude towards the Europeans, influenced by his urgent need to relieve himself and the excruciating pain caused by his new shoes, is somewhat modified. The events following the ceremony confirm Meka's revised estimation of the white man. Politely ignored at the reception, he gets dead drunk, staggers back to his village in a violent tropical storm, loses his medal and is arrested and imprisoned for vagrancy. Eventually recognized and released he returns home cursing the Europeans, his attitude to the colonial administrators vastly changed.
'. . . a devasting indictment of colonialism in fictional terms . . . the point is that Oyono's critique of the colonial set-up is made a hundred times more effective by its brilliance as literature.'
K. W. – *West Africa*
'. . . has the quality, so rare in modern African writing, of bringing together both the comic and the sad elements in the situation of preindependence Africa . . . makes thoroughly enjoyable reading . . . the translation from the original French by John Reed is excellent.'
Jeanette Kamara – *African Literature Today*

Chemin d'Europe
Paris: Juillard, 1960. 196 pp. o/p
Paris: Union Générale d'Editions, 1973 (Coll. 10/18, 755). 189 pp. FF13.00
Dakar: Nouvelles Editions Africaines, 1980 (Club Afrique Loisirs, 8). CFA1,900 cased
The hero of Oyono's third novel, set in colonial times, is a former seminarian who has had to leave school in order to earn a living for himself and his widowed mother and who is as obsessed with Europe and Europeans as he is oblivious to the patent racism of the latter. His obsession includes, until he is abruptly dismissed, the mother of a young girl he has been hired to tutor. His one aim is to get to Europe to finish his studies but all doors are closed to him. As the novel ends, however, he discovers an ingenious way to fulfil his dreams. Originally published in 1960 by Juillard, the book is available in hard cover from NEA as a bookclub offering.

Oyônô-Mbia, Guillaume

Trois prétendants, un mari
Yaoundé: C.L.E., 1962. 128 pp. CFA720

A light-hearted play, with music and dancing, that tells of the efforts of a father to obtain the best bride-price for his educated daughter. In English *translation*, see next entry.

Three Suitors: One Husband; and Until Further Notice
London: Methuen, 1974 (2nd ed.). 100 pp. £2.60 cased £1.75 p/b
The author, himself, has translated the preceding entry which is published here with another play, *Until Further Notice,* which he wrote in English. The action focuses on a group of villagers waiting in vain for the triumphal return of an educated daughter of the village, who has married an important government official. The villagers want to 'cash in' on their 'investment' but the young couple are reluctant to share the material rewards of their success. The play won first prize in the 1967 BBC African Service Drama competition.
'Three Suitors: One Husband *is a delightful comedy, which although entertaining to read, should surely be seen to be fully appreciated.'*
A. M. – *West Africa*

Notre fille ne se mariera pas!
Paris: O.R.T.F.-D.A.E.C., 1973 (2nd ed.) (distr. by Les Nouvelles Editions Africaines, Dakar) (Répertoire théâtral africain, 9). 183 pp. CFA300
Charlotte, an educated young woman from Mvoutessi in Eastern Cameroon, must be prevented from marrying, for a husband would surely object to her helping the members of the family who have paid for her education. The problem is solved, however, when Charlotte's betrothed turns out to be 'an important man'. A comedy that won a prize in the 1969 Interafrican Theatre Competition and that was originally published in 1971.

Jusqu'à nouvel avis
Yaoundé: C.L.E., 1978 (New ed.). 48 pp. CFA300
Prompted by the success of the English edition of this comedy *(Until Further Notice),* Oyono-Mbia here presents an adaptation in French.

Chroniques de Mvoutessi 1
Yaoundé: C.L.E., 1979 (New ed.). 64 pp. CFA400
In this brief collection of stories, the first of three, Oyônô-Mbia continues the humorous portraits of the inhabitants of Mvoutessi in Southern Cameroon that he had begun in his three plays. In this volume, containing, 'Le sermon de Yohannes Nkatefoe,' 'La petite gare', and 'Les sept fourchettes', we meet the village catechist, the stationmaster, and the village chief.

Chroniques de Mvoutessi 2
Yaoundé: C.L.E., 1979 (New ed.). 64 pp. CFA400
Oyônô-Mbia's second 'Chronicle', and authentic story, makes gentle fun of a certain type of 'emancipated' young women in Africa. In it he relates a fortuitous encounter with one of his former students, a Miss Marie-Thérèse Medjô, an astonishing young lady who plans a film career.

Chroniques de Mvoutessi 3
Yaoundé: C.L.E., 1972. 48 pp. CFA230
Contains a single story. Here we meet Madame Matalina who has managed to climb the social ladder thanks to her inventiveness in exploiting her daughter, Charlotte's, natural charms.

Le train spécial de Son Excellence
Yaoundé: C.L.E., 1979. 144 pp. CFA990
A high-ranking official is arriving by train in a small town and everyone has come to the station to greet him. What a disappointment when he finally gets there! This play is presented in bilingual text (English-French).

Penda [Nedi-Penda, Patrice]
La corbeille d'ignames
Yaoundé: C.L.E., 1971. 64 pp. CFA210
By disguising himself as a beggar and hiding in a basket of yams good King Foué-So learns how corrupt his kingdom is and sets about to reform it.
'. . . a very traditional African tale, still faithful to oral narrative techniques and devices.'
Edouard Roditi – *Books Abroad*

Pfouma, Oscar
Siang
Yaoundé: C.L.E., 1971. 42 pp. CFA210
Siang leaves his village in order to get away from the uncle who has raised him but tragedy awaits him.

Philombe, René [pseud. for Ombede, Phillipe Louis]
Lettres de ma cambuse
Yaoundé: C.L.E., 1965. 68 pp. o/p
In English *translation*, see next entry.

Tales From my Hut
(Trans. from the French by R. Bjornson)
Yaoundé: Buma Kor, 1977. 79 pp. CFA450 ($2.75)
Awarded the Prix Mottart de l'Académie Française, this book of 'letters' or short stories was written whilst Philombe was in seclusion in a small Cameroonian village, recovering from an illness. The nine tales record events that really took place. The English language edition

was prepared for use in secondary schools in Cameroon.

'*These short stories show the wit, humor, the penetrating insight and the compassion of the Cameroonian author . . . The themes of colonialism and modernization and the contrasts between city and village, virtue and vice, make the stories real and help the reader peep into contemporary Africa and Cameroon.*'

Mario Azevedo – *African Book Publishing Record*

Sola ma chérie
Yaoundé: C.L.E., 1966. 124 pp. o/p
Sola leaves old Nkonda, the husband her parents had chosen for her, to go off with Tsango, the man she loves. A novel which criticizes marriage customs.

Un sorcier blanc à Zangali
Yaoundé: Ed. C.L.E., 1969. 187 pp. o/p
Father Marius arrives in the Beti village of Zangali where his predecessor had lost his life. The task is hard but through understanding, tact, and tolerance he gains the trust of the inhabitants – until the day the colonial administrator has the chief shot. Missionaries, the priest learns, are there to help the colonizer.

Les époux célibataires
Yaoundé: Ed. A.P.E.C., 1971. 54 pp. CFA250
Philombe's first play, a comedy, concerns a young man who goes off to France to study and who discovers upon his return how ill-suited his illiterate village wife is to his new way of life. All ends well, however, when she realizes that education might be a good thing if it can help her keep her husband! Contains a short essay by the author about the problems facing an African playwright.
'*This extremely amusing play was enthusiastically received and particularly by the youth of his country.*'
Rodney E. Harris – *Books Abroad*

Histoires queue-de-chat
Yaoundé: C.L.E., 1971. 112 pp. CFA500
In this collection of five contemporary short stories, the author attacks those who make a business of playing on the superstitions of their fellow Africans. Such practices, he says in the preface, 'impede the progress of young African nations'. In one tale, a clever young Cameroonian doctor puts superstitions to good use, however, in 'curing' a patient who has nothing medically wrong with him but who believes himself to be the victim of witchcraft. Contains a glossary of Cameroonian expression used.

Les Blancs partis, les nègres dansent
Yaoundé: Semences africaines, 1973. 23 pp. o/p
Bafoussam, Cameroon: La Librairie Populaire, 1978 [?]. 40 pp. CFA490
A collection of verse which criticizes African governments for making the same errors that the former colonizer had.

Petites gouttes de chant pour créer l'homme
Yaoundé: Ed. Semences Africaines, 1977. 54 pp.
The author's first collection of poems published by his own publishing house. The underlying theme of all these poems is man's isolation from man.

Africapolis
Yaoundé: Ed. Semences Africaines, 1978. 64 pp. CFA750
In this play, Philombé attacks unpopular African dictatorships symbolized here by the despot, King Ekamtid. The revolt against him is led by Boki, the intellectual, who uses his position as head of the National Development Bank to grant financial aid to the poor. In the final scene the people put down the King and his corrupt counsellor.

Choc anti-choc
Yaoundé: Ed. Semences Africaines, 1978. 40 pp. CFA450
These nine poems were originally written in 1960 when Philombé was in prison for belonging to the outlawed Cameroonian revolutionary party, the U.P.C.

Sanduo, Lazare
Une dure vie scolaire
Yaoundé: C.L.E., 1972. 93 pp. o/p
A Cameroonian pastor recalls, with a certain amount of bitterness, his primary school years in the forties.

Sengat-Kuo, François
Collier de cauris
Paris: Présence Africaine, 1970. 61 pp. FF25.00
The cowry shells in the author's 'necklace' are the famous Africans and Afro-Americans to whom he has dedicated most of these poems: Ahidjo, Senghor, de Andrade, Myriam Makeba, Chaka, Louis Armstrong, Luther King. The author is currently a minister in Cameroon. Contains a postface by Thomas Melone.

Fleurs de latérite. Heures rouges
Yaoundé: C.L.E., 1971. 54 pp. CFA300
This volume of verse of a militant nationalist

contains two short collections which were originally published in 1954 under the pseudonym of Nditsouna, Francesco. The theme of *Heures rouges* is the tragic events of autumn 1945 in Douala.
'Fleurs de latérite *regroupe des poémes écrits sous le signe de la révolte, de la libération, du souvenir mais aussi de la fraternité.*'

Afrique Littéraire et Artistique

Tale, Kume [pseud. for Mbida, King-Martin]

Le journal d'une suicidée
Yaoundé: Ed. Le Flambeau, 1978. 83 pp.
CFA580
Sidonie, a bright young lady, whose life is full of promise, commits suicide at the age of sixteen when she discovers how cruelly she has been deceived by Leopold, the university student.

La rose d'une nuit de rêves ou une cruche de sang pour Prétoria
Yaoundé: Ed. Le Flambeau, 1980. 112 pp.
CFA600

Tchakoute, Paul

Corps jumeaux: poèmes
Bafoussam, Cameroon: Librairie Populaire, 1978. 41 pp. CFA475
A collection of love poetry.
'*Un courant romantique circule à travers ses vers . . . Les accents de Tchakoute émeuvent, ce recueil figurera dans la bibliographie poétique de l'Afrique*'.

Maurice A. Lubin – *African Book Publishing Record*

Les femmes en cage: tragédie politique en Rhodésie
Bafoussam, Cameroon: Librairie Populaire, 1979. 43 pp. CFA300
A play.

Samba
Bafoussam, Cameroon: Librairie Populaire, 1980. 95 pp. CFA500
A play based on the life of Martin Paul Samba a former guide and interpreter for the Germans in Cameroon who was executed in 1914 for plotting against them.

Journal d'un matin: poème
Bafoussam: Librairie Populaire, 1979. 24 pp.
CFA300

Tioguep, Poincaré

Le triomphe de l'amour
Yaoundé: Ed. Semences Africaines, 1979.
38 pp. CFA500
In this play inter-ethnic marriages are seen as

the means of fostering national unity in young African countries.

Toko, Jérémie

Chants d'amour et d'espoir
Paris: La Pensée Universelle, 1980. 154 pp.
FF30.00
Poetry.

Tsino [pseud. for Tsoungui Ngono, Vincent-de-Paul]

Nyia bariba
Paris: O.F.T.F.-D.A.E.C., 1973 (Répertoire théâtral africain, 19) (distr. by Nouvelles Editions Africaines, Dakar). 72 pp. CFA300
A traditional tale about a brave mother who triumphs over a bad genie (her mother-in-law) which was rewritten for the stage in the form of a folk-opera and which was performed at the first Pan-African Cultural Festival of Algiers. Choral parts are all in Ewondo although the narrative is in French. The title means 'The Mother of Bariba'.

Um Nyobe, Ruben

L'innombrable symphonie
Yaoundé: Imp. du Gouvernement, 1959.
43 pp.
Poetry []. The author was the founder of the Union of Cameroonian People, a revolutionary party. He was assassinated on the eve of independence and inspired many of Mongo Beti's novels.

Werewere-Liking

On ne raisonne pas avec le venin: poèmes
Paris: Ed. Saint Germain-des-Prés, 1977.
64 pp. FF30.00

La puissance de UM
Abidjan: C.E.D.A., 1979. 63 pp.
A play about ritual death. An African community has recourse to the supernatural to settle a crucial matter of guilt and innocence.

Une nouvelle terre
Dakar: Nouvelles Editions Africaines, 1980.
92 pp. CFA600
The actors in this play, a form of ritual theatre, seek to eliminate an evil force, by studying, as a group, the slightest deed of each member. In this way unity prevails and a new equilibrium ensues.

Yanou, Etienne

L'homme-dieu de Bisso
Yaoundé: C.L.E., 1974. 155 pp. CFA700
Winner of the 1975 Grand Prix Littéraire de l'Afrique Noire, Yanou's novel is about Man'Si, a handsome young man who has been

deified in order to purify his village which has been stricken by tragedy. But he chooses voluntarily to step down from his divine pedestal to marry Silla, a childhood friend who converts him to Christianity. Parallel to this tale is that of a French family to whom a son is born after the wife drinks water blessed by Man'Si. The son grows up to revolt against the ways of his parents and to adopt the local religion.

'*Par-delà le combat métaphysique entre deux civilisations symbolisées ici par deux religions, le roman d'Etienne Yanou, quelque féerique soit-il, pose un problème humain: celui d'une personne qui refuse d'être un sur-homme.*'

Fame NDongo – *Cameroon Tribune*

Chad

Bangui, Antoine
Prisonnier de Tombalbaye
Paris: Hatier, 1980 (Monde noir poche, 1).
160 pp FF19.00
A former minister under the regime of President Tombalbaye tells how he survived three years in prison.

Bruneau, Xavier
Roboa-Nat, le sorcier malgré lui
Yaoundé: C.L.E., 1972. 72 pp. CFA400
A play.

Djimet, Kari [also known as Kari Garang, Ko-Tourou]
Le crime de la dot: Drame en quatre actes
Ndjamena: Commission Nationale Tchadienne pour l'UNESCO, n.d. 28 pp.
A four-act play: 'The Crime of the Bride-Price.'

Moustapha, Baba [pseud. for Moustapha, Mahamat]
Le maître des djinns
Yaoundé: C.L.E., 1977. 71 pp. CFA670
In this play the author tries to answer the question of how to prevent the people from being manipulated by customs and beliefs that have become meaningless. It relates the plight of Dansou and her new husband who are threatened with a curse by Dansou's mother if they do not supply her with all the money she needs. A friend of the husband plays the master of the spirits to solve the dilemma.

'*The story is well narrated with much humour and interesting dialogues and setting . . . The superficiality of certain situations is overshadowed by the final message.*'

Evelyne Accad – *African Book Publishing Record*

Makarie aux épines
Dakar: Nouvelles Editions Africaines, 1979 (Répertoire théâtral africain, 25). 116 pp. CFA500
Yaoundé: C.L.E., 1979. 116 pp. CFA500
Born and raised in Europe, Barka returns to Makarie, the country of his origins, with romantic ideas about Africa. Thanks to Zirega, a young woman who has chosen to remain in the village away from the artificial life of the capital, he discovers the true image of Africa – Africa of the burning sun, or drought, dust and thorns. This is, indeed, subversive knowledge for those in power who do not hesitate to pull this particular 'thorn' out of their feet.

Seid, Joseph Brahim
Un enfant du Tchad
Paris: Ed. SAGEREP, 1967 (Dossiers littéraires de l'Afrique actuelle, 1). 112 pp. o/p
The story of Abakar, a young boy from Chad.

Gabon

Magang Ma Mbuju Wisi
Le crépuscule des silences
Paris: P. J. Oswald, 1975 (distr. by L'Harmattan, Paris). 83 pp. FF18.00
Poetry.

Ndouna-Depenaud, Pascal
Passages: essais poétiques
Libreville: Lettres Gabonaises, Institut Pédagogique National, 1975. 50 pp.
Poetry.

Rêves à l'aube
Libreville: Lettres Gabonnaises, Institut Pédagogique National, 1975. 13 pp.
Poetry.

Nkoghe-Mve, Moïse
Fables et poèmes choisis
Libreville: Lettres Gabonnaises, Institut Pédagogique National, 1975. 19 pp.

Ntyugwetondo, Rawire
Elonga
Paris: EDITAF, 1981. 261 pp. FF50.00
A man of mixed ancestry who was born in the West returns to Africa to search for his origins. The first novel of the author, a young Gabonese woman.

Nyonda, Vincent de Paul
La mort de Guyfaki suivi de Deux albinos à la M'passa et du Soûlard
Paris: L'Harmattan, 1981. 192 pp. FF42.00

Three plays. The first one, *La mort de Guyfaki*, was performed at the Dakar Festival of Negro Arts in 1966.

Pounah, Paul-Vincent
Chant du Mandolo alias Pégase
Fontenay-le-Comte, France: Imp, Loriou, 1978. 132 pp.
A collection of verse in five parts.

Ratanga-Atoz, Ange
Regards sur Gabao
Libreville: Institut Pédagogique National, 1977. 50 pp.
Poetry.

Rawiri-Bouroux, Georges
Chants du Gabon
Paris: EDICEF, 1975. 48 pp. o/p
Poetry.

Zotoumbat, Robert
Histoire d'un enfant trouvé
Yaoundé: C.L.E., 1971. 60 pp. CFA230
An abandoned child discovers little by little the unhappy tale of his past.

Guinea

Adama, Sékou
Soleils
Paris: Ed. Saint-Germain-des-Prés, 1980. 64 pp. FF28.00
Poetry.

Aidra Fodekaba, Chérif
Le Royaume de Sinaban
Yaoundé: C.L.E., 1973. 64 pp. CFA210
Sinaban wins a kingdom for obeying his genie.

Bokoum, Saïdou
Chaîne: une déscente aux enfers
Paris: Denoël, 1974. 316 pp.
Kanaan Niane, an African student in Paris, has cut himself off from his relations. One day as he is thinking of committing suicide he finds himself helping to fight a fire that has been set by an arsonist in a run-down hotel for African immigrants. From then on he devotes himself to trying to better the lot of African workers in France.

Camara, Lanciné
Les inachevés
Soissons, France: Imp. Saint-Antoine, 1967. 32 pp.
Poetry.

Camara, Sikhé
Poèmes de combat et de vérité
Paris: P. J. Oswald, 1967 (distr. by L'Harmattan, Paris). 80 pp. FF16.00
Poems of a Guinean militant.

Clairière dans le ciel
Paris: Présence Africaine, 1973. 91 pp. FF25.00
A collection of verse which is largely militant in nature. Its themes include Sékou Touré and the Guinean Democratic Party, Martin Luther King and black power, Albert Luthuli.

Cissé, Ahmed-Tidjani
Pollen et fleurs
Paris: Nubia, 1981. 91 pp. FF29.00
Poetry. The first volume of verse of the lead dancer of the Grands Ballets d'Afrique Noire, Guinea's national dance troop.

Doumbouya, Alpha Kabine
Liberté de la femme, ignorance du péché
Paris: La Pensée Universelle, 1974. 126 pp. o/p
A novel.

Fantouré, Alioum [pseud.]
Le cercle des tropiques
Paris: Présence Africaine, 1972. 256 pp. FF40.00
This first novel by a Guinean writer in exile won the Grand Prix Littéraire d'Afrique Noire in 1973. As the colonizer prepares to leave the African country of Southern Lakes the tension grows between the partisans of the Club of Workers, led by Monchon, a true patriot, and the Social Party of Hope, led by Baré Koulé, an ambitious politician. Monchon is assassinated while on trial for fomenting an insurrection against colonial authorities. Both the uprising and assassination are a plot of Koulé to slander the Club. The plot works, for Koulé wins the elections and comes to power in the newly independent state. A reign of terror begins as a new 'religion' sweeps the country – 'Messiahkoism' named after the 'divine leader'. The Club's work is carried on, however, under the leadership of Dr Malekê and Mellé Houré, despite the arrest and torture of the latter. The novel ends with Koulé's overthrow. In English *translation* see next entry.
'Le récit d'Alioum Fantouré, qui est une des fines plumes du 'nouveau roman nègre', se caractérise par un style alerte, sobre, précis'.
Fame Ndongo – *Cameroon Tribune*

Tropical Circle
(Trans. from the French by Dorothy S. Blair)
London: Longman, 1981. 256 pp. £1.60

Le récit du cirque
Paris: Buchet/Chastel, 1976. 150 pp.
Fantouré's second book is a 'play within a novel'. A captive audience locked literally into a theatre become gradually involved in the devastating spectacle being acted out on stage, a 'circus' of horror and suffering in an African dictatorship complete with political trials and concentration camps. There is no final curtain, only newsreel shots being projected onto a screen as the actors turn to watch the panic-stricken spectators seek an exit which is not there.
'[le] *livre de Alioume Fantouré* . . . *n'est pas un récit d'événements, mais un assaut aux moyens de perceptions: vue, ouïe, nerfs, un affrontement de l'entendement par une prostestation volcanique, une explosion d'images corrosives, la danse macabre de monstreux symboles organisées autour d'un thème: Laissez vivre mon peuple.'*   – *Africa*

L'homme du troupeau du Sahel
Paris: Présence Africaine, 1979. 297 pp. FF52.00
A young man, Maingual, a victim of racism, is expelled from Lycée and becomes a soldier in a disciplinary regiment somewhere in French Equatorial Africa. He works for a while at the conference of Brazzaville and finally ends up at Mare in Ivory Coast in charge of border troops whose mission is to prevent herds of cattle from going into Liberia. This work is the first of a projected trilogy to be called *La cité des termites*.

Fodeba, Keita
Aube africaine
Paris: Seghers, 1965. 85 pp. o/p
Poetry.

Le mâitre d'école, suivi de *Minuit*
Paris: Séghers, 1952. o/p
Plays.

Poèmes africains
Paris: Seghers, 1958 (2nd ed.). 63 pp. o/p
A volume of verse that was first published in 1950.

Fodekaba Chérif, Aïdra
Le royaume de Sinaban
Yaoundé: C.L.E., 1973. 64 pp. CFA230
The tale of the legendary founder of the Kingdom of Seven Hills who was awarded his kingship for obeying strictly the orders of his genie and successfully overcoming a number of ordeals.

Gaye, Mamadou
Caméléon
Paris: Pierre-Jean Oswald, 1976 (distr. by L'Harmattan, Paris). 67 pp. FF18.00
Poetry.

Laye, Camara
L'enfant noir
Paris: Plon. 1953. 256 pp. FF30.00
Paris: Presses Pocket, 1976 (Presses pocket, 1249). 221 pp. FF8.50
Paris: France Loisirs, 1976. 217 pp. FF20.00 cased
In English *translation*, see next entry.

The Dark Child/The African Child
(Trans. from the French by James Kirkup)
New York, Noonday Press, 1954. 188 pp. o/p
Glasgow: Fontana/Collins, 1955 [publ. as *The African Child*] 159 pp. 85p
New York: Farrar, Straus and Giroux, 1969 (Noonday paperbacks, N365: with an introduction by Philippe Thoby-Marcelin). 188 pp. $5.95 cased $3.95 p/b
Camara Laye's autobiographical recollections of childhood days in Guinea are recreated with nostalgia. He describes his life in chronological order: his early childhood days, portraying his father with great respect and his mother with love and tenderness, his attainment of manhood, his initiation and circumcision ceremonies. After finishing primary school he entered a Technical College in Conakry, and four years later was offered a scholarship to study engineering in Argenteuil near Paris. In France Camara Laye's funds soon ran out. Confronted with serious financial difficulties, he was obliged to interrupt his studies and seek work in the Simca car factories. Lonely and unhappy, he was spurred to put down on paper these vivid memories of an African childhood, which he dedicated to his mother.
'It is not often that any reviewer gets the chance to read a simple and natural work of art like this work . . . this book is high art, springing straight from first sources, and woven instinctively into a flowing pattern of deeply poetic prose. The book has rightly made a sensation in France.'
Mercedes Mackay – *African Affairs*

L'enfant noir
Ed. by Joyce Hutchinson
London and New York: CUP, 1966. 196 pp. £2.25/$4.95
Another edition, presented here in the original French, with an introduction, a bibliography, and notes in English.

Le regard du roi
Paris: Plon, 1954. 255 pp. o/p
Paris: Presses pocket, 1975 (Presses Pocket,
1209). 252 pp. FF10.50
This is a paperback re-issue of the original
1954 edition. In English *translation*, see next
entry.

The Radiance of the King
(Trans. from the French by James Kirkup)
London: Collins, 1956. 318 pp. o/p
Glasgow: Fontana/Collins, 1965 (Fontana
Books, 1208). 284 pp. p/b
New York: Macmillan, 1970. 256 pp.
Clarence, the white hero of this symbolic
novel, is in search of the briefly glimpsed king
whom he wishes to serve. Having lost all his
money at cards, his financial resources exhausted, the bankrupt Clarence is thrown out
of his hotel. Without any support from his
fellow white men, he is forced to beg for help
and sustenance. Clarence pins his hopes on the
African king in whose service he hopes to find
peace. The novel follows his search for the
king, his gruelling trek through the forest, his
companions – the beggar, the eunuch, the
blacksmith and the fortune-teller – to his life
in Anzia, where Clarence ultimately sees the
full radiance of the king and has his long-
awaited encounter with him. A great many
interpretations have been offered of *The
Radiance of the King*. The English publishers
claim that the book is an allegory of 'Man's
search for God', while critics have interpreted
it as 'a search for identification' (Gerald
Moore), 'a tentative approach to the mystery of
our being – an approach which suggests that a
journey into the primitive, and apparently
utterly strange, can result in a self-discovery
altogether startling but none the less illuminating' (John Ramsaran), or, 'a lesson in African
wisdom' (Janheinz Jahn). The American
paperback reissue has an introduction by
Albert Gérard.

Dramouss
Paris: Plon, 1966. 253 pp. o/p
Paris: Presses Pocket, 1974 (Presses pocket,
1123). 256 pp. o/p
A paperback re-issue of the original 1966
edition. In English *translation*, see next entry.

A Dream of Africa
(Trans. from the French by James Kirkup)
London: Fontana/Collins, 1970. 191 pp. 85p
New York: Collier Books, 1971. 191 pp. $1.50
In this translation of Laye's third novel,
Dramouss, the narrator returns from six
arduous years in Paris, where he had fought
poverty and hunger, to his homeland in Africa,
now on the verge of independence. Through

his family, his friends, and his new wife, he
rediscovers his own country, and sees its
magic, religion and the ancient skills of his
people replaced by political violence. A vision
reveals to him a terrifying period of unrest in
the immediate future. The novel is dedicated
to young people of Africa in general, and of
Guinea in particular; it is a call to them to
revive and restore 'native ways of thinking'.
The American edition has an introduction by
Emile Synder.
'. . . as with Laye's other works, one is struck by the
beauty of this poetic prose which loses nothing in Mr
Kirkup's admirable translation from the French.'
                              S. K. Dabo – *African Affairs*

Le maître de la parole: Kouma Lafôlô Kouma
Paris: Plon, 1978. 314 pp. FF40.00
Paris: Presses Pocket, 1980 (Presses pocket,
1905). 286 pp. FF16.00
In English *translation*, see next entry.

The Guardian of the Word
(Trans. from the French by James Kirkup)
Glasgow: Fontana/Collins, 1981. 223 pp.
£1.35
The last work Laye published before his death
in 1979. It is another version of the legend of
Sun Jata, the thirteenth century Manding ruler
as told to Laye in 1963 by a ninety-year-old
griot, Babou Condé, known as *Belêm-Tigui*, the
Master of Words.
'Though there are epic and biblical overtones
throughout much of the narrative – especially with the
hero motif and the extended genealogies – it is Laye's
affinities with the modern novel that shape his epic
and render it into a work of beauty.'
                     Charles Larson – *Times Literary Supplement*

Monenembo, Tierno
Les crapauds-brousse
Paris: Ed. du Seuil, 1979. 186 pp. FF37.00
Having been trained as an electrician in
Hungary, Diouldé comes home to an imaginary African republic full of idealism and
hoping to help his people. Much to his
disappointment he is appointed to a political
position as attaché in the Ministry of the
Interior in charge of relationships with Eastern
Europe. Soon after, he is arrested for plotting
against the regime. In an effort to help, his
wife accepts the sexual advances of one of his
'friends' then assassinates a leading politician
before going off to join the resistance. A novel
which is a violently critical assessment of Africa
today by a Guinean author living in exile in
Paris.
'. . . rien n'y manque, le tout conté dans un style
chargé d'images qui est une réussite incontestable.
Tierno Monenembo, délaissant le passé proche ou
lointain, nous entraîne à sa suite, au coeur des

problèmes les plus brûlants de l'Afrique aujourd'hui.'
        Maryse Condé – *Demain l'Afrique*
'Le Monde qu'il décrit est l'annexe tropicale de celui de Kafka . . . Le talent que met l'auteur a en faire le procès est époustouflant.'
        Conrad Detrez – *Le Matin*

Nenekhaly-Camara, Condetto
Lagunes
La Courneuve, France: Académie Populaire de Littérature et de Poésie, 1956. 23 pp. o/p
Poetry.

Continent Afrique suivi de *Amazoulous*
Paris: P. J. Oswald, 1970 (Théâtre africain, 7). 100 pp. o/p
The first play in this volume focuses on a certain number of historical events and social problems in Africa which are meant to be acted out against a background of film clips. *Amazoulous,* the second one, is based on the life of Chaka. Mario de Andrade, Minister of Cultural Affairs in Guinée at the time of publication prefaced the volume.
'Political and social comment finds its way into the theater in the form of caricature and cartoon, those stylized and frozen symbols of angry humor . . . The Guinean author . . . uses the idiom masterfully.'
        Eric Sellin – *Books Abroad*

Niane, Djibril Tamsir
Méry: nouvelles
Dakar: Nouvelles Editions Africaines, 1975. 80 pp. CFA550
Two stories in this collection deal with the theme of culture conflict. In the title story, set in the colonial period, two intellectuals forsake their village, and in 'Kakandé', a teacher, who claims not to believe in witchcraft, goes mad. The third one evokes historical figures, the Princess of Segou and her husband, Prince N'Ki, who had a canal built to bring water from the Niger to the fortress of Bambougou.

Sikasso ou la dernière citadelle suivi de *Chaka*
Paris: P. J. Oswald, 1976 (Théâtre africain, 15) (distr. by L'Harmattan, Paris). 97 pp. FF20.00
The heros of these two plays are great figures of African history – Ba Bemba Traoré, king of the fortified city of Sikasso in what is now Mali that was one of the last strongholds of resistence to French penetration at the end of the nineteenth century: and Chaka, the Zulu warrior-king.

Sacko, Biram
Dalanda ou la fin d'un amour
Dakar: Nouvelles Editions Africaines, 1976. 179 pp. CFA950
A novel of star-crossed love, set in indepen-

dent Guinea. The son of a *griot,* a traditional bard, refuses the calling of his father in order to become a painter just as he refuses to marry Dalanda, his cousin, who by custom should be his wife. Then he falls in love with her, only to be separated from the young woman by fate.

Saidou, Conté
Au fil de la liberté
Paris: Présence Africaine, 1966. 64 pp. o/p
Poetry.

Sara, Alphonse Tylé
Actes de conscience: poèmes
Paris: Ed. Saint-Germain-des-Prés, 1973. 88 pp. FF17.00

Sassine, Williams
Saint Monsieur Baly
Paris: Présence Africaine, 1973. 223 pp. FF41.00
Thanks to the perseverance and dedication of an elderly school teacher an African village finally gets a primary school. A novel.

Wirriyamu
Paris: Présence Africaine, 1976. 207 pp. FF41.00
In English *translation,* see next entry.

Wirriyamu
(Trans. from the French by John Reed and Clive Wake
London: HEB, 1980 (AWS, 199). 160 pp. £1.95/$5.50
The destruction of the village of Wirriyamu at the hands of the Portuguese during the war of liberation seen through the eyes of Kabalango, a European-trained writer who is terminally ill with T.B. and who has come home to die. He throws himself into the struggle and dies, ironically, under the guns of rival African forces.
'With a deep concern for the lives of individuals caught in the web of barbarism and inhumanity, Sassine explores the heart of the problem of existence.'
        F. Ojo-Ade – *World Literature Today*

Le jeune homme de sable
Paris: Présence Africaine, 1979. 185 pp. FF41.00
Oumarou detests his country's repressive regime as much as he detests his father, a prominent politician. An unconscious gesture of the young man's provides the spark which, it is hinted, will eventually topple the regime. In a central symbol of the novel Oumarou is compared to the individual grains of sand which are gradually turning his drought-stricken country into a desert – insignificant in

themselves yet capable of triggering great events when combined with other forces. Oumarou dies but others will be born, it is said, to carry on the struggle.

'Williams Sassine décrit avec un rare talent des réalités bien connues de l'Afrique – et du monde: répression aveugle, complots maraboutages, etc. Il trace aussi l'intéressant protrait d'une certaine classe politique.'   Sylviane Kamara – *Jeune Afrique*

Thiam, Djibi
Ma soeur la panthère: roman
Paris: Robert Laffont, 1978 (Plein vent, 127). 205 pp. FF16.00
What appears to be an insignificant event – the killing and eating of a dog by a panther – is, in fact, highly dramatic for the inhabitants of a small African village. The panther is their totem and must not come to harm. How, then, can they defend themselves? A novel.

Touré, Ahmed Sékou
Poèmes militants
Conakry: Parti Démocratique de Guinée, 1964. 80 pp.
The poetry of Guinea's Head of State.

Youla, Nabi
Moussa, enfant de Guinée. Mussa, ein Kind aus Guinea
Regensburg, West Germany: J. Habbel, 1964. 68 pp.
A story of childhood in Guinea, in bilingual text (French-German). The translation is by the late Jahnheinz Jahn.

Ivory Coast

Adiaffi, Jean-Marie
La carte d'identité
Paris: Hatier, 1980 (Monde noir poche, 7). 159 pp. FF16.10
In this first novel the search of a blind old man, a descendant of the royal family of the Agni of Bettié, for his lost identity card becomes the mythical quest of all Africans for the identity that has been usurped by the colonizer.

D'éclairs et de foudres: chant de braise pour une liberté en flammes
Abidjan: C.E.D.A., 1980. 106 pp. CFA790
Adiaffi's second book is a volume of prose poetry that is the antithesis of lyric verse. It gives free rein to the rage, pain and horror that have marked the African experience – past and present – and which are announced by the book's title, itself – *Thunder and Lightning: A Smouldering Song for Freedom in Flames*.

Amoi, Fatho
Mon beau pays d'Ivoire: poèmes
Saint-Genix-sur-Guiers, France: Ed. Marc Pessin et Paul Desalmand, 1967. 63 pp.

Amoi, Fatho and Clavreul, J. Y.
Chaque aurore est une chance
Abidjan: C.E.D.A., 1980. 64 pp. CFA900
Lyric poetry inspired by the natural setting of Abidjan and the Bay of Lagos. Illustrated by photographs by J. Y. Clavreul.

Amon d'Aby, François-Joseph
Kwao Adjoba ou procès du régime matriarcal en Basse Côte d'Ivoire: drame en trois actes et huit tableaux
Paris: Millas-Martin, 1958. 51 pp. o/p
In this play the author raises the problems of unjust inheritance customs. Followed by a short study of the rights of fathers in the matriarchal society of the Agni-Ashanti.

La couronne aux enchères: drame social en trois actes et six tableaux
Paris: Millas-Martin, 1958. 47 pp. o/p
This play has been reprinted in Amon d'Aby and Dadié et al., *Le Théâtre populaire en Côte d'Ivoire*.

Analla, Gnoussira
Morte saison
Dakar: Nouvelles Editions Africaines, 1980. 38 pp. CFA350
Poetry.

Anoma Kanié, Léon Maurice
Les eaux du Comoé: poèmes
Paris: Ed. du Miroir, 1951. 64 pp. o/p
Poetry.

La grande Samoko
Dakar: Nouvelles Editions Africaines, 1977. 61 pp. CFA600
The love story of a great African queen: a three-act play.

Les malheurs d'Amangoua
Dakar: Nouvelles Editions Africaines, 1978. 303 pp. CFA2,000
The problems of a young man who has had to fend for himself early in life in an urban milieu.

Anouna, Joseph
Les matins blafards
Paris: P. J. Oswald, 1977 (Poésie/prose africaine, 20) (distr. by L'Harmattan, Paris). 70 pp. FF21.00
The verse of a young Ivorian who is better known as an artist than as a poet.

Pas cadences suivi de *Champs magnétiques*
Paris: Ed. Silex, 1981. 63 pp. FF25.00
Poetry.

Assoi Adiko, Célestin Virgile
L'Epopée de la Reine Abla Pokou
Abidjan: Imp. commerciale, 1971. 40 pp.
CFA200
A dramatic representation of the legend of
Queen Pokou. In the end the queen flees – the
only way to resolve the conflict between right
and duty.

Atta Koffi, Raphaël
Les dernières paroles de Koimé
Paris: Nouvelles Editions Debresse, 1961.
144 pp. o/p
A desperate mother commits suicide when her
son leaves home to continue his education in a
far-away place.

Le trône d'or
Paris: O.R.T.F.-D.A.E.C., 1969 (Répertoire
théâtral africain, 6) (distr. by Nouvelles
Editions Africaines, Dakar). 109 pp. CFA300
A historical play that was a runner-up in the
1968 African Theatre Competition sponsored
by Radio-France Internationale. Adingra, the
ruler of the Abron gives his golden throne to
the king of the Ashanti, his liege lord. But
Adingra's sister sets herself up as Queen
Yangouman and declares war against the
Ashanti, but because of the treachery of her
own son the Abron lose. The queen kills her
brother and commits suicide and the Ashanti
king will execute Yangouman's son on the
tomb of his mother.

Bamba, Daouda
Eloges et amours
Paris: Ed. Saint-Germain-des-Prés, 1979.
58 pp. FF19.30
Poetry.

Berté, Mamadou
La colère de Baba
Paris: O.R.T.F.-D.A.E.C., 1969 (Répertoire
théâtral africain, 5) (distr. by Nouvelles
Editions Africaines, Dakar). 62 pp. CFA300
A play set in a rural milieu which was a
runner-up in the 1967-68 African Theatre
Competition organized by Radio-France Internationale. Baba, a farmer, kills a bull that
Sadio, a herder, lets wander onto his land. He
is convinced of his right for it is common
knowledge that cattle are always spoiling
farmers' crops. The law, however, decides
otherwise.

Bognini, Joseph-Miézan
Ce dur appel de l'espoir
Paris: Présence Africaine, 1960. 127 pp. o/p
A volume of poetry.
'. . . shows all the virtues of true simplicity . . . the
controlled fervour, quality of melody and innocence of
language give Bognini's poems great depth and
significance.'
                              Jacques Howlett – *Présence Africaine*

Herbe féconde: poèmes
Paris: P. J. Oswald, 1973 (Poésie/prose
africaine, 5) (distr. by L'Harmattan, Paris).
67 pp. FF15.00
A collection of verse in four parts which
represent the 'stations of the cross' the poet
goes through to save his people.

Bolli, Fatou
Djigbô
Abidjan: C.E.D.A., 1978. 93 pp. CFA530
A young lady is troubled by what seems to be
witchcraft.

Brou de Binao, Komenan
Mensonges de soirs d'Afrique
Yaoundé: C.L.E., 1973. 64 pp. CFA210
The hero of four of these tales is Jean Abafri,
the Spider. The last tale is about a leper who
helps a cripple, goes through several ordeals
and ends up a rich, respected man. Two of
these tales are traditional in format but
contemporary in setting.

Dadié, Bernard B.
Afrique debout!
Paris: Séghers, 1950. 43 pp. o/p
Poems.

Climbié
Paris: Séghers, 1953. 191 pp. o/p
In English *translation*, see next entry. The
French text remains available in a combined
volume of Dadié's poetry and prose, see
below.

Climbié
(Trans. from the French by Karen C. Chapman)
London: HEB, 1971 (AWS, 87). 157 pp. £1.25
New York: Africana Publishing Corp., 1971.
196 pp. $9.75 cased $5.50 p/b
Dadié's first novel is largely autobiographical
in content, reminiscent of Camara Laye's
African Child. It recounts the childhood,
upbringing, daily life and social environment
of a boy living in pre-independent Ivory Coast.
In its later chapters it is also concerned with
the struggle of African trade unionists and
nationalists under the French colonial administrators with their determined assimilation policies.

Un nègre à Paris

Paris: Présence Africaine, 1959 (reprinted 1976). 219 pp. FF25.00

Long out of print, this book was reissued in 1976. A satirical view of Paris and Parisians, seen through the eyes of an African student. In the novel Dadié makes repeated comparisons between his own culture and customs and those of the French people.

Patron de New York

Paris: Présence Africaine, 1964 (Coll. Chronique). 311 pp. o/p

Dadié's personal and satirical account of life and society in New York in particular, and of American civilization in general. The book is the result of the author's four-month stay in the U.S. and is perhaps the francophone equivalent to John Pepper Clark's *America their America.*

Légendes et poèmes: Afrique debout!; Légendes africaines; Climbié; La ronde des jours

Paris: Séghers, 1966 (reprinted 1973). 257 pp. FF18.00

An anthology of previously published folk tales and poetry, including *La ronde des jours* which was published in a separate volume by Séghers in 1956, together with the novel *Climbié* in its entirety.

Hommes de tous les continents

Paris: Présence Africaine, 1967. 103 pp. o/p

A book of poetry.

La ville où nul ne meurt

Paris: Présence Africaine, 1969. 212 pp. o/p

A sequel to *Patron de New York,* presenting Dadié's view of Rome, and the way of life in contemporary Roman society.

'. . . *c'est un récit agréable et bien enlevé par un écrivain doué et qui a le don de raconter, la grace d'observer et de rendre, ce qui n'est pas donné a tout le monde.'* Paulin Joachim – *Bingo*

Sidi Maître Esroc; Situation difficile; Serment d'amour

Yaoundé: C.L.E., 1969 (C.L.E. Théâtre, 4). 32 pp. o/p

Three short plays.

Béatrice du Congo: pièce en trois actes

Paris: Présence Africaine, 1970. 149 pp. FF28.00

This was the first play by an African author to be performed at the Avignon Festival in France (1971). It concerns the life and martyrdom of Beatrice, the founder of the first Christian sect in the Congo in the sixteenth century, and her struggles to rid her people of a foreign exploiter claiming to bring the 'true religion', Henry the Navigator.

'*Ce qu'il y a de nouveau dans ce théâtre, c'est le rôle de la femme africaine . . . Dadié a mis sur la scène une courageuse héroïne qui mène le jeu.'*
Femi Ojo-Ade – *Afrique Littéraire et Artistique*

Monsieur Thogo-Gnini

Paris: Présence Africaine, 1970. 115 pp. FF24.00

A satirical play that was first performed – with considerable success – at the first Pan-African Cultural Festival in Algiers in 1969. The title means 'The Opportunist' in Malinké. The scene is a West-African village in the nineteenth century. The central character is a freed slave who has returned to Africa and who gains wealth and power by winning the confidence of the local king in encouraging his dealings with European slave traders.

'*a clever comedy . . . a first-rate social and political comedy.'* Eric Sellin – *Books Abroad*

Les Voix dans le vent; tragédie

Yaoundé: C.L.E. 1970. 168 pp. o/p

In an imaginary African country Nahoubou revolts against the leader, the Macadou, and comes to power dreaming of a regime of peace and prosperity. But he becomes an exploiter himself and is eliminated, just as his predecessor had been.

Iles de tempête: pièce en sept tableaux

Paris: Présence Africaine, 1973. 144 pp. FF25.00

A play about a historical subject: colonization and slavery in the West Indies, which focuses in the final scenes on General Toussaint L'Ouverture and his struggle against the forces of Napoleon to win the independence of Santo Domingo.

Papassidi maître-escroc: comédie

Dakar: Nouvelles Editions Africaines, 1975. 80 pp. CFA600

Aka, a public scribe, is penniless and has no work. He lets himself be taken in by Papassidi who practises the fine 'art' of multiplying banknotes. But thanks to Aka's wife, Djouna, Papassidi is uncovered for what he really is and arrested.

Mhoi-Ceul: comédie en cinq tableaux

Paris: Présence Africaine, 1979. 101 pp. FF24.00

Dadié's latest play continues the satirical vein of *Monsieur Thogo-Gnini* and *Papassidi.* The egocentric bureaucrat Mhoi-Ceul (from the French: *moi, seul,* 'me, myself') rules over his staff with utter disregard for civil service regulations. 'The rules are not for me,' he says, especially concerning his dealings with his

Very Private Secretary, Chérie Beauzieux ('Miss Prettyeyes'). But when his accountant Cendiplaume ('Mr. Nodegree') is arrested the truth will inevitable be revealed.

Assémien Dahylé: roi du Sanwi
Abidjan: C.E.D.A., 1979. 48 pp.
A re-issue of the play Dadié wrote when a student at the William Ponty Normal School and that appeared in the journal *Education Africaine* in 1937. The volume includes an introduction by Nicole Vincileoni who writes about Dadié and the theatre troupe at the William Ponty School.

Opinions d'un nègre
Dakar: Nouvelles Editions Africaines, 1980 (Club Afrique Loisirs, 6). 190 pp. CFA1,900 cased
A series of aphorisms written between 1934 and 1946 and which Dadié has regrouped under six headings: the human condition, virtue and vice, the world as it is, those who govern, a profile of those who are governed, the milk of human kindness.

Les jambes du fils de Dieu
Paris: Hatier, 1980 (Monde noir poche, 8). 159 pp. FF16.10
Fifteen short stories.

Contes de Koutou-as-Samal
Paris: Présence Africaine, forthcoming 1981. Folk-tales.

Commandant Taureault et ses nègres
Abidjan: C.E.D.A., 1981. 122 pp.
A novel that draws a portrait of a French colonial official at a time when forced labour still existed and the economy was in the hands of the colonial trading companies but also when nationalist sentiment was beginning to take form.

Dem, Tidiane
Masseni: roman
Dakar: Nouvelles Editions Africaines, 1977. 251 pp. CFA950
A novel set in the Mandingue culture just before World War II which evokes the despair of a childless couple and the unscrupulous dealings of those who claim to be able to solve their problem.

Dervain, Eugène
La reine scélérate, suivi de La langue et le scorpion
Yaoundé: C.L.E., 1968. 106 pp. o/p
Two historical legendary plays set in the kingdom of Ségou in ancient Mali during the latter part of the eighteenth century.

Abra Pokou
Yaoundé: C.L.E., 1969 (C.L.E. Théâtre, 3). 15 pp. o/p
This short one-act play – inspired by a short story by Bernard Dadié – centres around Abra Pokou, chief of the Amansi tribe.

Termites
Paris: P. J. Oswald, 1976 (Théâtre africain, 32) (distr. by L'Harmattan, Paris). 61 pp. FF15.00
The top floor of a building disappears mysteriously as soon as it is rebuilt. The police chief suspects the opposition, but it is only termites. A satirical play.

Diallo, Mamadou M.
Tam-tam noir
Abidjan: Ed. Africaines, 1970. 44 pp.
This book of verse won the 1970 Houphouët-Boigny prize for poetry.

Pleurs et fleurs pour Méliane: poèmes
Dakar: Nouvelles Editions Africaines, 1974. 76 pp. o/p
Another collection of verse.

Dodo, Jean
Symphonie en noir et blanc: poèmes
Paris: P. J. Oswald, 1974 (distr. by L'Harmattan, Paris). 47 pp. FF14.00
A collection of verse which was awarded the 1976 prize of the Broquette-Gonin Fondation by the Académie Française and which had received the previous year the prize for young African and Malagasy poets given by Radio Netherlands.

Wazzi: la 'mousso' du forestier
Dakar: Nouvelles Editions Africaines, 1977. 154 pp. CFA700
A novel about the tribulations of a young woman weighed down by custom.

Sacrés dieux d'Afrique
Dakar: Nouvelles Editions Africaines, 1978. 143 pp. CFA900
After making a customary marriage a young man leaves for Europe to continue his studies. A novel.

Fatho-Amoy
Chaque aurore est une chance
Abidjan: C.E.D.A., 1980. 64 pp.
Poems celebrating life and nature's beauties.
' . . . stands out for its lyrical optimism and warmth . . . recommended for purchase for general poetry and African poetry collections.'
Janis L. Pallister – *African Book Publishing Record*

Halilou, Mohamadou Sabbo

Abboki ou l'appel de la côte
Dakar: Nouvelles Editions Africaines, 1978
(2nd ed.). 57 pp. CFA700
The adventures of Amadou, a Niger countryman, in an unnamed African city. Like
many others he is lured to the coast in hopes of
quick riches but soon discovers the sad truth:
gainful employment is out of the question.
Then follows a series of jobs, all more or less
illegal. After an accident in which he loses a leg
he is caught in a police raid and deported as an
'undesireable' and returns home a hero.

Kablan, Ahoussi

Le temps de l'école
Abidjan: C.E.D.A., 1978. 120 pp. CFA930
A young man from the Ivory Coast recall his
schooldays.

Kakou, Konan

Le matin sera rouge
Yaoundé: C.L.E., 1980. 145 pp.
A novel that relives an episode of the
beginnings of the nationalist period.

Kakou, Julian

*Trafic d'âmes: une aventure de Scorpion
l'Africain*
Paris: A.B.C., 1976. (Archives secrètes du
B.S.I., 7). 95 pp. FF7.00
One in a series of detective thrillers.

Bis Le Scorpion noir contre le pouvoir pâle
Paris: A.B.C., 1976 (Archives secrètes du
B.S.I., 9). 95 pp. o/p

*Le Scorpion noir contre la diabolique Mme
Attaway*
Paris A.B.C., 1976 (Archives secrètes du B.S.I.,
11). 80 pp. o/p

Kaya, Simone

*Les danseuses d'Impe-Eya: jeunes filles à
Abidjan*
Abidjan: INADES, 1976. 127 pp. CFA1,500
FF30.00
An account, part fiction, part autobiography,
of a young girl growing up in Comikro, a
district of Treichville in the suburbs of
Abidjan, and her exposure to both European
customs (from her schooling) and African ones
(from her neighbourhood).

*'I believe Simone Kaya is capable of developing into
a writer of considerable skill. Her sober style, her
sense of proportin and the sincerity with which she
expresses the sentiments of youth prefigure an
outstanding career.'*

Christophe Dailly – *World Literature Today*

Koné, Maurice

La guirlande des verbes
Paris: Grassin, 1961 (Poésie nouvelle, 22).
32 pp. o/p
(Reprinted in *African Poems in French*. Nendeln,
Liechtenstein, Kraus reprint, 1970. $27.00)

Au bout de petit matin: poèmes
Bordeaux: Jean-Germain, 1962. 66 pp.
Poetry.

Le jeune homme de Bouaké
Paris: Grassin. 1963. 64 pp. o/p
A novel.

Au seuil de crépuscule: poèmes
Rodes: Subervie, 1965. 40 pp. o/p

Poèmes
Abidjan: Imp. Commerciale, 1969. 32 pp.
Poetry.

Poèmes verlainiens
Millau, France: Imp. Maury, 1969. 40 pp.
Poetry.

Argile du rêve
Dakar: Nouvelles Editions Africaines, 1979.
83 pp. CFA1,000
Poetry.

Koulibaly, Isaïe Biton

Les deux amis
Abidjan: Nouvelles Editions Africaines, 1978.
71 pp. CFA550
Most of the stories in this collection of eleven
are only three or four pages long. They range
in tone from the comic to the tragic, from the
letter of a poor peasant to his son in France to
the suicide of a young mulatto girl who is not
allowed to marry the man of her choice, a full-
blooded African. There is the cynical educated
man who witnesses a political assassination
and agrees to say nothing but also the young
teacher who is 'exiled' to a school in the
country for 'subversive' ideas. The title story,
set in a traditional milieu, is about a test of
friendship successfully passed.

Kourouma, Ahmadou

Les soleils des indépendances
Montréal: Les Presses de l'Univerité de Mon-
tréal, 1968. 171 pp. Can.$2.50
Paris: Seuil, 1970. 205 pp. o/p
In English *translation*, see next entry.

The Suns of Independence
(Trans. from the French by Adrian Adams)
London: HEB, 1981 (AWS, 239). 144 pp.
£2.50

New York: Africana Publishing Company, 1981.
A deposed chief has to adjust himself to living among the proletariat. It is the story of Fama, the last legitimate ruler of Horodougou in the Malinke region, exiled after losing his chieftaincy to his cousin Lacina, who proved to be more acceptable to the colonial administrators.
'. . . *a variation of the familiar 'things fall apart' theme . . . Kourouma manages to create an atmosphere of intimacy . . . he does not hesitate to let the images, the rhythms, the words of his mother-tongue pierce the polished surface of polite prose . . . an exciting first novel.*'
Willfried Feuser – *The New African*
'. . . *the narrative is sustained by vivid and highly figurative language, most effective when conveying the subtle relationship between the African village and its surrounding forests.*'
John Mukele – *South*

Loba, Ake
Kocoumbo, l'étudiant noir
Paris: Flammarion, 1960. 269 pp. o/p
An African student thrust into a working-class environment in Paris.
'. . . *profoundly original and of considerable significance.*' Guy de Bosschère – *Présence Africaine*

Les fils de Kouretcha
Nivelle, Belgium: Ed. de la Francité, 1970. 72 pp. FB180
The authorities of a newly-independent African country have decided to build a dam on the Kouretcha, a sacred river, but they must face the attacks of Damno, a former government worker in colonial times who is also a candidate for elections. It is a losing battle and it will end tragically. Damno kills his 'advisor', Moussa Dombyia, the fetish priest, and turns himself in. This novel won the 1969 Houphouët-Boigny prize.

Les dépossédés
Brussels: Ed. de la Francité, 1973. 228 pp. FB110
This novel also appeared in serialized form in *Fraternité Matin* in 1974. Set in Abidjan between 1930 and 1950 it is the story of a peasant turned museum attendant who settles in the city when he is 20 and who changes over the years, just as the city changes. Other important protagonists are his wives (including Marie, the 'City Woman'), Douézo, his best friend (who was his 'traditional enemy' in the village), the catechist, and two Europeans: the police chief and the priest. All in one way or another are 'dispossessed' or alienated.

Niangoran, Porquet
Soba ou grande Afrique
Dakar: Nouvelles Editions Africaines, 1978. 98 pp. CFA600
Moussa, a strong young man, suddenly falls ill and his mother begins a desperate search for a healer. She sees a number of imposters before finding a real healer who saves her son just in time and discovers that witchcraft is the cause of it all. A play.
'*La critique des vieux qui profitent du changement et exploitent les jeunes n'est pas nouvelle, mais en centrant sa pièce sur ce sujet "social" Niangoran dévoile l'un des drames de l'Afrique moderne*'.
Afrique Asie

Nokan, Charles [pseud. for Konan, Zégoua]
Le soleil, noir point
Paris: Présence Africaine, 1962. 71 pp. FF20.00
The autobiographical account of a young man from the Ivory Coast who comes to France to study, leaving his fiancée, Amah, behind. In France he becomes involved with Sarah, the daughter of his landlady, until an accident makes him impotent. Back home, he confesses all to Amah, releases her from her promise and throws himself into the task of organizing evening classes for adults. The novel is presented as a series of sixty brief *tableaux* centring around the themes of love, rebellion, despair and hope.

Violent était le vent
Paris: Présence Africaine, 1966. 181 pp. FF27.00

Les malheurs de Tchakô: pièce en cinq tableaux
Paris: P. J. Oswald, 1968 (Théâtre africain, 3) (distr. by L'Harmattan, Paris). 98 pp. FF18.00
A play.

Abraha Pokou suivi de *La voix grave d'Ophimoi*
Paris: P. J. Oswald, 1971 (Théâtre africain, 9) (distr. by L'Harmattan, Paris). 89 pp. FF18.00
A historical play about the Baoulé queen, Pokou, who saved her people by sacrificing her child. Followed by a series of poems.

Nokan, Zégoua [Charles]
La traversée de la nuit dense suivi de *Cris rouges*
Paris P. J. Oswald, 1972 (Théâtre africain, 19) (distr. by L'Harmattan, Paris). 75 pp.
A play about the exploitation of African workers in Europe. In his preface the author talks about the evolution of African literature.

Harmattan is preparing a new edition of this play.

'*Le propos fondamental de Nokan ne varie pas: il s'agit de créer un théâtre et une poésie qui s'adaptent à l'époque historique que vivent les africains afin de servir de moyens de connaissance destinées à impulser une prise de conscience politique . . . le principal personnage n'est plus un individu, mais un peuple pris dans sa globalité.*'

Noureini Tidjani-Serpos – *Présence Africaine*

Ouassenan, Gaston Koné

L'homme qui vécut trois vies: roman
Issy-les-Moulineaux, France: Eds. Saint-Paul, 1976 (Les classiques africains, 710). 112 pp. FF13.00
The three lives in the title of this novel refer to the three Africas the hero comes in contact with over the years: colonial Africa, Africa of the past and post-independent Africa. During World War II the hero flees into the bush to escape recruitment and settles with an isolated group still living as in the past. He returns to his village thirty years later and discovers independence has come.

Aller-retour
Issy-les-Moulineaux, France: Eds. Saint-Paul, 1977 (Les classiques africains, 714). 136 pp. FF16.00
A novel about a mixed marriage which ends unhappily.

Oussou-Essui, Denis

Vers de nouveaux horizons
Paris: Ed. du Scorpion, 1965. 190 pp. o/p
The problems of a young man who leaves his village to go off to school in Bouaké.

La souche calcinée
Yaoundé: C.L.E., 1973. 204 pp. CFA630
Once in France, the hero of this novel must abandon his studies in order to earn his living because a compatriot has 'forgotten' a monetary transaction. And the job market in Paris is ruthless for an African who has no skills. Only the strongest of wills and the help of a few other countrymen enable him to survive.

Le temps des hymnes: poèmes
Paris: José Millas-Martin, 1975. 72 pp. FF17.00
Most of these poems were written in the late fifties, early sixties, including one, 'La souche calcinée' which served as the title for the author's second novel. Part I 'Hymne à la nuit ou Poèmes d'Exil' was written during a stay in France.

Les saisons sèches
Paris: L'Harmattan, 1980. 192 pp. FF39.00

Aguié, a civil engineer, is full of enthusiasm and idealism when he returns home to the Ivory Coast after completing his studies in France. He is shocked to discover how much his country has changed. A novel.

Sery D., Gaston [pseud. for Atta Koffi, Gabriel]

Commissaire K contre Dragax, no. 1: le premier roman policier ivoirien
Dakar: Nouvelles Editions Africaines, 1975. 58 pp. CFA250
Dragax is the diabolic seducer who 'collects' beautiful women like others collect butterflies. One more time he eludes Police Commissioner Koua Koffi Kadar.

Teya, Pascal Koffi

Une victoire indésirable
Dakar: Nouvelles Editions Africaines, 1976. 72 pp. CFA550
Three tales about the ironies of human relationships: the young wrestler who, by miracle, defeats the champion; the wife who cannot keep a secret – but only because her husband refuses to confide in her; and the El Hadji, more quack than saint, who disrupts a peaceful pagan village.

Timité, Bassori

Les bannis du village
Dakar: Nouvelles Editions Africaines, 1974. 132 pp. CFA550
Written about 1964 these six stories first appeared in serialized form in *Fraternité Matin* in 1972. Their settings vary widely, from a small village in Ivory Coast to post-independent Abidjan, but the themes share a similar ironic approach ranging from the title story about a jealous mother who is led to commit incest to the tale of 'Monsieur Dubois', a prosperous French baker in pre-war Abidjan who loses his fortune but gains a sense of the common humanity he shares with the African customers he had so despised.

Touré, Kitia

L'arbre et le fruit: nouvelles
Issy-les-Moulineaux, France: Ed. Saint-Paul, 1979 (Les classiques africains, 718). 103 pp. FF16.00
Six short stories around the theme of relationships between parents and children, about the world of yesterday and that of today.

Vabe, Alain Gérard

Mes premiers mots
Paris: Ed. de l'Athanor, 1975. 77 pp.
The first book of poetry of a young teacher.

Wanne, Tegbo
Enfants d'Afrique
Dakar: Nouvelles Editions Africaines, forth-
coming 1981

Zadi Zaourou, Bernard
Fer de lance: livre 1
Paris: P. J. Oswald, 1975 (Poésie, prose
africaine, 11) (distr. by L'Harmattan, Paris).
51 pp. FF15.00
A long poem.

Les sofas suivi de *L'oeil*
Paris: P. J. Oswald, 1975 (Théâtre africain, 26)
(distr. by L'Harmattan, Paris). 125 pp. FF21.00
Two plays.

Mali

Bâ, Amadou Hampaté
*L'étrange destin de Wangrin ou les roueries
d'un interprète africain*
Paris: Union Générale d'Editions, 1973 (Coll.
10/18, 785). 440 pp. FF22.50
The extraordinary life of an extraordinary
man, Wangrin, who served for over fifteen
years as interpreter to French colonial administrators in what is now known as Mali.
Wangrin first met the author, briefly, in 1912
and many years later told him the story of his
life which he hoped would be both entertaining and edifying. One of the first Africans to
learn to read and write, Wangrin had attended
the 'School of Hostages' at Kayes in the early
years of this century. A daring opportunist
who used his position as interpreter to gain a
fortune and become one of the first African
businessmen, Wangrin was a man of great
contradictions. Wit and cunning were equally
matched by generosity and sincerity, the
consequence, the author says of his having
dedicated his life to the Bambara deity of
opposites – Gongoloma-Sooké. French colonial practices and relationships between
colonizer and colonized are the backdrop to
this true story. This novel won the Grand Prix
Littéraire de l'Afrique Noire in 1973.

Badian, Seydou
Sous l'orage: Kany, roman suivi de *La Mort de
Chaka: pièce en 5 tableaux.*
Paris: Présence Africaine, 1973. 253 pp.
FF15.00
A re-issue in a combined volume of two of
Badian's previously published works. *Sous
l'orage* is a novel with pre-independence Sudan
as a setting which was first published by Les

Presses Universelles in 1957 and later by
Présence Africaine in 1963. It tells the story of
Kany's struggle to marry the man of her
choice. Education, her parents fear, has made
her headstrong. A friend of the family
intervenes to solve the problem. The novel is
followed by a play about the Zulu prince,
Chaka (see next entry) which Présence Africaine first published in 1962.

The Death of Chaka. A play in five tableaux
(Trans. from the French by Clive Wake).
Nairobi: OUP, 1968 (New Drama from Africa,
1). 52 pp. o/p
An English translation of Badian's play based
on Thomas Mofolo's *Chaka* which narrates in
dramatic form the death, by assassination at
the hands of his brothers, of Chaka, the
founder of the Zulu nation.

Le sang des masques
Paris: Robert Laffont, 1976. 251 pp.
A novel written while the author, former
minister of Modibo Kieta, was in prison
following the 1968 coup in Mali. Its hero,
Bakari, returns to his village after three years
in the city working as a mechanic and is
greeted with suspicion and hostility: has he not
succumbed to new ways? He falls in love with
Nandi who is courted by Namakoro. The latter
plots against Bakari with other members of his
age group. The clan, however, comes to
Bakari's defence and, as a sign of trust, invests
him with the responsibility of seeing that
Nandi remains pure until her marriage. Later,
he leaves for the city where Nandi and her
husband, Amadou, a brute of a man, have
come, too. In the tragic climax Bakari kills his
former employer to save Nandi's husband who
owes the man a lot of money and then takes his
own life.

*'Seydou Badian ne cherche ... pas à idéaliser
l'univers villageois dont il connaît trop bien la
complexité pour n'en restituer qu'un pâle reflet. Les
amateurs d'exotisme, que pourrait allécher la
tapageuse couverture du livre, resquent d'être déçus
par ce roman qui ... rend parfaitement compte de
l'atmosphère d'une petite communauté rurale à
l'époque de la colonisation.'*
                              Jacques Chevrier – *Le Monde*
*'The style is austere, offering many fine passages and
a sharpness of image.'*
                              Hal Wylie – *World Literature Today*

Noces sacrées: les dieux de Kouroulamini
Paris: Présence Africaine, 1977. 150 pp.
FF35.00
Set in the French Sudan (Mali) during later
colonial times, the novel is the tale of Besnier,
a Frenchman, who has returned to Africa with

his fiancée in order 'to give back' a mask to the people from whom it had been stolen. Haunted by the god N'Tomo ever since he acquired the mask, Besnier is on the verge of a nervous breakdown. The African doctor who narrates the story seems to be the only person who can help him, providing the rightful owners of the mask can be found.

'*Badian a traité avec intelligence et sensibilité un sujet véritablement grand . . . Il évite aussi bien les mocqueries faciles que les naïvetés.*'

Robert Kanters – *Le Figaro*

'*Le récit est conduit avec vivacité. L'auteur a construit son récit de telle sorte que le cercle des blancs se trouve être convaincu et fasciné: blancs et noirs ayant leur place dans la société secrete.*'

Salem Jay – *Afrique Littéraire et Artistique*

Cissé, Ahmen-Tidjani
Pollen et fleurs
Paris: Nubia, 1981. 91 pp.
Poetry.

Couloubaly, Pascal Baba F.
Les angoisses d'un monde
Dakar: Nouvelles Editions Africaines, 1980.
125 pp. CFA1,200

A group of young men led by Yiriba, a mechanic home from Bamako, revolt against the initiation rite of the *konmen* in the Malian village of Fougakéné. Perhaps useful in times past, the *konmen* symbolizes in the present the repressive authority of a gerontocracy which includes the power of life over death, something young people like Yiriba, whose father had suffered ritual death years before, can no longer tolerate. Other young people, like Massa, the schoolteacher, desire initiation for intellectual reasons, as a means of gaining knowledge about their culture, but they cannot help admiring Yiriba's courage and determination and wonder if perhaps he is not right. The author's first novel.

Dembele, Nagognimé Urbain
Tchagona né d'un défunt
Bamako: Ed. Populaires du Mali, 1980.
156 pp. FM685

A novel set in the Minianka region of Mali with a glossary of Minianka terms at the end.

Diabaté, Massa Makan
Kala Jata
Bamako: Ed. Populaires du Mali, 1970. 96 pp.
FM635

In relating this version of the Sunjata legend, which comes from the griot, Kele Monson, a descendent of a hunting companion of the thirteenth century Manding ruler, Diabaté has respected the oral nature of the tale and the drama of its telling. Narrative portions are interspersed with poems and songs meant to be accompanied by the *nkoni*, a string instrument.

Une si belle leçon de patience
Paris: O.R.T.F.-D.A.E.C., 1972. (Répertoire théâtral africain, 15) (distr. by Nouvelles Editions Africaines, Dakar). 123 pp. CFA300

A historical play set in nineteenth century Mali which won the 1970 African Theatre Competition organized by the French broadcasting corporation. Samory, the Emir of Ouassoulou stands at the gate to Sikasso with his troops ready to attack his rival, Ba-Bemba, the King of Kenedougou. But Ba-Bemba, who is, in theory, an ally of the French, refuses to fight and tries to convince Samory to join forces with him against the foreign invader.

L'aigle et l'épervier ou La geste de Sunjata
Paris: Pierre-Jean Oswald, 1975 (Poésie/prose africaine, 13) (distr. by L'Harmattan, Paris).
90 pp. FF18.00

The legend of Sunjata, founder of the thirteenth century Manding empire, as told to the author by his uncle, the griot Kélé Monson Diabaté.

'*This version of the Sunjata epic is important because it comes from Mali itself and from the very historical and geographical context of the Sunjata legend.*'

J. D. Gauthier – *World Literature Today*

Le lieutenant de Kouta
Paris: Hatier, 1979. 127 pp. FF33.95

Diabaté's first novel centres around Siriman Keïta, a lieutenant in the French colonial army, who returns home to Kouta in Mali at retirement and in a manner of speaking 'occupies' the village. His vanity and his extravagant behaviour involve him in a number of incidents which almost bring about his downfall. His conversion to Islam will restore his dignity.

'*Un joli récit qui se lit avec plaisir . . . Mais en fait, le vrai personnage de ce récit, c'est le village de Kouta.*' Tahar Badraoui – *Afrique-Asie*

'*Derrière la gaîté salubre, et parfois même un peu salace, qui préside aux tribulations de ce soldat fanfaron, se dessine peu à peu la figure grave et pathétique d'un homme secrètement blessé dans sa dignité.*' Jacques Chevrier – *Le Monde*

Le coiffeur de Kouta
Paris: Hatier, 1980 (Monde noir poche, 2).
160 pp. FF19.00

Siriman Keïta has died a peaceful death and
been buried in the mosque and the village goes
on as before until a new barber arrives,
upsetting the monopoly which Kompè, a
colourful character in his own right, had
enjoyed until then. Kompè's private intrigues
to ruin his rival, added to the lesson which the
village as a whole intends to give the visiting
Secretary General of the Party, contribute to
the comic matter of the novel which is the
second of an announced trilogy on Kouta. The
'cast' of characters includes Solo, the blind
man, N'dogui, the leper, old Soriba, a village
elder, Togoroko, the idiot, Namori, the
butcher, Father Kadri, the priest of the local
parish, and the Iman of the Mosque.

Comme une piqûre de guêpe
Paris: Présence Africaine, 1981. 159 pp.
FF35.00
Diabaté's latest novel deals with the ritual of
circumcision and the way it effects both family
and community.
'. . . *l'auteur descendant de griots est un merveilleux
et délicat conteur, et l'on admirera son art de rendre
présents les moindres faits et gestes de chacun et la
pyschologie fouillée des personnages.*'
                        Guillevic – *Le Monde*
'*Le style simple et limpide porte la marque d'un rite
qui se déroule en mineur et qui respire en des silences
de sonate . . . Le livre se situe dans l'oralité. Aussi les
phrases s'articulent sur la ligne sinueuse, l'inflexion de
la voix du conteur, à la veillée.*
            Jean F. Brierre – *Afrique Nouvelle*

See also Folklore & Oral Tradition

Diakité, Yoro
Une main amie
Bamako: Ed. Populaires du Mali, 1969.
325 pp. FM1200
The tale of a waitress, a young Frenchwoman,
and her marriage and move to Africa. The
author was at one time President of the
provisional government in Mali.

Diarra, Mandé-Alpha
Sahel! sanglante secheresse
Paris: Présence Africaine, 1981. 176 pp.
FF39.00
A village in Mali is dying from drought and
corrupt officials get rich from the relief
supplies. Boua, an educated young man,
returns to his village only to discover the
extent of his people's misery and the role
played by authorities. With the help of his
uncle and other educated young people he
organizes a revolt. The author's first novel.

Diawara, Gaoussou
L'aube des béliers
Paris: Radio-France Internationale, 1975
(Répertoire théâtral africain, 25) (distr. by
Nouvelles Editions Africaines, Dakar). 78 pp.
CFA300
In the land of the Bazozos, somewhere in
Africa, the sheep, the eternal sacrifical victims,
revolt against man. An allegorical play.

Gologo, Mamadou
Le rescapé de l'Ethylos
Paris: Présence Africaine, 1963. 278 pp. o/p
A novel written in 1952 and not published
until ten years later which would seem to be
autobiographical. It tells the story of M.G.B.,
an 'African doctor' in French Sudan who
becomes an alcoholic and who later recovers,
thanks to his mother and to a famous
marabout.

Kaba, Alkaly
*Nègres, qu'avez-vous fait? Tragédie en trois
actes*
Bamako: Ed. Populaires du Mali, 1972. 72 pp.
FM770
A tragedy in three acts evoking the social and
political problems of the black people. Set first
in the United States, then in Guinea-Bissau,
and finally in the Republic of Guinea.

Kaba, Diama and Alkaly
Les hommes du Bakchich
Paris: O.R.T.F.-D.A.E.C., 1973 (Répertoire
théâtral africain, 16) (distr. by Nouvelles
Editions Africaines, Dakar). 154 pp. CFA300
The 1971 prize-winning play in the annual
theatre competition organized by the French
broadcasting corporation, this work is a
symbolic representation in six acts of African
history from conquest and colonization to the
post-independence era. The principal characters, all women, are Africa of the Past, Africa
Yesterday, Africa Today and Europe. Asia,
America, and Oceania appear in the final two
acts.

Kaba, Alkaly
Mourir pour vivre: tragédie
Paris: Ed. Saint Germain-des-Prés, 1976.
85 pp. FF9.50
Produced by the French broadcasting corporation in 1972, with considerable success, this
play concerns a traditional African monarch
awaiting ritual death. The kings of the
Somonobozos are strangled every seven years
and now it is Kalaï's turn. His Queen revolts
against the custom and manages to convince
the King, but the people are scandalized.

Amour et haine: poèmes 1959-1971
Paris: Ed. Saint Germain-Des-Prés, 1976.
45 pp. FF9.50
Poetry.

Walanda: la leçon
Paris: Ed. Saint Germain-des-Prés, 1976.
96 pp. FF8.50
A humble fisherman and a wealthy man try to
win the heart of the same woman, the 'Queen
of Bara', a dancer. The novel was made into a
film in Mali by the author himself.

Konaké, Sory
Le grand destin de Soundjata
Paris: O.R.T.F.-D.A.E.C., 1973 (Répertoire
théâtral africain, 17) (distr. by Nouvelles
Editions Africaines, Dakar). 89 pp. CFA300
A historical play which won the listeners' prize
in the 1971 African Theatre Competition
sponsored by Radio France. It is based on the
life of Sunjata, the thirteenth century founder
of the Manding empire.

Konaté, Moussa
Le prix de l'âme
Paris: Présence Africaine, 1981. 153 pp.
FF37.00
A novel set against the drought years in Mali.
A young man and his sister leave the village for
the city to improve their living. He fails and
she succeeds – but only by becoming a
prostitute. Back home their village is dying but
officials continue to make the people pay 'the
price of the soul'. Konaté's first novel.

Koné, Amadou
Les frasques d'Ebinto
Paris: Hatier, 1980 (Monde noir poche, 3).
128 pp. FF16.00
A new co-edition of the novel originally
published in 1975 by La Pensée Universelle. It
is the dramatic account of the sexual awakening of Ebinto, an African adolescent who is
torn between the past, represented by
Monique, and the future, represented by
Muriel.

De la chaire au trône
Paris: Radio-France Internationale, 1975
(Répertoire théâtral africain, 24) (distr. by
Nouvelles Editions Africaines, Dakar). 64 pp.
CFA300
A university professor agrees to become the
monarch of an African kingdom even if it
means dying after twelve years, as custom
dictates. He has hopes that in that period he
will be able to use his wealth and power to
initiate reforms. The fatal day arrives when his
reign must come to an end, and not even the
most enlightened ruler dares transgress custom. This play won a prize in the 1972 African
Theatre Competition sponsored by Radio-
France Internationale.

Jusqu'au seuil de l'iréel: chroniques
Dakar: Nouvelles Editions Africaines, 1976.
144 pp. CFA850
Black magic pursues Karfa, the Dioula, with its
tragic consequences. Despite conversion to
Islam and flight to a new region with his son
Lamine, Karfa cannot seem to escape his
destiny. When Lamine dies mysteriously along
with his beloved Tie'nic, the chief's daughter,
Karfa, enlists the help of her father to have
done once and for all with witches and their
horrible craft. A novel set against the background of French efforts after World War I to
impose groundnut farming as a cash crop in
Upper Volta.

Le respect des morts
Paris: Hatier, 1980 (Monde noir poche, 5).
125 pp. FF16.10
The title play in this volume of two was a
runner-up in the 1974 Interafrican Theatre
Competition organized by Radio-France Internationale. In it the inhabitants of a small
village learn that a dam to be built nearby will
flood their homes. The ancestors demand a
human sacrifice, a child, to stop the construction and the chief's son, an educated man, has
no choice but to offer his own son. This he
does, even while teaching his people a lesson
on the meaning of tradition and progress.

Les liens
Abidjan: C.E.D.A., 1980. 80 pp. CFA990

Sous le pouvoir des Blakoros I: Traites
Abidjan: Nouvelles Editions Africaines, 1980.
96 pp. CFA950
Poor farmers, like old Mamadou, the coffee
grower from northern Ivory Coast, have no
choice but to submit to the power of the
'Blakoros'. The word comes from Bambara
and means 'the uncircumcized, the un-
initiated,' and refers to all those who have
prospered since independence. In the village
that means people like El Hadj, the chief, who
deliberately let the Cooperative die when
hardly born, and like Akafu who has grown fat
lending money. As for town dwellers, they all
want their 'cut', from Habib, the merchant
who buys up the coffee crop, to the school
principal who enrolls pupils, for a fee, and
finally to the hospital attendant who lets
Mamadou's little son, Issa, die for lack of
money to buy medicine. But Mamadou has
one source of hope – a grown son, Lassinan,

who has been to school and who is determined
to make things change.

Ouane, Ibrahima Mamadou
L'énigme du Macina
Monte-Carlo: Ed. Regain, 1952. 192 pp. o/p
A novel.

Fadimâtâ, la princesse du désert suivi de
Drame de Déguembéré
Avignon: Les Presses Universelles, 1955.
109 pp. o/p

Lettres d'un Africain
Monte-Carlo: Ed. Regain, 1955. 61 pp. o/p

Le collier de coquillages
Andrézieux, France: Impr. Moderne, 1958.
72 pp. o/p
Poetry.

Pérégrinations soudanaises
Lyon: Ed. du Capricorne et du Lion, 1960.
192 pp. o/p
Poetry.

Les filles de la reine Cléopâtre
Paris: Millas-Martin, 1961. 191 pp o/p
Poetry.

Ouologuem, Yambo
Le devoir de violence
Paris: Seuil, 1968. 208 pp. o/p
Ouologuem, the first African writer to receive
a major French literary award, won the Prix
Renaudot 1968 for this first novel. In English
translation, see next entry.

Bound to Violence
(Trans. from the French by Ralph Manheim)
New York: Harcourt, Brace, Jovanovich, 1971
London: Secker and Warburg, 1971. o/p
London: HEB, 1972 (AWS, 99). 182 pp.
£1.95/$4.00
The English translation of Ouologuem's novel
first appeared in 1971 in London in a Secker
and Warburg edition and has since been reissued in paperback in the African Writers
Series. The novel is a kind of epic of a fictitious
Sudanese empire. The author's main thesis is
that the black man has been created and
formed by violence, and that three forces in his
history are largely responsible for the black
man's 'slave' mentality and character: first, the
African emperors and notables; then the
Arabs; and lastly, since the mid-nineteenth
century, the European colonial administrators.
'. . . the young Malian Yambo Ouologuem in his
fascinating first novel . . . presents the white colonialist as a mere pawn of the native poten-

tate . . . Yambo Ouologuem has succeeded in blending the legendary and the real without over lapsing
into pomposity or sentimentality.'
Hena Maes-Jelinek – *African Literature Today*

Lettre à la France nègre
Paris: Edmond Nalis, 1969. 220 pp. o/p
Contains 'Lettre au Président de la République
Française', 'Lettre aux couples mixtes', 'Lettre
à tous ceux qui fréquentent les Nègres', 'Lettre
aux femmes nègrement seules', 'Lettre à tous
les racistes', and several others.
'. . . the essays are primarily addressed to Europeans,
especially bogus liberals and paternalists, and probe
in particular the seamy side of the noble sentiments
sometimes expressed in France about Africa. I am told
even to a French reader he is sometimes obscure and
convoluted, but the brilliance of his style, his verbal
acrobatics and brazen handling of language illuminates the occasional profundities.'
K. W. – *West Africa*

Rodolph, Utto [pseud. for Ouologuem, Yambo]
Les mille et une bibles du sexe
Paris: Ed. du Dauphin, 1969. 368 pp.

Sangaré, Yadji
Naïssa
Bamako: Ed. Populaires du Mali, 1972. 91 pp.
MF685
The theme of this novel is the problems arising
over marriage customs in a society in which the
old and the new co-exist.

Sissoko, Fily-Dabo
Crayons et portraits
Mulhouse: Imprimerie Union, 1953. 79 pp.
o/p

Harmakhis: poèmes du terroir africain
Paris: Ed. de la Tour du Guet, 1955. 80 pp.
o/p
Poems from the treasures of 'the soil', inspired
by oral traditions.

La passion de Djimé
Paris: Ed. de la Tour du Guet, 1956. 115 pp.
o/p

La savane rouge
Avignon: Les Presses Universelles, 1962.
141 pp. o/p
Recounts the story of French repression of a
Tuareg uprising during the First World War.

*Poemes de l'Afrique noire; Feux de brousse;
Harmakhis; Fleurs et chardons*
Paris: Debresse, 1963. 171 pp. o/p
A collection of poetry.

Les jeux du destin
Paris: J. Grassin, 1970 (Club J.G., 11). 48 pp.
FF30.00
A posthumous collection of verse. The author, a political prisoner, was executed in 1964.

Au-dessus des nuages: de Madagascar au Kenya
Paris: J. Grassin, 1970. 120 pp. o/p
A second posthumous collection.

Traoré, Issa Baba
Koumi-Diossé, un héros: plutôt mort que la honte
Bamako: Ed. Populaires du Mali, 1962. 64 pp.
MF615
Subtitled 'A Hero: Better Dead than a Life of Shame.'

Ombre du passé
Bamako: Éditions Populaires, 1972. 152 pp.
FM695
A novel.

Quand la drogue s'en mêle
Bamako: Editions Populaires, 1974. 20 pp.
A short story: *Drugs Complicate Matters.*

Traoré, Seydou
Vingt-cinq ans d'escaliers ou La vie d'un planton
Dakar: Nouvelles Editions Africaines, 1975.
144 pp. CFA1100
The autobiographical account of a man who spent twenty-five years of his life as houseboy, butler, and office messenger in the service of the colonialist. His style recalls in many ways that of the Nigerian, Amos Tutuola.

Mauritania

Ba, Oumar
Poèmes peul modernes
Nouakchott: Imp. Mauritanienne, 1965.
47 pp.
Modern Fulani poetry, translated into French by the author that was first published in Pierre F. Lacroix, 'Dix-huit poèmes peul modernes' in *Cahiers d'Etudes Africaines*, II, 8, 1962.

Dialogue d'une rive à l'autre: poèmes
Saint Louis, Senegal: I.F.A.N., 1966. 23 pp.
A collection of verse dedicated to the Fulani peoples living on the Senegalese and Mauritanian sides of the Senegal River.

Presque griffonnages ou la francophonie
Saint-Louis, Senegal: I.F.A.N., 1966. 136 pp.

A poetic evocation of the themes that Ba wrote about in a pamphlet entitled 'Should We Keep the French Language' published that same year by the Institut Fondamental d'Afrique Noire in Saint-Louis.

Témoin à charge et à décharge: poème
Dakar: Imp. Saint-Paul, n.d. 98 pp.

Paroles plaisantes au coeur et à l'oreille
Paris: La Pensée Universelle, 1977. 63 pp.
FF19.30
Another collection of verse.

Odes sahéliennes
Paris: La Pensée Universelle, 1978. 160 pp.
FF30.00
The latest collection of poetry by a dedicated scholar of the Fulani of the Fouta-Foro who has recently translated the Koran into Fulani for Nouvelles Editions Africaines.

Diallo, Assane Y.
Leyd'am: poèmes
Honfleur, France: P. J. Oswald, 1967. 46 pp.
o/p
The title poem, dedicated to the poet's uncle, expresses a yearning for a simple life without the burden of a borrowed culture. In another poem, 'Blues', he sings about Afro-Americans and in yet another he calls to the Atlantic Ocean to calm the hatred and hostility in Africa.

Guèye, Youssouf
Sahéliennes
Dakar: Nouvelles Editions Africaines, 1975.
24 pp. o/p
Poetry.

Les exilés de Goumel: drame historique
Dakar: Nouvelles Editions Africaines, 1975.
59 pp. CFA600
A historical play set in the early sixteenth century. Boukar Siré, pious Muslim ruler of the Foûta in Senegal, has been chased from his throne by his brother, a pagan, thanks to the meddling of the French colonial company. But he will eventually recover his throne and his brother will convert to Islam – and a treaty will be signed with the French abolishing the slave trade at N'Dar (Saint Louis).

A l'orée du Sahel
Dakar: Nouvelles Editions Africaines, 1975.
127 pp. CFA600
Two short stories, one set in colonial times and the other in the present-day, dominated by the desert landscape of Mauritania. In the first one, Sall, a nurse, wanders in the desert like a

lost soul. He had left his station to look for food for his family and is caught by the head doctor, a Frenchman. In his rush back, his water bag empties. In the second story a lake mysteriously appears, disappears and appears again to the confusion of the civil authorities who consult religious leaders.

'*Youssouf Guèye a manifestement du talent; il sait raconter, rendre l'atmosphère, bref, il nous fait croire à ces deux nouvelles fort bien enlevées.*'

Afrique Contemporaine

Sall, Djibril
Cimetière Rectiligne
Nouakchott: Société Nationale de Presse et d'Edition, n.d. [1977] 31 pp.
A collection of verse of a young Mauritanian Police Commissioner. The title poem evokes the servitude and misery of black people everywhere.

Les yeux nus
Dakar: Nouvelles Editions Africaines, 1978. 31 pp. CFA350
Poetry.

Niger

Diado, Amadou
Maïmou ou le drame de l'amour: roman suivi de poèmes
Niamey: Impr. Générale du Niger, 1972. 88 pp
A novel about the problems of bride price and marriage which was first published in serial form in *Le Niger* in 1972. It is followed by poems.

Hama, Boubou
Kotia-Nima
Paris: Présence Africaine, 1968 and 1969
vol 1: *Rencontre avec l'Europe,* 168 pp. o/p
vol 2: *Rencontre avec l'Europe,* 192 pp. FF35.00
vol 3: *Dialogue avec l'Occident,* 280 pp. FF37.00

This is Boubou Hama's autobiography which won the 1970 Grand Prix Littéraire de l'Afrique Noire. Only volume 1, which relates how the young Fulani boy from the village of Dori grew up to become a 'black-white' man whose job was to explain Europe to Africans, is strictly speaking autobiographical. Volumes 2 and 3 are more books of essays as Kotia-Nima, Hama's childhood name, lives through the anti-colonialist struggle and finally independence with its political and economic problems.

L'aventure extraordinaire de Bi Kado, fils de Noir
Paris: Présence Africaine, 1971. 630 pp. o/p
An extended version of *L'aventure d'Albarka,* see next entry.

Hama, Boubou and Clair, Andrée
L'aventure d'Albarka
Paris: Juillard, 1972. 247 pp. o/p
The adventures of Albarka, a little boy from Niger, which take him from his village to the European school in Tera, then on to Dori, Gao, Ouagadougou and finally Dakar and Niamey. It is at the same time a book of legends, proverbs and stories of witchcraft as well as a criticism of colonization especially as perceived through its educational system. Albarka is, in reality, Boubou Hama, himself.

Hama, Boubou
Cet 'autre' de l'homme
Paris: Présence Africaine, 1972. 215 pp. FF36.00
An account of growing up in the Songhay village of Fonéko in Niger through the imaginary dialogue of a sixty-year-old man and two-year-old child that he once was. Also contains a 35-page section of Songhay legends and tales.

Le double d'hier rencontre demain
Paris: Union Générale d'Editions, 1973 (Coll. 10/18, 784). 445 pp. o/p
The old African who guides the child on a journey of mystery and enchantment through the realm of the spirits before setting him off with an Atakourma, a dwarf, to complete his learning in the realm of men, is none other than Bi ('Yesterday'), and the child is Souba ('Tomorrow'). As for the dwarf, it is Bi Bio, Bi's 'Shadow' or his Other Self from the spirit world. The journey, itself, is a lesson in the eternal truths of the world that the black people of Africa still harbour in the peace and calm of their souls.

Hon si suba ben: aujourd'hui n'épuise pas demain
Paris: P. J. Oswald, 1973 (Poésie/prose africaine, 4) (distr. by L'Harmattan, Paris). 153 pp. FF26.00
A sequel to *Le double d'hier rencontre demain.*

Bagouma et Tiégouma 2 vols
Paris: Présence Africaine, 1973. 285 pp. and 216 pp.
These two volumes have not yet been released since their printing in 1973.

Issa, Ibrahim

Grandes eaux noires
Paris: Ed. du Scorpion, 1959. 125 pp. o/p
A novel.

La vie et ses facéties: poèmes
Niamey: Imp. Nationale du Niger, 1979.
117 pp.
Poetry. Two other unpublished works,
Clameurs d'antan et soleil présents and *Les boutures du soleil* received the 1978 prize for literature of the French Agency for Cultural and Technical Cooperation.

Mamani, Abdoulaye

Poèmerides
Honfleur: P. J. Oswald, 1972 (distr. by L'Harmattan, Paris). 51 pp. FF11.00
Poetry about friendship, love, liberty, exile, but also about taboos in Africa and the overly fastidious Western culture.

Sarraounia: le drame de la reine magicienne
Paris: Harmattan, 1980 (Encres noires, 4).
160 pp. FF38.00
A novel.

Oumarou, Idé

Gros plan
Dakar: Nouvelles Editions Africaines, 1977.
160 pp. CFA550
Oumarou's novel, which won the 1978 Grand Prix Littéraire de l'Afrique Noire, is a 'close up' of Niger in the first years of independence as narrated by Tahirou, an early Party militant and driver for the head of a large business concern in Niamey. The world of privilege, power and hypocrisy which Tahirou observes daily in his job contrasts sharply with his own miserable existence.

15 ans, ça suffit
Niamey: Impr. Nationale du Niger, 1977.
163 pp.
Set against the backdrop of the drought in the Sahel, this novel relates how Sidi Balima, the owner of a firm of lorries, comes to be accused of selling for his profit the relief goods he is supposed to deliver into the interior. His own son, back from legal studies in France, undertakes to defend him in court. Prefaced by Idé Oumarou.

Outman, Mahamat

Les sahels
Paris: P. J. Oswald, 1972 (distr. by L'Harmattan, Paris). 29 pp. FF13.00
A collection of verse.

Salifou, André

Tanimoune: Drame historique en 7 actes
Paris: Présence Africaine, 1973. 122 pp.
FF24.00
The author, a historian, based this play on real events in central Sudan in the nineteenth century. It relates the struggle of Tanimoune, the sultan of Damagaram (region of Zinder) to unite his people and free them from their feudal links to the throne of Bornou. In his preface Salifou talks about the importance of theatre as an instrument of education in Africa where people are still largely illiterate.

Zoume, Boubé

Les souffles du coeur
Yaoundé: C.L.E., 1977. 64 pp. CFA700
The first verse collection of a young poet.

Nigeria
(writing in French, see also English-speaking Africa)

Balogun, Ola

Shango suivi de *Le roi-éléphant*
Paris: P. J. Oswald, 1968 (Théâtre africain, 4)
(distr. by L'Harmattan, Paris). 90 pp. FF18.00
These two short three-act plays are among the few books in French to have so far come from Nigeria. *Shango* is a historical play based on a Yoruba myth; and *Le roi-éléphant* takes place in the animal world, with an elephant and a cock confronting each other.

Biakolo, Anthony O.

L'étonnante enfance d'Inotan
Paris: L'Harmattan, 1981 (Encres noires, 7).
183 pp. FF41.00
A novel in which the beliefs and conceptions of the Urhobo people of the Niger delta play a major role.

Senegal

Anta Ka, Abdou

Théâtre
Paris: Présence Africaine, 1972. 203 pp.
FF31.00
Contains four plays: *La fille des dieux* (an adaption of Sidiki Dembelé's *Le Chant de Madhi*); *Les Amazoulous* (the story of Chaka); *Pinthioum Fann* (set in Dakar's psychiatric hospital); and *Gouverneur de la rosée* (an adaptation of the novel by the Haïtian, Jacques Roumain).

Mal: nouvelles
Dakar: Nouvelles Editions Africaines, 1975.
30 pp. CFA450
The heros of these four short stories are the
educated 'misfits' of big African cities: an
alcoholic writer about to start another useless
day in his room in the psychiatric ward of a
Dakar hospital; a poverty-stricken writer,
awaiting his destiny on a railroad platform; a
wealthy businessman tired of being a token
black; and a successful lawyer married to a
Frenchwoman who learns a lesson from his
long-lost brother, a poor peasant.

Bâ, Mariama

Une si longue lettre
Dakar: Nouvelles Editions Africaines, 1979.
131 pp. CFA1,200
Winner of the 1980 Noma Award for Publishing in Africa this book is Mariama Bâ's first
published novel. Written in epistolary form, it
deals with the themes of polygamy and the
problems of social inequality faced by women
in present-day Africa. After thirty years of
marriage, the last ten of which she has been
separated from her husband who has moved in
with   a   much   younger   second   wife,
Ramatoulaye, the heroine, finds herself a
widow. The suffering she has gone through
over the past few years and now goes through
in mourning prompts her to take up her pen
and pour out her misery to her friend,
Aïssatou. The lives of both women are
strikingly similar. Both are well-educated,
both married for love to men who became
prominent citizens of Dakar, and both were
eventually deserted by their husbands. Aïssatou, however, preferred divorce, making a
new life for herself as an interpreter at the
Senegalese Embassy in New York, whereas
Ramatoulaye tried bravely to go on living as
before. She remained in the same home with
her twelve children and continued to teach in
the same primary school but with severely
limited financial means since her husband now
spent all he earned and more to maintain his
second   wife   in   luxury.   How   could
Ramatoulaye have known when she married
what a wretched destiny awaited her? In
English *translation*, see next entry.

*'It is not often that a first novel gives the impression
of an achieved thing as this one . . . It is not only the
fact that this is the most deeply felt presentation of the
female condition in African fiction which gives
distinction to this novel, but also its undoubted
literary qualities, which seem to place it among the
best novels that have come out of our continent.'*
                              Abiola Irele – *West Africa*
*'La polygamie, les dépenses somptuaires lors des
cérémonies, la situation faite à la femme africaine, les*

*problèmes de l'éducation sexuelle des jeunes, les
préjugés de castes . . . rien n'échappe à la sagacité de
Mariama Bâ qui fustige sans pitié dans une langue
riche, belle, gonflée d'images et de vie.'*
                         Moudjib Djibril – *Afrique Nouvelle*

So Long a Letter
(Trans. from the French by Modupé Bodé-
Thomas)
London: HEB, 1981 (AWS, 247). 96 pp. £1.95
p/b
London: Virago Press, 1982. 96 pp. £5.50
cased; £2.50 p/b. U.K., Australia, N.Z. only
Ibadan: New Horn Press, 1981. ₦3.00 p/b
The English translation of Mariama Bâ's prize-
winning book published jointly by Heinemann
and Nigeria's New Horn Press, with a cased
edition produced by Britain's leading feminist
publisher Virago Press. Mariama Bâ's novel,
winner of the 1980 Noma Award for Publishing in Africa, has now been translated into
sixteen languages. (For an outline of the novel
see preceding entry.)

Le chant écarlate
Dakar: Nouvelles Editions Africaines, 1981.
272 pp. CFA1,850
Published after her death in August, 1981,
Mariama Bâ's second novel is the story of a
mixed marriage, that of a French woman and
a Senegalese man, and the problems encountered by the wife in her efforts to adapt to her
husband's culture.

Bâ, Thierno

Bilbassy: drame en six tableaux
Dakar: Nouvelles Editions Africaines, 1980.
83 pp. CFA600
A historical play about a Fulani prince of the
eighteenth century, Samba Gueladio Diegui,
and his struggle to keep the throne of Diôvol
which his uncle was trying to usurp.

Ciss, Jean Gerem

Le cri des anciens
Dakar: Nouvelles Editions Africaines, 1980.
217 pp. CFA1,350
A novel which illustrates, through the example
of a Catholic Serer community near Thies, the
concrete problems confronting today's Senegalese society: the younger educated generation who disdain working in the field and yet
who expect to be fed while home for the school
holiday and the still unresolved conflict
between customary law and the laws of a
modern state. If the second problem leads to a
tragedy in which the two parties in a land
dispute case, one a Serer and the other a Fulbe,
both die, the first problem is partially solved
when the young people decide to listen to the

'elders' outcry' and resolve to begin studying ancient ways 'while holding on to book knowledge'.

Coly, Adam Loga

Kahoténor
Dakar: Nouvelles Editions Africaines, 1977. 38 pp. CFA350
The poems of a career officer in the Senegalese army from Casamance.

Karambakin
Dakar: Nouvelles Editions Africaines, forthcoming 1981.

Dia, Amadou Cissé

Les derniers jours de Lat Dior: La mort du Damel
Paris: Présence Africaine, 1965 (reprinted 1978). 98 pp. FF24.00
A play about the last Wolof king (or *Damel*) of the region of Cayor in Senegal. He was defeated by the French in 1886.

Dia, Malick

L'Impossible compromis: récit
Dakar: Nouvelles Editions Africaines, 1979. 102 pp. CFA1,000
A first novel, told autobiographically. The 'impossible compromise' that faces Salmone, a Paris-trained doctor, is that between his proud background as a descendent of one of the feudal chiefs of the Baol in Senegal and the world of the *tubaab* (the white man), which some people accuse him of preferring. It is the painful choice between two women he both loves: Monica, the French woman whose interest in African history helped fill the gaps in his education which had been left by the colonial school system, and Fama, the village girl whose grace and beauty remind him of the nobleness of his people.

Diaïté, Moustapha

Cous rompus
Dakar: Nouvelles Editions Africaines, 1978. 64 pp. CFA600
An old peasant cannot possible win out in the confrontation with the government-run peanut cooperative. In a rage because he is told to return two weeks later for payment for the peanut crop he has just sold, Boubacar assaults the director of the cooperative: his son is dying and he needs money to buy medicine. The judges in court care little about attenuating circumstances and he is sent to prison. This play won the 1976 prize of the Senegalese association of authors.

Diakhaté, Lamine

La joie d'un continent
Alès, France: Ed. P.A.B., 1954. o/p
Poetry.

Primordiale du sixième jour
Paris: Présence Africaine, 1963. 61 pp. FF18.00
Poetry.

Temps de mémoire
Paris: Présence Africaine, 1967. 64 pp. o/p
A further volume of poetry, illustrated by Senegalese artist Papa Ibra Tall.

Nigérianes: poèmes
Dakar: Nouvelles Editions Africaines, 1974. 47 pp. CFA350
A collection of verse in honour of Nigerian women written during the author's stay in that country.

Prisonnier du regard: nouvelles
Dakar: Nouvelles Editions Africaines, 1975. 89 pp. CFA550
Contains two short stories. In the title story a Senegalese peasant relives the ordeal of the German war camp where he and his age mates were held captive during World War II. Was this not but a prolongation of their initiation rites? In 'Le Madihou de Pikine', a self-proclaimed Muslim holy man claiming to be the Redeemer, settles in Pikine on the outskirts of Dakar and for a while does good business, indeed.

Chalys d'Harlem
Dakar: Nouvelles Editions Africaines, 1978. 232 pp. CFA1,200 FF31.20
Diakhaté's first novel, which won the 1979 Grand Prix Littéraire d'Afrique Noire, tells the story of a Senegalese man's life in Harlem. In 1919 Amadou Leye, the Chalys of the title, leaves Rufisque for New York with several of his countrymen. The owner of a lunchroom in Harlem which he runs with his wife, Marghret, a black American, and his two daughters, Chalys is an active figure in black self-identity movements, especially pan-africanism, from 1919 to the end of World War II. His return to Senegal after independence, where he meets Omar Fall, the narrator of the tale, is a disappointment. In Harlem he had been known as 'Pater Africa', the authentic African, but in Rufisque he is 'the American' and the 'toubab' (the 'white man').
'*Lamine Diakhaté n'analyse guère, mais expose, décrit et fait voir en jugeant le moins possible . . . son humour au vitriol, la perspicacité de son regard et la férocité de sa raillerie.*'
Olympe Bhêly-Quénum – *Eurafrique*

Diakhaté, Ndèye Coumba Mbenghue
Filles du soleil
Dakar: Nouvelles Editions Africaines, 1981.
42 pp. CFA500
Poetry.

Diallo, Bakary
Force Bonté
Paris: Rieder, 1926. 211 pp. o/p
Considered by some as the first African novel
(the honour has since gone to Togolese author
Félix Couchoro for his novel, *L'Esclave*),
Diallo's book is in reality an autobiographical
account of his life as a soldier in the French
colonial army.

Diallo, Nafissatou
De Tilène au Plateau
Dakar: Nouvelles Editions Africaines, 1976.
128 pp. CFA1,100
The story of the author's childhood and
adolescence and her move from village to city
(the 'Plateau' is Dakar).

Le fort maudit
Paris: Hatier, 1980 (Monde noir poche, 6).
125 pp. FF19.00
Nafissatou Diallo's second book is a historical
novel set in pre-colonial Senegal. The favourite daughter of a high-ranking nobleman in
the kingdom of Cayor, Thiane Sakher Fall sees
her happy existence take on nightmarish
proportions overnight when her village is
invaded by the neighbouring King of the Baol.
But she rises above tragedy to carry out, alone,
a plan of revenge.

Diop, Birago
Leurres et lueurs: poèmes
Paris: Présence Africaine, 1967 (2nd ed.).
87 pp. o/p
An anthology of Diop's verse, presenting
poems written as early as 1925, and as recently
as 1966. The first edition was published by
Présence Africaine in 1960.
'... the style is rhythmical and perfectly in tune with
the climates of expression ... Birago Diop is by
temperament a lyric poet ... an important contribution to contemporary African poetry.'
Guy de Bosschère – *Présence Africaine*

La plume raboutée: mémoires I
Paris: Présence Africaine, 1978. 253 pp.
FF56.00
Dakar: Nouvelles Editions Africaines, 1978.
253 pp. CFA2,450
Part I of Birago Diop's autobiography covers
the period 1906-1945: his upbringing in
Dakar, his studies at the School of Veterinary
Medecine in Toulouse where he met Paule

Pradère who was to become his wife, his years
in the Colonial Service in French Sudan before
the war. It is a book full of names and faces,
including those of his contemporaries, the
illustrious members of the Négritude generation.

L'os de Mor Lam
Dakar: Nouvelles Editions Africaines, 1976.
72 pp. CFA600
This play, which was first performed in Senegal
in 1967-68, is adapted from a tale in Diop's *Les
nouveaux contes d'Amadou Koumba* and is today
in the repertory of Peter Brook's troupe of the
Bouffes du Nord Théâtre in Paris. Mor Lam
refuses to share his supper (the bone) with his
initiation brother who has shown up un-
invited. He pushes his selfishness to feigning
first, sickness, and then death, and even agrees
to be buried – thus losing all, including his
life!
'... an artistic triumph. It will be appreciated as
evidence of the kinship of oral narrative and drama,
as a genuine and endearing reflection of African
culture and, above all, as a work of wit and wisdom.'
Eileen Julien – *World Literature Today*

See also Folklore and Oral Tradition

Diop, David Mandessi
Coups de pilon
Paris: Présence Africaine, 1973 (2nd revised
ed.). 62 pp.
Diop died tragically in an air-crash in
September, 1960. This slim volume of poems
of protest in the Négritude vein, and poems of
love, originally published in 1961, and reissued with eight poems discovered since his
death, would appear to be the definitive
collection of his works, though several of his
earlier poems appeared in the Senghor anthology (see p. 93), and in the journal *Présence
Africaine*. In English *translation*, see next entry.
'... David Diop's poetry ... is difficult to analyse by
reason of its singular poetic compactness and its high
content of poetry. The work is complete in itself and
perfectly impervious. It is like those works of art
whose beauty is beyond question but defies explanation.'   Guy de Bosschère – *Présence Africaine*

Hammer Blows and Other Writings
(Trans. and ed. by Simon Mpondo and Frank
Jones)
Bloomington, Indiana: Indiana Univ. Press,
1973. 88 pp. $5.00
London: HEB [publ. as *Hammer Blows*], 1975
(AWS, 174). 64 pp. £1.95/$4.00
The Bloomington edition contains the original
French of the *Présence Africaine* edition and the
English translation on facing pages in addition

to several of Diop's prose pieces originally published in *Présence Africaine* and followed by a biographical note and a critical essay. The African Writers Series edition contains only the English translation and includes five earlier Diop poems from the pages of *Présence Africaine* which had not been printed in *Coups de pilon* but omits the prose pieces.

Diop, Mamadou Traoré

Mon Dieu est noir
Dakar: Nouvelles Editions Africaines, 1975.
32 pp. o/p
Poetry.

La patrie ou la mort
Dakar: Nouvelles Editions Africaines, forthcoming 1981.

Fall, Bilal

L'intrus
Dakar: Nouvelles Editions Africaines, forthcoming 1981.

Fall, Kine Kirama

Chants de la rivière fraîche
Dakar: Nouvelles Editions Africaines, 1976.
64 pp. CFA350
Poems set in the landscape of northern Senegal evoking the river, the forest and the Lake of Guiers.

Les élans de grâce
Yaoundé: C.L.E., 1979. 48 pp. CFA880
Poetry of a religious inspiration.

Fall, Malick

Reliefs
Paris: Présence Africaine, 1964. 103 pp. o/p
A volume of poems, with an introduction by Léopold Senghor.

La plaie
Dakar: Nouvelles Editions Africaines, 1980
(Club Afrique Loisirs, 5). CFA1,900 cased
A hard-cover, luxury edition for NEA's new book club, 'Club Afrique Loisirs', of the original 1967 volume published by Albin Michel, Paris, and now o/p. In English *translation*, see next entry.

The Wound
(Trans. from the French by Clive Wake)
London: HEB, 1973 (AWS, 144). 160 pp.
£1.50/4.00
The hero was attracted by the illusory opportunities of life in Dakar. But on the way he was badly injured in a lorry crash. The result is a festering sore on his foot which enables him to exist as a beggar. He forges a

new personality as the 'madman' of the market of N'Dar (Saint-Louis). Removed from the market for a time by a stay in prison followed by a stay in hospital, he returns one day with his foot cured: no one recognizes him. The only novel of a Senegalese poet and diplomat who died in July 1978.
'. . . *a dense and complex novel. This is compounded by a brilliant poetic style and a multi-level structure.*
Frederic Michelman – *Books Abroad*
'. . . *oeuvre d'apprentissage, oeuvre charnière au regard de l'évolution du roman africain.*'
Mohamadou Kane – *Le Soleil*

Fall, Sidiki

Les affameurs: une aventure de Scorpion l'Africain
Paris: A.B.C., 1976 (Archives secrètes du B.S.I., 4). 95 pp. FF6.00
A detective novel.

Faye, N. G. M.

Le débrouillard: souvenirs
Paris: Gallimard, 1964. (L'Air du temps, 187).
224 pp. FF16.40
The adventures of a carefree and cunning young boy in Dakar as a porter, cocoa-vendor, photographer, and poster-hanger.

Goundiam, Ousmane

Le procès du pilon: pièce en quatre tableaux
Dakar: Nouvelles Editions Africaines, 1980.
61 pp. CFA600
The trial of Malang Draame who uses a magic pestle to identify thieves is, in reality, the trial of modern justice, based on written codes of law, and traditional justice, based on the occult sciences. It ends, however, on an inconclusive note. The author of this play is Prosecutor in the Supreme Court of Senegal.

Haïdar, Nabil Ali

Silence cimetière!
Dakar: Nouvelles Editions Africaines, 1979.
65 pp. CFA700
Tales of horror and of the fantastic, by an admirer of Edgar Allan Poe.

Ibrahima, Issébéré Hamadoun

Clameurs d'antan et soleils présents
Dakar: Nouvelles Editions Africaines, 1980.
101 pp. CFA700
Poetry.

Irele, Abiola ed.

Selected Poems of Leopold Sédar Senghor
London: CUP, 1977. 134 pp. £10.50 cased
£3.95 p/b
This volume aims to provide a representative sample of Senghor's poetry from his first four

collections. For the English-speaking reader who may have difficulty understanding the poems, which appear in the original French, Irele has supplied an extensive introduction to Senghor and his works as well as notes on the poems themselves.

'*The preface is quite general and serves as a good initiation to African poetry and the concept of Negritude. However, the notes are the most valuable part of the book. Here Irele has, in short concise phrases, clarified references and imagery which might be obscure.*' Eric Sellin – *World Literature Today*

Kane, Cheikh Hamidou
L'aventure ambiguë
Paris: Union Générale d'Editions, 1971 (Coll. 10/18, 617). 192 pp. FF13.00
Dakar: Nouvelles Editions Africaines, 1980 (Club Afrique Loisirs, 2) CFA1,900 cased
The Paris edition is a reissue of the original one published in 1961 by Juillard. The Dakar edition is a luxury volume published for NEA's new book club, 'Club Afrique Loisirs'. In English *translation*, see next entry.

Ambiguous Adventure
(Trans. from the French by Katherine Woods)
New York: Macmillan, 1969. 166 pp.
London: HEB, 1972 (AWS, 119). 192 pp.
£1.95/$4.00
Kane's autobiographical novel was first published in English translation by Walker of New York in 1963. Samba Diallo, the son of a Fulani nobleman living in Paris is caught between his belief in the traditional Islamic faith and the Western European culture and life encountered in his new environment. The original French edition won the Grand Prix Littéraire d'Afrique Noire in 1962. The Macmillan paperback re-issue has an introduction by Wilfred Cartey.
'*. . . In some ways this is the most powerful statement of the complexity of the cultural 'ambiguity' of the French assimilé . . . Diallo faces the most acute of cultural divisions, between his tradition and the new Western imposition of values.*'
John Povey – *African Studies Review*

Kébé, M'Baye Gana
L'Afrique a parlé
Paris: O.R.T.F. D.A.E.C., 1972 (Répertoire théâtral africain, 12) (distr. by Nouvelles Editions Africaines, Dakar). 96 pp. CFA300
Paulin, a European who has been befriended by an African king, is accused of stealing a mask and condemned to death. On hearing the news, the king's daughter, who loves Paulin, commits suicide. African wisdom and justice will finally prevail and Paulin will be

saved. As the play ends the European proclaims a message of peace, friendship and understanding between Africa and Europe. Winner of the Listeners' Prize in the 1970 African Theatre Competition of Radio France.

L'Afrique une
Paris: Radio-France Internationale, 1975 (Répertoire théâtral africain, 22) (distr. by Nouvelles Editions Africaines, Dakar). 111 pp. CFA300
A play set 'somewhere in Africa'. Betrayed by her own sons and threatened by Europe, Africa can only be saved by sacrificing a young virgin. The genie decrees the victim must be Princess Niéli who willingly and bravely agrees. Impressed by her courage the genie grants her life on the condition that Africa unites, forgetting internal struggles, and negotiates with the Red Ears (the white man). The final scene is one of friendship and fraternity between Europe and Africa, once Europe has recognized Africa's great contribution to humanity.

Ebéniques: poèmes
Dakar: Nouvelles Editions Africaines, 1975. 48 pp. CFA350
Poems evoking symbolic figures of Africa, its legendary heroes – Sunjata, Guélâdio, Giêgui, Kaya Magan – and its women.

Kaala Sikkim: nouvelles
Dakar: Nouvelles Editions Africaines, 1976. 64 pp. CFA550
The five portraits in this collection of short stories are all drawn from contemporary Senegalese society. There is the false marabout who gets his comeuppance, and an older man who leaves his wife and six children for a younger woman who wears *Némali*, a potent love perfume, and who lives to regret it. There is also 'Madame Civilization', a village woman married to a civil servant in Dakar who puts on airs. If Kébé satirizes these characters he also writes with sympathy about a peasant who gets a medal and who realizes that a bag of rice and a modern plough would have been a better prize, and the educated young lady who refuses to let her parents pressure her into marrying a bearded old millionaire.

Guirlande
Paris: Ed. Saint-Germain-des-Prés, 1978. o/p
Poetry.

Le blanc du nègre
Dakar: Nouvelles Editions Africaines, 1980 (Club Afrique Loisirs, 9). CFA1,900 cased.

Mahamadou, Halilou Sabbo

Abboki
Dakar: Nouvelles Editions Africaines, 1978.
57 pp. CFA500
The disastrous adventures of a young man from the inland who comes to the big city on the coast.

M'Bengue, Mamadou Seyni

Le procès de Lat Dior
Paris: O.R.T.F.-D.A.E.C., 1972 (Répertoire théâtral africain, 14) (distr. by Nouvelles Editions Africaines, Dakar). 154 pp. CFA300
Lat Dior, the last 'Damel', or ruler, of Cayor fiercely resisted French penetration in Senegal in the nineteenth century. In this play, which was a runner-up in the 1970 Interafrican Theatre Competition, M'Bengue brings back the African sovereign to be judged before the 'Court of Posterity'. He will be declared a hero and martyr of national independence.

Le Royaume de sable
Dakar: Nouvelles Editions Africaines, 1976.
240 pp. CFA950
A historical novel set in nineteenth century Senegal. Madior Fall, prince of Cayor resists colonialization, represented by a perfidious French colonial officer who is mentally unbalanced. But there is also the loyal, tolerant captain who gradually succeeds in gaining the confidence of the people of Cayor. Having joined the French army Madior Fall dies in battle during World War I.

Morisseau-Leroy, Félix

Kasamansa
Dakar: Nouvelles Editions Africaines, 1977.
40 pp. CFA350
A collection of verse of a poet with a political and social conscience.

Ndao, Cheik Aliou

L'exil d'Albouri suivi de *La décision*
Paris: P. J. Oswald, 1967 (Théâtre africain, 1) (distr. by L'Harmattan, Paris). 134 pp. FF23.00
Two plays: the first one, a historical play that won first prize at the 1969 Festival of Algiers, is set in the middle ages in what is now called Senegal. *La décision* is set in the American South. Bakari Traoré has contributed a foreword.

Mogariennes
Paris: Présence Africaine, 1970. 54 pp. o/p
Poems to the women in Ndao's life – African and European – and to the cities in his life – those of Mali and of France. But there are also poems of a more pointed political message like 'Hello Joe', about America of the almighty dollar and ever-ready troops. One poem, 'Nkrumah's Voice', is in English.
'Langue et images neuves et pures contribuent à faire naître des poèmes les plus beaux . . . Avec Les Mogariennes *[Ndao] est parmi les plus grands poètes de la littérature africaine.'*
Jean F. Brierre – *Afrique Littéraire* et *Artistique*

Buur Tileen: roi de la Médina: roman
Paris: Présence africaine, 1972. 110 pp.
FF19.00
Set in the slums of Dakar, this novel is the tragic tale of Raki who dies giving birth to an illegitimate child after having been repudiated for her 'sins' by her outraged father. He had refused to let her marry the child's father who is none other than the son of his best friend.
'L'auteur . . . a composé une toute simple chanson, douce et amère comme la vie.'
Guy Kouassi – *Fraternité Matin*

Le fils de l'Almamy suive de *La case de l'homme*
Paris: P. J. Oswald, 1973 (Théâtre africain, 20) (distr. by L'Harmattan, Paris). 77 pp. FF16.00
A play about the son of Samory Touré, the nineteenth century Manding ruler, who was said to have betrayed his father to the European invaders. A dramatic poem set in a men's initiation hut follows.
'The main themes . . . and the moments of high poetry are reminiscent, in a less developed way, of Ndao's wildly acclaimed first-published play. This perplexing fact becomes understandable, however, when one learns that the plays in the later volume were written first. The promise that is apparent here was to be fulfilled in L'exil d'Albouri.'
Frederic Michelman – *Books Abroad*

L'Ile de Bahila: drame en 5 actes
Paris: Présence Africaine, 1975. 66 pp.
FF20.00
A play set on an island-state with its dictator, its military chief, its police force, its intellectuals and its rebel forces.

Le Marabout de la secheresse: nouvelles
Dakar: Nouvelles Editions Africaines, 1979.
69 pp. CFA700
Ndao's first collection of short stories offers a series of portraits drawn from life in contemporary Senegal. The heros of three are students in France. One has to confess to his French girlfriend that his wife is arriving and another is a pious Muslim who is shocked by French mores. In the title piece there is a fake holy man, a harmless-enough fellow, who has stumbled upon his 'calling' as a result of the drought. In the others there is a young widow, newly arrived from the country, who takes up

prostitution to earn a living for herself and her son; a recent city dweller who loses his meagre savings when the government levels the shanty-town in which he had been living; and a villager, a man of uncertain origins, who meets death along with all the members of his family, when he knowingly violates a Muslim custom.

Ndiaye, Mamadou

Le sceau du sang
Paris: La Pensée Universelle, 1980. 160 pp. FF30.00
A novel.

Assok ou les derniers jours de Koumbi
Dakar: Nouvelles Editions Africaines, 1973. 181 pp. CFA950
The love story of Assoka and Tounka, two young Songhay people, set against the back-ground of the last days of the ancient empire of Ghana whose capital, Koumbi, fell to the hands of Sunjata, the Manding ruler, around 1240. A historical novel.

Ndiaye, Papa Guèye

Ethiopiques: poèmes de Léopold Sédar Senghor. Edition critique et commentée
Dakar: Nouvelles Editions Africaines, 1974. 113 pp. CFA800
An extensively annotated edition of Senghor's *Ethiopiques* for classroom use. Each poem is preceded by a page of presentation.

Ndiaye, Sada Weïndé

Le retour de l'aïeul
Dakar: Impricap, 1972. 74 pp. o/p
A collection of short stories and poems.

La fille des eaux
Dakar: Nouvelles Editions Africaines, 1975. 64 pp. CFA550
These short stories set in the drought-stricken Sahel, in a fishing village, and in a hospital ward won second prize in the short story competition organized by Radio France Inter-nationale.

L'épée et la fleur
Dakar: Nouvelles Editions Africaines, 1978. 32 pp. CFA350
Poetry.

Ndong, Assane

La trahison
Dakar: Nouvelles Editions Africaines, 1977. 40 pp. CFA550
A humorous account of the daily life of Senegalese villagers written by a former school principal.

Niang, Lamine

Négristique
Paris: Présence Africaine, 1968. 86 pp. o/p
A personal philosophy of Négritude is ex-pressed in this volume of verse, which is prefaced by Léopold Senghor.

Ousmane, Sembène

L'Harmattan
Paris: Présence Africaine, 1964. (Reprinted 1980). 312 pp. FF20.00
A re-issue of the original 1964 novel which was the first volume of an envisaged trilogy on contemporary Africa. Its theme is the national referendum of 2 September 1965. The vote asked for a 'oui' or 'non' for De Gaulle's French Community, the 'yes' meaning the continued presence of the colonial ad-ministrators, the 'no' deciding for total independence.

Le docker noir
Paris: Nouvelles Ed. Debresse, 1956. 223 pp. o/p
Paris: Présence Africaine, 1973. 219 pp.
In the early 1950s Sembène Ousmane found employment as a docker in the Marseille harbour. An accident there forced him to leave work for several months, during which time he put down on paper his personal experiences as a docker, resulting in this, his first (auto-biographical) novel.

O pays, mon beau peuple
Paris: Amiot-Dumont, 1957. 236 pp. o/p
Paris: Presses Pocket, 1975 (Presses pocket, 1217). 187 pp. FF8.50
A paperback re-issue of Ousmane's second novel originally published in 1957. After serving in the French army the hero, Faye, returns home to Senegal, accompanied by a French wife. Difficulties ensue as Faye's community objects to the white woman and to his newly acquired progressive ideas, such as his model farm. When Faye is ultimately killed by African mercenaries hired by the white men, he is seen as a hero.
'. . . there is much in it that is worth our attention.'
Ulli Beier – *Black Orpheus*

Les bouts de bois de Dieu: Banty Mam Yall
Paris: Le Livre Contemporain, 1960. 383 pp. o/p
Paris: Presses Pocket, 1971 (Presses pocket, 871). 383 pp. FF10.50
A paperback re-issue of the original 1960 edition. In English *translation*, see next entry.

God's Bits of Wood
Trans. from the French by Francis Price)

New York: Doubleday, 1962. 333 pp. o/p
London: HEB, 1969 (AWS, 63). 288 pp. £1.75
New York: Doubleday/Anchor, 1971. 288 pp.
$3.95
Doubleday first brought out an English translation of *Les bouts de bois de Dieu* in 1962 and it is currently available in these two paperback editions. The novel is set against the background of the strike on the Dakar-Niger railway from October 1947 to March 1948 and follows the struggles of the strikers in Dakar, Thiès and Bamako by concentrating on the hardships encountered by individual families in these three towns.
'*Falling in the middle of Sembène's literary canon, before he turned to film-making, it is in some ways his most outstanding, and certainly most ambitious work of fiction . . . Most of the characters are triumphantly real.*' K. W. – *West Africa*

Voltaïques. La noire de . . . nouvelles
Paris: Présence Africaine, 1971 (2nd ed.).
221 pp. FF15.00
A collection of short stories that Présence Africaine first brought out in 1962. In English *translation*, see next entry.

Tribal Scars and Other Stories
(Trans. from the French by Len Ortzen)
London: HEB, 1973 (AWS, 142). 128 pp. o/p
Washington D.C.: Inscape Corp., 1974.
116 pp. $12.50
Most of the stories in this collection of thirteen are concerned with the social and political problems of contemporary Africa and many deal with women, such as the well-known 'La Noire de . . .' about an African maid in France who commits suicide which Ousmane has made into a film, 'Lettres de France' about a young African woman married to an immigrant worker – an old man – living in Marseille, and 'Ses trois jours' about a wife in a polygamous household who waits in vain for her husband's promised visit. But there is also the portrait of a trade-unionist turned parliamentarian who has betrayed the cause of workers and that of an African born in Algeria who is arrested as a 'revolutionary' during the Algerian war. The title story, however, is a sort of latter-day legend on how Africans got their tribal scars – originally self-inflicted wounds as a means of dicouraging slave hunters who only took unmarred 'merchandise'.

'. . . *this collection presents an artistic reality of the author's private world. His cynicism, bitterness and humor, though slightly stilted by the translation, place Ousmane – the modern* griot – *among the best* conteurs *of modern Africa . . . will hopefully open to*

Ousmane *a wide new world of readers which he definitely merits.*'
Victor Carrabino – *Books Abroad*

Le Mandat et Véhi Ciosane
Paris: Présence Africaine, 1969 (2nd ed.).
192 pp. FF15.00
Présence Africaine first published these two short stories in 1965 under the title *Véhi Ciosane ou blanche genése suivi du Mandat*. In English *translation*, see next entry.

The Money Order with White Genesis
(Trans. from the French by Clive Wake)
London: HEB, 1971 (AWS, 92). 160 pp.
£1.50/$4.00
In *White Genesis*, the first story in this collection, a Senegalese girl is with child and the inhabitants of her village try to guess who the author of the foul deed is, hardly thinking the girl's own father could be the culprit. In *The Money Order* an illiterate city-dweller has received a money order from his nephew in France but his happiness is short-lived as he runs into problems first, to cash it, and second, to keep the news away from his creditors. The original French edition was awarded the literature prize at the first Festival of Negro Arts in Dakar in 1966 and *The Money Order* has been adapted for the screen by Ousmane and was presented for the first time at the 1968 Venice Film Festival.
'*Sembène's writing is strong and clean, and he shows where Wolof's words can be introduced into another text with advantage (there is a good glossary).*'
K. W. – *West Africa*
'. . . [*shows*] *how deep Ousmane's imagination can delve into the lives of people, how close he is to them.*'
A. U. Ohagbu – *Présence Africaine*

Xala: roman
Paris: Présence Africaine, 1973. 171 pp.
FF38.00
In English *translation*, see next entry.

Xala
(Trans. from the French by Clive Wake)
London: HEB, 1976 (AWS, 175). 128 pp.
£1.75
Westport, Conn.: Lawrence Hill, 1976.
112 pp. $6.95 cased
On the eve of his marriage to his third wife El Hadj Abdou Kader Beye, a rich businessman, falls victim to *Xala*, the curse of sexual impotency, and soon all of Dakar knows about it. Ousmane uses this theme to trace a satirical portrait of Senegal's privileged class; as for *Le Mandat* he has also produced a film version of this novel.
'*the satirical and realistic depiction of the individuals who constitute the world of El Hadj: his three wives,*

his colleagues, his secretary, a marabout, the beggars and the cripple.'

Martin O. Dechênes – *World Literature Today* 'Much of the distinction [of this book] is provided by Sembène's sharp eye for the revealing detail: the wedding party with the guests working out the cost of the reception, the strange meetings with the seers . . . These are images that will remain in the mind and confirm the already acknowledged skill of Sembène Ousmane as a major West African writer.'
John Povey – *African Arts*

Le dernier de l'empire 2 vols.
Paris: L'Harmattan, 1981. (Encres noires, 8–9). 225 pp. and 212 pp. FF44.00 ea.
The author calls his latest novel a work of 'political fiction'. Léon Mignane, an imaginary president, organizes a *coup d'état* in a real country – Senegal.
In English *translation*, forthcoming 1983

Sadji, Abdoulaye

Modou-Fatim: roman
Dakar: Impr. Abdoulaye Diop, 1960. 54 pp. o/p
A novel.

Tounka: nouvelle
Paris: Présence Africaine, 1965. 95 pp. o/p
A short novel that was first published in Dakar in 1952.
'. . . combines an epic account of the settlement of Cap Vert by the Lebou tribe with an African version of the Undine theme, in which a hero marries a sea nymph and then makes her the laughing stock of the village by revealing her frigidity . . . the reader's interest is held by the rapidity and economy of narrative, as well as by Sadji's success in recreating the style of the African epic in French.'
Thomas Cassirer – *African Forum*

Maïmouna: petite fille noire
Dakar: Les Lectures Faciles, 1953. o/p
Paris: Présence Africaine, 1965 (reprinted 1980). 253 pp. FF13.00
Chronicles the life of a beautiful, naïve young village girl in a working-class environment. Living in the city of Dakar she meets with ultimate disgrace. In English *translation*, see next entry.

Maïmouna
London: Sydenham Books, 1972. 200 pp.
This volume, which was edited and abridged by Alec Bessey, was prepared for use in French classes in Anglophone Africa.

Nini: mulâtresse du Sénégal
Paris: Présence Africaine, 1965. (2nd ed.). 189 pp. o/p
Nini is a young half-caste who despises her

African heritage and searches for total assimilation in European society. This, in the end, results in her downfall. First published in 1954 in a special issue of *Présence Africaine* entitled 'Trois écrivains noirs'.

Sall, Amadou Lamine

Mante des aurores
Dakar: Nouvelles Editions Africaines, 1979. 28 pp. CFA450
A collection of poetry.

Sall, Ibrahima

La génération spontanée
Dakar: Nouvelles Editions Africaines, 1975. 40 pp. CFA350
A volume of verse by a man who claims in one of these poems to be 'black by vocation' and 'a poet by birth'. At the same time he speaks out against doctrines which limit and categorize: 'I've had enough of your negritude, white-itude, yellow-itude, red-itude'.

Crépuscules invraisemblables
Dakar: Nouvelles Editions Africaines, 1977. 100 pp. CFA750
Thirteen short stories which are linked by the series of tragedies they relate.

Le choix de Madior
Dakar: Nouvelles Editions Africaines, forthcoming 1981

Samb, Amar

Matraqué par le destin ou la vie d'un talibé
Dakar: Nouvelles Editions Africaines, 1973. 200 pp. o/p
The apparently autobiographical account of the tormented life of a young boy whose early years were spent suffering from the strict educational practices of Koranic schools. The book lashes out violently against such schools and the marabouts who run them and defends Westernized educational systems. The hero is 'saved' when he goes to the French school.

Sangaré, Moussa Ly

Sourd-muet, je demande la parole
Dakar: Nouvelles Editions Africaines, 1978. 175 pp. CFA900
An autobiographical novel which relates the suffering and hardship of a young man growing up in a Muslim family in Dakar after World War I and who manages at last to come to terms with his physical disabilities (loss of hearing and muscular coordination) and personal tragedies (loss of his parents). Told in three parts entitled 'The Golden Age', 'The Bronze Age', and 'The Iron Age'.
'Sangaré's style is rich with a vibrant vocabulary,

sensuous description and sensitive dialogue, which lend a freshness to the familiar themes.'
Esther Y. Smith – *African Book Publishing Record*

Sangaré, Dono Ly
Sucre, Poivre et Sel
Dakar: Nouvelles Editions Africaines, 1980.
97 pp. CFA700
The protagonists of these eight short stories are all losers: Olèle who cleans a minister's office in Dakar and who for a time pretends to be the minister, himself ('Monsieur le Ministre'); Ndoya, the Dakar lady who plays at being a pious Muslim before going pop and then going broke ('L'Elue du Seigneur'); Oussou, who falls victim to a con artist and loses the fat sheep he had bought to sacrifice for the Muslim festival of *Tabaski* ('Inch-'Allah'); the crowd who literally die of curiosity ('Cheveux de manege'); Ndig, the illegitimate son of a rich man who finally 'becomes someone' the day his name is in the headlines after dying in an accident ('Psychose'); Djimbôti, the Senegalese boxer in his first pro fight who almost knocks out the killer from Uganda but gets knocked out instead ('Etre Mohamed Ali'); Saranthia, the young leper whose father decides he is not a member of the family any more; and Valdiodio, the aging shoemaker who finally marries, becomes the father of twins, and is ruined by the baptismal expenses forced on him by the family ('Pour des jumeaux'). Sangaré, who also wrote *Sourd muet je demande la parole*, has dropped the name 'Moussa' for that of 'Dono'.

Seck, Cherif Adrame
Njangaan
Dakar: Nouvelles Editions Africaines, 1975.
37 pp. CFA550
This is the screenplay of the film which was produced by Mahama (Johnson) Traoré and which relates the life and death of a young boy who, as part of his Koranic training, has been sent out into the streets to beg. Illustrated with stills from the film.

Seck, Ibrahima
Jean le fou: théâtre
Dakar: Nouvelles Editions Africaines, 1976.
94 pp. CFA600
Who is the mad man in this play – Jean, the central figure, or all the mediocre characters around him who push him to his tragic destiny through their fear, hatred and vice?

Ibrahima Seck raconte: les meilleures histoires de l'humour cannibale
Paris: Mengés, 1979 (distr. by Hachette, Paris).
178 pp. FF24.00
A collection of short stories entitled 'The Best Tales of Cannibal Humour'.

Senghor, Léopold Sédar
Chants d'ombre
Paris: Seuil, 1945. 78 pp. o/p
Senghor's first volume of poetry.

Hosties noires
Paris: Seuil, 1948. 86pp. o/p
Senghor resided in Paris at the outbreak of World War II. *Black Victims*, his second verse collection, contains the poems both written in and concerned with these war years. They substantially reflect the impact the war had on Senghor and his personal reactions to the conflict.

Chants pour Naëtt
Paris: Séghers, 1949. 49 pp. o/p
'Songs for Naëtt' – a set of love poems.

Chants d'ombre, suivis de *Hosties noires*
Paris: Seuil, 1956. (2nd ed.). 157 pp. o/p
A new edition combining the first two published verse collections.

Ethiopiques
Paris: Seuil, 1956. 126 pp o/p.
A further volume of poetry by the chief exponent of Négritude. This book includes his long dramatic poem 'Chaka', Senghor's adaption of Thomas Mofolo's historical novel. *Ethiopiques* has since been reissued in the 1974 collection of Senghor's poetry, also published by Seuil.

Nocturnes
Paris: Seuil, 1961. 94 pp. FF6.00
This collection contains Senghor's 'Elégies', a series of poems that deal with the nature of poetry and the role of the poet himself. In English *translation*, see subsequent entry.

Poèmes
Paris: Seuil, 1964. 255 pp. FF50.00
This comprehensive volume contains Senghor's first four poetry collections: *Chants d'ombre* (first published by Seuil in 1945); *Hosties noires* (poems first published by Seuil in 1948 and whch concerns Senghor's personal reaction to World War II); *Ethiopiques* (a third collection that Seuil originally brought out in 1956 containing a long dramatic poem 'Chaka', Senghor's adaption of Thomas Mofolo's historical novel); *Nocturnes* (in English *translation*, see next entry); and *Poèmes divers*.

Nocturnes: love poems
(Trans. from the French by Clive Wake and
John Reed)
London: HEB, 1969 (AWS, 71). 64 pp.
£1.95/$4.00
New York: The Third Press, 1971. 96 pp. $6.95
cased $2.95 p/b
Contains Senghor's 'Elegies', a series of poems
that deal with the nature of poetry and the role
of the poet himself. Several of the poems are
grouped under the heading 'Songs for Signare'
('Chants pour Signare') and are a translation
of the revised version of *Chants pour Naëtt*, a set
of love poems published by Séghers in 1949
and which have since gone out of print. The
French edition of this volume received the
Grand Prix International de Poésie.
'... the poetry of Léopold Sédar Senghor is an
exclusive gathering place of words ... the theme of
the poet is sumptuously African ... his poetry is not
one of the dispute, or even of discussion, but one of
taking root.'
                Guy de Bosschère – *Présence Africaine*

Selected poems
(Trans. from the French and introduced by
John Reed and Clive Wake)
London: OUP, 1964. 120 pp. o/p
New York: Atheneum, 1964. 99 pp. o/p
A selection of the outstanding poems from
each of Senghor's five volumes of verse, with
an introduction by the translators, who also
provide a glossary defining African words
frequently used by Senghor. A less extensive
sample of the poems in this volume is available
in the African Writers Series edition (see next
entry).
'... the sights, sounds, smells, motions, music and
texture of tropical landscapes populated with
creatures living and dead, present and familiar,
distant and mysterious; the sensuous maternal
warmth, the loving sternness of father and uncle; the
proud heritage of forebears, these are the Africa his
poems evoke. Senghor's genius and what will make
his poetry endure is his extraordinary lyric and
imaginative power.'
                Ellen Conroy Kennedy and Paulette
                J. Trout – *Africa Report*

Prose and Poetry
(Selected and trans. by John Reed and Clive
Wake)
London: OUP, 1965. 192 pp. o/p
London: HEB, 1976 (AWS, 180). 192 pp.
£2.25/$5.00
Presents the English-speaking reader with a
wide range of Senghor's writings. A detailed
introduction by the translators discusses
Senghor's achievements and his career as a
politician. There are translations from

Senghor's scattered prose writings and
speeches, and from his book *Nation et voie
africaine du socialisme*. These are arranged in
such a fashion as to show in outline his
thinking on cultural, political and artistic
matters. The second part of the book consists
of a selection of his poetry. A glossary of
African names often used by Senghor and a
bibliography complete the volume.

*Elégie des alizés. Avec une lithographie
originale en trois couleurs de Marc Chagall*
Paris: Seuil, 1969. 32 pp. o/p

Lettres d'hivernage
Paris: Seuil, 1973. 59 pp. o/p
Dakar: Nouvelles Editions Africaines, 1973.
59 pp. o/p
In these 'letters' addressed to women, everywhere, the poet compares Africa's *hivernage*,
the season of rains and growth but also the
time when the dry season approaches, to that
season in a woman's life when she grows older
and replaces the passion of younger years with
the longer-lasting feelings of tenderness and
friendship. Illustrated with original drawings
by Marc Chagall.
'Le peintre et le poète se sont rencontrés ... pour
chanter, dans la même note, le doux plaisir d'aimer,
et l'innocence de l'amour ... une calme mélancolie se
dégage souvent de ces poèmes, des regrets parfois, de
voir le jour tomber trop tôt, la mer se retirer, les
bateaux partir ... et partir la femme, au versant de
l'âge.'
                Yves Delatour – *Afrique Littéraire et Artistique*

Poèmes
Paris: Seuil, 1974 (Points, 53). 256 pp. FF14.00
Dakar: Nouvelles Editions Africaines, 1974.
248 pp. CFA550
This low-priced volume of Senghor's poems,
co-edited by NEA and Seuil, has been
especially prepared for the African market and
regroups poems from *Chants d'ombres, Hosties
noires, Ethiopiques* and *Lettres d'hivernage*.

Selected Poems/Poésies choisies
(Trans. from the French and introduced by
Craig Williamson)
London: Rex Collings, 1976. 148 pp. £4.50
cased £2.95 p/b
The poems included in this bilingual edition
have been taken from *Chants d'ombre, Hosties
noires, Ethiopiques*, and *Nocturnes*. In addition to
the 20-page introduction to Senghor's works,
the translator also provides a short glossary of
African terms used in the poems.

Elégies majeures suivi de *Dialogue sur la poésie francophone*
Paris: Seuil, 1979. 124 pp. FF38.00
Contains the full text of *Elégies des alizés* that had originally been published by Seuil with illustrations by Chagall plus five other elegies that are published here for the first time: the Elegy for Jean-Marie (a young Frenchman who died in Senegal); the Elegy for Martin Luther King; the Elegy for Georges Pompidou (France's former president); the Elegy for Carthage (dedicated to the president of Tunisia); and the Elegy for the Queen of Sheba. The second half of the volume contains contributions by three French poets on the subject of francophone poetry (Alan Bosquet, Jean-Claude Renard, Pierre Emmanuel) as well as Senghor's 'Letter' to the three men.

see also: Irele, Abiola ed.
Selected Poems of Léopold Sédar Senghor
Ndiaye, Papa Guèye
Ethiopiques. Poèmes de Léopold Sédar Senghor

Signaté, Ibrahima
Une aube si fragile
Dakar: Nouvelles Editions Africaines, 1977. 189 pp. CFA1200
A novel of post-independent Africa. A young man, having finished his university studies in Europe, returns home to Africa with his French wife and becomes involved with other young intellectuals in a plot to overthrow the regime.

Socé, Ousmane
Karim, roman Sénégalais, suivi de *Contes et légéndes d'Afrique noire*
Paris: Nouvelles Editions Latines, 1949. 239 pp. FF18.00
Karim is an early African novel originally published in 1935 and now in its third edition. It is the story of a young man attracted to the prospects of big-city life in Dakar, its pleasures and fascinations, who eventually returns to his village up-country and his traditional garb. The second part of the book consists of traditional folk-tales and legends. It has a foreword by Robert Delavignette.

Mirages de Paris
Paris: Nouvelles Editions Latines, 1964. 188 pp. FF18.00
Socé's second novel, a love story between an African and a European, was originally published in 1937 and later reprinted by Nouvelles Editions Latines in 1956 in a combined volume with *Rhythmes du khalam*, a collection of verse. It has since been reissued as a separate volume.

Rhythmes du Khalam
Paris: Nouvelles Editions Latines, 1962. 61 pp. FF12.00
Poetry.

Sourang, Ibrahima
Auréoles
Monte-Carlo: Ed. Regain, 1961 (Poètes de notre temps, 255). 61 pp. o/p
Poetry.

Chants du crépuscule
Monte-Carlo: Ed. Regain, 1962 (Poètes de notre temps, 273). 62 pp. o/p
Another collection of verse.

Aubades
Monte-Carlo: Ed. Regain, 1964 (Poètes de notre temps, 318). 45 pp. o/p
Sourang's third collection has a preface by Léopold Sédar Senghor.

Sow, Samba
Vacances chargées: une aventure de Scorpion l'Africain
Paris: A.B.C., 1976 (Les Archives Secrètes du B.S.I., 8). 94 pp. FF6.00
A detective story centred around the character of Scorpion the African.

Sow-Fall, Aminata
Le revenant
Dakar: Nouvelles Editions Africaines, 1976. 128 pp. CFA950
Bakar, the hero of this novel recalls in many ways the hero of Achebe's *No Longer at Ease*. Having successfully passed the post-office civil service exam, he prepares for the good life. He marries, lavishly, and proceeds to live beyond his means. The inevitable happens: he loses his job and ends up in prison for embezzlement. On his release he is but the 'ghost' of his former self and has his death announced to his family. On the day of his 'funeral' he suddenly appears, seizes the money mourners have given his parents, and disappears forever.

La grève des Battu ou les déchets humains
Dakar: Nouvelles Editions Africaines, 1979. 131 pp. CFA1200
Aminata Sow-Fall's second novel had the distinction of being pre-selected for the Prix Goncourt. A high civil servant in an imaginary African country decides to rid the capital of beggars. They in turn revolt and go on strike when one of their numbers is struck down by a car, refusing to come out on the streets when, ironically, the same official discovers he needs them – in order to distribute the alms his marabout said was the necessary pre-condition

to his being appointed to the vice-presidency of the state. The book was the winner of the 1980 Grand Prix Littéraire d'Afrique Noire. An English translation by Dorothy Blair will soon be published in Longman's Drumbeat series under the title *The Beggar's Strike*.
'*Aminata Sow-Fall aborde un problème aïgu. C'est qu'en marginalisant une catégorie de sa population, une société perd une partie fonctionelle d'elle-même . . . touche aussi à d'autres plaies: la polygamie, l'utilisation du pouvoir à des fins personnelles, l'exploitation des talibés par les marabouts, la dilapidation des biens de l'Etat, le "magouillage" politique.'* Sylviane Kamara – *Jeune Afrique*
'*Avec* La grève des Battu, *Aminata Sow-Fall se confirme comme un écrivain chevronné. Elle entre ainsi à grands pas . . . dans le cercle de la nouvelle génération des écrivains sénégalais.'*
J. B. Kouamé – *Fraternité Matin*

Sy, Boubacar
Pas si fou
Dakar: Nouvelles Editions Africaines, 1979. 160 pp. CFA1050
An autobiographical novel about a life of misery and solitude. The narrator grew up in the slums of Dakar where he was orphaned at an early age and ended up as an adult in a Dakar prison cell.

Wade, Amadou Moustapha
Présence: poèmes
Paris: Présence Africaine, 1966. 48 pp. o/p

Wane, Abdoul Baïla
Les habitués du paradis
Dakar: Nouvelles Editions Africaines, 1977. 102 pp. CFA600
The 'Paradise' of the title of this novel is the bar in Dakar where Nabou and her friends – the lawyer, the teacher, the male-nurse, the high civil servant's widow – gather to seek solace for their unhappy lives and try to find personal solutions to the difficult relationships between men and women in modern Senegalese society.

Le tourmenté
Paris: La Pensée Universelle, 1978. 93 pp. FF37.50
A Senegalese in Paris who is obsessed with the ideas of sin and purity commits a murder. A novel.

Willane, Oumar
Pasteur King: tambour-major de paix
Paris: Nouvelles Editions Debresse, 1969. 47 pp. o/p
A volume of verse written in honour of Martin Luther King.

Ce monde nu
Paris: Nouvelles Editions Debresse, 1969. 89 pp. o/p
Another book of poetry.

Togo

Adotévi, Adovi John-Bosco
Sacrilège à Mandali
Yaoundé: C.L.E., 1980. 230 pp.
A heroic love story set in a politically agitated country. The hero, Ernest Viwatonou Koffi, is a sort of modern Christian martyr.

Aladji, Victor
Akossiwa mon amour
Yaoundé: C.L.E., 1971. 52 pp. CFA230
Féli, a young schoolteacher about to take up his first post in a far-off city (Ouagadougou), visits the scenes of his childhood – his mother's village and Aunt Mouna's where he spent three happy years – and falls in love with Akossiwa, his former playmate. The novel first appeared in serialized form in *Togo Presse* in 1970.
'*Le récit d'Aladji ne se borne pas à nous restituer son enfance, mais il nous oblige à une réflexion personnelle sur ce monde qui nous entoure'.*
Afrique Littéraire et Artistique

L'équilibriste
Yaoundé: C.L.E., 1972. 64 pp. CFA230
The story of Koumi, a big-hearted thief who steals only from banks and businesses, never from the people. Every time he is arrested he always manages to escape. One day a police inspector falls in love with his daughter and it is around her that the action of the novel will finally be resolved.

Almeida, Modeste d' and Lacle, Gilbert
Keteyouli, l'étudiant noir ou le drame des jeunes élites africaines
Lomé: Ed. de la Lagune, 1966. 59 pp.
Keteyouli returns from France with a degree in engineering and must choose beteen a young Togolese peasant girl and a Frenchwoman. The book is subtitled: 'The Problems of the Young African Elite'.

Ananou, David
Le fils du fétiche
Paris: Nouvelles Editions Latines, 1971 (2nd ed.).
219 pp.
A child is born to Sodji and his wife, Avlessi, who despaired of having children. He is named Danson in honour of the serpent totem

to whom sacrifices had been made, although the pregnancy is the result of Avlessi's having been treated in a Lomé hospital. The boy grows into a fine, handsome young man, marries Afiavi against his parents' wishes and prepares to devote his life to the gods. Then he goes to Ghana with his wife and twin children and is converted to Christianity. First published in 1955. '

Couchoro, Felix
L'esclave
Paris: La Dépêche Africaine, 1929. 306 pp. o/p
A prolific writer, Couchoro only published four novels in book form. The eighteen others were serialized in *Togo-Presse* between 1962 and 1970. Couchoro's first novel (generally considered as being the first novel from francophone Africa) is about Mawoulawoe, the ambitious slave who had been adopted into the family which had bought him as a child. Mawoulawoe ruins his life and that of his mistress, Akoeba, the wife of his adopted brother, starting from the murder of their respective spouses. The death of these two remains a mystery until another son of the family comes home. A power struggle ensues in which Mawoulawoe is the loser.

Amour de féticheuse
Ouidah, Benin: Imp. de Mme P. d'Almeida, 1941. 74 pp. o/p
Anassi, a pretty village girl, tries to catch the heart of Pierre, a medical attendant, but her inclination for juju practices displeases him. Later she is taken in for training by the chief priest and becomes his mistress. When it is learned that she is pregnant she must agree to abortion, against her will, and goes to Pierre for help. Pierre also counters the diabolic designs of the chief priest's son. In the end Pierre marries a mid-wife.

Drame d'amour à Anecho
Ouidah, Benin: Imp. de Mme P. d'Almeida, 1950. 168 pp. o/p
Gilbert and Mercy are in love but Mercy's family is violently opposed to their marriage because Gilbert comes from a rival family which, like Mercy's seeks the chieftainship of Anecho. Mercy flees when her family tries to marry her by force to another. Her uncle from Lomé intervenes to settle the matter. The marriage of the two young people is the beginning of political unity.

L'Héritage, cette peste: les secrèts d'Eléonore
Lomé: Editogo, 1963. 160 pp.
When old John Alson dies Léon learns with stupefaction that he is not his son. His 'brothers' contrive to disinherit him but their sister, Eléonore foils the plot, saving their father's estate from squander and ends by marrying Léon.

Dogbé, Yves-Emmanuel
Affres!
Porto-Novo, Benin: Rapidex, 1966. 24 pp.
Sixteen poems.

La victime
Le Mée-sur-Seine, France: Ed. Akpagnon, 1979. 238 pp. FF46.00/CFA2,600
In this novel, set on the palm-tree covered beaches of Saborou, the capital of an imaginary West African country, Dogbé explores the problems of black-white relationships. The love affair between Solange, the French woman and Pierre, the African, ends tragically for Solange, but there will be a happy ending to Pierre's encounter with Maryse. This is one of the first publications of the new publishing house, Editions Akpagnon, owned by the author.

Le divin amour suivi de *Paix et bonheur*
Le Mée-sur-Seine, France: Ed. Akpagnon, 1979. 112 pp. CFA220
Dogbé's third book of verse which won the 1979 Charles Vildrac poetry prize and which was originally published by P. J. Oswald in 1976.

Flamme blême
Le Mée-sur-Seine, France: Ed. Akpagnon, 1980 (2nd rev. ed.). 86 pp. FF45.00/CFA2,200
A collection of poetry that was first published in 1969 by the Editions de la Revue Moderne. '*Malgré certaines défaillances qui sont inévitables dans toute oeuvre de début, même corrigée,* Flamme Bleme *merité qu'on lui porte de l'attention. C'est un bel écho de la poèsie togolaise.*'
Maurice A. Lubin – *African Book Publishing Record*

L'incarcéré: roman
Le Mée-sur-Seine, France: Ed. Akpagnon, 1980. 204 pp. FF59.00/CFA2,800
A novel focusing on conditions in African prisons which is at the same time a call to African intellectuals to assume their responsibilities.

Typamm, Paul Akakpo
Rythmes et cadences
Le Mée-sur-Seine, France: Ed. Akpagnon, 1980. 100 pp.
Short stories and verse.

Viderot, Toussaint Menash
Courage: poèmes
Paris: Ed. Hautefeuille, 1957. 93 pp. o/p

Courage si tu veux vivre et t'épanouir, fils de la grande Afrique
Monte-Caro: Ed. Regain, 1960 (Les Cahiers des poètes de notre temps, 234). 159 pp. o/p
Poetry.

Zinsou, Sénouvo Agbote
On joue la comédie
Paris: Radio-France Internationale, 1975 (Repertoire théâtral africain, 20) (distr. by Nouvelles Editions Africaines, Dakar). 114pp. CFA300
A play that takes the form of a musical comedy although its theme is tragic: that of the genocide black people have suffered down through the ages. A central figure called Chaka plays the role of a black saviour.

Upper Volta

Boni, Nazi
Crépuscule des temps anciens: Chronique du Bwamu
Paris: Présence Africaine, 1962. 256 pp. FF31.00
The defeat of the Bwamu rebellion in Upper Volta by French colonial troops in 1916 serves as the culminating point of this novel which traces three centuries of Bwamu history. It is the sorrowful tale of the downfall of a once proud people subjected to the combined onslaught of foreign invaders, natural catastrophe and internal pressures.

Coulibali, Augustin-Sondé
Les dieux délinquants: roman
Ouagadougou: Ed. Coulibaly Frères, 1974. 227 pp.
Tibila, a young man, comes to Ouaga to seek his fortune.

Coulibaly, Issaïe B.
Ma joie en lui
Dakar: Nouvelles Editions Africaines, 1977. 160 pp.
A novel.

Les deux amis
Dakar: Nouvelles Editions Africaines, 1979. CFA550
Short stories.

Dabire, Pierre
Sansoa: Drame en six actes
Paris: O.R.T.F.-D.A.E.C., 1969. (distr. by Nouvelles Editions Africaines). 65 pp. CFA300
A prize-winning play in the 1967–68 African Theatre Competition organized by the French broadcasting corporation. It evokes the problems of forced labour and in particular the use of African porters under colonization.

Guégane, Jacques Boureima
Poémes voltaïques: Appels, Yé Vinu Muntu, Nativité
Dakar: Nouvelles Editions Africaines, 1978. 53 pp. CFA350
Poetry.

Nikiéma, Roger
Dessein contraire
Ouagadougou: Presses Africaines, 1967. 172 pp.
A novel.

Deux adorables rivales. Les soleils de la terre
Yaoundé: C.L.E., 1971. 51 pp. o/p
In the first story of this collection two women who love the same man, Cyrille, a doctor, manage to remain friends even when one of them marries him. The second story has a traditional setting and tells how Tougtouenga becomes the 'mother' of the Mossi after her marriage to the Chief of the Dagoumba and the birth of her son, Oubri, who becomes a Mossi chief.

Noaga, Kollin
Haro! Camarade Commandant
Ouagadougou: Ed. Presses Africaines, 1977. 110 pp.
A novel about the reactions of the young elite of Upper Volta to certain aspects of local bureaucracy.

Le retour au village: roman
Issy-les-Moulineaux, France: Eds. Saint-Paul, 1978 (Les classiques africaines, 76). 139 pp. FF16.00
A novel about the problems facing Africans from the inland who emigrate to the coast (Abidjan) in search of work and who return home many years later.

Sawadogo, Etienne
La défaite du Yargha
Paris: La Pensée Universelle, 1977. 155 pp. FF28.00

Titinga, Pacéré
Refrains sous le Sahel
Paris: P. J. Oswald, 1976 (Poésie-prose
africaine, 14) (distr. by L'Harmattan, Paris).
89 pp. FF18.00
Sixteen poems prefaced by Joseph Ki-Zerbo.
'. . . *strongly rhythmic and almost palpable. One
feels the presence of a performer (a dancer?) who has
become entranced by his own chanting.*'
              David K. Bruner – *World Literature Today*

Ça tire sous le Sahel: satires nègres
Paris: P. J. Oswald, 1976 (Poésie-prose
africaine, 15) (distr. by L'Harmattan, Paris).
64 pp. FF16.00
The ironies of contemporary Africa are the
major themes of this collection of verse.
'. . . *the infrequency of specifically African referents
and words extend the applicability well beyond the*

*Sahel . . . the structural intricacies of the longer
poems and the charming sardonic humour must
appeal to many readers not ordinarily concerned with
African literature*'.
              D. Dorsey – *World Literature Today*

Quand s'envolent les grues couronnées: poèmes
Paris: P. J. Oswald, 1976 (distr. by
L'Harmattan, Paris). 66 pp. FF15.00
Titinga's third collection of verse is a long
lamentation on the death of an old man from
his village of Magega in Upper Volta whose
passing away symbolizes Africa's loss of
wisdom and prefigures the parched, drought-
stricken days to come.

Zongo, Daniel
Charivaris: poèmes
Tours: Impr. Pinson, 1977. 47 pp.

EAST & CENTRAL AFRICA

Central African Republic

Bamboté, Pierre Makombo
La poésie est dans l'histoire
Paris: P. J. Oswald, 1960. 42 pp. o/p
Poetry.

*Chant funèbre pour un héros d'Afrique précédé
d'un Chant populaire adapté par Sembène
Ousmane*
Paris: P. J. Oswald, 1962 (J'exige la parole,
11). 75 pp. o/p
Poetry.

Le dur avenir
Bangui: Imp. Centrale d'Afrique, 1965. 55 pp.
Poetry.

Les deux oiseaux de l'Ubangui
Paris: Ed. Saint Germain-des-Prés, 1968.
75 pp.
A young man, Ombambi, and a young
woman, Naloto, leave their village to go to
Bangui and can never go home again. A tale in
verse.

Princesse Mandapu
Paris: Présence Africaine, 1972. 187 pp.
FF34.00
Independence has come to Central Africa and
Monsieur Boy, a civil servant, is the lord of the
land in Uandja, 1000 km from Bangui. He is

rich, powerful, and feared, and his mortal
enemy is Mokta, the 'arab' trader, the second
most important man in the region, to whom
Mandapu, Boy's youngest daughter has nonetheless been promised since birth. Boy's
transfer to Bangui signals the end of his 'reign'
and Mokta's ascension, but the move to
Bangui will end tragically for little Mandapu.
'*Il s'agit d'un roman d'une grande originalité, écrit
dans une langue étonnante dans un réalisme étrange.*'
              Patrick Mérand – *Afrique Asie*

*Technique pour rien, suivi de Civilisation des
autres*
Paris: Ed. Saint Germain-des-Prés, 1973.
142 pp.
Poetry followed by a long tale, the 'Journal of
a Central African peasant', in which an old
man sitting under a tree weaving a rooftop
comments on life, people he knows, familiar
objects around him: his destiny is as parched
as the dry season itself.

Nouvelles de Bangui
Montreal: Les Presses de l'Université de
Montréal, 1981. 168 pp. Can.$12.00
Fourteen short stories that won the 1980 prize
of the journal *Etudes Françaises*.

Ipeko-Etomane, Faustin-Albert
L'ombre des interdits: comédie en trois actes
Yaoundé: C.L.E., [n.d.] (Clé-Théâtre, 14).
19 pp. and 24 pp. o/p
A play.

Le Lac des sorciers
Yaoundé: C.L.E., 1971. 48 pp. CFA230
Four short stories evoking the mysteries of
contemporary life as well as traditional
legends.

Mariage mixte à Bangui
Paris: Agence de Coopération Culturel et
Technique and le Méridien, 1981. 96 pp.
An African engineer and a French school
teacher decide to get married, despite the
problems that entails. A novel.

Sammy, Pierre
L'odyssée de Mongou
Paris: Hatier, 1977. 128 pp. FF48.00
Mongou, the chief's son, suddenly discovers
the existence of another culture when he is sent
to Europe to fight in the war.

*'Se plaçant délibérément à contre-courant de la
pensée africaine actuelle, Sammy soutient, obstiné-
ment, que, sans l'arrivée des Européans, l'horizon de
Mongou – le héros – se serait borné aux rives de
l'Oubangui et ne les aurait jamais dépassées.'*
                     Patrick Mérand – *Afrique Asie*

Siango, Benoit Basile
A Molengue ti independance
Bangui: Compagnons du Théâtre, 1967.
53 pp.
The theme of this play, the first from the
Central African Republic, is the refusal of a
young educated girl to marry the wealthy
suitor whose generosity has enabled her
parents to pay off their debts.

Yavoucko, Cyriaque Robert
Crépuscule et défi
Paris: Ed. L'Harmattan, 1979. 160 pp.
FF30.00
A novel which describes the first contact of the
people living along the Ubangui River with the
Europeans who land in their 'floating huts'.
The foreigners are greeted enthusiastically as
living gods, but the enthusiasm cools when the
missionaries arrive and begin their assault on
local religious practices. Revolt spreads among
the people and the missionaries, personified
by Father Boussin, will be, temporarily,
defeated.

*'Dans l'histoire de cette mise au pas manquée . . . il y
a une certaine densité et, surtout, l'interpretation, par
les noirs, de ce qu'ils perçoivent de la présence blanche
en fonction de leur culture et de leurs normes. . . Yavoucko le romance bien.'*
                     J.C.P. – *Le Monde*

Congo Popular Republic

Bemba, Sylvain
L'Homme qui tua la crocodile: tragicomédie
Yaoundé: C.L.E., 1972. 72 pp. CFA360
The crocodile of the title of this play is a tyrant
of a man who mistreats his wife and exploits
local people. Everyone falls into his 'teeth',
except the schoolteacher, who alone is
courageous enough to denounce him.

Une eau dormante
Paris: Radio-France Internationale, 1975
(Répertoire théâtral africain, 21) (distr. by
Nouvelles Editions Africaines, Dakar). 103 pp.
CFA300
A play, set in the Congo around 1930, which
won the 1972 Listeners' Prize in the annual
African Theatre competition organized by
Radio-France Internationale. Olessa, a young
fisherman, dares to defy tradition, represented
by Olouo, village chief and witch-doctor, and
Sosso, a wealthy man, owner of a local pond,
to defend his right to the just fruits of his
labour.

Tarentelle noire et diable blanc
Paris: P. J. Oswald, 1976 (Théâtre africain, 28)
(distr. by L'Harmattan, Paris). 136 pp. FF21.00
Through the private story of Ibouanga and his
family, this play, covering the period
1890-1930, evokes the abuses of colonial
trading companies and the role they played in
exploiting the people and the resources of the
former French Congo.

*Un foutu monde pour un blanchisseur trop
honnête*
Yaoundé: C.L.E., 1979. 48 pp. CFA770
A runner-up in the 1977 African Theatre
Competition of Radio-France Internationale.
In a world where 'dishonesty is normal' the
utter scrupulousness of Raphaël, the poor
laundry man whose life is devoted to cleaning
filth, appears somehow suspicious to everyone,
including his family, and makes him an easy
prey for 'dirty dealers'. Even two years in
prison where he is detained on false charges do
not seem to cure him of his 'strange' affliction.
Much of this play is written in pidgin which,
according to the author, may cause purists to
'cover their faces and plug their ears' but 'that
won't stop such language . . . from existing.'

Rêves Portatifs
Dakar: Nouvelles Editions Africaines, 1979.
208 pp. CFA1,200 FF31.20

In Bemba's first novel spectators seated in a darkened movie house watch a film about post-independent Africa, about an era of freedom and of intrigue, political and sexual, that has gone sour. They see images of a dictatorship which concentrates power and wealth in the hands of a few. There are political opponents in dank prison cells and assassinated patriots. Women are both victims and profiteers of the system. The ambiguity between what the people see on the screen and in the streets is deliberate as they carry the film away with them in their minds like so many 'portable dreams'.
'. . . at times the narrator is experimenting with a new genre. However, the work is expressive and strong, and the narrative reveals clear and detailed observations of a society in transition and torn by many contradictions.'
Evelyne Accad – *African Book Publishing Record*

Bilombo-Samba, Jean-Blaise
Témoignages
Paris: Pierre-Jean Oswald, 1976 (distr. by L'Harmattan, Paris). 85 pp. FF18.00
Bilombo-Samba's first book of verse is prefaced by Henri Lopès.
'. . . a keen sense of metaphor which tends to the surreal. A first effort which, despite its flaws, suggests that Bilombo-Samba is a poet in the making.'
Eileen Julien – *World Literature Today*

Biniakounou, Pierre
Chômeur à Brazzaville
Dakar: Nouvelles Editions Africaines, 1977. 78 pp. CFA500
A tale of misery and joblessness in the slums of a large African city.

Dongala, Emmanuel
Un fusil dans la main, un poème dans la poche
Paris: Albin Michel, 1973. 284 pp. FF24.00
Mayéla dia Mayéla is a young African revolutionary who has studied in Europe. He decides one day to put his words into action and he leaves university to go to Southern Africa and fight in the guerrilla war in Zimbabwe. Then he returns to his country, comes to power and is finally faced with political reality. He, too, like his predecessor will be overthrown and executed. The novel was awarded the Ladislas Dormandé prize for the best foreign book.

Kodia, Noël-Ramatta
Les conjurés du 17 janvier 1961
Brazzaville: Ed. Héros dans l'Ombre, n.d. 39 pp.
In this play Africa brings suit against Europe and her sons East and West in an International Court of Justice for plotting and carrying out the death of Patrice Lumumba. The presiding judges are Asia and Latin America.

Letembet-Ambily, Antoine
L'Europe inculpée: drame en quatre actes
Yaoundé: C.L.E., 1977. 116 pp. CFA540
Originally published in Paris in 1970 by the French broadcasting corporation, then known as O.R.T.F., in the series 'Répertoire Théâtral Africain'. The Biblical figure, Noah, comes back to earth to testify before judge Humanity in a court suit involving his grandchildren. Europe, the daughter of Noah's son Haphet, and her own daughter America stand accused of exploiting Africa, the daughter of Ham. This play won the 1969 Interafrican Theatre Competition in France.

Les aryens: tragédie en trois actes
Yaoundé: C.L.E., 1977. 60 pp. CFA540
Letembet-Ambily's third play is a symbolic attack on fascism and racism, represented by Hito and Dol, the father and son of aryanism. Victory against these two will only come about when the 'non-aryans', all races combined, realize that they must either live together or die.

Lopes, Henri
Tribaliques
Yaoundé: C.L.E., 1971. 104 pp. CFA720
This collection of eight short stories about the ironies and dilemmas of life in contemporary Africa won the Grand Prix Littéraire d'Afrique Noire in 1972. In it we meet people such as the young African who goes to France for training and who never returns; a university student who must turn away her fiancé, another student, to marry a man from her village who can help her family; the hypocritical parliamentarian who pronounces fine speeches about the liberation of women and who lives otherwise; the honest government worker whose report about the crooked dealings of a French businessman must be hushed up; and the African maid whose son is dying and who dare not interrupt her mistresses' fancy-dress party to ask for an advance on her wages.
'Henri Lopes refuse de pleurer ou de rêver: il ausculte la nouvelle société africaine. Ses outils: le sens de l'observation, la perspicacité, une langue alerte qui tord le cou à la rhétorique grandiloquente et sinueuse pour privilégier la concision et la pertinence.'
Fame Ndongo – *Cameroon Tribune*

La nouvelle romance
Yaoundé: C.L.E., 1976. 196 pp. CFA1,200
Dakar: Nouvelles Editions Africaines, 1980 (Club Afrique Loisirs, 10). CFA1,900

Wali is married to Bienvenue N'Kama, called 'Delarumba', an ambitious football hero turned banker who treats her as nothing better than a slave. When he loses his job at the bank (for irresponsibility) he uses his influence to obtain a position as cultural attaché at the embassy in Belgium. There Wali meets a Belgian couple, trade-unionists, who act as catalysts in her growing awareness of her exploitation as a woman. When her husband is declared *persona non grata* she refuses to follow him home, going instead to Paris where she continues her education (while supporting herself as a maid) in order to prepare herself for a future in which she can be useful to her people.
'. . . ce n'est pas seulement la chanson d'un couple, c'est celle de l'homme face à une vie qui ne serait plus un simple simulacre.'
Jacques Vignes – *Jeune Afrique*
'. . . an excellent literary work which provides a poignant picture of the universal dilemma of the young educated wife of the twentieth century.'
Philip A. Noss – *World Literature Today*

Sans tam-tam
Yaoundé: C.L.E., 1977. 126 pp. CFA990
In Lopès's second novel, written in epistolary form, a young schoolteacher dies of cancer, having preferred his far-off village school where he can serve his people to a prestigious position as cultural attaché in Paris.
'. . . apparaît ainsi comme un hymne à la brousse et au petit peuple, hymne sombre et simple.'
Jacques Fame Ndongo – *Cameroon Tribune*

Mabassi, Enoch
Balbutiements
Brazzaville: Ed. Héros dans L'Ombre, 1977. 90 pp.
Poetry.

Macouba, Auguste
Boutou grand soir: poèmes affiches
Paris: Saint Germain-des-Prés, 1978. 43 pp. o/p
Poetry

Makouta-Mboukou, Jean-Pierre
En quête de la liberté: ou une vie d'espoir
Yaoundé: C.L.E., 1970. 168 pp. CFA570
The life of a young man growing up in the Congo in the forties who is marked by personal tragedies (death of a young cousin and then of his parents) and by the injustice, cruelty and racism of the colonizer. He leaves school to earn his living and is sent to Bordeaux to work in a bookstore. Befriended by the owner he is able to complete his law studies. Fifteen years later he returns home

only to discover that independence has not made his country any more just or free. His outspokenness puts a stop to a budding political career as he and his family are forced into exile.

Les initiés
Yaoundé: C.L.E., 1970. 88 pp. o/p
A tragic love story. Ravimanari comes to Paris from Madagascar and soon forgets all the lessons of morality his mother, a strict Lutheran, had taught him. When his girlfriend, Rosine, gets pregnant he advises abortion. Then he is stricken by remorse and decides to marry her to pay for his 'fault'. But it is too late; she dies. He dies, himself, soon after.

L'Ame-bleue: poèmes
Yaoundé: C.L.E., 1971. 112 pp. CFA500
Poetry.

Le contestant
Paris: La Pensée Universelle, 1973. 256 pp. o/p
To atone for their adulterous love affair Jean Kayilou, a university professor, and Myriam turn to religion, he as a Protestant minister and she as a Catholic nun. But Kayilou's vision of his ministry is too radical for the church establishment and the regime, and he will eventually have to pay for his 'deviancy' with his life, dying from torture wounds in the convent where he is being looked after by Myriam.

Cantate d'l'ouvrier
Paris: P. J. Oswald, 1974 (Poésie/prose africaine, 9) (distr. by L'Harmattan, Paris). 70 pp. FF16.00
Poetry

Les exilés de la forêt viérge ou le grand complot
Paris: P. J. Oswald, 1974 (Poésie/prose africaine, 10) (distr. by L'Harmattan, Paris). 210 pp. FF30.00
Paris: L'Harmattan, 1981 (2nd ed.) (Encres noires, 10). 206 pp. FF30.00
In the imaginary African republic of Durmen a condemned poet flees into the forest to escape death. Several years later he meets the deposed president who had sentenced him to death and who also has been forced into exile. The forest setting becomes a place of reconciliation in the author's fourth novel that was originally published by P. J. Oswald in Paris in 1974.

Malinda, Martial [pseud. for Bemba, Sylvain]
L'enfer c'est Orféo: pièce en trois actes
Paris: O.R.T.F.-D.A.E.C., 1970 (Répertoire

théâtral interafricain, 10). 120 pp. o/p
The struggle for the liberation of Guinea-Bissau gives Orféo, a rich medical doctor who becomes disgusted with himself and the privileged milieu in which he lives, the opportunity to escape the hell of his existence, This play won third prize in the 1969 Inter-african Theatre Competition in France.

Malonga, Jean
La légende de M'Pfoumou ma Mazono
Paris: Présence Africaine, 1973 (2nd ed.).
155 pp. FF15.00
The plot for this novel which was first published by Présence Africaine in 1954 is based on a traditional Congolese tale. Hakoula commits adultery with her husband's slave who loses his life when Bitouala, the husband, finds them out. A war ensues between the two clans of the couple. Meanwhile Hakoula flees into the forest where she lives fifteen years under supernatural protection. While in exile she gives birth to a male child, Bitouala's son, who will eventually discover the mystery of his birth and be reunited with his father's clan, becoming a great chief whose aim is to abolish all forms of traditional injustice, including slavery. In 1976 the author was awarded the Grand Prix of the President of the Republic of Congo for all his works.

Mamonsono, Léopold P.
Héros dans l'Ombre
Brazzaville: Ed. Littéraires Congolaises, 1976 [?] (distr. by Ed. Héros dans l'Ombre). 48 pp.
A collection of poems dedicated to the memory of a Congolese schoolteacher who died while on official business, and to teachers everywhere, those unsung 'heroes in the dark'!

Luzingu-Lua-Liadi: une vie d'enfer
Brazzaville: Ed. Héros dans L'Ombre, 1976 [?] 138 pp.
A novel.

Mutantu: ou la tragédie de l'enfant naturel
Brazzaville: Ed. Héros dans L'Ombre, 1976 [?] 150 pp.
An autobiographical novel.

Tembe na mundele Alongui; malheur d'Irace
Brazzaville: Ed. Héros dans L'Ombre,1977 [?] 253 pp.
A social tragedy.

Light-Houses: Poems
Brazzaville: Ed. Héros dans L'Ombre, 1978. 52 pp.

Poems in English. The poet sings of the Congo of his ancestors while proclaiming himself a citizen of the world.

Le regard du fou
Dakar: Nouvelles Editions Africaines, forthcoming 1981
A play.

Manki Man Tséké
Echo
Paris: P. J. Oswald, 1977 (distr. by L'Harmattan, Paris). 54 pp. FF15.00
Poetry.

Menga, Guy [pseud. for Bikouta-Menga, Gaston-Guy]
La palabre stérile
Yaoundé: C.L.E., 1968. 138 pp. CFA1,100
The title, 'fruitless palavers', refers not only to the hero's supposed sterility, but to all the hapless events which beset him: his exile to the city for having violated village customs, his unhappy marriage (his wife gets pregnant by another man), his sixteen years in a hard-labour camp in Chad for 'nationalist activities', the result of his membership in the Matswa sect. The book was awarded the Grand Prix Littéraire de l'Afrique Noire for 1969.
'Guy Menga ne cherche pas à faire du style et c'est bien ainsi: il écrit dans une langue claire, adaptée aux diverses situations de son récit . . . l'expression de la 'difficulté d'être' dans un monde où les forces de la tradition et celles de l'oppression coloniale conjuguent leurs actions pour écraser l'individu.'
J. B. Tati-Loutard – *Sentiers*

Les aventures de Moni-Mambou. Les nouvelles aventures de Moni-Mambou
Yaoundé: C.L.E., 1975. 126 pp. CFA810
A combined volume of the first two series of Moni-Mambou tales which were originally published separately by C.L.E. in 1971.
'. . . a refreshingly simple and direct gift of narrative and a colourful French style . . . comes as a pleasant surprise to weary readers of le nouveau roman.'
Edouard Roditi – *Books Abroad*

Adventures of Moni-Mambou
(Adapted from the French by Malachy Quinn)
London: Evans, 1979. 64 pp. 85p
The extraordinary escapades of a Congolese folk hero who fights evil and defends the oppressed, accompanied by his talking parrot, Yengui.

L'oracle: comédie en trois actes
Paris: O.R.T.F.-D.A.E.C., 1969 (Répertoire théâtral africain, 1). 90 pp. o/p
A father tries to make his daughter give up her

studies and marry, against her will, a wealthy old man. But grandfather, the oracle of the family, will find an acceptable solution. A three-act comedy which won (with *La Marmite de Koka M'Bala*) the 1967-68 Interafrican Theatre Competition in France. Reprinted with *La Marmite de Koka-M'Bala*.

Les indiscrétions du vagabond: contes et récits du Congo
Sherbrooke, Canada: Ed. Naaman, 1974. 96 pp. Can.$4.00 FF24.00
The narrative unity in this book of tales (seven traditional and four contemporary) is provided by the story-teller, a traveller from afar, who entertains a Congolese village for six nights in a row with his fire-side stories told to the sound of his *nsambi* (a musical instrument).

Les Aventures de Moni-Mambou 3
Yaoundé: C.L.E., 1975. 64 pp. CFA210
Menga's third volume of Moni-Mambou tales.

La marmite de Koka-Mbala. L'Oracle
Monaco: Ed. Regain, 1966. o/p
Yaoundé: C.L.E., 1976. 96 pp. CFA450
These two plays won the 1967-68 Interafrican Theatre Competition in France. They were originally published as separate volumes: *La Marmite de Kolo-Mbala* in Monaco by Ed. Regain in 1966 and again in 1969 by the O.R.T.F. in Paris. In *La marmite . . .* a king dares to violate custom by refusing to condemn to death a young man who had seen a woman bathing in a river.

Kotawali
Dakar: Nouvelles Editions Africaines, 1976. 288 pp. CFA1,400
The title of Menga's first novel means 'great woman' in Sango. Set in the imaginary African republic of Kazalunda, it is the love story of Kotawali, a revolutionary young woman fighting a tyranical regime, and Belindao, a taxi-driver known for his kindness and generosity. They meet when Belindao finds her wounded on the road one day. Belindao's wife, Pemba, eventually turns Kotawali in to the police, but will, herself, along with the two others, be condemned to death only to be rescued by Kotawali's companions. Belindao and his wife cross the border to safety and Kotawali continues the struggle to liberate her people.

M'Fouillou, Dominique

La soumission: roman congolais
Paris: L'Harmattan, 1977. 150 pp. FF32.00
This novel which covers the years 1935-45, or the passage of the hero from childhood to adulthood, is a critical examination of colon-

ialization. In his words it speaks of 'the unhappiness, the suffering and the human sacrifices on which colonial life was based.'

Les corbeaux
Le Mée-sur-Seine, France: Ed. Akpagnon, 1980. 240 pp. FF52.00
The 'Crows' are followers of the prophet Matsoua who are preparing the revolution which will liberate the Congolese people from both local and foreign exploiters. A novel of contemporary Africa.

Mouangassa, Ferdinand

N'Ganga Mayala: tragédie en trois actes
Yaoundé: C.L.E., 1977. 78 pp. CFA540
In this play, a wise king, open to new ideas, attempts to modify the Conseil of Elders by inviting in young, progressive members. It will end tragically.

N'Debeka, Maxime

Soleils neufs
Yaoundé: C.L.E., 1969. 107 pp. o/p
Poetry.

Le président: drame satirique en trois actes
Paris: P. J. Oswald, 1970 (Théâtre africain, 8) (distr. by L'Harmattan, Paris). 95 pp. FF18.00
An African president who cynically declares that governing is stealing from the people should not be surprised when the people decide to overthrow him. A play, prefaced by Henri Lopès.

L'oseille et les citrons
Paris: P. J. Oswald, 1975 (Poèsie/Prose africain, 12) (distr. by L'Harmattan, Paris). 70 pp. FF16.00
Poetry.

Les signes du silence
Paris: Ed. Saint-Germain-des-Prés, 1978. 57 pp. o/p

Ngoie-Ngalla, Dominique

Lettre à un étudiant africain suivi de La sonate des derniers veilleurs
Brazzaville: Ed. Mbonda, 1981. 34 pp.
Two philosophical essays disguised as short stories which express the author's concern for the future of Africa. The first takes the form of a letter to an African student advising the elite of the future to heed the common needs rather than the needs of self, expressing concern over Arab domination of Africa, and recalling that a religious attitude is not incompatible with revolutionary ideas. The second one is a plea for Africa to become adult, to avow her faults and control her violence before it is too late.

Nkouka, Alphonse
Deuxième bureau
Yaoundé: C.L.E., 1980. 150 pp.
The sorry love affair of Jyl, a single girl.

N'Zala-Backa, Placide
Le tipoye doré: récit
Paris: P. J. Oswald, 1976 (distr. by
L'Harmattan, Paris). 80 pp. FF17.00
African history from colonial days to independence is the backdrop of this story of a man
growing to adulthood to become a civil servant
in an independent Congo. The title refers to
the sedan chair used by African rulers to travel
in, and later adopted by French colonial
administrators. First published in 1968 in
Brazzaville.

'... *the author may be credited* ... *with having
recreated, in an unaffected but appealing and
sensitive style, a concise and yet quite complete vivid
description of an African civilization* ... *He also
adeptly depicts the degrading realities of colonialism.*'
Martin O. Deschênes – *World Literature Today*

Obenga, Théophile
Stèles pour l'avenir
Paris: Présence Africaine, 1978. 79 pp.
FF29.00
The first book of poetry of the Congolese
historian-cum-politician.

Owi-Okanza [pseud. for Okanza, Jacob]
*La trilogie déterminante, Sélé-Sélé le mauvais
cadre agricole, Tokolonga ou le socialisme
triomphera*
Bucarest: Ilexim, n.d. [1975] (Témoignage de
L'Afrique contemporaine). 138 pp.
Three plays set in independent Africa in which
workers and peasants seen as agents of the true
socialist revolution win out over the parasitical
and corrupt bureaucrats and expatriates who
have mismanaged affairs. *Sélé-Sélé* is being
republished with *Oba l'instituteur* in a forthcoming Présence Africaine volume.

Oba l'instituteur, Les Sangsues
Bucarest: Ilexim, n.d. [1975] (Témoignage de
l'Afrique contemporaine). 189 pp.
Two plays. In the first a young teacher is sent
to fight in World War II by a local recruiter
seeking revenge and comes back a fervent
Marxist and anti-colonialist. The second play
gives a portrait of an African parliamentarian
who is one of those 'bloodsuckers' who profit
from colonialism.

Sama, Eugène
Poèmes diplomatiques
Paris: P. J. Oswald, 1976 (distr. by

L'Harmattan, Paris). 111 pp. FF27.00
Poetry.

Sinda, Martial
Premier chant du départ
Paris: Seghers, 1955 (Poésie 55, Cahiers 'P.S.',
454). 61 pp. o/p
A collection of verse.

Sony Labou Tansi
La vie et demie
Paris: Ed. du Seuil, 1979. 192 pp. FF43.00
In a newly-independent African state
(Katamalanasie), a brutal dictator comes to
power under the ironic title of 'Providential
Guide'. He assassinates his chief political rival
and has his body made into pâté and fed to the
man's family. But the victim, an agent of the
prophet Mouzédiba, continues to haunt the
regime through the body of his daughter,
Chaïdana, the prostitute, who systematically
does away with its officials after a night with
them in the hotel whose name serves as the
book's title. Years later, Chaïdana's followers,
who have managed to set up a state within a
state deep in the forest, will be strong enough
to challenge the regime. A fable of power and
politics in modern-day Africa that won the
jury's prize at the Festival of Francophonie in
Nice in 1979.
'... *il faut se laisser emporter dans le déchaînement
bouillonnant d'une prose torentielle* ... *donne une
idée des immenses possibilitiés de la jeune littérature
nègre. Un chef-d'oeuvre de surréalisme tropical.*'
Grégory Pons – *Figaro Magazine*
'*Pour cette chronique des régimes dictatoriaux, Sony
Labou Tansi a choisi le mode de la fable: énorme,
burlesque, satirique et féroce.*'
Brigitte Salino – *Nouvelles Littéraires*

Conscience de tracteur
Dakar: Nouvelles Editions Africaines, 1979
(Répertoire théâtral africain, 26). 116 pp.
CFA500
Yaoundé: C.L.E., 1979. 116 pp. CFA500
On the eve of the 35th anniversary of the
Republic of Coldora somewhere in Central
Africa in the year 1995 an old scientist, who
considers himself a Noah of modern times,
begins to carry out his final plans to save
humanity through death and selective re-birth.
And people start dying mysteriously in the
capital of San-Mérina. Sony's play won 4th
prize in the 1973 Interafrican Theatre Competition. Henri Lopes has supplied an introduction. Two other plays, (not yet published) also won prizes in the Interafrican Theatre
Competition: *Je soussigné cardiaque* in 1976 (not
yet published) and *La parenthèse de sang* in 1978
(see subsequent entry).

L'Etat honteux
Paris: Ed. du Seuil, 1981. 160 pp. FF40.00
Labou Tansi continues to explore the absurdities of certain African states in his latest novel. The central figure, a head of state, resembles Alfred Jarry's King Ubu in many ways. As the narrator says, 'this is the true story of my ex-colonel, Martillimi Lopez, son of Mother Nation and commander of His Hernia' whose entire political philosophy is based on considerations to be found under the belt. Serious problems arise one day when all the ministers resign. As they say, 'We have a duty to leave this country to the children of our children but not in the wretched state it's in.'

La parenthèse de sang
Paris: Hatier, 1981 (Monde noir poche, 11). 156 pp. FF16.10
A play.

Tati-Loutard, Jean-Baptiste
Poèmes de la mer
Yaoundé: C.L.E., 1968. 64 pp. o/p
A first collection of verse by this poet-politician (he is the Congolese Minister of Culture). It is followed by an essay entitled 'Poésie nègre et retour aux sources'.

Les racines congolaises précédé de *La vie poétique*
Honfleur, France: P. J. Oswald, 1968 (distr. by L'Harmattan, Paris). 77 pp. FF17.00
This second volume of verse also contains a critical essay. Here the author discusses the nature of his muse.
'Tati-Loutard is at home in this literary syndrome [of orthodox Négritude themes], but his offerings are refreshingly individualistic. Lyric values are not marred by political or chauvinistic preoccupations'.
Dwight O. Chambers – *Books Abroad*

L'envers du soleil
Honfleur, France: P. J. Oswald, 1970 (distr. by L'Harmattan, Paris). 69 pp. FF17.00
Tati-Loutard's third book of poetry.
'L'auteur est à la recherche de ceux qui pour les raisons diverses préfèrent tourner le dos au soleil. Il ramène du fond de leur nuit de nombreux déclassés sociaux dont il reconstitue le poids de souffrances. La mer, la terre, le ciel, le vent et surtout le soleil sont intimement mêlés à l'univers lyrique de l'auteur où l'espoir et l'amour trouvent aussi leur place.'
L'Afrique Littéraire et Artistique

Les normes du temps
Kinshasa: Ed. du Mont Noir, 1974 (Jeune littérature, 1). 70 pp.
Poetry.

Chroniques congolaises: nouvelles
Paris: P. J. Oswald, 1974 (Poésie-prose africaine, 6) (distr. by L'Harmattan, Paris). 135 pp. FF25.00
Short stories

Les feux de la planète
Dakar: Nouvelles Editions Africaines, 1977. 41 pp. CFA350
Poetry.

Nouvelles chroniques congolaises
Paris: Présence Africaine, 1980. 188 pp. FF39.00
Disappointment due to the irony of circumstance is a major theme in Tati-Loutard's latest collection of twelve short stories, like the regret experienced by the young wife with an unfaithful husband who misses the chance for a love affair of her own, or the emotional letdown of a political prisoner who discovers, upon release, that his wife has left him. There can be tragic twists too, as seen in the story of the man who takes his car to meet a friend and who meets death or in that of the old woman in Brazzaville whom poverty drives mad.

Tchicaya U Tam'si, Gérard Félix
Le mauvais sang
Paris: Caractères, 1955. 45 pp. o/p
U Tam'si's first volume of poetry.

Feu de brousse
Paris: Caractères, 1957. 86 pp. o/p
In English *translation*, see next entry

Bush Fire
(Trans. from the French by Sagodare Akanji; pseud. for Ulli Beier)
Ibadan: Mbari, 1964. unpaged [96 pp.] o/p
The first volume of verse by U Tam'si to be translated into English.

A triche coeur
Paris: Ed. Hautefeuille, 1958. 82 pp. o/p
A volume of poetry.

Le ventre
Paris: Présence Africaine, 1964 (Collection Poésie). 136 pp. o/p
A further collection of verse. U Tam'si was awarded first prize for poetry at the first World Festival of Negro Arts held in Dakar in 1966.

Epitomé
Honfleur, France: P. J. Oswald, 1968 (2nd ed.). 137 pp. o/p
A fourth book of poetry, with an introduction by Léopold Senghor.

Arc musical précédé de *Epitomé*
Honfleur, France: P. J. Oswald, 1970 (P.J.O. Poche, 10) (distr. by L'Harmattan, Paris).
172 pp. FF22.00
This combined collection of verse includes an earlier volume, *Epitomé*, originally published in 1962.

Selected Poems
(Trans. from the French by Gerald Moore)
London: HEB, 1970 (AWS, 72). 96 pp.
£1.50/$5.00
Includes poems written both before and after U Tam'si's first English volume *Bush Fire* was published by Mbari in 1964.
'Moore's collection reveals that Tchicaya's dominant themes continue to be his quest for roots and self-identity. Moore translates closely and sensitively, but of course can only refract Tchicaya's vision. He admits his problems with the puns and surreal elements . . . will be of great value in increasing Tchicaya's audience.' Richard F. Bauerle – *Books Abroad*

La veste d'intérieur suivi de *Notes de veille*
Paris: Nubia, 1977. 111 pp. o/p
U Tam'si's most recent collection of verse won the Louise Labe Poetry Prize in 1979, the equivalent for poetry of the Fémina Prize for fiction.

Le Zulu suivi de *Vwène le fondateur*
Paris: Nubia, 1977. 149 pp. o/p
The first of these two plays is U Tam'si's version of the Chaka legend that was presented at the Festival of Avignon in 1976 and again the following year in Paris by J. Rosette's Théâtre Noir company.

Le ventre suivi de *Le pain ou la cendre*
Paris: Présence Africaine, 1978. 171 pp. FF36.00
In addition to *Le ventre*, which Présence Africaine originally published in 1964, this volume contains two new poems, 'La Conga des mutins' and 'La mise à mort' under the collective title, 'Le pain ou la cendre'.

Le mauvais sang suivi de *Feu de brousse* et *A triche-coeur*
Paris: Ed. Harmattan, 1978 (Poésie-prose africaine, 25). 137 pp. FF25.00
Tchicaya U Tam'si's first three collections of verse, originally published in 1955, 1957 and 1958 respectively, and reissued in 1970 in a combined volume by P. J. Oswald have again been made available by Editions Harmattan who have taken over Oswald.
'Le talent de Tchicaya U Tam'si, sa puissance évocatrice restent toujours aussi denses et aussi remarquables . . . un ouvrage poétique fondamental de notre temps'. – *Afrique Contemporaine*

Le destin glorieux du Maréchal Nnikon Nniku, Prince qu'on sort: comédie-farce-sinistre en trois plans
Paris: Présence Africaine, 1979. 112 pp. FF24.00
In the Kingdom of the Blind, the one-eyed man is King – so goes a French saying to which U Tam'si has given his own peculiar twist in this pun-filled satire of contemporary African dictatorships which recalls in many ways Alfred Jarry's *Ubu Roi*. There is the power clique led by Nnikon Nniku, the Supreme Guide and principal mentor of the Philosophy of Regression, and his cohorts, Nkha Nkha Dou and Mphi Ssans Po. There is Shese, prison guard and latrine cleaner who finds himself at the head of the country when Nnikon is overthrown. And on the side-lines, observing this 'sinister farce' are Lheki and Nniya, the young 'counter-revolutionary' and 'anti-reactionary' couple.
'. . . va très au-delà de la satire. C'est un hymne à la liberté que Félix Tchicaya a dédié à dessein à son père . . . le doyen et plus combatif des militants nationalistes du Congo dont il domina la vie politique jusqu'en 1958 en s'y faisant le champion de la démocratie parlementaire.'
Philippe Decraene – *Le Monde*

Les cancrelats
Paris: Albin Michel, 1980. 320 pp. FF55.00
In *The Cockroaches*, his first novel, U Tam'si continues his uneasy investigation of contemporary African society. This is no satire, but a real world of misery, injustice, dashed dreams and unfulfilled promise: the world of Africa's losers. The principal protagonists are Sophie and Prosper, the orphaned children of a man who had high hopes for them and whose death sets them on the downward path.

La main sèche
Paris: Laffont, 1980. 208 pp. FF49.00
Several of these eleven stories evoke historical black messiah figures of the Congo like Dona Béatrice, André Matswa or Simon Mpadi. Another story, entitled *Noces*, has animals as the main characters and satirizes receptions and social gatherings of VIP's in Africa today – and all over the world.

Tchichellé Tchivéla
Longue est la nuit
Paris: Hatier, 1980 (Monde noir poche, 4).
127 pp. FF16.00
Most of the eight stories in this collection have political undertones. One of them recalls, tragically, the colonial period when the white master had the power of life, and death, over the black man. Others offer critical portraits of

figures of the post-independence era: the high-level civil servant who collects young mistresses with threats; the corrupt agricultural engineer who is moved by a peasant strike to return to the ideals of his youth – when it is too late: the medical doctor, an opponent to the regime, who is arrested one day for no apparent reason; the young man who is shot to death during a student demonstration and whose girlfriend vows revenge. The setting for all is the imaginary country of Tongwétani, the former colony of Eurique, and now a one-party state ruled by the 'Almighty Dynast', Yéli Boso.

Tiemele, Jean-Baptiste
Chansons païennes
Paris: P. J. Oswald, 1969 (distr. by L'Harmattan, Paris). 46 pp. FF15.00
Poetry.

Rwanda

Naigiziki, J. Saverio
Escapade ruandaise: journal d'un clerc en sa trentième année
Bruxelles: G. A. Deny, 1949. 210 pp. o/p
A narrative of life in Rwanda

L'optimiste. Mes transes à trente ans
Nendeln, Liechtenstein: Kraus Reprint, 1977. These two works, originally published separately, have been bound together by Kraus in a reprint volume. *L'optimiste*, a three-act play, was first published in Astrida in Rwanda in 1955, and *Mes transes à trente ans* in 1956. The second work is an expanded form of *Escapade ruandaise* in two volumes entitled *De mal en pis* and *De pis en mieux*.

Somalia
(see also English-speaking Africa)

Syad, William F. J.
Khamsine
Paris: Présence Africaine, 1959. 72 pp. o/p
Love poems. With a foreword by Léopold Senghor.

Cantiques
Dakar: Nouvelles Editions Africaines, 1976. 176 pp. CFA750
The greater part of this collection, which is divided into three parts or three 'Songs', is love poetry, some of which has been inspired by traditional Somali verse. A few poems are in English. The author is a Somalian diplomat.

Harmoniques
Dakar: Nouvelles Editions Africaines, 1976. 168 pp. CFA750
Many of the love poems of this volume, like those of the previous collection, are free translations of *Malidy*, traditional Somalian verse. They are followed by a long radio poem entitled, 'The Angel with Broken Wings or The Legend of Good and Evil'.

Naufragés du destin
Paris: Présence Africaine, 1978. 123 pp. FF40.00

Zaïre Republic

Bolamba, Antoine-Roger
Esanzo: chants pour mon pays
Paris: Présence Africaine, 1955. 45 pp. o/p
In English *translation*, see next entry.

Esanzo, Songs for My Country: poems
(Trans. from the French by Jan Pallister)
Sherbrooke, Cananda: Ed. Naaman, 1977. 80 pp. Can.$5.00
Contains the original French text published by Présence Africaine, in 1955 and now out of print, and the English translation on facing pages. Prefaced by Léopold Senghor.
'. . . another orphic voice that comes out of Africa . . . Esanzo joins the general themes of Négritude with lyricism, sensitivity and rhythm.'
          Victor Carrabino – *World Literature Today*

Elébé, Lisembe (Philippe)
Mélodie africaine: poèmes
Laon, France: Ed. l'Etrave, Revue de la Nouvelle Pléiade, 1970. 119 pp. o/p
A collection of verse.

Uhuru: poèmes
Paris: Debresse, 1970. 53 pp. o/p
Poetry.

Rythmes
Kinshasa: Ed. du Mont Noir, 1971 (Jeune littérature, 5). 35 pp. 20k
Poetry.

Orphée rebelle
Paris: Ed. Saint Germain-des-Prés, 1972. 116 pp. FF20.00
Part I of this collection of verse is the title poem – a long poem in sixteen parts about Angola's struggle for sovereignty. The poems in part II are in a more personal vein, containing works written in honour of his

daughter, his German wife, Uta, his child-hood, a pet monkey, but also poems lamenting the death of Mobutu's mother.

Simon Kimbangu ou le messie noir suivi de *Le sang des noirs pour un sou*
Paris: Nouvelles Editions Debresse, 1972.
128 pp. FF15.00
The common theme of these two plays is the revolt against colonial authority. The first one deals with Simon Kimbangu, a Congolese prophet who was sentenced to life imprison-ment by the Belgiums in 1921; and the second one is a tale of black workers trapped in a South African mine after a cave-in and the subsequent arrest of one of the miners for inciting his fellow miners to strike for better working conditions.

Solitude: poèmes
Paris: P. J. Oswald, 1973 (distr. by L'Harmattan, Paris). 54 pp. FF15.00
A fifth collection of verse.

Chant de la terre, chant de l'eau
Paris: P. J. Oswald, 1973 (distr. by L'Harmattan, Paris) (Théâtre africaine, 24).
78 pp. FF15.00
Elébé's play is a free adaptation of the novel, *Gouverneurs de la roseé*, by the Haïtian author, Jacques Roumain. It is the tragic tale of Manuel who returns home after 15 years abroad with ideas about how to pull his village out of misery and who is killed by a local official who is jealous of him and his love for Annaïse. Despite his death, however, his project, a water scheme, will be carried out.

Souvenirs d'enfance
Paris: La Pensée Universelle, 1975. 156 pp. FF21.40
A book about the author's childhood.

La Joconde d'Ebene
Paris: Ed. Saint Germain-des Prés, 1977.
86 pp. o/p
Elébé's latest anthology of verse is prefaced by Maurice Carème.

Stations du monde: poèmes
Paris: Les Paragraphes Littéraires de Paris, 1979. 167 pp.

Kabatanshi Mulamba
Flammèches
Kinshasa: Ed. du Mont Noir, 1973 (Jeune littérature, 15). 31 pp. 30k
Poetry.

Kaboke Kolomoni [pseud. for Mamadu, Valentin]
Chroniques katangaises
Paris: La Pensée Universelle, 1976. 128 pp.
FF23.60
Tales of an historical nature: the feats of M'Siri and the strike of African miners in Upper Katanga in 1941.

Kadima-Nzuji Mukala (Dieudonné)
Les ressacs: poèmes
Kinshasa: Ed. Lettres Congolaises, Office National de la Recherche et du Développe-ment, 1969. 40 pp. o/p
Poetry.

Préludes à la terre
Kinshasa: Ed. du Mont-Noir, 1971 (Jeune littérature, 2). 48 pp. o/p
Poetry.

Redire les mots anciens
Paris: Ed. Saint Germain-des-Prés, 1977.
45 pp.
A collection of verse, with a preface by Jacques Rabemananjara, containing new poems in addition to those which appeared in his two previous collections, now out-of-print, *Les ressacs* and *Préludes à la terre*.

Kal'ngo Kinuana-Ngo Wayisa Yebeni
Lettres sans cendres: poèmes et prières
Kinshasa: Centre Africain de Littérature, 1973.
31 pp. 50k CFA250
Fifteen poems by one of the founding members of the Ndoto literary circle.

Lomami-Tshibamba, Paul
Ngando: le crocodile
Brussels: Ed. Georges A Deny, 1948. o/p
(reprinted with Mutombo, Dieudonné, *Victoire de l'amour*, and Malembe, Timothée, *Le mystère de l'enfant disparu*, Nendeln, Liechtenstein: Kraus Reprint, 1970. 327 pp. S.Fr.51.00)
One of the first Zaïrois novels. A child who falls into a river and is captured by a crocodile must be saved without violating traditions.

La récompense de la cruauté suivi de *N'Gobila des M'swata: nouvelles*
Kinshasa: Ed. du Mont-Noir, 1972 (Jeune littérature, 10). 94 pp. 70k
The first of these two stories is set in later colonial times. In the sacred forest, near what is now Kinshasa, a strange beast has everyone in a panic. The Europeans who have chased away all the fetish priests think their religion and their guns will get the better of it. But they fail. The second story recounts the massacre

that takes place at Stanley's station at Kimpoko on the Congo by King N'Gobila and his people when they realize their foreign 'guests' are exploiting them.

Ngemena
Yaoundé: C.L.E., 1980. 145 pp.
The comic adventures of a 'civilized African' from Léopoldville who travels through the Congo during the days of Belgian colonization.

Luamba, N.-K.
L'ecclésiastique
Paris: La Pensée Universelle, 1979. 288 pp. FF37.50
A priest must face nasty insinuations about his conduct. A novel.

Malembe, Timotheé
Le mystère de l'enfant disparu
Kinshasa: Bibliothèque de L'Etoile, 1962. 82 pp. (reprinted with Lomami-Tshibamba, Paul, *Ngando* and Mutombo, Dieudonné, *Victoire de l'amour*. Nendeln, Liechtenstein: Kraus Reprint, 1970, 334 pp. S.Fr.51.00).
The story of an adolescent boy who is taken hostage by an enemy village and how he is finally reunited with his family after a long series of adventures. Set in the early days of colonialization in the region of Kasai.

Matala Mukadi Tshiakatumba
Réveil dans un nid de flammes: poèmes
Paris: Seghers, 1969. 88 pp. o/p
Poetry.

Mayengo, Kulanda Tsi Mwela (François Médard)
Mon coeur de saisons: poèmes
Kinshasa: Ed. du Mont-Noir, 1972 (Jeune littérature, 8). 34 pp. 20k
Poetry.

Mbiango Kekesse, Ngatshan
La Confession du sergent Wanga
Kinshasa: Ed. du Mont-Noir, 1973 (Jeune littérature, 16). 95 pp.

Mikanza Mobiem Mangangi-Kidah (Norbert)
Pas de feu pour les antilopes
Kinshasa: Congolia, 1970. 56 pp.
A play written in collaboration with Paul Mahamwe Mushiete.

La bataille de Kamanyola ou bataille de la peur et de l'espoir
Kinshasa: Les Presses Africaines, 1975. 64 pp.
A play.

Muamba Kanyinda
La pourriture: roman
Kinshasa: Ed. EDIMAF, 1978. 304 pp. Z4.50
A popular novel which presents a broad canvas of life in present day Zaïre. The story concerns a young artist, Tshikida, who has been set upon by the family of a young girl he has been accused of raping. Tala Ngai, a lawyer, and hero of the novel, takes up his case in the conviction of his innocence, and the development of his handling of the case affords an insight into the methods of the police and the whole process of administration of justice in Zaïre. The novel is essentially a satire of modern Zaïre, and especially of Kinshasa society.

Mudimbe, Vumbi Yoka (Valentin Yves)
Déchirures: poèmes
Kinshasa: Ed. du Mont-Noir, 1971 (Jeune littérature, 3). 48 pp. 20k
Love poems structured in fifteen parts like the fifteen Stations of the Cross.

Entre les eaux: Dieu, un prêtre, la révolution
Paris: Présence Africaine, 1973. 192 pp. FF35.00
Mudimbe's novel about a young African priest caught between his spiritual and his political beliefs won the Grand Prix Catholique in 1975. Written in 1967 but not published until 1973, the book portrays a priest who forsakes his calling to join the resistence, out of respect for the Biblical message, and then ends up in a Trappist monastery having lost his faith in God and men.

Entretailles précédé de *Fulgurances d'une lézarde*
Paris: Ed. Saint Germain-de-Prés, 1973. 79 pp. o/p
Kinshasa: Ed. du Mont-Noir, 1973. 79 pp.
A collection of verse.

Carnets d'Amerique: journal
Paris: Ed. Saint Germain-de-Prés, 1974. 204 pp. o/p

Les fuseaux parfois: poèmes
Paris: Ed. Saint Germain-de-Prés, 1974. 48 pp. FF15.00
Mudimbe's third collection of poetry.

Le bel immonde
Paris: Présence Africaine, 1976. 175 pp. FF40.00
Set against the 1965 rebellions in Zaïre, Mudimbe's novel is written in twenty sequences and told mainly in the second and third persons. Its heroes are the Minister and

the Prostitute, named only by the roles they play. He yearns for true freedom which she symbolizes for him, and she seeks help for the rebellion, led by her father. But the minister, himself, will be a victim of the state's powers of repression. With a preface by Jacques Howlett.

L'écart
Paris: Présence Africaine, 1979. 159 pp. FF35.00
Mudimbe's latest work is not fiction at all – or so he claims in the preface – but rather the posthumous account of the 'fantastic schism of a heart' as recorded in the seven notebooks of a young man, Ahmed Nara, who died mysteriously.

Mutombo, Dieudonné
Victoire de l'amour
Leverville: Bibliothèque de L'Etoile, 1954 o/p (reprinted with Lomami-Tshibamba, Paul, *Ngando* and Timothée Malembe, *le mystère de l'enfant disparu*. Nendeln, Liechtenstein: Kraus Reprints, 1970. 334 pp.)
A young man who had been out of work and who had come to Léopoldville and managed to secure employment in a jewellery store almost loses his job and the girl he loves when he is falsely accused of theft.

Mwamba'a Musas Mangol
Muzang
Kinshasa: Ed. Ngongi, 1977. 77 pp.
A play presented by the National Theatre of Zaïre at the 2nd World Black and African Festival of Arts and Culture in Lagos in 1977 evoking the struggle of legendary Zaïrois people, the Mbal and the Hang, to free themselves from an invader – an obvious parallel to colonialism.

Mweya, Tol'Ande (Elizabeth-Françoise)
Remous de feuilles
Kinshasa: Ed. du Mont-Noir, 1972 (Jeune littérature, 9). 46 pp. 20k
Poetry.

Ahata suivi de *Récit d'une damnée*
Kinshasa: Ed. Bobiso, 1977. 92 pp.
Two stories. In 'Ahata', a young woman with a promising future learns her fiancé has chosen to marry a white woman but then she falls in love and marries Polo, the best friend of her ex-fiancé.

Ngal, Mbwil a Mpaang
Giambatista Viko ou le viol du discours africain: récit
Lubumbashi: Eds. Alpha-Omega, 1975. 113 pp.

In Part I of this novel, the personality of Professor Giambatista, internationally known author, gradually takes form. He is an intellectual who despises the African culture of his birth. In Part II we attend the 'trial' of the writer and that of his disciple and alter-ego, the mulatto, Niaiseux (Mr Inane). Giambatista is accused of the most hideous of crimes: desecrating African discourse by trying to transfer it artificially into a foreign-inspired literary genre, the novel, after attempting to undergo an initiation rite under false pretences. The writer is sentenced to 'return to his origins' and wander throughout Africa in search of its eternal wisdom.

L'errance
Yaoundé: C.L.E., 1979. 146 pp. CFA1,300
In the sequel to the previous volume, Giambatista and Niaiseux having completed their time in 'convents of African culture' throughout the continent and come out new men, settle in a quiet hotel in order to write the 'spontaneous account' of their experiences. Through discussion and monologue they review the lessons they have learned (the most valuable being cultural relativism) and seek the key by which their new insights can be transferred onto paper.

Ngandu Nkashama (Pius)
La délivrance d'Ilunga
Paris: P. J. Oswald, 1977 (Théâtre Africaine, 33) (distr. by L'Harmattan, Paris). 152 pp. FF26.00
A play about the struggle between the inhabitants of a village and the authorities of a newly-independent African country.

Ngenzi Lonta Mwene Malamba
La fille du forgeron
Kinshasa: Ed. Bobiso, 1969. 58 pp.
This play, which attempts to come to terms with the problem of individual freedom, was presented by the National Theatre of Zaïre at the 1976 second World Black and African Festival of Arts and Culture in Lagos. Sengula, the daughter of the village smithy, unrepentently violates two taboos by first daring to declare her love for her father and then by entering his forge where arms and masks are made. She even has the audacity to rebel against the death sentence the fetish priest places on her head and convinces the elders to withdraw it.

Njinji ou une fille de Ngola sauvera le peuple Ngola
Kinshasa: Ed. Bobiso, 1976. 36 pp.

A play. Njinji becomes the heroine of the Ngola people when she seduces the chief of the invaders to learn the secret of their military success.

Aimer à en mourir
Kinshasa: Ed. Bobiso, 1976. 59 pp.
Four short stories which weave together the themes of love and death.

La tentation de Soeur Hélène
Kinshasa: Ed. Bobiso, 1977. 42 pp.
A play about a nun whose vocation is not a real one.

Ngombo Mbala
Deux vies, un temps nouveau: roman
Kinshasa: Ed. Okapi, 1973. 190 pp.
A study in generations: the life of a father and then of his sons – one a minister, another a painter, and a third a singer. This novel won the 1970 Mobutu Grand Prix Littéraire.

Ngonda, Bempu Moyela
Appel et méditation d'Afrique
Paris: La Pensée Universelle, 1981. 112 pp.
FF32.10
Poetry

Nguwo, André B.
Chants intérieurs
Kinshasa: Ed. du Mont-Noir, 1972 (Jeune littérature, 6). 32 pp. 20k
Poetry.

Nsimba Mumbamuna
Lettres kinoises: roman épistolaire
Kinshasa: Centre African de Littérature, 1974. 32 pp. CFA250/50k
A short epistolary novel. A young customs worker and would-be-poet corresponds with Longo, the student, and Mumbamuna, the nurse. It is the end of one love and the beginning of another.

Nzuji, Madiya (Clémentine)
Le temps des amants
Kinshasa: Ed. Mandore, 1969. 45 pp.
Poetry. (This item, and the next two originally published under the name Faik-Nzuji, Madiya-Clémentine).

Kasala: poèmes
Kinshasa: Ed. Mandore, 1969. 54 pp.
Poetry.

Lianes
Kinshasa: Ed. du Mont-Noir, 1971 (Jeune littérature, 4). 31 pp.
Poetry.

Gestes interrompus: poèmes
Lumbumbashi: Ed. Mandore, 1976.
Another collection of verse with illustrations by the author.

Sangu, Sonsa
La dérive ou la chute des points cardinaux
Paris: O.R.T.F.-D.A.E.C., 1973 (distr. by Nouvelles Editions Africaines, Dakar) (Répertoire théâtral africain, 18). 145 pp. CFA300
A play set in a convent located on an African river island which is completely isolated during the rainy season. It is a haven of peace for the African and European nuns living there, including Sister Monyama, a well-known scholar from Germany, until the arrival of an African monk who has come on retreat. The dialogue which ensues will shake the very foundations of their beliefs.

Sumaili N'Gaye Lussa (Gaby)
Testament poèmes
Kinshasa: Ed. du Mont-Noir, 1971 (Jeune littérature, 1). 47 pp.

Tshimanga Membu Dikenia
Fleurs de cuivre: poèmes
Kinshasa: Centre Africain de Littérature, 1973. 31 pp. 50k/CFA250
Love poetry.

Tshinday-Likumbi, Etienne
Marche, pays des espoirs: poèmes
Paris: Présence Africaine, 1967. 56 pp. o/p
Poems. André Terrisse contributes a foreword.

Tuyinamo-Wumba
Pour une noix de palme
Yaoundé: C.L.E., 1974. 60 pp. CFA210
Five short stories about life in the different neighbourhoods of Kinshasa.

Wembo-Ossako
Amour et préjugés
Kinshasa: Centre Africain de Littérature, 1973. 48 pp. 50k/CFA250
The tragic tale of Mote and Shama, two young lovers from different social classes who are prevented from marrying and whose death leads to the social awareness of Mutamba, Shama's wealthy father. A play.

Withankenge Walukumbu-Bene (Edouard)
Les ancêtres zaïrois: poèmes
Kinshasa: Ed. Belles-Lettres, 1964 (Belles-lettres, 5). 23 pp.

La kinoise
Kinshasa: Ed. Belles-Lettres, 1965 (Belles-

lettres, 8). 19 pp.
Poetry: *The Girl from Kinshasa.*

Le filet
Kinshasa: Ed. Belles-Lettres, 1968 (Belles-lettres, 19). 46 pp.
Poetry.

Le déformateur
Kinshasa: Ed. Belles-Lettres, 1976. 36 pp.
The mental anguish of a man who is considering marriage.

Yisuku Gafudzi, Tito
Cendres et lumière
Kinshasa: Ed. Propoza, 1977. 55 pp.
Each poem in this very personal collection is preceded by a prose piece which, as the author

says, is meant to help 'keep the memory of the poem alive'.

Zamenga Batukenzanga
Les hauts et les bas
Kinshasa: Ed. Saint-Paul, 1971. 92 pp.
A young man defies the members of his family in order to get an education. In so doing he becomes a sort of 'black-white man' who belongs to neither the African nor the colonial society. He later plays an important role, however, in the independence struggle in Zaïre.

Sept frères et une soeur
Kinshasa: Ed. Saint-Paul, 1975. 60 pp.
Tragedy strikes the members of a family, one by one, in the form of suicide, madness, and then fratricide.

INDIAN OCEAN ISLANDS

Madagascar

Andria, Aimée
Brouillard
Paris: Ed. L. Soulanges, 1967. FF20.00
A novel

L'Esquif
Paris: Ed. L. Soulanges, 1968. 130 pp. FF20.00

L'année en fleurs
Paris: Ed. de la Revue Moderne, 1973. 55 pp.
o/p
A collection of verse organized around the theme of the seasons.

Dréo, Pélandrova
Pélandrova
Montvilliers, France: Eds. du C.E.D.S., 1975 (distr. by Chiron, 40 rue de la Seine, Paris). 401 pp. FF39.00
The heroine of this novel, set among the Antandroy peoples in the southern part of Madagascar, is a fetish priestess. Prefaced by two former Malagasy ambassadors to France.

Rabéarivelo, Jean-Joseph
La coupe de cendres
Tananarive: Pitot de la Beaujardière, 1924. o/p
The first book of poems by the man who is considered to be the father of modern literature in Madagascar.

Sylves
Tananarive: Imp. de l'Imerina, 1927. 103 pp.
o/p
Verse. Contains 'Nobles dédains', 'Fleurs mêlées', 'Destinée', 'Dixains', and 'Sonnets et poèmes d'Iarive'.

Volumes
Tananarive: Imp. de l'Imerina, 1928. 108 pp.
o/p
This third collection of poetry includes 'Vers le bonheur', 'La guirlande à l'amitié', 'Interlude rythmique', 'Sept quatrains', 'Arbres', 'Au soleil estival', and 'Coeur et ciel d'Iarive'.

Imaitsoanala – Fille d'oiseau – Cantate
Tananarive: Imp. Officielle, 1935. 236 pp. o/p
Poems.

Traduit de la nuit
Tunis: Ed. de mirages, 1935. 69 pp. o/p
Poems transcribed from the Hova. In English *translation*, see next entry.

Translations from the Night
(Trans. and ed. by John Reed and Clive Wake)
London: HEB, 1975 (AWS, 167). 96 pp.
£1.50/$5.00
This AWS edition contains poems from the original French edition plus some poems published posthumously.
'The short introduction is an excellent commentary and guide to the discovery of Rabéarivelo.'
J. D. Gauthier – *Books Abroad*

Chants pour Abéone
Tananarive: Henri Vidalie, 1937 [?]
A volume of poetry published just before Rabéarivelo committed suicide in 1937 at the age of thirty-six.

Des stances oubliées
Tananarive: Imp. Live, 1959. 24 pp. o/p
More posthumous poems.

Presques-Songes et Traduit de la nuit
Tananarive: Imp. Officielle, 1960. 221 pp.
A reissue in a combined volume of two previously published collections.

24 Poems
(Trans. from the French by Ulli Beier and Gerald Moore)
Ibadan: Mbari, 1962. Unpaged [40 pp.] o/p
Contains 'The white bull', 'Three birds', 'Valiha', 'Cactus', 'Birth of day', 'Zebu', and several others.

Vieilles chansons du pays Imerina
Tananarive: Ed. Madprint, 1980. 53 pp.
FMG2,350
This posthumous collection was originally published in Tananarive in 1939. It contains prose poems, most of which are translations or transpositions of an ancient poetic form in Madagascar called *hainteny*. Both the 1939 and the 1980 editions contain a biographical study of the author by R. Boudry, and the 1980 edition also includes a literary analysis of the verse in the volume by Professor Adrianarahinjaka of the University of Madagascar. The Madprint edition was awarded an honourable mention by the jury of the 1980 Noma Prize. It is printed on handcrafted Madagascar papyrus with dried wild flowers encrusted on the cover.

Rabémananjara, Jacques

Sur les marches du soir
Gap: Ed. Ophrys. 1942. 76 pp. illus. o/p
Verse.

Rites millénaires
Paris: Séghers. 1955 (Cahiers bimensuels, 55). 33 pp. o/p
Verse.

Les boutriers de l'Aurore
Paris: Présence Africaine, 1957. 232 pp. o/p
A three-act historical play set in Madagascar.

Antidote
Paris: Présence Africaine, 1961. 48 pp.
FF17.00
For actively partaking in the national libera-

tion movement in Madagascar, Rabémananjara was imprisoned from 1947 to 1950. The poems were written during this time; their central themes are Négritude, ancestry, and Rabémananjara's political hopes.

Agapes des dieux: Tritiva – tragédie malgache
Paris: Présence Africaine, 1962. 226 pp. o/p
Set in the ancient kingdom of Ambohimena, this historical play tells the tragic story of two young lovers, Hanta and Ratrimo.

Antsa
Paris: Présence Africaine, 1962. 70 pp. o/p
A further collection of verse reprinted in *Oeuvres Complètes*; see subsequent entry.

Les dieux malgaches (version destiné à la scène)
Paris: Hachette. 1964. 165 pp. o/p
A reissue of a play first published in Paris in 1947 now again o/p

Lamba
Paris: Présence Africaine, 1966. 85 pp. o/p
This book of poems has a foreword by Aimé Césaire; reprinted in *Oeuvres Complètes*, see subsequent entry.

Les ordalies: sonnets d'outre-temps
Paris: Présence Africaine, 1972. 62 pp.
FF24.00
Poetry.

Oeuvres complètes: poèsie
Paris: Présence Africaine, 1978. 356 pp.
FF68.00
All of Rabémananjara's previously published volumes of poetry, most of which are now o/p, are included here: *Les marches du soir* (first published by Ed. Ophrys in 1942); *Rites millénaires* (Séghers, 1955); *Lamba* (Présence Africaine, 1956); *Antes* (Présence Africaine, 1962); *Antidote*; and *Les ordalies*.

Ranaivo, Flavien

L'ombre et le vent
Tananarive: Imp. Officielle, 1947. 30 pp. o/p
Antananarivo, 1967 (new edn) 32 pp. illus.
(Reprinted in *The Poetic Works of Flavien Ranaivo*. Nendeln, Liechtenstein: Kraus Reprint, 1970. S.Fr.24.00)
Verse.

Mes chansons de toujours
Paris: Author, 1955. 31 pp. o/p
(Reprinted in *The Poetic Works of Flavien Ranaivo*. Nendeln, Liechtenstein: Kraus Reprint, 1970. S.Fr.24.00)
Ranaivo's second book of poems. There is a foreword by Léopold Senghor.

Le retour au bercail
Tananarive: Imp. Nationale, 1962. 36 pp.
(Reprinted in *The Poetic Works of Flavien Ranaivo*. Nendeln, Liechtenstein: Kraus Reprint, 1970. S.Fr.24.00)

Ratsitohaina, Harisata
Je ne savais pas . . .
Paris: T.M.T., 1969. 146 pp. o/p
A novel set in the upper classes of Malagasy society which aims to prove that marriages based on any other premise than mutual love and attraction are bound to fail.

Szumski
Sous le signe du Zébu
Metz, France: Ed. le Lorrain, 1970. 96 pp.
A collection of short stories.

Pas de girafe dans le sud
Finanarantsoa, Madagascar: Imp. Saint-Paul, 1972. 112 pp.
Short stories. The author has also published a volume of verse in Madagascar entitled *Sud alors*.

Mauritius
(See also English-speaking Africa)

Berthelot, Lilian
Intemporelles
Port-Louis: Ed. Chien de Plomb, 1973.
Rs12.00
A collection of poems illustrated with woodprints by Hervé Masson. The author is a regular contributor to the daily newspaper, *Le Mauricien*.

Le participe futur
Port-Louis: Imp. Père Vaval, n.d. [1979?].
Rs15.00
A story belonging to the genre that the author calls the 'contrevelle', half way between the short story ('conte') and the novelette ('nouvelle').

Cabon, Marcel
Kélibe-Kéliba
Port-Louis: Ed. Croix du Sud, 1951. 16 pp.
o/p
A long incantatory poem for narrator and chorus inspired by the culture of Malagasy peoples of African ancestry.

Namasté
Port-Louis: Ed. Le Cabestan, 1965. 94 pp. o/p
The tragic story of Ram, an Indian immigrant to Mauritius, who disembarks on the island with hardly anything more than the ritual greeting of his people, 'Namasté'. The efforts at integration followed by the death of Ram's wife in a cyclone unsettle his mind and lead to his own death. A re-issue is expected in the near future.

Le pain de chaque jour
Port-Louis: Royal Printing, 1966.
A radio play. The author, who was head of News Services of Mauritius radio and television, died in 1972.

Chasle, Raymond
Le corailleur des Limbes précédé de *Versos interdits*
Paris: P. J. Oswald, 1970. o/p
Poetry.

Vigiles Irradiées
Paris: Eds. Saint Germain-des-Prés, 1973.
110 pp.
The second part of a poetic trilogy.

Le rite et l'extase
Brussels: Eds. l'Etoile et la Clef, 1975 (distr. by Librairie Trèfle, Port-Louis, Mauritius). 55 pp.
Rs35.
Poems written in the form of calligrams. Some have already appeared in the journal, *L'Etoile et la Clef*.

L'alternance des solstices
Brussels: Eds. l'Etoile et la Clef, 1976. 92 pp.
A further volume of verse.

Chazal, Malcolm de
Sens plastique II
Port-Louis: General Printing and Stationery Co., 1947. 592 pp. o/p
Paris: Gallimard, 1948, 316 pp. o/p
This collection of verse remains the best known of Malcolm de Chazal's works. It was first published in Mauritius in 1947. On an earlier trip to France de Chazal met André Breton who had admired the verse to be included in this collection.

La vie filtrée
Paris: Gallimard, 1949, 300 pp. o/p

Iésou: théâtre mythique en 6 actes
Port-Louis: Imp. Aletophile, 1950. 63 pp.

Le rocher de Sisyphe
Port-Louis: Al-Madinah Printing, 1951.
48 pp.

Mythologie de crève coeur
Port-Louis: Al-Madinah Printing, 1951.
106 pp.

Petrusmok: mythe
Port-Louis: Standard Printing Establishment,
1951. 579 pp.

L'Evangile de l'eau
Port-Louis: Imp. al-Madinah, 1952. 115 pp.
o/p

Les Désamorantes, Le Concile des poétes
Port-Louis; Mauritius Printing Co., 1954.
80 pp.

L'Espace ou Satan: discours sur l'illusion
Port-Louis: Standard Printing Establishment,
1954. 35 pp.

Sens magique
Port-Louis: Al-Madinah Printing, 1957.
140 pp.

Apparadoxes
Port-Louis: Al-Madinah Printing, 1958.
84 pp.

Sens unique
Port-Louis: Ed. Le Chien de Plomb, 1958 [?]
Poetry.

Poèmes
Paris: J. J. Pauvert, 1968. 64 pp. FF8.50

Fanchette, Jean
Alpha du Centaure
Paris: Buchet-Chastel, 1975. 161 pp. FF50.00
Back in France after a trip to Mauritius the
hero of this novel tries to make sense of his life
by evoking the women he has loved and the
places he has lived in. The author won the Prix
des Mascareignes in 1972.
*'Oeuvre ambitieuse, sans doute déroutante, qu'il
faudrait lire comme une méditation sur l'exil et
l'enracinement: c'est-à-dire sur l'expérience cruciale
de beaucoup d'intellectuels mauriciens.'*
              Jean-Louis Joubert – *Notre Librairie*

Fragments pour un théâtre
Port-Louis: Imp. Esclapon, 1959 (distr. by
Librairie Allot, Curepipe, Mauritius). 34 pp.
Rs30.00
A play set in the context of World War II about
a man who willingly gives up his life so that his
wife and the man who has fathered her son
may live.

Hart, Robert-Edward
see **Hazareesingh, K.** ed.

Hazareesingh, Kissoonsingh ed.
Anthologie poétique de Robert-Edward Hart
Paris: F. Nathan and Ed. de l'Océan Indien,
1976. 127 pp. FF40.00
Poems by Robert-Edward Hart, one of
Mauritius' most prolific poets who died in
1954, are currently available in this anthology.
Practically unknown outside of Mauritius,
Hart published a number of poetry collections
locally ·during his lifetime, including *La vie
harmonieuse*, *Les voix intimes*, *L'ombre étoilée*,
Poèmes choisie, *Insula Beata*, *Poèmes anglais*
(translations of Marlowe, Spenser,
Shakespeare, Webster, Keats, Shelley, Byron,
Poe), *Bhagavad Gita* and *Poèmes védiques* (Hart's
Hindi poems). A bibliography of his works is
contained in Prosper's *Histoire de la littérature
mauricienne* (see page 48).

Anthologie poétique de Léoville L'Homme
Paris: F. Nathan, 1976. 127 pp. FF00.00
An anthology of the poetry of a man who is
considered to be the 'Father of Mauritius
Poetry'. Léoville L'Homme (1857-1928) published his verse locally between 1881 and 1928,
except for one collection, *Poèmes épars* published by Jouve et Cie., Paris, in 1921. Other
collections include *Poèmes païens et bibliques*
(1887). This volume contains a bibliography of
the poet's works and a general, annotated
bibliography. A bibliography of Léoville
L'Homme's writing can also be found in
Prosper's *Histoire de la littérature mauricienne* (see
page 48).

L'Homme, Léoville
see **Hazareesingh, K.** ed.

Humbert, Marie-Thérèse
A l'autre bout de moi
Paris: Stock, 1979. 468 pp. FF41.30
The twins, Anne and Nadège, are the heroines
of this novel set in Mauritius in the period
1936-1956. They may look alike but are
completely different. One accepts herself and
her background – that of a multi-racial, multicultural society – whereas the other rejects it.
*'La peinture d'une société multiraciale, avec toute sa
charge de préjugés, ses cloisonnements, ses espoirs, ses
déceptions.'*   Norbert Benoit – *Notre Librairie*

Lagesse, Marcelle
La diligence s'éloigne à l'aube
Paris: Julliard, 1955
Port-Louis: General Printing and Stationery
Co., 1971. 259 pp. Rs30.00
In this historical novel a young French planter
dies mysteriously in Mauritius in the early
nineteenth century, and his cousin, Nicolas

Kerubec, travels out to the island to claim his inheritance, falling in love, as had his deceased relative with the young widow in the neighbouring plantation. The novel won the Robert Bargues prize awarded by the P.E.N. club for the best novel from the Indian Ocean.

Sont amis que vent emporte
Port-Louis: General Printing and Stationery Co., 1973. 175 pp.
The members of an Air France flight crew sit out a cyclone in an airport on the island of Réunion, living together different moments in their lives.

Une lanterne au mât d'artimon
Port-Louis: General Printing and Stationery Co., 1979. Rs50.00
An historical novel written around a murder mystery. The heroine, an orphan, is one of the great number of young ladies that were sent out to Mauritius, the 'Isle of France', in the late eighteenth century to help populate the island.

Masson, André

Un temps pour mourir
Paris: Calmann-Lévy, 1962. 297 pp. o/p
Masson's first novel was one of the works nominated for the Prix Goncourt in 1962. It tells of the tragedy of man in the apocalyptic setting of a tropical cyclone.

Le chemin de pierre ponce
Paris: Calmann-Lévy, 1963. 324 pp. FF14.00
Masson's second novel is set in a sugar cane factory that is meant to be a microcosm of Mauritius society, where economic injustice and social barriers have full reign. In this context the young hero's search for perfect love becomes a mystical quest for salvation.

Le temps juste
Paris: Calmann-Lévy, 1966. 269 pp. FF13.00
Caught in a present where time no longer has any meaning, the hero of Masson's third novel relives different moments out of his past.

Chants de l'exil et photos mystiques
Port-Louis: Henry et Cie, 1974 [?] Rs50.00
Masson was forced to leave Mauritius in 1971 for political reasons and these poems, published locally thanks to an unidentified sponsor, carry the scars of that separation.

Le verrue
Dakar: Nouvelles Editions Africaines, 1977. 224 pp. CFA1,400
A novel written in 1971, when Masson had to go into exile from Mauritius, that raises the question of the freedom of individuals when confronted by an implacable institution.

Masson, Loys

Les autres nourritures
Port-Louis: T. Esclapon, 1938. 197 pp. o/p
An early collection of prose poems published before Masson left to settle in France. A prolific writer, Masson published thirty-one works before his death in 1969 and one posthumous volume. Only two of his books were published in Mauritius; the others were brought out by the major Paris publishing houses like Séghers, Gallimard, and Robert Laffont. For a complete bibliography of his works see Prosper, *Histoire de la littérature mauricienne* p. 48.

Poèmes d'ici
Neuchâtel, Switzerland: Ed. de la Baconnière, 1943. 76 pp. o/p
Poems written while the author was fighting for the French Resistance in World War II.

L'étoile et la clef
Paris: Gallimard, 1945. 366 pp. FF20.00
The hero of this autobiographical novel set on a sugar plantation in Mauritius is a white man who combats oppression and racism. In the background are the strikes and revolts of the Indian workers which shook the island in the late thirties.

Les vignes de septembre
Paris: Séghers, 1955
Poetry.

Les tortues
Paris: Robert Laffont, 1956. 268 pp.
A novel.

Christobal de Lugo. Le Pape. La résurrection des corps
Paris: Robert Laffont, 1960. 352 pp.
Theatre.

Les anges noirs du trône
Paris: Robert Laffont, 1967. 288 pp.
The adventures of a black pastor named Wake and his shipmates aboard Captain Hodgson's Ellery Prince who set out to save the lives of men.

Le notaire des noirs
Paris: Robert Laffont, 1969 (2nd ed.). 256 pp.
A paperback edition of one of Masson's best selling novels that was first published in 1961. It tells of the death of a young child, separated from his parents and surrounded by hypocritical adults, who dreams of his father as a

liberator. Set in Mauritius in the thirties against a background of strikes and popular revolts and narrated by a law clerk who had been one of the few adults to befriend the child.

Des bouteilles dans les yeux
Paris: Robert Laffont, 1970. 364 pp.
Short stories published a year after Masson's death.

Maunick, Edouard J.
Ces oiseaux de sang
Port-Louis: Regent Press, 1954. o/p
Maunick was working as a librarian on his native island of Mauritius when he published his first collection of verse. The book was a critical success, receiving a prize from the Académie Française, and in 1961 Maunick was encouraged to move to Paris to attempt to earn his living as a man of letters.

Les manèges de la mer
Paris: Présence Africaine, 1964. 101 pp.
A second volume of poetry, with an introduction by Pierre Emmanuel.

Mascaret ou le livre de la mer et de la mort
Paris: Présence Africaine, 1968. 142 pp. o/p
In these nine long poems Maunick continues to work out some of the themes that he took up in *Manèges de la mer*: the ambiguities of his birth on an island, of his mixed ancestry, of his life 'in exile' in Paris. Jacques Howlett has provided a preface.
'. . . *un recueil qui constitue un événement dans le domaine de la nouvelle poésie.*'
                    Marc Alyn – *Le Figaro Littéraire*

Fusillez-moi
Paris: Présence Africaine, 1970. 59 pp. o/p
A collection of poetry inspired by the Nigerian Civil War.

Ensoleillé vif: 50 paroles et une parabase
Paris: Ed. Saint Germain-des-Prés, 1976.
120 pp. FF30.00
Dakar: Nouvelles Editions Africaines, 1976.
120 pp. CFA1,500
In a 27-page introduction to this volume of verse that won the 1977 Guillaume Appolinaire Prize Léopold Senghor declared that 'few poets have a vision of the world which is as new and as profound as Maunick's.'

Africaines du temps jadis
Paris: A.B.C., 1976. 48 pp. FF9.10
Poems about great women in African history which were published to coincide with UNESCO's International Women's Year.

En mémoire du mémorable suivi de *Jusqu'en terre Yoruba*
Paris: L'Harmattan, 1979. 92 pp. FF22.00
Maunick's latest collection is meant to be a sort of poetic reckoning of the twenty-five years the poet has spent in trying to come to terms, in each successive volume of verse, with his identity as a man of mixed racial and cultural ancestry. The first part of this book contains Maunick's most recent verse whereas *Jusqu'en terre Yoruba* is a much earlier piece that was first published in *Présence Africaine* in 1965. It was inspired by a visit to a temple of the goddess Oshun in Nigeria.

Renaud, Pierre
Les balises de la nuit
Port-Louis: Ed. Le Chien de Pomb, 1974.
A long poem for which the author was awarded, posthumously, the Prix des Mascareignes. Renaud died in 1976.

Réunion

Azéma, Jean Henri
Olographe: poèmes mascarins
Saint-Denis, Réunion: Ed. des Trois Salazes, 1978. 89 pp.
Poetry in French and Creole.

Cheynet, Anne
Les muselés
Paris: L'Harmattan, 1977. 159 pp. FF33.00
A novel.

Debars, Riel
Sirène de fin d'alerte
Sainte-Clotilde, Réunion: Ed. Chemins de la Liberté, n.d. FF15.00
Poetry.

Gauvin, Axel
Quartier Trois-Lettres
Paris: L'Harmattan, 1980. 148 pp. FF39.00
The author's first novel, set in Réunion. Ti-Pierre, the son of an itinerant mason, succeeds in becoming a real fisherman thanks to his 'uncles', 'ton Kaêl and 'ton Maxime.

Kichenapanaïdou, Marc
L'Ivrogne
Sainte-Clotilde, Réunion: Ed. Chemin de la Liberté, 1974.
A play.

La demande en mariage
Sainte-Clotilde, Réunion: Ed. Chemin de la Liberté, 1975.
A play.

L'esclave
Sainte-Clotilde, Réunion: Ed. Chemin de la
Liberté, 1976.
A play.

Lacpatia, Firmin
Boadour
Sainte-Clotilde, Réunion: Ed. Chemin de la
Liberté, n.d. 140 pp. FF35.00
A novel about Indian labourers in Réunion.

Lorraine, Alain
*Tienbo le rein et Beaux visages cafrines sous la
lampe*
Paris: P. J. Oswald, 1975 (distr. by
L'Harmattan, Paris). 96 pp. FF26.00
A collection of verse that was originally
published in Saint-Denis (Réunion) by
Témoignage Chrétien de la Réunion.

Marimotou, Carpanin
Arracher cinquante mille signes
Sainte-Clotilde, Réunion: Ed. Chemin de la
Liberté, n.d. FF15.00

Fazele
Sainte-Clotilde, Réunion: Ed. Chemin de la
Liberté, n.d. 56 pp. FF15.00
Poems in Creole and French.

Sam-Long, Jean-François
Empédocle
Saint-Denis, Réunion: Nouvelle Imp.
Dionysienne, 1975. 29 pp.
Poetry and stories.

Crucifixion
Saint-Denis, Réunion: Nouvelle Imp.
Dionysienne, 1977. 64 pp.
A collection of verse prefaced by Gilbert
Aubry.

Treuthard, Patrice
20 désann et d'entre tous les zanzibar
Sainte-Clotilde, Réunion: Ed. Chemin de la
Liberté, n.d. FF15.00
Poetry in French and Creole.

Seychelles

Abel, Antoine
Paille en queue
Mahé, Seychelles: Saint Fidèle Press, 1969.
49 pp.
Poetry.

Coco sec: récit
Paris: P. J. Oswald, 1977 (Poésie-prose
Africaine, 21) (distr. by L'Harmattan, Paris).
139 pp. FF25.00

Une tortue sa rappelle
Paris: P. J. Oswald, 1977 (Poésie-prose
Africaine, 22) (distr. by L'Harmattan, Paris).
125 pp. FF27.00

Contes et poèmes des Seychelles
Paris: P. J. Oswald, 1977 (Poésie-prose
Africaine, 23) (distr. by L'Harmattan, Paris).
70 pp. FF16.00

LUSOPHONE AFRICA

Editor's note:
This section, which has been contributed by Donald Burness – and which he wishes to be dedicated to Gerald Moser – gives a *selection* of creative writing by authors from Angola, Cape Verde, Mozambique and the twin islands of São Tomé e Principe. Donald Burness has also provided details, and annotations, on a number of critical works and anthologies. These, however, are included in the appropriate sections on pp. 12–96 and are listed together with English and French titles.

Angola

Abreu, Antero
A Tua Voz Angola
Luanda:União dos Escritores Angolanos, 1978 (Cadernos Lavra e oficina 11). 22 pp.
20 Kwanzas (70c)
A collection of twelve poems, hymns to Angola, written in a direct and simple style that at times achieves remarkable resonance. Two lyrical elegies, 'Camarada Comandante' and 'Requiem' highlight the volume.

Albuquerque, Orlando de
O Homem Que Tinha a Chuva
Lisbon: Agência-Geral do Ultramar, 1968. 140 pp. o/p
Awarded the Fernão Mendes Pinto Prize of 1967, this novel of conflict between Mussulo, a witch-doctor called upon by the people to bring much needed rain, and his hated enemy, Chief Chipala, ends in tragedy. Nandololo, an elderly woman, remembers that years ago Chipala banished his rival in love, Mussulo. The drought years later provides Mussulo with an opportunity to gain revenge; he blames the chief for the absence of rain and demands the death of Chipala. The inevitability of the tragedy stems from the hopelessness of Chipala, who cannot tell the people that, in fact, personal rather than supernatural forces are at work. The simple, direct style of the novel reinforces the simplicity of the action.

António, Mário
Mahezu: Tradições Angolanas
Lisbon: Serviço de Publicações Ultramarinas, 1966. 70 pp. o/p
'Mahezu' is a Kimbundu word spoken by the story teller when he has concluded his tale. The folk-tales in this collection include trickster stories, moral fables and myths.

Rosto de Europa
Braga, Portugal: Editora Pax, 1968 (Metropole e Ultramar, 40). 76 pp. 50 escudos
Poems, portraits in words, in which Mário António captures a mood or an experience through a series of apparently gratuitous images. Mário António's early poetry dealt solely with Africa; these abstract poems are inspired by Europe.
'*Todo ele e suavamento belo, . . . lírico e equilibradamente moderno.*'
Armando Ferreira – *Jornal de Comércio*

Assis Junior, António de
O Segredo da Morta – Romance de Costumes Angolenses
Luanda: A Luzitana, 1934. o/p
Lisbon: Edições 70, 1979 (2nd ed.) (Autores Angolanos, 21), 285 pp.
One of the early Angolan novels by a black or mestiço. The author describes Angolan society in towns and villages along the Cuanza River at the end of the 19th century. A great deal of ethnographic information is presented in this story of two enterprising women, Ximinha Belchoir and her friend Kapaxi. The spirit of Ximinha Belchior lives on after her death, punishing those companions who stole her ring, her money and her cloths as she lay dying.

Barbeitos, Arlindo
Angola Angolê Angolema
Lisbon: Sá da Costa, 1976 (Vozes do Mundo, 6) 76 pp.
In an interview that precedes this collection of poems Arlindo Barbeitos affirms that his poetry is a compromise between the word and silence.
'*A técnica paralalística, a discursividade prosaica, são subvertidas e aplicadas em proveito dos pequenos episodias, que afloram e se deixam aprender mas não supreender.*' Pires Laranjeira – *África*

Nzoji (Sonho)
Lisbon: Sá da Costa, 1979 (Vozes do Mundo, 13) 56 pp. 70 escudos

'Nzoji' is a Kimbundu word for 'Dream'. The poems in this collection are rooted in traditional imagery. In his second volume Barbeitos continues to suggest through metaphor emotional states and social values.
' . . . a concepção cíclica do tempo e a integração do homen no espaço como um organismo cosmogónico total.'   Ana Mafalda Leite – *África*

Bessa Victor, Geraldo
Mucanda
Braga, Portugal: Editora Pax, 1964 (Metropole e Ultramar, 2) 1965 (2nd ed.) 74 pp. o/p
Reprinted with two other volumes of poetry, *Debaixo do Ceu* and *Cubata Abandonada* by Kraus Reprint, Nendeln, Liechtenstein, 1970.
A book of lyric poems in three parts: 'Menino Negro,' 'O Negro e o Amor,' and 'Um Homem Negro no Mundo.' Bessa Victor, a lawyer living in Lisbon, uses traditional Portuguese poetic forms to express an African vision of brotherhood.

Monandengue
Lisbon: Livraria Portugal, 1973. 54 pp.
Bessa Victor's last book of poems was awarded the Camilo Pessanha Prize in 1972. Returning in 1970 to Angola after twenty-four years of absence, the poet recaptured instinctively memories of his African chidhood. This volume is dedicated to those memories.

Cardoso, António
21 Poemas da Cadeia
Luanda: União dos Escritores Angolanos, 1979 (Cadernos lavra e oficina, 16). 30 pp. 20 Kwanzas (70c)
Poems written in prison between 1970 and 1973 by a leading member of 'The Generation of '50'. Cardosa frequently combines classical form, freshness of rhyme, and symbolic richness in these poems of love, sorrow and art.

Cardoso, Boaventura
Dizanga Dia Muenhu
Lisbon: Edições 70, 1977 (Autores Angolanos, 12), 95 pp. 90 escúdos
Ten lively short stories show various aspects of life in the musseques of Luanda. Influenced by the modern Angolan prose of Luandino Vieira, Cardoso is faithful to the spoken language of the people rather than traditional Portuguese syntax and spelling.
'Haverá, seguramente, uma enorme alegria nesta palavra'   João de Melo – *África*

Carvalho, Ruy Duarte de
Exercicios de Crueldade
Lisbon: Publicações Culturais Engrenagem,

1978. 65 pp.
These poems celebrate in unrestrained elation love of life, love of country, love of woman. The poet, a cinematographer, expresses his visions through a visual imagery that is often punctuated by the erotic.

Costa Andrade, Fernando
Poesia com Armas
Lisbon: Sá da Costa, 1976 (Vozes do Mundo, 4) 155 pp. 95 escudos
This book of poems is largely concerned with the war of Angolan independence. It is a hymn to heroes, living and dead; it is also a song of love to Angola, its landscapes and its people. There is a preface, 'O Canto Armado do Povo Angolano' by Mário de Andrade.
'Poesia com Armas de Costa Andrade é o maior documento épico da primeira guerra de libertagao.'
Manuel Rui – *Lavra e Oficina*

Jacinto, António
Vôvô Batolomeu
Lisbon: Edições 70, 1979 (Autores Angolanos, 17), 41 pp. 50 escudos
In this didactic tale written in 1946, the young narrator refuses to accept the fatalistic position of the elder Vôvô Bartolomeu that nothing can be done about the poor lot of the blacks.

Lima, Manuel dos Santos
As Lágrimas e o Vento
Lisbon: Africa Editora, 1975. 296 pp. 90 escudos.
A war novel set in Northern Angola in the early sixties when popular resistance to Portuguese colonialism manifested itself in armed rebellion.
'Na relação violenta colonizador/colonizado assenta parte da estrutura deste livro . . .'
João de Melo – *África*

A Pele do Diabo
Lisbon: Africa Editora, 1977 (Dossier Angola, 4), 66 pp. 60 escudos
Dos Santos Lima's play is set in St Louis in 1970. Jim Blackman, a hero returning from Vietnam, struggles to find identity and self-esteem in racist America. He tries passing as white, but when he realizes that a white mask cannot cover his black soul, he joins the militant Black Panthers.
'Jim encontra-se dividido entre duas alternativas contrárias – o protesto não-violento, simbolizado pelo seu amigo Jack, ou a revolução aberta simbolizado pelos Panteras Negras.'
Donald Burness – *África*

Macedo, Jorge
Clima do Povo
Lisbon: Edições 70, 1977 (Autores Angolanos, 5), 43 pp. 50 escudos
A book of poetry in two parts, 'Clima do Exílio' and 'Clima Regressado'. Macedo captures the spirit of optimism of a new day in independent Angola. This is an oral poetry characterized by frequent use of consonance and repetition of word and phrase.
'Terá acontecido ao poeta o que em 1922 era confissão de Maiakovski: versos e revolução como que se associaram na minha cabeça.'
Vergílio Alberto Vieira – *África*

Mestre, David
Do Canto à Idade
Coimbra, Portugal: Centelha, 1977 (Poesia Nosso Tempo, 14), 80 pp.
Twenty-eight poems composed between 1972 and 1976 by one of Angola's important contemporary writers. Although several of Mestre's poems make direct social statements, the majority, deliberately vague, are constructed through the use of private symbols and an imagistic logic that goes beyond reason.
'Há aqui a assinalar uma grande riqueza substantiva, resultado dum privilégio concedido, no trabalho semântico, aos nomes simbólicos das coisas.'
Luis de Miranda Rocha – *África*

Neto, Agostinho
Sagrada Esperança
Lisbon: Sá da Costa, 1974 (Vozes do Mundo, 1) 138 pp.
In English *translation,* see next entry.

Sacred Hope
Trans. from the Portuguese by Marga Holness
Dar es Salaam: Tanzania Publ. House, 1974.
84 pp. T.shs.17.00 ($3.00)
The first complete Portuguese edition (1974) of the principal collection of poems of Agostinho Neto was awarded the Poetry of Combat Prize by the University of Ibadan in 1975. The forty-eight poems were written between 1945 and 1960. Neto, a medical doctor as well as a writer, devoted much of his life to his country's struggle for freedom and after independence; as first president of Angola, worked for the development of a just socialistic society in which black, white and mulatto Angolans participated equally. These committed poems reflect an increased consciousness of the people's need to win independence through self-assertion. Many poems speak of love, harmony, freedom and the humiliation caused by colonialism, in particular forced labour and the Massacre in São Tomé. (Lusophone

Africa's Sharpeville). During the MPLA's active struggle for freedom, soldiers would sing poems of their leader Agostinho Neto that Rui Mingas had put to music. Like former President Senghor of Senegal, Neto subordinated his career as poet once his political responsibilities demanded his complete attention.

Pepetela [pseud. for **Pestana, Artur**]
Muana Puó
Lisbon: Edições 70, 1978 (Autores Angolanos, 14), 171 pp.
An allegory. Bats rebel against crows in order to create their own future; a man and a woman seek harmony through love. The two plots are woven together through the theme of a quest for Utopia.
'A unidade dos três planos da narrativa – o colectivo, o individual e o utópico – é realizado pela máscara de Muana puó.' Fernando Martinho – *África*

Pimentel, Carlos
Tijolo a Tijolo
Luanda: Instituto Nacional do Livro e do Disco, 1980. 69 pp. 125 Kwanzas ($4.15)
A collection of poems in which the author fuses personal experience and communal aspirations. This is frequently a poetry of equivalence, a poetry of indirection, but the metaphors are so simple that one cannot fail to see that Pimental's volume, like the struggle of Angolan people, proceeds 'tijolo a tijolo', brick by brick.

Ribas, Oscar
Uanga-Romance Folclórico Angolano
Luanda: Lello, 1969 (2nd ed.). 260 pp.
When Catarina wins Joaquim for her husband, her jealous rival Joana will stop at nothing, including the use of witch-craft, to recapture the man she loves. This novel, set in and around Luanda in the 1880s, presents a portrait of the age, its customs and values. Ribas is primarily concerned with capturing the essence of traditional life. His novel is more than a romantic tale; it is an ethnographic repository punctuated with Kimbundu riddles, myths and fables.

Tudo Isto Aconteceu
Luanda: Ediçao do Autor, 1975. 641 pp.
Ribas calls this an autobiographical novel. An extensive dictionary of Angolan regional words and phrases is found at the conclusion of the novel.

A Praga
Luanda: União dos Escritores Angolanos, 1978 (Cadernos lavra e oficina, 9). 25 pp.
20 Kwanzas (70c)

This short story first appeared in 1952 in *Escos da Minha Terra: Dramas Angolanas,* one of many works of popular folklore written by the blind Oscar Ribas. Awarded the Margaret Wong prize from the International Committee on Christian Literature for Africa, *A Praga* is inspired by oral literary traditions. Senhora Donana, the protagonist of the story, calls for a curse to fall on the person who has found but not returned her lost money. Ironically, Senhora Donana becomes a victim of her own curse, for a plague strikes her village.

Rocha, Jofre

Estória de Kapangombe
Luanda: União dos Escritores Angolanos, 1978 (Cadernos lavra e oficina, 13). 19 pp.
20 Kwanzas (70c)
In this political story, Kapangombe, an educated youth, teaches factory workers that one must trust the leaders, for their decisions, which may not be understood by all, are in the best interest of the people. Rocha's use of Kimbundu words and expressions and his predilection for spelling words as they are pronounced in the musseques shows the influence of Luandino Vieira.

Rui, Manuel

Regresso Adiado
Lisbon: Edições 70, 1978 (2nd ed.) (Autores Angolanos, 7). 155 pp. 130 escudos
A collection of five stories with a preface and concluding comment by Manuel Ferreira. Manuel Rui, poet and storyteller, writes in colloquial language of the alienation of assimilated Angolans who feel superior to 'unenlightened' Africans. In 'Mulato de Sangue Azul,' Luís Alvim, a mulatto who denies his African heritage, is mysteriously killed. The stories 'Com ou Sem Pensão' and 'O Aquário' narrate the lives of alienated whites, caught in a web of poverty or boredom.
'Todos os contos passam a ser lidos em função dum regresso incumbente que pressupõe uma alteração das situações que os motivaram.'
Manuel Simões – *África*

Soromenho, Castro

Terra Morta
Rio de Janeiro: Livraria-Editôra da Casa do Estudante do Brasil, 1949. 228 pp.
Lisbon: Arcadia, 1961. 267 pp. (banned upon publication)
Lisbon: Sá da Costa, 1975 (Vozes do Mundo, 3) 261 pp.
Soromenho's novel, set in the outpost of Camaxilo in the diamond rich province of Lunda in the 1930s, depicts the injustice and

suffering caused by the Portuguese colonial policy of 'pacification' in Angola. Joaquim Américo, a white man with democratic ideas, opposes minor Portuguese officials who sanction excessive taxation and brutal life in the mines. Through a series of flashbacks we learn of the horrors caused by forced labour. In the ninth chapter an old chief, who had the courage to stab a sepoy (a black man who supports the Portuguese) to death when his village was raided in search of fugitives from forced labour, subsequently hangs himself. This classic of Angolan writing is so convincing that Léopold Senghor is supposed to have been surprised when he learned that Soromenho was not a black man.

Camaxilo
Trans. from the Portuguese by Violante do Canto
Paris, Présence Africaine, 1955. 1963 (2nd ed.). 322 pp. o/p

Vieira, José Luandino

Luuanda
Luanda: ABC, 1963. 103 pp. o/p
Lisbon: Edições 70, 1974 188 pp. 130 escudos
In English *translation*, see next entry.

Luuanda
Trans. from the Portuguese by Tamara L. Bender
London: HEB, 1980 (AWS, 222). 128 pp. £1.95/$5.00
In 1965 this collection of three stories was awarded by the Portuguese Writers Society first prize for the best prose fiction of the year produced in Portugal and the overseas provinces. However, the authorities banned the book and the society itself was dissolved. Opposition to the awarding of the prize to *Luuanda* ostensibly centred on the negative literary quality of Luandino's prose which frequently includes regional expressions. However, the fact that the author was at the time a political prisoner undoubtedly upset the authorities far more than they were publicly willing to admit. The three stories, set in the musseques or suburbs of Luanda, show the lives of African people, their dreams, their sorrow, their laughter. The third story 'Estória da Galinha e do Ovo' is a social and political allegory in which various villagers each claim the ownership of an egg. In the end the police come to try to settle the public dispute, and determine that they shall keep the egg. *Luuanda* represents the beginning of a new direction in Angolan writing. Luandino's enriching of traditional Portuguese by bringing to it an African originality opened the way for modern

writers to free themselves from the confines of classical Portuguese.
'*Highly recommended for all collections of African literature.*'   – *Library Journal*

La vrai vie de Domingos Xavier followed by *Le complet de Mateus*
Trans. from the Portuguese by Mário de Andrade and Chantal Tiberghien
Paris: Présence Africaine, 1971. 159 pp. o/p
The French translation was the first published edition of this novel. It was not published in the original Portuguese until 1974, when the Armed Forces Movement in Portugal had wrought a radical change in colonial policy.

A Vida Verdadeira de Domingos Xavier
Lisboa: Edições 70, 1974. 128 pp. 120 escudos
In English *translation*, see next entry.

The Real Life of Domingos Xavier
Trans. from the Portuguese by Michael Wolfers
London: HEB, 1978 (AWS, 202). 84 pp. £1.50/$4.00
This first novel, written in 1961, was not published in Portugal until 1974. The central character of the novel, Domingos Xavier, a truck driver and member of the MPLA, is arrested and imprisoned for political activity by Portuguese authorities. Despite the fact that he is brutally tortured, Domingos Xavier refuses to betray his friends and their cause. He dies peacefully in jail, a martyr to a cause of freedom for his people. His friends include Mussunda, an intellectual tailor with socialist inclinations, Chico João, an athlete and ladies' man, and Mr Silvester, a white Angolan, completely sympathetic to the goals of the liberation movement. The novel concludes with celebration, with music and dancing as a tribute to the courage of Domingos Xavier and the vitality of a cause that will eventually rid Angola of colonialist oppression. Luandino Vieira's novel reveals the awakening of consciousness of the Angolan people in the direction of armed struggle for independence. Shortly after completing this novel, the author himself was sentenced by a military court to many years in prison for his nationalism.
'. . . *a remarkable novel, in many ways a quite unique novel, and altogether a most compulsively readable novel . . . And perhaps the greatest success of this novel is that Luandino has been able, without the least forcing of probability, and even with a stark realism, to present this life and death as an occasion for pride and even joy.*'
Basil Davidson – *West Africa*

Nós, os do Makulusu
Lisbon: Sá da Costa, 1974 (Vozes do Mundo, 2) 140 pp. 85 escudos

This lyrical novel about a family of colonialists living in Makulusu, a district of Luanda, was written in April, 1967, when Luandino was a political prisoner in Tarrafal, Cape Verde. The narrator, a white man like the author, comes to identify with African victims of exploitation. The action is set during the time of armed revolutionary struggle.

No Antigamente na Vida
Lisbon: Edições 70, 1974. 220 pp. 140 escudos
Three autobiographical stories set in the musseques of Luanda recollect the magical and fanciful realm of childhood. These stories are of particular import, for they reflect an unrestrained stylistic freedom that furthers a linguistic revolution begun with *Luuanda*.

Vidas Novas
Porto, Portugal: Afrontamento, 1975. 111 pp. 70 escudos
Lisbon, Edições 70, 1979 (2nd ed.). 110 escudos.
Awarded the João Dias Prize by the Casa dos Estudantes do Império in Lisbon in 1962, this collection of eight stories, written before *Luuanda*, presents a pantheon of heroic figures who inspire the people by their bravery and dedication. One of the stories 'O Fato Completo de Lucas Matesso' was published by *Présence Africaine* in conjunction with *A Vida Verdadeira de Domingas Xavier*.

João Vêncio: Os Seus Amores
Lisbon: Edições 70, 1979. 144 pp. 140 escudos
Luandino calls this, the confessions of a small time Don Juan of the musseques, a literary circumlocution written in slang and jargon. João Vêncio, the anti-heroic picaresque figure, recaptures in his narration disparate images of childhood. In a language as unpredictable and varied as is the nature of the protagonist, the author captures the vitality, the sorrow and the laughter of poor districts of Luanda. There is a substantial introduction by Fernando Martinho.

Xitu, Uanhenga (de Carvalho, Agostinho Mendes de)

Manana
Lisbon: Edições 70, 1978 (Autores Angolanos, 11), 185 pp. 150 escudos
Felito Bata de Silva, an assimilated Angolan, gets caught up in a series of lies in his quest to win the love of the innocent Manana. In this comic novel, the anti-heroic protagonist becomes increasingly alienated from his wife, from his community and from Manana.
'*Manana é mais um exemplo da vitalidade das letras angolanos.*'   Fernando Martinho – *África*

Cape Verde

Amarilis, Orlanda
Cais-do-Sodré té Salamansa
Coimbra, Portugal: Centelha, 1974 (Ficção-Nosso Tempo, 2). 124 pp.
Orlanda Amarilis, the Cape Verdean wife of critic and novelist Manual Ferreira, has written a collection of seven short stories in which the dominant figures are usually women dreaming of what might be or remembering past days on Cape Verde.
'As personagens de Orlanda Amarilis, através do protexto do diálogo com o outro, fazem o dialogo consigo mesmas.' Maria Lúcia Lupecki – *África*

Lopes, Baltasar
Chiquinho
Sâo Vicente, Claridade, 1947. 298 pp. o/p
Lisbon: Prelo, 1970 (3rd ed.). 300 pp.
Written by one of the founders of the Cape Verdean journal *Claridade, Chiquinho* expresses the quality of being Cape Verdean. This novel tells the sad story of Chiquinho – his father works in America in order to provide the family with money; he, his mother, his friends seek to survive in a land where repeated droughts make life a continual struggle. Lopes introduces a gallery of characters including Andrézinho, a young political activist and liberator, Euclides Varanda, an elderly poet, and Parafuso, the sickly Latin scholar who dies of tuberculosis before he can contribute to the success of the school football team.

Lopes, Manuel
Chuva Braba
Lisbon: Instituto de Cultura e Fomento de Cabo Verde, 1956. 309 pp. o/p
Lisbon: Ulisseda, 1965 (2nd rev. ed.). 262 pp. o/p
The first novel of Manuel Lopes, who along with Baltasar Lopes and the poet Jorge Barbosa, gave birth to the first issue of the Cape Verdean journal *Claridade* in 1936. Mane Quim, the adolescent protagonist, is torn between a call for adventure to other lands and a refusal to abandon the land. A driving rain convinces him that the land will, in fact, yield again; unlike the hero of Baltasar Lopes' novel *Chiquinho,* Mane Quim chooses to remain.

Tavares, Eugénio
Mornas: Cantigas Crioulas
Lisbon: J. Rodrigues Ca., 1932. 108 pp. o/p
The morna, a unique expression of the Cape Verdean soul, is not merely poetry put to music; it is dancing and gestures as well. Tavares' collection of mornas, all composed in Crioulo language, is of historic import, for Cape Verdean writers have continued to cultivate Crioulo poetry over the past four decades. Moreover, in his emotional preface, the author calls on Portugal to recognize the culture of his people. A few years after Tavares published his *Mornas,* the journal *Claridade* took up the same theme, the confident expression of a Cape Verdean essence that was different from but not inferior to Portuguese culture.

Mozambique

Azevedo, Mario J.
The Returning Hunter
Thompson, Conn.: Inter Culture Associates, 1978 (The African Sketches Series). 60 pp. $1.95
Dr Azevedo, born in Mozambique, teaches history at Jackson State University in Mississippi. His novella, written in English, tells the story of Bento who seeks a comfortable life as an 'assimilado', a Portuguese African. His childhood friend N'gando and his own son Vasco, a secret member of FRELIMO, combine to shatter Bento's confidence in the colonial government.

Craveirinha, José
Chigubo
Lisbon: Casa dos Estudantes d Império, 1964 (Autores Ultramarinos 14). 35 pp. o/p
Lisbon: Edições 70, 1980 (2nd ed.).
This slim volume by Mozambique's most celebrated poet takes its title from a traditional Ronga dance. Vivid imagery and a pulsating rhythm achieved through repetition of sound, word and line are dominant qualities of Craveirinha's verse.

Honwana, Luís Bernardo
Nós matamos o cão tinhoso
Lourenço Marques: Sociedade de Imprensa de Moçambique, 1964. 135 pp. o/p
Porto, Portugal: Afrontamento, 1972 (2nd ed.). 147 pp.
Lourenço Marques: Livraria Académica, 1975 (3rd ed.). 125 pp.
In English *translation,* see next entry.

We Killed Mangy-Dog and other Mozambique stories
Trans. from the Portuguese by Dorothy Guedes
London: HEB, 1969 (AWS, 60). 117 pp. 90p/$3.00
This was the first Lusophone African book to

be published in the Heinemann 'African Writers Series'. In the title story the cruelty and humiliation endured by the stray mangy dog suggests the suffering of Mozambicans under colonialism. Honwana chooses to present an indictment of Portuguese policy not by vigorous declamation but through softness of tone and understatement. The other six stories in the collection also depict lives of humiliation.

São Tomé e Principe

Costa Alegre, Caetano da
Verses
Lisbon: Livraria Ferin, 1916. 163 pp. o/p
Lisbon: Fernandes, 1950 (2nd ed.). 163 pp.

Lisbon: Ferin, 1951 (3rd ed.). 155 pp.
Ed. by Norberto Cordeiro Nogueira Costa Alegre
The ninety-six poems in this collection were written between 1882 and 1889 by an African poet who spent much of his short life in Portugal. Many of his poems emphasize the pain he suffered because his blackness caused women to reject him in love.

Tenreiro, José Francisco
Ilha de Nome Santo
Coimbra,Portugal: Colecção Novo Cancioneiro, 1942. 55 pp. o/p
This collection of poems constitutes the first book by a lusophone African written in the spirit of Négritude. Tenreiro, a mulatto and former high official in the Portuguese Overseas Ministry, shares with other apostles of Négritude a universal sense of the brotherhood of black people.

Children's literature – a selection

The following section presents a *selection* of books for children and young adults written by African authors, the bulk of them actually published *in* Africa. A small number of collections edited by non-African authors are included also, and the listing is preceded by details of a number of checklists and bibliographies of children's literature on and from Africa.

Bibliographies of children's literature

Commonwealth Institute
Commonwealth Children's Literature
London: Commonwealth Institute, 1979 (Checklists on Commonwealth Literature, 1). 56 pp. £1.00
Provides a catalogue to the collection of children's imaginative literature from the Commonwealth and Third World countries at the Commonwealth Institute. Pp. 7–19 cover books from and about Africa

Rauter, Rosemarie comp.
Printed for Children. World Children's Book Exhibition
Munich: K. G. Saur, 1978. 448 pp. DM42.–
This catalogue was produced to provide a permanent record of an exhibition first shown at the Frankfurt Book Fair 1978, when the Fair's central theme was 'The Child and the Book'. It gives a country-by-country bibliography of children's books published in many parts of the world, together with introductory essays on the state of children's book publishing in each nation. There are listings from the following African countries: Cameroon, Egypt, Ghana, Ivory Coast, Liberia, Madagascar, Mauritius and Nigeria.

Schmidt, Nancy J. comp.
Children's Books on Africa and their Authors: an annotated bibliography
New York: Africana Publ. Co., 1976 (African Bibliography series, 3). 290 pp. $24.50 cased
837 annotated entries by author/title of children's books about Africa, published in the US and elsewhere. Includes folk-tales, fiction, biography, geography, ethnography, adventure and animal stories, and has six indexes according to geographic location, name, subject, series, title and ethnic group.
'. . . recommended highly because it will cause more people to take a critical approach to children's literature about the continent . . . a unique and valuable educational resource for schools, parents, and libraries.'
Olive Pearl Stokes – *ASA Review of Books*

Supplement to 'Children's Books on Africa and their Authors: an annotated bibliography'
New York: Africana Publ. Co., 1979 (African Bibliography Series, 5). 273 pp. $19.50 cased
Lists a further 501 titles.

Children's Literature and Audio-Visual Materials in Africa
Buffalo, N.Y.: Conch Magazine, 1977. 109 pp. $15.00
A series of reviews by teachers, librarians, and Africanist scholars, covering a wide range of children's material about Africa. It 'attempts to present the multiplicity of viewpoints which are needed for evaluating children's material about Africa.' It covers largely American titles and A/V materials, but there are also several reviews and review articles on African published material.

Children's literature by African authors

Abanga, D.
Affa
Tema, Ghana: Ghana Publ. Corp., 1978. 33 pp. illus.
A picture story of several days in the life of a northern Ghanaian boy, in which his activities are traced from the time he wakes until he goes to sleep.

Abbs, Akosua [pseud. for E. Nockolds]
Ashanti Boy
London: Collins, 1959. 256 pp.
The story of Kofi Boetang's struggles to obtain a formal education despite his illiterate father's opposition and indifference. Revealing the character and attitude of European teachers in the Ghana schools system, the story ends on the eve of Ghana's independence in 1957, with Kofi's resolution to become a doctor.

Abessolo, Jean Baptiste
Les aventures de Biomo
Paris: L'Arbre du voyageur, 1975 (Contes de la gazelle, 6). 63 pp.
The Adventures of Biomo were originally published by the Institut Pédagogique National in Libreville.

Ablorh-Odjidja, J. R.
Adventures of Olatunde in Ghana
Accra: Waterville Publ. House, 1974. 36 pp. illus. ₵2.50

Adventures of Yaw Kantinka
Accra: Waterville Publ. House, 1975. 44 pp. illus. ₵2.50
Two stories in pictures.

Achebe, Chinua
Chike and the River
London and New York: CUP, 166. 64 pp. illus. 95p
A first children's book by the distinguished Nigerian novelist. It recounts Chike's adventure on the River Niger that 'brought him close to danger and then rewarded him with good fortune'.

The Flute
Enugu, Nigeria: Fourth Dimension Publ. Co., 1978. 24 pp. illus. ₦1.25
A traditional Igbo tale with a moral lesson, for children and adults alike.

The Drum
Enugu, Nigeria: Fourth Dimension Publ. Co., 1978. 24 pp. illus. ₦1.50
A tale of drama and adventure containing undertones of political satire. With four-colour illustrations.

Achebe, Chinua and Iroaganachi, John
How the Leopard Got his Claws
Enugu, Nigeria: Nwamife Publ., 1972. 35 pp. illus. ₦1.23
New York: Third Press, 1973. 35 pp. illus. $4.95
Nairobi: EAPH, 1976 (Lioncubs). 48 pp. illus. K.shs.10.00
A Nigerian fable which tells of the happy life the animals of the forest enjoyed under King Leopard, until a sharp-toothed and selfish dog began to terrorise the community ... With colour illustrations by Per Christiansen.

Acquaye, Saka
Obadzeng goes to Town
London: Evans, 1945. 32 pp. 80p
A cautionary play with a cast of thirteen males and two females.

Ade-Ajayi, Christie
Ade, our Naughty Little Brother
Ibadan: Onibonoje Press (Junior African Literature Series), 1976. 65 pp. illus. 65k
Five short stories about Ade and his middle-class family, which includes four sisters older than himself.

Adedeji, 'Remi
Four Stories about the Tortoise
Ibadan: Onibonoje Press, 1973 (Junior African Literature Series). 25 pp. illus. 50k
Contains 'Why the Tortoise Has No Hair On His Head' (it was burnt off by hot porridge he had stolen), 'The Tortoise and the Elephant' (he saves a king by killing an elephant), 'The Tortoise and Gourd of Wisdom' (he learns he cannot collect all the wisdom in the world), and 'Why the Tortoise's Back is Crooked' (he was crushed collecting palm wine).

The Fat Woman
Ibadan: Onibonoje Press, 1973 (Junior African Literature Series). 7 pp. illus. 45k
A good doctor helps the fat woman grow thin. 'Eat less, and work very hard,' he says.

Papa Ojo and His Family
Ibadan: Onibonoje Press, 1973. 9 pp. illus. 35k

Ajose, Audrey
Yomi's Adventures
London and New York: CUP, 1964. 90 pp. illus. £1.15
An adventure story set in Nigeria and London by a Nigerian journalist.

Yomi in Paris
London and New York, CUP, 1966. 92 pp. illus. £1.15
Yomi, the heroine of Audrey Ajose's previous story, goes to Paris and becomes involved in a mystery. Includes a list of French words used in the dialogue.

Aka, S. M. O.
Stories from an African Village
Lagos: Longman Nigeria, 1976. 75 pp. illus.
African tales which fall into the class of 'stories that actually happened'.

Akinsemoyin, Kunle
Stories at Sundown
London: Harrap, 1965. 71 pp. illus. 50p
Stories of 'Simple, the Elephant', 'Ika, the Ungrateful Lion', 'Slaka, the Poet', and other folk tales.

Twilight Tales
Lagos: African Univ. Press, 1965 (African Readers Library, 10). 80 pp. illus. 75k
More traditional stories, simply told.

Twilight and the Tortoise
Lagos: African Univ. Press, 1963 (African Readers Library, 3). 80 pp. illus. 75k
The author conveys the village atmosphere in a prelude: twilight is story-time in Nigeria. In those last rays of daylight the village children gather round the feet of the story-teller, begging for a tale before bedtime. These are the stories of the wily Tortie the tortoise, a not unfamiliar figure in African folklore.

Akinsemoyin, Kunle and Egunjobi, L.
The Door. The Crafty Tailor. The Bundle of Sticks
Lagos: West African Book Publ., 1977. 32 pp. illus. ₦1.20.
Three stories with an African setting. Illustrated in colour.

Akpabot, Anne
Aduke Makes her Choice
Walton-on-Thames: Nelson, 1966 (Rapid Reading series, higher level, 4). 57 pp. illus. 90p
The dreams and ambitions of a young Nigerian girl.

Sade and her Friends
Walton-on-Thames: Nelson, 1967 (Rapid Reading series, higher level, 6). 62 pp. illus. 90p
Sade is a young Yoruba girl whose parents neglect her education, but she finally succeeds in obtaining one after many setbacks.

Akpan, Ntieyong Udo
Ini Abasi and the Sacred Ram
London: Longman, 1966. 26 pp. illus. 45p
Ini Abasi, son of Okon and Nko, is an incredibly strong champion wrestler, who apparently was born dumb. He miraculously recovers his voice when falsely accused of killing the village's sacred ram.

Alagoa, E. J.
King Boy of Brass
Nairobi: HEB (East Africa), 1975. 36 pp. K.shs.9.00
A story set in the Rivers State of Nigeria.

Alor, Igbonne
The Magic Apple Tree
Enugu, Nigeria: Fourth Dimension Publ. Co., 1980. 32 pp. illus. ₦1.50

A new version of a traditional Igbo tale about an orphan boy who is favoured by the spirits in a special way.

Amarteifio, Victor
Bediako the Adventurer
Accra: Waterville Publ. House, 1979. 156 pp. illus. ₵7.50
A biographical adventure story which presents a picture of the day-to-day Ghanaian way of life.

Amoaku, J. K.
Badu goes to Kumasi
Tema, Ghana: Ghana Publ. Corp., 1970. 46 pp. illus. 30pes.
A village boy visits the city for the first time.

The Christmas Hut
Tema, Ghana: Ghana Publ. Corp., 1970. 28 pp. illus. 40pes.
A group of playmates decide to build a traditional hut for the Christmas season, which gives them a lesson in co-operation.

Amu-Nnadi, S. E.
The Magician
Enugu, Nigerian: Fourth Dimension Publ. Co., 1981. 56 pp. illus. ₦1.50
The story of a magician who tricks two youngsters into giving away their possessions.

Anane, F. K.
Kofi Mensah
Tema, Ghana: Ghana Publ. Corp., 1968. 60 pp. illus. 35pes.
The experiences of a country boy who finds himself in a large city.

Anizoba, Rose
The Adventures of Mbugwe the Frog
London and Ibadan: OUP, 1965 (The Little Bookshelf series). 94 pp. illus.
The many adventures of an enterprising frog from Enugu in eastern Nigeria, in search of an education.

Ankrah, E.
Mutinta Goes Hunting
Lusaka: Neczam, 1972. 24 pp. illus. 50k
A story of a girl who kills a lion about to attack her three elder brothers.

Anametemfiok, Emman
Beautiful Voices
Calabar, Nigeria: Scholars Press, 1980. 22 pp. ₦1.20
Poetry for children.

Aniakor, Chike
Ojadili: the clever wrestler
Enugu, Nigeria: Fourth Dimension Publ. Co.,
1980. 56 pp. illus.
Tells the story of a boy who dared to wrestle
with the spirits.

Anta Ka, Abdou
La création selon les noirs
Dakar: Nouvelles Editions Africaines, 1975.
20 pp. illus.
No, says grandfather, for Africans the first
man was not Adam. He was the Moon and he
had two wives, the Morning Star and the
Evening Star. An African creation tale with
colour illustrations by B. Camara.

La princesse noire
Dakar: Editions Muntu, 1979. 26 pp. illus.
A black princess asks her husband for a river
for a present and this causes a canal to be dug,
bringing water from the River Niger to the
arid region of her husband's domain. An
engaging transposition into the folk-tale idiom
of what is a current national concern not only
in Senegal, but the entire Sahel region of West
Africa, the subject of drought. With striking
colour illustrations.

Apraku, L. D.
A Prince of the Akans
Accra: Waterville Publ. House, 1979. 58 pp.
illus. ₵3.00
An adventure story.

Asare, Meshack
Tawia Goes to Sea
Tema, Ghana: Ghana Publ. Corp., 1970.
34 pp. illus. ₵2.00
Tawia watches the activities of elderly fishermen on the beach and pleads to be allowed to
go to sea with them. His uncle refuses to take
him along because Tawia is only a little boy.
Tawia meanwhile makes a toy canoe with twigs
as fishermen, and launches his canoe. This
earns him a trip to sea with his uncle. (One of
the first picture-story books from an African
publisher, and now also available in Japanese
and Russian editions.)

I am Kofi
Tema, Ghana: Ghana Publ. Corp., 1972.
16 pp. illus. 10pes.
One of a series of picture books designed to
help teach young children.

Mansa Helps at Home
Tema, Ghana: Ghana Publ. Corp., 1972.
16 pp. illus. 20pes.
Especially for the younger child.

The Brassman's Secret
Accra: Educational Press, 1981. Unpaged
[40 pp.] illus.
After helping his father turn wax figures into
brass ones by the 'lost wax' process, Kwajo
befriends one of them. Through this story the
author introduces the young reader to two
important aspects in the cultural life of the
Asante people of Ghana, namely its gold-
weights and its traditional architecture, both of
which have virtually succumbed to new forms
and are almost forgotten. *The Brassman's Secret*
was the winner of the 1982 Noma Award for
publishing in Africa.

Asheri, Jedida
Promise
Lagos: African Univ. Press, 1969 (African
Readers Library, 17). 96 pp. illus. 75k
The story of a girl growing up thirty years ago
in rural Cameroon. It tells of her family and
her friends, her schooling, and her training in
teaching and nursing, and depicts the influence of environment on an adolescent girl.

Asiedu, Michael
Rookie the Unlucky Hen
Tema, Ghana: Ghana Publ. Corp., 1977.
35 pp. illus. ₵1.50
The unlucky experiences of a mother-hen, told
in simple English for the younger reader.

Esi Goes for Water
Tema, Ghana: Ghana Publ. Corp., 1978.
32 pp. illus. ₵.25
The adventures of a village girl on her way to
collect water from a stream.

Okpoti's First Day at School
Tema, Ghana: Ghana Publ. Corp., 1978.
33 pp. ₵2.00
Okpoti looks forward to the prospect of
attending school, and he excels in class when
the teacher introduces the first lesson.

Ba, Amadou Hampaté
Petit Bodiel
Dakar: Nouvelles Editions Africaines, 1976.
72 pp. CFA550

Ba, Ngagne
Le coq, l'ane et la chien
Dakar: Nouvelles Editions Africaines, 1977.
16 pp. illus. CFA350

A tale of the time when animals spoke to men. Illustrated in colour.

Banks Henries, A. Doris
Once Upon a Time; Spider Stories
London: Evans, 1975. 48 pp. illus. 95p.
Spider's adventures with his friends and foes: suitable for upper primary school children.

Beier, Ulli, and Gbadamosi, Bakare eds.
The Moon Cannot Fight
Ibadan: Mbari, 1964. Unpaged [46 pp.] o/p
Yoruba children's poems, with explanatory notes.

Beier, Ulli
The Stolen Images
Cambridge: CUP, 1979. 55 pp. illus. 95p
A story about a priest's son who helps to recover two important carvings stolen from a Yoruba shrine in Nigeria and sold to an American art dealer.

Bhêly-Quénum, Olympe
Un enfant d'Afrique
Paris: Larousse, 1970. 256 pp.
A novel for 10- to 14-year-olds written in collaboration with Roger Guiffray and R. Delamadeleine. Entitled *A Child of Africa*.

Bolling, Ellen L.
Kwabena
Accra: Waterville Publ. House, 1979. 44 pp. illus. ₵2.00
The story of a Ghanaian boy.

Boyd-Harvey, Julia
Tutti and the Magic Bird
Johannesburg: Ravan Press, 1980. Illus. R7.50 cased R3.50 p/b
Tutti is a young black boy who comes to live in the house of an archaeologist, and his magic bird transorts him into the rich, ancient past of the region. The illustrations are by Marjorie Bereza.

Bracey, Dorothy and Lieta, Peter
'Longman Reading Scheme'
Letter Sounds – Introductory Book, 32 pp. illus.
Hare is Here – Book 1, 20 pp. illus.
Hare's House – Book 2, 32 pp. illus.
Hare is Bad – Book 3, 31 pp. illus.
Where is Hare? – Book 4, 18 pp. illus.
The Party – Book 5, 21 pp. illus.
Gum on the Gate – Book 6, 50 pp.
The Woman and the Millet – Book 7, 24 pp.
Crocodile Stories – Book 8, 45 pp.
Tortoise's Wings – Book 9, 48 pp.
No Feast for Kiundu – Book 10, 56 pp.

Nairobi: Longman Kenya, 1975–1979.
K.shs.3.50–7.50
A reading scheme which draws on local traditional stories, told very simply for the young reader. Many of the tales put across a simple morality common to many traditional stories. Splendidly illustrated in colour by Terry Hirst.

Brown, Godfrey N.
'All Africa Readers'
Lagos: African Univ. Press, 1970. 16 pp. ea. illus. 35k ea.
A series of twelve simple story books with strip pictures by Prue Theobalds, each telling a folk-tale from a different African country. For example, from Kenya comes the story of *The Jackal and the Camel*; from Senegal a trickster tale *The Hare and the Termites*; from Sierra Leone *Ee Ar Ee*, a tale about two travellers one of whose snoring is thought to be nice singing by villagers; from Zambia *The Clever Hare and the Terrible Lion*, another trickster tale; or from Ethiopia *The Tower of Baboons*, which tells the story how the baboons tried to take their dead king to the god of animals in the sky. A book of teacher's notes and a wall map of Africa go with the series and are available separately.

Calame-Griaule, Geneviève
Le lièvre et le tambour: fable dogon
Paris: Présence Africaine, 1958. Unpaged [12 pp.] illus.
A Dogon tar-baby story about how the hare outsmarts the other animals who had caught him playing the tam-tam – which he had been forbidden to do. An edition for children with a two-page commentary on Dogon culture and beliefs at the end.

Cavally, Jeanne de
Papi
Dakar: Nouvelles Editions Africaines, 1978. 32 pp. illus. CFA400
Papi, the little Baoulé boy, introduces young readers to his family and his countryside.

Chahilu, Bernard P.
The Herdsman's Daughter
Nairobi: EAPH, 1978. 283 pp. K.shs.12.00 ($3.50)
A portrait of young womanhood in Africa.

Chibule, Anderson
The Broken Branch
Nairobi: EAPH, 1968. 48 pp.
A young East African boy caught in the midst of conflict between the traditional views of his parents and those he has assimilated at school.

Chigbo, Thomas
Odenigbo
London: Evans, 1978. 64 pp. 95p.
An adventure story centred around an Igbo village in the early part of the century where ancient traditions display their power over village life.

Clair, Andrée and **Hama, Boubou**
La savane enchante
Paris: Ed. La Farandole, 1972. 92 pp. illus.
African tales for children, illustrated with children's drawings.

La Baobab merveilleux
Paris: Ed. La Farandole, 1971. 29 pp.

Kangue ize
Paris: Ed. La Farandole, 1974. 44 pp.

Clinton, J. V.
The Rescue of Charlie Kalu
London: HEB, 1970 (Heinemann Secondary Reading Scheme, 2). 64 pp. 60p.
The story of the rescue of a kidnapped boy in the creeks of Nigeria.

Cole, Aaron
Animal Palaver
Walton-on-Thames: Nelson, 1965 (Rapid Reading series, lower level, 5). 48 pp. illus. 90p
The animals meet to elect their king, but events take an unexpected turn. A story from Sierra Leone.

Cole, Robert Wellesley
Kossoh Town Boy
London and New York: CUP, 1960. 192 pp. illus. £2.10
The first African to be elected a Fellow of the Royal College of Surgeons of England looks back on his childhood days in Freetown, Sierra Leone, seventy years ago.

Combet, Sabine
Boubacer découvre la ville
Dakar: Nouvelles Editions Africaines, 1978. 32 pp. illus. CFA650
A little village boy discovers the big city for the first time.

Coulibali, A. and **Kouassi, D.**
Contes et Histoires d'Afrique: vol. 1
Dakar: Nouvelles Editions Africaines, 1977. 28 pp. illus. CFA800
This three-volume series of African tales and legends, with vividly coloured comic-book inspired illustrations, was sponsored in part by the French Government's Agency of Co-operation in the framework of their pro-

gramme for the promotion of cultures and national languages. The collection is meant for adolescents and adult readers. Volume 1 contains the story of why the sky is so high (Man became mean and sick and chased the Heavens away from the Earth). There is also a Senoufo legend explaining why the sun shines during the day and the moon and stars at night; the moon and stars are a mother and her children who had to flee an angry husband and father, the sun. In 'The Palm Tree and the Humming Bird' the tiny creature has the audacity to ask God to make him bigger and think he can fulfil the conditions. Finally, in the legend 'Tchad' the wandering tribe of Alifa, the only survivors of the great disaster, come to a huge lake where friendly giants invite them to make their home. The land is named 'Tchad' meaning 'land of abundance, of happiness, of love'.

Contes et Histoires d'Afrique: vol. 2
Dakar: Nouvelles Editions Africaines, 1977. 28 pp. illus. CFA800
Contains four tales. 'Mame Coumba' tells how the waters of the two branches of the Senegal River around the town of Saint Louis were calmed. 'Téré and the Rainbow' explains how Man captured the Fleeing Rains with the help of Rainbow – and was rewarded with the hand of Turtle Dove's daughter. In 'Gouai' a hunter is killed by animals; that is why the Dida people of Divo hunt very little nowadays. And in 'N'Djama' a beautiful, but wretched orphan fearlessly seeks death until she is told her time has not yet come.

Contes et Histoires d'Afrique: vol. 3
Dakar: Nouvelles Editions Africaines, 1977. 28 pp. illus. CFA800
The four stories here are: 'The Devil and the Young Lady' about a beautiful, proud princess who finally finds a brave husband – the man who kills the devil; 'Coniyara' about a prince with magic powers who almost loses his lovely wife and child when she wants to know what the origins of her husband are; 'The Lake of Witches' about a bereaved mother who avenges in a terrible way the death of a son who had died during initiation rites; and 'Mandjambe' about how Man triumphs over the Ogre who monopolizes fire. The colour illustrations in this volume are by Daniel Marteaud and Nguyen Ngoc My.

Crowder, M. and **Ladan, Umaru**
Sani Goes to School
Lagos: Africa Univ. Press, 1979 (African Readers Library). 64 pp. 75k
Can Sani overcome the difficulties which stand in the way of his going to school?

Amon d'Aby, François Joseph

Le regard mortel
Dakar: Nouvelles Editions Africaines, 1978.
16 pp. illus. CFA400
With the help of his animal friends young Koui triumphs over the ordeals his elder brothers had cunningly devised in the hope of seizing the fortune which he alone had inherited from their dying father. Illustrations by F. Hanes.

La mare aux crocodiles
Dakar: Nouvelles Editions Africaines, 1973.
128 pp. CFA600
Traditional fireside tales with animal heroes.

Le singe noir et la tortue
Dakar: Nouvelles Editions Africaines, 1977.
15 pp. illus. CFA400
Tortoise teaches monkey a lesson about courtesy and consideration for others. Colour drawings by Georges Lorofi.

Dahal, Charity

The Orange Thieves, and other stories
Nairobi: EAPH, 1966 (East African Readers Library, 5). 76 pp. illus. K.shs.3.00 ($1.00)
Stories of magic, mystery and adventure with one thing in common – they are all about giants.

Danka-Smith, H.

Some Popular Ananse Stories
Accra: Waterville Publ. House, 1979. 114 pp. illus. ₵7.00
Further stories of the crafty spider.

Decker, Thomas

Tales of the Forest
London: Evans, 1968. 72 pp. illus. 90p
Twenty-six stories, simply told, based on traditional West African folk-tales.

De Graft-Hanson, J. O.

The Secret of Opokuwa
Accra: Anowuo Educational Publ., 1967.
72 pp. illus.
When Opokuwa, Agyeman and Boafo, three children in a Ghanaian village, learn that the British Governor in Cape Coast plans to seize the State Stool during the yam festival, they set out to work to defeat the plan. 'Written for the entertainment of both children and adults', says the sub-title.

Papa and the Animals
Tema, Ghana: Ghana Publ. Corp., 1973.
20 pp. illus. 50pes
The experiences of a Ghanaian schoolboy, Papa, with creatures like the Pig, the Vulture and the Monitor Lizard, each telling a tale.

Papa Ewusi and the Magic Marble
Tema, Ghana: Ghana Publ. Corp., 1973.
48 pp. illus. 75pes
A book which recounts the adventures of Papa Ewusi when he finds a magic marble which controls a dwarf who serves whoever possesses the marble.

The Little Sasabonsam
Tema, Ghana: Ghana Publ. Corp., 1973.
64 pp. illus. 75pes
Papa Ewusi's encounter with a family of legendary wild creatures.

The Fetish Hideout
Tema, Ghana: Ghana Publ. Corp., 1975.
100 pp. illus. ₵1.20
An adventure story based on a legend about a Fánti shrine.

Dickson, Timothy

David and the Gangsters
Walton-on-Thames: Nelson, 1965 (Rapid Reading series, lower level, 1). 80 pp. illus. 95p
An adventure story.

Diong, Cheikhou Oumar

La fin héroïque de Babemba roi du Sikasso
Dakar: Nouvelles Editions Africaines, 1980.
22 pp. illus. CFA800
A comic-strip volume for younger readers that tells of the heroic end of the kingdom of Sikasso (Mali) under the reign of Babemba.

Diop, Birago

Contes d'Awa
Dakar: Nouvelles Editions Africaines, 1977.
40 pp. illus. CFA550
The five tales in this volume have colour illustrations by Alpha Diallo. Leuck the Hare has a prominent role in the first three but there is also Bouki the Hyena, and 'the son of Ngor' which recalls the Tar Baby story of Uncle, Remus.

Dladla, Mboma

Mboma (as told to Kathy Bond)
Johannesburg: Ravan Press, 1980. 48 pp. 96c
The 14-year-old Mboma's life story as told to Kathy Bond – it is the adventurous story of a boy who grows up herding cattle in the rugged and barren Msinga district of South Africa.

Dogbe, Anne

Afi à la campagne
Dakar: Nouvelles Editions Africaines, 1978.
28 pp. illus. CFA400
Two little city dwellers spend a few days in the country. Colour illustrations by Ansoumane Diédhiou.

Dzovo, E. V. K.
Salami and Musa
London: Longman, 1967. 72 pp. 50p
The story of Salami, a Northern Ghanaian boy, who against his family's advice leaves home to seek his fortune.

Edwards-Tack, A.
Ngoni's Dream and Other Stories

Ekwensi, Cyprian
The Passport of Mallam Ilia
London and New York: CUP, 1960. 80 pp. illus. £1.10
A tale of intrigue and revenge. The first of several children's books by the prominent Nigerian novelist.

The Drummer Boy
London and New York: CUP, 1960. 88 pp. illus. £1.10
Tells the story of Akin, a blind beggar boy, who is a superb drummer.

An African Night's Entertainment
Lagos: African Univ. Press, 1962 (African Readers Library, 1). 96 pp. illus. 75k
An adventure story of betrayal and vengeance, which centres on the African custom of betrothing girls when they are very young.

The Rainmaker, and other stories
Lagos: African Univ. Press, 1965 (African Readers Library, 6). 80 pp. illus. 75k
A collection of adventure stories and tales featuring schoolboys of Nigeria as its heroes.

The Great Elephant-Bird
Walton-on-Thames: Nelson, 1965 (Rapid Reading series, lower level, 2). 80 pp. illus. 95p
A collection of Nigerian folk-tales, 'to be told only at night, for it was believed that the narrator's mother would die if they were told by day.'

The Boa Suitor
Walton-on-Thames: Nelson, 1966 (Rapid Reading series, lower level, 6). 64 pp. illus. 95p
A sequel to *The Great Elephant-Bird*: more popular tales.

Trouble in Form Six
London and New York: CUP, 1966. 76 pp. illus. £1.10
Things begin to go wrong at Ilubi College when a popular boy is not made a prefect.

Juju Rock
Lagos: African Univ. Press, 1966 (African Readers Library, 11). 110 pp. illus. 75k
Rikku Sansaye's adventures when he joins in the search for the missing Captain Plowman, lost in an expedition to find gold at Juju rock.

Coal Camp Boy
Lagos: Longman Nigeria (Palm Library), 1973. 66 pp. illus. 62k
The problems of a family starting life again after the Nigerian Civil War.

Samankwe in the Strange Forest
Lagos: Longman Nigeria (Palm Library), 1975. 58 pp. illus. 50k
Samankwe thinks he has killed his schoolteacher and runs away into the strange forest.

Samankwe and the Highway Robbers
London: Evans, 1979. 48 pp. illus. 78p
While travelling on holiday Samankwe falls victim to a gang of robbers and is taken prisoner. He manages to escape and tells the police, but nobody wants to believe his story.

Motherless Baby
Enugu, Nigeria: Fourth Dimension Publ. Co., 1980. 96 pp. ₦1.50
A morality tale about a Nigerian secondary school girl who falls in love with a band leader, abandons their illegitimate baby son, and is then later unable to bear a child when she wants one; she dies. For young adults.

The Rainbow-Tinted Scarf and Other Stories
London: Evans, 1979. 48 pp. 78p
Five stories set in Nigeria during the colonial period.

Elliot, Geraldine
The Long Grass Whispers
Johannesburg: Macmillan South Africa, 1981 (p/b ed.). 132 pp. illus. R4.95
African animal stories based on folk-tales, superstitions and customs. Illustrated by Sheila Hawkins.

The Hunter's Cave
Johannesburg: Macmillan South Africa, 1981 (p/b ed.). 174 pp. illus. R5.95
A further paperback reissue of another of Geraldine Elliot's popular animal stories, again illustrated by Sheila Hawkins.

The Singing Chameleon
Johannesburg: Macmillan South Africa, 1981 (p/b ed.). 168 pp. illus. R5.95
Tales woven around the proverbs and customs

of Central Africa, with illustrations by Sheila Hawkins.

Where the Leopard Passes
Johannesburg: Macmillan South Africa, 1981 (p/b ed.). 134 pp. illus. R4.95
Stories based on African tales, featuring Kalulu the Rabbit, the Greedy Spider, the Leopard and the Tortoise. Illustrated by Sheila Hawkins.

Emecheta, Buchi
Titch the Cat
London: Allison and Busby, 1980. 96 pp. illus. £2.50
A black family in North London has its domestic peace shattered by a kitten.

Nowhere to Play
London: Allison and Busby, 1981. 366 pp. illus. £3.75
The children of a black family living in London search for a place to play.

Enin, T. Y.
The Gongon Man
Tema, Ghana: Ghana Publ. Corp., 1975. 32 pp. 50pes
A book in verse for the young primary school child.

Seidu Drives his Father's Cow
Tema, Ghana: Ghana Publ. Corp., 1975. 75 pp. illus. 95pes
A simple story for children, which also portrays the culture of the people of Northern Ghana.

Eshun, J. O.
The Adventures of the Kapapa
Tema, Ghana: Ghana Publ. Corp., 1976. 116 pp. illus. ₵3.00
The story of Mr Afful, a physics lecturer, who invents an anti-gravitational theory on which the Kapapa Space Cargo Craft is built. For the secondary school reader.

Forde, W.
Air Force Cadet
Lagos: African Univ. Press (African Readers Library, 18), 1971. 125 pp. illus. 75k
The adventures of a young Sierra Leonean who joins the Royal Air Force as an officer cadet.

Fulani, Dan
The Hijack
Walton-on-Thames: Nelson, 1979 (Authors of Africa). 64 pp. 65p
A fast moving account of a hijack, involving

Nigeria and the imagery African state of Tibesti. For secondary school level.

Gachago, David
The Scapegoat
Nairobi: EAPH, 1971. 36 pp. K.shs.5.00 ($1.50)
A play for schools with an industrial setting.

Gichuru, Stephen
The Fly Whisk, and other stories
Nairobi: EAPH, 1968 (East African Readers Library, 10). 72 pp. illus. K.shs.2.00 ($1.00)
An anthology of stories and folk-tales from Masailand, Kenya.

Gicoru, Nereas and Hirst, Terry
Take Me Home
Nairobi: EAPH (Lioncub Books), 1974. 20 pp. illus. K.shs.4.50
A story of a young African boy, his friend Mr Tumbo and a red bus called 'Take Me Home'. With colour illustrations.

Gwengwe, J. W.
Sulizo Achieves Greatness
London: Evans, 1968. 62 pp. 21p, illus. 85p
The adventures of young Sulizo, from his schooldays to early manhood.

Hoh, I. K.
Prodigal Brothers
London: Evans, 1968 (Plays for African Schools). 48 pp.
The reverend Doe and his wife have two troublesome sons. This play tells the story of their many adventures and misfortunes.

Ibongia, John M. and Bobrin, M.
The Magic Stone, and other stories
Nairobi: EAPH, 1967 (East African Readers Library, 12). 50 pp. illus. K.shs.2.50 ($1.00)
Stories told by a grandmother from the Kisii highlands in western Kenya.

Igboanugo, P. S. C.
My Tana Colouring Book
Enugu, Nigeria: Flora Nwapa Co., 1979. 20 pp. illus. 40k
A first colouring book.

My Animal Colouring Book
Enugu, Nigeria: Flora Nwapa Co., 1979. 20 pp. illus. 50k
A colouring book that includes drawings of common animals.

Ijioma, Wendy
A Child's Book of African Poetry

London: Macmillan, 1978. 46 pp. illus.
For pupils in Upper Primary level, intended to
encourage children's enjoyment of poetry.
Most poems, each illustrated with two-colour
drawings, are by African authors.

Inem, Uwana
The Gift: Ekpe
Enugu. Nigeria: Fourth Dimension Publ. Co.,
1980. 16 pp. illus. ₦1.25
The small girl in this story receives a very
unusual present.

Iroaganchi, John
Night and Day
Lagos: African Univ. Press, 1977 (African
Junior Library, 10). 32 pp. illus. 50k
The succession of events which occur when Ijiji
the Tombo fly buzzes in Mbe the tortoise's ear.
For younger readers.

The Sunbird's Drum
Lagos: African Univ. Press, 1977 (African
Junior Library, 11). 32 pp. illus. 50k
An animal fable featuring tortoise again, with
line drawings by Prue Theobalds.

Irungu, Daniel
The Powerful Magician, and other stories
Nairobi: EAPH, 1969 (East African Readers
Library, 24). 46 pp. illus. K.shs.3.00 ($1.00)
Daniel Irungu recounts the stories told to him
by his grandmother.

Iyatemi, Phebean and Dove-Danquah, Mable
The Torn Veil and other stories
London: Evans, 1978. 48 pp. 78p
Four stories which are concerned with the
liberation of women in Africa.

Japuonjo, Roeland
Mzee Nyachote
Nairobi: EAPH, 1967 (East African Readers
Library, 6). 56 pp. illus. K.shs.3.00 ($1.00)
Told as a series of anecdotes, these are tales of
the adventures of a mischievous boy in Kenya.

Kaban, Ahoussi
Le temps de l'école
Abidjan: C.E.D.A., 1980. 119 pp.
A story of childhood, in the Ivory Coast.

Kabui, Joseph
The Coconut Girl
Nairobi: EAPH, 1971. 52 pp. illus. K.shs.4.90
($1.50)
A collection of traditional stories from Central
Kenya.

Kagiri, Samuel
Leave Us Alone
Nairobi: EAPH, 1978. 132 pp. K.shs.10.00
($3.20)
An African ballad of youth – from childhood
to adolescence, and to adult life.

Kago, F. K.
Lucky Mtende and other stories
Nairobi: Equatorial Publ., 1968. 27 pp. illus.
K.shs.4.50

Mango's Grass House and other stories
Nairobi: Equatorial Publ., 1969. 27 pp. illus.
K.shs.4.50

Kala, John
The Adventures of Musa Kaago
Nairobi: EAPH, 1968. 99 pp. K.shs.4.00
($1.50)
An attempt by Musa Kaago's stepmother to do
away with him brings tragedy and the death of
her own daughter.

Valley of Flames
Nairobi: EAPH, 1976. 92 pp. illus. K.shs.9.00
($3.00)
A story of young love, adventure and tragedy.

Kamau, George A.
The Adventures of Pongo
Nairobi: EAPH, 1976. 84 pp. illus. K.shs.7.00
($2.60)
The hazards that face Pongo and his uncle in
their search for Pongo's kidnapped mother.

Kamen, Tony
Nigerian Life in Colour
Enugu, Nigeria: Nwamife Publishers, 1978.
Unpaged [24 pp.] illus. ₦1.00
A colouring book for Nigerian children.

Karanta, Issaka Soumaila; Coulibali, Augustin Sondé; Nikiema, Roger Théodore
Poèmes pour enfants
Dakar: Institut Culturel Africain, 1976. 48 pp.
The authors of this anthology of poetry for
children won, respectively, first, second and
third place in the 1975 Grand Prix of the
Institut Cultural Africain at Malgache. The
aim of the competition was to encourage
African writers to furnish African-inspired
poetry for use in the classroom.

Kareithi, Peter Munuhe
Kigo in England
Nairobi: Equatorial Publ., 1968. 74 pp. illus.
K.shs.2.00 ($1.25)
An adventure story.

Kariuki, E. M.

The Sun's Daughter
Nairobi: EAPH, 1976. 35 pp. illus. K.shs.7.00
($2.00)

Ziki my Monkey Boy
Nairobi: Longman Kenya, 1979. 30 pp. illus.
K.shs.8.00
The story of James Muiga who, despite his
dislike of monkeys, when he finds one that has
been injured, takes it home and cares for it.

Kawegere, Fortunatus

Inspector Rajabu Investigates
Nairobi: EAPH, 1968 (East African Readers
Library). 36 pp. illus. K.shs.2.00 ($1.00)
Set in Tanzania, an inspector of police on leave
in Mwanza gets onto the trail of a gang of bank
robbers.

Kay, Kwesi

The Treasure Chamber
London: HEB, 1970 (Heinemann Secondary
Reading Scheme, 6). 96 pp. illus. 40p
An historical play about Egypt, written by a
Ghanaian.

Kébé, Mbaya Gana

Colombes
Dakar: Nouvelles Editions Africaines, 1979.
32 pp. CFA3.50
Poetry for children.

Rondes:
Dakar: Nouvelles Editions Africaines, 1979.
34 pp. CFA3.50
A second volume of verse for children.

Keelson, M. B.

Kofi Goes Back to Farm
Tema, Ghana: Ghana Publ. Corp., 1978.
111 pp. ₵5.50
A biographical novel aimed at the teenager,
telling of a land-working Ghanaian youth who
completes middle school, becomes a mechanic
and serves his community by combining motor
repairs and farming.

Khiddu-Makubuya, K.

The Newcomer and other stories
Lagos: African Univ. Press, 1973 (African
Readers Library, 19). 96 pp. 75k
Men's relations with one another and the
satisfaction of their desires set in a village
atmosphere. For older children.

Kimenye, Barbara

The Smugglers
Walton-on-Thames: Nelson, 1968 (Rapid
Reading series, lower level, 9). 64 pp. illus. 95p
An eventful adventure awaits three African
boys who stray across the Congo-Uganda
border.

Moses
Nairobi: OUP, 1967. 88 pp. illus. K.shs.9.00
The first of several titles recounting the various
adventures about Moses, a Kenyan school boy.

Moses and Mildred
Nairobi: OUP, 1968. 80 pp. illus. K.shs.5.50

Moses in Trouble
Nairobi: OUP, 1968. 88 pp. illus. K.shs.5.00

Moses and the Ghost
Nairobi: OUP, 1971. 88 pp. illus. K.shs.5.00

Paulo's Strange Adventure
Nairobi: OUP, 1971. 70 pp. illus. K.shs.4.75

Moses and the Penpal
Nairobi: OUP, 1973. 80 pp. illus. K.shs.5.25

Sara and the Boy
Nairobi: OUP, 1973. 16 pp. illus. K.shs.3.00

The Gemstone Affair
Walton-onThames: Nelson, 1978 (Authors of
Africa). 72 pp. 65p
A story about emerald mining in East Africa.
For older children.

The Scoop
Walton-on-Thames: Nelson, 1978 (Authors of
Africa). 72 pp. 65p
The kidnapping of a rich businessman's
daughter means a 'scoop' for *Standard* journalist Kosaro. But has Grace Ndungu really been
kidnapped . . . ? For secondary school level.

Kimeto, Arap Zaccheaus

The Battle of Mogori
Nairobi: EAPH, 1972. 39 pp. illus. K.shs.4.00
($1.50)
A collection of stories of olden days from the
Kerich District in Western Kenya.

Kokiri, Oguda

The Jungle Star
Nairobi: East African Lit. Bureau, 1974.
142 pp. K.shs.15.75 (£1.50/3.70)
A collection of Kenyan folk-tales

Kola, Pamela

East Africa When? stories
Nairobi: EAPH, 1968. 32 pp. illus. K.shs.1.70
($1.00)
Traditional folk-tales.

Koné, Amadou
Terre ivoirienne
Abidjan: C.E.D.A., 1979. 187 pp.
Young Tikilikau discovers his country, its riches, its past, and its inhabitants.

Kor, Buma
Sense-Pass-King
Yaoundé: Buma Kor, 1981. 32 pp. illus.
The first of a graded series of readers for children aged five to ten in which the hero, Sense-Pass-King, triumphs over the many tricks of the King who wants to kill him.

Koulibaly, Isaïe Biton
La légende de Sadjo
Abidjan: C.D.E.A., 1975. 64 pp. CFA496
The tale of a friendship between a little girl and a hippopotamus.

Kuguru, Felix M.
Kimi the Joker
Nairobi: EAPH, 1972. 56 pp. illus. K.shs.4.00 ($1.00)
The comic adventures of a young boy.

Kuguru, Peter
The Tales of Wamugumo
Nairobi: EAPH, 1976 (East African Readers Library, 7). 73 pp. illus. K.shs.4.00 ($1.50)
The stories of Wamugumo, retold by a young Kenyan. Wamugumo was one of the most famous story-tellers among the Kikuyu people of Kenya.

Kyendo, Kalondu
Cock and Lion
Nairobi: EAPH, 1969. 32 pp. illus. K.shs.1.60 ($1.00)
Seven traditional stories from central Kenya.

Lantum, Daniel
Tales of Nso
Lagos: African Univ. Press, 1969 (African Readers Library, 18). 80 pp. illus. 75k
A number of tales from the Nso area of Cameroon, primarily evolving around a wicked character named Wanyeto.

Leshoai, B. L.
Masilo's Adventures
London: Longman, 1968. 48 pp. 50p
Four tales from Lesotho concerning giants, monsters, warriors and a beautiful princess, as told to the author by his grandmother.

Lubega, Bonnie
The Great Animal Land
Nairobi: East African Lit. Bureau, 1971.

48 pp. illus. K.shs.18.50 (£1.70/$4.25)
An animal story about East African national parks.

The Burning Bush
Nairobi: East African Lit. Bureau, 1971.
98 pp. illus. K.shs.7.65 (95p/$2.00)
Evening tales told by elders, about the East African environment.

Cry Jungle Children
Nairobi: East African Lit. Bureau, 1974.
79 pp. illus. K.shs.6.00 (80p/$2.00)
The preservation of African wildlife is the theme of this story.

Pot of Honey
Nairobi: East African Lit. Bureau, 1974.
131 pp. illus. K.shs.6.50 (£1.30/$3.20)

McDowell, Robert E. and Lavitt, E.
Third World Voices for Children
New York: Third Press, 1972. 156 pp. illus. $6.95
Folk-tales from Africa and other Third World nations, with illustrations by Barbara Kohn Isaac.

Maillu, David
Kisalu and his Fruit Garden, and other stories
Nairobi: EAPH, 1972. 64 pp. illus. K.shs.3.00 ($1.00)
A collection of stories which teach the virtues of unselfish love, the punishment that meets malicious evil, and the dangers of spoiling children.

Makumi, Joel
The Children of the Forest
Nairobi: EAPH, 1968 (East African Readers Library, 18). 42 pp. illus. K.shs.4.00 ($1.50)
A shepherd finds two little children abandoned in a deserted hut in a forest, and he and his wife decide to bring them up as part of their family.

The Feather in the Lake
Nairobi: EAPH, 1969. 32 pp. illus. K.shs.2.50 ($1.00)
A collection of tales from the Central Province of Kenya.

The Good Medicine Bird
Nairobi: Longman Kenya, 1976. 52 pp. illus. K.shs.7.00

Malaika Nyanbura and Ward, Leila
The Flame Tree
Nairobi: Transafrica Publ., 1976. (Bushbabies, 3). Unpaged [34 pp.] illus. K.shs.10.00

The legend of the flame tree as told by Owl to his friends the butterflies. The tree grew up on the spot where two lovers lay united in death; Mbumbi, the beautiful young girl, and Tutu, the handsome warrior who had needlessly died in battle thanks to his jealous, conniving Chief.

Manji, Akberali
Valley of the Dead
Nairobi: EAPH, 1972. 55 pp. illus. K.shs.4.50 ($1.00)
Adventure stories which feature young boys.

Manley, Deborah ed.
Growing Up
Lagos: African Univ. Press, 1967 (African Readers Library, 15). 80 pp. illus. 75k
West African childhood memories. Includes extracts from the writings of Adelaide Casely-Hayford, Prince Modupe, Camara Laye, William Conton, Mabel Segun and others.

Matindi, Anne
The Lonely Black Pig
Nairobi: EAPH, 1968 (African Junior Library 5). 30 pp. illus. K.shs.1.70 ($1.00)
Stories and folk-tales from East Africa.

The Sun and the Wind
Nairobi: EAPH, 1968 (African Junior Library 7). 28 pp. illus. K.shs.1.65 ($1.00)

Matindi, Anne and Hunter, Cynthia
The Sun Men, and other plays
Nairobi: EAPH, 1971. 80 pp. illus. K.shs.6.00 ($1.50)
Plays with a background of East African life.

M'Baye d'Erneville, Annette
Chansons pour Laity
Dakar: Nouvelles Éditions Africaines, 1976. 16 pp. illus. CFA350
Poems and songs for Senegalese children.

Menga, Guy
Adventures of Moni-Mabou
London: Evans, 1978. 64 pp. 95p
The escapades of Moni-Mambou and Yengui the parrot. Adapted from the French by Malachy Quinn.

Meniru, Teresa
Unoma
London, Evans, 1976. 80 pp. 95p
Unoma is one of the few girls in her village to attend school and this tale describes her adventures there.

Mensah, J. S.
Kofi Baah's Cat

Tema. Ghana: Ghana Publ. Corp., 1975. 24 pp. 60pes
A story for very young children.

Nimbo the Driver
Tema, Ghana: Ghana Publ. Corp., 1974. 58 pp. illus. 65pes
Nimbo begins a career as a driver against his parents' wishes and gets into trouble on the first day of his new job.

Mlagala, Martha
Yasin's Nightmare Week
Nairobi: EAPH, 1976. 42 pp. illus. K.shs.5.00 ($2.00)
A mischievous schoolboy becomes the school's head prefect.

Moneke, Obiora
How Plants Scattered
Enugu, Nigeria: Flora Nwapa Co., 1979. 18 pp. illus. ₦1.20

Muhire, E.
Wake Up and Open Your Eyes
Nairobi: EAPH, 1976. 127 pp. illus. K.shs.9.00 ($3.00)

Mukunyi, Dickson
The Pet Snake and other stories
Nairobi: EAPH, 1968 (East African Readers Library, 19). 47 pp. illus. K.shs.2.50 ($1.00)
Ten short stories.

Kikuyu Tales
Nairobi: EAPH, 1969. 100 pp. illus. K.shs.5.00 ($2.00)
Tales from Kenya's Kikuyu country.

Mureithi, C. M.
Adventures of Thiga
Nairobi: EAPH, 1971. 69 pp. illus. K.shs.4.80 ($1.50)
An allegory showing the trials of achieving manhood.

Muthoni, Susie
Florence the Blue Flamingo
Nairobi: EAPH, 1973. 17 pp. illus. K.shs. 3.50
A fairy story with illustrations by Beryl Moore.

The Hippo Who Couldn't Stop Crying
Nairobi: EAPH, 1972 (Lioncub, 1). Unpaged [22 pp.] illus. K.shs. 7.50
None of the antics of Harold the Hippo's animal friends can cheer him up – until he happens to catch a glance one night of Leary the long-eared, leaf-nosed bat.

Mutia, Ba'bila
Fireside Tales
Yaoundé: Burma Kor, 1981. 46 pp.
A collection of fifteen traditional animal
stories for the young reader, in which Tortoise
plays a prominent role.

Mutua, Jamlick
Njogu the Prophet
Nairobi: EAPH, 1971. 46 pp. illus. K.shs.3.50
($1.50)
A story of the occult world.

Mwangi, Crispin
The Secret of the Waterfalls
Nairobi: EAPH, 1977. 130 pp. illus.
K.shs.15.00 ($5.00)
A novel of suspense and intrigue, mystery and
miracle.

Mwaurah, David M.
The Circle of Revenge
Nairobi: EAPH, 1976. 78 pp. illus. K.shs.9.00
A vicious circle of revenge threatens a village
until the gods intervene.

Nagenda, Musa
Dogs of Fear
London: HEB, 1970 (Heinemann's Secondary
Reading Scheme, 1). 96 pp. illus. 40p
New York: Holt, 1972. 122 pp. illus. $4.95
A short story of a boy who, having failed his
initiation rites, finds school a more hospitable
place than home.

Nagenda, Sala
Mother of Twins
Nairobi: EAPH, 1971. 52 pp. illus. K.shs.4.90
($1.00)
A wife and her twins are deserted by her
husband, who takes a second wife.

Ndiaye, Théodore Ndock
Si j'étais . . . Rêve d'enfant
Dakar: Nouvelles Editions Africaines, 1974.
16 pp. illus. CFA250
'What if I were . . . ?' dreams the little child in
this story. The colour work is by Arona Dabo.

Le beau voyage de Biram
Dakar: Nouvelles Editions Africaines, 1975.
Unpaged [18 pp.] illus. CFA400
The school year has ended and Biram's uncle
takes him on a trip through Senegal to reward
him for his good marks. It takes him from
Dakar to Saint-Louis in the north and down to
Casamance in the south and the national park
in eastern Senegal.

Ndirangu, Eutychus
Island of Yo
Nairobi: EAPH, 1976 (Lioncub, 8). Unpaged
[24 pp.] col. illus. K.shs.6.50
The island of Yo disappears under the sea for
ever when Tristo refuses to have his sister
sacrificed to the god Cirio.

Ndong, Assane
La trahison
Dakar: Nouvelles Editions Africaines, 1977.
39 pp. illus. CFA550
A father takes pity on his son, Ngor, and
restores the wealth the young man has lost on
the condition that he promises to remain
grateful. But the promise is soon forgotten and
Ngor becomes mean and dishonest. In the
end, however, he realizes his error. A tale for
older children and adults that is illustrated by
A. Diallo.

Ndoro, Joyce
The Hare's Horns
Nairobi: EAPH, 1968 East African Readers
Library, 16). 36 pp. illus. K.shs.2.00 ($1.00)
Six stories from the Baringo district in Kenya.

Ndungu, Frederick
Beautiful Nyakio
Nairobi: EAPH, 1968 (East African Readers
Library, 17). 34 pp. illus. K.shs.2.00 ($1.00)
The main story in this collection centres
around the ugliest man in the village, who very
nearly succeeds in winning the hand of the
beautiful Nyakio, a girl who has refused to
speak to any man.

Ngibuini, Peter Kuguru
Tales of Wamugumo
Nairobi: EAPH, 1967(East African Readers
Library, 7). 70 pp. illus. K.shs.4.00 ($1.50)
Traditional tales of a giant named
Wamugumo, a man of fantastic strength and
an enormous appetite.

Ng'osos, David
*The Man who Stopped Hunting, and other
stories*
Nairobi: EAPH, 1968 (East African Readers
Library). 100 pp. K.shs.4.00 ($1.50)
Stories of the Tugen people of the Baringo
district in Kenya.

Travels of a Raindrop
Nairobi: EAPH, 1973. 47 pp. illus. K.shs.3.00

Njoroge, J. K.
The Greedy Host and other stories
Nairobi: EAPH, 1968 (East African Readers

Library, 11). 36 pp. illus. K.shs.2.00 ($1.00)
Stories of zebras, tortoises and hyenas, simply
told.

The Proud Ostrich and other tales
Nairobi: EAPH, 1968 (East African Readers
Library, 9). 49 pp. illus. K.shs.2.00 ($1.00)
Six simple folk-tales from East Africa.

Tit for Tat
Nairobi: EAPH, 1969 (East African Senior
Library). 101 pp. illus. K.shs.4.50 ($2.00)
Traditional folk-tales from Kenya. 'These
stories deal with human beings and animals in
all their glory, folly, agony and wisdom,' writes
the author.

Njururi, Ngumbu
Tales from Mount Kenya
Nairobi: Transafrica, 1975. 113 pp. illus.

Ntabgoba, J.
My Goodnight Book
Nairobi: EAPH, 1978. 28 pp. illus. K.shs.7.50
($2.00)

Nwakoby, Awele
Ten in the Family
London: Evans, 1975. 64 pp. 95p
The adventures of each of ten members of a
Nigerian family.

Nwankwo, Nkem
Tales out of School
Lagos: African Univ. Press, 1963 (African
Readers Library, 2). 80 pp. illus. 75k
The adventures of two Nigerian schoolboys,
Bayo and Ike – two great friends although of
different tribes – during their first term of
grammar school.

More Tales out of School
Lagos: African Univ. Press, 1965 (African
Readers Library, 7). 80 pp. illus. 75k
In this sequel to *Tales out of School* Bayo
becomes an amateur detective.

Nwapa, Flora
Journey to Space
Enugu, Nigeria: Flora Nwapa Co., 1980.
20 pp. illus. ₦1.20
Eze and his sister Ngozi were playing in the lift
one afternoon and pushed the alarm button,
which promptly set them off on a journey into
space!

The Miracle Kittens
Enugu, Nigeria: Flora Nwapa Co., 1980.
19 pp. illus. ₦1.20
Madam Bum Bum has got big problems – rats

have invaded her kitchen. Two kittens come to
the rescue.

Mammy Water
Enugu, Nigeria: Flora Nwapa Co., 1979.
32 pp. illus. ₦1.50
A folk-tale woven around the water and its
mysteries.

Nyokabi, Sally
*The Chameleon Who Couldn't Stop Changing
His Mind*
Nairobi: Transafrica, 1974. Unpaged [22 pp.]
illus. K.shs.6.00
Chris the Chameleon learns to live with
himself thanks to the wise old Eagle Owl.

Nzekwu, Onuora, and Crowder, Michael
Eze Goes to School
Lagos: African Univ. Press, 1963 (African
Readers Library, 4). 80 pp. illus. 75k
The trials of an Ibo boy determined to go to
school and get an education, despite all the
odds against him.

Odaga, Asenath
Jande's Ambition
Nairobi: EAPH, 1966. 72 pp. illus.
K.shs.3.50 ($1.00)
A young girl is determined to complete her
education and become a teacher.

The Diamond Ring
Nairobi: EAPH, 1967. 52 pp. illus. K.shs.2.00
($1.00)
The adventures of a boy lost in the forest.

The Hare's Blanket
Nairobi: EAPH, 1967. 28 pp. illus. K.shs.1.70
($1.00)
Short stories about a clever hare.

The Angry Flames
Nairobi: EAPH, 1968. 48 pp. illus. K.shs.2.50
($1.00)
A girl escapes being sacrificed to gods by the
elders.

Sweets and Sugar Cane
Nairobi: EAPH, 1969. 24 pp. illus. K.shs.1.60
($1.00)
The adventures of a little boy and his younger
sister.

Kip on the Farm
Nairobi: EAPH, 1969. 16 pp. illus. K.shs.6.50
($2.00)
The adventures of a boy on his grandparents'
farm in the Nandi Hills of Kenya.

Odoi, N. A.
The Adventures of Esi Kakraba
Accra: Waterville Publ. House, 1980. 55 pp.
illus. ₵4.00
A country girl leaves her home to go to the
town and meets with temptations which almost
ruin her life.

Ofosu-Appiah, L. H.
Eight Stories for Children
Tema, Ghana: Ghana Publ. Corp., 1976.
60 pp. illus. STC1.20
Tales for school-age children.

Ogot, Pamela
East African How Stories
Nairobi: EAPH, 1968 (East African Junior
Library, 2). 44 pp. illus. K.shs.2.50 ($1.00)
A collection of traditional tales, containing
'How the hawk and the crow came to hate each
other', 'How the leopard got his spots', 'How
the hyena got an ugly coat', and other stories.

East African When Stories
Nairobi: EAPH, 1968 (East African Junior
Library, 8). 35 pp. illus. K.shs.2.50 ($1.00)
This book includes 'When death began',
'When people stopped killing twin girls',
'When the guinea-fowl stopped living with
people', and other tales.

Okoro, Anezi
The Village School
Lagos: African Univ. Press, 1966 (African
Readers Library, 13). 112 pp. illus. 75k
A picture of life in a primary school in Nigeria.
A soccer match between the school's first and
second elevens is of particular importance.

New Broom at Amanzu
Lagos: African Univ. Press, 1967 (African
Readers Library, 14). 96 pp. illus. 75k
The village school gets a new headmaster, and
his methods arouse strong feelings locally.

The Village School
Lagos: African Univ. Press, 1971 (African
Readers Library, 13). 77 pp. illus. 75k
School life in south-eastern Nigeria in the
1930s.

Febechi and Group in Cave Adventure
Enugu, Nigeria: Nwamife Publ., 1971. 98 pp.
illus. 50k

One Week One Trouble
Lagos: African Univ. Press, 1973 (African
Readers Library, 21). 112 pp. illus. 75k
The adventures of a boy in his new secondary
school.

Febechi Down the River
Enugu, Nigeria: Nwamife Publ., 1975. 116 pp.
illus. ₦1.45

Okoro, N.
The Twin Detectives
London: Evans, 1978. 48 pp. 85p
Two schoolboys become involved in searching
for a gang of robbers.

Okoye, Ifeoma
The Adventures of Tulu the Little Monkey
Enugu, Nigeria: Flora Nwapa Co., 1980.
15 pp. illus. ₦1.20
Tulu the monkey escapes from the zoo only to
find that life is hard outside.

Eme Goes to School
Enugu, Nigeria: Flora Nwapa Co., 1979.
19 pp. illus. ₦1.00
A story about a little girl who is reluctant to go
to school, but then finds it quite enjoyable in
the end.

No Supper for Eze
Enugu, Nigeria: Fourth Dimension Publ. Co.,
1980. 16 pp. illus. ₦1.25
The consequences of Eze refusing to take an
afternoon nap.

No School for Eze
Enugu, Nigeria: Fourth Dimension Publ. Co.,
1980. 16 pp. illus. ₦1.25
Eze thinks that staying at home will be more
fun than going to school – until he tries it.
Illustrated in colour.

Only Bread for Eze
Enugu, Nigeria: Fourth Dimension Publ. Co.,
1980. 16 pp. illus. ₦1.25

Okpaku, Joseph
Jojo
New York: Third Press, 1976. 46 pp. $5.95
A story which aims to teach Nigerian children
national unity. With colour illustrations.

Olagoke, D. Olu
The Incorruptible Judge
London: Evans, 1967 (Plays for African
Schools). 48 pp. 50p
A judge withstands all temptations of bribery.

The Iroko-man and the Wood-carver
London: Evans, 1963 (Plays for African
Schools). 44 pp. 50p
A play based on a local Nigerian legend that a
wood-carver can never get rich through such a
trade. The play, taking this superstition into

account, gives it a happy turn by making a wood-carver prosper.

Olela, Henry and Neuendorffer, Mary Jane
Beyond Those Hills
London: Evans, 1966 (Evans Children's Library). 134 pp. 75p
Juma is a young boy who lives with his family on Rusinga Island in Lake Victoria. He has great dreams of going to Kisii on the mainland to further his education and to see more of the world. The story tells how he achieves this. The late Tom Mboya contributes a foreword, in which he says 'this is a book that will contribute much to our efforts in education'.

Oludhe-Macgoye, M.
Growing Up at Lina School
Nairobi: EAPH, 1971. 77 pp. illus. K.shs.5.25 ($2.00)
A story for girls which tells of the school life of Grace, and of her efforts to re-adapt to life in Africa after having lived abroad.

Omanga, Clare
The Girl Who Couldn't Keep a Secret
Nairobi: EAPH, 1969 (East African Readers Library, 23). 34 pp. illus. K.shs.1.75 ($1.00)
Traditional stories from Kissi in Kenya.

Omolo, Leo Odera
Onyango's Triumph
Nairobi: EAPH, 1968 (East African Readers Library, 14). 47 pp. illus. K.shs.3.00 ($1.00)
A Kenyan schoolboy's adventurous career, from new boy to senior prefect.

The Talking Devil
Nairobi: EAPH, 1969 (East African Readers Library, 26). 39 pp. illus. K.shs.4.50 ($1.00)
Stories from Masailand, the Central Province of Kenya, and the animal kingdom.

The Rain Maker, and other stories
Nairobi: Longman Kenya, 1971. 46 pp. Traditional stories from Kenya.

Onadipe, Kola
The Adventures of Souza
Lagos: African Univ. Press, 1963 (African Readers Library, 5). 80 pp. illus. 75k
The adventures, deeds and misdeeds of a Nigerian boy in his home village, told by Souza himself.

Sugar Girl
Lagos: African Univ. Press, 1964 (African Junior Library, 1). 72 pp. illus. 50p
A kind of West African *Little Red Riding Hood*,

this is the story of Ralia, the 'sugar girl' who follows a little bird and finds herself lost in the forest.

Koku Baboni
Lagos: African Univ. Press, 1965 (African Junior Library, 3). 80 pp. illus. 50k
A brave woman and a little boy bring to an end the fear of twin births in their community.

The Boy Slave
Lagos: African Univ. Press, 1966 (African Readers Library, 12). 112 pp. illus. 75k
The life story of a Nigerian boy taken as a slave by Sheikh Maitama's men to the edge of the Sahara in the mid-nineteenth century.

Magic Land of the Shadows
Lagos: African Univ. Press, 1971 (African Junior Library, 6). 64 pp. 70k
An orphan girl finds herself in the strange land of the Shadow people living under the earth.

The Return of Shettima
Lagos: African Univ. Press, 1973 (African Readers Library, 22). 94 pp. illus. 75k
The sequel to *The Boy Slave* in which Shettima grows up and wins his freedom from slavery.

A Pot of Gold
Ijebu-Ode, Nigeria: Natona Press, 1980. 32 pp. illus. ₦1.00

Sweet Mother
Ijebu-Ode, Nigeria: Natona Press, 1980. 64 pp. illus. ₦1.00

Happy Birthday
Ijebu-Ode, Nigeria: Natona Press, 1980. 40 pp. illus. ₦1.00

Sunny Boy
Ijebu-Ode, Nigeria: Natona Press, 1980. 104 pp. illus. ₦1.60

Onyonah, Eric Nyakiti
Where There is Smoke and other stories
Nairobi: Longman Kenya, 1972. 27 pp.

Opare, Agyei
The Cock, the Hen and the Chicks
Accra: Waterville Publ. House, 1975. 16 pp. ₡1.00

Oppong-Affi, A. M.
Powers of Darkness
London: HEB, 1970 (Heinemann Secondary Reading Scheme, 4). 96 pp. illus. 60p
A Ghanaian Roman Catholic schoolboy is attracted by a Muslim magician, and this leads to conflicts with his teachers.

Osahon, Naiwu
"Obobo Story Series"
Apapa, Nigeria: Obobo Books, 1981. 24 pp.
ea. illus. ₦1.95 ea.
The first fifteen titles in this new series of story
books are scheduled for publication late in
1981. Titles include *Right-on Miss Moon, Laruba
and the Two Wicked Men, Madam Universe Sent
Man, Odu and Onah, The Blue Cowrie, Giant
Alakuku, Ada and the Hunchback Child*, and
Amina. Each booklet is illustrated, some pages
in colour.

"Obobo Colouring Series"
Apapa, Nigeria: Obobo Books, 1981. 30 pp.
ea. illus. ₦1.95 ea.
A series of new colouring books for very young
children, the first five titles of which are to be
published late in 1981.

"Obobo Adventure Series"
Apapa, Nigeria: Obobo Books, 1981. 24 pp.
ea. illus. ₦1.95 ea.
Yet a further new children's series from Obobo
Books, all written by Naiwu Osahon. The first
five titles are promised for late 1981.

Osogo, John
The Bride Who Wanted a Special Present
Nairobi: East Africa Lit. Bureau, 1966. 63 pp.
illus. K.shs.3.00 (60p/$1.50)
Thirteen folk-tales from Western Kenya.

Ossai, Anji
Tolulope
Walton-on-Thames: Nelson, 1979 (Authors of
Africa). 108 pp. 65p
The story of a young girl growing up in
Ibadan, Nigeria, caught between the fast
lifestyle of her boy friend and her stern father's
disapproval. For young adults.

Owolabi, O.
Ngozi Goes to Market
Ibadan: Onibonoje Press, 1978. 29 pp. 55k
One in a series of books about the day-to-day
life and adventures of Nigerian children.

Hassana Goes to Lagos
Ibadan: Onibonoje Press, 1978. 20 pp. 70k

The Cat and the Rat
Ibadan: Onibonoje Press, 1978. 29 pp. 55k

Adebola's School
Ibadan: Onibonoje Press, 1978. 20 pp. 70k

Adamu and his Cow
Ibadan: Onibonoje Press, 1978. 29 pp. 55k

Ade and his Drum
Ibadan: Onibonoje Press, 1979. 28 pp. 55k

Owusu, Martin
The Story Ananse told
London: HEB, 1970 (Heinemann Secondary
Reading Scheme, 5). 64 pp. 50p
A play about Ananse the spider, one of the
central figures of West African folklore.

*Adventures of Sasa and Esi. Two plays for
children*
Tema, Ghana: Ghana Publ. Corp., 1968.
24 pp. 50pes
Based on short stories of a little boy and his
sister and their experiences with a giant and a
witch.

Owusu-Nimoh, Mercy
Kofizee Goes to School
Tema, Ghana: Ghana Publ. Corp., 1978.
60 pp. illus. ₵2.50
Kofizee looks forward to his first day at school
and is not disappointed.

Stories of Kofizee
Tema, Ghana: Ghana Publ. Corp., 1979.
55 pp. ₵2.50
Aspects of Kofizee's life from his birth until he
is old enough to attend school.

The Walking Calabash and other stories
Tema, Ghana: Ghana Publ. Corp., 1977.
71 pp. illus. ₵1.75
Seven stories set in Ghana which are mainly
about animals.

Pepetela [pseud. for Pestana, Artur]
Ngunga's Adventures
London: Liberation/Young World Books,
1980. £1.50
A simply written tale, by an Angolan author, of
the discovery of adulthood in a time of war
and liberation. It is illustrated with drawings
and a photo-essay from the liberated areas of
Angola during the war.

Tales of Mozambique
London: Liberation/Young World Books,
1980. £2.30
A large, A4-size book of stories from the
African oral tradition in Mozambique. It
contains fables, human stories, allegories and
realistic tales. The collection is based upon an
anthology published by FRELIMO in 1977,
which was designed to stimulate the Mozambique tradition of popular story telling.
Eighteen artists from all over the world
contribute illustrations.

Poland, Marguerite
The Mantis and the Moon
Johannesburg: Ravan Press, 1980. 128 pp.
illus. R7.50 cased R3.95 p/b
A book of animal stories inspired by San
('Bushman') mythology. Illustrated by Leigh
Voigt, the book was a recent winner of the
Percy Fitzpatrick Award.

Prather, Ray
A is for Africa. A colouring book of Africa
Nairobi: East African Lit. Bureau, 1976.
Unpaged [40 pp.] illus. K.shs.5.60
Forty full-page drawings depicting the various
peoples of Africa, accompanied by small maps
showing their geographical locations.

Ririani, Rachel
The Lazy Hyena
Nairobi: Njogu Gitene Publ., 1972. 13 pp.
illus. K.shs.4.00

The Naughty Hyena
Nairobi: Njogu Gitene Publ., 1972. 13 pp.
illus. K.shs.4.00

The Sisters Who Were Afraid
Nairobi: Njogu Gitene Publ., 1972. 19 pp.
illus. K.shs.6.00

The Burning House
Nairobi: Njogu Gitene Publ., 1972. 23 pp.
illus. K.shs.6.00

Ruheni, Mwangi
In Search of Their Parents
Nairobi: Longman Kenya, 1973. 41 pp. illus.
Two boys in search of their parents find they
are in danger themselves.

Ruhui, Wahome
Mole, Rat and the Mountain
Nairobi: EAPH, 1973. 19 pp. illus. K.shs.4.00

Sankawulo, Wilton
*The Marriage of Wisdom and other Tales from
Liberia*
London: HEB, 1974 (Heinemann Secondary
Readers). 89 pp. illus. 60p
Songs and tales from Liberia, about humans
and animals.

Saritti, Tony
The Little Orphan Boy
Yaoundé: Buma kor, 1981. 24 pp. illus.
A story for young children about how an
orphan was abandoned by his step-parents for
faults committed by his step-sisters and
brothers. He goes to the kingdom of the

animals where an elephant gives him the egg
that enriches him.

Segun, Mabel
My Father's Daughter
Lagos: African Univ. Press, 1965 (African
Readers Library, 8). 80 pp. illus. 75k
Portrays the experiences of a young Nigerian
girl, the daughter of a versatile father, a
doctor, judge and postal agent.

Senghor, Léopold Sédar, and Sadji, Abdoulaye
La belle histoire de Leuk-le-Lièvre
Paris: Hachette. 1953. 176 pp. FF15.00
A collection of short folk-tales. They are aimed
primarily at younger readers, featuring Leuk
the hare as the main character in all the stories.

La belle histoire de Leuk-le-Lièvre
Edited by J. M. Winch
London: Harrap, 1965. 154 pp.
An English edition with an introduction, notes
and a vocabulary. Difficult and unusual points
of grammar and syntax are noted and
explained.

Sidibe, B. K.
The Animals Go Strange Farming
Banjul, Gambia: Oral Hist. Ant. Division,
1976. 16 pp. illus. D2.50 ($1.50)

Suleiman, L.
The King's Picture
Lagos: West African Book Publ., 1977. 26 pp.
illus. ₦1.00
The hero is an artist who makes a picture of
God at the King's request. With striking colour
illustrations.

The Gold Digger
Lagos: West African Book Publ., 1977. 26 pp.
illus. ₦1.00
The Protector of the Forest rescues the gold
digger from the pit in which he found the gold,
on condition he uses his wealth for the benefit
of others. When he disobeys . . .

Sutherland, Efua
Vulture! Vulture!
Tema, Ghana: Ghana Publ. Corp., 1968.
32 pp. illus. ₡1.00
Two rhythm plays for use in schools.

Playtime in Africa
New York: Atheneum, 1962. 58 pp. illus. $5.50
cased
A picture essay combining rhythmic verse with

photographs depicting playtime activities of children in Ghana. With photographs by Willis E. Bell.

Taiwo, Oladele
The King's Hair
Walton-on-Thames: Nelson, 1965 (Rapid Reading series, lower level, 4). 80 pp. illus. 95p
A collection of stories, riddles and proverbs from Nigerian folklore, reflecting the traditional beliefs, customs and attitudes of Nigerians.

The Hunter and the Hen
Lagos: African Univ. Press, 1965 (African Junior Library, 2). 80 pp. illus. 50k
Twenty-four stories and folk-tales from Nigeria

Tetteh-Lartey, A. C. V. B.
The Schooldays of Shango Solomon
London: CUP 1965. 80 pp. illus.
A school story set in Ghana.

Toweet, T.
Tears Over a Dead cow, and other stories
Nairobi: African Book Services (distr.), 1970. 63 pp. illus. K.shs.5.50

Tsaro-Wiwa, K. B.
Tambari
Lagos: Longman Nigeria, 1973 (Palm Library). 96 pp. illus. 70k (60p)
At first, Tambari does not wish to move to Port Harcourt, but soon finds much to interest him.

Tambari in Dukana
Lagos: Longman Nigeria, 1973 (Palm Library). 102 pp. illus. 60k (65p)
Tambari lives in a big town, but returns to the small village of Dukana in which he was born for a holiday, and comes to appreciate the simple life.

Tuitoek, William Arap
The Boy Who Learnt a Lesson and other stories
Nairobi: Longman Kenya, 1975. 32 pp. illus. K.shs.3.50
Rabbit trickster and other tales from the Kericho Valley of Kenya.

Ukoli, Neville
The Twins of the Rain Forest
Lagos: Longman Nigeria, 1968 (Palm Library). 70 pp. illus. 60k
Oshare's mother gives birth to twins. This was considered to be a curse and the babies were set adrift in the creek. Oshare rescues them and arranges for his mother to feed them.

Ukoli, Neville and Olomu, M.
The Antelope that Hurried
Benin-City: Ethiope Publ. Corp, 1975. 16 pp. 50k

Umeh, R. E.
Why the Cock Became a Sacrificial Animal
Enugu, Nigeria: Fourth Dimension Publ. Co., 1981. 32 pp. ₦1.25

Uwemedimo, Rosemary
Akpan and the Smugglers
Lagos: African Univ. Press, 1965 (African Readers Library, 9). 78 pp. illus. 75k
A detective story involving Akpan Bassey in an attempt to foil a smugglers plot.

Vatsa, Mamman J.
Children's Stories and Riddles in Verse
Enugu, Nigeria: Fourth Dimension Publ. Co., 1978. 56 pp. illus. ₦1.50
A collection of poems for children in junior classes.

Children's Rhymes
Enugu, Nigeria: Fourth Dimension Publ. Co., 1978. 56 pp. illus. ₦1.50
A verse collection for children, with colour illustrations.

ABC Rhymes
Enugu, Nigeria: Fourth Dimension Publ. Co., 1979. 16 pp. illus. ₦1.25
Rhymes for the very young, designed to help them to master the alphabet.

The Lion in the Cage
Enugu, Nigeria: Fourth Dimension Publ. Co., 1979. 16 pp. illus. ₦1.25
A short story for children in the spirit of the oral tradition.

Soldier's Children as Poets
Enugu, Nigeria: Fourth Dimension Publ. Co., 1979. 32 pp. illus. ₦1.50
An anthology of poetry by and for children which in many ways is a companion to Vatsa's anthology of the poems of soldier-poets, *Voices from the Trench.*

Stinger the Scorpion
Enugu, Nigeria: Fourth Dimension Publ. Co., 1979. 16 pp. illus. ₦1.25
Illustrated in colour, this is a short story in verse for the young about the habits and characteristics of scorpions

Drought
Enugu, Nigeria: Fourth Dimension Publ. Co., 1980. 16 pp. illus. ₦1.25
A narrative describing the causes and effects of drought.

Waciuma, Charity

Mweru the Ostrich Girl
Nairobi: EAPH, 1966 (East African Readers Library, 1). 48 pp. illus. K.shs.2.50 ($1.00)
Mweru the ostrich girl runs away from home into a world of magic, alien creatures and strange adventures.

The Golden Feather
Nairobi: EAPH, 1966 (East African Readers Library, 4). 48 pp. illus. K.shs.2.50 ($1.00)
A search for a lost cow leads little Keru to the home of the great giant after a series of exciting adventures.

Daughter of Mumbi
Nairobi: EAPH, 1969. 153 pp. illus. K.shs.8.00

Merry-Making
Nairobi: EAPH, 1972 (Lioncub, 2). Unpaged [15 pp.] K.shs.6.50 ($2.00)
Grandfather Kaguru helps the children prepare for the merry-making season when the rains have stopped and the planting has been done by telling stories and riddles to them and by encouraging them to learn traditional skills – hunting for the boys and household duties for the girls.

Who's Calling?
Nairobi: EAPH, 1973 (Lioncub, 3). 15 pp. illus. K.shs.6.50 ($2.00)
A story involving a little girl, some African friends and the echoing hills.

When I awoke

Nairobi: EAPH, 1968 (East African Senior Library). 69 pp. illus. K.shs.7.50 ($2.50)
A collection of stories by young East African school children, this is the outcome of a literary competition sponsored by the Associated Tea Growers of East Africa and the Brooke Bond Tea Company. One of the rules of the competition stated that all essays had to begin with 'When I awoke . . .'

Wiredu, Anokye

Queen Amina
Tema, Ghana: Ghana Publ. Corp., 1973. 29 pp. illus. 50pes
A story for the younger child, telling of King

Ali who married two women – Salamatu and Amina.

Sons of a Fisherman
Tema, Ghana: Ghana Publ. Corp., 1979. 76 pp. ₵2.50
An adventure story telling of the exploits of Akyeri and his younger brother on an island.

Yari, Labo

A Visit to Grandmother
Enugu, Nigeria: Fourth Dimension Publ. Co., 1981. 32 pp. illus. ₦1.25

Yassin, Mohammed

Tales from Sierra Leone
London: OUP, 1967. 55 pp.
These stories from Sierra Leone in West Africa were collected over a long period from different people of various dialects.

Yemitan, O.

The Bearded Story-Teller
Ibadan: Fagbamigbe, 1980. 128 pp. ₦1.50
A novel for ten to fourteen year olds.

Youdeowei, T.

My Alphabet Book
Ibadan: Onibonoje Press, 1978. 53 pp. ₦1.00

My Animal Book
Ibadan: Onibonoje Press, 1978. 50 pp. ₦1.00

Zacchaeus, Arap Kimeto

The Battle of Mogori and other stories
Nairobi: EAPH, 1972. 39 pp. illus. K.shs.4.00
Historical tales of the Kipsigi's of Kenya.

Zirimu, Elvania N.

Kamasiira and other stories
Nairobi: EAPH, 1980. 68 pp. K.shs.12.50
Short stories which re-create the African oral tradition and African folklore.

MAGAZINES

This section is divided into three parts: part I features major literary and cultural periodicals; part II provides details on other periodicals which include contributions on African literature from time to time, and also lists the major bibliographic tools for African studies; part III, finally, is a short listing of a number of non-Africanist journals which have published special issues on African literature since the first edition of the *Guide* was published. Full ordering information is provided for each journal, and in part I subscription rates (surface mail) are also given, though these are of course subject to change.

I. Literary and cultural periodicals

Literary journals, anywhere, tend to live a somewhat precarious existence, and almost a third of the journals in the listing that follows have ceased publication, or certainly have been dormant for some time. Nevertheless, we have attempted to include all the important ones, even though a number of them are only modestly produced. The listing does *not* pretend to be complete however, and we have excluded, for example, a number of very short-lived African magazines such as *Expression* (Limbe), *Mila* (Nairobi), *Muse* (Nsukka), *Moran* (Morogoro), or *Penpoint* (Kampala).

Although defunct, or dormant, back numbers of many of the journals given in this list may be found in major university and in some public libraries who maintain sizeable African collections. The reader who would like to have access to these journals – other than by subscribing where it is possible – should consult the section 'Directory of Libraries with African Literature Collections' on page 525. Thus a reader in, say Los Angeles, who would like to consult copies of, for example, *Présence Africaine* will find this on the shelves of both the Los Angeles Public Library, as well as at the University of California at Los Angeles Library. Or a reader in, say, Leeds, England, will find that the University of Leeds Library has copies of, for example, *Black Orpheus*, but if he or she would like to examine copies of e.g. *Abbia* a visit to a library in Birmingham or London may be required, unless journal back numbers are available on inter-library loan.

Abbia. Revue Culturel
Camerounaise/Cameroun Cultural Review
BP 879, Yaoundé, Cameroun
1963 - quarterly
Editor: Bernard Fonlon
Subscription rates: CFA1,600 in Cameroun,
CFA4,000 elsewhere (early back issues available
from Kraus Reprint)

This important literary and cultural magazine has been dormant for a number of years, but publication recommenced with a triple number (nos. 31-32-33), and an issue combining four numbers (nos. 34-35-36-37) was published in June 1979. Articles appear both in English and in French, covering a wide variety of cultural activities. There are frequent essays on both traditional and modern African literature, supplemented by short stories, plays, poetry and book reviews.

África. Literatura – Arte e Cultura
Africa Editora Lda., R. de Santa Cruz, Lote 9–3,
Oeiras, Portugal
1979 – three times yearly
Editor: Manuel Ferreira
Subscription rates: Esc.450$00 in Portugal and
lusophone Africa, Esc.550$00 elsewhere
Devoted to literature, arts, and culture throughout the lusophone African world. Original poems and stories are featured along with critical articles, substantial book reviews, which include pictures of each book under discussion, and a section presenting news about African literature from Africa, Brazil, the United States, and Eastern and Western Europe. Articles on anglophone and francophone literatures appear from time to time. Numerous photos, some of which are full paged, and frequent sketches make *África* a visually attractive journal.

African Arts

African Studies Center, Univ. of California,
Los Angeles, Ca. 90024, USA
1967 – quarterly
Editor: John Povey
Subscription rates: $16.00 in the US, $18.00
elsewhere

A lavishly produced scholarly journal, which is aimed at both general and academic audiences. Its subject area spans the entire field of the African arts – drama, pure and applied art, sculpture, cinema, literature, literary criticism, music and dance, and each issue is richly illustrated with many full-colour plates. The journal aims to record Africa's traditional art and stimulate its contemporary art. African arts are thus viewed from a dual perspective, i.e. their origins and their directions. '*African Arts* has a double mission – to act as a catalyst to the contemporary African artist and to gain a wider audience for the arts of all Africa *in* Africa and *beyond* Africa.'

African Literature Today

Heinemann Educational Books Ltd., 22 Bedford
Square, London WC1B 3HH
1968 – annually
Editor: Eldred Jones
prices vary, see pp. 30–1

An annual survey and forum for the examination of the literature of Africa. Each number now concentrates on a particular area of literature. For full details see pp. 30–1.

L'Afrique Littéraire et Artistique

Société Africaine d'Edition, BP 1877, Dakar,
Senegal (in France: 32 rue de l'Echiquier, Paris 10)
1968 – quarterly
Editor: Paulette Ph. Decraene
Subscription rates: CFA6,000 in Africa, FF150.00
elsewhere

Written entirely in French, this cultural magazine surveys literature, drama, art, music and cinema as well as history; it also includes creative writing, essays, and reviews. Considerable attention is devoted to the development of African theatre. Tourism, gastronomy and news stories make up additional features.

ALA Newsletter

c/o Stephen Arnold, Department of Comparative
Literature, University of Alberta, Edmonton, Alberta,
Canada T6G 2E6
1977 – quarterly
Editor: Stephen Arnold
Subscription rates: $12.00 for individuals ($4.00 for
students), $18.00 for institutions

This newsletter is the official publication of the (US) African Literature Association, an independent professional society that 'exists primarily to facilitate the attempts of a worldwide audience to appreciate the creative efforts of African writers and artists'. Each issue provides a variety of notes and news, together with a round-up of reports on conferences, and activities of the Association.

Arts and Africa

BBC African Service, British Broadcasting
Corporation, PO Box 76, Bush House, Strand,
London WC2B 4PH
1970 – irregular [about two transcripts monthly]
Subscription rates: on application, limited circulation

These are the mimeographed transcripts (mostly 5–6 pages in length) of the BBC's regular 'Arts and Africa' programme, which is widely broadcast throughout Africa. The programmes provide news and reports on cultural events in and about Africa, and, for the researcher in African literature, particularly valuable are the frequent interviews with major African writers.

Asemka

c/o French Department, University of Cape Coast,
Ghana
1974 – twice yearly
Editor: Y. S. Kantanka Boafo
Subscription rates: ¢2.00 in Ghana, $5.00 elsewhere

A literary journal of the University of Cape Coast, *Asemka*, which means 'food for thought' in Akan, is a joint venture between the departments of English and French, and includes scholarly articles both in English and French, as well as creative writing.

Ba Shiru

866 van Hise Hall, Univ. of Wisconsin, Madison,
Wi. 53706
1970 – twice yearly
Editors: Margaret Brualdi and Zinta Konrad
Subscription rates: $5.00 for individuals, $15.00 for
institutions

A semi-annual journal devoted to African languages and literatures, which, as stated in their first issue, 'presents facts in terms of the African perspective, not the European, in terms of the African interest, not the European.' Recent issues have focused on Swahili and Creole literatures, and the two numbers of volume 12 are on 'The Oral Tradition' and 'Women Writers and Artists in Africa/African Diaspora'.

The Benin Review

Ethiope Publishing Corp., PMB 1192, Benin City,
Nigeria
1974, Vol. I, no. 1 [all publ., ceased]
Editors: Abiole Irele and Pius Olehe

This impressive magazine was poised to

become a significant addition to the growing number of African cultural magazines, but unfortunately (for the time being at least) it never went beyond volume I, number 1. Its intended scope was to cover all the arts in Africa, both traditional and modern, and cultural life in the Black World generally.

Black Orpheus

University of Lagos Press, PO Box 132, Yaba, Lagos State, Nigeria
1957 – twice yearly
Editor: Theo Vincent
Subscription rates: ₦8.00 in Nigeria,
£8.00/$16.00 (Back issues available from Kraus Reprint)
Black Orpheus, the first literary journal of black Africa to appear on African soil, has had a chequered career. Its first number was published in 1957, and for many years it was the most important vehicle for the expression of all forms of African literature and art. Its founding editors were Ulli Beier and Janheinz Jahn, and other editors have included Ezekiel Mphahlele, Wole Soyinka, Abiola Irele, and John Pepper Clark. However, the magazine has been dormant for several years now, and its last issue (under J. P. Clark's editorship) was volume III (New Series), number 4, published in December 1976. The University of Lagos Press has now announced that it will recommence publication late in 1981, under the editorship of Theo Vincent. Produced as the university's main journal of the arts and the humanities, it will continue to include both creative writing and criticism, as well as covering music, painting, sculpture, and other art forms.

The Bloody Horse

Bateleur Press (Pty.) Ltd., PO Box 6690, Johannesburg 2000, South Africa
1980 – six times yearly [ceased?]
Editor: Patrick Cullinan
Subscription rates: R9.75 in Southern Africa, £7.00/$15.00 elsewhere
A lively and attractively produced new literary magazine which 'is open to all writing and art which is innovative, original, and combative.' 'No writer', said an editorial statement in the first number, 'whatever his background, his views, his politics, will be barred from the magazine.' Contributions come both in English and in Afrikaans, and include short stories, poetry, essays and commentary, plus photographs and graphic work.

Bulletin of the Association for African Literature in English

1964-1966 [all publ., ceased]

Editor: Eldred Jones
(Back issues of nos. 1–4 available from Kraus Reprint)
This mimeographed bulletin was the forerunner of *African Literature Today*, see pp. 30–1.

Busara [formerly Nexus]

Kenya Literature Bureau, POB 30022, Nairobi, Kenya
1968 – twice yearly [ceased?]
Editor: Kimani Gecau (editorship rotates from year to year)
Subscription rates: K.shs.10.00 in Kenya, $5.00 elsewhere
This is one of several East African literary journals which has been affected by the collapse of the East African Community, and the consequent suspension of activity by the East African Literature Bureau. The successor of the latter is the Kenya Literature Bureau, but who, thus far at least, have not recommenced publication, and the last issue was volume VIII, no. 2, published in 1976. Published under the auspices of the Department of Literature at the University of Nairobi, *Busara* (which superseded *Nexus*) presented original creative writing and critical articles, including material discussed at the university's Writers' Workshop.

Le Cahiers du Cercle Littéraire de Brazzaville

Centre Culturel Français, BP 2141, Brazzaville, Congo Popular Republic
1979 – irregular
Editor: Caya Makhele
Subscription rates: free
A modestly produced literary and cultural magazine, containing poetry, short stories, and essays.

Le Cameroun Littéraire

1964, nos. 1 & 2 [all publ., ceased]
(Nos. 1 and 2 available from Kraus Reprint)
A short-lived magazine which was the official journal of the Association Nationale des Poètes et Ecrivains Camerounais, and the two numbers published include some early writing by authors such as René Philombé and Francois Evembe.

Ch'indaba [formerly Transition]

Transition Limited, PO Box 9063, Accra, Ghana
1961–1975 [as Transition], vol. I, no. 1, October 1975 – [as Ch'indaba] [ceased]
Editor: Wole Soyinka
Subscription rates: ₵3.20 in Ghana, $8.00 elsewhere
(Back issues available from Kraus Reprint)
Founded in October 1961 by Rajat Neogy, *Transition* was for a long time Africa's most influential and most outspoken cultural and political magazine, and Abiola Irele once aptly

wrote that '*Transition* is not merely reporting about Africa or feeling its pulse, but is charting the directions of its mind.' Every point of view was tolerated as *Transition* reflected the heartbeat of the African continent, its articles treating subjects as diverse as politics, poetry, sex, literature, sociology, business, racial discrimination, and more. Among its widely known contributors were writers such as Chinua Achebe, Wole Soyinka, J. P. Clark, Christopher Okigbo, Ali Mazrui, Kofi Awoonor, and statesmen such as Julius Nyerere, Kenneth Kaunda, and Milton Obote. In October 1968, *Transition* was banned by one of those selfsame contributors, Milton Obote, who had its editor arrested and detained on charges of publishing seditious material. During Neogy's detention the journal ceased publication and several issues were confiscated by the Ugandan authorities.

In 1971 Neogy moved to Ghana and resumed publication from Accra. Wole Soyinka took over as editor in 1974, and with the publication of the 50th issue its name was changed to *Ch'indaba*, an invocation composed of 'Indaba', a Matabele word meaning the Great Assembly, Council, or Colloque, and 'Cha' which stands for 'to dawn' in Swahili. Sadly, however, this splendid journal seems to have ceased publication (there were some plans to publish it from London, which did not materialize) and the last issue was no. 2, July/December 1976.

Coloquio-Letras

Calouste Gulbenkian Foundation
Lisbon, Portugal
1971 – six times yearly
Editor: Jacinto do Prado Coelho
Subscription rates: $22.00
Features critical essays, fiction, and poetry from the lusophone world as well as a book review section. Although there is a greater concentration on traditional and modern writing from Portugal and Brazil than on African literatures, much original and scholarly African material is presented. Some recent issues, such as number 39 (September, 1977), are devoted specifically to Africa.

The Conch

Conch Magazine Ltd., 102 Normal Avenue
Symphony Circle, Buffalo, N.Y. 14213, USA
1969 – twice yearly |irregular in recent years|
Editor: Sunday Anozie
Subscription rates: $9.00 for individuals, $12.00 for institutions
This journal derives its title from William Golding's novel *Lord of the Flies* – 'Hear him! He's got a conch!' The initial two issues were sub-titled 'A Biafran Journal of Literary and Cultural Analysis', but as from volume 2, no. 1 it was changed to 'A Sociological Journal of African Cultures and Literatures'. *The Conch's* editorial policy 'emphasizes the need for a close analytical study of specific African social and cultural environments in relation to specific African languages and works of art . . . it favours the use of modern structuralist methods and theories.' Emphasis is laid on critical writings and interpretations, but some poetry is also included in each issue, along with book reviews.

CRNLE Reviews Journal

Centre for Research in the New Literatures in
English, Flinders Univ. of South Australia, Bedford
Park, South Australia 5042
1979 – twice yearly
Editors: Haydn Moore Williams and Paul Sharrad
Subscription rates: $A6.00 for individuals, $A9.00
for institutions
Aims to provide a critical guide to English-language literary publishing from the post-colonial societies of the Commonwealth and beyond. It covers creative writing and literary criticism – but deliberately avoids long scholarly articles – and each issue includes a large number of book reviews.

Cultural Events in Africa

1965 – monthly |ceased|
Editors: Dennis Duerden and Maxine Lautre
Subscription rates:
A handy news bulletin which comprehensively covered cultural events and general trends in all areas of African arts and literatures, published in the form of short notices, news stories or reviews. A particularly valuable feature in each number were the regular interviews with African artists and writers, some of which have since been published in book form (see p. 78; Duerden, D.).

Darlite – see *Umma*

Dhana

Kenya Literature Bureau, PO Box 30022, Nairobi,
Kenya
1971 – |ceased?|
Editor: Adminola Ocitti
Subscription rates: K.shs.10.00/£1.00/$2.50
Features creative writing from East Africa – prose, poetry, drama – together with critical essays and book reviews.

Dombi

BP 3498, Kinshasa-Kalina, Zaïre Republic
1970 – twice yearly |ceased?|
Editor: Philippe Masegabio
Subscription rates: Z2.00

Subtitled 'Revue Congolaise des Lettres et des Arts', this cultural journal contains poetry, short stories, and essays.

Ethiopiques. Revue Socialiste de Culture Négro-Africaine

10 rue El Hadi Amadou Assane Ndoye, Dakar, Senegal
1975 – quarterly
Editors: Abdou Galam Kane and Makhily Gassama
Subscription rates: CFA 5,000 in Africa, FF160.00 elsewhere
A major scholarly journal which aims to provide a platform for a dialogue for committed socialism, as well as analysis of African arts and cultures. Each issue is divided into two distinct sections: 'Développement et sociétes' includes essays, and 'Culture et civilisations' features prose, poetry, and reviews, as well as containing art and graphics.

The Greenfield Review

PO Box 80, Greenfield Center, N.Y. 12833, USA
1970 – twice yearly
Editors: Carol and Joseph Bruchac
Subscription rates: $6.00
A non-profit-making literary magazine which features the work of a wide range of contemporary poets, both new and well established. Although the journal covers poetry from all parts of the world, it publishes (as a double number) an attractively produced 'African Poetry Issue' every other year. The most recent one, the fifth (volume VII, nos. 1 & 2, Spring 1980), featured work by Arthur Nortje, Ifeanyi Menkiti, Michel Kayoya, Oswald Mtshali, Chinua Achebe, and others, plus poetry of Akpalu (translated by Kofi Awoonor) and Domegbe (translated by Kofi Anyidoho). *The Greenfield Review* is the journal that has probably done the most in promoting poetry by new and sometimes still unknown African writers.

The Jewel of Africa

Mphala Creative Society, University of Zambia, PO Box 2379, Lusaka, Zambia
1965 – 1969[?] [ceased]
Editor: Steven Mayo
A short-lived journal that aimed to promote literary development in Zambia, and which included fiction, drama, poetry, folk-tales, as well as essays and criticism.

Joliso. East African Journal of Literature and Society

Kenya Literature Bureau, PO Box 30022, Nairobi, Kenya
1973 – twice yearly [ceased?]
Editor: Chris Wanjala
Subscription rates: K.shs.24.00 in Kenya, £2.10/$5.20 elsewhere
Following the collapse of the East African Community and suspension of activity by the East African Literature Bureau, *Joliso* has been dormant for several years now, though it is possible that it may be revived. It included short stories and articles, and aimed to provide a platform for criticism, analysis and comment, not only for the literary critic, but also for social scientists, historians, philosophers, and educationists.

Journal of African and Comparative Literature

Heinemann Educational Books (Nigeria) Ltd., PMB 5205, Ibadan, Nigeria
1981 – twice yearly
Editors: Isidore Okpewho and Femi Osofisan
Subscription rates: ₦5.00/£4.00/$10.00 for individuals, ₦12.00/£10.00/$20.00 for institutions
Published on behalf of the Nigerian Association for African and Comparative Literature, this new journal is devoted to 'exploring issues in African literature in their wider implications.' It is largely of a comparatist nature, i.e. a journal of literary theory with a focus on Africa. The editors put a strong emphasis on 'inter-connectedness' which, they state, 'should be recognized as a first principle in a piece of creative African literature.'

The Journal of Commonwealth Literature

Hans Zell Publishers, An imprint of K. G. Saur Verlag, PO Box 56, Oxford OX1 3EL, England
1965 – twice yearly
Editors: Alastair Niven and Angus Calder
Subscription rates: DM36.-/£8.00/$19.00 for individuals, DM54.-/£12.50/$29.00 for institutions
Published since 1965 and for a long time under the editorship of Arthur Ravenscroft, this well-established journal provides a focal-point for discussion of literatures in English outside Britain and the USA. The first number of each volume consists of an issue of critical studies and essays; the second is the bibliography issue, providing an annual checklist of publications in each region of the Commonwealth. Volume XV, number 1, August 1980, was a special 'Africa issue'.

Journal of the New African Literature and the Arts

Third Press, 444 Central Park West, New York, N.Y. 10025, USA
1966 – quarterly [ceased?]
Editor: Joseph Okpaku
Subscription rates: $10.00
Publishes plays, short stories, poetry, as well as

scholarly articles on African literature, music, fine art, dance, and other aspects of African culture. No issues have been published, however, for several years now.

Journal of the Performing Arts
School of Performing Arts, Univ. of Ghana,
PO Box 19, Legon, Ghana
1980 – twice yearly
Editor: Nissio Fiagbedzi
Subscription rates: not known
The official journal of the School of Performing Arts at the University of Ghana, this mimeographed publication carries articles on all aspects of music, dance, and drama, as well as covering television and the media.

Kaafa
Society of Liberian Authors, c/o Ministry of Education, Monrovia, Liberia
1970 – [?]
Editors: Osborne K. Diggs and Doris Bank Henries
Subscription rates: 75c per issue
A modestly produced (mimeographed) journal and newsletter of the Society of Liberian Authors.

Kiabara. Journal of the Humanities
School of Humanities, University of Port Harcourt, PMB 5223, Port Harcourt, Nigeria
1978 – twice yearly
Editor: I. N. C. Aniebo
Subscription rates: ₦5.00/£4.00/$9.00 for individuals, ₦7.00/£5.00/$12.00 for institutions
Kiabara takes its name (in Khana) from the Kingfisher, a bird which pervades the oral traditions of the Rivers people of Nigeria in many diverse forms. The journal thus does not restrict its scope to a single academic discipline, but aims to cover the whole of the humanities relating to Africa and the black diaspora. Contents in each issue include folklore, short stories, poetry, drama, book reviews, as well as critical essays. The first number of each volume is sub-titled the 'Rains issue', whereas the second is the 'Harmattan issue'.

Kunapipi
Dangaroo Press, Department of English, University of Aarhus, Denmark
1978 – twice yearly
Editor: Anna Rutherford
Subscription rates: DKr.30.00/£3.00/$6.00 for individuals, DKr.50.00/£5.00/$10.00 for institutions
Kunapipi (a continuation of the *Commonwealth Newsletter*) is a journal of creative and critical writing concerned with the new literatures in English. The major concentration is on the present and former Commonwealth countries, though this is by no means exclusive. The journal is the bulletin for the European branch of the Association of Commonwealth Literature and Language Studies, and as such it offers a wide variety of news and information about courses, conferences, scholarships, and literary competitions. Interviews with major writers are another regular feature.

Kwanza Journal
PO Box 42, Pretoria 0001, South Africa
1979 – irregular [normally quarterly]
Editor: Risimati j'Mathonsi
Subscription rates: not known
Modestly produced, *Kwanza Journal* features poetry and other creative writing by as yet little-known black South African writers. It also aims to inform local writers about literary activities outside South Africa, and includes a regular column of notes and news, as well as book reviews.

Légitime Defense
1932, no. 1 [all publ., ceased]
Editors: Jules Monnerot and René Ménil
(Available in reprint from Kraus. Reprint, and also re-issued by J. M. Place, Paris, in 1979 at FF40.00 per copy)

The one and only issue of this celebrated journal. It was a manifesto of political and literary doctrines, to spur young Africans and West Indians living in Paris into action, and which thus marked the birth of the Négritude movement.

Lotus. Afro-Asian Writings
104 Kasr El Aini Street, Cairo, Egypt
1968 – quarterly
Editor: Youssef El Sebai
Subscription rates: not known
Published by the Permanent Bureau of Afro-Asian Writers, containing articles, poems, short stories, folklore and graphics by African and Asian artists and writers.

Marang
Department of English, University College of Botswana,
Private Bag 0022, Gaborone, Botswana
1977 – twice yearly
Editor: Bob Leshoai
Subscription rates: 75 Thebe per issue
An attractively produced literary magazine that presents a major effort to stimulate and encourage creative writing in Botswana. Each number includes poetry, fiction, drama, and, occasionally, essays.

Mzalendo
Literature Department, University of Nairobi,
Nairobi, Kenya
1981 – irregular [about two issues annually]
Editors: Machayo wa Olilo and J. A. O. Teyie
Subscription rates: K.shs.5.00 per issue
This is a modestly produced (mimeographed)
but lively new student's journal from the
Literature Department of the University of
Nairobi. It includes poetry, short stories, and
essays, most of them in English, but also with
some material in Kiswahili.

The New African
2 Arundel Street, London WC2
1962 – monthly [ceased]
Editor: Mukhtar Mustapha
This now defunct radical magazine (originally
published from Cape Town) has served as
an important voice of opposition to South
Africa's apartheid regime, and a great many
South African writers, such as Dennis Brutus,
Lewis Nkosi, and Ezekiel Mphahlele have
expressed themselves in its columns. It contained political and social commentary, along
with essays on African arts and culture, short
stories, poetry, and extensive book reviews.

New Classic [formerly *The Classic*]
Ravan Press (Pty.) Ltd., PO Box 31134,
Braamfontein 2017, South Africa
1975 – quarterly [ceased]
Editor: Sipho Sepamla
Publication of the *New Classic* marked the re-
emergence of *Classic*, the journal founded by
the late Nat Nakasa in the early 1960s.
Unfortunately it became dormant once again
only two years after recommencing publication. It included poetry, fiction, essays, as
well as graphics and photography. It may
reappear on the scene in the near future, for as
an editorial statement in the first issue of the
New Classic aptly put it, 'the beat of our hearts
is too strong for our silence to be true and
real.'

**New Culture. A Review of Contemporary
African Arts**
New Culture Studios, N6A/532A Adeola Crescent,
Oremeji, PMB 5162, Ibadan, Nigeria
1978 – monthly
Editor: Demas Nwoko
Subscription rates: ₦12.00 in Nigeria,
£24.00/$36.00 elsewhere
New Culture – one of the most exciting new
magazines to have come out of Africa for a
long time – is the product of an extraordinary
venture by the well-known Nigerian artist,
Demas Nwoko. The New Culture Studios,
which he founded some years ago, is a

development of the imaginative cultural centre
which he designed, and began to construct, in
1967 to fill the gap created by the demise of the
Mbari Club with which he had been closely
associated. The New Culture Studios has now
become an active centre of artistic work under
the general direction of Nwoko himself,
assisted by three other full-time professionals
in charge of its principal areas of interest – the
plastic arts, the performing arts and children's
art. *New Culture* has been produced as its house
journal.
    Each issue is splendidly illustrated, and
features separate sections on the plastic arts,
architecture and environmental design, the
performing arts, reports and news items on the
American and European scene (especially
covering the work and activities of black
artists), and also includes stories and creative
material in a special children's section.

New Writing from Zambia
New Writers' Group, PO Box 1889, Lusaka,
Zambia
1966 – 1975[?] [ceased]
Editor: Godfrey Kasoma
Another small literary magazine from Africa
that has ceased publication. It included short
stories, poetry, plays and book reviews, and
aimed to stimulate literary activities in Zambia.

Nexus – See *Busara*

Nsukka Studies in African Literature
Department of English, University of Nigeria,
Nsukka, Anambra State, Nigeria
1978 – twice yearly
Editor: E. N. Obiechina
Subscription rates: ₦5.00/£4.00/$6.00
Sponsored jointly by the Departments of
English and Modern Languages at the University of Nigeria, Nsukka, this journal is devoted
to the study and debate of African literature in
a very broad sense. Its scope embraces English
and Francophone African literatures, the oral
tradition, as well as containing scholarly
articles on Black American literatures and the
African diaspora in general.

Odi. A Journal of Literature from Malawi
Department of English, Chancellor College, Univ. of
Malawi, PO Box 280, Zomba, Malawi
1976 – twice yearly
Editor: Robin Graham
Subscription rates: K1.00 in Malawi, £2.00/$5.00
elsewhere
Odi – not to be confused with *Odu*, published
in Nigeria – aims to bring together and to
publicize the best in creative writing from
Malawi. Short stories, drama, and poetry are

supplemented by critical essays and book reviews. The English department at Chancellor College also publishes an irregular bulletin on literature entitled *Kalulu*.

Oduma

Rivers State Council for Arts and Culture, 74/76 Bonny Sreet, PMB 5049, Port Harcourt, Rivers State, Nigeria
1973 – twice yearly |ceased?|
Editor: Theo Vincent
Subscription rates: ₦4.50/$8.00
A cultural publicaton that covers a wide spectrum of the arts, history, language, philosophy, literature, and oral tradition, with an emphasis on material by writers originating from the Rivers State (Gabriel Okara and Elechi Amadi have been recent contributors), or research carried out in the State.

Okike. An African Journal of New Writing

PO Box 53, Nsukka, Anambra State, Nigeria
1971 – quarterly
Editor: Chinua Achebe
Subscription rates: ₦12.00 in Nigeria, £12.00/$24.00 elsewhere
Now in its tenth year of publication, this celebrated journal has been aiming to dictate a new pace for African writers for the past decade. Handsomely produced, it has provided an important forum for authors, readers, and critics of African literature, and most of all the well-known African writers of today have appeared in its pages. However, *Okike* (Creation) has also significantly helped to discover new writers, publish them, and to set a new school of thought for critical standards of African literature. It has promoted new and experimental writing, believing that in form and content African literature is still groping towards its self-realization.

Each number includes essays, short stories, poetry, book reviews, and occasional artwork. In 1979 Okike introduced a special 'Educational supplement', with the idea to expand the magazine's interests and audience, and to appeal to young readers and teachers of African literature, particularly post-primary students in West Africa.

Okyeame

Writers Workshop, Institute of African Studies, University of Ghana, Legon, Ghana
1964 – irregular |ceased|
Editor: Efua Sutherland
This journal has been defunct for many years now, though there have been promises, from time to time, that it would recommence publication. It carried creative writing, as well as essays on various aspects of African literature, language, and music.

Ophir

Ravan Press (Pty.) Ltd., PO Box 31134, Braamfontein 2017, South Africa
1967 – 1976 |all publ., ceased|
Editors: Peter Horn et al.
Sadly, this fine journal ceased publication with its 23rd issue, a double number published late in 1976. Published since 1967 *Ophir* provided a major outlet for South African poets, both aspiring and established and both black and white.

Ozila

BP 73, Yaoundé, Cameroun
1970 – quarterly |ceased|
Editor: Jean-Pierre Togolo
This now defunct magazine was influential in stimulating literary activities in Cameroon. Contributions were both in English and French, and each number contained creative writing as well as articles and papers of a critical nature.

Peuples Noirs/Peuples Africains

3 rue de l'Asile-Poincourt, 75011 Paris, France
(distr. by L'Harmattan, 18 rue des Quatre-Vents, 75006, Paris)
1978 – six times yearly
Editor: Mongo Béti
Subscription rates: FF120.00
A radical magazine controlled by militant black writers and intellectuals, and edited by the distinguished Cameroonian writer Mongo Béti, who has been living in exile in France for some time now. In addition to papers of a political nature, there are frequent scholarly contributions on African literature, articles on literature and society, and the committed African theatre.

Présence Africaine

25 bis rue des Ecoles, 75005 Paris, France
1947 – quarterly |English version since 1959: bilingual version as from no. 61, January 1967 |
Editors: Geoffrey Jones and Muhala Kadima-Nzuji; et al.
Subscription rates: FF100.00 in France and Africa, FF110.00 elsewhere
(Early back issues available from Kraus Reprint)
Présence Africaine has undoubtedly been the pioneer among African literary and cultural magazines. It has been published for thirty-four years, first entirely in French and then from 1957 in English also. Since 1967 it has been published as a bilingual magazine. Founded by a Senegalese intellectual, the late Alioune Diop (who died in 1980) with the support of a distinguished group of patrons, the first issue containing 198 pages was launched in November 1947 with very little financial support. Alioune Diop had long

advocated a debate between Africa and the West in his contacts with leading French intellectuals. This had attracted the attention of such prominent French men of letters as André Gide, Jean-Paul Sartre and Albert Camus, as well as the black American Richard Wright, Diop's compatriot Léopold Senghor, and Aimé Césaire from Martinique. With the establishment of *Présence Africaine* Diop aimed to provide a journal open 'to all contributors of good will (white, yellow or black) who might be able to help define African originality and to hasten its introduction into the modern world'. Jean-Paul Sarte, too, felt a need for an African presence, 'which would be among us not like that of a child in the family circle but like the presence of a remorse and a hope'. *Présence Africaine* opened its columns not only to black intellectuals but also to religious leaders of both Christian and non-Christian denominations, socialists, communists, historians, anthropologists and political commentators. African students were invited to express their views in a special number.

In the issues of the late forties and early fifties contributions from virtually all leading black intellectuals from Africa, the Americas and the Caribbean had appeared. During 1950–1954 the first in a series of special issues was published. Among these there appeared a volume examining African art, and another containing Cheik Anta Diop's now highly significant essay, 'Nations Nègres et Culture'.

The 'new series' of *Présence Africaine* was inaugurated in the spring of 1955, followed by two special issues covering the First International Conference of Negro Writers and Artists held in September 1956 in Paris, and the subsequent Second International Conference held in Rome in March/April 1959. Earlier, in 1956, the Society of African Culture was created, and *Présence Africaine* became its official organ. A separate publishing division was added, which has published well over two hundred titles to date. Since 1965 *Présence Africaine* has been published as a single bilingual review, with articles, poetry, prose, and drama appearing either in English or in French.

An *Analytical Index of Présence Africaine (1947-1972)*, compiled by Femi Ojo-Ade, was published by Three Continents Press in 1977 (see p. 8).

The Purple Renoster

87 Roberts Avenue, Kensington, Johannesburg, South Africa
1956 – 1978 [?] [ceased?]
Editor: Lionel Abrahams
Many distinguished black and white South African writers made an appearance in this important magazine, which has been battling with South Africa's repressive publications' law for many years, and which aimed to keep the names of the banned and gagged writers alive. It included stories, poems, essays, humorous sketches, letters, dramatic excerpts, one-act plays, and more.

Research in African Literatures

University of Texas Press, Box 7819, Austin, Texas 78712
1970 – quarterly [since 1980, previously twice annually, thereafter three times annually]
Editor: Bernth Lindfors
Subscription rates: $16.00 for individuals ($12.00 for students and retired), $28.00 for institutions
This interdisciplinary journal, covering all aspects of the oral and written literatures of Africa, has perhaps been the most important forum during the past decade for the debate and critical analysis of African writing. Illustrated by noted African artists, each issue features articles (in English and French) by widely known writers on the subject, and there is a lively and influential book-review section. In addition to publishing critical articles, *Research in African Literatures* also aims to serve the wider need of the academic community by including a variety of extra features, such as descriptions of research in progress, accounts of university and school literature programmes, listings of theses and dissertations, reports from libraries and archives, conference reports, and more. From time to time special issues of *RAL* focus on particular topics of interest, such as African song, West African popular culture, and African folklore in the New World.

RAL is the official journal of both the African Literature Association and the African Literatures Division of the Modern Language Association.

Revue de Littérature et d'Esthétique Négro-Africaines

Nouvelles Editions Africaines, BP 20615, Abidjan, Ivory Coast
1977 – twice yearly [ceased?]
Editor: N'Guessan di Djangone
Subscription rates: CFA 3,600
A scholarly journal from francophone West Africa, covering the arts and culture.

Snarl

Ravan Press (Pty.) Ltd., PO Box 31134, Braamfontein 2017, South Africa
1974 – [ceased]
Editor: Joyce Ozynski
Yet another short-lived South African literary magazine, which aimed to provide informed

criticism in all areas of the arts, featuring theoretical articles, as well as cartoons and photographs.

Staffrider
Ravan Press (Pty.) Ltd., 35 Jorissen Street, PO Box 31134, Braamfontein 2017, South Africa
1978 – monthly
Editor: edited by an editorial collective
Subscription rates: R12.00
Staffrider is surely the most interesting venture on the South African literary scene for years; it is a magazine with a unique rationale and unique problems. It takes its name from the young men who ride 'staff' on the crowded commuter trains from Johannesburg's black townships, by climbing perilously on the roofs of the carriages or standing on the steps – with daring, skill and considerable folly – entertaining and alarming their more sedentary fellow passengers. The name of the magazine therefore reflects the precarious lifestyle of young urban blacks.

The magazine is put out by Ravan Press, a radical white publishing house established in 1973, which has somehow managed to survive despite various moves against it by the South African government. Both the original directors have been banned, the press has been prosecuted under the Suppression of Communism Act, its offices have been subjected to police searches, and several publications have been banned (including two issues of *Staffrider*) or had to be withdrawn. The magazine is under the control of an informal editorial collective and it publishes poetry, fiction, extracts from plays in progress, interviews, book reviews, as well as photography and graphic art. Well-known writers such as Miriam Tlali, Mothobi Mutloatse, Mtutuzeli Matshoba, Es'kia Mphahlele, Nadine Gordimer appear in its pages, but for the most part it publishes, and was conceived for, the work of new young black writers.

Transition – see Ch'indaba

Two Tone
PO Box MP 79, Mount Pleasant, Salisbury, Zimbabwe
1964 – quarterly
Editor: O. H. Robertson
Subscription rates: Z$4.00
A quarterly of poetry from Zimbabwe, and occasionally South Africa, in English, Shona, and Ndebele (the last two with English translations).

Umma [formerly *Darlite*]
Kenya Literature Bureau, PO Box 30022, Nairobi, Kenya
1965 – twice yearly [ceased]
Editor: Clement Ndulute
(Some back issues of Darlite *available from Kraus Reprint)*
Another victim of the break-up of the East African Community (and cessation of activities of the East African Literature Bureau), this was the journal of the Department of Literature at the University of Dar es Salaam. It carried short stories, plays, and poetry, both in English and in Swahili.

Umma. Africa's Social and Entertainment Monthly Magazine
Directories Africa Ltd., PO Box 50618, Nairobi, Kenya
1976 – monthly [ceased?]
Editor: Arthur Kemoli
Subscription rates: K.shs.45.00 in Kenya, K.shs.100.00 elsewhere in Africa, K.shs.160.00 elsewhere
It is not clear whether this *Umma* is in fact the successor to the journal originally published by the East African Literature Bureau (see previous entry). This version presents a variety of creative writing – short stories, poetry, folktales – together with features on African art and essays on African literature, all in an attractively produced format.

West African Journal of Modern Languages/Revue Ouest Africaine des Langues Vivantes
University of Maiduguri, Maiduguri, Borno State, Nigeria
1976 – twice yearly
Editor: Conrad-Benedict Brann
Subscription rates: ₦7.50/£5.25/$12.00 for individuals, ₦12.00/£8.40/$20.00 for institutions
This scholarly periodical is the official publication of the West African Modern Languages Association, providing an outlet for discussion, research and documentation, on aesthetic, historical, psychological, and sociolinguistic aspects of modern languages and literatures, in the linguistic and cultural context of West Africa. Each issue focuses on a specific topic, and articles are supplemented by book reviews, notes on the activities of the Association, bibliographies, and other items.

World Literature Written in English
Department of English, University of Guelph, Guelph, Ontario, Canada N1G 2W1
1971 – twice yearly
Editor: G. D. Killam
Subscription rates: $10.00 for individuals, $12.00 for institutions
WLWE is a well-established scholarly journal devoted to criticism and discussion of Com-

monwealth literature, Third World writing in English, and New World literature in English. Each issue includes a substantial number of book reviews.

Zuka. A Journal of East African Creative Writing
Oxford Univ. Press, Eastern Africa branch, PO Box 72532, Nairobi, Kenya

1967 – [ceased]
Originally edited by Ngugi wa Thiong'o this now defunct magazine provided an important platform for the wealth of literary activities in East Africa in the sixties. It included short stories, poetry, critical essays and book reviews, as well as occasional articles on African art.

II. Other periodicals and magazines in brief

The listing below gives details – in briefer form than in the previous section – of general Africanist and other periodicals which feature contributions on African literature (critical or creative writing, or both) from time to time. Also included are the major bibliographic tools which provide coverage of new African studies, and in some cases African *published*, material.

ACLALS Bulletin
Department of English, University of Queensland, St. Lucia, Queensland 4067, Australia
1975 – irregular
A newsletter and bulletin of liaison of the Association for Commonwealth Literature and Language Studies.

África
Africa Journal Ltd., Kirkman House, 54a Tottenham Court Road, London W1P 0BT
1971 – monthly
Editor: Raph Uwechue
A glossy *Newsweek*-style magazine published from London by African staff. Features mainly business, economic, and political items, but there are articles and reports about African arts and culture from time to time.

Africa
Fac. de Filosofia, Letras e Ciencias Humans, Univ. de São Paulo, CP 8191, São Paulo, Brazil
1979 – quarterly
Editor: Fernando Mourao
The only major journal on African studies to be published in South America. It focuses on comparative Afro-Brazilian studies, and there are frequent contributions on African art and cultures, and on lusophone African literature.

Africa Now
Pan-African Publishers Ltd., Dilke House, Malet Street, London WC1E 7JA
1981 – monthly
Editor: Peter Enahoro
Lively current affairs magazine; news and analysis, with a regular 'Arts and Culture' section.

Africa Today
c/o Graduate School of International Studies, University of Denver, Denver, Colo. 80208, USA
1954 – quarterly
Editor: Edward A. Hawley
Essays and articles on the political, social and economic currents in Africa. There are frequent essays on the art, and literature, and there is an extensive book-review section. A recent thematic issue that focused on 'African Literature and Literature about Africa' was volume XXVII, no. 3, 1980.

Africana Journal [formerly *Africana Library Journal*]
Africana Publishing Co., 30 Irving Place, New York, N.Y. 10003
1970 – quarterly
Editor: Judith Ambrose
A major review tool for new Africana published in all parts of the world. There are also regular bibliographic essays (some on literary topics), and the numerous in-depth book reviews are the journal's main feature.

African Affairs
Oxford University Press, Press Road, Neasden, London NW10 0DD
1901 – quarterly
Editors: Anthony Atmore and Michael Twaddle
A long-established scholarly journal that covers largely the social sciences and history, but there are frequent book reviews of literary items.

The African Book Publishing Record
Hans Zell Publishers, An imprint of K. G. Saur Verlag, PO Box 56, Oxford OX1 3EL

1975 – quarterly
Editor: Hans M. Zell
Provides comprehensive coverage of new and forthcoming African publications in English and French, as well as significant new titles in the African languages. *ABPR* is the major review outlet for African published material, including very frequent reviews of African literature. Also included are articles, reports, and interviews about book trade activities and developments in Africa.

African Forum
American Society for African Culture, 101 Park Avenue, New York N.Y. 10017
1965 – quarterly [ceased]
This now defunct periodical included regular contributions and reviews on the arts and literature.

African Notes
Institute of African Studies, University of Ibadan, Ibadan, Nigeria
1964 – twice yearly
Editor: Robert Armstrong
Covers traditional African culture, language, music, art, history, and anthropology.

Afrique Contemporaine
Centre d'Étude et de Documentation sur l'Afrique et l'Outre-Mer, 31 quai Voltaire, 75340 Paris Cedex 7, France
1962 – monthly
Editor: Robert Cornevin
Presents wide-ranging documentation about African current affairs, economics, the social sciences, and arts. It features a valuable and extensive book-review section, with short, concise reviews of new Africana material in English, French, and German, including literary items.

Afriscope
Pan Afriscope (Nigeria) Ltd., PMB 1119, Yaba, Lagos State, Nigeria
1971 – monthly
Editor: Uche Chukumerije
Largely a current-affairs journal devoted to in-depth analysis of African economic and political developments, but also carries a regular 'Literary scene' column.

Afro-Asian Theatre Bulletin
American Educational Theater Association, Inc., John F. Kennedy Center, 726 Jackson Place, Washington, D.C. 20566, USA
1965 – twice yearly [ceased?]
Research reports, conference papers, bibliographies and checklists, plus African and Asian theatre news.

Ambario. Revue d'Animation Culturelle et Scientifique
Association Ambario, Académie Malgache, BP 6217, Antananarivo, Madagascar
1978 – quarterly
Editor: Bakoly D. Ramiaramanana
Aims to promote cultural development in Madagascar and to project an image of Madagascar's culture and literature to an overseas audience. Each issue – which has illustrations, photographs, and artwork supplementing the text – contains a wide variety of contributions on the history, literature, culture, and ethnic groups of the country, together with poetry and short stories.

Bingo
Société Africaine de Publicité et d'Edition, BP 176, Dakar, Senegal
1952 – monthly
Editor: B. Soelle [?]
A widely circulated popular magazine, with occasional literary contributions.

Cahiers de Littérature et de Linguistique Appliqué
Université National du Zaïre, Campus de Lubumbashi, BP 1825, Lubumbashi, Zaïre Republic
1970 – quarterly [ceased?]
Mainly for teachers of literature and linguistics in secondary schools.

Cahiers de Littérature Orale
Publications Orientalistes de France, 4 rue de Lille, 75007 Paris, France
1976 – twice yearly
Editor: Naiade Anido et al.
Articles and discussions on all aspects of the oral tradition.

The Conch Review of Books
Conch Magazine Ltd., 102 Normal Avenue, Symphony Circle, Buffalo, N.Y. 14213, USA
1975 – quarterly
Editor: Sunday Anozie
In-depth reviews of books, films, and music relating to the Third World, together with bibliographic essays.

Contrast
211 Long Street, Cape Town, South Africa
1960 – quarterly [ceased]
Essays, fiction, poetry. Book reviews in English and Afrikaans.

A Current Bibliography on African Affairs
African Bibliographic Center, PO Box 13096, Washington, D.C. 20009, USA
1965 – quarterly

Editor: Daniel G. Matthews

Features topical bibliographies and bibliographic essays, plus comprehensive listings of new books and periodicals articles on Africa. The African Bibliographic Center is a black non-profit making organization, which also provides an information service about Africa to schools and colleges and the general public.

Demb ak Tey. Cahiers du Mythe

Centre d'Etudes des Civilisations de Dakar, Dakar, Senegal
1972 – quarterly
A scholarly periodical that provides analysis and investigations into the different forms of oral traditions in Africa.

Drum

62 Eloff Street Extension, Johannesburg 2000 West African ed.: Drum Publications (Nigeria) Ltd., PMB 2128, Lagos, Nigeria
1951 – monthly [South African ed. ceased?]
Editor: P. Selwyn-Smith (Olu Adetule for West African ed.)
Widely circulated popular magazine. Includes short stories, reports, and interviews.

East Africa Journal

East African Publishing House, PO Box 30571, Nairobi, Kenya
1964 – monthly [ceased]
Now defunct, this journal covered East African affairs, politics economics, sociology, and education. A number of special 'Ghala' literary issues devoted to East African writing were published in the late sixties.

Ecriture française

Editions Naaman, CP 457, Sherbrooke, Québec, Canada J1H 5J7
1979 – quarterly [as from 1982; previously three times yearly]
Editor: Leo A. Brodeur
A cultural quarterly of French writing, that also aims to serve as an outlet for francophone authors born or living outside France. There are frequent essays on aspects of francophone African literature (including the Maghreb countries), together with news items of interest.

English in Africa

Institute for the Study of English in Africa, Rhodes University, PO Box 94, Grahamstown 6140, South Africa
1974 – twice yearly
Editor: Andre de Villiers
Critical articles on aspects of African literature written in English, and the use of English language in Africa, with relevant pedagogic developments.

English Studies in Africa

Witwatersrand University Press, 1 Jan Smuts Avenue, Johannesburg 2001, South Africa
1958 – twice yearly
Editor: B. Cheadle
Scholarly articles on topics relevant to the study of the English language and literature on the continent of Africa.

Ibadan Review

Ibadan University Press, University of Ibadan, Ibadan, Nigeria
1977 – twice yearly [ceased?]
Editor: N.J. Udoeyop [?]
A forum for critical and perspective views in the humanities and social sciences, with special reference to the place of Africa and the black race in world culture and civilisation.

ICA Information

African Cultural Institute, 14 Avenue Pdt. Lamine Gueye, BP 01, Dakar, Senegal
1975 – quarterly
Editor: Basile T. Kossou
This bilingual quarterly provides regular information on cultural policies and activities in member states of the ACI. It includes news, articles, and reports about festivals, seminars, etc. on the arts and cultural development in Africa. Each issue focuses on a particular aspect of African art or the African cultural heritage; issue no. 10 was on 'The role of the theatre in the African cultural development'.

International African Bibliography. Current Books, Articles and Papers in African Studies

Mansell Publishing, 3 Bloomsbury Place, London WC1A 2QA
1971 – quarterly
Editor: David Hall
Covers monographs and pamphlets, proceedings and symposia, as well as periodical articles, and is based on new material received and scanned at the Library of the School of Oriental and African Studies, University of London.

Jeune Afrique

51 Avenue des Ternes, 75827 Paris Cedex 17, France
1947 – weekly
Editor: Bechir Ben Yahmed
Widely read illustrated general interest and news magazine. Regular features on the arts and culture, and several book reviews in each issue.

Joe. Africa's Entertainment Monthly

1973 – monthly [ceased?]
Editor: Terry Hirst

Good-humoured social commentary, cartoons, contemporary literature, and satire. This is by far the best popular magazine published in Africa, and past contributors have included some of the liveliest creative writers from East Africa. Owing to chronic financial problems, publication has been somewhat erratic recently.

Limi
University of South Africa, PO Box 392, Pretoria, South Africa
1966 – annually
Articles on African languages and literatures, including biographical sketches of writers and book discussions.

Literature East and West
Carney 446, Boston College, Chestnut Hill, Ma. 02167, USA
1956 – quarterly
Editor: Louis Hartley
Comparative literature studies. Book reviews, and some coverage of African writing.

Maktaba
Kenya Library Association, PO Box 46031, Nairobi, Kenya
1974 – twice yearly
Editor: R. Wanja Thaitu
The official journal of the Kenya Library Association, with papers on librarianship, documentation and information, publishing and the book trade; there are also occasional items of literary interest, and bibliographies.

Mawazo
Institute of Social Research, PO Box 16022, Kampala, Uganda
1967 – twice yearly [ceased]
Editor: A. B. K. Kasozi
This journal has been dormant for several years now; it covered the arts and social sciences, and included frequent book reviews on African literature.

MLA International Bibliography
see p. 7

New African [formerly *New African Development*]
International Communications, 63 Long Acre, London WC2E 9JH
1965 – monthly
Editor: Alan Rake
A news magazine providing largely coverage on business economics, and international affairs, but there are occasional contributions on African arts and cultures.

Newbreed
35 Ogunlana Drive, PO Box 5414, Lagos, Nigeria
1972 – twice monthly
Popular Nigerian current affairs magazine, with frequent literary contributions, short stories, etc.

New Coin
Institute for the Study of English in Africa, Rhodes University, PO Box 94, Grahamstown 6140, South Africa
1965 – quarterly
Editor: Andrew de Villiers
Publishes previously unpublished poems by South African poets, both well-established and unknown.

Nigeria Magazine
Cultural Division, Federal Ministry of Information, PMB 15524, Lagos, Nigeria
1932 – quarterly
Editor: Garba Ashiwaju
A well-established cultural quarterly (though appearing somewhat irregularly during the past few years), carrying a wide variety of features on the modern and traditional arts in Nigeria, together with poetry and short stories. There are occasional special literary issues.

Notre Librairie
Club des Lecteurs d'Expression Française, 66ter rue Saint-Didier, 75116 Paris, France
1970 – five times annually
Editor: Marie-Clotilde Jacquey
Sub-titled 'Livres, Lectures et Bibliothèques Afrique, Madagascar, Maurice', this attractively produced journal is devoted to books, reading, and libraries in francophone Africa and the Caribbean. Each issue includes articles on African literature, book reviews, bibliographic notes and listings, and reports or features about libraries and library development.

Obsidian. Black Literature in Review
Department of English, Wayne State University, Detroit, Mi.48202, USA
1975 – three times yearly
Editor: Alvin Aubert
Aims to bring together the best writing in English by black writers worldwide. It includes poetry, fiction and short plays, together with critical articles, interviews, bibliographies and book reviews.

Odu. A Journal of West African Studies
University of Ife Press, Ile-Ife, Nigeria
1964 – twice yearly
Editor: O. O. Oyelaran
Contains largely contributions on West African culture, religions, archaeology, and

linguistics, but includes occasional articles on literature, particularly the oral tradition.

Pan African Book World
Fourth Dimension Publishers, PMB 1164, Enugu, Anambra State, Nigeria
1981 – quarterly |?|
Editor: Jane Nwankwo
Recently launched new magazine that aims to serve the African book professions. It includes articles and reports on publishing and book development, together with book reviews. The first issue featured a long interview with Chinua Achebe.

Positive Review
c/o Department of African Languages and Literatures, University of Ife, Ile-Ife, Nigeria
1978 – quarterly |publ. irregularly|
Editors: Biodun Jeyifo et al.
A radical magazine – with frequent literary items – that aims to provide a platform 'for the free and unfettered discussion of ideas and issues in contemporary black African society.'

Présence Francophone
C.E.L.E.F., Faculté des Arts, Université de Sherbrooke, Sherbrooke, Québec, Canada J1K 2R1
1970 – twice yearly
Editor: Rodalphe Lacasse et al.
A journal of information and liaison among scholars in the francophone world; includes occasional papers on francophone African literature.

Raizes
CP 98, Praia Santiago, Republic of Cape Verde
1971 – quarterly
Editor: Arnaldo Franca
Raizes (Roots) continues an examination of the cultural and literary heritage of the islands that was begun in 1936 with the publication of the first issue of *Claridade*. Each issue includes a wide variety of contributions on the arts, cultures, languages and literatures, and the history of the Cape Verde Islands, together with verse and short stories by Cape Verde writers.

S'ketsh'
PO Box 78, Dube 1800, South Africa
1975|?| – quarterly
Provides reviews of the arts – mainly black arts – essays, scripts, and book reviews.

South African Literary Journal
PO Box 3841, Cape Town 8000, South Africa
1960 – irregular |ceased?|
Editor: Jack Cope

Studies in Black Literature
c/o Department of English, Mary Washington College, Fredericksburg, Va. 22401, USA
1970 – three times yearly |ceased?|
Editor: Raman K. Singh
Critical studies of Afro-American and African literatures, together with bibliographies and book reviews.

Third World First. A Review of Arts and Letters of Committed Afrika
Third World First Publications, 10/14 Calcutta Crescent, PO Box 610, Apapa, Lagos State, Nigeria
1978 – six times yearly
Editor: Naiwu Osahon
A bi-monthly journal of opinion, reviews and analysis on subjects of current intellectual and cultural interest in Africa. Short stories, poetry, and essays on African literature are a regular feature.

Umoja. A Scholarly Journal of Black Studies
Black Studies Program, Campus Box 294, Univ. of Colorado, Boulder, Col. 80309, USA
1977 – three times yearly
Editor: William M. King
A multidisciplinary journal of Black studies, with occasional contributions on African literature.

Ufahamu
African Activist Association, African Studies Center, Univ. of California, Los Angeles, Ca. 90024, USA
1970 – three times yearly
Editor: varies from year to year
An interdisciplinary journal, radical in outlook, run and produced entirely by students. Includes occasional contributions on topics relating to African literature.

UNISA English Studies
University of South Africa, PO Box 392, Pretoria 0001, South Africa
1965 – twice yearly
Editors: S. G. Kossick
Contains literary papers and reviews, and there is also some creative writing (mainly poetry) together with graphics.

West Africa
West Africa Publishing Co. Ltd., Bath House, 53 Holborn Viaduct, London EC1A 2FD
1971 – weekly
Editor: Kaye Whiteman
An influential weekly, which reports on a wide range of topics relating to African current affairs, economics, social problems, the arts and literature. There are regular features of literary interest, and in recent years *West Africa* has also begun publishing short stories and poetry. Its title is somewhat misleading, for the magazine covers news and events well beyond West Africa.

World Literature Today |formerly *Books Abroad*|
University of Oklahoma Press, 1005 Asp Avenue, Norman, Oklahoma 73069, USA
1927 – quarterly
Editor: Ivar Ivask
Commentary and extensive book reviews on new literary publications. Provides good coverage of African literature.

Zambezia
University of Zimbabwe, PO Box MP167, Salisbury, Zimbabwe
1969 – twice yearly
Editor: R. S. Roberts
Scholarly articles on all aspects of South Central Africa, mostly sociological, but papers on literary topics are often included also.

III. Special issues

The following non-Africanist journals have recently (i.e. since 1971) published special issues on African writing, or on folklore and the oral tradition.

Arts & Lettres (Nascodoches, Texas) — vol. 6, no. 2, Fall 1972
Black Academy Review (Buffalo, N.Y.) — vol. 2, nos. 1 & 2, Spring-Summer 1971
Cahiers d'Études Africaines (Paris) — vol. 12, no. 45, 1972
The Dalhousie Review (Halifax, Canada) — vol. 53, Winter 1973–74
Europe. Revue littéraire mensuelle (Paris) — no. 618, October 1980
Ethnopsychologie (Le Havre) — April–September 1980
Pacific Quarterly (Hamilton, New Zealand) — vol. 6, nos. 3–4, July/October 1981
Poésie (Paris) — no. 43–45, 1976
Revue de Littérature Comparée (Paris) — nos. 3–4, 1974
Revue d'Histoire du Théâtre (Paris) — no. 1, January–March, 1975
Spectrum (Atlanta, Georgia) — vol. 3, June 1973
Yale/Theatre (New Haven, Conn.) — vol. 8, no. 1, Fall 1976

BIOGRAPHIES

Peter Abrahams

born 1919   SOUTH AFRICA

From 1930 to 1946 no black South
African had published a novel. Peter
Abrahams brought this situation to an
end with the publication of *Mine Boy* in
1946. It followed upon the earlier release
of his collection of short stories *Dark
Testament* (1942), and has since been
succeeded by novels published in New
York and London: *Song of the City* (1945),
Path of Thunder (1948), *Wild Conquest*
(1950), *A Wreath for Udomo* (1956), *A Night
of their Own* (1965), and *This Island Now*
(1966) in addition to his autobiographical
Tell Freedom: memories of Africa (1954), and
an essay, *Return to Goli* (1953).

Born Peter Henri Abrahams to a 'Cape
Coloured' mother and Ethiopian father
in the slums of Vrededorp, Johannesburg, the young Abrahams spent his
youth in part with relatives in Elsenburg
before returning to live with his brother,
sister, and mother in Johannesburg.
When he was ten years old and working
in an office a 'short-sighted Jewish girl
. . . looked at me and then began to read
from Lamb's *Tales from Shakespeare*',
Abrahams records in *Tell Freedom*.

> The story of Othello jumped at me and
> invaded my heart and mind as the young
> woman read.
>   I attended school regularly for three years
> [after that]. I learned to read and write.
> Lamb's *Tales from Shakespeare* was my favour-
> ite reading matter. I stole, by finding,
> Palgrave's *Golden Treasury*. These two books,
> and the European edition of John Keats,
> were my proudest and dearest possessions,
> my greatest wealth. They fed the familiar
> craving hunger that awaits the sensitive
> young and poor when the moment of
> awareness comes.
>   With Shakespeare and poetry, a new world
> was born. New dreams, new desires, a new
> self-consciousness, were born. I desired to
> know myself in terms of the new standards
> set by these books. I lived in two worlds, the
> world of Vrededorp and the world of these
> books. And, somehow, both were equally
> real. Each was a potent force in my life,
> compelling. My ear and mind were in
> turmoil. Only the victory of one or the other
> could bring me peace.[1]

Abrahams continued to attend school
sporadically after that. Though he did go
to St Peter's College in South Africa, in
1939 he was counted among Durban's
unemployed. If 'life had a meaning that
transcended race and colour' Abrahams
'could not find it in South Africa'. He felt
'the need to write, to tell freedom and for
this I needed to be personally free', he
says.[2] So in 1939 he signed on as a stoker,
and after two years aboard ship, he
decided to settle in Britain, where he was
on the editorial staff of the communist
newspaper, *The Daily Worker*. It was in
England that Abrahams began to write,
and even though he was living abroad, it
was his home that he returned to for his
plots. When *Mine Boy* was published in
1946, it was one of the first books to draw
attention to the blacks' situation in South
Africa, and it simultaneously established
Abrahams as an important novelist.
'Most of Peter Abrahams' other books
recreate the social climate of this country
of racial segregation', Claude Wauthier
notes. The exception, *A Wreath for Udomo*,
'caused a considerable stir in the Gold
Coast [now Ghana] in 1956. Appearing a
few months before Independence, it
looked like a gloomy prediction since
similarities between Udomo's career
and the early career of Nkrumah had
not escaped notice . . .'[3] In the 1940s
Abrahams had been part of a group of
black intellectuals which also included
Kenyatta, Nkrumah and Padmore; he
was also one of the organizers of the 1946
Pan-African Conference in Manchester.

Abrahams' most recent novel, *This
Island Now*, is set in the Caribbean (his
present home); 'its concerns are those
that face most of the states which used to
be colonies, the terms in which they are
presented (with great emphasis on black-
white race relations) remain essentially
African', comments Arthur Ravenscroft.
Ravenscroft also finds that both *A Wreath
for Udomo* and *This Island Now* 'show an
extraordinary awareness of personal and
public dilemmas in a newly independent
country. The central figure in each is a
political leader who is fired with an
almost impersonal vision of his country's
potential greatness, once it is truly free
from colonialism.'[4]

Abrahams returned to Africa in 1952 to do a series of articles on Kenya and South Africa for the London *Observer*. The series was also printed in the Paris *Tribune* and in the European edition of the *Herald Tribune*. The experience of returning to South Africa proved to be traumatic for Abrahams, recounted with bitterness in *Return to Goli*: 'As I wandered about the country and saw how the Blacks lived in the Reserves, it seemed to me that one did not have to die to go to hell. This was hell.'[5]

In 1957, after he had been to Jamaica to prepare an official report on the British West Indies, Abrahams moved to the island with his wife and family. He became editor of the *West Indian Economist*, controller of the daily radio news network *West Indian News*, and a commentator on Jamaica's radio and television.

Abrahams' works have all been translated into numerous languages: *The Path of Thunder* alone is available in 26 languages. There have been two critical studies of him written recently; Michael Wade, writing in 1972, said of Abrahams:

He is a skilful, if flawed, writer, and there is evidence that he finds the writing of fiction arduous. What is most apparent about his fiction is the complete sincerity and honesty of the author. He has not chosen an easy path; he feels every word he writes and seems incapable of writing conscious pot-boilers.[6]

In his 1979 study, Kolawole Ogungbesan evaluates the response by Abrahams to the socio-political problems of South Africa in terms of his 'liberal belief that it is only in the hearts of individuals that freedom from racism must come about'. He had adhered consistently to a belief 'that in the final analysis the problem can only be satisfactorily settled on the personal level'.[7] Considering the writer's philosophy in the context of current systems of thought in African literature, Ogungbesan looks at Abrahams' characters, who

have faith in the future; as a part of the oppressed majority, they have the force of morality at their back. Because they are already sure of victory, even if it doesn't come in their own lifetime, Abrahams'

characters do not voice the despair common in most novels by the oppressed. For this reason Abrahams' novels will probably survive the present mood of confrontation.[8]

[1] Peter Abrahams. *Tell Freedom* (New York, 1954), pp. 171–2, 189
[2] *Ibid.*, p. 370
[3] Claude Wauthier. *The Literature and Thought of Modern Africa: A Survey* (London, 1966 and 1980), pp. 158–9
[4] Arthur Ravenscroft, 'African literature. V: Novels of disillusion', *The Journal of Commonwealth Literature*, no. 6, Jan. 1969, p. 128
[5] Peter Abrahams, *Return to Goli* (London, 1953), p. 108
[6] Michael Wade, *Peter Abrahams* (London, 1972), p. 6
[7] Kolawole Ogungbesan, *The Writing of Peter Abrahams* (London, 1979), p. 147
[8] *Ibid.*, pp. 149–50

Chinua Achebe
born 1930   NIGERIA

The most prominent novelist writing in Africa today is Chinua Achebe. His first novel, *Things Fall Apart*, has been translated into nearly 30 languages and has sold more than a million copies in its different editions since it was published in 1958. It is on the compulsory reading lists of schools and universities not only in Africa but all over the world. Achebe has been nominated for a Nobel Prize in literature.

Born on 15 November 1930 in the large village of Ogidi in Eastern Nigeria, Achebe grew up in a Christian family, the son of a retired Christian churchman and the grandson of one of the first men in Nigeria to embrace Christianity. The precolonial era of his grandparents' generation had not yet been completely eclipsed during the early years of Achebe's life. He says:

> I think I belong to a very fortunate generation in this respect . . . the old hadn't been completely disorganized when I was growing up . . . it was easy, especially if you lived in a village, to see, if not in whole, at least in part, these old ways of life. I was particularly interested in listening to the way old people talked and the festivals were still observed; maybe not in the same force, but they were still there.[1]

At six his formal education began. He later attended a leading Government Secondary School in Umuahia, and received a scholarship to pursue studies in medicine at the University College of Ibadan. After a year, however, he switched his course to literature and received his B.A. in 1953, in one of the first graduating classes. He taught for several months after graduation, and then in 1954 embarked on a career with the Nigerian Broadcasting Company in Lagos. He was Director of External Broadcasting from 1961 to 1966.

Chinua Achebe is thus the product of three eras. With vestiges of traditional practices still existing in his childhood, his youth was spent in a predominantly colonial society, in a village where Christians and non-Christians maintained their distance; he reached maturity in a newly independent state (1960) beset by the problems that traditionally accompany liberation. His four novels, which have received universal acclaim, are drawn from and reflect this span of history. And this is perhaps deliberate; Achebe says:

> I would be quite satisfied if my novels (especially the ones I set in the past) did no more than teach my readers that their past – with all its imperfections – was not one long night of savagery from which the first Europeans acting on God's behalf delivered them. Perhaps what I write is applied art as distinct from pure. But who cares? Art is important but so is education of the kind I have in mind. And I don't see that the two need be mutually exclusive.[2]

Achebe's first novel, *Things Fall Apart*, published by Heinemann in 1958, was reissued four years later in paperback, inaugurating Heinemann Educational Books' African Writers Series for which Achebe later became Editorial Advisor. The novel was the winner of The Margaret Wrong Prize. A sequel, *No Longer at Ease* (originally conceived as one novel in combination with his first), appeared in 1960 and won the Nigerian National Trophy. This was followed by *Arrow of God* in 1964, the first recipient of the *New Statesman* Jock Campbell award, and in 1966 by *A Man of the People*, a novel Achebe considered 'a rather serious indictment – if you like – on post-independence Africa. But I don't despair because I think this is a necessary stage in our growth.'[3] The following year Achebe commented:

> Right now my interest is in politics or rather my interest in the novel is politics. *A Man of the People* wasn't a flash in the pan. This is the beginning of a phase for me in which I intend to take a hard look at what we in Africa are making of independence – but using Nigeria which I know best.[4]

That this is Achebe's on-going concern more than ten years after that statement is attested by a new book, *What's Wrong with Nigeria*, to be brought out soon by the young Nigerian publishing house, Fourth Dimension Publishing Company, headed by Arthur Nwankwo.

During the seventies a different facet of Achebe's public image appeared – that of the poet and storyteller and, more than ever, of the lecturer and essayist. The reasons for Achebe's retreat from the novel genre date back to the Nigerian civil war in which Achebe was actively involved in the Biafran cause. Those years of conflict not only gave Achebe no leisure for writing a full-length book but transformed his artistic sensitivities and made him seek other media of expression. Interviewed in the United States in 1969 while on a speaking tour on behalf of Biafra (in which he was accompanied by Gabriel Okara and Cyprian Ekwensi), Achebe said:

> I think there is a myth about creativity being something apart from life, but this is only a half truth. I can create, but of course not the

kind of thing I created when I was at ease. I can't write a novel now; I wouldn't want to. And even if I wanted to, I couldn't. ... I can write poetry – something short, intense, more in keeping with my mood. I can write essays. I can even lecture.[5]

The poems that Achebe wrote during and just after the war were first published in Nigeria in 1971 in a collection entitled *Beware Soul Brother*. A revised, expanded version appeared in London the following year in Heinemann's African Writers Series and that year (1972) Achebe won the Commonwealth Poetry Prize for the collection. The volume appeared in the United States in 1973 under the title *Christmas in Biafra and Other Poems*. In referring to his new image as a poet Achebe says, '. . . I was always a surreptitious poet; I was always a poet in my prose. I don't think you can really separate the two as rigidly as some people think . . . if one has a good prose style, the chances are that there would be poetry in his work even if he wasn't writing poems.'[6] In 1978 Achebe collaborated with Dubem Okafor in presenting an anthology of poetic tributes to the memory of Christopher Okigbo, *Don't Let Him Die*, published by Fourth Dimension Publishing Company.

In the early seventies Achebe also published a major collection of short stories, *Girls at War and Other Stories*. (A slim volume of stories, *The Sacrificial Egg and Other Stories* had appeared in Nigeria in 1962.) One of Achebe's stories, 'The Madman', was also included in the anthology, *The Insider: Stories of War and Peace from Nigeria*, that Nwankwo-Ifejika and Co. of Enugu brought out in 1971.

He continued to write critical essays on African literature and gathered together both earlier and later essays in the collection, *Morning Yet on Creation Day* published by Heinemann in 1975. This includes the well-known pieces (published separately in the sixties) that contain his oft-quoted statements on the role of the writer in Africa and on his use of language ('The novelist as teacher' and 'The African writer and the English language'). It also includes essays published between 1972 and 1974 during the

first two years of a four-year stay in the United States, which deal with Achebe's concern about current criticism of African literature ('Colonialist criticism', 'Africa and her critics', 'Thoughts on the African novel'). When questioned by the Nigerian journalist, John Agetua, about the meaning of the title, *Morning Yet on Creation Day*, Achebe replied: 'Well, it means that we cannot be dogmatic about art and literature. We must avoid saying: African literature is this . . . I'm saying that we are very early in the day.'[7]

Achebe also used that same occasion to reply to younger Nigerian writers, like Kole Omotoso, who have criticized him and his generation for dealing too much with the past:

It does not require too much sophistication to know that we have a past and a present and a future. Now some people may not be able to write about the past because they don't know a thing about it. That's understandable. You can't write about what you don't know ... But don't make your inability into a virtue. New writers have a whole wide range of choices and also the work of older writers to build on. It is really stupid to waste their energies on the peculiarly Western father/son confrontation. I prefer to see history as a growth, as a cumulative process in which we make use of the things in our past, even our mistakes without waging war, like adolescent children of another culture, on anybody and anything over thirty.[8]

If Achebe has changed as a writer over the years by venturing into new media of expression one can note a reaffirmation, even a strengthening, of the basic concerns that inform all of his writing – that of the responsibility of a writer to be the conscience within his society, in a word to be *committed*. Achebe had voiced this idea more than ten years before when speaking about his involvement in the Biafran cause: 'It is clear to me that an African creative writer who tries to avoid the big social and political issues of contemporary Africa will end up being completely irrelevant – like that absurd man in the proverb who leaves his burning house to pursue a rat fleeing from the flames.'[9] He reiterated this idea in 1978 in a paper read at a conference at the University of

Kent which concludes with these words: 'A writer who feels a strong and abiding concern for his fellows cannot evade the role of social critic which is the contemporary expression of commitment to the community. And this concern is at the very heart of African literature, past and present.'[10]

Another leitmotif of Achebe's early essays, and in particular 'The novelist as teacher', which continues to inspire Achebe's work today, is the commitment of a writer to be an educator in his society. This explains Achebe's devotion over the past few years to contributing to children's literature, a concern that arose, in part, from his perception of the needs of his own children:

> I discovered that my daughter, in Lagos, was receiving all kinds of strange notions that were not coming from me or my wife. So we tried to get down to the books she was reading, to the school she was going to. The school we could deal with; the books – we were responsible for that! We went into the supermarket and bought attractive looking books and simply threw them at her, you see, and many of those books had in-built prejudices ... Once she discovered this, it was easy enough to get persuaded to move in the direction of children's writing.[11]

In 1966 Achebe had already published in London a first story for children, *Chike and the River*, and planned to have another published by the firm which he launched with Christopher Okigbo in 1967; but the war intervened and Okigbo was killed. The story, *How the Leopard Got its Claws*, written in collaboration with John Iroaganachi, was eventually published by Nwamife in Enugu and by The Third Press in New York after the war. Since then, Achebe has written two more children's stories, *The Drum* and *The Flute*, both published by the Nigerian firm, Fourth Dimension Publishing Company in 1977.

The publication of these two books by a Nigerian publisher points to another growing concern that Achebe shares with many of the younger generation of Nigerian writers: the need to encourage local publishers as the condition *sine qua non* of a 'genuine literary tradition':

if you are going to have a genuine literary tradition, then the entire book business should have an indigenous base. Not just writers being here, but their publishers, editors, bookshops, printers ... if we are going to grow at all, we won't grow by shuttling between Lagos and London, or Lagos and Paris and New York. I think London, Paris and New York will, in future, come here and take what catches their fancy from what we produce. Like anybody else, they'll compete for what we have and reissue abroad works which originate with local publishers.[12]

But publishers would have nothing to publish if there were no writers, and Achebe spent much of his time in the 1970s in making sure Nigeria continued to produce writers by offering them a forum for expression through the pages of *Okike*, the literary journal he edits. Subtitled 'An African journal of new writing', *Okike* was founded in 1971 when Achebe was Director of African Studies at the University of Nigeria at Enugu. From 1972 to 1976 he edited it from the United States while a visiting professor, first at the University of Massachusetts and then, for a final year, at the University of Connecticut. *Okike* is now based in Nsukka where Achebe is Professor of Literature.

Nigerian writers, Achebe feels, would also benefit from an association. There was a Society of Nigerian Authors in the mid-60s, but the war disrupted its activity. As the Society's last chairman, Achebe feels it is his personal mission to bring Nigerian authors together, and he was instrumental in re-activating the Society in 1981, when a writer's convention took place at Nsukka.

Chinua Achebe's works are the subject of three full-length critical commentaries, G. D. Killam's *The Writings of Chinua Achebe* (revised 1977), Arthur Ravenscroft's *Chinua Achebe* (second edition, 1977), and David Carroll's *Chinua Achebe* (1970). In addition, an anthology of critical studies on Achebe appeared in 1978 in the United States and the following year in England. Edited by C. L. Innes and Bernth Lindfors it is entitled *Critical Perspectives on Chinua Achebe*.

[1] 'Conversation with Chinua Achebe', *Africa Report*, vol. 9, no. 5, July 1964, pp. 19–20.

[2] Chinua Achebe, 'The novelist as teacher', in *Commonwealth Literature* (London, 1965), p. 205, and reprinted in Chinua Achebe, *Morning Yet on Creation Day* (London, 1975), p. 45.

[3] Achebe interviewed by Robert Serumaga, *Cultural Events in Africa*, no. 28, Mar. 1967 and reprinted in Dennis Duerden and Cosmo Pieterse, eds., *African Writers Talking* (London, 1972), p. 13.

[4] 'Chinua Achebe talking to Tony Hall', *Sunday Nation* (Nairobi), 15 Jan. 1967, p. 15

[5] 'Interview with Chinua Achebe', in Bernth Lindfors *et. al.*, eds., *Palaver: Interviews with Five African Writers in Texas* (Austin, Texas, 1972), p. 12

[6] 'Interview with Chinua Achebe', in John Agetua, ed., *Critics on Chinua Achebe: 1970–76* (Benin City, Nigeria, 1977), p. 36

[7] *Ibid.*, p. 40

[8] *Ibid.*, p.41

[9] Chinua Achebe, 'The African and the Biafran cause', in *The Conch*, vol. 1, no. 1, Mar. 1969, p. 8.

[10] Chinua Achebe, 'The uses of African literature', *Okike*, no. 15, p. 17

[11] 'An interview by Professor Chinua Achebe', *Pan African Book World*, vol. 1, no. 1, August 1981, p. 3.

[12] *Ibid.*

Ama Ata Aidoo

born 1942   GHANA

This Ghanaian poetess, playwright, and short-story writer was born Christina Ama Aidoo. She began to write professionally after winning a prize in a short-story competition organized by Ibadan's Mbari Club. At that time she was an undergraduate reading English at the University of Ghana in Legon. *The Dilemma of a Ghost*, her first play, was initially presented by the Students' Theatre in March 1964. Later that year, after its production in Lagos, Eldred Jones wrote.

> Miss Aidoo displays a gift – very useful to a social dramatist – of showing both sides of the coin at the same time. She shows the reverence of African village society towards motherhood while at the same time exposing the inherent cruelty of a system which makes the childless woman utterly miserable ... This play should be speedily published.[1]

In 1965 *The Dilemma of a Ghost* was published by Longmans. Thereafter her poems, short stories and book reviews appeared frequently in a variety of African journals, among them *Black Orpheus, Okyeame, The Journal of the New African Literature and the Arts, Zuka, Présence Africaine*, and *The New African*. Her stories 'are written primarily to be heard'. A firm believer in the potency and positive aspects of oral communication, she would like to see a theatre in which stories are recited or related to the audience. 'If I have any strong conception of what else could be done in literature today it is this,' she says.[2]

However, Ms Aidoo believes it is also important to cultivate a wider African readership, which she sees as vital to the emergence of a critical audience – 'If you're writing from a certain background, it's only the people from that background can tell the world whether this is good or bad.' She does not see 'any validity in having someone who does not belong to the society from which the literature itself springs telling you how to write'.[3]

The Institute of African Studies at the University of Ghana granted Ama Ata Aidoo a research fellowship which enabled her to continue writing and to conduct research into contemporary Ghanaian drama, 'a kind of drama in Fanti which has been going on since the thirties. It caters to a clear 80% of the people.'[4] Ms Aidoo feels, regretfully, that her writing can reach perhaps only one-fifth of the people, and she says,

> I feel almost guilty myself writing the type of thing I write, but my own sort of alibi for wanting to continue writing in English is that one gets the chance to communicate with other Africans outside Ghana. Even in Ghana alone, if you are writing in English you are more able to carry yourself over, and if you have a message, to carry your message over to more people outside.[5]

Ms Aidoo's second play, *Anowa*, was originally a story-song she had heard from her mother. Published in London in 1969, it is a dramatization of an old Ghanaian legend to which she gives her own interpretation.

Ama Aidoo spent two years away from Ghana, travelling in the United States,

England and East Africa. She spent a year at Stanford University on a creative-writing fellowship, and she has taught at the universities of Nairobi and Cape Coast, Ghana. In 1970 her short stories were collected in *No Sweetness Here*. Although written over a period of four to five years, they have an essential unity of theme, in which Aidoo surveys

> present-day Ghana with the involved, sympathetic eye of a critical patriot and her conclusion in every instance is that there is 'no sweetness'. There is no lack of gaiety or of playful quarrelsomeness, no lack of glitter, no lack of wine, women and song. But even at its merriest, there is no quintessential sweetness.[6]

She castigates the elite of Ghana and their imitators, but to the inherent problems 'she offers no easy solutions'.[7] The creative strength of the stories is due in part to the duality of her perceptions and techniques; she combines 'traditional story-telling techniques . . . as the media for the traditional viewpoints in a rural society' with a 'Westernized female consciousness'.[8]

Ms Aidoo's novel, *Our Sister Killjoy*, although published in 1977, has a 1966 copyright date. The narrator is indeed a killjoy;

> she constantly underlines weaknesses and faults and frailties. Quite consciously, she nags. She complains. She 'wails and screams' about a great many ills, in the main those that result from the various moral, social and political problems of Africa. For example, the so-called 'big men' and their cocktail parties vs. the children of the streets for whom there are no schools; the endless desire for consumer goods; the clashes of nations in the race for power; the exploitation of Africa by foreigners . . .[9]

[1] Eldred Jones, 'A note on the Lagos production of Christina Aidoo's *Dilemma of a Ghost*', *Bulletin of the Association for African Literature in English*, no. 2, n.d., pp. 33–4
[2] Ama Aidoo, interview in *Cultural Events in Africa*, no. 35, Oct. 1967, p. 1
[3] *Ibid.*, p. 11
[4] *Ibid.*
[5] *Ibid.*
[6] Dapo Adelugba, '*No Sweetness Here*: literature as social criticism', *Ba Shiru*, vol. 6, no. 1, 1974, p. 15
[7] Lloyd W. Brown, 'Ama Ata Aidoo: the art of

the short story and sexual roles in Africa', *World Literature Written in English*, vol. 13, no. 2, 1974, p. 182
[8] *Ibid.*, p. 172
[9] Anita Kern, 'Ama Ata Aidoo: *Our Sister Killjoy*', *World Literature Written in English*, vol. 17, no. 1, 1978, p. 56

Timothy M. Aluko
born 1918   NIGERIA

In the 1940s Timothy Aluko received a number of prizes in short-story competitions organized by the British Council in Nigeria, but it is as a novelist that he has made his reputation. His first novel, *One Man, One Wife*, appeared originally in 1959 and was the first novel to be published by a Nigerian publisher, the Nigerian Printing and Publishing Company in Lagos. Mr Aluko has since written five further novels, *One Man, One Matchet* (1964), *Kinsman and Foreman* (1966), *Chief the Honourable Minister* (1970), *His Worshipful Majesty* (1973), and his most recent work, *Wrong Ones in the Dock*, published in 1982 after an interruption of eight years in his writing career.

Margaret Laurence has said of him, 'Aluko's work as an engineer has enabled him to understand in profound detail the clash between cultures and the difficulties involved in social change. These are the chief themes in his novels.'[1] Eustace Palmer notes that Aluko is only concerned with exploring the consequences of this clash in more recent times, not in the distant past:

> [Aluko] confines himself to the more modern period immediately preceding and succeed-

ing independence, the period of adjustment and redefinition of values. Like Achebe, his main theme is the clash between the old and the new, but although the old is traditional society, the new is not the white man's civilization, but the efforts and ideologies of educated Africans who are striving to bring a measure of order into their society and take it into the modern world. The opponents of traditionalism here are not the white administrators ... but the mainly Western-educated African professionals – the doctors, engineers, lawyers and civil servants.[2]

Aluko has been criticized by some, including fellow Nigerian writer Kole Omotoso, for his failure to take a moral stand in his novels. He concedes that this is true, saying it comes from 'his own helplessness of preventing others from being corrupt'.[3] In his defence, however, he affirms that the act of writing, in itself, can be helpful to a society. He uses the bulldozer image, as an engineer might, to make his point more forcefully: 'It digs up and exposes the muck under the bush. And one hopes that someone comes along, someone of authority who will decide what to do to clear up the muck.'[4]

A Yoruba born in Ilesha on 14 June 1918, Aluko received his secondary school education at the Government College in Ibadan and also attended the Higher College in Yaba, Lagos. He was then trained in civil engineering and town planning at the University of London from 1946 to 1950. Returning to Nigeria he spent the next ten years working as an engineer for the Public Works Department (like Titus Otis, the hero of *Kinsman and Foreman*). In that period he served as district engineer in a number of western Nigerian localities and as town engineer for Lagos. He later became Director of Public Works for western Nigeria and also had an appointment as Senior Research Fellow in Municipal Engineering at the University of Lagos. He was State Commissioner for Finance in the Ministry of Finance, Ibadan, and is now a consulting engineer and writer in Lagos.

[1] Margaret Laurence, *Long Drums and Cannons* (New York, 1968), p. 170
[2] Eustace Palmer, *The Growth of the African Novel* (London, 1979), pp. 102–3
[3] Kole Omotoso, 'Interview with Timothy M.

Aluko, *Afriscope*, vol. 3, no. 6, 1973, p. 52
[4] *Ibid.*

Elechi Amadi
born 1934   NIGERIA

Elechi Amadi's first novel, *The Concubine*, published in London in 1966, was greeted as a 'most accomplished first performance',[1] and as an 'outstanding work of pure fiction'.[2] In his recent study guide devoted to the novel Alastair Niven speaks of it as 'an example of how an absence of conscious sophistication or experimentation can result in a novel of classic simplicity ... Rooted firmly among the hunting and fishing villages of the Niger delta, *The Concubine* nevertheless possesses the timelessness and universality of a major novel.'[3]

Elechi Amadi, an Ekwerri, was born in Aluu near Port Harcourt in Eastern Nigeria and educated at Government College, Umuahia. He graduated with a degree in mathematics and physics from University College, Ibadan. He was employed for a time as a land surveyor and later as a teacher in the Nigerian army at the Military School in Zaria, where he attained the rank of captain. In 1965 he left the army to teach at the Anglican Grammar School, Igrito, Port Harcourt.

In 1969 Elechi Amadi's second novel appeared. *The Great Ponds*, set in precolonial Eastern Nigeria, concerns a battle between two village communities over the possession of a pond.

During the Nigerian Civil War, Mr Amadi was twice detained in Eastern Nigeria. Upon his second release (despite Biafran pressures), he joined the Federal army and was later appointed District Officer in Ahoada. A third work, *Sunset in Biafra* (1973) records Amadi's experiences during the civil war. Although autobiographical in content, the book, in Alastair Niven's words, 'is written in a compelling narrative form as though it were a novel'.[4]

When the war ended Amadi joined the Rivers State Government as head of its Ministry of Information. He is now in charge of the Ministry of Education. He has also continued to write fiction, publishing a third novel, *The Slave*, in 1978. It is a work which shows Amadi's ongoing concern with the effects of belief in the supernatural upon individual destiny. In one of his few recorded comments about his concept of the novel, Amadi says,

> I think the novel, the so-called Western novel, is really a universal form. It is storytelling . . . [but] our problem is: Are we exploiting this universal form enough from the African point of view? . . . an African writer who really wants to interpret the African scene has to write in three dimensions at once. There is the private life, the social life, and what you may call the supernatural.[5]

Amadi has also written an article on 'The novel in Nigeria' which appeared in *Afriscope*.[6] It was originally written for the 1973–4 session of the International Writing Program at the University of Iowa, in which Amadi participated.

Since the early seventies Amadi has revealed a new facet of himself – that of playwright. He published *Isiburu*, a play about a wrestler for secondary schools, with Heinemann in 1973, and three other plays, *Peppersoup* and *The Road to Ibadan* (a combined volume) and *Dancer of Johannesburg* with Onibonoje Publishers (Ibadan) in 1977 and 1978 respectively.

[1] Eustace Palmer, 'Elechi Amadi and Flora Nwapa', *African Literature Today*, no. 1, 1969, p. 56
[2] Eldred Jones, 'African Literature 1966–1967', *African Forum*, vol. 3, no. 1, p. 5
[3] Alastair Niven, *A Critical View on Elechi Amadi's 'The Concubine'* (London, 1981), p. 7
[4] *Ibid.*, p. 5
[5] Quoted in Theophilus Vincent, ed. *The Novel and Reality in Africa and America* (Lagos, 1974), pp. 13–14
[6] 'The novel in Nigeria', *Afriscope*, vol. 1, no. 11, November 1974

I. N. C. Aniebo
born 1939   NIGERIA

Like Captain Benjamin Onwura, one of the heros of his first novel, *The Anonomity of Sacrifice*, I. N. C. Aniebo trained as a career army officer. He joined the Nigerian Army in 1959 and attended cadet schools in Ghana and, again like his hero, in England. Both Aniebo and the fictional Onwura fought in the Nigerian Civil War on the side of Biafra, although the resemblance between the two probably stops here. Onwura does not survive his war experience, meeting death, not at the hands of the enemy but, ironically, at those of a fellow Biafran, a non-commissioned officer who believes him to be a traitor. Aniebo, the author, however, was discharged from the Nigerian Army in 1971 and completed his education at the University of California at Los Angeles, pursuing a new career as a university teacher and as a writer. His first novel, a tale of the clash of two men from different social and educational backgrounds who are fighting for the same cause, was published in 1974. The focus of *The Anonymity of Sacrifice* is much less the war itself than the conflicting personalities of Captain Onwura and his subordinate, Sergeant Agumo. An Indian critic, Kirpal Singh, notes how unrelentingly Aniebo pushes such differences to tragic proportions in his desire 'to rid the reader of any complacency in human nature and in life generally . . . The raw style and the intense narration eliminate any comfort we may want to derive from [the novel's] moral.'[1]

The heros and heroines of Aniebo's second novel, *The Journey Within*, are involved in a battle of another kind taking place on another front, but they are as torn apart by seemingly irreconcilable differences as are the soldiers Onwura and Agumo. The novel portrays the sort of warfare that goes on between married couples and it is fought out against the background of an emerging African urban culture as seen in the early forties in Port Harcourt, the city where Aniebo was born in 1939. His novel seems to suggest that the only marriages that can achieve lasting peace are those in which the woman 'warrior' surrenders silently by learning to put up with a wayward partner whose belligerency will cease for lack of provocation. Such is the case for the marriage of Nelson, the railway worker and Ejiaka, whereas the union of the educated Janet and Christian fails.

Aniebo left Los Angeles in June 1979 to take up his current position teaching literature in the School of Humanities of the University of Port Harcourt. In addition to completing his reasearch and writing up his doctoral dissertation he plans to devote time to his writing, which means, in his own words that he is,

> panting to finish a play set in Nigeria in 1915; struggling to wrap up any one of three novels-in-progress, and putting together a collection of short stories (especially those that won literary prizes in Nigeria and UCLA). Not to mention picking up my life where I left it in 1972 to take refuge in the anonymity that is UCLA![2]

The short story collection referred to is the one entitled *Of Wives, Talismans and The Dead* that will appear shortly in Heinemann's African Writers Series. The volume contains 22 stories that had previously appeared in such publications

as *Black Orpheus, Nigeria Magazine, Okike*, the *Sunday Times* (Lagos), *Spear Magazine*, and *Ufahamu*. Some, like 'Rats and Rabbits', date back as early as 1963 when Aniebo was still a career officer in the Nigerian army and bear the mark of a highly aware social critic. Aniebo often used a pseudonym in this period to avoid being censored or reprimanded by his army superiors. The Nigerian Civil War is present in other stories, and still another category is concerned with the private stress of individual lives – like the pains experienced in growing up or in confrontations with members of the opposite sex. But there are also stories on higher philosphical and mystical planes. *Of Wives, Talismans and The Dead* helps to complete the image that readers had already formed of I. N. C. Aniebo, the novelist.

[1] Kirpal Singh, 'An essay on Aniebo's *The Anonymity of Sacrifice*', *Dhana*, vol. 6, no. 1, 1976, p. 61

[2] Correspondence with the editors, 4 March 1980

Ayi Kwei Armah
born 1939   GHANA

Upon the New York publication of his first novel in 1968, *The Beautyful Ones are Not Yet Born*, Ayi Kwei Armah was internationally greeted as an important new writer. The distinguished African literary critic Abiola Irele wrote:

> there is enough evidence in the novel of the writer's tremendous talent, of a profound imaginative perception coming through in

sensitive language, which is the mark of a great writer.

The novel itself seems to have been meant as a kind of metaphysical novel with which readers of contemporary European fiction have become familiar and in its description of the vague existential *ennui* of his unnamed hero, recalls Sartre's *La Nausée*.[1]

Born in Takoradi, this Ghanaian writer has lived in several parts of his country. After his education at Achimota School, Armah spent one year at Groton School in Massachusetts and afterwards, on a scholarship, majored in social studies at Harvard, where he graduated *cum laude*. He has been variously employed as a French–English translator in Algiers, in Ghana as a television scriptwriter, as an English teacher and as an editor-translator for the Paris-based international news magazine, *Jeune Afrique*. Ayi Kwei Armah attended Columbia University's Graduate School of Fine Arts, and later joined the staff of the University of Massachusetts. Before the publication of his first novel, Armah wrote for such magazines as *The New African*, *Drum Magazine*, *Atlantic Monthly* and *The New York Review of Books*.

Armah's second novel, *Fragments*, was published in 1970. Autobiographical in nature, it concerns a child whose parents are disappointed in him. 'He is like a ripple on the water, spreading further and further out and not bringing back the material possessions that might have been expected from his early promise,' Armah says. 'My family was unhappy because I was too full of ideas, not actions ... I found it very traumatic writing this book because of my family's attitude.'[2]

Publishers' Weekly called *Fragments* 'powerful and poetic'[3] and Christopher Lehmann-Haupt of the *New York Times* wrote:

Mr Armah's descriptive powers are formidable: There are passages that actually left me feeling nostalgic for Ghana, and I've never even been in Africa. His sense of structure is worthy of a Swiss watchmaker. Near the book's beginning there's a 17-jewel scene describing the slaughter of a mad dog that symbolically foreshadows the action of the novel's mainspring with gleaming pre-

cision. He is inventive and perceptive and wickedly satirical. I grant I'll remember many of the scenes and characters in *Fragments* next week, next month, next year.[4]

In 1970 Armah was able to fulfil a long-standing plan to travel in East Africa, where he spent five years writing, learning Kiswahili, and later teaching at the College of National Education of Chang'ombe in Tanzania. From 1976 he went further south to the National University of Lesotho where he taught African literature and creative writing. During his time there he wrote his next three novels. The first, *Why Are We So Blest?* 'moves from the tight circle of largely Ghanaian concerns to embrace a world view, a total vision of the contemporary world whose limits of reference are defined as America, the Muslim Maghreb and sub-Saharan Africa'.[5] In a complex and abstruse way he traces the interactions and tensions of three people – a failed revolutionary, a Ghanaian, and an American girl meeting in a North African city. The language and imagery are powerful, the events startling, and a critic observes: 'He is one of those writers who articulate in bold language what others are too modest or too nice to put in print.'[6]

To move to his next novel, *Two Thousand Seasons*, is to be plunged into the realms of myth and racial memory and to confront 'the whole history of exploitation of BLACK people ... in the Armah "gut" style',[7] as the author chronicles the passage of a thousand years in the history of a black people. Nazareth sees the significance of the book as being 'socialist in a very deep sense; it presents a positive socialist vision for Africa, just as *The Beautyful Ones Are Not Yet Born* documented bitterly the betrayal of a socialist vision in Africa'. He sees the advent of socialism as depending not merely on slogans or economic policies, but as the 'tapping of the people's boundless, ageless communal wisdom and energy and their desire to live in co-operation and with human dignity.'[8] The characterization is minimal; one does not seek to identify with the people involved; he is speaking for 'We, us, the Black people –

the plural narrative voice of the novel.'[9]

Both of these books have evoked a heated debate about whether, in exploring the psychological effects of racism, he has been racist himself. For one appraiser Armah clearly has a different function:

> *Two Thousand Seasons* is not . . . a racist tract. The ferocious onslaught which it makes on the destructive intrusion of alien nationalities soon falls into place as a preparatory exercise designed to liberate the mind of those to whom the book is obviously and purposefully addressed and make them consider, perhaps for the first time, the validity of what existed before the alien impositions on society.'[10]

The East African Publishing House published his next epic work, *The Healers*, in 1978. The spiritual diseases of the community are the concern of a fringe group of people in the Asante empire of the nineteenth century. Lindfors speaks of Armah in this novel as

> fleshing out his nightmare vision of the past by substituting concrete substance for abstract symbol. If *Two Thousand Seasons* was his theory of history, *The Healers* is an adumbration of the theory using actual recorded events as proof of the hypotheses advanced. Armah takes the fall of the Ashanti Empire as emblematic of Africa's destruction, and he attributes the calamity not only to the rapacity of the West but also to the disunity within Africa itself. It is towards the reunification of Africa tomorrow that Africans must work today if they wish to repair the damage done yesterday. History is again seen as a guide to a better future.[11]

Indeed, the 'remythologizing' of Africa is so important a task that – concludes the critic – this is Armah's most important book 'and certainly his healthiest. One can no longer complain that his vision is warped or his art sick.'[12]

Armah himself chooses not to be interviewed or to discuss his work. 'I have no personal contact whatsoever with any Western critic of African Literature. I have never granted any interviews about my person or my work, no matter how prestigious the publication asking for it. That is my choice.' He has not made any lecture tours or accepted invitations to writers' workshops, and only his extreme annoyance at the American critic Charles

Larson prompted him to break his silence. Armah objected to a number of points in Larson's analysis of his writing in *The Emergence of African Fiction*. Armah coined the term 'larsony' to describe 'the judicious distortion of African truths to fit Western prejudices . . .'[13]

Ayi Kwei Armah returned to the United States for a period at the University of Wisconsin and is now living in Dakar in Senegal.

[1] Abiola Irele, 'A new mood in the African novel', *West Africa*, 20 Sept. 1969, p. 1119
[2] *Cultural Events in Africa*, no. 40, March 1968, p. 5
[3] *Publishers Weekly*, vol. 196, no. 18, 3 Nov. 1969, p. 48
[4] Christopher Lehmann-Haupt, 'Books of the Times', *The New York Times*, 16 Jan. 1970, p. 45
[5] Robert Fraser, *The Novels of Ayi Kwei Armah* (London, 1980), p. 48
[6] Charles E. Nnolim, 'Dialectic as form: pejorism in the novels of Armah', *African Literature Today*, no. 10, 1979, pp. 222–3
[7] Peter Nazareth in *Busara*, vol. 6, no. 1, 1974, p. 31
[8] *Ibid.*
[9] S. Nyamfukudza, 'Drought and rain', *New Statesman*, 17 March 1980
[10] Bai Kisogie in *Transition*, no. 45, p. 75
[11] Bernth Lindfors, 'Armah's histories', *African Literature Today*, no. 11, 1980, p. 91
[12] *Ibid.*
[13] Ayi Kwei Armah, 'Larsony or fiction as criticism of fiction', *Positive Review*, no. 1, 1978, p. 14, reprinted from *Asemka*, no. 4

Kofi Awoonor
born 1935   GHANA

Kofi Awoonor started writing under the name George Awoonor-Williams. His

poems are considered to be among the most exciting African verse, and have been extensively anthologized and translated into French, Russian, Chinese, and German. He established his literary reputation with the poetry volume *Rediscovery and Other Poems* published by Mbari in 1964.

Born in Wheta, Awoonor received his education at Achimota School and the University of Ghana in Legon, where in 1959 he won the university's Gurrey Prize for the best original creative writing, and obtained a degree in English language and literature. Following graduation, Awoonor lectured in English at the School of Admministration in the University of Ghana (1960–3) and thereafter became a research fellow and lecturer in African literature at the university's Institute of African Studies.

Kofi Awoonor's activities have extended far beyond the university campus. Although he resided in Ghana until 1967, his travels took him to the Soviet Union, Cuba, Indonesia and China, where he was a guest of the Writers Union of the People's Republic of China. He served as managing director of the Ghana Film Corporation, founded and chaired the Ghana Playhouse, where he produced plays for stage and television, was editor of the Ghanaian literary review *Okyeame*, which published some of his own writings, and in 1967–8 was an associate editor of *Transition*.

In 1967 Kofi Awoonor left Ghana. A Longman's fellowship took him to the University of London, and he began work on his M.A. in modern English (with emphasis on the linguistic features of English in West Africa). He then received a Fairfield fellowship, and in 1968 went to the University of California at Los Angeles. The following year Awoonor broke new ground at the State University of New York at Stony Brook by starting a course in African literature. He was chairman of the department of comparative literature and taught there for six years.

As a participant in the 1967 African–Scandinavian Writers Conference in Stockholm, Kofi Awoonor made clear his view of the writer's role in contemporary African society:

> He is going to provide in his writings a certain articulate vision, which must order his society because otherwise social life would be a very sterile and a very futile exercise ... whether he writes poetry or whether he writes a piece of drama or whether he writes fiction, he must, through his writings, provide a vision for those who are going to order his society ... he must be a person who has some kind of conception of the society in which he is living and the way he wants the society to go.[1]

With Adali-Mortty he edited an anthology of Ghanaian poetry called *Messages*. His own poetry was maturing: 'I have gone through the trauma of growth, anger, love and the innocence and nostalgia of my personal dreams ... Now I write out my renewed anguish about the crippling distresses of my country and my people ...'[2] *Night of My Blood*, a collection which appeared in 1971, contains many of the new poems plus a selection of poems from *Rediscovery*. Apronti later evaluated the work, maintaining that the poems provided

> much evidence that Awoonor has expanded his range of expression without sacrificing those insights that emanate from his fidelity to the tradition of oral poetry that launched him in the first place. This is still poetry of the speaking voice, of the narrator cognizant of the presence of his evidence.[3]

This Earth, My Brother is Awoonor's venture into prose, although the prose passages are interspersed with poetry. What he was trying to do, he explained, was 'to provide myself with a very expansive, a very wide genre form in which to push my poetic awareness. I do not think that I was essentially writing fiction as such, but rather a very long prose poem.'[4] The lawyer, Amamu, in a sequence of events complex, abstruse and allegorical, relating to his life in the past and present, finally confronts a mythical death-figure. Awoonor did not perceive Amamu as a sort of everyman, but as a 'more sensitive, a more aware, a more spiritual person'. And of Amamu's responses to Ghana, he is again emphatic: 'As to his dilemma, I'm not talking about a political neo-colonialist condition, and I'm not talking about the colonial condition itself, I'm talking about the whole totality of the experience of being in that context'.[5]

Awoonor returned to poetry in his next publication, *Ride Me, Memory*, which records his experiences of America. He had absorbed and incorporated this into his work:

I'm no longer the poet using the traditions *per se*. Now I'm a poet using both the traditions and the rhythm of everything that is around me. I have, for example, talked to the American poets, I have gone into their way of thinking, I have gone into their awareness and their consciousness.[6]

He also found some positive aspects to exile. Living outside Africa imposed 'a certain burden of sorrow' on his work; but he feels that it 'sharpens my articulation in many ways'.[7]

He returned to Ghana in 1975 joining the University of Cape Coast. Shortly afterwards he was arrested and imprisoned for harbouring a fugitive from justice. He has written about the experience in an as yet unpublished manuscript called *The Cistern's End*. On a tour of the United States after he had been released he assessed what he had gained from this experience:

The poet has always been a commentator on the political condition of his people. As Neruda puts it, the poet soils his hands in the despair of his people. The poet is not separate from his people and thus can articulate their pain, hunger and suffering. Prison taught me humility, absolute humility. I found that I was able to deal with myself alone, naked. What sustained me was the realization that there were people outside prison who loved me . . .[8]

The prison poems were sent out of the country and incorporated finally in *The House by the Sea* (1978). The following year found him once again teaching at Cape Coast.

He has written two plays, included in Pieterse's *Short African Plays*; and he has a couple of non-fiction works to his credit. *The Guardians of the Sacred Word* and *The Breast of the Earth*, a survey of African art from a socio-historical perspective. A

collected volume of his poetry is in preparation and he has recently completed a second novel called *Comes the Traveller at Last*.

[1] George Awoonor-Williams, quoted in Per Wästberg, ed., *The Writer in Modern Africa* (New York, 1969), p. 31
[2] Kofi Awoonor and G. Adali-Mortty, eds., *Messages: Poems from Ghana* (London, 1971), p. 183
[3] Jawa Apronti, 'Ghanaian poetry in the 1970s', in Kolawole Ogungbesan, ed., *New West African Literature* (London, 1979) p. 35
[4] 'Interview with Kofi Awoonor', in Bernth Lindfors *et al.* eds., *Palaver, Interviews with Five African Writers in Texas* (Austin, Texas, 1972) p. 54
[5] *Ibid.*, p. 56
[6] *Ibid.*, p. 50
[7] John Goldblatt interviewing Kofi Awoonor, *Transition*, vol. 8, no. 4, 1972, p. 42
[8] *West Africa*, 17 April 1978, p. 750

Mariama Bâ

1929–1981   SENEGAL

Mariama Bâ suddenly appeared on the African literary scene in 1979 when her first novel, *Une si longue lettre*, was published. In the following year she won the first Noma Award for Publishing in Africa. As her second novel was about to appear, she died in Dakar after a long illness.

Makilily Gassama wrote in *Le Soleil* on the day after her funeral, 'Mariama Bâ has crossed the constellation of African letters like a meteor'.[1] In the same issue Bara Diouf wrote:

Mariama Bâ could have been the first

Senegalese woman judge, professor, even engineer if she had wanted. Used to winning school honours, at a time when meeting the challenges of the West, and therefore of colonization, meant necessarily acquiring a higher education, she preferred a calm life as a mother, although she had everything she needed to succeed.[2]

But he did her less than credit, for he neglected to take into consideration her career as a schoolteacher and as a school inspector. He also overlooked her pioneering of women's rights.

Mariama Bâ's grandfather and father were highly educated people. Her paternal grandfather was an interpreter for the French colonial office and her father a civil servant, becoming the first Senegalese Minister of Health in 1956. Her mother died when Mariama Bâ was quite young, and she was raised by her maternal grandparents, a well-to-do Dakar family. In an interview published in 1979 she speaks about her upbringing as a little girl:

Normally I should have grown up in the midst of this family without ever having gone to school, my only education being a traditional one including initiation rites. I had to know how to cook, to wash up, to pound millet, to make couscous from flour. I had to know how to wash clothes, iron the ceremonial boubous, and would end up, when the right time came – with or without my consent – in another family, that of a husband.[3]

Thanks to her father, Mariama Bâ did go to school. On each trip home to Dakar from his different postings in, then, French West Africa, he made her grandparents keep her in school. It was against their opposition that Mariama Bâ attended the Ecole Normal for girls in Rufisque, on the outskirts of Dakar. Her grandparents thought that 'a primary school certificate [was] good enough for a girl'.[4] Characteristically, Mariama Bâ had not thought about attending the Ecole Normal. She had enrolled in a secretarial course, and it was her principal who, seeing her promise, had her prepare the 1943 entrance examination which, also characteristically, she passed with the highest mark of all candidates in French West Africa.

Mariama Bâ's first efforts at writing were the essays and compositions she did while at the Ecole Normal. One of her essays was published in the journal *Après* and another, about her happy childhood in Dakar, was anthologized in a volume prepared by Maurice Genevoix of the French Academy. The essay received a great deal of attention when it was published, for it amounted to an implicit rejection of the French policy of assimilation. She recalls saying in the essay 'my mind has been whitened and my head remains black, but the blood surges, unrestrained, through my civilized veins . . . I was eight years old and I shouted "drum, carry me away".'[5]

Apart from the newspaper articles which she began writing much later when she became involved in Senegalese women's associations, Mariama Bâ published nothing until *Une si longue lettre* appeared. A number of her friends, and especially Annette Mbaye d'Erneville, formerly of Radio-Sénégal, had encouraged her to write. Annette d'Erneville, in fact, announced to the editors of Nouvelles Editions Africaines, before the book was even written, that Mariama Bâ intended to submit a manuscript. And it was pride as a women that set her to work. 'I began thinking about these men sitting around a table making fun of a woman who failed to submit a manuscript. I began immediately to write *Une si longue lettre*.'[6] By winning the 1980 Noma Award for Publishing in Africa the novel – now available in no less than sixteen different editions or translations – brought instant fame to its author, and revealed to the world of African letters a new woman writer of immense talent.

Taking the form of a letter written to a friend, the novel records how an educated woman perceives the inferior status society has traditionally assigned to her. After long years of marriage and bringing up twelve children, Ramatoulaye, the heroine, is forced into a separation with her husband when he marries a much younger woman. What pains her most is not his taking a second wife, but his secrecy and complete lack of concern for her feelings.

Like her heroine, Mariama Bâ had separated from her husband. The mother of nine children, she had been married to Obèye Diop, a parliamentarian and a former Senegalese minister. Madame Bâ repeatedly claimed that her novel was not autobiographical. It is evident, however, that her own life experiences and sensitivity contributed in an important way to fashioning the novel, even if its plot is not patterned directly on the events of her own life.

Mariama Bâ believed that the writer has a crucial role to play in the building of a truly democratic society in Africa. Writing in Africa, she said, has always been an essentially political act. This was true during the colonial era and it continues to be true today. Writers contributed directly to shaking the foundations of colonialism and today they must contribute to eradicate the ills that remain:

> the writer plays an important role in guiding people and making them aware. He has a duty to convey the aspirations of all social categories, especially the most underprivileged. Denouncing the evils and scourges that eat away at our society and delay its full development and striking out at the archaic practices, traditions and customs that are not a real part of our precious cultural heritage – this is the sacred mission the writer must carry out with steadfastness and faith and whatever the obstacles. He can also recommend solutions.[7]

Mariama Bâ ends with a fervent call to the women of Africa to assume their responsibilities and commit themselves to the struggle to end 'the glaring inequality between men and women in Africa':

> The nostalgic songs dedicated to African mothers which express the anxieties of men concerning Mother Africa are no longer enough for us. The black woman in African literature must be given the dimension that her role in the liberation struggles next to men has proven to be hers, the dimension that coincides with her proven contribution to the economic development of our country. [But] women will not be given this place without their real participation.[8]

Mariama Bâ hoped that *Une si longue lettre* would help to arouse women to the awareness of their inferior status, and also set men thinking. The warm reception she had received to her book in Africa, by men as well as by women, made her hopeful that her aim had, in part at least, been reached. She was quite lucid, however, about the capacity of society to resist change and realised the process would take more than one generation. Men will not willingly relinquish their power, she said: 'To abandon these advantages all of a sudden – it really requires a great, great effort.'[9]

For a number of years Mariama Bâ had been attempting to contribute concretely to the promotion of women in Africa through her work in Senegalese women's associations and, in particular, in the Dakar chapter of the International Association of Soroptimists. So much needed to be done, she said; 'Up to now there have really been no laws for women.'[10] Although apolitical, in theory, she felt women's associations could offer a political outlet for the women 'who want to play a role in building the nation' and, in any case, they offered women greater freedom for self-expression than 'the male-dominated political parties' which tended to draw women in only at election time 'as campaign arguments'.[11]

Mariama Bâ's second novel, *Le Chant écarlate*, was finished but not published when she learned she had won the Noma prize for her first work. Although extremely pleased about the award she felt concerned that she might not meet her readers' expectations in the second novel, which is about a racially mixed marriage in Senegal (a European wife and an African husband). It will no doubt be read, along with *Une si longue lettre*, as Mariama Bâ's testament to men and women everywhere.

[1] Makilily Gassama, *Le Soleil*, no. 3396, 19 August 1981, p. 5 (editors' translation)

[2] *Ibid.*

[3] Alioune Touré Dia, 'Succès littéraire de Mariama Bâ pour son livre: *Une si longue lettre*', *Amina*, no. 84, 1979 (editors' translation)

[4] *Ibid.*

[5] *Ibid.*

[6] *Ibid.*

[7] Mariama Bâ, 'La fonction politique des littératures africaines écrites', *Ecriture Française*, vol. 3, no. 5, 1981, p. 5 (editors' translation)

[8] *Ibid.*
[9] *African Book Publishing Record*, p. 211
[10] 'Mariama Bâ prix Noma 1980: écho des voix féminines de détresse', *Le Soleil*, 13 June 1980, p. 2 (editors' translation)
[11] *Ibid.*

Seydou Badian

born 1928   MALI

Seydou Badian has led a triple existence as author, doctor and politician. Born on 10 April 1928 in Bamako as Seydou Badian Kouyaté, he was educated first at Lycée Terrasson de Fougères in Bamako and finished his secondary studies in Montpellier, France. His first work, the short novel *Sous l'orage* was written in 1954 while he was completing his medical studies at the University of Montpellier. It was published in 1956, a year after he had returned to Mali to practice medicine, by the Presses Universelles in Avignon.

In 1962 Badian was appointed Minister of Rural Economy and Development in the socialist government of President Modibo Keita, and from 1965 to 1966 was Mali's Minister of Development. He became a member of the political bureau of Keita's party, l'Union Soudainaise.

In the same year that he entered politics, Badian's play, *La Mort de Chaka*, was published by Présence Africaine. (It has since been translated into English and published by Oxford University Press.) The focus of his verion of the Chaka legend is the betrayal of the Zulu warrior-king by his chiefs, so that the play may be said to be 'a symbol of the anti-colonial struggle and the pan-African aspirations'.[1]

Seydou Badian has experienced the rise and fall of political fortune. Although he left politics in 1966 to return to his private medical practice, he was among those arrested in 1968 when Modibo Keita was overthrown. He spent the next seven years – until 2 June 1975 – imprisoned in an isolated region of Mali. It was during this period that he wrote a second novel, *Le Sang des masques*, which was published the year after his release. A third novel, *Noces sacrées*, came out in 1977. Badian outlined his political philosophy and his concept of African socialism in a book entitled *Les Dirigeants africains face à leur peuple*, which was awarded the Grand Prix Littéraire d'Afrique Noire in 1965.[2] The essential aim of socialist construction in Africa, he says, should be to eliminate under-development. The education of the people is an important first step towards that goal, but it must be an education that 'eradicates from our young people the disdain for land and work that the colonial educational system had fostered in them'.[3] Another vital aim of this 'first step towards the awareness of dignity' is to 'rehabilitate the cultural heritage so that our people, who have been led to resignation and despair by the colonial regime, might understand that their fathers' past already contained values that have their place in the tower of universal values'.[4]

Seydou Badian's novels can be viewed as works meant to illustrate the ideas he expounded in *Les Dirigeants africains face à leur peuple*. His heroes (and heroines) are 'new men' who 'must feel concerned and committed'.[5] They are people who have had contact with the world of the colonizer but who remain faithful to a certain vision of the past as symbolized by the village. The important idea to retain from *Sous l'orage*, Badian's first novel, is not so much the rigidity of a social system inherited from the past which prevents two young people in love from marrying, as the fact that the society already contains visionaries in its midst who symbolize all that is inherently wise therein. These people are also among the few who view with empathy the desire of the young people, Samou and Kany, to marry.

Bakari, the hero of *Le Sang des masques*, is also a 'new man'. Trained as a mechanic in the city, he does not let himself be lured by the temptations of urban life but returns to his village. The stay in the city has given Bakari new ideas, but he also holds fast to the values that tradition has taught him – honour, integrity and humanity. Although his age group shows him nothing but hostility, the village elders recognize his worth by agreeing to make him the *ton-mousso* of the young woman, Nandi. This means the two are condemned to a platonic relationship, for henceforth Bakari has the responsibility of making sure Nandi remains a virgin until her marriage with Amadou. Bakari carries his sense of honour and duty to the highest degree, sacrificing himself to save Nandi and her husband – a scoundrel and a spendthrift – from a threatening creditor who demands repayment of the debts Amadou has made. Like all Badian's novels, *Le Sang des masques* is set in late colonial times and the city – here Bamako – is the symbol of the degradation of values brought about by the introduction of an economy which measures everything in terms of money. Although Badian's village is no idyllic paradise, it does remain the repository of the values on which Africa can build its future.

In Seydou Badian's first interview since his release from prison, recorded just as *Le Sang des masques* was coming out, he spoke at length about the symbolism of the village in his novel. He was *not* talking about a 'return to origins', he said, nor about the keeping of 'obsolete customs'. 'Fixation with the past was never a motor of revolution.'[6] But, he added,

Africa will never be free if she doesn't recover the identity that was torn into pieces by four centuries of colonization, if she doesn't recreate national unity by the communal organizing of everyone's destiny that is symbolized by the village. Being independent also means assuming one's culture while remaining receptive to universal contributions.[7]

Seydou Badian's most recent novel, *Noces sacrées*, symbolically picks up the pieces of Africa's torn culture by having a mask that had been taken to Europe brought 'home', and replaced in the sanctuary from whence it had been stolen. Besnier bought the mask from a dealer during a stay in Mali and he is haunted by it when he returns to France. He feels compelled to go back to Mali in order to find the mask's rightful owner. The search is successful, thanks to an African doctor who is treating Besnier's nervous disorder, and the novel ends in a village somewhere in Mali with a rite of integration. Besnier gives up the mask but receives in turn a better understanding of what Africa's contribution to mankind could be.

Seydou Badian has been living in Dakar since his release from prison.

[1] *Littératures de langue française hors de France: anthologie didactique*, Gembloux (Belgium), 1976. (This and the following quotations translated by the editors.)
[2] Paris, 1965 (Cahiers libres, 65).
[3] Quoted in S. and M. Battestini, eds., *Seydou Badian: écrivain malien* (Paris, 1968), p. 61
[4] *Ibid.*, pp. 61–2
[5] *Ibid.*
[6] 'Un entretien avec Seydou Badian', *Politique Hebdomadaire*, no. 248, 6–12 December 1976, p. 45
[7] *Ibid.*

Francis Bebey
born 1929   CAMEROON

Francis Bebey has an international reputation as both musician and writer. As a guitarist and composer of considerable talent he has recorded many of his compositions and he has travelled worldwide to give concerts which include performances of his own music and readings in French from the works of Africa's most prestigious poets. Interest in African music has led Bebey to write several articles, including 'La musique africaine moderne' published by Présence Africaine in 1967 in the volume of collected papers from the colloquium on

Negro Art held in Dakar in 1966. Bebey has also authored the full-length work, *Musique de l'Afrique*, which was translated into English as *African Music* by Josephine Bennett for an American edition in 1975.

As an author Bebey has attempted every genre except play-writing. He has published three novels with Editions C.L.E. in Yaoundé: *Le Fils d'Agatha Moudio* (1967), *La Poupée ashanti* (1973), and *Le Roi Albert d'Effidi* (1976). All of them have appeared in English translation in both English and American editions, and *Le Roi Albert d'Effidi* has been translated into German. Bebey's immensely successful first novel, *Le Fils d'Agatha Moudio*, winner of the 1967 Grand Prix Littéraire d'Afrique Noire, is soon to be made into a film.

Bebey's short stories have appeared in *Embarras & Cie* (1968), a collection of nine stories, each followed by a poem. In addition he has written a tale about the adventures of three little shoeshine boys in a big West African city: *Trois petits cireurs* (1972). In talking about his stories, Bebey says, 'I tell stories which are very simple but in which I try to convey the message of an African who is not just an African but a man living within the human community.'[1]

Francis Bebey is also a poet, and his verse has appeared in many reviews and anthologies. The only full-length collection to appear so far, however, is the volume that Nouvelles Editions Africaines brought out in 1980, *Nouvelle saison des fruits*.

Gifted with outstanding abilities in two creative media, Bebey draws a distinction between them:

> As far as writing is concerned, I do have a strong feeling that I can write only when I remain an African in the full sense of the word. It's quite different from my feeling about music, really quite different, because the spoken language, or the written language, is much stronger actually than the dream which you have when you think about music. So you remain yourself. At least I remain more personal, more African if you like, when I tell a story or when I write it down, than if I just let my memory wander about and find some notes and arrange them in a melody.[2]

There have been times when the literary vision failed to materialize and Bebey turned to music. For example, refering to *Le Chant d'Ibadan*, one of the compositions on the recording, *Pièces pour guitare seule*, Bebey said, 'For me, it is a poem which I failed to write, because I could not find the words. Perhaps the music will redeem this original intention.'[3] And words, in the sense that Bebey uses the French language in his work, at one time proved a problem to him, as they have for many African writers. But he overcame this.

> There are sometimes difficulties in putting the right expressions which would correspond exactly to what African expressions would have meant. This, to me, was one of the main difficulties when I started, but I was lucky because I am a radio man basically and writing for radio, is, to me, very African-like. Writing for radio is like telling things to the radio, to the microphone, as we tell things to other people in Africa. So, little by little, I came to combining both media. I found that every time I tried to write what we call 'literature' which is very polished, very clean, I couldn't tell my story like an African would have told it. But if I considered my reader as a listener, then I could tell him the story in a more African way.[4]

Born in Douala on 15 July 1929, Francis Bebey learned to play several instruments even before he learned to read. After primary and secondary schooling in Cameroon, he studied English at the Sorbonne in Paris and trained in Paris and New York as a radio broadcaster. Bebey worked for UNESCO in Paris from 1961 to 1974, first in the Information Department and then as head of musical programmes in the Department of Culture. He left UNESCO in 1974 to devote himself full-time to music, writing and management of his record company.

Recently Bebey has felt compelled to integrate his activities as musician and creative writer more closely than he has in the past by writing the long poem, *Concert pour un vieux masque*, published jointly in 1980 by Editions Harmattan and the Agence de Coopération Culturelle et Technique in Paris. The title comes from an original musical composition that

Bebey has performed on many occasions since 1965. Before each performance Bebey would recite the story of an old African mask that had been 'abducted' from its homeland only to end up committing suicide in a museum in Brazil. One day in 1975, however, after performing the piece at the International Guitar Festival in Fort-de-France, Martinique, Bebey was accosted by a young black man who had been confused by the 'message' of the musical version of *Concert pour un vieux masque*: did Bebey mean that black people of the diaspora should commit suicide like the mask? The young man's question so disturbed Bebey that he decided to give words to *Concert pour un vieux masque*:

> In the place of a response, I started to scribble a letter . . . This letter to a stranger became the present poem – a long gush like the ink that I couldn't stop flowing from my pen.[5]

And Bebey's response to the young man – not death, but life:

Ma mort est un suicide
une résurrection
et la vive intensité d'une vie qui ne
    finira jamais
Ici se termine ma quête
qui partait du fond de l'Afrique vièrge
au luxe d'un musée de Bahia

My death is a suicide
a resurrection
and the spirited intensity of a life that will
    never end
My quest ends here
from the depths of virgin Africa
to an opulent museum in Bahia.[6]

[1] 'Arts and Africa', no. 143, BBC African Service transcript (London, n.d.), p. 4
[2] Francis Bebey interviewed in *Cultural Events in Africa*, no. 40. March 1968, p. 1
[3] Back sleeve of Bebey, *Pièces pour guitare seule*, Disque Ocora 27 Oct. (Paris, 1965)
[4] Bebey interviewed in *Cultural Events in Africa*, p. 11
[5] Francis Bebey, *Concert pour un vieux masque* (Paris, 1980), p. 9 (editors' translation)
[6] *Ibid.*, p. 72 (editors' translation)

Mongo Beti
born 1932   CAMEROON

Beti's works have variously been called comic, humorous, ribald, boisterous, and Rabelaisian; 'Beti was the master of a scalding and amazing comic talent,' wrote Gerald Moore.[1] Underneath these adjectives, however, A. C. Brench discerned an 'inexpressible sadness, as if a great deception had made life bitter and cynical humour was the only relief'[2] and he found that essentially 'Beti is a pessimist'.[3]

These words, written in the past tense, were applied to the Beti of the fifties, the man who had written four novels in the short period from 1955 to 1958 – *Ville cruelle* (1955), *Le Pauvre Christ de Bomba* (1956), *Mission terminée* (1957), and *Le Roi miraculé* (1958) – and who suddenly stopped publishing. This was the man who was thought to have given up creative writing and who, more than fifteen years later, came back in 1974 to publish two novels in quick succession – *Perpétue ou l'habitude de malheur* and *Remember Ruben* (the title is in English in the original French edition). Another novel, thematically linked to the two others came out in 1979, *La Ruine presque cocasse d'un polichinelle*.

Alexandre Biyidi, who took the pen-name of Mongo Beti, was born some 25 miles south of Yaoundé in Mbalmayo, Cameroon. A Béti, he was educated at the local Catholic mission until 1945 when he was expelled for insubordination. He went to a French school in Yaoundé and in 1951 at 19 years of age took his *baccalauréat*. Beti obtained a scholarship and left for France to continue his education. Studying first in the Faculty of Letters at the University of Aix-en-Provence, he completed his *licence* at the Sorbonne. Later he received his *agrégation* and began a career in France teaching classics and French literature at school and university levels.

While Beti, now aged 22, was studying at Aix, a chapter of his first novel was published in *Présence Africaine* under the title 'Sans haine et sans amour'. The novel itself, *Ville cruelle* (written under the pen-name Eza Boto), was released by Présence Africaine in 1954. However, Beti was doubtful of its literary quality. He decided to drop the Boto pseudonym and adopted 'Mongo Beti', the name he used thereafter for all his novels.

His second novel, *Le Pauvre Christ de Bomba*, created something of a furore in Paris, for its unfavourable portrayal of colonialist France and the Catholic Church's missionary activities in Africa. Gerald Moore says, 'With this book . . . the author emerged as a formidable satirist and one of the most percipient critics of European colonialism . . . we see the greed, the folly and tragic misunderstandings of a whole epoch in Africa's history.'[4] Strangely enough, the novel's original publisher, Robert Laffont, allowed the book to go out of print and sold reprint rights to Kraus Reprints in Lichtenstein, who marketed the book outside France. It was not until 1976 that the novel was again available in France – this time under the Présence Africaine imprint. The English version of the novel, translated by Gerald Moore and entitled *The Poor Christ of Bomba*, was issued in Heinemann's African Writers Series in 1971.

In 1957 Beti's reputation was firmly established with his third and very successful novel, *Mission terminée*, which received the 1958 Saint Beuve literary award and was nominated for the *Prix Renaudot*. *Mission Accomplished* (*Mission to Kala* in the British edition) appeared the following year in New York and London. The hero of the novel is a young man who, because he has been educated (but has ironically just failed the *baccalauréat* examination), has been entrusted by his village with the awesome task of bringing home a wayward village woman. It is a process that turns into a quest for self-knowledge, and the hero learns that he does not fit into either the traditional or the colonial order. Abiola Irele considers *Mission terminée* to be Beti's best work:

His satire is at its most cutting in this novel in which the verve and exuberance of the writing are given the fullest play in an unrelenting interrogation of the traumas and frustrations of the colonial experience. And in the way in which the novel captures the atmosphere of the African setting, Beti gives a special effect to the indirectness of his attack on the colonial system.[5]

When *Mission terminée* was published, the indirectness of Beti's approach was perceived as a welcome change. ' "Here at last is an African novel which has no political motive." This was the sigh of relief of the French publisher who brought [it] out,' says Claude Wauthier.[6] This is a statement that has since proven to be ironic. Beti considers all of his works as political and has been (and continues to be) outspoken on the subject of Western intervention in Africa, past and present.

Beti's third novel, *Le Roi miraculé* (translated as *King Lazarus* as early as 1960 and reissued in the African Writers Series in 1970), continues his satirical examination of the impact of colonialism on African societies as its hero, a traditional African monarch, is wooed by the local missionary into becoming a Christian convert.

Then Beti fell silent. Not only had his four novels gone out of print (all were again reprinted in the seventies, but only after being unavailable for a long period), but he himself had stopped writing. In 1962 Gerald Moore wrote that Beti

seems to have entered a mood of disenchantment with literature and with what it can achieve. He believes that the new nations can only shake free from colonialism by a double revolution; the revolution of formal political independence is now complete in most of tropical Africa, but the more painful and drastic revolution which will produce truly independent societies is only just beginning. Mongo Beti is throwing himself into this second revolution as a publicist through such articles as his *Tumultueux Cameroun* which appeared in the *Revue Camerounaise* in 1960. His conversation, especially since the Congo débâcle, reveals the same restlessness and disquiet.[7]

Whatever the reasons for his former silence, Beti has found his voice again, and it is as biting and caustic as ever, if not more so. Beti's primary concern in his first four novels was to denounce colonialism as a political and social order, and in his latest three novels – *Perpetua and the Habit of Unhappiness* (the African Writers Series edition dates from 1978), *Remember Ruben* (African Writers Series, 1979), and *La Ruine presque cocasse d'un polichinelle* (not yet translated) – Beti focuses sharply on the post-independent Africa of dictatorships, one-party states and misery. *Perpetua* takes the form of the quest of a young man for his lost sister:

> Poor Perpetua has in fact been sold off to a no-hoper whose only prospects are in his zeal as local police and party tyrant: a mediocre being at the service of a regime whose only service is to itself and foreign interests. All this comes out in the story of how Perpetua died in childbirth (her third) having found love for the first time with a nationally popular footballer called Zeyang, or The Vampire. It is suggested that Perpetua died from the sheer habit of unhappiness, but the real story is the society in which this misery was allowed to take the life of a strong being.[8]

With *Remember Ruben* Beti takes his readers back to the days just prior to Independence in Cameroon when the revolutionary party, l'Union des Peuples Camerounais, was an active force. The title of the novel comes from the name of the leader of the UPC, Ruben Um Nyobé, who was assassinated in 1958, but the novel's central character is not Um Nyobé but the 'rubenist' Mor Zamba. It is Mor Zamba who is again the central figure in the sequel to *Remember Ruben*, *La Ruine presque cocasse d'un polichinelle*. The novel was published by Beti's own publishing house in Paris in 1979 and first serialized in the journal he edits, *Peuples Noirs/Peuples Africains*.

Beti, a very vocal opponent of the regime of Ahidjo, last visited Cameroon in 1959 just before Independence, and all of his recent novels have been banned there (as was *Le Pauvre Christ de Bomba* when it was published). In 1972 Beti published a polemical study of post-independent Cameroon entitled *Main basse sur le Cameroun*, that was banned in France soon after it appeared. After a long battle in French courts Beti succeeded in having the ban lifted and the book was reissued by Maspéro in 1977. It was the book's initial banning that prompted Beti to write *Remember Ruben*; he says:

> I wanted to put into a novel form all the ideas I had written in essay form in *Main basse sur le Cameroun*. Why? Because in France there is a tradition of not seizing anything that is a novel, that is a work of art . . . it is certain that in these two books [*Main basse sur le Cameroun* and *Remember Ruben*], and in the following, too, I am a witness to the truth of decolonization in Cameroon and in Africa . . . I show the truth of this process that was, in fact, to reinforce French presence – French colonization – in Africa.[9]

Having been the object of censorship, both in Cameroon and in France, Beti is more firmly convinced than ever of the necessity of not compromising on his beliefs. In the past he has not hesitated to criticize the great names of African literature like those of the negritude school, and particularly Camara Laye, for having a 'folkloric' vision of Africa that only served to give the colonizer a good conscience. Beti has also attacked authors like Ferdinand Oyono and Ahmadou Kourouma for having published brilliant works and then becoming staunch defenders of the *status quo* in Africa today.

Beti is not a man to mince his words – the role of the writer is much too important. This is a concept Western writers have lost:

> What always astonished me when I find myself in the presence of my white 'confrères' is the impression that we don't have the same profession. In Europe writing has become the pretext of sophisticated uselessness, of gratuitous vulgarity, whereas in our land it can ruin tyrants, save children from

massacres, tear a whole people away from ageless slavery, in a word, serve. Yes, for us writing can serve a purpose, and therefore must serve a purpose.[10]

[1] Gerald Moore, *Seven African Writers* (London, 1966), p. 91
[2] A. C. Brench, *The Novelists' Inheritance in French Africa* (London, 1967), p. 48
[3] A. C. Brench, *Writings in French from Senegal to Cameroon* (London, 1967), p. 56
[4] Moore, *Seven African Writers*, pp. 77–8
[5] Abiola Irele, *The African Experience in Literature and Ideology* (London, 1981), p. 155
[6] Claude Wauthier, *The Litterature and Thought of Modern Africa* (London, 1966), p. 157
[7] Moore, *Seven African Writers*, p. 91
[8] N.B-E., 'Habit of unhappiness', *West Africa*, 11 Dec. 1978, p. 2490
[9] 'Entretien avec Mongo Beti', *Peuples Noirs/Peuples Africains*, no. 10, July–Aug., 1979, p. 105
[10] Mongo Beti, 'Choses vues au Festival des arts africains de Berlin-Ouest (du 22 juin au 15 juillet 1979)', *Peuples Noirs/Peuples Africains*, no. 11, Sept.–Oct. 1979, p. 91

Dennis Brutus
born 1924   SOUTH AFRICA

Although born in Salisbury, Rhodesia, Dennis Brutus spent his childhood in the township of Dowerville in Port Elizabeth, South Africa. Of mixed descent, a 'Coloured' by South African definition, he was one of four children; his parents were both teachers by profession. His father was engaged in a continuous battle against poverty, and Dennis Brutus today suggests it was this struggle that forced his father to abandon his family. Though in his childhood he did not attend school

regularly, he did spend much time reading and participating in family poetry recitations led by his mother. Her favourite poems, Tennyson's 'Lady of Shalott' and 'The Round Table' and Wordsworth's narrative poems, were to become his favourites as well. Acknowledging this early influence on his career, Brutus has written.

I discovered something that linked my adult work with the beginnings of my literary knowledge; there recur in my poetry certain images from the language of chivalry – the troubadour, in particular. The notion of a stubborn, even foolish knight-errantry on a quest, in the service of someone loved; this is an image I use in my work, because it seems to me a true kind of shorthand for something which is part of my life and my pursuit of justice in a menacing South Africa. But it only made sense to me when in prison another image came to me; of my mother, in the afternoon sunlight, reading of Sir Galahad's search for light and beauty, with the sunlight falling on the page, and on the glowing colours of a picture of a knight entering a dark forest.[1]

An arts graduate from Fort Hare University College, Dennis Brutus taught English and Afrikaans in South African high schools for fourteen years – ten of those years at the Government High School in Port Elizabeth. Dismissed from that post in 1962, he moved to Johannesburg and enrolled in the University of Witwatersrand to study law.

Brutus, however, was an activist, a leader in the struggle against racialism in South African sport, and involved in anti-apartheid campaigns. Because of this, he was arrested early in 1963. He was released on bail, but his activities did not cease and he was soon banned by the South African government from attending social or political meetings. When the No Trial Act took effect Brutus moved to Swaziland, where he was ultimately refused a residence permit. On his way to an Olympic committee meeting in Germany he was detained in Mozambique, and secretly handed over by the PIDE to the South African police. He was afraid that he might 'disappear'. He therefore made a bolt for freedom in the centre of Johannesburg and was shot at and wounded outside the Rand Club. He was sentenced to 18 months' hard labour on Robben Island.

During his imprisonment his first volume of poetry, *Sirens, Knuckles, Boots*, was awarded the 1962 Mbari prize for poetry; the following year it was published by Mbari. Essentially protest poetry, the critic Ulli Beier found it 'transfigured by a quiet fortitude'.[2] Brutus, however, judged the competition as racially discriminatory in that it was open only to black writers, and rejected the money prize.

He was freed from prison in 1965, but new bans prohibited him from writing, from being published, even from being quoted. In 1966 Dennis Brutus obtained a Rhodesian passport and left for England on a one-way exit permit.

His second collection of poetry was published in 1969 under the title *Letters to Martha and Other Poems from a South African Prison*. They are chiefly inspired by his experiences as a prisoner on Robben Island and were originally written as letters to his sister-in-law, Martha – it was a crime for Brutus to write poetry. *Library Journal* notes that,

> They express his fear, loneliness, and deprivation (especially the lack of music), and they are peopled by figures from his nightmares – brutal prison wardens, fellow prisoners, former friends, and so on. A few written earlier in 1962 and 1963, or later in 1966, when the poet was outside South Africa, are somewhat different in tone, but they are equally successful in conveying his feelings – tender, angry, puzzled, mystical.[3]

Even after his oppressive life in South Africa, Dennis Brutus looks back on his home with affection. 'It's a suffering people and a suffering land, assaulted, violated, raped, whatever you will, tremendously beautiful and I feel a great tenderness for it,' he says.[4]

After staying in England for a while, Dennis Brutus spent some time on the staff of the University of Denver. He remains vigorously involved in anti-apartheid activities, serving as Director of the World Campaign for the Release of South African Prisoners. President of the South African Non-Racial Open Com-

mittee for Olympic Sports, and Campaign Director of the International Defence and Aid Fund. He was largely responsible for South Africa's exclusion from the Olympic Games, and in March of 1970 the United Nations' Special Committee on Apartheid granted him a hearing. His testimony concerned apartheid in sport and the conditions of political prisoners in South Africa.

By 1970 Brutus had been away from South Africa long enough to feel doubts about being invited to the Pan-African Cultural Festival in Algiers. He speaks of 'misgivings about my right to be called an "African Voice": how far were my ideas and opinions and art at all particularly African?' These concerns are reflected in *Poems from Algiers*. He resolved the problem

> in a series of answers about Africa – some in discarded (or lost) verse, – in assertions of myself and my (South) African experience, but especially in my rediscovery of the 'variousness' of Africa and the extent to which my own difference was a part of it. And especially in a sense of 'belonging' – as far as it is possible for a loner like me to remain belonging for anytime.[5]

In 1972 *A Simple Lust* was published. Besides containing selections from previous works, the book also contained new poetry which points to the agony of exile. Edwin Thumboo indicates the new pressures on Brutus:

> Confrontations with apartheid *in situ* cease with exile. One set of pressures diminish, another develop. Exile is never easy, never free from trauma, and for a patriot committed to the land, loved ones and friends with such fervour as Brutus is, the rupture must have been very profound. The moment of personal freedom is paradoxically also a moment of personal loss.[6]

A Simple Lust also contains a political joke against the South African censorship. Dennis Brutus had been circulating a small collection of his poetry in South Africa under the name John Bruin, and it is in this collection that his true identity is revealed.

For the last decade and a half, the poet has sought a greater simplicity of style. 'I felt my work was too clotted, too thick, there were too many strands knotted together, I was trying to make the language do too many things at the same time.'[7] When he visited China in 1973 he was therefore happy to experiment with the *haiku* form, producing 'spare, succinct utterances', successfully 'tight-fisted with words', observes Lindfors.[8]

Troubadour Press brought out a collection of poems called *Strains* in 1975, which

> represents thirteen years of growth and experience, and the poems are various kinds of equipment for living through thirteen years of change. So revolution and liberation are the major themes, and the poems talk quietly of dying and enduring, of will and despair, and of the embracing of the world as a totality – the motive of the revolutionary heart.[9]

In the 1970s he received various awards, including the Freedom Writer's Award (1975) and the K. D. Kaunda Award for Humanism (1979). Since 1971, Brutus has taught at the Northwestern University in the USA, with a year as visiting professor at the University of Texas in Austin. In spite of his having tenure at Northwestern University, the United States Government has denied him residence rights, and in 1981 a Defense Committee was set up to appeal. At the time of writing he was still not granted permission to remain, even as a political exile.

His stature and achievement as a poet and prominent exile is summarized by Romanus Egudu:

> in his intellectual protest without malice, in his mental agony over the apartheid situation in South Africa, in his concerns for the sufferings of the others, and in his hope which has defied all despair – all of which he has portrayed through images and diction that are imbued with freshness and vision – Brutus proves himself a capable poet fully committed to his social responsibility.[10]

[1] Dennis Brutus, 'Childhood reminiscences' in Per Wästberg, ed. *The Writer in Modern Africa* (New York, 1969), p. 98
[2] Ulli Beier quoted in Anne Tibble, *African English Literature* (London, 1965), p. 55
[3] *Library Journal*, Aug. 1969, p. 2790
[4] Dennis Brutus, 'New poems', *African Arts/Arts d'Afrique*, vol. 1., Summer 1968, p. 12

[5] Dennis Brutus, *Poems from Algiers* (Austin, Texas, 1970), pp. 21–2
[6] Edwin Thumboo, 'Dennis Brutus: apartheid and the Troubadour', *Umma*, vol. 8, Feb. 1978, p. 31
[7] Interview with Brutus in C. Pieterse and D. Duerden, eds., *African Writers Talking* (London, 1972), p. 57
[8] Bernth Lindfors, 'Dennis Brutus' mousy tongue', *World Literature Written in English*, vol. 15, no. 1, 1976, p. 7
[9] Jerry Ward, review of *Strains*, *Okike*, no. 11, 1976, p. 160
[10] R. N. Egudu, 'Pictures of Pain: the poetry of Dennis Brutus', in C. Heywood, ed., *Aspects of South African Literature* (London and New York, 1976), p. 143

John Pepper Clark

born 1935   NIGERIA

J. P. Clark has spoken of himself as

> that fashionable cultural phenomenon they call 'mulatto' – not in flesh but in mind! Coming of an ancient multiple stock in the Niger Delta area of Nigeria from which I have never quite felt myself severed, and going through the usual educational mill with the regular grind of an English school at its end, I sometimes wonder what in my make-up is 'traditional' and 'native' and what 'derived' and 'modern'.[1]

Thus Clark introduced *A Reed in the Tide* (1965), his second volume of verse, in which he also noted his gratitude to his friend and fellow poet Christopher Okigbo who, he says, 'was the first to take my poetry seriously enough to want to publish a volume of it at a time when I

was still at college. His constant encouragement and criticism have been a
great help.'[2]

A Reed in the Tide was the first volume
of verse by a single African poet to be
published internationally. Before that,
Clark's poetry, like that of other African
writers, had been published in anthologies, and a first collection, simply
entitled *Poems*, was brought out in
Nigeria by Mbari in 1962. Clark has since
published two further volumes of verse.
In 1970 Longman in England and
Africana Publishing Corporation in the
United States simultaneously released
Clark's volume of war poems, *Casualties:
Poems 1966/1968*. His most recent collection is *A Decade of Tongues*. The volume,
published in Longman's Drumbeat Series
in 1981 contains selected poems from
Clark's three previous collections.

Critics have reacted unevenly to Clark's
poetry. In reviewing his first collection,
Poems, Ulli Beier found his technique
resulted in a

> poetry that makes heavy reading, but which
> is moving, because it is always nourished by
> immediate experience and because the
> author's harassed, tormented and irrepres-
> sible personality is present in every line . . .
> Some of his moving poems are touched off
> by a specific moment from the past which is
> suddenly remembered . . . and very often, as
> one might expect, it is love . . . Whatever it is,
> there is always immediacy, urgency and
> spontaneity in his work.[3]

Another critic, Paul Theroux, says,

> There is a thin line between Clark's good
> poems and his bad ones. The poor poems
> are obscured by the use of pyrotechnic and
> imprecise language. The good poems are
> illuminated by simple and direct language.
> Ambiguity exists in both kinds, although it is
> hard to take in the poor poems.[4]

In an article published after *A Reed in
the Tide* came out, John Povey noted the
'significant presence' in Clark's poetry 'of
the influence of the English literary
tradition', notably the poetry of Hopkins
and Eliot, but also the way Clark skilfully
combines these influences with his
African experience: 'Clark begins with
the African scene, charges it with his style
forged out of the discipline of English

poetry and then leads the reader to his
personal, even intimate, revelation.'[5]

The volume entitled *Casualties* contains the poem, 'Death of a Weaverbird',
that refers implicitly to the death of
Christopher Okigbo. The title poem is
dedicated to Chinua Achebe. In it Clark
reminds his readers that 'we are all
casualties'. The Nigerian critic Ime Ikiddeh says of the collection: 'Of the poetry
written during the war, J. P. Clark's
Casualties is among the most substantial
volumes. Clark was safely outside the war
area, but his poetry shows he was not
emotionally out of it.'[6]

In 1961 Clark established himself as a
playwright as well, with Mbari's publication of his first drama, *Song of a Goat*.
Performed at Ibadan and Enugu the
following year, it was well received
throughout Africa and Europe, and at the
Commonwealth Festival of the Arts in
London in 1965, along with his drama
The Masquerade. In 1964, Oxford University Press issued Clark's *Three Plays*, which
included the two pieces already mentioned, plus *The Raft*. Said one of his
fellow Nigerian writers: 'Clark's three
plays are tragedies and critics have
attempted to show how close to Greek
tragedies they are.'[7] Clark spoke of the
influence of classical Greek writing in an
interview with Lewis Nkosi in 1962 but
several years later he expressed his
impatience with those who carry the
exercise of influence-seeking too far:

> There are times when you are well aware
> you're doing a double-take, and it doesn't
> take a very clever critic to detect that . . . this
> business of looking for sources can be
> misleading . . . the influences may be there,
> but there are coincidences, too, because we
> are all human beings with the same basic
> emotions and experiences.[8]

On the question of the place of the
writer in society Clark has a more careful,
nuanced position than many African
writers. Like every other member of
society, he says, the writer has his own
role to play, but Clark objects to people
'creating for the writer an almost super-
stitious role':

> I find [it] unbearable, as if he were a special
> kind of human being who has certain duties,

functions, privileges mystically set apart from other human beings. I don't at all assume that kind of romantic position. I'm not impressed with the social or political life a poet leads outside of his profession if he doesn't produce poems.[9]

The point is that in producing art you are ordering material and creating something new which you hope will not just show life, not just help to interpret life, but also probably help to direct life. This is where the commitment is.[10]

J. P. Clark was born on 6 April 1935 in Kiagbodo, in the Ijọ region of the Niger Delta. He was educated in Okrika and Jeremi, at Warsi Government College in Ughelli, and at the University of Ibadan. In Ibadan Clark founded the student poetry magazine *The Horn*, which published some of his first verse. After receiving his B.A. Honours degree in English in 1960, he began work in journalism, first as Information Officer for the government of Nigeria for a year, then on the staff of the Nigerian *Daily Express* in Lagos as a features and editorial writer. In 1963 he travelled to America as a Parvin Fellow at Princeton University. The record of his experiences that year are contained in a satirical volume, *America, their America*, that André Deutsch published in 1964. The book has been the subject of some controversy for the way Clark relentlessly criticizes American life and manners. In 1969 it was reissued in London in Heinemann's African Writers series and also published for the first time in the United States.

Upon returning from his year's study at Princeton, Clark became a Research Fellow, working on Ijọ traditional myths and legends at Ibadan's Institute of African Studies. That work led to the publication, in 1966, of a play, *Ozidi*, based on an epic tale of the Ijọ people; it was also the beginning of a 15-year project to record the Ozidi legend in its entirety. This was an undertaking of monumental proportions, for the legend requires seven days to be performed in full. During the course of the project Clark also made a film, *The Ozidi of Atazi*, under the sponsorship of the University of Ibadan and the Ford Foundation. The project was finally completed and published jointly in 1978 by the presses of the Universities of Ibadan and Oxford as *The Ozidi Saga*. The volume was singled out for special commendation in the 1980 Noma Award for Publishing in Africa. In a review of the book, another Nigerian author, Femi Osofisan, wrote:

Everything about this latest book of Clark's is in large proportions. Perhaps not unexpectedly: the subject itself is huge. The egregious drama of Ozidi, in its local Ijo setting, normally takes seven full days of performance, and to have succeeded in capturing its literature here, in some four hundred pages of print, is no mean feat.[11]

Clark's activities have also included critical writing. In the sixties he published a number of articles in such magazines as *Transition*, *Black Orpheus*, and *Présence Africaine*. Some of these have been reprinted in a volume of essays entitled *The Example of Shakespeare*. Published in 1970, the volume includes essays on the use of language by African writers ('The Legacy of Caliban') and on the relationship between the poet and his reader ('The communication line between poet and public').

John Pepper Clark is currently professor of English at the University of Lagos where he has been teaching since 1966. In 1981 the British Council made available in its Nexus Books Series a study guide to John Pepper Clark's selected poems, edited by Kirsten Holst Petersen.

[1] John Pepper Clark, from the introduction to *A Reed in the Tide* (London, 1965).
[2] *Ibid.*
[3] Ulli Beier, 'Three Mbari poets', *Black Orpheus*, no. 12, p. 48
[4] Paul Theroux, 'A study of six African poets' in Ulli Beier, ed., *Introduction to African Literature*, quoted in Kirsten Holst Petersen, ed., *A Critical View of John Pepper Clark's Selected Poems* (London, 1981), p. 28
[5] John Povey, 'Two hands a man has: the poetry of J. P. Clark', *African Literature Today*, vol. 1, 1968, p. 37
[6] Ime Ikiddeh, 'Literature and the Nigerian civil war', *Présence Africaine*, 98, 1976, p. 169
[7] Oladele Taiwo, *An Introduction to West African Literature* (London, 1967), p. 76
[8] 'Interview with John Pepper Clark', in Bernth

Lindfors *et al.*, eds., *Palaver: Interviews with Five African Writers in Texas* (Austin, Texas, 1972), p. 16
[9] *Ibid.*, p. 20
[10] *Ibid.*, p. 21
[11] Femi Osofisan, 'The trail of Ozidi', *Positive Review*, vol. 1, no. 3, 1979, p. 36

José Craveirinha
born 1922   MOZAMBIQUE

For nearly three decades José Craveirinha has been the most important poet from Mozambique. Born on 28 May 1922 in Maputo, Craveirinha has written poetry from the early 1950s to the present. His first volume *Chigubo* (the title is the name of a traditional Ronga dance) published in 1964, contains poems that have been incorporated in the following collections in English: Gerald Moore and Ulli Beier's *Modern Poems from Africa*; Margaret Dickinson's *When Bullets Begin to Flower* and Wole Soyinka's *Poems of Black Africa*. These protest poems are characterized by a virile elan that celebrates with rhythmic power landscapes of the body and soul of Mozambique. The themes of Mother Africa and labour in the mines of South Africa also recur frequently.

Three other books of Craveirinha's poems have been published: *Cantico a un Dio de Catrame* (1966) in a bilingual Portuguese and Italian edition, *Karingana Ua Karingana* (1974), and *Cela I* (1980). The last work appears as the initial volume in the Mozambican Authors Series initiated by Ediçoes 70 in Lisbon. Volume number four in the series, *Xigubo*, is a revised version of *Chigubo*. Many of the poems in *Cela I* reflect the moods and dreams of four years (1965–9) that Craveirinha spent in prison for political dissent. In his poetry, whether as lover or political combatant, Craveirinha identifies with the joys and sufferings of the people of Mozambique.

A journalist by profession, Craveirinha has written articles and essays for *O Brado Africano*, *Notícias*, *A Tribuna*, *Notícias da Beira*, *O Jornal*, and *Voz de Moçambique*. Winner of literary prizes in Italy, Portugal and Mozambique, he was a member of the Mozambican delegation at the 6th Conference of Afro-Asian Writers in Luanda, Angola, in the summer of 1979, where he was elected a permanent member of the Lotus Prize jury.

Russell Hamilton has called Craveirinha 'the master of the power of the word and the most important cultivator of African themes and stylistic features in the poetry, not only of Mozambique, but of all Portuguese Africa.'[1] Luís Bernardo Honwana praised his countryman as 'the true expression of the poetry of Mozambique' in dedicating to him *We Killed Mangy Dog*. Although critics have extolled the work of Craveirinha, there is no major study of his writing to date.

[1] Russell Hamilton, *Voices from an Empire* (Minneapolis, 1975) p. 212

Bernard Binlin Dadié
born 1916   IVORY COAST

Few African authors have published more than Bernard Dadié, one of the major names of the first generation of francophone African authors. He is a prolific writer and has publications in every genre – the novel, poetry, plays and the short story. The list includes essays and critical pieces as well as his lesser-known political writings of the early fifties (sometimes published under a pseudonym), when he was a militant nationalist. And it is no mean feat that, despite Dadié's high-level political responsibilities – he is Minister of Culture and Information in Ivory Coast – he has continued to write creatively. Other authors of his generation who have equally high-ranking positions – Cheikh Hamidou Kane and

Ferdinand Oyono, for example – have long stopped writing. Not so Dadié. Four new plays were published in the seventies, bringing the total to nine, and in 1980 and 1981 Dadié brought out a fourth collection of stories and a fifth novel. Reissues of his earlier works have also appeared in the decade 1970–1980.

Dadié became known to an anglophone public when translations of his poems appeared in several African anthologies. His autobiographical novel *Climbié*, which first appeared in New York in 1953, also became available in English in 1971, translated by Karen Chapman. As yet none of his plays have appeared in English.

Dadié's first poetry collection, *Afrique debout*, published in Paris in 1950, launched his literary career. The poems were published shortly after Dadié was released from a 16-month prison stay for having participated in the 'Treichville events' of February 1949. In the field of poetry he has produced two additional volumes: *Ronde de jours* (1956) and *Hommes de tous les continents* (1967). Of his poems, Clive Wake has said that they 'remind one of Reverdy in style, but his themes are all African. They deal very simply and without pretension or anger of Africa and the African's desire to proclaim his equality with other peoples.'[1] For A. C. Brench, Dadié's best poems are 'equal to Senghor's best'.[2]

Following these collections of verse Dadié published two books of traditional tales from the rich and varied oral literature of Africa – *Légendes africaines* (1954) and *Le Pagne noir* (1955). The stories, proverbs and legends that make up this collection are a distinct genre are 'a lesson in prudence, generosity, patience and wisdom, indispensable to the guidance of mankind and the stability of society',[3] according to Dadié; 'these stories and legends are our museums, monuments and street names – our only books, in fact. This is why they have such an important place in our daily lives . . .'[4] In 1966 Seghers reissued Dadié's legends and poems in a combined volume that also included his novel, *Climbié*. A third edition appeared in 1973.

Dadié's prose writing from that period also included the accounts of visits he made to Paris, New York and Rome, rewritten in novel form: *Un nègre à Paris* (1959); *Patron de New York* (1964), winner of the 1965 Grand Prix Littéraire d'Afrique Noire; and *La Ville ou nul ne meurt* (1968). Not novels in the strict sense, they are satirical works 'rather in the tradition of Montesquieu's *Lettres persanes*', says Martin Banham. Long out of print, the first of these volumes, *Un nègre à Paris*, was reissued by Présence Africaine in 1976. In describing the book, which is written in letter form, A. C. Brench said:

> Its real significance is that, published in 1959, it is the first example of a novel by a committed writer to be set outside Africa, in which the African hero is not forced to live within the limitations set by colonial domination . . . colonialism and racial prejudice are hardly present; this is not in character with the novels which precede or follow it. Yet, it does preclude a new development in the novel. Not only does Paris become the background for later novelists to use but, more important, the African hero becomes an objective observer, freed from the restraint of his inferior position in society. In the novels which follow *Un nègre à Paris*, the hero has, also, to accept the responsibility of his new freedom.[5]

It is as a playwright, nonetheless, that Dadié has made his most important contribution to African letters. His interest in the theatre dates from his schooldays. In 1934 he wrote a short skit, *Les Villes* (never published), to be played by the pupils of Bingerville at the First Children's Feast of Abidjan held concurrently with the celebration of the move of the colonial capital from Bingerville to Abidjan. The 'towns' in the play's title are Assini, Bingerville and Abidjan, which are vying with one another for the title of capital. A second play, *Assemien Déhylé*, an epic of the Agni people, dates back to 1935–6 when Dadié was a student at the famous William Ponty school on the island of Gorée near Dakar. The play was performed by students at the school and in 1937 at the Theatre des Champs-Elysées in Paris during the Colonial Exposition. *Assemien Déhylé* was published in a Catholic church newsletter in 1936, in *Education Africaine* in 1937, and republished in 1965 in *L'Avant-Scène Théâtre*. It has recently been made available by CEDA (1979).

It was not until 1956, however that he began writing plays in earnest. His immediate aim was to produce something that the theatre group of the cultural centre he founded could act in a competition organized by colonial authorities. From 1956 to 1960 he wrote a number of plays for these competitions, including the short pieces *Serment d'amour*, *Situation difficile*, and *Papassidi: maître escroc*. The plays were published collectively by CLE in 1968. *Papassidi: maître escroc*, a comedy about a confidence man who preys on the gullibility of poverty-stricken people by claiming to multiply banknotes, was reissued separately by Nouvelles Editions Africaines in 1975.

With *Monsieur Thôgô-gnini* (1970) Dadié's talents as a playwright were confirmed. In the late sixties the play toured a number of African and French cities and was staged in 1969 at the First Pan-African Cultural Festival in Algiers. Set in the mid-nineteenth century, *Monsieur Thôgô-gnini* is a satirical study of a slave, returned from the Americas, who seeks to enrich himself by encouraging a local monarch to conclude lucrative deals with European slave traders. For Jacques Nantet the play is 'very well constructed and fiercely clever'.[6]

Dadié returned to a historical theme for his next play, *Béatrice du Congo*, published by Présence Africaine and staged by Jean Serreau, the French director, with African actors at the Festival d'Avignon in 1971. The play, in Dadié's words, is a tragedy about 'the meeting of the first Europeans with Africans . . . the history of the conquest of the Kingdom of Zaire'.[7] Another play, *Les Voix dans le vent*, also came out in 1970. The play's main character, Nahoubou, 'comes closer to Jarry's Ubu than Thôgô-gnini does', notes Martin Banham: 'Dadié's play is about a man of no importance who is so tired of being pushed around and exploited by the

macadou's (king's) men, that he takes up the suggestion of one of them that he become the *macadou* himself.'[8]

With *Iles de tempête* (1973), a play about the West Indian Toussaint l'Ouverture, Dadié again shows his fondness for setting his plays in the past. He justifies his reasons for doing so by saying;

> You are more at ease in treating such subjects . . . You are not part of it, no one is part of it. On the contrary, if you choose a present-day subject, someone might recognize himself, even if the author didn't intend it.'[9]

In explaining Dadié's success as a dramatist, Martin Banham writes:

> He has quickly become the one dramatist who really stands out, and this is largely because he recognizes and uses the theatre imaginatively as a total medium in its own right. He writes plays to be acted and to be enjoyed by an audience, not just to be read. He is able to see beyond the printed page of his text in a way no other French-speaking African dramatist is able to equal. He is the only playwright to have written historical plays which are thoroughly meaningful to a modern, post-independence audience.[10]

Bernard Dadié's latest play, *Mhoi ceul* (1979), again offers a satirical portrait of a power-hungry leader in the form of an Ubu-like character. But for the first time both setting and characterization offer clear indications that Dadié meant to pattern his play after contemporary African political realities – an entirely new feature of his writing. *Les Jambes du fils de Dieu*, a collection of short stories, followed in 1980, and a new novel, *Commandànt Taureault et ses nègres*, in 1981. Astonishingly, the novel takes up a theme – anti-colonialism – that might be thought to be outdated. It draws a portrait of a French colonial official whose duties include enrolling Africans in compulsory public-works projects. It is a theme that attests to Dadié's desire as a writer to be free to choose any subject, including subjects previously thought to be 'exhausted'. One must recall here words that Dadié pronounced back in 1964 in referring to works being written at that time:

> The titles of most of the works clearly reveal

the situation in which the Negroes are placed, and the reason why they take to writing. Certainly they are quite capable of singing of rain and birds. This is a point that has obviously escaped the notice of persons who criticise Negro-African writers for producing far too many works in which a definite stand against the system of government to which they are subjected becomes a constant refrain. Surely these critics forget that Negro writers are men who in fact have lost everything – lands as well as independence ... they desire to be genuine producers, convinced ... they are contributing something specific and regenerative. They are in fact defending their right to live, the beauty of life, the excellence of life as compared with death, whether we conceive of death in terms of disease, poverty, injustice, slavery or racial segregation. It is important that this essential aspect of the work of Negro-African writers should be grasped.[11]

When queried in 1971 about the central concern of his works Dadié replied:

[it is] Man ... and all the excesses that are committed in the name of God or others. We, who have been in certain situations in certain countries, have been despised by certain people and that's very serious. Those kicks in the pants – even if they weren't given literally, were felt even so.[12]

Born in Assinie, Ivory Coast, in 1916, Bernard Binlin Dadié attended the local Catholic school in Grand Bassam and then the Ecole William Ponty where he became active in a drama and folklore movement. In 1939 he received his civil servant's diploma in the colonial administration and worked at the Institut Français d'Afrique Noire (now called the Institut Fondamental d'Afrique Noire) in Dakar until 1947, when he returned to the Ivory Coast. He spent the next few years working full-time on the newspaper of the nationalist party, the Parti Démocratique de Côte d'Ivoire, and was imprisoned for 16 months for participation in a nationalist demonstration.

Since 1957 Bernard Dadié has been successively First Secretary of the Ministry of Education, Director of Information Services, Director of Cultural Affairs and Inspector-General of Arts and Letters.

He has also been vice-president of the executive committee of UNESCO and has travelled widely throughout the world. He holds honorary doctoral degrees from several European and American universities. For a number of years he has been Minister of Culture and Information of the Ivory Coast.

[1] Clive Wake, *An Anthology of African and Malagasy Poetry in French* (London, 1965), p. 19
[2] A. C. Brench, *The Novelists' Inheritance in French Africa* (London, 1967), p. 86
[3] Bernard Dadié, 'Le rôle de la légende dans la culture populaire des noirs d'Afrique', *Présence Africaine*, XIV-XV, p. 167, trans. and quoted in Claude Wauthier, *The Literature and Thought of Modern Africa* (London, 1966 and 1978), p. 67
[4] Dadié, 'Le rôle de la légende' p. 165; Wauthier, *Literature and Thought*, pp. 64–5
[5] Brench, *The Novelists' Inheritance*, pp. 90–1
[6] Jacques Nantet, *Panorama de la littérature noire d'expression française* (Paris, 1972), p. 72 (editors' translation)
[7] François Prelle, 'A batons rompus' (interview with Bernard Dadié), *Bingo*, October 1971, p. 42 (editors' translation)
[8] Martin Banham, *African Theatre Today* (London, 1976), p. 77
[9] Prelle, 'A batons rompus', p. 42 (editors' translation)
[10] Banham, *African Theatre Today*, p. 74
[11] Bernard Dadié, 'Folklore and literature', (trans. by C. L. Patterson) in Lalage Bown and Michael Crowder, eds, *The Proceedings of the First International Congress of Africanists* (Illinois, 1964), pp. 215–6
[12] Prelle, 'A batons rompus', p. 43 (editors' translation)

Massa Makan Diabaté
born 1938   MALI

The descendant of a long line of *griots* or *namen kala*, the troubadours and praise-singers in the Manding culture who have the responsibility of preserving and transmitting the oral tradition, Massa Makan Diabaté is Mali's *griot* of modern times. Through the legends and songs of the Manding people that he has published (*Si le feu s'éteignait, Janjon et autres chants populaires du Mali*) and especially through his transcriptions of the epic tales of the thirteenth-century Manding empire of Sundiata (*Kala Jata*, and *L'Aigle et l'épervier ou La geste de Sunjata*) and his historical play about another illustrious empire-maker, the nineteenth-century warrior-king Samory Touré (*Une si belle leçon de patience*), he has made the oral traditions of Mali available in written form not only for Malians but for readers all over the world.

Although *Janjon et autres chants* was awarded the Grand Prix Littéraire d'Afrique Noire in 1971, Diabaté says, 'My talent comes from the elders . . . I am a tool. I am a craftsman who works with words.'[1] The words may be French, but Diabaté tries to use them in a way that recalls the rhythms and the images of the Manding language: 'It's an adulterous relationship, for I take the French language without marrying it. Pardon the expression, but I make little bastards.'[2]

As for the elders Diabaté refers to, one of them is his uncle, Kélé Monson Diabaté, one of Mali's most celebrated *griots* and the man who taught the Sundiata legends to his nephew. Massa Makan Diabaté describes his uncle's storytelling: 'His recitals are half-sung, half-spoken. My uncle is practically total theatre in himself. He is also the melting-pot where the soul of the Malian people is forged, for when Kélé Monson speaks on the radio every Malian feels concerned.'[3]

Other 'elders' who have inspired Diabaté are Boubou Hama, the former president of the National Assembly of Niger and the former ambassador of Niger to France (who has published oral traditions in French), and Amadou Hampaté Bâ with whom Diabaté has worked in collecting data.

Diabaté admits that his insistence on the importance of the oral tradition is sometimes criticized, but he believes that a modern Africa cannot be defined 'without defining the past'. 'It's not a question of choosing. It's a continuity.'[4] His work in reviving the culture of Mali's past is his way of being committed; it is his contribution to the political struggle:

I have an aim and that is to say to Malians, 'We have been a great empire' . . . I transmit to the young people what the elders have deposited with me. If the young people accept my message, very well, if not, I will have fulfilled my responsibility . . . I have

defined development as a structural process that concerns the economic, political, cultural and social areas. I work essentially in the cultural field and the work I do is useful for society.[5]

Diabaté explains that his reason for wanting to rescue oral traditions from oblivion stems from having spent so many years away from Mali in his youth. As is customary in Mali, he was raised not by his parents but by his uncle, a doctor, who was required to travel all over what was then French West Africa. And Diabaté was still quite young when he came to France to complete his education: 'The fact of being away helped to make me aware of the oral tradition in Mali. Perhaps telling me to find myself in this tradition. I returned to the oral tradition because I needed it.'[6]

Diabaté has two degrees from French universities, one in political science and the other in sociology. He wrote a dissertation on the role of the *griot* as social memory in Mali, and has carried out research in the Institute of Human Sciences in Bamako. From 1969 to 1970 he was Mali's Director General of Information and subsequently the head of the government's Cultural Division. He lived in Abidjan for a number of years as Head of Information for UNICEF in West Africa, but is now back in Bamako in the Office of Higher Education.

He first began writing for his own pleasure, with no thought of publication, when he was living in France. He tells how he found the title for his first collection of stories and legends, *Si le feu s'éteignait*. The book was written when his wife, who is French, was expecting a child:

We had an old stove that you had to keep filled with coal. My wife would say, 'Go and get some coal or the fire will go out', and in the morning she would say, 'Get up or the fire will go out'. And so I found the title for my collection.[7]

Besides being a *griot* who transmits the ancient culture of his people, Massa Makan Diabaté is also a novelist who brings to life scenes from Mali today. He has finished a trilogy which paints a comic fresco of the village of Kita (or Kouta as it is named in the novels) where he was born in 1938. Two novels have already appeared, *Le Lieutenant de Kouta* and *Le Coiffeur de Kouta*. A third novel will be centred on the penny-pinching butcher of Kouta who turns into a do-gooder when the *imam* of the local mosque makes him give half his fortune away to atone for selling donkey meat to the poor. When he dies he will be revered as a saint.

A novel which is not part of the Kouta trilogy has also been published recently. Entitled *Comme une piqûre de guêpe*, the novel tells the story of a little boy who is being prepared for the ritual of circumcision by his parents. It is a work in which the craft of the novelist is reinforced by that of the storyteller who is nurtured by traditions: 'I think a good novelist,' affirms Massa Makan Diabaté, 'is above all a good storyteller.'[8]

[1] 'Radioscopie de Jacques Chancel avec Massa Makan Diabaté', a cassette recording of a programme broadcast on 14 March 1977 from Paris (Radio France) (this and the following quotations translated by the editors)
[2] 'Massa Diabaté: conteur, griot', *Afrique-Asie*, no. 183, 1979, p. 71
[3] 'Radioscopie'
[4] *Ibid.*
[5] *Ibid.*
[6] *Ibid.*
[7] *Ibid.*
[8] 'Massa Diabaté: conteur, griot'

Lamine Diakhate

born 1927   SENEGAL

Like his friend, Léopold Sédar Senghor, Lamine Diakhate has combined a career as a statesman with that of a poet, and more recently, short-story writer and novelist. Born in 1927 in Longa near Saint Louis in northern Senegal, Diakhate was Minister of Information just after Independence and then began a long career in the Diplomatic Service as ambassador to a number of African countries, including Nigeria and Morocco. For the last few years he has been a member, with rank of Minister, of the permanent Senegalese delegation to UNESCO in Paris.

In the early fifties Diakhate belonged, with the Frenchman Jean Breton, to a group of poets who called themselves 'hommes sans épaules' ('men without shoulders') and published his first collection of poetry (now out of print), *La Joie d'un continent*. A decade went by before he published his second collection of verse, *Primordiale du sixième jour* (1963), although several of his critical studies on African poetry and on myth in popular Senegalese poetry appeared in that time, notably in the journal *Unité Africaine*. He has published two further volumes of verse, *Temps de mémoire* (1967) and *Nigérianes* (1974). Inspiration for the latter, written in honour of the women of Nigeria, came to him while he was Senegal's ambassador there. Two years after *Nigérianes*, Diakhate returned to critical writing with the publication of a presentation of two of Léopold Sédar Senghor's early poetry collections, *Lecture libre de Lettres d'hivernage et d'Hosties noires de Léopold Sédar Senghor*.

Diakhate has become identified with the members of the negritude generation who are his near-contemporaries, and critics invariably want to know whether, like some other writers, he views negritude as an out-dated concept. Interviewed in 1976 on this point, he responded by saying;

> Negritude is linked to a period in history . . . the history of black African people and West Indian people who were dominated by the French . . . This is what was at the bottom of the negritude movement: [it was] a question of the defence and the illustration of the values of the black world. . . . the quarrel about negritude astonishes me a little. People say negritude must evolve, must be surpassed, but Senghor defines negritude as all the values of the civilization of the black world . . . So for me, the problem of going beyond negritude or of readjusting it is a false problem, in that it is a matter of starting with our own values and seeing essentially what we can do with the contributions of modern techniques, with the contributions of others.[1]

A lyrical poet in the neo-classical vein, Diakhate believes poetry should be 'accessible to everyone'. In Africa, he says, poetry is, above all, defined as 'words pleasing to the heart and the ear'.[2] The creator – the poet, the writer, and the artist in general – is traditionally someone who is close to the people, who comes from the people. It is someone who 'says aloud what everyone says under his breath'.[3] In this context concepts like commitment have no meaning: 'The problem of commitment is a Western notion . . . where we live the notion of a poet is a notion of tradition that makes the poet someone who has the gift of foresight, and what he says through this gift of foresight must, and can, apply to all'.[4]

If Diakhate is not what can be termed 'an angry poet', a relatively new facet of the man as a writer is revealed in the fiction he has brought out since 1975. The two short stories published in *Prisonnier du regard* (1975) show that Diakhate can also be an astute observer of social ills in contemporary Senegal – such as the antics of religious quacks who take advantage of people's credulity, which is the theme of 'Le Madihou de Pikine', the second story in the collection. This new impression of Diakhate has been reinforced by the novel he published in 1979, *Chalys d'Harlem*. The book of an experienced poet but a newcomer to the novel genre, *Chalys d'Harlem* won the 1979 Grand Prix Littéraire d'Afrique Noire. It is the saga of a man from Rufisque in Senegal who emigrates to New York in the early twenties and becomes a major figure in the Black Renaissance and Pan-African movements of his day and who returns to Senegal after Independence, only to discover that the 'authentic African' he had been in Harlem is now considered to be a 'white man' in his country of origin.

Diakhate has plans for a new collection of verse, and a second novel on the daily lot of people in Africa is about to be published. Diakhate says, 'There is still a lot to be written on the life of the people. Africa is not just about questions of culture conflict and the affirmation of the African personality. Besides, that is sociology, not literature.'[5]

[1] *Poésie I: Nouvelle poésie négro-africaine*, Paris, 1976, pp. 95–6 (this and the following quo-

tations translated by the editors)
[2] *Poésie I*, p. 92
[3] *Ibid.*, p. 94
[4] *Ibid.*, p. 94
[5] 'Le Grand Prix Littéraire d'Afrique Noire', *Jeune Afrique*, p. 80

Birago Diop
born 1906   SENEGAL

Birago Diop was born and raised in Dakar, one of the four 'communes' in Senegal in which the populace was accorded French citizenship. His father, a Wolof, died when Diop was an infant and he grew up under the strong influence of his mother's side of the family. Her family originated from the Senegal–Mali border area where the Senegal and Faléme rivers meet. It was there many years later that Diop, in his inspection tours as a vet in the French colonial service, met the old family *griot* (story-teller), Amadou Koumba, who was to inspire his tales.

Diop was educated in Dakar and later attended the Lycée Faidherbe in the former capital of Senegal, St Louis. Moving to France, he studied veterinary science, at the University of Toulouse until 1933. It was while Diop was furthering his studies at the Institut d'Etudes Vétérinaires Exotiques in Paris the following year that he met and collaborated with his fellow countryman, Léopold Senghor, in the publication of the single, yet highly influential, issue of the journal *L'étudiant noir*.

In France Diop began writing much of the poetry that was later to appear in *Leurres et lueurs*. Several of his poems were included in Senghor's *Anthologie de la nouvelle poésie nègre et malgache de langue française* (1948), thus introducing him to a wide audience.

From 1937 to 1939 Diop worked as a veterinary surgeon in the Sudan, after a brief return to Paris in the early forties, he continued his work in the Ivory Coast, Upper Volta, and in the early fifties, in Mauritania.

Diop tells us that during his travels,

beneath other skies, when the weather was dull and the sun was sick I often closed my eyes and there would arise from my lips the *Kassaks* which used to be sung in the 'Men's Huts'; and I would hear my mother or my grandmother recounting once again the rebuffs of Bouki-the-Hyena, that conceited coward, or the misfortunes of Khary-Gaye, the orphan girl, the tricks of that *enfant terrible* Djabou N'Daw, the triumphs of the diabolical Samba Seytane, and the misadventures of Amary-the-Devout.

This momentary return to my childhood tempered my exile . . . On my return to my own country, having forgotten little of what I had learnt as a child, I had the great good fortune to meet by chance old Amadou-Koumba, our family *griot*.

. . . Amadou-Koumba recounted to me the tales which had lulled me to sleep as a child. He taught me others, too, studded with maxims and morals, in which can be found all the wisdom of our ancestors.

These same tales and legends – with slight variations – I also heard in the course of my travels along the banks of the Niger and across the plains of the Sudan, far from Senegal.[1]

The first product of such avid and attentive listening was a volume in which Diop rendered these memorable tales into French, *Les Contes d'Amadou Koumba*, published in Paris in 1947. This volume (which has been translated into Russian and Lithuanian) was followed by two more books of tales: *Les Nouveaux contes d'Amadou Koumba* (1958), with a preface contributed by Senghor, and *Contes et lavanes* (1963), winner of the 1964 Grand Prix Littéraire d'Afrique Noire. A hardcover edition of *Contes et lavanes* was recently one of the initial offerings of Africa's first book club, Club Afrique Loisirs, which Nouvelles Editions Africaines inaugurated in April 1980.

In *Tales of Amadou Koumba*, published in 1966, Dorothy S. Blair has translated into English 19 of Diop's traditional folk tales. Joyce Hutchinson has also produced a volume of selected stories from Diop's two volumes, with an introduction in English. An anthology of world literature written in French has this to say about Birago Diop's tales:

From one collection to the next he remains faithful to the teachings of the old master, but shows a growing awareness for novel techniques and the writer's craft. In other words, he endeavours to conciliate both his concern to remain true to traditions and his desire to create a personal body of work. His writings remain a particularly rich source of information on the life and the beliefs of people in the bush. They also teach us about the affinities of traditional oral literature with certain modes of thought, certain forms of sensitivity.[2]

As for the exact role played by Amadou Koumba in Diop's tales, he himself noted in 1976:

Amadou Koumba Ngom was only a borrowed name, a convenient banner to cover the 'goods' which came to me from several sources, and which first and last were family sources. For I owe more to my brother Youssoupha than to the *griot* of my maternal grandmother.[3]

Diop also recalled at that time that it was Senghor who suggested that he retain the name of Koumba in his second book, for the work was originally titled *L'Os* after its first tale.

Over the years many of Birago Diop's tales have been adapted for the stage in Senegal by both professional and school groups. Diop has himself rewritten one of his stories as a play, *L'Os de Mor Lam*. An immensely successful comedy, the play was first performed in Senegal as early as 1966, although not published until 1976. It has become part of the repertoire of Peter Brooke's company at the Bouffes du Nord Theatre in Paris.

Diop's other publications in the seventies include the book of tales for children, *Contes d'Awa*, which Nouvelles Editions Africaines published in 1978 and which were originally meant as monthly contributions to the Senegalese children's magazine, *Awa*, founded by Annette M'Baye. A more significant publication is Diop's voluminous autobiography, *La Plume raboutée* (1978), published jointly by Nouvelles Editions Africaines and Présence Africaine. This was an important event, for Diop had long sworn that his 'quill was broken'. In addition to the interesting comments on Diop's personal life – which included marriage in 1936 to a French woman at a time when black–white marriages were almost unheard of – the book is valuable for the glimpses it gives of the birth of the negritude generation in Paris in the early thirties.

In the interview that appeared in *Le Soleil* in December 1976 on the occasion of his seventieth birthday, Diop recalls the importance of the negritude movement, but also notes the necessity of evolution:

> The black man must stop looking behind himself. And the negritude that claims to be a movement must arrange to go beyond itself and open up to the world of tomorrow. As for African literature today, it is not yet a rising spiral, but it has stopped being the snake that eats its own tail.[4]

When Senegal achieved Independence in 1960 Birago Diop, upon Léopold Senghor's insistence, became ambassador to Tunisia, a post he remained in until 1965 when he returned to Dakar to open a private veterinary clinic.

Three studies of Diop and of his writings have appeared thus far: *Birago Diop: écrivain sénégalais*, edited by Roger Mercier and Monique and Simon Battestini (Paris, 1964); and two works by Mohamadou Kane, *Les Contes d'Amadou Coumba* (Paris, 1969) and *Birago Diop: l'homme et l'oeuvre* (Paris, 1971).

[1] Translated and quoted by Dorothy S. Blair, *Tales of Amadou Koumba* (London, 1966), p. xxii
[2] *Littératures de langue française hors de France: anthologie didactique* (Sèvres, France, 1976), p. 41
[3] Birago Diop: 'Je me supporte', interview with Mohamadou Kane and Pierre Klein, *Le Soleil*, 11 December 1976, p. 2
[4] *Ibid.*

David Diop
1927–1960   SENEGAL

David Diop had published only one small verse collection, *Coups de pilon*, in 1956, before his untimely death in 1960. He has nevertheless been called 'the most promising of West Africa's younger French poets'[1] and 'a leader of the younger generation of "negritude" writers, those who reached their twenties in the postwar years.'[2] Gerald Moore finds that this one volume 'was enough to establish David Diop as the most interesting and talented new African poet of the fifties.'[3]

Although recognized as a West African poet, Diop was born in Bordeaux. His mother came from Cameroon and his father was a Senegalese doctor. After his primary education in Senegal, the remainder of his schooling took place in France, where he earned two *baccalauréats* and a *licence-és-lettres*. He was a semi-invalid for most of his life, and frequently in hospital. Diop lived only a brief time during his childhood in Senegal and Cameroon, and spent most of his life in France.

Diop witnessed the suffering of many of his compatriots in World War II. Later, in the fifties, he followed the moves for Independence in many parts of Africa. His exile from his native country exerted a decisive influence on his work, as did Aimé Césaire (a writer from Martinique). His vehement and critical opposition to European society, its position in and effect on Africa, stood in contrast to his love for Africa and his African brethren, and his vision of a sovereign Africa. These are the dominant motifs in his poetry.

In the latter part of the fifties Diop returned to Senegal. In Dakar he taught for a year at the Maurice Delafosse school, and in 1958 he went to Kindia, Guinea, where he was principal of a secondary school. Two years later he was killed with his wife in an air crash near Dakar. Since his manuscripts were destroyed in the crash, Diop left only the volume published by Présence Africaine. During his life, his work had appeared in *Présence Africaine* and had been included in Senghor's *Anthologie de la nouvelle poésie nègre et malgache de langue française*.

In a 1968 issue of the *Journal of the New African Literature and the Arts*, Paulette Trout and Ellen Kennedy translated ten of Diop's poems and accompanied them with a short biographical essay. A complete English version of *Coups de pilon* has become available since then, however, in a volume translated by Simon Mpondo and Frank Jones and published in the United States with Indiana University Press in 1973 as *Hammer Blows and Other Writings*. A British edition (entitled simply *Hammer Blows*) appeared in Heinemann's African Writers Series in 1975.

[1] Gerald Moore, *Seven African Writers* (London, 1962), p. 18
[2] Paulette Trout and Ellen C. Kennedy, 'Profile of an African artist. David Diop: negritude's angry young man', *Journal of the New African Literature and the Arts*, Spring and Autumn 1968, p. 77
[3] Moore, *Seven African Writers*, p. 18

R. Sarif Easmon

born 1913   SIERRA LEONE

A prominent Sierra Leonean, Dr R. Sarif Easmon is a medical practitioner in Freetown, professionally educated in England, and a leading voice in political matters in Sierra Leone. Half Creole and half Susu (a people from Guinea), he says, 'I have a very large and interesting family – I don't need to go outside my family at all to find plots.'[1]

He is the author of two published plays. *Dear Parent and Ogre* was initially performed in Lagos by the '1960 Masks' in 1961. It was the first prize-winner in a London playwriting contest organized by *Encounter* magazine. It was published in 1964, and was followed in 1965 by *The New Patriots*, a play dealing with corruption in the civil service. This opened in Ghana in the period following President Nkrumah's deposition, and after several presentations along the west coast of Africa, was performed in Sierra Leone in 1968.

Dr Easmon is the author of two further plays: *Mate and Checkmate*, produced by the Nigerian Television Service, and *Dilys Dear Dilys*. Of his four plays he has said. 'One tries to write not only on a theme that is of passing interest but on the basic themes of humanity that interest people at all times. My plays are wildly different.'[2]

Easmon also has to his credit two novels: *The Burnt-out Marriage*, which appeared in London in 1967, and *Geneviève*, submitted to the 1968 *African Arts/Arts d'Afrique* literary competition (excerpted in the winter 1969 issue), and noted as being a 'close runner up to the prize-winning novel of Ezekiel Mphahlele'.[3]

A thirteen-year gap ensued before the publication of Dr Easmon's next book,

The Feud, which comprises short stories that are cosmopolitan in origin and passionate in theme. Of the title story, a reviewer comments:

> Easmon, who is an established writer by any standard, is at his best when he places the pre-colonial era of the Susu tribe of West Africa under the literary microscope ... Using sharp imagery and drawing the characters in bold relief ... Easmon paints with unrelenting urgency and vividness, the inhumanity of the slave trade in all its blood-curdling ramifications.[4]

[1] *Cultural Events in Africa*, no. 44, 1968
[2] Ibid.
[3] *African Arts/Arts d'Afrique*, vol. 2, Winter 1969, p. 30
[4] Maxwell Nwagboso, 'African book of the day', BBC African Service, 7 Oct. 1981

Obi Egbuna

born 1938   NIGERIA

In an interview with Bernth Lindfors in Enugu in February 1973, Obi Egbuna candidly referred to his reputation as 'the bad boy of Nigerian literature' which he earned among Western publishers after the publication of his first novel, *Wind versus Polygamy* (reissued by Fontana in 1978 as *Elina*).[1] According to Egbuna this reputation resulted from his refusal to follow the 'literature of conflict' trend of writing in favour of a novel set in the present, whose character is a traditional African monarch, a sort of 'black Solomon' who rationally defends the institution of polygamy in modern times. G. C. Mutiso claims that the novel is, indeed, 'unrepresentative of African writing since most of the literature shows men and women in mainly non-polygamous settings'.[2] Critics certainly do not agree at all on the artistic merits of Egbuna's novel. Mbella Sonne Dipoko says 'he has never had so much fun reading a work on this institution ... Mr Egbuna has written an extraordinary novel with world-wide implications.'[3] For Ronald Dathorne, however, the book is 'the worst African novel I have ever read'.[4] Oladele Taiwo has harsh words about Egbuna's 'stilted language' and about the main character's 'empty philosophising'.[5] Vladimir Klima, on the other hand, although conceding that the author of *Wind versus Polygamy* is an 'inexperienced' writer, finds 'some remarkable ideas' in the novel.[6]

In his own defence Egbuna dates the novel from his period of 'self-discovery' as a writer. His only published play, *The Anthill*, also dates from this period, which he says was an important time in his life but he admits that he is not 'terribly proud of those early works now'.[7] Critical commentary on *The Anthill*, a comedy built around a case of mistaken identity, has been quite consistently favourable. It inspired S. Ramaswamy to write an article entitled 'A well-made Nigerian play' and Joseph Bruchac to say that it is 'light and frothy' and 'the most entertaining and the best constructed of all Egbuna's plays'.[8]

Egbuna has remained, nonetheless, a controversial figure, not so much for his drama or fiction as for his outspoken involvement in the Black Power movement in London, where he went on a scholarship in 1961 and remained until 1973. During this period he edited *The Voice of Africa*, a militant journal linked to ex-president Nkrumah of Ghana, and served as president of the Universal Coloured Peoples' Association, an organ of the British Black Power movement. Arrested on a number of occasions, Egbuna spent six months in Brixton prison awaiting trial on a charge of inciting to murder police officers (a charge stemming from a speech made at Speaker's Corner in Hyde Park). He was given a three year's suspended sentence. A non-fiction volume, *Destroy This Temple: The Voice of Black Power in Britain* published in London in 1971 records in part Egbuna's prison experience, although the first two parts of the original manuscript dealing with Egbuna's trial and related matters were dropped in the final version as being 'too revolutionary'. Over the next three years Egbuna's notoriety caused him to be the victim of several attacks. His car was set on fire, his house sprayed with bullets and he himself severely stabbed by a group of white thugs. This period left him angry and embittered. In an article appearing in *The*

Renaissance, a Nigerian weekly newspaper published in Enugu, Egbuna wrote that: 'Fifteen years in England has taught me that any black man seeking legal redress in a WASP-controlled white country like Britain is merely confessing his naivety and ignorance concerning the contradiction between law and justice in that land.'[9]

Back in Nigeria in 1973 Egbuna rediscovered the land and the family and friends he had been away from for so many years. *The Menace of the Hedgehog*, a sequel to *Destroy the Temple* which says 'everything that book should have said about the history of the black movement in England' also devotes a section to the prose poems Egbuna wrote to express the emotions homecoming inspired in him, particularly after the visit to his mother and the village of Ozubulu near Onitsha where he was born.[10] The return to Nigeria also gave Egbuna the opportunity to use his skills and interest in writing in the service of apprentice authors as Director of East Central State's Writers Workshop and producer of a weekly radio series called 'Writers Workshop Hour'. He later became director of East Central State Broadcasting System Television. In an interview with Bernth Lindfors, made just as the writers' workshop was taking form, Egbuna speaks enthusiastically about the project as a means of giving young Nigerians 'an equal opportunity to create':

> There has to be a good atmosphere to encourage literary growth. People like Achebe and the other great writers in Nigeria are accidents because if someone's father hadn't been what he was or if the person never had the opportunity to go to school, he wouldn't have become a writer.[11]

Egbuna also viewed his homecoming as a way to renew contacts and stimulate dialogue with other Nigerian writers, notably those at the University of Nsukka, where Achebe is based.

In talking about his own need to create, Egbuna declared in the 1973 interview his impatience with people who think he is 'angry and writes only about politics', and his desire to bury the myth that has grown up around him as a firebrand revolutionary: 'I'm not interested in playing politics. I am not even interested in being a revolutionary. I just want to write and get people to think.'[12] In Egbuna's mind this does not mean, of course, that a writer does not have a role to play in his time for 'it is the writer who ultimately puts flesh on the personality of his period.'[13]

It is certainly true that since the time of this interview Egbuna has more than fulfilled his self-appointed task of writing in order to get others to think. A second volume of short stories, *Emperor of the Sea and Other Stories* followed two years after a first collection published in 1972: *Daughters of the Sun and Other Stories. Emperor of the Sea* marks what Egbuna feels is his 'new style' of writing, one showing that 'Africa, not the Africa of Lagos or Port Harcourt or Calabar, but the real Africa in the interior' can be presented 'beautifully'.[14]

A second novel, *The Minister's Daughter*, a parody of contemporary African politics, appeared in 1975, and a volume of memoirs, *The Diary of a Homeless Prodigal* (Enugu: Fourth Dimension Publishing Co.) came out in 1978. Two new books were published in 1980, *The Rape of Lysistrata* and *Black Candle for Christmas*, a third collection of stories, and *The Madness of Didi*, a third novel. Egbuna finished the manuscript of *The Madness of Didi* while completing work on a doctorate at Howard University in Washington DC. (He also holds a Master's degree in English from the University of Iowa.) It is interesting to speculate on the source of Egbuna's inspiration for his most recent novel, for the experiences of the main character echo many of his own. The central figure of *The Madness of Didi* is a man who was thought to be dead and who returns home from a long stay in England (including time in prison) to become the centre of controversy. For the younger generation Didi is a hero and a visionary, but for the older generation he is a dangerous subversive.

Egbuna has had to answer attacks from fellow Nigerians for remaining out of the country during the civil war. He defends himself by saying that his contribution took the form of an essay called 'The murder of Nigeria' and by pointing out the relevance of his work in England helping to correct the plight of 'the dispossessed sons of Africa'.

A kind of lone-wolf figure among Nigerian authors, Obi Egbuna feels a writer must chart his own literary path and that imitation is a dangerous thing. Although an Igbo, he has studiously avoided association with the Achebe school of writers while maintaining cordial, if sometimes quarrelsome, relationships in literary circles at Nsukka. Egbuna believes, however, that disagreement can be healthy and beneficial: 'I admire the relationship Lenin and Gorky had, for example. They were always telling each other off yet at the same time they were advising one another. I like that kind of thing happening, and I want it to happen here, too.'[15]

[1] 'Interview with Obi Egbuna', in Bernth Lindfors, ed., *Dem-Say: Interviews with Eight Nigerian Writers* (Austin, Texas, 1974), p. 15
[2] G. C. Mutiso, 'Women in African literature', *East Africa Journal*, March 1971, p. 11
[3] Quoted in Donald Herdeck, *African Authors: A Companion to Black African Writing* (Washington DC, 1973), p. 119
[4] Review of Egbuna's *Wind versus Polygamy*, *Black Orpheus*, no. 17, 1965, p. 59, also quoted in Herdeck, *African Authors*
[5] Oladele Taiwo, *Culture and the Nigerian Novel* (London, 1976) p. 39
[6] Vladimir Klima, *Modern Nigerian Novels* (Prague, 1969), pp. 103 and 141
[7] Lindfors, *Dem-Say*, p. 18
[8] S. Ramaswamy, 'A well-made Nigerian play', *Literary Half-yearly*, vol. 17, no. 2, 1976, pp. 109–13; Joseph Bruchac in Vinson, ed., *Contemporary Dramatists* (London, 1973), p. 238
[9] Obi Egbuna, 'I am no Medusa on ice', *The Renaissance* (Enugu, Nigeria), 18 March 1973, p. 8
[10] Lindfors, *Dem Say*, p. 20
[11] *Ibid.*, p. 22
[12] *Ibid.*, p. 21
[13] *Ibid.*, p. 21
[14] *Ibid.*, p. 19
[15] *Ibid.*, p. 21

Cyprian Ekwensi
born 1921   NIGERIA

Cyprian Ekwensi is a prolific writer. To date he has published seven full-length novels, three novellas, twelve children's books, three collections of short stories, and numerous articles and stories that have appeared in newspapers and magazines throughout the English-speaking world. His works have been translated into several languages and he himself has toured Africa, Europe, and America extensively. He is certainly one of the best-known African writers, and in 1968 was awarded the Dag Hammarskjöld International Prize in Literature.

He is a *popular* novelist, saying, 'I don't regard myself as one of the sacred writers, writing for some audience locked up in the higher seats of learning.'[1] He has described his audience as consisting of 'the ordinary working man ... the masses'.[2]

Ekwensi has been called an African Defoe, the chronicler of contemporary African city life, but he objects to being stereotyped exclusively as an urban writer. Although many of his novels are set in the city, one of them (*Burning Grass*) deals with the cattle-herding peoples of the savannah region of northern Nigeria, and his children's books are set in all parts of the country. Ekwensi defines himself as a 'national novelist', 'because I know Nigeria backwards. I have driven

throughout the length and breadth of this country. There is no part of Nigeria I have not been to.'[3]

Even though he writes in a popular style and does not hesitate to entertain his readers with vivid, often titillating, descriptions of low-life in West Africa, Ekwensi weaves deeply serious topics into his novels: concern about the loss of values in today's money-mad Africa, concern about political violence and instability, and, more recently, concern about the effects of the civil war on people's day-to-day lives. Writing for Ekwensi is a way to mirror society and to expose social ills:

> directly or indirectly the writer in today's Africa must be a committed writer. He must be committed to truth. He must be committed to the exposure of the ills of society. And he must be committed to pointing the direction towards the future, as he understands it.[4]

Ekwensi works into his novels and stories the notes and observations that he has the habit of jotting down in his diary. The gathering process for a book can take years but the actual writing is done quickly, sometimes even in just a few days. As Ernest Emenyonu points out in the full-length study on Ekwensi that he published in Evans' Modern African Writers Series, Ekwensi can write literally at any time and in any place:

> Those who know Cyprian Ekwensi very well reveal that writing has become a part of his life. There is no separate schedule and often no preparation for it. It happens in the office, over telephone conversations, at meals, at conference tables, wherever a typewriter can be fitted for action. At least one of his novels was sketched in a moving car. Orlando Aguocha, the secretary who typed most of his novels, and who knows him better than most people, remarks that to work for or with Ekwensi on his writings is to work twenty-four hours of the day.[5]

Ekwensi is an Igbo, born in Minna in the northern part of his country on 26 September 1921. Educated in Nigeria, Ghana and London, he attended Government College, Ibadan; Yaba Higher College; Achimota College in Ghana (when Yaba was used as an Italian P.O.W.

camp during World War II); the School of Forestry, Ibadan; and on a government scholarship at the Chelsea School of Pharmacy, London University. In Ekwensi's checkered career he has worked as a Forestry Officer in northern Nigeria and as a teacher in subjects as diverse as English, science, and pharmacy. His main career, however, has been in broadcasting and journalism. From 1957 to 1961 he was Head of Features at the Nigerian Broadcasting Corporation and from 1961 to 1966 he was Federal Director of Information Services. Just before the Nigerian Civil War broke out he transferred to eastern Nigeria to take up the same position on the regional level. During the war Ekwensi was a prominent campaigner on behalf of the Biafran cause and Chairman of the Bureau for External Publicity in Biafra.

Ekwensi dates his interest in writing from his school days in Ibadan. Students were taught to read extracts from the works of famous authors like Oliver Goldsmith and Charles Dickens:

These extracts stimulated the appetite and made you want to go to the original source. Before that, in my primary school days, I had won as a prize a volume called *Highroads of Literature* ... it contained extracts from Dickens, Jonathan Swift, Lord Tennyson's 'Morte d'Arthur' showing the sword flung into the lake and an arm catching it before it sank – it was that kind of thing that got me very excited about literature. I did a lot of under-the-desk reading during mathematics lectures, and by the time I left secondary school I was prepared to start scribbling things down.[6]

It was during Ekwensi's days as Forestry Officer in the early forties, when he was alone most of the time, that he started to write short stories. Later, when he had left forestry work for teaching, he began to read his stories on a weekly radio programme. One of the regular listeners to the programme, and a neighbour of his in Lagos (the setting for the collection *Lokotown and Other Stories*), was Mr Chuks, a bookshop owner. Chuks urged him to write a story to be sold in his shop. The result was the extremely successful novella, *When Love Whispers*, which was published in 1948. Before that Ekwensi had also published five of his stories in *African New Writing* (1947). Ekwensi also collected Igbo folk tales and an early collection, *Ikolo the Wrestler and other Igbo Tales* was published in London in the same year.

People of the City, originally published in 1954, was Ekwensi's first full-length novel. It is generally considered to be the first contemporary African novel, and was reissued in Britain in 1963. Ekwensi followed this with more novellas and children's stories (many of which date back to his forestry days), and the full-length novels, *Jagua Nana* (perhaps his most popular), *Burning Grass* (also dating back to his forestry days), *Beautiful Feathers*, and *Iska*, Ekwensi's post-war publishing includes four children's stories, two novels (*Survive the Peace* and *Divided We Stand*), a novella (*Motherless Baby*), and a collection of short stories (*Restless City and Christmas Gold*). He has also edited an anthology of new writing from Nigeria (the FESTAC anthology) which grew out of his directorship of Nigeria's participation in the Second World Black and African Festival of Arts and Culture held in Lagos in January 1977.

When the civil war ended Ekwensi opened a pharmacy in Enugu and involved himself in reorganizing Biafra's former radio station at Orlu (an experience that is undoubtedly reflected in *Survive the Peace*, whose central character is a radio broadcaster for Biafra). In 1971 Ekwensi returned to public service as chairman of the East Central State Library Board and following that he became managing director of the state-owned Star Printing and Publishing Company, the publishers of the *Daily Star*. He wrote a weekly column for the *Daily Star* and a monthly column for *Drum* magazine. In 1979 he set up his own consultancy business, and in 1981 was appointed managing director of a new newspaper published in Imo State, *The Weekly Eagle*.

[1] 'Interview with Cyprian Ekwensi', in Bernth Lindfors, ed., *Dem-Say: Interviews with Eight*

Nigerian Writers (Austin, Texas, 1974), p. 28
[2] 'Cyprian Ekwensi', in Lee Nichols, ed., *Conversations with African Writers* (Washington DC, 1981), p. 44
[3] *Ibid.*, p. 43
[4] *Ibid.*, p. 44
[5] Ernest Emenyonu, *Cyprian Ekwensi* (London, 1974), p. 12
[6] 'Interview with Cyprian Ekwensi', p. 24
[7] Cyprian Ekwensi, 'Literary influences on a young Nigerian', *The Times Literary Supplement*, 4 June 1964, p. 475, quoted in Bernth Lindfors, 'Cyprian Ekwensi: an African popular novelist,' *African Literature Today*, no. 3, Omnibus edition, 1972, p. 3

Buchi Emecheta
born 1944   NIGERIA

Emecheta's voice has been welcomed by many as helping to redress the somewhat one-sided picture of African women that has been delineated by male writers. Theirs has often been an idealized view, presenting women as 'one-dimensional, romanticized images . . . primarily mothers'.[1] Similarly, the 'good-time girl' has also received a facile treatment. Emecheta's perspective is complex, often difficult and challenging. 'Rather than simply portraying the African woman symbolically as part of the warm and secure past, she offers faithful portrayals, patterns of self-analysis and general insight into the female psyche . . .' She asks for, and gives, a diverse approach; for writers not to typecast women, not to simplify – 'we should be respected in our different roles. We should not be regarded as appendages of men but as

individuals.'[2] Hers is not a strident or unbalanced voice about feminist issues (indeed she has recently denied that she is a feminist at all), but she none the less plays a valid and significant role in that she 'writes to raise the images of Nigerian women to a level commensurate with historical truths'.[3]

She was born in Lagos. Her father, a railway porter, died when she was very young. She attended the Methodist Girls' High School from the age of ten when she won a scholarship. As soon as she left school she married and had a child by the age of seventeen. Retrospectively she observes, 'I had to get married because both my parents were dead and nobody was going to look after me.'[4] She accompanied her husband to London where he was a student. She finally left him and, supporting her five children in unsatisfactory conditions, she gained an honours degree in sociology and wrote in the early hours of the morning.

Her writing at this stage consisted of imaginative stories and was rejected by publishers. Emecheta recollects wryly:

I happen to be one of the unluckiest would-be authors that ever had lived. I spent almost every week of 1968, 1969, and 1970 trying to persuade publishers just to read my work. I did not care whether I was paid for their publication or not, my only wish was that someone would share in my dreams . . .[5]

Nobody did, however, and she forlornly contemplated having to return to work in the British Museum. At that stage she started writing 'observations', her opinions and views of social aspects of London. After several vague letters from the *New Statesman*, she burst in and confronted the editor, the late Richard Crossman, in his office and he agreed to publish her articles; they appeared as a column called 'Life in the ditch'. Doors were suddenly opened to her and a book of the observations, *In the Ditch*, was accepted for publication. The book details 'her wretched experiences while living in London as a poor single-parent raising her children'. She dwells not only on her own crises, but also

establishes her views on the plight of vulnerable women in an over-industrialized, male-dominated society. Multiple images emanate from the book, the author's convictions on race relations, social services, housing and male–female relations from a woman's point of view are forcibly stated. As a result, it is with this book that Emecheta establishes herself as a feminist writer.[6]

In her next novel, *Second Class Citizen*, she delves into her turbulent marriage and past, and three-quarters of it, she maintains, is autobiographical. The result was the expression of the 'cumulative oppression resulting from being alien, black and female'. She was the spokesman for many of the under-privileged: 'The indignities of poverty, discrimination, and oppression are vividly chronicled . . .'[7]

For her next three books she turned to a Nigerian setting. *The Bride Price* (1976) is about marriage and the payment of betrothal fees; it insists on the potency of tradition and taboos which still exist in Nigeria. The people who are the vehicles for her message are the young lovers, Aku-nna and Chike, who marry despite opposition – but Aku-nna dies in childbirth. Emecheta claims; 'I had to kill her at the end because she went against our tradition. So to me, deep down inside, I'm still a traditionalist . . .'[8] On this very important topic, one critic evaluated her contribution:

Emecheta . . . maintains the equilibrium between the artist's involvement and the sociologist's judicious disinterest that offers the reader a deeply moving, yet detached experience. Being herself a woman living out of the tribal culture but still touched and affected by her knowledge of it, she brings a special clarity to her treatment of the all-important tradition of bride price. For the first time, perhaps, a writer examines this concept from the viewpoint of the person most directly concerned but least considered – the woman.[9]

Implicit in the book is an understanding of the dynamics of the society she is describing. 'She probes with tenderness and sadness into the mores of a culture slowly crumbling under the onslaught of European and American influence . . .'.[10]

For *The Bride Price* and her next novel, *The Slave Girl*, 'a hauntingly beautiful story, mainly about religious hypocrisy and the hardships of being a woman',[11] she received the *New Statesman* Jock Campbell Award for 1978. The levels of domination that the young girl, Oje-beta, is subjected to include her sale at the age of seven by her brother, to finance his coming-of-age ceremony; her exploitation by Pa Palagada and by her relative Eze: '. . . all seek to dominate her. Emecheta illustrates in a most compelling manner her victimization of women on many levels.'[12]

The stringently uncompromising *Joys of Motherhood* was published in 1979. The necessity for a woman to be fertile, and above all to give birth to sons, is the basis of the novel. And yet in a transitional society there are none of the rewards that a mother might have received from a traditional society. Emecheta here looks at the realities of motherhood, not an idealized version; she 'breaks the prevalent portraitures in African writing . . . It must have been difficult to draw provocative images of African motherhood against the already existing literary models, especially on such a sensitive subject.'[13]

Destination Biafra is Emecheta's latest book, published in 1981. In it she has tried with mixed success to extend her writing, which is strong on individuals, to the greater sweep of political events. She has had a play, *A Kind of Marriage*, produced by BBC television. Using her daughter's diaries as a basis she has branched into children's literature with *Titch the Cat*, and more children's books are expected. She returned to Nigeria to an academic post at the University of Calabar, but stayed only briefly, because of '. . . frustration with Nigerian society, its inefficiency, the chauvinism of the men and the treachery of the educated women (in knowingly sacrificing their independence to materialism)'.[14] One cannot accuse her of abdicating her duty, however. 'It is through Buchi Emecheta,' points out a critic, 'that the souls of Nigerian women in the various social strata are revealed. The aspirations and fear of her characters are, to some extent, those of every woman.'[15]

[1] Marie Umeh, 'African women in transition in the novels of Buchi Emecheta', *Présence Africaine*, no. 116, 1980, p. 190
[2] *Ibid.*
[3] *Ibid.*, p. 191
[4] *Africa Woman*, no. 2, Jan. 1976
[5] Buchi Emecheta, 'Out of the ditch and into print', *West Africa*, 3 April 1978, p. 671
[6] Umeh, 'African women in transition', p. 191
[7] Roberta Rubenstein, 'Buchi Emecheta. Second class citizen', *World Literature Written in English*, vol. 15, no. 1, 1976, p. 72
[8] 'Arts and Africa', no. 127, BBC African Service transcript (London)
[9] Margaret R. Lauer, 'Buchi Emecheta. The Bride Price', *World Literature Written in English*, vol. 16, no. 2, 1977, p. 310
[10] Peter Tinniswood, *The Times*, 24 June 1976
[11] *Matchet's Diary*, *West Africa*, 6 Feb. 1978, p. 238
[12] Umeh, 'African women in transition', p. 196
[13] *Ibid.*, p. 199
[14] Wendy Davies, 'Two Nigerian women writers', *Centrepoint*, vol. 3, no. 9, Nov./Dec. 1981
[15] Umeh, 'African women in transition', p. 201

Nuruddin Farah

born 1945   SOMALI REPUBLIC

Nuruddin Farah himself claims, 'I'm a problem to most reviewers'[1] and indeed his work, while receiving wide acclaim in Britain, has been almost totally ignored in Africa and to a large extent in America. He does not conform comfortably to any particular mould. Politically he has challenged both right and left. While he has written more sympathetically about women than almost any other African writer, he has also portrayed them harshly enough to have been accused of misogyny; his books have been regarded as thrillers but also as 'writing in the best traditions of Solzhenitsyn and Gabriel Garcia Márquez . . .'[2]

He was born in Baidoa in what was then Italian Somalia, and educated at secondary level at Shashamanne School in Ethiopia and at the Institutio di Magistrale di Mogadishu. He worked briefly in the Ministry of Education in Somalia before studying abroad. In 1966 he moved to India and studied philosophy and literature at the Panjab University at Chandigarh for four years.

He left India in 1970, the year in which *From a Crooked Rib* was published. Its heroine, the young nomadic girl Ebla, breaks away from traditional society – which regards women as no better than Adam's 'crooked rib' – and acts upon her 'resentment of the role she must play as a woman in Somali culture, with its subordination, vulnerability, and constant dreary labour'.[3] A speaker at the Horizons '79 Festival in Berlin said: 'There is no single African novel about women that poses the question of women's status and dignity as sensitively as *From a Crooked Rib*. Why is it that a writer from Somalia, above all one with an Arab cultural background, should be successful in this?'[4] In an interview Nuruddin Farah said: 'I am conscious of the role that women should play in societies.' He is critical of societies which use only half their human potential, and observes that 'Whether it is in the most technologically advanced societies or the least-informed societies, you will find that women are given a very minor role. They are chained hand and foot to domestication, to household chores.'[5]

He taught in Mogadishu for the next four years, at the Dhagaxtur and Wardhigley Secondary Schools and at the National University of Somalia. During this time he wrote in Somali. A novel and a novella were serialized (as had been the novel *Why Dead So Soon*) in the *Somali News* in 1965.

From 1974 to 1976, Nuruddin Farah resided in Britain studying at the Universities of London and Essex. He was also attached to the Royal Court Theatre in London for eight months. *The Offering*, a play, was accepted in lieu of an M.A. thesis by Essex University. He had started writing plays while in India, and had had a revue – *Doctor and Physicist* – broadcast in 1968. A three-hour stage play and two plays commissioned by the BBC followed. The short-story genre has also attracted him, and over 20 stories have been published in India, Somalia, the United States and Britain.

In 1976 he published *A Naked Needle*, an attempt to assess the state of Somalia in the mid 1970s, viewed through the lens of Koschin, the central protagonist. 'It is an intellectual novel, thoroughly cosmopolitan in its approach and assumptions; no excuses are made for its Somali origins or setting . . .'[6] Koschin, says Nuruddin Farah, is confused, and

> he finds himself in an ideologically confused country – a man who has no priorities whatsoever apart from the primary essence of day to day survival, a man whose only function is to think. But since he lives in squalor, and in an ideologically confused society, he becomes inarticulate. He is also full of hate, not only towards himself but towards women – towards everything else.[7]

Nuruddin Farah moved to Rome in 1976, and lived there for three years. His aim was to research into Italian culture, but the book arising out of that stay was rooted in Somalia – *Sweet and Sour Milk* (1979). It is the first part of a trilogy and 'tells the tale of those who do *not* compromise'. *Sardines* (1981) 'is about those who do compromise', and the third part will be about the traditional elements of the society, the patriarchy.[8] A military coup in 1969 brought Siad Barre to power in Somalia. *Sweet and Sour Milk* (which won the 1980 English Speaking Union Literary Award) is derived from Nuruddin's experiences then: 'I lived in Somalia during that period and I remember the pain on people's faces. This inspired me to write the novel.'[9]

The mysterious death of Soyaan, economic adviser to the president, involves his brother Loyaan in Machiavellian intrigues as the novel unfolds. It is not a simple thriller, for, as a reviewer observes,

> the movement of this novel does not hinge on the mechanics of plot, rather it is an evocation of the confusion and terror created by living in a police state. This evocation derives its brilliance from the fact that the plot never actually materialises – it is a plot that Loyaan is searching for and never finds.[10]

It may be the Russian-backed Siad Barre regime which receives Nuruddin Farah's condemnation in this novel, but he draws a careful distinction: 'I didn't attack society here; I attacked a regime. A regime is not a society.'[11] His distaste for the ideological basis of such regimes is clear:

> The Russians were the ones who built this cemented structure for Siad Barre. If the Russians had not come in, the Americans would . . . Siad Barre would use whatever means that are in his possession in order to continue remaining in power. One day Islam, the next day Communism, the third day Africanism, the fourth day Siadism, the fifth day Tribalism.[12]

This prolific writer has several works in the pipeline, including a completed film script which has not yet been put into production due to financial difficulties. He has been awarded a UNESCO Fellowship, and also a Fellowship from the United States Endowment for the Arts and Humanities.

His work, apart from *A Crooked Rib*, is not available in his own country. He lives abroad, has taught briefly at the University of Connecticut, and was visiting scholar at the African Studies Center at UCLA. He has been guest professor at Bayreuth, West Germany, and has now taken up an appointment at the University of Jos in Nigeria. He 'sees himself both as a nomad and as a cosmopolitan. This is by no means paradoxical, for a nomad carries his world with him wherever he goes. His country is everywhere.'[13]

---

[1] Personal communication
[2] C. Larson, *World Literature Today*, vol. 54, no. 3, May 1980, p. 395

[3] David F. Beer, 'Somali literature in European languages', *Horn of Africa*, vol. 2, no. 4, Oct./Dec. 1979, p. 33

[4] Al Imfeld, 'Portraits of African writers', no. 3, Deutsche Welle transcript (Cologne, 1979), p. 1

[5] 'Nuruddin Farah: committed writer', *New African*, Jan. 1979, p. 85

[6] Beer, 'Somali literature', p. 34

[7] 'Nuruddin Farah', p. 85

[8] 'Arts and Africa', no. 305P, BBC African Service transcript (London)

[9] *Ibid.*

[10] Leonie Rushforth, review in *Bananas*, Feb. 1980

[11] 'Arts and Africa', no. 305P, BBC African Service transcript (London)

[12] *Ibid.*

[13] Imfeld, 'Portraits of African writers', p. 2

Joe de Graft

1924–1978   GHANA

Born into a Fante family in Cape Coast in the 1920s, Joe de Graft grew up in one world; he was to win a reputation as playwright, poet and actor in another – the dramatic years of Ghana's independence. His work drew upon this breadth of experience, and in his own vivid metaphor: 'My imaginative life is like a fire that feeds on more than charcoal: butane gas, electricity, palm-oil, petrol as well as dry cow-dung and faggots have kept it burning.'[1]

De Graft received his early education at Mfantsipim and Achimota Schools. Then at the University College of the Gold Coast he was one of the first undergraduates to take English Honours. His degree work included a special paper on drama, and when he returned to Mfantsipim as a teacher, de Graft made a point of developing drama at the school. The University of Science and Technology lured him away to initiate their drama programme. In 1961 he was seconded to serve as director of the newly established Ghana Dance Studio. The demands were diverse:

> Being director of this studio meant producing plays, acting in them, training young Ghanaians who wanted to be related to the theatre, doing radio plays, trying to encourage school drama programs, and carrying out general research. It was an amorphous program that gave me a lot of scope.[2]

Arising out of that, de Graft instituted the theatre arts programme for the School of Music and Drama at the University of Ghana in 1963. The same year also saw the publication of his play *Sons and Daughters*. Of his intentions in writing his study of conflict between generations, he says: 'I was trying to make young people aware that their lives were important and could be looked at in this way, that they had a right to examine life as they saw it from their own perspective.'[3] Another successful venture of this period was the staging of his *Visitors from the Past* by the Ghana Dance Studio in 1963; a revised version was to be published as *Through a Film Darkly* seven years later.

A UNESCO grant enabled him to go to Nairobi in 1969 as a specialist in the teaching of English as a second language. His dramatic interests soon asserted themselves, and he joined the staff of the University of Nairobi to teach drama in the Faculty of Education. This was also a period which demonstrated de Graft's range as an actor. His performances on stage and television included a memorable Othello and the part of Muntu in his own play of that name. While at Nairobi he was commissioned to write this play, to convey the message of the African Churches to the World Council of Churches. *Muntu* was 'my first attempt at writing for a really adult audience'.[4] Of the play Simon Gikandi has observed: 'De Graft's greatest achievement in *Muntu* ... lies in his ability to bring onto one plane the whole history of the continent in spite of its expansiveness, and to present in one well woven organ a wide range of themes.'[5]

Whether writing, producing or acting, theatre obviously meant a great deal to de Graft over many years. Towards the end of his life he noted ruefully that African theatre was moving towards commercialism, 'to entertaining people for money', and he feared that this risked the loss of the essence of theatre. Specifically he thought that 'theatre at its most beautiful is ritual', and added,

It's closely related to religion, to rediscovering our lost selves, re-energizing ourselves. To put it simply, theatre at the centre is religion and ritual. To hell with all this business of shaking your bottom and getting money for it, or splashing light on fancy costumes![6]

Poetry, a complementary side of de Graft's creative expression, has provided a constant outlet for his ideas and responses. Some of his poems were included in *Messages*, a 1970 anthology of Ghanaian verse selected by Awooner and Adali-Mortty, and in 1975 a collection of his own work, *Beneath the Jazz and Brass*, brought together poems written over three decades – 'a sort of inner auto-biography'.[7]

De Graft died in November 1978 not long after returning from Kenya to his native Ghana. An obituary of this 'elder statesman of Ghanaian letters' recorded that a younger generation of the country's writers 'had learned to look up to him as a monumental figure, teacher and practitioner in one'.[8]

[1] K. Awoonor and G. Adali-Mortty, eds., *Messages: Poems from Ghana* (London, 1970), p. 179
[2] Bernth Lindfors, 'Interview with Joe de Graft', *World Literature Written in English*, vol. 8, no. 2, 1979, pp. 319–20
[3] *Ibid.*, p. 319
[4] *Ibid.*, p. 316
[5] Simon Gikandi, *Africa*, no. 79, March 1978
[6] Lindfors, 'Interview', p. 324
[7] Obituary in *West Africa*, 1 January 1979
[8] *Ibid.*

Bessie Head
born 1937   SOUTH AFRICA

Born in Pietermaritzburg, South Africa, of mixed parentage, Bessie was sent to foster parents until the age of thirteen. She then attended a mission school until she turned eighteen. Teacher training, a four-year stint of teaching, and a couple of years working on *Drum* magazine as a journalist were to follow. An unsuccessful marriage, together with involvement in the trial of a friend, led her to apply for a teaching post in Botswana. Her precarious refugee status lasted fifteen years until she was granted Botswanan citizenship in 1979.

The element of exile is important in her work, albeit in an indirect manner. Ogungbesan elaborates on this theme:

> She fits into a pattern which is now familiar to the whole world – the writer in exile – and, like other writers in exile, she has carried with her the mental stresses and strains of her home country, even while describing the landscape and people of her adopted country. Miss Head is remarkable among South African writers living in exile. Intensely urbanized, practically all of them ... have settled in the cities of America and Western Europe. But Miss Head has settled in Botswana where she has participated in an experiment in rural self-sufficiency. Her fierce determination to take root and grow in this unfamiliar terrain accounts for her distinctive vision of alienation.[1]

She was part of the refugee community

based at Bamangwato Development Farm in Botswana, and she says:

> My first novel, *When Rain Clouds Gather*, grew out of this experience . . . It is my only truly South African work, reflecting a black South African viewpoint. The central character in the novel, a black South African refugee, is almost insipid, a guileless, simple-hearted simpleton. But that is a true reflection of the black South African personality. We are an oppressed people, who have been stripped bare of every human right. We do not know what it is like to have our ambitions aroused, nor do we really see liberation on an immediate horizon. Botswana was a traumatic experience to me and I found the people, initially, extremely brutal and harsh, only in the sense that I had never encountered human ambition and greed before in a black form.[2]

By 1973 she had published two more novels, *Maru* and *A Question of Power*. *Maru* addresses the question of racialism although not between white and black: it is the despised Masarwa people who are the victims of discrimination by the Botswana people. Of the book, Head volunteers: 'With all my South African experience I longed to write an enduring novel on the hideousness of racial prejudice. But I also wanted the book to be so beautiful and so magical that I, as the writer, would long to read and re-read it.[3] As a so-called 'Coloured' she was able to envisage the position of Margaret, the heroic girl who chooses to announce that she is a Masarwan, and not a relatively privileged Coloured, as everyone had assumed.

One can discern common themes within her first two books, and *A Question of Power* (published in 1973) takes further the quest for good and evil, nobility, racism, the regenerative force of the land, and love. Ravenscroft points to the links:

> in *A Question of Power* we are taken nightmarishly into the central character's process of mental breakdown, through lurid cascades of hallucination and a pathological blurring of the frontiers between insanity and any kind of normalcy. It is precisely this journeying into the characters' most secret interior recesses of mind and (we must not fight shy of the word) of soul, that gives the three novels a quite remarkable cohesion

and makes them a sort of trilogy . . . It seems to me that . . . each novel both strikes out anew, and also re-shoulders the same burden. It is as if one were observing a process that involves simultaneously progression, introgression, and circumgression.[4]

Elizabeth, the central character, echoes experiences that Head herself endured – 'a private philosophical journey to the sources of evil'.[5] Once again, one sees the past looming up; in the words of Mzamane:

> Bessie Head's novel is certainly a powerful statement of the problem and process of evil as it has personally affected her . . . I see the insane element in the novel as a reflection of the evil world she has known . . . The novel is aimed at societies, black and white, where evil has been institutionalised and directed against individuals. It shows how evil can, when constantly and persistently willed upon one, lead to one's personality disintegration.[6]

The Collector of Treasures, a book of short stories, was published in 1977. In it she explores the position of women in Africa, a topic she had adumbrated in a guest column in *The Times* during the International Women's Year:

> The country is experiencing an almost complete breakdown of family life, and a high rate of illegitimate births . . . No one can account for it. It just happened somewhere along the line. A woman's place is no longer in the yard with her mother-in-law, but she finds herself as unloved outside the restrictions of custom, as she was within it.[7]

That she attributes the inferior position of women to history – 'frictions between men and women have a historical reason'[8] – and refutes the feminist label, has not diminished her popularity amongst feminists, which was evident during her four-month stay in Iowa in 1977 as a participant in the International Writers Program and during a visit to Denmark in 1980. The short stories also point to her growing interest in the past of Africa, where traditional society is examined without sentimentality.

Her creative interest in history was given full rein in *Serowe: The Village of the Rainwind*, which appeared in 1981. It consists of interviews with the people of

Serowe, falling into three categories: those talking about the period of Khama the Great (1875–1923), life in the era of Tshekedi Khama (1926–59), and life during the Swaneng Project, under Patrick van Rensburg, from 1963 onwards.

By recording for posterity the words of the traditional historian, the retired school-teacher, the traditional potmaker, tanner, farmer, basket-maker and hut-builder – alongside the experiences of those who have participated more recently in the school, the tannery brigade, the farmers' brigade and all the other offshoots of the Swaneng Project – Bessie Head has made a quite unique contribution to her country of refuge and to our understanding of how societies develop and change.[9]

By her own assessment, Bessie Head's involvement in the Swaneng Project brought her peace of mind. 'In South Africa, all my life I lived in shattered little bits. All those shattered bits began to grow together here ... I have a peace against which all the turmoil is worked out!'[10]

Finally one has to confront her impatience with politicians and politics in the conventional sense, and as one interviewer perceived:

The first encounter with Bessie Head is not easy. Many Africans cannot understand how, living so close to South Africa and with such a background, she always lays stress on unpolitical things. But, reading her work, one soon becomes aware of what she means by 'politics' – empty words, eternal promises, a short cut to Paradise, something unreal and therefore ineffective ... And one suddenly realises that she is leading one into new depths, new sources, into the 'village' and the countryside, towards a fresh start. Here, swords are turned into ploughshares, we learn to listen to our hearts instead of manifestos, start to live from the depths of inner feeling rather than empty words. Isn't this a form of politics – perhaps a more fruitful form?[11]

[1] Kolawole Ogungbesan, 'The Cape gooseberry also grows in Botswana: alienation and commitment in the writings of Bessie Head', *Présence Africaine*, no. 109, 1979, pp. 92–3
[2] Bessie Head, 'Social and political pressures that shape literature in Southern Africa', *World Literature Written in English*, vol. 18, no. 1, 1979, pp. 22–3
[3] *Ibid.*, p. 23
[4] Arthur Ravenscroft, 'The novels of Bessie Head', in C. Heywood, ed., *Aspects of South African Literature* (London, 1976), p. 175
[5] Head, 'Social and political pressures', p. 24
[6] Mbulelo V. Mzamane, *New Classic*, 4, 1977
[7] Bessie Head, *The Times*, 13 Aug. 1975
[8] Sasha Moorsom, 'No bars to expression', *New Society*, 19 February 1981, p. 35
[9] 'Arts and Africa', no. 392G, BBC African Service transcript (London) [1981]
[10] Betty McGinnis Fradkin, 'Conversations with Bessie', *World Literature Written in English*, vol. 17, no. 2, Nov. 1978 p. 429
[11] Al Imfeld, 'Portraits of African writers', no. 3, Deutsche Welle transcript (Cologne, 1979), p. 9

Luís Bernardo Honwana
born 1942   MOZAMBIQUE

With the publication in 1969 of the English version of *Nós Matamos o Cão Tinhoso* (We Killed Mangy-Dog and Other Mozambique Stories) in Heinemann's African Writers Series, Luís Bernardo Honwana instantly became known as an important lusophone prose writer. Yet as a budding author he was not at all sure of the literary merit of his work: 'I don't know if I really am a writer ... This book of stories is a testimony in which I try to portray a series of situations and proceedings that perhaps might be of interest.'[1]

In fact, as critics have pointed out, Honwana's modesty is not justified.

Russell Hamilton has noted that 'Honwana's work revealed a visible natural talent for storytelling'.[2] Donald Burness has alluded to his 'profound insight into the psychological dehumanization of both black and white living under a system that ultimately destroys the best instincts of all men'.[3]

Honwana's stories are characterized by understatement. He chooses to show the suffering caused by colonialism; but he does not overtly lecture the reader. In an as yet untitled novel that he has recently finished, a work set in 1924 in a Mozambican village near the South African border, Honwana has continued to express himself with his wonted objectivity and understanding.

One of nine children, Honwana was born in Maputo in November 1942, and until the age of seventeen he lived with his family in Moamba, a suburb of the capital. While completing his secondary education, Honwana worked as a journalist, and he also became interested in books and painting. Like many lusophone African writers, Honwana was imprisoned by colonialist authorities. He was released in 1967 after three years of confinement. He then went to live in Portugal, where he worked and studied for three years. He later went to Switzerland, Algeria and Tanzania before returning to Mozambique in order to work in the cabinet of the Prime Minister of the transitional government. Today Honwana works as Chief of Staff of the President of Mozambique.

Apart from his achievements in literature, Honwana has made several documentary films. One of them, made with Murillo Sales, and entitled *Estas São as Armas*, was awarded a prize at the Leipzig Film Festival in 1978. Honwana is also an accomplished photographer and one of the heads of the Organization of Mozambican Journalists.

[1] Introduction to *Nós Matamos o Cão Tinhoso* (Laurenço Marques, 1964)
[2] Russell Hamilton, *Voices from an Empire* (Minneapolis, 1975), p. 213
[3] Donald Burness, *Fire: Six Writers from Angola, Mozambique and Cape Verde* (Washington DC, 1977), p. 104

Chukwuemeka Ike
born 1931   NIGERIA

Satirist and chronicler of the many-faceted world of education in Nigeria, Chukwuemeka Ike, probably more than any other of his country's writers, has found the matter out of which he has fashioned his novels by delving directly into his professional experiences. As Assistant Registrar for student affairs at the University of Ibadan from 1957 and 1960, then as Deputy Registrar and Registrar of the young University of Nigeria at Nsukka from 1960 to 1971, Ike was a privileged onlooker of Nigerian university life. Both positions, to which one must certainly add the memory of his student days at University College Ibadan where he received his B.A., gave him valuable insights into the undergraduate community, the principle focus of *Toads for Supper*, and into the growing pains and power struggles at young Nigerian universities (involving expatriate and local elements on campus), the underlying theme of a second university novel, *The Naked Gods*. For Oyin Ogunba the intrigue and power play in this novel 'make the atmosphere . . . look more like that of a political electioneering arena rather than that of a university set up for the pursuit of knowledge and truth'.[1] Another critic, Gerald Moore, notes how Ike has managed to blend fact and fiction in this work:

> The strength of this book is that all the intrigues have a familiar ring, without its being a mere *roman à clef*. Anyone acquainted with the chief academic scandals of Nigerian universities in the past twenty years will recognize many of them here, but the mixture and the relish are Mr Ike's own.[2]

Ike has also examined the university through the practised eye of a social scientist, putting to profit his stay at Stanford University in California where he obtained an M.A., to complete research on an academic study of Nigerian universities, *University Development in Africa: The Nigerian Experience* (Oxford University Press, 1976).

During the Nigerian Civil War, Ike, an

Igbo born in Ndikelionwu near Awka in Eastern Nigeria, served the Biafran cause as Provincial Refugee Officer for Umahuia Province. His wartime experiences, not surprisingly, have surfaced in yet another novel, *Sunset at Dawn*. It is the story of Dr Kanu, an Igbo doctor who has been appointed Biafra's Director of Mobilization, and of his northern-born wife, Fatima, a trained hospital technician. Fatima learns to overcome personal tragedy and to become the best of Biafran patriots and the loving daughter-in-law of her husband's parents, offering her services as a refugee worker after the deaths of both son and husband and assuming the care of her elderly parents-in-law just as her husband would have done. The irony Ike deliberately creates, in building his novel around an Igbo–Hausa marriage amidst a war in which easterners were supposed to hate northerners, reveals the kinds of wartime complexities that Ike has tried to convey in his novel. This has led one critic to say: 'Mr Ike gives the impression that he is scrupulously fair, though passionately committed.'[3]

Ike's most recent novels, *The Chicken Chasers* and *Expo '77*, show traces of yet another aspect of his professional career – that of Chief Executive of the West African Examinations Council located in Accra, Ghana, a position he held from 1971 to 1979. In *The Chicken Chasers* Ike casts his satirist's eye on a pan-African cultural organization, noting how little time national delegates spend on planning cultural strategies for Africa and how much on plotting and womanizing. *Expo '77* is a mystery story with a difference. No ordinary tale of cops and robbers, it has a special inspector getting to the bottom of 'leaked' examination papers for the Nigerian Examinations Board. The Board is headed by the scrupulous Dr Buka who fears his appointment will not be renewed if the racket is not stopped. The novel gives elaborate details of the lengths to which ingenious Nigerian students go in order to get a pass mark in a national examination. One wonders if these were the sort of shenanigans Ike and his staff

of the West African Examination Council had to contend with!

Despite what would appear as overpowering evidence, Ike warns the reader to beware of finding too close a resemblance between his own life and the lives of his fictional heroes. In an interview published in 1976 (but recorded in 1973) Ike strongly resists the suggestion that his novels are autobiographical, admitting, however, that a writer 'draws from personal experiences, direct experience and also indirect experience. You chat with people and you pick up things from them. A writer has his eyes wide open all the time . . .'[4]

Ike means his warning in particular to apply to *The Potter's Wheel*, the only one of his novels set in the past. It is the account of the schooling – a maturing and toughening process – of a nine-year-old mama's boy. If Ike refuses to be identified with little Obu, he has surely incorporated into the novel memories of his own school days, which included studies at the prestigious Government College in Umuahia, the school to which the boy hero of *The Potter's Wheel* aspires to go to when he finally realizes that education is 'good for him'. The novel also undoubtedly draws upon Ike's intimate knowledge of the day-to-day life in a school that comes from having been a schoolmaster in elementary and secondary schools for six years up to 1956, prior to beginning his career in university administration.

In the 1973 interview with John Agetua of the *Sunday Observer* (Lagos) Chukwuemeka Ike spoke at length about his writing technique and style. He outlines his novels chapter by chapter and determines the physical appearance of his characters. He tries to be careful in choosing names of characters – a friend once chided him for using his name for a rather dubious character. He visually imagines the settings of his novels, and for a novel like *The Naked Gods* he even used a photograph as a reminder 'of the campus [he] intended to describe'.[5] As for his use of language, Bernth Lindfors calls Ike a follower of Achebe and has written about Ike's 'Igbo prose style' which is evident even in a non-village novel like *Toads for Supper.*[6] Ike's most recent novels, however, contain no Igbo mannerisms, seeming to corroborate what Ike says himself about his style: 'My style has grown from my literary upbringing, from what I was taught especially in the secondary school [but it also] depends on my subject matter . . . I don't think I have any literary antecedents. It's just something that has grown with me with time.'[7] Ike's sense of humour, however, he shared with his father who '. . . was a humorous man. I also find that humour is a good quality to have if you want to survive in a difficult world.'[8]

In the same interview Ike mentions plans for a novel about military rule in Africa, a subject that 'intrigues' him: 'I'm hoping to use contemporary events to project the reader into the future.'[9] It is almost ten years since that interview and there has been no sign so far of this novel although three others have appeared in that time. Ike gave up full-time public service in the summer of 1979, and we can perhaps expect him to fulfil his promise now.

[1] Oyin Ogunba, 'The image of the university in Nigerian fiction', *West African Journal of Modern Languages*, no. 2, 1976, p. 130
[2] Gerald Moore, review of *The Naked Gods*, *Okike*, vol. 1, no. 3, Sept. 1972, pp. 61–2
[3] D. A. N. Jones, 'The birth and death of Biafra', *Times Literary Supplement*, 9 July 1976, p. 860
[4] John Agetua, 'Interview with Chukwuemeka Ike' in *Interview With Six Nigerian Writers*, (Benin City, Nigeria, 1976), p. 40
[5] *Ibid.*, p. 36
[6] Bernth Lindfors, 'Yoruba and Igbo prose styles in English' in *Folklore in Nigerian Literature* (New York, 1973), pp. 153–75.
[7] Agetua, 'Interview with Chukwuemeka Ike', p. 36
[8] *Ibid.*, p. 36
[9] *Ibid.*, p. 39

Cheikh Hamidou Kane
born 1928   SENEGAL

Although not published until 1961, *L'Aventure ambiguë* (*Ambiguous Adventure* in Heinemann's African Writers Series edition), dates from 1952 when the author, like his fictional hero, Samba Diallo, was pursuing his university education in Paris. The novel first took the form of a diary or daily observations that Kane wrote to allay the anxiety and solitude he felt at being cut off from the cultural milieu in which he had been raised.[1] The autobiographical elements in the novel are striking. Like the hero of *Ambiguous Adventure*, Kane comes from the region of Matam along the Senegal River in north-eastern Senegal (called Diallobé country in the novel). And like Samba Diallo, Cheikh Hamidou Kane was brought up according to strict Muslim traditions. For the first ten years of his life he was educated entirely in a Koranic school and spoke only the Fulbe language of the Toucouleur people. In just three years after enrolling in the colonial school, however, Kane learned French and obtained his primary school leaving certificate. He then left his region to complete his secondary studies in Dakar and went to Paris in 1952 to study law and philosphy, earning a degree in both subjects in 1959. That same year he also graduated from a two-year professional training course for overseas administrators at the Ecole Nationale de la France d'Outre-Mer, writing his second-year dissertation on the 'Principles and means of French technical assistance'.

Ambiguous Adventure was awarded the Grand Prix Littéraire d'Afrique Noire in 1962. Its publication the previous year had been hailed as a major event in francophone African literature. In both content and form the novel goes beyond the specific social situation (the Toucouleur Muslim society) and historical context (French colonialism) which were its inspiration. The symmetry of the novel's two-part structure, and elegance and 'high seriousness' of Kane's French language and the gravity of its theme 'of which the profound truth is wholly sad',[2] fuse into an aesthetic whole and give the novel its classic proportions. 'The unusual strength, the exalting poetry, the constantly renewed beauty of the language, make *Ambiguous Adventure* that rare work that is unique in African literature, a work that is both a mystic drama and a philosophical tale – all within the apparently sparse framework of the *récit*.'³

The novel's hero is a young man who yearns for the spiritual unity that his koranic upbringing had instilled in him but who, nonetheless, leaves it behind and embarks – not out of personal choice but as an emissary of his society – on a quest for Western education that results in tragedy. Critic Lilian Kesteloot, says of the theme of acculturation that Kane 'poses with an art and profundity unparalleled to date in world literature'.⁴

Cheikh Hamidou Kane, to all appearances, has resolved for himself the dilemma of cultural ambiguity that pursues Samba Diallo to the end of the novel. In a literary meeting held in Dakar in 1965 and attended by such writers as Sembène Ousmane, Ousmane Socé, Tchicaya U Tam'si, Camara Laye, Birago Diop and Abdou Anta Ka, Kane made the following declaration:

> I am a Moslem; not every black man is a Moslem. I am a Toucouleur; not every black man is a Toucouleur. I have been schooled in the West; not every black man has been schooled in the West – by that I mean in the school of Western Europe. And there, I think, lies my problem. I cannot reject, I cannot deliberately get rid of these elements in myself. I am obliged to accept them, and that not just in theory but as part of my daily life. I think this is to some extent reflected in my book, and not only there but in all my actions. There is nothing deliberate about this; it is just my life.⁵

On that same occasion Kane gave his point of view on two much-debated issues, negritude and the language question:

> I believe there to be a Negro aesthetic, and perhaps black artists also have their own characteristic sensibility or way of approach; but to say that these permanent factors represent the whole dimension or characteristics of *Négritude* seems to me to be confusing the container with its contents ... I do not reject Négritude in any way ... but ... the time is coming when, without wishing to deny any of that we must nevertheless give up trying to bring everything down to it ... To act otherwise would itself, I think, be a

new form of imperialism. Moreover, it would also be to split the solidarity that unites us with the rest of mankind.⁶

As for the problem of African writers who are obliged to write in a non-African tongue, Kane takes a very pragmatic approach:

> our languages need modernizing and we need to learn to write them, we need to teach them, and to use them. But meanwhile, until this has all been done, are we to do nothing else? Are we not to live or express ourselves? Are we to call a halt to all evolution? My own answer would be no; nor do I think there is anyone whose answer would be yes. But without exactly saying yes to these questions, it is possible to adopt a kind of half-way attitude, especially with regard to the question of sitting with our arms folded and waiting until we have forged a language of our own.⁷

One may legitimately wonder whether Kane will ever publish a second novel or whether *Ambiguous Adventure* will remain a lone masterpiece. Kane has spoken of a second novel that 'like *Ambiguous Adventure* will show the effects of the collision of divergent cultures, but concern itself as well with the emergence of traditional Africa into the contemporary world.'⁸ One explanation for Kane's failure to produce the second novel could be lack of writing time. Since his return to Africa in 1959 he has had an absorbing career in public service. He has been Director of the Department of Economic Planning and Development for Senegal, Governor of the region of Thiès, and Commissioner of Planning in Mamadou Dia's government. Kane also worked for a number of years in the seventies as an official for UNICEF in Lagos and Abidjan. He is at present Senegal's Minister of Industrial Development.

¹ Roger Mercier and M. and S. Battestini, eds., *Littérature Africaine 1: Cheikh Hamidou Kane, écrivain sénégalais* (Paris, 1967)
² *Ambiguous Adventure*, translated from the French by Katherine Woods (London, 1972), p. 51
³ Mercier and Battestini, *Cheikh Hamidou Kane*, p. 14 (editors' translation)
⁴ Quoted in John Erickson, *Nommo: African Fiction in French South of the Sahara* (York, South Carolina, 1979); p. 187

⁵ G. D. Killam, ed., *African Writers on African Writing* (London, 1973), p. 153
⁶ *Ibid.*, pp. 152–3
⁷ *Ibid.*, pp. 153–4
⁸ Erickson, *Nommo*, p. 189

Legson Kayira

born *c*.1940   MALAWI

Legson Kayira was born in a village in the bush country of pre-Independence Nyasaland (now Malawi). Educated by Presbyterian missionaries in Nyasaland's Livingstonia mission school, Legson Kayira decided that he, like the Abraham Lincoln he had studied, would somehow rise above his childhood penury and serve the interests of his country and people. He decided to go the United States to be educated. Lacking funds and passport, but carrying a Bible and a copy of *Pilgrim's Progress*, he set out on foot to travel 2,500 miles across Africa, from Nyasaland to Khartoum. Here, with the assistance of the US consul, he was accepted for study at Skagit Valley Junior College in Washington. Legson adopted the motto of his Nyasaland secondary school, 'I Will Try', for the title of his autobiography, a book recounting his determined struggle and his adventurous two-year 2,500-mile trek. The winner of the Northwest Non-fiction Prize, it was initially published in 1965, and was reissued by Longman in an abridged, simplified edition suitable for lower secondary-school students.

After completing the two-year course at Skagit, Kayira enrolled in the University of Washington, majoring in political science. He obtained his degree and went on to Cambridge University on a two-year postgraduate scholarship.

Legson Kayira is the author of two novels: *The Looming Shadow*, published in 1968 and reissued in paperback in Collier's African/American Library in 1970, and *Jingala*, released in 1969 in both London and New York. Of *The Looming Shadow*, Kayira says 'it fills up what I probably missed out in *I Will Try*, namely my background. This is a story of a village and its people.'¹ Ezekiel Mphahlele finds it

> a tale of scalding malice . . . it leaves little or no room for romanticism . . . He captures the quality of village life, a life that is changing even while the shadow of the past lingers. Kayira is good at sketching the surface of things in this village life: the landscape, festivities, physical appearances, of people, the ordeal etc.²

Kayira would have liked to write this book in his native language, for as he says, 'I was sitting on my mother's verandah for a good part of the writing, looking at the system, and if I had been able to get a publisher to put it out in Timbuka, I would have written it in Timbuka.'³

Of *Jingala*, the author notes, 'The story is basically a feud between a 50-year-old man and his 18-year-old son. The theme is similar – the conflict of old and new.'⁴

When asked his opinion on the role to be played by the writer in Africa, Legson Kayira said:

> Certainly the writer is serving a purpose – books by and about Africans for schools are very important. Now that the way is being opened up for these writers to come up and write their own books, I think that their chances of playing a large role in society have increased so that a writer has just as much role to play in society as a politician.⁵

In 1971 Longman published Kayira's novel, *The Civil Servant*. The writer's fifth novel, *The Detainee*, published in 1974 in the African Writers Series, deals with the pertinent question of dictatorship. The insidious way in which innocent and ignorant people are trapped in the machinations of tyranny is poignantly dealt with.

¹ 'Legson Kayira from Malawi, author of *I Will Try* and *The Looming Shadow*, interviewed by Margaret Henry', *Cultural Events in Africa*, no. 41, 1968, p. 1
² Ezekiel Mphahlele, 'The Looming Shadow, L. Kayira', *The Jewel of Africa*, vol. 2, no. 1, 1969, p. 40
³ *Cultural Events in Africa*, no. 41
⁴ *Ibid.*
⁵ *Ibid.*

Keorapetse William Kgositsile

born 1938   SOUTH AFRICA

Kgositsile is an exile from South Africa, who has achieved a remarkable degree of assimilation into the American black intelligentsia. He places a good deal of importance on geographical origins and ethnic roots, and remains a vociferous spokesman for Africa. 'The major difference', he maintains, 'between the condition of the African and that of the Afroamerican in relation to the oppressor' is the question of land:

> when the African gets sick of the oppressor and finally decides to do something about it, he can fight to reown his land and establish his veritable social institutions. The Afroamerican, uprooted, uncertain about the right to own a specific bit of land, when he gets sick of the oppressor, he has to withdraw within himself to search for a system of values to strike the necessary balance to enable himself to breathe under the sun.¹

He feels that it is important to establish one's genesis; 'until you are clear about your identity and roots there can be no self-respect'. Without such self-respect, respect for others is also impossible. Only through historical and social self-awareness – 'until you know who you are in Our Time . . . until you know who you are ethically and aesthetically' – can the individual 'do anything of useful value to your community'.²

He went to Madibane High School in Johannesburg, and then wrote for the radical Cape Town journal *New Age* before leaving South Africa. There followed a stint in Tanzania, during which he worked for *Spearhead* magazine in Dar es Salaam. In the early sixties he began his association with America. He has been attached to a number of US institutions, including Lincoln University, the University of New Hampshire, Columbia University, and the New School for Social Research in New York. He was the recipient in 1969 of a National Endowment for the Arts grant, and served as poet-in-residence at the North Carolina Agricultural and Technical State University in Greensboro.

Kgositsile's poetry has been published in many journals including *Présence Africaine*, *Transition*, *Journal of Black Poetry*, and *The New African Literature*. He has been African editor-at-large for *Black Dialogue*. The first anthology of his own poems, *Spirits Unchained*, was published in 1969, and for it he was awarded the second Conrad Kent Rivers Memorial Prize. In the following year *For Melba* appeared, and in 1971 *My Name is Afrika*, which evoked this response:

> reading Kgositsile is to plunge into the maelstrom. The anger is . . . palpable, defiant, aggressive. The verse matches the tone with its sharp febrile lines, jumpy with a rhythm part deliberate, part merely agitation.³

A fourth anthology was published in 1975 – *The Present is a Dangerous Place to Live* – and this prolific poet added *Places and Bloodstains* in 1976, the year in which he was awarded the Harlem Cultural Council Literature Poetry Award. Kgositsile says of his own writing:

> I wrote, first of all, because I enjoyed writing. I also considered writing relevant to our goals, that is, instrumental in taking me closer to taking up arms against the oppressor after my consciousness had brought me to a more concrete level of creativity, collective social action, the only way to our liberation.

And of his aims, he declares:

> When I write every line I write will contain particles of poison for the oppressor; every line will either be an element of entertainment for us or it will be part of an attempt at commenting on or exploring where we are today, bringing out the uglinesses of this place and time in such a precise manner that,

hopefully, I will be adding something of use to the forces among us who try to persuade us through what they do to be people, to live again.[4]

He returned to Africa to teach at the University of Dar es Salaam in 1975. In 1980 he published *Herzspuren* (poems in German with English translations) and the proceeds from this went to the financial rescue of *The Voice of Women*, a magazine of the exiled African National Congress. He has also edited an anthology of poetry called *The Word is Here: Poetry from Modern Africa* (1973) and a substantial selection of his work is available in *Seven South African Arts*, edited by Cosmo Pieterse.

Kgositsile's is 'a very individual voice', concludes Oscar Dathorne:

> not merely an Afro-American poet or an African poet. He fuses the two roles into one, and the two experiences are one. His work shows that he is never at loggerheads with the Black society he describes. His is the truly universal Black voice.[5]

[1] Keorapetse Kgositsile, 'More steps toward our freedom', *Pan-African Journal*, vol. 11, no. 2, Spring 1969, p. 155
[2] *Ibid.*, p. 154
[3] John Povey, 'I am the voice: three South African poets', *World Literature Written in English*, vol. 16, no. 2, 1977, p. 271
[4] G. Brooks *et al.*, eds., *A Capsule Course in Black Poetry Writing* (Detroit, 1975), pp. 12, 15
[5] O. R. Dathorne, *African Literature in the Twentieth Century* (London, 1976), p. 215

Ahmadou Kourouma

born *c.*1927 IVORY COAST

Called 'undoubtedly one of the finest novels ever written by an African' by the Ghanaian critic Kwabena Britwum,[1] *Les Soleils des indépendances* (*The Suns of Independence*) is Ahmadou Kourouma's only published work to date, although he has also written a play, *Tougnantigui ou le diseur de vérité* which was performed in Abidjan in December 1972.

Kourouma was completely unknown when, in 1967, he submitted the manuscript for *The Suns of Independence* to the literary competition sponsored by *Etudes Françaises*, a French-Canadian publication. The novel subsequently won the journal's Prix de la Francité, and Kourouma was awarded his prize at the 1967 World Fair in Montreal. *The Suns of Independence* was published the following year by the Presses de l'Université de Montreal and in 1970 Seuil in Paris brought out the edition which is currently available in French. The novel has been translated into English by Adrian Adams for Heinemann's African Writers Series.

The Suns of Independence belongs thematically to the post-Independence 'novels of disillusion' that began to be written by both French-speaking and English-speaking Africans in the mid-sixties. Fama, the hero of the novel, is the last descendent of a long line of Malinke rulers. In the past a man of his birth would have known wealth, honour and glory. Modern times, however, have turned a once-noble prince into an illiterate *dioula* trader. He is hardly better than a beggar and has nothing to sell except the prestige of his name which, with luck, may bring in a few coins at funerals in the capital of the imaginary republic of Ebony Coast. Decreptitude is also the word that describes the present state of the ancestral home of the Doumbouya dynasty to which Fama belongs. Located up north in Malinke country, the royal court has been reduced to a few huts in an impoverished village peopled by a handful of toothless old men and women. Fama had eagerly awaited Independence as the time when the injustices he had suffered during colonialism – including forced labour and the supreme injustice of having his cousin appointed chief in his stead by the French – would be righted. But when the suns of Independence finally dawn, as the Malinke say, nothing changes for Fama. Worse, as portrayed in one of the novel's central images, he will become like the frail plant that withers and dies in the burning hot sun when the giant silk cotton trees which had overshadowed it is cut down. F. Salien calls the novel 'extremely appealing, not so much for its political satire, which other writers – like Fantouré – have successfully conveyed, as for the picture of the annoyances and problems, big and little, of the insignificant events of daily life of humble black people . . . who fatalistically scoff at their misery.'[2]

Critics have pointed out the originality of Kourouma's style in *The Suns of Independence*. The novel attempts to re-create Malinke speech patterns in the French not only through the use of images and proverbs but also in linguistic devices such as syntax. Nor does Kourouma hesitate to create words in French when he deems it necessary. He has explained the reasons for his experiments with language:

> When I wrote the book, I noted that Fama did not stand out well enough in the classical [French] style. I was not able, if you like, to express Fama from the inside, and that is when I tried to find a Malinke style. I would think in Malinke and put myself in Fama's skin to present things.[3]

For Jacques Chevrier the result of Kourouma's experiment is original and successful:

> [he] gives the impression of perfect mastery over his linguistic tool. Through a whole series of verbal interferences, collisions and borrowings he succeeds in bridging the gap between the depth of his imagination, on the one hand, and the language in which he relates his experience, on the other.[4]

Some African writers have reacted very negatively to *The Suns of Independence*, claiming that the novel's message is, at best, ambiguous and confusing, and at worst, reactionary. As proof they point to Kourouma's current life style – he is an actuary and heads the Inter-African Insurance Institute in Yaoundé – and the fact that he has seemingly abandoned

literature. In a radio interview recorded on the occasion of the First Festival of World Culture, held in Berlin in the summer of 1979, Kourouma answered his critics by honestly admitting that, however deeply Africa's problems affect him, he has been unable to find any personal solution for them: 'I am not happy, as I am very conscious of all the problems and I keep on thinking, "What happened – where are we going?" At the moment, of course, I cannot see any solutions.'[5]

Born in about 1927 in Boundiali, the Malinke area of northern Ivory Coast, Ahmadou Kourouma spent his early childhood in Guinea. He then studied at the Higher Technical School in Bamako from 1947 to 1949 but was expelled for his leadership in a student strike. He was drafted into the army by the French and sent to Abidjan and later transferred, for disciplinary reasons, to Indo-China after having refused to take part in actions to quell demonstrations organized by nationalist movements. He was able eventually to leave his combat unit and spent the remainder of his stay in Saigon working as an interpreter and radio broadcaster for the army. He retired from the army in 1954 and went to France to finish his studies. Intending to study aeronautical engineering at the Ecole Nationale d'Ingénieurs in Nantes he successfully passed the very rigorous entrance examination, but could not obtain a scholarship. He entered, instead, the Institute for Actuaries in Lyon. Upon graduation in 1959 he worked for a time in a bank in Paris before returning to the Ivory Coast in 1961. Ahmadou Kourouma has held important positions in the insurance and banking fields in Paris and Abidjan and was in charge of setting up Algeria's national insurance plan from 1964 to 1969.

A recording of an interview with Kourouma with Jacques Chevrier and of selected passages from his novel has been produced jointly by CLEF and Radio France Internationale in the 'Archives Sonores de la littérature noire' series.

[1] Kwabena Britwum, 'Tradition and social criticims in Ahmadou Kourouma's *Les Soleils des indépendances*', in Kolawole Ogungbesan,

ed., *New West African Literature* (London, 1979), p. 80

[2] F. Salien, 'Un anti-héroes: Fama', *Notre Librairie*, no. 60, June–August 1981, p. 69 (editors' translation)

[3] Quoted by Jacques Chevrier in 'Une écriture nouvelle', *Notre Librairie*, no. 60, June–August 1981, p. 70 (editors' translation)

[4] *Ibid.*, p. 75 (editors' translation)

[5] Al Imfeld, 'Portraits of African writers. 12: Ahmadou Kourouma', Deutsche Welle transcription, p. 5 (translated from the French by Jan Klingemann)

Mazisi (Raymond) Kunene

born 1930   SOUTH AFRICA

The true interpreters of African oral literature can only be Africans themselves. This literature cannot adequately be understood without the full knowledge of the language, customs and thought systems that are part of the ancient history of southern Africa, indeed of Africa as a whole.[1]

Kunene is himself a testament to his beliefs, and he has steeped himself in the Zulu heritage. In 1953 he took Zulu and History as the main subjects of a B.A. degree at the University of Natal. For his M.A. he undertook a survey of traditional and modern Zulu poetry. He followed this by studying Zulu literature at the School of Oriental and African Studies in London. He then became involved in politics and ran the London office of the African National Congress as the UK and European representative.

In 1970, his first collection, *Zulu Poems*, was published. He writes in Zulu and then translates his work. The poems contain a mixture of elements, 'the note of protest places him in the modern Black

South African tradition; the references to the ancestor make him a traditional poet'.[2] Another critic is struck by the way the book 'is rich in its illustration of African (Zulu) concepts of life, the universe, and pointedly, in its reaction to white domination'.[3]

Kunene has successfully combined the academic and political worlds: he was a founder member of the anti-apartheid movement; director of education for the South African United Front; and director of finance for the African National Congress in 1972. In his academic career, he was head of African Studies at the University of Iowa; he has taught at Stanford, and lectured widely. He now is associate professor in African Literature at the University of California, Los Angeles. His poetry has been published in many journals and anthologies, and his philosophy has recently been expressed in an article on the relevance of African cosmology.[4] He also wrote an introduction to a new edition of Césaire's *Return to my Native Land*.

In 1979 Kunene's epic work, *Emperor Shaka the Great*, was published, a mammoth praise-song which the poet himself has translated, but which has not yet been published in the original Zulu. The seventeen books comprising the epic encompass not only Kunene's conception of the legendary Shaka, differing in many respects from previous characterizations, but also Kunene's exploration of Zulu culture within an historical perspective. He spoke, in a 1966 interview with La Guma, of the wish 'to create, in the artistic and perhaps in the political world, a national ego'. His vision extends beyond the glorification of the Zulu empire, to encompass the experience of mankind in general, as he explained to La Guma,

> that general experience . . . must emphasize the oneness and the unity of man. And I think the important thing in doing this is that you in fact release the energies of the particular community, and it's able to reflect and create perpectives for its development, and its expression in general, realizing its context in the whole history of mankind.[5]

The fruits of many years labour were

seen in 1981 when his next epic, *Anthem of the Decades*, was published. In it the poet tells of the creation, the origin of life as conceived by an African community. He says

> And, since this is a discussion, basically, about a philosophy of life (which I think is what any religion is), the social expression of the philosophy of life of a particular community; the epic then deals with this philosophy, the beliefs in the ultimate destinies of man, and the belief in the actual history of the community itself.[6]

This work was influenced, Kunene says, by his great-grandmother, Maqandeyana, who told him early in life that 'knowledge is of the Ancestors', and left him to ponder these words: 'The secret of ancient wisdom lies in the name of things and their forgotten meanings'.[7]

K. L. Goodwin, in a new study of ten poets, evaluates Kunene's achievements highly:

> he has written the two most ambitious poems to come out of modern Africa. With modest confidence in the face of much discouragement, he has created from his Zulu inheritance two epics (and others that have not been translated or published yet) that are both thoroughly African and at the same time of international significance. His achievement may mark the end of the period when African poetry in English turned to Britain and America for its style and allusions. It may even mark the beginning of a reverse process, for his work is more substantial and inspired than that of other poets currently writing in English.[8]

In 1981 Doris Lessing chose *Anthem of the Decades* as one of her choice of three outstanding books of the year:

> A marvellous epic poem, like the same author's *Emperor Shaka the Great*. I suppose it goes without saying that the Zulu view of their history does not much resemble ours.[9]

A new volume of his poetry will be published in 1982 by Heinemann, *The Ancestors & the Sacred Mountain*. And of those poems which deal with the political situation in South Africa, Goodwin notices that Kunene 'has the confidence of the poet who speaks on behalf of the clan rather than as an individual agonized voice.'[10]

[1] Mazisi Kunene, 'South African oral traditions', in C. Heywood, ed., *Aspects of South African Literature* (London and New York, 1976), p. 41

[2] O. R. Dathorne, *African Literature in the Twentieth Century* (London, 1976), p. 215

[3] Tayo Olafioye, 'South African thoughts in poetry', *Ba Shiru*, vol. 6, no. 1, 1974, p. 7

[4] Mazisi Kunene, 'The relevance of African cosmological systems to African literature today', *African Literature Today*, no. 11 (London and New York, 1980), pp. 190–205

[5] Kunene interviewed by A. La Guma in D. Duerden and C. Pieterse, eds., *African Writers Talking* (London, 1972), p. 89

[6] *Ibid.*, p. 88

[7] Mazisi Kunene, *Anthem of the Decades* (London, 1981), p. ix

[8] K. L. Goodwin, *Understanding African Poetry: A Study of Ten Poets* (London, 1982), p. 209

[9] *The Observer* (London, 6 December, 1981)

[10] Goodwin, *op. cit.* p. 209

Alex La Guma

born 1925   SOUTH AFRICA

Jimmy La Guma was one of the leading figures in South Africa's non-white liberation movement. His son Alex was therefore raised in a politically conscious environment and likewise plotted a politically active course, a dangerous thing for a 'Coloured' in South Africa.

As a young man Alex La Guma joined the Communist party and became a member of its Cape Town district committee until 1950, when it was banned by the government. The authorities learned of his activities in 1955 when he helped to organize the South African representatives who drew up the Freedom Charter, a declaration of rights. Consequently in 1956 he was among the 156 people accused in the notorious Treason Trial, a charge which was dropped five years later.

His professional career took root in 1960, when he joined the staff of *New Age*, a progressive newspaper for which he wrote until August 1962. Always simultaneously involved in politics, by 1960 he was an executive member of the Coloured People's Congress and thus became one of 2,000 political prisoners detained for five months as a state of emergency was declared by the government after the violent incidents at Sharpeville and Langa. During this imprisonment, La Guma read voraciously and wrote. A year later he was again arrested, this time for his part in organizing a strike in protest against the Verwoerd republic. When South Africa's Sabotage Act was passed in the early sixties, it enabled the government to detain its opponents under house arrest without trial; in December 1962, La Guma became its victim. He was confined to his house for twenty-four hours a day, every day, for five years. Nothing he said or wrote was allowed to be quoted or printed in the republic. Before the five years elapsed, however, a No-Trial Act was passed in South Africa and La Guma and his wife were arrested and confined to solitary imprisonment. Though his wife was soon released, a longer time elapsed before La Guma himself was, and then on bail, for he was now charged with possessing banned literature, and again subjected to house arrest.

Though his work was not allowed to be published in South Africa, in 1962 Mbari in Ibadan issued Alex La Guma's first novel, *A Walk in the Night*. It was reissued by Heinemann and Northwestern University Press simultaneously in 1967 together with six of his short stories, three of which had appeared previously in *Black Orpheus*. This short work 'has distinct Dostoevskian overtones', claims Lewis Nkosi, himself a black South African who finds it 'inexcusable that European and American publishers who are in such indecent haste to put into print any mediocre talent from Africa have ignored this novel'.[1] Robert July describes it as 'a story on which is built a picture of such vividness and verisimilitude that one can almost taste and smell the air, the streets, the buildings against which the characters move in sure and full three-dimensional reality.'[2]

During his initial house arrest La Guma wrote his first full-length novel, *And a Threefold Cord*, published in 1964 in East Germany. While this dealt with events in a ghetto on the periphery of Cape Town, his experiences in prison thereafter prompted him to dedicate his novel *The Stone Country* 'to the daily 70351 prisoners in South African goals in 1964'.[3] This novel was published in 1967, at a time when his East German publishers, Seven Seas Books, were happy to announce that the La Guma family had arrived safely in Britain.

La Guma first established his literary career as a short-story writer with 'A Glass of Wine' and 'Slipper Satin', which appeared in early issues of *Black Orpheus* (7 and 8 respectively). Later years saw 'At the Portages', 'Blankets', and 'Tattoo Marks and Nails' appear in its pages. 'A Matter of Honour' was published in *The New African*, and magazines in South America, Germany, the United States and Sweden have featured his stories as well. They also appear in numerous collections, including Richard Rive's *Quartet*. Bernth Lindfors writes that 'the most accomplished non-white short-story writers in South Africa today are Richard Rive and Alex La Guma', and summarizes the latter's technique and subject matter:

> La Guma's style is characterized by graphic description, careful evocation of atmosphere and mood, fusion of pathos and humor, colorful dialogue, and occasional surprise endings. His stories most often concern lawbreakers – criminals, prisoners, prostitutes and apartheid offenders – who possess either an unusual sensitivity or a sense of honor or morality which redeems them as human beings and raises them to heroic stature.[4]

In the Fog of the Seasons' End was published in 1972 and in it La Guma 'reminds us that South Africa is not merely an "issue", some abstract fixture to arrange in the liberal conscience: it is a complicated country full of living people and able to retain the love of those who suffer in it.'⁵ While no one can quibble with his political commitment, Nadine Gordimer takes issue with his exile's perception of a changing society:

> La Guma, in the gentle, beautifully written *In the Fog of the Seasons' End*, writes, like so many black exiles, as if life in South Africa froze with the trauma of Sharpeville . . . he cannot from abroad quite make the projection, at the deeper level, into a black political milieu that has changed so much since he left.⁶

The forcible removal of communities and their resettlement, the theme of La Guma's *Time of the Butcherbird* (1979), was, however, politically timely, coming as it did at the height of the South African Government's enforced resettlement schemes. The dynamics of the political process are perceived through La Guma's examination of the specific; we are shown the oppressed, and also 'those in the camp of the oppressor who are caught up in the intricate network of oppression – the small cogs without which the big wheel could not turn'.⁷

The Afro-Asian Writers' Association awarded La Guma the Lotus Prize for Literature in 1973. Two non-fiction works are included in his output: *Apartheid* and *A Soviet Journey*. He is at present the African National Congress representative in Cuba.

¹ Lewis Nkosi, 'Fiction of black South Africans', in Ulli Beier, ed., *Introduction to African Literature* (Illinois, 1967), p. 127
² Robert July, 'The African personality in the African novel', in Beier, *Introduction to African Literature*, p. 219
³ Alex La Guma, *The Stone Country* (Berlin, 1967), p. 7
⁴ Bernth Lindfors, 'Form and technique in the novels of Richard Rive and Alex La Guma', *Journal of the New African Literature and the Arts*, no. 2, Autumn 1966, p. 11
⁵ Angus Calder, 'Living objects', *New Statesman*, 3 Nov. 1972
⁶ Nadine Gordimer, 'English-language literature and politics in South Africa', in C. Heywood, ed., *Aspects of South African Literature* (London and New York, 1976), p. 114
⁷ Scarlet Whitman, 'A story of resistance', *The African Communist*, Spring/Summer, 1979, p. 111

Camara Laye
1928–1980   GUINEA

Camara Laye, one of the first black African authors to receive world-wide recognition, died in Dakar on 4 February 1980 at the age of only 52. The ill-health which had plagued him since the mid-sixties and the tensions of life in exile had taken their toll. In the interview which proved to be Laye's last, Denis Herbstein noted how difficult exile had been for Laye – both financially and in terms of his art:

> Few modern writers can be less well-suited to living in exile than Camara Laye. He is ill, with a kidney complaint and high blood pressure. 'I usually earn enough from writing to sustain my entourage,' he says. 'But when a domestic financial crisis occurs, I don't work well. I get blood pressure from the worry.'¹

And Herbstein quotes Laye's words about what his life might have been like:

> Had I continued to live in Kouroussa, I would have worked in tranquility. The Malinke family is a collective. I have seven full and half brothers and sisters there. The sons and daughters would have worried about the house, while I spent my days writing.²

Laye's childhood was spent in an essentially traditional society in the ancient city of Kouroussa in Upper Guinea where he was born on 1 January 1928. As the son of a family of goldsmiths, on both his father's and his mother's side, Laye grew up aware of the full weight of tradition. His was a society in which magic was revered, a familiar part of everyday life. It was a society where the smith, a person reputed to possess supernatural gifts, was a powerful and respected figure. And this remained true despite the Muslim religion which the Malinke had embraced.

The young Laye went first to the local koranic school and then to the Government Primary School before leaving Kouroussa to attend Conakry's technical college, Ecole Poiret, where he received a scholarship to study in France. Against his mother's protestations, he left Guinea for Argenteuil (near Paris) to train as an engineer. Upon finishing his studies there, Laye wanted to carry his education still further, but financially hampered from doing so, he was only able to attend evening classes at the Conservatoire des Arts et Métiers while he worked as a mechanic at the Simca car factory. At this point in his life Laye says,

Having lived for years far from my native Guinea and my parents in almost complete isolation in Paris, I carried myself off in my thoughts to be near my people. And then one day I realized that these memories that were once so fresh might well, if not entirely fade away – how could they do that? – at least lose some of their freshness. So I began to write them down. I was living alone, in my poor student's room, and I would write. I remember I would write as if in a dream. I would write for my pleasure, and it was an extraordinary pleasure, one that the heart never tired of.[3]

The culmination of this effort established Camara Laye's reputation. When the autobiographical novel *L'Enfant noir* was published in Paris in 1953 it was welcomed 'by some as a minor masterpiece' and by others, chiefly African nationalists, as 'a colonialist pot-boiler'.[4] The following year it won for Laye the famed Prix Charles Veillon, and was subsequently published in the United States as *The Dark Child* (translated by James Kirkup) in 1954, and in Great Britain as *The African Child* in 1955.

Janheinz Jahn later wrote:

In *The Dark Child* Camara Laye shows the new spirit of French West Africans towards tradition. He did not consider his African childhood as something remote, primitive, something to be ashamed of. On the contrary: looking back on it from a distance, and having the technical skills European education had to offer, he discovered that these skills had been animated, and had been more closely related to man in his native civilisation.[5]

Laye's first novel continues to be widely read, and remains today the subject of heated literary discussion, particularly on the part of more militant African writers like Mongo Beti. Laye chaffed at these attacks and in interview after interview he felt it necessary to defend his notion of commitment. In 1972 he stated:

One does not have to talk about specific political problems in order to be political. All literature is, in a sense, 'committed' in the way in which it asserts the style of a particular culture and way of life, and a writer who deals with his culture and history for the purpose of bearing witness to its greatness is certainly a committed writer.[6]

At the Berlin Festival in 1979, which he attended, Laye was once more attacked for writing irrelevant works. Although obviously ill he jumped to his feet saying:

Again and again this old question of whether literature is committed or not. I tell you, all literature is committed, even the uncommitted kind ... My commitment is subtle, concealed, in the background ... When I write about our lost values, about the great empire and people of Mali, it's true, these things have passed away, but I'm trying to bring them back to life ... Not only Mali, other great civilisations should be brought back to life ... that is the important thing today.[7]

In 1954 Camara Laye published his second work, a symbolic novel, 'usually considered as an ingenuous allegory about man's search for god'.[8] *Le Regard du roi*, open to widely different interpretations, appeared in English as *The Radiance of the King* in 1956; it was released again late in 1970 in Collier's African/American Library.

Camara Laye returned to Guinea in 1956 and for two years worked as an engineer. When Guinea achieved Independence in 1958 Laye entered the political arena and was appointed Director of the Centre de Recherches et d'Etudes for the Ministry of Information in Conakry.

Twelve years elapsed between the appearance of *Le Regard du roi* and *Dramouss*, his third and last novel. In the interim he wrote short stories for *Black Orpheus*, *Présence Africaine*, *Paris–Dakar*, and *Bingo*, and contributed a paper, 'L'âme de l'Afrique dans sa partie Guinéenne', to the *Colloque sur la littérature africaine d'expression française*. Returning again to autobiography, in *Dramouss* (long scheduled for publication as *Retour au pays natal*) his 'emphasis changes from fiction narration to direct social comment,' noted A. C. Brench.[9] First published in 1966 after Laye had left Guinea for Senegal, it appeared in English in 1968 as *A Dream of Africa*. Laye dedicated this book 'to the young people of Africa . . . I write this book in order that African ways of thinking, re-integrated and restored . . . may be a new force – not aggressive but fruitful.'[10] Brench records that here Laye reintroduces the characters from *L'Enfant noir*. 'This time, however, he is a stranger looking at a world he knows imperfectly. His memories are blurred and idealized while the country has changed considerably during his absence. He looks at his country critically and seems to deplore what he sees.'[11]

Laye's growing hostility for the Guinean regime and his enmity for Sékou Touré personally (he is satirized in *A Dream of Africa* as the 'Big Brute') forced Laye into exile in 1965. On the pretext of needing urgent medical attention in Paris he left Guinea and never returned. Laye's troubles with Guinea continued into exile when his first wife, Marie (his childhood girl-friend in *L'Enfant noir*), was detained for a time by Sékou Touré when she returned to Conakry in 1970 to visit her ailing mother. In talking with Denis Herbstein about *A Dream of Africa* (the only one of Laye's novels to be banned in Guinea) after fifteen years in exile, Laye bluntly assessed Sékou Touré's regime:

> I reproach Sékou Touré for destroying a society which is 1,000 years old, and replacing it with the worst aspect of Russia and Hitler's Germany. Before him, we did not have concentration camps, dictatorships and torture . . . that's not my country, the most beautiful in Africa. I do not say that I want colonialism back. But I don't want black people in its place who destroy our liberty.[12]

Upon leaving Guinea, Laye lived for a time in the Ivory Coast but then settled permanently in Senegal where he was offered a position at the Institut Fondamental d'Afrique Noire in Dakar as a researcher in the oral traditions of the Malinke peoples. It was this work that led to the publication in 1978 of his last book, *Le Maître de la parole*, which contains another version of the legend of Sun Jata (or Sundiata), the thirteenth-century Malinke ruler, as told by the *griot*, Kouma Lafôlô Kouma. Translated by James Kirkup (the man who has translated all of Laye's other works) as *The Guardian of the Word*, the work appeared in London in 1981 in a Fontana edition. In his review of the book Charles Larson said, 'Perhaps the most interesting aspect of *The Guardian of the Word* is the title that Laye chose for his work. One would expect that the epic would be named after its hero, Sundiata . . . Instead, Laye has shifted the emphasis to the oral historian, the griot . . .'[13] And Larson quotes from Laye's introduction to his book: '[the griot] is above all an artist, and, it follows, his chants, his epics and his legends are works of art.'[14]

Camara Laye, the man, is no longer among us, but his works, like those of the *griot*, will live on after him. At his death he left seven children by his first wife, Marie, and a young daughter by his second wife, Ramatoulaye, a woman from the Malinke area of Senegal. Adele King's study of Camara Laye's fiction, *The Novels of Camara Laye*, was published by Heinemann in 1980.

[1] Denis Herbstein, 'Camara Laye – involuntary exile', *Index on Censorship*, vol. 9, no. 3, June 1980, p. 8

[2] *Ibid.*, p. 8

³ From a paper read by Camara Laye at the *Colloque sur la littérature africaine d'expression française. Faculté des Lettres de Dakar, 26–29 Mar. 1963*, quoted in Joyce A. Hutchinson, ed., *L'Enfant noir* (London, 1966), p. 7 (Editor's translation)
⁴ A. C. Brench, 'Camara Laye: idealist and mystic', *African Literature Today*, no. 2, Jan. 1969, p. 11
⁵ Janheinz Jahn, 'Discussion on Camara Laye', *Black Orpheus*, no. 6, Nov. 1959, p. 35
⁶ 'Laye: Commitment to timeless values', interview by J. Steven Rubin, *Africa Report*, May 1972, p. 22
⁷ Al Imfeld, 'Portraits of African writers', no. 2, Deutsche Welle transcript [Cologne 1979], p. 5 (English translation by Jan Klingemann)
⁸ Jahn, 'Discussion', p. 36
⁹ Brench, 'Camara Laye: idealist', p. 31
¹⁰ Camara Laye, *A Dream of Africa* (London, 1968), pp. 7–8
¹¹ Brench, 'Camara Laye: idealist', p. 28
¹² Herbstein, 'Camara Laye – exile', p. 7
¹³ *Times Literary Supplement*, no. 4085, 17 July 1981, p. 802
¹⁴ Camara Laye, *The Guardian of the Word* (London, 1981)

Taban lo Liyong

born 1939   UGANDA

Taban lo Liyong is one of the most candid and stimulating African men of letters. His poetry and prose have called on a wide range of traditions from both Africa and the West. His output of critical writing has been prolific and, frequently, controversial.

The Last Word was the first book of literary criticism to be published in East Africa. Many of its essays originally appeared in African and American journals; their compilation provides a composite picture of lo Liyong's idea of 'cultural synthesism', as he calls it in the collection's subtitle. A review by Basil Busacca in *Africa Report* found *The Last Word* 'a Magna Carta for African greatness', and called lo Liyong 'an East African writer and critic who genuflects before no idols – European, Nigerian or local – and who proves that he is right to exercise the prerogatives of genius. With this slim book of essays he introduces himself as a powerful voice, a spectacular and audacious intelligence.'¹

One section in *The Last Word* is autobiographical, others discuss the blacks in the United States, but the majority of essays concern African literature. lo Liyong's stimulating commentaries have led some to call him 'a *bad African* in the sense that recalls a term like *un-American*'.² lo Liyong is not a chauvinist. He rejects the philosphy of negritude and black mysticism in any form. He also opposes another current trend, in that he feels 'it is folly to imagine that an African, any African, is the best critic of things African . . . it is the height of folly for Africans to declare that African culture or literature is the one branch of knowledge beyond the attainment of all non-Africans'.³ If black people have a monopoly on 'soul' lo Liyong asks, does it follow that only white people can appreciate classical music, art, and literature?

The British, too, do not escape his criticism. In 1965 lo Liyong saw East Africa as a literary wilderness and he wrote:

I blame the British. The education they came to offer was aimed at recruiting candidates for a Christian Heaven and eliminating others for a Christian Hell; they sought to teach clerks, teachers, servants and administrators. Culturally, they stood aloof . . . Not only that, the British went about castrating the Africans. Culturally our dances, including songs became Satanic . . . Poetry writing and the art of fiction were not taught us though we debated and reasoned.

This led directly to early writings which were of a quarrelsome nature; political grievances (about land, mostly) and answering back the white racist charges through pamphlets, and biographies and anthropological works.[4]

However, when lo Liyong returned to East Africa in 1968 after his studies abroad, he found that during his absence the output of literature had proliferated. Now, his previous call for the incorporation of African literature into the curricula has become a reality. But for him the study of the world's literature is vital as well, because 'we need to know how our works stand in relation to other contemporary works throughout the world; we also need to compare our works with those by past societies.'[5]

Although Taban lo Liyong realises that African writers will have to write in a European language to attain a wide readership, he points out that if the language is English, 'we will not have to stick to Queen's English . . . we have to tame the shrew and naturalize her . . .'[6] 'The new languages such as English and French have to pay a price for their absorption into the African's thought process.'[7]

Eating Chiefs. Lwo culture from Lolwe to Malkal was published in the African Writers Series in 1970. Here Taban lo Liyong utilized Africa's cultural heritage to forge a new literary medium. His aim was to 'induce creative writers to take off from where the anthropologists have stopped . . . This book is merely an attempt to show what can be done. If it inspires other artists or, better still, provokes them to treat their tribal literature as raw material, or artistic forms for containing their views on the past and the present, then our legacy from the past will have been accepted and our forefathers rewarded by multiplication of their efforts.'[8] *Eating Chiefs* was part of lo Liyong's research at the Institute of African Studies, University of Nairobi, where he had a Tutorial Fellowship and edited their newsletter of cultural research, *Mila*. He also lectured in the English department.

Taban lo Liyong was born in northern Uganda. He attended Gulu High School and Sir Samuel Baker School. Upon graduating from the National Teachers College, Kampala he was awarded two scholarships. Under the influence of his father, he chose a political science course in the United States where he attended Howard University and Knoxville College. He took his graduate degree when at the writer's workshop at the University of Iowa, the first African writer to attend this school.

In addition to the two volumes discussed. Taban lo Liyong has produced a collection of short stories entitled *Fixions*, also published in the African Writers Series. This was followed in the next three years by *Meditations in Limbo, Frantz Fanon's Uneven Ribs: Poems More and More, The Uniformed Man* and *Another Nigger Dead*. The East African Literature Bureau published his *Ballads of Underdevelopment* in 1976 and Rex Collings his *Meditations* two years later.

Liyong was invited to the University of Papua New Guinea to teach and since 1978 he has been at the Faculty of Literature at Juba in the Sudan. In addition to collecting oral literature, teaching in a writing school, and working in theatre, Liyong would like to stimulate more locally relevant material for use on television in Southern Sudan.

As a writer Liyong has provoked fierce criticism as well as fulsome praise; his vitality is undeniable. One observer measures his contribution to Africa:

> as a phenomenon he is not easy to grasp. He doesn't fit into any category. One thing, though, is certain: modern African literature would be infinitely poorer without Taban lo Liyong. His many works are a measure of this. What cannot be measured is what he has done for others, by provoking, stimulating and inspiring them.[9]

[1] Basil Busacca, review of *The Last Word, Africa Report*, Nov. 1970

[2] *Ibid.*, p. 35

[3] Taban lo Liyong, *The Last Word* (Nairobi, 1969) p. 63

[4] Taban lo Liyong, 'Can we correct literary barrenness in East Africa?', *Transition* no. 19, and *East Africa Journal*, June 1965, and *The Last Word* (Nairobi, 1969) pp. 31–2

[5] Taban lo Liyong, *The Last Word*, p. 36

[6] *Ibid.*, p. 79

Lopes

[7] *Ibid.*, p. 81
[8] Taban lo Liyong, *Eating Chiefs* (London, 1970) pp. xi–xii
[9] Al Imfeld, 'Portraits of African writers', no. 6, Deutsche Welle transcript (Cologne, 1979)

Baltasar Lopes
born 1907   CAPE VERDE

Baltasar Lopes has played a pivotal role in the development of modern Cape Verdean letters. Born in the town of Ribeira Brava on the island of São Nicolau on 23 April 1907, Lopes earned degrees from the Faculties of Law and Letters at the Univerity of Lisbon. He returned to Cape Verde to become a teacher at the Gil Eanes High School on the island of São Vicente. A director of the school for many years, he retired in 1972.

That Baltasar Lopes, a lawyer, spent his life working in Cape Verde testifies to his commitment to his native land, for he could easily have remained in Portugal teaching at the Univerity of Lisbon, where, in fact, he was offered a position in 1945. As an educator, philologist, essayist, short-story writer and poet, Baltasar Lopes has devoted much of his life to the revitalization and study of Cape Verdean culture. In 1936, along with Jorge Barbosa and Manuel Lopes, he gave birth to the first issue of *Claridade*, a journal whose main purpose was an examination of the roots of Cape Verdean identity. He has contributed as well to other journals, including *Atlântico*, *Vértice*, *Colóquio*, *Cabo Verde*, *Mensagem* and most recently *Raízes*.

As a poet, he has written under the pseudonym Osvaldo Alcântara. Lopes' poetry, written over five decades, celebrates the African mother of Cape Verde, whose sons and daughters must suffer from poverty, droughts, starvation and self-exile.

Lopes' first and only novel, *Chiquinho*, was first published in 1947, and re-issued in 1961. Commenting on the importance of this, the first modern novel in the history of Cape Verdean literature, Donald Burness has noted that:

> To appreciate the impact of *Chiquinho*, one must realize that it is to the literature of Cape

Verde what *Things Fall Apart* is to Nigerian fiction and *L'Enfant Noir* is to Francophone African prose. Moreover, Lopes' novel was written a decade before the appearance of the two above mentioned pivotal works in African fiction.[1]

In 1960, exactly 500 years after the discovery of Cape Verde, Lopes edited an anthology of 23 Cape Verdean stories, *Antologia de Ficção Cabo-Verdiana Contemporânea*, a collection which includes six of his own stories. As in *Chiquinho*, Lopes introduces into his stories Creole words and expressions, an affirmation of the validity of this language as a manifestation of the identity and unity of Cape Verdeans. This is most important since the vast majority of Cape Verde's population is 'mestiço' or mulatto, and a debate has continued for decades as to whether the islands' culture is European or African, or both. Lopes' essays, including *Cabo Verde Visto por Gilberto Freire* (1956) and his preface to the second edition of Manuel Ferreira's *A Aventura Crioula* (1973), study the important contributions of Creole culture and language.

Baltasar Lopes has been the subject of considerable scholarly investigation. Donald Burness,[2] Norman Araujo[3] and Russell Hamilton[4] have commented extensively on his work. Although some modern Cape Verdeans have lamented the fact that Baltasar Lopes and the *Claridade* generation failed to emphasize, sufficiently, the islands' African roots. Manuel Ferreira, among others, has shown that Lopes and his fellow authors initiated the first *poesia de raiz* (grass-roots poetry) in the African lands colonized by the Portuguese.[5]

Lopes' poems and stories have appeared in numerous anthologies including Mário de Andrade's *Antologia de Poesia Negra de Expressão Portuguesa* (Paris, 1958) and Manuel Ferreira's *No Reino de Caliban*, vol. 1 (Lisbon, 1975).

Baltasar Lopes resides today in Cape Verde.

[1] Donald Burness, *Fire: Six Writers from Angola, Mozambique and Cape Verde* (Washington DC, 1977), p. 81
[2] *Ibid.*

[3] Newman Araujo, *A Study of Cape Verdean Literature* (Boston, 1966)
[4] Russell Hamilton, *Voices from an Empire* (Minneapolis, 1975)
[5] Manuel Ferreira, *No Reino de Caliban*, vol. 4 (Lisbon, 1975), p. 88

Henri Lopes

born 1937   CONGO

In an interview published in 1977, Henri Lopes, the Congolese novelist and short-story writer, speaks about the 'new period' that is opening up for African literature, one in which young writers need to 'retain the substance, the marrow of Négritude without considering [themselves] as members of that school'. 'Our elders,' he says, 'must understand that the best way to follow their example is not to re-do what they had done but rather to propose something else'.[1] Lopes refuses to be hampered by any preconceived notion of what constitutes the proper subject for African literature: 'You must allow each artist to express himself in the form he finds best and treat the subjects that he finds the most interesting.'[2] In his opinion, it is the 'personal sensitivity', and the 'particular culture' that a work of creative writing expresses that gives it its specificity. As a consequence, the first important requirement for a writer is to have 'a temperament, a personality, and a style'. The second requirement is that he work hard and beware of the word 'inspiration': 'Africans in particular must forget all those clichés about being "born artists". No! We have to invest in our art just as you have to invest in anything.'[3]

Like many African writers of the younger generation, Henri Lopes is concerned with the issues confronting present-day, independent Africa. He believes he has a duty to say 'what he feels in his gut' and to protest against 'what [he] cannot stand, particularly the contradictions of society'.[4] A writer must educate people and contribute to their awareness 'in order for them to get rid of the different forms of oppression that suffocate them'.[5]

However responsive the writer must be to the needs of his society, which for Lopes means all of Africa, not just the

Congo, he none the less has an obligation to his craft. Creative writing is not the same thing as political writing, and a writer must 'work with art'.[6] The critical response that has greeted Lopes' first two books indicates that this imperative has been uppermost in his mind. *Tribaliques*, the collection of short stories that he published in 1971, had the distinction of winning the Grand Prix Littéraire d'Afrique Noire for 1972, and his novel, *La Nouvelle romance*, published in 1976, has been described by Fame N'Dongo as a 'work which from the outset classes [Lopes] among the tenors of the "new black African novel" ... who look beyond the present-day reality that they feel is too paralysing towards new horizons that are more favourable to an authentic progress of Africans'.[7] The themes of the stories that make up *Tribaliques* are, indeed, the contradictions of contemporary Africa. Lopes invented the title from the word 'tribe', although the theme of tribalism plays only a minor role in the collection, on equal footing with other problems: the 'brain drain' that deprives Africa of the talented, educated people it sorely needs; corrupt bureaucrats and hypocritical politicians; acute social inequality and crippling superstitions out of the past that Africa would be unwise to perpetuate. In one of the stories of the collection, 'Ancien combattant', Lopes even recalls how a moment out of the colonial past can resurge painfully many years later and spoil human relations. In it an African diplomat realizes with sorrow that he fought with French troops in the battle against Algerian freedom fighters, in which the mother of his Algerian mistress lost her life.

The theme of *La Nouvelle romance*, as Lopes describes it, is not only the problem of the relationship between men and women in Africa today, but that of a society which allows unqualified people with political contacts to obtain positions of responsibility.

In contrast to *Tribaliques* and *La Nouvelle romance* Lopes' third book, *Sans tam-tam*, also a novel, portrays a young educated African who has decided to serve his country and his people as a humble schoolteacher in a rural area and who dies as he had lived, quietly unattended, 'undrummed'.

Unlike the hero of *Sans tam-tam*, Lopes has felt the need for direct political action. He has held several ministerial appointments in the Congo Republic as Minister of Education, Minister of Foreign Affairs, and Minister of Finance. For two years, from the beginning of 1973 to the end of 1974, he was prime minister.

Born on 12 September 1937 in Kinshasa, Lopes received his primary education in Brazzaville and Bangui. At the age of twelve he went to France, where he completed his secondary school and university education. He has a graduate and postgraduate degree in history. In 1965 he returned to the Congo Republic to teach history at the Ecole Normale Supérieure d'Afrique Noire in Brazzaville, but was soon afterwards appointed Minister of Education. He is currently in Paris working for UNESCO and has just been appointed Director of the UNESCO Press.

[1] 'Rencontre avec Henri Lopes, écrivain', *Bingo*, January 1977, p. 58 (this and the following quotes translated from the French by the editors)
[2] 'Henri Lopes: L'écrivain doit prendre position, ou se taire', *Fraternité Matin*, 26 October 1976
[3] *Ibid.*
[4] *Ibid.*
[5] *Ibid.*
[6] *Ibid.*
[7] Fame N'Dongo, *La Nouvelle romance* d'Henri Lopes: fleuron du nouveau roman nègre', *Afrique Littéraire et Artistique*, 41, 1976, p. 43

Yulisa Amadu Maddy

born 1936   SIERRA LEONE

Maddy is one of a younger generation of Creole writers who – in taking a critical look at society – are examining their cultural heritage, emphasizing the positive elements and revealing the sham. Palmer states that, in depicting the Creole aristocracy in *No Past, No Present, No Future*.

Maddy spares no pains . . . to expose their snobbery, their contempt for the provincial peoples, their religious hypocrisy, their sterile striving for respectability and their regard for English culture. Maddy takes his characters from low life – the drop-outs from school, the under-privileged orphans, the prostitutes and the pimps – and he sets his scenes in brothels or amidst the corruption of a railway goods shed. Their language is earthy, realistic and almost crude; they have no hesitation in using four-letter words and quite often make use of Krio as it would be spoken in the fleshpots of Freetown.[1]

Maddy is quite consciously writing for the common person, as he made clear in an interview:

I'm writing for the man in the street. I'm writing for the kids who don't know whether they should go home when they've had a fight with their parents. I'm writing for the laborer who is now being taught what is self-help and he wants to help himself. I'm writing for those people who all over the world really want to make something out of their own lives by working for themselves, and doing what they want to do, not the person who's waiting for someone to come and do something for him. So in a word I mean I'm going to the masses. It is they I'm interested in because they have got a rich culture, they have got tradition, they have got their gods, they have got their indigenous way of life. And this is rich, this is what I want to touch. I'm not interested in the still-born or archaic traditions of imported culture. I love original cultures as they are.[2]

Maddy was educated in Sierra Leone until the age of 22, when he went to France to study literature and drama. Two years later he continued his studies in England. During the sixties he was involved in drama at many levels: he produced African plays for Danish radio and had his own plays produced for television and radio in England and Denmark. In London he started a lunch-time theatre, *Gbakanda Teater*, and was Director of Drama at the Keskidee Centre. Two of the four plays which have appeared in *Obasai and Other Plays*, published by Heinemann in 1971, were performed at both locations. 'Theatre is a very effective platform,' asserts Maddy, 'to catch people's attention, to make them aware that in this part of the world, or in that part of the world, atrocities are going on.'[3]

He lived in Denmark in the mid-sixties, teaching African literature. A book of his poetry, *Ny afrikansk prosa*, was published in Denmark in 1969. On his return to Sierra Leone in 1968 he became head of drama on Radio Sierra Leone. A stint as features editor for the Unity Press followed, and a period as editor of *Konomanda*. He subsequently worked in Zambia, directing ZADACO (the national dance troupe) and training them for the Montreal World Fair in 1970.

His first novel, *No Past, No Present, No Future*, appeared in 1973. In it he returns to a topic – love – which preoccupied him in the play 'Alla Gbah', published in *Obasai*:

And here again I was dealing with this theme of love where you have three characters, three boys who have been to the Catholic mission, three boys who are ambitious, three boys from the same country, but from different backgrounds, from different parts of the country who wanted the best for themselves and hoped to get the best for their families. But eventually as time goes by it did not happen that way. And why is that? I don't think it's destiny. I think there's something more to it. What that is I have yet to find out. Maybe the intrigues in Africa, the lust for money.[4]

His collaboration with Alem Mezgebe, an Ethiopian writer, resulted in *Pulse*, a play which won first prize at the Edinburgh International Festival. Maddy produced and acted in the play, which deals with the question of dictatorship. On that subject he speaks bitterly, having himself been imprisoned in Sierra Leone: 'I was living an experience which I will never forget, I will never forgive.'[5] He objects to the lack of status writers are accorded in his society, and feels that politicians

fail to understand that culture, literature is the mother of politics. If there is no culture, if there is no literature, I cannot see how politics can really be strong. Because any sensible politician will work from the premise of his culture. Any sensible politician should be a father and mother of the artist because that is where his strength lies.[6]

The production of *Big Berrin* (big

burying), staged recently in Freetown, received wide acclaim. It provides an insight into social and political habits, and in the words of the author 'looks at the present condition in which some of us live'. After taking 'a long and critical look', Maddy finds that although everyone complains, 'nobody seems to really know who to take their problems to', and he attempted to write a play mirroring the ills of the society and advocating self-awareness.[7] *Big Berrin* makes ample use of songs, as do his other plays; indeed, he places great importance on traditional material. Discussing the use of Temne and Krio songs, parables and sayings, he explains:

as soon as people pick up the book they recognise these phrases. And some people say, 'But you shouldn't have put that down in a book.' But why? If I'm going to educate my own kids as to the morals of our society I have to let them know by the tradition of the society what the morals of the past were and then they will understand the morals of the present in order for them to formulate a moral for the future. And this is one of the reasons why a certain class of society don't like my book. But most of the students, you know, kids around, young people, they really dig it.[8]

He has recently been teaching drama in Nigeria at the universities of Ibadan and Ilorin.

[1] Eustace Palmer, 'The development of Sierra Leone writing', in B. King and K. Ogungbesan, eds., *A Celebration of Black and African Writing* (Zaria and Ibadan, 1975), p. 254
[2] Quoted in Lee Nichols, ed., *Conversations with African Writers* (Washington DC, 1981), p. 112
[3] 'Arts and Africa', no. 307P, BBC African Service transcript (London)
[4] Nichols, *Conversations*, p. 111
[5] 'Arts and Africa', no. 307P
[6] Nichols, *Conversations*, pp. 114–15
[7] 'Arts and Africa', no. 130
[8] Nichols *Conversations*, p. 112

David G. Maillu
born 1939   KENYA

Maillu is a controversial writer of popular novels; his numerous books, mostly published by his own publishing company, Comb Books, sell extremely well, but 'a long debate rages about the acceptability of the values he portrays . . .'[1] His interest in writing stories began when he was very young, and he received encouragement at school, for, he says,

> I started going to school when I was already grown up, so I was a good story teller. I began with traditional stories, but as I progressed with my own education and began to read other books, I also became interested in other kinds of stories and decided to try writing them . . .
>
> I just kept on writing, first traditional stories, and then fiction, even science fiction, and then poetry and then anything else. At a later stage I developed an interest in philosophy and practical psychology

and 'human relations are what I mainly write about now'.[2]

Publishers rejected the work he sent to them, and apart from short stories which magazines printed, he accumulated the work he wrote. During this time he worked as a graphic designer for the Voice of Kenya, the broadcasting service. He also acted in comic roles on television. In 1972 he took a gamble, resigned his job, and set up Comb Books. His first venture, a book written in Kikamba, was not a success. The next, *Unfit for Human Consumption*, was. *My Dear Bottle* and *Troubles* were his next publications, and the latter has sold 50,000 copies.

The content of the novels is urban in character. Prostitutes, layabouts, the unfaithful and drunks feature largely and sex is explicit. Maillu declares '. . . I write boldly about sex as well as about everything else. I don't go around subjects. I am quite direct . . . Life does not hesitate to say anything so why should I hesitate?'[3]

He himself leads a fairly isolated life. He 'prefers the peace and quiet of his suburban Langata residence west of Nairobi to the hurly-burly of city life.'[4] He takes his work seriously: 'I want to point out some of the issues that people have to deal with in life';

> if an alcoholic reads *My Dear Bottle* and decides not to go out for drinks that night, it gives me satisfaction in the sense that I know that I have helped him by occupying his mind with something else. So maybe I write

under the delusion that I may be making a fair contribution to society. I rather like to believe that I am an educator as well as an entertainer and that my books have a moral purpose.[5]

Tanzania banned his books in 1976 on the alleged grounds of their often cheap morality. He accepts their decision philosophically, and remarks disarmingly that 'I am not in a position to know whether my books are bad or not, but I would assume that if they were bad, they would have made me bad.'[6]

In the first volume of *The Kommon Man* he included a questionnaire to elicit readers' responses to the book, asking them to answer brief biographical questions about themselves. He received 285 replies, and the results were analysed by Apronti in the *African Book Publishing Record*. From the results – although based upon a self-selecting sample – one can get a profile of the readers who contribute to his vast popularity and sales. The ten most common occupations listed were: teacher, clerk, civil servant, secretary, driver, surveyor, salesman, train guard, policeman and businessman; over 60 per cent of the respondents had educational attainments of O-level or above. The majority were between 20 and 30 years old. Forty per cent said they enjoyed the man–woman relationships best. The questionnaire confirms Maillu's claim that he writes with a realism that his readers can identify with, and 'whatever vulgarity one can point to in his work can also be found in real life'.[7]

Meanwhile the author has 30 unpublished works, he writes several books at a time, and his publishing house (now called David Maillu Publishers) produces books on a wide range of subjects from religion to accountancy. Macmillan have published two of his books, *For Mbatha and Rabeka* and *The Equatorial Assignment*, in their Pacesetters Series. Maillu himself plans to fill a gap in the school world by printing a magazine that will cater for young people and 'concentrate on the things that school doesn't bother with. School education has been made very miserable because it is so serious and people don't learn about themselves.'[8]

[1] E. O. Apronti, 'David G. Maillu and his readers – an unusual poll of readers' evaluation of a popular writer's work', *African Book Publishing Record*, vol. 6, nos. 3 & 4, 1980, p. 220

[2] Bernth Lindfors, 'Interview with David G. Maillu', *African Book Publishing Record*, vol. 5, no. 2, April 1979, p.85

[3] *Ibid*, p. 86

[4] Apronti, 'David G. Maillu and his readers', p. 220

[5] Lindfors, 'Interview', p. 87

[6] *Ibid.*, p. 86

[7] Apronti, 'David G. Maillu and his readers', p. 220

[8] Lindfors, 'Interview', p. 88

Jean Pierre Makouta-Mboukou

born 1929   CONGO

A novelist and a poet, Jean Pierre Makouta-Mboukou is one of the few African writers who is also a critic. In addition to a number of articles, he has published two full-length critical studies of African literature, *Introduction à la littérature noire*, published by CLE in 1970, and a study of the francophone novel, *Introduction à l'étude du roman africain de langue française*, published jointly by Nouvelles Editions Africaines and CLE in 1980. In the introductory chapter to the latter he regrets that there is no proper African school of literary criticism and blames African writers for neglecting this field. In a shorter critical study presented at a colloquium on the criticism of African literature, held at the Sorbonne in March 1978,[1] he contends that both African and Western critics are responsible for the 'amateurish' quality of current critical analysis. There is now an abundance of the survey type of study, he says, and not enough serious analysis of individual authors, and especially of lesser-known writers. Moreover, critics are often blinded by their own culture and are handicapped by what Makouta-Mboukou terms their 'ecology' – the geographical, historical, ethno-religious, sociological, political and linguistic background of a particular work and of its author. Western critics are particularly at fault, he contends, but even African

critics lack knowledge of African cultures other than their own. For Makouta-Mboukou the critic is above all someone who 'is responsible for the intelligence of an entire society'.[2] He 'teaches people how to read', and it is his duty to make sure that he does not distort an author's message by letting himself be influenced by a subjective, or partisan viewpoint. 'The role of a critic,' he says, 'is neither to be the director of conscience for writers nor their hangman, but to give a faithful report of a finished work.'[3]

In the same article Makouta-Mboukou defines African literature as being 'realistic', 'utilitarian', and 'committed'. It is not a bourgeois literature. African authors have no time or paper to waste. Their writing is 'a contribution to and a sign of the struggles resulting from the building of a society.'[4] In Makouta-Mboukou's own creative works the concept of 'commitment' includes commitment not only to a society in which justice and equality reign, but also commitment to a Christian ideal. The hero of his novel, *Les Initiés* (1970), a young Malagasy student in Paris, comes to a tragic end for having ignored the teachings of the Church and having lived a dissolute existence. He repents, but will die none the less. The central figure of another novel, *Le Contestant* (1973), is an African pastor whose teachings are too 'radical' for the establishment.

Makouta-Mboukou's first novel, *En quête de la liberté* (1970), is about a young man who spends 15 years in France and who returns to the Congo after Independence, only to discover that although his country is now being run by African politicians, liberty has still not come. The novel ends on a note of chaos and despair. *En quête de la liberté* was banned in the Congo when it was first published and Makouta-Mboukou, who had been a member of parliament from 1963 to 1968, left the Congo to teach in France, where he still lives.

In the perspective of the first three novels, a fourth novel, *Les Exilés de la forêt vierge*, published by P. J. Oswald in 1974 and reissued by L'Harmattan in 1981, would appear to be a work of reconcili-

ation. It is set in an imaginary independent African state where a resistance
fighter, who had fled into the forest to
escape a death sentence, meets up many
years later with the president who condemned him to death and who is,
himself, in exile after being overthrown.

Makouta-Mboukou has also published
two verse collections, *L'Ame bleue* (1971)
and *La Cantate de l'ouvrier* (1974). Two of
his plays have yet to be published, *Un
ministre nègre à Paris* and *Le Lèpre du roi*.

Jean Pierre Makouta-Mboukou was
born on 17 July 1929 in Kindamba in the
region of Pool and attended secondary
schools in Libamba, Cameroon, and in
Brazzaville. He did his undergraduate
work in literature at the University of
Grenoble from 1957 to 1960. He also
obtained a secondary-school teaching
degree at the Ecole Normale Supérieure
de Saint-Cloud and a postgraduate
degree in literature from the Sorbonne.
He has written a doctoral dissertation on
the works of the Haïtian author, Jacques
Roumain and has a subsidiary doctorate
(*doctorat de spécialitée*) in linguistics. Jean
Pierre Makouta-Mboukou has taught at
the University of Dakar (1960–1) and at
the Centre d'Enseignement Supérieur de
Brazzaville. He is an active member of the
association of authors writing in French
which awards the annual Grand Prix
Littéraire d'Afrique Noire.

[1] 'Tatonnements de la critique des littératures
africaines', *Afrique Littéraire et Artistique*, no. 50,
1979, p. 8
[2] *Afrique Littéraire et Artistique*, no. 50, p. 8 (this
and the following quotations translated from
the French by the editors)
[3] *Ibid.*, p. 14
[4] *Ibid.*, p. 13

Dambudzo Marechera
born 1955   ZIMBABWE

'It is no good pretending this book is an
easy or pleasant read. More like over-
hearing a scream.' So wrote Doris
Lessing[1] of Marechera's first book, *The
House of Hunger*, which won the writer *The
Guardian* Fiction Award in 1979.

Born the son of a lorry driver in a small
Zimbabwean town, Marechera went to a
mission boarding school, supported by
scholarships. Shortly after he left the
school, a number of pupils deserted to
join the guerrillas in Mozambique; of his
own generation's political involvement
the author's wry comment is, 'In our
time, we thought demonstrations were
more to the point. We were more learned
in political argument than in working it
out physically, in violence. So in a way we
were easy fodder for the police.'[2]

The House of Hunger describes life in a
Zimbabwean township, and, says the
author,

> is about the brutalisation of the individual's
> feelings, instincts mental processes – the
> brutalisation of all this in such a way that you
> come to a point where, among ourselves in
> the black urban areas, that is ordinary
> reality. We then inflict it on ourselves,
> husbands on wives, wives upon wives, wives
> beating their children, children beating up
> the cats.[3]

And yet, in writing about the essence of
violence, Marechera rises above mere
reporting or sensationalism. Lessing per-
tinently remarks that

> *The House of Hunger* is not polemical writing,
> far from it: and what a miracle that it isn't.
> But writer and book are both of the nature of
> miracles. Hard for anyone to become a
> writer, but to do it against such handicaps?
> It seems that he was held together partly by
> great literature, which can nourish, in the
> world's cultural deserts, in a way not easily
> understood by the more advantaged.[4]

While at the University of Rhodesia (as it then was), Marechera edited a student magazine. Following a protest demonstration he was expelled from the university, and was due to be arrested when he was helped to escape, and then remained in hiding for four months. A scholarship took him to the University of Oxford in 1974. The attitudes to education that he encountered in Oxford were novel – and shattering: 'I was suddenly among people who didn't give a damn about hard work . . . You came out with your whole mind concussed.'[5] He remained at the university for two years, after which he was given the option of leaving or of submitting to voluntary psychiatric treatment, according to an interview in *The Guardian*.

A period as a resident writer in the University of Sheffield, and several years of roughing it in London, Cardiff and Oxford followed. This experience, and the knowledge of the war in Zimbabwe and the uncertain fate of friends and family, went into the writing of *The House of Hunger* (a novella and short stories) and *Black Sunlight*, his first published novel which emerged out of a constellation of mini-novels. He has also written some poetry. Asked to what extent his work is autobiographical, Marechera has answered:

I based *The House of Hunger* on fact . . . in Southern Africa we have always had the difficulty of writing about racialism, fascism, black township life, without appearing to write documentary novels rather than actual fiction. I tried to find a style whereby I could actually use the facts which everybody knows in such a way that the fiction emanated, as it were, from the basic facts. In *The House of Hunger* I do not preach about politics, I do not preach about anything at all. I merely state exactly what 'The House of Hunger', Zimbabwe, is like.[6]

Black Sunlight, published in 1980, deals with urban guerrillas operating in a society in chaos. One reviewer has written:

Personal breakdown is the theme as much as political breakdown – indeed the two are inseparable. And Marechera makes ambitious use of many of the methods that one associates with 'experimental' fiction to present this sense of complete collapse.

There are abrupt shifts of time and place, streams – or rather torrents – of consciousness, and verbal extravagance, all drafted to the service of an attitude that insists upon depredation as the present norm of human existence.[7]

Marechera has created very considerable impact with his first two books. One assessment, from Germany, is not untypical:

There is perhaps no other African writer who has described the permanent persecution, the process of brutalisation and the domination of others over the most secret cells of one's personality so powerfully, so intensely and so realistically as Dambudzo Marechera.[8]

A television study of him and his return to Zimbabwe has been made for the new British fourth television channel.

[1] Doris Lessing, 'A cultural tug-of-war', *Books and Bookmen*, June 1979, p. 62
[2] *The Guardian*, 30 Nov. 1979
[3] Al Imfeld, 'Portraits of African writers', no. 9, Deutsche Welle transcript (Cologne, 1979), p. 2
[4] Lessing, 'A cultural tug-of-war'
[5] *The Guardian*, 30 Nov. 1979
[6] 'Arts and Africa', no. 288P, BBC African Service transcript (London)
[7] James Lasdun, 'Sunlight and chaos', *New Statesman*, Dec. 1980
[8] Imfeld, 'Portraits of African writers', p. 3

Edouard Maunick
born 1931   MAURITIUS

'My little island', says Mauritian poet, Edouard Maunick, 'is not on most maps':

When I went into the world, I was taught to speak about my country. But how? One of the first things I used to say was not that in Mauritius there are black people. Africans came there. Indians came there . . . I did not say that we were very proud to belong to Africa. I was told by my mother, by my teachers, and by other people not to take heed of this side of myself. What I used to say was : 'Oh, you don't know Mauritius? . . . This is the island where the stepfather of Baudelaire sent him. Baudelaire came to Mauritius . . .' This is the way I was behaving. I was just that sort of half-breed that they wanted me to be in that society.[1]

One of the major concerns of Edouard

Maunick as a poet has been to forge an identity out of the paradoxes of his birth on 23 September 1931 of mixed African, Indian and French ancestry on that tiny island lost in the Indian Ocean. For the first 29 years of his life, which he lived entirely in Mauritius, he was taught to ignore his African and Indian forebears and claim only his French background. As he grew up, however, schooled in both English and French traditions (passing the junior and senior Cambridge examinations and the diploma of the Alliance Française and later studying at the Teacher's Training College in Port Louis) he learned to hate the white man for rejecting him, just as his mother, the daughter of a Frenchman and a black woman, had hated the white man who had refused to marry her mother and give her child a name. In one of his poems Maunick tells the world he cannot afford to mourn over the facts of his existence: 'What do you want me to do about this, except to laugh at the crime and build my body stronger than bereavement?'[2]

Faced with the dilemma of his very existence, which means that he is 'not black enough to be a Black Man, and not white enough to be a White Man, and not Hindu enough to be a Hindi',[3] Edouard Maunick has had to seek out and proclaim his own identity. 'I am Negro, by preference,' he says in an oft-quoted remark.

One of Maunick's earliest memories was the day in 1936 when, as a five-year-old, he heard his father announce sadly that a great poet had committed suicide. He was referring to the Malagasy writer, Jean-Joseph Rabéarivelo, who, says Maunick, had taken his life because the French had refused him the opportunity to go to Paris:

He had read about the universality of what is called French culture and the Occidental world, he wanted to go there. He wanted to touch, to go to the very flesh of that metropolis, and it was *then* he became the Negro. *Then* he was the black man who couldn't go there because there was no place for him. So he killed himself.[4]

A little over a quarter of a century later, in 1961, Edouard Maunick had the opportunity that Rabéarivelo did not have. After the success of *Ces oiseaux de sang*, his first poetry collection, published in Mauritius in 1954 and awarded a prize by the Académie Française, Maunick left his island and his job as director of the municipal library of Port Louis and moved permanently to Paris. The six verse collections that he has published since then have confirmed his stature as a poet.

For Edouard Maunick poetic discourse is as natural a function of mankind as speech. 'The words of a man, a woman or a child who says exactly his dream or his reality are a poem.'[5] You do not talk about or define poetry, he says, you make poetry. A certain amount of analysis can be a good thing, but too much can ruin poetry and signal 'the beginning of death': 'In the last reading the discourse of man does not seek to re-discover the *original* word so much as it seeks to partake of cosmic rumblings.'[6]

A central image in Maunick's poetry is the sea – the sea that has defined the existence of the island where he grew up but that also can narrow and circumscribe human existence. In working out his identity Maunick has felt compelled to beware of insularity and to extend his gaze across the sea, first to the African continent, and then on to those other islands in the world where black people live.

Maunick has also had to assume the apparent contradiction of his life in voluntary 'exile' in the French capital where he speaks and writes in French and is surrounded by French culture. In talking with a group of students at the California Institute of Technology in 1971 Maunick explained that, like Shakespeare's Caliban, he intended to use French and English as a weapon: 'If I am going to bring most of what I am to the world, and explain myself to the world, these languages are a weapon you have given me, and I am going to use them against you.'[7]

Since his move to Paris Edouard Maunick has become an eminent spokesman for francophone African writers, notably through his work as a journalist for publications like *Demain Afrique* (now defunct) and *Nouvelles Littéraires* and as producer of radio and television broadcasts for Radio France Internationale, aimed at audiences in Africa and the Indian Ocean. His interviews and book reviews of the major writers in francophone African literature have contributed to his renown, not only as a poet, but as a critic. In addition, two of his radio plays (*Noël perdu et retrouvé* and *Un soir une source*) have been broadcast by Radio France Internationale. Maunick has also travelled throughout the world to speak before university communities.

Edouard Maunick has been closely linked with the Société Africaine de Culture, and its publishing house, Présence Africaine, which brought out his second, third, and fourth collections of verse. He has also developed intimate friendships with the founders of negritude, Léopold Sédar Senghor and Aimé Césaire. Maunick has interviewed Senghor for radio, and in 1963 he published a critical piece on Césaire's poetry for *Preuves Informations*. The Senegalese Government has made Maunick an officer of the Order of the Lion.

One would be wrong to fix a label on Maunick as an orthodox proponent of negritude. For him negritude is 'neither a school nor an institution'. It has 'no canons, no credos'. 'A black poet,' affirms Maunick, 'naturally partakes of Négritude.'[8] By that he means that negritude was simply the fact of the black man discovering his true identity:

> The important 'lesson' of the phenomenon of Négritude is that, suddenly, men became aware of belonging naturally in the world, as themselves, and they finally listened to their inner urges and brought out that aspect of themselves that would make the world a whole. In so doing [however] they do not exile themselves from others; they do not go into a museum filled only with mirrors; they do not scratch their navel to touch the centre of the earth; they do not turn to the past; they simple *recognize* themselves.[9]

Maunick has no respect for 'black intellectuals' who want to make political slogans or war cries out of negritude. He speaks as sarcastically about them as he does of those who have attempted to define degrees of negritude. The black man's struggle for identity, in his view, must not blind him to the struggles faced by men elsewhere in the world: 'As for me, I cannot stop thinking about Latin America or South Africa and all those other places on the earth where man is still an *object* and a curse.'[10]

[1] *Edouard Maunick: A Black Mauritian Poet Speaks* (Pasadena, California, 1971) p. 4
[2] *Ibid.*, p. 17
[3] Edouard J. Maunick: Comme si on pouvait encoure chauffer le soleil!' *Poésie I: Nouvelle poésie négro-africane*, nos. 43–45, 1976, p. 100 (translated from the French by the editors)
[4] Maunick, *A Black Mauritian Poet Speaks*, p. 3
[5] Maunick, *Poésie I*, p. 104
[6] *Ibid.*, p. 105
[7] Maunick, *A Black Mauritian Poet Speaks*, p. 18
[8] Maunick, *Poésie I*, p. 99
[9] *Ibid.*, p. 100
[10] *Ibid.*, p. 101

Guy Menga
born 1935   CONGO

The unifying theme of the novel and the two plays that Guy Menga published between 1966 and 1969 are the young men and women who defy traditions and who get away with it. In the comedy, *L'Oracle* (1969), a young woman obtains the right to marry whom she pleases. In an earlier play, *La Marmite de Koka-Mbala*, which is much more serious in tone, young Bitala is brought before the elders for sentencing, after having seen a woman bathing in the river. According to custom he must be put to death but is absolved in the end, thanks to his own courage and determination and the intervention of the king's favourite wife whom the monarch had allowed to speak before the elders – a thing unheard of in itself. Bitala and a group of young men, all armed, had burst in on the assembled elders and declared, 'We won't leave this palace before you satisfy us that the cauldron [the symbol of tradition] here be broken, and that the assembly of elders be dissolved, for it is the origins of all the wrongs done to young people, we are sure.'[1] *L'Oracle* and *La Marmite de Koka-Mbala* won the 1967–8 *Concours*

Théâtral Interafricain sponsored by the French broadcasting corporation and were published in a combined volume in 1969 by CLE. *La Marmite de Koka-Mbala* had first been issued in 1966 by Editions Regain in Monaco and was performed at the First Festival of Negro Arts in Dakar that same year.

Vouata, the hero of Menga's novel *La Palabre stérile*, winner of the 1969 Grand Prix Littéraire d'Afrique Noire, is also an individual who refuses to accept customs that he believes unjust. Unlike the heroes of Menga's plays, however, he has to pay a high price for his stubbornness in the beginning, but is eventually rewarded. He is exiled from his village for having cried when his father died after being suspected of witchcraft and undergoing trial by poison. The move to the city is made smoothly, however, and he finds a job and marries. What does throw him into an emotional turmoil is that his wife leaves him after getting pregnant by another man in order to prove that their childless marriage is his fault, not hers. Vouata joins the Matswanas, a religious sect-cum-nationalist movement, but is deported by the authorities to Tchad when the sect is outlawed. Fortunately, all ends well. He is reunited with his wife upon his return and discovers that he had, in fact, sired three children – by his wife and two other women.

Fame N'Dongo, the literary critic of the *Cameroon Tribune*, is very harsh on the novel's contents, while praising its clearness of language and purity of style. The novel, he claims, is nothing less than 'soporific' because it magnifies trite problems (outdated customs, the hero's sterility) and avoids the real issues of contemporary Africa. *La Palabre stérile*, he says, is not even an illustration of the troubled nationalist era since it is clear the hero joined the Matswa movement as a result of a broken heart rather than out of real commitment.[2] Several years earlier, in an article that appeared just after *La Palabre stérile* had been published, Tati-Loutard had been much kinder to the novel, praising it for expressing the 'difficulty of existence in a world where the forces of tradition and of colonial

oppression join together to crush the individual'.[3]

With the publication of Guy Menga's latest novel, *Kotawali* (1977), it would be very difficult to accuse him of glossing over present-day political issues in Africa. The central figure of the novel is a young woman who is a resistance fighter in an independent African country and who contributes to arousing the political awareness of the taxi-driver who discovers her wounded and helps her go into hiding. As a result he too becomes involved in the resistance.

Since 1971 Guy Menga has also turned to the more traditional genre of story-telling with the three 'Moni-Mambou' collections which have all been published by CLE. The hero of each of these tales is the wanderer, Moni-Mambou, who says the whole world is his home and who spends his life going from place to place, adventure to adventure, and who never refuses to help the poor and oppressed. A fourth collection of stories, *Les Indiscretions du vagabond*, in which another wandering hero entertains a Congolese village for six nights in a row, form the substance of the volume Menga published in 1974 with Editions Naaman. Menga has written three other plays: *Tsia Mbuala ou le griot insoumis* which is to come out soon, *Okouele*, staged in Brazzaville in 1971, and *Ndako ya Ndélé*, a play written in Lingala. Two short stories which are not part of the Moni-Mambou series or of his most recent collection have also appeared in print. *Un bambou précieux* was published in an issue of *Bingo*, and *Le Cicerone de la Médina* in the first volume of *10 nouvelles de . . .*, a work published by the Agence pour la Coopération Culturelle et Technique in Paris.

Guy Menga's professional career has been devoted to journalism and broadcasting work, after a short period as a primary school teacher upon completion of his secondary studies. He spent two years in training in Paris at the Office de Coopération Radiophonique (1961–2 and again in 1963–4) and was director of programmes and then General Director with the Radiodiffusion Télévision Congolaise from 1967 to 1971. Born as

Gaston-Guy Birouta-Menga in 1935 in Mankonongo, a village south of Brazzaville, he attended St Joseph's school in Brazzaville from 1945 to 1951 and Collège Cheminade, a Catholic secondary school in Brazzaville, from 1951 to 1956. He has been living in Paris since 1971 when he left his position in broadcasting in the Congo and went to France for further training.

[1] Quoted in Jean-Baptiste Tati-Loutard, ed., *Anthologie de la littérature congolaise d'expression française*, Yaoundé, 1976, p. 84 (editors' translation for this and following quotations)

[2] Fame N'Dongo, 'Le roman soporifique, III: *La Palabre stérile* de Guy Menga', *Cameroon Tribune*, no. 841, 10–11 April 1977

[3] Jean-Baptiste Tati-Loutard, 'Guy Menga: du théâtre au roman', *Sentiers*, September–October 1969, p. 24

Es'kia Mphahlele
born 1919   SOUTH AFRICA

Es'kia (Ezekiel) Mphahlele emerged from the slums of Pretoria to become a novelist, essayist and teacher, and one of the leading voices from South Africa. The hard work and sacrifice of his grandmother and aunt, with whom he lived in Pretoria's Second Avenue, enabled the young Mphahlele to attend primary school and later escape the ghetto to board at Johannesburg's St Peter's Secondary School, an institution noted for its high standards of academic freedom

and scholarship, and from there to Adams College in Natal.

Having been banned from a teaching career for his outspoken opposition to the government's Bantu Education Act, Mphahlele worked as a messenger for a while, but then returned to Pretoria. Here he began his literary career as a reporter for *Drum*, a picture magazine designed for a black African audience, while simultaneously studying externally for his B.A. and M.A. from the University of South Africa. However, Mphahlele was not really a journalist; he did not believe in 'a press for whites and a press for non-whites'; he was mostly interested in 'the editing of short stories'.[1] His first collection of short stories *Man Must Live* was published by the pioneering *African Bookman* in Cape Town in 1947.

In 1957, at the age of 37, Mphahlele left South Africa for Nigeria, where he taught at a grammar school; he then lectured in English language and literature in the University of Ibadan's Department of Extra-Mural Studies.

In 1959 his first full-length autobiographical work, *Down Second Avenue*, met with critical acclaim. In 1961 his second collection of short stories, *The Living and the Dead*, was published by Mbari. By 1957 Mphahlele had found that his perspective had changed from escapist to protest writing and hopefully, he said, 'to something of a higher order, which is the ironic meeting between protest and acceptance in their widest terms.'[2]

From Nigeria Mphahlele went to Paris, where at the Congress for Cultural Freedom he was director of the African programme. In the meantime, together with Wole Soyinka and Ulli Beier, he co-edited issues 7 (June 1960) to 13 (November 1964) of the literary journal *Black Orpheus*. Returning to Africa in 1963, Mphahlele founded Chemchemi, a new cultural centre for writers and artists in Nairobi, and directed its activities up to 1965.

Living his life in exile, Mphahlele described himself as 'the personification of the African paradox, detribalized, Westernized, but still an African'.[3] His outlook toward himself and South Africa was revealed in a 1964 National Educational Television interview:

These two ways of living, the African and the European, I think in South Africa are much more integrated than you will find outside South Africa . . . the black tar has rubbed off on to the white man and . . . the stuff of whiteness has rubbed off on to the black . . . we have influenced one another so much . . . I have reconciled a good number of these disparate elements in me . . . My African values continue to remain a top, solid thing inside me, the African humanism . . . wanting to be one of a community which is very African; this individualism also . . . the European part of one; but at the same time . . . you get to this middle point where you can reconcile the disparate elements. And I think I have done so in me . . .

I feel very gloomy about the whole situation as far as creative writing is concerned. I think right now we are being sucked into this battle between the ruling whites and the Africans . . . our energies go into this conflict to such an extent that we don't have much left for creative work. One might ask the question – why could this not be a spur towards creative writing? . . . We are in two ghettos, two different streams . . . and you can't get really dynamic art in this kind of society. You won't get a great, white novel, I don't think, and you won't get a great black novel until we get to a point where we . . . [are] integrated.[4]

Mphahlele's odyssey took him to the United States in 1967 to lecture in English at the University of Denver, where he also acted as editor of *Africa Today* and worked for his doctorate which was awarded in 1968. He returned briefly to Africa in the autumn of 1968 to lecture in the English department at the University of Zambia in Lusaka. In June 1970 Mphahlele returned to the University of Denver.

The 1968 *African Arts/Arts d'Afrique* literary competition awarded *The Wanderers* its first prize. Subtitled *A Novel of Africa*, this autobiographical novel describes Mphahlele's 'experiences as a wanderer with his family, as he moved across the continent seeking for those essential roots which a writer must have'.[5] This four-part novel was released by Collier in 1971.

Ezekiel Mphahlele's output has been considerable: he has written numerous articles, essays, book reviews and short stories, including the volume *In Corner B* published in 1967, and *The African Image*, a collection of essays growing out of his M.A. thesis. He is the editor of two anthologies, *Writing Today in Africa* and *Modern African Stories*, the latter produced in association with Ellis Komey. *Voices in the Whirlwind*, a new critical work, was published in 1972. Apart from one new essay, it brought together articles published in periodicals and continued the themes picked up in *The African Image*. These are far from dry literary pieces. His biographer points out that when Mphahlele 'writes on a literary theme, he produces not so much a literary essay as a commentary on writers with whom he is closely involved intellectually'.[6]

Mphahlele moved again in 1974, joining the staff of the University of Pennsylvania as professor of English literature. His next novel *Chirundu* was written by this time, but it was not to be published until 1980. It arose out of his stay in Zambia; 'I've always wanted to be able to get the feel and smell of a place before I write about it. And now I want to do this thing set in Zambia . . .'[7] In it, he takes a careful look at African independence, and traces the feelings of optimism and disillusionment through the relationships of Chirundu and other characters.

In mid-1977 he left Pennsylvania and returned to South Africa. The government vetoed his appointment as Professor of English at Turfloop, the University of the north. Instead, he became an inspector of schools at Lebowa returning, he remarked, after 20 years of exile to live in a town 'seven miles from where at ages 5–12 I herded goats and cattle'.[8] The sense of alienation as an exile had never left Mphahlele and his wife:

Towards the end of our nine years stay in the US, I became painfully aware that I was not contributing meaningfully to American education and cultural goals . . . you can cuddle up in an American university atmosphere, become engrossed in your intellectual pursuits, and forget, simply insulate yourself against the sound of human concerns out there.[9]

Apart from intellectual considerations, his work was affected by the sense of exile. He found it possible to write critically and even to write poetry, for it 'can overlook diversities or try to unify them if one wants to produce public poetry; because the poetic sensibility strives to put things together, explores the quality of relationships'. Fiction is different. It 'thrives on conflict, even though the final product demonstrates a single total focus. For conflict and diversity, you need to be intensely familiar with particulars, place. I did not have these, and could not fake them if I wanted to.'[10] Like so many South African exiles, he never lost his commitment to the country. It represented a reality 'so deeply rooted in my life that I could never lose it, dare not lose it. That is its tyranny and its value as the root of commitment to its culture.'[11] He has written poetry too, which has appeared in *Black Orpheus, The Gar, South African Voices, New African Literature and the Arts*, and *Poems from Black Africa*.

Once in South Africa he noticed changes, mostly for the worse. Soweto, he observed, was a 'real great big slum, in the sense it wasn't when I was still there . . .'. Detentions, tension and suffering had increased, he thought.[12] When a post was offered to him as a Senior Research Fellow at the African Studies Institute at the University of the Witwatersrand, he accepted. Besides teaching African and comparative literature, he conducts his own research, particularly into the oral poetry of the northern language groups of the Venda, Sotho and Tsonga peoples. His and his wife's return to South Africa (their children have remained in the United States) has provoked both immense admiration and stringent criticism. Perhaps Mphahlele should have the last word on the subject:

My very return is a compromise between the outsider who did not *have* to be bullied by place and yet wanted it badly, and the insider who has an irrepressible attachment to ancestral place anywhere from a rural to an urban setting. The teacher and the writer in me made a deal: that as we both want place, you to teach among our people and regain a

sense of relevance, I to create a metaphor out of physical place and its human environment, we should return to the country of our birth. Just don't you breathe down my neck, teacher, and tell me how to write. Because you're an almost irresistible pedagogue, and soon I shall be dragged before a tribunal accused of writing bad verse and worse fiction. Just stick to the classroom and let me take care of the metaphors, understand![13]

[1] Ezekiel Mphahlele, *Down Second Avenue* (Berlin, 1962), p. 187
[2] *Ibid.*, p. 217
[3] 'African writers of today', National Educational Television, Program no. 3, 1964
[4] *Ibid.*
[5] *African Arts/Arts d'Afrique*, vol. 2, no. 2, Winter 1969, p. 12
[6] Ursular A. Barnett, *Ezekiel Mphahlele* (Boston, 1976), p. 123
[7] 'Interview with Ezekiel Mphahlele', in Bernth Lindfors *et al.*, eds., *Palaver: Interviews with Five African Writers in Texas* (Austin, Texas, 1972), p. 44
[8] Es'kia Mphahlele, 'Exile, the tyranny of place and the literary compromise', *Studies in English*, University of South Africa, April 1979, p. 44
[9] *Ibid.*, p. 40
[10] *Ibid.*, pp. 40–1
[11] *Ibid.*, p. 41
[12] 'Arts and Africa', no. 271, BBC African Service transcript (London)
[13] Mphahlele, 'Exile, the tyranny of place', p. 44

Oswald (Joseph) Mbuyiseni Mtshali

born 1940   SOUTH AFRICA

Mtshali, the first black South African to publish a book of poetry inside the country for 20 years, and the first poet writing from within the country to have a book published abroad, has been the subject of several controversies. Critics overseas have protested at this lack of vehemence, due to the 'restraints placed on a poet who writes within South Africa', and castigated his performance as 'cramped by the knowledge of existing censorship and banning laws'.[1] Within South Africa he was a *cause célèbre* of a different kind: debates, lectures, and letters turned on 'literary standards', incorrect grammar, and whether he writes verse, songs, or poetry. One critic wrote: '. . . our responsibility towards art should prevent us from celebrating something as poetry which is not quite poetry',[2] while another patronizing academic judged: 'It is good, small-scale poetry and its sales chiefly denote a taste on the part of the public as healthy as that of children for boiled sweets.'[3]

Mtshali's reply is succinct: '. . . we have got an urgent message to deliver to any one who cares to listen to it. We have not got the time to embellish this urgent message with unnecessary and cumbersome ornaments . . . and an ornate and lofty style.'[4] Or, as a perceptive critic summed up in a 'defence' of Mtshali, contributed in an exchange in a South African publication:

> When a man can do for African township life, even imperfectly, what Carl Sandburg did for the sprawling industrialism of the United States in the thirties (*The People, Yes*); when African after African can hold up Mtshali's book and say 'This is *it*, this is how it *is*!' because their world and their experience have been so clearly articulated, then it is time for the academic pundits . . . to get off their high horses and reconsider their whole aesthetic,[5]

The poet was born and educated in Vryheid, Natal, and came to Johannesburg after matriculation. On a visit to the city when he was young, he was horrified by it; now he sees it as 'the centre of all things'.[6] He wrote some poetry while still at school, and received encouragment from his teachers. His wish to attend the University of the Witwatersrand was thwarted when the separate universities legislation was introduced, and he rejected the alternative 'tribal colleges'. Instead he worked as a messenger and in his spare time wrote poetry which was printed in various journals: *Ophir*, *New Coin*, *The Purple Renoster*, *The Classic*, and *Unisa English Studies*.

The fruits of his labours were collected in the anthology *Sounds of a Cowhide Drum*, published in South Africa in 1971. It was an overnight success; 16,000 copies were sold in the first year, as the book ran through six impressions. An American edition appeared in the following year, and a British one in 1974. The book was further honoured by the award of the 1974 Olive Schreiner Poetry Prize. Remarked a journalist: '. . . it suggests there is either something remarkable about the poet, or something peculiarly receptive about the time in which he writes. Both would be true of Oswald Mtshali.'[7]

The success of the book was received with mixed feelings by the poet. 'This attempt to communicate has had a traumatic effect on me and badly bruised my soul.' He concedes that several blacks have written poetry successfully, 'but my position was different', he explains: 'I was innocently and genuinely employed as a "messenger". This was seized upon, glamourised, romanticised, and, presto, I became an underprivileged Black who was "gifted" but had to do menial work. Most of these newspaper write-ups were genuine, but some were quite patronising.'[8]

Despite the reservations he felt, he none the less was held by many to have served black South Africans well. 'He's given a real impetus to local poetry as no other poet has ever done', says Mzamane.[9] He 'brilliantly depicts the hypocrisy, hatred, violence and murder that permeate South African society',[10] Mtshali aligned himself with the Black Consciousness attitudes in South Africa. 'I am pessimistic about the purpose of inspiring and influencing people here in South Africa', he wrote:

> Many Whites don't care a damn about the feeble efforts I make. I once thought I could evangelise and convert Whites to give us back our dignity . . . I have now turned to inspire my fellow Blacks to be proud, to strive, to seek their true identity as a single solid group.[11]

Mtshali's second volume, *Fireflames*, was long awaited. Its publication in 1980 was immediately followed by its banning. Mphahlele sees Mtshali as having donned the mantle of 'poet-priest-prophet', like other African and Afroamerican writers. He adds:

> To the extent the poetry is powerful words expressing powerful feelings, the 'powerful' word also meaning the 'beautiful', this heroic verse is moving. The beautiful, the

powerful, also increases the reader. Built into this is also poetry as a way of perceiving. Mtshali's imagery which sends signals in various directions excites our sense of the heroic. His metaphor of the fire flames recurs throughout to reinforce this sense.[12]

Mtshali was awarded a fellowship in the International Writers programme at Iowa, and has attended Columbia University. At the British Poetry International in 1973 he shared the platform with W. H. Auden and Allen Ginsberg. He worked for a time on a Johannesburg daily newspaper on his return to South Africa, and then accepted the appointment as vice-principal of a privately funded school (PACE) which has been set up in Soweto. He continues to write in both English and his mother tongue, Zulu.

The Soweto uprising in 1976, and the changing consciousness in South Africa has lent hope and inspiration to blacks. Mthsali's is one of the articulate voices on the subject: '. . . our feelings as black people have become more and more vocal. For too long we have been muffled by our unfounded fears which we cannot contain any more . . . Now we have seen through this smokescreen and we know the truth.'[13] An irreversible step has been reached in the history of South Africa, and the poets are in the forefront of change:

> We capture history as it is made by our people. Politicians think they can rewrite or even hold the turning wheel of history, but they are always proved wrong. If this earth were ruled by poets, there would be no wars to turn the course of history. I am convinced that my poetry echoes the feelings, aspirations, hopes, disappointments of many Blacks here in South Africa, rural as well as urbanised.[14]

[1] Tayo Olafioye, 'South African thoughts in poetry', *Ba Shiru*, vol. 6, no. 1, 1974, p. 10
[2] Alan James, 'Mtshali – a discordant view', *New Nation*, Oct. 1971, p. 22
[3] Philip Birkinshaw, 'Afro-English poetry', *New Nation*, Jan. 1973, p. 18
[4] Oswald Mtshali, 'Black poetry in Southern Africa: what it means', in C. Heywood, ed., *Aspects of South African Literature* (London and New York, 1976), p. 127
[5] Walter Saunders, 'Mtshali: a defence', *New Nation*, June 1972, p. 21
[6] Mtshali quoted in the *Rand Daily Mail*, 12 June 1971
[7] Hugo Young, 'Stranger's voice', *The Sunday Times*, 6 May 1973
[8] Oswald Mtshali, 'Mtshali on Mtshali', *Bolt*, no. 7, 1973, p. 2
[9] Mbulelo Mzamane, 'The 50s and Beyond: an evaluation', *New Classic*, no. 4, 1977, p. 30
[10] Louis Barron, *Library Journal*, 15 Jan. 1973
[11] Ursula Barnett, 'Interview with Oswald Joseph Mtshali', *World Literature Written in English*, 12, 1973, pp. 29–30
[12] Es'kia Mphahlele, 'Mtshali's strident voice of self-assertion', *Rand Daily Mail*, 19 Dec. 1980
[13] Mtshali in Heywood, *Aspects*, p. 123
[14] Barnett, 'Interview with Mtshali', p. 34

Dominic Mulaisho
born 1933   ZAMBIA

Mulaisho has managed to combine writing with some of the most powerful and influential posts in Zambia; his most recent is economic adviser to President Kaunda. He was born at Mkando in Zambia, and received his education at Katondwe Mission, Canisius College and Chalimbana Teachers College. He graduated from the (then) University College of Rhodesia and Nyasaland in English, economics and history. The educational experience of Africans in mission schools is one of the themes of Mulaisho's first novel, *The Tongue of the Dumb*, which was published in 1971. The book explores the impact of colonial rule upon the structure and dynamics of politics in a tribal village. The position of Chief Mpona, flexible in his responses to change, is threatened by the wily but often insightful Lubinda. Mulaisho himself is not 'terribly nostalgic about the past' where 'the past did not make for a better life for people';[1] and Dathorne comments on this distinctly balanced view:

> *The Tongue of the Dumb* is impressive as a novel that describes conflict within the group itself. Few writers have attempted this and managed to maintain Mulaisho's neutrality. This is no pretty picture of a romanticized Africa; the passages dealing with hunger have a pathetic realism about them. At the conclusion one feels that Chief Mpona triumphs because he represents order, while Lubinda, who had flirted with the forces of evil, fails because his success would have brought disorder.[2]

Asked how autobiographical this first novel was, Mulaisho confirmed that while most was 'sheer imagination', as a child he 'had very personal experiences of what hunger can mean' while his father was working in Rhodesia.[3]

The young Mulaisho won rapid promotion in his career in education; he was successively a teacher, an inspector, and the principal of a teacher training college. Since 1965 he has held a number of senior administrative positions in Zambia. In that year he became the permanent secretary in the Office of the President – a post which he also occupied in the Ministry of Education. During the sensitive period which saw the nationalization of the Zambian copper mines he was chairman of the Mining Development Corporation, and subsequently general manager of the Marketing Board and managing director of the Industrial Development Corporation.

A number of critics have speculated on the relationship between the author's public life and his creative work. In his second novel, *The Smoke that Thunders* (1979), politics is again well to the forefront. The novel depicts the frantic attempts of big business to protect its interests during the battle for Independence in a fictitious country. Many readers would agree with the reviewer who commented:

> Although the author says all his characters are fictitious, the reader familiar with Zambia's pre-independence politics cannot help but notice that in many ways Kawala is President Kaunda, the President of Zambia. However, Mulaisho is not retelling the story of Zambia's fight for black rule. If the reader cannot avoid this impression, it is because the author is relating a story about the independence struggle in any African country.[4]

Mulaisho has said that he considers he has a duty to write. First, as an educationalist, 'if we were serious about an African-oriented educational system it was not the teachers' responsibility alone to produce the books out of which our children should be taught'. Secondly, he feels that although a number of books were being written by Africans, 'some of

these books did not bring out the nobleness of the African'. Particularly, politicians were 'invariably painted as either lecherous, corrupt or ignorant'. Further, he objects to the predominance in African literature of 'folklore and tales about rabbits, tortoises and so on' and so he seeks rather to present 'the people of Africa . . . first and foremost essentially as human beings no different from any others . . . motivated by the same instinct'.[5] Asked whom he intended as an audience, this politician–writer replied: 'I would like to write primarily for the Zambian audience, then the wider African audience and thereafter for humanity as a whole.'[6]

[1] Lee Nichols, ed., *Conversations with African writers* (Washington DC, 1981), p. 178
[2] O. R. Dathorne, *African Literature in the Twentieth Century* (London, 1979), pp. 149–50
[3] Nichols, *Conversations*, p. 178
[4] *The Rhodesian Herald*
[5] Nichols, *Conversations*, p. 181
[6] *Ibid.*, p. 182

John Munonye
born 1929   NIGERIA

John Munonye is often described by critics as a leading member of the 'Achebe school' of Igbo novelists for the way he has emulated Achebe's use of Igbo language, culture and history in his fiction. Munonye freely admits, moreover, to having been inspired by the example of a man who is not only a compatriot but a friend: 'I felt an urge to burst out into something new [other than his inhibiting civil service job], to start doing something different, and when Chinua got a novel published, I thought, "Here is a possibility." So I began to write. This was around 1963–64.'[1]

Munonye also shares a similar background with his friend Achebe. He was born in 1929 in the eastern Nigerian village of Akokwa which is near Ogidi, Achebe's birth-place. After secondary-school studies at Christ the King College in Onitsha, Munonye, like Achebe, attended University College, Ibadan, reading classical languages and history and obtaining a B.A. in 1952. But whereas Achebe went into broadcasting work following his matriculation from Ibadan and only entered the field of education later in his career, Munonye chose to go directly into education. He completed a Masters degree at the Institute of Education of the University of London in 1953 and worked for the Nigerian Ministry of Education from 1954 to 1977. For the latter part of that period he was principal of the Alvan Ikoku College of Education in Owerri (until 1973, known as the Advanced Teacher Training College), and then Chief Inspector of Education in Imo state.

Education – and Christianity – are major themes of four of Munonye's novels, three being set in the early days of colonialism (*The Only Son*, *Obi*, *The Oil Man of Obange*) and one that has a near-contemporary setting (*Bridge to a Wedding*). The struggle to acquire an education, which means converting to Christianity and renouncing traditional Igbo ways, places heavy strains on the family relationships of Munonye's characters and the consequences are invariably tragic. Jeri, the pathetic oil man of Obange, has one piece of bad luck after another, beginning with the loss of his wife, and literally works himself to death in order to provide an education for his five children. The desire for education pushes Nnana, the young hero of Munonye's first novel, *The Only Son*, to sever ties with his widowed mother, a woman who had dreams of her son's taking his

rightful place in the traditional community and righting the wrongs she had suffered since her husband's death. Disappointment nearly drives her mad. The dramatic conflict in *Obi*, the sequel to *The Only Son*, can be traced in part to the role played by Christian values in moulding the personality of the hero. In this novel Nnana, now a grown man, goes by the name of Joe. He has given up his job in the forestry service and returned to his village with his wife, Anna, a convent-raised orphan, and plans to start a modern plantation. The couple are childless but their devout, almost fanatic, Catholic faith prevents them from adopting traditional solutions to the problem (such as Joe's marriage to a second wife), and this is one of the indirect reasons why Joe is later exiled from the village. As tension increases among Joe's relatives, fueled also by a family land dispute case, Joe's temper flares and, in a momentary loss of control, he strikes the sister-in-law who had been taunting him. The woman dies some time after and Joe is held responsible for precipitating her death and is forced to leave the village.

Obi also focuses on the rivalry of the older and younger generations as seen from the angle of Church membership. For O. R. Dathorne this is a situation in which Munonye makes full use of his talent as a writer: 'The clash within the church is also one of individuals and personalities. And it is here that Munonye is at his best. He brings ideological institutional conflicts down from their high intellectual level and makes them personal . . .'[2]

As though sensitive to the criticism of his Nigerian readers who have reproached him for making his novels 'gratuitously tragic', Munonye finally puts an end to old quarrels growing out of the white man's educational system and religion in *Bridge to a Wedding*, published in 1978. Though not stated as such, the novel must be seen as the final work in the trilogy that started with *The Only Son* and *Obi*. *Bridge to a Wedding* ends on a note of reconciliation as Joe and Anna (now called Mr and Mrs Kafo, and the parents of five children) marry their daughter to the son of a leading citizen of the village that had banished Joe so many years before.

One of the themes of *Bridge to a Wedding* is the impatience of the younger generation with the unprogressive attitude of their elders, and Munonye, a member of Nigeria's first generation of novelists, has ironically come in for his own share of criticism from some younger writers who feel his themes are out of date. In a BBC broadcast devoted to *Bridge to a Wedding*, the Nigerian Peter Enahoro, author of *You Gotta Cry to Laugh*, bluntly declared:

They say in the blurb that 'Achebe opened the way for a whole series of Nigerian writers to investigate the cultural clash between the traditional pagan and the modern Christianized way of life. The best of them apart from Achebe himself is John Munonye' – fine, but they've been doing this now since the 50s.[3]

Munonye would undoubtedly feel Enahoro is being unfair, having himself stated in 1973 that Nigerian writers have finished recreating their past:

When we started writing, we felt a sense of mission about reconstructing our history, but now we must write about the present. We must go into our society – its strong and weak points, its problems, the prescriptions we would like to offer, casting these into art form. We cannot ignore such subjects. We must deal with them because if we do not, nobody will.[4]

In the same interview he said that he felt authors should begin writing about the civil war, its human dimension and its ironies. This is precisely what he did in a novel published three years after the war ended, *A Wreath for the Maidens*. Although the setting and the place names are fictional the novel is indeed Munonye's record of the Biafran conflict as seen through the eyes of two young men who watch with concern as their country heads towards civil war. When the inevitable occurs they feel duty-bound to take sides in favour of the seceding state but soon realize that their leaders are as self-interested and power-hungry as those of the former nation. In a recently published critical anthology on West African literature, Olalere Oladitan writes about *A Wreath for the Maidens*:

Munonye's work bears an indelible moral imprint which is sustained by the heroes and narrators. Although these itinerant witnesses are ready to participate in the actions when invited, they stand out of the common run of political leadership and remain at that remove of objectivity which allows for a critical analysis of the successive events and a just assessment of the other actors.[5]

With *A Dancer of Fortune*, a novel which is completely different in conception from his others, Munonye adds to the growing body of satirical novels coming out of Nigeria, a tradition that began with Achebe's *A Man of the People*. *A Dancer of Fortune* offers a tongue-in-cheek study of business practices in contemporary Nigeria where *caveat emptor* reigns and no one has ever heard of consumer associations, fair-trade commissions or ethical guidelines for publicity. The successful businessman is he who manages to outwit both his customers and his business rivals. The dancer of the title is Ayasko, a picturesque hero who earns his living dancing in itinerant market shows for patent-medicine dealers and whom everyone takes for a fool – until the day he fools the others by opening his own patent medicine shop after playing off his employers one against the other. Munonye has referred to his earlier novels as 'confrontation stories about people with high principles who pursue these principles, ideals or objectives unbendingly. These persons physically fail . . .'[6] No one in *A Dancer of Fortune* fails physically. True, Ayasko ends up in a courtroom at the novel's close but he walks out a free man. As unscrupulous as his business rivals, he nonetheless has redeeming human qualities which they lack. He is a good husband and father and has obvious charisma: 'His character is mainly ambiguous; his conduct mainy dubious. None the less he appears in no wise blameworthy since he is in keeping with the world around him, a world of shady undertakings, of semblance, of downright deceit.'[7]

In the 1973 interview Munonye complained about being caught in the dilemma of not being able to write full-time and spoke of having to serve 'two very demanding masters – my career in education and my career in writing'.[8] He retired from his Ministry of Education career, partly to have more time to devote to his writing, but he has now returned to teaching.

[1] 'Interview with John Munonye', in Bernth Lindfors, ed., *Dem-Say: Interviews with Eight Nigerian Writers* (Austin, Texas, 1974) p. 35
[2] O. R. Dathorne, *African Literature in the Twentieth Century* (London, 1976) p. 114
[3] 'Arts and Africa', no. 232, BBC African Service transcript (London)
[4] Lindfors, *Dem-Say*, p. 40
[5] Olalere Oladitan, 'The Nigerian crisis in the Nigerian novel', in Kolawole Ogungbesan ed., *New West African Literature* (London, 1979) p. 12
[6] Lindfors, *Dem-Say*, p. 37
[7] J. Stanhope Robb, '*A Dancer of Fortune* by John Munonye', *The Literary Half-yearly*, vol. 20, no. 1, Jan. 1979, p. 108
[8] Lindfors, *Dem-Say*, p. 38

Rémy Gilbert Médou Mvomo

born 1938   CAMEROON

The hero of Rémy Médou Mvomo's first novel, *Afrika Ba'a* (1969) is a young man who revives his dying village thanks to the new ideas and methods he brings home after a stay in the city. The city in Médou Mvomo's novel is certainly not the reference point. It is named, symbolically, Nécroville. What is evident in the novel, however, is that the move from home and the experience of different ways were crucial factors in the growth of the hero's self-awareness. In an interview published in *Abbia* in 1978 Médou Mvomo confirms the importance he places in a writer being well-travelled. The best way for an artist to 'be himself', he says, 'is by wandering throughout the world': 'You must make the thinkers, the great writers, the great artists travel because it is in moving around that they acquire their "muscle tone", in a word, their genius.'[1]

Médou Mvomo himself spent ten years away from Cameroon, going to France when he was still quite young and remaining there for his entire secondary school education and early adulthood. When he returned to Cameroon he devoted himself first to a project of popular education before enrolling in 1963 at the Faculty of Law in Yaoundé. He left without finishing his studies to go into journalism. In 1971 he founded the printing business which he still runs today.

The years in France, which included four years in the Massif Central, provided the background and setting for Médou Mvomo's second novel, *Mon amour en noir et blanc*, a tale about an African student and a French girl who fall in love. Unable to overcome the resistance of both sets of parents they ultimately give up their plans for marriage. It is a different sort of failure that is the central theme of a third novel, *Le Journal de Faliou*, published in 1972, a year after *Mon amour en noir et blanc*. *Le Journal de Faliou* records 16 dreary months in the life of a young man who goes to Douala hoping to earn enough money as a musician in order to continue his university studies – 16 months of occasional success but mainly failure, including the loss of his wife to another man. Even when hungry with no place to stay, Faliou continues to pursue his dream of an education by reading whenever he can.

In addition to three novels, Rémy Médou Mvomo has also recently published a play, *Les Enchaînés*, that received honourable mention in the 1973 Concours Théâtral Interafricain and that was published jointly by CLE and Nouvelles Editions Africaines in 1979. The play's hero, Zibi, is a former schoolteacher who 'chains himself up' when he borrows money to live in the grand manner that befits his new position as high civil servant in the 'Ministry of Planning and Various Affairs'. The play is a comedy and Médou Mvomo eventually finds a way to get his hero out of his predicament. If the audience is entertained at poor Zibi's expense, Médou Mvomo also wants them to retain the play's 'message'. 'You cannot have literature that is pure entertainment in Cameroon', he affirms.

'We have not yet reached the time when a literature of pure imagination is needed. You cannot be simple dreamers in a country that needs to build itself and that also has to struggle to solve so many problems.'[2] As a writer Médou Mvomo minimizes the role played by his imagination and emphasizes that he is above all an 'observer': 'We examine exactly the way things are and why they are, and we try to put down what we have seen and what we have thought about what we have seen.'[3]

The events recorded in *Africa Ba'a*, he says, really took place, and he participated in them. The reader may then wonder whether his other novels are autobiographical: a love affair he may have had while in France like the hero of *Mon amour en noir et blanc*, and his own unsuccessful search for a university education like Faliou in *Le Journal de Faliou*.

A member of the second generation of Cameroonian authors, Rémy Médou Mvomo speaks about the necessity for Africans today to adopt a 'third way' that is neither the wholesale adoption of Western values nor the sort of 'museum' culture that the negritude school would suggest:

> Our civilization must not be mummified for we do not have a dead culture. We did not start from nothing and we must not make coffins for our culture. The third way is, therefore, a way that encourages people to revive the culture that is already latent in them. However, one must not turn one's back on international civilization. I did not say European civilization, but international civilization.[4]

Rémy Médou Mvomo was born on 25 December 1938 near Sangmélina in southern Cameroon. He is one of the founding members, along with René Philombe and seven others, of the Association of Cameroonian Poets and Writers, an organization which over the years has played an important role in breaking the isolation surrounding writers in Cameroon but which, since 1975, has been inactive for lack of financial support. All of Médou Mvomo's works have been published in Cameroon by CLE.

[1] Richard Bjornson, 'Interview avec deux écrivains camerounais', *Abbia*, no. 31–33, February 1978, p. 222 (translated from the French by the editors)
[2] *Ibid.*, p. 215
[3] *Ibid.*, p. 215
[4] *Ibid.*, pp. 217–18

Meja Mwangi
born 1948   KENYA

Meja (David) Mwangi was born in Nanyuki, Kenya, and was a child during the Mau Mau emergency. He was confined, as were many Africans, to a camp to prevent contact with the Mau Mau. The restriction policy did not have much effect however: 'Everybody growing up at that time ... couldn't help getting involved ... You just couldn't help feeling the tension of the conflict between the forest fighters and the colonial government. Everyone was caught up in this big movement.'[1] His first book, *Taste of Death* (not published until 1975) arises out of that period. It is 'not actually an historical novel, but it is based on historical events, on more or less true story, and I thought this experience ought to be shared with other Kenyans ...'[2] The book deals with a group of forest fighters who are exterminated by British forces. Despite their apparent defeat, Mwangi sees the book in terms of a victory for the Mau Mau:

> What I was trying to say is that these people never gave up, even though they were no match for the colonial forces. Let's face it: there is no way they could have won the war

militarily. Yet, in spite of being outnum-
bered, outgunned and overwhelmed, they
kept on fighting, hoping that something
would come to their rescue, would help them
out of the situation. Eventually, when
Haraka, the hero of the novel, gets killed, his
spirit symbolically lives on. This was the
point I was trying to stress: the spirit of
resistance lived on. The fact that one little
band was wiped out did not mean that the
movement died.[3]

Mwangi's schooling was completed
after he attended Kenyatta College to do
A level science. He was then employed by
French television in Nairobi. He has also
worked as an audio-visual aide for the
British Council. By the mid-1970s he was
managing to live as a writer, submitting
short stories to magazines as well as
writing books.

The second major aspect of Mwangi's
concerns is evident in *Kill Me Quick*
(1973), namely his committed and
sensitive response 'to the problems of the
poor and downtrodden of his own
generation'.[4] The two main characters are
young lads who have been to middle
school through the sacrifices of their
families and who believe they will get jobs
in Nairobi and return home in glory.
They soon realize the hopelessness of the
situation and resort to begging, scroung-
ing and eventually thieving to survive.
One dies, the other embarks upon a
career of crime. Mwangi claims that
living in ghetto conditions during his
childhood days gave him an insight into
the way boys had to live out of dustbins.
He is optimistic that writing coming out
of East Africa now will affect the readers:
'You get a feeling walking down the street
that everybody's living in his own little
hut'; but despite their seeming isolation
Kenyans 'are very receptive to this kind of
thing. They have an idea of what's
happening but they don't know what's
happening and they're quite ready to
read something like that ... They didn't
know it was so hard. That's the kind of
realization I'm trying to bring out.'[5] *Kill
Me Quick* was awarded the 1974 Kenyatta
Prize for Literature.

In his next book, *Carcase for Hounds*
(1974), Mwangi reverted to his involvement with the Mau Mau. He thinks every

Kenyan should want to write about the
struggle at least once. Conscious of
comparison and parallels drawn between
the approach of various writers to the
conflict, Mwangi defines the difference
between himself and Ngugi. While Ngugi
wrote 'personal tragedies of a number of
people who were active in Mau Mau from
the social viewpoint', focusing on how
individuals were affected, 'what I wanted
to write was the impersonal mechanism
in itself'.[6] The result, to one critic, was
'little more than a novel of action with
slight plot and characterization',[7] but to
another it was a valuable account of the
logistics of the campaign:

> Mwangi tells us how the actual fighting took
> place: what the engagements were like, how
> the guerrillas obtained their weapons, what
> these weapons were like, what it was like to
> move in the forests with heavy guns, what
> happened when it rained, how the captain of
> the British anti-guerrilla force plotted and
> planned to defeat the Mau Mau, how the
> movement was finally defeated, and so on.[8]

Two more novels on the social problems of post-Independence Kenya have
followed, *Going Down River Road* (1976)
and *The Cockroach Dance* (1979). The
former, 'set in Nairobi's seething brothel,
pub, and cheap nightclub area', is
another example of Mwangi's 'characteristic qualities – a touching compassion
for the social or political underdog, a
quietness of tone which emphasises
rather than obscures the very serious
problems being analysed, and a remarkably controlled prose style'. However, the novelist is not merely being a
propagandist, for 'his preoccupation with
the social realities of the city does not
prevent him from creating some interesting characters and exploring some significant relationships'.[9] *The Cockroach
Dance* presents the despair and revolt of
one Dusman Gonzaga. He lives among
and identifies himself with the people of
the slums against the bureaucracy of the
controlling elite.

Nazareth suggests an aspect of Mwangi's writing – the element of suspense –
that is common to all his books:

> His stories are like thrillers: it is difficult
> to put them down because we want to

know what happens next. Underlying the details is a series of dualities in Mwangi's novels: hunter/hunted, policeman/criminal, educated/uneducated, selfishness/generosity, growth/decay, well-fed/hungry, greed/honesty, wealthy/dispossessed. The contradiction and conflict between these dualities created the tension in the novels, building up a movement toward resolution.[10]

He has turned a film script into a novel called *The Bushrangers* and a film has been made of *Carcase for Hounds* under the title *Cry Freedom.*

[1] Bernth Lindfors, 'Meja Mwangi', *Kunapipi*, vol. 1, no. 2, 1979, p. 68
[2] *Ibid.*
[3] *Ibid.*, pp. 69–70
[4] Lee Nichols, ed., *Conversations with African Writers* (Washington DC, 1981), p. 195
[5] *Ibid.*, p. 197
[6] Satoru Tsuchiya, 'Modern East African literature: from *Uhuru* to *Harambee*', *World Literature Today*, vol. 52, no. 4, 1978, pp. 570–1
[7] J. Burns, *Books Abroad*, vol. 49, no. 2, 1975
[8] Peter Nazareth, *Afriscope*, vol. 6, no. 4, 1976
[9] Eustace Palmer, 'Two views of urban life', *African Literature Today*, no. 9, 1978, p. 105
[10] Nazareth, *Afriscope*

Agostinho Neto

1922–1979   ANGOLA

Dr Agostinho Neto's life was intimately tied to the history of Angola during the transition from Portuguese colony to independent African state. Born in September 1922 in the village of Kaxikane in the region of Icolo e Bengo about 40 miles from Luanda, Dr Neto was raised in a Christian household. His father was a Protestant pastor and his mother was a teacher. In 1947 after working in the colonial health service, he was given a grant to study medicine at the University of Coimbra in Portugal. He later transferred to the University of Lisbon where he received his medical degree in 1958.

Imprisoned twice in the fifties by the colonial authorities because of his involvement in demonstrations, Neto was again arrested in 1960. This action by the Portuguese resulted in vociferous protests from around the world. Amnesty International spoke out on his behalf, as did writers such as Basil Davidson, Doris

Lessing, C. Day Lewis, Angus Wilson and John Osborne.

When he was finally released, Dr Neto joined the exiled MPLA (People's Movement for the Liberation of Angola) becoming its president in 1962. When, after a decade and a half of armed resistance, Angola gained Independence on 11 November 1975, Dr Neto became the first president of a free Angola. During the difficult period of his presidency, a time of civil strife, Dr Neto successfully guided the MPLA, always stressing the necessity of creating a multiracial socialist society based on tolerance and a dream of brotherhood. When the world heard that he had died of cancer in September 1979, leaders from socialist and capitalist countries alike hailed the gentle, soft-spoken man who dedicated his life to his people and the cause of peace.

Dr Neto, an active poet from 1945 to 1960, articulated in his verse the concerns and aspirations of Angola. A small volume of 48 of his poems was first published in Italy in 1963 under the title *Con Occhi Asciutti*; Sá da Costa published the first Portuguese edition, *Sagrada Esperança*, in 1974 as the first number in its Vozes do Mundo (Voices of the World) Series. It was awarded the Poetry of Combat Prize by the University of Ibadan in 1975. A voice of negritude, Dr Neto decries the injustices and loss of African self-respect that resulted from foreign political and cultural oppression. In his poems written in the late fifties and again in 1960, the gynaecologist from rural Angola speaks openly of independence, of a return to traditions and rivers and homes and beaches. Like Léopold Sédar Senghor, Dr Neto abandoned his poetic calling when political responsibilities demanded his entire attention. Dr Neto, however, remained an active member of the Angolan Writers Union, commenting from time to time on the writer's role. On one such occasion, he asserted his moral calling:

> I think that all of us will agree that writers should situate themselves in their times and exercise their function as formers of consciousness. They should be active agents in

the improvement of humanity ... Today, it will be necessary for Angolan literature to insert itself well into and be a reflection of Angolan culture.[1]

Socialism, for Dr Neto, did not mean blind adherence to preconceived ideas. Literature serves the revolution, but national culture is not static. He warned against cultural chauvinism and fixed socialistic positions.

Agostinho Neto's poems have been translated into many languages and are available in several collections. Donald Burness has devoted a chapter to him in his critical study, *Fire: Six Writers from Angola, Mozambique and Cape Verde*, and other critics have commented on his artistic achievement. As poet-president Agostinho Neto made a significant impact on African letters and the history of Angola. A day after his death António de Figueiredo appropriately summed up his life in an obituary that appeared in *The Guardian*: 'Angola, Africa, and the world have lost a great man who not only wrote history and poetry, but made it.'[2]

[1] Agostinho Neto, *On Literature and National Culture* (Cadernos Lavra e Oficina no. 20) (Luanda, 1979), pp. 10–11
[2] António de Figueiredo, 'A poet who wrote himself into the history of Africa', *The Guardian*, 12 Sept. 1979, p. 15

Ngugi wa Thiong'o
born 1938   KENYA

One must listen to the beat of the drums. If a singer is out of tune with the drums, he is a poor singer. He is a sweet singer when everybody joins in. The sweet songs last longer, too. They have more meaning and more emotion.[1]

Ngugi wa Thiong'o has himself amply borne out his premise. His sounds have been listened to so keenly that he is regarded as a threat by those whom he criticizes in his own country.

Ngugi wa Thiong'o's novel *Weep Not, Child* was written under the name James Ngugi. It was the first English language novel to be published by an East African writer and won him international praise as well as awards from the 1966 Dakar Festival of Negro Arts and from the East African Literature Bureau. Written during his student days in Uganda, it is divided into two parts: the first deals with the period just before the Mau Mau emergency, the second with the emergency itself, as it affected the life of a Kenyan family. 'Written in a simple, lyrical style, it creates a song about a society in transition ... Like the transition of the hero from youth to adulthood, the movement of society is inevitable. The kind of movement and the direction of the movement are not, however, predetermined. That is in the hands of the people affected.'[2] In 1969 *Weep Not, Child* was also published in an American edition.

In fact, this was Ngugi's second novel, for *The River Between*, although published a year later in 1965, was written first. In it he establishes the legend of land being given to the Kikuyu people, a legend which is 'the cornerstone of Ngugi's art, reiterated in each of his novels. His fiction is a systematic fictional examination of the consequences of the alienation of the people from their land, thus effectively from life.'[3]

When his third novel was published in 1967 it received high praise. *A Grain of Wheat* was, commented Lewis Nkosi, 'a prolonged meditation on the theme of national struggle, the courage, sacrifices and loyalties it requires, and not surprisingly some of the opportunism and failure of nerve which are brought to the surface by such momentous events'.[4] Eldred Jones declared that it was difficult to think of Kenyan Independence in the same way after reading Ngugi's novel 'which has the stature of art that changes and transforms our vision'.[5]

An historical pattern has emerged in these three novels which Ngugi claims is accidental. They do, however, represent

a history of colonialism. They start with the alienation of Gikuyu land and end with the alienation of the social and individual psyche of the colonised. The first begins at a time when the Gikuyu have their land, and the colonial presence is little more than one of missionaries and mission schools, a force which divides the people but does not yet dispossess them. In the second novel they are the dispossessed, tenant farmers, landless labourers or fighters seeking to regain the land which is home. In the third novel the white colonial landlords are going, leaving behind them the traumatised victims of the struggle and the new black landlords who threaten to perpetuate the system of alienation which colonialism set up.[6]

By 1967 Ngugi felt that the African writer had failed and he pointed out a future course, saying at the African Scandinavian Writers' Conference in that year:

When we, the black intellectuals, the black bourgeoisie, got the power, we never tried to bring about those policies which would be in harmony with the needs of the peasants and workers. I think it is time that the African writers also started to talk in the terms of these workers and peasants.[7]

Speaking on the same point in a 1969 interview Ngugi said,

Meanwhile I think the African writers ought to be addressing themselves more and more fully to the present needs, especially what I call the crisis or conflict between the emergent African bourgeoisie and the African masses.[8]

Ngugi is a Kikuyu, born in Limuru to one of his peasant father's several wives. After graduating with honours in English from (the erstwhile) Makerere University College in 1964 he worked on Nairobi's *Daily Nation* for several months before he left to do graduate work at the University of Leeds. Upon his return to Africa, Ngugi became a special lecturer in English at Nairobi's University College, a

post he held for a year and a half. In January 1969 the students went on strike. He resigned from his position in protest following the College's closure on 27 January and the alleged dictatorial attitude taken towards the student body both during and after the strike. He was editor of *Zuka: A Journal of East African Creative Writing*. (During his student days he had edited *Penpoint*, a periodical published by the Department of English at Makerere.) He dropped his Christian name of James and assumed the traditional Kikuyu name by which he is now known.

His literary career has encompassed playwriting, short stories, and journalism. *The Black Hermit*, his first play, was expressly written for the Uganda National Theatre as part of the 1962 Independence celebrations. *This Time Tomorrow*, a second play, is included in Pieterse's *Eleven Short African Plays* and was also published separately. Essays have appeared in *Transition*, *Penpoint*, *The New African*, and *Zuka*. Some of these, on African and Caribbean literature, culture and politics, were collected in *Homecoming* (Heinemann, 1972). In 1972 Ngugi was appointed head of the Department of Literature at the University of Nairobi. The thoughts of the previous twelve years gave rise to a set of short stories, *Secret Lives*, published in 1975. The themes in the stories often parallel those in his novels, but he does not regard the genre as a draft or literary experiment:

you cannot really separate your moods or your preoccupations if you write in a certain period. If you write a short story and then a play and a novel at about the same time, you'll find that some of the themes that are in my plays or short stories in a certain period reappear in the novel.[9]

His next play, *The Trial of Dedan Kimathi*, was co-scripted with Micere Mugo in 1976, and was performed at the 77 Festac in Lagos. Ngugi felt bitter about the fact that the Ministry of Social Services had to intervene before the play was allowed to run at the National Theatre in Nairobi, and then only for a few performances, during 'Kenyatta Day' week.

It was, after all, the month in which some Mau Mau and KAU leaders were arrested and detained. It was the month in which the Mau Mau armed struggle against British colonialism started. What could be more relevant for the week than a play about one of the most heroic leaders of the Mau Mau resistance? Kenyans needed to remind themselves that their independence had been won through sweat and blood.[10]

The emotional reaction of those in the audiences, some of whom travelled miles to see the play, bore out his contention.

1977 was an eventful year for Ngugi. It began highly successfully with the acclaim given to *Petals of Blood*, published by Heinemann simultaneously in Nairobi and London. Its origins lie in the late 1960s, as the author relates:

> I started writing *Petals of Blood* in 1970, although the idea had been conceived a year before. So between 1970 and 1976 I was fully engaged in writing that novel so that my development as a writer is related to the development of *Petals of Blood* in that period. It was not a very easy novel to write. It kept changing all the time. I grew with it all the time. And that is why it took so long to write. In that period I don't think I wrote much else in the way of creative writing except occasional articles and occasional public lectures in which I tried to define my outlook on literature.[11]

The book

> begins with a fire – arson? – in which there are killed three prominent, corrupt figures of the new Kenya. It ends with our knowing exactly what happened and why. But its journey, which has at its heart an actual journey taken by the drought-stricken people of the village of Ilmorog in order to beg for help from the city-world of its MP and of the national conscience, takes it back through all the sufferings of the fight for national freedom.[12]

The power of the book is conveyed by Baraka:

> Ngugi does not bite his tongue, he lays it out. He has upheld his responsibility so breathtakingly that one is given to putting the book down as one reads, starting up exclaiming, shouting out loud, that yes, yes, this is exact. A powerful book.[13]

Ngugi's commitment to the people of his country is clear:

> I am not as a Kenyan ashamed of speaking and writing about the peasants and workers who have built Kenya and who, through their blood and sweat, have written a history of grandeur and dignity and fearless resistance to foreign economic, political and cultural domination, a history of which we should be proud. If *Petals of Blood* can convey at least that message to us Kenyan readers, I shall be satisfied. Hopefully out of *Petals of Blood* we might gather petals of revolutionary love.[14]

Putting theory into practice, Ngugi was one of a committee that founded the Kamiriithu Educational, Cultural and Community Centre. Adult literacy courses were followed by the writing and production of a play in Gikuyu – devised jointly by Ngugi wa Thiong'o and Ngugi wa Mirii – entitled *Ngaahika Ndeenda*. It broke theatrical traditions by selecting actors among peasants and workers. The play opened in October 1977, in a theatre built by the Kamiriithu community, to packed houses. After a month the licence was revoked on the grounds that the play was provocative and potentially subversive. Three years later, when the play was published in Gikuyu by Heinemann in Nairobi, it went into three printings in as many months. The English edition, entitled *I Will Marry When I Want*, is shortly to appear in the African Writers Series. Far from being daunted by the banning, Ngugi drew encouragement from the experience:

> I saw how the people had appropriated the text . . . so that the play which was finally put on . . . was a far cry from the tentative awkward efforts originally put together by Ngugi and myself. I felt one with the people. I shared in their rediscovery of their collective strength and abilities, and in their joyous feeling that they could accomplish anything.[15]

It 'showed me the road along which I should have been travelling on all these past seventeen years of my writing career'.[16]

The crowded year of 1977 ended with Ngugi in prison. No charges were brought against him; he was not brought to trial; and it was about a year before he was released. 'To be arrested for the power of your writing is one of the highest compliments an author can be paid, if an unwelcome one . . . Ngugi says he wouldn't wish the experience of prison on anyone, certainly not on himself.'[17] While jailed he remained totally defiant, as is clear in his *Detained: A Writer's Prison Diary*, published by Heinemann in Nairobi and London in 1981. Detention without trial, he says, 'is not only a punitive act of physical and mental torture of a few patriotic individuals, but it is also a calculated act of psychological terror against the struggling millions'.[18] In an excerpt from Ngugi's prison diary, his view of the link between his art and his punishment is clear:

> I have not been charged or told so, but I am convinced in other words that I am where I am because I have written about and believed in a Kenya for Kenyans, because I have attempted to hold up a mirror through which Kenyans can look at themselves in their past, their present and perhaps in their future. I am here because a tiny section of that society – but more influential because of the political and ill-gotten economic power it wields over the labouring majority – has not particularly liked the image of its role in Kenya's history. They have therefore struck with vengeance at the hand that raised a mirror which showed them what they did not like to see, or what they did not like seen by the ordinary folk. To them, the hand which held the mirror and the mirror itself, were what created the reality therein reflected.[19]

Not cowed at being imprisoned for writing a play in Gikuyu, he also started a novel in the same language while in prison. It was written secretly on the sheets of interleaved toilet paper, the written pages being carefully hidden at the bottom of the pack. The author recounts an occasion in prison when the manuscript was found and confiscated: 'It was as if I had been drained of blood . . . With this novel I had struggled with language, with images, with prison, with bitter memories, with moments of despair, with all the mentally and emotionally adverse circumstances in which one is forced to operate while in custody . . .'[20] The manuscript was returned to him three weeks later. The result, *Caitaani Mutharaba-ini*, Heinemann in Nairobi brought out in 1980; it was, like the play,

thrice reprinted. His English translation is being published under the title *Devil on the Cross* by Heinemann in Nairobi and London in 1982. It was optimistically placed as No. 200 in the African Writers Series before his imprisonment and some 50 further titles will have been published before it is issued.

Ngugi says that the effect of the availability of the Gikuyu version led to all sorts of surprising consequences. For instance a public reader in a bar would go on reading aloud until his glass was empty. He would then put the book face downwards on the counter until another drink was bought for him. He would then continue to read.

The works written in Gikuyu are the product of deep-seated convictions held by the writer. In his time at Leeds he felt doubts about his writing. The realization that the peasantry who were the basis of *A Grain of Wheat* could not read it 'was very painful. So I really didn't see the point of writing anything at all.'[21] Ngugi has sought to resolve the problem by writing in his own language. A Kenyan national literature, he says, 'can only get its stamina and blood by utilising the rich national traditions of culture and history carried by the languages of all the Kenyan nationalities'. Literature, 'a process of linking images', utilizes language and the history embodied in it:

> In writing one should hear all the whisperings, all the shouting, all the crying, all the loving and all the hating of the many voices in the past, and those voices will never speak to a writer in a foreign language. For us Kenyan writers, we can no longer avoid the question, whose language or history will our literature draw upon.[22]

Ngugi has never been reinstated in his post as head of the Department of Literature in the University of Nairobi. *Writers in Politics*, a second book of essays, appeared at the same time as *Detained*. It incorporates ten years of speeches and articles which consider the relevance of literature to life.

In his forty-two years he has found much to be angry about. To state that as a writer he has reported sensitively on the winds of change that have been blowing through Africa since independence is not to say enough. Rather say that in a clutch of powerful novels, short stories, and plays, he has been unequalled as chronicler of elemental change. Certainly there are several African writers of a very high order – but few have matched Ngugi's ability to get to the heart of a matter, say, that Yeats did with his diagnosis that 'things fall apart, the centre cannot hold'.[23]

[1] Interview with Dr B. J. Parker in *Black Books Bulletin*, vol. 6, no. 1, 1978
[2] Martin Tucker in the introduction to Ngugi, *Weep Not, Child* (New York, 1969), p. 17
[3] G. D. Killam, *An Introduction to the Writings of Ngugi* (London, 1980), p. 20
[4] Lewis Nkosi, 'A voice from detention', *West Africa*, 20 Feb. 1978, p. 334
[5] Eldred Jones, 'African literature 1966–1967', *African Forum*, vol. 3, no. 1, Summer 1967, p. 16
[6] Andrew Gurr, 'The fourth novel', *Hekima*, no. 1, Dec. 1980, p. 15
[7] Per Wästberg, ed., *The Writer in Modern Africa* (New York, 1969), p. 25
[8] Ngugi in an interview in *Cultural Events in Africa*, no. 50, 1969
[9] Reinhard Sander and Ian Munro, ' "Tolstoy in Africa": an interview with Ngugi wa Thiong'o', *Ba Shiru*, vol. 5, no. 1, 1973, p. 28
[10] Ngugi wa Thiong'o, *Writers in Politics* (London, 1981), p. 50
[11] Ngugi wa Thiong'o, *The Weekly Review*, 9 Jan. 1978, p. 9
[12] Christopher Ricks, *The Sunday Times*, 26 June 1977, p. 41
[13] Amiri Baraka, 'Ngugi', *The Literary Review*, no. 23, Aug./Sept.1980, p. 6
[14] Ngugi, *Writers in Politics*, p. 98
[15] Ngugi wa Thiong'o, *Detained: A Writer's Prison Diary* (London, 1981), p. 78
[16] Interview with Margaretta wa Gacheru, *The Weekly Review*, 5 Jan. 1979
[17] Sasha Moorsom, 'No bars to expression', *New Society*, 19 Feb. 1981, p. 334
[18] Ngugi, *Detained*, p. 14
[19] *Ibid.*, p. 188
[20] *Ibid.*, p. 164
[21] Sander and Munro, 'Tolstoy in Africa', p. 23
[22] 'Arts and Africa', no. 295, BBC African Service transcript (London)
[23] Michael Simmons, 'Chronicler of the winds of change', *The Guardian*, 7 Jan. 1981, p. 8

Lewis Nkosi
born 1936   SOUTH AFRICA

Lewis Nkosi is primarily an essayist and critic of African letters, and perhaps one of the most distinguished to have emerged in this area. In 1955 he embarked on a career in journalism with the *Ilanga lase Natal* (Natal Sun), a Zulu-English weekly, and the following year joined the staff of South Africa's highly popular *Drum* magazine. When he went to Johannesburg to work for *Drum*, Nkosi records:

> On the whole I was very sober, very young and fiercely ambitious. I was reading an incredible amount; reading always badly ... My sense of honour was propounded out of the romantic novels of Dumas, Kingsley and Marryat and the love I knew best was the love of knights and ladies in the drawing rooms of fifteenth-century Europe. What was happening under my eye was filtered through the moral sieve provided by this foreign literature. It was clear I was using literature as a form of escape; I was using it as a shield against a life of grime and social deprivation.[1]

Speaking for his entire generation, Nkosi feels 'the decade of the fifties was the most shaping influence of our young adulthood'; it was a time in which 'we had no literary heroes, like generations in other parts of the world' and 'we longed desperately for literary heroes we could respect and with whom we could identify'.[2]

While working for *Drum* as chief reporter and later for the *Post*, Nkosi lived in Sophiatown, a ghetto in Johannesburg; a city which Nkosi describes as 'totally without an inner life', where 'people loved quickly . . . lived fitfully; so profligate were they with emotion, so wasteful with their vitality, that it was very often difficult for them to pause and reflect on the passing scene'.[3] And this is partially the reason behind the significant lack of novels as well as plays to come out of South Africa, according to Nkosi.

> It is not so much the intense suffering (though this helped a great deal) which makes it impossible for black writers to produce long and complex works of literary genius as it is the very absorbing, violent and immediate nature of experience which impinges on individual life. Unless literature is assumed to be important in itself, for its own sake, unless it is assumed to be its own justification, there was no reason why anyone in our generation should have wanted to write.[4]

Furthermore:

> Language must be inhabited, it must be enlarged by usage; South Africans abridge it and stop it from referring too closely to those emotions which they spend almost all their lives trying to obliterate or deny. We cannot be cowards in the lives we live and be brave in the act of creating plays, novels and paintings.[5]

The school year 1960–1 saw Lewis Nkosi in the United States, a student of journalism at Harvard University. For accepting his Nieman Fellowship to study in the US, South Africa issued him with a one-way exit permit and thus barred him from returning. Lewis Nkosi's works are no longer allowed to be published or quoted in his native country. He has since been living in exile.

As a journalist, his articles have appeared in *The New Yorker*, the London *Observer* (for which he toured the south of the US), *The Spectator*, *The Guardian*, *The New Statesman*, *Africa Report*, *Africa Today*, and *Black Orpheus*, among others. His numerous, outspoken, and sometimes controversial articles dealing with African literature have included: 'Where does African literature go from here?', 'Fiction by black South Africans', 'African fiction: Part I – South African protest', and 'African literature: Part II – English-speaking West Africa'.

Home and Exile, a collection of Nkosi's essays and articles published in London in 1964, was awarded a prize at the Dakar World Festival of Negro Arts. It revealed his background and his thoughts on Johannesburg, apartheid, identity, and New York, as well as eight literary topics. The following year Nkosi's *The Rhythm of Violence*, a play set in Johannesburg, was published in England; reportedly it was the first English-language play to be written by a black South African since 1936.

For a number of years Nkosi lived in London. He was the literary editor of *The New African* and in 1964 served as moderator and interviewer for the 'African Writers of Today' series, produced by the National Educational Television network in conjunction with London's Transcription Centre.

Lewis Nkosi has expressed views on virtually every aspect of African literature; his opinions have often provoked considerable discussion and controversy. Thus it is perhaps appropriate to give Nkosi's answer to the question, 'What is African literature?':

> it seemed to me that, ultimately, what linked various African peoples on the continent was the nature and depth of colonial experience; and this was the final irony. Colonialism had not only delivered them unto themselves, but had delivered them unto each other, had provided them, so to speak, with a common language and an African consciousness; for out of rejection had come an affirmation.[6]

The Ethiope Publishing Company in Nigeria produced the next book by Nkosi in 1975. *The Transplanted Heart* contains 20 essays covering the areas of art, politics and travel. Of his perception of recent political events in South Africa, a critic comments on his perspicacity: 'Nkosi proceeds to write lovingly about what most of us have only managed to read about. He makes art out of suffering and thus blurs the line of action.'[7]

His latest work, *Tasks and Masks: Themes and Styles of African Literature*, was published by Longman in 1981. In it Nkosi ranges over sub-Saharan Africa in his critique of African literature. He focuses on two characteristics of literature, as he sees it, first the perception and presentation of African society, and secondly, the desire for social and political change. The interaction of the two elements is seen by him as germane to the understanding of the literature.

Nkosi has now returned to Africa and is currently senior lecturer in literature at the University of Zambia.

[1] Lewis Nkosi, *Home and Exile* (London, 1965), pp. 9–10
[2] *Ibid.*, pp. 9, 7, 8
[3] *Ibid.*, p. 17
[4] *Ibid.*
[5] *Ibid.*, p. 119
[6] *Ibid.*, p. 117
[7] Kole Omotoso, *African Book Publishing Record*, vol. 3, no. 3, 1977, p. 145

Arthur Nortje
1942–1970   SOUTH AFRICA

Nortje's voice has been relatively little heard and he is only now receiving more of the acclaim due to 'that brilliant young luminary of the South African poetic firmament . . .'[1] He died at the age of 27, and three years later a volume of his poetry, *Dead Roots*, was brought out posthumously. Several hundred poems of his are still unpublished. Bateleur Press in South Africa is in the process of bringing out an anthology of as yet unpublished

work, edited by Hedy Davis. His work has been published in journals such as *New Coin*, *Sechaba* and *Lotus*, and has been included in various anthologies, *Seven South African Poets* (Pieterse, ed.), *Modern Poetry from Africa* (Gerald Moore and Ulli Beier, eds.), and *New Anthology of Poetry from South Africa* (Butler and Mann, eds.).

He was born in Oudtshoorn, in the Cape Province, but went to Port Elizabeth with his mother while still very young. At school he was a brilliant all-rounder and struck up a close and lasting friendship with Dennis Brutus who was his English teacher. Later he attended the segregated University of the Western Cape, where he obtained a B.A. in English and psychology, followed by a post-graduate teacher's certificate. Before taking up a scholarship to Oxford he taught briefly at Port Elizabeth. At this stage his poetry laments the agonies and contradictions of the country:

> All one attempts is talk in the absence
> of others who spoke and vanished
> without so much as an echo.
> I have seen men with haunting voices
> turned into ghosts by a piece of white paper
> as if their eloquence had been black magic.[2]

After completing an Oxford B.A. degree, he chose to work in Canada, teaching at the Hope High School in Columbia. He was not happy, one factor being the strain of exile which he incorporated into his work. However, he 'drew upon his immediate environment and matters of global significance for many of his images and themes', so demonstrating 'the breadth and power of his poetic vision'.[3] By this time he had suffered a nervous breakdown and had an unhappy love affair. Two of his poems are dedicated to Sylvia Plath, another casualty of mental stress, wherein 'he cites personal betrayal and the insane destructiveness of civilization as conditions for madness'. As Charles Dameron put it: 'Nortje's world at these moments is a bleak and excruciatingly painful one.'[4]

Instead of taking up the place at Toronto University which was offered him, he returned to Oxford for further postgraduate study. Nine months later he was dead, having taken an overdose of barbiturates. A fellow South African's assessment, a decade after the poet's death, concludes:

> It is true that his rhetoric is a solitary, even an individualistic one; and it is true that his poetry is cerebral, his images 'metaphysical' in Johnson's sense, and his view of man's plight a metaphysical one – a view of man adrift in the universe. At the same time, this self-centered poetry gives a vision of every-man's soul in its despair and exultation, gives a measure of man's aspiration to be not only free in society, but intact within himself ... He is fighting out the quarrel with himself ... and he is making of it poetry.[5]

[1] E. O. Apronti, 'The tyranny of time: the theme of time in the artistic consciousness of South African writers', *African Literature Today*, no. 8, 1976, p. 110

[2] Arthur Nortje, *Dead Roots* (London, 1973), p. 5

[3] Charles Dameron, 'Arthur Nortje: craftsman for his muse', in C. Heywood, ed., *Aspects of South African Literature* (London and New York, 1976), p. 159

[4] *Ibid.*, p. 161

[5] Gessler Moses Nkondo, 'The human image in South African English poetry', *Africa Today*, vol. 27, no. 3, Dec. 1980, pp. 17–18

Nkem Nwankwo
born 1936   NIGERIA

Nkem Nwankwo's highly successful first novel was published in the mid-sixties. *Danda* is about a 'simple, happy-go-lucky village poet and social misfit who spreads mirth and confusion all about', in the words of Nigerian critic Emmanuel Obiechina.[1] It was followed a little more than ten years later by a second novel, *My Mercedes is Bigger than Yours*. Onuma, the hero of Nwankwo's second work, is a handsome, educated young man who misuses his obvious talents. Unlike Dan-da whose waywardness is always forgiven – by his villagers as well as by the novel's readers – the hero of *Mercedes* has nothing to recommend him. He does indeed take a vow near the end of the novel to mend his ways but it is as easily forgotten as it was taken. If both Danda and Onuma ultimately get their own way it is due not to the similarities between the two heroes but to the profound differences in their

characters and in the societies in which they live. Danda leaps up just as the initiator's knife begins the traditional incisions which are to allow him to enter the society of men (a ceremony he had been avoiding for years) and disappears for twelve months, only returning after his father's death to take possession of the family compound and live just as he pleases. His life will be unconventional, but honest. Not so Onuma's. As he drives off at the end of the novel in the Mercedes he finally managed to get (after wrecking a Jaguar obtained in rather dubious circumstances), he leaves behind him the dead body of the car's rightful owner, a man who is, moreover, a distant cousin. Onuma's amorality is but a reflection of that of the society around him, the money-mad world of contemporary Nigeria where old values, like ties of kinship, no longer operate. As John Fletcher puts it:

> What kind of world is this, Nwankwo seems to be asking accusingly, in which one man can ride around in a de luxe Mercedes while another makes perhaps £10 a year? The answer, bleak enough in all conscience, is that it is a world in which a beautiful butterfly like Onuma, a rogue and a scoundrel straight out of the picaresque tradition, can prosper and flourish.[2]

Born in 1936 in Nawfia-Awka in what was then Nigeria's East-Central State, and trained in English at University College, Ibadan, after secondary studies at King's College, Lagos, Nwankwo has followed a path similar to that taken by many Nigerian writers. At various times in his career he has been an English teacher, a radio producer, and a journal-ist (for *Drum* magazine before the civil war and the *Daily Times* in Lagos after the war). By the time Nwankwo's second novel came out he had made the decision to return to the university and work for a higher degree, enrolling in a doctoral programme in comparative literature at the University of Indiana at Bloomington where he moved with his wife and his son.

Nwankwo's early writing has included two volumes of short stories for children, *Tales Out of School* and *More Tales Out of School* (both published by Pilgrim Books), in addition to a play entitled *Eroya* (published in a mimeographed edition by University College, Ibadan, in 1963). A musical comedy based on the novel *Danda* was performed at the First Festival of Negro Arts in Dakar in 1966.

[1] Emmanuel Obiechina, *Culture, Tradition and Society in the West African Novel* (London, 1975), p. 88

[2] John Fletcher, *The International Fiction Review*, 4, 1977, p. 90

Flora Nwapa

born 1931   NIGERIA

Florence Nwanzuruaha Nwapa was the first Nigerian woman to have published a novel and the first woman in Africa to have a work of fiction published in London. *Efuru*, her first novel, was published in 1966 by Heinemann in their African Writers Series. In it, says Nwapa, 'I tried to present a dignified woman, who suffered in silence, who was good and gentle and understanding, but was badly rewarded by fate'.[1] Her next novel, *Idu* (1970), is the story of a woman in a small town in Nigeria who wants more from life than just bringing up her children.

Flora Nwapa was raised in Oguta in eastern Nigeria, the eldest in a family of six. First educated at Archdeacon Crowther's Memorial Girls' School, and in Lagos at the CMS Girls' School, in 1953 she travelled to Britain to attend Edinburgh University for studies culminating in a diploma in education.

Returning to Nigeria, she has since held several administrative posts in educational institutions. In Calabar she accepted an appointment as a Woman Education Officer; in Enugu she taught English and geography at Queen's School; at the University of Lagos she was assistant registrar. Before the outbreak of the civil war in Nigeria, Flora Nwapa returned to eastern Nigeria.

The war interrupted her writing, but her reactions to it were subsequently recorded in *Never Again* (1976). Written in the first person, it 'repeatedly affirms the importance of Biafra's women in sustaining their fighting men and the rudiments of their society'.[2] Nwapa's scrupulously honest appraisal of the evils of war and of propaganda has been praised; she takes

> a severe glance at relations between the ordinary people who find themselves as the unarmed majority of Biafra-at-war and its soldiers, war propaganda, suspicion and deprivation. These in turn provoke glimpses of both the poisoning of social relations as the reaffirmation of an indelible fact, the attachment of people to the land of their birth and their basic impulse to recreate the conditions for simple survival.[3]

After the war she assumed a cabinet post in the Ministry of Health and Social Welfare in the war-battered east-central state. Looking back over the five years she spent in the government, she remembers her most difficult problem as coping with the two thousand orphans after the war.

After a period as Commissioner for Lands, Survey and Urban Development in her state, she retired. Six months later she founded her own printing press and publishing company, Tana Press and the Flora Nwapa Company. Her aims include the publishing of works in other African languages, and the distribution of books throughout the continent. So far nine children's books have been published, three written by Nwapa herself. The illustrations are important, and the stories didactic; they 'aim to teach moral lessons, such as obedience and humility, or to make children appreciate school . . .'[4] Flora Nwapa laments Western ignorance and would like to fill the gap – 'we shall continue to write for our children . . . but our second objective will be to write for European, American and Asian children *about* African children'. Her third objective, she says, 'is to inform and educate women all over the world, especially Feminists (both with capital F and small "f") about the role of women in Nigeria, their economic independence, their relationship with their husbands and children, their traditional beliefs and their status in the community as a whole'.[5]

This is Lagos and Other Stories (1971) and *Wives at War and Other Stories* (1980) demonstrate the writer's skill in the short-story genre. The reaction of the character Soha in 'This is Lagos' to the exploitation she suffers is dealt with very differently from, say, Ekwensi's *Jagua Nana*, observes one critic, and these stories 'spell the agony of her sex – the disdain in which they are held in society; the exploitation of their virtues and qualities by men who in return jeer and scorn them. She looks at the problem of her sex from a passionate and yet realistic and intimate angle.'[6] Her own company is shortly to publish her latest novel, *One is Enough*.

[1] Flora Nwapa, interviewed in *African Woman*, no. 10, July/Aug. 1977, p. 9
[2] J. V., *West Africa*, 5 Jan. 1981
[3] *Ibid.*
[4] Nancy J. Schmidt, review in *African Book Publishing Record*, vol. 7, no. 3, 1981, p. 191
[5] Hans M. Zell, 'Frankfurt Book Fair 1980', *African Book Publishing Record*, vol. 7, no. 1, 1981, p. 6
[6] Tony Nnaemeka, 'Problems of African women', *Daily Times* (Lagos), 25 Aug. 1971, p. 16

Onuora Nzekwu
born 1928   NIGERIA

Onuora Nzekwu is the author of three novels and co-author with Michael Crowder of the highly successful children's book *Eze Goes to School*. His first two novels, *Wand of Noble Wood* and *Blade among the Boys*, published in 1961 and 1962 respectively (and later reissued in Heinemann's African Writers Series), revolve around the traditional conflict between old and new values. According to John Povey, they expose 'the dilemmas of the young African with all his longings and anger as he seeks a tenable morality amid the conflicting pressures of the pragmatism of his education and the beliefs of his traditions'.[1] His third novel, *Highlife for Lizards*, published in London in 1965, is the story of Agom, a woman childless for many years who 'finally after adversity and various magic spells . . . has a child and becomes a loved wife and an influential and admired woman'.[2] O. R. Dathorne calls *Highlife for Lizards* 'the most ambitious of Nzekwu's works' and Agom 'a symbol of Onitsha maidenhood' and 'a poetic character with mythological ramifications'.[3]

Born in Kafanchan in north-eastern Nigeria on 19 February 1928, Nzekwu received his education in various northern and eastern Nigerian schools. He studied at St Anthony's Elementary Teacher's College in 1943 and at St Charles' Higher Elementary Teacher Training College from 1944 to 1946. Upon graduation he entered the teaching profession, and for the next nine years taught in Oturkpo, Onitsha, and Lagos. In 1956 his career took a new direction when he joined the staff of *Nigeria Magazine* as an editorial assistant. He became editor-in-chief of the publication in 1962, holding that position until 1966 when he joined the Eastern Region Public Service. During the Nigerian Civil War he was a Biafran patriot but returned to the Federal Public Service in 1970 as senior information officer. At the present time Nzekwu is deputy director with the Federal Ministry of Information in Lagos.

He was the recipient in 1961 of a Rockefeller Foundation Fellowship to study the methods of American magazine production, and of a 1964 UNESCO fellowship to study copyright administration.

[1] John Povey, 'The novels of Onuora Nzekwu', *Literature East and West*, vol. 12, no. 1, Mar. 1968, p. 74
[2] *Ibid.*, p. 81
[3] O. R. Dathorne, *African Literature in the Twentieth Century* (London, 1976), p. 91

Grace Ogot
born 1930   KENYA

Grace Emily Akinyi Ogot occupies a distinctive position as one of the very few female writers from East Africa thus far. She was the first woman to have had her fiction published by the East African Publishing House. Born in Kenya's Central Nyanza district, she attended Ng'iya Girls' School and Butere High School, after which she trained as a nurse both in Uganda and England. Working in Maseno Hospital as a nursing sister and midwifery tutor, and later in Makerere at University College with the Student Health Service, Ogot's career thereafter took various routes. For 15 months she was employed as a script-writer and broadcaster for the BBC Overseas Service, as a community development officer in Kisumu, and in Nairobi as a public relations officer for the Air India Corporation of East Africa. She has had an ambassadorial role to play too, as a delegate to the General Assembly of the United Nations in 1975, and as a member of the Kenya delegation to UNESCO the following year. She was a founder member of the Writers' Association of Kenya, as well as serving as its president. A weekly radio programme in her mother tongue, Luo, has been extremely popular. Howard University, Washington DC, honoured her for her contribution to African humanities in an award made in 1975. She married the historian Bethwell Ogot in 1959, and has also helped him in his research.

Her major contributon to African literature is primarily as a short-story writer. Her stories have appeared in *Black Orpheus*, *Transition*, *Présence Africaine*, and *East Africa Journal*. Her first volume of short stories was published in 1968 under the title *Land Without Thunder*. Two years earlier her first novel, *The Promised Land*, appeared. In her stories, Ogot is loyal to tribal laws and wisdom, believing them to be immutable moral laws, and 'she is devoted to the task of passing on the folktales of the Luo tribe to the younger generation and thus instructing them'.[1]

Her production of short stories has been prolific. *The Other Woman and Other Stories* (1976) was seen by one critic as a 'masterly combination of the techniques of flashback, foreshadowing and discovery, [which] makes for reading with breathless attention and sustained interest'.[2] *The Island of Tears* (1980) is a recent collection of short stories, while *The Graduate*, published in the same year, shows that she is still interested in the novel as a genre.

Grace Ogot has recounted the incidents which led her to take pen in hand:

Authors from other parts of Africa and beyond had brought in their works, and these were on display, while there was nothing from East Africa [at the 1962 African Writers' Conference in Kampala]. I read my short story 'The Year of Sacrifice' but this was like a speck of salt dropped into the sea. A feeling of literary barrenness in East Africa arising from the helplessness of East African writers at this conference was later echoed by Taban lo Liyong. Through sheer embarrassment Ngugi and I took the challenge without any delay.[3]

The lack of outlets for fictional writing once produced was a serious hindrance. When she took some of her stories to the East African Literature Bureau, 'They really couldn't understand how a Christian woman could write such stories, involved with sacrifices, traditional medicines and all, instead of writing about Salvation and Christianity'. She feels strongly that this discouraged potential writers, who 'received no encouragement from colonial publishers, who were perhaps afraid of turning out radical writers critical of the colonial regime'.[4]

Now, she merely wishes to have enough time to continue writing:

I would like to write numerous short stories on various aspects of life if I can find enough time. This may mean dropping out of some of my voluntary organization duties and cutting down on social commitments. I have a burning desire to write a book depicting the social, economic, and political situation of my people before the colonial era. And I hope that one day I will be able to write a book about my childhood.[5]

[1] Satoru Tsuchiya, 'Modern East African litera-

ture from *Uhuru to Harambee'*, *World Literature Today*, vol. 52, no. 4, 1978, p. 573
[2] Romanus N. Egudu, *World Literature Today*, vol. 52, no. 1, 1978, p. 165
[3] Bernth Lindfors, 'Interview with Grace Ogot', *World Literature Written in English*, vol. 18, no. 1, 1979, p. 58
[4] *Ibid.*, p. 59
[5] *Ibid.*, p. 68

Wale Ogunyemi
born 1939   NIGERIA

The Nigerian playwright, Wale Ogun-yemi, came to work in 1962 as an actor for the Nigerian Broadcasting Corporation Television, where he quickly assumed the leadership of the Nigerian Theatre Group. Ogunyemi's knowledge of the theatre has been acquired on stage. His only formal training was in 1966–7 when he spent a year at the School of Drama of the University of Ibadan, five years after his début as a professional actor and after he had already begun writing plays. In Ogunyemi's opinion insistence on formal qualifications for an actor can actually stifle theatre in Nigeria, preventing gifted people who lack education from daring to join theatre groups: 'I believe strongly that you don't need high qualifications and degrees for good drama ... If you do not insist on these qualifications you will find many people coming in to do professional drama.'[1]

For all that, Ogunyemi has had the best training one could possibly obtain through his many long years' association with Nigeria's internationally famous playwright, Wole Soyinka. He was a founding member of the Orisun Theatre Troupe which Soyinka started in 1964 and was also associated with another Soyinka troupe, The 1960 Masks.

As an actor Ogunyemi has an imposing list of international performances to his credit. But despite his talent for acting, it is as a playwright that Ogunyemi feels he can make his greatest contribution to Nigerian theatre. He began writing plays in the late fifties, before becoming an actor, admitting that he had submitted a play to the Nigerian Independence Cele - bration Competition in 1960 – a competi-

tion that Soyinka won for his *A Dance of the Forests*. *The Vow*, one of Ogunyemi's early plays (actually a film script), dates from his Nigerian Theatre Group days with NBC Television, and it later became part of the Orisun Theatre's repertoire. *The Vow* deals with the tragic events surrounding the return home from America of a Nigerian student with his American wife. The play, as yet unpublished, won the 1971 drama prize of *African Arts* magazine.

Ogunyemi says his desire to write plays came as a result of having seen an Indian film whose language he could not understand: 'When I came home, I wrote a play of it, imagining what they'd said through the action.'[2] While Soyinka was in prison from 1967 to 1969 during the Nigerian Civil War Ogunyemi was responsible for writing a new play every two weeks for the Orisun Television series which Dapo Adelugba produced, as well as for the Armchair Theatre series. It was a straining period but Ogunyemi is grateful for the experience it gave him: 'I really thank my God that I had that opportunity to turn out plays every week.'[3]

The themes of most of Ogunyemi's plays are taken from the history and legends of the Yoruba people which he uses, according to Martin Banham, 'in an illuminating way'.[4] Ogunyemi is well versed in Yoruba culture. He was born on 12 August 1939 in Igbajo, 90 miles from Ibadan, and as a child he frequently visited Yoruba shrines and sacred groves with his grandmother, the Iyalode of Igbajo. She taught him the fundamentals of traditional Yoruba religious practices, and although his mother was a Christian he was allowed to have his own mask.[5]

Ijaye War, a play which Ogunyemi published in 1970, is a historic drama of the nineteenth-century war of rivalry between the Yoruba rulers of Ijaye and Ibadan. *Eshu Elegbara*, published the same year, is based on the Yoruba creation myth. In *Obaluaye*, Ogunyemi's only Yoruba-language play (an English version also exists), the Yoruba god of smallpox takes revenge on a village chief for converting to Christianity.

Ogunyemi's most ambitious undertaking to date is *Kiriji*, an epic play (published by Pilgrim Books in 1976) on the Ekitiparapo war in the nineteenth century with a cast of over a hundred that includes musicians, singers and dancers. The play was produced in December 1971 during the All-Nigeria Arts Festival by the Department of Theatre Arts of the University of Ibadan in cooperation with the Institute of African Studies where Ogunyemi is currently research assistant. *Kiriji* was also taken on tour to places in Ibadan, Ile-Ife and Yaba (Lagos) from January to March, 1972.

Ogunyemi researches his historical plays thoroughly, making full use of the staff and resources of the Institute of African Studies. The idea for Ijayi, for example, came from an old newspaper clipping dating back to 1869 that Ogunyemi saw in the Institute library. He does not hesitate to consult traditionalists like the priest of Ifa, the god of divination, who supplied him with the ideas that went into a still unpublished play entitled, *Orunmila* (the name of the father of Ifa). Another unpublished play, *Oloronbi*, derives from a traditional Yoruba tale that Ogunyemi had to piece together from several sources: 'I tried to ask people, "Do you know the story?" None of them seemed to know the story. So I had to go home, I asked people in my home town. One man told me about half of it and said, "That's all I know".'[6]

Ogunyemi's language, as well as his themes, shows signs of his Yoruba heritage. He makes use of Yoruba proverbs and modes of expression as well as 'Yoruba English'. The result is a language that may sound quaint or even incorrect to native speakers of English, prompting Dapo Adelugba, the director of the *Kiriji* performances, to write: 'how do we define "correctness"? . . . Perhaps the time has come to reappraise the whole yardstick of normality, and accept the fact that different species of English inevitably make different demands on actors and audiences.'[7] Adelugba has defined this kind of language as 'Yorub-anglish'. It is 'the many-sided attempt to catch the flavour, tones, rhythms, emotional and intellectual content of Yoruba

language and thought in an adventurous brand of English'.[8]

Not all of Ogunyemi's plays deal with historical or traditional subjects. *The Divorce*, written in 1974 while on a year's secondment to the Workshop Theatre at the University of Leeds and published in 1978 with Onibonoje Publishers in Ibadan, is a comedy in a contemporary setting involving a jealous husband and a case of mistaken identity. *The Divorce* was staged by the Unibadan Masques company of the University of Ibadan in June 1975 and was one of the plays chosen for performance by the Rivers State National Theatre Workshop Seminar at Port Harcourt in June 1975.

The number of Ogunyemi's published plays is hardly indicative of his output. Only eleven have been printed so far. Five are in separate volumes (*Ijayi War*, *Eshu Elegbara*, *Obaluaye*, *Kiriji* and *The Divorce*). *The Scheme* is one of Ulli Beier's *Three Nigerian Plays*, and two other plays have appeared in issues of *Nigeria Magazine*: *Be Mighty Be Mine*, about the rivalry of the Yoruba gods Shango and Ogun, in June 1968, and *Aare Akogun*, an adaptation of *Macbeth*, in April 1969. Also in collections are *Sign of the Rainbow*, a radio play about a mythical water spirit that won the 1972 BBC African Theatre Prize (it has been broadcast in Finnish on Radio Helsinki), and *Poor Little Bird*, about a Nigerian schoolteacher who refused to leave his fiancée's village to avoid a traditional ceremony that 'foreigners' must not see, and who ultimately suffers death.[9]

Unpublished plays include *Obatala* and *Ojiya*, both produced by the Black Studies Department of Fisk University in Nashville, Tennessee, in 1972. *Langbodo* has been adapted from Soyinka's translation of a novel by the Yoruba writer, Daniel Fagunwa, and it was the official Nigerian Festac entry. *We Can Always Create* won second prize in the Nigeria Broadcasting Corporation National Day Playwriting Competition. Ogunyemi's most recent play, *The Night of the Oro Cult*, is a tragedy about a Western-educated teacher who refuses to marry his late brother's wife, as custom requires.

Theatricality for Ogunyemi means

putting to use all the dramatic elements at a playwright's disposal: speech, gesture, costumes, setting, props, music, dance. For the Nigerian director Dapo Adelugba, a man who knows Ogunyemi's works well, the playwright's major contribution to Nigerian drama comes from his 'pervasive, all-round sense of theatre'.[10]

[1] Maxine Lautre, 'Wale Ogunyemi interviewed', *Cultural Events in Africa*, no. 51, 1969 (recorded May 1968)
[2] *Ibid.*
[3] *Ibid.*
[4] Martin Banham, *African Theatre Today* (London, 1976), p. 46
[5] From an unpublished interview with Ogunyemi referred to by Dapo Adelugba, 'Three dramatists in search of a language' in Ogunba and Irele, eds., *Theatre in Africa* (Ibadan, 1978)
[6] Lautre, 'Wale Ogunyemi interviewed'
[7] Dapo Adelugba, '*Kiriji*: the concept of theatre as exploration' in *African Notes*, vol. 7, no. 1, 1971-2, pp. 114, 115
[8] Dapo Adelugba, 'Three dramatists', p. 216
[9] 'Sign of the rainbow' in G. Henderson, ed., *African Theatre: Eight Prize-winning Plays for Radio* (London, 1973); 'Poor Little Bird' in Moody, *The Study of Literature or Literary Studies and Creative Writing* (London, 1972)
[10] Dapo Adelugba, 'Three dramatists', p. 217

John Atukwei Okai
born 1941   GHANA

'Atukwei's poetry resounds with music. He acquired this quality in his early life in Northern Ghana where redolent, low-pitched drums feature prominently in courtly as well as recreational music.'[1] This assessment by Jawa Apronti points to the most striking feature of Okai's poetry: its musical, mellifluous quality. Okai even employs musical terminology in naming sections of the poems. His work is meant primarily to be listened to and his public recitals have been called 'mesmerizing, convincing in the most part and utterly unforgettable'.[2]

Born in Accra, Okai was educated at Gambaga Native Authority School and Nalerigu Middle Boys' School before going on to Accra High School where he received encouragement in his writing from William Conton, the headmaster and author of *The African*. In 1961, the

year after he left school, Okai – a member of the Young Pioneer Movement – left Ghana to study literature at the Gorky Institute in Moscow. He received an M.A. in 1967. The contact he had with Russian poets while there influenced him in various ways. Apronti traces its course: '. . . the greatest contribution that his Russian experience made to his growth as a poet is the method of public recital that he has used to revolutionize poetry in Ghana . . . He brings to his public performances a severe theatrical discipline.'[3]

He has given poetry readings in Europe, Africa, and at the Pan-African Cultural Festival at Algiers in 1969. He combines dancing, drumming, chanting and recitation in these performances, which incorporate oral traditions and emphasize the sound of the words. The effect is not solely auditory, as 'his preoccupation with social problems, his imagery, sense of humour and dramatic presentation of ideas and events'[4] engages the audience intellectually as well. The chants are cast in a variety of languages which reflect Okai's polyglot background: 'the range of his linguistic competence is amazing, spanning as it does his own mother tongue Ga, Akan, Hausa, Yoruba, Swahili, Russian, French and, of course, English.'[5]

The poet received a postgraduate scholarship in 1967 to attend the University of London where he completed an M.Phil. in Russian literature. Afterwards he was appointed as a lecturer in modern languages at the University of Ghana.

His work has appeared in numerous journals, and has been translated into several languages. *Flowerfall* was published in 1969, and two years later *The Oath of Fontomfrom and Other Poems* appeared. A third collection, *Lorgorli Logarithms* (1974) provoked strong reactions, some favourable and others highly critical. His use of proverbs and of striking imagery demand attention. 'His new images are startling', writes a Ghanaian critic. 'There is nothing wrong in calling his imagery revolutionary, so long as we bear in mind that Okai has his roots in literary tradition, both native and foreign.'[6]

Similarly, Anyidoho finds Okai's imagery 'is stark naked and shocks with its unchecked eroticism . . .'[7]

Even though his language contains these challenging and novel elements, Okai's work 'must be seen as being in the very mainstream of African poetry', maintains Nwoga in the Introduction to *Lorgorli*. Okai's verse has not, Dseagu feels, suffered the 'dissociation of dance and song which has taken place in Western lyrical poetry'.[8] The sense of continuity or tradition is keenly felt by Okai himself:

> in our traditional society, poetry has always been a living part of the living society. It is part of the nature of the modern society that we have the printed word . . . that is good. But within a society that we are trying to balance in terms of that which was and that which is now, it is also necessary for us to try to keep poetry as a living art by not only locking it up in books that are printed but also by carrying it to the people and letting it live within our society because through poetry the people talks to itself, converses with its soul and maintains a very vital and healthy dialogue of the spirit.[9]

He is a member of the Society of Authors of Great Britain, the Royal Society of Literature (UK) and the Royal Society of Arts, and since 1971 he has been President of the Ghana Association of Writers. His poetry has appeared in many journals, including *The New African*, *African Arts*, *Atlantic Monthly*, the *New American Review*, *Okyeame*, and the *Legon Observer*. Throughout his career one can discern the importance of pan-Africanism to him, and when asked his nationality recently he replied 'I am an African from Ghana'.[10]

This radical and committed poet – in his persona as 'Oshamraku Atukwei . . . by appointment the organ-grinder to God and Man' – has composed a note to posterity:

> And when they ask who the hell I was
> And what the hell on earth
>   I did, remind them I cared
>   enough to rise at dawn and
>   roll my mat, and I, too, during
> the festival of the soul, sang our
> world.[11]

[1] Jawa Apronti, 'John Atukwei Okai: the growth of a poet', *Universitas*, vol. 2, no. 1, 1972, P. 123
[2] *Ibid.*, p. 118
[3] *Ibid.*, p. 118
[4] Kofi Anyidoho, 'Atukwei Okai and his poetic territory' in K. Ogungbesan, ed., *New West African Literature* (London, 1979), p. 50
[5] Apronti, 'John Atukwei Okai', p. 118
[6] Kwei Orraca-Tetteh, 'Atukwei Okai revisited', *Legacy*, vol. 1, no. 3, 1973, p. 34
[7] Anyidoho, 'Atukwei Okai', p. 50
[8] Quoted in Amanor Dseagu, introduction to *Lorgorli Logarithms* (Accra, 1974), p. xv, *African Literature Today*, no. 10, 1979, p. 50
[9] 'Arts and Africa', no. 314G, BBC African Service transcript (London)
[10] *Africa*, no. 100, Dec. 1979, p. 49
[11] Atukwei Okai, *The Oath of Fontomfrom and Other Poems* (New York, 1971), p. 119

Gabriel Okara
born 1921   NIGERIA

Until 1964 Gabriel Okara was known primarily as a Nigerian poet. Before that date his verse had appeared in numerous magazines (in particular in *Black Orpheus*, including its maiden issue), had been translated into several languages, and had been read by the author in Africa, America, and Europe. His poems were widely anthologized. Among the most often quoted were 'The Call of the River Nun', which won for Okara an award at the 1953 Nigerian Festival of Arts, and 'The Snow Flakes Sail Gently Down', which he wrote from his experience of an American winter. As a prose writer, his short stories included 'The Crooks', again published in *Black Orpheus*.

Then in 1964 André Deutsch issued *The Voice*. This first novel was greeted with mixed reactions. Arthur Ravenscroft, in his introduction to the paperback edition (reissued in both London and New York in the early half of 1970), reviews its initial reception:

> some African reviewers found its unconventional use of English unacceptable; they seemed to see it as a novel in a line of development from Amos Tutuola's books. Reviewers abroad were also partly nonplussed by the language, and uncomfortable about its strange symbolism and apparently naive simplicity, which seemed old-fashioned in a world of Western European sophistication. But there were discerning voices . . . In 1968 the Canadian novelist Margaret Laurence wrote of it in her book on Nigerian literature, *Long Drums and Cannons*: 'It is certainly one of the most memorable novels to have come out of Nigeria'. I share this view.[1]

The core of this criticism centred largely around Okara's unique and experimental use of the English language: his English translation of some linguistic characteristics of his native Ijọ tongue. Okara himself had already written of his technique in 1963:

> As a writer who believes in the utilisation of African ideas, African philosophy and African folk-lore and imagery to the fullest extent possible, I am of the opinion the only way to use them effectively is to translate them almost literally from the African language native to the writer into whatever European language he is using as his medium of expression . . . In order to capture the vivid images of African speech, I had to eschew the habit of expressing my thought first in English. It was difficult at first, but I had to learn. I had to study each Ijaw expression I used and to discover the probable situation in which it was used in order to bring out the nearest meaning in English. I found it a fascinating exercise.[2]

Paradoxically, despite Okara's renown as a poet, no collection of his verse was available in book form until 1978 when *The Fisherman's Invocation* was published in Heinemann's African Writers Series. The volume, which shared the 1979 Commonwealth Poetry Prize with Brian Turner, contains many of Okara's early works, including the title poem, which had previously been anthologized; but it also contains poems written during and since the Nigerian Civil War. Theo Vincent provides an introduction to Okara and his poetry in *The Fisherman's Invocation*:

> these poems are generally marked by alluring lyricism and superficial simplicity of diction which are reminiscent of oral traditional songs . . . even the most esoteric of his poetry appears easily accessible while making profound statements and comments. This ability to combine these two aspects of the communicative force of poetry without attracting any of the familiar accusations of incomprehensibility is the mark of Okara's greatness as a poet.[3]

The Fisherman's Invocation is surprisingly slim (only 52 pages) considering the great number of poems Okara has written over the years. The reason, Vincent explains, is that many were lost during the war. In an interview with Bernth Lindfors in 1972 Gabriel Okara revealed that the completed manuscripts for two novels also disappeared during those troubled years.

Gabriel Imomotimi Gbaingbain Okara, the son of an Ijọ chief, was born on 21 April 1921 at Bumoundi in the Niger delta. Educated at Government College, Umuahia, his secondary studies were interrupted by World War II but he managed to finish them at Yaba Higher College, passing the Senior Cambridge examination in 1940. The plastic arts (particularly water colours) first attracted Okara rather than writing. In his school days he had been a student of the celebrated Nigerian artist, Ben Enwonwu. Okara also completed a course in bookbinding and worked in this trade for a number of years starting in the mid-forties. From a modest start as a bookbinder Okara's professional career led him to the publishing business and into the information division of the civil service. He studied journalism at Northwestern University in the United States in the late fifties and worked, for most of the sixties, before the outbreak of the civil war, as Information Officer for the Eastern Nigerian Government Service.

During the civil war he actively supported Biafra, serving as Director of the Cultural Affairs Division of the Biafran Ministry of Information. In 1969 he toured the United States to promote the Biafran cause with his compatriot and fellow novelist, Chinua Achebe.

After the war Okara founded the Rivers State Government newspaper *The Nigerian Tide*, and was its general manager for a number of years. For a period of about ten months he was Commissioner for Information and Broadcasting, and he has also been Writer-in-Residence of the Rivers State Council on Arts and Culture. Okara is now head of the Rivers State Cultural Centre.

In addition to his poetry and fiction Gabriel Okara has written plays and features for use in broadcasting. Widely regarded as a thoughtful man, self-developed by extensive private reading, Okara has translated a great deal of the folklore and poetry of his Ijo heritage. He believes that '. . . the African writer, just as any other writer anywhere in the world, should incorporate the culture of his people into his writing':

Somebody has said literature is the soul of a country because it reflects the culture, the beliefs, the philosophy, the total being of the people of that country. That, I think should be the first commitment or the role of a writer – to express the soul of his country.[4]

[1] Gabriel Okara, *The Voice* (New York and London, 1970), p.4
[2] Gabriel Okara, 'African speech . . . English words', *Transition*, vol. 3, no. 10, 1963
[3] Gabriel Okara, *The Fisherman's Invocation* (London, 1978), p. xiii
[4] 'Interview with Gabriel Okara', in Bernth Lindfors, ed., *Dem-Say: Interviews with Eight Nigerian Writers* (Austin, Texas, 1974), p. 46

Christopher Okigbo
1932–1967   NIGERIA

In the nearly fifteen years since he died in action while serving as a major in the Biafran army during the Nigerian Civil War, the poet Christopher Okigbo has become legendary in the field of African poetry and a source of inspiration for young Nigerian and, indeed, African, writers. Major Nigerian writers, like Chinua Achebe, Wole Soyinka and John Pepper Clark, have dedicated poems to his memory, and Okigbo's voice continues to speak out as critics read and re-read the slim volume of verse, *Labyrinths with Path of Thunder* which was published posthumously in 1971.

The volume is a near-complete collection of Okigbo's previously published works, containing the definitive versions of 'Heavensgate' and 'Limits' which appeared in Mbari editions in 1962 and 1964 respectively. It also contains the two-part poem, 'Silences', which was first printed in three issues of *Transition* in 1962, as well as 'Distances' that *Transition* printed in 1964. *Labyrinths* also includes six poems that *Black Orpheus* published posthumously in 1968. Missing from the volume, however, are the 'Four Canzones' which appeared in an early issue of *Black Orpheus*, 'Dance of the Painted Maidens' which was anthologized in *Verse and Voice* in 1965, and 'Lament of the Masks' which was included in a book of contributions honouring the centenary of the death of W. B. Yeats.[1]

Okigbo had planned for the re-edition of his poems under the title *Labyrinths* as early as 1965 and he supplied the four-page introduction which is published with the poems. In it he wrote that 'although these poems were written and published separately, they are, in fact, organically related'.[2] Readers also learn from the introduction that 'Limits' was written after a journey that turned out to be pointless, that 'Distances' was inspired by the emotions produced after surgery under general anaesthesia, and 'Silences' by the imprisonment of Chief Obafemi Awolowo, a Yoruba politician, and the death of Awolowo's son. Okigbo wanted the poems in *Labyrinths* to be 'a fable of man's perennial quest for fulfilment':

> a poet-protagonist is assumed throughout . . . a personage for whom the progression through 'Heavensgate' through 'Limits' through 'Distances' is like telling the beads of a rosary; except that the beads are neither stone nor agate but globules of anguish strung together on memory.[3]

Christopher Okigbo wrote his first poem, 'Song of the Forest', in 1957 but the discovery of the fact that 'he couldn't be anything else than a poet' dates from the following year:

> . . . the turning point came in 1958, when I found myself wanting to know myself better, and I had to turn around and look at myself from inside . . . And when I talk of looking inward to myself, I mean turning inward to examine myselves. This of course takes account of ancestors . . . Because I do not exist apart from my ancestors.[4]
>
> . . . I am believed to be a reincarnation of my maternal grandfather, who used to be the priest of the shrine called Ajani, where Idoto, the river goddess, is worshipped. This goddess is the earth mother, and also the mother of the whole family. My grandfather was the priest of this shrine, and when I was born I was believed to be his reincarnation, that is, I should carry on his duties. And although someone else had to perform his functions, this other person was only, as it were, a regent. And in 1958, when I started taking poetry very seriously, it was as though I had felt a sudden call to begin performing my full functions as the priest of Idoto. That is how it happened.[5]

Okigbo is not an easy poet. His images are often personal and his symbolism complex, calling forth all the influences that have worked on him. In speaking about these influences Okigbo said, 'I think that I've been influenced by various literatures and cultures, right from Classical times to the present day, in English, Latin, Greek and a little French, a little Spanish'.[6] By his own admission, his work was also affected by his childhood in Ojoto, an Igbo village near Onitsha, and Igbo mythology. Literary critics have moreover noted that his sources and models are to be found in Pound, Eliot, the Bible and the French surrealistic poets.

One critic, the East African Ali Mazrui, has taken Okigbo to task for being deliberately obscure. After Okigbo's death, Mazrui went on to restate his criticism in fictional terms in a work entitled *The Trial of Christopher Okigbo*. The book also accuses Okigbo posthumously for having betrayed his art by allowing himself to die for a less noble cause. Coming to Okigbo's defence, Dan Izevbaye, the Nigerian critic, asserts that Okigbo's 'allusiveness' results from his having had to tie together elements from a variety of cultures as a 'response to a situation that required the poet to fashion a literary tradition for himself'.[7]

The British poet Peter Thomas, recounting his friendship with Okigbo, wrote that Okigbo's father had made certain that his sons received a good education and had the freedom to plan their own vocational directions. Educated at Government College in Umuahia, Okigbo then studied classics at Ibadan University. After receiving his degree there in 1956, he acted as Private Secretary to Nigeria's Federal Minister of Research and Information for the following two years, taught for another two years, and then served as Acting Librarian of the University of Nigeria at Nsukka. Although his aspiration was to be a poet, Okigbo continued to gain his livelihood through various means: from Nsukka he moved to the library on the Enugu campus, then became the West African representative of Cambridge University Press and West African editor of

Transition magazine, as well as an editor of Mbari Publications.

In 1972 a full-length study of Christopher Okigbo was published by the Nigerian critic, Sunday Anozie, a close personal friend, under the title, *Christopher Okigbo: Creative Rhetoric*. An anthology of poetic tributes to Okigbo, entitled *Don't Let Him Die* and edited by Chinua Achebe and Dubem Okafor, was published in 1978 by the Fourth Dimension Publishing Company of Enugu.

The impression Okigbo has left on African letters is undeniable. 'His apprenticeship was long', says Gerald Moore, 'but the completion of his visionary sequence from *Heavensgate* to *Distances* in only three years (1961–4) is an achievement that African poetry will not easily surpass.'[8]

As testimony to his outstanding achievement, the 1966 Festival of Negro Arts in Dakar had awarded Christopher Okigbo its First Prize for Poetry which, however, he declined, saying, 'There is no such thing as Negro art',[9] confirming a statement he had made two years earlier, 'There is no African literature. There is good writing and bad writing – that's all.'[10]

[1] D. E. Maxwell and S. B. Bushrui, eds., *W. B. Yeats 1865–1965* (Ibadan, 1965)
[2] Christopher Okigbo, *Labyrinths with Path of Thunder* (New York and London, 1971), p. xi
[3] *Ibid.*, p. xiv
[4] Marjory Whitelaw, 'Interview with Christopher Okigbo, 1965', *The Journal of Commonwealth Literature*, July 1970, no. 9, p. 35
[5] *Ibid.*, p. 36
[6] 'Death of Christopher Okigbo', *Transition*, vol. 7, no. 33, p. 18
[7] Dan Izevbaye, 'From reality to the dream: the poetry of Christopher Okigbo', in Edgar Wright, ed., *The Critical Evaluation of African Literature* (London, 1973), p. 124
[8] Gerald Moore, *The Chosen Tongue: English Writing in the Tropical World* (New York and Evanston, 1969), p. 176
[9] 'Death of Christopher Okigbo', p. 18
[10] *Ibid.*, p. 18

Kole Omotoso
born 1943   NIGERIA

Kole Omotoso is probably the most widely published of the second generation of Nigerian authors. All his publications (five novels, a collection of short stories, two plays, plus an impressive body of critical writing) have appeared since the end of the Nigerian Civil War.

Omotoso's earliest contact with literature was written in Yoruba not English (a language never spoken in his family). He grew up in the midst of a flourishing Yoruba literary culture reading the novels of D. O. Fagunwa and seeing plays produced by the professional Yoruba theatre companies. As a child Omotoso read a Yoruba magazine called *Aworerin* which was, until recently, the only children's magazine in Nigeria. The importance of Yoruba heritage in Omotoso's family was also a major part of his upbringing. He learned the Yoruba myths and legends at the regular evening storytelling sessions held in his grandfather's house where his mother moved when he was still a young boy after the death of his father.

In spite of his great familiarity with the Yoruba oral tradition, Omotoso's works show no signs of what one might call traditional aspects of Yoruba culture. Instead, his literary style is the result of his English-language university training and his own reading, and his themes are those of a writer concerned with present-day issues in Africa.

Omotoso admits to being luckier than his elders who had to forge their own literary tradition and make their way carefully through the often irrelevant reading material colonial society had offered them as children. The authors of Omotoso's generation, on the contrary, have been nurtured not only on the classics of English literature but also on those of their own literary masters, such as Achebe, Soyinka, and Ekwensi. One of Omotoso's earliest memories as a reader of English is coming across Ekwensi's Onitsha publication, *When Love Whispers*, in 1958.

As a schoolboy Omotoso eagerly devoured all the English storybooks in the Oyemekun Grammar School in his home town of Akure in western Nigeria where he was born on 12 April 1943. His voracious reading habits continued during the two years he spent at Kings College, Lagos, from 1961 to 1963 where he also involved himself in editing the school literary magazine. As Omotoso describes it, he had by that time so completely initiated himself into the classics of English literature and so intensely desired to discover new languages and literatures that, when he was accepted to read English at the University of Ibadan in 1964 and discovered he already knew the books in the syllabus, he decided instead to take his degree in Arabic with French as a second language. Interest in writing for Omotoso began in his school days. He says:

My first published stories were written in English and were continuities from classroom compositions and essays [for] school magazines and daily newspapers and monthly magazines. I was in the sixth form at Kings College Lagos when my first stories were published by *Radio Nigeria* magazine.[1]

While pursuing his degree in Arabic at the University of Ibadan he was active in writing for *Horizon*, the English Department's literary magazine, and regularly supplied expatriate and Nigerian publishers with manuscripts that were just as regularly rejected. Omotoso remembers the discouragement he felt during this period but also what he calls 'a significant point' in his writing career when his

short story, 'The Honourable Member', appeared in the last issue of *Black Orpheus* to be edited by Ulli Beier.

Determined to make a career in writing, Omotoso put off graduate work after receiving his B.A. and accepted a teaching position in English, French and Arabic at a Muslim secondary school in Ikare in western Nigeria. He directed the school drama society in a staging of his play, *Pitched Against the Gods*. In September 1969, 'because he had not got anything worthwhile published' (although *Pitched Against the Gods* had won second prize in an Oxford University Press competition), Omotoso decided to do a post-graduate course in Islamic studies and left for the University of Edinburgh where he stayed for three years, writing his doctoral dissertation on the modern Arabic novelist and playwright, Abi Ahmad Bakathir, and completing his first novel, *The Edifice*, which was published in 1971 by Heinemann.

Although the novel is not autobiographical it does draw on Omotoso's experiences in Britain, painting the portrait of a Nigerian student whose marriage to an English girl is largely the result of his need to overcome the isolation and hostility he feels in the society around him. The marriage ultimately fails, after the couple's move to Nigeria, but not for reasons of racial incompatibility. In 1972 Omotoso published a second novel with Heinemann, *The Combat*, an allegorical tale of the Nigerian Civil War, through the story of two friends fighting over the paternity rights to a child born to the mistress they shared, a young market girl who later becomes a high-class prostitute.

All of Omotoso's works since this date have been published in Nigeria, the result of a deliberate choice on his part. In 1973 Onibonoje Publishers of Ibadan brought out *Miracles and Other Stories*, a collection of largely tragic short stories that are 'centred around children but not . . . for children', as the blurb on the cover states. The book appears in the African Literature Series collection which Omotoso edits. A third novel, *Fella's Choice*, described by Omotoso as 'the first Nigerian detective novel', was published in 1974 under the imprint of the Ethiope Publishing Corporation. The hero is a Nigerian undercover agent who foils South Africa's attempt to ruin the Nigerian economy by flooding the country with counterfeit Naira notes.

Omotoso's fourth novel, *The Sacrifice*, about a medical doctor who rejects his mother who was forced into prostitution in order to raise and educate him, was published by Onibonoje in 1974, and it was followed two years later by a fifth novel, *The Scales*, a detective story on a socially significant theme, the exploitation of beggars for private profit.

Two plays came out in 1976 and 1977. The first one, *The Curse*, was the second publication of a new Ibadan venture, New Horn, which Omotoso helped to set up and whose maiden publication was Femi Osofisan's novel, *Kolera Kolej*. In both *The Curse* and Omotoso's second play, *Shadows in the Horizon*, property owners and the dispossessed are at odds, showing signs of Omotoso's growing social commitment and his concern to level social inequality. Omotoso returned to Nigeria in September 1972 to take up first, a position in modern Arabic literature at the University of Ibadan, and subsequently that of senior lecturer in the Department of African Languages and Literature at the University of Ife. As Literary Editor for the journal *Afriscope* since 1974 he has had the opportunity to propound his ideas on the role of writers and literature in Africa. For Omotoso, art has never been and never can be a leisurely pastime in African societies. The notion of art for art's sake belongs to the capitalistic West. The artist has a vital role to play in African societies, particularly in contemporary Africa in which 'the old order has been destroyed and the new has not been chosen'.[2]

Omotoso describes African societies today as being 'ideologically committed'. Art and literature in this context, he says, are means for the society 'to provide some light by which we can see more clearly the foreign element in our present-day culture'.[3] Although he warns that literature 'must not be subservient to any

political system'[4] its function as art is to help society discover its ills. The artist, himself, is the oracle of the people, the self-ordained priest who can help make society aware of itself and know where it is going: '. . . the Artist forms the mind of his community, training it to know and acclaim Truth, teaching it to reject Evil and Lies, performing the role of the Priest'.[5]

Omotoso maintains that the writer must know his society by living in it. He is a harsh critic of those African writers who choose to live in 'voluntary exile' abroad. West Africans are more guilty of this offence than East Africans, and francophone writers, 'those who live in chateaux and only go back to the jungle once or twice to check their data', more than anglophone writers.[6] The writer must also seek out his audience and it must be a home audience. He defines the task facing writers nowadays as that of rediscovering the audience, the 'missing apex' of the triangle whose two other points are the writer and the publisher.[7] Writers, Omotoso says, must agree to publish their works first at home, before allowing publication abroad. He says that the excuse that they often give for publishing abroad – that publishing at home does not pay – is a myth. He claims to have earned much more from works published in Nigeria than from the two novels published in London.

The literary needs of 'ideologically-committed societies' impose certain obligations on writers which have vital consequences for their art, the first being that content is more important than form. Omotoso does not deny that the form a work of literature takes can and does entertain, but he insists on the necessity of the educative value of the content. He sees the literature of the West as being in a decadent phase for having lost sight precisely of this imperative; 'the whole of the aesthetics of Capitalism in as far as it exists, is constructed around the issue of the form while the content is given no place of importance'.[8] Giving content its proper emphasis means that African writers need new themes. The time has come, says Omotoso, for writers to stop explaining Africa to others: 'The new generation of writers are concerned with explaining ourselves to ourselves'.[9] Preoccupation with the past, and the 'culture-conflict hero' are irrelevant topics in present-day Africa and Omotoso severely castigates writers who continue to churn out exotic anthropoligica or culture-clash fiction:

It is high time we had a new generation of African writers whose concern would be with the society at large, with the teeming millions of Africans who are putting together both their African past and their Western present to build a viable future for themselves and for those around them.[10]

Finally, in order for literature in Africa to answer the needs of society, 'it must seek to reconcile the general and the particular by choosing the typical' which 'must be the basis of realism in prose writing'.[11] A writer concerned with realism does not 'satirize the community in favour of the individual'.[12] The implications on the structure and characterization of Omotoso's own writing are obvious. In the fiction that Omotoso has published since *The Combat* his characters have gradually been stripped of their individuality and reclothed as the embodiment of ideas or concepts. The two 'brothers' fighting one another to death in *The Combat* are the Federal forces and secessionist Biafra fighting a fratricidal war. The ungrateful son in *The Sacrifice* represents the elite of Africa who have been educated at public expense and have refused to acknowledge what they owe society.[13] The protagonists of *The Curse* and *Shadows in the Horizon* are embodiments of the haves and the have-nots in Nigerian, and African, society. Even the heroes of Omotoso's detective novels are concept figures. The central character of *Fella's Choice* represents black Africa combating the evils of apartheid, and the hero of *The Scales* is the reincarnation of true justice in a society which has fallen into the clutches of evil individuals whose power and wealth have been usurped from the people.

Concerning questions of language, Omotoso refuses to let himself be caught in a debate which he sees as the stock-in-trade of critics of African literature for too long and which should finally be put to rest. A writer's desire to write in any language which comes easily to him should be respected, and the only requirement the writer has, in any language, is to avoid obscurity.[14]

Since the overwhelming majority in Nigeria are not literate in English, Omotoso has begun to prepare the way for the future by encouraging literacy in local languages among the young. He has been involved in producing a number of children's books in Yoruba, translations of stories from other literatures and histories of the achievements of black peoples all over the world. Futhermore, as one of the leaders of the Union of Writers of African Peoples, an association that Omotoso helped to found in Accra in June 1975, he would agree that Africa ultimately needs its own continent-wide tongue. The obvious choice, for members of the Union, is Swahili: 'It is absolutely necessary, and we have to face it sooner or later, that Africa will need a language of its own and the earlier this decision is taken and pursued, the better.'[15]

Novelist, playwright, critic, Kole Omotoso's output shows no signs of letting up. In 1979 Fagbamigbe Publishers brought out a critical essay, *The Form of the African Novel*, and have published a new novel, *To Borrow a Wandering Leaf*. He is currently working on an introduction to African writing for 'beginners' in African literature, to be published by Ikenga Publishers, Enugu, in 1982 under the title *Discovering African Literature*. In preparation also is an autobiographical novel, tentatively entitled *Memories of Our Recent Boom*, about 'growing up moderately well-to-do in a situation of general poverty', a novel that would appear to heed the programme that Omotoso, the critic, has set out for writers.

[1] Omotoso, 'Writing and publishing in an African country: a personal experience' (unpublished manuscript, Barbados, 9 Feb. 1979), p. 6
[2] Omotoso, 'Politics, propaganda and prostitution', *Afriscope*, vol. 1, no. 11, Nov. 1974, p. 47
[3] Omotoso, 'Form and content in ideologically committed societies', *Afriscope*, vol. 5, no. 12,

Dec. 1975, p. 40

[4] Omotoso, 'Literature and society in Africa', *Afriscope*, vol. 6, no. 9, Sept. 1976, p. 9

[5] Omotoso, 'Ritual dreams of art', *Afriscope*, vol. 5, no. 6, June 1975, p. 40

[6] Omotoso, 'Need for new horizons', *Afriscope*, vol. 3, no. 5, 1973, p. 45

[7] Omotoso, 'The missing apex' in Oluwasanmi *et al.*, eds., *Publishing in Africa in the Seventies* (Conference proceedings of the 1973 Ife Conference on publishing in Africa) (Ile-Ife, Nigeria, 1975)

[8] Tola Adeniyi, 'Writers' search for audience in Africa' (interview with Kole Omotoso), *Daily Times* (Lagos), 14 Mar. 1974, p. 12

[9] Omotoso, 'Form and content', p. 41

[10] Omotoso, 'Need for new horizons', p. 44

[11] Omotoso, 'Literature and society', p. 9

[12] *Ibid.*

[13] Omotoso, 'Politics, propaganda', p. 47

[14] 'Interview with Kole Omotoso', in Bernth Lindfors, ed., *Dem-Say, Interviews with Eight Nigerian Writers* (Austin, Texas, 1974), p. 55

[15] *The African Book Publishing Record*, vol. 2, no. 1, 1976, p. 12

Femi Osofisan

born 1946   NIGERIA

A prominent member of the post-Achebe and post-Soyinka generation of Nigerian writers, Femi Osofisan has come upon the literary scene only since the end of the civil war. Osofisan (whose full name is Babafemi Adeyemi Osofisan) calls himself 'more of a playwright than a novelist',[1] although his first published work (1975) was a novel, *Kolera Kolej*. A stage version of the novel was performed in 1975 by the Unibadan Masque Theatre and has been described by Gerald Moore as 'an effective play'.[2]

As an author Osofisan acknowledges his debt to the older generation of writers, especially Soyinka whose disciple he once was. His play, *The Chattering and the Song*, is dedicated to Soyinka and to Christopher Okigbo, the Igbo poet who died fighting for Biafra. Osofisan admires the first generation of writers but he also attacks them on two points. First, he says, by seeking an international reputation, they have put their private interests as authors over the needs of their society which is involved in an urgent struggle 'against neo-colonization and the insidious spread of fascism', and the consequence is that the works of these authors 'are not immediately relevant to our people'.[3]

In his published essay, 'Anubis resurgent: chaos and political vision in recent literature',[4] and the debate with Odei Ofeimum in *Afriscope* following his article 'Literature as suicide',[5] Osofisan has gone even further, taking older African writers to task for the cynical souring of their vision. He refers explicitly to Soyinka's *Season of Anomy* and Mongo Beti's *Remember Ruben*. What is worse, Osofisan argues, many members of the older generation are guilty of creating what he calls 'an escapist literature'. Without naming any names, Osofisan identifies such a writer as one who 'fails to grapple with the reality of his society in any meaningful way'.[6] If it is clear that Soyinka does not fall into this category, Osofisan is nevertheless very critical of the man whom he once felt to be his literary master (and whom he continues to respect), due to Soyinka's use of mythology and ritual. Although Osofisan is wary of labels such as 'revolutionary', he does define himself as a man with socialist convictions 'without being dogmatic about Marxism' and for whom the use of mythology in literature is 'mere mystification'.[7] Osofisan believes he and his fellow progressive artists 'must begin to confront history at its empirical points' and 'move our people away from superstition'.[8] What this means in terms of Osofisan's art is not the refusal to adopt elements of mythology and ritual, but to use them 'from a subversive perspective': 'I borrow ancient forms specifically to unmask them'.[9]

In a radio programme Andrew Horn, the former Head of Performing Arts at Nigeria's Ahmadu Bello University, questioned how radical Osofisan's vision really is in a play like *The Chattering and the Song*. The script calls for the use of a play-in-the-play device centred around a traditional African monarch who urges his subjects to return to 'ancestral roots' and to reaffirm values out of the past.[10] For Gerald Moore, however, Osofisan's use of the inner play in which the characters act out traditional roles is a means by which they expose themselves (and by extension the roles they have assumed). 'More than any play of Soyinka's *The Chattering and the Song* offers a model of the new society as well as a condemnation of the old.'[11] Gerald Moore feels that it is in the field of drama that Femi Osofisan will make his contribution to Nigerian letters, 'bringing it to a more specific political commitment than was evident in the first wave of Nigerian dramatists'.[12]

Commitment is certainly evident in the works Osofisan has published so far and which include the novel, *Kolera Kolej*, and three plays – *A Restless Run of Locusts*, *The Chattering and the Song*, and *Who's Afraid of Solarin?* His two most recent plays are also the works of a committed artist. They were performed in 1979 in the Arts Theatre at the University of Ibadan where Osofisan is senior lecturer in African and Comparative Literature in the Department of Modern Languages. Both plays were staged by the Kakaun Sela Kompany, a semi-professional group which Osofisan founded and directs. The first of these plays, *Once Upon Four Robbers* (soon to be published by BIO Press, Ibadan), is built around the double metaphor of a robbery and symbolic cannibalism. In it a motley crew of thieves cast a spell on market-goers in order to rob them, and they in turn are robbed by the soldiers sent to arrest them. In *Morountodun*, the second play, Osofisan elicits dramatic interest from the myth of Moremi, the legendary Yoruba heroine who let herself be captured by the enemy in order to bring about their defeat and which has already inspired a play by Duro Ladipo. In Osofisan's version, however, the myth is twisted and the message reversed. The context is a peasant uprising and the main character, Titubi, a true believer in the ideology of the power establishment, dreams of becoming a latter-day Moremi by letting herself be captured by the peasants in order to hasten the fall of their revolt. In the end, however, she realizes her error and sincerely adopts their cause, after which she is renamed Morountodun ('I have found a sweet thing').

Osofisan also extends commitment to literary criticism, and he was one of the organizers of a conference on 'Radical perspectives in African criticism' held in Ibadan. For Osofisan literature must be 'a social force, an ideological weapon'. The primary virtue of literature is 'its subversive potential, that explosive charge which lies hidden behind the facade of entertainment'.[13]

In addition to his academic duties Osofisan helps edit *Opon Ifa*, the Ibadan 'Poetry Chapbooks'. The journal offers a forum for young unknown poets but, due to lack of finance, it unfortunately remains a sporadic publication. Osofisan notes bitterly that there is money available for older established writers, but no one, he says, is interested in young writers.

Still a young writer himself, Osofisan continues his output, despite what he considers to be the lack of official encouragement and the obvious publication difficulties which he and his generation encounter for being determined to publish in Nigeria. Work in progress includes another play on the theme of armed robbery, *Once Upon Other Robbers*, and a sequel to *Kolera Kolej*, *Kolera Kolej Goes to War*. He is also working on two other plays, *Another Raft* and *Aringindin and the Nightwatchmen*, and on a collection of poetry entitled *A Girl is Going into Saturday*. In addition to *Morountodun* three other plays have already been performed but have still to find a publisher: *Oduduwa, Don't Go!*, *You Have Lost Your Fine Face* and *Behind the Ballot Box*.

Osofisan was born on 15 June 1946 at Ijebu Ode in Western Nigeria (now Ogun State) and holds a doctorate in French from the University of Ibadan after studying at the Universities of Ibadan, Dakar and Paris.

[1] Ossie Onuora Enekwe, 'Interview with Femi Osofisan', *The Greenfield Review*, vol. 8, nos. 1/2, Spring 1980, p. 79
[2] Gerald Moore, 'Against the Titans in Nigerian literature', *Afriscope*, vol. 7, July 1977, p. 21
[3] Enekwe, 'Interview', pp. 80, 77
[4] *Ch'Indaba*, July–Dec. 1976
[5] *Afriscope*, vol. 7, no. 1, 1977
[6] Osofisan, 'Criticism as homicide, a brief

reply', in *Afriscope*, vol. 7, no. 8, 1977, p. 36
[7] Enekwe, 'Interview', p. 77
[8] *Ibid.*, p. 77
[9] *Ibid.*, p. 79
[10] 'Arts and Africa', no. 262, BBC African Service transcript (London)
[11] Moore, 'Against the Titans', p. 21
[12] *Ibid.*
[13] Enekwe, 'Interview', p. 80

Yambo Ouologuem
born 1940   MALI

The son of a school inspector and a member of a traditional Dogon ruling-class family, Yambo Ouologuem was born on 22 August 1940 in Bandiagara in the region of Mopti. As a consequence of his family's position, Ouologuem speaks several African languages in addition to his own Dogon; he is also fluent in French, English and Spanish. He studied at schools in Bamako and Paris and holds university degrees in literature, philosophy and sociology. He also has a gradu-ate certificate in English.

Yambo Ouologuem received lavish praise upon the publication of his first novel, *Le Devoir de violence*, in 1968, and was awarded the coveted Prix Renaudot. Within the next two years the novel was translated into German, Danish, Norwegian, Swedish, Dutch and Japanese (with editions planned for Italy and Argentina), and an English edition (*Bound to Violence*) appeared in New York and London in 1971. The following year the novel became available in Heinemann's African Writers Series. The year after the publication of his first work Ouologuem brought out a series of 'letters', entitled *Lettres à la France nègre*, in which he violently denounced the hypocrisy of Europeans and Africans. Guilty Africans included the 'concierges de la négritude' (the 'innkeepers' or the 'doormen' of negritude). In 1969, under the pseudonym of Utto Rodolph, Ouologuem also published a pornographical novel, *Les milles et une bibles du sexe*, that was issued by his own publishing house, Editions du Dauphin.

When *Le Devoir de violence* appeared it was greeted as 'perhaps the first African novel worthy of the name' by *Le Monde*.[1]

But the prominent Nigerian literary critic Abiola Irele described it as 'a meandering succession of sordid happenings, excesses and extravagances, presented as an historical narrative of a fictitious but "typical" African empire . . .' He found the novel's salient idea is 'that the past has only bequeathed to the present generation of Africans a legacy of crime and violence'.[2]

Soon after publication *Le Devoir de violence* was caught up in a nasty controversy. At issue was whether or not Ouologuem had plagiarized André Schwarz-Bart's *Le Dernier des justes*, Graham Greene's *It's a Battlefield*, and perhaps others. Eric Sellin suggested that Ouologuem's French publisher, Editions Seuil, had commissioned Ouologuem to write an African version of Schwarz-Bart's novel (published by Seuil in 1959) and accused Ouologuem of borrowing whole passages from it.[3] He produced passages from both works to prove his point. The *Times Literary Supplement* of 5 May 1972 claimed (by again comparing parallel passages) that Ouologuem had lifted several paragraphs from Graham Greene's novel. In answer to the first accusation Seuil denied that they had commissioned *Le Devoir de violence* and Schwarz-Bart played down the idea of plagiarism, reportedly saying, 'I am especially touched, even overwhelmed, to think that a Black writer should have relied on *Le Dernier des justes* in creating a book like *Le Devoir de violence*. Thus Mr Ouologuem is not indebted to me, but rather I to him.'[4] The resemblances between the novels of Ouologuem and Greene, however, were hard to deny. Seuil sent a letter of apology to Greene and asked Ouologuem to rewrite certain passages – which has never been done. Ouologuem, interviewed in the midst of the furore, admitted having quoted from a certain number of authors but insisted that the quotation marks had been edited out in the publication process.

In the ensuing years a number of critics have spoken up, not to condone Ouologuem's borrowings, but to defend the originality of the overall conception of his novel. In *Myth, Literature and the African World*, while admitting 'it would have been preferable if Yambo Oulouguem (sic) had acknowledged his sources', Wole Soyinka writes:

> The charges of plagiarism in Oulouguem's work appear to be well substantiated; it would be futile to deny this. The literary question remains, however, whether or not we are confronted with an original contribution to literature, in spite of the borrowings. The *drama* of the novel is original; this, I believe, has not been disputed. The stylistic 'griot' propulsive energy and the creative vision are unquestionably Oulouguem's.[5]

More recently John Erickson has tried to put Ouologuem's borrowings in their proper perspective. Not only have great authors of the past 'borrowed' from others, Erickson says – and the list includes Shakespeare, Montaigne, Voltaire and Victor Hugo – but as an African, Ouologuem comes from an oral tradition where 'the custom of anonymity presupposes that all oral expression is the common property of all people'.[6] The real point to be considered, according to Erickson, is that of the *impact* of Ouologuem's novel: '. . . the fact remains that [the materials and methods of composition] were *combined* by Ouologuem into a narrative structure that did not exist prior to its combination and one that succeeded powerfully'.[7]

The issue of borrowings aside, the personality of Ouologuem alone would seem to attract controversy. He is 'a small, mercurial man with a mocking sense of humour and a scathing intellect . . . a supreme conversationalist'.[8] He seems to revel in the shock effect created, not only by the violence of his tone in the novel, but also by his outspoken declarations on the subject of African literature and on the 'language dilemma' of African writers. On the question of language he 'rejects the snobbery which claims that it is not possible to think "African" in French. I am not a victim of French culture', he maintains. When he writes in the French language, the language itself is 'simply a tool'.[9]

Speaking of the 'black man' he has said,

> For me there is no 'Negro' problem, there are only problems of class and of human

conflict. The French worker with his minimum wage, tied to certain activities, restricted, in some ways ostracised, is a Negro. For me a Jew is simply a badly whitened Negro. I deliberately chose as one of my central characters a Negro who was also of Arab and Jewish background.[10]

As for 'African literature', it does not exist. There are only national literatures – the result of the desire of governments to create a 'national folklore':

> The problem of African literature is fundamentally linked to that of African unity. It is certain that if these racial and political barriers existing among African people could be pulled down the literature would respond. It is because we haven't yet succeeded in this big step that we have shut ourselves in ghettos of a sort.[11]

That was in 1969. Seven years later, in 1976, Ouologuem builds on this idea:

> The independence that has been achieved, in theory, and that could have brought about a renewal of ideas and of literature in Africa, only served to castrate both literature and the living forces that should have been the sap of the young generation. And even if one wanted to give Africa the opportunity to express herself, there is such chaos, such cracks in the basic structures that it is difficult for anything to emerge.[12]

The scandal surrounding *Le Devoir de violence* may indeed have ruined Ouologuem's career, as Erickson suggests, for he published almost no creative writing in the seventies. Three of his poems (and an interview) did appear in a special issue of *Poésie I* alongside the verse of such prestigious names as René Depestre, Lamine Diakhaté, Edouard Maunick, V. Y. Mudimbé and Tchicaya U Tam'si. Ouologuem also co-edited in the late sixties and early seventies three textbooks on African literature for primary and secondary schools. However, the novel that *West Africa* announced as 'completed' in 1971, *The Pilgrims of Copernaum*, has never appeared, presumably as a result of the taint on Ouologuem's name. The novel was to be a sort of immense fresco with, according to *West Africa*, '250 characters from five continents covering a time span from before Abraham to 1971'.[13]

Since the *Poésie I* interview in 1976 nothing has been heard from Ouologuem. He is listed by the 1981 *Annuaire de l'ADELF* (Association des Ecrivains de langue française) as residing in Europe (probably meaning France), but unlike other writers in the ADELF yearbook no home address is given for him.

[1] *The Guardian*, 28 Nov. 1968, quoted in *Cultural Events in Africa*, no. 47, 1968, p. 6

[2] Abiola Irele, 'A new mood in the African novel', *West Africa*, 20 Sept. 1969, p. 1115

[3] Eric Sellin, 'Ouologuem's blueprint for *Le Devoir de violence*', *Research in African Literature*, vol. 2, no. 2, Fall 1971, pp. 117–20

[4] Quoted by Eric Sellin, 'The unknown voice of Yambo Ouologuem', *Yale French studies*, no. 53, and reproduced in John Erickson, *Nommo: African Fiction in French South of the Sahara* (York, South Carolina, 1979), p. 245

[5] Wole Soyinka, *Myth, Literature and the African World* (London, 1976), pp. 98–9

[6] Erickson, *Nommo*, p. 228

[7] *Ibid.*, p. 229

[8] *West Africa*, 13 Aug. 1971, p. 930

[9] *Cultural Events in Africa*, no. 47, 1968, p. 6

[10] *Ibid.*, p. 6

[11] 'Yambo Ouologuem (Mali) interviewed by Dr S. Okechukwu Mezu during the African Studies Association, Montreal, October 1969', *Cultural Events in Africa*, no. 61, 1969, p. i–ii

[12] 'Yambo Ouologuem (Mali): La conscience malheureuse', *Poésie I: Nouvelle Poésie Négro-Africaine: La parole noire*, nos. 43–44–45, Jan.–June 1976, p. 124 (editors' translation)

[13] *West Africa*, 13 Aug. 1971, p. 930

Sembène Ousmane
born 1923   SENEGAL

From a fisherman, mason, mechanic, and dock-worker to a novelist, short-story writer, and film director of international repute, Sembène Ousmane has travelled a long, varied, and still promising route. Born in the southern region of Senegal in Ziguinchor (Casamance) on 1 January 1923, essentially self-educated, he initially became a fisherman, just like his father. 'I have earned my living since I was 15', Sembène says.[1]

When he moved to Dakar, he worked at manual jobs until the outbreak of World War II. In 1939 he was drafted into the French army and saw action in Italy and in Germany. Returning to Senegal for a brief time, Sembène Ousmane realized that in order to further his literary ambitions he would need to move to France. His intense political commitment also dates from this time. After working as a docker in Marseilles, he became the trade-union leader of the dockers and joined the French Communist party, remaining a member until Senegal became independent in 1960. He also began writing.

His first semi-autobiographical novel dating from this period is aptly titled *Le Docker noir* (1956). This work was followed one year later by *Oh Pays, mon beau peuple!* about the problems of re-adaptation encountered by an African who returns home from Europe with a French wife and new ideas. In 1960 *Les Bouts de bois de Dieu* appeared in which, once again, Ousmane utilized actual historical events as a basis for his novel: this time, the Niger–Dakar railway strike of 1947. An English version of the novel, translated by Francis Price, became available as early as 1962 in the United States and appeared in Heinemann's African Writers Series in 1969. In 1962, *Voltaïque*, a collection of Ousmane's short stories, was published. The volume contains the story 'La noire de ...' ('Black Girl') which Ousmane later turned into a prize-winning film. The stories were translated into English by Len Ortzen as *Tribal Scars and Other Stories* and appeared in the African Writers Series in 1973 and under an American imprint in 1974. 'Black Girl' has been translated by Ellen Conroy

Kennedy and appears in *African Short Stories* (New York, 1970).

A fourth novel, *L'Harmattan*, was released in 1964 (reissued by Présence Africaine in 1980). In the original edition Ousmane wrote:

> I do not theorize about the African novel. I recall just the same that once in this Africa that may be called 'classique' (or traditional), the griot professional singer was not only the dynamic element in his tribe, clan, village, but also the obvious testimony or 'witness' of every event. It was he who captured, and laid out before everyone under the tree of talk the deeds and mannerisms of each. The conception of my work will spin out in that manner: to remain as close as possible to the reality and to the people.[2]

A new avenue of expression was open to Ousmane when the Moscow Film School invited him to study there. Returning to Dakar, he continued his activities in the field of cinema and completed *Barom Sarret*, a short feature about the driver of a donkey-drawn taxi-cart, a familiar sight in the slums of Dakar.

Two short novels, *Véhi Ciosane ou blanche genèse*, and *Le Mandat*, were published in one volume by Présence Africaine in 1965. The latter was reissued in 1969 and a fellow African writer, Mbella Sonne Dipoko, claimed this short novel to be 'a minor masterpiece'.[3] Of Ousmane he wrote: 'He is the leader of the new dynamic realism which is developing in French African writing'.[4] It was this story, when made into a film, that established Sembène Ousmane as an internationally prominent film director. After winning a prize at the Venice Film Festival, it was presented in 1969 as part of the seventh New York Film Festival at Lincoln Center and hailed in the *New York Times* as 'the surprise hit of the festival'.[5] It also brought its director to New York, where he was interviewed by the *Times*.

In this interview Ousmane states, perhaps giving the key to his entire artistic orientation, 'The thing I was trying to do in it was to show Africans some of the deplorable conditions under which they live. When one creates, one doesn't think of the world; one thinks of

his own country. It is, after all, the Africans who will ultimately bring about change in Africa – not the Americans or the French or the Russians or the Chinese.'[6]

Throughout the seventies Ousmane has continued to express himself on the written page and on the screen, and both his writing and his latest films reveal a heightened sense of his duty as a committed artist to contribute to social awareness:

> this is the most difficult and therefore the most important aspect of my effort as an artist – to guide them [the people] to feel, to understand and perhaps to discover deep within themselves that they and only they have the real and sure possibility of changing [their living conditions], to improve them, and even to destroy some aspects of these conditions if such is required for their well-being, which is a natural and legitimate aspiration of all men.[7]

In 1973 Ousmane published a new novel, *Xala*, which three years later came out under the same title in English and American editions in a translation by Clive Wake. The full-length feature film based on the novel which Ousmane produced in 1974 was the object of some controversy in Senegal, for the corrosive picture it presents of the Senegalese bourgeoisie, and ten scenes were cut (without Ousmane's consent) before the film was authorized for showing there. *Xala* is a Wolof word meaning 'temporary sexual impotence', and it is used in the film as a symbol of the privileged class in Africa today that is, in Ousmane's words, 'culturally, politically, economically impotent; impotent in terms of the very sources of the life of a society'.[8]

All Ousmane's most recent films have been subjected to some form of censorship – either in his own country or in other African states. *Emitaï*, a film he made in 1971 about a resistance movement to colonialism that took place in the region of Casamance in Senegal in the forties, was almost banned in Senegal – under pressure of the French government – and has not been shown in Ivory Coast. Ousmane's latest feature film, *Ceddo* (or *Cedo* in the officially authorized spelling) has still not been seen to this day in

Senegal even though it dates from 1977. The official explanation for the ban is Ousmane's refusal to conform to the authorized spelling for the film's title, but the real reasons go much deeper. Again set in the past, the film studies another kind of historical resistance movement, that of animists who refused conversion to Islam – an explosive theme in Senegal today where 90 per cent of the people are Muslim.

Ousmane has always considered his writing and film-making as complementary activities, and he has no intention of giving up literature even if he is aware that film-making puts him in more direct contact with people. And the problems he has encountered with censorship make his writing all the more necessary. After his troubles with Senegalese authorities over the film *Xala*, he declared:

> I like to write and I like to film. A film obviously has more viewers than readers for a book, especially in Africa ... But as I wonder if I'm going to be able to make films in Senegal after the *Xala* affair, and as I don't want to go into exile, it is wiser to continue to write books (for people are less wary of books than of images since their impact is not so great). However, *Xala*, the novel, is in its third printing and has already reached 10,000 readers in Francophone black Africa.⁹

Since that interview Sembène Ousmane, fortunately, was able to make the film *Ceddo*. He has also produced a new novel, the massive two-volume work, *Le Dernier de l'empire*, published in 1981. Called a work of 'political fiction' by the author himself, the novel takes place in a real country – Senegal – but one that is governed by imaginary politicians, suggesting that fiction and reality are strangely intermingled in Africa today.

¹ Guy Flatley, 'Senegal is Senegal, not Harlem', (Interview with Ousmane Sembène), *The New York Times*, 2 Nov. 1969, p. 17
² Ousmane, *L'Harmattan* (Paris, 1964), p. 10, trans. and quoted by A. C. Brench in *Writing in French from Senegal to Cameroon* (London, 1967) and reproduced in Donald Herdeck, *African Authors: A Companion to Black African Writing, 1300–1973* (Washington DC, 1973), pp. 392–3
³ *Africa Today*, Aug.–Sept. 1968
⁴ Per Wästberg, ed., *The Writer in Modern Africa* (New York, 1969), p. 70
⁵ Flatley, 'Senegal is Senegal', p. 17
⁶ *Ibid.*
⁷ Tahar Cheriaa, 'The artist and revolution: interview with Ousmane Sembéne', excerpt from *Cinema-Quebec*, nos. 9–10, pp. 12–17, trans. by Jibs Akinkoye and reproduced in *Positive Review*, vol. 1, no. 2, 1978, p. 4
⁸ *Ibid.*, p. 3
⁹ Sembène Ousmane, 'Denoncer la nouvelle bourgeoisie', *Afrique-Asie*, no. 79, 24 Mar. 1975, p. 64 (editors' translation)

Ferdinand Oyono

born 1929   CAMEROON

There are similarities between the lives and works of Ferdinand Oyono and Mongo Beti. Like his Cameroonian compatriot, Ferdinand Oyono is a Béti, educated in his native land and abroad in France, a satirical novelist who during the late fifties directed his attack primarily toward colonial rule and oppression. And according to at least one critic, they are 'both precursors in African literature'; both their works mark 'a watershed in contemporary African literature in French. There is a new element of assurance in their treatment of colonialism as a political force. Although oppressed, the African can turn his back and laugh heartily at his masters. Their biting satire and sarcasm is softened by this frank humour.'¹ In his later writing, however, Mongo Beti has gone on to include post-independent Africa, and specifically Cameroon, in his satirical scope, and as an outspoken opponent to the regime of Ahidjo, Beti has felt it necessary to live in exile in Paris. On the other hand, all of Oyono's novels date back to the days of colonialism, and Oyono's entire professional career has been devoted to serving the state of Cameroon.

Ferdinand Oyono was born in the small village, N'goulemakong, near Ebolowa on 14 September 1929, and began his education at the local primary school. His father practised polygamy; his mother, however, was a devout Catholic, and refusing to share her husband, left him and went to work as a seamstress to support her children. The young Oyono worked at the local mission, as did his younger sister, and

was introduced to a conventional education in the French colonial tradition. It
was here, too, that he first became
acquainted with what it meant to be the
'boy' of the local missionaries. After
attending the local provincial school, his
father sent him to France, where Oyono
first attended the Lycée de Provins, and
later studied in the Faculté de Droit, and
then the École Nationale d'Administration in Paris. While a student in France –
lonely and living under circumstances
similar to those of Camara Laye –
Ferdinand Oyono was prompted to write
his first two novels, *Une vie de boy* and *Le
Vieux nègre et la médaille*, both in 1956.

The two works were, in fact, written
concurrently. In an article based on an
interview with Oyono that appeared in
Cameroon Tribune in February 1976,
Oyono is reported to have said that *Une
vie de boy* was a hard book to write. It did
not flow easily from his pen, and it was
while he was trying to write that novel
that the idea for *Le Vieux nègre et la
médaille* came to him. He dashed off the
novel in three days and then went back to
finish *Une vie de boy*, which explains the
reasons the works were published almost
simultaneously. At the time of their
publication neither work attracted more
than moderate attention from critics.
Paradoxically, Oyono was enjoying much
more success as an actor in the title role
in Louis Sapin's *Papa bon Dieu* which
played at the Théâtre d'Aujourd'hui of
the Alliance Française in Paris in 1959.

Today ranked as classics of modern
African literature Oyono's novels are
among those books which are required
reading in introductory courses to
African literature. *Une vie de boy* has been
translated into five languages and *Le
Vieux nègre et la médaille* into ten.

In his introduction to the American
edition of *Une vie de boy* (titled simply, *Boy*)
Edris Makward points out that the novel
'denounced openly the excesses of colonial society and above all it showed the
awareness of the African and his capacity
to see with lucidity the vanity and
unfounded claim to "superiority" of the
European in Africa'.[2] The French critic,
Jacques Chevrier, notes that Oyono

cleverly uses the structures and techniques of the French colonial novel that
was enjoying a certain vogue in those
days, as an exotic exercise in the rein-
forcement of colonial ideology, to produce exactly the opposite effect 'by
ripping apart the factitious décor of
exoticism'.[3]

Oyono's second novel is probably his
most successful among readers, if one
judges from the number of translations it
has been through. *The Old Man and the
Medal* (translated and published in London in 1967) is the pitifully comic tale
of Méka, the old peasant upon whom
colonial authorities decide to bestow a
medal for his exceptional 'devotion' to
France. The irony of the situation is that
devotion includes, in Jacques Chevrier's
words, having two sons 'die for France on
battlefields in far-off Europe and having
most of his land distributed to the
Catholic mission'.[4] 'The art of Ferdinand
Oyono', concludes Chevrier, 'is to have
made his hero Méka into a Cameroonian
Huron whose naïveté reveals the gap
between what is said and what is done.'[5]
The result is a novel that is 'an irrefutable
document on African colonial society'.[6]

Four years went by before his third
novel was released. Gerald Moore finds
that *Chemin d'Europe* (not as yet translated
into English) 'is more ambitious, for it
depicts a situation which is in itself diffuse
and hard to grasp, the situation of the
young man educated beyond his fellows
but still not sufficiently so to assure him
of a career'.[7] Summarizing Oyono's
works, Moore writes:

Ferdinand Oyono's novels celebrate the
disillusionment of the African with the white
man's world. His heroes set out in a state of
innocent enthusiasm; then comes the moment of truth, opening the door into a new
world of bitterness or corrosive resignation.
Despite the brilliance of his comic writing,
this fatal *consequence* gives a kind of tragic
intensity to his plots as a whole, particularly
in *Une vie de boy*, his first novel. He is
probably the greatest master of construction
among African novelists now writing.[8]

Oyono's only other piece of published
fiction is the short story 'Un lépreux sur
une tombe' that was included in the

anthology *Hommes sans épaules* in 1958. Although a fourth novel, *Le Pandemonium*, has long been announced, it has not as yet appeared. In the 1976 interview in *Cameroon Tribune* Oyono is said to have given the work to a publisher – not Julliard, he specifies. His own dissatisfaction with the novel, however, had led him to revise and rewrite it so much that he feels it is still not ready for publication. *Le Pandemonium* is described in this article as having more than 500 pages and a hundred characters and as being a criticism of occidental society as seen from the inside.[9]

Since the Independence of Cameroon in 1960 Ferdinand Oyono has spent his career in the diplomatic service. He has represented his country at the European Common Market (1961–2 and 1965–8) and has been ambassador to Liberia, France and the United States. In 1977 he became Director General of UNICEF at the United Nations headquarters in New York, a position he still holds. Roger Mercier and Monique and Simon Battestini edited a study guide to Oyono's works with Nathan in 1964 and more recently Jacques Chevrier has presented (1977) a critical analysis of Oyono's *Une vie de boy* in Hatier's collection 'Profil d'une oeuvre'.

[1] A. C. Brench, *The Novelists' Inheritance in French Africa* (London, 1967), pp. 49, 48
[2] Edris Makward in introduction to Ferdinand Oyono, *Boy* (New York, 1970), p. vi
[3] Jacques Chevrier, *Une vie de boy – Oyono: analyse critique* (Paris, 1977), p. 73 (this and following quotations translated by the editors)
[4] *Ibid.*, p. 7
[5] *Ibid.*, p. 68
[6] *Ibid.*, p. 68
[7] Gerald Moore, 'Ferdinand Oyono and the colonial tragi-comedy', *Présence Africaine*, vol. 18, no. 46, 1963, p. 70
[8] *Ibid.*, p. 61
[9] *Cameroon Tribune*, 23 Feb. 1976, p. 2

Guillaume Oyono-Mbia
born 1939   CAMEROON

Completely bilingual, Guillaume Oyono-Mbia is that unusual author who writes his plays in both English and French, and the process of going from one language to the other he calls 'rewriting' rather than 'translation'.

> I never translate my plays. I hate it when people refer to my translations. I take into account the different mentalities of English and French speakers. And the theater experiences of the French-speaking and English-speaking audiences are so widely different that I always try to make not only linguistic but staging differences.[1]

Oyono-Mbia was born in 1939 in the Cameroonian village of Mvoutessi near Sangmélima, the village setting that has inspired both his plays and his short stories. He attended the Collège Evangélique of Libamba, and it was here he began to write 'by mere accident', as he says. 'I was preparing for the French *baccalauréat* and this, in fact, led me to write in dramatic dialogue.'[2]

He went to England in 1964 on a British Council scholarship to prepare a diploma as translator/interpreter and the following year entered the University of Keele to study French and English, graduating in 1968.

The theatre is to this essentially comic playwright 'the only means which can reach illiterate as well as literate people'; he would like to specialize in a kind of participatory theatre where people are 'allowed to take part'.[3]

Thus far Oyono-Mbia has published four comic plays. *Trois prétendants . . . un mari* (*Three Suitors: One Husband*), first published in Yaoundé in 1964, is the work that goes back to his secondary school days, and the play's first production was by Oyono-Mbia's classmates. 'The story stems from something that happened to one of my cousins', Oyono-Mbia says, 'who got married in almost exactly the same way as described in *Three Suitors*. I just happened to attend the palava where they decided all this. And I was interested in the fact that nobody had consulted her at all . . . So my first play started as a sort of taking down of everything which was being said during the palava.'[4] In the introduction to the English version, Oyono-Mbia wrote: 'Throughout the comedy, the audience will learn something about the major problems facing Africans today: is it possible to make room for the new while at the same time facing the old?'[5]

Produced widely through the whole of Cameroon (particularly at school graduation ceremonies), the French version of *Three Suitors: One Husband* has sold more copies than any other book published by CLE. The English version of the play was published in 1968 in a Methuen play script along with *Until Further Notice*, a radio play written in English that received first prize in a drama competition organized by the BBC African Service. Early in 1970 it was awarded the newly established El Hadj Ahmadou Ahidjo literary prize, and was issued in a French edition entitled *Jusqu'à nouvel avis* (again rewritten by the author himself) by CLE in 1970.

Oyono-Mbia's third play, *Notre fille ne se mariera pas!* (1971 and reissued 1973) is the only one of his plays that has yet to appear in English. Winner of the 1969 Inter-African theatre competition sponsored by Radio-France Internationale, the play comically reverses the theme of *Three Suitors: One Husband*. In that play the educated daughter had to be married at all costs to 'the highest bidder'. In *Notre fille ne se mariera pas!* (*Our Daughter must not marry*), the family is concerned to prevent the daughter's marriage in order to make sure that her earnings as an educated person will be channelled directly into the family coffers.

A fourth play, *His Excellency's Train* (*Le train spécial de Son Excellence*), was published in English and French editions by CLE in 1978. Originally meant for radio production, it was broadcast by the BBC in 1969. The comic element in this play centres on the gap between people's expectations and their perceptions as they anxiously await the arrival of a very important dignitary. How disappointed they will be when he turns out not to look very important at all!

Oyono-Mbia has also published (1971 and 1972) three collections of short stories entitled *Chroniques de Mvoutessi I, II* and *III*. He says he chose his own village as a setting so as not to anger people:

> I'm chiefly a satirical writer and it wouldn't have done me any good to do satirical

writing about someone else's village. But it would be a mistake to say it concerns only my village. My village is taken as a typical village in southern Cameroon.[6]

The themes that interest him, he adds, are those that concern contemporary society:

> My short stories are concerned with the days after independence. I'm not concerned with the times before. So many good writers have written about those times, my cousin Ferdinand Oyono and others like Mongo Beti. I don't think it's really worth going back and exploring what was wrong. It's about time we began looking for what may be wrong in our days or what may be right, why not?[7]

Although concerned with social problems, he says, 'I don't write about politics' and 'I'm not a man with slogans. I don't believe in clear-cut solutions to problems'.[8] Nor does he have any inflated idea as to the role of the writer:

> I suppose you would expect me to say [he is] a sort of guide. I don't like the word guide or messiah. I think a writer is like yourself [the interviewer], a reporter, a man who perhaps has a gift not only for seeing but also for telling people what he saw and they may have missed. I think a writer ought to be true not only to himself but to his age, and nothing pleases me more than to have people with no literary pretensions pick up my book and say, 'Yes, this is what happened in my village'.[9]

Guillaume Oyono-Mbia has been teaching English for a number of years at the Federal University of Cameroon in Yaoundé. From 1972 to 1975, in addition to his academic duties, he was head of the cultural affairs division of the Ministry of Information and Culture.

[1] 'Guillaume Oyono-Mbia', transcript of an interview with Lee Nichols recorded in Yaoundé on 24 July 1975
[2] *Cultural Events in Africa*, no. 55, p. ii
[3] *Ibid.*, p. iii
[4] *Ibid.*, p. ii
[5] Guillaume Oyono-Mbia, *Three Suitors: One Husband. Until Further Notice* (London, 1968), p. 7
[6] Nichols, 'Guillaume Oyono-Mbia', p. 237
[7] *Ibid.*, p. 237
[8] *Ibid.*, pp. 237–8
[9] *Ibid.*, pp. 238–9

Okot p'Bitek
1931–1982   UGANDA

Ugandan-born Okot p'Bitek attended his native Gulu High School in the northern part of his country and went on to King's College, Budo. He was a young man of diverse talents: at Budo he composed and produced an opera, he later toured Britain with Uganda's football team, and his first literary work, *Lak Tar Miyo Wi Lobo*, a novel written in Acoli, was published in 1953.

Okot p'Bitek went on to receive a Certificate in Education from Bristol University, and then an LL.B. from the University College of Wales, Aberystwyth. His next step was to work for a B.Litt. at the Institute of Social Anthropology in Oxford, where in 1963 he presented his thesis on Acoli and Lango traditional songs.

Returning to his native Uganda, he joined the staff of the Department of Sociology at Makerere University College in 1964, and two years later became a tutor with the Extra-Mural Department.

'It may seem ironical that the first important poem in English to emerge in Eastern Africa should be a translation from the vernacular original',[1] wrote Gerald Moore. He was referring to p'Bitek's *Song of Lawino*, originally written

in Luo. Although turned down by several British publishers, it became the best-selling title of the East African Publishing House, which issued this highly praised volume in 1966. The World Publishing Company of Cleveland issued a separate American edition in 1969.

Founder of the Gulu Festival and Director of Uganda's National Theatre and National Cultural Centre, p'Bitek subsequently accepted a position with Nairobi's University College as director of the Western Kenya section of the Extra-Mural Department. Here, at the close of 1968, he initiated and organized the successful Kisumu Arts Festival. For Okot p'Bitek, the local artists and writers in attendance represented a small percentage of available talent; hundreds of creative artists remained obscure in rural areas; to p'Bitek 'these were the real artists'.[2]

A frequent contributor to *Transition* and other journals, Okot p'Bitek's poems and articles displayed the same diversity of interests as did his varied career. They range from poems such as 'Return the Bridewealth' and 'Harvest', to essays such as his early 'Acholi folk tales and Fr. Tempels' *Bantu Philosophy*', to literary criticism, as for example, 'The self in African imagery'. Okot p'Bitek published *Song of Ocol*, his second verse collection in 1970. In this, Ocol, the modern west-ernized African, replies to Lawino. The writer has commented on the reactions that the poem has evoked: 'I think most African reviewers have not been very fair to Ocol because they see themselves in him, and Western reviewers have not been very fair to him because they don't like the human creature they have pro-duced in Africa, which is Ocol'.[3]

Song of a Prisoner and *Song of Malaya* were further extensions of the writer's comments on society. *Song of a Prisoner* was written following the death of his friend, the politician Tom Mboya, and a week after he himself had been arrested for disorderly conduct. He comments: 'So the opening . . . is my own experience really. You sleep on that stone floor and the light is there and they never put it out. But it was as if it were me arresting the killer of this famous man and putting him in my office.'[4]

He attacked the hypocrisy of the elite, who simultaneously use and condemn prostitutes, in *Song of Malaya*. For these two works he received the 1972 Kenyatta Prize for Literature.

In 1970 the East African Literature Bureau released his study *African Religions and Western Scholarship*, 'which takes sharp issue with the way African religion is discussed by Western writers', and this was followed by his *Religion of the Central Luo*, another of his 'efforts to show how he felt such studies should be done'.[5] Heinemann produced his collection of Acholi songs in 1974 as *Horn of my Love*, followed by *Hare and Hornbill*, a collection of folk tales.

Apart from writing, p'Bitek continued teaching. In 1978 he left Nairobi for the University of Ife in Nigeria. He had been a visiting lecturer at various universities including Texas and Iowa, where he was writer in residence in 1971. He then returned to Makerere University as Professor of Creative Writing, but died within five months of taking up the appointment.

In his writings p'Bitek continued to probe, to stir. He saw the writer's role as

> challenging ourselves to ask basic questions about the ideal society, about the value of human life, about how we should organize ourselves ... I really hold very strongly that an artist should tease people, should prick needles into everybody so that they don't go to sleep and think everything is fine.[6]

Ngugi would agree with p'Bitek. In an introduction to a book of essays by p'Bitek he speaks of the psychological wound inflicted on their generation by colonialism and Christianity, and declares: 'It is a hidden wound and hence more dangerous because we are not always aware of it. Okot p'Bitek's concern, like that of a good African surgeon, is with this wound. We can ignore a surgeon's advice only at our peril.'[7]

His death has left a gap in the African literary scene, which will not be filled. 'He could be sourly argumentative, he drank too much, he sometimes disappointed people with his casualness, but

he was alive to the tips of his fingers and in every utterance he made. His death is like the splitting of a drum.'[8]

[1] *Transition*, no. 31, June–July 1967, p.52
[2] *Cultural Events in Africa*, no. 50, 1969
[3] Bernth Lindfors, 'An interview with Okot p'Bitek', *World Literature Written in English*, vol. 16, no. 2, Nov. 1977, p. 289
[4] Lee Nichols, ed., *Conversations with African Writers* (Washington DC, 1981), p. 249
[5] *Ibid.*, p. 250
[6] *Ibid.*
[7] Ngugi wa Thiong'o, introduction to Okot p'Bitek, *Africa's Cultural Revolution* (Nairobi, 1973), p. xiii
[8] Alastair Niven, *Africa Now*, October 1982

Lenrie Peters
born 1932   THE GAMBIA

Poet, novelist, and doctor, Lenrie Peters was born in Bathurst, The Gambia. After receiving his basic education there, in 1949 he moved to Sierra Leone, his parents' native home, where he obtained a Higher School Certificate from Freetown's Prince of Wales School. In 1952 Peters began medical studies at Trinity College, Cambridge; a Pan-Africanist, he became President of the African Students Union. After obtaining his medical degree in 1959, Dr Peters went on to specialize in surgery at a hospital in Northampton, England.

On his return to The Gambia, he worked for the government as a surgeon specialist for two years before setting up in private practice. A versatile man, Dr Peters' talents also extend to singing and broadcasting. He has participated in BBC programmes, notably 'Calling West Africa', and was Chairman of its 'Africa Forum'.

Dr Peters is essentially an urbanized poet writing in English within the European tradition though concentrating on African themes and images. He is primarily known for his verse, of which the first was published in *Poems* in 1964 by Mbari, and his poetry has since appeared in both African and British journals. In 1967 Heinemann published *Satellites*, a volume containing 21 poems from the Mbari collection and an additional 34 previously unpublished ones. Lenrie Peters has also written a novel, *The Second Round*, set in Freetown. It is partly autobiographical. His central character, Dr Kawa, returns to Freetown 'bringing with him not only medical skills but also a strong sense of service and a sensitivity to the inadequacy of materialism'.[1] A turtle hunt takes place in the course of the novel, which Peters sees as symbolic of the Vietnamese refugees; furthermore

one is using a symbol of the great against the weak. And the turtle seemed to me an example of endurance such as the black people have endured over the centuries and in their long life they have no protection, apart from the shell and the attempt to escape. And therefore it was a cloistered creature. And man and all the forces of evil are pursuing those that are naked, that are unable to protect themselves.[2]

In 1971 the collection, *Katchikali*, was published in Heinemann's African Writers Series. The sacred grove of Katchikali, the Gambian god of fertility, protection, and procreation, is in Peters' village, Bakau. Among the poet's concerns are the desire to lament the loss of institutions under the impact of colonialism, and to advocate African self-recognition – before he can redeem himself, a man must see himself as 'a being whose soul has been bruised by the colonialists, neo-colonialists and African politicians'.[3]

Selected Poetry (1981) has items from the two previous anthologies as well as new poetry. His concerns have always been for Africa the continent, as Romanus Egudu notes:

Of all the modern poets of English expression, he is the least concerned about his own country and most concerned about the fate of the continent as a whole. He considers himself first an African and secondly a Gambian. Although Peters has not used the techniques of African oral literature, or African linguistic devices, his poems reflect the African spirit and sensibility in their handling of socio-political problems.[4]

[1] Thomas R. Knipp, 'Black African literature and the New African state', *Books Abroad*, vol. 44, no. 3, Summer 1970, p. 373
[2] Al Imfeld, 'Portraits of African Writers', no. 10, Deutsche Welle transcript (Cologne, 1979)
[3] Romanus N. Egudu, 'The colour of truth: Lenrie Peters and African politics', in K. Ogungbesan, ed., *New West African Literature* (London, 1979), p. 60
[4] *Ibid.*, p. 70

René Philombe
born 1930   CAMEROON

'In reality the writer does not invent anything. He arranges what he has heard, what he has seen, and with all that he makes an original work.'[1]

These are the modest words of one of Cameroon's most prolific authors, the man who has been called by the *Cameroon Tribune* 'one of the most influential personalities in the new wave of creative writing in Cameroon'. Philombe is described as a writer whose vision 'is deeply rooted in African life and whoselanguage is full of local images and expressions, making of him a certain incarnation of the conscience of the people'.[2]

René Philombe's renown has grown constantly, both in Cameroon (despite his opposition to the regime) and abroad, since the publication in 1964 of his first collection of short stories, *Lettres de ma cambuse*. The collection was awarded the French Academy's Mottart Prize and the Interallié short-story prize. Philombe's publications to date also include another collection of stories (*Histoires queue de chat*, 1971), two novels (*Sola, ma chérie*, 1966, and *Un sorcier blanc à Zangali*, 1970), two dramatic works (*Les Époux célibataires*, 1971, a comedy, and *Africapolis*, 1978, political satire), plus three verse collections (*Les Blancs partis, les nègres dansent,*

1972; *Petites gouttes de chant pour créer l'homme*, 1977, and *Choc anti-choc*, 1978).

Philombe's work as the General Secretary of the Association of Cameroonian Poets and Writers which he founded in 1960 with seven other writers, including Rémy Médou-Mvomo, has also made him an active, vocal, figure in the cultural life of Cameroon, especially through his editorship of the association's journal, *Le Cameroon Littéraire*, which Philombe launched in 1964. (He later also founded and edited the short-lived journal, *Ozila*.) The aim of the association, as Philombe said, was to 'contribute actively to the elaboration of a national literature, to make the people aware of Cameroonian culture and also to contribute to the writing of a history of the national literature by collecting useful documents'.[3] The association remained active for 15 years, during which time the membership expanded from the original eight to 120, but due to inadequate financial support it ceased functioning in 1975.

The association's lack of official encouragement may be traced, in part, to its strong identification with its leader, who has lived in uneasy peace with the government of President Ahidjo since Independence. In the early sixties Philombe was subject to regular police searches and was even imprisoned for six months for his involvement in an association of farmers and workers that he started in his home town of Batchenga. He had also been linked with the outlawed revolutionary party, L'Union des Populations Camerounaises (UPC), whose leader Ruben um Nyobé was killed in 1958.

During the fifties René Philombe had already attracted attention to himself for his political ideas. He had joined the national police force in 1949, a decision provoked by his urgent need to earn a living, but his outspoken involvement in his professional trade union put him constantly at odds with his superiors and caused him to be moved from city to city during his entire career with the police. Stricken by polio in 1955 (an illness which has left him crippled and unable to

walk without the help of crutches), Philombe spent two years in convalescence. *Lettres de ma cambuse*, stories based on the daily life of the inhabitants of the humble neighbourhood of Nlongkak in Yaoundé where Philombe lived, was written in 1957 when he was in hospital. 'I had written these letters during my hours of solitude – simply not to have morbid thoughts and without the intention of publishing them one day.'[4] It was also in 1957 that Philombe began a career in journalism by founding two newspapers, one in French, *La Voix du citoyen*, and one in Fwondo, *Bebela Ebug*. These activities led to his arrest and to a first stay in prison.

Since the publication of *Lettres de ma cambuse* (*Tales from my Hut* in the English language edition) in 1964 and the winning of the Mottart Prize which brought Philombe international recognition, there would appear to be a sort of 'truce' in the relationship between the writer and the Cameroonian government. In 1967 Philombe was suspected of having reconstituted the UPC and again arrested and imprisoned for a short time. No charges were brought against him, however, and the following year he was appointed to the jury to award the El Hadj Ahmadou Ahidjo Prize for Literature, Arts and Science, something which amounted to 'official recognition'. Philombe also scripted the Cameroon national anthem, but despite this, he no doubt continues to worry the authorities of his country for, in the summer of 1979, he was denied the exit visa which would have allowed him to participate in the Festival of African Arts held in Berlin.

In a 1978 interview René Philombe noted how important travelling can be for a writer as a means to prevent him from living in a 'vacuum' and as a way of helping him see his own culture better. Philombe, himself, however, has had none of the opportunities of the other African authors of his generation. Illness, as well as material and political problems, have kept him cloistered in Cameroon, unable to travel. The same problems have prevented him from acquiring a university education which

African writers of his generation almost all have. None the less, the lack of formal education has certainly been no handicap to Philombe as a writer and Jacques Rial acknowledges him as 'one of the writers from whom one can expect the most'.[5]

The son of an interpreter in the French colonial administration, René Philombe (his real name is Phillippe-Louis Ombede) was born in 1930 in Ngaoundéré where his father had been posted. He moved to the family's home in Batchenga at the age of six, when his father left the service to devote himself to his coffee plantation. Philombe was educated at Catholic missions, first in Efok and then in Bafia, but obtained his primary school leaving certificate from the public school in Bafia in 1942 after being expelled from the mission school. He completed his studies at the Ecole Primaire Supérieure in Yaoundé in 1944 where he helped edit the school journal, 'Appel du Tam-Tam'. His first position upon leaving school in 1947 was that of secretary to the native court of Saa which was presided over by his father. The following year he founded a cultural association in Saa and was awarded a prize by the Committee of Cultural Expansion of France Overseas for a short story entitled 'Nden bobo'. Then began his career in the police force and his trade union activities. During the fifties, Philombe sympathized with the revolu-tionary ideas of the UPC but was not involved directly in its activities. Nor did he participate in the struggle for Independence. It was not until 1960 that his commitment took concrete shape. One of his poems, 'Sur la tombe de mon père', suggests the bitterness Philombe felt for having been on the sidelines during this crucial era, for reasons of ill health, certainly, but also probably because of the ambiguity of his position in the police force.

Commitment to social reform – the problems of dowry, of superstition, of the heavy heritage of missionary education – is an obvious trait of Philombe's writing. He says: 'A writer is led to talking about all subjects – political, economic, cultural, everything. In this way the writer sometimes touches on political issues in Cameroon. It cannot be avoided. And when you avoid it, you lie.'[6]

Philombe's short stories and novels are certainly not political tracts. His literary style in these works is that of the painter endeavouring faithfully to record scenes from everyday life – but with ironic twists. The publication in 1978 of his play, *Africapolis*, and of his book of verse, *Choc anti-choc*, seem to mark a new departure in his writing. Both works have been published by Editions Semences Africaines, the publishing firm run by Philombe. In an article appearing in *Peuples noirs, peuples africaines* Eloise Brière suggests that the more explicit political content of these works made them unacceptable to CLE who had published Philombe's writings up to then, prompting him to found his own publishing concern.[7] In her bibliography of Cameroon authors and artists Thérèse Baratte Eno Belinga lists one of Philombe's poems, *N'Krumah n'est pas mort*, as having been published in 1972 by Editions Semences Africaines,[8] leading one to deduce that Philombe's publishing house dates from the early seventies (no official date of founding is available). If this is the case, and if *Choc anti-choc* and *Africapolis* were not printed until 1978, then one must suppose that Philombe felt he could not, for political reasons, release these works any earlier.

Africapolis, written in 1973, is set in an imaginary African state ruled over by a despot-king who is overthrown in the last scene thanks in part to the spirit of reform brought about by Boki. The young man returns home from studies in France to become Director of the National Bank of Development and his policies encourage a more equal distribution of national revenue. The play has only been performed once, in Bafoussam in 1974, and in the introduction to the published edition Philombe lashes out at directors and the Cameroonian broadcasting system for, in effect, censoring his play by refusing to stage it.

The book of verse, *Choc anti-choc*, contains nine long poems that Philombe wrote while in prison in 1960 and that had been held back all these years.

468

Philombe/Pliya

Originally entitled *Peuple debout: monstre sans age* from the refrain in 'Vision', a five-part poem in the collection, *Choc anti-choc* is a chant to liberty and to its martyrs (specifically, the assassinated leaders of the UPC) and a reaffirmation of the revolutionary potential of the people. It remains to be seen, however, whether *Africapolis* and *Choc anti-choc* mark a real turning point in Philombe's literary production, and a sign of the liberalization of the Cameroonian regime, which has allowed these works, at last, to be published. Another novel, *L'Ancien Maquisard*, has been ready for a number of years and has still to be published.

While continuing to manage the affairs of Editions Semences Africaines René Philombe has lived a retired existence since 1975 in his home town of Batchenga.

[1] Richard Bjornson, 'Interview avec deux écrivains camerounais', *Abbia*, no. 31–33, Feb. 1978, p. 214 (this and the following quotations translated from the French by the editors)
[2] 'La passion de refaire l'âme noire', *Cameroon Tribune*, no. 107, 4 Nov. 1974
[3] Bjornson, *Abbia*, p. 213
[4] *Ibid.*, p. 214
[5] Jacques Rial, *Littérature camerounaise de langue française*, Lausanne, 1972, p. 37
[6] *Ibid.*, p. 223
[7] Eloise A. Brière, 'La littérature camerounaise: nouvelles tendances ou faux espoirs?', *Peuples noirs, peuples africaines*, no. 9, May–June 1979, pp. 69–80
[8] Thérèse B. E. Belinga, *Ecrivains cinéastes et artistes camerounais* (Yaoundé, 1978)

Jean Pliya
born 1931   BENIN

The author of two plays and two collections of short stories, Jean Pliya has also led a varied career as teacher and, for a time, politician. Trained at the Universities of Dakar and Toulouse, where he obtained a degree in history and geography in 1955 and a secondary-school teaching diploma in 1957, he taught at the Lycée Béhanzin in Porto-Novo, later at the Lycée Technique in Cotonou, and from 1965 to 1969 at a secondary school in Lyon, France. Returning to Africa, he

became professor of geography at the young university in Lomé, Togo, from 1969 to 1972 and then went home to teach at the National University of Benin in 1975. The same year he was appointed the university's vice-chancellor, and later chancellor, a position he still holds. From 1961 to 1963, between his first two teaching appointments, Jean Pliya was head of cabinet in the Ministry of Education and Culture in Benin (then called Dahomey) and thereafter became Minister of Information and Tourism. The following year he was elected to the National Assembly of Benin from the constituency of Abomey and served as the assembly's first secretary.

Alain Ricard has said that Jean Pliya's political career was 'not the road to ambition but the road to deception'.[1] This was probably inevitable for the author of *Kondo le requin* and *La Secrétaire particulière*, two plays that evoke problems and ambiguities of power in Africa past and present. The first play is a historical tragedy set in the early days of colonialism, and the second amodern satire. Unlike works by other African writers of the time, both plays were first published locally before being reissued in international collections. They are, states Ricard, profoundly rooted in the soil and the experiences of Dahomey (Benin). The corrupt, ambitious bureaucrat of *La Secrétaire particulière* is a composite figure of the social types Pliya encounterd when working in the Ministry of Education in the early sixties. It was a position, Jean Pliya says, that enabled him 'to know the life of offices' and 'to make a lot of observations'.[2]

Kondo le requin, a play which won the Grand Prix Littéraire d'Afrique Noire in 1967 (along with *Sur la terre en passant* by François Borgia Evembe), is about the defeat by the French of King Béhanzin, the last ruler of Abomey, in the late nineteenth century. It is without doubt the most successful of Pliya's works and was written in 1965 while he was teaching in Porto Novo at the school named after the monarch. It was first performed by the school's theatre group and has been a regular part of their repertoire ever since.

Performances have been given as far away as Nigeria and the Ivory Coast. Alain Ricard affirms that 'it is not an exaggeration to say that modern Dahomean theatre was born with *Kondo*'.[3]

Being at Lycée Béhanzin served as a daily reminder to Pliya of the historical importance of the last monarch from Abomey, but there is another, much more personal reason that explains why Pliya chose Béhanzin as the central figure of his first play. Pliya was born on 21 July 1931 in Djougou in north-west Dahomey and his great-grandfather was Béhanzin's *Migan*, or prime minister, and his mother-in-law is Béhanzin's granddaughter. Pliya was fifteen years old when his great-grandfather died in 1950, and he often had the opportunity to hear him talk about 'Kondo, the shark', Béhanzin's other name. Pliya, who is trained in history, made careful use of other historical sources, however, and we may recall that he is also the author of the text on national history in current use in schools in Benin.

Like many African playwrights, Jean Pliya feels that theatre is a privileged medium of education in a society where illiteracy remains high. 'Theatre', he says, 'enables you to transmit a message rapidly when you think that you have something to say to your compatriots or to your contemporaries, lessons to give them.'[4]

Kondo le requin, like Pliya's other works, is, of course, written in French, raising the inevitable question of the language barrier. Pliya admits that this is a problem. He recommends as a starting point that works of authors who are unable to write in their national tongues be translated but concedes that if the majority of people are not literate, translations are unlikely to be read. The situation is different for theatre, however. *Kondo* has been translated into Fon and performed to enthralled audiences on a number of occasions. Pliya confesses to a feeling of excitement at such performances: 'It's the first time I realized what popular theatre could be. I had never felt such an emotion.'[5]

Jean Pliya's first effort at creative writing was not a play but a short story, a genre he also feels is particularly well suited to the needs of an African audience 'that comes from a civilization of the tale' and that 'doesn't like to read anything long'.[6] 'L'Arbre fétiche', the title story in the collection *Pliya* published in 1971, was written in 1963 when he was working in the Ministry of Education. It was originally published in the journal *Preuves*, after winning first prize in the journal's short-story competition jointly with a work by the Congolese author Sylvain Bemba. In 'L'Arbre fétiche' a sacred Iroko tree has to make way for a modern highway, but the lumberman who cuts it down is struck by the falling tree and dies. Pliya's story is no simple tale of the gods of ancestral Africa 'punishing' those who dare choose modernity over tradition. 'The work', writes the critic U. Edebiri, 'is less that of an illusionist than of a realist',[7] meaning that Pliya, although a practising Catholic, recognizes that Africa cannot build its future except by reference to its past. In a 1978 interview with David Akaachir, Pliya refers to the paper on traditional economy in eighteenth-century Benin that he presented at FESTAC in Lagos in 1977:

> I showed how animistic religious structures were the basis of an economic organization that mobilized the whole population. Animism is a very profound form of thought that I greatly respect as a way station or a starting place towards belief in one God ... I worked into my short stories the observations I made on the activities of this animist religion simply in order to show that animism controls certain forces and that it is a profound reality of African societies ... This is why, as someone who wants to be a realistic observer of these societies, I also wanted to show the manifestations of that force.[8]

Although Pliya believes theatre gives him 'the best opportunity to show society its own image or the reflection of itself' and his role is to be a realistic writer whose 'inspiration is always fed by observation', he does not intend to abandon the short-story medium. It is a genre which allows an author 'to rapidly give a finished form to themes [on everyday life] you want to develop'.[9] A second collection of stories, *Le Chimpanzé amoureux*, came out in 1977, and he has plans for another collection which would be inspired by, but not a direct transcription of, traditional tales. He has also begun work on a novel, saying 'there are things one can say in a tone that needs greater amplification than in short works. There are great problems. There are characters I would like to develop more than is possible in short stories.'[10]

[1] Alain Ricard, 'Jean Pliya: écrivain dahoméen', *Afrique Littéraire et Artistique*, no. 27, Feb. 1973, p. 3 (translation of this and following quotations by the editors)
[2] 'Entretien avec Jean Pliya', *Présence Francophone*, no. 23, Autumn 1981, p. 177
[3] Ricard, 'Jean Pliya: écrivain dahoméen', p. 5
[4] 'Entretien avec Jean Pliya', p. 178
[5] *Ibid.*
[6] *Ibid.*
[7] U. Edebiri, 'L'espérence tacite de Jean Pliya, écrivain dahoméen', *Afrique Littéraire et Artistique*, no. 37, 1975, p. 10
[8] 'Entretien avec Jean Pliya', pp. 183–4
[9] *Ibid.*, pp. 178, 181
[10] *Ibid.*, p. 186

Jean-Joseph Rabéarivelo
1901–1937   MALAGASY REPUBLIC

Jean-Joseph Rabéarivelo lived and worked in an era when 'Madagascar did not regard itself as part of the African world, a world of which it was only dimly aware'.[1] It was a time in which negritude (the philosophy that pervades a number of the works of francophone African writers presented in this volume) was as yet unborn.

Rabéarivelo was born in Antananarivo, Madagascar. He was reared in a poor family by his father, a tailor, and his mother, a woman of noble caste. His formal education ceased when he was only 13 years old, and thereafter he taught himself. He mastered both Spanish and French and used the latter for most of his literary work. Rabéarivelo married young, fathered three children, and supported himself and his family by working as a proof-reader at Imerina Printing Press.

A passionate devotee of French culture and literature, his primary goal was to get to France. When all his efforts failed, Rabéarivelo (known to be of a romantic and melancholy temperament in addition to being addicted to drugs) committed suicide at the age of 36.

During his short life he wrote seven volumes of poetry, six published in his lifetime, and *Vieilles chansons des pays d'Imerina* published posthumously in 1939. The work was reissued in 1980 by Madprint in Tananarive in a collectors' edition which won an honourable mention when submitted for the 1980 Noma Award for Publishing in Africa. The volume is printed on locally handcrafted papyrus and has a cover incrusted with wild flowers from the region.

Of Rabéarivelo's entire opus it is generally agreed that *Presque-songes* and *Traduit de la nuit* – written in French and Hova – are his greatest works, 'the most important', 'the poems of his maturity'. Ulli Beier writes that in these collections alone, particularly the later one, 'he liberated himself completely from French models',[2] and therein lies his contribution to African poetry.

Tracing Jean-Joseph Rabéarivelo's literary development to this pinnacle of achievement Clive Wake writes,

Rabéarivelo's early poetry is influenced by Baudelaire on the one hand and his own contemporaries in French poetry on the other . . . Many of them belonged to a group known as the *Fantaisistes*. Their poetry was full of vague melancholy and a sense of futility much like the poetry of the early French Romantics, although in form they are disciples of Baudelaire and his successors. Rabéarivelo calls them 'les poètes les plus délicieux et les plus parfaits de leur génération'. He was fortunate in having as his friend and counsellor in literary matters the poet Pierre Camo who was a civil servant in Madagascar at the time. He encouraged Rabéarivelo to publish and included some of his earliest poems in his review *18° Latitude Sud*. But Camo's most important role was gradually to wean Rabéarivelo from a style which revealed too obviously the influence of his favourite French poets. From Baudelaire and the *Fantaisistes* he acquired however a strong sense of form which is very striking in *Presque-Songes* and *Traduit de la Nuit*. These are the poems of his maturity.[3]

Ulli Beier and Gerald Moore have found Jean-Joseph Rabéarivelo to be 'a poet of genius'.[4] Ulli Beier has called him 'one of the greatest French-speaking African poets', 'a poet of cosmic visions'.

The themes of his poems are death, dissolution, catastrophe and sometimes resurrection ... The dominant vision of Rabéarivelo is a vision of death ... The death he sees is not a specific individual death; it is a cosmic universal death ... Rabéarivelo's poems are clear and precise visions of a strange and personal world. Like Baudelaire, his favourite French poet, Rabéarivelo had a disgust of reality. In his poetry he has destroyed and dismembered reality. And out of the fragments he has built a new mythical world; it is a world of death and frustration, but also transcended by a sad beauty of its own.[5].

During his lifetime his poetry and critical articles on it were published in *La Vie, Le Divan, Les Nouvelles Littéraires,* and *La Dépêche de Toulouse.* Along with Gabriel Razafintsambia he founded and edited (1930–1931) a literary review, *Capricorne.*

Ulli Beier's and Gerald Moore's translations of Rabéarivelo's poems appeared in *Black Orpheus, Transition, Modern Poetry from Africa,* and in *Jean-Joseph Rabéarivelo: 24 poems* published by Mbari in 1962 but long out of print. A full-length volume of Rabéarivelo's verse in English translation has recently become available, however. It is the work entitled *Translations from the Night,* containing a wide-ranging selection of both Rabéarivelo's early and later poems which John Reed and Clive Wake translated for publication in Heinemann's African Writers Series in 1975.

[1] Gerald Moore and Ulli Beier, eds., *Modern Poetry from Africa* (Harmondsworth, 1963), p. 17
[2] Ulli Beier, 'Rabéarivelo', *Black Orpheus,* no. 11, p. 10
[3] Clive Wake, ed., *An Anthology of African and Malagasy Poetry in French* (London, 1965), pp. 12–13
[4] Moore and Beier, *Modern Poetry,* p. 16
[5] Beier, 'Rabéarivelo', pp. 10–12

Oscar Ribas
born 1909 ANGOLA

The distinguished ethnologist, folklorist and short-story writer, Oscar Ribas, has written 14 books in Portuguese. Born in Luanda in 1909, the son of a Portuguese father and an African mother, Ribas first wrote romantic tales and essays: *Nuvens que Passam* (Passing clouds), 1927; *O Resgate duma Falta* (Atonement), 1929; *Flores e Espinhos* (Flowers and thorns), 1948. They were inspired primarily by Portuguese writers of the late nineteenth century.

The publication of *Uanga* (Enchantment), a folkloric romance, in 1951, and *Ecos da minha terra* (Echoes of my land) in 1952, marked a new direction in Oscar Ribas' literary career. These African dramas depicting traditional Kimbundu wisdom are inspired by oral literature. In later works Ribas continues to retell Kimbundu stories in a fresh style marked by keen psychological insight.

Although most of Oscar Ribas' books have been published at his own expense, he has gained international esteem and recognition, particularly in Brazil, a country he visited in 1963 and later in 1968. These visits inspired him to use popular speech habits in his writings.[1] *Sunguilando* (Story-time) (1967), *Misoso I* (Tales) (1961), and *Quilanduquilo* (Pastime) (1973), three volumes of stories, are infused with dialogue and description that captures in Portuguese the flavour of the Kimbundu world. Perhaps his most celebrated African story is 'A Praga' (The Curse), which was awarded the Margaret Wrong prize in 1952 from the International Committee on Christian Literature for Africa.

Despite the fact that he has been blind since the age of 21, Ribas has devoted his life to research and writing. In fact, literature has been his *métier*.[2] His autobiography, *Tudo isto Aconteceu* (All of this happened), begun in 1962 and completed in 1974, confirms his spiritual attachment to Angola and to mankind in general. He has sympathy for the two races that produced him. He declared in 1965 before a Portuguese audience: 'I shall always stand between the two races, loving both equally well.'[3] And in 1979, commenting on the then President of Angola, Agostinho Neto, Oscar Ribas said, 'He is an ideal representative of our country. He is black, his wife is white, and his children are mestizo.'[4]

Respected by younger writers not only for his literary productivity but for his loyalty to the cause of the MPLA, Oscar Ribas nevertheless remains intellectually isolated in his country where contemporary writers see literature primarily as a tool to build socialism. All the same, there has not been a more important figure in the literature of Angola in this century. Mário António has paid tribute to Oscar Ribas in an essay, 'The literary work of Oscar Ribas',[5] as has Gerald Moser in 'The Career of Oscar Ribas, a Writer of Angolan Stories'.[6] Russell Hamilton also has cited the significant role of the gentle old man of Angolan letters.[7]

Oscar Ribas continues to research and write in Luanda. Most recently he has published an amended edition of *Misoso I* (1979) and he is working on a *Dictionary of Angola Regionalisms.*

[1] Gerald Moser, 'The career of Oscar Ribas as a writer of Angolan stories', paper presented at the African Literature Association Meeting, Madison, Wisconsin, Mar. 1977

[2] Mário António, *Luanda, 'Ilha' Crioula* (Lisbon, 1968), p. 154

[3] Moser, 'Career of Oscar Ribas', p. 11

[4] Conversation with Donald Burness, Luanda, Angola, Summer, 1979

[5] Mário António, *Luanda*, pp. 151–62

[6] Moser, 'Career of Oscar Ribas'

[7] Russell Hamilton, *Voices from an Empire*, (Minneapolis, 1975), pp.45–8

Richard Rive

born 1931   SOUTH AFRICA

Unlike most black South African writers of his generation, Richard Rive continues to live and write in his native country. Designated 'Coloured' under his country's racial classification, he was born and raised in District Six, an impoverished but vital slum in the heart of Cape Town. After attending local schools, he won a municipal scholarship to high school at the age of thirteen, the commencement of an impressive academic career. Rive – who began writing short stories while still a student – graduated in 1949 with a B.A. degree in English from the University of Cape Town and began teaching at Hewat Training College.

Essentially a short-story writer, his early works first appeared in South African journals. They received favourable critical recognition and have since been translated into fifteen languages, appearing in *Transition, Contrast, Classic, Présence Africaine*, and several other magazines and anthologies. Bernth Lindfors considers him and Alex La Guma to be 'the most accomplished non-white short story writers in South Africa today'. He found Rive's style to be 'characterized by strong rhythms, daring images, brisk dialogue and leitmotifs (recurring words, phrases, images) which function as unifying devices within stories'. Rive's subject-matter was 'tsotsis, life in the slums, the consequences of overt protest and the ironies of racial prejudice and color snobbery'.[1]

A volume of Rive's short stories, *African Songs*, was published in East Germany in 1963. In the same year he edited *Quartet*, a collection of stories by four South Africans, one white and two black writers in addition to himself. The following year he edited *Modern African Prose*, an anthology intended for school use. Rive had come to the conclusion after years of teaching high-school English literature in Cape Town that 'important as Shakespeare, Dickens and Sir Walter Scott are, students needed something much more recognizable and immediate in addition (not instead of) in order to synthesize their literary experiences'. It was foolhardy, he added, 'to assert that all writers not produced out of the African experience are unacceptable, in favour of local material'.[2]

In 1964 Rive's novel, *Emergency*, was published in England. Taking its title from the state of emergency declared by the South African government after the Sharpeville massacre, it recounts three days in the life of a Coloured schoolteacher in Cape Town – the days between the massacre and the emergency. *Emergency* was reissued in 1970 in paperback by Macmillan in New York.

By the time that his novel was published, Rive had embarked upon what was to become a considerable amount of travel and study overseas. In 1962 he was awarded a Farfield Foundation travel fellowship, on which he toured parts of Africa and Europe. In September 1963 he returned to South Africa: he was already extremely conscious of what he considered the personal price to be paid for life in exile, and determined to live in South Africa. He had been back only a few months when his novel suffered the same fate as his poetry (*African Songs*) – both were banned. Rive was, he comments wryly, 'part of a small elite of South African writers not allowed to read their own works in case they became influenced by them'.[3]

In 1965–6, Rive attended the University of Columbia in New York, where he was awarded an M.A. He returned again to Cape Town where he continued to teach English and Latin in a large high school.

He continued to write, although he describes his own output during these years as 'a mere trickle'. In 1970 he won the *Argus* 'Writer of the Year' award with a short story called 'The Visits'. In August 1971, he took up a Junior Research Fellowship at Magdalen College, Oxford. There he worked on the life and works of Olive Schreiner, earning a D.Phil. in 1974.

On his return to Cape Town, he lectured in English at a training college for two years, and in 1977 published *Selected Writings*, which comprised essays, short stories and two plays (including 'Make Like Slaves', which won the BBC African Theatre Competition in 1972). In 1979 he accepted a Fulbright fellowship in order to conduct research at the University of Texas in Austin, and to lecture widely in the USA. His keynote address at the African Literature Association conference in March 1979 – 'The ethics of an anti-Jim Crow' – incorporated a number of autobiographical memories. Rive was subsequently encouraged to expand this address to book form, and in 1981 it appeared as *Writing Black*. The book traces his academic and literary careers, with particular emphasis on the years of foreign travel. It also contains a number of pen-pictures of, and anecdotes about, African and American writers. Implicit in the work is Rive's own commitment to universal and timeless literary standards, his belief that 'African literature can only be understood in terms of universal creativity, without allowances or concessions. It cannot be judged in terms of its own yardstick, or dictate its own terms of reference.'[4] Rive is thus unconvinced by the case for negritude, and spells out the cultural and literary implications for his creative self:

> I cannot be what the propounders of negritude or the African Personality cult would have me be. I am Johannesburg, Durban and Cape Town. I am Langa, Chatsworth and Bonteheuwel. I am discussion, argument and debate. I cannot recognise palm-fronds and nights filled with the throb of the primitive. I am buses, trains and taxis. I am prejudice, bigotry and discrimination. I am urban South Africa.[5]

[1] Bernth Lindfors, 'Form and technique in the novels of Richard Rive and Alex La Guma', *Journal of the New African Literature and the Arts*, no. 2, Autumn 1966, p. 11

[2] Richard Rive, ed., *Modern African Prose* (London, 1964), p. xi

[3] Richard Rive, *Writing Black* (Cape Town, 1981), p. 109

[4] Richard Rive, *Selected Writings: Stories, Essays, Plays* (Johannesburg, 1977), p. 67

[5] Rive, *Writing Black*, p. 23

Ola Rotimi

born 1938   NIGERIA

Prize-winning Nigerian playwright Ola Rotimi's interest in drama can be traced, in his own words, to 'hereditary sources . . . a home naturally inclined to the arts'.[1] As a young boy he took part in amateur plays directed by his father, principal of the Engineering Training School of the Ports Authority in Lagos, making his stage debut at the age of four, and his mother had her own traditional dance troupe. Moreover, Rotimi's ethnically mixed background (his father, a Yoruba, comes from western Nigeria, and his mother, an Ijo, from Rivers State in Eastern Nigeria) has had direct consequences on his theatre, inspiring some of his themes. His play, *The Gods Are Not to Blame*, first staged at Ife in 1968 and awarded the following year first prize in *African Arts* magazine's annual competition, is more than an African Oedipus tale. Although the author used the Greek myth as a conscious model, adapting it to an African setting, he was also concerned to show the tragic effects of ethnic and regional animosity. The hero of the play, whom the oracle had predicted at his birth would be doomed to kill his father and marry his mother, acts out his tragic destiny, not so much out of irascibility like his Greek counterpart, but out of distrust for a community he has been called to lead and whom he does not consider his own. *The Gods Are Not to Blame* was written in 1967 while Nigeria was in the throes of a civil war. Rotimi describes what his play was attempting to convey:

> The title . . . does not refer to the mythological gods or mystic deities of the African pantheon. Rather it alludes to national, political powers such as America, Russia, France, England, etc. – countries that dictate the pace of world politics. The title implies that these political 'gods' shouldn't be blamed . . . for our own national failings . . . In essence, the war took strength from tribal animosities, which had been fostered by the politics of the day, and compounded by insatiable corruption in high quarters. So I asked: why hold outside powers responsible for the resultant bloodshed?[2]

A pan-Nigerian by birth and education (he attended primary school in Port Harcourt in eastern Nigeria and the Methodist Boys' High School in Lagos in western Nigeria), Rotimi's heterogeneous background also inevitably dictated the medium in which he would later write – English. Surrounded by four languages – Ijo Yoruba, English and pidgin – he claims to have learned Nigerian languages only imperfectly. As he himself put it, 'My knowledge of the vernacular is miserable.'[3] English as a language of expression was, therefore, an inevitable choice for him, but like other Nigerian writers Rotimi is convinced that English must be adapted to suit the unique Nigerian character, 'A carbon copy of Oxford or even London English would be rather stiff for us.'[4]

From 1959 to 1966 Rotimi was in the United States where he studied for a B.A. in playwriting and directing at Boston University on a Nigerian Federal Government scholarship and an M.A. at Yale University on a Rockefeller Foundation Scholarship. In his final year at Yale his comedy, *Our Husband Has Gone Mad Again*, was honoured as 'Yale Major Play of the Year' and Rotimi had the privilege of staging his play under the direction of a New York professional, the late Jack Landau. He recalls what a valuable experience this was for him:

> You see, it is one thing to learn directing in a classroom situation where you're called upon to stage a short scene or a one-act play with fellow drama students. Now, to work with someone who has had years of experience in professional directing is, indeed, a different phenomenon altogether, an entirely challenging exposure.[5]

Rotimi is the author of two historical tragedies, *Kurumi* (first performed at Ife in 1969 and published by Oxford in 1972) and *Ovonramwen Nogbaisi* (produced at Ife in 1971 and published by Oxford in 1974). For one who epitomizes the new generation of Nigerian dramatists in making free use of Yoruba oral traditions, it is ironic that Rotimi came into contact rather late, relatively speaking, with traditional drama. It was not until he returned to Nigeria with his American wife in 1966, to become senior research fellow at the Institute of African Studies at the newly founded University of Ife, that the opportunity was even presented to him – and he is the first to regret it:

> Could you believe I never saw or heard the traditional bata drum or appreciated the linguistic beauty, of say, the Apala lyrics until 1967 and 68 respectively. But before then I could tell you about the joys of Handel, and Haydn. Shameful wasn't it?[6]

Rotimi also regrets having been absent from Nigeria in the late fifties and early sixties, during 'the first renaissance of Nigerian culture', as he puts it, 'when people like Clark, Soyinka, Chris Okigbo, Ulli Beier and others were contributing to the emergence of a new literary culture through *Black Orpheus*, Mbari and so on'.[7] Rotimi did not even have the chance to meet fellow playwright Wole Soyinka in person until December 1969.

Rotimi credits the University of Ife, where he remained from 1966 until recently (he is now at the University of Port Harcourt) with providing the material and psychological conditions in which his talent could develop. In addition to his duties as research fellow, he also directed the university theatre company, the Ori-Olokun Players, coaching them into a first-rate professional company which had the honour of being invited by the French Government to the World Festival of Theatre at Nancy in 1971. The Ife theatre group was truly a living laboratory where Rotimi could carry out his creative experiments in the best possible conditions. Rotimi is very concerned that his productions reflect what he calls 'total African theatre in the

contemporary idiom' bringing together 'music, dance, acting, mime and of course, the communicative aspect of language'.[8] And for him this cannot be accomplished without the support of two of the most basic aspects of traditional African drama – the setting in the round and audience participation.

Author, producer, director and actor, Ola Rotimi is a total man of the theatre. As he playfully remarked to Bernth Lindfors in 1973:

> My ultimate artistic ambition is to *write* a full-length massiveness in music, dance and movement lasting two whole hours and half *directed* by me, mobilizing a 500-man cast. *And then?*, queried Lindfors.
> I collapse and die after making my last exit on stage *acting* in it![9]

[1] John Agetua, ed., *Interviews with Six Nigerian Writers* (Benin City, 1976), p. 29
[2] Bernth Lindfors, ed., *Dem-Say: Interviews with Eight Nigerian Writers* (Austin, Texas, 1974), pp. 61–2
[3] *Ibid.*, p. 59
[4] Robert M. Wren, 'Ola Rotimi: a major new talent', *Africa Report*, Sept.–Oct., 1973, p. 31
[5] Lindfors, *Dem-Say*, p. 58
[6] Agetua, *Interview*, p. 29
[7] Lindfors, *Dem-Say*, p. 59
[8] 'Arts and Africa', no. 25, BBC African Service transcript (London) [1978]
[9] Lindfors, *Dem-Say*, p. 68

Stanlake Samkange
born 1922   ZIMBABWE

Stanlake Samkange's literary career reveals an abiding and deep-seated feeling for the past, whether he is writing as a historian or as a novelist. Indeed, it is through his novels as well as in his academic writing that he has pursued his investigations into the early colonial period in Zimbabwe (then Southern Rhodesia) and into the customs and beliefs of the Zimbabwean peoples.

Son of a Methodist minister, Samkange was educated in Waddilove Institution, S. Rhodesia, and then in South Africa, where he attended Adams College and Fort Hare University College. He received a B.A. Honours degree in history from the University of South Africa, and then returned to Rhodesia. There he assumed the dual responsibilities of teacher and political organizer, becoming the General Secretary of the African National Congress. He was instrumental in the founding of Nyatisme College, a self-help venture offering a broad range of subjects.

In 1957–8 he resumed his educational studies at the University of Indiana, where he worked on a Masters degree in education. He returned to Indiana in 1965 to complete a doctorate in history. In the intervening years he combined his research work with a variety of enterprises in Rhodesia; he worked in journalism, producing a newspaper for businessmen, and directed an advertising and public relations firm. His doctoral thesis was published as *The Origins of Rhodesia*, which was awarded the prestigious Herskovits Prize in 1970. The subsequent *African Saga: Introduction to African History* is a highly personal introduction to the history of the continent.

Dr Samkange taught at Tennessee State University in 1967 and 1968, followed by three years at Fisk University and a spell in the Afro-American Studies Department at Harvard. He then became Professor at Northeastern University in Boston. He is married to an American psychologist.

His first novel, published in 1966, was *On Trial for My Country*. This work effectively used some of the material collected for *The Origins of Rhodesia*, and is an imaginative recreation of the clash between Cecil Rhodes and Lobengula, the Ndebele king, setting the desperate struggle of the king in the context of the wiles and political pressure which attended the occupation of the country by the Chartered Company.

More recently two other novels have been published, melding historical facts and fictional narratives. *The Mourned One* (1975) is set in 1935, and explores the pressures and prejudices of colonial society through the eyes of a condemned man. In *The Year of the Uprising* (1978) Samkange deals with the events leading up to the great uprising by Shona and Ndebele groups in 1896, with the rebellion itself, and its brutal suppression.

A review of this novel sums up Samkange's strengths: 'The writer is deeply imbued with the customs and spiritual life of the people of Zimbabwe. Some passages have a mesmeric quality, like something from the Old Testament.'[1]

Much that is implicit in the novels is made explicit in some of the reflective passages of *African Saga*. In the novels the reader is alerted to the powers of traditional priests, soothsayers and traditional doctors, and the resilience that they confer on black society. In *African Saga* Samkange proposes that modern African societies should draw upon the social philosophy of *Hunhuism* or *Ubuntuism*. *Ubuntuism* (explained Samkange in an interview) 'is the attitude of the Bantu, and their political, social and cultural philosophy. I believe they are distinguished by their own peculiar attitude toward life and something that motivates them and something which they would rather die than do.'[2]

[1] K. M., *West Africa*, 1 May 1978
[2] 'Arts and Africa', no. 328G, BBC African Service transcript (London)

Léopold Sédar Senghor
born 1906   SENEGAL

A man who has embraced poetics, philosophy, and politics, Léopold Sédar Senghor, the recently retired President of Senegal, has been accorded the tribute of being 'the greatest of the African poets to write in a European language'.[1] Along with Aimé Césaire and Leon Damas, whom he met in Paris in 1928, Senghor's reputation as an apostle of negritude is renowned. He defines it in the following manner:

Négritude is the awareness, defense and development of African cultural values. Négritude is a myth, I agree. And I agree there are false myths, myths which breed division and hatred. Négritude as a true myth is the very opposite of these. It is the awareness by a particular social group of people of its own situation in the world, and the expression of it by means of the concrete image . . . However the struggle for négritude must not be a negation but affirmation. It must be the contribution from us, the peoples of sub-Sahara Africa, to the growth of Africanity, and beyond that, to the building of the Civilization of the Universal. Négritude is part of Africanity, and as such is part of human civilization . . . More deeply, in works of art, which are a people's most authentic expression of itself, it is sense of image and rhythm, sense of symbol and beauty.[2]

Quite simply, négritude is the sum total of the values of the civilization of the African world. It is not racialism, it is culture.[3]

It is this spirit of Negro-African civilization based on the earth and Negro hearts, which is offered to the world – both beings and things – to unify it, to understand and to show it.[4]

Senghor was born to Christian parents belonging to the Serer tribe in the small village of Joal, on the Senegalese coast, about 75 miles south of Dakar. His formal education commenced when his father sent him to the nearby Catholic mission at Ngazobil 'to punish me and "straighten me out" '.[5] From there he moved to a seminary and then to the school at Dakar. In 1928 he received a government scholarship and left for France, studying first at the Lycée Louis-le-Grand and then at the Sorbonne, where in 1934 he received his *licence-ès-lettres*.

Through the personal intervention of the Senegalese deputy Blaise Diagne, Léopold Senghor became a French citizen. He was the first African to obtain his *agrégation*, a prerequisite for lycée and university teaching in France. In the following years he held French teaching posts at the Lycée Descartes in Tours, and Lycée Marcelin Berthelot at St-Maur des Fosses, near Paris. It was largely during this time that Senghor wrote the poetry that was to appear in his first volume of verse, *Chants d'ombre*, released in 1945.

Clive Wake points out that 'when Seuil published Senghor's first volume of poems . . . African poetry as distinct from West Indian poetry made its first appearance in the literary world'.[6] John Reed and Clive Wake find its 'main themes . . . are exile, the loneliness and homesickness of an African student in Paris in the 1930s. He recalls his childhood . . . This nostalgia for the paradise of childhood with its "innocence of Europe" brings an awareness of a conflict between his African heritage and European culture.'[7] Senghor himself later noted 'that almost all the beings and things which my poems call up for me belong to my canton, a few Serer villages . . . I have only to name them to relive the Kingdom of Childhood . . .'[8]

When World War II broke out, Senghor joined the French army. He was captured by the Germans and for two years (1940–1942) he remained a prisoner of war. During this time he wrote much of the verse that appeared in *Hosties noires*, published in 1948. Here 'the poet discovers that he is not alone in his exile, but that he is involved in it with those of his compatriots . . . fighting a white man's war in Europe, but because of their black skin, treated as inferiors. He discovers his solidarity with the black race but he also realizes that with his education and his poetic gifts he not only can but he has a duty to speak for them.'[9]

The year 1948 also saw the publication of what has been called 'probably the most influential single work of the whole [negritude] movement':[10] Senghor's *Anthologie de la nouvelle poésie nègre et malgache de langue française*, with a preface by Jean-Paul Sartre (which was later made available separately as *Orphée noir*). 'The poets of the *Anthologie*', according to its editor, 'like those of the oral tradition are above all *auditives*, singers.'[11] Until then, they were for the most part unknown names;

today they are part of the canon of French African literature.

Chants pour Naett, published in 1949, celebrates Senghor's 're-discovery of Africa, symbolized as the woman he loves'.[12] Six years passed before his next volume, *Ethiopiques*, appeared, which includes the now famous poetic transformation of Thomas Mofolo's historical novel *Chaka*. Also in 1956, *Chants d'ombre – Hosties noires* was released in one volume, and in 1961 *Nocturnes*, a sequence of love poems, (which includes the earlier *Chants pour Naett*) was published. Three further volumes of poetry have appeared since then. *Elegies des alizés* came out in 1969 in a limited edition with an original illustration by Marc Chagall. *Lettres d'hivernage* followed in 1973 and *Elegies majeures* (containing the full text of *Elegies des alizés* and five new poems) in 1979. Poetry to Senghor

> is song even when not actual music . . . The poem is like a jazz score, where the execution is as important as the text. As I have published each of my collections, this idea has become stronger. And when at the head of a poem I indicate the instruments to be used, this is not mere form of word . . . I still consider that the poem is only complete when it becomes song, speech and music at the same time.[13]

This is aptly illustrated in *Elegies majeures*, which contains precise indications of the music meant to accompany each poem.

After World War II Senghor returned to his teaching post at the Lycée Marcelin Berthelot and in 1944 joined the staff at the Ecole Nationale de la France d'Outre-Mer. With his election as Senegal's deputy to France's Constituent Assembly in 1945 his political career took root. In 1948 he broke with the French Socialist Party (the SFIO) and their leader in Senegal, Lamine Guèye, to found the first of a number of African political parties whose elected representative he became under France's Fourth and Fifth Republics until Senegal gained Independence in 1960. Abiola Irele summarizes this period of Senghor's political career:

> His activities in the French parliament were marked by a ceaseless effort to gain recognition for African rights and attention for

African interests, within the context of the colonial relationship. But Senghor did not take the colonial arrangement for granted; he campaigned tirelessly for its transformation, advocating a French Union as the model and nucleus of a vaster relationship between Europe and Africa (*Euro-Afrique* as he termed it) in which the essential bond would be mutual respect between civilisations, in an almost spiritual union of peoples who would no longer see each other as antagonistic, but rather as complementary. His political views thus rested on a cultural foundation.[14]

When Senegal acquired Independence in 1960 Senghor was elected its first president, a position he held until his retirement from politics in December 1980. In 1969 he was honoured with membership in the French Academy of Moral and Political Sciences, where he took the seat of the late German Chancellor Dr Konrad Adenauer. The previous year he received the 1968 Peace Prize, the distinguished award made annually by the German book trade on the occasion of the international Frankfurt Book Fair.

Senghor's extensive writings reflect his career not only as a poet, but as a major spokesman of the negritude movement, as a literary critic, and as a political thinker. In 1961 he published *Nation et voie africaine du socialisme* with Présence Africaine which appeared the following year in English translation by Mercer Cook as *Nationhood and the African Road to Socialism*. Abridged American and British editions appeared later as *On African Socialism*. The complete French version was reissued by Seuil in 1971 as volume II of the *Liberté* series in which Senghor planned to publish, in alternating volumes, his collected writings on cultural and political subjects. *Liberté I: Négritude et humanisme*, containing articles published between 1937 and 1963, had already come out in 1964, and *Liberté III: Négritude et civilisation de l'universel*, another volume of cultural and literary writings, in 1977. Recent publications in the field of literary criticism include *La parole chez Paul Claudel et chez les négro-africains*, containing the text of a paper presented at the international convention organized by the Friends of Paul Claudel, which Nouvelles Editions Africaines brought out in 1973. As for other non-literary works, the list comprises *Les Fondements de l'africanité ou Négritude et arabité*, a speech delivered at the University of Cairo in February 1967 and published the same year by Présence Africaine (translated into English by Mercer Cook in 1971). More recently, Senghor published *Pour une relecture africaine de Marx et Engels* with Nouvelles Editions Africaines in 1976. Senghor's lengthy conversations with the Tunisian writer, Mohammed Aziza, appeared in 1980 under the title *La Poésie de l'action*.

Léopold Senghor's work has been translated into many languages, he has provided prefaces to numerous books, and he has been the subject of several critical studies, some of which are listed in the bibliographical section of this volume. In 1976 Présence Africaine published the voluminous *Hommage à Léopold Sédar Senghor: homme de culture*, containing contributions of more than 30 African and French writers and scholars in honour of Senghor's seventieth birthday. Biographies in French of Senghor include Armand Guibert's *Léopold Sédar Senghor* (Paris, 1961), Jean Rous' *Léopold Sédar Senghor: un président de l'Afrique nouvelle* (Paris, 1967), S. O. Mézu's *Léopold Sédar Senghor et la défense et l'illustration de la civilisation noire* (Paris, 1968), and E. Milcent and M. Sordet's *Léopold Sédar Senghor et la naissance de l'Afrique moderne* (Paris, 1969). Two biographies of Senghor have appeared in English: Irving Markovitz's *Senghor and the Politics of Negritude* (New York and London, 1969) and Jacques Hymans', *Léopold Sédar Senghor: An Intellectual Biography* (Edinburgh, 1971).

The British scholars, John Reed and Clive Wake, have been especially active in translating Senghor's prose and poetry into English. They are the joint editors of *Léopold Sédar Senghor: selected poems* (1964), and *Léopold Sédar Senghor: prose and poetry* (1965), and have contributed detailed and lucid introductions to both volumes and, an extensive bibliography to the latter. John Reed and Clive Wake were also responsible for the English translation

of Senghor's *Nocturnes*, published in the Heinemann African Writers Series in 1969. More recently Craig Williams has translated Senghor's poetry for a bilingual edition, *Selected Poems/Poèmes choisis*, published by Rex Collings in 1976, and Abiola Irele has introduced and annotated a volume of Senghor's verse in French, entitled *Selected Poems of Léopold Sédar Senghor* (London, 1977), in an edition meant, in particular, for the English-speaking student of French.

[1] John Reed and Clive Wake, eds., *Senghor: Prose and Poetry* (London, 1965, reissued 1976), p. 1

[2] *Ibid.*, p. 97 (from *Discours devant le parlement de Ghana*; unpublished, dated Feb. 1961)

[3] *Ibid.*, p. 99 (from *Pierre Teilhard de Chardin et la Politique Africaine*, 1962)

[4] Léopold Senghor, 'Négritude and the concept of universal civilization', *Présence Africaine*, vol. 18, no. 46, Mar. 1963, p. 11

[5] Reed and Wake, *Senghor: Prose and Poetry*, p. 4

[6] Clive Wake, ed., *An Anthology of African and Malagasy Poetry in French* (London, 1965), p. 1

[7] John Reed and Clive Wake, eds., *Senghor: Selected Poems* (London, 1964), p. xi

[8] Reed and Wake, *Senghor: Prose and Poetry*, p. 92 (from 'Comme les lamantins vont boire à la source', in *Ethiopiques*, 1956)

[9] Wake, *Anthology*, pp. 15–16

[10] Gerald Moore, *Seven African Writers* (London, 1962), p. xv

[11] Reed and Wake, *Senghor: Prose and Poetry*, p. 93 (from 'Comme les lamantins vont boire')

[12] Wake, *Anthology*, p. 16

[13] Reed and Wake, *Senghor: Prose and Poetry* pp. 95–6 (from 'Comme les lamantins vont boire')

[14] Abiola Irele, *Selected Poems of Léopold Sédar Senghor* (London, 1977), p. 4

Sipho Sidney Sepamla
born 1932   SOUTH AFRICA

One of the so-called 'township poets', Sepamla is totally urban, something the South African government, in its efforts to assign every Black to a Bantustan, sought to deny. 'My inspiration is urban', says the poet, 'completely urban. I can't say my roots, for instance, are in the homelands.'[1]

He was born in Krugersdorp, a typical mining town on the Witwatersrand, and trained as a teacher. At the age of eighteen, Sepamla tried his hand at short stories, but seems not to have written anything further until he was 35. The lack of an accessible tradition affected him (Mphahlele was the only indigenous South African whose work he read); the previous generation of writers are (or were) banned, exiled, or censored. 'It is very, very difficult to write in South Africa today', says Sepamla. This is partly because the truth is difficult to establish:

> truth can be what the white man says it is . . . relating it to the historical process . . . There is also truth according to the so-called militants. These are the people who think they have seen the light in terms of what the white man has been offering the black people.

Further, there are barriers of ignorance, brought about by such things as censorship, to be overcome:

> It means – because of the laws that govern the lives of people, one is not able to expand one's mental horizons. I've always regretted the fact that we have this reasoning in South Africa . . . where people cannot read whatever they'd like to read, and then decide whether they'd like to continue reading that type of material or not. This is an ignorance that is imposed upon the people.[2]

The consequences of a segregated and inadequate education for Blacks has led to impoverishment and confusion in language instruction and skills. Sepamla considers that he was at an advantage in learning English early: 'I write only in English. That's the only language I work in. I haven't written a single thing in my mother tongue. All the writing I've done, all the dreaming I've done, has been in English . . .'[3]

This inaccessibility of one's literary heritage, the lack of free conversation, has produced a particular kind of isolation for the poet. One critic likens it to a state of exile.

> Yet, paradoxically, or more understandably, the sense of exile can be even more bitter when the exiled remains in South Africa, isolated in prison or restricted in some way by government action. Sepamla's poem 'Home' describes this restriction as one in which home becomes 'a dungeon rewombing its children'.[4]

Sepamla was inspired to start writing after seeing the now-famous production of *King Kong*, and after reading Alan Paton's *Sponono* and *Cry the Beloved Country*. And there was a deeper motivation – 'The pounding of incidents around me was so strong, I couldn't help but react'.[5] A play, which was never produced, was followed by serious poetry writing. The result, *Hurry Up to It!*, appeared in 1975, for which Sepamla shared the 1976 Pringle Award. Two more anthologies followed rapidly: *The Blues is You in Me* came out in the same month that Soweto erupted (June 1976). It is 'spare, ironic, pungent and deadpan'.[6] The following year, Sepamla's response to the riots was voiced in *The Soweto I Love*. Predictably it is banned in South Africa. The gap between riots and publication was deliberate. 'I reacted almost impulsively to what was happening, but I had to give myself a little time, so that I don't cry over the page, I don't bleed over the page.'[7] The apparent simplicity and naivety of the poems in *The Soweto I Love* hides a 'deeper, more profound meaning . . . The poet's anger is contained with poise, and does not spill over into bitterness, vituperation.'[8]

He has worked in the art world, as a promoter of exhibitions, and in industry, and he has spent several years bringing *The Classic* to life again as *The New Classic*. The magazine was founded in the sixties by Nat Nakasa and Nimrod Nkele, and is 'a symbol of the spirit which refuses to die, it is a beacon for those who are coming'.[9] Simultaneously, the editorship of *S'ketsh*, a Black theatre magazine, landed in his lap. Without secretarial help, and battling constantly to produce, distribute, and sell these journals in perpetual financial difficulties, Sepamla none the less raised the readership considerably. Censorship was a constant factor in the production of the journals, and he remarks bitterly:

> I hate it because it has destroyed my mind. I churn bitterness in my heart because my heart has grown more through hurtful things than through those things that might have helped to develop my spiritual being to its full capacity.[10]

Fortunately, FUBA (Federated Union of Black Arts) appointed him full-time director, and eased his financial position somewhat.

Sepamla is not only occupied with writing and editing, but he has also played a central role in the arts generally. The assessment of one critic is

> that Sepamla has had an enormous seminal influence ... Sepamla has been not only a poet but also an impresario of sorts. His example in helping to organize poetry readings, conferences, and workshops throughout 1975 and 1976 seems in part to have generated the present proliferation of writers' groups, readings, and general interaction among Black writers.[11]

Three applications for a passport were turned down. The German government successfully put pressure on the South African authorities to allow him to attend the 1980 Frankfurt Book Fair. He took the opportunity of visiting London where he toured cultural centres on an invitation that had been extended years before. He was also able to take up a 1981–2 fellowship of the Iowa University Writers' Program. In 1979, he had a novel published, *The Root is One*, the story of a man who becomes a police informer, set against the background of township clearance. *A Ride On the Whirlwind*, his second novel, has a 1980 imprint. It deals with Soweto and is banned in South Africa.

Sepamla is aware of the increased militancy of the young Blacks in South Africa: 'I have attended readings, you know, where young chaps have read their works and they have frightened even me who's one of them ...'[12] He can nevertheless still write yearningly, despite everything,

> but a wish of mine remains
> peace at all times with all men.[13]

[1] Avril Herber, *Conversations* (Johannesburg, 1979), p. 140
[2] *Ibid.*, pp. 138–9
[3] *Ibid.*
[4] Sheila Roberts, 'The black South African township poets of the seventies', *Genève-Afrique*, vol. 18, no. 2, 1980, p. 85
[5] Joyce Ozynski, 'Writing is a painful exercise – Sepamla', *South*, 1980, p. 46
[6] David Wright, *The Times Literary Supplement*, 10 Oct. 1977
[7] Stephen Gray, 'Spirit which refuses to die', *Index on Censorship*, vol. 7, no. 1, 1978, p. 3
[8] Vernon February, review of *The Soweto I Love*, *African Literature Today*, no. 10, 1979, p. 257
[9] Gray, 'Spirit', p. 4
[10] Sipho Sepamla, 'A note on *The New Classic* and *S'ketsh*', *English in Africa*, vol. 7, no. 2, 1980, p. 84
[11] Roberts, 'Black South African township poets', pp. 81–2
[12] 'Arts and Africa', no. 388, BBC African Service transcript (London)
[13] Sipho Sepamla, *The Soweto I Love* (Cape Town and London, 1977), p. 53

Mongane Wally Serote

born 1944   SOUTH AFRICA

'I am quite aware of the restrictions in my life, but I go on as if they are not there. When I write it's just the same way,'[1] says Serote, the South African poet. Like the other Black township poets who made such an impact in the 1970s, he writes prolifically despite considerable pressure and risks. He spent nine months in solitary confinement in a South African jail in 1969 and was then released without being charged. Of his books, his second anthology is banned.

The situation has scarred him, as Lionel Abrahams points out: 'His painfully intense utterances show him caught, perhaps more consciously than any of the others, in the struggle to clear his personal being from a lethal morass of his Black experience'.[2] He has had poetry published in such journals as *Classic*, *Purple Renoster*, *New Coin Poetry*, and *Ophir*. In 1972 Renoster Books brought out his first anthology, *Yakhal'inkomo* (literally translated: the cry the cattle make at the slaughter-house). The urban environment, however, is central to his imagery and it permeates his consciousness; through his writing he addresses

> My brothers in the streets,
> Who holiday in jails,
> Who rest in hospitals,
> Who smile at insults.[3]

In 1973 he was awarded the Ingrid Jonker Poetry Prize.

Serote was born in the tough but vibrant community of Sophiatown, and went to school in Alexandra Township. For eighteen months he was at school in Leribe, Lesotho. He completed his education at the Morris Isaacson High School in Soweto.

In 1974, *Tsetlo* was published and banned in South Africa. *No Baby Must Weep* appeared the following year, and *Behold Mama, Flowers* in 1978. Serote and his contemporaries Mtshali and Sepamla 'are not (so far) men of letters in the sense that Mphahlele and Nortje are', remarks a critic, further observing: 'It seems to me that their very lack of formal instruction in European eloquence has left them freer to employ African modes of expression. This dearth of revered models may well be an advantage.'[4]

Nadine Gordimer pinpoints the strengths of his writing:

> generalised definitions of blackness, or anything else, are not for him. He puts a craftsmanlike agony to making-by-naming (Gerald Moore's and Ulli Beier's definition of the particular quality of African poetry) in a vocabulary and grammar genuinely shaped by black urban life in South Africa. There is a piercing subjectivity in his work, in which 'black as struggle' becomes at times an actual struggle with the limits of language itself.[5]

Serote, like Sempala, feels strongly about the lack of literary roots available to black people in South Africa due to the stringent banning and censorship laws: 'The only way I can describe black South African writing', says the poet, 'is to say it's a very tragic thing. The writing seems to have no continuity . . .'[6] Despite their truncated literary heritage, the poets have enriched the craft with a devotion to parents, family, and friends, together with a reverence for ancestors, 'something we have not seen from England and America for many decades', suggests another poet.[7] Or, as a kinsman puts it, Serote 'touches the delicate webbing of human perceptions'.[8]

Serote was a Fulbright scholar, and attended the University of Columbia where he completed a Fine Arts degree in 1979. Since then he has been living in Gaberone, Botswana, attached to the Nedu Arts Ensemble. A selected edition of his poetry is due to appear in 1982, and he has a major contribution in an anthology, *Voices from Within: Black Poetry from South Africa*, and a casebook, *Soweto Poetry*, both to be published in 1982. A novel called *To Every Birth Its Blood* is to be published by Ravan Press also in 1982; it will also appear in the African Writers Series.

He is a man of his times, 'basically a painfully reserved man', says Livingstone, 'whose sensibilities, far from being brutalised by his circumstances, have been maintained, even heightened by these circumstances so that his pitch or tone of voice, in his best work, is tragically resonant, deeply felt and very sad'.[9]

[1] Mongane Serote, quoted in *Issue*, vol. 6, no. 1, 1976, p. 32
[2] Lionel Abrahams, 'Black experience into English verse', *New Nation*, vol. 3, no. 7, p. 13
[3] Mongane Serote, 'My Brothers in the Streets', *Yakhal'inkomo* (Johannesburg, 1972), p. 19
[4] Guy Butler, 'The language of the conqueror on the lips of the conquered is the language of slaves', *Theoria*, vol. 45, Oct. 1975, p. 5
[5] Nadine Gordimer, *The Black Interpreters* (Johannesburg, 1973), p. 62
[6] Serote, *Issue*, p. 25
[7] Douglas Livingstone, 'The poetry of Mtshali, Serote and Sepamla and others in English', *New Classic*, no. 3, 1976, p. 56
[8] Gessler Nkondo, 'The human image in South African poetry', *Africa Today*, vol. 27, no. 3, p. 17
[9] Livingstone, 'The poetry of Mtshali, Serote and Sepamla', p. 56

Robert Serumaga
1939–1980   UGANDA

Robert Serumaga's primary interest was in the theatre. He was the inspiration behind Theatre Limited, a professional acting company based in Uganda, while his business background (an M.A. in economics from Trinity College, Dublin) helped to keep the venture financially sound.

Speaking of the theatre in East Africa, Robert Serumaga found it necessary to point out that it does not operate

> with the same level of formalization as in Europe. On the other hand, the practice of

people getting together to watch the story-teller act out his story, or to hear a musician like the famous Sekinnoomu of Uganda relate a tale of trenchant social criticism, dramatized in voice, movement and the music of his Ndingidi, has been with us for centuries. And this is the true theatre of East Africa.[1]

Serumaga worked hard to provide the incentive necessary to give birth to a professional theatre. He realized that 'first and above all, whatever theatrical movement there is must be integrated with and inspired by the society in which it is growing'. Secondly, mass involve-ment 'will only come about when plays, with their roots firmly embedded in the Africa of today, can be written and produced'.[2]

In the latter part of 1969 at least one such play was produced by Theatre Limited, namely Serumaga's *Elephants*, a play he originally titled *The Fish Net*, and which he said is

> about a man who creates a certain kind of world around himself with the help of friends. He is not aware of having created this world until the holes in its artificiality are blocked up by someone else. I am interested in this idea of a man living in an artificial environment which he has created unknowingly perhaps. We might see all sorts of weaknesses in this life form, but do we stop to contemplate the possibility that if we destroy it, we might destroy the man?[3]

Elephants, with Robert Serumaga in the lead role, was warmly received in Ugan-da. In April of 1970 Theatre Limited brought the production to Nairobi, where it was welcomed as 'the greatest happening on the East African stage this decade'.[4]

Serumaga not only acted in his own plays but he gave numerous perform-ances in London and Uganda in plays as diverse as Edward Albee's *Who's Afraid of Virginia Woolf?* and Wole Soyinka's *The Trials of Brother Jero*.

A man of many talents, Robert Serumaga was at one stage with London's Transcription Centre, where he was producer of a radio programme, *Africa Abroad*. For a while he was a fellow in creative writing at Makerere University,

and was secretary and treasurer of the Commonwealth Literature Association. His commercial bent led to his forming 'Kiyingi Productions Limited', a private recording studio for songs and plays. He wrote *A Play*, first presented at the National Theatre in Kampala in 1968, and published in the same year by Uganda Publishing House. His poetry has appeared in *Transition*, and in 1969 his first novel *Return to the Shadows* was published by Heinemann in London and the following year by Atheneum in New York.

In the mid-seventies, Serumaga visited the United States to negotiate the staging of *A Play* in New York, while trying to raise funds for Theatre Limited. *Majan-gwa* was performed in the Philippines in the following year for the Third World Theatre Conference.

In 1975 a world theatre season was organized in London. Serumaga and *Abafumi* (as Theatre Limited was now called) staged his 'Renga Moi'. The experimentation in which *Abafumi* had been involved, to create 'a theatre which is language itself and does not have to rely on other languages',[5] was successful. In addition to stressing the sound qualities of language, Serumaga stated:

> We also did a lot of psychological immersion of ourselves in our cultural milieu, and we came up with a kind of theatre which is not a deliberate attempt to integrate music, dance and drama but a rediscovery of how our forefathers spoke. Motivations have to bear on the psychological needs of an African society.[6]

Initially he favoured the Amin takeover but he became totally disillusioned, and in 1977 he left Uganda. He was arrested by the Kenyans for, allegedly, anti-Amin activities. Previously he had led a band of guerilla fighters against Amin. In the brief period that Yusufu Lule governed Uganda, Serumaga assumed ministerial responsibility, then followed him into exile. Serumaga died from a brain haemorrhage in Nairobi in September 1980.

Of the dual elements discernible in his life and art, a critic remarks:

There is . . . a profound discrepancy between the doctrine of disengagement elaborated in Serumaga's writing and the political activism into which he has thrust himself. But through it all – in both plays and politics – one may discern the figure of the Olympian romantic, the self-dramatising individualist, the playhouse solipsist, besieged.[7]

[1] Robert Serumaga, 'Uganda's experimental theatre', *African Arts/Arts d'Afrique*, vol. 3, no. 3, Spring 1970, p.52
[2] *Ibid.*, p. 53
[3] Robert Serumaga, *Uganda Argus*, Sept. 1960, quoted in *Cultural Events in Africa*, no. 61, 1969, p. 3
[4] *Daily Nation* (Nairobi), quoted in *Cultural Events in Africa*, no. 63, 1969, p. 2
[5] 'Arts and Africa', no. 269, BBC African Service transcript (London)
[6] *The Times* (London), 21 Apr. 1975
[7] Andrew Horn, 'Individualism and community in the theatre of Serumaga', *African Literature Today*, no. 12, 1981, p. 40

Zulu Sofola

born 1935   NIGERIA

Zulu (short for Nwazulu) Sofola, Nigeria's only woman playwright, has written eight plays, five of which have been published. Almost all of her works have been performed in Nigeria, either for western Nigerian Television broadcasts or for productions in the Department of Theatre Arts of the University of Ibadan where she has been a lecturer since 1969. Diversity in genre, setting and theme is the characteristic feature of her plays. Her scope extends from social and domestic comedy to historical tragedy. She feels equally at ease, whether depicting contemporary or traditional society. Thematically, Zulu Sofola's plays are as wide-ranging as her settings. In *King*

Emene and *Old Wines are Tasty* she evokes the misuse of political power, in both past and present. In *The Wedlock of the Gods* she deals with problems of free-will and individual determination in traditional society (especially as concerns women) and in *The Disturbed Peace of Christmas* the problems of adolescence and growing up in today's Nigeria. *The Sweet Trap* pokes fun at the shallowness of Nigeria's academic community, and *The Wizard* satirizes the excessive materialism of Nigerian urban society. An as yet unpublished play, *The Operators*, which was performed in May 1979 at the Arts Theatre of the University of Ibadan, is about organized crime in Nigeria.

Of Igbo parentage, from Issele-Uku in mid-western Nigeria, Zulu Sofola is married to a Yoruba and has lived in Ibadan for many years. She is familiar with traditional Igbo culture, for she wrote her master's thesis for the Catholic University of America on the theatrical elements of a traditional Igbo rite. Dapo Adelugba, the Nigerian director with whom Zulu Sofola has collaborated for many years, says,

> Mrs Sofola's dramatic efforts to date indicate a strong interest in the dramatic and ritual heritage of her people and an involvement in the life styles and social modes of contemporary Nigerians. Her theatrical idiom shows a determination to create a new language that will reflect the dignity of traditional modes and the reality of contemporary ones, not only in speech but in gesture, costumes, décor and staging.[1]

In the task of creating a new language for Nigerian theatre, Zulu Sofola has been particularly attentive to speech usage, varying the speech patterns to suit the historical and social requirements of her plays. The atmosphere of traditional Igbo society in *King Emene* and *Wedlock of the Gods* is created by the use of traditional imagery and proverbs. In a work such as *The Wizard*, however, which she adapted from the mediaeval French farce, *Pierre Pathelin*, she playfully weaves into the dialogue the contemporary modes of expression of the Yorubas of Ibadan (a combination of English, Pidgin and Yoruba) to produce a language which 'opens up avenues of comic expressiveness'.[2] For *The Sweet Trap*, on the other hand, a satirical study of Nigeria's university community, Mrs Sofola strikes at various registers of standard English to caricature, as Adelugba puts it, 'the artificiality and varying degrees of emotional callowness' of Westernized Nigerians.[3]

Zulu Sofola's versatility and her refusal to limit herself to any one dramatic style is indicative of her approach as a playwright. For her, theatre must be more than mere entertainment. In the way that it can mirror life on the stage it can heighten the spectator's sense of understanding and play an important educational role in developing societies. She wants her plays to be true to life and views herself as an artist who gives practical reality to ideas. Drama is 'the practical aspect of philosophy':

> drama well used has greater power over any other mass educating media because drama has a way of engrossing the totality of the observer and the performer. So deep on the stage, life is truly mirrored in a genuine and serious manner. The viewers' minds, psychology and emotion can be directed. But on the other hand if trivial stuff, time killers are fed to the public, the usefulness of the theatre would be lost and the people themselves will be misguided and misdirected.[4]

At the same time, however, theatre should avoid becoming a vehicle for propaganda or a podium for moralizing. In the opinion of the Nigerian author and critic, Kole Omotoso, this concern has led Sofola in some of her plays, *Wedlock of the Gods* in particular, to overemphasize the deterministic elements in man's destiny and thus perpetuate the very superstitions that contemporary writers have been fighting against. But Omotoso is candid enough to observe that Sofola does not agree with his interpretation of her play. She feels her plays should be true to historical reality, undistorted by the imposition of any overt message: 'She does not believe in writing thesis plays. She does not write to propagate any particular idea, philosophy or line of thought.'[5]

Zulu Sofola does not admit to having any 'special problems' because of her sex, only saying that 'one has to work twice as hard to be given a chance, 'but I think that once a break-through is made one is freer'.[6] Although she feels deeply that she performs services for African women that few male writers are capable of doing, Zulu Sofola cannot easily be labelled a feminist writer. Rebellious women in her plays are seldom victorious. At best they are gently put in their place, like silly Mrs Clara Sotubo, the wife of the university professor in *The Sweet Trap*, but the consequences can also be tragic, as for the young widow in *Wedlock of the Gods* who refuses to marry her dead husband's brother as custom dictates, and seeks openly to marry another.

Wedlock of the Gods has been staged for Western Nigerian Television as well as for a Department of Theatre Arts production at the University of Ibadan and is probably the best known of Sofola's plays in Nigeria. It was first performed in 1971 at the University of Missouri at Columbia. The production phase is vitally important for Mrs Sofola and she often rewrites passages from her plays once rehearsals have begun.

Zulu Sofola was educated in the United States where she lived for a number of years from adolescence to young womanhood. She attended Southern Baptist Seminary in Nashville, Tennessee, and studied English at Virginia Union University in Richmond, Virginia. In 1965 she obtained an M.A. in drama from the Catholic University of America in Washington DC. She returned to Nigeria in 1966 with her husband, a Nigerian, whom she married while in America. She has four sons and a daughter.

[1] Dapo Adelugba, 'Three dramatists in search of a language', in Ogunba and Irele, eds., *Theatre in Africa* (Ibadan, 1978) p. 212
[2] *Ibid.*, p. 211
[3] *Ibid.*, p. 212
[4] Interview with Zulu Sofola in John Agetua, ed., *Interview with Six Nigerian Writers* (Benin City, Nigeria, 1976) p. 20
[5] Kole Omotoso, 'Interview with playwright Zulu Sofola', *Afriscope*, vol. 3, no. 12, 1973, p. 59
[6] Agetua, *Six Nigerian Writers*, p. 20

Castro Soromenho
1910–1968   ANGOLA

Castro Soromenho has been called the
first Portuguese writer to do justice to
Africans,[1] and Léopold Senghor was
surprised to learn that he was not a Black
African writer. His first job as a recruiter
of African contract labour for a powerful
mining company in north-eastern Angola
gave him a chance to know and to respect
traditional African life.

Fernando Monteiro de Castro Soromenho was born on 31 January 1910 in
the coastal town of Chinde, Mozambique.
His childhood was spent in Angola,
where his parents took him in 1911. His
father, a colonial administrator, and his
mother, the daughter of a judge on the
Supreme Court in Lisbon, sent him to
school in Portugal when he was six, but
Soromenho returned to Angola in 1925
and remained there until 1937. Like his
father, he became a colonial administrator, but this apparently did not
satisfy Soromenho, for he gave it up to
become a journalist with the *Diário de
Luanda*. He moved to Lisbon in 1937
where he edited the weekly *Humanidade*.
In 1943 he abandoned his second career,
journalism, to devote himself to publishing. He started his own publishing
house, Sociedade de Intercâmbio Luso-
Brasileiro, then later Ediçôes Sul.

Trips to South America, where he
visited Brazil and Argentina, brought
him into close contact with such Afro-
Brazilian scholars as Arthur Ramos. His
great interest in African life resulted in
Soro-menho's adopting a fourth profession, that of a writer.

Nhári, a collection of stories, appeared
in 1938 in Luanda. This work earned him
the Prize for Colonial Literature, a prize
he would win again. His novels and
stories deal with life in Lunda Province in
the interior of Angola. *Terra Morta*, ready
in manuscript since 1945 but published
four years later in Brazil, was banned
by the Portuguese authorities because it
severely censured the hypocritical policy
of 'pacification'. Moreover, the government prevented the distribution of books
published by Soromenho. In 1960 to

escape arrest he left for France and exile.

Castro Soromenho travelled a great
deal from 1960 to 1968, the year of his
death. He taught at the University of
Wisconsin in 1961; he then lived in Paris
where he worked for the publishers
Gallimard, as a reader of Portuguese and
Spanish, and he also contributed to the
journal *Présence Africaine*. In December
1965 Soromenho returned to Brazil to
teach sociology in São Paulo. While there
he completed a novel, *A Chaga*, sequel to
A Viragem which had been published in
the late fifties. The projected third novel
in the trilogy was never written. Soromenho died of a brain haemorrhage in
São Paulo at the age of 58.

Castro Soromenho's literary works
include four completed novels, *Noite de
Angústia* (1939), *Homens sem Caminho*
(1942), *Terra Morta* (1949) and *A Viragem*
(1957); he also wrote four volumes of
stories, *Nhári* (1938), *Rejada e outras
histórias* (1943), *Calenga* (1945) and *Histórias da terra negra* (1960). His non-
literary achievements include several
sociological studies and travel books.
Gerald Moser's study 'Castro Soromenho, an Angolan realist'[1] helped bring
the Angolan author to the attention of
the English-speaking world. Scholarly
interest in Soromenho continues; recently the Angolan novelist, dramatist and
poet Manuel dos Santos Lima, published
in Portuguese a study of Castro Soromenho, who can be considered as one of
the founders of Angolan written literature.

[1] Gerald Moser, 'Castro Soromenho, an
Angolan realist', in his *Essays in Portuguese-
African Literature* (University Park, Pa., 1969),
p. 42

Aminata Sow-Fall
born 1941   SENEGAL

Aminata Sow-Fall attracted critical attention when her first novel, *Le Revenant*, was
published in 1976, for being the first
woman novelist in francophone black
Africa, and she managed to sustain that
attention by publishing a second novel,
La Grève des bàttu, two years later. It was

one of the nine works pre-selected by the prestigious Académie Goncourt for their annual prize. This was only the second time that a Black writer has been so honoured. Although Aminata Sow-Fall did not ultimately obtain the 1979 prize, its selection for consideration was an enviable achievement for so young a writer. *La Grève des bàttu* was awarded, however, the 1980 Grand Prix Littéraire d'Afrique Noire, and has since been translated into English, Russian, and Spanish.

Born on 27 April 1941 in Saint-Louis, Senegal, Aminata Sow-Fall received her *baccalauréat* in 1962 after studying at Lycée Faidherbe in Saint-Louis and at Lycée Van Vollenhoven in Dakar. She travelled to Paris for her university training and obtained a degree in French literature from the Sorbonne in 1967.

Both of Aminata Sow-Fall's novels are concerned with the realities of present-day Africa. The hero of *Le Revenant* (*The Spectre*) is a familiar figure in African literature – the over-ambitious young man who ruins his life because he cannot measure up to the intolerable demands for success that his society places on him. His solution to the problem is to drop out of society by faking his death. The theme of her second novel, beggars in an urban community, is relatively new in francophone African literature. In *La Grève des bàttu* the beggars in Dakar go on strike, upsetting the plans of a would-be politician whose marabout has advised him to have recourse to charity in order to ensure political success. Aminata Sow-Fall meant her novel as a study in contemporary mentalities, that of beggars and of those who give to beggars, saying: 'There are beggars who forsake their dignity and who cultivate a certain form of guilt, and there are people who cultivate a certain form of conceit by encouraging begging.'[1]

The idea for the novel came to her one day when she saw a group of beggars fighting over a bowl (*bàttu* in Wolof) of cous-cous that someone had given them. Whoever gave them the food, she thought, had felt the need to give and she wondered what people would do if beggars began to refuse their offerings.

By setting her novels in post-colonial society Aminata Sow-Fall has deliberately chosen what she calls a literature that is 'rooted' in the present ('literature enracinée') and that is 'inspired by our realities': 'Our literature must raise the questions that invite one to find solutions to certain problems that are specifically ours, problems that, while existing elsewhere, take on a particular dimension in our country.'[2]

Aminata Sow-Fall defines commitment as being concerned about present-day social ills:

The African writer cannot and must not take up the pen only to offer beautiful expressions and beautiful sentences. The product of a society that has its problems, he can and must contribute to revealing them, to making everyone clearly aware of them so that people think about them and find solutions to them. If this is what it means to be a committed writer then that is what I am.[3]

However unflattering her portrait of Senegalese society may be, Aminata Sow-Fall has apparently been able to convey her concern to her African audience. She has received letters from readers of many different social groups, and her first novel, *Le Revenant*, has already gone into a second printing. Her third novel, *L'Appel des arènes*, is to be published shortly by Nouvelles Editions Africaines.

Aminata Sow-Fall was employed for a time by the Senegalese National Commission for the reform of the teaching of French, and has collaborated in the writing of school texts for the teaching of literature and grammar. She formerly taught French in a number of schools in Senegal as well as in two of Senegal's prestigious professional training schools or *grandes écoles*. Her current job is that of Director of Letters and Intellectual Ownership in Senegal's Ministry of Culture.

[1] 'Aminata Sow-Fall: *La Grève des bàttu*', *Afrique Nouvelle*, 1–7 Aug. 1979 (this and the following quotations translated from the French by the editors)
[2] 'Huit questions à Aminata Sow-Fall', *Le Soleil*, 20 June 1979
[3] 'Aminata Sow-Fall: *La Grève des bàttu*'

Wole Soyinka

born 1934   NIGERIA

'Like his Renaissance progenitors, Soyinka is something of a Universal man: poet, playwright, novelist, critic, lecturer, teacher, actor, translator, politician and publisher. He is all of these', according to the British publisher Rex Collings.[1] D. A. N. Jones has written 'I doubt if there is a better dramatic poet in English',[2] and Gerald Moore calls Soyinka a 'major tragic imagination'.[3] The Nigerian critic, Abiola Irele, acknowledges 'the special quality of greatness' of Soyinka's writing that imposes itself upon our minds'.[4]

As a poet Soyinka, who published his first verse in an early issue of *Black Orpheus*, has been extensively anthologized. He has also brought out two major collections, *Idanre and Other Poems* (1967), and *A Shuttle in the Crypt* (1971), a volume containing poems written while Soyinka was imprisoned during the Nigerian Civil War. In 1969 while he was still in detention Rex Collings published a leaflet containing two poems Soyinka had managed to smuggle out of prison – 'Live Buriel' and 'Flowers for My Land' – which are reprinted in *A Shuttle in the Crypt*. More recently, Rex Collings, in association with Opon Ifa, brought out Soyinka's *Ogun Abibiman* (1976), a long poetic tribute to the struggle for liberation on the African continent that he dedicated to 'the dead and the maimed of Soweto'.

Most of Soyinka's creative energies,

however, have been directed to the theatre. As a playwright his output has been both prolific and widely praised. In just over two decades Soyinka has written nearly 20 plays of which 14 are published. His works have been staged on numerous occasions, not only in Africa but in major theatres in Europe and North America.

Soyinka got his first break in the theatre while working as play-reader at the Royal Court Theatre from mid-1958 to the end of 1959. *The Swamp Dwellers* and *The Lion and the Jewel* had already been written at that date, and *The Swamp Dwellers* was performed in the autumn of 1958 at the University of London Drama Festival. Both plays were taken to Nigeria by Geoffrey Axworthy, then teaching English at the University of Ibadan, and produced in the Arts Theatre there in 1959. That same year another play, *The Invention* (unpublished) was performed at the Royal Court Theatre in London along with excerpts of what would seem to be an early version of *A Dance of the Forests*, a play conceived by Soyinka as his contribution to Nigerian Independence, that won the competition organized for the occasion by the magazine *Encounter* (London). *A Dance of the Forests* created something of a furore. And 'no wonder', comments Robert MacDowell, 'for Soyinka here, as elsewhere, is anti-conservative, anti-Négritude, anti-social deadening habits'.[5] The play has such a massive cast and makes such demands on production that it has yet to be performed a second time.

Soyinka's intense interest in Nigerian theatre involved him not only as playwright, but also as actor, director-producer – and talent scout. Through his various companies, which included The 1960 Masks, and the Orisun Theatre founded in 1964, he has contributed in the creation of a thriving and original English-language theatrical tradition in Nigeria. J. P. Clark's plays were first produced by Soyinka, and the Nigerian director, Dapo Adelugba, was associated with Soyinka from these early days, as was the playwright, Wale Ogunyemi. Ogunyemi originally joined Soyinka's company as an actor and later began writing his own plays under Soyinka's encouragement and guidance.

In 1963 Mbari published the first collection of Soyinka's plays in a volume entitled *Three Plays*, containing *The Swamp Dwellers*, *The Trials of Brother Jero*, and *The Strong Breed*. The following year Oxford produced a more substantial collection, *Five Plays*, in which the previous three were included in addition to *A Dance of the Forests* and *The Lion and the Jewel*. Soyinka's plays were not only being published, they were being widely performed as well. In the two theatre capitals of the world, London and New York, Soyinka's plays have been successfully introduced to an international audience. *The Road*, published in 1965, was performed in London the same year in association with the Commonwealth Arts Festival and subsequently won the prize for published drama at the First Festival of Negro Arts at Dakar. The Royal Court Theatre in 1966 followed with a presentation of *The Lion and the Jewel*. In 1967 and 1968 three of Soyinka's plays opened in New York: *The Trials of Brother Jero* and *The Strong Breed* at the off-Broadway Greenwich Mews Theatre, and the following year *Kongi's Harvest* was performed by the Negro Ensemble Company. *Kongi's Harvest* was already the recipient of a prize at the 1966 Dakar Festival of Negro Arts, where it was performed jointly by *The 1960 Masks* and the *Orisun Theatre*. It has been made into a film by Omega Films under the direction of Ossie Davis, with Wole Soyinka as Kongi.

Later plays include *Madmen and Specialists* (1971), Soyinka's first post-war publication, which Abiola Irele describes as a pivotal work: it

> holds a special significance within the body of Soyinka's work, not simply as his form of commentary on the war itself, but also as an indication of the new dimension that his awareness has acquired. We have here no longer a direct preoccupation with social problems and human types, but rather a passionate and consuming obsession with the problem of evil.[6]

In 1973 followed the second 'Jero' play, *Jero's Metamorphosis*. The work was printed in *The Jero Plays*, issued in the Methuen Modern Plays Series, a combined volume which also includes the earlier piece, *The Trials of Brother Jero*. Another play, *Death and the King's Horseman* was also issued in 1975, also in the Methuen Modern Plays Series. It is a tragedy based on an event of contemporary history when, in 1946, the colonial District Officer in Oyo (the ancient Yoruba city in western Nigeria) prevented the Elesin, or horseman of the Oba, from committing ritual suicide in order to join his royal master in his life in the hereafter. Soyinka warns readers against interpreting *Death and the King's Horseman* as a statement about 'the conflict of cultures' resulting from the colonial situation. In a note appended to the play Soyinka writes: 'The confrontation in the play is largely metaphysical, contained in the human vehicle which is Elesin and the universe of the Yoruba mind – the world of the living, the dead and the unborn, and the numinous passage which links all: transition.'[7]

Soyinka's growing use of theatre as a ritualistic exploration of the mind of man can be seen in his adaptation of *The Bacchae* of Euripides, which he published with Methuen in 1973. Performed by London's National Theatre at the Old Vic in August 1973, the play retains the Greek setting but changes Dionysus from a drunken deity into 'the god of the people – an elixir for the suffering'.[8] Soyinka's Dionysus is someone who bears more resemblance to Ogun, the Yoruba god of iron (and thus of war) but also of creativity, someone who incarnates both the complexities and the ambiguities of mankind. On the other hand Pentheus, the King of Thebes, is portrayed as a power-hungry monarch whose death at the end of the play signals the promise of liberation, not only for the chorus of male slaves (Soyinka's addition to the original play) but for the free-born citizens. The parallels that can be drawn between the play and the contemporary Nigerian situation are obvious. The blood that flowed during the civil war continued to flow afterwards in the public executions that were held regularly on Bar Beach in Lagos:

We're back to Roman decadence ... To
watch these bloody circuses in the name of
public morality is to unite and identify with
the guilty men of power ... The war no
longer united people in stoicism; so they're
trying to unite them in bestiality and guilt by
the titillation of the power-cravings of the
meanest citizen.[9]

From *The Bacchae* and his other plays it
is evident that one of Soyinka's conscious
aims is to establish a parallel between a
classical Yoruba world-view and that of
the European (particularly Greek) tradition. He has exposed this at length in a
volume of essays published in 1976, *Myth,
Literature and the African World*, which
grew out of a lecture series that Soyinka
delivered while fellow of Churchill College, Cambridge, in 1973 (one of a
number of positions that Soyinka took up
when he went into voluntary exile after
being released from prison). The volume
also contains a slightly revised version of
'The Fourth Stage', an early essay on the
Yoruba concept of tragedy which had
first appeared in 1969 in *The Morality of
Art* (ed. D. W. Jefferson).

In the early seventies Soyinka also
published two plays which were written
several years previously. The radio play,
Camwood on the Leaves was first broadcast by the Nigerian Broadcasting Corporation in 1960. Subtitled 'A rite of
childhood passage', the play centres on
the revolt of a young man against the
authority and religion of his father, a
doctrinaire Christian minister. *Before the
Blackout*, published in 1971 in an Orisun-
Acting edition, goes back to the chaotic
mid-sixties. Not a play in the strict sense,
it reproduces the text of a satirical revue
that Soyinka and his players staged at the
University of Ibadan in 1965. It represents a lesser-known aspect of Soyinka's
concept of theatricality – the use of the
dramatic media to comment on and
ridicule contemporary political actuality.
Similarly *Opera Wonyosi* (London, 1980),
Soyinka's adaptation of John Gay's *The
Beggar's Opera* and Brecht's *Threepenny
Opera*, uses elements from the Gay and
Brecht works, including the famous
musical themes, but adapts them to the
context of the contemporary African

political scene. *Opera Wonyosi*'s dramatis
personae, for example, includes Emperor
Bokassa, Idi Amin, and members of
military governments from all over
Africa. Writing in *The Positive Review*, a
young Nigerian publication, Biodun
Jeyifo makes this comment on *Opera
Wonyosi*:

> the play's real affinities go back to Soyinka's
> *Before the Blackout* [which] ... reflects the
> power, arrogance, cowardice and institu-
> tionalised sycophancy which characterised
> life in the social order (or disorder, if you
> will) created by the Nigerian civilian bour-
> geoisie. *Opera Wonyosi* reflects the 'order'
> created by the military bourgeoisie. But a
> civil war which enriched many and an
> oil boom stand between the two social
> orders ... The decadence, the vulgarity, the
> brutalisation, the sycophancy, the criminality
> and obscenity are all magnified. This is the
> difference between the artistic universes of
> *Before the Blackout* and *Opera Wonyosi*.[10]

In both his comedies and his tragedies
Soyinka is essentially a satirist. 'Satire
is at the heart of Soyinka's theatre', says
Martin Banham,[11] 'and is expressed not
only verbally but also visually.' In order
to achieve his dramatic effects Soyinka
uses a wide variety of techniques. Robert
MacDowell notes that Soyinka

> makes use of fascinating devices in his own
> expressionistic plays: dancing, singing, mim-
> ing, speeches in verse, flashbacks (sometimes
> covering eons of time), and characters from
> the spirit world. He employs techniques
> familiar at Nigerian festivals, and utilizes any
> poetic methods which enforce the emotional
> and intellectual impact of his dramas; in
> short he has no slavish attachment to the
> merely naturalistic level of presentation.[12]

Critics have repeatedly insisted on the
universal appeal of Soyinka's works,
which despite their African, and even
Yoruba, elements can be immediately
apprehended by a world audience.

> The essential ideas which emerge from a
> reading of Soyinka's work are not specially
> African ideas although his characters and
> their mannerisms are African. His concern is
> with man on earth. Man is dressed for the
> nonce in African dress and lives in the sun
> and the tropical forest, but he represents the
> whole race.[13]

Soyinka's plays attest to his familiarity, through training and extensive reading, with theatrical conventions from all parts of the world. Nonetheless, it is apparent, as Eldred Durosimi Jones goes on to note, that Soyinka is also a *Yoruba* writer. His plays abound with images and references from Yoruba culture and cosmology. The god Ogun, in particular, has a special symbolic value for Soyinka as the representation of man's potential for both creation and destruction.

In 1966 Wole Soyinka shared with Tom Stoppard the John Whiting drama prize, and while imprisoned in 1969 he was awarded the Jock Campbell *New Statesman* literary prize.

With the publication of his first novel in 1965, Soyinka had embraced every traditional literary genre. *The Interpreters* received for the most part superlative reviews, although some critics reproached Soyinka with obscuring meaning by over-indulging in word play. D. A. N. Jones compared the novel to James Joyce's *Ulysses*:

> Soyinka's novel *The Interpreters* contains some guidance about the Yoruba gods, but will be best remembered for its Joycean scatology and dashing language: the first sentence – 'Metal on concrete jars my drinklobes' – stands in my head alongside 'stately plump Buck Mulligan'.[14]

In 1973 Soyinka published a second novel, an allegorical work, *A Season of Anomy*. Critics have noted parallels between the hero Ofeyi's quest for Iriyise, the cocoa princess who has been abducted by a cruel and cunning politician, and that of Orpheus for Eurydice. There are enough references in the novel to indicate that Soyinka meant it to be a statement on the devastating civil war his country had just been through:

> Generally, the novel is meant to be a parable of the events in Nigeria both before the coup and during the military regime. Soyinka is expressing his detestation and horror at the cruelty and injustice that characterised the conduct of government in his country during both periods.[15]

As a literary critic Wole Soyinka has been an outspoken and controversial figure. He has often been quoted as making the now familiar denunciation of negritude, in which he supposedly said in caustic rebuttal of this philosophy, 'I don't think a tiger has to go around proclaiming his tigritude'. However, in a recording made by Janheinz Jahn at a conference in Berlin in 1964, Soyinka said his words had been distorted by reviewers:

> to quote what I said fully, I said 'A tiger does not proclaim his tigritude, he pounces'. In other words: a tiger does not stand in the forest and say: 'I am a tiger'. When you pass where the tiger has walked before, you see the skeleton of the duiker, you know that some tigritude has been emanated there. In other words: the distinction which I was making at this conference [in Kampala, Uganda 1962] was purely a literary one: I was trying to distinguish between propaganda and true poetic creativity. I was saying in other words that what one expected from poetry was an intrinsic poetic quality, not a mere name-dropping.[16]

At the African–Scandinavian Writers Conference in Stockholm in 1967 Soyinka spoke out violently about the sorry state of African letters, for which he said both foreign publishers and African writers were to blame. Foreign publishers 'hovered like benevolent vultures over the still-born foetus of the African Muse' and 'at a given signal they tore off bits and pieces, fanned up with powerful wings delusions of significance in commonness and banality'.[17] As for the 'average published writer', whom Soyinka called 'the most celebrated skin of inconsequence to obscure the true flesh of the African dilemma', he was to blame for having ignored the pressing social and political problems of the day: 'He was content to turn his eye backwards in time and prospect in archaic fields for forgotten gems which would dazzle and distract the present. But never inwards, never truly into the present . . .'[18] Soyinka concluded his talk on that occasion by defining his concept of the role of the writer in Africa: 'The artist has always functioned in African society as the record of the mores and experience of his society *and* as the voice of vision in his own time. It is time for him to respond to this essence of himself.'[19]

Soyinka has followed his own preachings to the letter, as Irele notes:

No serious consideration of Soyinka's writing can fail to perceive the central position and even the explicit character of the social awareness that runs through all his work . . . And it is the logical development from this fundamental interest in the realities of social experience implicit in his writings to an active sense of social responsibility, that seems to define the relationship of Soyinka himself to his own work as well as the elements of his individual career and indeed, of his personal drama.[20]

Soyinka has not hesitated to give active forms to his sense of commitment, even to the point of risking his own life. A fellow Nigerian playwright calls Soyinka his country's 'first modern incarnation of the Malvarian idealist and activist, the romantic who voluntarily risks his own security and even survival in a daring, physical intervention in political violence'.[21] In 1965 Soyinka had been detained on a charge that he had substituted his own tape for one supposed to be broadcast by the Prime Minister. Later in 1967, in the midst of Nigeria's Civil War, Soyinka, although a Yoruba, was arrested by the Federal Government for alleged pro-Biafran activity and detained in Kaduna prison. Despite international pleas for his release, he spent two years there. 'Whatever it was I believed in before I was locked up, I came out a fanatic in those things', Soyinka said upon his release in early October 1969.

A statement made to John Agetua in 1976 helps to tie together Soyinka's concerns not only as a man but as a writer:

You must know of course about my fascination with the symbol figure of my society – Ogun. He represents this duality of man: the creative, destructive aspect. And I think this is the reality of society, the reality of man, and that one would be foolish not to recognise this. I cannot sentimentalise revolution. I recognise the fact that it very often represents loss. But at the same time I affirm that it is necessary to accept the confrontations which society creates, to anticipate

them and try to play a programme in advance before them. The realism which pervades some of my work and which has been branded pessimistic is nothing but a very square, sharp look.[22]

Born in Abeokuta in Western Nigeria on 13 July 1934, Soyinka attended Government College and University College in Ibadan. In 1954 he left for the University of Leeds where he graduated in 1958 with an honours degree in English language and literature. He then trained with the Royal Court Theatre in London for another two years.

After his five-year stay in England Soyinka returned to Nigeria in 1960 and was offered a Rockefeller Foundation grant to research into African dramatic arts, thus enabling him to travel extensively throughout Nigeria. From 1960 to 1966 he lectured at the Universities of Ibadan, Ife and Lagos, and was always involved in theatrical productions. He served for a time as co-editor of *Black Orpheus*. With his different theatre companies he directed and produced plays (his own and those of others) at a dizzy pace.

Then began the sombre period in Soyinka's career – his first, brief, arrest in 1965 and his two-year detention from August 1967 to October 1969 during the civil war. During his imprisonment Nelson published Soyinka's free translation from the Yoruba of the late Chief D. O. Fagunwa's novel *Ogboju ode ninu Igbo Irunmale*, under the title *The Forest of a Thousand Daemons: a hunter's saga*.

In 1969 Wole Soyinka returned to the post he had held immediately before his imprisonment as head of the department of drama at the University of Ibadan, where he used a $1,000 grant awarded to him by the Farfield Foundation to help establish a School of Drama. During the summer of 1970, Soyinka was at the Eugene O'Neill Memorial Theatre Centre in Waterford, Connecticut with a troupe of fifteen actors from Nigeria to produce *Madmen and Specialists*, one of the three plays he wrote during his imprisonment, and which was published early in 1971.

Then in 1972 Soyinka published his account of his prison experience, *The Man*

Died. In the characteristically outspoken manner of its author, the book does not hesitate to name names and make indictments. It was, in Soyinka's words, 'very pointedly political and ... geared towards re-educating the minds of Nigerians by relating things which they thought they knew about and shaping their ways of looking at so-called public leaders and figures'.[23]

In April 1972 Soyinka resigned his position at the University of Ibadan and went into a sort of self-imposed exile, not returning until 1976, after Gowon had been overthrown. Interviewed while still away he explained his reasons for leaving:

A lot of people think that the main reason for my staying away is the book [*The Man Died*] and some kind of official reaction to it. That's only a small fraction of the causes why I'm staying away. Most people are not aware first of all, of the pressures which attach to the existence of individuals like myself not merely from the fact that they become famous or notorious but also because of their participation in the political life of their countries ... I have, as you know, been actively involved in all sorts of political activities ... I was also involved in the insurrection which took place in the West and again I was involved in what I call the Third Movement which was an attempt to find a third ground for the resolution of the civil war. The point of it is that I recognized a long time ago that the problem of Nigeria has moved beyond the remedy of debate and controversy, that the options are very clear. I find it impossible to return at this stage.[24]

During his absence from Nigeria Soyinka lectured at various universities both in Africa and in Europe and America. He also served as editor of *Transition* (renamed *Ch'Indaba*) in Accra where the journal had been moved from Uganda, and as Secretary-General of the Union of Writers of African Peoples. Soyinka is now the head of the Department of Comparative Literature at the University of Ife and has recently published *Ake: the Years of Childhood* (1981), the autobiography of the first twelve years of his life.

Two full-length studies have been devoted to Soyinka's writings: Gerald Moore's *Wole Soyinka* (first issued in 1971 and revised in 1978); and Eldred Jones' *The Writing of Wole Soyinka* (1973). In 1981 Martin Banham brought out a study-guide on Soyinka's *The Lion and the Jewel* in the British Council's newly established Nexus Books Series published by Rex Collings. No complete bibliography of works by and about Soyinka has yet appeared although Lindfors' *Black African Literatures in English* (Detroit, 1979) lists critical writings on Soyinka up to the end of 1976, and James Gibbs has published in manuscript form at the Department of English of the University of Ibadan his *Wole Soyinka: a Select Bibliography in Progress.*

[1] Rex Collings, 'A propos', *African Arts/Arts d'Afrique*, vol. 2, no. 3, Spring 1969, p. 82

[2] D. A. N. Jones, 'Tribal gods', *New York Review of Books*, 31 July 1969, p. 8

[3] Gerald Moore, *Wole Soyinka* (New York, 1971), p. 6

[4] Abiola Irele, *The African Experience in Literature and Ideology* (London, 1981), p. 211

[5] Robert McDowell, 'African drama: West and South', *Africa Today*, vol. 15, no. 4, Aug./Sept. 1968, p. 26

[6] Irele, *The African Experience*, p. 202

[7] Wole Soyinka, *Death and the King's Horseman* (London, 1975), [p. 7]

[8] Henry McGee, 'Soyinka goes Greek', *Newsweek*, 13 Aug. 1973, p. 49

[9] Soyinka quoted in Albert Hunt, 'Amateurs in horror', *New Society*, 9 Aug. 1973, p. 37

[10] Biodun Jeyifo, review of Wole Soyinka's *Opera Wonyosi*, *The Positive Review*, no. 1, 1978, p. 22

[11] Martin Banham with Clive Wake, *African Theatre Today* (London, 1976), p. 24

[12] McDowell, 'African drama', p. 25

[13] Eldred D. Jones, *The Writing of Wole Soyinka* (London, 1973), p. 11

[14] Jones, 'Tribal gods', p. 8

[15] Eustace Taiwo Palmer, 'Wole Soyinka's *Season of Anomy*', *World Literature Written in English*, vol. 17, no. 2, 1978, p. 447

[16] Soyinka quoted in Janheinz Jahn, *Neo-African Literature* (London, 1966), pp. 265–6

[17] Wole Soyinka, 'The Writer in a modern African state', in Per Wästberg, ed., *The Writer in Modern Africa* (New York, 1969), p. 17

[18] *Ibid.*, p. 17

[19] *Ibid.*, p. 21

[20] Irele, *The African Experience*, p. 198

[21] Femi Osofisan, 'Tiger on stage: Wole Soyinka and Nigerian theatre', in Oyin Ogun-

ba and Abiola Irele, eds., *Theatre in Africa* (Ibadan, 1978), p. 155
[22] 'Interview with Wole Soyinka in Accra, Ghana, 1974' in John Agetua, ed., *When the Man Died: Views, Reviews and Interview on Wole Soyinka's Controversial Book* (Benin City, Nigeria, 1975), p. 39
[23] *Ibid.*, p. 34
[24] *Ibid.*, p. 45

Efua Theodora Sutherland
born 1924   GHANA

I'm on a journey of discovery. I'm discovering my own people. I didn't grow up in rural Ghana – I grew up in Cape Coast with a Christian family. It's a fine family, but there are certain hidden areas of Ghanaian life – important areas of Ghanaian life, that I just wasn't in touch with; in the past four or five years I've made a very concentrated effort to make that untrue. And I feel I know my people now.[1]

Efua Sutherland more than knows her people. She has contributed extensively to their lives through her accomplishments in the literary, dramatic, and teaching professions.

The years 1958–1961 saw the birth of an Experimental Theatre and the Ghana Drama Studio in Accra, both founded by Mrs Sutherland, the latter with the assistance of grants from the Rockefeller Foundation and the Arts Council of Ghana. She conceived the Drama Studio 'as a centre for vigorous experimentation in drama ... as eventually being a formative process in developing writers.' As she says:

The Drama Studio has really come as another expression of my desire to have more and more people interested in writing – primarily for children. But later on it

turned out that not everyone is interested in writing for children, although there are a great many interested in writing. To give another reason why people would want to write I started to build the Drama Studio and develop the experimental threatre programme.[2]

In 1962 two of Mrs Sutherland's plays, *Foriwa* and *Edufa*, were performed at the Drama Studio for the first time. Later published in *Okyeame* (a Ghanaian literary magazine she helped establish) in 1964 and 1966 respectively, they have both since been issued in book form. Productions at the studio have also included Efua Sutherland's one-act play *You Swore an Oath* and *Odasani*, a Ghanaian interpretation of *Everyman*. A versatile playwright, her publications also include *The Marriage of Anansewa*, a fantasy *The Pineapple Child*, and *Nyamekye*. Combining her lifelong interest in children with her literary abilities, she has written several children's plays as well: *Tweedledum and Tweedledee*, *Two Rhythm Plays: Vulture! Vulture!* and *Tahinta* (published in Ghana's State Publishing Corporation in 1968) and *Ananse and the Dwarf Brigade*.

Efua Sutherland feels that the language problem in Ghana will ultimately force English to become the national language. She is therefore 'pushing with the objective of a bilingual society in ... mind'.[3]

Some of my writing for children is in both English and Akan; I am anxious that children are started off bilingually in the schools. This can't happen unless there is literature in support of it. So this is all part of my experimental programme – to find out what can be translated in both languages towards this end.[4]

In 1961 Efua Sutherland's first book, a pictorial essay for children entitled *The Roadmakers*, was published. A joint endeavour in the same genre, *Playtime in Africa*, was issued the following year, with photographs contributed by the American Willis E. Bell (who later also supplied photographs for the publication of *Two Rhythm Plays*) and text by Efua Sutherland. Published in New York by Atheneum, this highly popular volume has been reprinted numerous times.

In 1963 Efua Sutherland was granted a research appointment in African literature and drama at the University of Ghana's Institute of African Studies. She is connected with the School of Drama in Legon and directs the Kusum Agormba, a theatre group based on the Ghana Drama Studio, which performs at Accra schools, churches, and training colleges, and travels throughout the country.

Efua Sutherland received her formal education at Ghana's Saint Monica's School and Teacher Training College, Homerton College in Cambridge for teacher training, and as a linguistics student at the University of London's School of Oriental and African Studies. Returning to her native country in the early 1950s, she married the American William Sutherland, had three children, taught in Ghana, and assisted her husband in the establishment of a school in the Transvolta.

Her work in the establishment of village theatres has had a welcome feedback. In one sense the village communities provide a vital link with the past: 'They have minded the culture. These are the people whom we ought to thank for what has been maintained of the culture.'[5] In an equally valid way, Sutherland regards them as the true critics of art and culture, and is recording their reactions to her theatrical experiments. 'We don't need anybody's hackneyed criteria for criticizing the work we are trying to develop. The ordinary criteria for literary criticism that somebody lifts out of a book or from another culture won't do.'[6]

The writer combined her literary skills with her awareness of the community in her play *The Marriage of Anansewa*, published in 1975. In this 'rich and vigorous example of her valuable work'[7] she draws on the conventions of the Anansesem musical performances, in which Ananse 'appears to represent a kind of Everyman, artistically exaggerated and distorted to serve society as a medium for self-examination . . . a medium for society to criticize itself'.[8]

[1] *Cultural Events in Africa*, no. 42, 1968, p. iii
[2] *Ibid.*, p. i
[3] *Ibid.*, p. ii
[4] *Ibid.*, p. iii
[5] Lee Nichols, ed., *Conversations with African Writers* (Washington DC, 1981), p. 280
[6] *Ibid.*, p. 285
[7] *British Book News*, Dec. 1975
[8] Efua Sutherland, *The Marriage of Anansewa* (London, 1980), introduction, p. v

Sony Labou Tansi

born 1947   CONGO

Parisian critics hailed Sony Labou Tansi's novel, *La Vie et demie*, a 'fable of contemporary Africa', published by Seuil in 1979, as an important literary event of the season. Their judgement was confirmed later that same year when the novel was awarded the special jury's prize at the first International Festival of *francophonie* held in Nice.

At that time little was known of Tansi other than that he was relatively young (he was born on 5 July 1947 in Zaire), had taught English at Collège Tchicaya in Pointe Noire, and was then employed in the Ministry of Cooperation in Brazzaville. Jean-Paul Morel, writing in *Le Matin*, said about *La Vie et demie* that

one thinks inevitably about Rabelais (with the Providential Guide's 'grotesque appetite'), about King Ubu in his murderous folly, about Vian's *Goûter des généraux* for the military parade . . . But can one be sure that this is his cultural horizon? Rather is it elsewhere; he continues to use the French language – and with what instinct for the nuances of the tongue! – but he manages to recreate an authentic new vision of the world.[1]

What Morel and other critics omitted to mention was that if *La Vie et demie* was

Sony Labou Tansi's first published novel it was not, strictly speaking, an only novel. Three other novels were also ready in 1979 – *La Raison et le béret*, *La Natte*, and *L'Etat honteux*. Nor was Tansi just a novelist. By 1979 he had written four as yet unpublished plays, three of which had won prizes in the annual African theatre competition sponsored by Radio-France Internationale. He had also written a short story, *Le Malentendu*, awarded second prize by the Agence de Coopération Culturelle et Technique in their 1976 competition, and several unpublished collections of poetry.

In the short period since the publication of *La Vie et demie* readers have come to know Sony Labou Tansi a little better as an author, however, for two of his plays (*Conscience de tracteur* and *La Parenthèse de sang*) and a second novel (*L'Etat honteux*) are now available. None the less, a certain mystery continues to surround him, and it has hardly been solved by interviews published in *Demain l'Afrique* and *L'Afrique Littéraire et Artistique*.[2] Tansi's manner of speaking in metaphor and parable, which resembles the way he writes, and his reticence to speak about himself, maintain that aura of mystery. In the interview with Maunick, for example, he dismisses the question of individual literary influences on his writing as one which 'negrologues' inevitably ask and then goes on to say: 'I have to say that my body is a flag, that every man's body is a flag, and that nothing or no one influences a flag better than the wind, than breath . . .'[3] In one of his plays Tansi has a character say, 'I have no other diploma than the fly on my trousers because I speak about what people know the least about, life. I don't need any other diplomas than my entrails and my water.' In the same way Tansi feels his identity as a man who writes is all one really need know of him: 'Who am I, when was I born, how and why? I don't think that is the essential thing. It will be said one day. In short, what counts now is my act of writing. My job of being mad but clear-headed [*"dingue sans déconner"*].'[4]

Sony Labou Tansi describes himself as a compulsive writer, using the French word, *étourderie*, to describe the state of light-headedness or giddiness that propels him, and all black authors, to write because, he says, 'our civilization is one of the Word' (*la Parole*).[5] In the interview with Guy Daninos he says, paradoxically, 'it is not I who write but "*the other me*". "*The self who reasons*" does not have much to do with "*the self who writes*". Simply because art does not reason. It breathes.'[6]

As a black man Tansi says he would be honoured if Senghor were to read his works and say, 'That's negritude'. But he also insists on being viewed not just as a black man, but as a simple *man*: 'I am the black man who goes far on the road of men . . . define me, if you really have to, as . . . a little sum of all men'.[7]

Because he feels intimately bound to all of mankind, Tansi would upbraid readers who see nothing more in *La Vie et demie* than a grotesque fable of the King Ubus of contemporary Africa – the Amin Dadas and Emperor Bokassas of recent times:

> To all of you I say 're-read!' In reality, *La Vie et demie* is a book about life. The life that we have ceased respecting . . . When Bokassa the First gobbles up Negroes out there in the former Ubangui-Chari, all the media here have a good laugh as if Hitler the First had never existed. And as if modern cannibals who turn human meat into money didn't gobble up men.[8]

The author of *La Vie et demie* speaks at length about his cult of life, and what the concept of new humanism means for him, in the interview with Guy Daninos. Man is gradually killing life, he affirms, because reason has replaced wisdom:

> We are all assassins. The Earth is full of assassins . . . We are preparing the death of mankind . . . This is what I call elsewhere in my writing 'The Shameful State' . . . It's Descartes fault . . . today man is a cripple who faces the world with only one eye – his reason. He has thrown all the other parts of his body overboard and only kept his reason. What an error! . . . Maybe we need to create schools where people learn to be alive.[9]

Sony Labou Tansi is now with the Ministry of Culture in Brazzaville and also directs a theatre troupe called 'Le

Rocado Zulu Théâtre'. Readers can expect to hear a great deal more of him in the future.

[1] Jean-Paul Morel, '*La Vie et demie* de Sony Labou Tansi', *Le Matin*, 12 Sept. 1979, p. 14 (this and the following quotations translated from the French by the editors)

[2] Edouard Maunick, 'Sony Labou Tansi: l'homme qui dit tous les hommes', *Demain l'Afrique*, 17 Nov. 1979; Guy Daninos, 'Entretien avec l'écrivain congolais Sony Labou Tansi, dramaturge, poète et romancier', *L'Afrique Littéraire et Artistique*, no. 57, 1980, p. 50

[3] Maunick, 'Sony Labou Tansi', p. 84

[4] *Ibid.*

[5] *Ibid.*

[6] Daninos, 'Entretien avec l'écrivain congolais', p. 50

[7] Maunick, 'Soni Labou Tansi', p. 82

[8] *Ibid.*

[9] Daninos, 'Entretien', pp. 51–3

Jean-Baptiste Tati-Loutard
born 1938   CONGO

For me, a poem is almost a physiological need that comes over me just like the need to drink. It is not violent like the sexual need. It is a vague element of the instinct for survival. Images, sounds, ideas only become clear little by little as they uncover the source from which they have sprung. This is why poetry is an adventure during the creative phase. Craftsmanship then comes in as the poem receives its aesthetic shape.[1]

This is how the poet-politician, Jean-Baptiste Tati-Loutard described the poetic process in a short article that appeared in the Dakar daily newspaper, *Le Soleil*. The article is an important statement that summarizes in 41 lines what Tati-Loutard, the man, feels is the essence of Tati-Loutard, the poet. In it he touches briefly on the sources of his inspiration – the sea, and the countryside, the city, and time – that have produced, in turn, his first four poetry collections.

The ocean and nature, the landscape of Tati-Loutard's childhood, have profound-ly affected his poetic sensitivities and they form the theme of his first collection, *Les Poèmes de la mer* (1968). He was born in Ngoyo near Pointe Noire on 15 December 1938 and says, 'between the ages of three and seven I lived out in nature with my mother and my sisters, far from other dwellings. The sight of nature has left its mark on me, and especially the sight of the sea that continues to resound within me.'[2] But the sea is more than a symbol of his happy childhood: 'The sea in the past was a sort of road to Calvary for the Congolese and for Africans in general and now there is another vision of the sea that an African could have today.'[3]

As Tati-Loutard grew up and was educated first in Pointe Noire and then at the Collège Cheminade in Brazzaville, a secondary school run by Marianist Fathers, the city began to leave its mark on him and served as the major inspiration for *L'Envers du soleil* (1970). The themes of *Les Racines congolaises* (1968) partake of both sources of inspiration – the sea and the city. In 1974 Tati-Loutard brought out a fourth collection in Kinshasa. Entitled *Les Normes du temps*, the collection allowed him, in his own words, 'to become reconciled with [the passage of] time, something that up to then had been rather painful for me'.[4]

Tati-Loutard recalls the various influences, both African and non-African, that have worked on him: 'I have read widely. African poets as well as foreign poets. Césaire, Perse, Maïakovski, Montale, Séféris, have inspired me.'[5] He also reiterates his declaration of independence as a writer: 'I have not belonged to any literary group. I have never contributed regularly to any journal.'[6] The implicit reference here, of course, is to negritude. Since the publication in 1968 of his first collection of poetry, *Poèmes de la mer*, which contained an essay on African poetry and a return to origins ('Poésie nègre et retour aux sources'), Tati-Loutard has been known for his studied opposition to negritude as a poetic theory. In an interview with Marc Rombaut in a special issue of *Poésie I* he repeats the reasons which have led him to reject negritude:

My reproach to negritude? For being, above all, an essentialist or substantialist doctrine . . . It is essentialist because it considers that there is a black soul or an immutable Negro soul whose values – rhythm, emotion, solidarity, union with cosmic forces – make an unchanging whole that goes through time and space ... I reject such a conception because, although these values produce behaviours that are quite obvious in the present, in my opinion, they can be modified by the simple fact of education.[7]

Tati-Loutard goes on to point out the dangers of such thinking for literature. An African writer is judged 'not for what his writing, his personality or his artistic individuality is worth', but out of deference to a 'racial specificity'.[8] Ultimately, he claims, the concept of negritude 'constitutes an inhibiting force to creation'.[9] In his view, the décor of a typical negritude poem with its metaphors of tam-tam and balafon is profoundly atypical in Africa today and does not correspond to contemporary African experience.

Through Tati-Loutard's declarations one detects, however, the impatience he shares with many younger African writers with the critics' inevitable questions on negritude. In the article appearing in *Le Soleil*, the newspaper of the homeland of negritude, he bluntly asserts, 'I no longer discuss negritude. My point of view is in the postscript to the *Poèmes de la mer*'.[10]

Jean-Baptiste Tati-Loutard completed his undergraduate training at the University of Bordeaux, France in 1963 with a degree in French, another in Italian the following year, and a secondary-school teaching diploma in 1965. In 1969 he was awarded a doctoral degree in comparative literature from the same university, writing his dissertation on French influences on contemporary African poetry. He taught the first courses on African literature to be offered in the Congo at the Ecole Normale Supérieure d'Afrique Centrale in Brazzaville in 1966, and the following year he became Professor of Literature at the Centre d'Enseignement Supérieur (which later became the University of Brazzaville). He was director of the Centre from 1972 to 1973 and then Dean of the Faculty of Letters of the University of Brazzaville in 1973. He has been Director of Higher Education and Research in the Congo

and since 1975 has been Minister of Culture and the Arts.

In addition to his creative writing Tati-Loutard has made several scholarly contributions to the field of African literature, publishing a study on African poetry in French in 1975 with the Editions du Mont Noir in Kinshasa (*Le Poète africain*), and an anthology of Congolese literature in French in 1976 with CLE (*Anthologie de la littérature congolaise d'expression française*).

[1] J.-B. Tati-Loutard, 'Réponse rapide à un littérateur', *Le Soleil*, 19 May 1976, p. 5 (this and the following quotations translated from the French by the editors)
[2] *Ibid.*
[3] 'Jean-Baptiste Tati-Loutard: Des reproches au concept de Négritude', *Poésie I: Nouvelle Poésie Négro-Africaine*, nos. 43–5, 1976, p. 127
[4] Tati-Loutard, 'Réponse rapide à un littérateur', p. 5
[5] *Ibid.*
[6] *Ibid.*
[7] 'Jean-Baptiste Tati-Loutard: Des reproches', p. 129
[8] *Ibid.*, p. 130
[9] *Ibid.*
[10] Tati-Loutard, 'Réponse rapide à un littérateur', p. 5

José Francisco Tenreiro
1921–1963   SÃO TOMÉ and PRÍNCIPE

Born in 1921 on the island of São Tomé, Tenreiro, the son of a Portuguese father and an African mother, went to Lisbon at an early age to complete his formal education. He gained a doctorate in geography from the University of Lisbon and was subsequently a professor at the Instituto Superior de Ciências Sociais e Política Ultramarina. Eventually he became a high official, a deputy representing São Tomé and Príncipe in the Portuguese National Assembly.

A scholar of merit, a literary critic and a poet, José Francisco Tenreiro published in 1942 the first book of negritude poetry in lusophone Africa, *Ilha do Santo Nome*. Inspired by his reading of black poets of the US Harlem renaissance (he authored a study, *Panorama de Literatura Norte-Americana*, in 1945) and by the literary vitality of the francophone negritude poets in Paris, Tenreiro identified with the culturally and politically exploited Africans of his homeland. The history of São Tomé and Príncipe explains why negritude took root on these islands more easily than in other Portuguese colonies. For centuries the islands' population consisted of indentured black workers or slaves exploited by a relatively few whites seeking to develop the cocoa and coffee crops.

Tenreiro's second volume of poems, *Coraçao em Africa*, published in 1964, a year after his death, voices a fraternal bond with oppressed blacks in Harlem, Brazil's Bahia and the Sudan. He speaks, in an essay, of his wish to help construct 'a humanist philosophy that will serve as a renewal and stimulus in relation to Africa'.[1] Richard Preto-Rhodas has commented on this catholic aspect of Tenreiro's vision: 'In keeping with his pan-African concept of negritude Ten-reiro, like Césaire, often goes beyond his island to other lands to attack the injustices which the black suffers in a white world'.[2]

In 1958 Tenreiro co-edited with Mário de Andrade the *Antologia de Poesia Negra de Expressão Portuguesa*; his own poetry has appeared in numerous anthologies published in Portugal, France, Italy, Algeria and Czechoslovakia.

[1] José Francisco Tenreiro, 'Acerca da literatura "negra" ', *Estrada Larga*, vol. 3, pp. 472–81
[2] Richard Preto Rodas, *Negritude as a Theme in the Poetry of the Portuguese-Speaking World* (Gainesville, 1970), p. 48

Miriam Tlali
born *circa* 1930   SOUTH AFRICA

Tlali's first novel, *Muriel at Metropolitan*, is autobiographical fiction, wherein Muriel, who works as a clerk in a Johannesburg store selling electrical wares, is forced to exploit her fellow Blacks while enduring insulting behaviour from the Whites also working there. This reflects her own experiences closely:

> I was actually between two fires . . . clashes with the whites on the one side because of the type of work I do, and on the other side with

my own people because they mistook me for someone who is prepared to try and get as much money as possible out of them.[1]

Although she finished writing the book in 1968, it was turned down by many publishers and only appeared in 1975. The novel is circumscribed in action and the plot is negligible, but its creative strength lies elsewhere: 'the texture and quality of the life she leads there are vividly conveyed. Her observations are minute and dispassionate . . . and this viewpoint is a new one in South African literature.'[2]

Miriam Tlali was born in Doornfontein, Johannesburg, and was a pupil at St Cyprian's Anglican School and then Madibane High School. She attended the University of the Witwatersrand until it was closed to Blacks, whereupon she studied at the University in Roma, Lesotho. Lack of funds forced her to leave there and to learn office skills which enabled her to become a clerk. The encouragement she has had from the success of her book and from her attendance at the Iowa Writer's Workshop have made her keen to write on a full-time basis.

Apart from her novels, Tlali is well known to the readers of *Staffrider* – the radical arts journal with mass circulation in the townships – for the series of interviews 'Soweto speaking'. These are graphic and demotic accounts of her conversations with working men and women, 'to find out how they work, how they feel, and that kind of thing'.[3]

She is also the South African associate editor of a new literary magazine for women to be published in the United States, *Straight Ahead International*. Several of her own stories have appeared in *Staffrider*. Her second novel, *Amandla* (1980), adds to the growing corpus of literature on Soweto. The lives of the people living there were fused by the events of 1976, and from the tumult Tlali hears the cry 'Amandla', 'power'.

[1] 'Arts and Africa', no. 267, BBC African Service transcript (London)
[2] Marie Dyer, *Reality*, vol. 7, no. 6, Jan. 1976, p. 15
[3] 'Arts and Africa', no. 267

Amos Tutuola
born 1920   NIGERIA

I am a native of Abeokuta . . . Abeokuta is 64
miles to Lagos. When I was about 7 years
old, one of my father's cousins whose name
is Dalley, a nurse in the African hospital,
took me from my father to his friend Mr
F. O. Monu, an Ibe man, to live with him as
a servant and to send me to school instead
of paying me money.

I started my first education at the Salvation Army School, Abeokuta, in the year
1934, and Mr Monu was paying my school
fees regularly . . .

But as I had a quicker brain than the other
boys in our class . . . I was given special
promotion . . .

Having spent two years with my master, he
was transferred to Lagos in 1936, and I
followed him through his kindness . . .

A few weeks after we arrived in Lagos, I
was admitted into a school called Lagos
High School . . .

I attended this school for a year, and my
weekly report card columns were always
marked 1st position . . . the Principal of this
school promoted me from Std. II to Std. IV
and he also allowed me to attend the school
free of charge for one year.

But having passed from Std. IV to V the
following year, I was unable to remain with
my master any longer, because the severe
punishments given me at home by this
woman were too much for me . . . When
I reached home, I refused to go back to
Lagos . . .

Again, I started to attend the school at
Abeokuta . . . At the end of that year, I
passed from Std. V to VI, and after I spent
nine months in Std. VI my father, who was
paying the school fees, etc., died unexpectedly (1939). Now, there was none of my family
who volunteered to assist me to further my
studies.[1]

Amos Tutuola, the first African writer
to achieve international fame, signed this
part of his autobiography on 17 April
1952, and in 1953 it was appended to the
Grove Press edition of *The Palm-wine
Drinkard*. Twelve years later he elaborated
on his life:

> Having failed to further my education, I
> went to my father's farm. I planted plenty of
> corn on which I put all my hope that when
> they yielded, I would sell them and pay my
> school fees, etc. out of the money realised.
> But to my disappointment, there were no
> sufficient rains that year which could make
> the crops to yield well. Then having failed to
> help myself to further my education, I went
> back to Lagos in the early part of 1940.
> I stayed with my brother when I came back
> to Lagos in 1940. In the same year, I started
> to learn smithery. At the end of 1942, I
> joined the R.A.F. as a blacksmith and
> discharged as a grade two blacksmith.
> . . . I got employment in the Department
> of Labour, Lagos, in 1946, as a messenger. I
> was still in this hardship and poverty, when
> one night, it came to my mind to write my
> first book – *The Palm-wine Drinkard* and I
> wrote it within a few days successfully
> because I was a story-teller when I was in the
> school. So since then I have become a
> writer.[2]

Amos Tutuola submitted *The Palm-wine
Drinkard* to the United Society for
Christian Literature, who passed it on to
the London publisher, Faber and Faber.
It was written in a somewhat unconventional, if not extraordinary English:
Faber's smoothed out its roughest edges
and the book was published almost
entirely in its original form in 1952.

Two months later, Dylan Thomas,
writing in *The Observer*, gave it a highly
laudatory review, calling it a 'brief,
thronged, grisly and bewitching story . . .
Nothing is too prodigious or too trivial
to put down in this tall, devilish story.'[3]
English and American critics alike hailed
it a remarkable success. An American
edition followed in 1953 and by the time
Janheinz Jahn published his bibliography
in 1965, he was able to note six translated
editions. Tutuola's most severe critics
were his fellow Nigerians, who criticized
him for his lack of education, his
imperfect English, his adaptations from

Yoruba oral literature, and for presenting a disparaging image of Nigeria. Over the years, however, Tutuola has slowly been 'rehabilitated' at home, thanks in part to the efforts of Chinua Achebe, Wole Soyinka and others. Kole Ogunmola, the late Yoruba folk opera director, produced a Yoruba-language version of *The Palm-wine Drinkard* for the stage at Ibadan in 1965. (Tutuola himself had previously collaborated with Professor Harold Collins in rewriting *The Palm-wine Drinkard* in English for the stage.)

Since *The Palm-wine Drinkard*, Tutuola has written *My Life in the Bush of Ghosts* (1954), *Simbi and the Satyr of the Dark Jungle* (1955), *The Brave African Huntress* (1958), and *Feather Woman of the Jungle* (1962). The last work is meant to be a collection of tales as told by an old Yoruba chief in ten successive nights. In 1967 Tutuola brought out *Ajaiyi and his Inherited Poverty*. Then followed a long period of silence which Tutuola has only recently broken by publishing, in October 1981, *The Witch-Herbalist of the Remote Town*. Interviewed by Molara Ogundipe Leslie for the BBC 'Arts and Africa' radio programme, Tutuola describes his latest work as a version of the famous tale about the tortoise:

> The materials from which I wrote the thing, it's quite simple even a child knows each one in Nigeria. The tortoise was so greedy. When his wife did not conceive in time, he went to a witch doctor and the witch doctor gave him some soup but the tortoise was so greedy that he ate from this soup and then he gave the rest to his wife. And then he conceived as well as his wife! So this was a sort of punishment from the witch doctor.[4]

The themes of Tutuola's books are drawn unmistakably from the Yoruba oral tradition but are then reworked in his own unique style. Tutuola's images, for example, reveal his fascination with modern technology and the mass media. As for other influences, Bernth Lindfors has written that Tutuola had read *Pilgrim's Progress* and *The Arabian Nights* two years before writing *The Palm-wine Drinkard*. Lindfors adds, 'He has also told Eric Larabee that he enjoyed reading

Joyce Cary's *Mister Johnson* and Edith Hamilton's *Mythology* which presumably is the book responsible for enlarging his folkloric vocabulary.'[5]

While continuing to write and publish his books Tutuola worked for most of the sixties and the seventies as a storekeeper for the Nigerian Broadcasting Service in Ibadan where he was one of the founders of the Ibadan Mbari club. Tutuola is now self-employed. He has opened his own baking business and has plans to start a poultry-farm. His plans also include writing another novel, but 'not just because of money', he says.[6]

Tutuola's style of writing has been called a 'fascinating literary cul-de-sac' by Eldred Jones.[7] What Jones means is that Tutuola's manner of writing is inimitable because it derives in part from his imperfect knowledge of English. Tutuola says he is not a full-time writer and is aware of his own special place in literature. He admires Achebe and Soyinka, the great names in Nigerian literature, but refuses to compare himself with them. Soyinka's writing, he says, is 'very beautiful'. 'He is very advanced in English, he knows English just like his own mother tongue, you see. So I cannot compare myself with him.'[8]

A full-length study of Amos Tutuola has been made by Harold Collins in a book entitled *Tutuola*, in Twayne's World Authors Series. Michèle Dussutour-Hammer has also published a book-length study of Tutuola in French under the title *Amos-Tutuola: Tradition orale et écriture du conte* (Présence Africaine, 1978).

[1] Amos Tutuola, *The Palm-wine Drinkard* (New York, 1953), pp. 126–8
[2] Amos Tutuola, 'A short biography' (a letter written to Faber and Faber, London), 14 July 1964
[3] Dylan Thomas, *The Observer* (London), 6 July 1952, p. 7
[4] 'Arts and Africa', no. 391G, BBC African Service transcript (London, 1981), p. 3
[5] Bernth Lindfors, 'Amos Tutuola and his critics', *Abbia*, May–Aug. 1969, pp. 115–16
[6] 'Arts and Africa', p. 4
[7] Eldred Jones, 'Jungle drums and wailing pianos', *African Forum*, vol. 1, no. 3, Spring 1966, p. 94
[8] 'Arts and Africa', p. 4

Adaora Lily Ulasi
born 1932   NIGERIA

Four of Adaora Lily Ulasi's five mystery novels are set in pre-independent Nigeria and have expatriate district officers or police inspectors involved in unravelling crimes or puzzling disappearances concerning Nigerians who often have recourse to the occult and the supernatural. Her fifth and most recent novel, *The Night Harry Died*, is set in the American South in the early twentieth century. In Adaora Ulasi's first two novels, *Many Thing You No Understand* and *Many Thing Begin for Change*, a traditional Igbo ruler, Oba Obieze III, who is suspected of having human sacrifices carried out on the occasion of the burial ceremony of his father, the former Oba, is pitted against two colonial officials. One is an older man who has lived for years in Africa and who recommends a cautious approach, and the other is a younger man just out from Britain with an inflexible sense of the law and justice. If Obieze comes out ahead in the first novel which ends with the disappearance of Mason, the older official, he is the obvious loser in the second novel when the extent of his unsavoury and criminal dealings are ultimately revealed – not by British officials, but by a Nigerian journalist.

The Man from Sagamu and *Who is Jonah?* also have pre-Independence settings. The Sagamu man who disappears in the former novel turns out to be the reincarnation of the Oshun deity, and Jonah of the latter novel is a master-thief who uses black magic and who ultimately eludes capture and conviction for the murder of his cohort, a British salesman and a dubious character in his own right. Adaora Ulasi explains her fondness for such themes and settings:

> My father, an Igbo Chief from the Royal House of Nnewi, but whose business was at Aba, where I was born, sat with the then colonial D.O.'s and A.D.O.'s at the Native Court at Nnewi to listen to cases, so that I had a privileged position to hear some of the details that went on in the Native Court in the form of children's tales from my father, hence the reason why my novels are set in pre-Independent Nigeria. The stories are tales from my background.[1]

The use of Pidgin is a prominent stylistic feature of Adaora Ulasi's novels and she says about this:

> I am always truthful to the backgrounds of the personalities in my books. I consider it ridiculous to put the Queen's English in the mouth of a nightwatchman or labourer. But I use Standard English which is the other name of the Queen's English when the personalities involved are educated.[2]

Born in Eastern Nigeria in 1932 Adaora Lily Ulasi is a journalist by training, having studied in Los Angeles, California, first at Pepperdine University and then at the University of Southern California where she obtained a B.A. in journalism. She began her career in the sixties as Women's Page editor of *The Daily Times* and *The Sunday Times* of Nigeria before marrying and moving to England where her three children were born. After her divorce in 1972 she returned to Nigeria to become editor of *Woman's World*, a popular West African woman's magazine. The circulation of *Woman's World* more than tripled under her editorship as she expanded its interests to include news of the achievements of women in Nigeria and around the world.

Since 1976 she has been in England, a country she has lived in at various periods for more than 15 years. She devotes her time to her novels and to a projected book of verse as well as to book reviewing for the BBC. She also writes for the *Nigerian Daily Star*, an Enugu publication, and has done radio work for The Voice of America.

[1] Correspondence with the editors, 14 Jan. 1980
[2] *Ibid.*

Tchicaya U Tam'si
born 1931   CONGO

The Congolese Felix Tchikaya U'Tamsi is the most prolific and gifted of the second generation of francophone poets. He is also the most difficult. His surrealism reaches back through Aimé Césaire to André Breton and others in the 1920s . . . his poetry, which in the hands of Gerald Moore, Sangodare Akanji and others seems to translate well, is oblique, fluid, suggestive, and replete with private symbols and symbolic motifs which accumulate meaning as they appear in poem after poem.[1]

Born Gérald Félix Tchicaya on 25 August 1931, this Congolese poet has adopted the pen-name of Tchicaya U Tam'si which, according to Janheinz Jahn, means 'the little bird who sings from home'.[2] U Tam'si has resided in Paris since 1946 when he accompanied his father, who was then his country's first Deputy, to France to take up his seat at the French National Assembly. Tchicaya U Tam'si thereafter went to school in Orleans and later at the Lycée Janson de Sailly in Paris. He disappointed his father, however, by not enrolling at a university and for the first few years after

he left school he supported himself with a variety of odd jobs as farmhand, doorman, mail sorter and carrier in the whole-sale market.

In 1967 Gerald Moore saw U Tam'si 'emerging as the outstanding poet of French expression among those who have been publishing since the war'.[3] Through both his critical articles and translations of his poetry, Gerald Moore has probably done more than anyone else to introduce U Tam'si to the English-speaking world, in particular to anglophone Africa. Moore's first English translation of his poetry appeared in early issues of both *Black Orpheus* (no. 13) and *Transition* (no. 9).

Critical assessment of U Tam'si as a poet is largely based on the six books of verse that he published between 1955 and 1969 – *Le Mauvais sang* (1955), *Feu de brousse* (1957), *A triche-coeur* (1960), *Epitome* (a volume published in 1962 that won the grand prize for Poetry at the Festival of African Arts in Dakar in 1966 and that has an introduction by Léopold Sédar Senghor), *Le Ventre* (1964), and *L'Arc musical* (1969) – all of which were reissued in the seventies. In 1964 Mbari published *Brush Fire*, containing English translations from *Feu de brousse* by Sangodare Akanji, and selected translations by Gerald Moore from U Tam'si's first four collections appeared in Heine-mann's African Writers Series in 1970 and in the American edition issued by Humanities Press in 1971. U Tam'si's publications from this first period of writing also include *Légendes africaines*, an anthology of traditional tales extracted from the works of Thomas Mfolo, Djibril Niane, Ousmane Socé and others, and including one of his own stories.

Gerald Moore has written that U Tam'si's poetry has been influenced by many things: 'the inspiration of Césaire and beyond him the technique and example of the Surrealists; the sculpture, music, dancing and poetry of the Congo; and not least his own poetic genius'.[4]

Each of his books is unified by the constant re-working and exploration of a fairly fixed vocabulary of images which he continually places in new relations to each other . . .

The physical intensity with which U Tam'si explores the landscape of the world and his own being cannot be fully matched by any other poet now working in Africa, but his general relationship to the elements of landscape and his insistence on the physical and temporal unity of all experience, with energy as the uniting principle, can be found equally in the work of many other African writers.[5]

U Tam'si himself has recorded that his poetry 'is a spoken poetry, not a written poetry, even though it is on paper. A spoken poetry does not obey the same laws as a written poetry which follows a grammatical logic. My logic is my own, it is a logic of reverberation in a way.' He admits of two different strains in his poetry:

There is a permanent feature in my writing which is a kind of black humour, an inner grin, a sort of chuckle. I laugh at myself when I can and this comes out in my writing ...
Certainly there is in my writing this universe, this loneliness, sadness of man – man everywhere, whether he be black, white, yellow.[6]

All of these self-described features of U Tam'si's writing are certainly discernible in the works he has produced in the seventies. His on-going interest in the poetic medium is attested by a new book of verse, *La Veste d'intérieur* (1977), a volume that won the 1979 Prix Louise Labé awarded by the jury of the Fémina Prize, as well as by the two new poems (grouped under the title 'Le pain ou la cendre') that he added to the new edition of *La Ventre* that Présence Africaine brought out in 1977. What is entirely new in U Tam'si's writing, however, is his venture into other genres – theatre and the novel. He produced three plays in the late seventies. One is *Le Zulu*, his own version of the Chaka legend, that was staged at the Festival d'Avignon in 1976 and published by Nubia the following year in a volume that also contains another work entitled, *Vwène le fondateur*. A third play, *Le Destin glorieux du Maréchal Nnikon Nniku Prince qu'on sort*, was issued by Présence Africaine in 1979. Like Bernard Dadié's *Mhoi Ceul*, this play

belongs to the *avant-garde* tradition of the theatre of the absurd, and the central characters of both plays are African cousins of Alfred Jarry's *Ubu-roi*.

His first novel, *Les Cancrelats*, brought out in 1980, continues the ferociously satirical vein of his play as he follows the lives of two young people, Sophie and her brother Prosper, whom society will prevent from living the lives of wisdom and prosperity that their father had wished for in naming them at birth. *La Main sèche*, a book of short stories, also appeared in 1980. One of the stories in the collection, reminiscent of George Orwell's *Animal Farm*, uses animal characters to ridicule human behaviour; the central characters of other stories are heroes of African history.

As a freelance writer and journalist, U Tam'si has contributed to both English and French reviews, and in 1960 he was editor of the short-lived journal *Congo* published in Kinshasa (then Leopoldville). He has written, produced, and directed many radio broadcasts, concentrating in particular on the adaptation of African stories and legends for this medium. He has been an officer of UNESCO in Paris since 1960.

At the 1967 African–Scandinavian Writers' Conference held in Stockholm, U Tam'si expressed his view of the writer in a modern African state:

I think the writer that I could be, that I am perhaps, should militate among 200 readers in the most strict intimacy and communicate to them what I think the message is rather than go say it in the town square ... Therefore, for me, I don't see any other task for a writer than to simply write and be a man.[7]

From the vision of Africa contained, particularly, in his more recent writings, it is clear that 'being a man' for U Tam'si means not failing to communicate to his readers his awareness of both the social and political dilemmas of contemporary Africa. His intention behind these words pronounced in Stockholm, is also to declare his independence from any ideology or school of thought that would shackle him as a writer. This would include negritude, of course, even though

Senghor supplied the preface to *Epitome*, U Tam'si's third volume of verse. U Tam'si has been reported as saying that he refuses to be 'the sandwich-man of Négritude'.[8] And in this he belongs very much to the younger generation of African writers, although in terms of age he is close to those of the first generation.

In 1978 Tchicaya U Tam'si was awarded the *Grand Prix des Lettres* of the President of Congo for his published works.

[1] Thomas R. Knipp, 'Negritude and negation: the poetry of Tchikaya U'Tamsi', *Books Abroad*, vol. 48, no. 3, Summer 1974, p. 511
[2] Janheinz Jahn, *Who's Who in African Literature* (Tübingen, 1972), p. 377
[3] Gerald Moore, 'The Negro poet and his landscape', *Black Orpheus*, no. 22, Aug. 1967, p. 35
[4] Gerald Moore, 'Surrealism and negritude in the poetry of Tchikaya U Tam'si', *Black Orpheus*, no. 13, Nov. 1963, p. 12
[5] Moore, 'The Negro poet', pp. 36, 38
[6] 'Tchikaya U Tam'si interviewed by Edris Makward during the African Studies Association Conference held at Montreal, October 1969', *Cultural Events in Africa*, no. 60, 1969, pp. ii, iii, iv
[7] Tchicaya U Tam'si, 'The writer in a modern African state', in Per Wästberg, ed., *The Writer in Modern Africa* (New York, 1969), p. 30
[8] Jacques Chevrier, ed., *Anthologie africaine* (Paris, 1981), p. 8

Luandino Vieira

born 1935   ANGOLA

Luandino Vieira, a patriarch of Angolan writing despite his relative youth, has forged a new and exciting path, and has inspired contemporary story-tellers. Luandino's life, like that of a good many writers in his country, has combined political and literary activism.

He was born José Vieira Mateus de Graça in Lagoa de Furadouro, Portugal, on 4 May 1935. The son of a shoemaker and a country woman who emigrated to Angola, Luandino lived his childhood and adolescence in the 'musseques' or suburbs of Luanda-Braga, Ramalho, Kinaxixi and Makulusu – sharing with other poor Whites, Mulattoes and Blacks a common lifestyle. He went to school until the age of 15, after which he was employed as a dealer in automobile parts and as a service engineer for trucks and heavy machinery. At the age of 26 he was arrested for the disclosure, during a BBC interview, of secret certified lists of army deserters from the Portuguese armed services fighting in Angola. Luandino was sentenced to a fourteen-year term, most of which was spent at the camp of Tarrafal in Cape Verde with the poets António Jacinto and António Cardoso. Released in June of 1972 on condition that he remain in Lisbon for five years, Vieira gained his freedom with the overthrow of the Caetano government by the military on 25 April 1974.

During his prison years Luandino, an active member of the MPLA, wrote stories and several novels, many of which were not published in Portugal until 1974. However, his first novel, *A Vida Verdadeira de Domingos Xavier*, and several stories including 'O Fato Completo de Lucas Matesso' were published abroad before this time.

The awarding by the Sociedade Portuguesa de Escritores of its highest prize to Luandino in 1965 for his collection of three stories, *Luuanda*, caused an uproar. The Portuguese government closed the society for its decision and in the process provided Vieira with significant public recognition. His volumes of stories, which include *A Cidade e a Infância, Duas Historias de Pequenos Burgueses, Vidas Novas, No Antigamente na Vida, Velhos Estorias* and *Macandumba*, depict the daily lives of those people living in and around the musseques of Luanda.

Luandino's contribution to Angolan letters stems primarily from his linguistic inventiveness. In *Luuanda*, he not only uses Kimbundu words and expressions, but he also reproduces unique linguistic features that occur when Kimbundu and Portuguese are spoken in the same society, thus recording in a realistic manner the spoken African–Portuguese of Luanda. Through his stories he is showing that the classical Portuguese of Camões is no more vital than the unique luso-African speech of Luanda. In later works he goes even further, using Portuguese as an ideogramic language. He invents words, stretches syllables, cuts off letters, creates neologisms. The freshness of Luandino's prose has, in fact, created a literary revolution in Angolan writing.

Luandino, a white Angolan writer like Castro Soromenho, António Jacinto, David Mestre and Costa Andrade, has articulated his strong belief that in his country, in the land where he fought for freedom, the question of race is supererogatory. He has remarked that

African literature is the literature of the people of Africa. Certainly a white man can be an African writer. There are African countries in which part of the population is of European origin. That population has a cultural background different from the traditional history and culture of black African people. But, for a long time they have shared an historical coming together, either in opposition to one another or in harmony, and this results in their national reactions being distinct because of diverse factors which also include inevitably their cultural backgrounds. A culture, like a literature, is never static; it is always being remade in historically determined and determin-ing space and time. For this reason, today, I am an Angolan writer, therefore an African writer.[1]

Luandino has been the subject of considerable scholarly study. Edições 70 published, in 1980, an anthology of critical essays on his writing. Donald Burness has devoted a chapter, 'Luandino Vieira and the World of the Musseque', to Luandino in his book *Fire: Six Writers from Angola, Mozambique and Cape Verde.*

Luandino Vieira lives in Luanda where he is actively involved in the selection of works published by the Union of Angolan Writers.

[1] From the introduction to Donald Burness, *Fire: Six Writers from Angola, Mozambique and Cape Verde* (Washington DC, 1977), p. xiii

Booksellers and Dealers in African Literature

This directory provides names and addresses of major Africana/Third World specialist booksellers, and other bookshops stocking African literature on a fairly regular basis and in some quantity.

GREAT BRITAIN

Africa Bookcentre
38 King Street
Covent Garden
London WC2E 8JT

Balham Book & Food Co-operative
2–16 Culmore Cross
London SW12

B. H. Blackwell Ltd
Broad Street
Oxford OX1 3BQ

Bookmarks
265 Seven Sisters Road
London N4

The Bookplace
13 Peckham High Street
Peckham
London SE15

Centerprise Bookshop
136–138 Kingsland High Street
Hackney
London E8 2NS

Central Books
37 Grays Inn Road
London WC1

Collet's London Bookshop
64–66 Charing Cross Road
London WC2

Collet's International Bookshop
129–131 Charing Cross Road
London WC2H 0EQ

Compendium
234 Camden High Street
London NW1

Dillon's University Bookshop
1 Malet Street
London WC1

W. & G. Foyle Ltd
119–125 Charing Cross Road
London WC2

Glasgow University Bookshop
John McIntyre Building
University of Glasgow
Glasgow G12 8PP

Grass Roots Bookshop
1 Newton Street
Manchester M1 1HW

Grassroots
101 Kilburn Square
London NW6

Grassroots Storefront
61 Golbothe Road
London W10

Haig & Hochland
University Precinct
Oxford Street
Manchester M13 9QA

Headstart Books and Crafts
25 West Green Road
London N15 5BX

W. Heffer & Sons Ltd
20 Trinity Street
Cambridge CB2 3NG

Hosains Books and Antiques
25 Connaught Street
London W2

Independent Bookshop
341 Glossop Road
Sheffield
South Yorkshire
S10 2HP

Kegan Paul Trench Trubner Ltd
39 Store Street
London WC1E 7DD

New Beacon Books
76 Stroud Green Road
Finsbury Park
London N4 3EN

Paperback Centre
10–12 Atlantic Road
London SW9

Arthur Probsthain
41 Great Russell Street
London WC1

Walter Rodney Bookshop
5A Chignell Place
London W13

Sabarr Books
378 Coldharbour Lane
London SW2

Soma Books
38 Kennington Lane
London SE11 4LS

Sussex University Bookshop
Falmer
Brighton
Sussex BN1 9QU

James Thin
King's Building
Edinburgh University
West Mains Road
Edinburgh

Third World Publications
151 Stratford Road
Birmingham B11 1RP

Harriet Tubman Bookshop
27/29 Grove Lane
Handsworth
Birmingham B21 9ES

CONTINENTAL EUROPE

Belgium

Lib. Générale des Sciences Humaines, 'Le Livre Africain'
35 rue van Elewyck
1050 Bruxelles

France

Le Marais Noire
44 rue Vieille du Temple
Paris 4

Librairie l'Harmattan
18 bis, rue des Quatre-Vents
75006 Paris

Librairie Présence Africaine
24 bis, rue des Ecoles
Paris 5

Germany (Federal Republic)

Afrika Buchhandlung
Volker Keller
8000 Munich 5
Klenzestrasse 32

Buchexpress GmbH
Habelschwerdter Allee 4
Berlin 33 Dahlem

Buchhandlung 'Drei
Kontinente'
Bochumerstrasse 1A
D-1000 Berlin 21

Convertrieb
Osterstrasse 36
D-2800 Bremen 1

Hans Heinrich Petersen
Buchimport GmbH
Rugenbarg 250
2000 Hamburg 53

Netherlands

Boekhandel Synthese
Lange Voorhout 96
The Hague

E. J. Brill N. V.
Boekhandel &
Drukkerijvoorheen
Oude Rijn 33a
Leiden

Dekker & Nordemann Bv.
O. Z. Voorburgwal 239
1012 E2 Amsterdam

Martinus Nijhoff F. B.
Lange Voorhout 9–11
Postbus 269
The Hague

Walter Rodney Boek Handel
1e Rozendwarsstraat 17
1016 PE Amsterdam

Portugal

Livraria Academica
Rua dos Martires da
Liberdade 10
Porto

Livraria Portugal
Rua da Carmo 70–74
Lisboa

Switzerland

Bücherkeller M. Fahas
Münstergasse 38
CH-3000 Bern 8

NORTH AMERICA

United States

Aburi Services
PO Box 130
Corona (a) Station
Flushing NY 11368

African Imprint Library
Services
Box 563
75 King Street
Falmouth Ma. 02540
*(this is the major library supplier
in the United States for African-
published material.)*

Ahidiana New Africa Book
Store
2303 Deslonde Street
New Orleans La. 70117

Africa Agency
Box 1118
Concord Ma. 01742

Book Center
518 Valencia Street
San Francisco Ca. 94110

The Cellar Bookshop
Box 6
College Park Station
Detroit Mi. 48221

Cody's Bookshop
2454 Telegraph Avenue
Berkeley Ca. 94704

Common Concerns
1347 Connecticut Ave. NW
Washington DC 20036

Dar al Kutab wal Nashrat al
Islamiyya
Box 207
New Brunswick NY 08903

Harvard Book Stores
12 Plympton Street
Cambridge Ma. 02138

Heritage Books
817 South Columbia Street
Chapel Hill NC 27514

Kitchen Table: Women of
Color Press
Box 592
Van Brunt Station
Brooklyn NY 11215

McBlain Books
Box 971
Des Moines Ia. 50304

Old Wives Tales
532 Valencia at 16
San Francisco Ca. 94110

Ottenberg Books
724 Pike Street
Seattle Wa. 98101

Pyramid Bookstore
2849 Georgia Ave. NW
Washington DC 20001

T'Olodumare Bookstore
4834 Telegraph Avenue
Oakland, Ca. 94609

Timbuktu Books
2530 S. Michigan Ave.
Chicago, Il. 60680

University Place Bookshop
821 Broadway
New York NY 10003

Canada

Mansfield Book Mart Ltd
2065 Mansfield Street
Montreal P.Q.
H3A 1Y7

AUSTRALIA &
NEW ZEALAND

Global Cultural Centre
8 Thomas Lane
Haymarket 2000
Sydney
New South Wales

AFRICA (South of
the Sahara)

Most bookshops in Africa
stock some literary items; we
have included a *selection* of
some of the larger
establishments. For more
extensive coverage of African
booksellers consult *The
African Book World and Press: a
directory*, see p. 12.

Angola

Instituto Nacional do Livro e
do Disco
CP 1281
Luanda

Lello S.A.R.L.
CP 1300
Luanda

Botswana

Botswana Book Centre
The Mall
PO Box 91
Gaborone

Burundi

Burundi Literature Center
BP 18
Gitega

Cameroun

The Bilingual Bookshop/
Librairie Bilingue
BP 727
Mvog-Ada
Yaoundé

Centre de Diffusion du Livre
Camerounais
BP 338
Douala

Librairie Populaire
BP 322
Baffoussam

Ethiopia

E.C.A. Bookshop Co-op
Society
PO Box 1236
Addis Ababa

Menno Bookstore
PO Box 1236
Addis Ababa

Gabon

Librairie Nouvelle
BP 612
Libreville

Ghana

Astab Books Ltd
Osu re
PO Box 346
Accra

The Atlas Bookshop Ltd
Ambassador Hotel Gardens
PO Box M160
Accra

University Bookshop
University of Ghana
University Square
PO Box 1
Legon

Ivory Coast

Centre d'Edition et de
Diffusion Africaines
BP 541
Abidjan 04

Maison des Livres
23 blvd. de la République
BP 4645
Abidjan

Kenya

Africa Book Services (EA) Ltd
Quaran House
Mfangano Street
PO Box 45245
Nairobi

S. J. Moore Ltd
Government Road
PO Box 30162
Nairobi

Prestige Booksellers &
Stationers
Prudential Assurance Building
Mama Ngina Street
PO Box 45425
Nairobi

Select Bookshop (Kenya) Ltd
Old Mutual Building
Kimathi Street
PO Box 40683
Nairobi

Text Book Centre Ltd
Kijabe Street
PO Box 45540
Nairobi

University of Nairobi
Bookshop
PO Box 30197
Nairobi

Lesotho

Mazenod Book Centre
PO Box MZ39
Mazenod

Liberia

Liberian Educational
Materials Supply
Corporation
PO Box 2088
Monrovia

Madagascar

La Librairie de Madagascar
38 ave. de l'Indépendance
BP 402
Antananarivo

Librairie Mixte
37 bis ave. du 26 Juin
BP 3204
Antananarivo

Malawi

Central Bookshop Ltd
PO Box 264
Blantyre

Times Bookshop Ltd
Victoria Avenue
BP 39
Blantyre

Mali

Librairie Populaire du Mali
Avenue Kasse Keita
BP 28
Bamako

Mauritius

Nalanda & Co. Ltd
30 Bourbon Street
PO Box 202
Port Louis

Mozambique

Instituto Nacional do Livro e
do Disco
Avenida 24 de Julho
CP 4030
Maputo

Nigeria

Ahmadu Bello University
Bookshop
PMB 11
Zaria
Kaduna State

Auchi Polytechnic Bookshop
PMB 0064
Auchi
Bendel State

Bendel Book Depot
6a Forestry Road
PMB 1127
Benin City
Bendel State

Benin University Bookshop
PMB 1154
Benin City

'The Bestseller'
Shop C5
Falmo Ikoyi Shopping Centre
Ikoyi
Lagos

Bisi Books (Nigeria) Ltd
720 Oyo Road
Mokola
PO Box 2785
Ibadan
Oyo State

Challenge Bookshops
Agege Motor Road
PMB 12256
Lagos

CSS Bookshops
Bookshop House
50–52 Broad Street
PO Box 174
Lagos
(branches throughout Nigeria)

Edekes Bookshops Stores Ltd
2 Falolu Road
PO Box 974
Surulere
Lagos

Elka Books (Nigeria) Ltd
49 University Road
PO Box 352
Nsukka
Anambra State

Florida Books and Library
  Equipment
5 Association Avenue
PO Box 7993
Lagos

Imedo Books and Stationery
  Centre
20 Shendam Road
PO Box 34
Pankshin

Jos University Bookshop
PMB 2084
Jos Plateau State

Nigerian Book Suppliers Ltd
28 Akinremi Street
PO Box 4440
Ikeja
Lagos State

Odusote Bookstores Ltd
68 Lagos Bye Pass
PO Box 244
Ibadan
Oyo State

University Bookshop (Nigeria)
  Ltd
University of Ibadan
Ibadan
Oyo State

University of Ife Bookshop
  Ltd
Ile-Ife
Oyo State

University of Lagos Bookshop
Akoka
Yaba
Lagos

University of Nigeria
  Bookshop Ltd
Nsukka
Anambra State

'Wunmi Ade Bookshop
29 Igboyegun Street
Akure
Ondo State

Senegal

Librairie Clairafrique
Place de l'Indépendance
BP 2005
Dakar

Librairie Sankore
25 ave. William Ponty
BP 7040
Dakar

Mamadou Traoré Ray Autra
BP 2380
Dakar

Sierra Leone

Fourah Bay College Bookshop
  Ltd
University of Sierra Leone
Freetown

The Sierra Leone Diocesan
  Bookshops Ltd
Cathedral House
1 Gloucester Street
PO Box 104
Freetown

South Africa

Academy Bookshop (Pty) Ltd
PO Box 2081
Cape Town 8000

Adams &.Co. Ltd
341 West Street
PO Box 466
Durban 4000

Campus Bookshop
PO Box 31361
Braamfontein 2017

Central News Agency Ltd
PO Box 1033
Johannesburg 2000
*(branches throughout South
  Africa)*

Constantia Books
PO Box 186
Constantia 7848

Exclusive Books Ltd
48 Pretoria Street
Hillbrow 2001

Haum Booksellers
303 Monarch House
58 Long Street
PO Box 1371
Cape Town 8000

Juta & Co. Ltd
PO Box 1010
Johannesburg 2000
(also at Cape Town and Durban)

Keegan's Bookshop
101–103 Main Road
Rondebosch
Cape Town

Logan's University Bookshop
  (Pty) Ltd
622 Umbilo Road
Durban 4001

Maskew Miller Ltd
7–11 Burg Street
PO Box 396
Cape Town 8000

Nasionale Boekhandel Ltd
386 Voortrekker Road
PO Box 122
Parow 7500
*(branches throughout South
  Africa)*

Shuter and Shooter (Pty) Ltd
PO Box 109
Pietermaritzburg 3200

C. Struik Booksellers (Pty) Ltd
Corner Loop and Wale Streets
PO Box 1144
Cape Town 8000

Frank Thorold (Pty) Ltd
PO Box 241
Johannesburg 2000

van Schaik's Bookstore
  (Pty) Ltd
Libri Building
Church Street
PO Box 724
Pretoria 0001

Sudan

The Khartoum Bookshop
PO Box 968
Khartoum

The Nile Bookshop
41 New Extension Street
PO Box 8036
Khartoum

Swaziland

Websters (Pty) Ltd
West Street
PO Box 292
Mbabane

Tanzania

Cathedral Bookshop
Mansfield Street
PO Box 2381
Dar es Salaam

Dar es Salaam University
  Bookshop
PO Box 35091
Dar es Salaam

International Publishers
  Agencies
Independence Avenue
PO Box 21341
Dar es Salaam

Pan-African Bookshop
Zambruarkis Building
PO Box 5068
Tanga

Uganda

Uganda Bookshop
Colville Street
PO Box 7145
Kampala

Zaire Republic

Librairie du Zaire
12 ave. des Aviateurs
BP 2100
Kinshasa

Librairie Universitaire
BP 1682
Kinshasa 1

Okapi Centre de Diffusion
10 ave. de la Caisse d'Epargne
BP 908
Kinshasa 1

Zambia

Malasa Book Service Ltd
Cairo Road
PO Box 1700
Lusaka

University of Zambia
  Bookshop
PO Box 2379
Lusaka

Zimbabwe

Alpha Books (Pvt) Ltd
Paget House
87 Union Avenue
PO Box 1056
Harare

The Book Centre
Textbook Sales Ltd
Colonial Mutual Buildings
Gordon Avenue
PO Box 3799
Harare

Dzidzo Yakanaka
106A Baker Avenue
Harare

Grassroots Bookshop
PO Box A-267
Avondale
Harare

Kingstons Ltd
PO Box 2374
Harare

The Literature Bureau
PO Box 8137
Causeway
Harare

Mambo Press Bookshop
28 Park Street
PB 6602
Harare

Matopo Book Centre
PO Box 3362
Harare

National Books of Zimbabwe
Morgan House
27 Gordon Avenue
PO Box 4828
Harare
(also at Bulawayo and Gweru)

Townsend & Co. (Pty) Ltd
PO Box 3281
Harare

Directory of Publishers

The directory below provides full ordering addresses of all publishers (as far as traceable) whose titles are listed in the *Guide*.

GREAT BRITAIN

The Africa Centre
38 King Street
London WC2 8JT

Africana Publishing Co.
Division of Holmes & Meier
  Publishers Ltd
131 Trafalgar Road
London SE10 9TX

Allen Lane Ltd
17 Grosvenor Gardens
London SW1W 0BD

Allen & Unwin
PO Box 18
Park Lane
Hemel Hempstead
Herts. HP2 4TE

Allison & Busby
6a Noel Street
London W1V 3RB

Edward Arnold Publishers Ltd
41 Bedford Square
London WC1B 3DP

Marion Boyars Publishers Ltd
18 Brewer Street
London W1R 4AS

Paul Breman Ltd
1 Rosslyn Hill
London NW3 5UL

John Calder Publishers Ltd
18 Brewer Street
London W1R 4AS

Cambridge University Press
The Edinburgh Building
Shaftesbury Road
Cambridge CB2 2RU

Frank Cass & Co. Ltd
Gainsborough House
11 Gainsborough Road
London E11 1RS

Collier Macmillan Ltd
Stockley Close
Stockley Road
West Drayton UB7 9BE

Rex Collings Ltd
6 Paddington Street
London W1M 3LA

Wm. Collins Sons & Co. Ltd
PO Box
Glasgow G64 2QT
(*see also Fontana Paperbacks*)

Commonwealth Institute
Kensington High Street
London W8 6NQ

André Deutsch Ltd
105 Great Russell Street
London WC1B 3LJ

Ad Donker Ltd
1 Prince of Wales Passage
117 Hampstead Road
London WN1 3EE

Edinburgh University Press
22 George Square
Edinburgh EH8 9LF

Eothen Books
129 Troughton Road
London SE7

Evans Brothers Ltd
Montagu House
Russell Square
London WC1B 5BX

Faber & Faber Ltd
3 Queen Square
London WC1N 3AU

Fontana Paperbacks
Wm. Collins Sons & Co. Ltd
14 St. James's Place
London SW1A 1PS

Victor Gollancz Ltd
14 Henrietta Street
Covent Garden
London WC2E 8QJ

Harper & Row Ltd
28 Tavistock Street
London WC2E 7PN

George Harrap & Co. Ltd
182–184 High Holborn
London WC1V 7AX

Harvard University Press
126 Buckingham Palace Road
London SW1W 9SD

Heinemann Educational
  Books Ltd
22 Bedford Square
London WC1B 3HH

Hickey Press Ltd
Unit 2.2
Pennybank Chambers
33–35 St. John's Square
Clerkenwell
London EC1

Hodder & Stoughton
PO Box 6
Mill Road
Dunton Green
Sevenoaks
Kent TN13 2XX

Holmes & Meier Publishers
  Ltd
131 Trafalgar Road
London SE10 9TX

C. Hurst & Co. Publishers Ltd
38 King Street
London WC2 8JT

Hutchinson Education
Hutchinson House
17–21 Conway Street
London W1P 6BS

Michael Joseph Ltd
44 Bedford Square
London WC1B 3DU

Liberation
313–315 Caledonian Road
London N1

Longman Group Ltd
Longman House
Burnt Mill
Harlow
Essex CM20 2JE

Lutterworth Press
Luke House
Farnham Road
Guildford
Surrey GU1 4XD

Macmillan Education Ltd
see Macmillan Publishers Ltd

Macmillan Publishers Ltd
4 Little Essex Street
London WC2R 3LF

Mansell Publishing Ltd
6 All Saints Street
London N1 9RL

Methuen & Co. Ltd
11 New Fetter Lane
London EC4P 4EE

John Murray Publishers Ltd
50 Albemarle Street
London W1X 4BD

Museum Press Ltd
see Pitman Publishing Ltd

The National Book League
Book House
45 East Hill
London SW18 2QZ

Thomas Nelson & Sons Ltd
Nelson House
Mayfield Road
Walton-on-Thames KT12 5PL

Outposts Publications
72 Burwood Road
Walton-on-Thames KT12 4AL

Peter Owen Ltd
73 Kenway Road
London SW5 0RE

Oxford University Press
Ely House
37 Dover Street
London W1X 4AH
(*and at Walton Street, Oxford
OX2 6DP*)

Palladio Press
99 High Street
Aberdeen AB2 3ER

Panther Books Ltd
Granada Publishing
PO Box 9
St. Albans
Herts. AL2 2NF

Penguin Books Ltd
Bath Road
Harmondsworth
Middx. UB7 0DA

Pergamon Press Ltd
Headington Hill Hall
Oxford OX3 0BW

Pitman Publishing Ltd
39 Parker Street
London WC2B 5PB

Davis Poynter Ltd
20 Garrick Street
London WC2E 9BJ

Regency Press Ltd
43 New Oxford Street
London WC1

Routledge & Kegan Paul Ltd
39 Store Street
London WC1E 7DD

Satellite Books
Kendall House
9 Kendall Road
Isleworth
Middx.

K. G. Saur Ltd
see Hans Zell Publishers

School of Oriental and
African Studies
Publishing Department
University of London
Malet Street
London WC1E 7HP

Martin Secker & Warburg Ltd
54 Poland Street
London W1V 3DF

Sphere Books Ltd
30–32 Gray's Inn Road
London WC1X 8JL

Standing Conference on
Library Materials on Africa
(SCOLMA)
c/o The Librarian
Institute of Commonwealth
Studies
27 Russell Square
London WC1V 3AU

Arthur H. Stockwell Ltd
Elms Court
Torrs Park
Ilfracombe
Devon EX34 8BA

Third World Publications
151 Stratford Road
Birmingham B11 1RD
(*distributes Kenya Literature
Bureau, NECZAM, and Ravan
Press titles in the UK; also stocks
some EAPH titles.*)

Tinga Tinga
R. C. Markham
The Windmill Press
Kingswood
Tadworth
Surrey KT20 6TG
(*distributes publications of
Heinemann Educational Books'
overseas companies*)

United Society for Christian
Literature
see Lutterworth Press

University of London Press
see Hodder & Stoughton

Virago Ltd
Ely House
Dover Street
London W1X 4HS

Westminster City Libraries
Marylebone Road
London NW1 5PS

Hans Zell Publishers
An imprint of K. G. Saur
Verlag
14 St. Giles
PO Box 56
Oxford OX1 3EL

CONTINENTAL EUROPE

Austria

Akademische Druck- und
Verlagsanstalt Dr. Paul
Struzl
Postfach 598
8011 Graz

Belgium

Centre d'Etude et
Documentation Africaine
(CEDAF)
7 Place Royale
1000 Brussels

Marcel Didier
1 Place de le Maison Rouge
1020 Brussels

Editions Complexe
24 rue de Bosnie
1060 Brussels

Editions de la Francité
21 blvd. des Archers
1400 Nivelles

Institut de Sociologie
Université Libre de Bruxelles
Parc Leopold
1040 Brussels

Les Nouvelles Editions
Marabout S.A.
65 rue de Limbourg
4800 Verviers

Musée Royale d'Afrique
Central
Tervuren

Czechoslovakia

Academia Publishing House
Vodickova 40
112 29 Praha 1

Oriental Institute
University of Prague
Ovocny trida 5
Prague

Denmark

Akademisk Boghandel
Universitetsparken
8000 Århus

Glydendalske Boghandel,
  Nordisk Forlag A/S.
Klareboderne 3
1001 Copenhagen

France

A.B.C.
(Afrique Biblio Club)
9 rue du Chateau d'eau
75010 Paris

Edition de l'Académie
  Populaire de Littérature et
  de Poésie
12 rue Racine
93120 La Courneuve

Agence de Coopération
  Culturelle et Technique
19 avenue de Messine
75008 Paris

Editions Akpagnon
678 ave. Bir-Hakeim
77350 la Mée sur Seine

Editions de l'Athanor
23 rue Vaneau
75007 Paris

Aubier Montaigne
13 quai de Conti
75006 Paris

Bibliothèque Nationale
58 rue de Richlieu
75084 Paris

Cercle International de la
  Pensée et des Arts Français
58310 Saint-Amand en
  Puisaye

Buchet Chastel
18 rue de Condé
75006 Paris

Calmann-Lévy
3 rue Auber
75009 Paris

Centre d'Etudes Africaines
  (C.A.R.D.A.N.)
54 blvd. Raspail
75006 Paris

Armand Colin-Bourrelier
103 blvd. Saint-Michel
75005 Paris

Conseil International de la
  Langue Française
103 rue de la Lille
75007 Paris

Corrêa (Bûchet-Chastel)
18 rue de Condé
75006 Paris

E.D.I.C.E.F.
Editions Classiques
  d'Expression Française
93 rue Jeanne d'Arc
75013 Paris

Edition Cujas
4, 6, 8 rue de la Maison
  Blanche
75013 Paris

Editions du Dauphin
43–45 rue de la Tombe-Issoire
75014 Paris

Denoël
19 rue de l'Université
75007 Paris

Didier
19 rue de l'Ancienne Comédie
75006 Paris

Droit et Liberté
89 rue Oberkampf
75011 Paris

Editions Louis Drouot-
  Soulanges
BP 442
75769 Paris

Editions de l'Ecole
11 rue de Sèvres
75006 Paris

E.D.I.T.A.F.
7 rue de l'Ecole Polytechnique
75005 Paris
(*distributed by l'Harmattan*)

Editions de l'Etrave (Révue de
  la Nouvelle Pléïade)
11510 Fitou

Fayard
75 rue des Saints-Pères
75006 Paris

Editions Federop
11 rue Ferrachat
69005 Lyon

Flammarion
26 rue Racine
75278 Paris

La Farandole S.A. Editions
11 bis rue de la Planche
75007 Paris

France Loisirs
123 blvd. de Grenelle
75015 Paris

Fédération Internationale des
  Professeurs de Français
Centre International d'Etudes
  Pédagogiques
1 ave. Léon Journault
92310 Sèvres

Editions de la Francité
20 rue du Louvre
75001 Paris

Gallimard
5 rue Sébastien-Bottin
75007 Paris

Paul Geuthner
12 rue Vavon
75006 Paris

Grassin
Moulin de l'Ecluse
28210 Nogent-le Roi

Hachette
254 blvd. Saint-Germain
75340 Paris Cedex 07

L'Harmattan
7 rue de l'Ecole Polytechnique
75005 Paris

Hatier
8 rue d'Assas
75278 Paris

Editions l'Hermès
31 rue Pasteur
69007 Lyon

Institut Pédagogique Africain
see E.D.I.C.E.F.

Istra
93 rue Jeanne d'Arc
75013 Paris

Julliard
8 rue Garancière
75006 Paris

Editions Karthala
22–24 blvd. Arago
75013 Paris

Editions Klincksiek
11 rue de Lille
75007 Paris

Robert Laffont
6 place Saint-Sulpice
75006 Paris

Larousse
13–21 rue de Montparnasse
75280 Paris

Le Livre Africain
13 rue de Sèvres
75278 Paris

Editions le Lorrain
14–16 rue des Clercs
37000 Metz

Luneau Ascot
9 rue Ampère
75017 Paris

Maisonneuve et Larose
15 rue Victor-Cousin
75005 Paris

Editions de la Marne
24 rue Louis Blanc
Paris
(no longer trading)

Albin Michel
22 rue Huyghens
75680 Paris

Minard
(Archives des Lettres
Modernes)
73 rue du Cardinal-Lemoine
75005 Paris

Fernand Nathan
9 rue Méchain
75014 Paris

A. G. Nizet
3 bis, place de la Sorbonne
75005 Paris

Nouveaux Horizons
11 rue de Lourmel
75015 Paris

Nouvelles Editions Debresse
7 rue Duguay-Trouin
75006 Paris

Nouvelles Editions Latines
1 rue Palatine
75006 Paris

Nubia
50 blvd de Port-Royal
75015 Paris

Editions de l'Orante
6 rue du Général Bertrand
75007 Paris

Editions Pierre Jean Oswald
7 rue de l'Ecole Polytechnique
75005 Paris
*(no longer trading; stocks
purchased by l'Harmattan)*

Peyronnet
8 rue de Furstenburg
75006 Paris

Paragraphes Littéraires de
Paris
*(no longer trading; refer orders to
José-Millas Martin, 14 rue Le
Bua, 75020 Paris)*

Jean-Jacques Pauvert
8 rue de Nesle
75006 Paris

Payot
106 blvd. Saint-Germain
75006 Paris

La Pensée Universelle
21 rue Charlemagne
75004 Paris

Editions Marc Pessin
La Galérie Saint Laurent
38380 Saint Laurent du Pont

Editions des Peuples Noirs
3 rue de l'Asile Popincourt
75011 Paris

Jean-Michel Place
12 rue Pierre et Marie Curie
75005 Paris

Plon
8 rue Garancière
75006 Paris

Présence Africaine
25 bis rue des Ecoles
75005 Paris

Presses Pocket
8 rue Garancière
75006 Paris

Presses Universelles Avignon
see La Pensée Universelle

Presses de l'UNESCO
7 Place de Fontenoy
75700 Paris

Presses Universitaires de
France
108 blvd. Saint-Germain
75006 Paris

Presses Universitaires de
Grenoble
BP 47X
38040 Grenoble Cedex

Publications Orientalistes de
France
2 rue de Lille
75007 Paris
*(distributed by INALCO, 4 rue de
Lille, 75007 Paris)*

Radio-France Internationale
116 ave. du Président Kennedy
75786 Paris Cedex 16

S.A.G.E.R.E.P. L'Afrique
Actuelle
*(distributed by DADCI, 41 rue de
la Chine, 75020 Paris)*

Saint-Germain des Prés
70 rue du Cherché Midi
75006 Paris

Editions Saint-Paul
(Les Classiques Africains)
184 ave. de Verdun
92130 Issy-les-Moulineaux

Seghers
31 rue Falguière
75725 Paris

S.E.L.A.F.
5 rue de Marseille
75010 Paris

Editions du Seuil
27 rue Jacob
75261 Paris Cedex 06

Editions Silex
56 bis rue du Louvre
75002 Paris

Stock
14 rue de l'Ancienne-Comédie
75675 Paris Cedex 14

Union Générale d'Editions
8 rue Garancière
75006 Paris

Germany (Democratic Republic)

Seven Seas Publishers
Glinkastrasse 13–15
108 Berlin

Germany (Federal Republic)

Ausstellungs- und Messe
GmbH des Börsenvereins
des Deutschen Buchhandels
Kleiner Hirschgraben 10–12
6000 Frankfurt am Main

Moritz Diesterweg Verlag
Hochstrasse 31
6000 Frankfurt am Main

Horst Erdmann Verlag für
Internationalen
Kulturaustausch GmbH
Hartmeyerstrasse 117
Postfach 1388
7400 Tübingen 1

Joseph Habbel Verlag
Postfach 339
8400 Regensburg 11

Otto Harrassowitz
Taunusstrasse 6
Postfach 2929
6200 Wiesbaden

B. Heymann Verlag
Bertramstrasse 21
Postfach 3065
6200 Wiesbaden

Institut für
  Auslandsbeziehungen
Charlottenplatz 17
D–7000 Stuttgart 1

Gunter Narr Verlag
Staufenbergerstrasse 42
Postfach 2567
7400 Tübingen 1

K. G. Saur Verlag
Postfach 71 10 09
8000 Munich 71

Schwiftinger Galerie-Verlag
Kirchberg 9
8911 Schwifting

Hungary

Afro-Asian Research Centre
Academy of Sciences/
  Akadémiai Kiadó
Alkotmány u 21
1054 Budapest

Kultura
PO Box 149
1389 Budapest

Liechtenstein

Kraus-Thomson Organization
  Ltd
Nendeln

Malta

Malta University Press
Valletta

Monaco

Edition Paul Bory
5 rue de la Poste
BP 313
Monte Carlo

Editions Regain
Palais Miami
10 blvd. d'Italie
Monte Carlo

Netherlands

Afrika-Studiecentrum
Stationsplein 10
Postbus 9507
Leiden

E. J. Brill N.V.
Oude Rijn 33a
Leiden

Mouton Publishers
Noordeinde 41
PO Box 290
2514 The Hague

Portugal

Agência-Geral do Ultramar
Praça do Comercio
Lisbon

S. da Costa
Rua Garrett 102
Lisbon

Edições 70 Lda.
Av. Duque d'Avila 69 r/c Esq.
Lisbon 1000

Edições Afrontamento
Rua Costa Cabral 859
Apdo. 532
Oporto

Editora Arcádia
Campo de Santa Clara 160
Lisbon 2

Editora Pax
Rua do Souto 75
Braga

Eduardo Fernandes
Ave. Marquẽs de Tomar 68
Lisbon 1

Instituto de Cultura
  Portuguesa
Rua Jau 54
Lisbon 1

Livraria Portugal
Rua da Carmo 70–74
Lisbon

Plántano Editora
Av. de Berna 31–2
Lisbon 1

Sweden

Almqvist and Wiksell Förlag
  AB
Brunnsgrand 4
PO Box 2120
103 13 Stockholm

Switzerland

World Council of Churches
Publications Division
150 Route de Ferney
1218 Geneva

Payot
4 Place Pepinet
1002 Lausanne

NORTH AMERICA

United States

African and Afro-American
  Research Institute
University of Texas
Austin Tx. 78712

African Studies Association
255 Kinsey Hall
University of California
405 Hilgard Avenue
Los Angeles Ca. 90024
see also Crossroads Press

African Studies Center
Indiana University
Bloomington In. 47401

African Studies Center
University of California
405 Hilgard
10244 Bunche Hall
Los Angeles Ca. 90024

African Studies Program
University of Wisconsin
1450 van Hise Hall
Madison Wi. 53706

Africana Publishing Co.
Division of Holmes & Meier
  Publishers Inc.
IUB Building
30 Irving Place
New York NY 10003

American Council on the
  Teaching of Foreign
  Languages
2 Park Avenue
New York NY 10016

Anchor Books
see Doubleday

Archon Books
995 Sherman Avenue
Hamden Ct. 06514

Ardis Publishers
2901 Heatherway Drive
Ann Arbor Mi. 48104

Atheneum Publishers
122 East 42nd Street
New York NY 10017

Bantam Books Inc.
666 Fifth Avenue
New York NY 10019

Barrons Educational Series
Inc.
113 Crossways Park Drive
Woodbury NY 11797

Black Academy Press Inc.
3296 Main Street
Buffalo NY 14214

Black Orpheus Press
322 New Mark Esplanade
Rockville Md. 20850

Boston College
116 McElroy
Chestnut Hill Ma. 02167

George Braziller Inc.
1 Park Avenue
New York NY 10016

Broadside Press Publications
74 Glendale Avenue
Highland Park Mi. 48203

Cambridge University Press
32 East 57th Street
New York NY 10022

Frank Cass & Co.
c/o Biblio Distribution Centre
81 Adams Drive
Totowa NJ 07512

Collier-Macmillan
see Macmillan Publishers

Columbia University Press
562 West 113th Street
New York NY 10025

Conch Magazine Ltd
102 Normal Avenue
Symphony Circle
Buffalo NY 14213

Crossroads Press
African Studies Association
255 Kinsey Hall
University of California
405 Hilgard Avenue
Los Angeles Ca. 90024

Thomas Y. Crowell Company
10 East 53rd Street
New York NY 10022

Crown Publishers Inc.
1 Park Avenue
New York NY 10016

John Day Company Inc.
666 Fifth Avenue
New York NY 10019

Department of Anthropology
University of Delaware
Newark De. 19711

Dodd, Mead & Co.
79 Madison Avenue
New York NY 10016

Doubleday & Co. Inc.
245 Park Avenue
New York NY 10017

Duke University Press
PO Box 6697
College Station
Durham NC 27708

E. P. Dutton & Elsevier Book
Operations
2 Park Avenue
New York NY 10016

The Eakins Press Foundation
155 East 42nd Street
New York NY 10017

Exposition Press Inc.
PO Box 2120
Smithtown NY 11787

Faber & Faber Publishers
99 Main Street
Salem NH 03079

Samuel French Inc.
25 West 45th Street
New York NY 10036

Friendship Press
c/o National Council of
Churches
475 Riverside Drive
New York NY 10027

Gale Research Co.
Book Tower
Detroit Mi. 48226

Georgia State University Press
University Plaza
Atlanta Ga. 30303

Ginn & Co.
191 Spring Street
Boston Ma. 02173

Greenfield Review Press
Greenfield Center NY 12833

Greenwood Press
88 Post Road West
Westport Ct. 06881

Grossman Publishers Inc.
625 Madison Avenue
New York NY 10022

Grove Press Inc.
196 West Houston Street
New York NY 10014

Guild of Tutors Press of
International College
Suite 105
1019 Gayley Avenue
Los Angeles Ca. 90024

G. K. Hall & Co.
70 Lincoln Street
Boston Ma. 02111

The HaPi Press
512 SW Maplecrest Drive
Portland Or. 97219

Harcourt Brace Jovanovich
Inc.
757 Third Avenue
New York NY 10017

Harper & Row Publishers Inc.
10 East 53rd Street
New York NY 10022

Harvard University Press
79 Garden Street
Cambridge Ma. 02138

Heinemann Educational
Books Inc.
4 Front Street
Exeter NH 03833

Hennessey and Ingalls
11833 Wilshire Boulevard
Los Angeles Ca. 90025

Hill & Wang
19 West Union Square
New York NY 10003

Lawrence Hill & Co.
24 Burr Farms Road
Westport Ct. 06880

Holmes & Meier Publishers
Inc.
IUB Building
30 Irving Place
New York NY 10003
see also Africana Publishing Co.

Hoover Institution Press
Stanford University
Stanford Ca. 94305

Houghton Mifflin Company
1 Beacon Street
Boston Ma. 02107

Howard University Press
2900 van Ness Street NW
Washington DC 20008

Indiana University Press
10th and Morton Streets
Bloomington In. 47405

Indiana State University Press
120 North Seventh Street
Terre Haute In. 47809

Inscape
2424 Gough Street
San Francisco Ca. 94123

Interculture Associates
PO Box 277
Thompson Ct. 08277

International
  Communications Agency
African Division
Washington DC 20547

Johnston Publishing Corp.
386 South Park Avenue
New York NY 10016

Judson Press
Valley Forge Pa. 19481

Alfred A. Knopf Inc.
201 East 50th Street
New York NY 10022

Lexington Books/D. C. Heath
  & Co.
125 Spring Street
Lexington Ma. 02173

Library of Congress
Africa and Middle Eastern
  Division
Washington DC 20540

Little, Brown & Co.
34 Beacon Street
Boston Ma. 02106

Longman Inc.
19 West 44th Street
New York NY 10036

Louisiana State University
  Press
Baton Rouge Lo. 70803

Macmillan Publishing Co.
  Inc.
866 Third Avenue
New York NY 10022

Manyland Books
84-39 90 Street
Woodhaven NY 11421

Maxwell School of Citizenship
  and Public Affairs
Syracuse University
119 College Place
Syracuse NY 13210

Julian Messner
1230 Avenue of the Americas
New York NY 10020

Modern Language Association
  of America
62 Fifth Avenue
New York NY 10011

Monarch Press
1230 Avenue of the Americas
New York NY 10020

Montclair State College Press
Upper Montclair NJ 07043

Munger Africana Library
California Institute of
  Technology
Pasadena Ca. 91109

Negro Universities Press
51 Riverside Avenue
Westport Ct. 06880

Thomas Nelson Inc.
405 Seventh Avenue
South Nashville Tn. 37203

The New American Library
  Inc.
1301 Avenue of the Americas
New York NY 10019

Nok Publishers International
150 Fifth Avenue
New York NY 10011

Northwestern University Press
1735 Benson Avenue
Evanston Il. 60201

October House
PO Box 454
Stonington Ct. 06378

Odyssey Press
c/o Bobbs-Merrill Company
  Inc.
4300 West 62nd Street
Indianapolis In. 46268

Ohio University Center for
  International Studies
Africa Program
Athens Oh. 45701

Ohio University Press
Scott Quad
Athens Oh. 45701

Orbis Books
Maryknoll NY 10545

Oxford University Press Inc.
200 Madison Avenue
New York NY 10016

Pantheon Books Inc.
201 East 50th Street
New York NY 10022

Penguin Books
625 Madison Avenue
New York NY 10022

Pennsylvania State University
  Libraries
University Park Pa. 16802

Pennsylvania State University
  Press
215 Wagner Buildings
University Park Pa. 16802

Pergamon Press Inc.
Maxwell House
Fairview Park
Elmsford NY 10523

Philosophical Library Inc.
15 East 40th Street
New York NY 10016

Praeger Publishers Inc.
383 Madison Avenue
New York NY 10017

Prentice-Hall Inc.
Englewood Cliffs NJ 07632

Press of the Langdon
  Associates Inc.
41 Langdon Street
Cambridge Ma. 02138

Princeton University Press
Box AAAA
Princeton NJ 08540

Random House Inc.
201 East 50th Street
New York NY 10022

Routledge & Kegan Paul of
  America
9 Park Street
Boston Ma. 02108

St. Martin's Press Inc.
175 Fifth Avenue
New York NY 10010

Scarecrow Press
52 Liberty Street
PO Box 656
Metuchen NJ 08840

Schocken Books Inc.
200 Madison Avenue
New York NY 10016

Scott, Foresman & Co.
1900 East Lake Avenue
Glenview Il. 60025

Charles Scribner's Sons
  Publishers
597 Fifth Avenue
New York NY 10028

Seton-Hall University Press
Room 213
Humanities Building
South Orange NJ 07079

Simon & Schuster Inc.
1230 Avenue of the Americas
New York NY 10020

Peter Smith
6 Lexington Avenue
Magnolia Ma. 01930

Stanford University Press
Stanford Ca. 94305

Temple University Press
Philadelphia Pa. 19122

The Third Press
Joseph Okpaku Publishing
Co. Inc.
444 Central Park
New York NY 10025

Third World Press
7524 Cottage Grove Avenue
Chicago Il. 60019

Three Continents Press
Suite 224
1346 NW Connecticut Avenue
Washington DC 20036

Troubadour Press
PO Box 14012
Austin Tx. 78761

Twayne Publishers
A Division of G. K. Hall & Co.
70 Lincoln Street
Boston Ma. 02111

Frederick Ungar Publishing
Co. Inc.
250 South Park Avenue
New York NY 10003

University of California Press
2223 Fulton Street
Berkeley Ca. 94720

The University of Chicago
Press
5801 South Ellis Avenue
Chicago Il. 60637

University of Minnesota Press
2037 SE University Avenue
Minneapolis Mn. 55455

University of Texas Press
PO Box 7819
Austin Tx. 78712

University of Washington
Press
Seattle Wa. 98105

University of Wisconsin Press
114 N. Murray Street
Madison Wi. 53715

University Press of America
PO Box 19101
Washington DC 20036

University Presses of Florida
15 NW 15th Street
Gainesville Fl. 32603

Vantage Press Inc.
516 West 34th Street
New York NY 10001

The Viking Press
625 Madison Avenue
New York NY 10022

Voice of America
United States International
Communications Agency
Washington DC 20547

Walker & Co.
720 Fifth Avenue
New York NY 10019

Washington Square Press
1230 Avenue of the Americas
New York NY 10020

Westview Press
5500 Central Avenue
Boulder Co. 80301

Yale University Press
92A Yale Station
New Haven Ct. 06520

Canada

Academic Press Canada Ltd
55 Barber Greene Road
Don Mills
Ontario M3C 2A1
(distributes Longman list in Canada)

Beauchemin Ltée
450 Avenue Beaumont
Montréal H3N 1T8

Book Society of Canada Ltd
4386 Sheppard Avenue East
PO Box 200
Agincourt
Ontario M1S 3B6
(distributes Heinemann list in Canada)

Editions Naaman
CP 697
Sherbrooke
Quebec J1H 5K5

Press Porcépic
70 Main Street
Erin N0B 1T0

Oxford University Press Canadian Branch
70 Wynford Drive
Don Mills
Toronto
Ontario M3C 1J9

Faculté des Arts
Université de Sherbrooke
Sherbrooke J1K 2R1

OTHER COUNTRIES (OUTSIDE AFRICA)

Brazil

Editora Atica
Rue Barao do Iguape 110
Liberdale
01507 São Paulo

India

Minerva Publishing House
24 Halls Road
Egmore
Madras 600 008

Lebanon

Longman/Penguin Arab
World Centre
PO Box 945
Beirut

AFRICA

Angola

Edições Maiaka
CP 1293
Luanda

Instituto Nacional do Livro e
do Disco
Rua Vereador Castelo
Branco 7
CP 1281
Luanda

Lello & Cia. Lda.
CP 1245
Luanda

União dos Ecritores
Angolanos
CP 1281
Luanda

Benin

Editions A.B.M.
BP 889
Cotonou

Botswana

Botswana Book Centre
The Mall
PO Box 91
Gaborone

Cameroun

Association des Poètes et
  Ecrivains Camerounais
  (APEC)
BP 2180
Yaoundé

C.E.P.E.R.
BP 808
Yaoundé

College Libermann
Centre Culturel
BP 5351
Douala-Akwa

Editions CLE
BP 1501
Yaoundé

Editions Le Flambeau
BP 113
Yaoundé

Editions Semences Africaines
BP 2180
Yaoundé

Imprimerie Nationale du
  Gouvernement
BP 1091
Yaoundé

Imprimerie Saint-Paul
BP 763
Yaoundé

Buma Kor & Co. Publishers
BP 727
Mvog-Ada
Yaoundé

Librairie Populaire
  Baffoussam
BP 322
Baffoussam

Université de Yaoundé
BP 1312
Yaoundé

Congo Popular Republic

Editions Héros dans l'Ombre
BP 1678
Brazzaville

Gabon

Editions Multipress
BP 3875
Libreville

Institut Pédagogique National
BP 813
Libreville

The Gambia

Oral History & Antiquities
  Division
c/o President's Office
Old National Library
Independence Drive
Banjul

Ghana

Afram Publications (Ghana)
  Ltd
Ring Road East
PO Box M18
Accra

Anowuo Educational
  Publications
2R McCarthy Hill
PO Box 3918
Accra
(*ceased trading?*)

Benibengor Book Agency
PO Box 40
Aboso

Catholic Mission Press
PO Box 60
Cape Coast

Department of Library and
  Archival Studies
University of Ghana
Legon

Educational Press &
  Manufacturers Ltd
PO Box 9184
Airport
Accra

Ghana Publishing
  Corporation,
Publishing Division
Private Post Bag
Tema

Presbyterian Book Depot Ltd
PO Box 195
Accra

Sedco Publishing Co.
PO Box 2051
Accra
(*distributor of Longman
  publications in Ghana*)

University of Ghana
  Bookshop
PO Box 1
Legon

Waterville Publishing House
PO Box 195
Accra

Guinea-Bissau

Imprensa Nacional
Bolama

Ivory Coast

Editions CEDA
BP 541
Abidjan 04

Institut Africain pour le
  Développment Economique
  et Social (INADES)
BP 8008
Abidjan

Nouvelles Editions Africaines
BP 20615
Abidjan

Université d'Abidjan
Secrétariat Général aux
  Publications
01 BP V34
Abidjan 01

Kenya

Africa Book Services (East
  Africa) Ltd
PO Box 45245
Nairobi

Books for Africa Ltd
see Macmillan Kenya Publishers

Comb Books Ltd
PO Box 20019
Nairobi
see also David Maillu Publishers

East African Literature Bureau
(*ceased operations; order from
  Kenya Literature Bureau,
  PO Box 30022, Nairobi*)

East African Publishing House
PO Box 30571
Nairobi

Eleza Services Ltd
PO Box 14925
Nairobi

Equatorial Publishers Ltd
Rooms 11–12 Mercury House
Victoria Street
PO Box 7973
Nairobi
(*ceased trading?*)

Heinemann Educational
  Books (East Africa) Ltd
PO Box 45314
Nairobi

Joe Magazine Ltd
PO Box 30362
Nairobi

Kenya Literature Bureau
PO Box 30022
Nairobi

Longman Kenya Ltd
PO Box 18033
Nairobi

Macmillan Kenya (Publishers)
  Ltd
PO Box 30797
Nairobi

David Maillu Publishers
PO Box 1300
Machakos

Thomas Nelson & Sons Ltd
PO Box 18123
Nairobi

Njogu Gitene Publications
PO Box 73989
Nairobi

Oxford University Press
Eastern African Branch
PO Box 72532
Nairobi

Textbook Centre Ltd
PO Box 47540
Nairobi

Transafrica Book Distributors
  Ltd
PO Box 42990
Nairobi
*(formerly Transafrica Book
  Publishers)*

Uzima Press
PO Box 48127
Nairobi

Lesotho

Lesotho Printing and
  Publishing Co.
PO Box 1345
Maseru 100

Liberia

Liberian Literary and
  Educational Publications
PO Box 2387
Monrovia

Madagascar

Editions Madprint
BP 953
Antsakaviro
Antananarivo

Imprimerie Nationale
BP 38
Antananarivo

Office du Livre Malagasy
BP 617
Antananarivo

Malawi

Dzuka Publishing Co. Ltd
Private Bag 39
˙Blantyre
*(distributor of Longman
  publications in Malawi)*

Popular Publications
PO Box 5592
Limbe

University of Malawi Library
PO Box 280
Zomba

Mali

Editions Populaires du Mali
BP 21
Bamako

Mauritius

Editions Croix de Sud
1 Barracks Street
Port Louis

Editions de l'Océan Indien
Mahatma Gandhi Institute
Moka

Dawn Printing Co.
39 Emmanuel Anquetil Street
Port Louis

Henry & Cie.
Les Pailles

Mauritius Printing Co. Ltd
PO Box 303
Port Louis

Regent Press
6 Chaussée
Port Louis

Standard Printing
  Establishment Ltd
Mallefille Street
Port Louis

Mozambique

Instituto Nacional do Livro e
  do Disco
CP 4030
Maputo

Niger

Centre for Linguistic and
  Historical Studies by Oral
  Tradition
BP 78
Niamey

Nigeria

African Designs Development
  Centre Ltd
PMB 5162
Ibadan, Oyo State

African Universities Press
see Pilgrim Books

Africana Educational
  Publishers (Nigeria) Ltd
PO Box 1639
Onitsha, Anambra State

Ahmadu Bello University
  Press
PMB 1094
Zaria, Kaduna State

Aromolaran Publishers
PO Box 1800
Ibadan, Oyo State

Ariya Productions
PO Box 318
Abule Ijesha
Yaba, Lagos State

Bendel State Newspapers
  Corporation
18 Airport Road
PMB 1334
Benin City, Bendel State

Black Academy Press
PO Box 255
Owerri, Imo State

Conch Magazine Publishers
  Ltd
113 Douglas Road
Owerri, Imo State

Cross Continents Press Ltd
PO Box 282
Yaba, Lagos State

Daystar Press (Publishers)
PO Box 1261
Ibadan, Oyo State

Delta Publications (Nigeria)
Ltd
PO Box 1172
Enugu, Anambra State

Department of African
Languages and Literatures
University of Ife
Ile-Ife, Ondo State

Deto-Deni Educational
Productions
PO Box 7317
Ibadan, Oyo State

Design Productions (Nigeria)
Ltd
PO Box 499
Yaba, Lagos State

Di Nigro Press
see Third World First Publications

Ethiope Publishing House
PMB 1332
Benin City, Bendel State

Evans Brothers (Nigeria) Ltd
PO Box 47610
Ibadan, Oyo State

Olaiya Fagbamigbe Publishers
PO Box 14
Akure, Ondo State

Fourth Dimension Publishing
Co.
PO Box 553
Enugu, Anambra State

Heinemann Educational
Books (Nigeria) Ltd
PMB 5205
Ibadan, Oyo State

Ibadan University Press
University of Ibadan
Ibadan, Oyo State

Institute of African Studies
University of Ibadan
Ibadan, Oyo State

Longman Nigeria Ltd
Private Mail Bag 1036
Ikeja, Lagos State

Macmillan Nigeria Publishers
Ltd
PO Box 1463
Ibadan, Oyo State

Mbari Publications
Ibadan, Oyo State
(no longer trading)

Ministry of Education
Publications section
Ibadan, Oyo State

Thomas Nelson (Nigeria) Ltd
Nelson House
8 Ilupeju Bye-Pass
PMB 21303
Ikeja, Lagos State

Natona Press
PO Box 423
Ijebu-Ode, Ondo State

New Culture Studios
*see African Designs Development
Centre Ltd*

New Horn Press Ltd
PO Box 4138
Ibadan, Oyo State

Nigeria Magazine Special
Publications
Department of Culture
Federal Ministry of Social
Development, Youth, Sports
and Culture
PMB 12524
Lagos, Lagos State

Nok Publishers International
PO Box 1005
Enugu, Anambra State
(also in New York)

Northern Nigerian Publishing
Co. Ltd
PO Box 412
Zaria, Kaduna State

Nwamife Publishers Ltd
PO Box 430
Enugu, Anambra State

Flora Nwapa Co.
see Tana Press Ltd

Obobo Books
PO Box 610
Apapa, Lagos State

Omoleye Publishing Co.
PO Box 1265
Ibadan, Oyo State

Onibonoje Press & Book
Industries (Nigeria) Ltd
PO Box 3109
Ibadan, Oyo State

Oxford University Press
Nigeria
see University Press Ltd

Pilgrim Books Ltd
PO Box 3560
Lagos, Lagos State
*(includes the imprint African
Universities Press)*

Scholars Press (Nigeria) Ltd
109 Mayne Avenue
Calabar, Rivers State

Tana Press Ltd
2a Menkiti lane
Enugu, Anambra State

Third World First
Publications
PO Box 610
Apapa, Lagos State
(formerly di Nigro Press)

University of Ife Press
Ile-Ife, Oyo State

University of Lagos Press
PO Box 132
University of Lagos Post
Office
Yaba, Lagos State

University of Nigeria Library
Nsukka, Anambra State

University Press Ltd
Oxford House
Iddo Gate
PMB 5095
Ibadan, Oyo State
*(formerly Oxford University Press
Nigerian branch)*

University Publishing Co.
PO Box 386
Onitsha, Anambra State

West African Book Publishers
Ltd
PO Box 3445
Lagos, Lagos State

Réunion

Bibliothèque Universitaire de
la Réunion
Sainte-Denis 97400

Editions Chemin de la Liberté
Sainte-Clotilde

Nouvelle Imprimerie
Dionysienne
BP 168
Saint-Denis

Rwanda

Editions Universitaires du
Rwanda
BP 54
Butare

Institut National de Recherche
Scientifique
BP 218
Butare

Senegal

Club Afrique Loisirs
see Nouvelles Editions Africaines

Centre d'Etudes des
  Civilisations
c/o Ministère de la Culture
Dakar

Editions Muntu
130 rue Blanchot
Dakar

Institut Culturel Africain
BP 01
Dakar

Institut Fondamental
  d'Afrique Noire
Université de Dakar
BP 206
Dakar

Les Nouvelles Editions
  Africaines
10 rue Assane Ndoye
BP 260
Dakar
*(also at BP 3525 Abidjan 01,
  Ivory Coast, and at BP 4862,
  Lomé, Togo)*

Sierra Leone

Fourah Bay College Bookshop
  Ltd
University of Sierra Leone
Freetown

South Africa

A. A. Balkema (Pty) Ltd
PO Box 3117
Cape Town 8000

Blac Publishing House
PO Box 17
Athlone
Cape

Department of African
  Languages
Rhodes University
PO Box 184
Grahamstown 6140

Department of Bibliography,
  Librarianship and
  Typography
University of the
  Witwatersrand
Jan Smuts Avenue
Johannesburg 2001

Ad Donker (Pty) Ltd
PO Box 41021
Craighall 2024

Drum Publications
62 Eloff Street Extension
Johannesburg 2000

Heinemann Educational
  Books
PO Box 61581
Marshalltown 2107

Knox Printing Co. (Pty) Ltd
4 MacDonland Road
Durban 4001

Longman/Penguin Southern
  Africa (Pty) Ltd
PO Box 1616
Cape Town 8000

Lovedale Press
PO Box
Lovedale 5702

Macmillan South Africa
PO Box 31487
Braamfontein 2017

Maskew Miller Ltd
PO Box 396
Cape Town 8000

Nasou Ltd
386 Vortrekker Road
PO Box 105
Parow 7500

Oxford University Press
Southern African Branch
PO Box 1141
Cape Town 8000

David Philip Publisher (Pty)
  Ltd
PO Box 408
Claremont
Cape Town 7735

Quagga Press Ltd
PO Box 86
Crown Mines 2025

Ravan Press (Pty) Ltd
PO Box 31134
Braamfontein 2017

Renoster Books
Johannesburg
(no longer trading)

Shuter & Shooter (Pty) Ltd
PO Box 109
Pietermaritzburg 3200

Spro-Cas Publications
see Ravan Press

University of Cape Town
  Library
Private Bag
Rondebosch 7700

University of Natal Press
PO Box 375
Pietermaritzburg 3200

University of South Africa
  Publishing Division
PO Box 392
Pretoria 0007

Witwatersrand University
  Press
1 Jan Smuts Avenue
2001 Johannesburg

Sudan

Khartoum University Press
PO Box 321
Khartoum

Swaziland

Macmillan Boleswa (Pty) Ltd
PO Box A 240
Swazi Plaza
Mbabane

Tanzania

Eastern African Publications
  Ltd
PO Box 1002
Arusha

Longman Tanzania
PO Box 3164
Dar es Salaam

Tanzania Mission Press
PO Box 399
Tabora

Tanzania Publishing House
PO Box 2138
Dar es Salaam

Togo

Editions Akpagnon
BP 3531
Lomé
see also under France

Editions Editogo
BP 891
Lomé

Ministère de la Culture
BP 40
Lomé

Uganda

Longman Uganda Ltd
PO Box 3409
Kampala

Uganda Publishing House
PO Box 2923
Kampala

Zaire Republic

Centre Africaine de
  Littérature pour l'Afrique
  francophone
c/o CEDI
BP 11398
Kinshasa 1

Centre d'Etudes des
  Littératures Romanes
  d'Inspiration Africaine
  (CELRIA)
Université Nationale du Zaire
Campus de Lubumbashi
BP 2896
Lubumbashi

Editions Alpha-Omega
BP 3278
Lubumbashi

Editions Bobiso
BP 1682
Kinshasa 1

Editions Dombi Diffusion
BP 3498
Kinshasa-Kalina

Editions de Kisantu
BP 3498
Kinshasa-Kalina

Editions de la Grue
  Couronnée
BP 3986
Kinshasa-Gombe

Editions du Mont Noir
BP 1944
Lubumbashi

Editions Edimaf
BP 16367
Kinshasa 1

Editions Lokole
Département de
  l'Information,
  Culture et Arts
Kinshasa-Gombe

Editions Mandore
BP 1607
Lubumbashi

Editions Ngoni
BP 858
Kinshasa-Limete

Editions Tigres Noirs
c/o L'Etincelle
BP 14946
Kinshasa 1

Les Presses Africaines
BP 12924
Kinshasa 1

Presses Universitaires du Zaire
BP 1682
Kinshasa 1

Zambia

National Educational Co. of
  Zambia (NECZAM)
PO Box 32664
Lusaka

Temco Publishing Ltd
PO Box 886
Lusaka
*(distributor of Longman
  publications in Zambia)*

Zambia Cultural Services
PO Box RW 335
Lusaka

Zimbabwe

The College Press (Pvt) Ltd
PO Box 3041
Harare

Gazebo Books Ltd
PO Box UA 544
Harare

The Literature Bureau
Ministry of Education
PO Box 8137
Causeway
Harare

Longman (Pvt) Ltd
PO Box ST 125
Southerton
Harare

Macmillan Publishers
PO Box 102
Union Avenue
Harare

Mambo Press
PO Box 779
Gwero

Poetry Society of Zimbabwe
PO Box A70
Avondale
Harare

Zimbabwe Publishing House
PO Box BW 350
Harare

A directory of libraries with African literature collections

This directory provides information on libraries in Europe, the United States, and in Canada, which hold sizeable collections on African literature. We have not included libraries in Africa, as most university and national libraries on the continent have substantial collections of African creative writing – in Nigeria, for example, there are particularly fine collections at the universities of Ibadan, Ife, and Benin.

Information for this section was collected by means of a questionnaire, which was sent to just over a hundred libraries. About 75 per cent responded and completed the questionnaires. A number of others replied to say that the size of their African literature sections were too small to warrant inclusion in the *Guide*.

Arrangement is alphabetical by country, and by town within countries (by state for the US). Information given includes the full name and address; telephone (and telex) number; name of the chief librarian; name of the person in charge of the African collection (if different from chief librarian); hours; conditions of access to and use of the library; loan and reference, and photocopying facilities; size of book and serials collections; special features of the collection; and publications (of relevance).

Details provided under *special features* may not necessarily pertain to African literature holdings, but we have included such additional details, or guidelines, if we felt the information provided was of interest to a potential user of the library.

With regard to details given of *book collections*, it should be noted that many libraries were unable to provide exact numbers or an actual shelf count. Therefore in many cases the figure indicated is that of *total* Africana holdings. This similarly applies to the *serials collections*. However, we have asked librarians to indicate, from a list of 60 titles (with some libraries adding extra titles), which journals were currently taken, and of which they held complete, or near-complete, runs. The list covers basic bibliographic tools and literary and cultural magazines (but *not* general Africanist periodicals), although a number of them have ceased publication or have been dormant for some time now. Some of the serials are given in abbreviated form, and a key to their full names appears below. More details about these periodicals (their ordering addresses, frequency, subscription rates, etc.) may also be found in the 'Magazines' section on page 326.

We hope to expand this section in future editions of the *Guide*, and we should be pleased to hear from libraries, omitted from the present list, who have significant collections of African creative writing.

Key to journals listed in abbreviated form:

ABPR	African Book Publishing Record	BH	The Bloody Horse
		BO	Black Orpheus
ACLALS Bulletin	Association for Commonwealth Literature and Language Studies Bulletin	CBAA	Current Bibliography on African Affairs
		CRNLE	Centre for Research in the New Literatures in English Reviews Journal
AfrA	African Arts		
AfrLJ	Africana Journal [formerly Africana Library Journal]	CulEA	Cultural Events in Africa
		Ecr franc	Ecriture française
ALA	L'Afrique Littéraire et Artistique	JCL	Journal of Commonwealth Literature
ALAC	Africa. Literatura, Arte e Cultura	JNALA	Journal of the New African Literatures and the Arts
ALA Newsletter	African Literature Association Newsletter	LAAW	Lotus: Afro-Asian Writings
ALT	African Literature Today		

NSAL	Nsukka Studies in African	SBL	Studies in Black Literature
	Literature	TT	Two Tone
PA	Présence Africaine	WAJML	West African Journal of
PFr	Présence Francophone		Modern Languages
PNPA	Peuples Noirs/Peuples	WLT	World Literature Today
	Africains		[formerly Books Abroad]
RAL	Research in African	WLWE	World Literature Written
	Literatures		in English
RLEN	Revue de Littérature et		
	d'Esthétique Négro-		
	Africaines		

AUSTRIA

Bibliothek
Institut für Afrikanistik der Universität Wien
Doblhoffgasse 5/9
A-1010 Wien
Tel: 0222-42-22-73
Chief Librarians: Walter Schicho and Erich
Sommerauer
Person in charge of African collection: Annie
Ogidan
Hours: Monday–Friday 09.30–19.00
Access: Open to the public.
Loan and reference facilities: Available.
Book collection: 800 volumes.
Special features:
The Library, officially part of the University
Library, is attached to the Institute of African
Studies which was established in 1978. A large
number of books in the African collection
which belong to the University Library are
housed at the Institute. The collection includes
literature written in African languages.
Serials collection: 13 titles.
APBR, AfrLJ, ALA, ALT, Conch, JCL,
Kiswahili, Mulika, Okike, PA, RAL, WAJML.
Publications:
Where they speak English in Africa (1981)

BELGIUM

Bibliothèque Générale
Université de Liège
Place Cockerill 1
B-4000 Liège
Tel: 041-420080
Chief Librarian: Paul Gorêt
Hours: 09.00–17.00
Access: Open to the public.
Loan and reference facilities: Available.
Book collection: 2,000 volumes (Africana total)
Special features:
The Library is strong on African fiction, but
the collection is not maintained separately.
Serials collection: 10 titles.
AfrA, ALA, ALAC, ALT, Annales des facultés

de Lettres des Universités de Côte d'Ivoire,
Dakar, et Madagascar, CulEA, Ecrivain Afri-
cain, JNALA, PA, PFr.
Photocopying facilities available.

CANADA

York University Libraries
4700 Keele Street
Downsview
Ontario M3J 1P3
Tel: 416-667-3428   *Telex:* 065-24736
Chief Librarian: Anne Woodsworth
Hours: Monday–Friday 08.45–24.00
            Saturday 10.00–18.00
            Sunday 13.00–24.00
Access: Open to the public.
Loan and reference facilities: Both are available,
but borrowing is permitted only after the
purchase of an extra-mural reader's card
available at $25.00 annually. Books may also
be borrowed through inter-library loan.
Book collection: 1,312 volumes.
Special features:
The bulk of the collection consists of literature
in French or English.
Serials collection: 55 titles.
Abbia, ABPR, AfrA, Afriscope, AfrLJ, ALA,
ALT, Ba Shiru, BO, CBAA, Ch'Indaba,
Conch, CRNLE, Dhana, Ecr franc, Ethiopi-
ques, Greenfield Review, JCL, JNALA, LAAW,
Mawazo, New Classic, New Coin, Odi, Okike,
Ophir, PA, PFr, RAL, SBL, Umma, WAJML,
WLT.
Photocopying facilities available.

Bibliothèque des Sciences Humaines et
Sociales
Université de Montréal
C.P. 6202 Succ. A
Montréal H3C 3T2
Tel: 343-7240
Chief Librarian: Richard Greene
Hours: Monday–Thursday 09.00–23.00
            Friday 09.00–19.00
            Saturday 11.00–17.00
            Sunday 13.00–17.00

Access: Open to students, lecturers and members of the public.
Loan and reference facilities: Available.
Book collection: 400 volumes.
Serials collection: 8 titles.
Abbia, ABPR, AfrA, AfrLJ, ALA, CBAA, Ethiopiques, JCL, PA, PFr, RAL, WLT, WLWE.
Photocopying facilities available.
Publications:
Mini-Guide Debroussailleur no. 21 – Afrique Noire

McLennan Library
McGill University
3459 McTavish Street
Montreal H3A 1Y1
Tel: 514-392-4943
Chief Librarian: Marianne Scott
Hours: 09.00–21.00 (Subject to slight seasonal variations).
Access: Open to faculty and university students, and members of the public wishing to carry out research.
Loan and reference facilities: Reference only, but books may be loaned on an inter-library basis.
Book collection: 1,650 volumes.
Special features:
African literature is not housed as a separate collection. There is a strong reference collection.
Serials collection: 20 titles.
ABPR, AfrA, Afriscope, AfrLJ, ALA, ALT, BO, Busara, CBAA, Conch, CulEA, JCL, Mawazo, Okike, PA, PFr, RAL, SBL, WLT, WLWE, Zambezia.
Photocopying facilities available.
Publications:
African Literature: guide to reference resources (1977)
Africa South of the Sahara: guide to reference resources (1981)

DENMARK

Aarhus University
Department of English
The Library
Bygning 325
DK-8000 Aarhus C
Tel: 06-13-67-11
Head of English Department: Dr. Anna Rutherford
Access: Open to students and members of staff of the University only.
Loan and reference facilities: Members of the public may borrow books by means of the inter-library loan through the State Library.
Book collection: Exact size unknown.
Serials collection: 13 titles.

ACLALS Bulletin, ALT, CRNLE, JCL, Kiabara, Kunapipi, NSAL, Okike, RAL, WLT, WLWE, Zuka.
Photocopying facilities available.
Publications:
'Monographs on Commonwealth Literature'
Kunapipi. Bulletin for the European branch of the Association of Commonwealth Literature and Language Studies. (Aarhus: Dangaroo Press)

Statsbiblioteket
Universitetsparken
DK-8000 Aarhus C
Tel: 06-12-20-22   *Telex:* 64515 STABIB DK
Chief Librarian: Karl V. Thomsen
Persons in charge of African collection: Judith Lund (African history and culture), and Vibeke Stenderup (Commonwealth literature)
Hours:
Reading room: Monday–Friday 09.00–19.00
                        Saturday 09.00–14.00
Lending dept.:   09.00–15.30
                        (not Saturday)
Access: Open to the public.
Loan and reference facilities: Both are available and any book which the State Library does not hold may be procured from Danish or foreign libraries through the Danish National Loan Centre in Copenhagen.
Book collection: Exact size unknown.
Special features:
The collection is substantial, though not maintained separately. Together with the English Department Library, the State Library has the most comprehensive collection of Commonwealth literature in Europe outside the UK. As a copyright deposit library, the State Library receives a large number of nationally published African works.
Serials collection: 18 titles.
AfrLJ, ALT, BO, CBAA, Ethiopiques, JCL, Kunapipi, Mawazo, Obsidian, Okike, PA, RAL, SBL, WLT, WLWE.
Photocopying facilities available.
Publications:
Overcentralkatalog (annually)
Nordic Library Guide to Documentation on Developing Countries (1981)

Det Kongelige Bibliotek (The Royal Library)
Chr. Brygge 8
DK-1219 Copenhagen K
Tel: 01-15-01-11   *Telex:* 15009
Chief Librarian: Palle Birkelund
Person in charge of African collection:
Dr. C. Steenstrup
Hours:
Reading room: 09.00–19.00
Lending dept.: Monday–Friday 12.00–16.00
Access: Open to the public.

Loan and reference facilities: Books may be loaned by registered readers, and are also available through inter-library loan.

Book collection: Exact size unknown.

Special features:

African literature is not kept as a separate collection. Following the establishment of the Scandinavian Institute of African Studies in Uppsala, the Library has tended to concentrate slightly more on Asian rather than African material in recent years.

Serials collection: Exact number not specified.

ABPR, ALT, AfrLJ, ALA, ALAC, ALT, BO, Busara, CBAA, JCL, JNALA, Mawazo, Okike, Okyeame, PA, RAL, WLT, WLWE.

Photocopying facilities available.

Publications:

Nyere Afrika-litteratur, marts 1962
Nyere Afrika-litteratur, supplement 1963
Nyere Afrika-litteratur, supplement 1965

FRANCE

Bibliothèque d'Afrique et d'Outre-Mer

29–31 Quai Voltaire
75340 Paris 07
Tel: 261-50-10   *Telex:* 204826 DOCFRAN
Chief Librarian: Professor Robert Cornevin
Person in charge of African collection: Agnes Lavagna
Hours: Monday–Friday 10.00–18.00
Access: Open to all with a reader's card.
Loan and reference facilities: Both are available and an inter-library loan service is provided.
Book collection: 60,000 volumes (Africana total).
Special features:
Since 1961 the Library has built up an extensive African collection.
Serials collection: 2,000 titles (Africana total).
Abbia, ABPR, AfrA, ALA, ALT, Annales des Facultés de Lettres des Universités de Côte d'Ivoire, Yaoundé, Dakar, et Madagascar, BO, Busara, CBAA, Conch, CulEA, Ecr franc, Ethiopiques, Greenfield Review, JCL, JNALA, LAAW, Mawazo, Notre Librairie, Ozila, PA, Pfr, PNPA, RAL, RLEN, Zuka.
Photocopying facilities available.
Publications:
Afrique Contemporaine

Bibliothèque Nationale

58 Rue Richlieu
75084 Paris 02
Tel: 261-82-83
Chief Librarian: Vacant
Person in charge of African collection: Paulette Lorderau

Hours: Monday–Friday 09.00–20.00
            Saturday (and month of August)
                09.00–18.00
            (closed for 15 days in Spring)
Access: Open to all over the age of 18 engaged in serious research and upon presentation of sufficient identification. There is a fee of FF10.00 for a 'laissez-passer' valid for two days. An annual pass costs FF60.00 (one for twelve visits FF25.00).
Loan and reference facilities: Reference only; national and international inter-library loan facilities are available.
Book collection: 4,000 volumes.
Special features:
African literature is not kept separately from the Library's collection of Africana, but the Bibliothèque Nationale has the most comprehensive African literature collection in France. It includes all material received as part of legal deposit, and there is a strong and growing number of books written in African languages. Since 1972 a card index catalogue has been maintained covering African material. Currently it consists of some 2,000 titles of which roughly half are in French and the remainder largely in English, with a small number of titles in Portuguese, Spanish, Afrikaans, Malagasy, Swahili, Yoruba, Ibo and other African languages.
Serials collection: 40 titles.
Abbia, ABPR, AfrA, Afriscope, AfrLJ, Annales des Facultés de Lettres des Universités de Côte d'Ivoire, Yaoundé, Madagascar et Dakar, Asemka, BO, CBAA, Ch'Indaba, Conch, Demb Ak Tey, Ecr franc, Ethiopiques, JCL, Joliso, Maktaba, Notre Librairie, Okike, Okyeame, PA, PFr, PNPA, RAL, RLEN, WLT, Zuka, (plus several literary and cultural magazines from francophone Africa and Madagascar).
Photocopying facilities available.

Centre d'Étude d'Afrique Noire
Institut d'Études Politiques, Bibliothèque

BP 101 Domaine Universitaire
33405 Talence
Tel: 80-60-57
Chief Librarian: F. Meynard
Hours: 09.00–1200; 14.00–18.00
            (closed in August)
Access: Open to lecturers, students and researchers.
Loan and reference facilities: Those holding a library card may borrow books. There is also an inter-library loan service.
Book collection: 150 volumes.
Special features:
The entire African collection numbers about 8,000 books. It consists mainly of works on

African economics, politics and sociology, with a small number of books on history, anthropology and literature (about 150 items). The Library is especially rich in its serials and African newspaper collection, as it subscribes to the African serials review service of the Foundation Nationale des Sciences Politiques.
Serials collection: 12 titles.
ABPR, AfrA, ALA, ALA Newsletter, BO, Ch'Indaba, Conch, Ethiopiques, Mawazo, PA, PNPA, RAL.
Photocopying facilities available.

Bibliothèque Interuniversitaire de Bordéaux Lettres et Sciences Humaines
Avenue des Arts
33405 Talence
Tel: 56-80-61-00
Chief Librarian: Elisabeth Traissac
Hours: Monday–Friday 09.00–18.30
　　　　Saturday 09.00–17.00
Access: Open to the staff and students of Bordeaux University.
Loan and reference facilities: Available.
Book collection: 100 volumes.
Serials collection: 7 titles.
ALA, JCL.
Photocopying facilities available.

Centre d'Études Littéraires Maghrébines, Africaines et Antillaise, Maison des Sciences de l'Homme
Esplanade des Antilles
33405 Talence
Tel: 80-84-43
Chief Librarian: Catherine Brisou
Hours: Monday–Friday 09.00–12.00
　　　　　　　　　　　14.00–18.00
　　　　(closed in August)
Access: Open to students, lecturers and researchers.
Loan and reference facilities: By arrangement. Inter-library loan facilities.
Book collection: 1,300 volumes.
Special features:
The collection consists mainly of francophone African literature, and material from the Caribbean.
Serials collection: 20 titles.
Abbia, Afrique et Culture, ALA, ALT, Annales des Facultés de Lettres des Universités de Côte d'Ivoire, Yaoundé, Brazzaville, et Madagascar, BO, Ecr franc, Ethiopiques, Notre Librairie, PA, RAL.
Photocopying facilities available.
Publications:
Liste des Thèses et Mémoires Africanistes (1981; deposited in the library)

GERMANY (FEDERAL REPUBLIC)

Universität Bayreuth
Universitätsbibliothek
Justus-Liebig-Strasse 8
Postfach 3008
D-8580 Bayreuth
Tel: 0921-608732
Chief Librarian: Dr. K. Wickert
Person in charge of African collection:
Dr. R. M. Kiel
Hours: Monday–Friday 09.00–1800
　　　　Saturday 09.00–12.00 (during term time only)
Access: Open to members of the University and to others by appointment.
Loan and reference facilities: Available. Inter-library loan facilities.
Book collection: 12,300 volumes (Africana total).
Serials collection: 248 titles (Africana total).
ABPR, AfrA, ALA, ALAC, ALT, CBAA, English in Africa, Ethiopiques, JCL, Kiabara, Kunapipi, NSAL, PA, PFr, PNPA, RAL, TT, WAJML.
Photocopying facilities available.
Publications:
Afrika. Bücher aus und über Schwarzafrika (1980)

Staatsbibliothek Preussischer Kulturbesitz
Potsdamer Strasse 33
Postfach 1407
D-1000 Berlin 30
Tel: 030-2661　　　　*Telex:* 183 160 STA D
Chief Librarian: Dr. Ekkehart Vesper
Person in charge of African collection:
Dr. D. George (Head, Oriental Collection)
Hours: Oriental Reading Room:
　　　　Monday–Friday 09.00–17.00
　　　　Saturday 09.00–13.00
Access: Open to the public.
Loan and reference facilities: The major part of the material may be borrowed through local lending or an inter-library loan service. The exception to this is the volumes housed in the reading rooms.
Book collection: 12,000 volumes (Africana total).
Special features:
African literature is systematically acquired but is not kept as a separate collection. It covers all African countries south of the Sahara with the exception of white South Africa. Acquisitions emphasis is on literature in European languages covering the arts, social sciences, linguistics, ethnology, history, politics, travel and exploration.
Serials collection: 10 titles.
ABPR, ALT, BO, CBAA, Ch'Indaba, JCL, PA, PFr, Umma, WLT.
Photocopying facilities available.

Stadt und Universitätsbibliothek Frankfurt am Main
Afrikaabteilung
Bockenheimer Landstrasse 134–138
D-6000 Frankfurt am Main 1
Tel: 0611-7907-247
Chief Librarian: Dr. K. D. Lehmann
Person in charge of African collection: Dr. Irmtraud Wolcke-Renk
Hours:
Lending dept.:	Monday–Friday 08.30–20.00
			Saturday 9.00–18.00
African dept.:	Monday–Friday 08.30–19.00
Access: Open to the public.
Loan and reference facilities: Available.
Book collection: 100,000 volumes (Africana total).
Special features:
In 1964 the Deutsche Forschungsgemeinschaft assigned to the Frankfurt Stadt- und Universitätsbibliothek the responsibility of establishing a special collection for 'Africa South of the Sahara'. As such the African Department of the Library aims to provide a collection of all relevant literature as comprehensively as possible, with materials being made available for lending purposes. The collection is very strong on African literature, and an attempt is made to obtain all relevant titles published in Europe, as well as in Africa itself. The private library of the late Janheinz Jahn was acquired by the Volkswagen Foundation and thereafter bequeathed to the Library, and the 1,000 or so titles made up a valuable addition to the collection.
Serials collection: 1,200 titles (Africana total).
Abbia, ABPR, AfrA, Afriscope, AfrLJ, ALA, ALAC, ALA Newsletter, ALT, Asemka, Ba Shiru, BO, Busara, CBAA, Ch'Indaba, Conch, CRNLE, CulEA, Dhana, Dombi, English in Africa, Ethiopiques, Greenfield Review, JCL, JNALA, Joliso, Kiabara, Kucha, Kunapipi, LAAW, Maktaba, Mawazo, New Classic, Odi, Oduma, Okike, Okyeame, Ozila, PA, PNPA, RAL, SBL, Staffrider, Umma, WAJML, WLT, WLWE, Zambezia, Zuka.
Photocopying facilities available.
Publications:
Current Contents Africa (quarterly; Munich: K. G. Saur)
Neuerwerbungen Afrika (quarterly)
Fachkatalog Afrika/Subject Catalog Africa/Catalogue matières Afrique vol. 3 Literatur, Literatur-Wissenschaft/Literature/Littérature (Munich: K. G. Saur, 1979)
Afrika-Zeitschriften in der Stadt- und Universitätsbibliothek Frankfurt am Main (1973, supplement 1977)
Literatur Schwarzafrikas in deutschen Übersetzungen (1980)

Bibliothek
Institut für Ethnologie und Afrika-Studien der Universität Mainz
Saarstrasse 21
D-6500 Mainz
Tel: 06131-392798
Chief Librarian: M. Krotky
Person in charge of African collection: Dr. Ulla Schild
Hours: Open during term time only (irregular).
Access: Open to members of the University only, and any member of the public wishing to visit the Library may do so only by prior arrangement.
Loan and reference facilities: Books may not be loaned outside the University.
Book collection: 6,000 volumes (Africana total).
Special features:
The Library houses the oldest African literature collection in the Federal Republic of Germany. It includes popular and children's literature, as well as many titles in African languages.
Serials collection: 50 titles.
Abbia, ABPR, AfrA, AfrLJ, ALA, ALAC, ALA Newsletter, ALT, Asemka, Ba Shiru, BH, BO, Busara, Conch, CRNLE, CulEA, Dhana, Dombi, Ecr franc, JCL, JNALA, Joliso, Kiabara, Kunapipi, New Classic, New Culture, Oduma, Okike, Okyeame, Ophir, PA, PFr, PNPA, RAL, Staffrider, TT, Umma, WLWE.
Photocopying facilities available.

Bayerische Staatsbibliothek München
Ludwigstrasse 16
Postfach 150
D-8000 München 34
Tel: 089-21981
Chief Librarian: Dr. Franz Georg Kaltwasser
Hours: Monday–Friday 09.00–20.00
			Saturday 09.00–17.00
(Many of the departments have varying hours and so it is advisable to check prior to making a visit.)
Loan and reference facilities: Available by arrangement. Inter-library loan.
Book collection: 35,000 volumes (Africana total).
Special features:
African literature is not kept separate from the general Africana collection, which numbers about 35,000 volumes and which includes some 450 titles of African creative writing. The Library also has a substantial amount of material concerned with African history, travel and exploration, particularly early literature.
Serials collection: 140 titles (Africana total).
ABPR, AfrA, Afriscope, AfrLJ, ALA, ALT, CBAA, CulEA, Ethiopiques, JCL, JNALA, Joliso, Maktaba, Mawazo, Okike, Okyeame, PA, RAL, WAJML.
Photocopying facilities available.

GREAT BRITAIN

National Library of Wales
Aberystwyth
Dyfed SY23 3BU
Tel: 0970-3816
Chief Librarian: Dr. R. Geraint Gruffydd
Hours: Monday–Friday 09.00–18.00
          Saturday 09.00–17.00
Access: Open to all with reader's tickets, which are available upon application.
Loan and reference facilities: The Library is for reference only. It does, however, offer a back-up service to the British Library Lending Scheme and also lends duplicate copies under the Welsh Regional Libraries Scheme.
Book collection: 500 volumes.
Special features:
The entire Africana collection numbers about 1,000 volumes, including a large amount of African language material such as dictionaries and grammars. Almost all the books have been published in the U.K. and as a copyright library it contains most African works published in Britain since 1911.
Serials collection: 4 titles.
ABPR, ALT, BO, CulEA, JCL.
Photocopying facilities available.

The Main Library
University of Birmingham
PO Box 363
Birmingham BL5 2TT
Tel: 021-472 1031
Chief Librarian: A. Nicholls
Person in charge of African collection: T. French
Hours:
Term: Monday–Friday 09.00–21.00
       Saturday 09.00–12.00
Vacation: Monday–Friday 09.00–19.00
August only: Monday–Friday 09.00–17.00
Access: Open to members of the University and visitors are also welcome, although prior written application is preferred especially when seeking access to special collections.
Loan and reference facilities: Items may be loaned only to those who have registered, or on an inter-library loan.
Book collection: 1,200 volumes.
Special features:
Since 1963 the Library has systematically built up its collection and it now specialises in material from West Africa, a large proportion of which was collected under the SCOLMA scheme. The collection includes approximately 500 eighteenth- and nineteenth-century monographs, theses from the Centre of West African Studies, and a number of mainly Nigerian pamphlets.
Serials collection: 26 titles.

Abbia, ABPR, AfrA, Afriscope, AfrLJ, ALA, ALT, BO, CBAA, Conch, CulEA, JCL, Kaafa, Mawazo, PA, RAL, WLT.
Photocopying facilities available.
Publications:
Select Basic Sources for West African Studies (1980)

Edinburgh University Library
George Square
Edinburgh EH8 9LJ
Tel: 031-667 1011   *Telex:* 727442 UNIVED G
Chief Librarian: Brenda E. Moon
Person in charge of African collection: L. A. Martin
Hours:
Term: Monday–Thursday 09.00–22.00
       Friday 09.00–19.00
       Saturday 09.00–12.30
Vacation: Monday–Friday 09.00–17.00
Access: Open to all members of the University and to non-members upon application to the University Librarian.
Loan and reference facilities: Available.
Book collection: 350 volumes.
Special features:
African literature is not stocked as a separate collection and the majority of the material is in English, with about 30 French items and a handful in Portuguese. Some additional material from Malawi has been collected under the SCOLMA scheme.
Serials collection: 15 titles.
ABPR, ALT, BO, Ch'Indaba, JCL, Mawazo, PA.
Photocopying facilities available.

National Library of Scotland
George IV Bridge
Edinburgh EH1 1EW
Tel: 031-226 4531   *Telex:* 72638 NLSEDI G
Chief Librarian: Professor E. F. D. Roberts
Person in charge of African collection: Dr. A. M. Cain
Hours: Monday–Friday 09.30–20.30
          Saturday 09.30–13.00
Access: Open to the public.
Loan and reference facilities: Books are for reference only, but may be loaned on an inter-library basis.
Book collection: Exact size unknown.
Special features:
African literature is neither housed nor catalogued as a separate collection within the Library. British copyright deposit books.
Serials collection: 10 titles.
ABPR, AfrLJ, ALT, CRNLE, JCL, Kunapipi, PFr, RAL, WLT, WLWE.
Photocopying facilities available.

The Library
University of Kent at Canterbury
Canterbury
Kent
Tel: 0227-66822
Chief Librarian: W. J. Simpson
Person in charge of African collection:
R. S. Holland
Hours: Term: Monday–Friday 09.00–22.00
	Saturday 09.00–19.00
	Sunday 14.00–21.00
	Vacation: Monday–Friday 09.00–19.00
	Saturday 09.00–17.00
Access: Open to members of the University.
Others free access for reference purposes.
Loan and reference facilities: Loan facilities are
not generally extended to external users.
Book collection: 1,000 volumes.
Serials collection: 22 titles.
ABPR, AfrLJ, ALA, ALT, Ba Shiru, BO,
Busara, Ch'Indaba, CRNLE, CulEA, Dhana,
English in Africa, JCL, JNALA, Kunapipi,
Mawazo, New Classic, NSAC, Obsidian,
Okike, PA, PFr, RAL, Staffrider, TT, WAJML,
WLT, WLWE, Zuka.

The Brotherton Library
University of Leeds
Leeds LS2 9JT
Tel: 0532-31751
Chief Librarian: D. Cox
Person in charge of African collection: Vanessa A.
Hinton
Hours:
Term: Monday–Friday 09.00–22.00
	Saturday 09.00–13.00
	Sunday 14.00–19.00
Vacation: Christmas and Easter
	Monday–Friday 09.00–21.00
	Saturday 09.00–13.00
	Summer
	Monday–Friday 09.00–17.00
	Saturday 09.00–12.30
Access: Open to members of the University, but
prior application must be made by members
of the public wishing to visit the Library.
Loan and reference facilities: Materials may be
borrowed by members of the University and
are available on inter-library loan. Serious
individual researchers may be granted borrowing privileges, but an annual fee of £5 is
required.
Book collection: 1,000 volumes.
Special features:
The main focus is on Commonwealth literature in English (from current as well as *former*
Commonwealth countries). The majority of
material is thus in English, with a smaller
amount in French, and the Library holds a few
works in African languages. The collection is

strong on South African literature (Afrikaans
writing excepted), with no distinction made
between black and white writers, and the
Library has almost as much South African
material in English as it does on Africa in
general.
Serials collection: 20 titles (some other titles in
incomplete runs).
ABPR, ALT, BO, Busara, Contrast, CRNLE,
Dhana, JCL, PA, Purple Renoster, RAL, SBL,
Umma, WLWE, Zambezia.
Photocopying facilities available.

Liverpool City Libraries
William Brown Street
Liverpool L3 8EW
Tel: 051-207 2147	*Telex:* 629500
Chief Librarian: Ralph Mallon
Person in charge of African collection:
Martin Walker
Hours: Monday–Friday 09.00–21.00
	Saturday 09.00–17.00
Access: Open to the public.
Loan and reference facilities: Available. On-line
service to computer data bases available on
application.
Book collection: 3,000 volumes (Africana total).
Special features:
The books are arranged on a country by
country basis and so the language, literature,
history and geography of each country are
treated together.
Serials collection: 10 titles.
Photocopying facilities available.

The Resource Centre
Africa Centre
38 King Street
London WC2E 8JT
Tel: 01-836 1973
Director: Dr. Alastair Niven
Person in charge of African collection: Wendy
Davies (Programme organiser)
Hours: 09.30–17.30 (sometimes later by ar-
rangement).
Access: Open to the public.
Loan and reference facilities: Reference only, no
loan facilities.
Book collection: 1,100 volumes.
Serials collection: 4 titles
APBR, JCL, Lotus.
Photocopying facilities available.

British Library Reference Division
Great Russell Street
London WC1B 3DG
Tel: 01-636 1544	*Telex:* 21462
Chief Librarian: A. Wilson
Hours:
Monday, Friday, Saturday 09.00–17.00

Tuesday, Wednesday, Thursday 09.00–21.00
Access: By application to the Reader Admissions Office. A pass is issued only upon proof of the intention to carry out research or reference work which cannot be reasonably conducted in other libraries.
Loan and reference facilities: Reference only.
Book collection: Substantial, exact size unknown.
Special features:
There is no separate African collection in the Library, but the width and depth of its intake of world literature has produced extensive African holdings. The Department of Printed Books has a very sizeable collection of material published in South Africa.
Serials collection: 42 titles.
Abbia, ABPR, AfrA, Afriscope, AfrLJ, ALT, Asemka, Ba Shiru, BO, Busara, CBAA, Ch'Indaba, Conch, CRNLE, Dhana, English in Africa, Ethiopiques, Greènfield Review, JCL, Joliso, Kiabara, Kunapipi, LAAW, Maktaba, Marang, New Classic, New Coin, New Culture, NSAL, Obsidian, Odi, Oduma, Okike, Okyeame, Ophir, PA, RAL, SBL, Staffrider, Umma, WLT, WLWE, Zambezia.
Photocopying facilities available.

Commonwealth Institute
Library and Resource Centre
Kensington High Street
London W8 6NQ
Tel: 01-602 3252 (ext. 242)   *Telex:* 8955822
Chief Librarian: Michael Foster
Person in charge of African collection: Christiane Keane
Hours: Monday–Saturday 10.00–17.30
Access: Open to all over the age of 14.
Loan and reference facilities: Books may be loaned to all U.K. residents over the age of 14. Visitors are welcome to use the Library for reference and study purposes. Facilities for the use of non-book materials are available.
Book collection: 2,100 volumes.
Special features:
The African collection is part of the special collection of Commonwealth literature. It is especially strong on the arts and cultural traditions of African countries, not only offering books and journals but also audio-visual material and items of interest such as BBC African Theatre scripts and a number of Onitsha Market pamphlets. The stock of children's literature is steadily increasing.
Serials collection: 80 titles.
ABPR, ACLALS Bulletin, AFRAM Newsletter, Afriscope, ALT, BO, Busara, CBAA, Ch'Indaba, CRNLE, Dhana, JCL, JNALA, Kunapipi, LAAW, Mawazo, New Writing from Zambia, Okike, Umma, WLWE, Young Zambian Writing, Zuka.
Photocopying facilities available.

Publications:
Commonwealth Bibliographies; New Materials on . . .; Checklists on Commonwealth Literature.

The Library
Royal Commonwealth Society
Northumberland Avenue
London WC2N 5BJ
Tel: 01-930 6733
Chief Librarian: Donald Simpson
Hours: Monday–Friday 10.00–17.00
Access: Open to members of the Society, others engaged in serious study of Commonwealth subjects may apply for a Reader's Ticket.
Loan and reference facilities: Open to members of the Society; others on application.
Book collection: Exact size unknown (total collection some 40,000 volumes).
Special features:
The Library holds some of the early works by African writers such as Thomos Mofolo, though it has not attempted to build up as extensive a coverage of texts as the Commonwealth Institute. It is particularly strong in critical works, biographies of writers, and in material on the cultural, social and political background against which such works were produced. Important articles in perodicals, including a good deal of literary material, is being catalogued.
Serials collection: several titles, exact number not specified.
Photocopying facilities available.
Publications:
Subject Catalogue of the Library of the Royal Empire Society, 4 vols.

The Library
School of Oriental and African Studies
Malet Street
London WC1E 7HP
Tel: 01-637 2388
Chief Librarian: V. T. H. Parry
Person in charge of African collection: M. D. McKee
Hours:
Term and Easter vacation:
    Monday–Friday 09.00–20.00
Christmas and Summer vacation:
    Monday–Friday 09.00–17.00
    Saturday 09.00–12.30
Access: Open to members of the School and to non-members upon application and the presentation of satisfactory references.
Loan and reference facilities: Borrowing is permitted upon payment of a £50 refundable deposit. Up to six books may be on loan at any one time.
Book collection: 1,800 volumes.
Special features:
The collection is extremely strong in African

language material. It has a substantial amount of Onitsha Market literature and some original manuscripts and typescripts of contemporary African writers.

Serials collection: 50 titles.

Abbia, ABPR, AfrA, AfrLJ, ALA, ALT, Asemka, Ba Shiru, BO, Busara, CBAA, Ch'Indaba, Conch, CulEA, Dhana, Dombi, Ethiopiques, JCL, JNALA, Joliso, Kiabara, LAAW, Maktaba, Mawazo, New Classic, New Culture, Odi, Oduma, Okike, Okyeame, Ophir, PA, RAL, Staffrider, Umma, WAJML, Zambezia, Zuka.

Photocopying facilities available.

Publications:

International African Bibliography. Current Books, Articles and Papers in African Studies (London: Mansell Publishing, quarterly)

University of London Institute of Education Library

11–13 Ridgmount Street

London WC1E 7AH

Tel: 01-637 0846

Chief Librarian: Dr. N. W. Beswick

Person in charge of African collection: Peter Moss

Hours:

Term: Monday–Thursday 09.30–20.00

         Friday 09.30–19.00

         Saturday 09.30–12.30

Vacations: Christmas and Easter:

         Monday–Friday 09.30–19.00

         Saturday 09.30–12.30

Summer:

         Monday–Friday 09.30–18.00

Access: Open to the public.

Loan and reference facilities: Members of the public may use the Library for reference purposes only and the loan facilities are usually restricted to the staff and students of the Institute.

Book collection: 150 volumes.

Serials collection: 15 titles.

Abbia, ABPR, ALT, BO, JCL, Mawazo, PA, Zuka.

Photocopying facilities available.

The Bodleian Library

Broad Street

Oxford OX1 3BG

Tel: 0865-44675

Chief Librarian: E. R. S. Fifoot

Person in charge of African collection: Peter Snow

Hours: Term: Monday–Friday 09.00–22.00

         Saturday 09.00–13.00

         Vacation: Monday–Friday 09.00–19.00

Access: Closed to the public.

Loan and reference facilities: Reference only.

Book collection: 3,000 volumes.

Special features:

The Library contains all relevant U.K. imprints received under the copyright deposit act, and it also acquires African published material.

Serials collection: 40 titles.

ABPR, AfrA, Afriscope, AfrLJ, ALT, Asemka, Ba Shiru, BO, Busara, Ch'Indaba, Conch, CRNLE, CulEA, Darlite, Dhana, English in Africa, Greenfield Review, JCL, Joliso, LAAW, Maktaba, Marang, Mawazo, New Classic, New Coin, New Culture, NSAL, Obsidian, Okike, PA, RAL, SBL, Staffrider, Umma, WLT, WLWE.

Photocopying facilities available.

Institute of Commonwealth Studies Library University of Oxford

Queen Elizabeth House

21 St. Giles

Oxford OX1 3LA

Tel: 0865-52952

Chief Librarian: R. J. Townsend

Hours:

Term: Monday–Friday 09.00–13.00

         14.00–19.00

         Saturday 09.00–12.30

Vacation: Monday–Friday 09.00–13.00

         14.00–17.00

Access: Open to the public.

Loan and reference facilities: Available.

Book collection: 600 volumes.

Serials collection: 17 titles (others transferred to Bodleian Library)

Abbia, ABPR, AfrLJ, ALA, ALT, BO, CBAA, Ch'Indaba, CulEA, Dhana, JCL, Mawazo, New Classic, Okike, Okyeame, PA, RAL, Staffrider.

Photocopying facilities available.

Publications:

Quarterly Select List of Accessions

University of Stirling Library

Stirling FK9 4LA

Tel: 0786-3171 (ext. 2227)   *Telex:* 778874

Chief Librarian: P. G. Peacock

Person in charge of African collection: D. S. Mack

Hours: Term: 09.00–22.00

         Vacation: 09.30–17.00

Access: Open to the public upon application to the University Librarian.

Loan and reference facilities: By arrangement only.

Book collection: 500 volumes

Special features:

The collection is part of the wider Commonwealth Literature section.

Serials collection: 10 titles.

BO, JCL, PA, PFr, WLT.

Photocopying facilities available.

The British Library
Lending Division
Boston Spa
Wetherby
West Yorkshire LS23 7BQ
Tel: 0937-843434   *Telex:* 557381
Chief Librarian: Dr. M. B. Line
Persons in charge of African collection: Dr. D. N.
Wood (Aquisitions) and E. S. Smith (Lending)
Hours: Monday–Friday 09.00–17.00
Access: On application, or by means of the
inter-library loan through local libraries.
Loan and reference facilities: Available.
Book collection: Exact size unknown.
Special features:
The collection does not include fiction,
textbooks, recreational, popular or children's
books. Monographs in English are readily
available and those in foreign languages are
acquired on demand.
Serials collection: Exact number not specified.
ABPR, AfrA, Afriscope, AfrLJ, ALT, Asemka,
Ba Shiru, Busara, CBAA, Ch'Indaba, Conch,
Ethiopiques, JCL, Kunapipi, Okike, PA, PFr,
RAL, Umma, WAJML, WLT, WLWE, Zam-
bezia.
Photocopying facilities available.

NETHERLANDS

Bibliotheek
Afrika-Studiecentrum
Stationsplein 12
Leiden
Tel: 071-148-333 (ext. 4040)
Chief Librarian: J. Van der Meulen
Hours: 08.00–12.30; 14.00–17.00
Access: Open to the public by arrangement.
Loan and reference facilities: Available.
Book collection: 1,200 volumes.
Serials collection: 36 titles.
Abbia, ABPR, AfrLJ, ALA, ALT, Annales de
l'Université d'Abidjan, Ba Shiru, BO, Busara,
CBAA, Ch'Indaba, Conch, Dombi, Ethiopi-
ques, Joliso, Kiabara, Maktaba, Mawazo, New
Classic, New Writing from Zambia, Oduma,
Okike, Okyeame, PA, PNPA, RAL, Umma,
WAJML.
Publications
Aanweirstenlyst (Accessions List)
Documentalieblad (Abstracts Journal)

SWEDEN

Scandinavian Institute of African Studies
The Library
P.O. Box 2126
Sysslomansgatan 7
750 02 Uppsala

Tel: 018-15-54-80
Chief Librarian: Birgitta Fahlander
Hours: Monday 10.00–21.00
                 Tuesday–Friday 10.00–15.00
Access: Open to the public.
Loan and reference facilities: Available, except for
reference works, serials, and government and
office publications.
Book collection: 1,000 volumes.
Serials collection: 40 titles
Abbia, ABPR, AfrA, Afriscope, AfrLJ, ALA,
ALT, Ba Shiru, BO, Busara, CBAA,
Ch'Indaba, Conch, CulEA, Dhana, JNALA,
Joliso, Kunapipi, Maktaba, Mawazo, New
Classic, Odi, Okike, Okyeame, Ophir, PA,
RAL, Snarl, Staffrider, Umma, Zambezia,
Zuka.
Photocopying facilities available.

SWITZERLAND

Institut Universitaire d'Etudes du
Développement Bibliothèque
24 Avenue Rothschild
CH-1202 Genève
Tel: 31-25-21
Chief Librarian: Jacqueline Clerc
Person in charge of African collection: René Barbey
Hours: Monday–Friday 09.00–18.00
Access: Open to the public.
Loan and reference facilities: Reference only.
Book collection: 7,000 volumes (Africana total).
Serials collection: 100 titles (Africana total).
Abbia, ABPR, AfrA, ALA, ALA Newsletter,
BO, CBAA, Ch'Indaba, Ethiopiques, Mawazo,
Odi, PA, PFr, PNPA, RAL, TT, Zambezia.
Photocopying facilities available.

Stadtbibliothek Winterthur
Museumstrasse 52
CH-8400 Winterthur
Tel: 052-84-51-41 (45 lending department)
Chief Librarian: Dr. Peter Sulzer
Hours:
Monday 10.00–12.00; 13.00–18.00
Wednesday, Friday 08.00–12.00; 13.00–18.00
Tuesday, Thursday 08.00–12.00; 14.00–18.00
Saturday 08.00–12.00; 13.00–16.00
Access: Open to the public.
Loan and reference facilities: Available by
arrangement. Inter-library loan facilities.
Book collection: 4,000 volumes (Africana total)
Special features:
The linguistic-literary collection of the Library
currently consists of over 1,700 titles, and is
constantly growing. The collection is particu-
larly strong on materials in the African
languages, and works on traditional litera-
tures. Supplementing the collection there are

extensive holdings of works on politics and history by African authors.

Serials collections: 183 titles (Africana total).

Abbia, ABPR, ALAC, ALT, Asemka, BO, Ch'Indaba, Conch, English in Africa, Ethiopiques, Greenfield Review, JNALA, Kiabara, Limi, New Classic, Odi, Okyeame, Ophir, Ozila, PA, PFr, PNPA, RAL, RLEN, Staffrider, Umma, WAJML.

Photocopying facilities available.

Publications:

Die Africana-Sammlung in der Stadtbibliothek Winterthur. Afrikanische Literaturen und Sprachen. The Africana Collection of the Municipal Library of Winterthur. African Literatures and Languages. (Basel: Basler Afrika Bibliographien, 1977; supplementary volume 1982).

UNITED STATES

Munger Africana Library
California Institute of Technology
201 E. California
Pasadena
Ca. 91125
Tel: 213-356-4468
Chief Librarian: Judith Nollar
Hours: Monday–Thursday 09.00–13.00 and by arrangement.
Access: Open to the public on application only.
Loan and reference facilities: Available.
Book collection: 27,000 (Africana total)
Special features:
The collection is strong on its seventeenth and eighteenth century works, its South African political pamphlets, and clippings on Africa south of the Sahara. African literature is not separated, however, into a specific section.
Serials collection: 110 titles (Africana total)
ABPR, CBAA.
Photocopying facilities available.
Publications:
Munger Africana Library News (six times yearly)

University Library
California State University Dominguez Hills
Carson
Ca. 90747
Tel: 213-516-3715
Chief Librarian: Phillip Wesley
Person in charge of African collection: Claudia A. Baldwin
Hours: Vary.
Access: Open to the public
Loan and reference facilities: Available. Interlibrary loan facilities.
Book collection: 200 volumes.
Serials collection: 8 titles.

APBR, AfrA, ALJ, ALT, CBAA, JCL, PFr, RAL, SBL, WLT.
Photocopying facilities available.

Los Angeles Public Library
630 W. Fifth Street
Los Angeles
Ca. 90071
Tel: 213-626-7461
Chief Librarian: Wyman Jones
Person in charge of African collection: Helene G. Mochedlover (Head, Literature Dept.)
Hours: Monday–Thursday 10.00–20.00
    Friday–Saturday 10.00–17.30
Access: Open to the public.
Loan and reference facilities: Available.
Book collection: 300 volumes.
Serials collection: 17 titles.
ABPR, AfrA, Afriscope, AfrLJ, ALT, Ba Shiru, BO, CBAA, JNALA, LAAW, Maktaba, Obsidian, Okike, PA, RAL, SBL, Umma, WLT.
Photocopying facilities available.

Stanford University Library
Cecil H. Green Library
Stanford
Ca. 94305
Tel: 415-497-1811   *Telex:* 910-3731787
Chief Librarian: David C. Webber
Person in charge of African collection: Dr. Peter Duignan and Karen Fung
Hours: Monday–Thursday 08.00–23.00
    Friday 08.00–18.00
    Saturday 09.00–17.00
    Sunday 12.00–23.00
Access: Open to the public.
Loan and reference facilities: Scholars may use material free for seven days in each year; if this period is exceeded or books are to be taken out on loan, a Visitors Library Card must be purchased. There is also inter-library loan service.
Book collection: 2,980 volumes (includes titles on linguistics).
Special features:
The Library has the 'Nigerian Collection of Simon Ottenberg' (15 microfilm reels). Most of the material covers the period 1940–1965. It consists primarily of market literature from Eastern Nigeria but also includes journals, etc. published elsewhere in Nigeria and some Nigerian government reports. There is an index: 'Nigerian Collection of Simon Ottenburg' (an inventory to the microfilm; 17 leaves).
Serials collection: 70 titles.
Abbia, ABPR, AfrA, Afriscope, AfrLJ, ALA, ALAC, ALA Newsletter, ALT, Asemka, Ba Shiru, BH, BO, Busara, CBAA, Cameroun Littéraires, Ch'Indaba, Conch, Contrast,

CulEA, Dhana, Dombi, English in Africa, Ethiopiques, Expression, JCL, JNALA, Kiabara, Kunapipi, LAAW, Maktaba, Marang, Mawazo, New Classic, New Coin, New Culture, New Writing from Zambia, NSAL, Obsidian, Odi, Oduma, Okike, Ophir, Ozila, PA, Penpoint, PNPA, Purple Renoster, RAL, SBL, Staffrider, TT, Umma, WAJML, WLT, WLWE, Zambezia, Zuka.
Photocopying facilities available.

The General Library
University of California at Berkeley
Berkeley
Ca. 94720
Tel: 415-642-6657 *Telex:* 910-3667337
Chief Librarian: Joseph A. Rosenthal
Person in charge of African collection: Phyllis B. Bischof
Hours: Monday–Thursday 08.00–20.00
       Friday 08.00–17.00
       Saturday 09.00–17.00
       Sunday 13.00–17.00
       (hours vary during vacations).
Access: Open to the public.
Loan and reference facilities: Available.
Book collection: 28,000 volumes (Africana total).
Special features:
The great strength of the Library lies in its collection of serials and documents. A vast number of African periodicals are subscribed to and conference proceedings are well represented. There is an extensive collection of African novels and poetry, as well as an excellent general reference collection.
Serials collection: Extensive, exact number not specified.
Abbia, ABPR, AfrA, Afriscope, AfrLJ, ALA, ALA Newsletter, ALT, Ba Shiru, BO, Busara, CBAA, Ch'Indaba, Conch, CRNLE, CulEA, Dhana, Dombi, Ethiopiques, JCL, Joliso, LAAW, Maktaba, Mawazo, New Classic, New Coin, New Culture, NSAL, Obsidian, Odi, Oduma, Okike, Okyeame, Ophir, PA, RAL, SBL, Staffrider, TT, Umma, WAJML, WLT, WLWE, Zambezia, Zuka (and others).
Photocopying facilities available.

University of California at Los Angeles Library
405 Hilgard Avenue
Los Angeles
Ca. 90024
Tel: 213.825-1201 *Telex:* 910-3426973
Chief Librarian: Russell Shank
Person in charge of African collection: Eric Siegel (Acting)
Hours: Monday–Thursday 08.00–23.00
       Friday 08.00–18.00
       Saturday 09.00–17.00
       Sunday 13.00–22.00

Access: Open to the public.
Loan and reference facilities: Loan facilities are free to University staff, faculties and students. Members of the public may borrow books upon purchase of a library card.
Book collection: 7,000 volumes (Africana total).
Special features:
The collection contains a large number of titles written in African languages.
Serials collection: 100 titles.
Abbia, ABPR, AfrA, AfrLJ, ALA, ALAC, ALA Newsletter, ALT, Annales de l'Université d'Abidjan, Asemka, Ba Shiru, BO, Busara, CBAA, Conch, CulEA, Dhana, Ecr franc, Ethiopiques, Greenfield Review, JCL, JNALA, Joliso, Kiabara, LAAW, Maktaba, Mawazo, New Classic, Odi, Oduma, Okike, Okyeame, Ophir, Ozila, PA, PFr, PNPA, RAL, SBL, Staffrider, Umma, WAJML, WLT, WLWE, Zambezia, Zuka.
Photocopying facilities available.

Yale University Library
130 Wall Street
New Haven
Ct. 06520
Tel: 202-436-8335 (Reference Dept.)
      202-436-1091 (African collection)
Chief Librarian: Rutherford D. Rogers
Person in charge of African collection: Moore Crossey
Hours: Monday–Thursday 08.30–24.00
(Hours are limited on Fridays and at weekends, and the Main Library closes at 17.00 during the vacations).
Access: Open to students and faculty members with valid identity cards.
Loan and reference facilities: Connecticut universities and inter-library loans are free to Research Libraries Group members, but a charge is made for most other loans. Most of the African literature collection is housed in the Main Library (the Sterling Memorial Library), with some in the Undergraduate Library (the Cross Campus Library) and the Rare Book and Manuscript Library. *Bona fide* researchers may make use of all materials.
Book collection: 5,000 volumes.
Special features:
Yale has the second largest African literature collection in the United States. There has been systematic acquisition of new titles and it currently holds about 3,000 titles in and on African languages. Many Nigerian and other titles are available on microfilm, and the Library has large holdings of colonial novels set in Africa. There is also a strong collection of relevant bibliographies and other reference works.

Serials collection: Extensive, exact number not specified.

Abbia, ABPR, AfrA, Afriscope, AfrLJ, ALA, ALAC, ALA Newsletter, ALT, Asemka, Ba Shiru, BH, BO, Bolt, Busara, CBAA, Ch'Indaba, Conch, CulEA, Dhana, Dombi, English in Africa, Ethiopiques, Greenfield Review, JCL, JNALA, Maktaba, Marang, Mawazo, New Classic, New Coin, New Culture, NSAL, Obsidian, Odi, Oduma, Okike, Okyeame, Ozila, PA, PFr, RAL, SBL, Snarl, Staffrider, Umma, WAJML, WLT, WLWE, Zambezia, Zuka.

Photocopying facilities available.

Northwestern University Library
Evanston
Ill. 60201
Tel: 312-492-7684   *Telex:* 910 2310872
Chief Librarian: John P. McGowan
Person in charge of African collection: Hans E. Panofsky
Hours: 08.30–17.00
Access: Open to the public.
Loan and reference facilities: Available. Interlibrary loan service.
Book collection: 11,000 volumes (Africana total).
Special features:
Large collection of African literary journals where only few issues were published.
Serials collection: 100 titles.

Abbia, ABPR, AfrA, African Writer, Afriscope, AfrLJ, ALA, ALAC, ALA Newsletter, ALT, Asemka, Ba Shiru, BH, BO, Busara, CBAA, Ch'Indaba, Conch, CRNLE, CulEA, Dhana, Dombi, Ecr franc, English in Africa, Ethiopiques, Greenfield Review, Jewel of Africa, JCL, JNALA, Joliso, Kiabara, Kucha, Kunapipi, LAAW, Maktaba, Marang, Mawazo, New Classic, New Coin, New Culture, NSAL, Obsidian, Odi, Oduma, Okike, Okyeame, Ophir, Ozila, PA, PFr, PNPA, RAL, RLEN, SBL, Staffrider, TT, Umma, WAJML, WLT, WLWE, Zambezia, Zuka (many others and single issues published).

Photocopying facilities available.
Publications:
Joint Acquisitions List of Africana (six times yearly)
Annual Cumulations (Boston: G. K. Hall, 1978–)

University of Illinois Library
1408 West Gregory Drive
Urbana
Ill. 61801
Tel: 217-333-6519 (African collection)
Chief Librarian: Hugh Atkinson
Person in charge of African collection: Yvette Scheven

Hours: African collection:
     Monday–Friday 08.00–17.00
Reference room and Circulation Dept.:
     Monday–Friday 08.00–22.00
     Saturday 09.00–22.00
     Sunday 13.00–22.00
     (hours vary during vacation)
Access: Upon application.
Loan and reference facilities: Both are available and an inter-library loan service is provided.
Book collection: 3,300 volumes.
Special features:
In addition to the specialised service available in Africana, and the rich collection in the stacks, the Modern Languages & Linguistics Library contains a good reference and circulating collection of materials in French African literature.
Serials collection: 175 titles. (Africana total).

Abbia, ABPR, AfrA, Afriscope, AfrLJ, ALA, ALA Newsletter, ALT, Annals Univ. Abidjan – Lettres, Annals Univ. Dakar – Lettres, Ba Shiru, BO, Busara, CBAA, Ch'Indaba, Conch, CulEA, Dhana, Dombi, Ecr franc, English in Africa, JCL, JNALA, Joliso, LAAW, Maktaba, Mawazo, Odu, Oduma, Okike, Okyeame, Ophir, PA, PFr, RAL, SBL, Ufahamu, Umma, WAJML, WLT, WLWE, Zambezia, Zuka.

Photocopying facilities available.
Publications:
Selected Africana Acquisitions (quarterly)

Indiana University Libraries
Indiana University
Bloomington
Ind. 47405
Tel: 812-337-1481
Chief Librarian: Elaine F. Sloan
Person in charge of African collection: David L. Easterbrook
Hours: Vary, depending upon time of the year, and therefore contact should be made with the Library prior to a visit.
Access: Open to the public
Loan and reference facilities: Any researcher may use the Library for reference purposes and may borrow material through inter-library loan. Books are readily available for loan to students, faculties and members of staff at the University and also to all resident in the state of Indiana.
Book collection: Exact size unknown.
Serials collection: 34 titles.

Abbia, ABPR, AfrA, Afriscope, AfrLJ, ALA, ALAC, ALA Newsletter, ALT, Ba Shiru, BO, Busara, CBAA, Ch'Indaba, Ecr franc, Ethiopiques, JCL, JNALA, Joliso, Maktaba, Mawazo, NSAL, Odi, PA, PFr, PNPA, RAL, RLEN, SBL, Umma, WAJML, WLT, WLWE, Zambezia, Zuka.

Photocopying facilities available.

African Studies Library
Boston University
771 Commonwealth Avenue
Boston
Ma. 02215
Tel: 617-353-3726
Chief Librarian: Gretchen Walsh
Hours: September–May:
   Monday–Saturday 09.00–17.00
   June–August:
   Monday–Friday 09.00–17.00
Access: Open to members of the University and
visiting scholars and researchers, upon ap-
plication for a visitor's card.
Loan and reference facilities: Books may only be
borrowed by members of the University,
although most circulating material may be
obtained by other libraries on inter-library
loan.
Book collection: 8,000 volumes (Africana total).
Special features:
Although the Library does not collect heavily
in African literature, it is strong in African
language materials and houses a substantial
African studies collection, with the major
emphasis placed on history and development.
Serials collection: 55 titles.
Abbia, ABPR, AfrA, Afriscope, AfrLJ, ALA,
ALAC, ALA Newsletter, ALT, Asemka, Ba
Shiru, BO, Busara, CBAA, Ch'Indaba, Conch,
CRNLE, CulEA, Dhana, Dombi, English in
Africa, Ethiopiques, JCL, JNALA, LAAW,
Maktaba, Mawazo, New Culture, Odi.
Oduma, Okike, Ozila, PA, RAL, SBL, Umma,
WAJML, Zambezia, Zuka.
Photocopying facilities available.
Publications:
Africana Libraries Newsletter (six times yearly)

The University Library
University of Maryland Baltimore County
5401 Wilkens Avenue
Catonsville
Md. 21228
Tel: 301-455-2232   *Telex:* 710-862-1456
Chief Librarian: Billy R. Wilkinson
Person in charge of African collection: Lawrence
Wilt
Hours: Monday–Thursday 08.00–23.00
    Friday 08.00–18.00
    Saturday 10.00–16.00
    Sunday 13.00–21.00
    (hours vary during the vacations).
Access: Open to the public.
Loan and reference facilities: Both are available
and there is inter-library loan.
Book collection: 400 volumes.
Special features:
Holds dictionary catalogues for several collec-

tions concerned with Africa and black studies
in the United States.
Serials collection: 12 titles.
AfrA, AfrLJ, Ba Shiru, Ch'Indaba, Conch
CBAA, Obsidian, Okike, PA, RAL, SBL, WLT,
Zuka.
Photocopying facilities available.

Michigan State University Library
East Lansing
Mich. 48824
Tel: 517-353-8816
Chief Librarian: Dr. Richard E. Chapin
Persons in charge of African collection: Dr. Eugene
de Benko, Onuma Ezera
Hours: Term: Monday–Friday 08.00–22.50
          Saturday 09.00–22.50
          Sunday 12.00–22.50
     Vacation: Monday–Friday 08.00–22.50
          Saturday 09.00–16.50
Access: Open to those resident of the State of
Michigan and to others upon application.
Loan and reference facilities: Michigan residents
can obtain a borrower's permit, but a special
permit is required by visiting researchers.
Book collection: 4,000 volumes (Africana total).
Special features:
African language material may be located in
the International Library pamphlet files.
Serials collection: 40 titles.
Abbia, ABPR, AfrA, Afriscope, AfrLJ, ALA,
ALT, Ba Shiru, BO, Busara, CBAA,
Ch'Indaba, Conch, CulEA, Dhana, Dombi,
Ethiopiques, Greenfield Review, JNALA,
Kiabara, LAAW, Maktaba, Mawazo, New
Culture, Obsidian, Odi, Oduma, Okike,
Okyeame, Ophir, Ozila, PA, PFr, RAL, SBL,
Staffrider, Umma, WLT, WLWE, Zambezia,
Zuka.
Photocopying facilities available.
Publications:
Africana. Select Recent Acquisitions List

Baker Library
Dartmouth College
Hanover
N.H. 03755
Tel: 603-646-2235
Chief Librarian: Margaret A. Otto
Person in charge of African collection: Helen M.
MacLam (Selection officer)
Hours: Term: Monday–Friday 08.00–22.00
          Saturday 13.00–18.00
          Sunday 14.00–22.50
     Vacation: Monday–Friday 08.00–17.00
Access: Open to members of the public upon
application of a Library card.
Loan and reference facilities: Both are available
and inter-library loan service is provided.
Book collection: Exact size unknown.

Special features:
There is no separate African collection *per se*, and these holdings are integrated with the rest of the humanities and social science materials. The bulk of African materials support instruction and research in history, anthropology, and political science.
Serials collection: 21 titles.
Abbia, ABPR, AfrA, Afriscope, AfrLJ, ALA Newsletter, ALT, BO, CBAA, Greenfield Review, JNALA, Mawazo, Obsidian, Oduma, Okike, PA, PFr, PNPA, RAL, RLEN, WLT.
Photocopying facilities available.

Herbert Lehman Library
Columbia University Libraries
313 International Affairs Building
New York
N.Y. 10027
Tel: 212-280-2271
Chief Librarian: Patricia M. Battin
Person in charge of African collection: Elizabeth A. Widenmann
Hours: Vary, details on application.
Access: Open to faculty, students, and members of the University; others by application.
Loan and reference facilities: Available to members of the University; other qualified scholars and researchers by application. A fee of $50.00 monthly is payable for extended use of the collection and borrowing privileges.
Book collection: 40,000 volumes (Africana total).
Special features:
The Libraries' collections on Africa south of the Sahara contain approximately 40,000 titles emphasizing the arts, economic development, geography, history, law, literature, political science, sociology and anthropology. Some materials are acquired in Arabic and African languages.
Serials collection: Exact number and details not specified.
Photocopying facilities available.
Publications:
Use of the Columbia University Libraries: Visiting Readers Guide No. 30, Africa South of the Sahara

New York Public Library
Schomburg Center for Research in Black Culture
515 Lenox Avenue
New York
N.Y. 10037
Tel: 212-862-4000
Chief Librarian: John Miller (Acting)
Hours:
Winter:
    Monday–Wednesday 12.00–20.00
    Thursday–Saturday 10.00–18.00

Summer:
    Monday, Wednesday 12.00–20.00
    Tuesday, Thursday, Friday 10.00–18.00
Access: Open to all adults, although identification with a home address is required. Admission to the special collections (i.e. Archives, Art and Artifacts) may only be granted after application and an interview.
Loan and reference facilities: Loans are made only to members of the Research Libraries Group, New York State inter-library loan and the United Nations. Music, oral history and audio material may be heard by remote control.
Book collection: 300 volumes (25,000 volumes Africana total)
Special features:
The total collection consists of 75,000 volumes, plus very substantial holdings of microforms, fiches and audio-visual materials – all relating to the Black experience throughout the world. The collection is strong in African linguistics, and there are sizeable stocks of materials in African languages.
Serials collection: 22 titles (187 titles Africana total).
ABPR, AfrA, AfrLJ, ALAC, Ba Shiru, BO, Busara, CBAA, Ch'Indaba, Conch, Dhana, Ethiopiques, Joliso, LAAW, New Culture, Obsidian, Odi, Okike, PA, RAL, Staffrider, Umma.
Photocopying facilities available.
Publications:
Catalogue of the Schomburg Collection (Boston: G. K. Hall)

E. S. Bird Library
Syracuse University
Syracuse
N.Y. 13210
Tel: 315-423-3715   *Telex:* 710-54104111
Chief Librarian: Donald Anthony
Person in charge of African collection:
Ann Biersteker
Hours:
Term: Monday–Thursday 08.00–22.00
         Friday 08.00–18.00
         Saturday, Sunday 10.00–18.00
Vacation: Monday–Friday 08.00–17.00
Access: Open to the public.
Loan and reference facilities: Books may be taken out by the faculties, students and staff of the University. Visitors wishing to borrow books may do so only by special permission.
Book collection: Exact size unknown
Special features:
The collection focuses mainly on East Africa. The only African language literature collected is Swahili.
Serials collection: 40 titles.
ABPR, AfrA, Afriscope, AfrLJ, ALAC, ALT,

BO, Busara, CBAA, Conch, English in Africa, Greenfield Review, JCL, JNALA, Maktaba, Mawazo, PA, RAL, Umma, WAJML, WLT, Zambezia.
Photocopying facilities available.

Paley Library
Temple University
Philadelphia
Pa. 19122
Tel: 215-787-7400
Chief Librarian: Joseph A. Boissé
Person in charge of African collection: Rosamond Putzel
Hours: Monday–Thursday 08.00–22.00
Friday–Saturday 09.00–17.00
Sunday 13.00–22.00
Access: Open to the public.
Loan and reference facilities: Available to staff and students of the University; inter-library loan.
Book collection: 1,000 volumes (Africana total).
Serials collection: 20 titles.
ABPR, AfrA, AfrLJ, ALA, ALT, Ba Shiru, BO, Busara, CBAA, Ch'Indaba, JCL, LAAW, Mawazo, Okike, PA, RAL, SBL, Umma, WLT, WLWE.
Photocopying facilities available.

Fisk University Library
17th and Jackson Street
Nashville
Tn. 37203
Tel: 615-329-8580 (ext. 646)
Chief Librarian: Jessie Carney Smith
Person in charge of African collection: Ann Allen Shockley
Hours: Monday–Friday 08.00–17.00
Access: Open to the public.
Loan and reference facilities: Reference only.
Book collection: Exact size unknown.
Special features:
African literature is included in the special Negro Collection.
Serials collection: Exact number not specified.
AfrA, ALJ, PA, SBL.
Photocopying facilities available.
Publications:
Dictionary Catalogue of the Negro Collection 6 volumes. (Boston: G. K. Hall, 1974).

The General Libraries
The University of Texas at Austin
Box P
Austin
Texas 78712
Tel: 512-471-3811   *Telex:* 910-8741304
Chief Librarian: Harold W. Billings
Person in charge of African collection: Richard Holland (History Bibliographer)
Hours: 08.00–24.00 (hours vary during vacations).

Access: Open to the public.
Loan and reference facilities: Available; inter-library loan.
Book collection: 3,500 volumes (Africana total).
Serials collection: 40 titles.
ABPR, AfrA, Afriscope, AfrLJ, ALA, ALAC, ALT, Asemka, Ba Shiru, Busara, CBAA, Conch, English in Africa, Greenfield Review, JCL, Joliso, Kunapipi, LAAW, Maktaba, NSAL, Obsidian, Odi, Okike, PA, PFr, RAL, TT, WAJML, WLT, WLWE, Zambezia, Zuka.

Alderman Library
University of Virginia
Charlottesville
Va. 22901
Tel: 804-924-3026/7849 *Telex:* 510-5875453 U
Chief Librarian: Ray W. Frantz
Person in charge of African collection: Mary Alice Kraehe
Hours: Monday–Thursday 08.00–24.00
Friday 08.00–22.00
Saturday 09.00–18.00
Sunday 12.00–24.00
Access: Open to the public.
Loan and reference facilities: Available; inter-library loan.
Book collection: 250 volumes.
Special features:
Although the collection covers the whole of sub-Saharan Africa, an emphasis has been placed on the countries of East Africa, and South Africa.
Serials collection: 32 titles.
ABPR, AfrA, AfrLJ, ALA, ALAC, ALT, Ba Shiru, BH, BO, Busara, Ch'Indaba, Conch, Dhana, Greenfield Review, JCL, LAAW, Mawazo, Obsidian, Okike, Okyeame, PA, PFr, PNPA, RAL, SBL, Umma, WAJML, WLT, WLWE, Zambezia, Zuka.
Photocopying facilities available.
Publications:
African Languages, a Guide to Materials in the Alderman Library of the University of Virginia (1981)

African Bibliographic Center
1346 Connecticut Avenue N.W.
Suite 901
Washington D.C. 20036
Tel: 202-223-1392
Chief Librarian: Gail A. Kostinko
Hours: Monday–Friday 09.00–17.00
Access: By appointment only.
Loan and reference facilities: Reference only.
Book collection: 500 volumes.
Special features:
All African literature indexing has been entered into the Center's computerized resource base.

Serials collection: 15 titles.
ABPR, AfrA, ALJ, Ba Shiru, Conch, CBAA, SBL.
Photocopying facilities available.
Publications:
A Current Bibliography on African Affairs (quarterly)

Moorland-Spingarn Research Center
Founders Library
Howard University
Room 109
Washington D.C. 20059
Tel: 202-636-7239
Chief Librarian: James P. Johnson
Person in charge of African collection:
Doris M. Hull
Hours: Term: Monday–Friday 09.00–20.00
           Saturday 09.00–16.30
      Vacation: Monday–Friday 09.00–17.00
Access: Open to the public, outside researchers must apply for a Visitor Research Card.
Loan and reference facilities: Reference only.
Book collection: 2,500 volumes (Africana total).
Special features:
The collection is rich in books and materials on black studies, the Caribbean, Africa, and the African diaspora. In addition to the Library, the Center is composed of a museum, a manuscript division, and a photography section.
Serials collection: 30 titles.
Abbia, ABPR, AfrA, AfrLJ, ALA, ALA Newsletter, Ašemka, Ba Shiru, BO, Busara, CBAA, Ch'Indaba, Conch, CulEA, Dhana, Dombi, Ethiopiques, Greenfield Review, JCL, JNALA, Mawazo, Obsidian, Odi, Oduma, Okike, Okyeame, Ozila, PA, RAL, SBL, Staffrider, Umma, WAJML, Zuka.
Photocopying facilities available.
Publications:
Current Contents: Africa (Aquisitions list)

African Section
African and Middle Eastern Division
Library of Congress
Adams Building, Room 1040C
Washington D.C. 20540
Tel: 202-287-5528
                Telex: 710-82201085 LIBCON
Chief Librarian: Dr. Daniel J. Boorstin
Person in charge of African collection: Beverley A. Gray
Hours:
Reading room: Monday–Friday 08.30–21.30
              Saturday 08.30–17.00
              Sunday 13.00–17.00
African section: Monday–Friday 08.30–16.40
Access: Open to all members of the public over the age of 18.

Loan and reference facilities: Available.
Book collection: 5,000 volumes (critical works only).
Special features:
Unusually rich and extensive research materials on sub-Saharan Africa are available to the researcher at the Library of Congress. One of the units of the African and Middle Eastern Division, the African Section, is the focal point of the Library's reference and bibliographic activities on sub-Saharan Africa, which excludes the North African countries of Algeria, Egypt, Libya, Morocco, and Tunisia. The Section plays a vital role in the Library's acquisitions programme, provides reference services for an international community, prepares bibliographic guides, and maintains liaison with other institutions in the United States and abroad. The Library's collections of Africana – material from or relating to Africa – are among the best in the world. They encompass every major field of study except technical agriculture and clinical medicine.
Serials collection: Extensive, exact number not specified.
Abbia, ABPR, AfrA, Afriscope, AfrLJ, ALA, ALAC, ALA Newsletter, ALT, Asemka, Ba Shiru, BH, BO, Busara, CBAA, Ch'Indaba, Conch, CulEA, Dhana, Dombi, Ecr franc, English in Africa, Ethiopiques, Greenfield Review, JCL, JNALA, Joliso, Kiabara, Kucha, LAAW, Maktaba, Marang, New Coin, New Culture, Obsidian, Odi, Oduma, PA, RAL, RLEN, SBL, TT, Umma, WAJML, WLT, WLWE, Zambezia, Zuka (and others).
Photocopying facilities available.
Publications:
As part of its continuing bibliographic programme, the African Section prepared thirty-eight studies for publication in the period 1960–1978, ranging in scope from general and topical guides on sub-Saharan Africa, to bibliographies of official publications of a country or region. A complete list of LC African Section publications is available on request.

Memorial Library
University of Wisconsin
728 State Street
Madison
Wi. 53706
Tel: 608-262-6397
Chief Librarian: Joseph H. Treyz
Person in charge of African collection: David Henige
Hours: Monday–Saturday 08.00–24.00
         Sunday 12.00–24.00
Access: Open to all serious researchers.
Loan and reference facilities: Loans are restricted

to those residents of the State of Wisconsin, except via inter-library loan.

Book collection: 3,000 volumes.

Serials collection: 47 titles.

Abbia, ABPR, AfrA, Afriscope, AfrLJ, ALA, ALA Newsletter, ALT, Ba Shiru, BH, BO, Busara, CBAA, Conch, CulEA, Dhana, English in Africa, Greenfield Review, JCL, JNALA, Joliso, Kiabara, Kucha, Kunapipi, LAAW, Maktaba, Mawazo, New Classic, New Coin, NSAL, Obsidian, Odi, Oduma, Okike, Okyeame, Ophir, Ozila, PA, PFr, RAL, SBL, Staffrider, TT, Umma, WAJML, WLT, WLWE, Zambezia, Zuka.

Index

This index lists all authors, editors and critics included in the bibliography. The abbreviation BIOG. followed by the relevant page number indicates that a biography of that author is included. Names of journals cited in parts I and II of the "Magazines" section are also indexed, and appear in *italics*. (The "Directory of Libraries with African Literature Collections" has not been indexed.)